S0-AFC-500

4th Edition

# Portfolio Construction, Management, and Protection

Robert A. Strong, CFA

*University of Maine*

Australia · Canada · Mexico · Singapore · Spain · United Kingdom · United States

**Portfolio Construction, Management, and Protection, Fourth Edition**
Robert A. Strong


**VP/Editorial Director:**
Jack W. Calhoun

**VP/Editor-in-Chief:**
Alex von Rosenberg

**Publisher:**
Melissa Acuña

**Executive Editor:**
Scott Person

**Developmental Editor:**
Leslie Kauffman, Leap Publishing Services

**Marketing Manager:**
Heather MacMaster

**Production Project Manager:**
Margaret M. Bril

**Manager of Technology, Editorial:**
Vicky True

**Technology Project Editor:**
John Barans

**Web Coordinator:**
Karen Schaffer

**Manufacturing Coordinator:**
Sandee Milewski

**Production House:**
Interactive Composition Corporation

**Printer:**
Courier Kendallville
Kendallville, Indiana

**Art Director:**
Chris Miller/Bethany Casey

**Internal Designer:**
Trish & Ted Knapke

**Cover Designer:**
Trish & Ted Knapke

**Cover Images:**
© Comstock.com &
© Gettyimages, Inc.





Printed in the United States of America
1 2 3 4 5 08 07 06 05

ISBN: 0-324- 23258-6





Library of Congress Control Number:
2005925624

For more information about our products, contact us at:

Thomson Learning Academic Resource Center

1-800-423-0563

**Thomson Higher Education**
5191 Natorp Boulevard
Mason, OH 45040
USA

# Summary of Contents

To BKKBR and K

# Contents

# PREFACE

The trend in investment management is to emphasize portfolio construction and to reduce the time spent on security selection. Though all portfolio managers should be familiar with the components of their portfolios, overwhelming evidence proves that asset allocation is what matters in the long run, with security selection playing a secondary role. Such is the focus of *Portfolio Construction, Management, and Protection*, Fourth Edition.

Prior study in investments is not a prerequisite—although many students will have had such a course—but I assume that the student has had a course in managerial or corporate finance. In schools without a "pure" portfolio course, this book will accomplish the objectives of both a traditional investments course and a portfolio theory course. The investments instructor who chooses to emphasize portfolio management rather than security selection will find the organization and spirit of this book especially appealing.

In schools that offer separate investments and portfolio courses, *Portfolio Construction, Management, and Protection*, Fourth Edition, enables the portfolio management instructor to develop a very rich course in which the students can discover the beauty, logic, and potential of modern portfolio management. I believe the strengths of this book are its application orientation and the transitions from theory to practice.

Although principles of portfolio construction and management have been taught at the university level for many years, students may find the subject uncomfortably quantitative, laden with mathematical proofs, intellectually inaccessible, and generally "user unfriendly." This book provides an alternative to the course's stereotypical approach.

## The Approach of This Edition

Some aspects of my own background helped form my ideas about what a useful course on portfolio management would need to cover. I am a firm believer in the utility of financial derivatives; five chapters of this book contain material on the sensible use of futures and options in portfolio management. I am also a Chartered Financial Analyst and chairman of a retail brokerage firm, and serve on a bank trust committee. My experience with these activities is largely responsible for two special chapters in this book. Chapter 4, "Investment Policy," covers an extremely important subject to which we often do not give sufficient attention in portfolio management courses. In order to manage money properly, money managers must have a statement of investment policy to guide their actions. They must also understand that investment policy is different from investment management, and that different people have responsibility for these two functions. Chapter 18, "Fiduciary Duties and Responsibilities," also discusses material that does not get much playing time in the classroom. I believe that instructors and students alike will find this material fascinating, and that for many people it will change their way of thinking about the investment process. The evolution of legal doctrine regarding proper fiduciary conduct is especially thought provoking. As chairman of a brokerage firm, I know that investment suitability is one of the NASD's principal areas of inquiry during firm audits.

Many chapters contain actual questions from past Chartered Financial Analyst exams. Participation in the CFA program is rapidly becoming a condition of employment at many firms. I am a staunch advocate of the CFA Institute, its Code of Ethics, and its Standards of Practice. I think we help our students by exposing them to this front-line sector of the industry.

Many adopters of the book have told me they find the Mutual Fund Evaluation Term Project (the appendix to Chapter 3) to be quite useful. I personally like the appendix on Stochastic Dominance (after Chapter 6) for the intellectual discussion it seems to promote.

## Supplements

### *Instructor's Manual and Test Bank (0-324-23259-4)*

An Instructor's Manual and Test Bank, prepared by Larry C. Holland of the University of Arkansas, is available to adopting instructors. It contains Key Points, Teaching Considerations, Answers to Questions, Answers to Problems, and a test bank of qualitative and quantitative multiple-choice questions.

### *Website (http://strong.swlearning.com)*

There are several Excel spreadsheet templates available on the text Web site at *http://strong.swlearning.com*. These are primarily time savers that can be incorporated into homework assignments or used as a take-home portion of an exam. The text Website also contains instructor and student resources, Internet applications from the text, links to relevant financial Websites, and other useful features. PowerPoint slides to accompany the text, prepared by Oliver Schnusenberg of the University of North Florida, are available to qualified instructors as downloads from the Website.

### *Thomson Finance Resource Center (http://finance.swlearning.com)*

The Thomson Finance Resource Center at *http://finance.swlearning.com* provides unique features that are frequently updated, including NewsWire: Finance in the News (summaries of the latest finance news stories) and FinanceLinks Online (directions to the best finance Websites), among others.

### *Business & Company Resource Center (http://www.swlearning.com/bcrc/bcrc.html)*

Put a complete business library at your fingertips with the *Business & Company Resource Center*. The BCRC is a premier online business research tool that allow you to seamlessly search thousands of periodicals, journals, references, sources of financial information, industry reports, company histories, and much more. The *Business & Company Resource Center* can be packaged with any Thomson textbook or coursepack at little or no additional cost. To learn how you can include BCRC in your course, visit the Website or contact your local Thomson representative.

## Acknowledgments

I received a great deal of help in writing this book from my academic and practitioner colleagues. Mike Reynolds and Scott Person of Thomson Business & Economics, my editorial team, are good folks to work with and very competent professionally. Leslie Kauffman of LEAP Publishing Services did an excellent job of shepherding me through the manuscript process. Marge Bril at Thomson, who also worked with me on the second and third editions of this book, was an able production editor who kept the project on schedule and did not let important details fall through the cracks. Also at Thomson, I'd like to thank Heather MacMaster, marketing manager; Chris Miller, art director; John Barans, technology project editor; and Karen Schaffer, Web coordinator. My former student, Christopher Whitford, checked all the mathematics in the book and contributed substantially to my peace of mind. His conscientiousness makes the book a better product.

In addition, the book has received thorough reviews from the following colleagues over the previous three editions:

S. G. Baldrinath
Northeastern University

James Buck
East Carolina University

John Burnett
University of Alabama in Huntsville

Natalya V. Delcoure
University of South Alabama

Thomas W. Downs
University of Alabama

Howard Finch
University of Tennessee–Chattanooga

H. Swint Friday
University of South Alabama

David Hall
Chicago Board of Options Exchange

Robert Hartwig
Worcester State College

Jon Hooks
Albion College

Philip A. Horvath
Bradley University

John S. Howe
Louisiana State University

Riaz Hussain
University of Scranton

Jau-Lian Jeng
Azusa Pacific University

Keith H. Johnson
University of Kentucky

Douglas Kahl
University of Akron

Peppi M. Kenny
Western Illinois University

Tom Krueger
University of Wisconsin, LaCrosse

Malek Lashgari
University of Hartford

Jeong W. Lee
University of North Dakota

Ralph Lim
Sacred Heart University

David Louton
Bryant College

Linda J. Martin
Arizona State University

Byron Menides
Worcester Polytechnic Institute

Mehdi Mohaghegh
Norwich University

Edgar Norton
Fairleigh Dickinson University

Prasad Padmanabhan
San Diego State University

Daniel E. Page
Auburn University

Luis Rivera
Dowling College

Mark Schaub
Texas A & M University

Thomas V. Schwartz
Southern Illinios University–Carbondale

Bill Swales, Esq.
Bangor Savings Bank Trust Department

Calvin True, Esq.
Eaton, Peabody

Bret Vicary
James W. Sewall Company

*Dr. Robert A. Strong, CFA*
University of Maine
Orono, ME
March, 2005

# PART ONE

# Background, Basic Principles, and Investment Policy

# 1 The Process of Portfolio Management

*The life of every man is a diary in which he means to write one story, and writes another; and his humblest hour is when he compares the volume as it is with what he vowed to make it.*

***J.M. Barrie***

## Introduction

The traditional investments course covers two principal topics: *security analysis* and *portfolio management*. Security analysis involves estimating the merits of individual investments while portfolio management deals with the construction and maintenance of a collection of investments.

Investment professionals often describe security analysis as a three-step process. First, the analyst considers prospects for the economy, given the stage of the business cycle. Second, the analyst determines which industries are likely to fare well in the forecasted economic conditions. Finally, the analyst chooses particular companies within the favored industries. Many people call this procedure *EIC analysis* for *economy*, *industry*, and *company*.[1]

In recent years the trend has been to move away from stock picking and toward portfolio management (Figure 1-1). Most of the academic literature from the last two decades generally supports the *efficient markets* paradigm. Market efficiency means that on a well-developed securities exchange, asset prices accurately reflect the trade-off between the relative risk and potential returns associated with the security. Markets are kept reasonably efficient because of the vast number of market participants who are quick to take advantage of security mispricing. This means that efforts to identify undervalued securities are generally fruitless. In other words, free lunches are difficult to find, and any quest for them is likely to wind up at a dead end.

The fact that markets are efficient does not mean that investment managers can just throw darts in making their investment decisions. Not all portfolios are created equal; some are clearly better than others. A properly constructed portfolio achieves a given level of expected return with the least possible risk. Portfolio managers have a duty to create the best possible collection of investments for each customer's unique needs and circumstances.

[1]This is a *top-down* approach, beginning with a large *security universe* and winding up with a smaller, more manageable number.

FIGURE 1-1

The Trend in Managerial Time and Focus

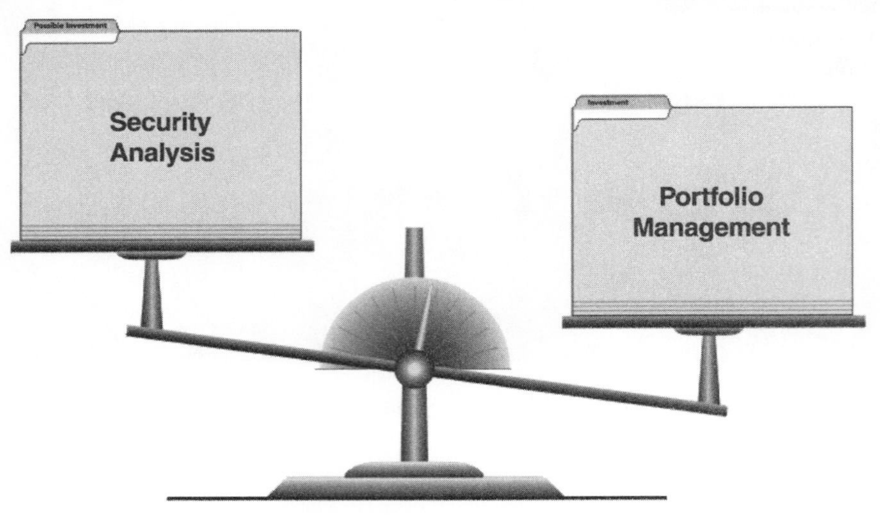


*Portfolio management primarily involves reducing risk rather than increasing return.*

By reducing the dispersion of an investment's returns while holding the mean return constant, the investor fares better. This is an important point. Figure 1-2 compares two $10,000 investments. One earned 10 percent per year for each of ten years, growing to a terminal value of $25,937. The arithmetic average of its annual returns is, of course, 10 percent. A second investment shows dispersion in its returns (9, –11, 10, 8, 12, 46, 8, 20, –12, and 10 percent), but it still has a 10 percent arithmetic average return. The terminal value of this investment, however, is only $23,642. It is a mathematical fact that the lower the dispersion in the returns, the greater the accumulated value of otherwise equal investments.

Before the portfolio manager can do the job, however, there needs to be a *statement of investment policy*. This outlines the return requirements, the investor's risk tolerance, and the constraints under which the portfolio must operate. It is absolutely essential for an investment manager to have this information before going about the business of asset allocation and security selection.

The portfolio management process has six steps, which are highlighted in Figure 1-3 and in the marginal notes. The remainder of this chapter previews things to come later in the book.

## Part One: Background, Basic Principles, and Investment Policy

*Step 1: Learn the basic principles of finance.*

A person cannot be an effective portfolio manager without a **solid grounding in the basic principles of finance.** This is the first aspect of portfolio management. At one time it may have been possible to get away with an ad hoc approach to managing money, but this is no longer the case. Modern portfolio management is too complex.[2]

[2]Also, our society is quite litigious these days, and investment managers sometimes have to explain their actions (or inaction) in court.

FIGURE 1-2

$10,000 Initial Investments

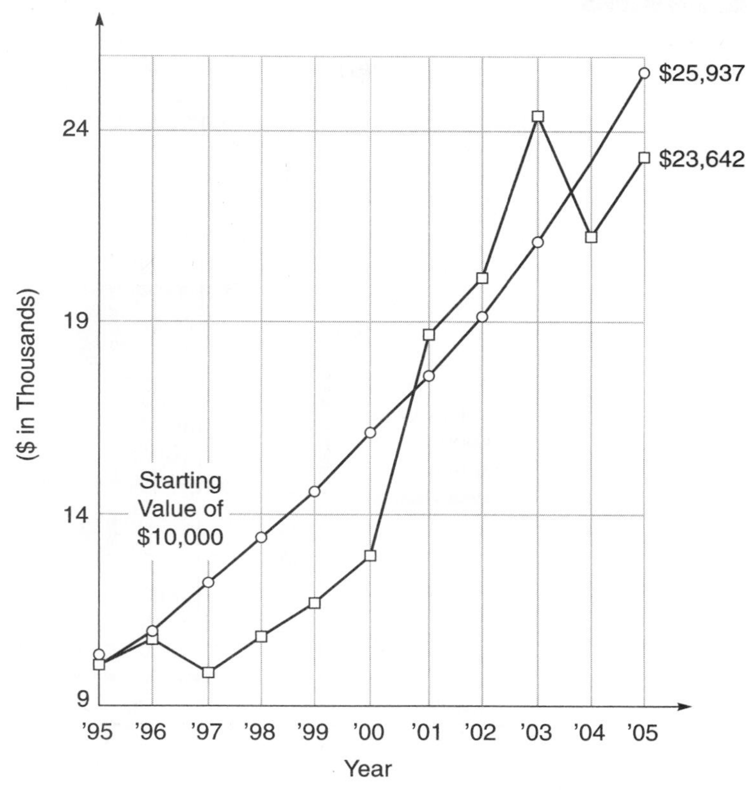


Both investments have a mean return of 10 percent.

*Talk is cheap in the investment business.*

Most people who read this book will have previously studied the fundamentals of finance. Finance is a very logical discipline with basic principles that are not difficult. The danger is that egos sometimes get involved, and people may be reluctant to spend much time reviewing "simple" material. One of the curious things about investment management is that the public's perception of its own competence seems bimodal: people are likely to believe that they know either *a lot* or *only a little* about this topic. Talk is cheap in the investment world. People can say that they know how to do something, but in the final analysis, it is deeds, not dialogue, that count.

The passage that follows is one of my favorite quotations. It is attributed to the Roman consul Lucius Aemilius Paulus as he addressed the people of Rome before the Pydna campaign (167 B.C.) of the Third Macedonian War:

> In every circle, and, truly at every table, there are people who lead armies into Macedonia; who know where the camp ought to be placed; what posts ought to be occupied by troops; when and through what pass that territory should be entered; where magazines should be formed; how provisions should be convoyed by land and sea; and when it is proper to engage the enemy, and when to lie quiet.
>
> And they not only determine what is to be done but if anything is done in any other manner than what they have pointed out, they arraign the consul, as if he were on trial before them.

FIGURE 1-3

Six Steps of Portfolio Management

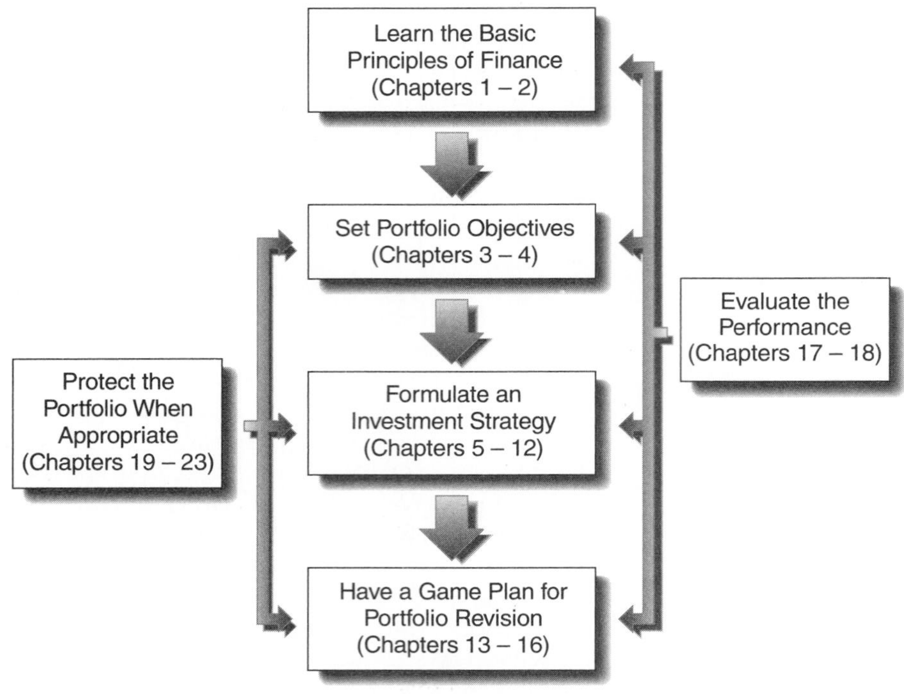


These are the great impediments to those who have the management of affairs; for everyone cannot encounter injurious reports with the same constancy and firmness of mind as Fadius did; who chose to let his own ability be questioned through the folly of the people, rather than to mismanage the public business with a high reputation.

I am not one of those who think that commanders at no time ought to receive advice; on the contrary, I should deem that man more proud than wise, who regulated every proceeding by the standard of his own single judgment. What then is my opinion? That commanders should be counseled. Chiefly, by persons of known talent; by those who have made the art of war their particular study, and whose knowledge is derived from experience; from those who are present at the scene of action; who see the country, who see the enemy; who see the advantages that occasions offer, and who, like people embarked on the same ship are sharers of the danger. If, therefore, anyone thinks himself qualified to give advice respecting the war I am to conduct, which may prove advantageous to the public, let him not refuse his assistance to the state, but let him come with me into Macedonia.

He shall be furnished with a ship, a horse, a tent; even his traveling charges shall be defrayed. But if he thinks this too much trouble, and prefers the repose of a city life to the toils of war, let him not, on land, assume the office of a pilot.

The city, in itself, furnishes abundance of topics for conversation; let it confine its passion for talking within its own precincts, and rest assured that we shall pay no attention to any councils but such as shall be framed within our camp.[3]

[3]Victor Duruy, *History of Rome and of the Roman People* (Boston: C.F. Jewett, 1883), 169–170.

In this quotation Paulus is emphasizing the fact that deeds are what count. This is good advice to modern portfolio managers as they do battle with the forces that would keep them from achieving their investment goals. If someone has a worthy idea to contribute, then let us hear it, but fluff and bluster have no place in the formation of investment policy or strategy. Many of those who feel that they know a lot about the investment business share the genes of the people Paulus was addressing. It is unlikely that someone who has never constructed a portfolio is qualified to give advice on the subject, and it is certain that a futures and options neophyte cannot speak intelligently on the prudent use of derivatives in portfolio protection. In the same fashion, a junior security analyst soon learns that a good *company* is not necessarily a good *investment*. The stock of a well-run company may simply be too expensive at the current price.

*A good company is not necessarily a good investment.*

This is true of anything we buy. The price tag hanging from an elegant business suit at a high-end clothing store may be $1,200. No one will argue that the suit is snazzy, but not everyone would consider it a good investment. At $350, however, the same suit would be a much more attractive investment. The same is true of a share of stock in a well-managed company. If the stock price comes down, it may *become* a good investment while remaining a good company.

Similarly, poorly run companies can be great investments if they are cheap enough. People buy old, beat-up stuff at yard sales because it is inexpensive, not because its quality is high. While most of us have a reasonably good understanding of value shopping, many people never figure out the distinction between good companies and good investments.

Part One of this book reviews the fundamental principles of finance and statistics that an analyst must understand before moving on to portfolio construction and management. Much of this material will be generally familiar to most readers, but virtually everyone will learn something from a review of these topics.

The two key concepts in finance are (1) a dollar today is worth more than a dollar tomorrow and (2) a safe dollar is worth more than a risky dollar. These two ideas form the basis for all aspects of financial management. In reviewing these two key concepts and some basic statistics in Chapter 2, readers will also get a refresher course on the importance of the economic concept of *utility* as it relates to risk and return. The whole point of investment management is for investors to get more of what they enjoy and get rid of what they dislike. Investors like *return*, be it in dollars or in intangible form, and they dislike *risk*. The goal is to get as much of the "good" while suffering as little of the "bad" as possible.

*The whole point of investment management is to get more of what you like and get rid of what you dislike.*

All of finance stems from the basic concepts of the risk/return trade-off and the time value of money. It is difficult to truly comprehend new investment products and risk-management practices without fluency in these principles. These first two chapters are a good review for every reader.

*Step 2: Set portfolio objectives*

According to an old saying, "It is difficult to accomplish your objectives until you know what it is you want to accomplish." Step 2 in portfolio management is setting portfolio objectives. Chapters 3 and 4 deal with setting objectives and determining investment policy. People think they understand words such as *growth* or *income*, but these terms often mean different things to different people. For some people reading this book, the discussion of the importance of objective setting will make the most lasting impression. Chapter 3 describes the difficulty people have in finding a balance between risk and expected return and provides a framework for determining portfolio objectives.

Chapter 4 focuses on investment policy. The separation of investment *policy* from investment *management* is a fundamental tenet of institutional money management. One group of people, such as a board of directors or an investment policy committee, establishes the rules of the game and hires someone to play the game. These people establish policy. The investment manager is the person who implements the plan. It is a mistake (sometimes a very serious one) and possibly a breach of legal duty to allow the investment manager also to set the rules and, by default, the investment policy.

*Investment policy is distinct from investment management.*

A formal statement of investment policy is a very useful tool. This document clearly outlines responsibilities and procedures. It is an important part of the investment process to make sure such a document exists.

## Part Two: Portfolio Construction

Once a person has been through financial boot camp and has a policy statement, it is time to begin **formulating an investment strategy** and constructing the portfolio itself. This involves more than simply buying a handful of securities so that all your eggs are not in one proverbial basket. There are many things to consider and to monitor.

*Step 3: Formulate an investment strategy.*

Portfolio managers need to understand the basic elements of capital market theory. The mathematical relationships underlying portfolio theory might seem forbidding, but their basic substance is not difficult. Unfortunately, concepts such as covariance and the appearance of double summation signs scare away many people. A special effort is made to keep Chapter 5 user friendly and to help readers appreciate the logical beauty of portfolio theory. Diversification *is* a good idea, both mathematically and logically. Chapter 6 discusses the risk-reduction benefits that accompany informed diversification. Portfolio construction deals with diversification. It surprises many people to learn that diversification is not oriented toward increasing return; its purpose is to reduce risk.

One of the most consequential pieces of academic research regarding portfolio construction is a paper by Evans and Archer showing the powerful risk-reduction benefits obtained through the *naive diversification* that comes from common sense in investment selection as opposed to some mathematical technique.[4] The implications of this research continue to be very important, even for the most sophisticated portfolio manager.

Chapter 6 then extends the basic principles of risk and return to a more general capital market theory. There the focus is on unavoidable risk, which is the type of risk that counts and the only type for which investors can reasonably expect additional return. Whereas naive diversification is beneficial, the informed portfolio manager can do even better with theoretical best-practice investing.

International investment is an important part of modern portfolio management. In Chapter 7 you will see why foreign securities are appealing and why the manager should think about the currency market as well as the global stock markets. Emerging markets, such as those in Central Europe, the Pacific Rim, and South America, carry special risks that investors should study before committing any money. Institutional portfolios frequently contain 15 percent foreign investments with at least a small portion in emerging markets; a money manager should be conversant with key aspects of this asset class.

[4]John Evans and Stephen Archer, "Diversification and the Reduction of Dispersion," *Journal of Finance*, December 1968, 761–77.

Unlike the emerging markets, the U.S. financial markets are informationally very efficient but not completely so. Chapter 8 explains the implications of this to the investor and the portfolio manager. The chapter also reviews the *beta* statistic arising from capital market theory, the way a portfolio manager might use it, and potential pitfalls with the number.

Many portfolios ultimately contain both equity and fixed-income securities. As you will see in Chapter 9, preferred stock is generally not a good investment for individual investors or endowment funds. It *is* appropriate, however, for many taxable corporations. There is some traditional security analysis in this chapter. There we see the categories of stock (such as blue chip, defensive, and cyclical) with their particular characteristics and investment appeal.

*Security screening reduces the list of eligible investments to a manageable number.*

Security screening, a topic most textbooks do not cover, describes a practice that most professional investors and individuals subconsciously follow. The world simply contains too many potential investments for a team of analysts to consider them all. Managers need a logical protocol to reduce the total to a workable number for closer investigation. We call such a technique a *screen*. As Chapter 10 shows, individuals use screens routinely in everyday life. Teachers tell children buying presents for school chums to spend less than $5, football coaches look for those who can run the 40-yard dash in under 5 seconds, admission officers look for Scholastic Aptitude Test scores over 1000, and investors might look for stocks with price-earnings ratios under 10 or those with listed options. All of these are examples of screens. What constitutes a good screen? We explore the question in Chapter 10.

*Understanding duration is essential to modern portfolio management.*

Chapter 11, "Bond Pricing and Selection," reviews basic principles regarding the pricing of debt securities. In addition, it introduces the concept of duration, which is critical in modern fixed-income security management. Duration enables the portfolio manager to alter the risk of the fixed-income component of a portfolio quickly and efficiently without having to perform complex calculations or trial-and-error iterations. In today's investment community, portfolio managers who are not fluent with duration are simply not current in their field and run the risk of becoming dinosaurs.

Having picked the equity players for a portfolio, how should the bonds be chosen? Does it matter? What does *bond diversification* really mean? This chapter provides a framework for answering these questions. It also examines the yield curve and the clues it provides about the future.

The set of investment possibilities includes assets other than stocks and bonds. Pension funds pay attention to gold and timberland; these are examples of *real assets*. Gold is an anecdotally familiar investment, sometimes with unusual merits as a portfolio component but frequently without. Many U.S. pension funds have significant percentages of their managed funds in timberland. In many respects, timberland is an ideal investment for long-term investors with no liquidity problems. Part of Chapter 12 is an investment primer on the terminology and characteristics of forestland investment.

## Part Three: Portfolio Management

Having formed a portfolio, an investor should not normally leave it untended. Conditions change, and portfolios need maintenance. **Developing a game plan for updating the portfolio** is the fourth step of portfolio management.

*Step 4: Have a game plan for portfolio revision.*

Chapters 13 and 14 deal with portfolio revision. An investor can manage a portfolio *passively* or *actively*. Passive management involves letting the chips fall where they may, either by doing nothing or by following a predetermined investment strategy that is invariant to market conditions. Active management requires the periodic changing of the portfolio components as the manager's outlook for the market changes. Chapters 13 and 14 also address considerations surrounding periodic contributions to the portfolio, either those generated internally through dividend and interest income or those arising from an outside source.

To be current, a modern portfolio manager should understand the basic principles of options and option pricing. This includes an understanding of where options come from, why they are a good idea, and what basic strategies portfolio managers might use. The Black-Scholes Option Pricing Model is one of the most important developments in finance in the last thirty years, earning its developers the Nobel Prize in 1997. We look at it in Chapter 15.

*Option overwriting seeks to increase the yield on a portfolio and to improve returns in a flat market.*

Option overwriting is a popular activity designed to increase the yield on a given portfolio and to improve performance in a flat market. People who do not understand options view these securities (and other *derivatives*) with a great deal of suspicion. The discussion in Chapter 16 gives examples of the intelligent and well-conceived use of stock options under various portfolio scenarios.

*Step 5: Evaluate the performance.*

The fifth step of the portfolio management process is **performance evaluation.** There are really two parts to performance evaluation. First, did the portfolio manager do what he or she was hired to do? If a pension fund hires a firm to be its large-cap value manager, this entity should not be investing in small-capitalization growth stocks. Someone needs to verify that the firm followed directions. The second step in performance evaluation is interpreting the numbers. How much did the portfolio earn, and how much risk did it bear? (See Figure 1-4.) Historically, the way the

**FIGURE 1-4** Investment Manager Performance Appraisal

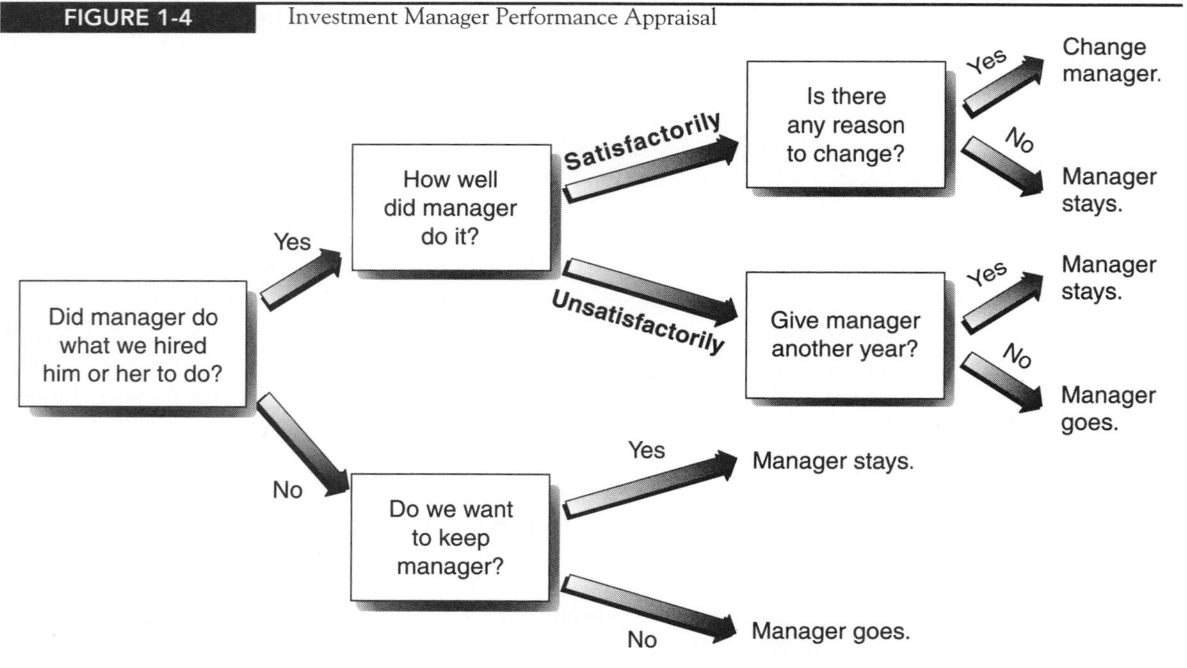

*To compare the historical performances of stocks and other investment alternatives, visit* http://www.duke.edu/~charvey/Classes/ba350/history/history.htm

investment community handles this issue has been problematic. The low-end financial press tends to imply that the manager whose portfolio had the highest return had the best performance. The common belief is that a portfolio that earned 20 percent outperformed another portfolio that earned 15 percent. These statements are incorrect. You must consider the return of a portfolio in conjunction with the riskiness of the portfolio. There are standard methods for doing so.

The performance evaluation problem is complicated when there are cash deposits and/or withdrawals from the portfolio and when the manager uses options to enhance the portfolio yield. Chapter 17 will explain how to deal with these situations.

*A fiduciary is responsible for the management of someone else's money.*

Many portfolio managers are *fiduciaries*. This means they are responsible for looking after someone else's money and have some discretion in its investment. The law specifies the duties of a fiduciary quite clearly. A breach of fiduciary duty can result in poor client relations or even a malpractice suit. Chapter 18 presents a discussion of the primary fiduciary duties and how they influence the investment process.

## Part Four: Portfolio Protection and Contemporary Issues

*Step 6: Protect the portfolio when appropriate.*

Portfolio *protection* was called portfolio *insurance* until the stock market crash of 1987. This is a powerful managerial tool designed to reduce the likelihood that a portfolio will fall in value below a predetermined minimum level. **Protecting the portfolio when appropriate** is the final aspect of the portfolio management process. Chapters 19 through 21 cover this topic.

The material in Chapter 19, "Principles of the Futures Market," is a cousin to the material on options in Chapter 15. Futures can play a very useful role in risk management. Some managers, in fact, will say they could not do their job properly if they could not hedge market risk with stock index futures.

Chapter 20, "Benching the Equity Players," covers popular methods of using options, futures, or both to reduce the risk of the equity components in the portfolio. As with options, the regulators and governing bodies that make decisions regarding investment funds do not always understand the economic purpose of futures contracts. The material in this chapter will enable you to carry on a fluent conversation about the merits of options or futures in a particular investment portfolio.

Chapter 21 covers similar issues with regard to interest rate risk. We revisit duration, seeing how intelligent duration management enables the bond manager to sleep more comfortably. A comprehensive review of the integration of futures and options with traditional portfolio management follows in Chapter 22. In some respects, this chapter is an extended case study showing how a portfolio manager can use derivative assets to generate additional income and to manage risk in an existing portfolio of stocks and bonds.

Chapter 23, the final chapter of the book, introduces some contemporary issues in portfolio management. The fact that derivative securities have faced such difficulty getting regulatory approval is a continuing problem. Despite what we know about risk-adjusted performance measurement, the idea has less than complete acceptance on the street. Chapter 23 also includes a review of the nuts and bolts behind program trading, stock lending, and the current dialogue regarding security analyst independence. All portfolio managers are aware of the Chartered Financial Analyst (CFA) designation; the book concludes with a strong endorsement of the program.

## INTERNET EXERCISE

The *Stockscreener* utility at *http://screen.finance.yahoo.com/newscreener.html* provides the ability to search and sort stocks by twenty different performance criteria. Identify ten stocks that match the criteria that are important for you using *Stockscreener*. Then, using the portfolio-tracking tool provided at *http://quote.yahoo.com*, *http://www.marketwatch.com/tools/stockresearch/screener/*, or some other Website, create a portfolio using the five stocks you have identified. Track the performance of your portfolio through the semester. At the end of the semester, you can reevaluate your portfolio creation strategy and assess its performance using the tools you will be introduced to in this book.

## PORTFOLIO MEMO

### Is the Stock Market a Good Place to Spend 2005?

You may be wondering if this is a good time to invest or where the stock market is headed. If so, Edward Jones has some answers for you—the same ones we've always had.

Successful investing depends on a strategy that includes buying high-quality equity investments and holding them for the long term. In other words, time in the market, not timing the market. Your strategy should also include diversification. Diversification involves investing in companies in different industries so that your success is not tied to a single industry's performance.

If you're considering the reasons not to invest in 2005, think about the reasons that kept others from investing in years past. Although past performance is no guarantee of future success, hesitation can be a costly decision. Our table shows what $10,000 invested in common stocks for the years noted would be worth today.*

You can probably think of a reason not to invest in 2005. But think about this instead—a buy-and-hold strategy that emphasizes diversification still offers tremendous value to investors, despite short-term fluctuations in the stock market. It was true 20 years ago and it's true today; the stock market is a good place for long-term investors.

| **$10,000 invested on Jan. 1** | **Value Today*** |
|---|---|
| 1974 | $332,850 |
| OPEC is in control. Nixon won't be for long. | |
| 1976 | $328,642 |
| New York City almost went bankrupt and we're wearing WIN buttons. | |
| 1978 | $286,295 |
| You can't make anything in this market. It's barely moved in two years. | |
| 1980 | $238,369 |
| Iran is holding America hostage. I'm holding on to my money. | |

*Based on the S&P 500. Assumes reinvestment of dividends. Ending values as of Dec. 31, 2004. The S&P 500 is an unmanaged index and cannot be invested directly.

PORTFOLIO MEMO

## Is the Stock Market a Good Place to Spend 2005? (continued)

1982 ............................................................ $189,211
The recession has started and it looks bad.

1984 ............................................................ $127,020
The Dow is over 1250. It's an all new high and I missed it.

1986 ............................................................ $90,739
The federal deficit is over $200 billion.

1988 ............................................................ $72,652
Where were you on Black Monday? I was out of the market.

1990 ............................................................ $47,358
The '80's are over but high yield bond problems aren't.

1992 ............................................................ $37,478
Invest in stocks? Maybe you haven't heard. We're in a recession.

1994 ............................................................ $31,651
Let the government run healthcare? American business will never recover.

1996 ............................................................ $22,714
The Dow sailed past 4000 and 5000. The tide's bound to turn and I'm afraid I'll get soaked.

1998 ............................................................ $13,855
The Dow went from 4000 to 8000 in less than three years. I'm getting out while the getting is good.

2000 ............................................................ $8,902
Y2K Doomsday? I'll wait until I know everything's O.K.

2002 ............................................................ $11,114
Sept. 11 changed everything. I'll wait out the war on terror.

2003 ............................................................ $14,265
We went to war with Iraq. I don't want to be in the market now.

2004 ............................................................ $11,087
Oil prices are soaring. I don't want to be in the market now.

Source: Bloomberg

PORTFOLIO MEMO

## Plan Sponsors

*Plan sponsors* are important players in the world of portfolio management. They may be corporations (such as General Electric or L.L. Bean) or a group of individuals (perhaps the partners of a medical practice or law firm). A plan sponsor is responsible for establishing and overseeing one or more investment programs for the benefit of others.

A pension fund is a common example. Employees of the firm participate in a retirement program with someone managing the fund's assets. The plan sponsor has a duty to see that someone handles the fund's assets in the best interests of the company's employees. While the corporate board of directors has the ultimate supervisory responsibility, the board frequently establishes an *investment committee* to do this. This committee often includes a few members from the board plus some outside experts or consultants if necessary. The committee ensures that there is a *statement of investment policy* providing objectives and constraints for the *investment manager*, the person or firm hired to make trades in the account. Setting investment policy is the responsibility of the plan sponsor; buying and selling securities is the responsibility of the investment manager. Although buying and selling sometimes happens by default in an unsophisticated organization, the investment manager should not be the one to prepare the investment policy statement.

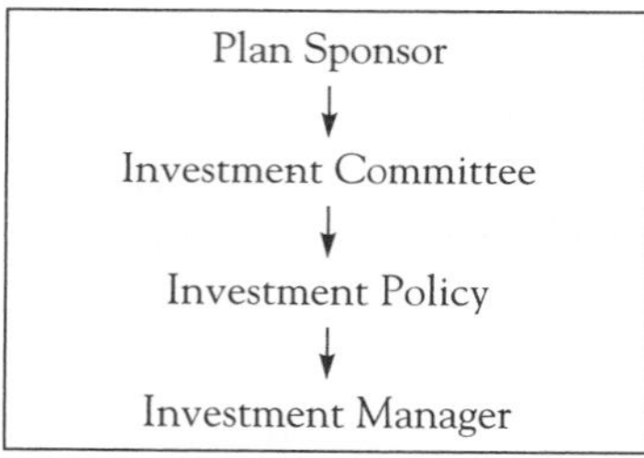


Managing money for a wealthy, tax-paying individual is quite different from managing the assets of a perpetual, nontaxable endowment fund. We expect the investment manager to follow the investment policy guidelines, and the law expects the plan sponsor to ensure that investment policy will work to the advantage of those who will benefit from the performance of the investment portfolio. Plan sponsors have a *fiduciary duty* to uphold; we will explore fiduciary duties and responsibilities in Chapter 18.

Portfolio management is not a "one-size-fits-all" process. As you study this topic, keep in mind any action you take should be for the express benefit of your client and that what works for one client may not be appropriate for another.

# 2 Valuation, Risk, Return, and Uncertainty

*It's what we learn after we think we know it all that counts.*
***Kin Hubbard***

## Key Terms

arithmetic mean
beta
bivariate
consumption decision
continuous
convenience risk
correlation
covariance
dependent variable
diminishing marginal utility of money
discrete
distribution
expected return
fair bet
geometric mean
growing annuity
growing perpetuity
holding period return
independent variable
logreturn
mean
median
mode
multivariate
opportunity cost
population
price risk
psychic return
qualitative
quantitative
R squared
return
return on assets (ROA)
return on equity (ROE)
return on investment (ROI)
return relative
risk
risk averse
riskless rate of interest
sample
sample statistic
semi-variance
skewness
St. Petersburg paradox
standard error
stochastic
total risk
uncertainty
univariate
utility

## Introduction

In many respects, this chapter functions as a crash course in the principles of finance and elementary statistics. Subsequent chapters amplify most of the points contained here or reinforce material from a more basic finance course.

We hope that you will pay close attention to this chapter and avoid the temptation to conclude, "I know all this; I don't need to read it." The occasional reading of basic material in your chosen field is an excellent philosophical exercise. Airline pilots know how to get their planes off the ground, but they still use a checklist to do

*The two key concepts in finance are that (1) a dollar today is worth more than a dollar tomorrow and (2) a safe dollar is worth more than a risky dollar.*

so. Ministers know the Ten Commandments but benefit from reading them frequently.

Remember that talk is cheap in the investment business. If someone were to say that she or he knows everything in Chapter 2, we would be tempted to put that person to the test. How many "experts" can do something as "simple" as finding the present value of a growing perpetuity that begins payments in five years? Treat this chapter seriously. Most readers will get their money's worth.

As Chapter 1 pointed out, two key concepts underlie all three divisions of modern finance (banking, corporate finance, and investments). These concepts are (1) a dollar today is worth more than a dollar tomorrow and (2) a safe dollar is worth more than a risky dollar. Anyone who has studied finance recognizes the universal application of these statements in rational decision making.

## Valuation

You can put forth a good argument that *valuation* is the most important part of the study of investments. We are accustomed to comparing something's price tag to the benefit we get from owning it. Someone shopping for a winter coat will consider the brand, the style, comfort, utility, and fit in deciding whether the benefit from owning the coat is sufficient to justify giving up the required fistful of dollars. From life experiences the shopper usually has a reasonable idea of what a winter coat costs and what you can expect from owning one.

Financial investments also have a price tag, but they are harder to interpret. You can buy shares of Harley Davidson (*HDI, NYSE*) common stock for $60 or you can buy Advanced Environmental Recycling Technologies (*AERTA, Nasdaq*) for $1.50. This does not mean, however, that HDI is forty times "as good" as AERTA. Stock prices cannot be directly compared the way you would consider price tags on winter coats. Security analysts make a career of estimating "what you get" for "what you pay," and recommending securities with attractive prices.

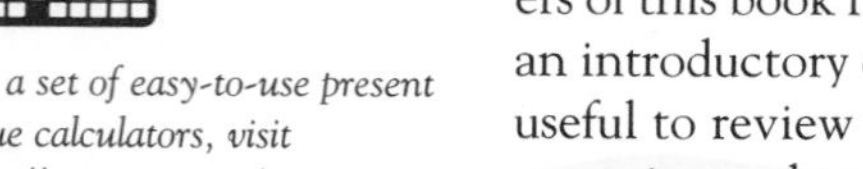

*For a set of easy-to-use present value calculators, visit* http://www.timevalue.com

The time value of money is one of the two key concepts in finance. Most readers of this book have previously studied basic present value/future value principles in an introductory course. While this chapter will not rehash that prior education, it is useful to review these concepts with *growing income streams* because of their importance in stock valuation.

### Growing Income Streams

A *growing* income stream is one in which each successive cash flow is larger than the previous one. A common problem in finance is one in which the cash flows grow by some fixed percentage.

**Growing Annuity.** A **growing annuity** is an annuity in which the cash flows grow at a constant rate $g$. It is of the following form:

$$PV = \frac{C}{1+R} + \frac{C(1+g)}{(1+R)^2} + \frac{C(1+g)^2}{(1+R)^3} + \cdots + \frac{C(1+g)^n}{(1+R)^{n+1}} \quad \textbf{(2-1)}$$

where C = cash flow and $R$ = interest rate.

The growing annuity formula is not common in finance textbooks, but it does appear in forestry applications. Timberland is a potentially important asset class for

PORTFOLIO MEMO

## Derivation of the Closed-Form Equation for the Present Value of a Growing Annuity

Let $C_1$ denote the first of a series of $n$ annual cash payments, with receipt of $C_1$ anticipated one year from today. Subsequent cash payments will increase at a constant rate $g$. Where $R$ denotes the discount rate, the general form of the present value equation for this growing annuity is

$$PV = \frac{C_1}{(1+R)} + \frac{C_1(1+g)}{(1+R)^2} + \frac{C_1(1+g)^2}{(1+R)^3} + \cdots + \frac{C_1(1+g)^n}{(1+R)^n}$$

A growing annuity with $N$ payments is equal to a growing perpetuity beginning at time 0 minus the value of a growing perpetuity beginning at time $N$. This can be readily seen on the time line in Figure 2-1.

The value of the growing annuity, then, is

$$PV = \frac{C_1}{(R-g)} - \frac{C_1(1+g)^N}{(R-g)(1+R)^N}$$
$$= \frac{C_1}{R-g}\left[1 - \left(\frac{1+g}{1+R}\right)^N\right]$$

This is the closed-form solution for the present value of a growing annuity.

**FIGURE 2-1**

The Value of a Growing Annuity

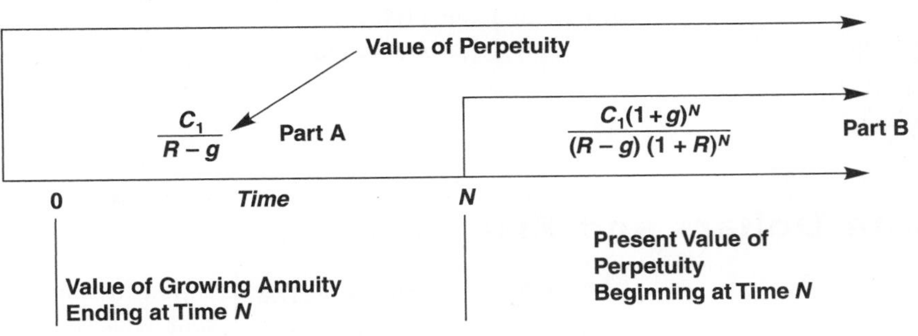


Subtract* part B from part A to get the value of the annuity.

certain institutional investors. Suppose a landowner decides to harvest the timber on a tract of land by cutting one-tenth of the trees each year for ten years (with no replanting). The wood volume grows each year as the trees get bigger, so each year's harvest is likely to be larger than the previous year. A timberland appraiser can estimate these growth rates, associate them with an appropriate required rate of return, and thereby estimate the value of the trees via the growing annuity formula.

**Growing Perpetuity.** If the cash flows continue indefinitely, the cash flow stream is a **growing perpetuity.** This means $n$ in Equation 2-1 equals infinity:

$$PV = \frac{C}{1+R} + \frac{C(1+g)}{(1+R)^2} + \frac{C(1+g)^2}{(1+R)^3} + \cdots + \frac{C(1+g)^\infty}{(1+R)^\infty} \qquad \textbf{(2-2)}$$

The growing perpetuity formula is especially important to security analysts. Many issues of common stock pay a dividend, and common stock has no maturity date: it is a perpetual security. Corporate earnings generally increase through time, leading to a growing dividend stream to the shareholders. If an analyst can estimate this future dividend growth rate, Equation 2-2 can be helpful in determining the value of the stock.

There will be more discussion of this in Chapter 9, Picking the Equity Players. For the moment, though, suppose a stock sells for $115.23 and pays a $1.20 quarterly dividend. If you project a 7 percent dividend growth rate and have a 12 percent required rate of return, you would not find this stock attractive. The present value of the dividends is

$$\frac{\$1.20 \times 4 \times 1.07}{.12 - .07} = \$102.72$$

By this calculation the stock is overpriced by $115.23 – 102.72 = $12.51. Note that to an investor with an 11 percent required rate of return the stock *is* attractive:

$$\frac{\$1.20 \times 4 \times 1.07}{.11 - .07} = \$128.40$$

This calculation indicates that the stock is undervalued by $128.40 – 115.23 = $13.17, or about 11.4%

Table 2-1 shows formulas for some useful mathematical identities related to present value and future value calculations.

## Safe Dollars and Risky Dollars

The second key concept in finance is that "a safe dollar is worth more than a risky dollar." The important point here is that we are talking about *one* safe dollar and *one* risky dollar. Anyone who invests in the stock market is exchanging bird-in-the-hand safe dollars for a chance at a higher number of dollars in the future.

Most investors are **risk averse.** This does not mean that people will not take a risk; it means they will take a risk only if they expect to be adequately rewarded for taking it. People have different degrees of risk aversion; some are more willing to take a chance than others.

### *Choosing Among Risky Alternatives*

Suppose you must choose between the following two alternatives:

Alternative A: $100 for certain
Alternative B: 50 percent chance of $100, 50 percent chance of $0

**TABLE 2-1** USEFUL MATHEMATICAL IDENTITIES IN CASH FLOW VALUATION

Given the following variables:

$R$ = discount rate per period

$g$ = growth rate in payment per period

$C_t$ = payment at end of period $t$

$N$ = total number of annuity payments

$t$ = period in which payment occurs

Annuity:
$$PV = \sum_{t=1}^{N} \frac{C}{(1+R)^t} = C\left[\frac{1}{R} - \frac{1}{R(1+R)^N}\right] \quad (2\text{-}3)$$

Perpetuity:
$$PV = \sum_{t=1}^{\infty} \frac{C}{(1+R)^t} = \frac{C}{R} \quad (2\text{-}4)$$

Growing perpetuity:
$$PV = \sum_{t=1}^{\infty} \frac{C_t(1+g)^{t-1}}{(1+R)^t} = \frac{C_1}{R-g} \quad (2\text{-}5)$$

Growing annuity:
$$PV = \frac{C_1}{R-g}\left[1 - \left(\frac{1+g}{1+R}\right)^N\right] \quad (2\text{-}6)$$

The present value equations for the annuities can be transformed into future value equations by multiplying them by $(1 + R)^N$.

**TABLE 2-2** FOUR INVESTMENT ALTERNATIVES

| A | | B | | C | | D | |
|---|---|---|---|---|---|---|---|
| [1–50] | $110 | [1–50] | $200 | [1–90] | $ 50 | [1–99] | $ 1,000 |
| [51–100] | $ 90 | [51–100] | $ 0 | [91–100] | $550 | [100] | –$89,000 |
| Average payoff | $100 | | $100 | | $100 | | $ 100 |

Number on lottery wheel appears in brackets.

No rational person would select Alternative B. Its average payoff is $50—only half what Alternative A offers for certain.[1]

Now consider another set of choices:

Alternative C: $100 for certain
Alternative D: 50 percent chance of $0, 50 percent chance of $200

Alternative D has an average payoff of $100—the same as Alternative C. Alternative C, however, is *safer* than Alternative D. People do not like risk, and after some thought, all rational individuals should choose the certain $100 over the risky $100.

Consider a more complicated example. Suppose you win the right to spin a lottery wheel one time. The wheel contains numbers 1 through 100, and a pointer selects one number when the wheel stops. Which payoff schedule would you choose from the four alternatives listed in Table 2-2?

Each of the choices has the same average payoff, but the consequences of the two possible outcomes with each choice vary widely. Choice A is the safe alternative in the minds of many people. Choice B offers a reasonable shot at $200. A person

[1] $(0.5 \times \$100) + (0.5 \times \$0) = \$50$.

PORTFOLIO MEMO

## Valuation Examples

*Annuity*

Given: Annual cash flow of \$500 ($C$)
10 years ($N$)
8 percent annual interest rate ($R$)

Find: Present value:

$$PV = C\left[\frac{1}{R} - \frac{1}{R(1+R)^N}\right]$$

$$= \$500\left[\frac{1}{0.08} - \frac{1}{0.08(1.08)^{10}}\right] = \$3,355$$

*Perpetuity*

Given: Annual cash flow of \$500 ($C$) in perpetuity
8 percent annual interest rate ($R$)

$$PV = \frac{C}{R} = \frac{\$500}{0.08} = \$6,250$$

*Growing Perpetuity*

Given: Initial cash flow of \$500 ($C_1$)
Cash flows grow perpetually at 3 percent annually ($g$)
8 percent annual interest rate ($R$)

$$PV = \frac{C_1}{R-g} = \frac{\$500}{0.08-0.03} = \$10,000$$

*Growing Annuity*

Given: Initial cash flow of \$500 ($C_1$)
Cash flows grow at 3 percent annually ($g$)
10 years ($N$)
8 percent annual interest rate ($R$)

$$PV = \frac{C_1}{R-g}\left[1-\left(\frac{1+g}{1+R}\right)^N\right]$$

$$= \frac{500}{0.08-0.03}\left[1-\left(\frac{1.03}{1.08}\right)^{10}\right]$$

$$= \frac{500}{0.05}[1-0.6225] = \$3,775.00$$

who chooses B often reasons, "If my number doesn't come up, at least I haven't lost anything." From an economic point of view, this is faulty logic: the person *did* lose something, and that something is the certain minimum payoff of $90 that is associated with Choice A. This is called an **opportunity cost.** An opportunity cost measures value forgone by choosing one alternative rather than another. In other words, a person who chooses A will get at least $90. The person gives that up by trying for a larger return with the other choices.

*An opportunity cost measures value forgone by choosing one alternative rather than another.*

Choice C offers a much higher possible return than B but ensures that the person will get at least $50. Some people select this alternative partly because of the fun of gambling. They feel that they are not risking much and have a chance at something significant.[2]

What about Choice D? This option has a very high likelihood of a $1,000 payoff. If the lottery wheel stops on the number 100, though, there is a huge loss. Some people (and some investment portfolios) cannot tolerate *any* chance of such a loss, and consequently they would not seriously consider Choice D.

Each of these alternatives has analogies in the investment world. Choice A is much like buying shares of a conservative utility stock. Choice B is akin to purchasing a stock option. Choice C might be a convertible bond that ensures a steady interest income and provides a chance for large gains if the underlying stock rises sharply. The last alternative, D, is similar to a program of writing out-of-the-money call options.[3] With such a program, there is a high likelihood that the options will expire worthless and the holder will keep the option premium, but there is also a small chance that the options will become extremely valuable, in which case the holder is in deep trouble.

## *Defining Risk*

**Risk** is an investment term that everyone knows, yet people often use it incorrectly.

**Risk Versus Uncertainty.** Among the worst culprits in using the word *risk* incorrectly are weather forecasters. They often speak of the risk of a shower tomorrow. Is this really a risky situation? There is a distinction between *risk* and *uncertainty*. Most dictionary definitions of risk say something about a "chance of loss." **Uncertainty** involves only a "doubtful outcome," as in what your parents will give you for a birthday present; there need not be any chance of loss.

*A risky situation must involve a chance of a loss.*

The key is that if a particular outcome does not present the possibility of a loss there is no risk. At a horse racetrack, you might decide that horse 4 is going to win. There is uncertainty about whether or not you are right, but there is no risk unless you make a bet.

The probability of rain is an interesting statistic to most of us. If you are lying in a hospital bed looking out the window, a little rain might be a welcome change and provide some viewing entertainment. However, if you are thinking about leaving some important office work early to paint your garage, the decision to leave work, given a 50 percent chance of rain, is a risky one. If it does rain, your painting plans will get washed out, and you will have wasted the afternoon.

**Dispersion and Chance of Loss.** Experimental psychologists are interested in how people make decisions or arrive at conclusions. Much of this work has been

---

[2]These people are getting utility from playing the game, as we shall see.

[3]This strategy is discussed in Chapter 14.

FIGURE 2-2

Perceptions of Risk

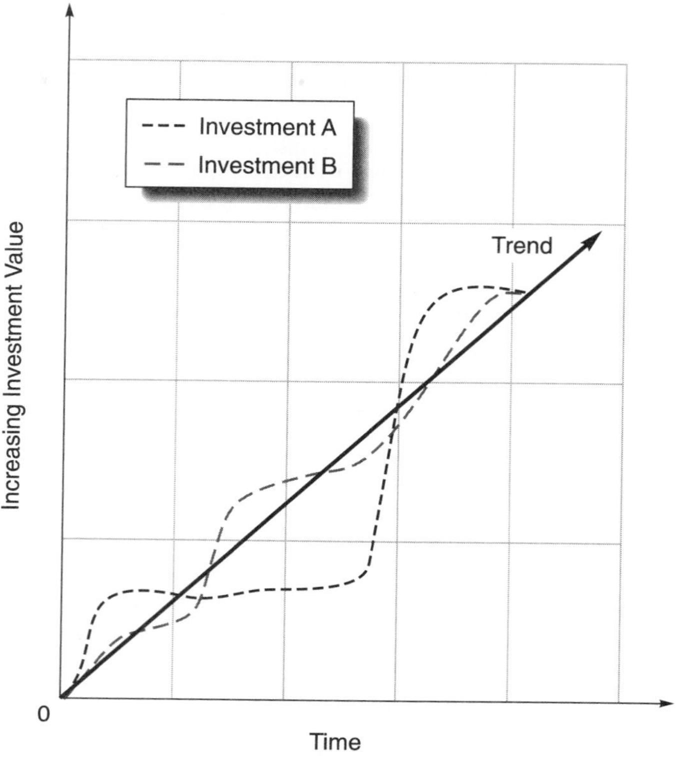


directed toward the general topic of risk assessment. Through this research, we have learned that the average outcome and the scattering of the other possibilities around this average are the two material factors most of us use in arriving at our attitude toward the riskiness of some event. Mathematically speaking, this means we need a measure of central tendency and some measure of dispersion around this mean in order to make a decision.

Consider Figure 2-2. Mathematically, Investments A and B show the same arithmetic mean return over the period shown, but A shows much wider variation around its mean. Even though the investment in A has periodically been worth more than the investment in B, most investors will view Investment B as less risky. This means that statistical dispersion (a quantifiable value) is very often a useful method of assessing risk in security returns.

**Types of Risk.** Risk has numerous subsets, and we will look at many of these in greater detail elsewhere in this book. **Total risk** refers to the overall variability of the returns of a financial asset.

Total risk has two principal components: the undiversifiable and the diversifiable risk components. *Undiversifiable risk* is risk that must be borne by virtue of being in the market. This risk arises from systematic factors that affect all securities of a particular type, such as all common stocks.

*Diversifiable risk* can be removed by proper portfolio diversification. The basic idea is that the ups and downs of individual securities due to company-specific events will cancel one another out. The only return variability that remains will be due to economic events affecting all stocks.

# Relationship Between Risk and Return

The fact that safe dollars are worth more than risky dollars is one of the most important ideas in finance. Understanding this relationship is crucial.

## Direct Relationship

Anyone involved with finance is quite familiar with the fact that there is a relationship between risk and expected return. Figure 2-3 shows this. The more risk someone bears, the higher the expected return. In time value of money problems, the appropriate discount rate depends on the risk level of the investment. Furthermore, some rate of return can be earned without bearing any risk. This is called the **riskless rate of interest,** or simply the *risk-free rate*, in finance theory.

*Riskier securities have higher expected returns.*

Figure 2-3 illustrates two important points. First, the risk/return relationship deals with **expected return.** The expected return is the weighted average of all possible returns with the weights reflecting the relative likelihood of each possible return. It is not correct to say that riskier securities have higher returns, although people often make this statement. If riskier securities *always* had higher returns, they would not be risky. Sometimes a person is hurt by a risk he took and "earns" a negative return. Such is the essence of the risk he is, on average, rewarded for bearing.

The second important point is that the risk we are talking about is unavoidable, or undiversifiable, risk. A person is not rewarded for bearing risk that could have been diversified away. Subsequent chapters elaborate on this point.

## Concept of Utility

**Utility** measures the satisfaction people get out of something. If you have a dollar in your wallet, you get utility from the sense of security the money gives you. You also get utility from pig-out pizza parties and from compact discs for your car's sound

FIGURE 2-3

The Direct Relationship between Risk and Expected Return

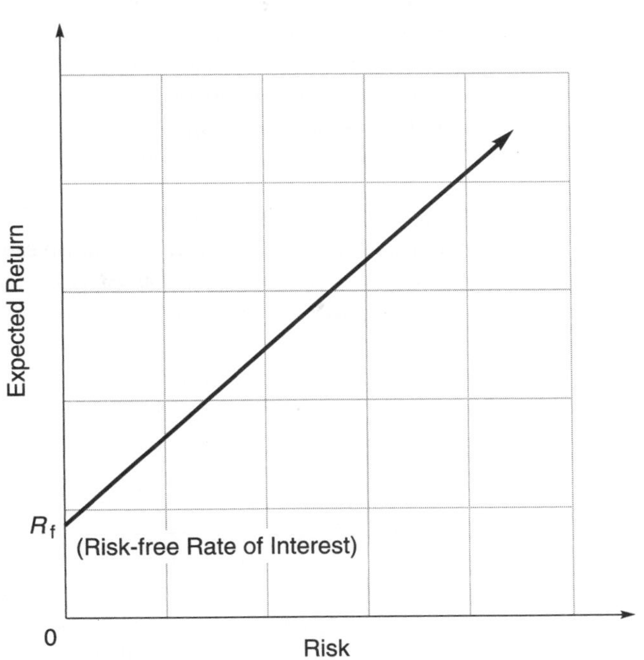

system. Vacationers at a casino know the payoff odds are against them, but still get utility from time at the gaming tables. The key economic fact is that we are individuals, and different individuals get different amounts of utility from the same event.

### Diminishing Marginal Utility of Money

Everything else being equal, rational people prefer more money to less money. The reason for this is that they get utility out of having money; it enables them to do things they otherwise could not. The greater their wealth, the more utility they can get. The economic concept of the **diminishing marginal utility of money** is very useful in explaining certain investor behavior. The concept comes from the fact that the relationship between more money and the consequent added utility is not linear. This is an intuitive result that is easy to illustrate with a few examples.

If a homeless person does not know when she will get the next meal, finding a $5 bill is a windfall gain. There is substantial utility from the discovery. Finding a second $5 bill a few minutes later will effectively double the utility for our impoverished person. In contrast, Bill Gates also feels good about finding a $5 bill and also gets utility but not very much. The extra money will not alter a billionaire's lifestyle in any appreciable way.

What about losing rather than winning? To see an example of this, let's replace our street person and billionaire with Division III and Division I-A collegiate baseball teams from the same city. If these teams schedule a game with each other, the Division I-A team is *supposed* to win. In most cases, it would not accomplish much by beating the team from the smaller school, but it would lose a lot if it were to be upset. For the I-A team, the lost utility from the defeat is much greater than the added utility from a win.

Figure 2-4 illustrates this concept. Starting with an initial wealth of $10,000, a gain of $10,000 might have an associated added utility of 2.7, whereas a loss of $10,000 involves a loss of 15.6 in utility. For a starting point of $50,000, however, the utility of a gain of $10,000 is nearly equal in magnitude to the utility of a loss of the same amount.

*"I hate to lose more than I like to win" is an example of diminishing marginal utility.*

Tennis player Ivan Lendl once made a statement that illustrates this same concept in a slightly different way. He said, "I hate to lose more than I like to win." At the time he made the statement, Lendl was winning most tournaments in which he played. He expected to win and was disturbed if he did not. There was utility associated with winning a tournament, but more was lost if a lower-ranked player upset him.

### St. Petersburg Paradox

*Expected utility is more consistent with human behavior than expected monetary value.*

The **St. Petersburg paradox** is a useful exercise illustrating the relationship among risk, expected return, and utility. Imagine a game in which participants pay an entry fee of $x$ dollars. Someone flips a coin repeatedly until a head appears, at which time the game ends. Prior to the appearance of the first head, there can be zero, one, two, ten, or conceivably an infinite number of successive tails. The payoff to the players is based on the number of tails (call this $n$) observed before the first head, and the payoff is calculated as $\$2^n$. What is the expected payoff from playing this game one time? To find out, we can construct a worksheet similar to Table 2-3.

It is mathematically possible that the players could have a very large number of successive tails before the appearance of the first head. In the limit, where the number of tails is infinite, the expected payoff from playing this game is also infinite. Here is the kicker: how much would you be willing to pay to play this game? Remember that its expected payoff is infinite. Would you pay $1 million? How about $10,000? In actual practice, few people will pay more than a couple of dollars for a chance at

FIGURE 2-4

Diminishing Marginal Utility of Money

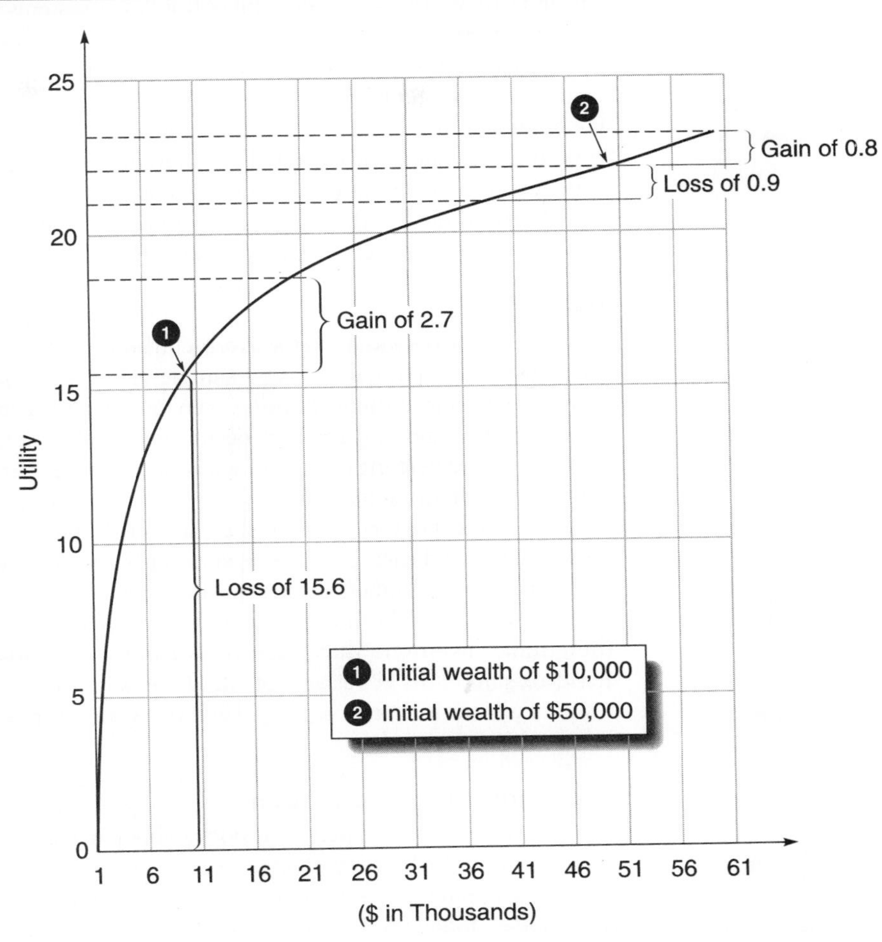


TABLE 2-3 ST. PETERSBURG PARADOX

| *Number of Tails before First Head* | *Probability* | *Payoff* | *Probability × Payoff* |
|---|---|---|---|
| 0 | $(1/2)^1 = 1/2$ | $ 1 | $0.50 |
| 1 | $(1/2)^2 = 1/4$ | $ 2 | $0.50 |
| 2 | $(1/2)^3 = 1/8$ | $ 4 | $0.50 |
| 3 | $(1/2)^4 = 1/16$ | $ 8 | $0.50 |
| 4 | $(1/2)^5 = 1/32$ | $16 | $0.50 |
| . . . | . . . | . . . | . . . |
| n | $(1/2)^{n+1}$ | $\$2^n$ | $0.50 |
| Total | 1.00 | | ∞ |

this infinite wealth. The best explanation for this stems from the fact that although each successive tail adds $0.50 to the expected payoff, the marginal utility of each additional $0.50 declines. Marginal *utility* refers to the incremental satisfaction associated with the additional payoff. An important column missing from Table 2-3 is a measurement of the added utility each additional $0.50 provides. The important statistic is not so much the expected payoff in dollars but the expected payoff in utility. The cost of playing the game represents an immediate loss of utility. Most players would determine that the expected future benefit is never great enough to outweigh the utility forgone when they pay the entry fee.

### Fair Bets

A **fair bet** is defined as a lottery in which the expected payoff is equal to the cost of playing. Matching quarters is an example of a fair bet game. Two people both toss quarters with one of them choosing even or odd. *Even* can occur (both heads or both tails), in two ways and *odd* can occur (head/tail or tail/head) in two ways. Each player has a 50 percent chance of winning the other person's quarter and a 50 percent chance of losing his own.

Instead of quarters, suppose the game deals with serial numbers on $100 bills. Two people could each pull one from his or her wallet and then bet on whether the sum of the serial numbers on the two bills is even or odd. There is still a 50 percent chance of winning, but most people probably would not play this game. It is likely they would determine that the utility they stand to lose exceeds the utility they stand to gain. This is because of the diminishing marginal utility of wealth. The result of all this is that most people will not take a fair bet unless the dollar amount involved is quite small.

*Most people will not take a fair bet.*

### The Consumption Decision

Libraries have shelves filled with books about what interest rates are, where they come from, and why they change. Interest rates are complicated statistics. In the simplest sense, an interest rate represents the extent to which people are willing to trade dollars today for dollars tomorrow. Economists talk about this in terms of our **consumption decision,** which is the choice we all make about whether to save or to borrow. If interest rates are high, we are inclined to open savings accounts or add to ones we already have. When interest rates are low, there is not much incentive to save, but borrowing looks attractive. We can afford a higher home mortgage, a new car, or a vacation in St. Barthelemy.

The term *consumption* does not necessarily have anything to do with food. In economic terms, if you have a dollar, you can do one of two things with it: *save* it or *consume* it. Consuming it simply means spending it; saving it amounts to a decision to consume it later.

The consumption decision needs to be made under the umbrella of the utility concept. Suppose that one hundred randomly selected people were asked this question: "Which would you prefer, $100 right now or $150 in one year?" These numbers reflect a 50 percent annual interest rate, and many people would recognize that there is a clear advantage to waiting a year for the higher amount. To a college student with little money, however, an extraordinary amount of utility might be associated with getting an unexpected $100 right now. It is a safe bet that many college students would take the money and run.

Let us revise the example slightly. Suppose we asked every person in the United States which he or she would prefer, $100 now or $100 in one year. Virtually all would take the money now; there is no reason to wait, because the interest rate associated with waiting is zero. Given the choice between $100 now and $106 in one year, we would find that some people would choose to wait. This means that they would forgo some current consumption in favor of future consumption. If the ante were upped to $108 in one year, many more would wait. Virtually everyone offered $10,000 in one year would wait.[4]

Banks, corporations, and individuals all want to borrow money as inexpensively as possible. Savers want to earn as much interest as possible. In essence, the entire country plays the game just described until the market clears. Zero percent is too low; 10,000 percent is too high. Somewhere in between is an equilibrium value. This equilibrium interest rate causes savers to deposit a sufficient amount of money to satisfy the borrowing needs of the economy.

## *Other Considerations*

Before this review ends, two other risk and return issues warrant a brief comment.

**Psychic Return.** **Psychic return** is something that people frequently experience. It comes from an individual disposition about something. Why, for instance, do so many people in the investment business wear Rolex watches? Why do people like designer jeans that may have no better quality than pants that cost one-third as much? A $20 watch will keep time to within a second a month. Is the Rolex more accurate? Are the designer jeans three times as comfortable? The answer, of course, is that people get utility from the watch and the jeans. They feel good about themselves when they wear these things. These benefits are called *psychic return* and are very real.

Someone once said that she could not see spending thousands of dollars on a vacation because when the trip was over, she would not have anything to show for it. A new car, however, is a tangible item; with this purchase she would have something to show for her money. There is a problem with this logic, of course. Many people say that vacations last forever; the good memories provide psychic return for a long time after an automobile is in the junkyard.

**Price Risk versus Convenience Risk.** As stated, *risk* refers to chance of loss. The loss, however, is not necessarily a financial one.

***Price Risk.*** **Price risk** refers to the possibility of adverse changes in the value of an investment because of changing market conditions, a change in the financial situation of the issuing firm, or a change in the public attitude toward a particular investment. When interest rates rise, bond prices decline. Rising interest rates also usually cause stock prices to fall. A change in the price of gold often accompanies a change in the value of the U.S. dollar. A bond's price will fall if Standard and Poor's lowers its bond rating. Stock prices tend to move as a group, so even though a particular firm may be very healthy, a large drop in the Dow Jones Industrial Average will probably cause its stock to fall in value as well. All of these events are examples of price risk.

***Convenience Risk.*** Convenience risk may not manifest itself directly in the value of a security. **Convenience risk** refers to a loss of managerial time rather than a loss of dollars. The level of convenience risk also may not be the same for the various security

---

[4]This assumes that the $10,000 is free of default risk.

holders. One example of convenience risk lies in the *call provision* that many bonds have. This feature permits the issuer to call in the debt early, meaning that a bondholder will have to replace the called bond with some other investment. This involves some research time and probably some added brokerage fees. For a portfolio manager with many accounts, replacing called bonds is a time-consuming nuisance.

South African Krugerrands provide a historical example. These coins were once the most popular form of private gold ownership. As part of the global sanctions against South Africa in the 1970s, however, the United States prohibited the importation of Krugerrands for a number of years, although those coins already here were permitted to remain. For the Krugerrand holder, selling the bullion coin at a reasonable price became more difficult. Some dealers did not want to bother with the coin at all, whereas others would do so only at a discounted price. Investment in Krugerrands became less convenient because of changes in government regulations and public policy.

## The Concept of Return

The relationship between risk and return is of foremost importance in finance. "Return" can mean various things, and it is important to be clear when discussing an investment.

### Measurable Return

Return is the ultimate objective in any investment program. A general definition of **return** is "the benefit associated with an investment." People invest money to get a return on it. In most cases, the bulk of their return is measurable; they can count it precisely. A $100 investment at 8 percent, compounded continuously, for instance, is worth $108.33 after one year. The return is $8.33, or 8.33 percent.

**Holding Period Return.** Many investments have two components to the measurable return: (1) a capital gain or loss and (2) some form of income. Suppose someone buys a bond for $950, receives $80 in interest, and later sells the bond for $980. The return equals the income received ($80) plus the capital gain ($30) all divided by your purchase price of $950:

$$\begin{aligned}\text{Return} &= \frac{\text{Income} + \text{Capital gain}}{\text{Purchase price}} \\ &= \frac{\$80 + \$30}{\$950} \qquad \textbf{(2-7)} \\ &= 11.58\%\end{aligned}$$

The return calculated in Equation 2-7 is a **holding period return** because its calculation is independent of the passage of time. We know only that there is a beginning and an end. The 11.58 percent might have been earned over one year or one week. It is important to be careful interpreting holding period returns in investment analysis, as we will see later in the book.

*The calculation of a holding period return is independent of the passage of time.*

**Arithmetic Mean Return.** Statistics useful in portfolio construction (such as covariance or standard deviation) deal with a series of holding period returns. It is important that all the holding periods be of equal length. You cannot meaningfully combine monthly and daily returns.

**TABLE 2-4** SAMPLE WEEKLY STOCK RETURNS

| *Week* | *Return* | *Return Relative** |
|---|---|---|
| 1 | 0.0084 | 1.0084 |
| 2 | –0.0045 | 0.9955 |
| 3 | 0.0021 | 1.0021 |
| 4 | 0.0000 | 1.0000 |
| 5 | 0.0059 | 1.0059 |
| 6 | –0.0063 | 0.9937 |
| 7 | 0.0043 | 1.0043 |
| 8 | 0.0072 | 1.0072 |
| 9 | –0.0067 | 0.9933 |
| 10 | 0.0063 | 1.0063 |

*A return relative is the return plus 1.

Suppose we observe the series of weekly stock returns shown in Table 2-4. To calculate the arithmetic average of these, also called the **mean** or **arithmetic mean,** we use Equation 2-8:

$$\text{Arithmetic mean} = \sum_{i=1}^{n} \frac{\tilde{R}_i}{n} \tag{2-8}$$

$\tilde{R}_i$ is the rate of return in period $i$. For the numbers in Table 2-4, the mean is 0.00167.

Arithmetic means are a useful proxy for the concept of expected return, but they are not especially useful for describing historical return data.[5] The problem is that it is unclear exactly what the number means once it is determined. To see why this is the case, first consider an alternate measure of the mean.

**Geometric Mean Return.** The **geometric mean** return is the $n$th root of the product of $n$ values, calculated via Equation 2-9:

$$\text{Geometric mean} = \left[\prod_{i=1}^{n}\left(1+\tilde{R}_i\right)\right]^{\frac{1}{n}} - 1 \tag{2-9}$$

The Greek capital letter pi ($\Pi$) stands for *product summation*. This means that instead of adding the values in the series, they are multiplied. The rest of the equation indicates that after multiplying the returns, we take the $n$th root of the product, where $n$ is the number of terms in the series.

Calculating the geometric mean of a series of returns has a potential problem because returns are often negative. If the number of negative returns in a series is odd, their product will be negative, and a negative number does not have an even root.

Fortunately, it is easy to eliminate the problems this would cause. It is common practice in finance to convert security returns into return relatives before calculating statistics on them. A **return relative** is simply the return plus 1.[6] Table 2-4 shows the return relatives.

---

[5]Other statistical moments such as variance also depend on the arithmetic mean.

[6]This means, then, that a 100 percent return (doubling the money) results in a return relative of 2.0.

The geometric mean return relative, then, is

$$(1.0084 \times 0.9955 \times 1.0021 \times 1 \times 1.0059 \times 0.9937 \times 1.0043 \times 1.0072 \times 0.9933 \times 1.0063)^{1/10} = 1.0167^{0.1} = 1.00166$$

Subtract 1 to turn this return relative back into a return, giving a geometric mean return of 0.00166 or 0.166 percent.

**Comparison of Arithmetic and Geometric Mean Returns.** An attractive feature of the geometric mean return is that its use reduces the likelihood of nonsense answers with financial rates of return. It is easy to show how this can happen.

Consider a $100 investment that falls in value by 50 percent in Period 1 but then rises by 50 percent in Period 2. What is the average rate of return? According to the arithmetic mean, it is 0: [(0.50) + (–0.50)]/2 = 0. This, however, is not logical. After one period, the value of the investment is down to $50. In the second period, it rises by 50 percent to become $75. It obviously did *not* break even, despite the fact that the "average" return was 0.

The geometric mean will yield a more meaningful result. After forming return relatives, we get the following answer:

$$[(1.50)(0.50)]^{0.5} = 0.866$$
$$0.866 - 1.000 = -0.134 = -13.4\%$$

The true average return on this investment was a loss of 13.4 percent per period. Most of the time in finance we are interested in the rate of return that equates a present value with a series of futures values. The geometric mean must be used to investigate this relationship.

*The greater the dispersion in a series of numbers, the greater the gap between the arithmetic and geometric means.*

The greater the dispersion in a series of numbers, the wider the gap between the arithmetic mean and the geometric mean. In essence, the geometric mean penalizes variance.[7] We can see this readily with an example. Consider Table 2-5 and Figure 2-5. All three series have the same arithmetic mean, 3.70. Their geometric means, however, differ widely. Series B has only a slight difference between the two measures (3.63 versus 3.70) because the components of this series have very little fluctuation. The widest gap occurs with Series C, containing numbers ranging from 1 to 9.

*In finance, what happened in the past is not as important as what happens in the future.*

**Expected Return.** In any financial application, what happened in the past is not nearly as important as what happens in the future. Security analysts are not paid to be historians; they are paid to be prophets.

**TABLE 2-5** COMPARISON OF ARITHMETIC AND GEOMETRIC MEANS

| *Series* | *Outcomes* | *Arithmetic Mean* | *Geometric Mean* |
|---|---|---|---|
| A | 5,3,5,4,3,3,2,4,3,5 | 3.70 | 3.56 |
| B | 4,4,2,4,4,4,4,3,4,4 | 3.70 | 3.63 |
| C | 8,7,9,1,1,1,1,3,3,3 | 3.70 | 2.59 |

[7]Note, however, that the order of the returns is irrelevant in the geometric mean return calculation.

FIGURE 2-5

Geometric Versus Arithmetic Mean

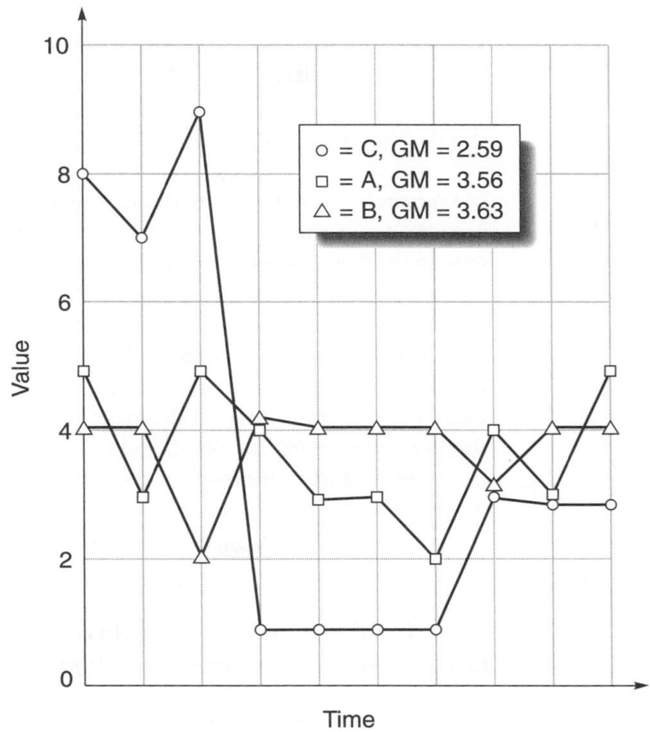


Arithmetic mean = 3.70. Lines show best fit through data points.

People often talk about a security's return in reference to the future. This can be confusing, because technically *return* refers to the past; *expected return* refers to the future. We do not know the future, but we can use past information to make some estimates about it. It is good practice to get in the habit of saying "expected return" when that is what is meant.

## Return on Investment

**Return on investment (ROI)** is a phrase widely used by both investment professionals and nonexperts. Unfortunately, the term very often causes confusion when someone uses it without elaboration.

Suppose a person buys a house for $100,000 by putting up a $10,000 down payment and getting a $90,000 mortgage. Two years later, the person has the house appraised and finds it is worth $120,000. What has been his return on investment? The answer depends on how we look at the problem. One person might observe that the value of the house rose $20,000. Relative to the $100,000 purchase price, this is a holding period return of 20 percent. Another person might view things differently. If the house were sold for $120,000, the owner would receive about $30,000 after paying off the mortgage. Investing $10,000 and walking away with $30,000 constitutes a 200 percent holding period return. So which return is correct: 20 percent or 200 percent?

*The use of leverage can dramatically shift an investor's return.*

The problem here is the use of two different measures of return. The first person calculated **return on assets (ROA);** the second calculated **return on equity (ROE).** Although someone might use return on investment to refer to either of these calculations, they are obviously quite different. ROE is a leveraged version of ROA. Avoid using the term ROI without first making sure that everyone understands what you mean.

**Measuring Total Risk.** Risk assessment is one of the most important aspects of modern financial management. Before embarking on any investment, a person should understand both the expected returns and the likely riskiness of those returns. The following sections discuss three important measures of total risk.

***Standard Deviation and Variance.*** Standard deviation and variance, two related statistics, are the most common measures of total risk. They measure the dispersion of a set of observations around the mean, or average, observation. Equation 2-10 shows the general formula for the calculation of variance. The standard deviation is the square root of the variance.

$$\text{Variance} = \sigma^2 = \sum_{i=1}^{n} \text{prob}(x_i)[x_i - \bar{x}]^2 \tag{2-10}$$

where $\bar{x}$ is the arithmetic mean return. If all possible outcomes are equally likely, then Equation 2-10 reduces to Equation 2-11:

$$\sigma^2 = \frac{1}{n}\sum_{i=1}^{n}[x_i - \bar{x}]^2 \tag{2-11}$$

Table 2-6 is a worksheet to calculate the variance of Series A from Table 2-5.

Most often in finance we are dealing with sample data rather than with the entire population of data. With sample data, the sum of the squared deviations should be divided by $n - 1$ rather than $n$. This statistical fine point ensures that our sample standard deviation or variance is an unbiased estimate of the true, or population, statistic. (With large samples, this adjustment makes little difference.)

**TABLE 2-6** CALCULATION OF VARIANCE

| $(x_i - \bar{x})^2$ | $prob(x_i)$ | $x_i \times prob(x_i)$ |
|---|---|---|
| $(5 - 3.70)^2 = 1.69$ | 0.10 | 0.169 |
| $(3 - 3.70)^2 = 0.49$ | 0.10 | 0.049 |
| $(5 - 3.70)^2 = 1.69$ | 0.10 | 0.169 |
| $(4 - 3.70)^2 = 0.09$ | 0.10 | 0.009 |
| $(3 - 3.70)^2 = 0.49$ | 0.10 | 0.049 |
| $(3 - 3.70)^2 = 0.49$ | 0.10 | 0.049 |
| $(2 - 3.70)^2 = 2.89$ | 0.10 | 0.289 |
| $(4 - 3.70)^2 = 0.09$ | 0.10 | 0.009 |
| $(3 - 3.70)^2 = 0.49$ | 0.10 | 0.049 |
| $(5 - 3.70)^2 = 1.69$ | 0.10 | 0.169 |
| | | Variance = 1.010 |

Standard deviation = $(\text{Variance})^{0.5} = 1.005$.

PORTFOLIO MEMO

## The Problem with Total Return

When asked to calculate total return, the majority of people would prepare a statistic like the holding period return in Equation 2-7:

$$\text{Return} = \frac{\text{Income} + \text{Capital gain}}{\text{Purchase price}}$$

Although this looks reasonable enough, the issue can be confounded in security analysis.

Consider the following example.* Companies A, B, and C are identical in every respect except for their dividend payout ratios. Company A pays 50 percent of its earnings as dividends, Company B pays 0 percent, and Company C pays 100 percent. Each company has earnings per share of $10.00 in the first year. Table 2-7 shows the associated values over a three-year period.

*This example is adapted from Marshall A. Geiger and David Kirch, "What Does 'Total Return' Really Mean? A Comment," *Journal of Portfolio Management*, Summer 1989, 80–81. This copyrighted material is reprinted with permission from Institutional Investor, Inc.

**TABLE 2-7** COMPARISON OF TOTAL RETURNS

| *Company A* | *Year 1* | *Year 2* | *Year 3* | *Total* |
|---|---|---|---|---|
| Earnings | $10.00 | $10.50 | $11.025 | |
| Dividends | 5.00 | 5.25 | 5.51 | $15.76 |
| Market price | 100.00 | 105.00 | 110.25 | |

$$\text{Total return} = \frac{(110.25 - 100.00) + 15.76}{100.00} = 26.01\%$$

| *Company B* | *Year 1* | *Year 2* | *Year 3* | *Total* |
|---|---|---|---|---|
| Earnings | $10.00 | $11.00 | $12.10 | |
| Dividends | 0 | 0 | 0 | $0.00 |
| Market price | 100.00 | 110.00 | 121.00 | |

$$\text{Total return} = \frac{(121.00 - 100.00) + 0}{100.00} = 21.00\%$$

| *Company C* | *Year 1* | *Year 2* | *Year 3* | *Total* |
|---|---|---|---|---|
| Earnings | $10.00 | $10.00 | $10.00 | |
| Dividends | 10.00 | 10.00 | 10.00 | $30.00 |
| Market price | 100.00 | 100.00 | 100.00 | |

$$\text{Total return} = \frac{(100.00 - 100.00) + 30.00}{100.00} = 30.00\%$$

Assume a constant price earnings ratio of 10.

PORTFOLIO MEMO

## The Problem with Total Return, *continued*

These three companies are similar in every respect except for their dividend payouts, yet the holding period returns calculated over this three-year period differ widely. For firms that are otherwise similar, this measure of return seems to produce the highest value for the firm with the highest dividend payout ratio.

The caveat behind the data in Table 2-7 is that the present value of growth opportunities is missing. This should be considered if you assume that the price/earnings ratio remains constant.†

†See Richard A. Brealey and Stewart C. Myers, *Principles of Corporate Finance*, 7th ed. (New York: McGraw-Hill, 2003) for a good elaboration of this important point.

***Semi-variance.*** **Semi-variance** is less familiar to most people than variance, but it has considerable appeal as a risk measurement tool. *Variance* considers the dispersion on both sides of the mean. *Semi-variance* considers the dispersion only on the adverse side. For instance, on a stock with an average monthly return of 1.4 percent, a week when the stock advances 5 percent contributes significantly to the variance of the price series. The windfall gain is not bad; it is a favorable outcome. A 25 percent loss, however, would be very unfortunate. The calculation of semi-variance throws out all observations that are greater than the mean and proceeds to calculate variance using only the remaining "bad" returns that are less than average.

Table 2-8 illustrates semi-variance using the data from Table 2-6. Semi-variance calculations are not common, but the concept is appealing in many ways. Given that *risk* means "chance of loss," we can argue that winning outcomes should not be included in the risk calculation. Substantial dispersion can actually come from positive outcomes, and this distorts the variance or standard deviation statistic as a measure of risk.

**Geometric Mean Return.** As previously mentioned, the geometric mean return captures both the mean and the dispersion around the mean in a single statistic. When we need to make comparisons among several series of data values, the geometric mean can measure risk and return simultaneously.

# Some Statistical Facts of Life

H.G. Wells said, "Statistical thinking will one day be as necessary for effective citizenship as the ability to read and write." Portfolio managers need statistical fluency *now*. The section that follows reviews the fundamentals.

### *Definitions*

Terminology is important in statistics. A few critical definitions are reviewed here.

**Constants.** A constant is a value that does not change. The number of sides of a cube is a constant, as is the number 8 and the sum of the interior angles of a triangle. A constant can be represented by a numeral (such as 6) or by a symbol (such as $x$ or $\pi$).

**TABLE 2-8** CALCULATION OF SEMI-VARIANCE

| $x_i$ | $prob(x_i)$ | | $x_i \times prob(x_i)$ |
|---|---|---|---|
| $(5-3.70)^2 = 1.69$ | | Ignore | |
| $(3-3.70)^2 = 0.49$ | 0.10 | | 0.049 |
| $(5-3.70)^2 = 1.69$ | | Ignore | |
| $(4-3.70)^2 = 0.09$ | | Ignore | |
| $(3-3.70)^2 = 0.49$ | 0.10 | | 0.049 |
| $(3-3.70)^2 = 0.49$ | 0.10 | | 0.049 |
| $(2-3.70)^2 = 2.89$ | 0.10 | | 0.289 |
| $(4-3.70)^2 = 0.09$ | | Ignore | |
| $(3-3.70)^2 = 0.49$ | 0.10 | | 0.049 |
| $(5-3.70)^2 = 1.69$ | | Ignore | |
| | | | Semi-variance = 0.485 |

**Variables.** A variable is a phenomenon with no fixed value. It is useful only when it is considered in the context of other possible values it might assume. If you go to your library and randomly choose a book from the card catalog, the number of pages it contains is a random variable, perhaps 44. The usefulness of this number lies in the fact that you have experience with other books, and based on that experience know that a book of 44 pages is short. In contrast, if you learn that the steam entropy inside a turbine engine is 1.2, this probably means very little unless you know the other values the variable might assume.

Technically, we determine a value for a variable by conducting an *experiment*. This might be as simple as looking at a car's instrument panel to see how fast the car is traveling. In finance, we formally call variables *random* variables, to further stress their nonfixed nature. A random variable is designated by a tilde (~, pronounced "TIL-duh") over it (for example, $\tilde{x}$). Constants appear without a tilde.

Random variables come from a **stochastic** process. This means that the variable might assume more than one possible value. Flipping a coin (with two possible outcomes) is a stochastic process, as is rolling a die (six possible outcomes) or guessing a football score (theoretically an infinite number of outcomes).

*Discrete random variables are counted; continuous random variables are measured.*

Variables can be **discrete** or **continuous.** We *count* discrete random variables; we *measure* continuous random variables. Length, for instance, is a continuous random variable. When you measure the length of a brook trout, you can be as precise as you wish, depending on the accuracy of your ruler. The number of trout you catch, however, is a discrete random variable. You catch only whole fish; the one that got away does not count as a half, nor does an unusually large one count double.

Variables can also be **quantitative** or **qualitative.** We measure quantitative variables by real numbers; numerical measurements are an example. Qualitative variables are categorical. Hair color, state of residence, and primary portfolio objective (such as growth) are examples.

Variables may be independent or dependent. A researcher observes the value of an **independent variable** directly, whereas determining the value of a **dependent variable** first requires the measurement of other independent variables.

The volume of a box is a dependent variable. To solve for it, we must first measure its length, width, and height. The height of the box, though, does not depend on any other measurement; it is independent of the box's other dimensions.

**Populations.** Random variables reside in a **population.** This is the entire collection of a particular set of random variables. The outcome of the throw of a single die is a

FIGURE 2-6

University of Maine Hockey Team (1977–2004)

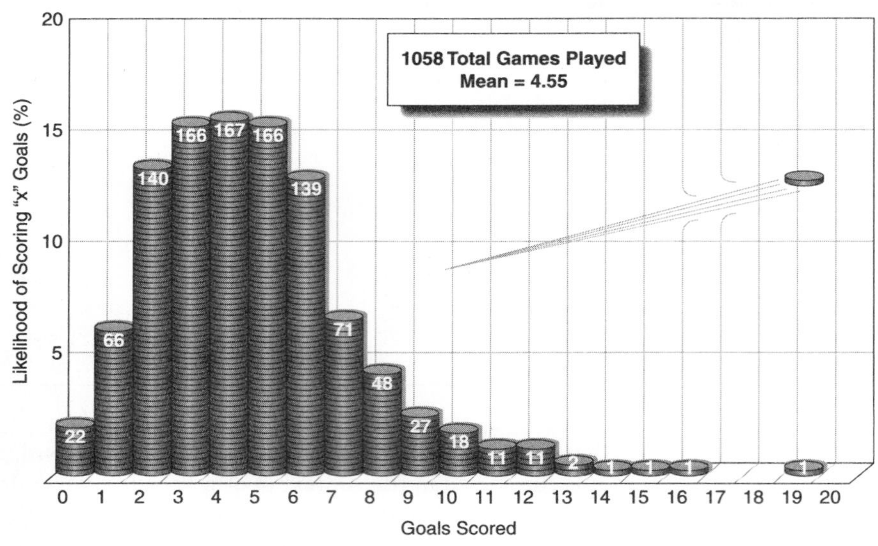


random variable coming from a population of six elements: 1, 2, 3, 4, 5, or 6. These are the only possible outcomes.[8] The nature of a population is described by its **distribution.** Figure 2-6 shows the distribution of goals the University of Maine hockey team has scored over its entire history through the end of the 2003–2004 season. The average number of goals scored in these 1058 games is 4.55. This is the arithmetic mean. Other measures of the central tendency of the distribution are the *median* and the *mode*. The point in a distribution where half the observations lie on either side is the **median** value. The value in a distribution that occurs most frequently is the **mode.** In this distribution of hockey scores, the median is 5 and the mode is 4.

Note that this distribution is not symmetrical. It shows **skewness,** because there is more dispersion on the high side of the mean than on the low side; it is skewed to the right.[9] A distribution that is skewed to the right has a mean that is greater than the median. This condition is also called *positive skewness*. Not surprisingly, a distribution that is skewed to the left has negative skewness and a mean that is less than the median. Stock returns are positively skewed because they are unbounded on the upside but can decline only by a maximum of 100 percent.

Some distributions are **binomial.** This means they contain only two random variables. Figure 2-7 shows the number of goals the University of Maine hockey team has scored during overtime. In ice hockey, overtime is sudden death. Once a team scores, the game is over. This means that during overtime, each team either scores one goal or does not score at all.

A card drawn at random from a deck yields an observation of a random variable from its distribution. A deck of cards is a *finite* population because we know in advance each of the possible outcomes. There are only fifty-two possibilities, and we know precisely what they are.

---

[8]These random variables come from a *uniform* distribution because they all have an equal likelihood of occurring. Other well-known distributions from statistics include the normal, binomial, Poisson, chi-square, exponential, and *F* distributions.

[9]Stock returns also have this characteristic, although only slightly. Stock can theoretically rise in value indefinitely, but it can fall only to zero.

FIGURE 2-7

Maine Hockey Team Goals Scored in Overtime (1977–2004)

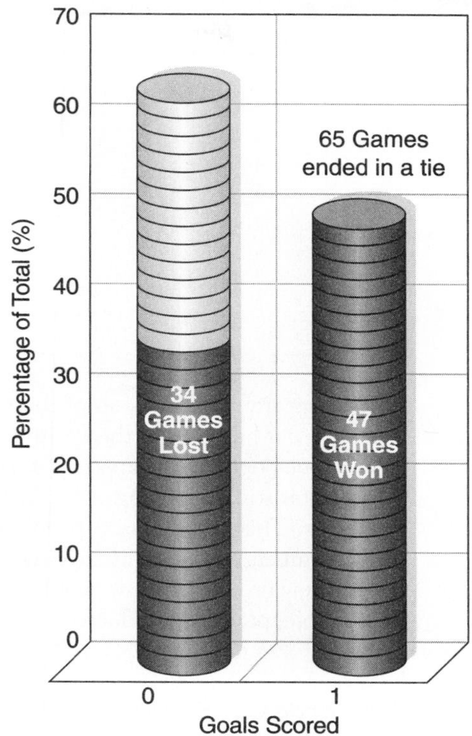


Some populations are *infinite*. For all practical purposes, the microorganisms in a cubic mile of ocean water constitute an infinite number of creatures, any of which might wind up under a zoologist's microscope. We could never count precisely how many of the little beasts are there.

Populations also may be **univariate, bivariate,** or **multivariate,** depending on the number of variables of interest. A univariate population has one variable of interest. A bivariate has two, and a multivariate has more than two. A jar might contain marbles of different colors, sizes, and weights. If we are interested in each characteristic of the marble, we take a sample marble from a multivariate population. If color does not matter, the population is bivariate. If only color matters, the population is univariate.

**Samples.** When the zoologist puts a dropper of ocean water on a microscope slide, she is sampling the population. A **sample** is any subset of a population. The zoologist can draw one or more samples as she attempts to learn about characteristics of the population.

A security analyst might be interested in measuring the standard deviation of returns of a particular common stock. To do this, the analyst might sample the past series of security price returns by using monthly closing prices over the past five years and then use these numbers to estimate the standard deviation statistic.

**Sample Statistics.** The beta thus determined is a **sample statistic.** Statistics are characteristics of samples. If an analyst samples the distribution properly, he will be

**TABLE 2-9** HYPOTHETICAL STOCK RETURNS

| *Month* | *Stock A* | *Stock B* |
|---|---|---|
| 1 | +2 % | +3 % |
| 2 | −1 | 0 |
| 3 | +4 | +5 |
| 4 | +1 | +2 |
| 5 | +2 | +3 |
| 6 | −2 | −2 |
| 7 | +5 | +5 |
| 8 | −1 | +1 |
| 9 | 0 | −1 |
| 10 | +3 | +4 |

able to specify the precision of the sample statistic compared with what would be discovered if he sampled the entire population.

A true population statistic is usually unobservable and must be estimated with a sample statistic. Checking the entire population is expensive and statistically unnecessary. This is the reason people involved in market research survey seemingly small numbers of people in arriving at conclusions about how the public is likely to view a new product or how people will vote in an election. A nationwide survey of 600 people, properly conducted, can result in very accurate information about how the other 293 million U.S. citizens probably feel.

### *Properties of Random Variables*

The mathematics of diversification stem from certain *properties* of random variables. To illustrate these properties, imagine that we have observed two new stock issues over the past ten months and that the information in Table 2-9 is the complete history of monthly returns for these two securities.

**Central Tendency.** Perhaps the most important characteristic of a population is its central tendency, or what one of its random variables "looks like," on average. This is what customers want from their car mechanics when they ask for cost estimates of brake jobs and engine tune-ups. If the repair shop is professional, its estimates are unbiased. They are sometimes low and sometimes high, but they are generally accurate.

The usual measure of central tendency is the population's expected value, or mean. This is merely the average value of all elements of the population. Some elements are larger and some are smaller, but they average out to some number. In finance, we often call this number the *expected value*.

The expected value of the returns of Stocks A and B in Table 2-9 is appropriately called the *expected return*.[10] There are ten return observations for each of the two securities. If we pick one observation at random, presumably each month stands an equal chance of being selected. To arrive at each security's expected return, we average the ten returns.[11] In symbols,

---

[10]Of course, we must be careful extrapolating the past into the future. There is no guarantee that the future distribution of stock returns will be identical to the past distribution.

[11]Technically,

$$E(\tilde{R}_i) = \sum_{i=1}^{n} \tilde{R}_i \text{prob}(i)$$

where prob($i$) = the probability of observing the particular return $R_i$. If all observations are equally likely, we arrive at Equation 2-12.

$$E(\tilde{R}_i) = \frac{1}{n}\sum_{i=1}^{n}\tilde{R}_i \qquad \textbf{(2-12)}$$

(The E with parentheses following it is common finance shorthand for the expected value operator.)

Summing the returns for Stock A gives a total of 13 percent. The expected return is therefore 1/10 × 13%, or 1.3%; for Stock B the value is 1/10 × 20%, or 2.0%. Symbolically,

$$E(\tilde{R}_A) = 1.3\%$$
$$E(\tilde{R}_B) = 2.0\%$$

**Dispersion.** Stock B's expected monthly return is 2 percent, but it has not always advanced by 2 percent. In some months it has risen more than this; in some months it has risen less or declined; and one month it did not change at all. Investors are interested in the best and the worst in addition to the average.

A common measure of dispersion is the variance or standard deviation. The standard deviation is the square root of the variance. In addition to Equations 2-10 and 2-11, we can also express variance in expected value notation via Equation 2-13:

$$\sigma_x^2 = E[(\tilde{x}_i - \bar{x})^2] \qquad \textbf{(2-13)}$$

or by $\sigma^2(\tilde{x})$ or var $(\tilde{x})$.

Table 2-10 shows how to calculate the variance of return for Stocks A and B. The variance for Stock A is $4.81 \times 10^{-4}$. The standard deviation is the square root of this, or 0.0219. For Stock B, the values are $5.40 \times 10^{-4}$ and 0.0232, respectively.

Note that standard deviation and variance will always be nonnegative, because squaring any number produces a positive result. The mean can be positive or negative.

Security analysts often move back and forth between variance and standard deviation of returns. They are both useful measures of dispersion that essentially measure the same thing. Analysts sometimes express variance and standard deviation as percentages. For instance, if the variance is 0.25, it might be expressed as 25 percent. This may be okay, but remember that the percent indication essentially counts as two decimal places. The standard deviation is the square root of the variance. What is the standard deviation if the variance is 25 percent? The first impression is 5 percent, but actually it is 50 percent. The square root of 0.25 is 0.50, or 50 percent. Forgetting this fact will inadvertently bias the analysis.

In the mathematics of portfolio theory, we frequently encounter a constant (such as $a$) multiplied by a random variable (such as $\tilde{x}$). If we multiply a series of random variables by the same constant, the resulting variance is the constant squared times the original variance:

$$\sigma^2(a\tilde{x}) = a^2\sigma_x^2 \qquad \textbf{(2-14)}$$

This means that if all the returns for Stock A in Table 2-10 were doubled, the resulting variance of return would be $4 \times 4.81 \times 10^{-4}$, or $19.24 \times 10^{-4}$.

**Logarithms.** When we consider security returns, especially in the context of the distribution from which they came, logarithms are helpful for several reasons. For one

**TABLE 2-10** CALCULATION OF VARIANCE

*Stock A (mean return = 1.3%)*

| *Observation* | $\tilde{x}$ (%) | $\tilde{x} - \bar{x}$ (%) | $(\tilde{x} - \bar{x})^2 \times 10^{-4}$ |
|---|---|---|---|
| 1 | 2 | 0.7 | 0.49 |
| 2 | −1 | −2.3 | 5.29 |
| 3 | 4 | 2.7 | 7.29 |
| 4 | 1 | −0.3 | 0.09 |
| 5 | 2 | 0.7 | 0.49 |
| 6 | −2 | −3.3 | 10.89 |
| 7 | 5 | 3.7 | 13.69 |
| 8 | −1 | −2.3 | 5.29 |
| 9 | 0 | −1.3 | 1.69 |
| 10 | 3 | 1.7 | 2.89 |
| | | | Total $48.10 \times 10^{-4}$ |

$$E[(\tilde{R}_A - \bar{R}_A)^2] = \frac{1}{10}(48.1) \times 10^{-4} = 4.81 \times 10^{-4}$$

*Stock B (mean return = 2.0%)*

| *Observation* | $\tilde{x}$ (%) | $\tilde{x} - \bar{x}$ (%) | $(\tilde{x} - \bar{x})^2 \times 10^{-4}$ |
|---|---|---|---|
| 1 | 3 | 1.0 | 1.00 |
| 2 | 0 | −2.0 | 4.00 |
| 3 | 5 | 3.0 | 9.00 |
| 4 | 2 | 0.0 | 0.00 |
| 5 | 3 | 1.0 | 1.00 |
| 6 | −2 | −4.0 | 16.00 |
| 7 | 5 | 3.0 | 9.00 |
| 8 | 1 | −1.0 | 1.00 |
| 9 | −1 | −3.0 | 9.00 |
| 10 | 4 | 2.0 | 4.00 |
| | | | Total $54.00 \times 10^{-4}$ |

$$E[(\tilde{R}_B - \bar{R}_B)^2] = \frac{1}{10}(54.0) \times 10^{-4} = 5.40 \times 10^{-4}$$

thing, logarithms reduce the impact of extreme values that might distort the true distribution. Takeover rumors, for instance, sometimes cause huge price swings, both up and down, in the value of a particular security. A stock that has not moved for ninety-nine days but doubles in one day will show an average daily gain of 1 percent over this one hundred–day period. If we take the logarithm of daily returns over this one hundred–day period, the average daily logreturn is 0.69 percent. This lower figure lessens the impact of the one big return. A **logreturn** is the logarithm of a return.

Logarithms also make other statistical tools more appropriate. The theory behind linear regression, for instance, assumes normally distributed random variables. Analysts frequently use linear regression of security returns on market returns to estimate beta. Logarithms reduce the effect of extraordinary deviations from normality.

Any time analysts are working on stock return distributions, it is good practice to take the raw returns, convert them to return relatives, and then take the natural logarithm of the return relatives.[12] Then you treat the logreturns as you would any other value for calculating statistics such as variance or correlation.

[12]With returns, logarithms also provide for continuous compounding.

**Expectations.** Three other important relationships deal with the product of constants and random variables. First, the expected value of a constant is the constant: $E(a) = a$. Second, the expected value of a constant times a random variable is the constant times the expected value of the random variable: $E(a\,\tilde{x}) = aE(\tilde{x})$. Third, the expected value of a combination of random variables is equal to the sum of the expected values of each element of the combination: $E(\tilde{x} + \tilde{y}) = E(\tilde{x}) + E(\tilde{y})$.

**Correlation and Covariance.** Correlation is a useful statistical concept that appears in colloquial speech. We often talk about things being correlated, or make statements such as "There was no correlation between what the professor covered in class and what was on the exam." **Correlation** is the degree of association between two variables. **Covariance,** however, is not a familiar concept. Formally, covariance is the product moment of two random variables about their means. Correlation and covariance are related, and they generally measure the same phenomenon. It is easiest to get an understanding of the difference between the two concepts by looking at the math behind them.

Let us look at covariance first; see Equation 2-15:

$$\text{COV}(\tilde{A}, \tilde{B}) = \sigma_{AB} = E[(\tilde{A} - \bar{A})(\tilde{B} - \bar{B})] \tag{2-15}$$

Note that covariance can be expressed either in the COV format or by subscripting the lowercase Greek letter sigma ($\sigma$). Table 2-11 calculates the covariance of returns for Stocks A and B (from Table 2-9).

The correlation coefficient for two random variables is closely related to their covariance; see Equation 2-16:

$$\rho_{AB} = \frac{\text{COV}(\tilde{A}, \tilde{B})}{\sigma_A \sigma_B} \tag{2-16}$$

**TABLE 2-11** CALCULATION OF COVARIANCE

| *Observation* | $\tilde{A}$ | $\tilde{A} - \bar{A}$ | $\tilde{B}$ | $\tilde{B} - \bar{B}$ | $(\tilde{A} - \bar{A})(\tilde{B} - \bar{B})$ |
|---|---|---|---|---|---|
| 1 | 0.02 | 0.007 | 0.03 | 0.01 | $7.00 \times 10^{-5}$ |
| 2 | −0.01 | −0.023 | 0 | −0.02 | $4.60 \times 10^{-4}$ |
| 3 | 0.04 | 0.027 | 0.05 | 0.03 | $8.10 \times 10^{-4}$ |
| 4 | 0.01 | −0.003 | 0.02 | 0 | 0 |
| 5 | 0.02 | 0.007 | 0.03 | 0.01 | $7.00 \times 10^{-5}$ |
| 6 | −0.02 | −0.033 | −0.02 | −0.04 | $1.32 \times 10^{-3}$ |
| 7 | 0.05 | 0.037 | 0.05 | 0.03 | $1.11 \times 10^{-3}$ |
| 8 | −0.01 | −0.023 | 0.01 | −0.01 | $2.30 \times 10^{-4}$ |
| 9 | 0 | −0.013 | −0.01 | −0.03 | $3.90 \times 10^{-4}$ |
| 10 | 0.03 | 0.017 | 0.04 | 0.02 | $3.40 \times 10^{-4}$ |
| | | | | | Total $4.80 \times 10^{-3}$ |

$$E[(\tilde{A} - \bar{A})(\tilde{B} - \bar{B})] = \frac{1}{10}(4.80 \times 10^{-3}) = 4.80 \times 10^{-4}$$

PORTFOLIO MEMO

## Correlation in Baseball: Pitches and Strikes

When a batter comes to the plate, one of three things results from the at-bat. He strikes out (three strikes), he walks (four balls), or he hits the ball onto the playing field (resulting in a hit, an error, or an out). If a pitcher stays in for the entire game, the fewer pitches he throws, the better he has performed in general. Many pitches usually means many balls (and walks) or many hits by the other team.

Whether a pitch is called a ball depends more on which umpire is behind the plate than Major League Baseball (MLB) officials would like. Umpires allegedly have a tendency to define their own strike zone rather than follow the prescribed definition in baseball's rules. Historically, people have said as long as they are consistent, that's okay. In the summer of 2001, however, Richard Anderson, MLB's executive vice president for baseball operations, sent a memo to the umpires instructing them to follow the rules.* MLB wants to reduce the average number of pitches per game to 270.

It seems logical that there will be more pitches per game when an umpire with a small strike zone is behind the plate. In fact, through August of the 2001 season, the averages for the individual MLB umpires ranged from a low of 262 pitches per game to a high of 312, with an average of 285. There is a statistically significant negative correlation, –0.44, between the number of pitches thrown in the game and the number of pitches called strikes by the umpires.

*Dan Seligman "Kill the Umps," *Forbes*, September 17, 2001, 92.

*A linear regression calculator/charter showing the effect of an outlier is provided at* http://www.stat.sc.edu/~west/javahtml/Regression.html

Previously we calculated the standard deviations for these two stocks and found them to be 0.0219 for Stock A and 0.0232 for Stock B. Their correlation coefficient is therefore

$$\rho_{AB} = \frac{4.80 \times 10^{-4}}{(0.0219)(0.0232)} = 0.945$$

An attractive feature of the correlation coefficient is the fact that it ranges from −1.0 to +1.0. This provides a frame of reference when you calculate the statistic. Two random variables that are *perfectly positively* correlated have a correlation coefficient of +1.0. For example, the returns on two different one hundred–share stock certificates of General Motors are perfectly correlated. *Perfectly negatively* correlated random variables move exactly opposite to each other and have a correlation coefficient of –1.0.

### *Linear Regression*

Linear regression is a mathematical technique used to predict the value of one variable from a series of values of other variables. For instance, we might have collected returns on the Standard & Poor's 500 stock market index at the same time we collected the data in Table 2-4 (see Table 2-12). These data appear in Figure 2-8. Linear regression finds the equation of a line through these points such that the best possible fit is obtained. The regression output indicates a slope of 0.91, meaning that

**TABLE 2-12** SAMPLE WEEKLY STOCK AND INDEX RETURNS

| *Week* | *Stock Return* | *Index Return* |
|---|---|---|
| 1 | 0.0084 | 0.0088 |
| 2 | –0.0045 | –0.0048 |
| 3 | 0.0021 | 0.0019 |
| 4 | 0.0000 | 0.0005 |
| 5 | 0.0059 | 0.0071 |
| 6 | –0.0063 | –0.0055 |
| 7 | 0.0043 | 0.0050 |
| 8 | 0.0072 | 0.0084 |
| 9 | –0.0067 | –0.0075 |
| 10 | 0.0063 | 0.0080 |

**FIGURE 2-8**

Linear Regression

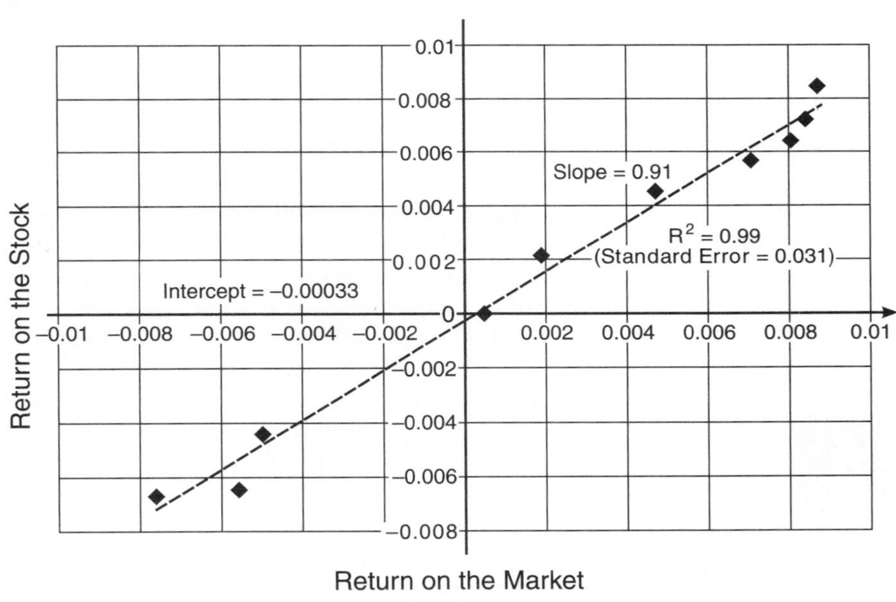


the returns on the stock, on average, are only 91 percent as volatile as those of the market index. Analysts call this slope **beta;** it is a helpful concept, as subsequent chapters will show.

## R Squared and Standard Errors

*R squared is a measure of goodness of fit.*

After calculating statistics, it is good practice to consider their accuracy before using them. **R squared** and the **standard error** are used for this.

**R Squared.** What about the $R^2$ statistic in Figure 2-8? What does this tell us? *R squared* is a measure of how good a fit we get with our regression line. If every data point lies exactly on the regression line, we will get an $R^2$ of 1.0, or 100 percent. In Figure 2-8, not every point is on the line, but visually the fit looks pretty good, and the $R^2$ statistic supports the impression.

**TABLE 2-13** RELIABLE AND UNRELIABLE BETAS

| *Company Name* | *Ticker Symbol* | *Industry* | *Beta 3-Year* | *R-Square 3-Year* |
|---|---|---|---|---|
| Morgan Stanley Dean Witter | MWD | Brokerage | 2.22 | 0.81 |
| Marsh & McLennan | MMC | Insurance | 1.42 | 0.76 |
| Republic New York | RNB | Bank | 1.56 | 0.75 |
| State Street Corp. | STT | Bank | 1.85 | 0.74 |
| BankAmerica Corp. | BAC | Bank | 1.63 | 0.72 |
| General Electric | GE | Electric Equipment | 1.15 | 0.68 |
| **4,478 Value Line stocks with 3-Year Beta Estimates** | — | — | **0.92** | **0.17** |
| Mauna Loa Macadamia Partners | NUT | Food Processing | –0.08 | 0.00 |
| Briggs & Stratton | BGG | Machinery | 0.06 | 0.00 |
| Maine Public Service | MAP | Electric Utility | 0.05 | 0.00 |
| Coors (Adolph) | ACCOB | Beverage (Alcoholic) | 0.04 | 0.00 |
| Cadbury Schweppes | CSG | Beverage (Soft Drink) | 0.09 | 0.00 |

Source: *Value Line for Windows*, September 1998.

R squared is also the square of the correlation coefficient between the returns on the security and the market; it ranges from zero to 1.0. Stated another way, $R^2$ measures the portion of the security's variability that is due to the market's variability. As an extreme example, we could run the regression line in Figure 2-8 from the upper left to the lower right, leaving about half the observations on either side of it. This would give us a poor fit, however, and the $R^2$ would be very low.

Table 2-13 shows three-year beta estimates from Value Line and the associated $R^2$. The table shows several well-known firms with reliable betas, and several other firms where the beta statistic tells nothing at all.

The point here is that we should not treat any financial calculation in "black box" fashion. We would be on shaky ground to state that Mauna Loa has a negative beta; statistically, the beta has no predictive or explanatory power. Note also that for the 4,478 stocks on which Value Line has an estimate of beta from the past three years, the average beta has an $R^2$ of only 0.17. Beta is much more reliable when applied to a portfolio rather than to a single stock because of the risk-reduction effects of diversification. There will be more discussion of this in Chapters 5 and 6.

**Standard Errors.** Figure 2-8 indicates that the slope of 0.91 has a **standard error** of 0.031. If we calculate regression statistics using Microsoft Excel, the regression output includes the standard error statistic. Mathematically, the standard error is equal to the standard deviation divided by the square root of the number of observations:

$$\text{Standard error} = \frac{\sigma}{\sqrt{n}} \tag{2-17}$$

The standard error enables us to determine the likelihood that the coefficient is statistically different from zero. According to The Survey Research Handbook, "the standard error is actually the standard deviation of a 'would be' distribution of the mean values computed from many different samples of exactly the same size from

**TABLE 2-14** STANDARD ERROR

| *Possible Pairs of Random Variables* | *Mean of Pair* |
|---|---|
| 3 & 5 | 4 |
| 3 & 7 | 5 |
| 3 & 9 | 6 |
| 5 & 7 | 6 |
| 5 & 9 | 7 |
| 7 & 9 | 8 |
| | Mean = 6.00 |
| Standard error = $\frac{\sigma}{\sqrt{n}} = \frac{1.29}{\sqrt{6}} = 0.53$ | Standard deviation = 1.29 |

Population of random variables: 3, 5, 7, 9.

precisely the same population."[13] According to the central limit theorem, such a distribution is very nearly normal. This means that about 68 percent of the elements of the distribution lie within one standard error of the mean, 95 percent lie within 1.96 standard errors, and 99 percent lie within 3.0 standard errors.

Suppose, for instance, that a jar contains four marked ping-pong balls numbered 3, 5, 7, and 9. If these balls are selected two at a time and then replaced, there are six possible outcomes of each drawing, as shown in Table 2-14.[14] If we apply the standard error to the values in Table 2-12, we can be 95 percent certain that the true beta coefficient lies within the range $0.91 \pm (1.96 \times 0.031)$, or between 0.85 and 0.97.

Alternatively, we can use the estimated statistic and its standard error to measure the statistical significance of the estimate. To do this, we divide the estimate by its standard error. The resulting statistic is approximately normally distributed with a mean of 0 and a standard deviation of 1.0. Dividing the Figure 2-8 estimate of 0.91 by the standard error of 0.031 gives 29.35. Values 29 standard deviations away from the mean virtually never occur by chance, and this is good support for the significance of the estimate of the coefficient.

## SUMMARY

It never hurts to review basic principles of finance. People often learn from "familiar" material. The two key concepts in finance are the time value of money and the fact that a safe dollar is worth more than a risky dollar. There is a direct relationship between expected return and unavoidable risk. Risky investments do not guarantee a return, nor does unnecessary risk warrant any additional return.

The St. Petersburg paradox is a famous example of a game with an infinite expected payoff, but one that most people won't pay much to play. People will generally not take a fair bet because of the diminishing marginal utility of money. Interest rates are determined by the consumption decisions of the public and their estimates of the utility of various choices facing them.

Elementary statistical concepts are important in investment theory and portfolio construction. Thus, an informed portfolio manager understands them.

---

[13]Pamela L. Alreck and Robert B. Settle, *The Survey Research Handbook* (Homewood, Ill.: Irwin, 1985), 339.
[14]This assumes that the order of the selection makes no difference: drawing a 3 followed by a 7 is the same outcome as a 7 followed by a 3.

We can measure return several ways. In most financial calculations dealing with investment returns, we should not use the arithmetic mean because it does not consider compounding and can give misleading results. The geometric mean is preferable because it captures the information contained in the dispersion of a stream of numbers; we use it, not the arithmetic mean, to calculate an average annual rate of return. Given two sets of numbers with an identical arithmetic average, the set with the highest variance will have the lowest geometric mean. The median and the mode are two other measures of central tendency.

The term *return on investment* can be ambiguous. It is generally a better idea to use *return on assets* or *return on equity* unless what you mean by return on investment is clear.

There are several ways to measure total risk, including the variance, the standard deviation, the semi-variance, and the geometric mean.

Many analysts use return logarithms to reduce the effect of returns that deviate significantly from the others. It is good practice to convert returns into logreturns before performing calculations on them.

Linear regression is useful in finance to predict likely future returns on a security from a series of past returns. An estimate of beta usually comes from a linear regression model. The R squared and standard error statistics provide information about the reliability of the estimate.

A constant is a value that does not change; a random variable is a phenomenon with no fixed value and whose value we discover by conducting an experiment. Random variables are generated by a stochastic process. Variables that we count are discrete, while those that we measure are continuous.

Variables reside in a population. Depending on the number of variable characteristics of interest, the population may be univariate (one characteristic), bivariate (two characteristics), or multivariate (three or more characteristics).

A portion of the population is a *sample*. Statistical tests usually involve taking a sample of the population and determining sample statistics that are then used to estimate the population statistics such as mean, standard deviation, and variance.

## QUESTIONS

1. "Utility measures the riskiness of an expected dollar payment." True or false, and why?
2. Refer to the information in Table 2-2. Suppose you had to pick only one of the four alternatives but were permitted to play the game ten times. Would the alternative you select be different than if you could play only once?
3. Refer to Table 2-2. Suppose you had to pay $50 to play this game and could play it only once. The $50 payment is also a sunk cost that you lose regardless of the outcome of the spin of the wheel. Which alternative would you select under these circumstances?
4. Is it possible for an ordinary annuity to have the same present value as a growing perpetuity if the discount rate and initial cash flows are the same?
5. Is it possible for an ordinary annuity to have the same present value as a perpetuity if the cash flows and discount rates are the same? (*Hint:* What is the difference between $1 received in 500 years and $1 received in 1000 years?)
6. Can the arithmetic and the geometric mean for a series of numbers ever be equal?
7. Can the arithmetic mean ever be less than the geometric mean for a series of numbers?

8. In simple terms that a nonexpert can understand, explain why an arithmetic average cannot combine monthly holding period returns with weekly holding period returns.
9. Why is it a good idea to do calculations with return relatives rather than simple returns?
10. What is the difference between ROA and ROE?
11. As a general policy, which measure, ROA or ROE, do you think should be preferred for evaluating investments?
12. In 250 words or less explain the logic of the concept of semi-variance in investment applications.
13. Comment on the following statement: "The correlation between a random variable and a constant must be perfect (+1.0) because no matter what random variable is chosen, I know the value of the constant. I can always predict the constant with perfect accuracy."
14. Comment on the following statement: "Semi-variance is good in theory, but in the real world it is a useless concept because we do not know until after the fact whether an outcome was favorable or not."
15. Bill and Joe are both fanatic sports bettors. They are both interested in a particular NFL game this coming weekend. Bill views the outcome of the game as a univariate distribution, whereas Joe considers it a bivariate distribution. Explain how they can both be correct.
16. Suppose you watch a stock over a period of two months and calculate its average daily return. Is the average a sample or population mean?
17. Do the returns of IBM common stock come from a univariate, bivariate, or multivariate distribution?
18. Do the returns of a twenty-security portfolio come from a univariate, bivariate, or multivariate distribution?
19. Will the geometric mean of a series of returns be greater or less than the geometric mean of the series of logreturns calculated from the same data?
20. Why must a standard deviation always be nonnegative?

## PROBLEMS

1. You sit on the board of directors of a local nonprofit corporation. At its last meeting, the board decided to begin to fund a very modest retirement pension for the organization's custodian. The details of the plan are as follows.
   - The custodian is 39 years old; the plan will begin to make annual payments to him 26 years from the date when funding for the plan begins. You assume the custodian will continue his employment with the corporation.
   - When payments begin, the custodian will receive a single cash payment each year for 15 years. The first payment will be \$5,000, and each succeeding payment will increase by 4 percent. Payments stop after the fifteenth payment.
   - Money paid into the fund collects interest at a constant 8 percent annual rate, and there is no tax liability on the account.
   - The annual contributions that the corporation makes to the fund will also increase at a 4 percent rate and will also earn 8 percent interest until withdrawn.

As chair of the personnel committee, you are responsible for determining the initial amount to fund this retirement stipend. If your figures are correct, all succeeding annual budget amounts will simply be increased 4 percent from the previous year's budget. How much do you need to deposit now to get the plan in motion?

2. An annuity will make a payment of $100 in one year; this is the first of a series of 20 payments. If each succeeding annual payment is 5 percent larger than the previous one, what is the present value of this annuity using a 12 percent discount rate?
3. What is the future value of the annuity in problem 2?
4. An investment will pay you $200 in one year and then pay annually forever. Each payment will be 3 percent larger than the previous one. If the investment costs $2,500, what rate of return do you expect to earn?
5. What is the present value of a $1,000 perpetuity that makes the first payment five years from today? Assume a 6 percent interest rate.
6. A stock just paid its annual dividend of $1; it has a dividend growth rate of 3.5 percent. What is the most you can pay for the stock to have an expected rate of return of 14.0 percent?
7. A perpetuity will make its first payment in ten years. The first payment will be $1,000, and future payments will increase at a 4 percent annual rate. What is the present value of this investment, assuming a 7 percent discount rate?
8. A cemetery just completed construction of a mausoleum to hold urns of ashes. The building cost $25,000 to erect, and its construction was just paid for. The mausoleum contains five hundred crypts. Maintenance costs associated with the building are estimated at $500 next year, and these costs are expected to rise by 5 percent annually. A person who buys a crypt pays cash for it once and incurs no other costs. How much should be charged for each crypt in order to earn a 12 percent return on this investment? Assume that the proceeds from the sale of the crypt will be received immediately.
9. An ordinary sheet of bond paper is 0.004 inches thick. The distance from the earth to the moon is 264,000 miles.
   a. Calculate the number of times you would have to double the paper to have a thickness sufficient to reach the moon. (If you double the paper once, the thickness is 0.008 inches. Doubled again, it becomes 0.016 inches, and 0.032 inches after the third doubling.)
   b. How does this problem relate to the St. Petersburg paradox?
10. Calculate the geometric mean of the following series of numbers: 1 2 3 4 5 6.
11. Calculate the semi-variance of the returns shown in Table 2-15.

**TABLE 2-15** SAMPLE RETURNS

| *Week* | *Return* |
|---|---:|
| 1 | 0.05% |
| 2 | 0% |
| 3 | –0.12% |
| 4 | 0.01% |
| 5 | –0.10% |
| 6 | –0.02% |
| 7 | 0.11% |
| 8 | 0% |

12. Prove that the variance is equal to the expected value of the square of the random variable minus the mean squared; that is, prove

$$E[(\tilde{x} - \bar{x})^2] = E(\tilde{x}^2) - \bar{x}^2$$

13. What is the covariance between a random variable and a constant? That is, $COV(\tilde{x}, a)$?
14. Suppose $Y = a + b\tilde{x}$. What do you think the variance of Y is?
15. Show that $COV(a\tilde{x}, \tilde{y}) = a\,COV(\tilde{x}, \tilde{y})$.
16. Using the returns in Table 2-15, construct an expanded table showing returns, return relatives, and logreturns.
17. Calculate the geometric mean of the returns in Table 2-15 using (a) returns and (b) logreturns.
18. Double the numbers for Stock A in Table 2-10. Then show that Equation 2-14 is true.
19. Calculate the standard error of the return series in Table 2-15.

Consider the information in the following table for Problems 20–23.

STOCK XYZ (END-OF-YEAR VALUES)

| | 2001 | 2002 | 2003 | 2004 | 2005 |
|---|---|---|---|---|---|
| Stock Price | \$20.50 | \$24.00 | \$36.25 | \$43.00 | \$56.50 |
| Dividends | \$0.23 | \$0.23 | \$0.25 | \$0.27 | \$0.31 |

20. Calculate the compound annual rate of return on the stock investment.
21. For the dividends, calculate the
    a. arithmetic average annual growth rate, and
    b. geometric mean growth rate.
22. Suppose you bought the stock for \$20.50 at the end of 2001 and still own it. You received dividends in 2002–2005. Calculate your holding period return.
23. Using the growing perpetuity model (also called the dividend discount model) and the growth rate you determined in the previous question, solve for the shareholders' required rate of return that is implied by the 2005 stock price. (This is the discount rate in the model.) If you were unable to solve problem 21b, assume a growth rate of 2.0 percent.
24. You know that a probability distribution has a mean of 23.20 and a variance of 2.56. You try four different sampling techniques and get the following results.

| *Technique* | *Mean* |
|---|---|
| A | 20.7 |
| B | 19.5 |
| C | 26.0 |
| D | 25.7 |

At the 95 percent confidence level, which (if any) of these results is unlikely to have happened by chance?

**25.** Ballplayers A and B both earn the same salary in 2005. They negotiate new three-year contracts providing for the following salary increases:

| | 2006 | 2007 | 2008 |
|---|---|---|---|
| Player A | 10% | 8% | 12% |
| Player B | 12% | 10% | 8% |

Indicate whether each of the following statements is true or false, and explain why.

a. Both players will have the same salary at the end of 2008.

b. From the players' perspective, Player B's contract is worth more than Player A's.

##  INTERNET EXERCISES

**1.** Calculate the year-by-year returns on German mark and Japanese yen between 1981 and 1990 using the historical data series at *www.triacom.com/archive/exchange.en.html*. Which currency seems to have provided a better return? Next, compute the semi-variance for each of the currencies over the same period. Which one seems to be less risky? Would your answer change if you had used variance as your measure of risk?

**2.** Use the linear regression calculator at *http://www.shodor.org/UNChem/math/lls/leastsq.html* to verify the intercept and the slope coefficient for the market return data in Table 2-12 on page 43.

##  FURTHER READING


Atkins, Allen B., and Edward A. Dyl. "The Lotto Jackpot: The Lump Sum Versus the Annuity." *Financial Practice and Education*, Fall/Winter 1995, 105–111.

Bernstein, Peter L. "What Does 'Total Return' Really Mean?" *Journal of Portfolio Management*, Spring 1988, 1.

Faustmann, Martin. "Berechnung des Werthes, Welchen Waldboden Sowie Noch Niet Haubare Holzbestände füspr die Waldwirtschaft Besitzen" ("Calculation of the Value Which Forestry Land and Immature Stands Possess for Forestry"). *Allgemeine Forst und Jagd-Zeitung* 25 (1849): 441–455. (English translation in W. Linnard and M. Gane, "Martin Faustmann and the Evolution of Discounted Cash Flow." Commonwealth Forest Institute Paper 42. Commonwealth Forest Bureau, University of Oxford.)

Francis, J.C., and S.H. Archer. *Portfolio Analysis*. Englewood Cliffs, N.J.: Prentice-Hall, 1971.

Geiger, Marshall A., and David Kirch. "What Does 'Total Return' Really Mean? A Comment." *Journal of Portfolio Management*, Summer 1989, 80–81.

Gressis, Nicholas, Jack Hayya, and George Philippatos. "Multiperiod Portfolio Efficiency Analysis via the Geometric Mean." *Financial Review*, 1974, 46–63.

Hassan, Mahamood M. "Arithmetic Mean and Geometric Mean of Past Returns: What Information Do These Statistical Measures Reveal?" *Journal of Investing*, Fall 1995, 63–69.

Latane, Henry A. "The Geometric Mean Criterion Continued." *Journal of Business Finance and Accounting*, Winter 1979, 309–311.

Latane, Henry A., and Donald L. Tuttle. "Criteria for Portfolio Building." *Journal of Finance*, September 1967, 359–373.

Markowitz, Harry. *Portfolio Selection*. New York: Wiley, 1959.

# 3 Setting Portfolio Objectives

*Today's put-off objectives reduce tomorrow's achievements.*
***Harry F. Banks***

## Key Terms

capital appreciation
cash drag
cash matching
duration matching
growth
growth of income
inconsistent objectives
infrequent objectives
investment policy
investment strategy
liability funding
liquidity
portfolio dedication
portfolio splitting
primary objective
secondary objective
stability of principal
total return concept

## Introduction

Setting objectives is important for every person and institution that uses the financial market. Too many investors have a casual attitude toward financial planning, including the management of their investment portfolios. It is easy for someone to be imprecise in communicating with the portfolio manager. Fund managers often hear their clients say, in essence, "We want a lot of return, we don't want any risk, and we need the money by Monday." The Gallup organization, in conjunction with UBS Paine Webber, once conducted a survey that found 39 percent of respondents believed stocks would deliver at least 15 percent annually for the next ten years. This belief is likely just wishful thinking and an historically unreasonable expectation.

In an article in *Pensions and Investments*,[1] the authors clearly state the importance of setting portfolio objectives:

> Over the years, the industry has learned two dominant factors contribute to a sponsor's successful investment program:
>
> - Suitable investment objectives and policy; and
> - Successful selection of the investment managers to implement policy.

[1]Edgar W. Barksdale and William L. Green, "Performance Is Useless in Selecting Managers," *Pensions and Investments*, 17 September 1990, 16.

This chapter discusses traditional portfolio objectives and presents a framework for formulating primary and secondary portfolio objectives in an operationally meaningful fashion. The following chapter considers the steps in the preparation of a formal investment policy statement.

## Why Setting Objectives Can Be Difficult

It is unlikely that any group of potential investors would argue against setting an investment objective before investing money. The unfortunate fact is that objective setting is frequently done in a casual fashion, or, worse yet, is not done at all. Setting objectives can be difficult, for several reasons.

### Semantics

Some of the language of investing has become part of everyday colloquial speech. Terms such as *growth*, *income*, *return on investment*, and *risk* are part of the common vocabulary. But these words mean different things to different people. You might, for instance, hear someone speak of the "growth" in their savings account. To an investment professional, a savings account provides income only; it has *no* growth potential.

*Not everyone has the same understanding of the meaning of the term "growth."*

The consequence of this is that when someone entrusts money to a fund manager or other fiduciary,[2] there needs to be clear understanding of the terms. For example, a client may tell a fund manager, "Here is $50,000 that I have had in a savings account. I would like to invest it and get some better growth." In this context, does *better growth* mean a higher rate of interest (perhaps through investing in a certificate of deposit), or does it mean capital appreciation (from investing in common stock)? The fund manager needs to sort this out and have the client clarify what she means.

Another semantic issue involves the interpretation of *principal* and *income*. To an attorney, the distinction may seem simple, but I have been personally involved in a number of situations in which there have been well-founded disagreements as to what these terms really mean.

Suppose a church receives a $10,000 bequest from a recently deceased church member. The bequest states that the "principal is to be kept in perpetuity, with the annual interest used to support the church library." Assume the church buys a one-year, 5 percent simple interest $10,000 certificate of deposit with the funds. When the CD matures, it is worth $10,500. Assume that $300 is spent acquiring a collection of books. The church treasurer then purchases a new one-year, 5 percent CD with the remaining $10,200. A year later this CD matures with a value of $10,710 ($10,200 principal and $510 interest earned).

How much can the church spend for the library at this point? The "annual interest earned" was $510 on a "principal" of $10,200. Here is where the problem begins. If the principal is restricted, this seems to mean that only the $510 can be spent. Another perspective, though, is that the intent of the benefactor was to restrict the original $10,000, and that accumulated interest should be eligible for spending at a later time. People holding this view would argue that $710 could be spent at the end of the second year.

The point is that even something as seemingly simple as determining principal and interest can be complicated. Whenever possible, these issues should be definitively addressed so as to reduce confusion and the length of committee meetings to discuss these matters.

---

[2]A fiduciary is a person or institution responsible for taking care of someone else's money.

PORTFOLIO MEMO

## The Total Return Concept

Modern money management embraces the **total return concept.** This is the notion that we should be able to enjoy some of the appreciation from a portfolio rather than just the dividends and interest it generates. The concept is especially relevant with charitable funds such as foundations and endowments.

Many firms establish a policy that provides an annual payout from the investment portfolio equal to some percentage of the average fund value over the past three or so years. The percentage usually ranges between 4 percent and 6 percent with an average around 5 percent. For instance, a portfolio might have been worth \$2 million two years ago, \$2.5 million last year, and \$2.4 million this year. If the target payout is 5 percent, the portfolio beneficiary would receive 5% × \$2.3 million, or \$115,000. A total return policy authorizes such a payout even if the total interest and dividends earned by the fund over the past year was much less than this.

Few investment managers would be comfortable with a payout rate higher than 6 percent except in extraordinary times of need. This is so because in some years the fund is likely to decline in value, yet there will still be a funds transfer to the beneficiary. Too high a payout rate will hinder the fund's ability to grow enough to sustain the payout in perpetuity.

Note that a policy of paying out a portion of the annual performance is not feasible. The fund will occasionally have a down year, and its manager cannot ask for the return of a previous payout.

### Indecision

Another occasional hurdle to effective investment management is the client's inability to make a decision. There is an old axiom that says "It is difficult to accomplish your objectives until you decide what it is you want to accomplish." Another equally relevant proverb is "You cannot have your cake and eat it, too."

A banker I know relates a story that illustrates the problem of client indecision. An elderly customer of the bank opened a sizable savings account with funds recently acquired from an insurance settlement. The customer was not interested in any of the bank's "fancy new products; an old-fashioned savings account would do just fine."

The problem arose when the customer wanted the interest the account earned sent home each month, but also wanted the interest compounded. The bank obviously cannot do this. The customer can spend the interest he earns, or he can leave it in the bank and let it earn more interest, but he cannot do both. The customer had substantial difficulty understanding why this was so. Once resigned to the inevitable, he had even more difficulty deciding whether to receive the interest or to leave it in the account.

### Subjectivity

*Investing is both an art and a science.*

Another thorn in the side of the objective-setting process stems from the fact that investing is both an art and a science. Instead of a black-and-white distinction among alternatives, there are inevitably shades of gray that involve subjective judgments.

A particular portfolio game plan may focus on "growth." In working toward this goal, the portfolio manager may choose to include some common stock of AT&T Corp. in the portfolio. Many people consider AT&T, or "Telephone," as it is called among investors, to be a growth stock. Others, though, would say that Telephone is purely an income stock and does not logically belong in a growth portfolio.[3] This is a subjective call, and disagreement is obviously possible.

### Multiple Beneficiaries

Investment portfolios often have more than one beneficiary. An endowment fund is a good example. It has a perpetual life and as such should benefit people today and people generations from now.[4] It is possible to increase the current income generated by a portfolio (to the benefit of today's beneficiaries), but this may well be at the expense of those who will benefit from the portfolio in the future.

This complicated issue is central to current debates about Social Security funding, workers' compensation rates, federal unemployment insurance, and the impact of entitlement programs on the federal budget deficit. An issue is, by definition, controversial, and concerns about multiple beneficiaries will not go away simply because they are irksome.

### Investment Policy versus Investment Strategy

*Investment policy is a long-term concept; investment strategy is short term.*

There is a distinction between *investment policy* and *investment strategy*. **Investment policy** deals with decisions that have been made about long-term investment activities, eligible investment categories, and the allocation of funds among the eligible investment categories. A pension fund, for instance, might decide never to place more than 10 percent of its assets in real estate or to place less than 20 percent in common stock. Another fund might have a policy constraint prohibiting the purchase of corporate bonds rated less than A.

**Investment strategy,** in contrast, deals with short-term activities that are consistent with established policy and that will contribute positively toward obtaining the objective of the portfolio. One manager might be required to maintain at least 20 percent in equities by policy but decide to put 75 percent into the stock market because of a belief that the market will advance in the near future. The increased equity exposure is part of the manager's strategy.[5]

## Portfolio Objectives

*Four principal objectives:*
1. *stability of principal,*
2. *income,*
3. *growth of income,*
4. *capital appreciation.*

Although the precise terminology varies among portfolio management firms, there are four main portfolio objectives. These are stability of principal, income, growth of income, and capital appreciation.

### Preconditions

Before getting into the nuts and bolts of objective setting and strategy formulation, you need to get some questions answered. First, you should assess the existing situation. What are the current needs of the portfolio beneficiary? Drastic, quick changes in the composition of the portfolio (especially the level of income generated) may not be feasible. Rather, it may be necessary to phase in any recommended changes.

---

[3]Categories of stock are discussed in Chapter 9.

[4]We will come back to this issue in the chapter on Fiduciary Duties.

[5]The word *tactics* is seldom used in investment management with the important exception of *tactical asset allocation*. To those with an understanding of military matters, *policy* and *strategy* are used here in the same fashion as army officers use the terms *strategy* and *tactics*, respectively.

PORTFOLIO MEMO

## NUPIA

"NUPIA" may sound like one of the many kingdoms Frodo Baggins marches through on his journey to Mt. Mordor, but it really stands for Maine's newly enacted "New Uniform Principal and Income Act." The Act became law in Maine on January 1, 2003, and will govern the rights of income and principal beneficiaries with respect to estates and irrevocable trusts. NUPIA is too vast to cover comprehensively here, but generally it lends welcome common sense to a previously murky area of law.

NUPIA may be more useful to the average investor than might first seem apparent, because the authors devoted much hard work and study to the perennial question: "How much can be withdrawn annually from a portfolio and still maintain the integrity of the capital?" This is a big issue for trustees trying to appease both income and remainder beneficiaries, but it is equally important to investors who want to make sure their capital continues to generate a sustainable annual distribution throughout their lifetimes. NUPIA provides the trustee with two solutions. One solution allows the trustee to convert the trust to a unitrust that assumes a reasonable annual income at 4 percent of a rolling three-year average of the portfolio value. A second solution vests the trustee with the power to adjust between principal and income in order to achieve an equitable result for all beneficiaries.

Maine's NUPIA authors relied heavily on extensive research compiled by Robert B. Wolf, who authored *Total Return Trusts Meeting Human Needs and Investment Goals through Modern Trust Design*. Mr. Wolf's 190-page treatise makes a strong case for focusing on the total return of a trust, and showcases the effect on the portfolio value over time of taking different distribution levels. It is a powerful educational tool, one that we expect will benefit trustees and individual investors alike in the quest for sustainability in portfolio management. NUPIA may not be a magic kingdom, but it may well chart the way to one for future retirees.

Source: *Investment Quarterly*, Year-end 2002, page 2. Reprinted by permission of Deighan Associates.

A second concern is the investment horizon. At a pension fund, for instance, the investment horizon is very long term.[6] The ups and downs of the market are not nearly as much a concern to a pension fund as they are to an individual investor who is investing for a child's college expenses or for retirement income. There may also be special liquidity needs or ethical investing concerns (explicit or subjective) established by the fund's owner or overseer.[7]

[6]This is one of the reasons timberland is rapidly becoming a popular pension fund asset (more about this in Chapter 12).

[7]Chapter 10 discusses subjective criteria in portfolio selection. Social investing encompasses an especially important set of subjective criteria. Some investors may ask that their portfolios not include tobacco stocks, brewing companies, or firms in the defense industry.

## *Traditional Portfolio Objectives*

The precise terminology that investment advisors use will differ, but many of them will identify four distinct portfolio objectives.

**Stability of Principal.** Sometimes the beneficiary of a portfolio cannot stand *any* chance of loss to the original principal. This might be because of bylaw provisions, statute, or the client's attitude toward risk. When someone says "I don't want any chance of losing the money I invest," the fund manager should interpret this person's objective as **stability of principal.** This is the most conservative portfolio objective, and over the long run, it will generate the most modest return.

The emphasis here is on preserving the "original" value of the fund. Perhaps a community foundation has received a bequest of $10,000 from the estate of a prominent member of the business community. The provisions of the bequest might stipulate that the annual interest be used in perpetuity to support the local symphony. You could logically interpret such a provision to mean that the $10,000 original principal should be maintained forever, with the interest generated by the gift varying each year as the level of interest rates changes.

*You can discover whether tax-exempt bonds are a good investment alternative for you and your tax bracket:* http://www.e-analytics.com/fp28.htm

When stability of principal is the objective, the appropriate investment vehicles include bank certificates of deposit and other money market instruments. One-year CDs might yield 5 percent, for instance, but are not marketable and can never sell for less than their original value.[8] A 5 percent yield means that the $10,000 bequest would produce annual income of $500 for the symphony's benefit.

**Income.** The **income** objective differs from stability of principal in that there is no specific proscription against periodic declines in principal value. A new issue of five-year Treasury notes might have a coupon rate of 6 percent. If the fund manager were to buy $10,000 of these at par, they would yield $600 per year, or $100 more than the 5 percent CD. This would be to the Symphony's benefit. However, these securities are marketable, and they are interest-rate sensitive. If the general level of interest rates rises, the market value of these securities will fall. On paper the foundation will show a *loss* on these securities relative to their purchase price. If the investor holds them until maturity, though, the redemption at par value causes the paper loss to disappear. If the bondholder finds it necessary to sell them prior to maturity, however, the sale could easily result in a loss.

The consequences of fluctuations in market value vary. In this example of a fund to benefit a public nonprofit organization, an income objective is probably more reasonable than one of stability of principal. When income is the chosen objective, appropriate investments include corporate bonds, government bonds, government agency securities, preferred stock, and perhaps some common stock.

**Growth of Income.** The *time value of money* is one of the two key concepts in finance. Dollars today are worth more than an equal number of dollars at any point in the future. The symphony will benefit materially if it receives $600 to support its operations this year.

Suppose, though, that over the next twenty years the average inflation rate turns out to be 4 percent. In today's dollars, $600 to be received in twenty years is worth only $600/(1.04)^{20}$, or about $274. Its purchasing power is less than half the

[8] Jumbo CDs are those of $100,000 or more. They can be marketable and consequently may be subject to interest rate risk if the owner chooses to sell them.

original $600 amount. The symphony's budget will not benefit nearly as much with this reduced amount.

*A growth-of-income objective sacrifices some current return for some purchasing power protection.*

An alternative approach to managing this fund would be to seek **growth of income.** This objective usually involves a reduced initial income payout, but a dollar payout that grows over time and eventually overtakes the level amount from an income objective.

The fund manager might, for instance, initially plan for annual income of $500 from the fund as well as an annual growth of 5 percent in the level of income generated. In ten years, the annual income from the fund will be $\$500 \times (1.05)^{10}$, or approximately $814. In twenty years, the annual income will be $\$500 \times (1.05)^{20}$, or $1,327.

*Funds with growth of income as the primary objective often seek to have the annual income increase by at least the rate of inflation.*

The present value of $1,327 in twenty years, given an average inflation rate of 4 percent, is $606. Note that this is more than the original income of $500. The amount the symphony receives will increase every year, and as long as inflation stays under control, its purchasing power will increase because the income growth rate exceeds the inflation rate. It is very common practice to establish a growth-of-income objective in which the annual income from the fund grows at a rate at least equal to the rate of inflation.

The client (and the fund manager) should clearly understand the difference between income and growth of income as objectives. An income objective seeks to generate as much current income as possible within the risk parameters established. Initially, this amount will be higher than that generated by a portfolio seeking growth of income. Eventually, though, income from the latter portfolio will overtake that generated by the former.

Figure 3-1 illustrates this phenomenon. Both portfolios A and B have an initial principal value of $100,000. We will assume that interest rates remain at a constant 10 percent per year over this fourteen-year period. Portfolio A has an *income* objective; it seeks to provide maximum income each year. Portfolio A is invested 100 percent in debt securities and generates $10,000 per year for each of the ten years.

Portfolio B seeks *growth of income* and contains both debt and equity securities. Because riskier securities, on average, produce higher returns, assume that Portfolio B

**FIGURE 3-1**

Income versus Growth of Income (GOI) (income in thousands)

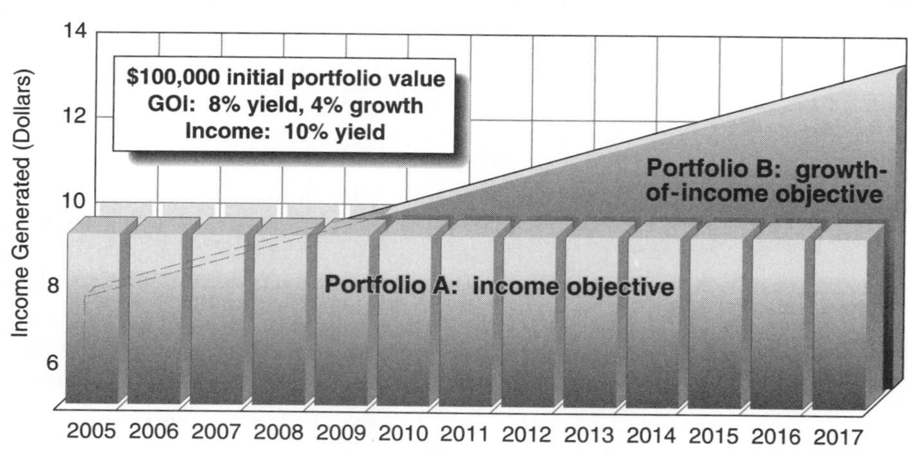

has an annual total return of 12 percent. In the first year it provides $8,000 in income (an 8 percent income yield) and experiences annual capital appreciation of 4 percent.

*A growth-of-income objective requires some investment in equity securities.*

The key point is this: a growth-of-income objective requires the fund manager to seek some capital appreciation in the original principal. This means that some of the fund needs to reside in equity securities. The common stocks purchased may generate some income from dividends, but the bulk of the income will come from fixed-income securities such as long-term bonds.

**Capital Appreciation.** Occasionally, it is not important that a portfolio generate any income at all. A retired couple, for instance, might receive pension and Social Security checks that are sufficient to finance their retirement lifestyle. If these people have an investment portfolio, they might be more interested in having it continue to grow in value rather than in getting additional income from it. Their objective is **capital appreciation.** Their intent may be to leave most of their estate to children and grandchildren.

*For a taxpayer, an unrealized capital gain is worth more than a dollar of income.*

There is also an income tax consideration. The government taxes interest and dividends immediately.[9] Capital gains are not taxable until they are realized. This means that unless the retired couple actually needs the income, a $1 capital gain is worth more than a dollar of income.

As an example, consider the case of an investor in the 28 percent federal income tax bracket.[10] Two $10,000 investments each have a 10 percent pretax expected return. Both involve the purchase of 500 shares of a $20 common stock. The first does not pay dividends, whereas the second has a constant dividend yield of 7 percent. (Commissions would be the same in both cases, so we can ignore them in the investment comparison.) Table 3-1 shows the projected cash flows. It is apparent that there is a cost associated with receiving the dividend income because 28 percent of the dividends goes to the tax man immediately, whereas the tax on capital gains occurs much later.

The difference between these two investments would be much less striking if the investor sold the shares at the end of year 5. Investment A would show a realized capital gain of $12.21, per share 28 percent of which would be lost to taxes. There would also be a capital gain with Investment B, but it would be much smaller. The internal rates of return (IRRs) are reduced to 7.56 and 7.32 percent, respectively, for Investment A and Investment B under this scenario.

The key point here is that unrealized capital gains are not taxed whereas dividend or interest income is. The investor can defer taxes for many years by successful long-term growth stock investing.

### Special Situation of Tax-Free Income

These four alternatives just discussed are the basic portfolio objectives. A common variation of the income-producing strategies is the additional stipulation that the income generated, or a portion of it, be tax free. This is accomplished by investing in municipal securities whose interest is free from federal tax and may also be free from state and local taxes.[11]

---

[9]Taxes are the largest component of transaction costs, far outweighing the impact of commissions for many investors.

[10]State and local income tax implications would make this example even more striking.

[11]Investors normally pay no state tax on municipal securities from their own state.

**TABLE 3-1** THE EFFECT OF TAXES ON INVESTMENT INTERNAL RATE OF RETURN

***Investment A (no dividends)***
***10% Pretax Annual Return***

| | *Year* | | | | | |
|---|---|---|---|---|---|---|
| | *(0)* | *(1)* | *(2)* | *(3)* | *(4)* | *(5)* |
| Price | $20.00 | $22.00 | $24.20 | $26.62 | $29.28 | $32.21 |
| Dividends | — | 0 | 0 | 0 | 0 | 0 |
| —Tax (28%) | — | 0 | 0 | 0 | 0 | 0 |
| Cash flow | $0 | $0 | $0 | $0 | $0 | $32.21[a] |

After-tax internal rate of return $(R): 20 = \frac{32.21}{(1+R)^5}$

$R = 10.00\%$

***Investment B (7% dividend yield)***
***10% Pretax Annual Return***

| | *Year* | | | | | |
|---|---|---|---|---|---|---|
| | *(0)* | *(1)* | *(2)* | *(3)* | *(4)* | *(5)* |
| Price | $20.00 | $20.60 | $21.22 | $21.85 | $22.51 | $23.19 |
| Dividends | — | 1.40 | 1.44 | 1.49 | 1.53 | 1.58 |
| —Tax (28%) | — | 0.39 | 0.40 | 0.42 | 0.43 | 0.44 |
| Cash flow | | 1.01 | 1.04 | 1.07 | 1.10 | 24.33[a] |

After-tax return:

$$20 = \frac{1.01}{(1+R)} + \frac{1.04}{(1+R)^2} + \frac{1.07}{(1+R)^3} + \frac{1.10}{(1+R)^4} + \frac{24.33}{(1+R)^5}$$

$R = 8.05\%$

[a]The year 5 cash flow includes the year 5 value of the stock.

If stability of principal is the objective, tax-free income can be earned by investing in a municipal bond mutual fund.[12] A direct investment in municipal bonds would be appropriate for a portfolio with income as its objective, whereas some mix of municipal bonds and common stock would be necessary for the growth-of-income objective. It would be unrealistic for an investor seeking capital appreciation from a portfolio also to expect the portfolio to generate tax-free income.

Figure 3-2 shows the relative riskiness of the four primary objectives. Stability of principal and income are substantially safer than growth of income and capital appreciation, because the latter two require the use of equity securities. A substantial range of risk/expected return characteristics can be associated with the capital appreciation objective. Higher-beta portfolios are obviously riskier, but over the long run, they tend to produce higher returns.

[12]There is a possibility of some price volatility with some tax-free mutual funds. This should be addressed before making such an investment.

### Portfolio Objectives and Expected Utility

Whether an investor seeks preservation of principal or long-term capital appreciation, there is one ultimate goal: to maximize the expected utility of the investment program. Utility is one of the most useful of all economic concepts. It may be difficult

FIGURE 3-2

Relative Riskiness of Portfolio Objectives: Average Annual Returns (1926–2004)

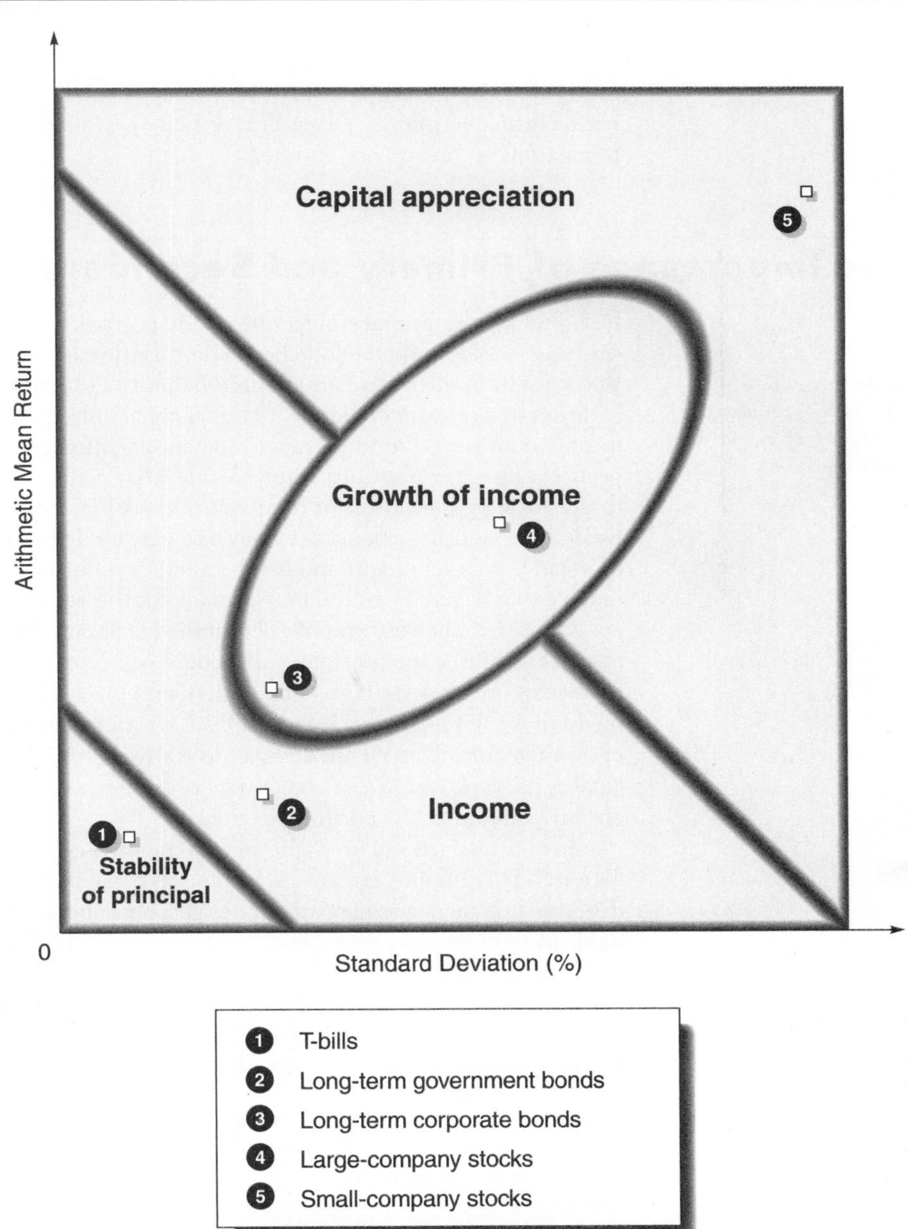


Source: Adapted from Ibbotson Associates, *Stocks, Bonds, Bills, and Inflation: 2000 Yearbook*. Chicago, 2000.

to explain completely, but everyone understands the concept: we seek out satisfying things and avoid things that cause us discomfort.

Mutual funds[13] are an excellent investment alternative for a great many investors. They are an economic and convenient means of achieving diversification and professional portfolio management for someone with limited investment capital.[14] Still, many people do not like mutual funds because they are "not exciting." These people argue that letting someone else pick the stocks removes the thrill of the hunt. Choosing your own stocks is fun; you get utility from the process if you enjoy it.

There is absolutely nothing wrong with this attitude. Investing should be fun rather than a chore. The utility from the investments comes from quantifiable and nonquantifiable sources. Regardless of how the investor perceives utility, she seeks to maximize it one way or another.

## The Importance of Primary and Secondary Objectives

*Establishing a secondary objective helps pin down the percentage to be invested in equity.*

Deciding on the **primary objective** of the portfolio is a major accomplishment for the fund manager and the fund beneficiary. Little can occur until you finish this task. But it is also prudent and enormously helpful to establish a **secondary objective** in addition to a primary objective. (The secondary objective, as the name suggests, indicates what is next in importance after specification of the primary objective.) The portfolio manager must ultimately decide what percentage of the investment funds to put into equities. Most of the remainder will go into debt securities; real estate, hard assets, or other asset classes may also play a role in some cases. If the fund manager can play psychologist and get the client to talk about secondary objectives, it is much easier to pin down the proper range for the equity percentage.

Consider a person who has determined that current income should be the primary objective of the portfolio. This could be accomplished by investing in money market securities, long-term debt, or dividend-producing common stock. The client might make statements such as "I really don't want to take any risk with this money," or "Is there any chance I am going to lose any of this?" In this case, stability of principal is probably the client's secondary objective, and the portfolio manager would put little, if any, of the portfolio in stock.

In contrast, the client might ask, "Is the income I get going to keep up with inflation?" This implies growth of income as a secondary objective. To accomplish this, the fund manager must attempt to get some appreciation in the principal of the fund, and this requires a greater investment in equities. Table 3-2 shows a useful matrix of primary and secondary objectives and typical debt/equity mixes to accomplish each combination.[15] The debt/equity percentages shown in the table are guidelines. A portfolio manager will often deviate from these because of attitudes toward the prospects for the market, an unusually high current level of interest rates, or temporary needs of the client.

---

[13]Mutual funds are existing portfolios of securities proportionately owned by a large number of investors. The appendix to this chapter also discusses the basic principles of mutual funds.

[14]Many rich investors also use mutual funds for their convenience and automatic diversification.

[15]A more detailed discussion of the objective-setting process is found in Robert D. Milne, "Determination of Portfolio Policies: Individual Investors," in John L. Maginn and Donald L. Tuttle, eds., *Managing Investment Portfolios* (Boston: Warren, Gorham, and Lamont, 1983), Chap. 5.

**TABLE 3-2** PRIMARY AND SECONDARY PORTFOLIO OBJECTIVES

| *Secondary Objective* | *Primary Objective* | | | |
|---|---|---|---|---|
| | *Stability of Principal* | *Income* | *Growth of Income* | *Capital Appreciation* |
| Stability of Principal | X | Debt and preferred stock | Unacceptable goals | ? |
| Income | Short-term debt | X | At least 40% equity | ? |
| Growth of Income | Unacceptable goals | Varies: often > 40% equity | X | At least 75% equity |
| Capital Appreciation | Unacceptable goals | ? | At least 75% equity | X |

? = unusual combinations involving a need to tailor a portfolio to a very specific need.
X = not applicable.

PORTFOLIO MEMO

## Total Return Unitrusts

As discussed earlier, at one time trustees were reluctant to distribute cash other than the dividends or interest a portfolio earned. Most managers now embrace the **total return concept.** As a consequence, state courts have begun to formally approve an investment vehicle called a **total return unitrust,** which permits trustees to convert decades-old trusts into a more modern version permitting the trustee to follow the total return concept in making portfolio distributions.

All states allow *new* trusts to be set up this way, but it will likely be a while before all states pass legislation allowing the conversion of existing trusts. A number of states also give trustees the "power of adjustment," enabling them to distribute a portion of principal to the trust beneficiaries. Regardless of the form of the legal authorization, legislatures, the legal community, and investment professionals are moving toward broad acceptance of the total return concept in determining prudent distributions.

# Other Factors to Consider in Establishing Objectives

### *Inconsistent Objectives*

Equally important in Table 3-2 is the fact that certain primary/secondary objective combinations are incompatible. An example of such **inconsistent objectives** is stability of principal as a primary objective and capital appreciation as a secondary objective. This, in effect, says, "I want no chance of a loss, but I do want capital gains." The world does not work this way.

*A good rule of thumb is to have 10 percent of your portfolio in fixed-income investments for each decade of your life.*
Charles Salisbury, T. Rowe Price Mutual Funds

Note also that investment managers cannot pair *growth of income* with *stability of principal*. There are two ways in which income can continue to rise. One way is for interest rates to increase continually. This occurs during inflationary times, but the government does everything it can to stop this. Investors cannot rely on increasing inflation to produce continually increasing income. It is also the case that the actual purchasing power of the higher income does not increase. The other way in which income can go up is through an increased value of the principal amount from which the income is generated. This means that some capital appreciation is necessary. Investment activities that potentially could provide capital appreciation carry a chance of loss, though, which is inconsistent with an objective of stability of principal.

### Infrequent Objectives

Table 3-2 indicates that some investment objective combinations are infrequent. **Infrequent objectives** are the cells containing question marks. Capital appreciation as a primary goal and stability of principal as a secondary goal appear at first glance to be patently incompatible. In most cases they are, but it is possible to construct a very specific type of portfolio that would generally accomplish this mission.

A wealthy individual in a high tax bracket might have no need for additional current income and might not be comfortable with the risk of equity investments. For this individual, investments in traditional fixed-income securities would produce unneeded income and a heavy tax bite in the year received.

An alternative would be to invest in low coupon bonds that are selling in the marketplace at a substantial discount from par. These bonds will produce less income than comparable grade issues with higher coupons and, therefore, a lower tax liability. As they approach their maturity date, these bonds will rise in value and, barring default, will be retired at par. The client will see this as a capital gain, which, depending on current tax laws, might receive favorable tax treatment. In any event, the tax liability will be incurred in the future, and its present value will be much smaller than if it occurred this year.[16]

*I like to think that there always are possibilities.*
Admiral James T. Kirk, Starship Enterprise

A material consideration with such a portfolio is the fact that low coupon bonds face *substantial interest rate risk.* If interest rates rise, the market value of low coupon bonds falls substantially, which might be considered inconsistent with an objective of stability of principal. The bonds will eventually recover, however, as they approach maturity. In this case, stability of principal happened to be the secondary objective rather than the primary.

Perhaps the important thing to keep in mind with infrequent combinations is largely philosophical: investment managers should look for ways to do things instead of explaining why they cannot be done. If clients want something unusual, the manager should not begin the conversation by telling them that their needs are bizarre and uncommon. It is better to verify that their situation does indeed call for something out of the ordinary, and if this is the case, try to work out a compromise. This is far better than a manager who throws up his hands saying, "It can't be done!"

### Portfolio Splitting

Occasionally, a fund manager will receive instructions that require that the portfolio be managed in more than one part. Perhaps a church's endowment fund has grown over the years to a current value of $4 million. One-fourth of this amount might be associated with restricted gifts providing that the annual income be used for a specific purpose. The remaining $3 million might have no restrictions on its use.

---

[16]Again, the current tax law may make this strategy ineffective. In some circumstances an investor must report "income" from the appreciation of bonds selling at a discount even though income has not actually been received.

In such a case, the fund manager and the church's board of trustees could decide to prorate the investment of the fund into two components with different objectives. Income is important with the restricted portion, and the board might select *income* as the primary objective of this portion of the fund. Income may be less important with the unrestricted portion, with *capital appreciation* being the primary objective of these remaining funds. Such **portfolio splitting** can be a more convenient way of administering the fund than trying to establish a single, overall objective.

*Portfolio splitting involves establishing separate objectives for portions of a single portfolio.*

Still, portfolio splitting has the potential to give people the opportunity to avoid making tough decisions about fund management. A board of trustees could be indecisive and decide it wants "a little of everything." Unless there is a good reason to do otherwise, the portfolio should be managed as a unit.

### Liquidity

In establishing portfolio objectives, another very real concern can overlay the objectives in Table 3-2. This is concern with *liquidity*. Liquidity is another term that often lacks consistent definition. Look up "liquid" in a dictionary and you will find "easily convertible into cash." **Liquidity,** then, is a measure of the ease with which something can be converted into cash. This is probably what most people mean when they use the word.

In establishing portfolio objectives, the client might mention a need to keep the funds reasonably liquid. Again, it is imperative for the fund manager to establish clearly what this comment means. Does the client anticipate a routine need to write checks against the funds? There are arrangements, such as money market mutual funds or the cash management accounts at a brokerage firm, that allow you to do this, but you cannot write a check against a self-assembled portfolio of short-term bonds.

One approach is to keep a portion of the investment portfolio in highly liquid form, perhaps with check-writing privileges, and to manage the remainder independently, free of liquidity constraints.

### The Role of Cash

The entries in Table 3-2 show only two asset classes; equity and fixed-income securities. Many investment management firms routinely prescribe portfolio proportions for these two asset classes and a third class, *cash*. Cash contributes to stability, especially during periods of rising interest rates.

In a portfolio context, *cash* does not refer to a wad of hundred-dollar bills. Rather, this term refers to any number of "near money" forms, such as money market instruments (for example, Treasury bills) or other short-term interest-bearing deposit accounts.

Many fund managers would prefer to see a chart such as Table 3-2 include the three dimensions of debt/equity/cash. Personal experience and preference dictate how the general guidelines of the table would be adjusted to accommodate these three asset classes.

Cash naturally arrives in portfolios through the receipt of dividends and interest. While this might be convenient, it is a problem for some portfolio managers. Consider an all-equity mutual fund whose comparison benchmark is the Standard & Poor's 500 index. Mutual funds seldom have less than 5 percent of their assets in cash because of the natural receipt of investment income and because shareholders mail in checks for additional purchases. Comparing a fund that is 95 percent in stock with an index that is 100 percent in stock results in a phenomenon called **cash drag.** (Chapter 22 will show how some managers use stock index futures contracts to fix this problem.)

## Portfolio Dedication

The topic of portfolio dedication could easily appear in the Portfolio Management part of this book rather than the Portfolio Construction part. The term has characteristics of both activities, and the fact that it is included here is simply a matter of personal preference. Portfolio dedication is really a form of portfolio management. It has objective-setting overtones, however, and appears here to show the richness that the objective-setting process may include.

**Portfolio dedication** involves managing an asset portfolio so that it services the requirements of a corresponding liability or portfolio of liabilities. Sometimes called **liability funding,** this is a specialized requirement overlaying the primary and secondary investment objectives. There are two principal methods of portfolio dedication: cash matching and duration matching.

### Cash Matching

*Cash matching involves assembling a portfolio such that its cash flows match the requirements of a liability stream.*

**Cash matching** is the most common form of portfolio dedication. With this technique, a manager assembles a portfolio of bonds whose cash flows match as nearly as possible the requirements of a particular liability.

A wealthy university alumnus might endow his alma mater with a set of ten four-year scholarships, each of which pays the recipient $2,000 every six months. This has an annual income requirement of $40,000. Assume for the sake of this example that the $2,000 payout will remain constant with no adjustment for inflation.

Such an endowment could be managed as a cash-matched, dedicated portfolio. The portfolio manager would choose bonds that pay interest semiannually just before distribution to the scholarship recipients. Perhaps the portfolio manager decides to structure this portfolio using the bonds listed in Table 3-3.

Table 3-4 is one possible combination of these bonds that meets the income requirement of $20,000 every six months. Cash matching seeks to match as nearly as possible a specific income need. The $3 shortfall is not a material difference.

### Duration Matching

The general idea behind **duration matching** is constructing a portfolio of assets that "pays the bills" associated with a liability or stream of liabilities.[17] Duration is

**TABLE 3-3** BONDS FOR DEDICATED SCHOLARSHIP PORTFOLIO

| *Bond*[a] | *S&P Rating* | *Price* | *YTM (%)* | *Duration* |
|---|---|---|---|---|
| Smith Enterprises 8¼ s17 | AA | 87⅝ | 9.97 | 7.49 |
| General Power 8½ s16 | AA– | 88⅝ | 10.16 | 7.10 |
| Consolidated Telephone 8¾ s26 | AA | 88¾ | 10.03 | 9.02 |
| Northeast Electric Service 7⅝ s15 | A+ | 79¾ | 10.82 | 6.82 |
| Airline Bank 8⅛ s20 | AA– | 78½ | 11.01 | 7.91 |

[a]These bonds all pay interest on March 1 and September 1.

[17]Duration matching is discussed further in Part Four, "Portfolio Protection and Emerging Topics."

**TABLE 3-4** CASH-MATCHED DEDICATED PORTFOLIO

| *Par* | *Bond* | | *Semiannual Interest* |
|---|---|---|---|
| $122,000 | Smith Enterprises 8 1/4s17 | | $5,033 |
| $117,000 | General Power 8 1/2s16 | | 4,973 |
| $131,000 | Northeast Electric Service 7 5/8s15 | | 4,994 |
| $123,000 | Airline Bank 8 1/8s20 | | 4,997 |
| | | Total | $19,997 |

Requirements: $20,000 income needed on September 1 and March 1.

a measure of interest rate risk that can be very helpful in fixed-income portfolio management. (We will look at this concept in detail in Chapter 11.) For the moment, accept the fact that the higher the duration, the greater the fluctuation in the price of a bond associated with a change in interest rates.

*In a duration-matched portfolio, the market value of the dedicated portfolio equals the present value of the liability cash flows, and the duration of the dedicated portfolio equals the duration of the liabilities.*

Rising interest rates will cause the market value of bonds to decline, but will enable reinvested interest checks to earn a higher return. In a duration-matched bond portfolio, a rise in interest rates results in a decline in the portfolio's value that is approximately offset by the additional income earned from the higher reinvestment rate. Similarly, if market rates fall, the increase in the market value of the portfolio will largely offset the decline in income from the reinvested funds.

There are two keys to duration matching. First, the duration of the asset portfolio must match the duration of the liabilities. Second, the present value of the liabilities to be paid must equal the market value of the asset portfolio.

Suppose another university benefactor decides to endow ten scholarships of $2,000 every six months for a period of twelve years. This means the liability is a series of outflows of $20,000 each, paid every six months, with a total of twenty-four payments. The benefactor will provide an initial sum that is sufficient to finance these future payments. Perhaps the university endowment office uses a 10 percent discount rate for calculations of this sort. The cost to the benefactor, then, is the present value of a stream of twenty-four payments of $20,000 each, paid every six months, using a 10 percent annual discount rate, which is $275,973.

Even though this cash flow stream is not from a bond, we can still find the duration of the payments. *Duration* is simply the weighted average of time until cash flows occur,[18] and for this liability stream, the duration is 5.19 years.

Most of the bonds in Table 3-3 have yields to maturity that are 10 percent or better, so these could satisfy the present value assumption in our example of a 10 percent discount rate. There appears to be a problem, however: each of the bonds has a duration greater than the target duration of 5.19 years.

Actually, this is not a problem if the manager has access to the money market. Three-month Treasury bills have a duration of one-fourth of a year, or 0.25. We can put part of the money there and pull duration down as needed. Alternatively, the manager can keep funds in a cash-equivalent account of the type offered by most brokerage firms and bank trust departments. These usually eliminate the whole-unit problems conventional securities carry. That is, although the manager cannot buy half a Treasury bill from the government, for all practical purposes he can do so through a broker or the bank.

Managers estimate the duration for a portfolio by computing the weighted average of the component durations, where the weights reflect current dollar values.

[18]Technically, this is only true if the bonds contain no embedded options such as a call provision.

**TABLE 3-5** BONDS FOR DURATION-MATCHED PORTFOLIO

| *Bond* | *Price* | *Value* | *Duration* | *Value-weighted Duration* |
|---|---|---|---|---|
| \$31,000 Smith Enterprises 8¼ s17 | 87⅝ | \$27,164 | 7.49 | 0.74 |
| \$30,000 General Power 8½ s16 | 88⅝ | 26,588 | 7.10 | 0.68 |
| \$79,000 Consolidated Telephone 8¾ s26 | 88¾ | 70,113 | 9.02 | 2.29 |
| \$34,000 Northeast Electric Service 7⅝ s15 | 79¾ | 27,115 | 6.82 | 0.67 |
| \$32,000 Airline Bank 8⅛ s20 | 78½ | 25,120 | 7.91 | 0.72 |
| \$106,737 90-day T-bill equivalents | 98.02 | 99,874 | 0.25 | 0.09 |
| | Total | \$275,973 | | D = 5.19 |

Suppose a 90-day Treasury bill currently sells for \$9,802. This security has a par value of \$10,000, and this price converts into an 8.19 percent bond equivalent yield.[19]

The chore then is to assemble a basket of the bonds in Table 3-3 plus Treasury bill equivalents (as needed) so that the basket has a market value of \$275,973 and a duration of 5.19. This problem is easily solved via linear programming. Table 3-5 presents one solution to the duration-matching problem. This portfolio has a duration equal to the duration of its associated liabilities, and its market value is within a dollar of the present value of the liability cash flow stream. Even if interest rates change, there should be sufficient cash flow generated by the portfolio to satisfy its needs. This is the whole point of portfolio dedication.

## SUMMARY

Setting objectives is a critical, and sometimes difficult, part of the portfolio construction process. Problems in setting objectives include confusion over the meaning of terms, inability of the client to make a decision, and different attitudes toward relative riskiness.

The four traditional portfolio objectives, in increasing order of risk, are stability of principal, income, growth of income, and capital appreciation.

In addition to the establishment of a primary portfolio objective, it is also useful to establish a secondary objective. This enables the portfolio manager to be an even better tailor in fitting the portfolio to the client.

Whatever the portfolio objective, the ultimate goal is maximizing expected utility. Utility can come from income, capital appreciation, the thrill of playing the game, and other intangible sources.

Hurdles to effective portfolio management include an impossible primary/secondary objective combination, uncommon objectives that require special allocation

19 $$\frac{198}{10{,}000-198}\times\frac{365}{90}=8.19\%$$

of the fund assets, and the occasional need to split the portfolio and manage each component separately. Liquidity, or the need to periodically get cash from the fund quickly, may also influence the construction of the portfolio.

Portfolio dedication involves managing an asset portfolio so that it services the requirements of a corresponding liability or portfolio of liabilities. Cash matching and duration matching are the two principal methods of doing this.

## QUESTIONS

1. What is the difference between the income objective and the growth-of-income objective?
2. Why is it useful to establish a secondary portfolio objective?
3. A client is definitely more interested in income than in capital appreciation. How would you help her discover whether the primary objective should be income or growth of income?
4. What role does common stock have in a portfolio whose primary objective is stability of principal? Would your answer be different if stability of principal were the secondary rather than the primary objective?
5. Does the income objective mean that the fund manager should seek to generate the maximum possible income from the fund? Why or why not?
6. When selecting bonds for a portfolio, what factors should be considered before choosing specific maturities and quality ratings?
7. Comment on the following statement: "In evaluating the suitability of a bond for a portfolio, I don't care about its maturity. Duration is all that matters."
8. Comment on the following statement: "I virtually never include AAA-rated bonds in portfolios I manage. AA-rated bonds are almost as safe, and they yield more."
9. When income is important, which is more relevant to the fund manager, current yield or yield to maturity?
10. Refer to Table 3-2. With which primary/secondary portfolio objectives could zero coupon bonds logically be used?
11. If a fund has an objective of income, is there anything wrong with buying five-year certificates of deposit?
12. Refer to Question 11. Suppose the objective were stability of principal. Would your answer be different?
13. Comment on the following statement: "There is still reinvestment rate risk in a duration-matched portfolio."
14. Explain the difference between *investment policy* and *investment strategy*.
15. Comment on the following statement: "Duration matching works better in practice during a period of rising interest rates because you do not have to sell any securities to make up for the income shortfall."
16. Suppose your small business prospers, and ultimately you incorporate, with 100 employees and annual sales of $25 million. You decide to establish a corporate retirement plan (never having had one before). Employees contribute up to 5 percent of their salary into the fund, and you match the contribution. There would be no tax implications until employees began to receive payments from the fund. If there is a single portfolio covering all employees, what primary/secondary objectives would you recommend?

17. What, in your opinion, should the primary and secondary portfolio objectives of the Social Security Administration fund be? Do you feel that these objectives are somehow different from those associated with corporate retirement funds in general?
18. From 1926 to the end of 1996, the annual standard deviation of returns for long-term government bonds was 9.2 percent, whereas that of intermediate-term government bonds was only 5.8 percent. Despite this, the average annual return on both groups of bonds was 5.4 percent. How can these results be explained to people who like return and dislike risk?

## PROBLEMS

Use the bonds in Table 3-6 to solve Problems 1 and 2.

1. A person wins $1 million in the state lottery. Actually, the person receives $50,000 per year every September 1. Using a 10 percent discount rate and the bonds in the table, construct a cash-matched dedicated portfolio that will service this need.
2. Use the bonds in the table plus 90-day Treasury bills with a price of $9,800 to assemble a duration-matched portfolio for the lottery payments in Problem 1. The Duration file on the text Website (http:// strong.swlearning.com) will calculate the individual bond durations. (This is easiest to do via a linear program with an objective function that minimizes the number of bonds used.)
3. A $100,000 bond portfolio generates exactly $9,000 per year in income. Another $100,000 portfolio currently yields $7,000 per year in income, but this amount is expected to grow at 4 percent annually. In about how many years will the two portfolios yield equal amounts?
4. A person is about to retire and must choose between three retirement plan options. One provides $55,000 per year for the remainder of his life. Another provides 85 percent of this amount and increases by 5 percent each year. A third option gives him a $400,000 lump-sum settlement. If his remaining life expectancy is twelve years, the prime interest rate is 8 percent, and he can ignore taxes, which should he choose?
5. Would your answer to Problem 4 be different if the prime interest rate were 15 percent and was expected to stay there for the foreseeable future?
6. The Bondport file at the text website will help in the solution of the following Church Endowment Fund Case Study. (This is an actual situation with the original market price data preserved.) In May 1990, Local Church had an

**TABLE 3-6** BONDS LIST FOR PROBLEMS 1 AND 2

| *Company* | *Maturity (Years)* | *Coupon (%)* | *Price* | *Yield to Maturity (%)* |
|---|---|---|---|---|
| ABC | 4 | 10 | 98 | 10.63 |
| DEF | 8 | 9 | 87 | 11.53 |
| GHI | 22 | 11 | 102 | 10.76 |
| JKL | 28 | 10 | 90 | 11.17 |

All bonds pay interest on March 1 and September 1.

endowment fund with a market value of about $750,000. This fund was managed by a bank trust department with a primary objective of growth of income and a secondary objective of income.

For calendar year 1990, the church had budgeted annual income of $54,600 from the endowment fund. Each month the bank forwarded a check for $4,550 (one-twelfth of the annual amount) to the church treasurer.

The church's board of trustees had formed the Investment Advisory Committee (IAC) in 1988 to oversee the management of the fund and to increase the regularity of communication between the bank and the church. Although the bank had made periodic presentations to the board of trustees, membership of this board changed annually. The IAC was intended to provide some constancy to the long-term administration of the endowment fund and regular communication between the bank and the church. The members of the IAC (all of whom were church members) were all investment professionals.[20]

In May 1990, the IAC discussed the feasibility of withdrawing the fixed-income portion of the endowment fund from the bank trust account and managing this portion of the fund themselves. The IAC members clearly had the capability to do so, and it appeared that this move would save the church about $3,900 in annual management fees.

The IAC considered managing the equity portion of the fund as well, but several members were concerned about the lack of precedent within the church for assuming such a level of fiduciary responsibility. The consensus was that it would be better to go slowly and let the precedent of internal management of any part of the fund develop before dealing with the equity securities.

During the spring of 1990 the church was also in the final stages of selecting a new minister. The search committee found a very talented man from out of state who seemed the perfect candidate. Finding suitable, affordable housing for the minister, his wife, his four children, and his two horses turned out to be a problem. As a consequence, the board of trustees agreed to loan him $50,000 from the endowment fund at an 8 percent interest rate, with the interest accruing (no payments being made) for a five-year period.[21] This development, coupled with the anticipated savings from moving the fixed-income portion of the fund, led the IAC to recommend to the church's board of trustees that the shift be made, and late in the year the funds were transferred to a custodial brokerage account at the stockbroker IAC member's firm. Table 3-7 shows the composition of the fund on January 1, 1991.

The growth-of-income objective called for the annual income generated by the endowment fund to grow at a 5 percent annual rate. The 1991 church budget showed anticipated revenue of $54,600 × 1.05, or $57,330. One-twelfth of this, or $4,778, was to be remitted from the brokerage firm account to the church treasurer each month. The chair of the IAC planned to call a meeting of the committee to do some planning for the next two years. Two things were especially important. First, the IAC knew that it would occasionally be

---

[20]A finance professor, a stockbroker, a retired bank president, a trust officer from another bank, and the owner of an insurance agency (who was also the president of the state university's foundation).

[21]At the end of the first year, for instance, he would owe $54,000.

**TABLE 3-7** ENDOWMENT FUND, JANUARY 1, 1991

| *Par* | *Bond* | | *Coupon (%)* | *Maturity Date* | *Price* |
|---|---|---|---|---|---|
| $25,000 | Ford Motor Credit | | 8.875 | 5/15/94 | 104.375 |
| $40,000 | Virginia Electric & Power | | 9.375 | 6/01/98 | 111 |
| $30,000 | Federal Home Loan Bank | | 8.15 | 4/27/92 | 101.312 |
| $25,000 | Federal Home Loan Bank | | 8.60 | 5/26/92 | 101.734 |
| $15,000 | Federal Home Loan Bank | | 8.80 | 11/25/92 | 103.859 |
| $30,000 | Federal Home Loan Bank | | 9.50 | 1/25/93 | 105.078 |
| $40,000 | Federal Home Loan Bank | | 10.75 | 5/10/93 | 107.906 |
| $40,000 | U.S. Treasury note | | 8.00 | 7/15/94 | 107 |
| $20,000 | Federal Home Loan Bank | | 8.875 | 6/26/95 | 110.281 |
| $50,000 | Federal National Mortgage Assn. | | 9.35 | 11/10/97 | 112.671 |
| $50,000 | Federal National Mortgage Assn. | | 9.55 | 11/10/97 | 115.469 |
| $30,000 | U.S. Treasury note | | 8.00 | 8/15/99 | 108.406 |
| | Mortgage: | 54,000 | | | |
| | Cash: | 7,000 | | | |

Common stock: $250,000 (dividend yield 3.0%).

necessary to transfer funds from the equity portion of the fund (at the bank) to the fixed-income portion (at the brokerage firm). The number and size of these transfers should be kept to a minimum because of the importance of equity growth (and growth of dividends) to a growth-of-income objective. Because the cash receipts from the bonds and the cash disbursements to the church treasurer were both known, it should be possible to find an appropriate, if not an optimum, transfer policy of funds from the brokerage firm.

Second, and of greater concern to the IAC, was the "lost income" from the $50,000 loaned to the minister. Although this interest continued to accrue, it was not currently payable and consequently could not be used to pay the bills. The 5 percent annual income growth rate meant that in 1992 the fund would be required to generate $60,196, and achieving this was going to require some advance planning.

What instructions should be given to the bank regarding the need for cash transfers, and how should the endowment fund be postured so as to generate the required $60,196 in 1992?

## INTERNET EXERCISES

The Mutual Fund Investor Center at *http://www.mfea.com* provides a step-by-step planning center that includes modules for retirement and college saving requirements. There is also a quiz to gauge the risk profile of investors. Using the planning center, do the following:

1. Determine your annual investment requirement to maintain a desired level of income flow during your retirement years. Note the various assumptions you have to make to fill out the worksheets.
2. Take the investor personality profile quiz to discover your risk-tolerance level. (This is under the "Getting Started/Understanding Risk" tabs.) Do you agree with the outcome?

## FURTHER READING

Asness, Clifford S. "Why Not 100% Equities?" *Journal of Portfolio Management*, Winter 1996, 29–34.

Baumann, W. Scott. *Performance Objectives of Investors*. Charlottesville, Va.: Research Foundation of Financial Analysts, 1975.

Bernstein, Peter L. "Are Stocks the Best Place to Be in the Long Run? A Contrary Opinion." *Journal of Investing*, Winter 1996, 9–12.

Bierman, Harold. "Why Not 100% Equities?: Comment." *Journal of Portfolio Management*, Winter 1998, 70–73.

Bierwag, G.O., George G. Kaufman, and Alden Toevs, "Immunization Strategies for Funding Multiple Liabilities." *Journal of Financial and Quantitative Analysis*, March 1983, 113–124.

Bierwag, G.O., George G. Kaufman, Robert Schweitzer, and Alden Toevs. "The Art of Risk Management in Bond Portfolios." *Journal of Portfolio Management*, Spring 1981, 27–36.

Black, Fischer. "The Investment Policy Spectrum: Individuals, Endowment Funds, and Pension Funds." *Financial Analysts Journal*, January/February 1976, 23–31.

Fabozzi, Frank J. *Bond Markets, Analysis, and Strategies*, 4th ed. Englewood Cliffs, N.J.: Prentice-Hall, 1999.

Fabozzi, Frank J., and Irving M. Pollack, eds. *The Handbook of Fixed Income Securities*. Homewood, Ill.: Dow Jones–Irwin, 1987.

Fisher, Lawrence, and Roman L. Weil. "Coping with the Risk of Interest Rate Fluctuations: Returns to Bondholders from Naive and Optimal Strategies." *Journal of Business*, October 1971, 408–431.

Fong, H. Gifford, and Oldrich Vasicek. "A Risk Minimizing Strategy for Multiple Liability Immunization." *Journal of Finance*, December 1984, 1541–1546.

Ibbotson, Roger G., and Rex A. Sinquefield. *Stocks, Bonds, Bills, and Inflation: 2004 Yearbook*. Chicago: Ibbotson Associates, 2004.

Klein, Robert A. and Jess Lederman, eds. *Controlling and Managing Interest Rate Risk*. New York: New York Institute of Finance, 1997.

Maginn, John L., and Donald L. Tuttle, eds. *Managing Investment Portfolios*, 2d ed. Boston: Warren, Gorham, and Lamont, 1990.

McEnally, Richard W. "Portfolio Management Policies for Fixed Income Investors." In *Advances in Bond Analysis and Portfolio Strategies*, ed. Frank J. Fabozzi and T. Dessa Garlicki. Chicago: Probus Publishing, 1987.

Milne, Robert D. "Determination of Portfolio Policies: Individual Investors." In *Managing Investment Portfolios*, ed. John L. Maginn and Donald L. Tuttle. Boston: Warren, 1983.

Price, Lee N. "Choosing between Growth and Yield." *Financial Analysts Journal*, November/December 1981, 57–67.

Strong, Robert A. "Linear Programming Solves Problem: Eases Duration Matching Process." *Pensions and Investment Age*, December 11, 1989, 21.

Thaler, Richard H. and J. Peter Williamson. "College and University Endowment Funds: Why Not 100% Equities?" *Journal of Portfolio Management*, Fall 1994, 27–37.

Vandell, Robert F. and Mark T. Finn. "Portfolio Objective: Win Big, Lose Little!" *Journal of Portfolio Management*, Fall 1981, 37–45.

# APPENDIX Mutual Fund Evaluation Term Project

*A small man—anyone with a portfolio of, say, under $100,000—is unlikely to do as well investing his own money as he can do in a no-load fund.*
***Paul Samuelson, winner of the Nobel Prize in Economics***

## Key Terms

closed-end fund
exchange-traded fund
fund manager
fund objective
investment company
load fund
management fee
mutual fund
net asset value
no-load fund
open-end fund
prospectus
redemption
redemption fee
sales charge
shareholder options

## Introduction

Many individual investors make their first entrance into the world of "real money" investing via a *mutual fund*. These are extremely popular investment vehicles for both the small and the large investor. Many institutions, in fact, place a substantial part of their money with mutual funds.

The Massachusetts Investors Trust, founded in 1924, was the first mutual fund. By the end of 2003 there were about 8,000 mutual funds in the United States, with assets totaling $7.4 trillion.

A **mutual fund** is an existing portfolio of assets into which someone may invest directly. We have seen that diversification makes sense. Mutual funds enable a person to achieve diversification instantly with a single investment. The following discussion is a primer on mutual fund fundamentals, terminology, and potential benefits.

## Classification of Mutual Funds

### *Open End versus Closed End*

Mutual funds are a type of **investment company.** There are two types of investment companies: *open end* and *closed end.*

An **open-end fund** may grow in size as new investors open accounts or as existing investors add to their accounts. Open-end funds have no set number of shares outstanding. The number may go up or down each day as new investments arrive or as *redemptions* occur. A **redemption** is a shareholder request to convert shares into cash. If I own shares in an open-end fund and decide to liquidate them, I redeem them with the mutual fund. No other person buys them from me, unlike the trading of a stock certificate. I simply inform the mutual fund administration that I want to redeem all or part of my shares. I can say that I "cashed them in," so to speak.

A *closed-end fund*, in contrast, does have a fixed number of shares that trade just like shares of common stock. The **closed-end fund** is an unmanaged portfolio of stock with each share representing partial ownership of the portfolio. Some closed-end funds trade on the New York Stock Exchange; others trade in the Nasdaq market. When an investor sells these shares, unlike the "redemption" of an open-end share another investor *does* buy them. Closed-end funds are much less popular than open-end funds. At the end of 2003, there were 586 closed-end funds in the United States with total assets of $214 billion.

People using the term *mutual fund* normally are referring to an open-end fund. This is the meaning intended in the remainder of this primer.

### Net Asset Value versus Market Value

You buy and sell an open-end fund on the basis of its **net asset value.** This equals the fund's assets minus its liabilities, all divided by the number of shares currently existing in the fund. It is analogous to the book value of the shares.

Closed-end funds, in contrast, trade at market-determined portfolio prices that may be more or less than the sum of the market values of the portfolio components.[22] Market value and net asset value are the same for an open-end fund.

### Load versus No Load

Some mutual funds have a *sales charge* associated with the purchase of new shares. The **sales charge** is a commission split between a mutual fund salesperson, that person's investment firm, and perhaps a national distributor. These funds are called **load funds.** The sales charge typically ranges from a low of 1 or 2 percent to a high of 8.5 percent.

The impact of a sales charge can be substantial. An 8.5 percent sales charge means that given a "$1,000 investment," a person actually invests only $915. The other $85 is a commission divided between the broker and the brokerage firm.[23] The size of this commission is actually larger than the stated rate. A person who pays $85 to invest $915 is really paying a rate of $85/$915, or 9.3 percent. This means that the value of the fund shares must appreciate 9.3 percent before the investment breaks even.

**No-load funds** have no sales charge. These shares are bought and sold at net asset value. The financial pages of many newspapers indicate whether a mutual fund has a load or not. Most papers give two columns of mutual fund price quotations, one labeled *NAV*, for net asset value, and another labeled *Offer*, which is the "ask" price, or the price that must be paid to acquire a new share. The difference between the "Offer" price and "NAV" is the sales charge. If the two numbers are the same, the fund is no-load. Some newspapers indicate *NL* (for no-load) in the Offer column for a no-load fund.

---

[22]The fact that the shares of closed-end funds very often sell at substantial discounts from their apparent "true" value is a continuing research puzzle.

[23]The commission may also be divided between a life insurance agent and the agency, and so on.

PORTFOLIO MEMO

## Exchange-Traded Funds

The concept of an **exchange-traded fund** (ETF) is relatively new. The first such fund was an S&P 500–index fund that began trading on the American Stock Exchange in January 1993. An ETF must register with the Securities and Exchange Commission and may be either an open-end fund or a unit-investment trust. An institutional investor creates an ETF by depositing securities with the fund custodian. The institutional investor receives, in exchange, a number of ETF shares that may be publicly traded on a stock exchange. According to the Investment Company Institute,* "The institutional investor may obtain its deposited securities by redeeming the same number of ETF shares it received from the ETF. Retail investors can only buy and sell the ETF shares once they are listed on an exchange, much as they can buy or sell any listed equity security. Unlike an institutional investor, a retail investor cannot purchase or redeem shares directly from the ETF, as with a traditional mutual fund or unit investment trust."

The majority of ETFs track major market indexes such as those Standard & Poor's and Dow Jones prepare. The following table lists the most actively traded ETFs in 2004.

*See its Website at *http://www.ici.org* for many statistics about the investment company industry.

**TABLE 3-8** EXCHANGE TRADED FUNDS

| *Fund* | *Ticker* | *YTD Return as of November 1, 2004* | *YTD Trading Volume (shares)* |
|---|---|---|---|
| Nasdaq 100 | QQQ | 1.21% | 100,832,000 |
| SPDR 500 | SPY | 2.88% | 48,824,800 |
| Semiconductor HOLDR | SMH | –22.03% | 19,171,700 |
| iShares MSCI Japan Index | EW | 3.01% | 7,101,900 |
| iShares Russell 2000 | IWM | 5.58% | 5,986,400 |
| DIAMONDS trust, series 1 | DIA | –2.61% | 5,306,500 |
| Energy Select Sector SPDR | XLE | 29.11% | 4,532,900 |
| Financial Select Sector SPDR | XLF | 3.25% | 1,944,500 |
| iShares Russell 2000 Growth | IWO | 1.43% | 1,661,800 |
| Consumer Discretionary SPDR | XLY | 3.51% | 1,289,000 |

SPDR = Standard & Poor's Depository Receipt (traded on the American Stock Exchange).
HOLDR = Holding Company Depository Receipt (created by Merrill Lynch, traded on the American Stock Exchange).
iShares = Index shares (created by Barclays Global Investors, traded on the American Stock Exchange, the Chicago Board Options Exchange, and the New York Stock Exchange).
Source: Morningstar.com

Near the end of 2004 there were 143 exchange-traded funds in the United States, with total assets of about $181 billion. Ninety-six of these were domestic funds, with 41 global/international firms and 6 bond index funds.

### Management Fees

There are expenses associated with the sale of shares, including postage costs, clerical time, and ultimately, commissions on the underlying assets of the mutual fund. Some funds, load and no-load alike, charge a **redemption fee** to offset this added cost. This fee is seldom more than 1 or 2 percent. Unlike a sales charge, this fee does not go to a salesperson; it remains a fund asset to pay the redemption expenses. Most funds do not have a redemption fee; some charge such a fee only on the redemption of shares that have been held less than a few months.

All mutual funds have a **fund manager,** who makes the decisions about what to buy or sell and when to do so. The fund manager receives a **management fee** for this service. The fee is normally a percentage of the fund's total assets, averaging about 0.75 percent. The individual investor never sees or pays the management fee. It is taken directly from the fund assets, and it results in a slight reduction in the overall performance statistics of the mutual fund.

### Buying Mutual Fund Shares

By law, a prospective fund investor must receive a fund **prospectus** before making an investment. This is a legal document outlining the fund's purpose, the management team, its mailing address, and its telephone number, and the fund's intended investment activity. All funds also provide descriptive brochures and a letter to anyone who inquires.

The actual purchase of shares is simple. The new account application asks only for name, address, tax identification number, and the investor's choice of several **shareholder options,** such as dividend reinvestment, automatic monthly investment, systematic withdrawal, individual retirement account designation, telephonic fund switching option, and so on. This one-page form, plus the investor's check, is all that is necessary if she purchases the shares directly from the fund. Unlike shares of stock, there is no such thing as an odd lot with mutual funds. The original value of a share is arbitrary, and, as we have seen, the number of shares changes daily. As a consequence of this, the fund's accounting department calculates the number of shares purchased to three decimal places. If the NAV of a no-load fund is $9.53, for instance, a $100 investment would buy $100/$9.53, or 10.493 shares.

Most no-load funds are not available for purchase through a brokerage firm because they generate no commission for the firm. Some brokerage firms have their own mutual funds, though, and a few of these can be purchased without a sales charge.

### Mutual Fund Objectives

The fund prospectus carefully outlines the type of investment anticipated in a statement of the **fund objective.** Figure 3-3 shows the relative proportion of mutual funds by type as of December 31, 2004.

*Capital appreciation* and *growth* funds both seek appreciation in the value of the fund shares; the former category is sometimes also called *aggressive growth. Income* funds seek current income from fixed-income securities and from common stock dividends. *Growth and income* funds seek a combination of both income and capital appreciation. *Balanced* funds are usually evenly split between growth and income securities. *Bond* funds invest in debt only and contain no preferred stock. *Money market* funds, the most numerous, generally seek stability of principal through investment in short-term debt instruments. *Tax-free* funds invest in municipal securities that are free from federal, and sometimes state, taxes. *Special-purpose* funds are not diversified across industries and may focus on precious metals, a particular industry, a region of the world, or special situations such as mergers or corporate reorganizations.

**FIGURE 3-3**

Mutual Funds by Type (December 31, 2004)

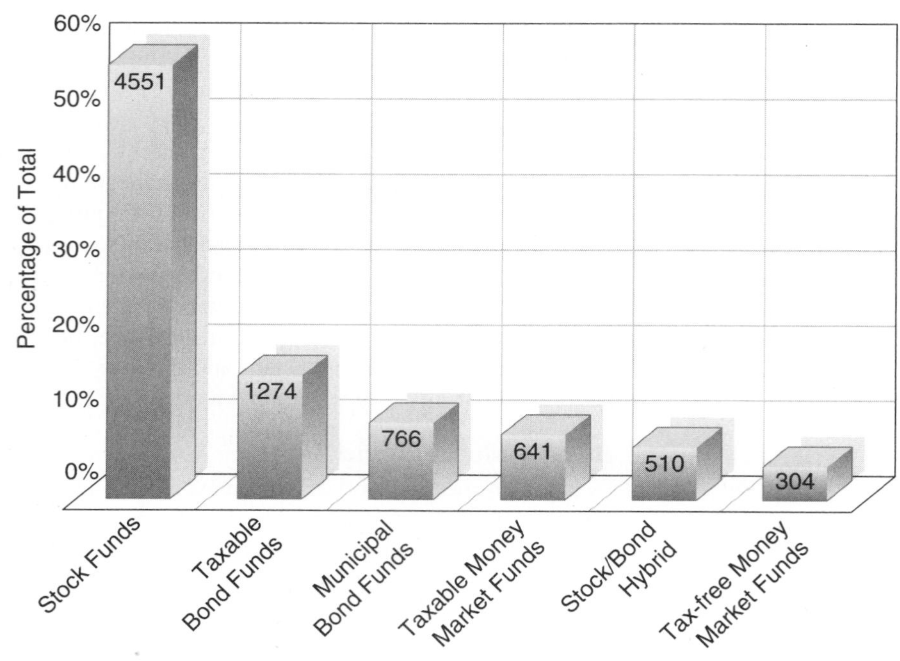


Source: Investment Company Institute.

## Term Assignment

Some parts of the requirements described in this assignment will be covered later in the book. You should, however, write for prospectuses and seek to identify the funds you will use in this project early. You may want to use the Cov, Runs, and Minvar files available on the text Website (*http://strong.swlearning.com*) while completing this assignment.

### *Part One*

Select five no-load mutual funds, each with a different objective. Do *not* use money market or tax-exempt funds. A mutual fund can specify whatever objective its management wishes, and the fund can use its own terminology. You will encounter many objectives other than those listed in this book. Common examples are "balanced," "growth and income," "small company growth," "BBB-rated bond," "precious metal," and "international." Just make sure you select five *different* objectives.

Also ensure that each fund you select has ten years of annual performance data available in the *Investment Company Yearbook*. Most library reference rooms subscribe to this well-known service. Alternatively, you can obtain historical mutual fund and stock index information via the "historical prices" option at *http://quote.yahoo.com*.

**A.** Prepare a single table showing the following for each of your five funds: [TABLE 1]

**1.** Fund name.

**2.** Annual total return statistics for the past ten years. Mutual funds must distribute a portion of their income and capital gains each year, so it is inaccurate to look only at changes in net asset value.

3. Arithmetic average of annual total returns.
4. Geometric average of annual total returns.
5. Standard deviation of annual total returns.
6. The current value of $1,000 invested 10 years ago, assuming all distributions were reinvested.

B. Prepare a covariance matrix of the five funds. [TABLE 2]
C. Prepare a correlation matrix of the five funds. [TABLE 3]
D. Write for a prospectus on each of your funds. Prepare a table showing the five largest holdings of each of your funds. You should specifically ask for this information, because some mutual funds do not automatically provide it. Show the stock ticker symbols. [TABLE 4]

### Part Two

A. Problem 1: Using end-of-the-year Treasury bill rates and the S&P 500 index, estimate the beta of each of your funds.[24]
B. Problem 2: Repeat Problem 1 using the Dow Jones Industrial Average instead of the S&P 500 index.
C. Show the T-bill rates and index levels in tabular form. [TABLE 5]
D. Problem 3: Write a 250-word essay on why your answers to Questions A and B in Part Two might be different.
E. Problem 4: Do a runs test on the annual changes in the level of the S&P 500 index. Write a 250-word essay on the interpretation of the results.

### Part Three

A. Construct an equally weighted portfolio of your five mutual funds. Prepare a table showing the arithmetic mean return, geometric mean return, and standard deviation of return for the five-fund portfolio over the ten years. [TABLE 6]
B. Using a spreadsheet package, prepare a graph showing the ten-year performance of each of your five funds and the five-fund portfolio. This chart should show the dollar value of an initial $1,000 investment over the ten-year period. [GRAPH 1]

### Part Four

Using the ten-year performance statistics of your five funds and the five-fund portfolio, determine and show graphically the efficient set using the following:

A. Mean-variance efficiency; this is merely a standard deviation/expected return plot showing six points, one for each fund and one for the five-fund portfolio. Identify the point that shows the best return per unit of risk. [GRAPH 2]
B. First-degree stochastic dominance. Identify any funds that are dominant under the first-degree stochastic dominance criterion. The technique of stochastic dominance is covered in the Appendix to Chapter 7. [GRAPH 3]
C. Second-degree stochastic dominance (SSD). Based on your plot in B, select the two funds that visually seem to have the greatest promise to show an

---

[24]The U.S. Government *Treasury Bulletin* is a convenient source of Treasury bill rates. It is compiled by Financial Management Service, Office of the Secretary, Department of the Treasury, Washington, D.C. *Standard & Poor's Security Price Index Record Statistical Service* has stock index information (Standard & Poor's Corporation, 25 Broadway, New York, NY 10004). You can also get treasury security rates from *http://www.publicdebt.treas.gov*.

example of SSD. Plot these two funds separately from the other funds. Include a few sentences indicating whether or not any dominance exists. [GRAPH 4]

### Part Five

Rank the performance of the five funds and the five-fund portfolio using the following: [TABLE 7]

A. The Sharp measure.

B. The Treynor measure.

C. The geometric mean return.
D. Stochastic dominance if you found any fund that dominated one or more of the others.

## FURTHER READING


Ang, J.S., and J.H. Chua, "Mutual Funds: Different Strokes for Different Folks?" *Journal of Portfolio Management*, Winter 1982, 43–47.

Baumol, W.J., S.M. Goldfield, L.A. Gordon, and M.F. Kohen. *The Economics of Mutual Fund Markets: Competition versus Regulation*. Boston: Kluwer Academic Publishers, 1990.

Blake, Christopher, and Matthew Morey. "Morningstar Ratings and Mutual Fund Performance." *Journal of Financial and Quantitative Analysis*, September 2000, 451–483.

Connor, G., and R.A. Korajczyk. "The Attributes, Behavior, and Performance of U.S. Mutual Funds." *Review of Quantitative Finance and Accounting* 1, 1991, 4–26.

Fortin, Rich, and Stuart Michelson. "Mutual Fund Trading Costs." *Journal of Investing*, Spring 1998, 66–70.

Garay, Urbi, and Philip Russell. "The Closed-End Fund Puzzle: A Review." *Journal of Alternative Investments*, Winter 1999, 23–43.

Indro, Daniel, Christine Jiang, Michael Hu, and Wayne Lee. "Mutual Fund Performance: A Question of Style." *Journal of Investing*, Summer 1998, 46–53.

Khorana, Ajay, and Edward Nelling. "The Determinants and Predictive Ability of Mutual Fund Ratings." *Journal of Investing*, Fall 1998, 61–66.

Lemak, David, and Peruvemba Satish. "Mutual Fund Performance and Managers' Terms of Service." *Journal of Investing*, Winter 1996, 59–63.

McDonald, J. "Objectives and Performance of Mutual Funds 1960–1969." *Journal of Financial and Quantitative Analysis*, June 1974, 311–333.

Oertmann, Peter, and Heinz Zimmermann. "U.S. Mutual Fund Characteristics Across the Investment Spectrum." *Journal of Investing*, Fall 1996, 56–68.

Reints, W., and P. Vandenberg. "A Comment on the Risk Discriminatory Powers of the Weisenberger Classifications." *Journal of Business*, April 1973, 278–283.

Sharpe, W. "Mutual Fund Performance." *Journal of Business*, January 1966, 119–138.

Taylor, Walton, and James Yoder. "How Diversified Are Stock Mutual Funds?" *Journal of Investing*, Spring 1996, 66–68.

# 4 Investment Policy

*We investment professionals also need to keep in mind that some who participate in our investment decisions will be younger and less experienced than we are; some, perhaps the most influential, will be older and more powerful but may be far less experienced with investing. They may care greatly about the fund being discussed but may not be expert in investing. We, as professionals, must manage their understanding.*

**Charles D. Ellis**

## Key Terms

asset allocation
asset class
benchmark
defined contribution plan
endowment fund
ERISA
fear of regret
fiduciary
foundation
investment management
investment policy
legal list
plan sponsor
prospectus
social investing
suitability
surplus
target return
total return

## Introduction

A sage once said that it is impossible to accomplish your objectives until you decide *what* it is you want to accomplish. While this statement seems logical, it is a fact of investment life that many investors, both individual and institutional, take the field without a game plan. Investment *policy* is different from investment *management*, and the same person should not be responsible for both. **Investment policy** is a statement about the objectives, risk tolerance, and constraints the portfolio faces. **Investment management** is the practice of attempting to achieve the objectives while staying within the established constraints.

In many situations, a statement of investment policy is not just a good idea, the law *requires* it. Retirement plans in the United States are subject to the provisions of the Employee Retirement Income Security Act of 1974, commonly called **ERISA**. Section 402(b)(1) of the act requires all pension plans to "provide a procedure for establishing and carrying out a funding policy and method consistent with the objective of the plan." The people making decisions about retirement funds may violate their legal duties if they fail to prepare and implement investment policy.

The purpose of this chapter is to see *why* an investment policy statement is important, *how* you go about creating one, and *what* should be in it.

## The Purpose of Investment Policy

*An investment policy statement should:*
*1. Outline expectations and responsibilities.*
*2. Identify objectives and constraints.*
*3. Outline eligible asset classes and their permissible use.*
*4. Provide a mechanism for evaluation.*

Procedure manuals that no one reads serve little purpose. The same is true with a statement of investment policy. If investors are going to have one (and they should), the policy ought to influence the investment process. A useful investment policy statement will do four things, ultimately resulting in better investment performance. *First,* it will outline expectations and responsibilities of the parties involved. *Second,* it will identify the investment objectives and relevant constraints. *Third,* it will address the choice of assets for the portfolio. *Fourth,* it will provide a mechanism for evaluation. In sum, it causes the parties involved to think about their responsibilities and their expectations. In addition, it increases accountability of both the client and the investment professional.

### Outline Expectations and Responsibilities

Investment *policy* is the responsibility of the client. The client might be an individual investor, the board of trustees of an endowment fund, or a corporate group that oversees the firm's pension fund. Investment *management* is the responsibility of the money manager, which might be a bank trust department, a brokerage firm, or an independent investment manager.

In a great many cases, one of two situations prevails: either there is *no* formal statement of investment policy, or the investment manager prepared it with little input from the client. Ideally, the client develops the policy statement and the manager carries it out. This is fundamental to effective long-term money management. Portfolio construction and maintenance unambiguously should be the responsibility of the investment manager.

*Investment policy is different from investment management, and different people should have responsibility for each.*

**Responsibilities and Knowledge Needs of Informed Clients.**[1] The client cannot delegate responsibility for investment policy to someone else. There are certain things only the client should do. First, he or she must set explicit investment policies consistent with their objectives. This means the person forming the policy must know what it is he or she is trying to do (the investment objective) and understand how the policy statement promotes the accomplishment of the objective.

Second, the client must define long-range objectives appropriate to the fund. The emphasis here is on *long range*. It is easy to set policy based on short-term needs or the "current outlook" for the market. Frequently this mistake leads to suboptimal investment performance. We will return to this topic later in the chapter.

Third, the client must ensure the managers are following the investment policy. The policy statement is the game plan. A deviation from the game plan should be made only after careful thought. To borrow an example from baseball, you do not

[1]The enumerated points in this section come from an excellent book by Charles D. Ellis, *Investment Policy: How to Win the Loser's Game*. This book is part of the required reading in the Chartered Financial Analyst program.

want the fund manager to swing away if you tell him to bunt. Sometimes performance evaluation focuses exclusively on "how well the investment performed." This is important, but it is also important to know whether or not the manager did what she was hired to do. There are plenty of horror stories about money managers who essentially rolled the dice with their clients' money hoping for an above average return, taking far more risk than the clients ever intended. This is especially true when a portfolio has been performing poorly; the manager feels a need to make up ground and attempts to do so by taking on more risk.

*Investment policy is the responsibility of the client, and this responsibility cannot be delegated to someone else.*

It is unlikely that any client can satisfactorily meet these requirements without some background and training in the business of investments. To begin with, clients need a genuine interest in developing an understanding of their own true interests and objectives. Some people are not talented at self-evaluation. Rationalizations are commonplace in the investment world, even among those who quickly recognize them in other people. Accountability is important; clients need to learn to accept responsibility for their decisions and to be honest when someone seeks to help them form an appropriate investment plan.

Clients also need an appreciation of the fundamental nature of capital markets and investments. There is an old story about the person who meets with his investment advisor to develop a statement of investment policy. When all is said and done, the advisor finds that what the person wants is simple: He wants a high return, he wants no risk, and he needs the money by Monday. The capital markets do not work this way. No amount of financial education will enable an investor to survey *The Wall Street Journal* every day and identify sure winners. The market is full of surprises that confound even the most informed analyst. Investors cannot eliminate risk from the marketplace unless they invest in short-term money market securities. Investors need to understand this.

Finally, clients need the discipline to work out the basic policies that will, over time, succeed in achieving their realistic investment objectives. An excellent game plan will fail if the investor abandons it. Many good things require discipline in order for them to be successful: completing the CFA program, a weed-free garden, a diet, athletic conditioning. Focusing on short-term results is seldom appropriate in the investment business. Investors need to understand that security prices fluctuate but that in the end, a well-diversified portfolio usually earns a return commensurate with its risk.

**The Investment Manager's Responsibilities.** The client is responsible for framing the investment policy while the investment manager is responsible for carrying it out. In this regard, the investment manager is responsible for a number of specific actions.

Before accepting the job and investing any money, the investment manager may need to educate the client about infeasible objectives. Sometimes the client's stated objectives are unrealistic or out of reach. Someone might say she wants to invest in stocks but needs liquidity, wants little risk, and will need to convert the entire portfolio to cash within six months. These requirements do not go together. Similarly, with fixed income securities, an investor cannot have interest compounded and mailed to him each month. He can reinvest it and let it grow, or he can take it and spend it, but he cannot do both.

With a reasonable statement of investment policy in place, the manager needs to develop an appropriate asset allocation and investment strategy. This step is a summary statement of how she intends to carry out the game plan. Next, the manager should communicate the essential characteristics of the portfolio to the client.

The investment manager should not operate secretly. Investment choices should be transparent[2] and individually identified.

The manager is also responsible for monitoring the portfolio and revising it as necessary. Investors often entrust money management to someone else because they do not want to spend time keeping up with the investments. The manager cannot be casual about this. Portfolio monitoring is part of what clients buy with the management fee. It is periodically necessary to revise the portfolio because of changes in market conditions, changes in the clients' financial or medical condition, changes in the outlook for a particular stock, or for tax reasons. Revising the portfolio as necessary is a responsibility of the investment manager.

Clients are entitled to progress reports from the investment manager. Just as the sportscaster reports "At the end of the first quarter, Penn State leads Ohio State 19–0," investment managers typically report "the score" at the end of each calendar quarter. Clients can ask for the score at any time just as fans can look at the scoreboard. After four quarters the football game is over, the calendar year ends, and both the game score and the portfolio performance get wide dissemination. Most money managers send their clients investment reports quarterly and give them oral presentations once a year, or more often if requested. The industry is cracking down on potentially misleading practices in portfolio performance presentation. Clients are entitled to know how well the investments did, and it is not fair for a smooth-talking investment manager to cover up poor performance. There is more on this topic in Chapter 17.

Finally, the manager needs to ensure there is a mechanism for learning when a client's needs change. When visiting a doctor for a checkup, one of the first questions a person will answer is "Has there been any material change in your health since your last visit?" If there has, this might cause the remainder of the examination to be different from what it otherwise would have been. Similarly, a material change in an investor's financial or family situation may require substantial changes in the portfolio asset allocation, the time horizon, the risk tolerance, or the return requirements. Examples of such events include marriage, the birth of children, changes in anticipated health expenditures, a substantial change in family income, or the inheritance of other assets. Some advisors send a short survey along with the quarterly account statement asking about any changes in these conditions.

### *Identify Objectives and Constraints*

The process of objective setting should determine both a target return and an appropriate level of risk. Risk and expected return go hand in hand, so both elements warrant consideration in the objective-setting process.

**Individual Investors.** In their book *Personal Money Management*, Bailard, Biehl, and Kaiser (BBK) propose looking at investors along two dimensions: the confidence they have in their decisions and the manner in which they make these decisions. Figure 4-1 shows these two dimensions and their extremes. This graphical representation can be very helpful in understanding an investor's personality and an appropriate investment policy.

Consider an investor who takes forever to make a decision and then worries constantly about it. BBK refer to such a person as a *guardian*. Often highly risk

[2]We say an investment or investment activity is *transparent* if it is obvious what the manager did. It is "easy to see through": You don't need someone to explain what is going on.

FIGURE 4-1

Individual Investor Classifications

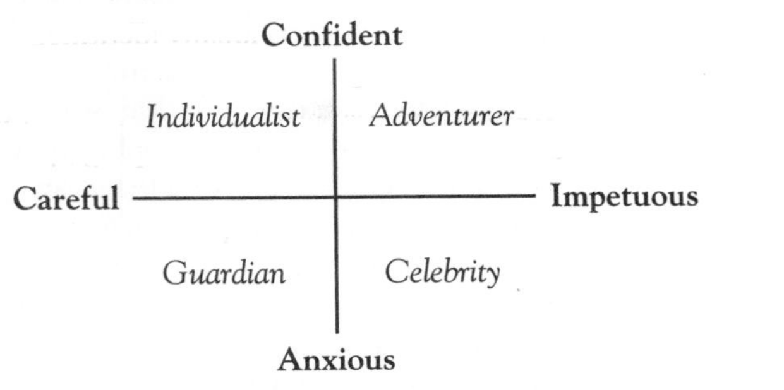


Source: Thomas E. Bailard, David L. Biehl, and Ronald W. Kaiser, *Personal Money Management*, 5th ed. (Chicago: Science Research Associates, Inc., 1986).

averse, guardians are very disturbed by declines in market value, and they find the stock market stressful. Frequently the appropriate portfolio objective for such a person is stability of principal or income.

Other worriers make their decisions quickly. BBK call them *celebrities*. These people are eager to jump on the current bandwagon. They like investment fads and worry about being left out. A celebrity would hate to admit he did not own any biotech stocks if others at the office party had them and were discussing them.

*Adventurers* make decisions quickly and feel good about them. They do not spend a lot of time second-guessing prior decisions. Adventurers often have substantial stock market experience and are quite familiar with the fundamental nature of the marketplace and its ups and downs, as well as the fact that the markets seldom offer free lunches. Adventurers typically seek capital appreciation and will occasionally speculate on a special situation.

*Individualists* are both careful and confident and are ideal clients for a money manager or stockbroker. Individualists will listen to advice, read research reports, and investigate investment alternatives on their own. They often have a longer-term investment horizon than the adventurer.

Some people are *straight arrows*; they do not fit conveniently into any single category. Depending on the circumstances, a straight arrow may move around on the two dimensions.

**Charitable Portfolios.** Many not-for-profit organizations have an endowment fund to help support them. An **endowment fund** is a perpetual portfolio designed to benefit both current citizens and future generations. Churches, the public library, the YWCA, environmental groups, and universities are examples of organizations that often have an investment portfolio of this type.

A **foundation** is an organization designed to aid the arts, education, research, or welfare in general. Plato, various Roman emperors, Benjamin Franklin, Henry Ford, John Rockefeller, and Andrew Carnegie all established foundations for favorite purposes, as have a number of modern-day sports figures and other celebrities. A foundation organizes as either a trust or as a nonprofit corporation. The trust format has fewer legal restrictions and is the more popular choice. The *assets* of a foundation may well be called its endowment.

These institutions typically have a board of trustees or directors that supervise the investments. Sometimes one or more of the members will have experience with institutional money management, but most of the time the members' personal investment experiences form the basis of their attitude toward the market. While this is understandable, it may lead the organization to develop suboptimal policies.

*A fiduciary is responsible for the management of someone else's money.*

Chapter 18 of this book deals with *fiduciary duty*. A **fiduciary** is someone responsible for the management of someone else's money. A board member for an endowment fund needs to recognize that managing money for the endowment fund is very different from managing personal funds. The legal literature speaks of the creative tension between the needs of current beneficiaries and future beneficiaries. This tension is easy to understand. Consider a local church. At one extreme, the organization could "spend all the money" because of all the pressing needs for charity in the community and throughout the world. This would benefit the current inhabitants of the planet but would provide no clear benefit to future generations. At the other extreme, the church could decide not to spend anything now, choosing instead to "let the money grow" to have more to distribute in the future. This is to the advantage of future generations and to the detriment of people living today.

In determining portfolio objectives, it is important to remember that an appropriate objective for people with their finite lifespans may well be inappropriate for a portfolio with a very long time horizon. Managers need to recognize this when preparing investment policy statements. They need to be particularly careful to avoid short-term thinking when, in fact, the portfolio needs are long term.

Richard Thaler is one of the foremost financial researchers on aspects of human behavior as it affects security prices. In an article he coauthored with Shlomo Benartzi, he coins the term *myopic loss aversion*. The term "loss averse" means that investors are more sensitive to losses than to gains. Some research, in fact, suggests that investors are twice as sensitive to losses as to gains. He finds that even long-term investors tend to value their portfolios far more often than they should. A short-term fluctuation may not matter in the long run, but loss-averse investors do not like it and may act to reduce this loss, even though the action may be inconsistent with their long-run best interests.

**Institutional Portfolios.** Institutional investors such as insurance companies and pension funds have their own special needs and concerns that deserve careful consideration in the establishment of investment objectives. A pension fund, for instance, sometimes promises a particular level of retirement benefits to employees. This is a defined benefit retirement plan. In an investment portfolio of this type, it is essential to minimize the likelihood that the fund will be unable to make the payments without additional contributions from the company. The total return on the fund is not nearly as important as the relationship between the current value of the fund and the present value of what the firm promised to the employees. This difference is the fund **surplus.** The investment manager's focus is on surplus management rather than total return. We will have a closer look at surplus management shortly.

**Other Considerations in Setting Effective Objectives.** Charles Ellis says there are six important questions for the client to think through during the objective setting process.[3]

1. *What is the real risk of an adverse outcome?* Risk means that there is a chance of a loss. The consequences of a loss vary widely, depending on the circumstances. If a well-paid professional person in his peak earning years sets a goal of having an investment portfolio worth $5 million at age 65,

[3]Ellis, 27–28.

what is the practical consequence of failing to achieve this goal by half a million? The shortfall will probably not make much difference in the person's retirement lifestyle, charitable giving, or eventual bequests. On the other hand, a 67-year-old widow who takes a lump-sum retirement benefit and invests it to earn an annual living wage of $25,000 would be seriously affected if the invested principal were badly eroded by adverse equity market conditions.

2. *What are the probable emotional reactions of clients to an adverse experience?* A guardian in the BBK taxonomy does not deal well with declining security values. This may be true even if the decline is immaterial. Consider the case of an individual investor's retirement fund that is predominately invested in U.S. Treasury bonds. A rise in market interest rates will cause the market value of the portfolio to fall, but this may actually be to the client's benefit because maturing securities can be reinvested at the current, higher interest rate. The fact that the bonds in the portfolio fall in value does not change the income they produce, and they will still eventually be redeemed at par. In many respects, the decline in value has no economic significance.

   Try telling this to a guardian, though. It may have no economic significance, but it has a clear psychological significance. A depressed portfolio value is impossible for a guardian to ignore. A fund manager should consider this when making a decision as to whether another 40 or 50 basis points adequately compensate for the added interest rate risk of a 20-year bond over that of a 5-year bond with the associated potential for client distress.
3. *How knowledgeable about investments and markets is the client's investment committee?* Statements that begin with "Everyone knows" or "I know someone who" have the potential to lead to bad decisions. In the Chartered Financial Analyst (CFA) program, one theme that comes through loud and clear in the code of ethics is the importance of differentiating between fact and opinion. People may *believe* that interest rates are coming down, but they do not know that for certain. Conventional wisdom is frequently assertive and without empirical support. An investment committee should be honest in assessing the committee's ability and seek professional assistance when appropriate.
4. *What other capital or income resources does the client have and how important is the particular portfolio to the client's overall financial position?* A manager may discover that a retired investor has a $50,000 brokerage account invested entirely in a single high-tech computer stock. Before branding such an investment as inappropriate and pointing out the lack of diversification, the manager should find out if there are other assets somewhere else. There is no requirement that an investor keep all of his money with one brokerage firm, trust department, or money manager.
5. *Are any legal restrictions imposed on investment policy?* Some states have a **legal list** outlining permissible investments. For instance, many insurance companies may not buy a corporate bond without an investment-grade rating (BBB or higher by Standard & Poor's). For many years, one state retirement plan prohibited the purchase of common stock because it was "speculative." This policy may not make any sense to an investment manager, but if it is the law, she has no option but to obey it (and perhaps to try to change it).
6. *Are there any unanticipated consequences of interim fluctuations in portfolio value that might affect policy?* A university endowment has an infinite time horizon, so interim fluctuations should not matter. This is easy to say but difficult for the endowment's board to swallow. One of the likely byproducts of the

*The average expected rate of return is not affected by time, but the range or distribution of actual returns around the average is greatly affected by time.*

endowment fund is an annual set of scholarships across the university. When the market is down and the fund value declines, the board will be inclined to reduce the number or size of the scholarships accordingly. This will have an immediate, adverse effect on the university community and may have a negative public relations impact, too. Investors might say fluctuations do not matter in the short run, but this may not be the case in practice.

### Outline Eligible Asset Classes and Their Permissible Uses

An **asset class** is a logical subgroup of the set of investment alternatives. **Asset allocation** is the relative proportion of money distributed across the various asset classes. The most commonly used asset classes are equities, bonds, and cash,[4] although there is no reason to limit the number to three. Some investment managers also establish separate asset classes for foreign equities, foreign bonds, real estate, corporate bonds, government bonds, and venture capital.

*The asset allocation decision is the single most important investment decision.*

There is substantial evidence showing that the asset allocation decision is the single most important investment decision investors make. The asset allocation decision affects long-term rates of return far more than security selection, market timing, or taxes. Consequently, investors should consider asset allocation requirements the single most important aspect of the investment policy statement.

### Provide a Mechanism for Evaluation

Performance evaluation is an involved topic. Done properly, it can provide substantial information about why a portfolio did as well (or as poorly) as it did.

**The Dual Aspects of Evaluation.** An effective performance evaluation should do two things. First, it should confirm that the manager managed in the way he was hired to manage. An equity manager should not be 75 percent in cash because of worry about a market downturn. Similarly, a small-cap, value-style manager should not be predominately buying large-cap growth stocks.

*Two aspects to performance evaluation:*
*1. What the manager did.*
*2. How well the manager did it.*

Having seen *what* the manager did, the next step is seeing *how well* the manager did it. In making this determination, an investor must consider the environment in which it operated. A stock portfolio that loses 2 percent for the year did quite well if the broad market was down 15 percent. Similarly, an annual return of 15 percent may seem good, but it loses its luster if the market was up 30 percent. The important thing is how the portfolio did *relative to other portfolios comparable in risk and security composition.* Investors can improve the evaluation process by carefully choosing the reference point against which to judge the fund's performance.

Performance evaluation over short periods of time is meaningless. Consider a $25 stock that rises by a point the first week in January. This is a 4 percent gain. If it rose by 4 percent each of the other 51 weeks in the year, it would sell for $192 by the end of December. A $25 stock occasionally rises by $1, but few ever show annual appreciation of 668 percent. Stock prices sometimes show jumps because of unexpected news; it is important not to assume the unusual price behavior will continue.

**Choosing the Benchmark.** One aspect of performance evaluation is an integral part of the act of setting investment policy. This is determining the *benchmark* against which the portfolio manager will be compared. A **benchmark** can be an *absolute* or a *relative* standard of comparison. An absolute standard might be a 10 percent rate of return. A relative standard might be top quarter.

---

[4]*Cash* means cash equivalents such as money market instruments.

We often hear people speak of how a portfolio did relative to the S&P 500 stock index. Such a comparison may or may not be appropriate. Why, for instance, would an investor rate a bond manager by comparing her performance against a stock portfolio? Similarly, if an investor hires someone to manage a portfolio of small-capitalization stocks, it usually does not make sense to compare performance to a large-capitalization index like the S&P 500.

A good benchmark should have the following characteristics.[5]

- *It should be* investable. This means it should be a viable investment alternative to the managed portfolio. Someone could have elected to invest in the benchmark rather than in the managed portfolio.
- *It should be* specified in advance. A common violation of this condition is a benchmark such as "median manager performance." This form of benchmark means the investor wants the manager to earn a return better than at least half of the other investment managers. With a performance gauge such as this, there is no way to tell how the manager is doing until the end of the evaluation period. There is also no way to tell what this person's portfolio looked like because there is no published information on the median performing portfolio. Consequently, a median performance benchmark is also not investable.
- *It should be* unambiguous. The securities that compose the benchmark and the relative proportion each occupies should be clearly stated. Statements such as "average security" or "market average" are not precise and will not work as a standard of comparison.

*Performance measurement is meaningless over short periods.*

## Elements of a Useful Investment Policy

The investment policy statement should be tailor-made for the specific circumstances the portfolio faces. Someone else's statement will seldom be exactly right for a specific investor. Still, there is an established framework that will work in most circumstances. This involves identifying risk and return objectives and the appropriate constraints that the portfolio must meet. It is the "filling-in-the-blanks" part that requires careful thought. The Appendix to this chapter contains several well-written actual investment policy statements.

### Return

The investment policy statement should say something specific about the **target return.** This is the level of performance the fund seeks to attain. The chosen target should be feasible and consistent with the facts of life in the marketplace.

**Reasonable and Unreasonable Objectives.** Reasonable return objectives might include these:

- Achieve a long-term average rate of return of 10 percent.
- Over a five-year period, achieve a rate of return of at least 80 percent of the return on the S&P 500 index.

[5]For an excellent overview of the characteristics of a good benchmark, see Jeffrey V. Bailey, "Are Manager Universes Acceptable Performance Benchmarks?" *Journal of Portfolio Management*, Spring 1992, 9–13.

- Generate a cash flow of $25,000 in the following 12 months, with subsequent annual cash flows growing at a 2.5 percent annual rate.
- Reach a terminal value of $1 million by the year 2015.

These objectives are not substitutes for each other. The return objective depends on individual circumstances, and, if stated in dollar terms, depends on the initial value of the investment.

Return objectives that are *not* feasible include these:

- *Maintain purchasing power with 100 percent probability*. Ensuring that the portfolio at least keeps up with inflation generally requires that some portion of the funds be invested in equities. There are no guarantees in the stock market, so the possibility that the portfolio will lose money or lose purchasing power cannot be eliminated.
- *Earn at least a 10 percent rate of return each calendar year*. Normally interest rates are not high enough to produce such a return without an equity investment. Investment managers cannot guarantee a positive return in the stock market every single year.
- *Ensure that the value of the fund never falls below the initial principal and that it produces an annual yield of 7 percent*. A requirement that the fund cannot fall below its initial value is highly restrictive. This essentially precludes investment in equities. A yield of 7 percent is normally not possible with short-term investments, and long-term bonds may well decline in value.

**A Note on Total Return.** As discussed earlier in this book, **total return** is a function of both income received and the realized or unrealized gains on the portfolio components. At one time, some portfolios operated under the rather severe restriction that principal must be preserved and only the "income" could be spent, with *income* defined as interest and dividends. Fortunately, this is no longer the norm. Most states have adopted the Uniform Management of Institutional Funds Act. Among other things, this act provides that an institution may spend the income plus a "prudent" portion of both realized and unrealized gains. Today most portfolios operate under some version of the total return concept.

### *Risk*

As discussed earlier in this book, risk is a very complicated topic. The investment manager should spend as much time as necessary with the client to ensure that all parties sufficiently understand the essential nature of risk and how it affects expectations and investment performance. Professional managers know that the presence of risk is a fact of investment life. They cannot get rid of it, but they can manage it.

Sometimes the risk decision boils down to a relative determination: the portfolio can take *less* risk than average, *more* than average, or the market *norm*. This requires some way to measure risk, and the measure is usually either beta or return variance.[6] In general, long-term investors can assume above-average risk. This is true for two reasons. First, market history indicates that over the long run, more risk leads to better returns.[7] Second, some investors are unable to take a long-term

---

[6]Or standard deviation.

[7]Remember that it is not correct to say that more risk means a higher return: It means a higher *expected* return. If more risk always meant more return, there would be no risk.

perspective because of liquidity needs or other constraints. This offers a competitive advantage to those who can invest for the long run and may mean that there is an extra return increment for those who are able to supply long-term capital.

**Views of Risk.** Suppose an investor has a ten-year investment horizon and $1 million in assets to invest. The investor might think of risk in several ways, depending on the circumstances.

- *Relative market risk.* A portfolio beta more or less than 1 means above or below average return volatility. This view of risk is dynamic in that it implies a concern with periodic fluctuations in portfolio value, especially relative to average market conditions.
- *Dispersion around the average outcome.* For a given asset allocation we can measure the historical mean return and the associated standard deviation. Ten years from now, the expected portfolio value might be $2 million, with a 95 percent confidence interval of $800,000 < final value < $3.2 million.
- *Dispersion around a target return.* This is a slight variation on the previous view of risk, with greater emphasis on holding dispersion down. One investment alternative, for instance, might be a zero coupon bond portfolio that is virtually certain to provide a 7 percent rate of return over the ten-year period. Another alternative might be expected to return between 6 percent and 9 percent, with a mean value of 7.5 percent. Some investors would take the "sure" 7 percent over the more uncertain alternative.
- *Likelihood of failing to achieve a certain level of return.* The client might say, for instance, "I want to minimize the likelihood that my portfolio fails to at least keep up with the cost of living." In this case, the investor is more concerned with the possibility of losses than potential gains. The goal is to minimize the area under the curve that corresponds to a return below the average inflation rate over the ten-year period.

**The Manager's View of Risk.** In one of the classic writings on the psychology of investing, Tversky and Kahneman[8] speak of the manager's **fear of regret.** The idea is that managers do not like having to apologize to clients, so they avoid risk. The risk they should be managing is the client's investment risk, not the risk to their own egos or personal comfort levels. Less risk in the client's portfolio means that less can go wrong from the manager's perspective, and this reduces the likelihood that the manager has to play spinmeister at a board meeting or otherwise explain what happened.

One fiduciary duty requires the investment manager to act in the sole best interest of the client. Managers who recommend a level of risk far below that which is prudent for the client likely violate this fiduciary duty. Managers cannot shortchange the client's financial interest in order to reduce the likelihood of their own embarrassment.

Managers frequently have numerous clients with numerous portfolios. In keeping with the old adage about the squeaky wheel getting oiled, an absentee or disinterested client may find that the dominant investment characteristic of the portfolio is inertia.

---

[8]Amos Tversky and Daniel Kahneman, "Rational Choice and the Framing of Decisions," *Journal of Business* 59, 4, part 2, 1986, 251–78.

## Constraints

Having determined a reasonable return objective and a statement about the appropriate level of risk, the investment manager's next step is to identify the special conditions under which he or she must operate.

**Time Horizon.** The length of time the investment will be at work is critical to proper asset allocation. A portfolio for someone who needs the money in six months should differ from a portfolio that will remain in the market for many decades.

*Earnings are the most important consideration to the long-term investor.*

The recent past may overly influence both the client and the manager. Recall the spectacular gains of technology stocks and the dot.coms in 1999. It was difficult *not* to buy some of them, even when they seemed substantially overpriced by historic standards. In the long run, daily fluctuations in security values do not matter. It is the long-term growth of earnings that is of paramount importance. Rapid changes in investor psychology, risk assessments, and the associated discount rate can cause dramatic short-term changes in security prices, but these changes even out over time. Earnings are not transient; they are the most important consideration to the long-term investor.

**Tax Situation.** For many investors, taxes are the largest component of trading costs. The combined federal, state, and local tax burden can exceed 50 percent. If this is the case, it may make sense to avoid taxable bonds and stocks with a high dividend yield. At such a rate, the after-tax current yield is only half the reported value. For the same reason, before selling a stock with a large capital gain, the fund manager should make sure the alternative use of the funds outweighs the substantial cost of the sale. When it is necessary to sell a stock and take a gain, the manager will often seek to sell some losing positions at the same time to minimize the tax consequences.

**Liquidity Needs.** Some portfolios must produce a steady stream of income to the owner or to a set of beneficiaries. The manager must ensure that the required funds are available in timely fashion. A manager would not, for instance, want an investment in an illiquid limited partnership that makes irregular cash payments if someone depends on a monthly draw from the fund for living expenses.

**Legal Considerations.** Some types of investment portfolios face a legal list of eligible assets. If the law prohibits the fund from holding high-yielding bonds (often called *junk bonds*), the fund manager needs to make sure that someone monitors bond rating changes. Another common requirement is a minimum payout rate. Some foundations, for example, face a minimum annual payout rate of 5 percent of average fund assets in order to maintain their tax-exempt status.

**Unique Needs and Special Circumstances.** Money under management does not belong to the investment manager; it belongs to the client. The client may have preferences quite different from those of the manager. This is the manager's problem, not the client's.

One contemporary issue in portfolio management is the broad topic of **social investing.** A client may state that he is unwilling to make any investments in tobacco stocks, for instance. Someone else may not want any investments in electric utilities that produce any power from nuclear sources.

Some Virginia state legislators recently asked the Virginia Retirement System to divest its holding of Seagram Co., Ltd. because one of the company's subsidiaries produces gangsta rap. One legislator said "When it comes to this type of music, I don't want it to be profitable, and I certainly don't want public employees and public money financing it." A similar measure has been proposed in Texas, seeking to ban public pension fund investing in companies that produce violent or sexually explicit music.

The empirical evidence is mixed on whether or not social investing influences realized investment returns. Although researchers have reached different conclusions, a number of studies show that limiting the investment universe does not hinder investment performance.[9]

There are also some legal considerations to think about with regard to social investing. Most important is the fact that a fiduciary cannot justify mediocre portfolio performance by the alleged social benefits of the fund's investment policy.[10] The Department of Labor, which oversees pension plans, has specifically stated that the retirement benefits of the participants cannot take a back seat to any "social purpose" of the fund.[11] In its Advisory Opinion 98-04, the department viewed its rules "as prohibiting a fiduciary from subordinating the interests of participants and beneficiaries in their retirement income to unrelated objectives. . . . A decision to make an investment, or to designate an investment alternative, may not be influenced by non-economic factors unless the investment ultimately chosen by the plan, when judged solely on the basis of its economic value, would be equal to or superior to alternative available investments."[12]

There is nothing wrong with social investing, but only if it occurs without an automatic strike against the portfolio. Many charitable portfolios have an investment policy constraint that can be construed as a social screen and many of these funds have decent performance.

In the current era the complications of international politics have spawned new questions, too. For example, in March 2003 the Montana Board of Investments

PORTFOLIO MEMO

## The Vice Fund

Some statements of investment policy specifically prohibit the fund manager from investing in "vice stocks" such as tobacco, alcohol, and gaming, or from firearms manufacturers or defense stocks. For those who actively seek these investments, however, the Vice Fund (ticker symbol *VICEX*) provides one-stop shopping and sports a performance record that is thought-provoking. This small, $15 million fund invests in 40 to 50 securities of the very type that a "socially responsible" fund would screen out. The fund was up 34.33 percent in 2003 and for the first ten months of 2004 the fund outperformed the S & P 500 index by more than five percentage points, largely due to good performance by defense contractors such as L-3 Communications and Northrop Grumman. For the one-year period ending September 2004, Lipper Analytical Services ranked the fund's performance 6th out of 684 multi-cap core funds.

---

[9]See, for instance, Louis D'Antonio, Tommi Johnsen, and Bruce Hutton, "Socially Responsible Investing and Asset Allocation," *Journal of Investing*, Fall 2000, 65–72; and Lorne Abramson and Dan Chung, "Socially Responsible Investing: Viable for Value Investors?" *Journal of Investing*, Fall 2000, 73–80.

[10] See Reish, Fred, "Doing Well While Doing Good," *Plan Sponsor*, May 2003, 76.

[11] Department of Labor Advisory Opinion 94-1.

[12] Department of Lable Advisory Opinion 98-04.

voted to sell nearly $15 million dollars worth of French stocks because of French opposition to the war in Iraq.[13] Other public pension funds have considered avoiding stocks in companies doing business in Iraq because of the potential for terrorist attacks against these companies and the likely negative impact on corporate earnings.

## Risk and Return Considerations: Different Investors

An important theme in developing appropriate investment policy statements is the issue of **suitability.** This is the general "fitness" of a particular investment vehicle or investment approach to a particular investor. Extremely speculative commodities strategies, for instance, are not suitable to low-income retirees. They are too risky and do not pass the straight-face test regardless of how the manager tries to explain their merit. At the other extreme, municipal bonds are probably not appropriate either because a low-income retiree's tax bracket is too low to benefit from the interest exclusion. Investment recommendations should always be made with full recognition of the suitability of individual investments for different investment situations.

### *Individual Investors*

**Range of Requirements.** One thing that sets investment policy for individual investors apart from investment policy for institutions is the extreme range of requirements. Endowment funds, for instance, are reasonably similar in their tolerance for risk and their return requirements. Individuals, however, are quite different. An investment policy and the associated asset allocation for one investor may be totally inappropriate for another. The consequence of this is that the investment manager must spend considerable time refining the investor's needs, risk tolerance, and comprehension of the realities of the marketplace.

**Portfolio Integration with Other Assets.** It is especially important with individual investors to consider any other assets that may be present in addition to the portfolio under construction. A manager who is responsible for the investor's entire portfolio may face a substantially different set of constraints than a manager who handles only part of the investor's assets. The presence of a defined benefit retirement plan, a separate investment account, or valuable real estate may well change the appropriate return objective and level of risk tolerance.

**Risk Education.** Risk is an extraordinarily complicated topic that defies precise definition. Some aspects of risk are not immediately logical, a fact that further complicates decision making by the client (and sometimes by the investment manager).

### *Institutional Investors*

**Mutual Funds.** A *mutual fund* is an existing portfolio of assets into which someone can invest directly. With one check, an investor acquires a portion of a diversified portfolio. All mutual funds have a stated investment objective and some discussion in the prospectus about the types of assets in which the fund will invest.[14] The **prospectus** is the legal document that describes the fund's purpose and investment policy. The manager of a mutual fund must comply with the information presented

---

[13] Schneyer, Fred, "French Toast," *Plan Sponsor,* May 2003, 20.

[14] One study finds that a mutual fund's investment policy explains 100 percent of its total return. See the Surz, Stevens, and Wimer article in the Further Reading section.

PORTFOLIO MEMO

## Faith-Based Investing

An important, and growing, variant of socially responsible investing is faith-based or morally responsible investing. This is a very personal issue that affects followers of Judaism, Hinduism, Buddhism, and Islam, as well as Christianity. One financial planning firm describes its mission as providing "personal financial advisory services within a biblical framework to those who desire to live life purposefully."* One of the fund advisors states, "We spend a lot of time looking at what the Bible has to say about a lot of different things from debt to investments, diversification, and generational wealth transfer."**

One of the earliest faith-based investing services was the Christian Brothers Investment Services, formed in 1981. Organized to "balance the needs of faith and finance," the organization today manages over $3.5 billion for Catholic institutions worldwide. The firm uses a "life ethics" screen to eliminate companies involved in contraception, abortion, the production of land mines or weapons of mass destruction, handguns, tobacco, and pornography.

It seems all faith-based screens weed out pornography, while Islamic funds also identify alcohol, companies that make pork products, and financial service companies because of the Islamic law prohibition against earning interest. The Dow Jones Islamic Index excludes defense companies. At least one fund also excludes companies that support Planned Parenthood or offer spousal benefits to unmarried couples.***

*National Planning Group, Atlanta, Georgia.
**Keane, Robert F., "Keeping the Faith," *Investment Advisor*, August 2004, 48–54.
***Ibid.

to the fund's investors. If, for instance, the fund prospectus states that the fund is a common stock growth fund, it should not be predominately invested in bonds because the manager fears a market downturn. This would frustrate attempts by individual investors to establish their own preferred asset allocation.

This does not preclude the fund manager from accelerating or delaying purchases. The aggregate mutual fund industry frequently holds cash positions ranging between 5 percent and 15 percent of total assets. The important thing is that the individual who chooses to use a mutual fund as an investment vehicle understands the conditions under which it will operate.

Mutual funds seek to earn the best return consistent with the requirements and constraints of the fund prospectus. For a chosen level of risk, the fund manager seeks to maximize the total return.

**Endowment Funds.** As described earlier, an endowment fund is a long-term investment portfolio designed to assist the organization in carrying out its charitable purpose. David Swenson, chief investments officer of Yale University, identifies three purposes of an endowment fund.[15]

[15]David F. Swenson. "Endowment Management," *Investment Policy*, AIMR Seminar Proceedings (Charlottesville, Va.: AIMR, 1994).

1. *Help maintain operating independence.* When the economy turns down, charitable giving often declines. Donors are usually a principal source of income for a not-for-profit organization. A decline in the level of giving may cause real problems for an organization that has no other source of income. A reliable cash flow from an investment portfolio can keep the charity in business during a recession.
2. *Provide operational stability.* Some organizations rely on short-term, temporary funds such as government grants for a portion of their operating income. These funds might not be renewed, or their availability may decline. An endowment relieves some of the pressure to continually find new funding sources or to have another fund-raising campaign.
3. *Provide a margin of excellence.* An endowment enables an institution to do something it otherwise would be unable to do. A university can attract world-class faculty by having endowed chaired positions or by providing laboratories and classroom facilities that would otherwise have to wait.

*Endowment funds frequently have an established payout rate based on the average level of fund assets.*

Endowment funds frequently have an established payout rate based on the average level of fund assets over the last few years. It would not make sense to establish the payout as a percentage of the fund's return because in some years the fund will lose money. An institution cannot reasonably be expected to give money back (i.e., a *negative* payout) when the market has an off year. Payout rates between 4 percent and 5.5 percent are common.

Endowments usually have at least 50 percent of their assets in equities. Nationally, the typical asset mix is 60 percent equities and 40 percent bonds. Some managers refer to the bond portion of the fund as the *anchor* that provides a steady stream of income and helps attenuate the adverse effects of a market downturn. The optimum level of equity investment in an endowment fund is a matter of debate. Some managers believe a perpetual investment fund should be 100 percent in equities.[16]

**Pension Funds.** There are two main types of pension funds: *defined contribution* and *defined benefit*. The organization establishing the fund is the **plan sponsor.**

1. *Defined contribution.* In a **defined contribution plan,** the employer establishes a set dollar contribution, usually made monthly, to be made on the employee's behalf. This might be 7 percent of the employee's monthly salary. The employee has a number of choices, typically mutual funds with different objectives, as to where to invest these funds. It is up to the employee to make the actual asset allocation decision. The employer might contribute $700 in the current month, with the employee splitting this amount between a U.S. growth mutual fund and an international equity mutual fund. The employer's only obligation is to contribute. There are no guarantees as to how well the chosen investments will do. As with a direct mutual fund investment, the employee wants to earn the maximum return possible consistent with his risk tolerance.
2. *Defined benefit.* A defined benefit plan differs materially from a defined contribution plan. With this type of program, the employer guarantees a specific level of retirement benefits regardless of the performance of the market. A firm might have a program that says upon reaching age 65, the firm

[16]See, for instance, Richard H. Thaler and J. Peter Williamson, "College and University Endowment Funds: Why Not 100% Equities?" *Journal of Portfolio Management*, Fall 1994, 27–37.

will pay its retirees 75 percent of the average of their three highest earning years annually for the rest of their lives.

The defined benefit pension plan is substantially more difficult to manage than a defined contribution plan. The performance monkey is on the employer's back. The employee makes no investment choices and counts on the firm to keep its promise. Firms tend to view these eventual pension payments as a corporate liability. The managerial focus is on surplus management. The *surplus* is the difference between the market value of the pension fund and the actuarial present value of the pension benefits the company is likely to pay in the future.

*The surplus is the difference between the market value of the pension fund and the actuarial present value of the pension benefits likely to be paid in the future.*

The firm hopes that the investment performance of the pension fund will be sufficient to cover the accrued pension benefit obligation. When the market declines and the fund value goes down, the employer may have to make additional contributions into the fund to make up for the shortfall. The market decline may result from an economic recession, which is likely to be the most inconvenient time for the firm to be making additional contributions out of its depressed earnings.

In late September 2002 financially troubled Delta Air Lines announced that it would be taking a charge of approximately $750 million to its equity to cover its pension payments. Under current law, if the ratio of a plan's current liabilities to its assets falls below 90 percent the company may be required to infuse cash to get the ratio up. A Watson Wyatt study predicted that two-thirds of U.S. pension plans would need cash contributions in 2003, and that only about one-fifth of all pension plans would be properly funded at the end of the year.[17]

Similarly, General Motors' pension fund was underfunded to the tune of $17.8 billion at the end of 2002. The plan had 645,000 participants and assets over $89 billion. In the summer of 2003 the firm floated the largest debt offering in the history of the world, $17.9 billion. $13.5 billion of the proceeds were headed straight for the pension fund. General Motors added another $5 billion, and by the end of 2003 the fund had a surplus of $300 million.[18]

**Life Insurance Companies.** Each state has an insurance commissioner responsible for regulating the activities of life insurance companies.[19] As with pension funds, people rely on their life insurance companies in their personal financial planning. It would be a disaster if a large life insurance company were to go bankrupt or otherwise be unable to pay on policies as required.

A life insurance company seldom has more than 10 percent of its assets in equities. Actuarial tables accurately predict life expectancies, so the company has a reasonably good idea of its future cash outflows stemming from the policies in force. Many life insurance products have a savings element combined with the insurance feature, but the guaranteed earnings rate is modest. Consequently, investment policy at a life insurance company is *liability driven;* the performance of the capital markets is secondary. The principal investment objective is to earn a competitive return on the surplus. This is similar to the concern in a defined benefit pension plan.

*The principal investment objective of a life insurance company is to earn a competitive return on the surplus.*

Taxes are also a concern with investment management at a life insurance company. The effective tax rate can exceed 50 percent. This impacts the manager's ability to take profits or otherwise actively manage the portfolio.

---

[17]Schneyer, Fred. "Two Thirds of US Pension Plans Will Need 2003 Contributions," *Plan Sponsor*, January 2003, 16.

[18]Ward, Judy, "Water Logged," *Plan Sponsor*, March 2004, 70–72.

[19]The National Association of Insurance Commissioners (NAIC) is the governing body for the U.S. insurance industry.

*Liquidity is especially important at a property and casualty company.*

**Property and Casualty Insurance Company.** Significant differences in investment management exist at a life insurance company and a property/casualty company. A major difference is that life expectancies and the associated policy payouts are relatively stable, but disasters strike without warning and vary enormously in their scope. With these policies, the issue is not "when" but "if." With many policies, such as fire insurance on a personal residence, there is *never* a claim. When there is a claim, though, it can be a corker. Consider the aftermath of a hurricane in Florida or an earthquake in California. Thousands of policyholders will file claims at the same time and will need money immediately. For this reason, liquidity is especially important at a property and casualty company, and it influences investment policy statements.

There is no earnings rate on this type of policy, so the company need not concern itself with this. Current industry practice is to focus on the after-tax yield on the fixed income portfolio. This type of insurance company may place 20 percent or more of its assets in stock.

## Critiquing and Revising the Investment Policy Statement

As with any policy statement, someone periodically needs to review the document, ensuring that it remains relevant. If it is not, steps should be taken to revise it.

### Characteristics of a Good Statement

Experience suggests that a good investment policy statement has three clear characteristics.

1. *It is realistic.* In particular, this means that the return objectives are reasonably attainable in ordinary market conditions. A target return that comes from a myopic view of the spectacular performance from the past few years will remain elusive unless the manager ratchets up the risk of the portfolio. The target return and the statements about risk should be logically consistent.
2. *The statement should be unambiguous to an outsider.* There should be no questions about what certain terms mean. Words such as *normal*, *average*, or *ordinary* should be scrutinized to ensure the meaning an outsider infers from them is the same meaning the writer intends to imply. It is a good idea to be especially careful in spelling out what *return* and *yield* mean in the context of the policy. A paragraph explaining the total return concept can be very helpful to future members of the investment management committee at an endowment fund.
3. *The policy should have been sustainable over the past.* A person's personal physical fitness regimen may, on paper, call for a daily morning run of two miles. Does she really adhere to such a policy regardless of the weather, vacations, houseguests, or illness? When she begins to tolerate frequent "exceptions" to the policy statement, she starts down the slippery slope toward having no real policy at all, only a document full of suggestions. A statement of investment policy should not contain language that everyone around the table fully expects to be ignored periodically.

### Revising the Policy

An investment policy statement is always a good idea, but, as stated earlier, it serves little purpose if it does not influence investment action. The Department of Labor has the responsibility for enforcing the ERISA regulations. The department has a

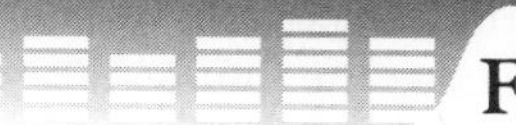

PORTFOLIO MEMO

## Family Investment Portfolios

At a recent AIMR conference* one speaker, James Hughes of the New York law firm Hughes and Whitaker, described the cultural danger of a family going from rags to riches and back to rags in three generations:

> "... if the first generation creates a fortune in a little village in China by working hard at planting rice and that family creates a financial fortune, the success usually does not significantly alter that generation's way of life. The family usually stays in the same village, for instance. Members of the second generation, however, are apt to move to the city, buy beautiful clothes, attend the university, participate in cultural activities, and evolve into prominent members of society. The third generation, with no work experience, consumes the wealth and winds up back in ... the rice paddy."**

Without professional guidance, the children and grandchildren may opt for a de facto investment policy focusing on stability of principal rather than a more appropriate long-term objective. People who inherit money may believe the prudent thing to do is to be conservative when, in fact, such a policy may not support the family standard of living. The family wealth will dissipate if the growth in the portfolio is insufficient to finance the outflow.

The third generation may lack both *investment* experience and *work* experience. It is a mistake to assume that someone with money necessarily knows how to manage that money. It may be necessary to develop the family's *human* capital in order to properly grow the *financial* capital. Money managers should be familiar with the three-generation rags/riches/rags story and help people develop appropriate statements of investment policy.

*"Investment Wealth Management: Investment Management, Taxes, Estate Planning and Wealth Transfer," March 27-28, 2001, Atlanta, Georgia.

**James H. Hughes, "Asset Allocation for Family Groups," *Investment Counseling for Private Clients III* (Charlottesville, Va.: Association for Investment Management and Research, 2001).

bulletin stating that maintaining a statement of investment policy does not relieve a fiduciary of responsibility for monitoring the investment manager.[20] The statement needs to be a familiar and consequential aspect of the portfolio management process. The body that formed the policy should review it regularly and revise it when circumstances warrant.

**Procedures for Modifying the Statement.** If circumstances change, the policy statement may well need changing. Changes should be made when necessary, and it is probably legally imprudent *not* to make them if they are required. The important thing investment managers should avoid is making changes to the policy because the previous policy has been violated, or "things are different now" and the investment manager wants to take advantage of a proverbial chance of a lifetime.

[20]DOL bulletin 92–2.

According to the chief investment officer at Yale University, the primary focus of the investment management process at Yale is the annual policy review. Many meetings suffer from a common malady: Far too much time is spent reviewing what has already happened and too little time trying to influence the future. Yale has it figured out; the people in charge of policy should be forward-looking rather than reactionary.

Changes to policy should be made carefully and sparingly, but they occasionally need to be made. An annual policy review provides a useful mechanism for discussing possible changes and ensuring that the relevant parties take the policy statement seriously.

**Changes in the Client's Financial Condition.** It may be necessary to accelerate the policy review if there are material changes in the client's financial situation. Identifying such a situation is the joint responsibility of the client and the investment manager. On the one hand, the manager cannot be a mind reader and know everything that happens to the client, but on the other hand, the manager should periodically inquire into whether or not material changes have occurred. Similarly, the client should not keep secrets about conditions that would logically influence the action of the investment manager.

## SUMMARY

A statement of investment policy is a necessary document in modern portfolio management. This document outlines responsibilities, and states the portfolio objectives and the rules under which the manager will function. Different people have responsibility for investment policy and for investment management.

An ultimate goal of the objective-setting process is determining an appropriate asset allocation. This is the single most important determinant of the long-run performance of an investment fund.

The return objectives for an individual can be quite different from those of an endowment fund, pension fund, or insurance company. Regardless of the objective, a good policy statement addresses risk and return objectives and constraints dealing with time horizon, taxes, liquidity, legal requirements, and unique circumstances.

A performance evaluation has two components: (1) identifying whether the manager did what he was hired to do, and (2) determining how well he did it. In assessing the second component, there should be an appropriate benchmark against which performance will be judged.

## QUESTIONS

1. Explain the difference between investment policy and investment management.
2. List four characteristics of a good investment policy statement.
3. List three client responsibilities regarding investment policy.

4. List six manager responsibilities regarding investment policy.
5. Contrast an individualist with a celebrity in the Bailard, Biehl, and Kaiser model.
6. Explain how someone might be a celebrity in one aspect of her life but a guardian in another.
7. Do you believe a guardian can logically invest in common stock? Explain.
8. Why is performance evaluation over short periods of time not particularly useful?
9. Explain the term creative tension with regard to an endowment fund.
10. Distinguish between an endowment and a foundation.
11. List three professions in which someone might act as a fiduciary.
12. Briefly explain the notion of myopic loss aversion.
13. Explain the difference between surplus management and total return management.
14. Why does it not make sense to establish an endowment's payout rate as a percentage of the annual return of the fund?
15. Distinguish between a defined benefit and a defined contribution pension plan.
16. Why is a defined benefit plan more difficult to manage than a defined contribution plan?
17. What is the principal investment objective of a life insurance company?
18. How are liquidity requirements different at a life insurance company and a property and casualty company?

## PROBLEMS

1. Get a copy of the article by Clifford Asness listed in the Further Reading section of this chapter. Briefly summarize his argument against an educational endowment investing 100 percent in equities.
2. Go to the Internet. Find and download a statement of investment policy for some governmental organization. Critique the statement and suggest changes.
3. Go to the Internet. Find and download a statement of investment policy for a foundation. Critique the statement and suggest changes.
4. FROM THE 1995 CFA LEVEL III EXAM (Question 1)

INTRODUCTION

Ambrose Green, 63, is a retired engineer and a client of Clayton Asset Management Associates ("Associates"). His accumulated savings are invested in Diversified Global Fund ("the Fund"), an in-house investment vehicle with multiple portfolio managers through which Associates manage nearly all client assets on a pooled basis. Dividend and capital gain distributions have produced an annual average return to Green of about 8 percent on his $900,000 original investment in the Fund, made six years ago. The $1,000,000 current value of his Fund interest represents virtually all of Green's net worth.

Green is a widower whose daughter is a single parent living with her young son. While not an extravagant person, Green's spending has exceeded his after-tax income by a considerable margin since his retirement. As a result, his non-Fund financial resources have steadily diminished and now amount to $10,000. Green does not have retirement income from a private pension plan, but does receive taxable government benefits of about $1,000 per month. His marginal tax rate is 40 percent. He lives comfortably in a rented apartment, travels extensively, and makes frequent cash gifts to his daughter and grandson, to whom he wants to leave an estate of at least $1,000,000.

Green realizes that he needs more income to maintain his lifestyle. He also believes his assets should provide an after-tax cash flow sufficient to meet his present $80,000 annual spending needs, which he is unwilling to reduce. He is uncertain as to how to proceed and has engaged you, a CFA Charterholder with an independent advisory practice, to counsel him.

Your first task is to review Green's investment policy statement.

AMBROSE GREEN'S INVESTMENT POLICY STATEMENT

Objectives:

- "I need a maximum return that includes an income element large enough to meet my spending needs, so about a 10 percent total return is required."
- "I want low risk, to minimize the possibility of large losses and preserve the value of my assets for eventual use by my daughter and grandson."

Constraints:

- "With my spending needs averaging about $80,000 per year and only $10,000 of cash remaining, I will probably have to sell something soon."
- "I am in good health and my non-cancelable health insurance will cover my future medical expenses."

QUESTION 1 HAS TWO PARTS FOR A TOTAL OF 16 MINUTES

**A.** **Identify and briefly discuss** *four* key constraints present in Green's situation not adequately treated in his investment policy statement.

**(8 minutes)**

**B.** Based on your assessment of his situation and the information presented in the Introduction, **create** and **justify** appropriate *return* and *risk* objectives for Green.

**(8 minutes)**

**5.** FROM THE 1995 CFA LEVEL III EXAM (Question 10)

INTRODUCTION

Giselle Donovan is the newly-appointed Chief Financial Officer of Bontemps International (BI), an import/export firm conducting a worldwide trading business from its principal office in New York. BI is a financially healthy, rapidly growing firm with a young work force. All liabilities are denominated in U.S. dollars. Its ERISA-qualified defined benefit pension plan is structured as shown in Table 1.

Donovan hopes to convince the Board to adopt a more global investment view and to reduce the plan's heavy emphasis on U.S. securities. She also wants the Board to consider several important aspects of the firm's non-pension financial affairs. BI's management asks you to help Donovan prepare for the extensive interaction with the Board that will result from her agenda.

**TABLE 1**

| | Percent Allocation | Prior-Year Total Return |
|---|---|---|
| ***Higher Risk Asset Classes*** | | |
| U.S. equities (large-capitalization) | 35.0% | 10.0% |
| U.S. equities (small-capitalization) | 10.0 | 12.0 |
| International equities | 5.0 | 7.0 |
| Total equities | 50.0% | |
| ***Lower Risk Asset Classes*** | | |
| U.S. Treasury bills (1 year duration) | 10.0% | 4.5 |
| U.S. intermediates and mortgage-backed securities (4 year duration) | 39.0 | 1.0 |
| U.S. long-term bonds (10 year duration) | 1.0 | 19.0* |
| Total fixed income | 50.0% | |
| Total | 100.0% | 10.0% |
| Present value of plan liabilities | $298 million | |
| Market value of plan assets | $300 million | |
| Surplus | $ 2 million | |
| Duration of liabilities | 10 years | |
| Actuarial return assumption | 7.0% | |
| BI Board's long-term total return objective | 9.0% | |

*Income element 7.0%; gain element 12.0%

QUESTION 10 HAS ONE PART FOR A TOTAL OF 6 MINUTES

The Board was surprised to learn that the pension plan's surplus had declined to only $2 million at the end of last year. This decline occurred despite the fact that the portfolio's return exceeded the Board policy's long-term total return objective (shown in Table 1).

Explain why the plan surplus declined despite the return achieved. Use *only* the information in Table 1 and the knowledge that it is BI's practice to discount plan liabilities at the market interest rate for bonds having the same duration as the liabilities.

**(6 minutes)**

**6.** FROM THE 1995 CFA LEVEL III EXAM (Question 12)

QUESTION 12 HAS TWO PARTS FOR A TOTAL OF 15 MINUTES

Donovan believes that the Board should emphasize the fundamental long-term considerations related to investment for BI's plan and de-emphasize the short-term aspects. Recognizing that a well-structured investment policy is an essential element in investing, Donovan requests your help in drafting such a document.

**A.** Discuss why the investment time horizon is of particular importance when setting investment policy for a corporate pension plan.

**(6 minutes)**

**B.** Briefly explain the importance of specifying *each* of the following when constructing an effective pension investment policy:
   i. an appropriate risk tolerance;
   ii. appropriate asset mix guidelines; and
   iii. the benchmarks to be used for measuring progress toward plan objectives.

**(9 minutes)**

**7.** FROM THE 1996 CFA LEVEL III EXAM (Question 13)

INTRODUCTION

The Help for Students Foundation (HFS) exists to provide full scholarships to U.S. universities for gifted high school graduates who otherwise would be denied access to higher education. Additional facts concerning the organization are as follows:

- Per-student full scholarship costs, which have been rising rapidly for many years, were $30,000 this year and are expected to grow at least 5 percent annually for the indefinite future.
- The market value of HFS's investment assets is $300 million, currently allocated as shown below:
  - 35 percent to long-maturity U.S. Treasury bonds;
  - 10 percent to a diversified portfolio of corporate bond issues;
  - 10 percent to U.S. bank certificates of deposit (CDs); and
  - 45 percent to large-capitalization, income-oriented U.S. stocks.
- HFS's entire annual administrative costs are paid for by donations received from supporters.
- An amount equal to 5 percent of the year-end market value of HFS's investment portfolio must be spent annually in order to preserve the foundation's existing tax-exempt status under U.S. law.

The Investment Policy Statement currently governing Trustee actions is unchanged since its adoption in the early 1960s and reads as follows:

> "The Foundation's purpose is to provide university educations for as many deserving individuals as possible for as long as possible. Accordingly, investment emphasis should be on the production of income and the minimization of market risk. As all expenses are in U.S. dollars, only domestic securities should be owned. It is the Trustees' duty to preserve and protect HFS's assets, while maximizing its grant-making ability and maintaining its tax-exempt status."

After a long period in which Board membership was unchanged, new and younger Trustees are now replacing retiring older members. As a result many aspects of HFS's operations are under review, including the principles and guidelines that have shaped investment decision making in the past.

QUESTION 13 HAS THREE PARTS
FOR A TOTAL OF 30 MINUTES

**A. Identify** *four* shortcomings of the existing HFS Investment Policy Statement and explain *why* these policy aspects should be reviewed.

**(12 minutes)**

**B.** **Create** a new Investment Policy Statement for HFS. In your response, be specific and complete with respect to objectives and constraints.

**(10 minutes)**

**C.** Using the policy created in Part B above, **revise** HFS's existing asset allocation and **justify** the resulting asset mix. You must choose from the following asset classes in constructing your response. (Calculations are not required.)

| *Asset Classes* | *Expected Total Return* |
|---|---|
| Cash equivalents | 4% |
| Medium- and long-term government bonds | 7% |
| Real estate | 8% |
| Large- and small-capitalization U.S. equities | 10% |
| International (EAFE) equities | 12% |

**(8 minutes)**

**8.** FROM THE 1997 CFA LEVEL III EXAM (Question 7)

QUESTION 7 HAS THREE PARTS FOR A TOTAL OF 16 MINUTES

The asset allocation objective of many corporate defined-benefit pension plan sponsors is to maximize returns while controlling risk, with risk defined as the volatility of returns. However, corporate pension plan sponsors may be concerned about other types of risk, such as:

- *surplus variance:* the potential for variance, over time, of the difference between the value of the pension plan's assets and value of its liabilities; or
- *corporate risk exposures:* risks in the pension plan portfolio that are similar to the risk exposures (operational, economic, or financial) of the corporate plan sponsor.

**A.** Identify two implications for asset allocation strategy of managing risk in the pension plan by controlling surplus variance.

**(6 minutes)**

**B.** Explain why a corporation might adopt a pension plan investment policy that seeks to manage corporate risk exposures.

**(5 minutes)**

**C.** Illustrate, by providing one example, how a corporation can manage corporate risk exposure in its pension plan.

**(5 minutes)**

**9.** FROM THE 1997 CFA LEVEL III EXAM (Question 18)

QUESTION 18 IS COMPOSED OF THREE PARTS FOR A TOTAL OF 21 MINUTES

BAC Associates is considering investments in international equities to diversify its U.S.-only stock portfolio. A consultant has recommended using the performance of the median manager from a broad universe of international common stock managers as the appropriate benchmark.

BAC Associates questions the use of median manager benchmarks because such benchmarks:

- lack validity because of conceptual shortcomings, and
- have statistical problems arising from survivor bias.

**A.** Discuss three conceptual shortcomings of using median manager performance as the benchmark for portfolio performance.

**(9 minutes)**

**B.** Discuss two statistical problems of using the median manager benchmark arising from survivor bias.

**(6 minutes)**

As an alternative benchmark for the international portion of the portfolio, the consultant now recommends using *either* a GDP-weighted or a market-capitalization-weighted index of all non-U.S. stock markets, such as the Morgan Stanley Capital International EAFE (Europe/Australia/Far East) Index.

**C.** Discuss two reasons that may cause an investor to prefer using a GDP-weighted international equity benchmark rather than a capitalization-weighted international equity benchmark.

**(6 minutes)**

**10.** FROM THE 2001 CFA LEVEL III EXAM (Question 6)

QUESTION 6 HAS ONE PART FOR A TOTAL OF 6 MINUTES

James Stephenson has accumulated a substantial investment portfolio without any clear long-term strategy in mind. His current investment advisor recommends that he develop an investment policy for his portfolio. Stephenson solicits advice from several friends with experience in the financial markets. Their advice includes:

- My firm, based on its experience with investors, has standard policy statements in five categories. You would be better served to adopt one of these standard policy statements instead of spending time developing a policy based on your individual circumstances.
- Developing a long-term policy can be unwise given the fluctuations of the market. You want your investment advisor to react to changing conditions and not be limited by a set policy.
- Because your investment advisor will retire in the next year or two, it would be inappropriate to commit to an investment policy before you solicit the input of your new advisor.

**State** whether you agree or disagree with *each* of the above comments. **Justify** *each* of your conclusions with *one* reason.

**Answer Question 6 in the Template provided.**

**(6 minutes)**

TEMPLATE FOR QUESTION 6

| *Comment* | *State agree or disagree (circle one)* | *Justify with one reason* |
|---|---|---|
| My investment firm, based on its experience with investors, has standard policy statements in five categories. You would be better served to adopt one of these standard policy statements instead of spending time developing a policy based on your individual circumstances. | Agree<br><br>Disagree | |
| Developing a long-term policy can be unwise given the fluctuations of the market. You want your investment advisor to react to changing conditions and not be limited by a set policy. | Agree<br><br>Disagree | |
| Because your investment advisor will retire in the next year or two, it would be inappropriate to commit to an investment policy before you solicit the input of your new advisor. | Agree<br><br>Disagree | |

11. FROM THE 1999 CFA LEVEL III EXAM (Question 12)

QUESTION 12 HAS TWO PARTS FOR A TOTAL OF 18 MINUTES

**Lindsay Corporation Pension Plan.** Michel Dumont is Chief Financial Officer of Lindsay Corporation, which is located in the United States, and chairs the Investment Committee for its $100 million defined-benefit pension plan. Lindsay operates exclusively in the U.S. market and has recently completed a five-year early retirement program. As a result of this program, many long-time employees decided to retire early at age 60 and receive full pension benefits. Lindsay's actuary has determined the following:

- 60 percent of all participants in Lindsay's defined-benefit pension plan are now retired and receiving their pensions;

- the required real rate of return based on actuarial assumptions for the pension fund is 5.5 percent annually;
- the average age of active employees who will eventually collect retirement benefits is 45 years;
- inflation has been stable at 2 percent annually, as measured by the U.S. Consumer Price Index (CPI), and is forecast to remain at this level for the foreseeable future; and
- the pension plan is currently fully funded, and Dumont would like to minimize the amount of company contributions required in the future.

**A.** Formulate and justify investment policy objectives for the Lindsay pension plan in the following three areas:
 i. return objective;
 ii. risk tolerance; and
 iii. time horizon.

**(9 minutes)**

**Mountain Top College Endowment Fund.** Dumont is a member of the Board of Trustees of the endowment fund at Mountain Top College. The fund was established to provide scholarships and currently has assets of US$ 1 billion. In addition to the U.S. campus, the college has recently amended as follows:

- the new payout level will increase the spending rate from 4 percent to 6 percent of assets each year; and
- 35 percent of the new payout level will be awarded in local currencies to students attending the college's foreign branches.

The fund's current asset allocation was structured to balance the objectives of near-term funding of scholarships and longer-term, inflation-adjusted preservation of capital. The overall volatility of the current portfolio is similar to the volatility of a domestic-only balanced portfolio. Annual increases in college tuition are forecast to average 3 percent globally over the long term, and inflation is forecast to remain at 2 percent annually as measured by U.S. CPI.

**B.** **Discuss** *each* of the following for the endowment fund. Specifically address the impact of the change in the fund's spending policy, where applicable:
 i. return objective;
 ii. risk tolerance; and
 iii. time horizon.

**(9 minutes)**

## INTERNET EXERCISE

Yahoo-Finance at *http://biz.yahoo.com/p/top.html* provides rankings of the top-performing mutual funds grouped by investment objective. Identify the leader in one of the categories for five-year performance. Click the *holdings* link. Evaluate the current portfolio composition of this fund to see if it seems consistent with its category.

## FURTHER READING


Abramson, Lorne, and Dan Chung. "Socially Responsible Investing: Viable for Value Investors?" *Journal of Investing*, Fall 2000, 73–80.

Asness, Clifford S. "Why Not 100% Equities?" *Journal of Portfolio Management*, Winter 1996, 29–34.

Bailard, Thomas E., David L. Biehl, and Ronald W. Kaiser. *Personal Money Management*, 5th ed. Chicago: Science Research Associates, Inc., 1986.

Bailey, Jeffrey V. "Are Manager Universes Acceptable Performance Benchmarks?" *Journal of Portfolio Management*, Spring 1992, 9–13.

Benartzi, Shlomo, and Richard H. Thaler. "Myopic Loss Aversion and the Equity Premium Puzzle." *Quarterly Journal of Economics*, February 1995, 73–92.

D'Antonio, Louis, Tommi Johnsen, and Bruce Hutton. "Socially Responsible Investing and Asset Allocation." *Journal of Investing*, Fall 2000, 65–72.

Ellis, Charles D. *Investment Policy: How to Win the Loser's Game*. Chicago: Irwin Professional Publishing, 1993.

Ennis, Richard M., and J. Peter Williamson. *Spending Policy for Educational Endowments*. Westport, Conn.: The Common Fund, 1976.

James H. Hughes, "Asset Allocation for Family Groups," *Investment Counseling for Private Clients III* (Charlottesville, Va.: Association for Investment Management and Research, 2001).

Kahneman, Daniel, and Amos Tversky. "Prospect Theory: An Analysis of Decision under Risk." *Econometrica* 47, 1979, 263–291.

Kritzman, Mark. "What Practitioners Need to Know about Time Diversification." *Financial Analysts Journal*, January/February 1994, 14–18.

Squires, Jan R., ed. *Investment Policy* (Seminar Proceedings). Charlottesville, Va.: Association for Investment Management and Research, 1994.

Surz, Ronald J., Dale Stevens, and Mark Wimer. "The Importance of Investment Policy." *Journal of Investing*, Winter 1999, 80–85.

Thaler, Richard H., and J. Peter Williamson. "College and University Endowment Funds: Why Not 100% Equities?" *Journal of Portfolio Management*, Fall 1994, 27–37.

Tversky, Amos, and Daniel Kahneman. "Rational Choice and the Framing of Decisions." *Journal of Business*, 59, 4, part 2, 1986, S251–78. Seminar Proceedings (Charlottesville, Va., 1994).

# APPENDIX Sample Statements of Investment Policy

## All Souls Congregational Church*

*All Souls Congregational Church*
*Endowment Fund*
*Investment Policy*
*March 2003*

### *General Purpose and Philosophy*

**Purpose.** There are two primary purposes to the All Souls Congregational Church endowment fund:

1. To provide a regular source of funds for maintenance of the church facilities and operation of the physical plant.
2. To provide stability within the operating budget when short-term funding sources are inadequate.

**Philosophy.** The fund should be managed so as to preserve the purchasing power of the assets through time and to provide for a consistent flow of income to the church budget. Future generations should be able to benefit from the endowment at the same level as the current generation. The Board of Trustees is responsible for managing the natural tension between the need for current income and the need for a growing stream of future income.

Because of the volatility of the marketplace, a policy that seeks to maintain purchasing power without exception is not feasible. There will be periods when the fund's allocation to the church's operating budget will exceed the realized rate of return on the fund.

---

*References: Association for Investment Management and Research, *Investment Policy* (Tokyo, Japan: Seminar Proceedings, April, 1994), 18–20.
Ellis, Charles D., *Investment Policy,* 2nd ed. (Chicago: Irwin, 1993).

### *Responsibilities*

**Board of Trustees.** The Board of Trustees has three undelegatable responsibilities:

1. Setting explicit investment policies consistent with the objectives of the endowment fund.
2. Defining appropriate long-range objectives.
3. Ensuring that the Investment Advisory Committee follows the established policy.

**Investment Advisory Committee.** The actual management of the endowment fund is the responsibility of the Investment Advisory Committee (IAC). The IAC may periodically advise the Board of Trustees on investment policy, but policy remains the responsibility of this latter group.

Given recent court decisions holding that proxy statements are an asset of the institution and that fiduciaries have an obligation to return them, the IAC will ensure that they are voted appropriately.

The Investment Advisory Committee should meet at least quarterly.

**Treasurer.** The church treasurer has the responsibility for any subsidiary or fund accounting the Board of Trustees deems necessary, as in, for instance, the Nason fund. The treasurer and the IAC will jointly determine the calculation of return allocations to any such subsidiary funds.

### *Objectives*

The fund should be managed on a total return basis under the assumption that it will persist in perpetuity. The long-term annual rate of return objective, including any distribution to the general fund, is 11% annually.

### *Constraints*

**Eligible Asset Classes.** The IAC may use any of the following asset classes:

1. Common stock.
2. U.S. government securities.
3. Corporate bonds in companies whose debt is rated at least BB by Standard & Poor's.
4. Convertible preferred stock.
5. Foreign equity securities, including those traded via American Depository Receipts.
6. Foreign fixed income securities.
7. Mutual funds.
8. Closed-end investment companies.
9. Covered call writing.

The following types of transactions are expressly prohibited:

1. Short sales.
2. Commodities.
3. Venture capital.
4. Purchase of securities on margin.
5. Direct real estate investment.

**Asset Allocation.** Because of the long-term time horizon, the fund should be predominately invested in equity securities. An allocation of less than 50 percent of the fund assets to equities must be approved by the Board of Trustees. As much as 15 percent of the entire portfolio may be invested in foreign securities. In general, no more than 5 percent of the fund assets should be held in the equity securities of any one company.

**Income.** In general, the annual allocation in support of the general operating fund of the church will be no more than 6 percent of the average of the year-end value of the endowment fund, less the value of the subsidiary funds, over the past three calendar years. Because there is no tax consequence to a realized gain, there is no requirement for any actual income yield from the portfolio.

### *Reporting*

The IAC will report verbally and in writing to the congregation at each annual meeting of the church and report verbally to the Board of Trustees at least twice a year.

---

## The Philadelphia Foundation*

***The Philadelphia Foundation, Inc.***
***Investment Policy***
***Approved—November 2003***

### *Mission*

The mission of The Philadelphia Foundation's (the Foundation) investment funds is to support current operations through a total return investment strategy and a spending policy set to maintain, and ideally increase, the purchasing power of the endowment, without putting the principal value of these funds at imprudent risk.

The level of the Foundation's grantmaking over time will be a function of:

1. An increasing body of assets as new contributions are added to existing endowment funds.
2. Successful investment performance using "total return" as the accepted measurement.
3. A conservative payout policy.

### *Investment Goals*

Investment goals for all investment funds of the Foundation, including both Trust and Corporate Assets, are to:

1. Meet payout requirements of Endowment Funds, calculated in accordance with a spending policy as established by the Board of Managers, currently 5%.
2. Provide sufficient liquidity to meet distribution requirements.
3. Earn a total return of 5% in excess of inflation as measured by the Consumer Price Index over a five-year time horizon.
4. Earn competitive returns relative to capital market measures, including broad market indices, as well as funds with similar objectives.
5. Investment goals and performance are to be computed net of investment management and independent investment consultant fees.

---

*The Philadelphia Foundation, © 2003.

### *Spending Policy*

Distributions will be made in accordance with a spending policy. The expected annual cash payout is 5% of the average market value, using a 20-quarter trailing average. This payout rate is established by the Board of Managers annually, for the following year. The cash payout includes cash required for the Foundation's grantmaking and for administrative costs.

### *Asset Allocation Strategy*

The general policy shall be to diversify investments to provide a balance that will enhance total return while avoiding undue risk concentration in any single asset class or investment category.

| *Asset Class* | *Target Allocation* | *Range* | *Index Benchmarks* |
|---|---|---|---|
| **Total Equity** | 50% | 40–60% | |
| Large Cap Domestic | 21% | 18–25% | S&P 500 |
| Mid/Small Cap Domestic | 12% | 9–15% | Russell 2000 |
| International EAFE | 12% | 9–15% | EAFE |
| Emerging Markets | 5% | 3–7% | MSCI Emerging Markets Free |
| **Total Fixed Income** | 27% | 23–31% | |
| Domestic Fixed Income | 22% | 18–26% | Lehman Aggregate |
| High Yield Fixed Income | 5% | 2–8% | Merrill Lynch High Yield Bond Index |
| **Alternative Investments** | 23% | 18–28% | |
| Absolute Return/Opportunistic | 10% | 6–14% | 91 Day T-Bills + 5% |
| Hedged Equity (Long/Short) | 10% | 6–14% | S & P 500 |
| Private Equity** | 3% | 0–5% | S & P 500 + 7% |
| **Cash/Short Term** | 0% | 0–10% | 90 T-Bills |

**Note that private equity performance figures are not meaningful until near the end of a partnership's life (8 to 12 years). In addition, as private equity assets are drawn down slowly, a large portion of the targeted assets will remain in the large/mid cap portfolio. Therefore, the benchmark will not include private equity until the investments become more mature and significant as a percentage of the Foundation's assets.

Should a manager deem it necessary to vary from these ranges, such variance shall be discussed with and approved by the Investment Committee.

### *Investment Guidelines*

1. The use of commingled funds/mutual funds is highly encouraged.
2. Equity holdings shall be readily marketable securities traded on the major stock exchanges, including NASDAQ. International equity investments of similar quality and marketability will be permitted.
3. Fixed income investments shall be readily marketable securities, including debt instruments of the U.S. Government and its agencies, corporations, and foreign denominated securities, so that the average portfolio quality is not less than AA. 80% of the bond portfolio value must be rated A or better.
4. Short term funds (under one year in maturity) shall be issues of high quality and marketability.
5. In order to enhance portfolio results, the Foundation may elect to invest in alternative investment strategies such as hedge funds, private equity or real estate. These investments are intended to raise portfolio returns and/or lower total portfolio volatility. In most cases, these investments will be implemented

via limited partnerships. Therefore, investment restrictions are established by the offering documents for each partnership. When investing in hedge funds, the Foundation will invest in fund of funds only, to effectively diversify manager risk in this asset class.

### Administrative and Review Procedures

1. The Investment Committee will review all policies, objectives and guidelines annually. Any changes will be presented to the Board of Managers for approval.
2. Each Investment Manager will keep the Investment Committee informed of any significant changes in the decision-making process, investment management style or personnel.
3. By the 15th of the month following the end of the quarter, each Investment Manager will provide reports on portfolio structure, performance and strategy.

### Investment Responsibility

1. The *Investment Committee* is responsible for:
   a. Overseeing the investment of trust assets.
   b. Establishing a recommended investment policy.
   c. Selecting and de-selecting Investment Managers as needed and making recommendations to the Board.
   d. Setting performance objectives and monitoring performance of Investment Managers in meeting these objectives.
   e. Reviewing investment policy and recommending changes as required.
   f. Reviewing investment objectives and expected returns and the portfolio's probability of supporting the annual spending policy.
2. *Independent Investment Managers* will be responsible for:
   a. Implementing the mandated strategy for the asset class under management, as directed by the investment committee.
   b. Acting in a prudent manner with respect to the investment of assets under management.
3. *Independent Investment Consultants* will be responsible for:
   a. Reporting monthly investment performance by manager account and asset class.
   b. Analyzing trends in manager performance, asset allocation and other objectives and making recommendations to the Investment Committee regarding same.
   c. Evaluating and proposing strategies relevant to the future of the portfolio.
   d. Assisting in the selection of investment managers.
   e. Modeling portfolios and calculating investment results under selected scenarios.
   f. Assisting in education of Board of Managers and donors about the Foundation's investment strategy and performance.
4. The *Foundation Staff* will be responsible for:
   a. Managing the investment activity to ensure sufficient Cash Flow to meet annual distribution requirements.
   b. Rebalancing portfolio in disciplined manner.
   c. Working with the independent investment consultants to compile information on investment return and performance for the Investment Committee's review.
   d. Staffing Investment Committee to ensure necessary action items are brought to the Committee and so that Committee decisions are implemented.

# Eastern Maine Healthcare*

## *Statement of Investment Objectives and Policy Guidelines for Eastern Maine Healthcare*

## *Pension Plan*
## *Endowment Fund Self Insurance Trust*
## *April 1998*

## *Amended by Eastern Maine Healthcare Board of Directors December 17, 2002*

### *Purpose*

The Statement of Investment Objectives and Policy Guidelines was developed to assist Eastern Maine Healthcare (EMH) in carrying out its fiduciary responsibilities for balancing conservation, growth and use of the assets of the pension, endowment and self insurance trust funds. Eastern Maine Medical Center (EMMC) has delegated to Eastern Maine Healthcare (the parent) authority to manage the assets of the EMMC Pension Plan on behalf of employees of EMMC, EMH, and other participating employers within the EMH system.

It is necessary that EMH, and those that manage assets on their behalf, have a clear mutual understanding of the purpose and objectives inherent in managing the assets of the funds. To this end, this statement of objectives will:

- Briefly outline the investment-related responsibilities of EMH, the Trustees and the investment advisor(s) retained to manage the assets of the funds.
- Address the funding and liquidity needs of the funds, recognizing the desire to protect the assets from inflationary erosion.
- Recognize current actuarial data and estimates of future plan requirements and characteristics for the self insurance trust and pension plan.
- Establish formal, yet flexible, investment guidelines incorporating prudent asset allocation and realistic total return goals.
- Provide a framework for regular constructive communication between EMH and all parties with responsibility for fund investments.
- Create standards of investment performance which have been historically achievable and by which the managers agree to be measured.

It is expected that this statement should be reviewed at least annually to assure that it continues to reflect the objectives of EMH.

### *Endowment Fund Spending Policy*

The Eastern Maine Healthcare Endowment supports the charitable, research, training, and capital needs of the healthcare system. The endowment is comprised of numerous pools of assets. Some of the pools are designated for a particular purpose, based on explicit restriction made by donors, while others are unrestricted and can be used for any board-designated purpose.

In establishing a spending policy for the endowment, EMH's primary goal is to balance long-term and short-term needs in carrying out its charitable purposes consistent with expected total return on its investments, price-level trends and general economic conditions. In addition, EMH desires to provide for a predictable spending pattern over an indefinite period of time.

To achieve these goals, the following guidelines are established:

**Spending Percentages.** Unless provided otherwise by the board, it is the intention of EMH to maintain an annual spending level generally in the range of three percent to six percent, with a target of five percent, of each endowment fund's moving five year average market value. In no event, however, may any distribution either: (i) decrease the value of any donor-restricted gift below its historic dollar value; or (ii) be made for a purpose other than that specified by the donor.

**Average Investment Balances.** The moving five year average market value is defined as the average of market values determined as of the close of the June accounting period over each of the five years preceding the fiscal year in which distribution is to be made.

**Permissible Universe.** Assets subject to the spending policy

1. Board-designated funds including all principal, accumulated appreciation, and accumulated interest and dividend income associated with these assets.
2. Accumulated appreciation and accumulated interest and dividend income generated from assets classified as permanently restricted whose income is unrestricted or temporarily restricted. For those endowment funds which lack an explicit donor prohibition against appropriation of appreciation, the appreciation may be appropriated by the Board and used for charitable purposes provided that the balance of any fund is not reduced below its historic dollar value (13 M.R.S.A. Chapter 97).

Assets not subject to the spending policy

1. All assets not included in the endowment investment portfolio.
2. Temporarily restricted assets.
3. Permanently donor-restricted assets.

Assets that are described in items 2 and 3 above are unavailable for distribution because the donor has restricted the use of the gift as to its purpose or time, or has restricted the original principal to remain intact for perpetuity.

**Decision Making.** The Eastern Maine Healthcare Chief Financial Officer and the Eastern Maine Charities Board of Directors must approve the expenditure of any endowment asset.

## *Objectives*

**A. Pension Plan.** The objective of the Eastern Maine Medical Center Defined Benefits Pension Plan is to assist in providing for the retirement security for employees and their beneficiaries. EMH has the responsibility to assure adequate funding to meet the Plan's benefit obligations.

The present strong financial condition of the Pension Plan combined with the young average age of the work force enables EMH to take a more long term, growth-oriented posture in the investment of Plan assets than might otherwise be warranted. This additional risk, however, must be weighed against the desire to maintain a non-contributory status by utilizing strong investment returns to offset any future contribution requirements.

Weighing these factors, EMH adopted a moderately growth-oriented investment policy. It is anticipated that as the Plan matures, the policy should move toward a more conservative posture.

The investment policy will conform with fiduciary standards of ERISA including (1) the safeguards and diversity to which a prudent investor would adhere and (2) that all transactions are undertaken for the sole interest of Plan participants and their beneficiaries.

**B. Endowment.** The objective of the endowment fund is to provide a source of funding for projects designed to enhance the delivery of Eastern Maine's health care services.

**C. Self Insurance Trust.** The self insurance trust provides initial funding for professional liability claims.

**D. Summary of Objectives.** EMH has the responsibility to assure that the funds are being used prudently and that they can continue to support these activities in the future. To control investment risk while maximizing total return, EMH has established the following investment guidelines:

- Assets of the Plan will be managed with the objective of achieving substantial gains while protecting principal from both market value and inflationary erosion. While it is understood that there may be sometime declines in fund value, the total fund is expected to achieve a positive return over a market cycle consistent with the returns of the appropriate selected indices.
- The primary focus of the investment strategy should be on capital growth. Income should be considered to the extent it is necessary to meet current cash flow requirements and to contribute to portfolio stability.
- Assets should be managed to achieve long-term consistency of performance. Excessive volatility of returns is not consistent with objectives.
- The investment policy for the funds will conform with all federal and state regulations pertaining to the investment of such assets.

Eastern Maine should review these objectives and guidelines periodically to ensure that they are consistent with fund goals.

### Asset Allocation/Manager Structure

EMH has determined that a diversified portfolio consisting of both equity and fixed income are the assets most likely to achieve the Funds' objectives. Under a moderately aggressive investment policy, a significant portion of the assets will be allocated to equities. A combination of active and passive strategies will be employed as the core equity investment. The Plan should also include active small capitalization and international equity products, as it has been shown that active managers can add significant value to these two asset classes. Fixed income should be used to provide a stable core, serving to mitigate overall portfolio return volatility. The fixed income assets should also be diversified among domestic and international markets.

It is understood that both the choice of asset classes and the targeted percentages will be reviewed periodically to ensure that the long-term needs of the funds are being met in an appropriate and prudent manner. EMH believes that the following asset mix should produce a pattern of returns over time that should conform to the desired return requirements and risk tolerance:

| | *Allocation %* | | | |
|---|---|---|---|---|
| *Asset Class* | *Minimum* | *Target* | *Maximum* | *Structure* |
| Large Cap Equity | 25 | 35 | 45 | Passive and Active |
| Small Cap Equity | 10 | 15 | 20 | Active |
| International Equity | 10 | 15 | 20 | Active |
| Core Fixed Income* | 25 | 35 | 45 | Active |

*Includes both domestic and international bonds with non-dollar bonds limited to a maximum of 25%.

International stocks are defined as highly liquid equity securities traded on the major international exchanges. Small capitalization U.S. stock holdings are defined as U.S. equity portfolios with weighted mark capitalizations under $2 billion. International bonds are high quality debt instruments issued by governments and companies domiciled outside of the United States.

Investment managers are engaged for their expertise in the management of equity and fixed income asset classes. It is recognized that in doing so, investment in cash equivalents may occasionally be necessary. However, the cash position for an equity manager's account should not exceed ten percent (10%) of the portfolio and for a fixed income manager's account, cash should not exceed twenty percent (20%) of the portfolio. It is expected that these guidelines will be strategic in nature and not change frequently.

## *Investment Guidelines*

The following investment guidelines have been established by Eastern Maine Healthcare in order to define the level of risk that is acceptable in the investment portfolios. It is expected that each investment manager will adhere to these guidelines, unless modifications have been authorized in writing by EMH. All commingled trusts, mutual funds or other pooled asset portfolios must conform to ERISA guidelines (for the Pension Plan) and to the restrictions set forth below, unless waived.

**Equities.** The following investment guidelines pertain to all types of equities. Specific sub-asset class guidelines follow.

***Commissions.*** Each manager will attempt to obtain the "best available price and most favored execution" with respect to all of the portfolio transactions.

***Permissible Investments***

- Common stocks listed or traded over the counter on a major U.S. exchange, foreign securities listed on U.S. exchanges, foreign securities listed on overseas exchanges (international equity managers only), and American Depository Receipts (ADRs).
- Preferred stocks or securities convertible into common stocks.
- Mutual or commingled funds investing in the above securities.

***Excluded Investments***

- Short sales.
- Margin purchases; lending or borrowing of funds.

- Letter stock, private or direct placements.
- Commodities contracts.
- Securities of the investment manager, the custodian, their parents or subsidiaries (excluding money market funds) or any other security that could be considered a self-dealing transaction. This restriction does not apply in the case of passive products where such investments are required to mimic the index.
- In separately managed vehicles, the portfolios may not contain companies whose primary revenue is derived from the manufacture or sale of alcohol or tobacco.

### Domestic Large Capitalization Indexed Equities

***Risk.*** The standard deviation of the quarterly returns over a three to five year period should not vary more than 0.5% from the standard deviation of the Russell 1000 Index.

***Diversification.*** Weightings in individual market sectors may not vary from the Russell 1000 sector weightings by more than two percentage points.

### Domestic Large Capitalization Equities

***Risk.*** The standard deviation of the quarterly returns over a three to five year period should not vary more than 120% of the standard deviation of the S&P 500 Index.

***Diversification.*** No more than 5% of the portfolio's market value may be invested in any one company at the time of purchase; however, should a position become more than 5% of the portfolio, the portfolio position cannot exceed 2% of the benchmark weight. No more than 25% of the portfolio may be invested in any one industry sector.

### Domestic Small Capitalization Equities

***Risk.*** The standard deviation of the quarterly returns over a three to five year period should not be greater than 140% of the standard deviation of the relevant benchmark index. Small cap value managers should be measured against the Russell 2000 Value Index, and small cap growth managers should be benchmarked to the Russell 2000 Growth Index.

***Diversification.*** No more than 5% of the portfolio's market value may be invested in any one company at the time of purchase; however, should a position become more than 5% of the portfolio, the portfolio position cannot exceed 2% of the benchmark weight. No more than 30% of the portfolio may be invested in any one industry sector.

### International Equities

***Risk.*** The standard deviation of the quarterly returns over a three to five year period should not be greater than 120% of the standard deviation of the Morgan Stanley Capital International (MSCI) All Country World International (ACWI) Ex U.S.

***Diversification.*** No more than 20% of the portfolio may be invested in emerging markets. No more than 30% of the portfolio may be invested in any one country; however, if a country comprises more than 30% of the benchmark, the portfolio weight may exceed 30%. No more than 5% of the portfolio may be invested in any one company at the time of purchase; however, should a holding become more than 5% of the portfolio, the portfolio position cannot exceed 2% of the benchmark weight.

**Fixed Income.** The following investment guidelines pertain to all types of fixed income securities.

***Risk.*** The standard deviation of the quarterly returns for the fixed income portfolio over a three to five year period should not be greater than 130% of the standard deviation of the Lehman Brothers Aggregate Bond Index.

***Diversification.*** Except for debt securities issued or guaranteed by the United States, its agencies or instrumentalities, no more than 5% of the portfolio's market value shall be invested in the securities of any one issuer. No more than 25% of the portfolio may be invested in non-dollar denominated bonds.

***Duration.*** The average effective duration of the bond portfolio may not differ by more than plus or minus 30% of the duration of the Lehman Brothers Aggregate Bond Index.

***Quality.*** The overall quality rating of the fixed income portfolio will be at least "A" as rated by a major rating agency. No more than 20% of the portfolio may be invested in issues rated below investment grade.

***Permissible Investments***

- Debt securities issued or guaranteed by the United States, its agencies or instrumentalities.
- Corporate bonds, debentures and other forms of corporate debt obligations.
- Indexed notes, floaters, variable rate obligations, and mortgage and asset-backed securities.
- Foreign bonds denominated either in U.S. dollars or foreign currencies.
- Mutual or commingled funds investing in the above securities.
- Private placement securities purchased under Rule 144A.

***Excluded Investments***

- Securities of the investment manager, the custodian, their parents or subsidiaries (excluding money market funds) or any other security that could be considered a self-dealing transaction.
- In separately managed vehicles, the portfolios may not contain companies whose primary revenue is derived from the manufacture or sale of alcohol or tobacco.

**Derivatives.** Financial derivatives may be used only with express written permission from EMH. EMH will approve their use only within prudent limits to manage risk, lower transaction costs, or gain market exposure. Under no circumstances should derivatives be used to leverage the portfolio or to materially increase portfolio risk. Specifically, use of derivatives should meet each of the following four criteria:

- Derivatives may be used to implement a strategy only when they provide a more cost-effective approach than can be achieved using approved securities.

- Derivatives will not be used to increase client-authorized risk above the level that could be achieved using only approved securities.
- Derivatives will not be used to acquire exposure to assets or indices that would not be purchased directly.
- No open-end liabilities should be created in the management of the portfolios which could expose EMH to unlimited or excessive risk.

**Cash and Equivalents.** Cash equivalents shall consist of instruments maturing in 360 days or less.

***Diversification.*** Except for United States government and agency holdings, no more than 5% of the portfolio's market value shall be invested in obligations of any one issuer.

***Quality.*** Commercial paper must be rated A-1 or better by Standard & Poor's or P-1 or better by Moody's.

***Permissible Investments.*** Approved cash equivalents include obligations of the United States government and its agencies, certificates of deposit, commercial paper, bankers acceptances, and prime quality short-term money market investment funds. International managers may invest in similarly rated securities of foreign issuers.

## Performance Standards

Investment managers are expected to achieve specified performance objectives. The objectives have both a short and long-term component, where short-term is intended to mean three years or less and long-term is a full market cycle of approximately three to five years. With the exception of mutual funds, performance comparisons should be made on a pre-fee basis. Manager performance will be reviewed quarterly to ensure compliance with these standards.

### Equities

***Long-Term.*** Passive domestic equity managers are expected to track the return on the Russell 1000 Stock Index within 10 basis points. Active large cap equity managers should aim at exceeding the S&P 500 by 100 basis points. Active small capitalization value managers should aim at exceeding the Russell 2000 Value Index by 150 basis points. Active small capitalization growth managers should aim at exceeding the Russell 2000 Growth Index by 150 basis points. Active international equity managers should aim at exceeding the Morgan Stanley Capital International (MSCI) All Country World International (ACWI) Ex U.S. by 150 basis points.

***Short Term.*** Active managers should rank in the top half of Mercer's appropriate equity universe composed of investment managers with similar risk characteristics and investment style.

### Fixed Income

***Long-Term.*** Active domestic fixed income managers should aim at exceeding the return of the Lehman Brothers Aggregate Index by 50 basis points or more on an annualized basis over the course of an interest rate cycle.

***Short-Term.*** Rank in the top half of Mercer's appropriate fixed income universe composed of investment managers with similar risk characteristics and investment style.

### Total Fund

***Long-Term.*** Exceed by 80 basis points the return on a composite index comprised of:

50% Russell 3000
15% MSCI ACWI Ex U.S.
35% Lehman Brothers Aggregate Bond Index

***Short-Term***

A. Pension—Rank in the top half of an appropriate universe for pension portfolios with market value between $20 and $250 million.
B. Endowment—Rank in the top half of an appropriate Master Trust universe.
C. Self Insurance Trust—Rank in the top half of an appropriate Master Trust universe.

## *Responsibilities*

**Eastern Maine Healthcare.** EMH acknowledges its responsibility as a pension plan fiduciary. In this regard, it must act prudently and for the exclusive interest of plan participants and their beneficiaries.

EMH acknowledges its fiduciary responsibility to attempt to balance conservation, growth, and prudent use of the endowment and self insurance trust assets.

More specifically, the corporation's responsibilities include:

***Compliance.*** Comply with the provisions of ERISA, and all pertinent federal and state regulations and rulings.

***Standards.*** Develop investment goals, objectives and performance measurement standards which are consistent with the goals of the funds.

***Spending.*** Approve a spending policy (distributions) for the endowment. In extenuating circumstances, EMH may limit endowment spending so as to preserve the purchasing power of the trust assets.

***Appointments.*** Evaluate and appoint investment managers to invest and manage fund assets. Appoint custodians and investment consultants.

***Communication.*** Communicate investment goals, objectives, and standards to investment managers, including any material changes that may subsequently occur.

***Manager Funding.*** Deploy existing assets and new monies to investment managers.

***Evaluation.*** Review and evaluate investment results in the context of established standards of performance and adherence to the investment guidelines.

***Corrective Action.*** Take whatever action is deemed prudent and appropriate, e.g. when the investment manager fails to meet mutually-accepted performance standards or significantly violates the investment guidelines.

**Investment Managers.** In recognition of their fiduciary responsibilities, investment managers must assume the following responsibilities:

***Investment Responsibility.*** Make all investment decisions with respect to the assets under its management.

***Compliance.*** Comply with this statement and any other written instructions provided by EMH. Adhere to the "prudent man" provisions of ERISA. Comply with all federal and state regulations pertaining to the investment of such assets.

***Voting of Proxies.*** Vote all proxy ballots for the exclusive benefit of the participants and beneficiaries of the Pension Plan. For all other funds, vote all proxy ballots in the best interest of EMH. Unless EMH provides information on how to vote a proxy, the manager shall vote the proxy in accordance with this policy on all shareholder issues. Upon request, the manager will provide EMH with the justification for any proxy vote.

***Notification of Changes.*** Inform EMH promptly of any material changes, e.g., in the manager's outlook, policy, or tactics or in the firm's structure including ownership, financial condition, and staff turnover.

***Reporting.*** Provide to EMH a monthly report listing all holdings and transactions. Additionally, provide a report comparing portfolio performance to the relevant indices on a quarterly and year-to-date basis, no less frequently than quarterly.

***Availability for Meetings.*** Meet at least annually or at other such times as EMH may reasonably request to discuss investment outlook, performance, strategy and tactics, organizational and personnel changes, and other pertinent matters.

**Custodian.** Eastern Maine Healthcare, in fulfillment of its fiduciary responsibilities, appoints one or more custodians to administer the funds' assets. The custodian has the responsibility to:

***Custody Securities.*** Receive, hold, manage, and invest, to the extent directed by EMH, the fund assets.

***Distributions.*** Make payments from the funds to such persons or organizations as designated in writing by authorized EMH personnel.

***Accounting.*** Keep accurate and detailed accounts of all investments, receipts, disbursements and other transactions.

***Reporting.*** Provide a written account of all holdings and transactions on a monthly basis.

**Investment Consultant.** The consultant will provide EMH with objective advice. The responsibilities will include:

***Reporting.*** Provide timely performance evaluation reports to EMH on a quarterly basis. Reports will include absolute and relative performance of each of the investment managers and the total fund. The consultant will utilize a meaningful database and market indices for comparisons.

***Consulting.*** Provide proactive advice to EMH on investment guidelines, asset allocation and manager structure. Assist in the selection of new investment managers and the termination of managers. Alert EMH of any adverse developments concerning the investment selection process, changes in the organization, and the performance of the managers.

***Availability for Meetings.*** Meet at least semiannually for a formal performance review or at other such times as EMH may reasonably request.

## Amendments

Eastern Maine Healthcare may amend this statement, subject to the approval of the Board of Directors. EMH also reserves the right to direct the investment managers to take any appropriate actions, whether or not consistent with this statement, if market conditions, liquidity needs or other circumstances so indicate.

1. These guidelines are waived for investments placed in pooled vehicles and mutual funds.
2. With respect to small capitalization growth investments actively managed by Waddell and Reed, the following guidelines apply:
   a. IV. Asset Allocation—After the initial investment positioning, cash should not represent more than 25% (waive the 10% limit stated in the policy) of the total portfolio at market value.
   b. V. Diversification—No more than 10% (waive the 5% limit stated in the policy) of the portfolio's market value may be invested in any one company at the time of purchase.

PART TWO

# Portfolio Construction

# 5 The Mathematics of Diversification

*O! This learning, what a thing it is!*
***William Shakespeare, The Taming of the Shrew***

## Key Terms

covariance matrix
efficient portfolio
industry effect
Markowitz model
minimum variance portfolio
multi-index model
single-index model

## Introduction

Ask some friends who have taken a course in portfolio theory what they most vividly remember about it, and one thing that is sure to be near the top of everyone's list is "all that math!" It is true; unwieldy equations underlie the theory behind portfolio diversification. The unfortunate thing is that deriving the formulas keeps some people from seeing the forest through the trees. The math is there to show why diversification is mathematically a good idea in addition to logically making sense.

Many books call Harry Markowitz "the father of modern portfolio theory." His pioneering work in the 1950s was the catalyst that accelerated the quantitative approach to portfolio construction. Markowitz's work centers on the quest for **efficient portfolios**—those providing the maximum return for their level of risk, or the minimum risk for a certain level of return. For this lifetime effort on portfolio construction, Markowitz shared the 1990 Nobel Prize in economic science.[1]

We know a good bit about utility and about people's attitude toward risk and return. People like return, they do not like risk, and presumably they want as much of the former with as little of the latter as possible.

This chapter covers the mathematics of diversification; the next chapter explores the practical logic. These pages will provide some guidance for people who are

[1] Markowitz's co-winners were Merton Miller and William Sharpe, both very influential in the development of modern financial theory.

intimidated by quantitative concepts. The math can be tedious, but the more of it you understand, the better your fluency in the theory and practice of portfolio construction and management.

## Linear Combinations

A portfolio's performance is ultimately the result of the performance of its components. When an investor distributes money across a handful of securities, the return realized on the investment is a linear combination of the returns on the individual investments. As you will see shortly, the portfolio's variance of return is more complicated; it is *not* a linear combination of component variances.

### Return

The expected return of a portfolio is easy to compute; it is a weighted average of the expected returns of the components. Equation 5-1 gives the general expression:

$$E(\tilde{R}_p) = \sum_{i=1}^{n} \left[ x_i E(\tilde{R}_i) \right] \tag{5-1}$$

where $x_i$ = proportion of portfolio invested in security $i$ and

$$\sum_{i=1}^{n} x_i = 1$$

*The expected return of a portfolio is a weighted average of the expected returns of the components.*

In this notation, the subscript $p$ indicates "portfolio," and $E(\tilde{R}_p)$ is the expected return on the portfolio. In other words, Equation 5-1 says that the expected return of a portfolio $E(\tilde{R}_p)$ equals the weighted sum of the component expected returns $E(\tilde{R}_i)$. The constraint that all the $x$'s add up to 1.0 is necessary because all the portfolio funds have to be invested somewhere. Every portfolio component contributes to the overall total, and this constraint ensures that all components get counted.[2] Even cash stuffed into a mattress is a portfolio component (with an expected return of 0).

Consider the data in Table 5-1. Suppose a portfolio is invested 40 percent in Stock A, with the other 60 percent in Stock B. The expected return of the two-security portfolio is then

$$\begin{aligned} E(\tilde{R}_p) &= \left[ x_A E(\tilde{R}_A) \right] + \left[ x_B E(\tilde{R}_B) \right] \\ E(\tilde{R}_p) &= \left[ 0.4(0.015) \right] + \left[ 0.6(0.020) \right] \\ &= 0.018 \\ &= 1.80\% \end{aligned}$$

The constraint to invest the money is met: 40% + 60% = 100%.

### Variance

*The variance of a linear combination of random variables is not a simple linear combination of their variances.*

Understanding the makeup of the variance of a linear combination of random variables is the essence of understanding the mathematics of diversification. Unlike the expected return, the variance of a linear combination of random variables is not a

[2] If short selling is permitted, some of the weights can be negative. This does not affect the computational method in any way; the weights must still total 1.0. The mechanics of short selling are reviewed in Chapter 23 in the section on stock lending.

**TABLE 5-1** STOCK A AND STOCK B STATISTICS

| | *Stock A* | *Stock B* |
|---|---|---|
| Expected return | .015 | .020 |
| Variance | .050 | .060 |
| Standard deviation | .224 | .245 |
| Weight | 40% | 60% |

Correlation coefficient = .50.

simple weighted average of the component variances. The Portfolio Memo "Derivation of the Variance of a Linear Combination of Random Variables" found on p. 133 in this chapter shows how to derive the formula for the variance of a linear combination. Many graduate students in finance learn how to derive this formula at some point in their academic studies.

Equation 5-2 shows the general form of the relationship for an $n$-security portfolio:

$$\sigma_p^2 = \sum_{i=1}^{n}\sum_{j=1}^{n} x_i x_j \rho_{ij} \sigma_i \sigma_j \tag{5-2}$$

where $x_i$ = proportion of total investment in Security $i$ and $\rho_{ij}$ = correlation coefficient between Security $i$ and Security $j$. This awkward-looking expression is easiest to understand by first looking at the simplest linear combination, the two-security case.

**Two-Security Case.** For a two-security portfolio containing Stock A and Stock B, the variance is this:

$$\sigma_p^2 = x_A^2\sigma_A^2 + x_B^2\sigma_B^2 + 2x_A x_B \rho_{AB}\sigma_A\sigma_B \tag{5-3}$$

The variance of the two-security portfolio in Table 5-1 is then

$$\begin{aligned}\sigma_p^2 &= (.4)^2(.05) + (.6)^2(.06) + 2(.6)(.4)(.5)(.224)(.245)\\ &= .0080 + .0216 + .0132 = .0428\end{aligned}$$

Figure 5-1 plots the expected returns for Stock A, Stock B, and the two-security portfolio containing both Stock A and Stock B.[3]

**Minimum Variance Portfolio.** In a two-security portfolio, some particular combination of the two securities will result in the least possible variance. This is called the **minimum variance portfolio.** You can find the proportions of the two securities in the minimum variance portfolio with some basic calculus. Finding the minimum of an equation requires taking the first derivative of the variance equation, setting it equal to 0, and solving for the value of the desired variable.

As shown in Equation 5-3, the variance of a two-security portfolio is as follows:

$$\sigma_p^2 = x_A^2\sigma_A^2 + x_B^2\sigma_B^2 + 2x_A x_B \rho_{AB}\sigma_A\sigma_B \tag{5-3}$$

[3] Be careful when you convert variances into standard deviations and vice versa. Suppose you calculate a variance of 0.04, which might also be expressed as 4 percent. The standard deviation is the square root of the variance. Without thinking, you might assume the standard deviation is 2 percent, because the square root of 4 is 2. This, however, does not work. The square root of 0.04 is 0.20, or 20 percent.

**FIGURE 5-1**

Risk and Expected Return

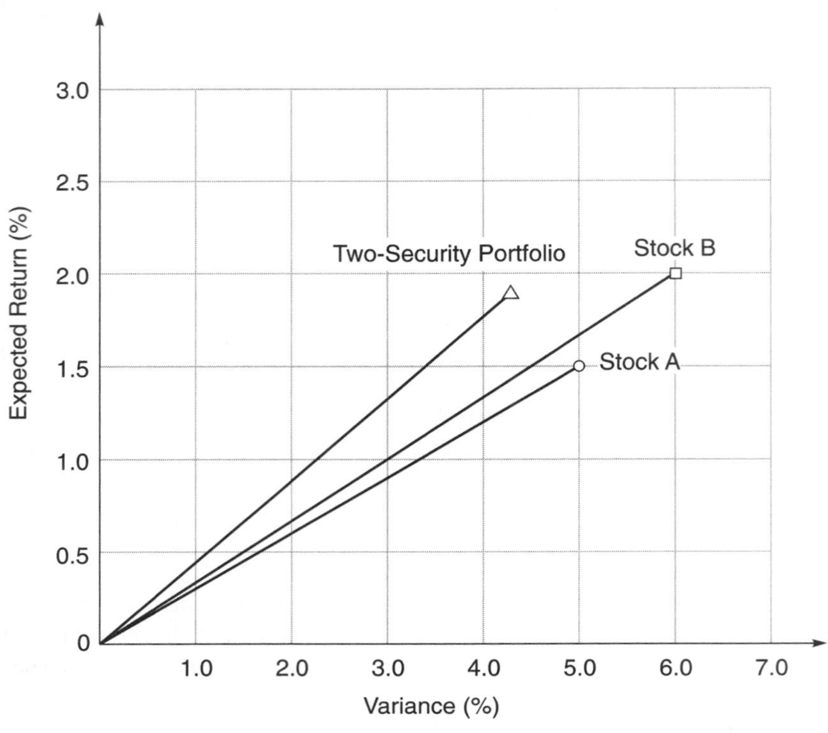


Because there are only two securities, whatever is not invested in Stock A must be invested in Stock B. That is, $x_A + x_B = 1$. This means that $x_B = 1 - x_A$. Substituting this expression for $x_B$ gives us this version of Equation 5-3:

$$\sigma_p^2 = x_A^2\sigma_A^2 + (1 - x_A)^2\ \sigma_B^2 + 2x_A(1 - x_A)\rho_{AB}\sigma_A\sigma_B \tag{5-3a}$$

To find the minimum value of this equation, we take the first derivative with respect to either $x_A$ or $x_B$. Differentiating with respect to $x_A$, the result is

$$\frac{\partial\sigma_p^2}{\partial x_A} = 2x_A\sigma_A^2 - 2\sigma_B^2 + 2x_A\sigma_B^2 + 2\sigma_A\sigma_B\rho_{AB} - 4x_A\sigma_A\sigma_B\rho_{AB} \tag{5-4}$$

Setting this equal to 0 and solving for $x_A$, we get

$$x_A = \frac{\sigma_B^2 - \sigma_A\sigma_B\rho_{AB}}{\sigma_A^2 + \sigma_B^2 - 2\sigma_A\sigma_B\rho_{AB}} \tag{5-5}$$

The minimum variance portfolio composed of Stocks A and B from Table 5-1 is therefore

$$x_A = \frac{.06 - (.224)(.245)(.5)}{.05 + .06 - 2(.224)(.245)(.5)}$$
$$= 59.07\%$$

FIGURE 5-2

Two-Security Portfolio Variance

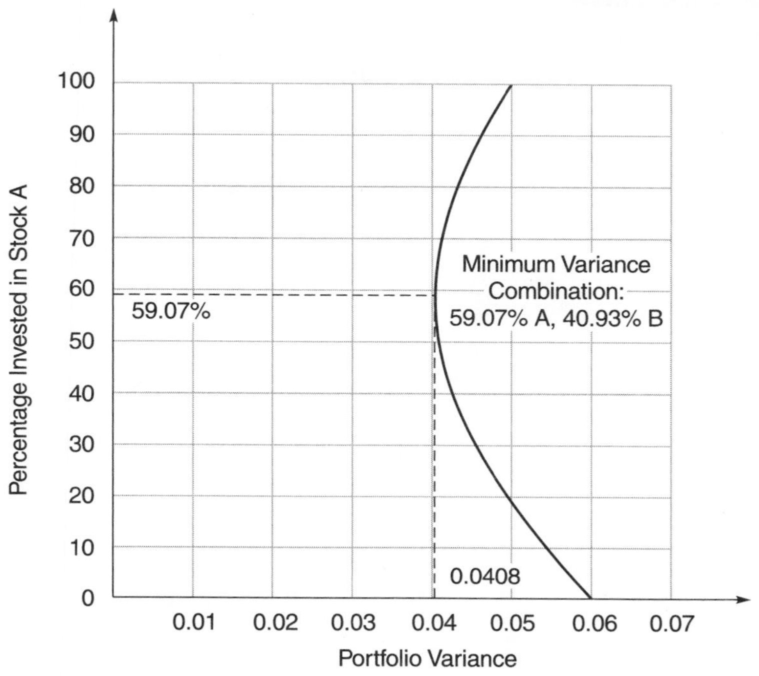


The minimum variance combination occurs when 59.07 percent of the investment is in Stock A and the other 40.93 percent is in Stock B. (Note: The proportions will change if the volatility of either stock changes or if the correlation in the returns changes.) Figure 5-2 shows this result.

**Correlation and Risk Reduction.** Figure 5-3 shows all possible combinations of Stocks A and B (beginning with 100 percent A and 0 percent B, and ending with 0 percent A and 100 percent B) for four different levels of correlation. The figure indicates that portfolio risk decreases as the correlation coefficient in the returns of the two securities decreases, and that risk reduction is greatest when the securities are perfectly negatively correlated.[4] Conversely, if the securities are perfectly positively correlated, there is no risk reduction via diversification effects.

**The *n*-Security Case.** Equation 5-2 is repeated here.[5]

$$\sigma_p^2 = \sum_{i=1}^{n}\sum_{j=1}^{n} x_i x_j \rho_{ij} \sigma_i \sigma_j \qquad (5\text{-}2)$$

where $x_i$ = proportion of total investment in Security $i$ and $\rho_{ij}$ = correlation coefficient between Security $i$ and Security $j$. From a portfolio construction perspective,

[4]In practice, we rarely find statistically significant negative correlations in the stock market. The performance of most firms is tied to the overall market. Over some time periods, however, certain commodities (such as gold, agricultural goods, and timberland) do seem to show negative correlation with a stock market index such as the S&P 500.

[5]As with the calculation for expected return, the weights ($x_i$) can be negative if short selling is allowed. The sum of the weights must still total 1.0.

FIGURE 5-3

Effect of Correlation on Variance

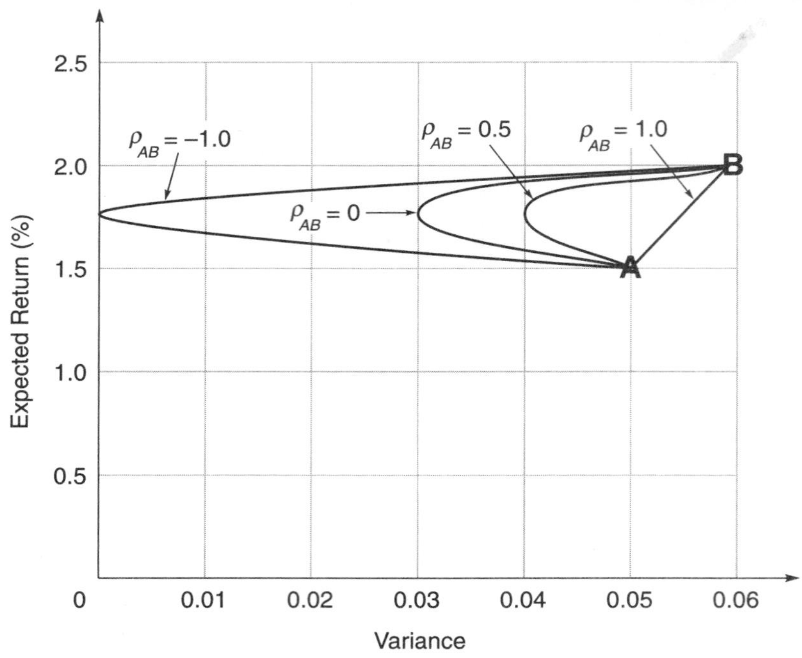


the important feature of this equation lies in the fact that it includes the correlation coefficient between all pairs of securities in the portfolio. Because $\rho_{ij}\sigma_i\sigma_j = COV(i,j)$, Equation 5-2 can be expressed in either covariance or correlation terms, and it is common to see it either way.

A **covariance matrix** is a tabular presentation of the pairwise combinations of all portfolio components. The Portfolio Memo "Building a Covariance Matrix" found on page 135 illustrates the steps taken to construct such a matrix.[6]

Recall from Chapter 2 that the covariance between two variables is the product of their expected deviations from their respective means:[7]

$$\sigma_{ij} = E\left\{\left[\tilde{R}_i - E(\tilde{R}_i)\right]\left[\tilde{R}_j - E(\tilde{R}_j)\right]\right\} \tag{5-6}$$

*The covariance of a random variable with itself is its variance*

Consider $COV(\tilde{A},\tilde{A})$. Substituting into Equation 5-6, this equals $E[(\tilde{A} - \bar{A})(\tilde{A} - \bar{A})]$, or simply

$$E\,[(\tilde{A} - \bar{A})^2]$$

the same as the formula for variance. Thus, the covariance of a random variable with itself is its variance.

[6]The COV file available at the textbook Website will calculate the covariance matrix from a series of security returns.

[7]Note that covariance is the expected value of the product of the deviations of two random variables from their means. These are different random variables, and their deviations can be positive or negative. This is why covariance can be positive or negative.

## Derivation of the Variance of a Linear Combination of Random Variables

Let $\tilde{Y} = a_0 + a_1\tilde{X}_1 + a_2\tilde{X}_2 + \cdots + a_n\tilde{X}_n$, where $a_0, a_1, \ldots a_n$ are constants and $\tilde{X}_i, \tilde{X}_j, i, j = 1, 2, \ldots, n$ are random variables with covariances $\sigma_{ij}$ and correlations $\rho_{i,j}$.

$$
\begin{aligned}
E(\tilde{Y}) &= E(a_0 + a_1\tilde{X}_1 + a_2\tilde{X}_2 + \cdots + a_n\tilde{X}_n) \\
&= E(a_0) + E(a_1\tilde{X}_1) + E(a_2\tilde{X}_2) + \cdots + E(a_n\tilde{X}_n)
\end{aligned}
$$

$$
\begin{aligned}
\tilde{Y} - E[\tilde{Y}] &= \left[a_0 - E(a_0)\right] + \left[a_1\tilde{X}_1 - E(a_1\tilde{X}_1)\right] + \left[a_2\tilde{X}_2 - E(a_2\tilde{X}_2)\right] + \cdots + \left[a_n\tilde{X}_n - E(a_n\tilde{X}_n)\right] \\
&= 0 + a_1\left[\tilde{X}_1 - E(\tilde{X}_1)\right] + a_2\left[\tilde{X}_2 - E(\tilde{X}_2)\right] + \cdots + a_n\left[\tilde{X}_n - E(\tilde{X}_n)\right]
\end{aligned}
$$

$$
\begin{aligned}
\left[\tilde{Y} - E(\tilde{Y})\right]^2 &= a_1^2\left[\tilde{X}_1 - E\left(\tilde{X}_1\right)\right]^2 + a_1a_2\left[\left(\tilde{X}_1 - E\left(\tilde{X}_1\right)\right)\left(\tilde{X}_2 - E\left(\tilde{X}_2\right)\right)\right] + \\
&\quad \cdots + a_1a_n\left[\left(\tilde{X}_1 - E\left(\tilde{X}_1\right)\right)\left(\tilde{X}_n - E\left(\tilde{X}_n\right)\right)\right] + \\
&\quad a_2a_1\left[\left(\tilde{X}_2 - E\left(\tilde{X}_2\right)\right)\left(\tilde{X}_1 - E\left(\tilde{X}_1\right)\right)\right] + a_2^2\left[\tilde{X}^2 - E\left(\tilde{X}_1\right)\right]^2 + \\
&\quad \cdots + a_na_1\left[\left(\tilde{X}_n - E\left(\tilde{X}_n\right)\right)\left(\tilde{X}_1 - E\left(\tilde{X}_1\right)\right)\right] + \cdots + a_n^2\left[\tilde{X}_n^2 - E\left(\tilde{X}_n\right)\right]^2
\end{aligned}
$$

$$
\begin{aligned}
E\left[\tilde{Y} - E\left(\tilde{Y}\right)\right]^2 &= a_1^2E\left[\tilde{X}_1 - E\left(\tilde{X}_1\right)\right]^2 + a_1a_2E\left[\left(\tilde{X}_1 - E\left(\tilde{X}_1\right)\right)\left(\tilde{X}_2 - E\left(\tilde{X}_2\right)\right)\right] + \\
&\quad \cdots + a_1a_2E\left[\left(\tilde{X}_1 - E\left(\tilde{X}_1\right)\right)\left(\tilde{X}_n - E\left(\tilde{X}_n\right)\right)\right] + \cdots + a_n^2\left[\tilde{X}_n - E\left(\tilde{X}_n\right)\right]^2
\end{aligned}
$$

By definition,

$$
\begin{aligned}
\sigma_X^2 &= E[\tilde{X} - E(\tilde{X})]^2 \\
COV\left(\tilde{X}, \tilde{Y}\right) &= E\left[\left(\tilde{X} - E\left(\tilde{X}\right)\right)\left(\tilde{Y} - E\left(\tilde{Y}\right)\right)\right] \\
COV\left(\tilde{X}, \tilde{X}\right) &= \sigma_X^2
\end{aligned}
$$

Then

$$
\sigma_Y^2 = \sum_{i=1}^{n} a_i^2\sigma_{xi}^2 + 2\sum_{i \neq j}^{n} a_ia_jCOV\left(\tilde{X}_i, \tilde{X}_j\right)
$$

But

$$
COV\left(\tilde{X}_i, \tilde{X}_j\right) = \rho_{ij}\sigma_i\sigma_j
$$

Rewriting as a double summation and substituting for $COV\left(\tilde{X}_i, \tilde{X}_j\right)$,

$$
\sigma_Y^2 = \sum_{i=1}^{n}\sum_{j=1}^{n} a_ia_j\rho_{ij}\sigma_i\sigma_j
$$

You can easily show that $COV(\tilde{A},\tilde{B}) = COV(\tilde{B},\tilde{A})$. This means that the required number of covariances is substantially less than the number of elements of the table. The actual number is given by $(n^2 - n)/2$. For a five-security portfolio, $(25 - 5)/2 = 10$ covariances are necessary, plus the five variances. With fifty securities, it would be necessary to calculate $(50^2 - 50)/2 = 1{,}225$ covariances, plus fifty variances.

You can convert a covariance matrix into a correlation matrix by dividing each covariance by the product of the two standard deviations.[8] The correlation between Securities B and C in the Portfolio Memo, for instance, is their covariance $(1.667 \times 10^{-4})$ divided by the product of their standard deviations $[(2.94 \times 10^{-2})(8.16 \times 10^{-3})]$, or

$$\rho_{BC} = \frac{1.667 \times 10^{-4}}{(2.94 \times 10^{-2})(8.16 \times 10^{-3})} = 0.69$$

Markowitz's pioneering work on the search for efficient portfolios uses the pairwise covariances of the portfolio components. We call any portfolio construction technique using the full covariance matrix a **Markowitz model.**

## Single-Index Model

*The single-index model compares all securities to a benchmark measure.*

While the Markowitz model makes use of the full covariance matrix with all its pairwise statistics, the **single-index model** simplifies matters by comparing all securities to a single benchmark.

### *Computational Advantages*

A fifty-security portfolio requires the calculation of 1,225 covariances to forecast portfolio variance. Thousands of stocks exist, and a pairwise comparison of them all would be a very unwieldy task.

Fortunately, we can avoid this problem. Instead of comparing a security with each of the others, why not compare each of the securities with a single benchmark? By observing how two independent securities behave relative to some third value, we learn something about how the two securities are likely to behave relative to each other.[9]

This is one of the merits of *beta*. We have seen that beta is a measure of how a security moves relative to overall market movements and that linear regression is a convenient way to estimate this statistic. If beta is greater than 1, the security tends to show price swings greater than the market average. A beta less than 1 means that the security moves less than the average.

A security's beta is a function of the variance of the market returns and the security's covariance with them. See Equation 5-7:

$$\beta_i = \frac{COV(\tilde{R}_i, \tilde{R}_m)}{\sigma_m^2} \qquad \textbf{(5-7)}$$

where $\tilde{R}_m$ = return on the market index; $\sigma_m^2$ = variance of the market returns; and $\tilde{R}_i$ = return on Security $i$.

---

[8]The COV file also calculates the correlation matrix directly.

[9]Nobel Prize winner William Sharpe was one of the first proponents of the single-index model.

PORTFOLIO MEMO

## Building a Covariance Matrix

Suppose we have the sample statistics for three securities as shown in Table 5-2. The covariance worksheet shows the steps to determine the covariances between A & B, A & C, and B & C. The covariance of a security with itself is exactly equal to its variance. The display of these values in tabular form is the covariance matrix (Table 5-3). Security variances are on the main diagonal. Because COV(A,B) = COV(B,A), only half the remainder of the matrix needs to be filled in; the other half is a mirror image, provides no additional information, and is frequently left blank.

**TABLE 5-2** SAMPLE RETURNS

| | *Stock* | | |
|---|---|---|---|
| | **A** | **B** | **C** |
| *Return Number* | | | |
| 1 | .010 | .050 | .025 |
| 2 | .020 | −.020 | .015 |
| 3 | .015 | .030 | .035 |
| *Sample Statistics* | | | |
| mean ($\bar{x}$) | .015 | .020 | .025 |
| standard deviation ($\sigma$) | $4.08 \times 10^{-3}$ | $2.94 \times 10^{-2}$ | $8.16 \times 10^{-3}$ |
| variance ($\sigma^2$) | $1.66 \times 10^{-5}$ | $8.64 \times 10^{-4}$ | $6.66 \times 10^{-5}$ |

***Covariance Worksheet***

| | $(x_i - \bar{x}_i)$: | | | *Columns Multiplied:* | | |
|---|---|---|---|---|---|---|
| | A | B | C | A × B | A × C | B × C |
| 1 | (.01 − .015) | (.05 − .02) | (.025 − .025) | $-1.5E^{-4}$ | 0 | 0 |
| 2 | (.02 − .015) | (−.02 − .02) | (.015 − .025) | $-2.0E^{-4}$ | $-5E^{-5}$ | $4E^{-4}$ |
| 3 | (.015 − .015) | (.03 − .02) | (.035 − .025) | 0 | 0 | $1E^{-4}$ |
| | | N = 3 | Σ | $-3.5E^{-4}$ | $-5E^{-5}$ | $5E^{-4}$ |
| | | | COV = Σ/3 = | $-1.167E^{-4}$ | $-1.667E^{-5}$ | $1.667E^{-4}$ |

**TABLE 5-3** COVARIANCE MATRIX

| | **A** | **B** | **C** |
|---|---|---|---|
| A | $1.66 \times 10^{-5}$ | | |
| B | $-1.167 \times 10^{-4}$ | $8.64 \times 10^{-4}$ | |
| C | $-1.667 \times 10^{-5}$ | $1.667 \times 10^{-4}$ | $6.66 \times 10^{-5}$ |

$COV(\tilde{A},\tilde{A}) = \sigma_A^2$; therefore, the diagonals of the matrix are the component variances.

Using a single index drastically reduces the number of preliminary calculations needed to determine portfolio variance. An analyst needs only one statistic per security instead of all the pairwise covariances. Rather than 1,225 covariances, a fifty-security portfolio requires only 50 betas.

### Portfolio Statistics with the Single-Index Model

*The beta of a portfolio is a weighted average of the component betas.*

This book does not go into the derivation of the relationships between beta and variance. For individuals who are interested in their origin, check out some of the source material listed in the Further Reading section at the end of this chapter. Four equations that describe portfolio characteristics are especially useful. These are in Table 5-4. Equation 5-8 indicates that the beta of a portfolio is merely a weighted average of the component betas, where the weights reflect the relative proportion of the total investment placed into each component. This equation greatly facilitates the calculation of a portfolio beta.

Equation 5-9 shows that if we know the variance of return on the market index and the betas of the portfolio components, we can calculate the portfolio variance. The last term in Equation 5-9 reflects unsystematic risk in the portfolio; this term approaches zero as the number of portfolio components increases. Unsystematic risk is the variance of the error term in the market model. For all practical purposes, this term is small after the portfolio size reaches about twenty securities. (The next

**TABLE 5-4** SINGLE-INDEX STATISTICS

***Beta of a Portfolio:***

$$\beta_p = \sum_{i=1}^{n} x_i \beta_i \qquad (5\text{-}8)$$

***Variance of a Portfolio:***

$$\sigma_p^2 = \left[\sum_{i=1}^{n} x_i \beta_i\right]^2 \sigma_m^2 + \sum_{i=1}^{n} x_i^2 \sigma_{ei}^2 \qquad (5\text{-}9)$$

$$= \beta_p^2 \sigma_m^2 + \sigma_{ep}^2 \qquad (5\text{-}9a)$$

$$\approx \beta_p^2 \sigma_m^2$$

***Variance of a Portfolio Component:***

$$\sigma_i^2 = \beta_i^2 \sigma_m^2 + \sigma_{ei}^2 \qquad (5\text{-}10)$$

***Covariance of Two Portfolio Components:***

$$\sigma_{AB} = \beta_A \beta_B \sigma_m^2 \qquad (5\text{-}11)$$

where $\sigma_m^2$ = variance of the market index;
$\sigma_{ei}^2$ = variance of the error term for Security $i$;
$\sigma_{ep}^2$ = variance of the error term for the portfolio; and
$x_i$ = proportion of total investment in Security $i$.

chapter amplifies this point.) In a well-diversified portfolio, unsystematic risk is negligible.

Equation 5-10 shows a method for determining the variance of a portfolio component. The last term of the equation indicates that some of the risk of a security is company specific and unrelated to market movements. This is the type of risk that diversification seeks to reduce. The first term on the right-hand side of Equation 5-10 measures systematic risk, whereas the second term measures unsystematic risk. Finally, Equation 5-11 shows how the covariance between two securities relates to their beta estimates.

## Multi-Index Model

Although beta is a very useful statistic in the construction of portfolios and in security analysis, it does not completely explain why security prices change. In fact, sometimes security price behavior deviates drastically from what is "supposed" to happen.

Numerous research projects have attempted to extend the single-index model to a more accurate **multi-index model** that considers independent variables other than the performance of an overall market index. Of particular interest are models that include an **industry effect,** which refers to factors associated with a particular line of business. We know that while stocks tend to move as a group, subgroups also tend to move together, and these subgroups often share industry characteristics. Retail food chains, for instance, are less susceptible to changes in the economy than are smokestack firms such as steel companies. People continue to buy groceries during a recession, whereas steel mills face reduced sales revenue and often have to lay people off. There should be a way to capture the information contained in a security's industry classification via some type of multi-index model. In the minds of many people, the single biggest drawback of the single-index model is its omission of industry effects.

Multi-index models generally have the form of Equation 5-12:

$$\tilde{R}_i = a_i + \beta_{im}\tilde{I}_m + \beta_{i1}\tilde{I}_1 + \beta_{i2}\tilde{I}_2 + \cdots + \beta_{in}\tilde{I}_n \tag{5-12}$$

where $a_i$ = constant associated with Security $i$; $\tilde{I}_m$ = return on the market index; $\tilde{I}_j$ = return on an industry index $j$; $\beta_{ij}$ = Security $i$'s beta for industry index $j$; $\beta_{im}$ = Security $i$'s market beta; and $\tilde{R}_i$ = return on Security $i$.[10]

Although the idea of a multi-index model employing industry (or other) effects is appealing, financial research has not uncovered much evidence that such models are particularly useful in forecasting security price behavior. There is ongoing work in this area, but the traditional market model, with its single index, continues to be the method of choice for the bulk of current portfolio management purposes.

## SUMMARY

When combined into a portfolio, the expected values of random variables combine linearly. One particular combination of securities yields the minimum variance portfolio. We find this combination by taking the first derivative of the variance

[10] Chapter 6 briefly discusses one especially important multi-index formulation, which is known as the *arbitrage pricing model*.

equation, setting it equal to 0, and solving for the value of the desired variable. The variance of return, however, is more complicated because it is necessary to collect pairwise covariances or correlations before computing the portfolio variance.

As the number of securities under consideration grows, the required number of covariances increases dramatically. This is the principal disadvantage of the Markowitz (full covariance) model.

The single-index model is computationally easy because it compares securities with a benchmark rather than with one another. We require only one beta statistic per security rather than numerous pairwise comparisons. The single-index model does not explicitly consider industry effects. The multi-index model seeks to include them, but as yet researchers have not discovered an efficient multi-index model.

## QUESTIONS

1. Explain how it is possible to have a portfolio with an infinite expected return if short sales are allowed.
2. Verify the derivative in Equation 5-4.
3. Refer to Figure 5-1. Which investment seems preferable to you: Stock A, Stock B, or the two-security portfolio?
4. In your own words, explain why covariance can be positive or negative.
5. Show that $COV(\tilde{A},\tilde{B}) = COV(\tilde{B},\tilde{A})$.
6. Write the equation for beta using correlation rather than covariance.
7. Suppose $\sigma_A^2 = 4$, $\sigma_B^2 = 6$, and $\rho_{AB} = 0.25$. What is $COV(\tilde{A},\tilde{B})$?
8. Refer to Equation 5–10. What do you think happens to $\sigma_{ei}^2$ as the number of components in the portfolio increases?
9. If the correlation between two series of returns is negative, their covariance is also negative. True or false, and why?
10. Comment on the following statement: For prediction purposes, a multi-index model like Equation 5-12 must be at least as good as the single-index model.

## PROBLEMS

1. There are 1,700 stocks in the *Value Line* index. How many covariances would have to be computed to use the Markowitz full covariance model?

Use the data in Table 5-5 for Problems 2 through 5.

**TABLE 5-5** SECURITY STATISTICS

| | *Security* | | | | | *Covariances* | | | |
|---|---|---|---|---|---|---|---|---|---|
| | A | B | C | D | | A | B | C | D |
| $E(\tilde{R})$ | 14% | 16% | 12% | 13% | A | 0.766 | 0.315 | 0.236 | 0.249 |
| $\sigma^2$ | 0.766 | 0.735 | 0.563 | 0.353 | B | 0.315 | 0.735 | 0.270 | 0.285 |
| $\beta$ | 1.050 | 1.200 | 0.900 | 0.950 | C | 0.236 | 0.270 | 0.563 | 0.214 |
| | | | | | D | 0.249 | 0.285 | 0.214 | 0.353 |

2. Calculate the proportions of Security A and Security B that represent the minimum variance portfolio.
3. What is the beta of an equally weighted portfolio of all four securities?
4. Assuming unsystematic risk equal to zero and a market variance of 0.25, what is the variance of the portfolio in Problem 3?
5. What is the expected return and variance of a theoretical portfolio made up of the following long and short positions in stocks A, B, and C?
    - 30 percent short A
    - 50 percent long B
    - 80 percent long C
6. Refer to Table 5-5, and assume that securities C and D are well-diversified portfolios. Suppose the market variance changes to 0.32. What new covariance between securities C and D does this change suggest?
7. A security has a variance of return of 25 percent. What is the standard deviation of its returns?
8. Using the data in Table 5-5, calculate the correlation between Securities B and C.
9. Given $\beta_1 = 1.10$, $\beta_2 = 1.25$, and $\sigma_{12} = 1.55$, find the variance of the market.

**TABLE 5-6** SECURITY RETURNS

| *Return Number* | *Sec. 1* | *Sec. 2* | *Sec. 3* | *Sec. 4* | *Sec. 5* |
|---|---|---|---|---|---|
| 1 | 0.027 | –0.023 | 0.056 | 0.002 | 0.033 |
| 2 | 0.012 | 0.000 | 0.013 | 0.004 | 0.017 |
| 3 | –0.022 | –0.010 | –0.015 | 0.002 | –0.045 |
| 4 | 0.013 | 0.034 | 0.015 | 0.010 | 0.008 |
| 5 | –0.011 | –0.023 | 0.012 | –0.029 | –0.019 |
| 6 | –0.033 | –0.061 | –0.035 | –0.022 | –0.024 |
| 7 | 0.029 | 0.026 | 0.002 | 0.000 | –0.001 |
| 8 | 0.055 | 0.045 | 0.047 | 0.020 | 0.056 |

Use the data in Table 5-6 for Problems 10 through 13.

10. Using the COV file and the Minvar file, what are the variance and expected return of a portfolio made up of 30 percent Security 2 and 70 percent Security 3?
11. Using the COV file, what are the variance and expected return of an equally weighted portfolio of all five securities?
12. Using the Minvar file, prepare a computer plot showing the minimum variance portfolio for each of the ten pairs of securities.
13. What is the minimum variance portfolio made up of the following three securities: Security 3, Security 4, and Security 5?
14. FROM THE 2001 CFA LEVEL II EXAM (Question 8).

INTRODUCTION

Abigail Grace has a $900,000 fully diversified portfolio. She subsequently inherits ABC Company common stock worth $100,000. Her financial advisor provided her with the forecasted information given in Table 5-7. The expected correlation coefficient of ABC stock returns with the original portfolio returns is 0.40. The inheritance changes her overall portfolio and she is deciding whether or not to keep the ABC stock.

**TABLE 5-7** RISK AND RETURN CHARACTERISTICS

| | *Expected Monthly Returns* | *Expected Standard Deviation of Monthly Returns* |
|---|---|---|
| Original Portfolio | 0.67% | 2.37% |
| ABC Company | 1.25% | 2.95% |

Assuming Grace keeps the ABC stock,

**A. Calculate** the:

i. expected return of her new portfolio that includes the ABC stock;

ii. expected covariance of ABC stock returns with the original portfolio returns; and

iii. expected standard deviation of her new portfolio that includes the ABC stock.

**(6 minutes)**

If Grace sells the ABC stock, she will invest the proceeds in risk-free government securities yielding 0.42 percent monthly. Assuming Grace sells the ABC stock and replaces it with the government securities,

**B. Calculate** the:

i. expected return of her new portfolio that includes the government securities;

ii. expected covariance of the government security returns with the original portfolio returns; and

iii. expected standard deviation of her new portfolio that includes the government securities.

**(6 minutes)**

**C. Determine** whether the beta of her new portfolio that includes the government securities will be higher or lower than the beta of her original portfolio. **Justify** your response with *one* reason. No calculations are required.

**(4 minutes)**

Based on conversations with her husband, Grace is considering selling the \$100,000 of ABC stock and acquiring \$100,000 of XYZ Company common stock instead. XYZ stock has the same expected return and standard deviation as ABC stock. Her husband comments, "It doesn't matter whether you keep all of the ABC stock or replace it with \$100,000 of XYZ stock."

**D. State** whether her husband's comment is correct or incorrect. **Justify** your response with *one* reason. No calculations are required.

**(4 minutes)**

In a recent discussion with her financial advisor, Grace commented, "If I just don't lose money in my portfolio, I will be satisfied." She went on to say, "I am more afraid of losing money than I am concerned about achieving high returns."

**E.** i. **Describe** *one* weakness of using expected standard deviation of returns as a risk measure for Grace.

ii. **Identify** *one* alternate risk measure that is more appropriate under the circumstances and **justify** your response with *one* reason.

**(6 minutes)**

## INTERNET EXERCISE

Retrieve monthly returns for S&P 500 and Small Cap 600 stock indexes from *http://finance.yahoo.com*. Calculate the expected return and the variance of a portfolio that is weighted 50 percent in each of these indexes.

## FURTHER READING


Arshanapalli, Bala, T. Daniel Coggin, and John Doukas. "Multifactor Asset Pricing Analysis of International Value Investment Strategies." *Journal of Portfolio Management*, Summer 1998, 10–23.

Block, Frank E. "Elements of Portfolio Construction." *Financial Analysts Journal*, May/June 1969, 123–129.

Connor, Gregory. "The Three Types of Factor Models: A Comparison of Their Explanatory Power." *Financial Analysts Journal*, May/June 1995, 42–46.

Elton, Edwin J., and Martin J. Gruber. "Modern Portfolio Theory." In *The Investment Manager's Handbook*, Sumner N. Levine. ed. Homewood, Ill.: Dow Jones–Irwin, 1980, 160–201.

———. *Modern Portfolio Theory and Investment Analysis*, 6th ed. New York: Wiley, 2002.

———. "Portfolio Theory When Investment Relatives Are Lognormally Distributed." *Journal of Finance*, September 1974, 1265–1273.

Fisher, Kenneth, and Meir Statman. "The Mean-Variance Optimization Puzzle: Security Portfolios and Food Portfolios." *Financial Analysts Journal*, July/August 1997, 41–50.

Frankfurter, George M., Herbert E. Phillips, and John P. Seagle. "Performance of the Sharpe Portfolio Selection Model: A Comparison." *Journal of Financial and Quantitative Analysis*, June 1976, 202–204.

Jeffrey, Robert H. "A New Paradigm for Portfolio Risk." *Journal of Portfolio Management*, Fall 1984, 33–40.

King, B.F. "Market and Industry Factors in Stock Price Behavior." *Journal of Business*, January 1966, 139–190.

Lofthouse, Stephen. "International Diversification." *Journal of Portfolio Management*, Fall 1997, 53–56.

Markowitz, Harry. "Markowitz Revisited." *Financial Analysts Journal*, September/October 1976, 47–52.

———. "Portfolio Selection." *Journal of Finance*, March 1952, 77–91.

———. "The Two Beta Trap." *Journal of Portfolio Management*, Fall 1984, 12–20.

Rosenberg, Barr. "Prediction of Common Stock Betas," *Journal of Portfolio Management*, Winter 1985, 5–14.

Sharpe, William F. "Factor Models, CAPMs, and the APT." *Journal of Portfolio Management*, Fall 1984, 21.

———. "A Simplified Model for Portfolio Analysis." *Management Science*, January 1963, 277–293.

# 6 Why Diversification Is a Good Idea

*The most important lesson learned is an old truth ratified.*
***General Maxwell R. Thurman***

## Key Terms

arbitrage pricing theory (APT)
borrowing portfolio
Capital Asset Pricing Model (CAPM)
capital market line (CML)
corner portfolio
dominance
efficient frontier
equity risk premium
lending portfolio
market model
market portfolio
market price of risk
Markowitz diversification
minimum variance portfolio
naive diversification
quadratic programming
security market line (SML)
security universe
stochastic dominance
superfluous diversification
systematic risk
total risk
unsystematic risk

## Introduction

Diversifying an investment portfolio is a logical idea. Even people who have never invested in anything seem to know that diversification is good. Diversification is indeed a good idea, and virtually all managers seek to diversify in one respect or another. This chapter discusses the logic of diversification and provides some intuition into why it is so important.

Some of the discussion here builds on the mathematical background presented in Chapter 5, "The Mathematics of Diversification." To get the best understanding of diversification, review this material if it has been a while since you read it.

## Carrying Your Eggs in More Than One Basket

*Don't put all your eggs in one basket is good advice.*

The saying "Don't put all your eggs in one basket" is familiar to everyone. It is a truism with global appeal. Still, this is a more powerful statement than it might first seem, and it is worth studying more closely. There are at least three psychological reasons why the saying constitutes good advice.

### *Investments in Your Own Ego*

Some people have a very difficult time admitting they made a mistake. A person might discover a particularly intriguing investment opportunity, or more likely, have someone point out to her a "good stock" or even the proverbial chance of a lifetime. It is virtually never a good idea to put a large percentage of investment funds into a single security such as this. Several things can happen if you do.

One possibility is that you hit a home run and make a pile of money. Although this is a positive short-term outcome, such investment success strokes the ego and can plant the speculative seed in people who should not be speculating. If people have been successful with a hot tip, they are in the minority of today's investors. Chasing hot tips with money is a good way to lose it.

*Investments that "break even" are really losers in an economic sense.*

A second possibility is that the investment never moves. People who own securities in this situation often say, "At least I didn't lose anything." From an economic point of view, the statement is not correct; you *did* lose something. You lost the certain income you would have received had your money been invested in a bank deposit or in short-term government securities. (You have an opportunity loss.) Your ego prefers to view this situation as neutral rather than as the loser it is.

A third possibility is that the investment declines in value. Holders of depreciated securities are prone to exercises in faulty logic. Statements such as "I can't afford to sell it now; it's down too much," or "If I sell now, I'll take a loss," or "It's a good stock; it'll go back up" are usually rationalizations that defy common sense. Your ego does not enjoy rejection from any quarter, be it from other people or from that amorphous entity "the market." When you put your faith and hopes in one security and it turns out to be a loser, your ego may have a very difficult time letting go. If, instead, your investments are varied, it seems that it is easier to lick your wounds and move on to something else.

### *The Concept of Risk Aversion Revisited*

Everyone understands why carrying all your eggs in one basket is not a good idea. It is too risky; if you drop the basket, you conceivably lose everything. During wartime, senior military leaders avoid assembling in groups or riding together in the same helicopter: they say, "One round will get us all." Families traveling together sometimes practice their own version of this diversification tactic. Lost luggage is a substantial inconvenience. Some people make it a practice to spread everyone's clothing throughout the family suitcases so that if one bag is lost, the inconvenience is reduced.

*Risk-averse people take risks only if they believe they will be rewarded for doing so.*

Diversification is not only logical but also a mathematically sound practice. Investors do not like risk, and enormous reductions in risk are associated with even modest diversification, as Chapter 5 showed. Most people are risk averse. This does not mean that they will not take a risk, however. Risk-averse people continually take risks but only when they believe there is a good reason for doing so. Stated another way, people take risks only if they believe they will be rewarded for taking them. Unnecessary risks are unattractive. It is easy enough to put our eggs in several baskets, and most of us do it instinctively.

Evidence indicates that diversification is more important now than ever before. A study in the prestigious *Journal of Finance*[1] found that while overall stock market volatility has not increased over time, the volatility of individual firms, on average,

---

[1]John Y. Campbell, Martin Lettau, Burton G. Malkiel, and Yexiao Xu, "Have Individual Stocks Become More Volatile? An Empirical Exploration of Idiosyncratic Risk," *Journal of Finance*, February 2001, 1–43.

*has* increased. The authors of the study show that this increased security volatility means that investors need more stocks to adequately diversify. Stated another way, rational portfolio construction is more important now than when Harry Markowitz first wrote about it.

### *Multiple Investment Objectives*

Another reason for the appeal of carrying your eggs in more than one basket stems from the presence of multiple investment objectives. Virtually all investors can find one or more mutual funds that would be consistent with their investment objectives. Some people, though, believe that mutual funds are not exciting. Similarly, someone might be disinterested in "unexciting" blue chip stocks despite their consistent long-term growth. Investment activity should be enjoyable rather than boring. If people want to practice aggressive stock selection on their own, it is perfectly okay. Many investors hold their investment funds in more than one account so that they can actively trade (i.e., play with) part of the total.

For instance, a person might split an individual retirement account between two mutual funds. In addition, she might maintain a separate brokerage account for trading individual securities and options and have another account holding funds for an upcoming European vacation.

## Role of Uncorrelated Securities

### *Variance of a Linear Combination: The Practical Meaning*

The previous chapter stressed the importance of selecting portfolio components that have low correlation in their returns.[2] This important section is worth another look.

We have seen how to calculate the variance of an $n$-security portfolio via the following equation:

$$\sigma_p^2 = \sum_{i=1}^{n}\sum_{j=1}^{n} x_i x_j \rho_{ij}\sigma_i\sigma_j \qquad \textbf{(6-1)}$$

where $\sigma_p^2$ = portfolio variance;
$x_i$ = proportion of funds invested in security $i$;
$\sigma_i$ = security standard deviation;
$\rho_{ij}$ = correlation in the returns of securities $i$ and $j$.

We also found that things are simpler to understand with the two-security form of the equation:

$$\sigma_p^2 = x_A^2\sigma_A^2 + x_B^2\sigma_B^2 + 2x_A x_B \rho_{AB}\sigma_A\sigma_B \qquad \textbf{(6-2)}$$

All else being equal, risk is something people want to avoid; one convenient (and economically justifiable) measure of risk is the variance of return. Return variance is a security's **total risk.** Presumably, most investors want portfolio variance to be as low as possible without having to give up any return.

Equation 6-3 shows that in a two-security portfolio, the total risk ($\sigma_p^2$) has three components: one from the variance of Stock A, another from the variance of Stock B, and a third from the relationship between the returns of Stock A and Stock B.

[2]The discussion here deals with nominal returns rather than those adjusted for inflation.

$$\sigma_p^2 = x_A^2\sigma_A^2 + x_B^2\sigma_B^2 + 2x_A x_B \rho_{AB}\sigma_A\sigma_B \tag{6-3}$$

Total Risk = Risk from A + Risk from B + Interactive risk

*The total risk of a portfolio comes from the variance of the components, as well as from the relationships among the components.*

As the number of securities in the portfolio increases, the number of terms on the right-hand side of the equation increases as well. With five securities, there will be five variance components and ten interaction components from the covariance matrix.

The portfolio manager has no control over the variance of an individual security but does have control over the portfolio components. If an individual decides to buy two securities, regardless of whether the securities are conservative or volatile she can try to select the securities so that their historical returns are largely independent. Their correlation will be low, and the third term in Equation 6-3 will be small. If the returns on two securities are completely uncorrelated (the correlation coefficient is 0), the third term drops out entirely. Two securities with *negative* correlation would be especially valuable, because they would reduce total risk rather than add to it.

### Portfolio Programming in a Nutshell

Suppose there are the five stocks listed in Table 6-1. From these returns, a correlation table like the one in Table 6-2 can be prepared.[3]

Perhaps an investor needs to create a two-security portfolio with an annual expected return of 12 percent.[4] As demonstrated earlier, the portfolio return is a linear combination of the component returns, so the expected return is

$$E(\tilde{R}_p) = x_1 E(\tilde{R}_1) + x_2 E(\tilde{R}_2)$$

where $x_1$ and $x_2$ are the proportions of the investment in Securities 1 and 2, respectively; $E(\tilde{R}_p)$ is the expected return on the portfolio, and $E(\tilde{R}_i)$ is the expected return on security $i$.

**TABLE 6-1** STOCK RETURN HISTORY

| *Year* | *Stocks* | | | | |
|---|---|---|---|---|---|
| | A | B | C | D | E |
| 1995 | .2 | .3 | .1 | .0 | –.1 |
| 1996 | –.1 | .0 | .0 | .1 | .2 |
| 1997 | .4 | .5 | .1 | .4 | .3 |
| 1998 | .1 | .2 | .3 | –.1 | .0 |
| 1999 | .2 | .3 | .3 | –.2 | .2 |
| 2000 | –.2 | –.2 | –.1 | .1 | .4 |
| 2001 | .5 | .5 | .0 | .3 | .3 |
| 2002 | –.1 | .1 | .2 | .3 | –.1 |
| 2003 | .0 | –.1 | .2 | .1 | –.2 |
| 2004 | .3 | .4 | .3 | .1 | .0 |
| $E(\tilde{R})$ | .13 | .20 | .14 | .11 | .10 |
| $\sigma$ | .219 | .232 | .136 | .176 | .195 |

[3]The COV file available at the text Website will do this.

[4]In practice, of course, it would be unusual to arrive at an objective this precise without considerable preliminary work.

**TABLE 6-2** RETURN CORRELATION COEFFICIENTS

| | A | B | C | D | E |
|---|---|---|---|---|---|
| A | 1.0 | | | | |
| B | 0.942 | 1.0 | | | |
| C | 0.195 | 0.286 | 1.0 | | |
| D | 0.226 | 0.220 | –0.436 | 1.0 | |
| E | 0.164 | 0.132 | –0.605 | 0.204 | 1.0 |

**TABLE 6-3** TWO-SECURITY PORTFOLIOS WITH AN EXPECTED RETURN OF 12 PERCENT

| *Combinations* | *Proportions (%)* | | | | |
|---|---|---|---|---|---|
| | A | B | C | D | E |
| 1 | 50.0 | 0 | 0 | 50.0 | 0 |
| 2 | 0 | 0 | 50.0 | 0 | 50.0 |
| 3 | 0 | 20.0 | 0 | 0 | 80.0 |
| 4 | 66.7 | 0 | 0 | 0 | 33.3 |
| 5 | 0 | 0 | 33.3 | 66.7 | 0 |
| 6 | 0 | 11.1 | 0 | 88.9 | 0 |

With the five securities in Table 6-1, an expected return of 12 percent can be achieved in many ways. There are two-security portfolios with this expected return, as well as portfolios with three, four, or all five securities. Table 6-3 lists the two-security proportions that do the trick.

*The point of diversification is to achieve a given level of expected return while bearing the least possible risk.*

The key question to the portfolio manager is this: which of the combinations in Table 6-3 is best? All of these combinations have an expected return of 12 percent; is one of them better than the others? Alternatively, is one of the portfolios clearly inferior to the other choices? The "best" portfolio is the one that provides the expected return of 12 percent with the least risk. For a given level of expected return, the risk-averse investor wants as little risk as possible.

We previously calculated the correlation coefficients between all pairs of these five securities, and we know their variances. Using Equation 6-2, we can determine the portfolio variances. Table 6-4 reports them. All six of these two-security portfolios have an expected return of 12 percent, but it is apparent that their relative risk varies substantially. Portfolio 2 has the least risk, with a variance of only 0.0061. Portfolios 1, 3, 4, and 6 have variances four times this much. A rational investor (one who does not like unnecessary risk) will prefer Portfolio 2 over the others. Figure 6-1 is a plot of the risk/expected return combinations.

## *Concept of Dominance*

**Dominance** is a situation in which investors universally prefer one alternative over another; it is one of the central ideas in the theory behind portfolio construction. As an analyst compares investment alternatives, one or more of them sometimes dominate some of the others. This means that all rational investors will clearly prefer some of the competing investments over some of the others.

To illustrate, some shoe stores in eastern Maine accept Canadian currency at par on purchases. The Canadian dollar is worth less than a U.S. dollar. The alternative of paying in Canadian currency dominates the alternative of paying in U.S. dollars because this results in a lower cost to the consumer.

**TABLE 6-4** TWO-SECURITY PORTFOLIO VARIANCES

| *First Variance* | | *Second Variance* | | *Interaction Variance* |
|---|---|---|---|---|
| | | **Portfolio 1: 50% A, 50% D** | | |
| $(.50)^2(.0480)$ | + | $(.50)^2(.0310)$ | + | $2(.5)(.5)(.226)(.0480)^{.5}(.0310)^{.5}$ |
| = 0.0120 | + | .0077 | + | .0044 |
| | | Total = .0241 | | |
| | | **Portfolio 2: 50% C, 50% E** | | |
| $(.50)^2(.0185)$ | + | $(.50)^2(.0380)$ | + | $2(.5)(.5)(-.605)(.0185)^{.5}(.0380)^{.5}$ |
| = .0046 | + | .0095 | – | .0080 |
| | | Total = .0061 | | |
| | | **Portfolio 3: 20% B, 80% E** | | |
| $(.20)^2(.0538)$ | + | $(.80)^2(.0380)$ | + | $2(.2)(.8)(.132)(.0538)^{.5}(.0380)^{.5}$ |
| = .0022 | + | .0243 | + | .0019 |
| | | Total = .0284 | | |
| | | **Portfolio 4: 66.7% A, 33.3% E** | | |
| $(.667)^2(.0480)$ | + | $(.333)^2(.0380)$ | + | $2(.667)(.333)(.164)(.0480)^{.5}(.0380)^{.5}$ |
| = .0213 | + | .0042 | + | .0031 |
| | | Total = .0286 | | |
| | | **Portfolio 5: 33.3% C, 66.7% D** | | |
| $(.333)^2(.0185)$ | + | $(.667)^2(.0310)$ | + | $2(.333)(.667)(-.436)(.0185)^{.5}(.0310)^{.5}$ |
| = .0021 | + | .0138 | – | .0046 |
| | | Total = .0113 | | |
| | | **Portfolio 6: 11.1% B, 88.9% D** | | |
| $(.111)^2(.0538)$ | + | $(.889)^2(.0310)$ | + | $2(.111)(.889)(.220)(.0538)^{.5}(.0310)^{.5}$ |
| = .0006 | + | .0245 | + | .0018 |
| | | Total = .0269 | | |

Figure 6-2 plots all combinations of Stocks B and E, ranging from a 100 percent investment in Stock B and nothing in Stock E to the other extreme of nothing in Stock B and 100 percent in Stock E. A vertical line through point E (which corresponds to a 100 percent investment in Stock E) crosses through another point on the graph, point X. This point corresponds to an investment of 80 percent in Stock B and 20 percent in Stock E.[5] Which would a rational investor prefer, point X or point E? The two points have the same level of risk, but X is associated with a higher level of expected return. As a consequence, Point X dominates a 100 percent investment in Stock E, and investors will choose X over E.

Figure 6-1 shows various two-security portfolios with an expected return of 12 percent. Portfolio 2 (with stocks C and E) is best because it achieves this expected return with the least risk; it dominates the others. Given that stocks C and E have negative return correlation, this result is not surprising. *A portfolio, then, dominates all others if, for its level of expected return, there is no other portfolio with less risk, or for its level of risk, there is no other portfolio with a higher expected return.*

---

[5]Finding these proportions is easiest using a spreadsheet package.

**FIGURE 6-1**

Two-Security Portfolios with $E(\tilde{R}) = 12\%$

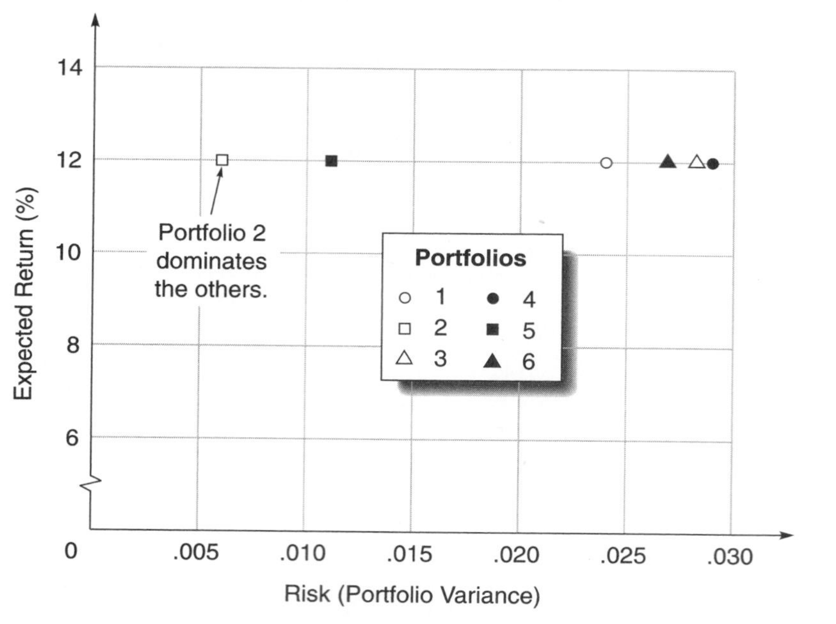


**FIGURE 6-2**

Varying Proportions of Stocks B and E

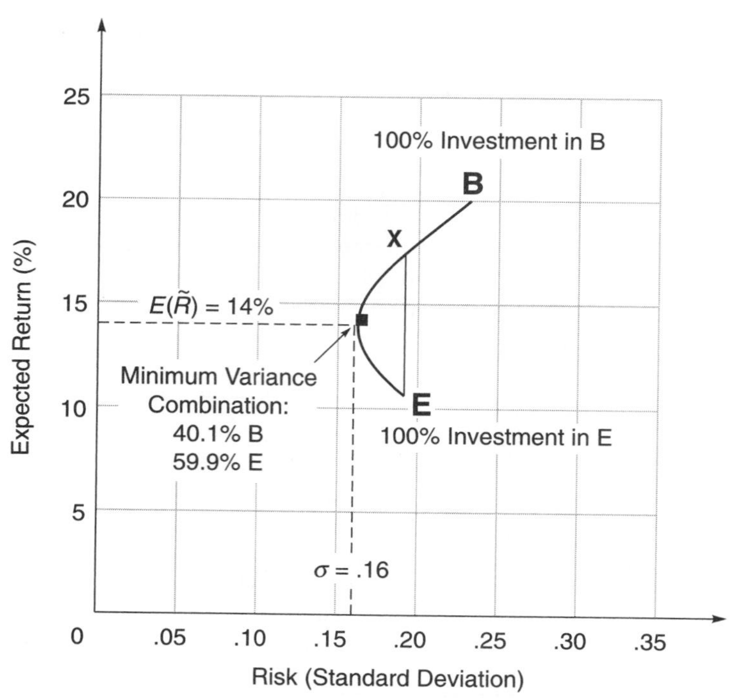

The whole idea behind dominance and portfolio theory boils down to the familiar activity of trying to get the best value for a dollar. Prospective car buyers visit various dealers and compare prices. The less consumers pay for something, whether it be a movie ticket, a new car, or a share of stock, the higher their return. When two people buy identical cars, the one who pays the least gets the best deal. The cost of an investment is really measured in terms of both dollar outlay and risk assumed.[6] For financial assets, expected return is a function of the dollars spent. Given the dollar cost, the goal is to "pay as little risk" as possible.

A formal theory of dominance, called **stochastic dominance**, is an alternative to conventional mean-variance portfolio analysis. Selection by stochastic dominance uses a set of alternative criteria that require no assumptions about the probability distribution of the possible outcomes. The ideas behind the formal theory are identical in spirit to the example just given. Although the application of stochastic dominance as a portfolio selection tool is cumbersome, computer algorithms exist to do the trick. The Appendix to this chapter provides a brief overview of the mathematics of stochastic dominance.

## Harry Markowitz: The Founder of Portfolio Theory

Harry Markowitz opened the door to modern portfolio theory when his article "Portfolio Selection" appeared in the March 1952 issue of the *Journal of Finance*. This was the first major publication indicating the importance of security return correlation in the construction of stock portfolios. Markowitz showed that for a given level of expected return and for a given **security universe** (the entire collection of alternatives from which specific investment choices are made), finding the specific portfolio that dominates the others requires knowledge of the covariance or correlation matrix between all possible security combinations.

*A portfolio dominates all others if no other equally risky portfolio has a higher expected return, or if no portfolio with the same expected return has less risk.*

Subsequent to the publication of this paper, numerous investment firms and portfolio managers began to program "Markowitz algorithms," which prescribed portfolio proportions so as to minimize portfolio variance. Even today the term **Markowitz diversification** refers to portfolio construction accomplished using security covariances.

**Terminology.** The theory arising from Markowitz's work produced some important new vocabulary for the portfolio manager.

***Security Universe.*** The security universe is the collection of all possible investments. For some institutions, only certain investments may be eligible components. The manager of a small capitalization stock mutual fund, for instance, would not consider large capitalization firms as portfolio components. For her, the relevant security universe consists of small cap firms.

*For a chronicle of the evolution of the Markowitz asset allocation model, see the article "Asset Allocation Using the Markowitz Approach" available at the Ibbotson knowledge center* http://www.ibbotson.com

***Efficient Frontier.*** A computer program can produce a plot of the expected return and risk characteristics of the possible portfolios. Many of these combinations will be dominated by others. Those portfolios that are *not* dominated constitute the **efficient frontier.** In general, the shape of the efficient frontier for risky assets such as common stock is similar to Figure 6-3. Note that the point at the lower left of the efficient frontier is *not* the security with the lowest variance. It is the **minimum variance portfolio.** (Refer to Figure 6-2 to see why this is so.) In general, the farther you move to the left on the efficient frontier, the greater the number of securities in the portfolio.

*Portfolios that are not dominated lie on the efficient frontier.*

[6]This will be discussed in detail later in Chapter 17, "Performance Evaluation."

**FIGURE 6-3**

Efficient Frontier for Risky Securities

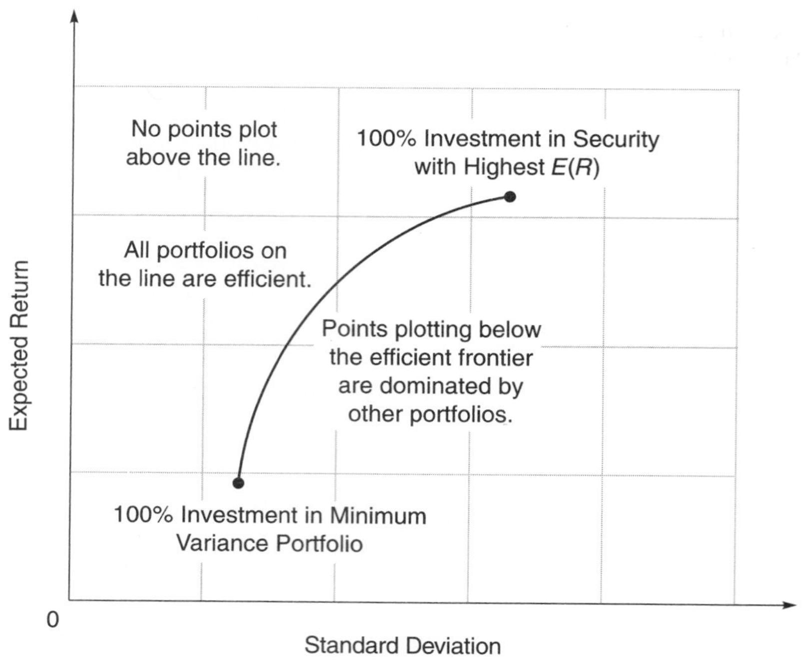

*The mean-standard deviation analysis tool at* http://www.duke.edu/~charvey/applets/EfficientFrontier/frontier.html *dynamically demonstrates the expansion of the efficient frontier by adding different securities into the portfolio. (Be sure to select at least two security groups.)*

*The availability of a risk-free rate changes the shape of the efficient frontier.*

When a risk-free investment is available in addition to risky securities, the shape of the efficient frontier changes markedly. The covariance between a random variable (such as the return on a stock portfolio) and a constant (such as the risk-free rate, by definition) is 0. The variance of a constant is also 0. This means that the expected return and variance (or standard deviation) of a constant/random variable linear combination are simply a weighted average of the two expected returns and variances, with the constant having a variance of zero.

The theoretical risk-free rate is a constant; there are no associated diversification benefits in the risk-reduction sense.[7] However, this does not mean that rational investors should not invest in the risk-free rate. It is easy to show that the optimum portfolio usually has some proportion invested in the risk-free rate.

Figure 6-4 shows the shape of the efficient frontier when a risk-free investment is available. It extends from the risk-free rate (point $R_f$) to point B and then follows the curve to point C. The straight portion of the line is tangent to the risky securities efficient frontier. You can extend other lines from $R_f$ but either the tangent line dominates them or they are not feasible. Point D, for instance, lies on one such line, but Point E clearly dominates it; E offers a higher expected return for the same level of risk. Points above the curved line do not exist, so there is no portfolio there to which the line from $R_f$ might extend.

***Capital Market Line and the Market Portfolio.*** The tangent line passing from the risk-free rate through point B in Figure 6-4 is the **capital market line (CML).** When the security universe includes all possible investments, capital market theory calls Point

[7]The risk-free rate is a theoretical concept. It is common practice in financial research to use the yield on a U.S. Treasury bill with 30 days remaining until maturity as a proxy for the theoretical value.

FIGURE 6-4

Efficient Frontier with a Risk-Free Rate

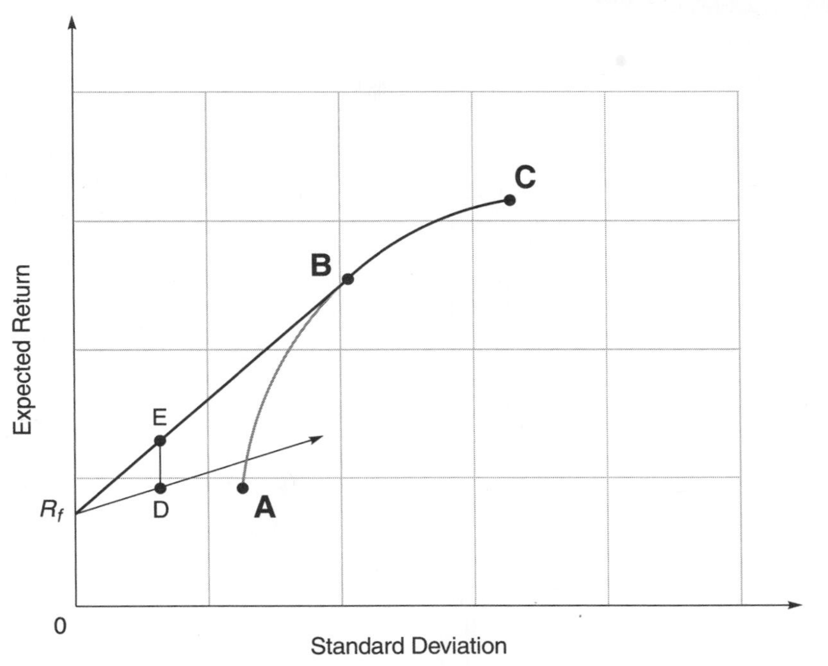


*In theory, the only risky asset that risk-averse investors will hold is the market portfolio.*

*The market portfolio is composed of all risky assets.*

B the **market portfolio.** Only efficient portfolios lie on the capital market line, and (in theory) the only risky asset that risk-averse investors will hold is the market portfolio. The reason for this is that investors seek to maximize their expected utility by optimally balancing risk and expected return. In other words, if there is a way to reduce risk while holding expected return constant, they will do so. When all investors do this, they face the same efficient frontier (Figure 6-4). Given this, theory shows that the market portfolio contains every risky asset and that the proportion each risky asset contributes to the market portfolio equals the market value of each asset divided by the aggregate value of all risky assets.

This has an important implication for investors. Regardless of the extent to which a person is willing to accept risk, *all investors should hold only two securities: the market portfolio and the risk-free rate.*[8] A conservative investor will choose a point near the lower left of the CML, whereas a more growth-oriented investor will stay near the market portfolio. Any risky portfolio that is partially invested in the risk-free asset is a **lending portfolio.**

An investor can construct an efficient portfolio with an expected return *greater* than that of the market portfolio. He does this by *borrowing money* to invest in the market portfolio.[9] Such a portfolio is a **borrowing portfolio.** Figure 6-5 shows the shape of the efficient frontier when the investor can both borrow and lend. It extends from the risk-free rate through and beyond the market portfolio.[10]

[8]This fact is sometimes called the *separation theorem.*

[9]Borrowing money to buy securities is called *buying on margin.* This involves financial leverage, which magnifies the risk and expected return characteristics of the portfolio.

[10]The length of the line segment extending beyond the market portfolio is determined by the extent of the leverage used in the margin transaction.

FIGURE 6-5

Efficient Frontier with Borrowing and Lending

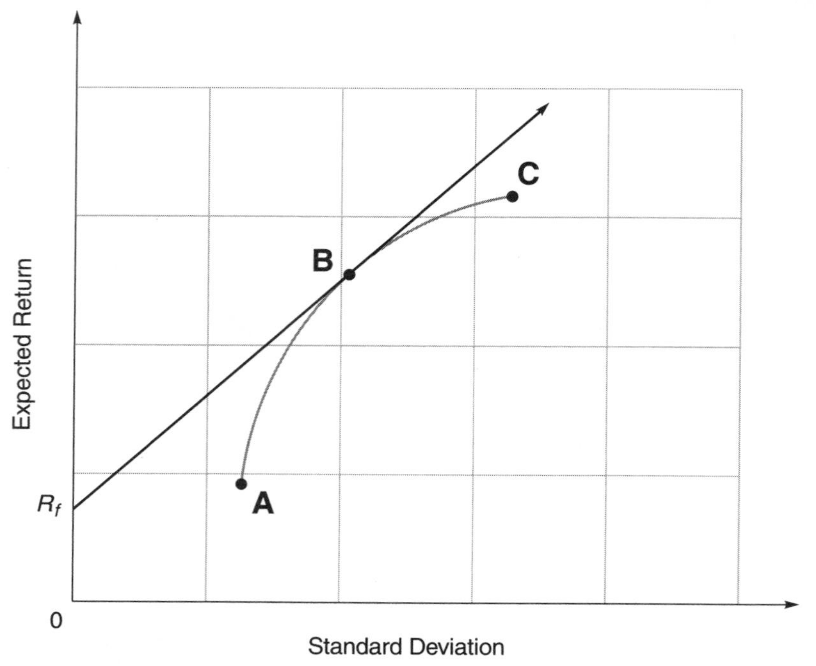


***Security Market Line.*** The market portfolio, by definition, has a beta of 1.0. As discussed earlier, all rational investors will restrict their risky investments to the market portfolio. The risk-free rate, being riskless, has a beta of 0.

Recall that betas combine in linear fashion (the beta of a portfolio is a weighted average of the component betas). This means that in the absence of arbitrage, there is also a linear relationship between the beta of an investment and its expected return. Given a security's beta and the expected return on the market, you can estimate any security's return over the next period if you know its beta. The graphical relationship between expected return and beta is the **security market line (SML);** see Figure 6-6. The SML is very easy to plot. One point on the SML corresponds to a beta of 1.0 and the expected market return.[11] We need two points to plot a straight line, and the second one is readily available. The risk-free rate of interest corresponds to a beta of 0. We connect the two points to form the SML.

Given any security's beta, find it on the horizontal axis, read up to the SML, and then read left to find the expected return that such a beta suggests. The higher the beta, the higher the expected return. As an example, assume the beta of a stock is 1.20, the risk-free rate (per period) is 0.0005, and the next-period return on the market is estimated to be 0.0020. What is the expected return on this stock? Using Figure 6-6, read up from 1.20 on the horizontal axis to the SML and then read over to the vertical axis, where we find an expected return of 0.0023.

Both the risk-free rate and the expected return of the market periodically change as economic conditions change, so the slope of the SML changes as well. We call the slope the **market price of risk** because it measures the cost of expected return in terms of risk.

[11]The SML is easy to plot if you know the market's expected return, but this can be an elusive statistic.

FIGURE 6-6

Security Market Line

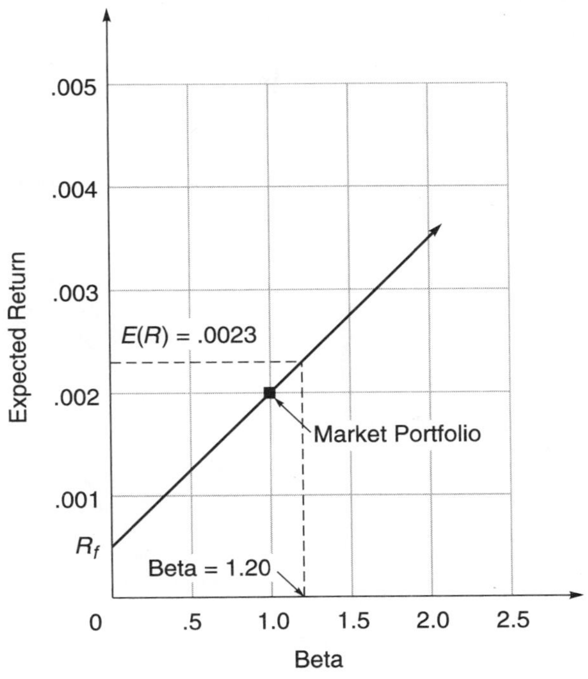


***Expansion of the SML to Four Quadrants.*** Although variances and standard deviations must be equal to or greater than 0, it is possible to have a negative beta.

Figure 6-7 extends the SML to all four quadrants. According to capital market theory, points on the SML are properly priced. Therefore, it is possible to have a security with a negative expected return yet still have it properly priced. The obvious question involves why anyone would buy something with a negative expected return.

*Securities can have a negative expected return and still be properly priced.*

The answer lies in the mathematics of diversification examined in Chapter 5. Variances and standard deviations cannot be negative numbers, so a negative beta means a negative covariance between the asset and the market portfolio:

$$\beta_i = \frac{COV(\tilde{R}_i, \tilde{R}_m)}{\sigma_m^2}$$

$$\beta_i < 0 \Rightarrow COV(\tilde{R}_i, \tilde{R}_m) < 0$$

where $\beta_i$ = beta of Security $i$; $\sigma_m^2$ = variance of the market returns. Negative covariance has powerful risk-reduction potential, and there is a value to this. A good real-world example lies in the risk-reduction characteristic of insurance. Most people do not feel bad if they "lose all their money" on their car insurance. Should they be upset if they do not have an accident? Similarly, people buy fire insurance on their homes, although they fully expect never to have a fire. The related question is this: Why would anyone buy insurance fully expecting to lose all the money paid for it and never to collect on the policy? The answer, of course, comes from an under standing of utility; there is advantage in reducing risk, and investors will pay f value for doing so.

FIGURE 6-7

Security Market Line in Four Quadrants

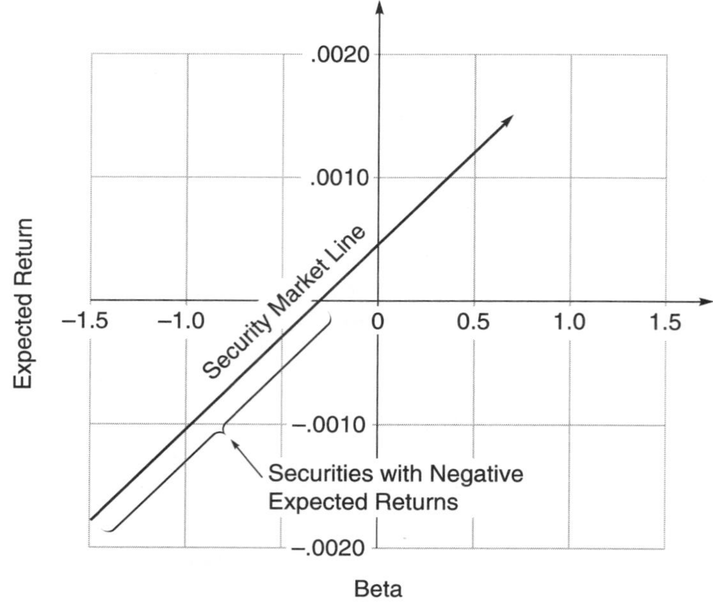


*Important terms in Markowitz programming include security universe, efficient frontier, and corner portfolio.*

***Corner Portfolio.*** When the security universe is large, the efficient frontier contains many thousands of different portfolio combinations.[12] Not all portfolios contain every security, however. Even in a ten-security universe, some portfolios on the efficient frontier may contain only eight or nine of the ten securities.

Imagine that you are on the upper right edge of the efficient frontier for risky securities. This point corresponds to the single security with the highest expected return, regardless of its risk. As you move down the efficient frontier to the left, new securities enter the portfolio mix. Continuing further down and to the left, more securities will enter, and some may leave. Remember that each point on the efficient frontier represents a specific, undominated portfolio.

Moving along the efficient frontier, a **corner portfolio** occurs every time a new security enters an efficient portfolio or an old security leaves. Returning to the example, as you continue down the efficient frontier from top right to lower left, securities come and go until you eventually arrive at the minimum variance portfolio. At this point you are as far to the left on the risk axis as you can get.

Computer programs designed to determine the efficient frontier often provide a printout listing the corner portfolios. Because the efficient frontier has an infinite number of points, it would be impossible to list the combination of securities making up each point. Knowing the composition of the corner portfolios usually provides as much information as necessary.

**Quadratic Programming.** Someone familiar with mathematical programming (linear programming, integer programming, and so on) can readily see that the Markowitz algorithm is an application of **quadratic programming** because the objective function involves portfolio variance, and the equation to calculate this

[12]If fractional shares are available, the efficient frontier contains an infinite number of different portfolio combinations.

statistic contains a squared term. An analyst will build and solve a quadratic program in essentially the same way as a linear program. Table 6-5 shows the Markowitz quadratic programming problem.

Table 6-6 is an example of the Markowitz quadratic program for a two-security universe. Given the statistics on the two eligible securities, we want to find the proportions $x_A$ and $x_B$ that minimize variance while providing a portfolio expected return of 11.5 percent. This is a simple example with only two securities. In any event, the quadratic program will ensure that we are fully invested, that the portfolio's expected return is 11.5 percent as required, and that the chosen portfolio has the least possible variance of return. When the security universe is more than three or four, the complexity of the problem increases dramatically. Quadratic programming is a major help in solving such a problem.

**TABLE 6-5** MARKOWITZ QUADRATIC PROGRAMMING PROBLEM

$$\min \sigma_p^2 = \sum_{i=1}^{n}\sum_{j=1}^{n} x_i x_j \rho_{ij} \sigma_i \sigma_j$$

Where $E(\tilde{R}_p)$ = expected portfolio return;

$\sigma_p^2$ = portfolio variance;

$E(\tilde{R}_i)$ = expected return on Security $i$;

$x_i$ = proportion of funds invested in Security $i$;

$\rho_{ij}$ = correlation between Securities $i$ & $j$;

$\sigma_i$ = standard deviation of Security $i$.

Subject to:

1. $$E\left(\tilde{R}_p\right) = \sum_{i=1}^{n} x_i E\left(\tilde{R}_i\right) = R^*$$

Establish the target return, $R^*$.

2. $$\sum_{i=1}^{n} x_i = 1$$

Ensure that the weights add to 100%.

3. $$x_i \geq 0$$

Ensure that the weights are positive; if short selling is allowed, this constraint is dropped.

**TABLE 6-6** MARKOWITZ QUADRATIC PROGRAM (TWO-SECURITY UNIVERSE)

| | | | |
|---|---|---|---|
| Given: | $E(\tilde{R}_A) = 10\%$ | $E(\tilde{R}_B) = 12\%$ | $\rho_{AB} = .56$ |
| | $\sigma_A^2 = .25$ | $\sigma_B^2 = .35$ | Target return = 11.5% |
| Minimize: | $x_A^2(.25) + x_B^2(.35) + 2x_A x_B(.56)(.25)^{.5}(.35)^{.5}$ | | |
| Subject to: | | | |
| 1. | $x_A(10\%) + x_B(12\%) = 11.5\%$ | | $(E(\tilde{R}_p) = 11.5\%)$ |
| 2. | $x_A + x_B = 1.0$ | | (Investments total 100%.) |
| 3. | $x_A \geq 0,\ x_B \geq 0$ | | (Proportions are positive.) |
| Solution: | $x_A = 25\%;\ x_B = 75\%$ | | |

PORTFOLIO MEMO

### Problems with Markowitz Modeling?

While the Markowitz model of portfolio optimization is one of the most significant contributions to the theory of finance, it does not provide the last word on how best to position portfolios for the future. The full covariance model relies on historical data: means, standard deviations, and correlations of the members of the security universe. There is no assurance that the future will look like the past. Frequently, there is very good evidence that the future will be quite different. Consider the deregulation of the airline industry, the Internet/technology bubble of the late 1990s, many electricity generators changing into pure distribution companies, and so on. The Markowitz efficient frontier is an ex post, or backward-looking, result, when the important thing is organizing the portfolio for the road ahead (an ex ante approach).

Another problem with the Markowitz model is its sensitivity to extreme values. If there is a security showing unusual price behavior over a period of time this usually shows up as a low correlation with other normally behaving securities. If a few securities in the universe have negative correlations with most of the others, for instance, the Markowitz model will often make heavy use of them. Similarly, if a security has had an unusually high return over the past, this desirable "expected return" gets considerable attention during construction of the efficient frontier. Company-specific events that have temporarily driven down a stock translate into a negative expected return, so the model largely ignores these stocks.

Extrapolating the past into the future is dangerous business in the world of investments. Portfolio managers know to make sure that historical statistics pass the straight-face test before using them as inputs in a portfolio construction algorithm.

## Lessons from Evans and Archer

In 1968, John L. Evans and Stephen N. Archer published an article in the *Journal of Finance* that is arguably the most consequential piece of academic research regarding portfolio construction.[13] This study shows how **naive diversification** reduces the dispersion of returns in a stock portfolio. This term refers to the selection of portfolio components randomly without any serious security analysis.

### *Methodology*

Evans and Archer sought to discover the effects of portfolio size on total portfolio risk when the securities are randomly selected common stocks. Using computer simulation, they measured the average variance of one-security portfolios, two-security portfolios, and so on up to portfolios with dozens of components.

[13]John L. Evans and Stephen N. Archer, "Diversification and the Reduction of Dispersion: An Empirical Analysis," *Journal of Finance*, December 1968, 761–767.

### Results

Figure 6-8 illustrates the general results of the famous research of Evans and Archer. It shows that as portfolio size increases, total portfolio risk, on average, declines. After a certain point, the marginal reduction in risk from the addition of another security is very modest. The level of risk that remains after no further diversification benefits can be achieved is pure **systematic risk.**

*Of total portfolio risk, about 75 percent can be eliminated through proper diversification.*

Risk reduction through diversification has been studied by other researchers as well, and the evidence indicates that perhaps three-fourths of total risk can be eliminated by properly diversifying a portfolio. In other words, of a single security's total risk, 25 percent is systematic risk (measured by beta), and 75 percent is unsystematic. **Unsystematic risk** is the part of total risk that is unrelated to overall market movements and that can be diversified away.

Capital market theory indicates that investors are rewarded only for bearing necessary risk and that diversifiable risk is unnecessary. This implies that rational investors should always diversify because diversification gets rid of a substantial percentage of portfolio risk.

The fact that rational investors should diversify also helps explain why beta is such an important concept in market analysis. Beta is a measure of systematic risk, and

**FIGURE 6-8**

Naive Diversification

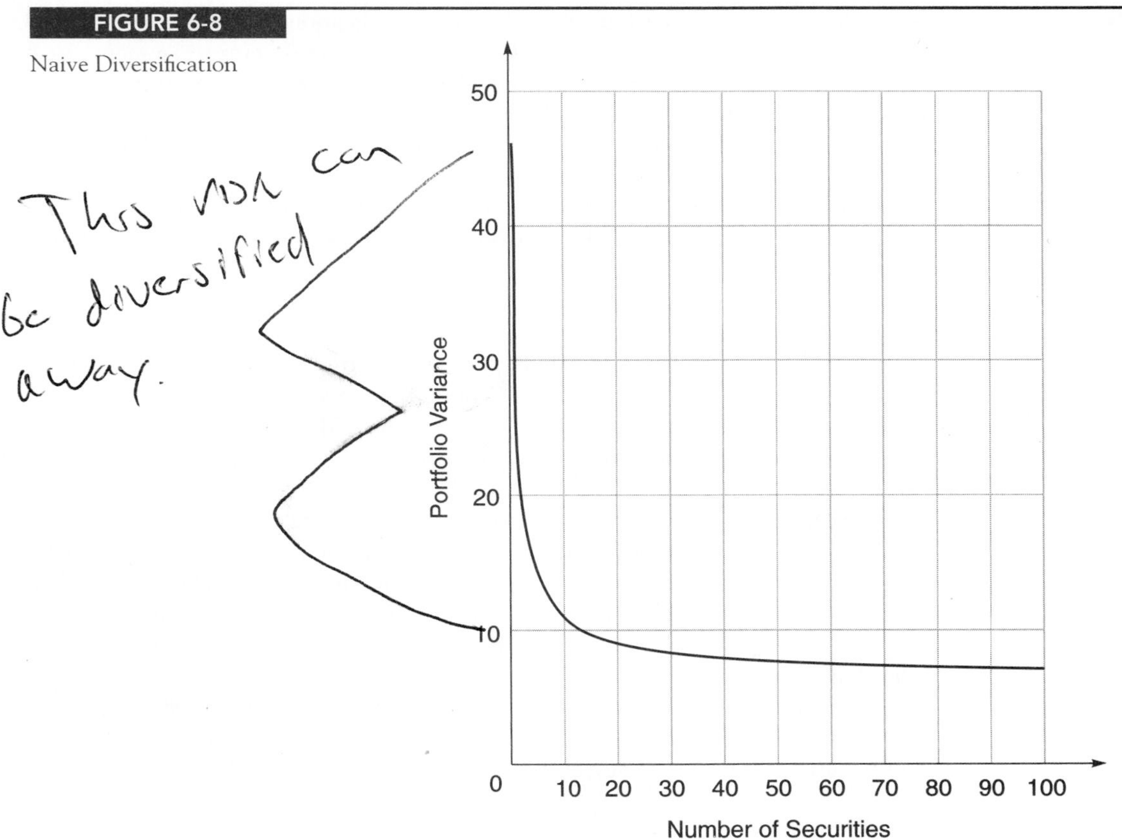


Source: Adapted from Edwin J. Elton and Martin J. Gruber, "Risk Production and Portfolio Size: An Analytical Solution," *Journal of Business*, October 1977, 415–437.

this is the only risk for which the investor is rewarded. Securities are priced on the basis of their beta coefficient, and prices are crucial to determining expected return.

Three principal results of the Evans and Archer research should be stressed. These are described in the following sections.

**Strength in Numbers.** One of the most obvious results of the Evans and Archer research is the fact that total risk, as measured by portfolio variance of return, declines as the number of securities included in the portfolio increases. This means that on average, a randomly selected ten-security portfolio will have less risk than a randomly selected three-security portfolio. Risk-averse investors should always diversify to eliminate as much risk as possible.

**Biggest Benefits Come First.** A second result of the Evans and Archer research is the fact that increasing the number of portfolio components provides diminishing benefits as the number of components increases. In other words, if an investor holds one security, adding a second one provides substantial risk-reduction benefits. If the investor holds twenty securities, however, adding a twenty-first provides only modest additional benefit. Some investment advisors go so far as to say that the nonexpert is better off selecting two securities at random rather than spending time searching for the single best.

*For an excellent discussion of risk (including a chat room), see* www.contingencyanalysis.com and www.riskchat.com

**Superfluous Diversification.** Superfluous diversification, a third result of the research, is related to the second result but sufficiently important to be mentioned by itself. **Superfluous diversification** refers to the addition of unnecessary components to an already well-diversified portfolio and deals with the diminishing marginal benefits of additional portfolio components. Note in Figure 6-8 that once a portfolio contains fifteen or twenty securities, there is little additional benefit (in a risk-reduction sense) to adding more components. The point here is that in large portfolios, the benefits of additional diversification may well be outweighed by the associated transaction costs.

### *Implications*

Capital market theory enables analysts to prove that the most complete diversification occurs when an investor owns some percentage of every asset there is. Normally, real-world correlations are such that the addition of one more security usually provides some reduction in risk.[14] In practice, of course, this is never done for three reasons.

First, the results of Evans and Archer show that very effective diversification occurs when the investor holds only a small fraction of the total number of available securities. An individual investor might be content with ten or twelve, whereas an institutional investor might find thirty or forty quite satisfactory. Technically, there is no reason why the optimum portfolio size for an individual should be different from that of an institutional investor. Capital constraints, however, usually prevent the individual investor from holding as many positions as might be desired.

It is interesting to note that for large institutional portfolios, superfluous diversification is unavoidable. Dividing a portfolio worth several billion dollars into only thirty

[14]The addition of another security to a portfolio will not always reduce portfolio risk. Total variance will be improved only if the correlation of the new asset and the existing portfolio is less than the ratio of the smaller standard deviation divided by the larger one.

or forty stocks would require the purchase of large ownership positions that would be extremely illiquid. Moreover, to minimize transaction costs, large institutions must concentrate their holdings in firms with stock issues large enough that substantial investments can be made without "buying the company." In addition, mutual funds are prohibited from holding more than 5 percent of a firm's equity shares.

A second reason that portfolios do not contain some investment in every security is that it would be expensive. Commission costs are incurred every time a new portfolio component is acquired. If an investor were to buy five hundred different stocks, she would pay five hundred commissions. These costs would aggregate to a considerable sum, and it is unlikely that any added benefit would be enough to justify the cost.

Finally, it would be difficult to follow so many stocks. It is hard enough to keep up with the news on a dozen common stocks. Holding hundreds of stocks would be very expensive in terms of the managerial time required to stay current with them. Of course, the manager could just ignore the news about his stocks and let the chips fall where they may, but then he faces the potential of some embarrassing questions from clients about company-specific news items they have noticed that he has not.

### Words of Caution

*Naive diversification usually provides good risk reduction but not always.*

It is important to remember that the Evans and Archer results arise from computer simulation over many different portfolios of various sizes. Simply selecting fifteen securities at random usually gives good diversification but not always.

Industry effects also should be mentioned here. Suppose an investor assembles a portfolio that includes the common stock of Daimler/Chrysler, General Motors,

PORTFOLIO MEMO

## An Update to Evans and Archer

The February 2001 issue of the *Journal of Finance* has a lead article* that provides a fresh look at the Evans and Archer research. The authors find that in recent years there has been a "noticeable increase in firm-level volatility relative to market volatility." Because of this they conclude that "the number of stocks needed to achieve a given level of diversification has increased."

For many years portfolio managers have followed the heuristic that investors need fifteen or twenty stocks to be well diversified. This *JF* paper suggests that this isn't enough to do the trick in 2001. In fact, a portfolio now needs almost 50 stocks to eliminate as much unsystematic risk as 20 stocks did thirty-five years ago. The study does not conclusively explain why this longstanding rule has changed, but speculates that "the trend may result in part from changes in corporate governance and in part from the institutionalization of equity ownership, but at this stage any such explanation can only be highly tentative."

Whatever the reason, the results have important implications for portfolio managers, financial planners, and individual investors.

*John Y. Campbell, Martin Lettau, Burton G. Malkiel, and Texiao Xu, "Have Individual Stocks Become More Volatile? An Empirical Exploration of Idiosyncratic Risk," *Journal of Finance*, February 2001, 1–43.

Ford Motor Company, and every other automobile company she can find. This portfolio is unlikely to show the risk-reduction benefits expected. Although the investor has bought stock in many different companies, she has not diversified effectively because the fortunes of these companies are highly correlated.

*Simply buying shares in many firms does not necessarily result in proper diversificaiton.*

Finally, although naive diversification reduces risk, it can also reduce return. This is unlike efficient diversification in the Markowitz sense when the return of the portfolio is held constant while risk is being reduced.

## Diversification and Beta

The point of diversifying is to reduce *total* risk so that only *systematic* risk remains. Beta measures systematic risk. Some people erroneously believe that "low betas are good" and that diversification seeks to reduce beta. This is not the case. All investors want to eliminate unnecessary risk, but because they have different degrees of risk aversion, they differ in the *extent* to which they will take risk.

It is possible to construct a well-diversified portfolio of stocks with a beta of 0.5 or with a beta of 1.5. A conservative investor would prefer the former, a more aggressive trader would opt for the latter. If an investor has a security universe made up entirely of stocks with a beta greater than 1.0, any portfolio drawn from this set will also have a beta greater than 1.0. Diversification does not reduce *beta*; it reduces *total risk*.[15]

PORTFOLIO MEMO

### Markowitz Diversification and the Real World

While virtually all portfolio managers are familiar with the basic principles of Markowitz diversification, few of them ever prepare a correlation matrix or calculate the covariance between two securities. This is not because they disbelieve the mathematics but because in the management of most institutional portfolios, the calculations are simply not necessary. A diversified common stock mutual fund manager might hold 75 or 100 individual stock positions. The naive diversification work of Evans and Archer shows that unsystematic risk dissipates quickly as the number of portfolio components increases. Purely by luck of the draw, a 100-security portfolio will be well diversified with its total risk approximately equal to its systematic risk.

If the manager has any skill at security selection, the expected returns of the portfolio's components will be competitive, and, ideally, above that predicted by financial theory. Given that the diversifiable risk is gone, the portfolio's characteristics should put it quite close to the efficient frontier.

[15]Think of total risk being like a person's total cholesterol count. There is "good cholesterol" (HDL) and "bad cholesterol" (LDL). A high total cholesterol count is a potential problem if most of it is "bad" but not a problem if much of it is "good." Similarly, a high portfolio variance is a symptom of risk, but if the elevated number is because of the portfolio's high beta, it is less a concern.

## Capital Asset Pricing Model

*Normative theories suggest how people should behave; positive theories explain how they do behave.*

The **Capital Asset Pricing Model (CAPM)** formalizes the current understanding about the relationship between expected risk and expected return. Behavioral scientists know that before prescribing a normative theory of behavior (how people *should* behave), it is important to understand the positive theory (how they *do* behave).

From observing years of human investment behavior, we know that most investors are risk averse and that attitudes toward consumption and utility play an important role in the determination of interest rates and rates of return in the stock market. Chapters 3, 4, and 5 showed the merits of holding a diversified portfolio and how beta measures the relevant risk of an investment.

Much of the current research in finance searches for a better understanding of the nature of risk and investigates investor attitudes toward future returns. An important consequence of this research is the capital asset pricing model, a widely used theoretical description of the way in which the market prices investment assets. The rest of this chapter is directed to helping you to understand the CAPM and its implications for security selection and portfolio construction.

### Systematic and Unsystematic Risk

*Investors are rewarded for bearing systematic risk only.*

Total risk (as measured by variance or standard deviation of return) has two components: systematic risk and unsystematic risk. The Evans and Archer results show how unsystematic risk can be diversified away until only systematic risk remains. Beta measures systematic risk, and the market rewards investors bearing this risk only.

Figure 6-9 shows randomly generated returns on four hypothetical stocks and on a portfolio composed of all four of them. Each of these stocks has a return variance of about 0.16. Individual returns on these stocks are plotted by symbols in the figure. The four-security portfolio appears as a jagged line and with less dispersion than the data points associated with the individual stocks. The portfolio has a variance of only 0.05, or about one-third the average of the individual stocks. This reduction in risk arises from the interaction of the unsystematic risk components of each of the four single securities. These components do not move in tandem with each other, and they tend to cancel themselves out when observed from a portfolio perspective.

Capital market theory assumes that rational investors get rid of unnecessary risk because unsystematic risk is unnecessary. The remaining risk is systematic and measured by beta. Beta determines the level of expected return on a security or portfolio, as illustrated by the security market line.

### Fundamental Risk/Return Relationship Revisited

The capital asset pricing model (CAPM) and the security market line (SML) succinctly capture the risk/return relationship.

**CAPM.** The essence of CAPM is this: the more systematic risk an investor carries, the greater his expected return. Table 6-7 formally states the CAPM. Several points are worth reinforcing. First, the CAPM deals with *expectations about the future*. We can always fit a regression line to past data or find some other way of modeling it. We do not, however, know the future but have only expectations about it.

Note also that the CAPM references the risk-free rate of interest, $R_f$. This is because it is possible to earn a return even when there is no risk. What counts is the return earned above the risk-free rate (i.e., the excess return.) The CAPM states that

FIGURE 6-9

Risk Reduction through Diversification

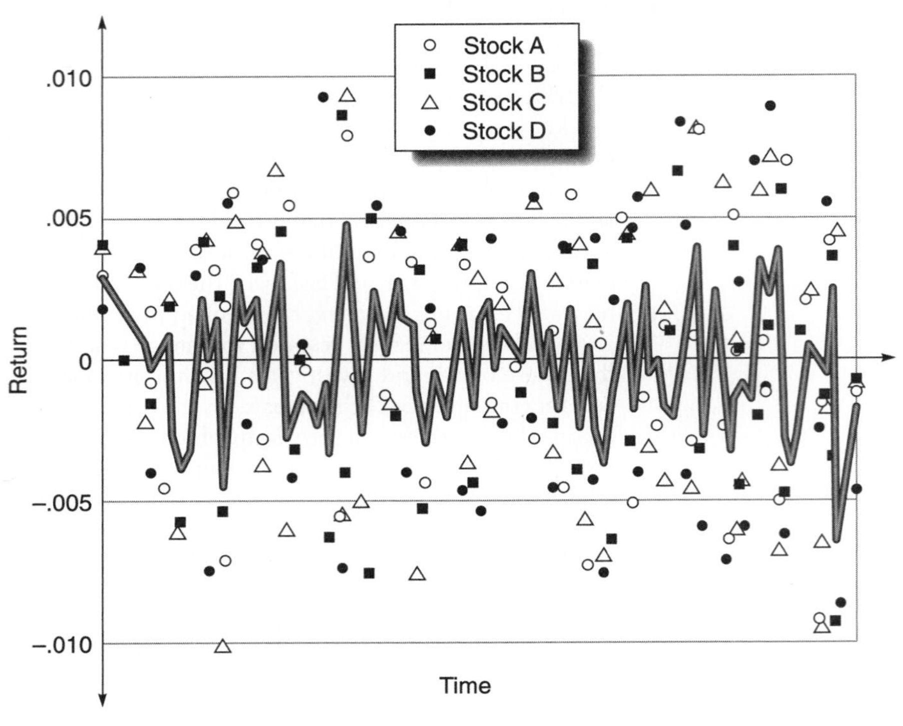


TABLE 6-7 CAPITAL ASSET PRICING MODEL

$$E(\tilde{R}_i) = \text{Riskless rate} + \text{Risk premium}$$
$$= R_f + \beta_i[E(\tilde{R}_m) - R_f]$$

where $E(\tilde{R}_i)$ = expected return on Security $i$;
$R_f$ = risk-free rate of interest;
$\beta_i$ = beta of Security $i$; and
$E(\tilde{R}_m)$ = expected return on the market.

Assumptions of the model:

1. Variance of return and mean return are all investors care about.
2. Investors are price takers; they cannot influence the market individually.
3. All investors have equal and costless access to relevant information.
4. There are no taxes or transaction costs.
5. Investors look only one period ahead.
6. Everyone is equally adept at analyzing securities and interpreting the news.

excess returns on a particular stock are directly related to the beta of the stock and the expected excess return on the market in the next period.

This raises a third point. The CAPM is a one-period model. The period used to calculate beta might be one week, one month, or one year. Whatever period is used, the CAPM considers expectations about the next period only. (There is ongoing academic research to find a multiperiod CAPM. As yet, no pricing model that accommodates expectations over more than one time interval is generally accepted.)

**SML and CAPM.** If we show the security market line with excess returns on the vertical axis, the equation of the SML is the CAPM. The slope of the line is the expected market risk premium, and the intercept is 0.

**Market Model versus CAPM.** Some people mistakenly use the phrase *capital asset pricing model* when they really mean the *market model*. The **market model** is a mathematical way to model past security price returns by regressing them on the returns of a market index. It is an ex post model in that it describes past price behavior. The CAPM, in contrast, is a theoretical, ex ante model. It predicts what a value should be, given other statistics.[16]

We can perform statistical tests only on events that have already occurred; we cannot test future events. It is possible, however, to attempt to predict future events using past data; that is what the market model does. From the past relationship between the price behavior of a security and the associated overall market activity, we learn something about the expected future relationship. Equation 6-4 is the equation for the market model:

$$R_{it} = \alpha_i + \beta_i(R_{mt}) + e_{it} \tag{6-4}$$

where $R_{it}$ = return on Security $i$ in period $t$;
$\alpha_i$ = intercept (called "alpha");
$\beta_i$ = beta for Security $i$;
$R_{mt}$ = return on the market in period $t$; and
$e_{it}$ = error term on Security $i$ in period $t$.

**Note on the CAPM Assumptions.** Several of the assumptions of the capital asset pricing model seem unrealistic. We know that people are concerned about taxes and that they do pay commissions to buy or sell their investments. We also know that many people look ahead more than one period, that particularly large institutions can influence the market, and that not all investors forecast the same distribution of returns for the market.

Theory is difficult to develop and useful to the extent that it helps us learn more about the way the world acts. All things considered, the assumptions of the CAPM constitute only a modest departure from reality. Empirical testing shows that the CAPM works reasonably well and that it is a useful representation of reality, although it may not capture everything that influences security prices.

**Stationarity of Beta.** Beta is central to the CAPM, but like expected return, it is not an observable value; beta is a statistic about the future. As we have seen, an analyst might use a past series of returns and the market model to estimate regression parameters. Here is the regression model (the market model) again:

$$R_{it} = \alpha_i + \beta_i(R_{mt}) + e_{it} \tag{6-4}$$

In words, the return on Security $i$ at time $t$ equals to a constant, $\alpha$ plus the security's beta multiplied by the return on the market at time $t$, plus an error term at time $t$. The error term is necessary because not all the data points lie exactly on the regression line. The *error term* is a plug value to make the equation hold. Sometimes the error term is positive, sometimes negative, and occasionally 0. The sum of all the

[16]If you wish, you can view the market model as a positive model and the CAPM as a normative model.

error terms in the regression is 0. Regression seeks to minimize the sum of the square of the error terms.

Suppose an analyst collects monthly stock returns on some company for the last twenty-five years. Using the market model on these data for the first ten years (120 observations) produces an estimate for beta. If, instead, the analyst used the *most recent* ten years, the beta estimate will almost certainly be different. The reason for this is that *beta is not stationary*. It changes as characteristics of the firm change. A higher debt ratio, for instance, usually causes beta to increase. Mergers or other acquisitions can also substantially alter a historical stock return/market return relationship.

*Because it is a measure of risk, beta should periodically change.*

Research into the stationarity of beta has uncovered a few important facts. A paper by Frank K. Reilly and David J. Wright provides some evidence that weekly betas are significantly less than monthly betas, especially for high-beta stocks.[17] The authors' study concludes that a major reason for the calculation of different betas from the same data is the intervaling effect, referring to the different time intervals used in the calculation.

A paper by Michael Theobald shows that the stationarity of beta is an increasing function of the length of the estimation period.[18] That is, the longer the interval used, the more stable the beta statistic. In practice, users of beta periodically re-estimate or otherwise validate their estimate. Betas change, and the informed investment manager knows this.

## Equity Risk Premium

Evidence shows that over long periods of time the average return on equity securities historically has exceeded the return on riskless government securities. The phrase **equity risk premium** refers to the difference in the average return between stocks and some measure of the risk-free rate, usually either the Treasury bill rate or Treasury bond rate.

In the CAPM, $E(\tilde{R}_m) - R_f$ corresponds to the equity risk premium. Since 1926 this value for large capitalization stocks has averaged about 8.4 percent relative to *Treasury bills*. A recent article in the *Journal of Applied Finance* finds that over the period 1982–1998, the risk premium was 7.14 percent relative to long-term U.S. Treasury *bonds*. Regardless of what we choose for the riskless rate, we can associate the risk premium with the prevailing riskless rate and a firm's beta to determine an estimate of its expected return.

Investors in the stock market are much more concerned with what will happen in the future than with what has happened in the past. Some researchers are proposing that the size of the equity risk premium is shrinking. One of the most important studies is by Jeremy Siegel; it appeared in the *Journal of Portfolio Management*.[19] Siegel argues that the historical risk premium is unlikely to persist in the future and that the future average level of return from equities is likely to decline from its historic levels. This is a subject of much debate.

[17]Frank K. Reilly and David J. Wright, "A Comparison of Published Betas," *Journal of Portfolio Management*, Spring 1988, 64–69.

[18]Michael Theobald, "Beta Stationarity and Estimation Period: Some Analytical Results," *Journal of Financial and Quantitative Analysis*, December 1981, 747–757.

[19]Jeremy J. Siegel, "The Shrinking Equity Premium," *Journal of Portfolio Management*, Fall 1999, 10–17.

## Using a Scatter Diagram to Measure Beta

Beta is a critical statistic in portfolio theory. In addition to understanding the concept mathematically, it is instructive to see beta graphically.

### *Correlation of Returns*

Some of the news arriving in the marketplace each day is company specific. Examples include reports of changes in top management, earnings reports, and corporate press releases. Much of the daily news, however, is of a general economic nature and affects all securities. This means that stock prices will move as a group. Some days stocks are up; other days they are generally down; and still others they are mostly unchanged.

PORTFOLIO MEMO

### Using Beta to Set Price Limits

Many investment research firms maintain a "focus list" of common stocks. Often the firm lists a twelve-month price target and a "buy limit" for the stocks on the focus list. The buy limit is the most they believe an investor should pay for the stock. Argus Research Company's newsletter states, "Buy Limits are calculated according to the Capital Asset Pricing Model."

Suppose we have the following data:

| | |
|---|---|
| Stock price | = \$20.07 |
| Current dividend | = \$1.22 |
| Estimated future dividend growth rate | = 6.1% |
| Stock beta | = 1.15 |
| 30-day Treasury bill rate | = 2.1% |
| Equity risk premium | = 8.4% |

Many analysts use the dividend discount model as part of their stock analysis. (Refer to Table 2-1.) If the DDM is used to solve for the stock price, a discount rate must be input. The CAPM can help determine what that rate should be.

For the stock in this example, the CAPM predicts an expected return of $E(R_{stock}) = R_f + \text{beta}[E(R_{market}) - R_f] = 2.1\% + 1.15(8.4\%) = 11.76\%$

If 11.76 percent is the expected return on the stock, it is also the rate at which the market discounts future dividends and earnings on the stock. Using this in the DDM, the stock is worth

$$P = D_0(1 + g)/(R - g) = \$1.22(1.061)/(.1176 - .061) = \$22.87$$

A firm might have a policy of establishing the "buy limit" at 95 percent of the DDM–determined intrinsic value of the stock, rounded down to the nearest half dollar. In this case, the buy limit would be 95% × \$22.87 = \$21.73, rounded to \$21.50.

Even though stocks tend to move as a group, some routinely move more than the others regardless of whether the market advances or declines. This happens because some stocks are more sensitive to changes in economic conditions than are others.

### Linear Regression and Beta

Beta is a relative measure that indicates how a particular security customarily behaves compared with the behavior of some other benchmark, or how sensitive a stock is to market movements. The benchmark is theoretically "the market," an abstract idea encompassing all the possible investments. In practice, we use a well-diversified index like the S&P 500 as a proxy for the market.

Figure 6-10 shows one way of measuring beta, using a scatter diagram, or scattergram. Here we plot 200 security returns against the returns on the market. Because most points lie in the first and third quadrants, the figure indicates that most of the time when the market is up, the security is up, too. Similarly, when the market is down, the security is usually down. The second and fourth quadrants of the figure have many fewer data points.

Linear regression finds the best-fitting straight line through the 200 data points in Figure 6-10. Using Microsoft Excel, we obtain the regression results in Table 6-8. The coefficient for the market return is the beta statistic. It indicates that the slope of the regression line is slightly more than 1, meaning that in general, this security tends

FIGURE 6-10

Measuring Beta with a Scattergram

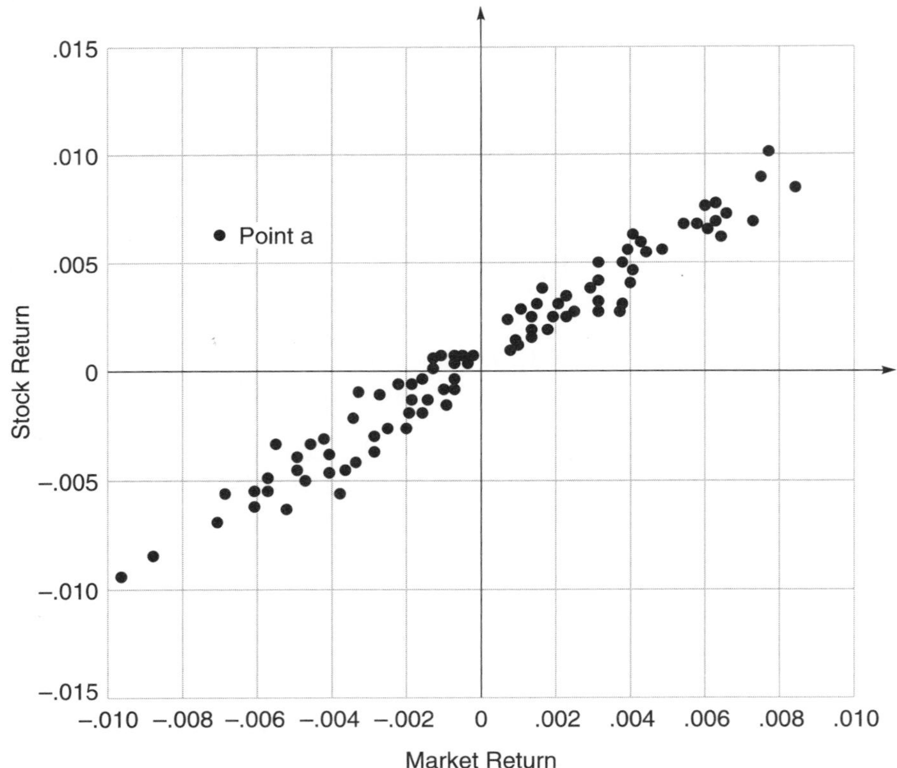

**TABLE 6-8** SCATTERGRAM REGRESSION RESULTS

| $Return_{stock} = 0.0010 + 1.0603\ (Return_{market})$ |
|---|

to move more than the market average. Specifically, the beta of 1.0603 means that this security tends to move 6.03 percent more than the overall market on any given day. (In practice, data services do not publish beta with more than two decimals.)

The intercept in the market model is *alpha*. This number is usually very close to zero. Alpha can be interpreted as a trend in the security price returns that is inexplicable by finance theory. A positive alpha means that returns tend to be higher than expected, given the beta statistic. Conversely, a negative alpha shows that the security is an underperformer.

PORTFOLIO MEMO

## Unlevering Beta

Imagine two firms, identical in every respect, except that one is debt free while the other has an amount of long-term debt on its balance sheet. Normally, the firm using leverage (i.e., the one with the debt) has a higher beta than the other. Stated another way, the stock in the levered firm is more volatile.

Sometimes analysts want to use beta in a comparison of two firms and want to remove the effects of any capital structure differences. In such a case it may be appropriate to *unlever* the beta. Equation 6-5 shows how.

$$\frac{\text{Equity}}{\text{Equity} + (1 - \text{Tax\%}) \times \text{Debt}} \times \beta_{equity} = \beta_{unlevered} \qquad \textbf{(6-5)}$$

where Tax% = the firm's corporate tax rate;
Equity = equity as a proportion of total assets;
Debt = debt as a proportion of total assets; and
$\beta_{equity}$ = the firm's standard beta.

An unlevered beta measures the sensitivity of a firm's equity without regard to the manner in which the firm finances its operations, that is, without regard to its capital structure. Suppose we have the following:

Tax% = 40%
Equity = 55%
Debt = 45%
Beta = 1.25

The unlevered beta is 0.84, about two-thirds the unadjusted beta:

$$\frac{0.55}{0.55 + (1 - 0.40) \times 0.45} \times 1.25 = 0.84$$

## Importance of Logarithms

An analyst might take the beta estimate of 1.0603 and run with it, but she can probably improve on it. Figure 6-10 indicates that at least one observation (Point a) is substantially out of the pack; the market had a bad day, but the stock rose significantly. Points like this are called outliers in that they distort the more general relationship seen in the bulk of the other points. In calculating beta, it is a good idea to reduce the effect of such outliers in order to get a more accurate measure of the stock's normal sensitivity to market movements. One convenient way to do this is by taking logarithms of the return relatives before doing the regression. Logarithms reduce the effect of outliers and, in the opinion of many analysts, generate better results. Doing this yields the revised regression results shown in Table 6-9.

Because it is common practice to round beta to one or two decimals, in this case the use of logarithms does not have much effect. Using logarithms has more effect the more outliers there are. Unless it is necessary to include the heavy influence of unusual data points, though, it is always a good idea to make calculations on the basis of logarithms of the return relatives.

### *Statistical Significance*

Chapter 2 pointed out the importance of looking at the statistical significance of regression coefficients. Beta is a regression coefficient. Just because some investment service publishes a beta of 1.20 for a stock does not mean that this number is useful. Individual securities show substantial unsystematic risk in their returns; they often behave quite differently than their betas predict. Portfolio betas are much better behaved because much of the unsystematic risk is diversified away.

Figure 6-11 shows the $R^2$ values associated with three-year betas computed by the Value Line Investment Survey, a well-known information service many investors use. As the figure indicates, the preponderance of these are below 0.25. An $R^2$ of 0.25 means that the regression explains only 25 percent of the variation in the stock returns. An investor should not place too much reliance on a statistic with this little explanatory power.

Figure 6-12 shows similar statistics for the industry groups that Value Line follows. You can view these as portfolios of securities ranging in size from a dozen firms to several hundred. The $R^2$ values are much higher than with the individual firms. The average is about twice the value from Figure 6-11. An $R^2$ value of 0.50 means the regression explains 50 percent of the variation, twice the explanatory power of the "individual beta" average.

**TABLE 6-9** REGRESSION RESULTS USING RETURN LOGARITHMS

$$\text{Return}_{stock} = 0.0010 + \underset{(0.0309)}{1.0564} \, (\text{Return}_{market})$$

$$R^2 = 0.8555$$

Standard errors are in parentheses.

**FIGURE 6-11**

Value Line Three-Year Beta R Square Value Ranges

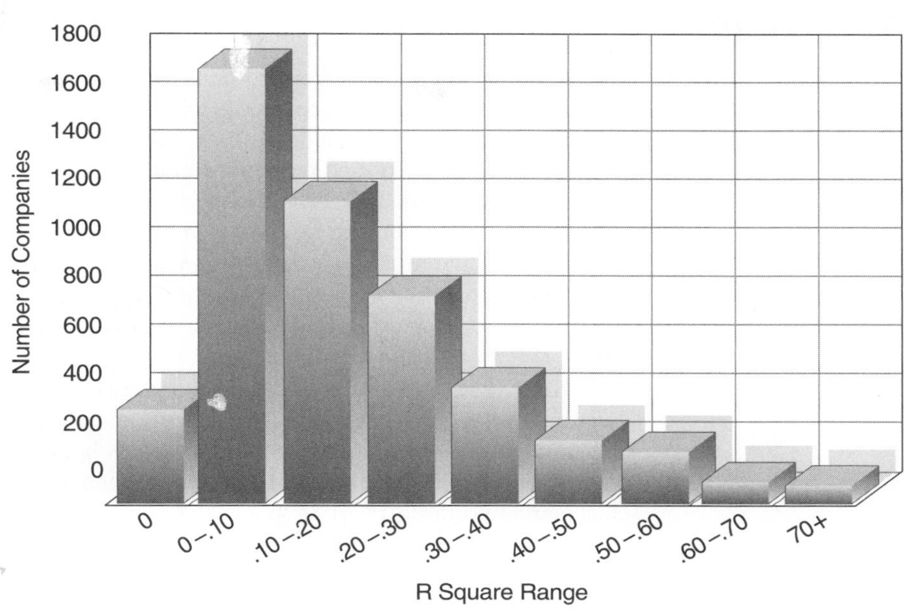


**FIGURE 6-12**

Value Line Three-Year Beta R Square Value Ranges by Industry Groups

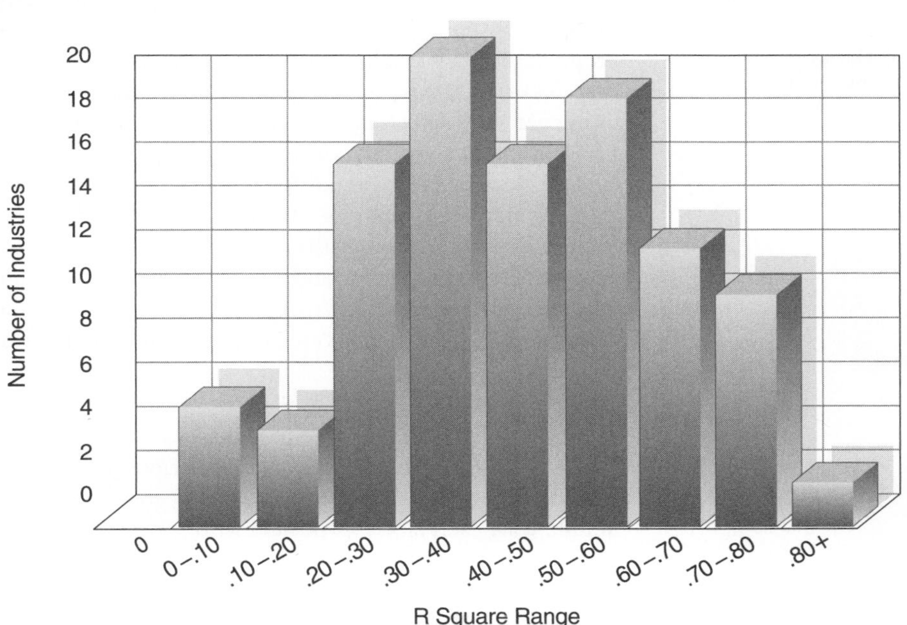

# Arbitrage Pricing Theory

Economic model builders are continually looking for better ways to mirror reality. The capital asset pricing model is a useful approximation of the process by which the market sets the price of a share of stock, but it is not perfect.

In 1976, Stephen Ross proposed a more complex model centered around **arbitrage pricing theory (APT).**[20] Although a generation has passed since the publication of Ross's paper, the model has yet to reach the practical application stage. Still, there is potential for it, and it may someday displace the CAPM. It is useful to know the basics of APT.

## APT Background

We know that stock prices often move together. We also know that certain stock sectors (or industries) sometimes show unusual volatility relative to the rest of the market, whereas other stock groups show less volatility. This seems to indicate that there is more to the cause of stock price movements than the behavior of a theoretical market portfolio.

Perhaps the key point behind the APT is the seemingly logical statement that a number of distinct factors (rather than just one) determine the market return. In an article in the *Financial Analysts Journal,* Richard Roll and Stephen Ross state specifically that APT assumes that a security's long-run return is

> directly related to its sensitivities to unanticipated changes in four economic variables—(1) inflation, (2) industrial production, (3) risk premiums and (4) the slope of the term structure of interest rates. Assets, even if they have the same CAPM beta, will have different patterns of sensitivities to these systematic factors.[21]

*The APT presumes that the market return is determined by a number of distinct macroeconomic factors.*

This seems reasonable. Analysts closely watch macroeconomic statistics such as the money supply, inflation, housing starts, interest rates, unemployment, changes in gross national product, political events, and many others. Analysts presumably watch these factors because of their belief that new information about them will influence future stock price movements.

Not all analysts are concerned with the same set of economic information. An analyst responsible for retail food chains, for instance, might not care much about housing starts but might be very interested in population density figures. An analyst for the forest products industry, in contrast, might be much more interested in housing starts (and the potential demand for construction lumber) than in shifting population centers. This seems to indicate that a single market measure (such as the CAPM beta) does not capture all the information relevant to the price of a particular stock.

## The APT Model

Table 6-10 shows the general representation of the arbitrage pricing theory model. A security's sensitivity to several macroeconomic factors determines the risk premium, with each factor associated with its own risk premium.

---

[20]See Stephen Ross, "The Arbitrage Theory of Capital Asset Pricing," *Journal of Economic Theory,* December 1976, 341–360.

[21]Richard Roll and Stephen Ross, "The Arbitrage Pricing Theory Approach to Strategic Portfolio Planning," *Financial Analysts Journal,* May/June 1984, 14–26.

MEMO

## Diversification and Enron

The energy giant Enron filed for bankruptcy on December 2, 2001, making it the largest bankruptcy in U.S. history. Earlier in 2001 Enron shares had sold for $84; they were $0.67 each in January 2002. While we will learn some interesting things from studying the reasons for this corporate failure, we have already heard one loud and clear: *diversify*.

A 401K plan is a popular retirement plan in which employees select from an array of investment alternatives (usually mutual funds with different objectives). In the Enron case, employees could voluntarily contribute up to 6 percent of their salaries to the plan, with the company matching 50 percent of the employees' contributions. Effectively, employees could put 9 percent of their annual salary into the plan. The company's contribution, however, was in *restricted Enron stock:* Employees could not sell the contributed stock until they were fifty years old. This meant that over time, Enron was likely to become an increasingly large proportion of an employee's portfolio, especially if the employee voluntarily bought more Enron stock, as many did. According to *The Wall Street Journal,** when Enron went bankrupt, the average employee had three-fifths of his 401K assets in the company's stock. The Profit Sharing/401K Council of America, representing the country's largest employers, reports that a national average of 43 percent of 401K assets is in company stock. Many statements of investment policy limit the equity investment in any one stock to 5 percent of total assets in "ordinary" portfolios. There is no reason that the prudent management of a retirement fund should be different.

A large part of the problem is that many employees do not understand the basics of prudent investment management. The *WSJ* article reports a study by John Hancock Financial Services finding that investors "believe a diversified stock fund is more risky than their company's stock." As we have seen, a single stock seldom offers a better risk/return package than a diversified portfolio. Many Enron employees learned this the hard way.

Aside from efforts to deal with the accounting and conflict of interest issues, two developments have resulted from the Enron disaster. Employees are learning about the need to diversify, and Congress has restricted the sale of stock in retirement plans.

---

*James K. Glassman, "Diversify, Diversify, Diversify," *The Wall Street Journal*, January 18, 2002, A10.

**TABLE 6-10** ARBITRAGE PRICING MODEL

$$R_A = E(\tilde{R}_A) + b_{1A}F_1 + b_{2A}F_2 + b_{3A}F_3 + b_{4A}F_4$$

where $R_A$ = actual return on Security A;
$E(\tilde{R}_A)$ = expected return on Security A;
$b_{iA}$ = sensitivity of Security A to factor $i$; and
$F_i$ = unanticipated change in factor $i$.

An infinite number of factors could presumably exist, although the empirical research done to date suggests that the four factors described by Roll and Ross capture a great deal of the information. Given that models are seldom 100 percent accurate and that a model with an infinite number of factors would be impractical, we can say that prices are a function of both macroeconomic factors and noise. The noise comes from the effects of minor factors with little routine influence.

*Price is a function of macroeconomic factors and noise.*

## Example of the APT

*As a comprehensive Website dedicated to APT,* http://www.aptltd.com *covers current issues related to the application of this theory.*

Consider the information in Table 6-11, which shows the expected returns for Treasury bills for Stocks A and B and for a two-security portfolio split 50–50 between T-bills and Stock B. We also see the factor 2 sensitivities for the stocks. T-bills, being riskless, have a factor sensitivity of 0. Both expected returns and betas combine in linear fashion, so the portfolio statistics are merely an average of the T-bill and Stock B figures.

Note that for both the portfolio and Stock A, $b_2 = 1.0$, yet their expected returns are different. Such a situation could not exist for long because it constitutes arbitrage. An arbitrageur could invest \$100 in the portfolio and sell \$100 worth of Stock A short, thereby creating a three-security portfolio with a $b_2$ of 0 and an expected return of 5 percent. This differs from an investment in the risk-free rate because the arbitrage portfolio would require no initial investment; the proceeds from the short sale would be sufficient to pay for the portfolio.[22] Investors would bid up the price of Stock B, thereby reducing its expected return. Similarly, the short selling of Stock A would cause downward pressure on it. This would cause prices to change until the two securities with the same beta sold for the same price.

The essence of the APT centers around this basic result. Securities can be formed into portfolios in such a way that all but one of their $b_i$ risks are 0, and all such securities should sell for the same price. You can form more complicated portfolios, but the law of one price still prevails: Identical securities should sell for the same price.

## Comparison of the CAPM and the APT

The capital asset pricing model is a single-index model and follows logically from the development of the security market line. Security returns are related to a well-defined measure (the return on the market portfolio), and the beta calculation is easy.

The practical problem of exact adherence to the CAPM is more difficult, however. It is one thing to specify a concept such as "the market portfolio," but constructing such a basket is challenging. Finance theory requires that all assets be included in the market portfolio, including nonfinancial assets such as real estate, gold, and so forth. This cannot be done conveniently, and consequently we use some proxy (often the S&P 500 stock index) for the theoretical portfolio. Betas calculated via the CAPM will be inconsistent if the market portfolio is incomplete.

**TABLE 6-11** SECURITY SENSITIVITIES AND EXPECTED RETURNS

| | *T-Bills* | *Stock A* | *Stock B* | *Portfolio (1/2 T-Bills 1/2 Stock B)* |
|---|---|---|---|---|
| $E(\tilde{R})$ | 5% | 10% | 25% | 15% |
| $b_2$ | 0 | 1.0 | 2.0 | 1.0 |

[22]"Investments" that require no dollar outlay should not earn any return. To earn the risk-free rate, funds must be committed.

The APT does not require identification of the market portfolio, but it does require the specification of the relevant macroeconomic factors. Much of the empirical APT research to date has focused on the identification of these factors, and the determination of the factor betas is still an unsolved problem.

The apparent computational problems of the APT may not be as severe as they seem. Mathematical techniques such as factor analysis and the calculation of eigenvalues can collapse a set of data into material and immaterial factors without having to specify precisely what the factors represent.

The CAPM and APT are not really at odds with each other. The two models together complement each other rather than compete. Both models predict that positive returns will result from factor sensitivities that move with the market and vice versa.

### Future Prospects for APT

*The rewards in business go to the man who does something with an idea.*
William Benton

The arbitrage pricing theory remains modestly controversial in academic circles. Some people doubt that it will ever become the norm within the investment community, largely because of the difficulties in associating names with factors and reliable numbers with the risk premiums and sensitivities. Still, some of the most respected finance academicians conduct the research in this area. Important economic developments are seldom easy. The jury is still out on the future role APT will play in portfolio management.

## SUMMARY

Diversification is a good idea, both logically and mathematically. Egos can get in the way of sound financial decisions, and spreading the investment dollars around can help prevent faulty reasoning in analyzing investment results.

People do not like risk; they are risk averse. They take risks only when they expect to get some positive benefit as a consequence. The central goal of careful portfolio construction is to achieve a return objective with as little risk as possible. We do this by choosing securities with returns that are largely uncorrelated.

A portfolio dominates all others if, for its level of expected return, no other portfolio has less risk, or, for its level of risk, no other portfolio has a higher expected return.

Harry Markowitz is the father of modern portfolio theory. His research shows the importance of security covariance and how proper security selection enables the portfolio manager to reduce risk without sacrificing expected return. The Markowitz algorithm is an application of quadratic programming.

A research paper by Evans and Archer is one of the most consequential contributions to portfolio theory. This paper shows that very thorough diversification is achieved with only fifteen or twenty securities and that random diversification eliminates a substantial amount of total risk. Current research suggests that closer to fifty may be necessary in today's market.

Random security selection usually leads to good diversification but not always. A portfolio manager should consider industry effects, and portfolio components ideally should be from unrelated industries.

The market model represents the relationship between a past series of security prices and the past level of a market index. The capital asset pricing model (CAPM) is a theoretical statement about the expected future relationship. Beta is an important element in the CAPM. Its value changes, and its estimation is partly a function of the time interval used in the calculation.

Beta is a measure of how sensitive a particular stock is to market movements. We can use scattergrams or linear regression to estimate beta. Betas greater than 1 indicate greater-than-average sensitivity. Changing market conditions or adjustments in a firm's capital structure can cause betas to change. Calculated betas are not always statistically significant, so it is a good idea to inspect the $R^2$ value along with the beta value. Portfolio betas are almost always more reliable than individual company betas.

The arbitrage pricing theory (APT) seeks to develop a model of security pricing that bases security returns on a number of macroeconomic factors rather than a single market index. Although the APT has little practical application at present, some of the leading academic researchers are proponents of this theory, and it may someday displace the CAPM as the best representation of how security prices are determined.

## QUESTIONS

1. In one hundred words or less, why is diversification a good idea?
2. How can your ego influence your investment decisions?
3. Some people believe that making a lot of money on a first investment is dangerous. Why is this?
4. What is meant by an *unnecessary* risk?
5. What are the three major components of risk in a two-security portfolio?
6. What is the relationship between beta and the risk of a well-diversified stock portfolio?
7. Suppose two securities have perfect negative correlation. Would it make sense to invest in these two securities only?
8. Two securities have the same expected return. According to capital market theory, what can you say about their risk?
9. Make up an example illustrating the concept of dominance.
10. What is the importance of the Evans and Archer study to the small investor?
11. How do industry effects influence portfolio construction?
12. What support does portfolio theory provide for the usefulness of the beta concept?
13. Why is the single security with least variance not necessarily on the efficient frontier of a risky security universe?
14. Why is the security with the highest expected return on the efficient frontier of a risky security universe?
15. In your own words, explain why the number of securities in an efficient portfolio generally increases as risk declines.
16. Why is superfluous diversification unavoidable for a large institutional investor?
17. What happens to the slope of the efficient frontier if the risk-free rate declines?
18. Suppose you pay a higher rate of interest to buy stock on margin than you receive when you invest at the risk-free rate. That is, the borrowing and lending rates are different. From your perspective, what does the efficient frontier look like? Draw a figure.

19. How is it possible for naive diversification to reduce *return* as well as risk?
20. What is the practical importance of corner portfolios?
21. The text states that the covariance between a constant and a random variable is 0. Given this, what is the correlation between a random variable and a constant?
22. Why do you think the "market price of risk" periodically changes?
23. What is the difference between the capital market line and the security market line?
24. What does *nonstationarity of beta* mean?
25. Explain the difference between the market model and the CAPM.
26. Comment on the following statement: You do not calculate beta; you estimate it.
27. What should you consider before making a decision to use daily versus weekly returns with the market model?
28. Why do you think it is necessary to know how people behave before proposing a normative theory of behavior?
29. What criteria would you use to determine when a data observation is an outlier that should be trimmed from the data set?
30. How does the CAPM differ from the APT model?
31. Suppose you hear someone make the following statement: "According to capital market theory, expected return is directly proportional to beta. You can increase beta by borrowing more money. Therefore, it makes sense for corporate treasurers to use as much debt as they can to increase the expected return to the shareholders." What is wrong with this logic?
32. You are a portfolio manager in an imaginary country where there are only three different investments: stock A, stock B, and a risk-free rate. Stocks A and B have a return correlation coefficient of 0.30. Knowing capital market theory, you are currently invested in an efficient portfolio made up of 20 percent the risk-free rate, 30 percent stock A, and 50 percent stock B. You also know that stock B is the riskiest of the three investments.

    Suppose the risk-free rate rises. You realize that in order for your portfolio to remain efficient you will have to adjust the proportions invested in the risky securities. You also decide to maintain 20% of the portfolio in the risk-free rate. Explain the adjustments you would have to make to the stock investments to keep your portfolio efficient and undominated by any other security combination. (No calculations are necessary.)

## PROBLEMS

1. Suppose you split your money 50–50 between the two securities shown in Table 6-12.
    a. What is the expected return of the two-security portfolio?
    b. What is the portfolio beta?
2. In Problem 1, what is the covariance between Security A and the market?
3. What is the portfolio variance in Problem 1?
4. Suppose you split your money between Securities A and B from Problem 1. What percentage of your portfolio variance comes from the interaction component of total risk?

**TABLE 6-12** SECURITY STATISTICS

| | *Security A* | *Security B* |
|---|---|---|
| $E(\tilde{R})$ | 12% | 13% |
| $\sigma$ | 0.021 | 0.029 |
| Beta | 1.10 | 1.20 |

Variance of the market = 0.0002; $\rho_{AB} = 0.6$.

**TABLE 6-13** SECURITY EXPECTED RETURNS AND BETAS

| *Security* | $E(\tilde{R})$ | *Beta* |
|---|---|---|
| 1 | 10% | 1.00 |
| 2 | 12% | 1.20 |
| 3 | 13% | 1.10 |

5. Refer to Table 6-6. Suppose there is a third security (C), with these characteristics: $E(\tilde{R}_C) = 10\%$; $\sigma_C^2 = .20$; $\rho_{AC} = .78$; and $\rho_{BC} = .56$. Construct the quadratic program that would minimize the risk of a three-security portfolio consisting of A, B, and C.
6. Suppose the risk-free rate is 8 percent. What is the expected return and variance of a portfolio containing 50 percent of the risk-free rate and 50 percent Security B from Table 6-12?
7. Refer to Tables 6-1 and 6-2. What is the least-risk *three-security* portfolio with an expected return of 12 percent?
8. Consider the data in Tables 6-1 and 6-2. What is the minimum variance portfolio composed of Securities C and E?
9. Consider the data in Tables 6-1 and 6-2. What is the minimum variance portfolio composed of Securities A and D?
10. Prove or disprove the following statement: If two securities are less than perfectly correlated, the minimum variance portfolio always contains some proportion of both securities.
11. Refer to footnote 14. Make up an example showing the truth of the statement.
12. Suppose there are three well-diversified portfolios, as shown in Table 6-13. An arbitrage opportunity is implied in these numbers. Show mathematically how to take advantage of it.
13. A portfolio has a $\sigma^2$ of 0.26. XXZ stock has a $\sigma^2$ of 0.20; the correlation between XXZ and the portfolio is 0.79. Refer to footnote 14; will the inclusion of XXZ in the portfolio reduce its risk?
14. A two-security portfolio contains Stocks B and C from Table 6-1. Using a spreadsheet package, do the following:
    a. Prepare a plot showing the portfolio variance for various combinations of Stocks B and C.
    b. Find the minimum variance portfolio.
    c. Find the proportions of Stocks B and C that constitute a portfolio with the same risk as Stock C alone.
15. Plot the excess returns in Table 6-14, and graphically estimate beta by hand.
16. Do Problem 15 using a spreadsheet package such as Microsoft Excel.
17. A security has a beta of 1.23. The risk-free rate of interest is 8 percent, and the market is expected to earn 14 percent. What is the expected return on the security?

**TABLE 6-14** HISTORICAL EXCESS RETURNS

| *Week* | *Stock* | *S&P 500 Index* |
|---|---|---|
| 1 | .06 | .08 |
| 2 | –.02 | .0 |
| 3 | –.03 | –.04 |
| 4 | .0 | .01 |
| 5 | .01 | .01 |
| 6 | .04 | .05 |
| 7 | –.01 | –.01 |
| 8 | .03 | .04 |
| 9 | –.02 | –.03 |
| 10 | .04 | .06 |

18. A portfolio with a beta of 1.0 has an expected return of 14 percent; the risk-free interest rate is 7 percent. Show that the expected return of a portfolio with a beta of 2.0 is *not* 28 percent.
19. Redo problem 15 using the following:
    **a.** The first five weeks only.
    **b.** The second five weeks only.
    Why might the beta you estimate from the two time periods differ?
20. Using a spreadsheet package, generate three series of 100 random numbers ranging from –1 to +1.
    **a.** Calculate the variance of each series.
    **b.** Calculate the variance of a portfolio containing all three series. (That is, calculate the variance of the sum of the three random numbers.)
21. You estimate beta and get the following output:
    $R_{stock} = -0.0022 + 0.9833R_{market}$
    Standard error of beta estimate = 0.3354
    What does the standard error tell you about your beta estimate?
22. You estimate beta to be 1.22 with a standard error of the estimate equal to 0.0400. What is the 95 percent confidence interval for the beta estimate?

## INTERNET EXERCISES

1. Using the *Stockscreener* at *http://screen.finance.yahoo.com/newscreener.html* search for stocks with a beta lower than –1. Then search for stocks with a beta higher than 4. Do you recognize any of the companies that result using these two criteria? Which group might be a valuable addition to a stock portfolio?
2. Use the "*Key Statistics*" tab at *http://finance.yahoo.com* to identify the 60 month historical betas of any four stocks. Now compute the expected return implied by CAPM on a portfolio weighted equally in these four stocks. Use the current annualized yield on three-month Treasury Bills as the risk-free rate. For the market return, use the 10-year annualized return on S&P 500 index from *http://www. barra.com/research/SummaryReturns.aspx.*

## FURTHER READING


Bierman, Harold. "How Much Diversification Is Desirable?" *Journal of Portfolio Management*, Winter 1981, 42–44.

Black, Fisher, Michael Jensen, and Myron Scholes. "The Capital Asset Pricing Model: Some Empirical Tests." In *Studies in Theory of Capital Markets*, ed. M.C. Jensen. New York: Praeger, 1972.

Brealey, Richard A., and Stewart C. Myers. *Principles of Corporate Finance*, 7th ed. New York: McGraw-Hill, 2003.

Brinson, Gary P., L. Randolph Hood, and Gilbert L. Beebower. "Determinants of Portfolio Performance." *Financial Analysts Journal*, July/August 1986, 39–44.

Brush, John S., and Michael E. Anselmi. "Practical Use and Misuse of Beta." *Journal of Investing*, Summer 1994, 42–47.

Chen, N., R. Roll, and S. Ross. "Economic Forces and the Stock Market." *Journal of Business*, July 1986, 383–403.

Dhrymes, P.J., I. Friend, and N.B. Gultekin. "A Critical Reexamination of the Empirical Evidence on the Arbitrage Pricing Theory." *Journal of Finance*, June 1984, 323–346.

Elton, Edwin J., and Martin J. Gruber. "Risk Reduction and Portfolio Size: An Analytical Solution." *Journal of Business*, October 1977, 415–437.

Evans, John L., and Stephen N. Archer. "Diversification and the Reduction of Dispersion: An Empirical Analysis." *Journal of Finance*, December 1968, 761–767.

Fisher, Lawrence, and James Lorie. "Some Studies of Variability of Returns on Investments in Common Stocks." *Journal of Business*, April 1970, 99–134.

Frankfurter, George M., and Herbert E. Phillips. "A Brief History of MPT: From a Normative Model to Event Studies." *Journal of Investing*, Winter 1994, 18–23.

Frost, Peter A., and James E. Savarino. "Portfolio Size and Estimation Risk." *Journal of Portfolio Management*, Fall 1985, 60–64.

Gehr, A. "Risk-Adjusted Capital Budgeting Using Arbitrage." *Financial Management*, Winter 1981, 14–19.

Harris, Robert, and Felicia Marston. "The Market Risk Premium: Expectational Estimates Using Analysts' Forecasts." *Journal of Applied Finance* 11, 1, 2001, 6–16.

Hawawini, Gabriel A. "Why Beta Shifts as the Return Interval Changes." *Financial Analysts Journal*, May/June 1983, 73–77.

Hudson-Wilson, Susan, and Bernard L. Elbaum. "Diversification Benefits for Investors in Real Estate." *Journal of Portfolio Management*, Spring 1995, 92–99.

Ibbotson, Roger C., Paul D. Kaplan, and James D. Peterson. "Estimates of Small Stock Betas Are Much Too Low." *Journal of Portfolio Management*, Summer 1997, 104–111.

Jennings, Edward. "An Empirical Analysis of Some Aspects of Common Stock Diversification." *Journal of Financial and Quantitative Analysis*, March 1971, 797–813.

Lintner, J. "Security Prices, Risk and Maximal Gains from Diversification." *Journal of Finance*, December 1965, 587–615.

Markowitz, Harry. "Portfolio Selection." *Journal of Finance*, March 1952, 77–91.

Olsen, Robert. "Sample Size and Markowitz Diversification." *Journal of Portfolio Management*, Winter 1984, 18–22.

Reilly, Frank K., and David J. Wright. "A Comparison of Published Betas." *Journal of Portfolio Management*, Spring 1988, 64–69.

Roenfeldt, R., G. Griepentrog, and C. Pflaum. "Further Evidence on the Stationarity of Beta Coefficients." *Journal of Finance and Quantitative Analysis*, March 1978, 117–121.

Roll, Richard, and Stephen Ross. "The Arbitrage Pricing Theory Approach to Strategic Portfolio Planning." *Financial Analysts Journal*, May/June 1984, 14–26.

———. "An Empirical Investigation of the Arbitrage Pricing Theory." *Journal of Finance*, December 1980, 1073–1103.

Rosenberg, Barr, and James Guy. "Beta and Investment Fundamentals." *Financial Analysts Journal*, May/June 1976, 60–72.

Ross, Stephen. "The Arbitrage Theory of Capital Asset Pricing." *Journal of Economic Theory*, December 1976, 341–360.

———. "A Simple Approach to the Valuation of Risky Streams." *Journal of Business*, July 1979, 254–286.

Sharpe, W.F. "Capital Asset Prices: A Theory of Market Equilibrium under Conditions of Risk." *Journal of Finance*, September 1964, 425–442.

Siegel, Jeremy J. "The Shrinking Equity Premium." *Journal of Portfolio Management*, Fall 1999, 10–17.

Smith, Keith V. "The Effect of Intervaling on Estimation Parameters of the Capital Asset Pricing Model." *Journal of Finance and Quantitative Analysis*, June 1978, 313–332.

Surz, Ronald J. "R-Squareds and Alphas Are from Different Alphabets." *Journal of Investing*, Summer 1998, 62–66.

Theobald, Michael. "Beta Stationarity and Estimation Period: Some Analytical Results." *Journal of Financial and Quantitative Analysis*, December 1981, 747–757.

Wagner, Wayne H. "Ten Myths and Twenty Years of Betas." *Journal of Portfolio Management*, Fall 1994, 79–82.

Whitmore, G.A. "Diversification and the Reduction of Dispersion." *Journal of Financial and Quantitative Analysis*, May 1970, 263–264.

# APPENDIX Stochastic Dominance

*What can be added to the happiness of a man who is in health, out of debt, and has a clear conscience?*

***Mark Twain***

## Key Terms

efficient
first-degree stochastic dominance (FSD)
second-degree stochastic dominance (SSD)

## Introduction

The Markowitz mean variance portfolio construction algorithm is an important portfolio management tool, but it is not every manager's algorithm of choice. If a manager does not have confidence in the correlation coefficients or in the stability of the standard deviation estimates, mean-variance portfolio construction can be flawed. In fact, Markowitz programming makes extensive use of extreme values. Stocks with very low correlations, expected returns, or unusual standard deviations will play a major role in the efficient portfolios that the algorithm determines. Stochastic dominance is an alternative, appropriate technique that can be employed in the portfolio construction process or used as an aid in performance evaluation.

The dictionary defines *stochastic* as "denoting the process of selecting from among a group of theoretically possible alternatives those elements or factors whose combination will most closely approximate a desired result."[23] Stochastic models are not always exact; they are, however, very useful shorthand representations of potentially complicated processes.

[23]*Funk & Wagnall's Standard College Dictionary* (New York: Harcourt, Brace & World, 1966), S.V. "Stochastic."

## Efficiency Revisited

As shown earlier, certain securities or portfolios of securities dominate others. If two competing investments have identical levels of risk, the one with the higher expected return dominates the other. Equivalently, if two portfolios (or securities) have identical expected rates of return, the one with the lower risk dominates the other.

Portfolios that are not dominated by any other portfolio are **efficient;** they are inefficient if at least one other portfolio dominates them. The concept of efficiency is important because we know from observing human behavior that all people like return and that most people dislike risk. If there is a way to increase return without adding risk, rational people do so; and if there is a way to reduce risk without sacrificing return, most people do that as well. Rational investors prefer efficient investments.

## First-Degree Stochastic Dominance

Regardless of a person's attitude toward risk, we know this: a rational investor always prefers more of a good thing to less. Given the choice, for instance, between receiving a riskless $100 and a riskless $200, a person logically picks the higher amount.

*Regardless of their attitude toward risk, investors prefer a higher return to a lower return.*

To investigate the concept of stochastic dominance, first consider a nonfinancial example. Suppose you are the sales manager for a car dealership, and you want to look into the performance of your five-member sales staff. You are especially interested in seeing if one of your people is clearly outperforming the others or if someone is not performing well relative to his or her colleagues. Table 6-15 shows the weekly car sales for each of the sales associates.

**TABLE 6-15** WEEKLY NEW CAR SALES

| *Week* | *Sales Associate* | | | | |
|---|---|---|---|---|---|
| | A | B | C | D | E |
| 1 | 5 | 4 | 6 | 3 | 3 |
| 2 | 3 | 6 | 4 | 4 | 5 |
| 3 | 4 | 5 | 5 | 4 | 3 |
| 4 | 5 | 6 | 3 | 7 | 2 |
| 5 | 4 | 5 | 4 | 4 | 3 |
| 6 | 6 | 4 | 6 | 5 | 3 |
| 7 | 3 | 2 | 3 | 4 | 1 |
| 8 | 1 | 2 | 6 | 5 | 7 |
| 9 | 3 | 2 | 3 | 3 | 2 |
| 10 | 1 | 5 | 6 | 4 | 7 |
| 11 | 2 | 3 | 5 | 5 | 3 |
| 12 | 5 | 5 | 5 | 5 | 3 |
| 13 | 4 | 3 | 4 | 4 | 1 |
| 14 | 6 | 4 | 2 | 4 | 3 |
| 15 | 1 | 3 | 5 | 2 | 7 |
| 16 | 5 | 6 | 6 | 4 | 3 |
| 17 | 2 | 1 | 2 | 5 | 5 |
| 18 | 6 | 6 | 7 | 7 | 3 |
| 19 | 3 | 5 | 3 | 5 | 7 |
| 20 | 5 | 2 | 2 | 7 | 3 |

Using stochastic dominance, you can see whether the performance of any of the sales associates dominates that of one or more of the others. To do this, you need to order the weekly sales figures from lowest (least desirable) to highest (most desirable) and then calculate the cumulative probability of obtaining each sales level or less. Table 6-16 shows the sorted sales figures.

Assuming that the weekly sales figures for each person are independent, each observation makes up one-twentieth, or 5 percent, of the twenty-week sample. You can then group the observations and assign a probability to them as in Table 6-17. Table 6-17 shows, for instance, that 60 percent of the time Sales Associate A sells

**TABLE 6-16** ORDERED WEEKLY SALES FIGURES

| *Observation* | *Sales Associate* | | | | |
|---|---|---|---|---|---|
| | A | B | C | D | E |
| 1 | 1 | 1 | 2 | 2 | 1 |
| 2 | 1 | 2 | 2 | 3 | 1 |
| 3 | 1 | 2 | 2 | 3 | 2 |
| 4 | 2 | 2 | 3 | 4 | 2 |
| 5 | 2 | 2 | 3 | 4 | 3 |
| 6 | 3 | 3 | 3 | 4 | 3 |
| 7 | 3 | 3 | 3 | 4 | 3 |
| 8 | 3 | 3 | 4 | 4 | 3 |
| 9 | 3 | 4 | 4 | 4 | 3 |
| 10 | 4 | 4 | 4 | 4 | 3 |
| 11 | 4 | 4 | 5 | 4 | 3 |
| 12 | 4 | 5 | 5 | 5 | 3 |
| 13 | 5 | 5 | 5 | 5 | 3 |
| 14 | 5 | 5 | 5 | 5 | 3 |
| 15 | 5 | 5 | 6 | 5 | 5 |
| 16 | 5 | 5 | 6 | 5 | 5 |
| 17 | 5 | 6 | 6 | 5 | 7 |
| 18 | 6 | 6 | 6 | 7 | 7 |
| 19 | 6 | 6 | 6 | 7 | 7 |
| 20 | 6 | 6 | 7 | 7 | 7 |

**TABLE 6-17** CUMULATIVE PROBABILITY OF ACHIEVING SALES LEVELS

| *Probability of Achieving Sales of No More Than:* | *Sales Associate* | | | | |
|---|---|---|---|---|---|
| | A | B | C | D | E |
| 0 | 0 | 0 | 0 | 0 | 0 |
| 1 | 0.15 | 0.05 | 0 | 0 | 0.10 |
| 2 | 0.25 | 0.25 | 0.15 | 0.05 | 0.20 |
| 3 | 0.45 | 0.40 | 0.35 | 0.15 | 0.70 |
| 4 | 0.60 | 0.55 | 0.50 | 0.55 | 0.70 |
| 5 | 0.85 | 0.75 | 0.70 | 0.85 | 0.80 |
| 6 | 1.00 | 1.00 | 0.95 | 0.85 | 0.80 |
| 7 | 1.00 | 1.00 | 1.00 | 1.00 | 1.00 |

FIGURE 6-13

Comparative Sales Performance

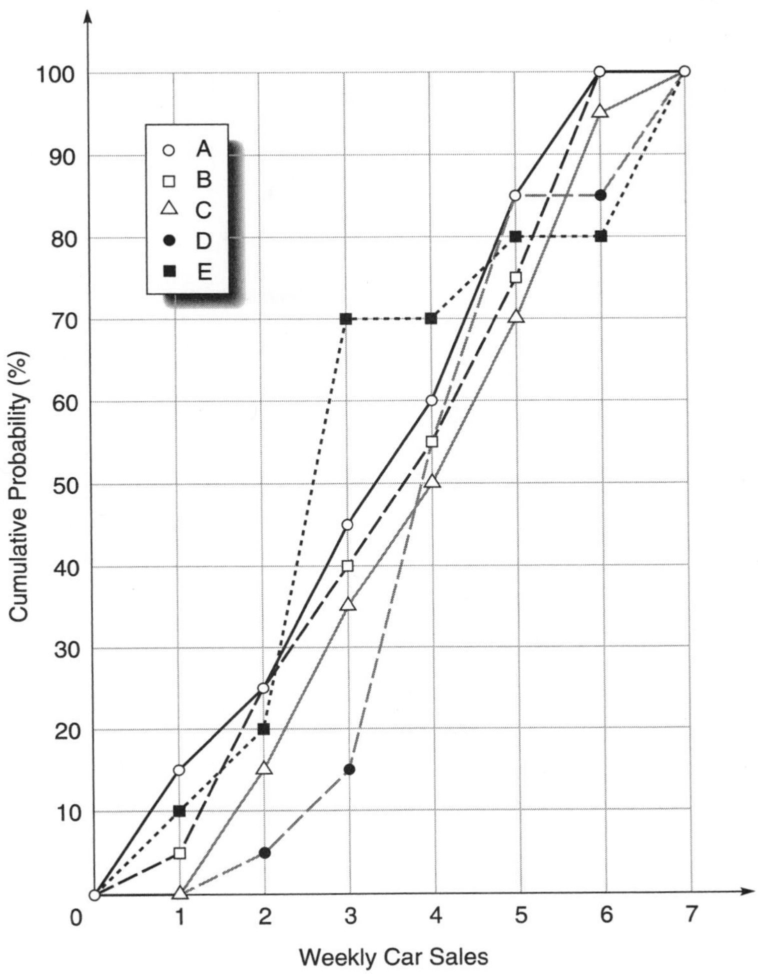


four cars or fewer in a week whereas Sales Associate C sells four or fewer 50 percent of the time. Alternatively, this means that 40 percent of the time Associate A sold more than four cars, and Associate C sold more than four 50 percent of the time. (Ideally, of course, each member of the sales staff would always sell more than four cars. The closer to 100 percent the actual figure gets, the better.) Figure 6-13 diagrams these cumulative probabilities.

*The First-Degree Stochastic Dominance Rule: Cumulative distribution A will be preferred over cumulative distribution B if every value of distribution A lies below or on distribution B, provided the distributions are not identical.*

What can you tell from Table 6-17 and Figure 6-13? Close inspection indicates that the performance of Associate C dominates that of both Associate A and Associate B. For every level of car sales, the likelihood that Associate C sold that many or fewer is less than that of Associate A or B. For instance, the likelihood that Associate C will sell three cars or fewer in a given week is 35 percent, whereas the corresponding likelihoods for Associates A and B are 45 and 40 percent, respectively. Associate C's cumulative probability is not higher than that of Associate A or B for any level of sales. This is the criterion for **first-degree stochastic dominance (FSD).**

FIGURE 6-14

Comparative Sales Performance (A, B, and C)

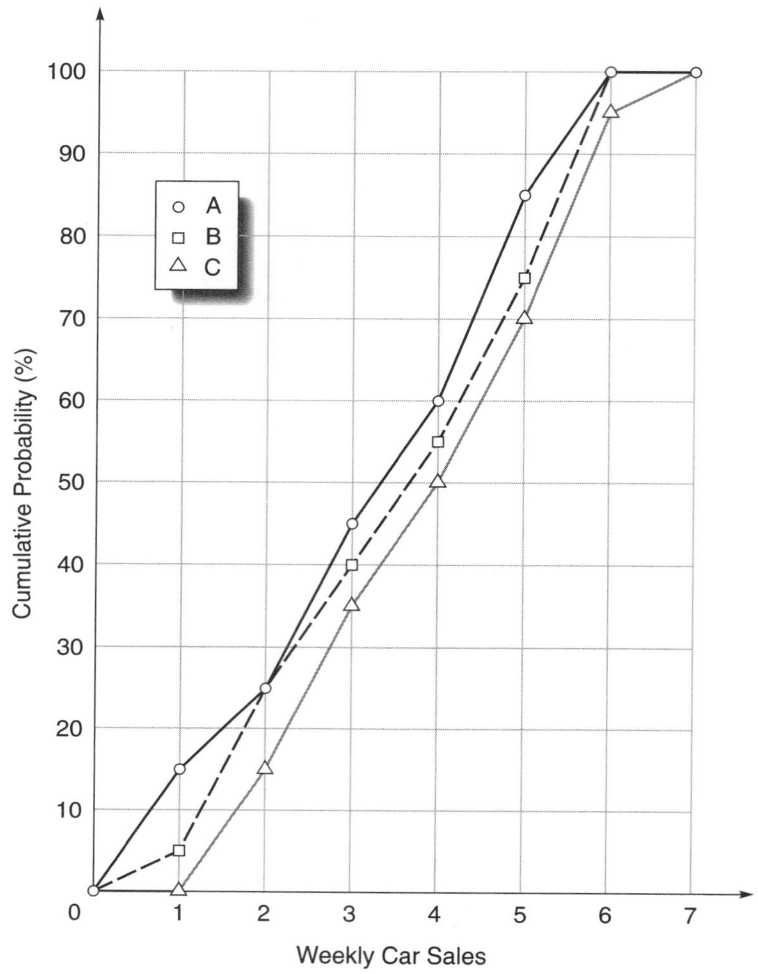


Figure 6-14 shows this more clearly. Every point on line C lies under lines A and B. Therefore, C shows first-degree stochastic dominance over A and B. Line B lies under line A except for one point where they coincide. This satisfies the criterion in the first-degree stochastic dominance rule, so B shows first-degree stochastic dominance over A. Rules of logic require that C then dominate A as well as B. The key graphic feature of FSD is that the lines do not cross, although there may be tangent points or areas where they coincide.

You can tell from these results that A and B are out of the running for best sales associate. This leaves you to choose between Sales Associates C, D, and E. Their lines, however, *do* intersect, so you cannot eliminate any of them by FSD: C, D, and E are consequently FSD efficient. They make up the FSD efficient set. You need to turn to *second-degree stochastic dominance* to investigate further.

## Second-Degree Stochastic Dominance

*The Second-Degree Stochastic Dominance Rule: Alternative A is preferred to Alternative B if the cumulative probability of B minus the cumulative probability of A is always nonnegative.*

The rule of **second-degree stochastic dominance (SSD)** states that we prefer Alternative A to Alternative B if for every observation X, the area under the cumulative distribution of A from minus infinity to X is less than the corresponding area under the cumulative distribution of B. An equivalent statement is that we prefer Alternative A to Alternative B if the cumulative probability of B minus the cumulative probability of A is always nonnegative.

Figure 6-15 shows the performance of the remaining three sales associates. Figure 6-16 compares Sales Associates C and E. Because the lines cross, neither person dominates the other by FSD. The cumulative area between the two lines, however, indicates that C dominates E by SSD. Associate E is not your best sales associate, either. This reduces the choice to Associate C or D; the corresponding

**FIGURE 6-15**

Comparative Sales Performance (C, D, and E)

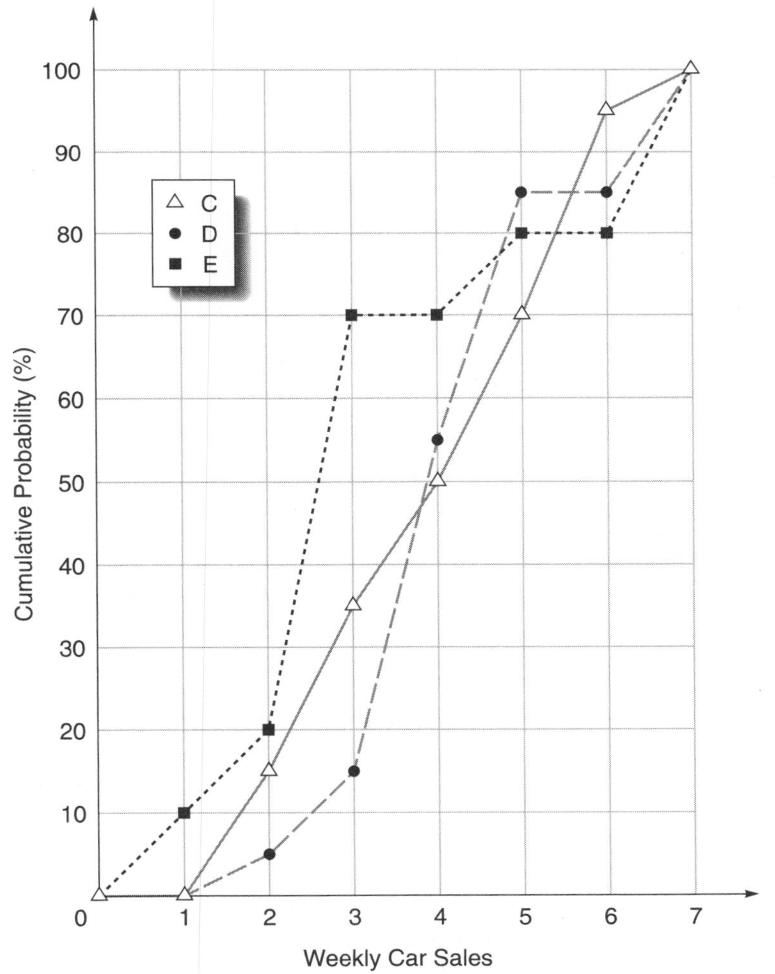

FIGURE 6-16

Comparative Sales Performance (C and E)

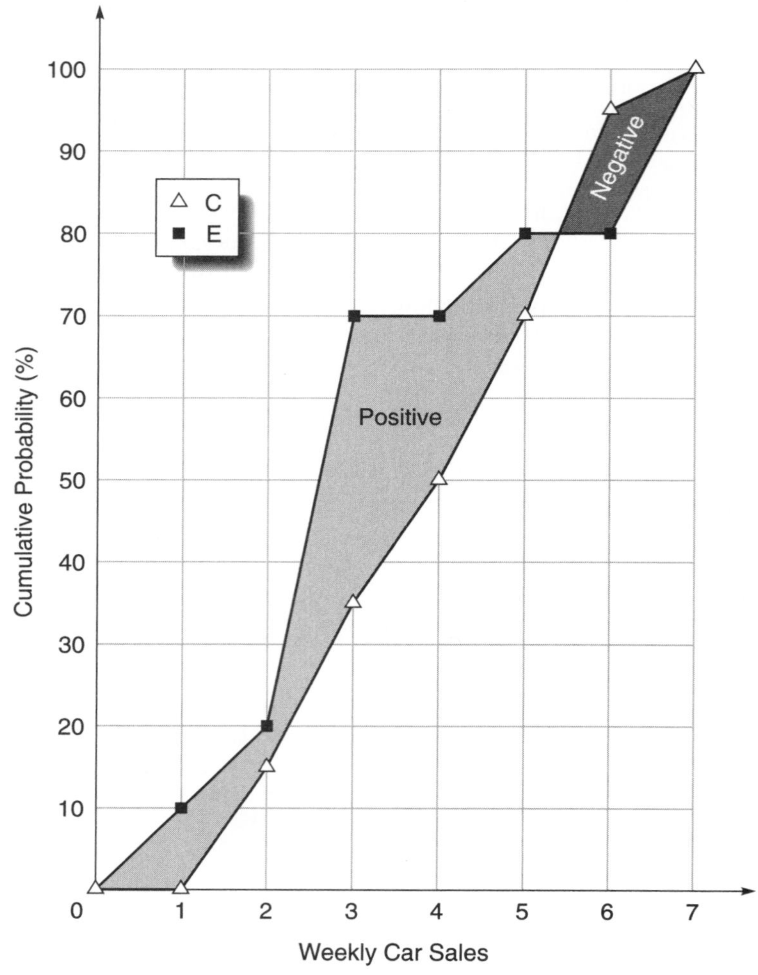


graph is Figure 6-17. This figure shows that D dominates C by SSD, so your highest-performing sales associate is Associate D. The SSD efficient set contains only one member, D. Associates A, B, C, and E are inefficient under SSD.

Now look at how someone might use stochastic dominance to compare investment alternatives. Table 6-18 shows actual annual percentage rates of return on two mutual funds (Mutual Shares and 44 Wall Street) over the period 1975 to 1988. These returns are ordered and processed in precisely the same way as in the sales associates example. This yields the cumulative probability diagram shown in Figure 6-18.

Because the cumulative probability plots for the two funds cross, neither fund is FSD dominant. Mutual Shares, however, is dominant by SSD because the cumulative area between the 44 Wall Street graph and the Mutual Shares graph is positive. By the SSD criterion, then, you can eliminate 44 Wall Street from the set of efficient alternatives facing a risk-averse investor. With potentially thousands of

FIGURE 6-17

Comparative Sales Performance (C and D)

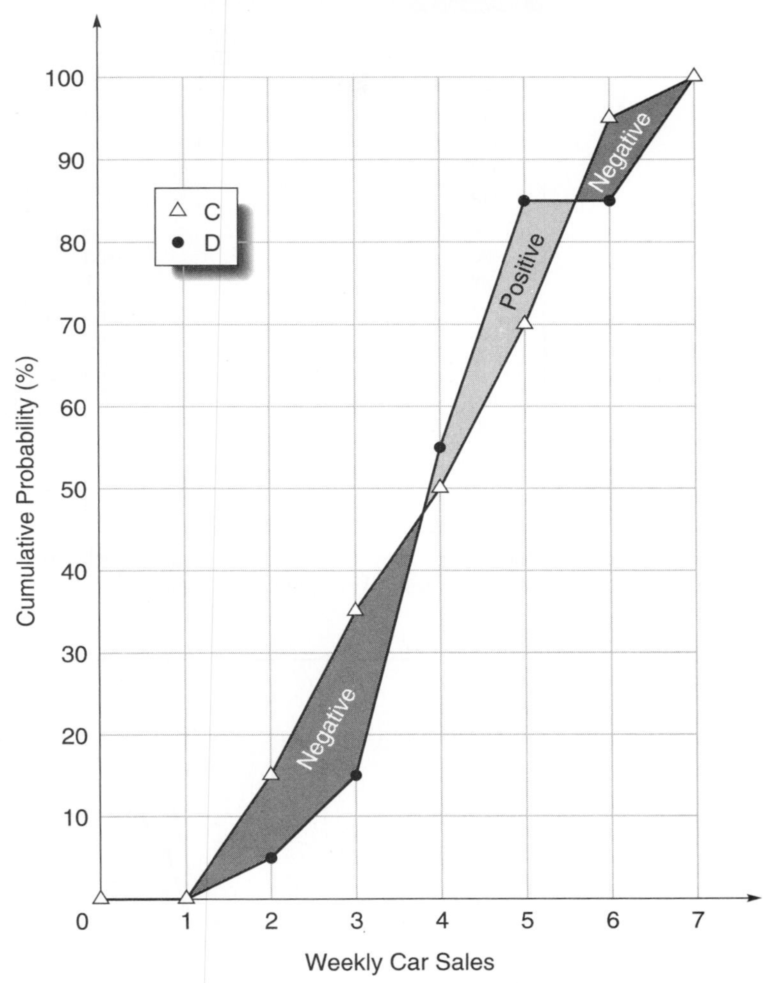


investment alternatives available, stochastic dominance (especially in the second degree) can be a significant aid in reducing the security universe to a workable number of efficient alternatives.

## Stochastic Dominance and Utility

*Both the conservative investor and the gambler prefer a first-degree stochastic dominant option over an FSD inefficient alternative.*

Stochastic dominance focuses on the expected return of an investment rather than on the risk of that investment. Economic theory shows that regardless of how much risk a person can tolerate, the first-degree stochastic dominance criterion is appropriate. Both the conservative investor and the gambler will prefer a first-degree stochastic dominant investment over an FSD inefficient alternative.

Most people are risk averse; they choose to take only those risks for which they expect to be properly rewarded. Those who are risk averse can use second-degree

**TABLE 6-18** SELECTED MUTUAL FUND ANNUAL PERCENTAGE RATES OF RETURN

| | *44 Wall Street* | *Mutual Shares* |
|---|---|---|
| 1975 | +184.1% | +24.6% |
| 1976 | +46.5 | +63.1 |
| 1977 | +16.5 | +13.2 |
| 1978 | +32.9 | +16.1 |
| 1979 | +71.4 | +39.3 |
| 1980 | +36.1 | +19.0 |
| 1981 | −23.6 | +8.7 |
| 1982 | +6.9 | +12.0 |
| 1983 | +9.2 | +37.8 |
| 1984 | −58.7 | +14.3 |
| 1985 | −20.1 | +26.3 |
| 1986 | −16.3 | +16.9 |
| 1987 | −34.6 | +6.5 |
| 1988 | +19.3 | +30.7 |
| Mean | +19.3% | +23.5% |

Change in net asset value, January 1 through December 31.
Source: Standard & Poor's *Stock Guide*, various years.

**FIGURE 6-18**

Second-Degree Stochastic Dominance

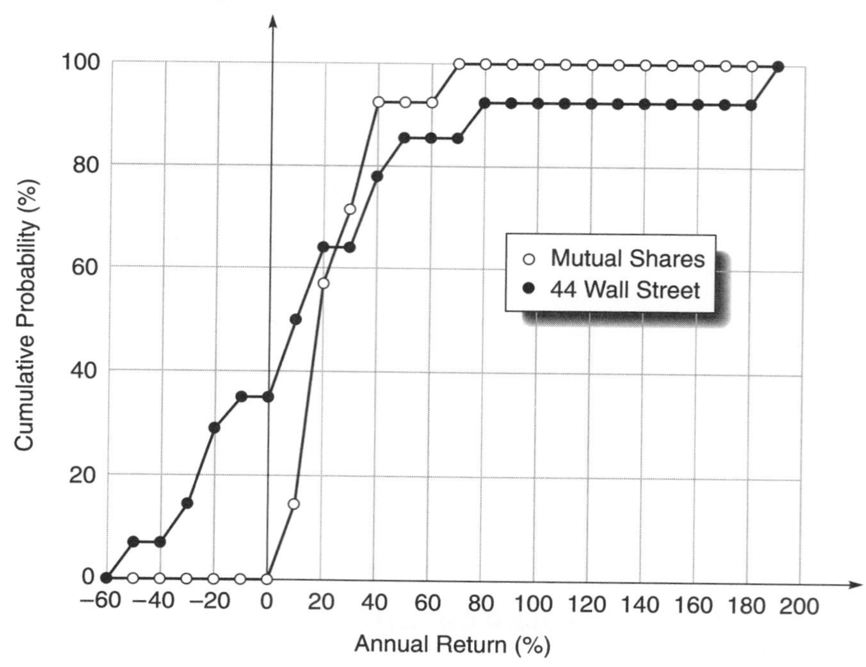


stochastic dominance to weed out inefficient alternatives from the choices available. Substantial research proves the validity of SSD in an economic theory framework. The Further Reading section at the end of the Appendix provides more information.

## Stochastic Dominance and Mean Return

A necessary condition for Alternative A to be FSD efficient over Alternative B is that the expected return of A must be no less than the expected return of B. If this is not the case, Alternative A cannot be FSD over Alternative B. It is also the case that security rankings based on the geometric mean are a necessary, but not a sufficient, condition for rankings based on stochastic dominance.[24] This means that if alternatives are ranked by both geometric mean and level of stochastic dominance efficiency, no FSD-efficient portfolio can have a higher geometric mean return than an SSD-efficient portfolio.

It is not appropriate to assume that the alternative with the highest arithmetic mean return is the dominant choice, although this is often the case. A simple example will show this. Figure 6-19 shows two alternatives with means of 4.5 and 5.0. Both are in the SSD-efficient set. The graph illustrates the fact that the alternative with the highest arithmetic mean cannot be assumed to be best.

## Higher Orders of Stochastic Dominance

*Higher orders of stochastic dominant sets are subsets of the lower orders.*

It is possible to calculate third and higher degrees of stochastic dominance, although we rarely encounter fourth and higher orders in the finance literature. For third-degree stochastic dominance (TSD) to be an appropriate selection criterion, there is

**FIGURE 6-19**

Unequal Means and Stochastic Dominance

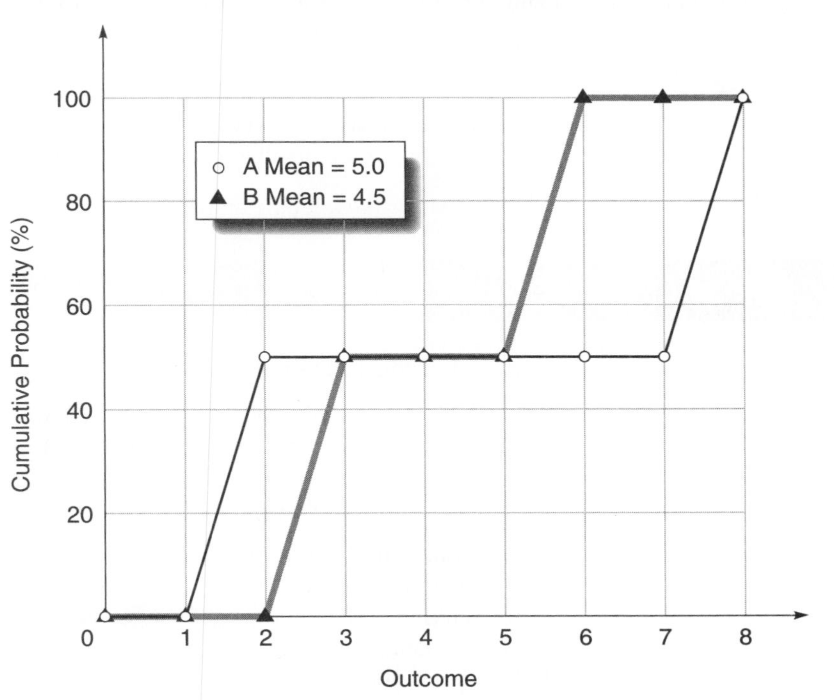


[24]See, for instance, William H. Jean, "The Geometric Mean and Stochastic Dominance," *Journal of Finance*, March 1980, 151–158.

a requirement that in addition to the investor being risk averse, the investor's degree of risk aversion decline as wealth increases.[25] Fourth and higher derivatives of a person's utility function are conceptually difficult and not very useful.

### *Practical Problems with Stochastic Dominance*

First-degree stochastic dominance is theoretically a sound decision criterion, but frequently it fails to reduce the security universe very much. Use of a lengthy history of returns does not identify many FSD securities. Second-degree stochastic dominance, in contrast, is often very useful in screening out inefficient choices from a universe of options. A study by Tehranian included five hundred randomly selected portfolios and found that seventy-two were efficient under the SSD rule, sixteen under TSD, fifteen under fourth-degree stochastic dominance, and thirteen under fifth-degree stochastic dominance.[26] The FSD efficient set was computationally too difficult to calculate, but it would have included virtually all five hundred portfolios.

## SUMMARY

Stochastic dominance is an alternative to the mean variance portfolio construction technique. First-degree stochastic dominance is an appropriate criterion for any investor regardless of attitude toward risk because any rational person prefers more wealth to less. If an investor is risk averse, as most are, the second-degree stochastic dominance criterion is appropriate. SSD is a much more powerful screening tool than FSD. Previous research shows that in a given universe, many, if not most, of the alternatives are FSD efficient.

It is possible to calculate any *n*th degree of stochastic dominance, although levels beyond the third do not appear often in the finance literature. In many instances, SSD eliminates a substantial number of investment alternatives from further consideration.

## PROBLEMS

Use the following data as needed:

Option A: 3, 3, 2, 2, 2, 3, 2, 4, 4, 4, 3, 3, 3, 5, 3, 6, 3, 3, 6, 6, 4, 3, 3, 3, 2
Option B: 4, 4, 1, 2, 2, 2, 5, 3, 6, 6, 8, 6, 6, 6, 4, 4, 7, 7, 7, 7, 3, 5, 3, 5, 5
Option C: 2, 1, 1, 2, 3, 3, 4, 2, 3, 2, 3, 3, 3, 2, 1, 2, 1, 2, 1, 2, 2, 3, 4, 2, 4
Option D: 3, 2, 2, 2, 3, 4, 3, 5, 5, 4, 5, 4, 2, 4, 3, 4, 4, 5, 6, 4, 6, 6, 4, 5, 3

1. Determine the FSD efficient set.
2. Calculate the geometric mean of the values. What is the relationship between the ranking of the options by their geometric mean and their ranking by stochastic dominance?
3. Determine the SSD efficient set.

---

[25]This is related to the notion of the diminishing marginal utility of money, discussed in Chapter 3.

[26]Hassan Tehranian, "Empirical Studies in Portfolio Performance Using Higher Degrees of Stochastic Dominance." *Journal of Finance*, March 1980, 159–171.

4. Suppose that an investment alternative has one outcome that is lower than any of the outcomes from the competing investments. Is it possible for this alternative to be in the FSD efficient set?
5. Suppose one of the options had an observation of 0. Is it possible for this option to be FSD efficient? To be SSD efficient?
6. Comment on the following statement: The problem with stochastic dominance is that it does not consider risk.

##  FURTHER READING

Elton, Edwin J., and Martin J. Gruber. *Modern Portfolio Theory and Investment Analysis*, 6th ed. New York: Wiley, 2003.

Hanoch, G., and H. Levy. "The Efficiency Analysis of Choices Involving Risk." *Review of Economic Studies* 38, 1969, 335–346.

Jean, William H. "Comparison of Moment and Stochastic Dominance Ranking Methods." *Journal of Financial and Quantitative Analysis*, March 1975, 151–161.

———. "The Geometric Mean and Stochastic Dominance." *Journal of Finance*, March 1980, 151–158.

Levy, Haim. "Stochastic Dominance among Log-Normal Prospects." *International Economic Review*, October 1973, 601–614.

Meyer, J. "Choice among Distributions," *Journal of Economic Theory* 14, 1977, 326–336.

Porter, R.B. "An Empirical Comparison of Stochastic Dominance and Mean-Variance Portfolio Choice Criteria." *Journal of Financial and Quantitative Analysis*, September 1973, 587–608.

Porter, R.B., and J.E. Gaumnitz. "Stochastic Dominance vs. Mean-Variance Portfolio Analysis." *American Economic Review*, June 1972, 438–446.

Tehranian, Hassan. "Empirical Studies in Portfolio Performance Using Higher Degrees of Stochastic Dominance." *Journal of Finance*, March 1980, 159–171.

Whitmore, G.A. "Third-Degree Stochastic Dominance." *American Economic Review*, June 1970, 457–459.

# 7 International Investment and Diversification

*All the people like us are We,*
*And everyone else is They.*
*And They live over the sea,*
*While We live over the way.*
*But—would you believe it?—*
*They look upon We*
*As only a sort of They.*

**Rudyard Kipling**

## Key Terms

absolute purchasing power parity
American depository receipts (ADRs)
country risk
cover
covered interest arbitrage
economic exposure
emerging market
Eurobond
foreign bond
foreign currency option
foreign exchange risk
forward rate
futures contract
hedging
inflation premium
interest rate parity
macro risk
micro risk
political risk
portfolio investment
purchasing power parity (PPP)
real investment
real rate
relative purchasing power parity
risk premium
spot rate
transaction exposure
translation exposure

## Introduction

Institutional investors are well aware of the possibilities international investments offer. U.S. equities, in fact, represent only about 51 percent of the world's equity capitalization. Over the period 1980–2000, the United States was the best-performing market only once. (In fact, in 1993 it was the *worst* of the ten largest developed countries.) In September 1999, each of sixty-six U.S. pension funds had more than $1 billion in actively managed international investment portfolios.[1] Table 7-1 shows the international equity commitment of U.S. investors around the globe.

[1]Bruce Kelly, "Active Foreign Equities Up Market-Adjusted 13%," *Pensions and Investments*, January 24, 2000, 75.

**TABLE 7-1** U.S. HOLDINGS OF FOREIGN SECURITIES ($ BILLIONS)

| *Country* | *Total* | *Debt* | *Equity* | *Equity percentage held in ADRs** |
|---|---|---|---|---|
| United Kingdom | 504 | 154 | 350 | 27 |
| Japan | 207 | 36 | 171 | 5 |
| Canada | 200 | 110 | 90 | 0 |
| Netherlands | 146 | 33 | 113 | 34 |
| France | 142 | 39 | 112 | 11 |
| Germany | 134 | 62 | 72 | 9 |
| Bermuda | 124 | 5 | 119 | 0 |
| Switzerland | 77 | 1 | 76 | 12 |
| Cayman Islands | 59 | 23 | 36 | 0 |
| Finland | 55 | 4 | 51 | 64 |
| Australia | 53 | 16 | 37 | 28 |
| Mexico | 48 | 22 | 26 | 73 |
| Everywhere else | 513 | 153 | 360 | 28 |
| **Total** | 2,262 | 649 | 1,613 | 20 |

*American Depository Receipts

Source: Department of the Treasury, *Report on U.S. Holdings of Foreign Securities as of December 31, 2001*, published May 2003.

William M. Mercer, a global investment consulting firm, reports, "In most asset allocation optimizations, the target allocation for international equity is in the range of 15–20% of total Plan. In practice, we observe allocations in the range of 10%–20%."[2]

While U.S. pension fund managers lag behind their overseas counterparts in the percentage of assets devoted to foreign stocks, both international equities and foreign bonds have become established asset classes. What role do the international markets play for portfolio management? Should U.S. managers invest more of their assets abroad? This chapter discusses key advantages and dangers of overseas investment. We will see that international investments carry additional sources of risk but that managers can reduce total portfolio risk via global investment.

This chapter also crosses the border into the field of international business a few times. A well-informed portfolio manager should understand the basics of international economics, international accounting, and political risk.

## Why International Diversification Makes Theoretical Sense

International diversification makes sense if it reduces portfolio risk without adversely affecting expected return.

### *Remembering Evans and Archer*

The mathematics of portfolio theory work to the investor's benefit even if he selects securities at random. Ideally, however, the portfolio manager does not select securities at random but selects them because of their investment promise and their fit with the rest of the portfolio. By choosing securities whose returns are poorly correlated, a manager can reduce total portfolio risk beyond the level achievable by luck.

[2]William M. Mercer, "International Equity Investing Discussion Guide," September 10, 2001.

FIGURE 7-1

Systematic and Unsystematic Components of a Portfolio's Total Risk

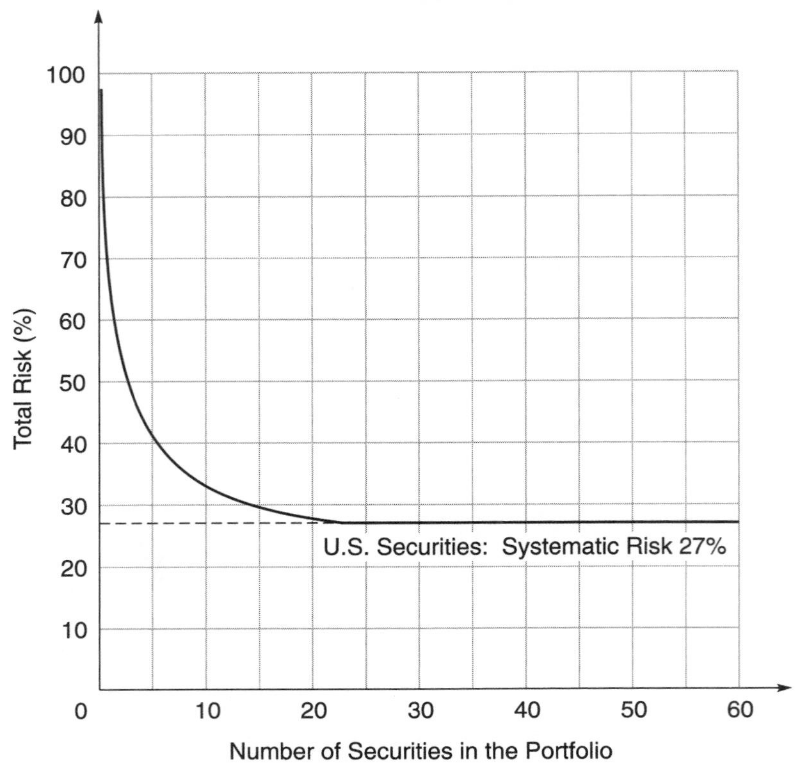


Recall that the total risk of an equity security contains both systematic and unsystematic components. The classic research of Evans and Archer (see Chapter 6) shows that holding fifteen or twenty equity securities substantially reduces the unsystematic risk of a portfolio. Figure 7-1 shows that portfolio total risk declines as the number of securities in the portfolio increases.

## *Remembering Capital Market Theory*

**Utility, Risk, and Return.** Having fifteen or twenty securities eliminates most of the unsystematic risk of a portfolio but not all of it. There will still be diversification benefits associated with the addition of other securities. For a given level of return (net of transaction costs), any reduction in risk, no matter how small, is a worthy goal. Given the opportunity to reduce risk further, a rational investor will do so if the expected return can be held constant.

**Variance of a Linear Combination.** *Capital market theory* tells us that as long as two assets are less than perfectly correlated, there will usually be diversification benefits. Chapter 5 showed the equation for the variance of a linear combination of two securities:

$$\sigma_p^2 = a_1^2\sigma_1^2 + a_2^2\sigma_2^2 + 2a_1a_2\sigma_1\sigma_2\rho_{12}$$

with all variables as previously defined. The last term of the equation, $2a_1a_2\sigma_1\sigma_2\rho_{12}$, is the critical component; it contains the correlation coefficient. Ideally, this is a very low (or negative) number. Presumably, the returns of none of the existing

FIGURE 7-2 Global Stock Market Correlations

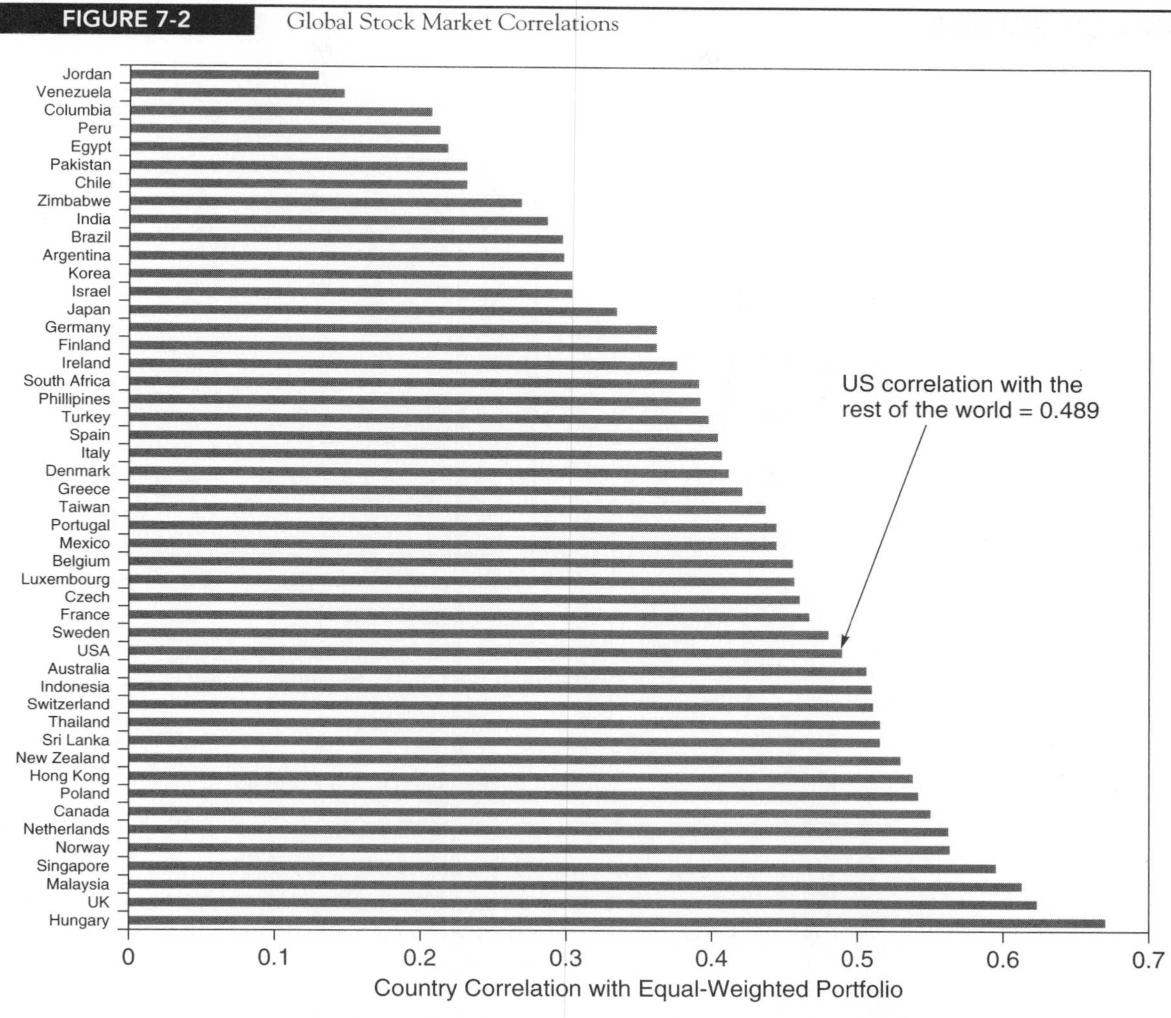


Source: Goetzmann, W. N., L. Lingfeng, and K. G. Rouwenhorst, "Long-Term Global Market Correlations." *Journal of Business* 78:1(2005), pp. 1–38. © 2005 University of Chicago.

shares on the stock exchanges march in perfect lockstep, so diversification benefits should generally accrue every time we add a new position to a portfolio.

*About 27 percent of the total risk of U.S. securities is systematic.*

**Relationship of World Exchanges.** For U.S. securities, market risk accounts for about one-fourth of a security's total risk.[3] In a country where the capital markets are less developed, this percentage tends to be higher because fewer securities make up that country's market basket, and those securities are exposed to more extreme economic and political events.

The potential advantages from international diversification stem from the fact that despite their growing global connections, the various international capital markets continue to show some degree of independent price behavior.

Figure 7-2 shows the results of a National Bureau of Economic Research study on the long-term correlations between global markets. This exhaustive study considers

[3]See, for instance, Bruno Solnik, "Why Not Diversify Internationally?" *Financial Analysts Journal*, July/August 1974, 48–54.

FIGURE 7-3

Portfolio Total Risk with International Investment

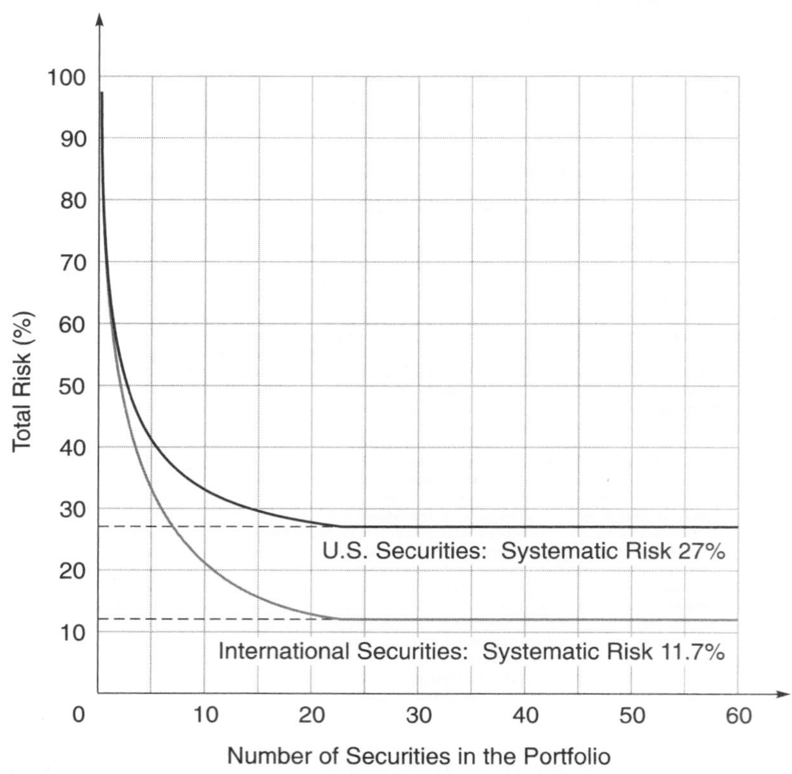


market returns over the past 150 years (ending in 2000). The figure shows correlations between each country and an equally-weighted portfolio of all the countries. Note that the correlation between the United States and everyone else is 0.489. This means that even naive diversification is likely to result in portfolio risk reduction.

When we expand the definition of *the market* to include all global securities and repeat the Evans and Archer methodology, the plot of total risk and portfolio size maintains its characteristic shape. Asymptotically, however, it approaches a lower level of systematic risk (see Figure 7-3). Table 7-2 sums up the fundamental logic of diversification, showing why rational investors should place some of their funds in foreign investments.

Various studies have replicated the original Evans and Archer research. Many people consider Bruno Solnik the guru of international diversification research. In a well-known *Financial Analysts Journal* article, he shows that expanding the security universe to include foreign companies can reduce systematic risk.[4] The "international securities" line of Figure 7-3 shows systematic risk approaching 11.7 percent of total risk. In other words, by diversifying internationally, seven-eighths of total risk can be eliminated. Solnik sums things up this way:

> "The gains from international diversification are substantial. In terms of variability of return an internationally well-diversified portfolio would be one-tenth as risky as a

[4]Ibid. 48–54.

**TABLE 7-2** FUNDAMENTAL LOGIC OF DIVERSIFICATION

1. Investors are, on average, rational people.
2. Rational people do not like unnecessary risk.
3. By holding one more security, an investor can reduce portfolio risk without giving up any expected return.
4. Rational investors, therefore, will hold as many securities as they can.
5. The most securities investors can hold is *all* of them.
6. The collection of all securities makes up the "world market portfolio."
7. Rational investors will hold some proportion of the world market portfolio.

typical security and half as risky as a well-diversified portfolio of U.S. stock (with the same number of holdings)."[5]

**Other Considerations.** We know that in practice, people do not possess a complete set of the securities making up the market portfolio. In the real world there are commissions and capital constraints; optimum portfolio size involves a trade-off of these costs against the benefits of additional diversification.

We incur trading fees when we buy securities. We cannot, however, pay a single commission to buy a portfolio of securities we pick; we pay a commission on each component of the portfolio. The number of securities in the United States runs well into five figures, and incurring this many commission costs would be imprudent. Globally, over a million equity securities may be available.

Also, most of us face capital constraints. This means that the funds we have available to invest are limited. We cannot purchase fractional shares of stock without some special arrangement such as a dividend reinvestment plan. In general, the smallest quantity we can buy is one share of each stock. Even ignoring commissions, the number of existing securities makes this prohibitively expensive and probably infeasible.

## Foreign Exchange Risk

When you, a U.S. investor, buy a foreign security, you are really making *two* relevant purchases. The actual purchase of the security is one of them, but before this purchase, you must exchange U.S. dollars for the necessary foreign currency. In essence, you are buying the foreign currency, and its price can change daily. The changing relationships among currencies of interest to you constitute **foreign exchange risk.** Modest changes in exchange rates can result in significant dollar differences. On a holding of 1 million units of foreign exchange, for instance, a price change of 1 cent per unit amounts to $10,000.

### *Business Example*

Suppose a U.S. importer has agreed to purchase forty New Zealand leather vests at a price of NZ$110 each for a total of NZ$4400. The vests will take approximately two months to produce, and the importer has agreed to pay for them before they are shipped.

[5]Ibid. 51.

*The Wall Street Journal* might indicate that today's spot exchange rate for New Zealand dollars is \$0.5855/NZ\$. The **spot rate** is the current exchange rate for two currencies. To the U.S. importer, this means that each vest costs NZ\$110 × \$0.5855/NZ\$, or \$64.41; the total cost for the forty vests is \$2,576.40. The importer has arranged to sell these vests to a local specialty shop for \$100 each; the shop owner is confident she can sell them for \$150. The importer's foreign exchange risk is obvious. If the U.S. dollar weakens between now and the time the vests are shipped, the cost of goods sold will go up. If the dollar strengthens, the importer's profit will increase.

To show the effect of fairly modest exchange rate changes, consider two different scenarios. In one case, if the dollar strengthens and the New Zealand dollar falls to \$0.5500, the cost of the vests becomes \$2,420. In the other case, if the dollar falls to \$0.6200/NZ\$, the cost of the vests translates into NZ\$4400 × \$0.62/NZ\$, or \$2,728. This is \$151.60 more than the original price.

The important thing to note here is that the vest manufacturer's published prices do not change with international exchange rates. A vest still costs NZ\$110. What does change is the U.S. price of the New Zealand dollar. This is the principal point in foreign exchange risk. Before a U.S. citizen can buy a foreign good, he must first buy the appropriate foreign currency. If a U.S. citizen sells goods abroad and receives payment in the local currency, he cannot spend the proceeds at home until converting them into his "currency of account," the U.S. dollar.

Also, note that the cost of the vests can increase or decrease as the result of *price volatility*, which constitutes risk. The fact that the volatility might work in the U.S. citizen's favor does not reduce the risk.

### An Investment Example

Through a broker, you might place a market order to buy 1,000 shares of Kangaroo Lager trading on the Sydney Stock Exchange. Assume you acquire the shares at AUD1.45. The brokerage statement will show the value of this purchase in U.S. dollars. The exchange rate might be \$0.7735/AUD at the time you buy the stock. This means the shares cost 1,000 × AUD1.45 × \$0.7735/AUD = \$1,121.58.

If the shares appreciate to AUD1.95, you have a holding period return of 34.5 percent. Over this same period, however, the value of the Australian dollar might fall to \$0.7000. If you were to sell the shares under this circumstance, you would receive 1,000 × AUD1.95 × \$0.7000/AUD, or \$1,365.00. From your perspective, the holding period return was not 34.5 percent but (1,365 – 1,121.58)/ 1,121.58, or 21.7 percent. This is still a nice return, but you were obviously hurt by the foreign exchange risk. One way to think of this is that an unhedged international investment had another cash flow—the eventual conversion to your home currency—embedded in it.

Consider another example with real data. During the first four months of 1993, a U.S. investor who bought a Japanese government bond earned a return of approximately 16.64 percent. To a Japanese investor holding the same bond, however, the return was only 2.72 percent. The U.S. investor benefited substantially from the appreciation of the yen relative to the dollar. This is an example of foreign exchange fluctuations dramatically improving investment performance.[6]

### From Whence Cometh the Risk?

It has been said that when the United States sneezes, the world catches a cold. Although this is a little parochial, the point is that events in one industrial country

[6]Reported in Constance Mitchell, "Beware of Currency Risk When Buying Foreign Bonds," *The Wall Street Journal*, April 27, 1993, p. C1.

affect the rest of the world. When a large player, such as the U.S. government, changes its economic policy, suffers a recession, or experiences high unemployment, this frequently has significant economic consequences elsewhere in the world. Interest rates are often a good barometer of these events. They are particularly relevant to an understanding of foreign exchange risk.

**Role of Interest Rates.** Students of finance learn that the stated interest rate (*nominal rate*) can be expressed as the sum of three components: the *real rate*, an *inflation premium*, and a *risk premium*.

***Real Rate of Interest.*** The **real rate** of interest is an economic abstraction that we cannot directly observe. Theoretically, it reflects the rate of return investors demand for giving up the current use of funds. In a world of no risk and no inflation, the real rate indicates people's willingness to postpone spending their money.

***Inflation Premium.*** The **inflation premium** reflects the way the general price level is changing. Inflation is normally positive, so the inflation premium measures how rapidly the money standard is losing its purchasing power. If the inflation rate is 5 percent per year, an average $100 purchase today will cost $105 in one year.

***Risk Premium.*** The **risk premium** is the component of interest rates that is toughest to measure; security analysts earn their pay by their efforts to decipher it. Risk-averse investors will not take unnecessary risks, and they expect to be compensated over the long run for any risks they do take. This is the reason that the average return on common stocks (which are risky) is higher than the average return on U.S. Treasury bills (assumed to have no risk). Investors will not purchase risky securities offering the same return as a riskless security. The price of a risky security must reflect a risk premium to entice someone to buy it. The magnitude of the risk premium is a function of how much risk the security carries. The more risk, the higher the risk premium, and therefore the lower the price. (Anything can become an attractive investment if its price falls low enough.)

*The spot rate is the current price of a foreign currency.*

**Forward Rates.** Before continuing to discuss interest rates, we look at the difference between *spot* and *forward* exchange rates. If the New Zealand importer cashes a U.S. dollar traveler's check while abroad, the exchange occurs at the spot rate.[7] This is the current exchange rate for two currencies; is the rate posted on signs at international airports and in banking centers. The spot rate changes daily, as we have seen, and can increase or decrease.

*The forward rate is a contractual rate between a commercial bank and a client for the future delivery of foreign exchange.*

The **forward rate** is a contractual rate between a commercial bank and a client for the *future* delivery of a specified quantity of foreign currency. Forward rates are normally quoted on the basis of one, two, three, six, and twelve months, but other terms can be arranged. Widely traded currencies have a forward market as long as five years.

Academic research shows that the forward foreign exchange rate is the best estimate of the future spot rate for foreign exchange.[8] The foreign exchange section of *The Wall Street Journal* can provide information on the direction the market

[7]That is, "on the spot."

[8]See, for instance, Bradford Cornell, "Spot Rates, Forward Rates, and Exchange Market Efficiency," *Journal of Financial Economics*, August 1977, 55–65.

**TABLE 7-3** FORWARD CONTRACT PREMIUM OR DISCOUNT

$$\text{Forward premium or discount} = \frac{\text{Forward rate} - \text{Spot rate}}{\text{Spot rate}} \times \frac{12}{n} \times 100$$

where $n$ = the contract length in months
(a negative value means a forward discount)

believes that relative currency values will travel in the months ahead. If forward rates indicate that the dollar is expected to strengthen, it makes sense for the importer to delay paying New Zealand dollars as long as possible. If the dollar is expected to weaken, the importer should lock in a rate now before the cost goes up.

The New Zealand dollar has no active forward market, so we consider an historical example using another currency, the Swiss franc (CHF). (With the European Union's general conversion to the euro at the beginning of 2002, the foreign exchange hedger's task becomes simpler. Hedging one currency, the euro, is obviously easier than hedging a dozen. Not all countries have adopted the euro, though, and the principles of hedging are the same regardless of the currency.) On November 19, 2004, *The Wall Street Journal* reported the spot exchange rate as $0.8542/CHF, and a six-month forward rate as $0.8610/CHF. Suppose a portfolio contained CHF120,000 par value in 8.33 percent Swiss corporate bonds that matured six months later. To avoid the foreign exchange risk, the portfolio manager could lock in the maturity value of these bonds by entering into a forward contract to deliver CHF125,000.[9] (He wants to *deliver* Swiss francs because he will *receive* them when the bonds mature.) This could be done at a local commercial bank.

Note that under the forward contract, the future dollar price of the Swiss franc is more than the prevailing spot rate. This means that the marketplace expected the value of the U.S. dollar to decline relative to the Swiss franc in the next six months. The difference between the two rates can be quoted as an annual forward contract premium or discount using the formula in Table 7-3.

We find a forward premium of 1.59 percent:

$$\frac{\$0.8610 - 0.8542}{\$0.8542} \times \frac{12}{6} \times 100 = 1.59\%$$

Having determined this, let us now see why we get the result.

*Forward rates reflect differences in national interest rates.*

**Interest Rate Parity.** The **interest rate parity** theorem states that differences in national interest rates will be reflected in the currency forward market. If there are no transaction cost differentials, two securities of similar risk and maturity will show a difference in their interest rates equal to the forward premium or discount, but with the opposite sign.

Continuing with our example, if six-month U.S. Treasury bills yield 2.00 percent, the interest rate parity theorem requires that Swiss T-bills yield 1.59 percent less, or 0.41 percent. (This assumes that the world considers the two securities equally risky. If this is not the case, a risk premium will be reflected in the riskier security's interest rate.)

[9]At maturity, the bonds will pay the principal (CHF120,000) plus six months interest (CHF4,998).

A Treasury bill rate for any country is a nominal rate. That is, it is the aggregation of the real rate, an inflation premium, and a risk premium. If some economic event causes interest rates in the United States or in Switzerland to change, the relative value of the two currencies will change; foreign currencies are risky.

**Covered Interest Arbitrage.** Suppose the conditions of interest rate parity are violated. We observe the spot and forward rates for the Swiss franc as previously stated: The spot rate is \$0.8542/CHF and the six-month forward rate is \$0.8610/CHF. On this date the U.S. six-month T-bill rate is 2.00 percent. Given the 1.59 percent premium we found, the equilibrium Swiss interest rate is 0.41 percent. Suppose instead the actual Swiss rate is 1.00 percent. An arbitrageur could take advantage of the situation by **covered interest arbitrage,** following the steps shown in Table 7-4.

Traders across the globe would spot this riskless opportunity and act upon it. Table 7-5 summarizes the likely price impact on the financial markets.

The actions in Table 7-5 would have the net effect of making the franc more valuable relative to the dollar and tightening the spread between U.S. and Swiss interest rates. An eventual equilibrium situation might be the values in Table 7-6.

At this point, the covered interest arbitrage steps are no longer profitable. Repeating the process from Table 7-4, the arbitrageur would earn nothing for her efforts, as Table 7-7 shows.

**TABLE 7-4** COVERED INTEREST ARBITRAGE

1. Borrow \$1 million for six months in the United States at 2.00 percent. \$1,010,000 will be due at maturity.
2. Convert \$1 million to francs at the spot rate:
   \$1 million/\$0.8542 per CHF = CHF1,170,686
3. Invest CHF1,170,686 in a Swiss bank for six months at 1.00 percent.
   Anticipated future receipt = CHF1,170,686 × 1.005 = CHF1,176,539.
4. Sell CHF1,176,539 forward six months at the forward rate of \$0.8610/CHF.
5. In six months, receive CHF1,176,539 from the German bank.
6. Deliver CHF1,176,539 against the forward contract, receiving CHF1,176,539 × \$0.8610/CHF = \$1,013,000.
7. Pay off U.S. bank loan with \$1,010,000, making an arbitrage profit of \$1,013,000 – \$1,010,000 = \$3,000.

**TABLE 7-5** ACTIONS TO ELIMINATE THE ARBITRAGE

| *Action* | *Impact* |
|---|---|
| Borrow dollars | Possibly increase U.S. interest rates due to added demand for money |
| Use dollars to buy francs | Upward pressure on the franc, downward pressure on the dollar |
| Sell francs forward | Downward pressure on the franc |
| Invest francs in Switzerland | Upward pressure on Swiss bonds, resulting in downward pressure on Swiss interest rates |

**TABLE 7-6** EVENTUAL EQUILIBRIUM

| | *Before* | *After* |
|---|---|---|
| Spot rate | $0.8542 | $0.8600 |
| 6 month forward rate | $0.8610 | $0.8650 |
| U.S. interest rate | 2.00% | 2.10% |
| Swiss interest rate | 1.00% | 0.94% |

**TABLE 7-7** FRUITLESS ARBITRAGE TRANSACTIONS

1. Borrow $1 million for six months in the United States at 2.10%. $1,010,500 will be due at maturity.
2. Convert $1 million to Swiss francs at the spot rate.
   $1 million/$0.8600 per CHF = CHF1,162,791.
3. Invest CHF1,162,791 in a Swiss bank for six months at 0.94%.
   Anticipated receipt = CHF1,162,791 × 1.0047 = CHF1,168,256.
4. Sell CHF1,168,256 forward six months at the forward rate of $0.8650.
5. In six months, receive CHF1,168,256 from the Swiss bank.
6. Deliver CHF1,168,256 against the forward contract, receiving
   CHF1,168,256 × $0.8650/CHF = $1,010,541.
7. Pay off U.S. bank loan with $1,010,500, making essentially no profit on the series of transactions. (The $41 discrepancy is mostly due to rounding.)

**Purchasing Power Parity.** In general, **purchasing power parity (PPP)** refers to the situation in which the exchange rate equals the ratio of domestic and foreign price levels. The *purchasing power parity theorem* is an extension of interest rate parity. It states that for two currencies that are initially in equilibrium, a relative change in the prevailing inflation rate in one of the countries will be reflected as an equal but opposite change in the value of its currency.

There are two versions of purchasing power parity. **Absolute purchasing power parity** follows from the economic principle of the "law of one price." This means that equivalent assets should sell for the same price, that is, a consumer should be able to buy just as much with two 10-dollar bills as with a 20. If absolute PPP holds, a basket of goods in one country should cost the same in another country after conversion to a common currency. In practice, this relationship is not particularly accurate because of transportation cost differentials, trade barriers, and cultural differences.

*Relative PPP is much more accurate than absolute PPP, especially over time.*

A more accurate version is **relative purchasing power parity.** This states that differences in countries' inflation rates determine exchange rates, as shown in the following equation.

$$\Delta S = \frac{1 + I_F}{1 + I_D} - 1$$

where $\Delta S$ = change in the spot exchange rate;
$I_F$ = foreign country inflation rate; and
$I_D$ = domestic country inflation rate.

This equation is absolute PPP expressed in "growth rate" terms. If, for instance, we expect German inflation to be 2 percent higher than U.S. inflation, the U.S. dollar will have better purchasing power relative to the mark. We would expect the dollar to appreciate 2 percent relative to the mark. In other words, the higher inflation in Germany will result in the U.S. dollar buying more German marks.

*Inflation causes the value of the home currency to fall.*

Consider two countries, A and B, whose currencies are in equilibrium, with 1 unit of Currency A equal to 2 units of Currency B. Countries A and B are contiguous, and people currently cross the border without interference to purchase goods from their foreign neighbors. If inflation in Country A suddenly rises by 2 percent more than that in Country B, Country A's currency will depreciate by 2 percent relative to Country B's currency. This means that the new equilibrium exchange rate will become 1.02A = 2B, or A = 1.9608B.

The reason for this change is the behavior of the international trading partners. People naturally want to buy a particular good for the least cost. In Country A, the higher level of domestic inflation causes the prices of goods to increase, making them less desirable to people in both Country A and Country B. Fewer people are now going to buy goods in Country A; it is cheaper to get them in B. The result is that Country A will export fewer goods, but Country B will sell more. This can cause Country A to develop a trade deficit with Country B. Less international trade means people in Country B will have less demand for Country A's currency because they are not buying as much in Country A. This reduced demand will cause the price of the currency to fall to a new equilibrium level at which residents of Country B are again motivated to cross the border to buy goods in Country A.

Table 7-8 provides a slightly tongue-in-cheek example of this phenomenon. By neglecting transactions costs such as airline tickets, it is apparent that customers can appease their Big Mac attacks at the lowest cost if they buy the burgers in China, Malaysia, or the Philippines, where they cost less than $1.35. Other relevant economic issues such as trade barriers on beef and sales taxes complicate this simple example substantially. The important point is the fact that differentials in international inflation rates can be a source of foreign exchange risk.

## *Dealing with the Risk*

Having seen some of the primary sources of foreign exchange risk, we now need to look at its operational meaning to the international investor.

**The Concept of Exposure.** Exposure is a measure of the extent to which a person faces foreign exchange risk. Unfortunately, there is not always a quick and convenient way to measure exposure. Accountants have fussed over this problem for years and have rewritten the rules several times, but it still remains a thorny issue. In general, there are two types of exposure: accounting and economic. The portfolio manager is primarily concerned with the latter type but should know something about the former, too.

***Accounting Exposure.*** Accounting exposure is of the greatest concern to multinational corporations that have subsidiaries in a number of foreign countries. It is also important to people who hold foreign securities and must prepare dollar-based financial reports on their portfolios' composition and performance.

A parent company must prepare consolidated financial statements "reflecting fairly" its current state of affairs. The financial statements, however, must be prepared in a single currency, that being the U.S. dollar for a U.S. firm. Turning foreign

See "Food for Thought," *Economist*, 5/29/2004 p. 71

**TABLE 7-8** THE HAMBURGER STANDARD

| | *Big Mac price in dollars** | *Implied PPP** of the dollar* | *Under (–)/ over (+) valuation against the dollar, %* |
|---|---|---|---|
| United States† | 2.90 | — | — |
| Argentina | 1.48 | 1.50 | –49 |
| Australia | 2.27 | 1.12 | –22 |
| Brazil | 1.70 | 1.86 | –41 |
| Britain | 3.37 | 1.54‡ | +16 |
| Canada | 2.33 | 1.10 | –20 |
| Chile | 2.18 | 483 | –25 |
| China | 1.26 | 3.59 | –57 |
| Czech Rep. | 2.13 | 19.5 | –27 |
| Denmark | 4.46 | 9.57 | +54 |
| Egypt | 1.62 | 3.45 | –44 |
| Euro area | 3.28§ | 1.06§§ | +13 |
| Hong Kong | 1.54 | 4.14 | –47 |
| Hungary | 2.52 | 183 | –13 |
| Indonesia | 1.77 | 5,552 | –39 |
| Japan | 2.33 | 90.3 | –20 |
| Malaysia | 1.33 | 1.74 | –54 |
| Mexico | 2.08 | 8.28 | –28 |
| New Zealand | 2.65 | 1.50 | –8 |
| Peru | 2.57 | 3.10 | –11 |
| Philippines | 1.23 | 23.8 | –57 |
| Poland | 1.63 | 2.17 | –44 |
| Russia | 1.45 | 14.5 | –50 |
| Singapore | 1.92 | 1.14 | –34 |
| South Africa | 1.86 | 4.28 | –36 |
| South Korea | 2.72 | 1,103 | –6 |
| Sweden | 3.94 | 10.3 | +36 |
| Switzerland | 4.90 | 2.17 | +69 |
| Taiwan | 2.24 | 25.9 | –23 |
| Thailand | 1.45 | 20.3 | –50 |
| Turkey | 2.58 | 1,362,069 | –11 |
| Venezuela | 1.48 | 1,517 | –49 |

*At current exchange rates ** Purchasing-power parity

†Average of New York, Chicago, San Francisco and Atlanta

‡Dollars per pound §Weighted average of member countries

§§Dollars per euro

Source:  http://www. economist.com

currencies into dollar equivalents involves two other accounting concepts: *transaction exposure* and *translation exposure*.

***Transaction Exposure.*** The Financial Accounting Standards Board provides a good explanation of the concept of **transaction exposure** in its *Statement No. 8*, "Accounting for the Translation of Foreign Currency Transactions and Foreign Currency Financial Statements": "A transaction involving purchase or sale of goods or services with the price stated in foreign currency is incomplete until the amount in dollars necessary to liquidate the related payable or receivable is determined."[10] This means that a promise to pay 4,400 New Zealand dollars for 40 vests constitutes transaction exposure until U.S. dollars are exchanged for enough New Zealand dollars to pay the bill.

***Translation Exposure.*** **Translation exposure** stems from the holding of foreign assets and liabilities that are denominated in currencies other than the U.S. dollar. The values of foreign real estate holdings and foreign mortgages, for instance, must be translated into U.S. dollars before they are incorporated into a U.S. balance sheet. A precise set of rules governs this translation, but fortunately these rules are for accountants to worry about and are not a routine portfolio management activity.

***Economic Exposure.*** The type of exposure measuring the risk that the value of a security will decline due to an unexpected change in relative foreign exchange rates is **economic exposure.** This is the type of exposure of greatest concern to security investors.

*The portfolio manager is most concerned with foreign exchange economic exposure.*

In determining the value of a financial asset, the security analyst seeks to measure the present value of all cash flows that will accrue to the security holder until the security is sold. The analyst should include expected changes in exchange rates in the forecasted cash flows. The present value comes from discounting these future cash flows using a well-conceived risk-adjusted discount factor. Determination of the discount rate is partly a subjective matter, as is the business of forecasting future exchange rates.

For the security investor, the importance of economic exposure is clear. An adverse foreign exchange movement since the security was purchased attenuates a prior gain, or may even turn it into a loss.

**Dealing with the Exposure.** Having identified foreign exchange exposure, the portfolio manager must decide what to do about it. In general, there are three choices: to ignore, to reduce or eliminate, or to hedge the exposure.

***Ignore the Exposure.*** An investor might be aware of the foreign exchange risk associated with a non-U.S. investment but consider that to be a fact of life with global investing. The choice to ignore the exposure is very often selected by default. This is also an appropriate strategy if the foreign exchange movements are expected to be modest or if the dollar amount of the exposure is small relative to the cost or inconvenience of doing something about it.

Ignoring the exposure would also be an appropriate action if the U.S. dollar were expected to depreciate relative to the country of the foreign security. This is so because the depreciation of the dollar would result in a gain to the U.S. holder of a security denominated in a foreign currency.

Some people use a diversification argument with currencies in the same fashion as they do with stocks. They say that, on average, the risks will balance out, so there is no reason to incur the expense of currency hedging. This may seem plausible, but it is not a good practice. In particular, negative currency returns come in bunches.[11]

---

[10]Financial Accounting Standard Board, *Statement of Financial Accounting Standards No.* 8, October 1975, paragraph 113. *Statement No.* 8 has been superseded by *Statement No.* 52, but the concept of exposure remains the same.

[11]See Stephen A. Gorman, *The International Equity Commitment*. Charlottesville, Va.: Research Foundation of the Institute of Chartered Financial Analysts, 1998.

The evidence does not support the notion that a diversified portfolio of currencies provides good risk reduction.

***Reduce or Eliminate the Exposure.*** An investor may decide to get rid of the foreign security or at least to reduce its holding. Certainly this is a way to deal with the problem, but a rather extreme one. Still, if the dollar is expected to appreciate dramatically, this approach should be considered.

***Hedge the Exposure.*** **Hedging** involves taking one position in the market that offsets another position. Buying fire insurance on your house, for instance, is a hedge. (To **cover** foreign exchange risk means to hedge the risk.) An investor can hedge foreign exchange exposure in various ways. The three most common methods are via the forward market, the futures market, or the currency options market. (You must be familiar with basic principles of futures and options to understand the last two alternatives. See Chapters 15 and 19.)

**Hedging with Forward Contracts.** As we noted earlier, a forward contract is a private, nonnegotiable transaction between a client and a commercial bank. We know that the CHF120,000 par value Swiss bonds in the earlier example will mature on a particular date, and if we choose, we can arrange with our bank to exchange those Swiss francs for dollars at an exchange rate to be determined now. No money changes hands until the Swiss francs are delivered, but we eliminate the foreign exchange risk. The rate the bank agrees to pay us reflects relative interest rates and associated risks, as we saw earlier.[12]

*A futures contract is a promise to buy or sell a specified quantity of a particular good at a set price by a predetermined delivery date.*

**Hedging with Futures Contracts.** A **futures contract** is a promise to buy or sell a specified quantity of a particular good at a predetermined price by a specified delivery date. Returning to the earlier example, we consider an example using Swiss franc futures. There were 125,000 Swiss francs in one futures contract.

Suppose that in December the price of a contract calling for delivery of Swiss francs the following March is \$0.6530/CHF. This means that the buyer of the contract is promising to pay \$0.6530/CHF × CHF125,000, or \$81,625, for CHF125,000 by the end of March. Similarly, the seller of the contract promises to deliver CHF125,000 at that time. Regardless of what happens to the dollar/Swiss franc relationship between now and March, the trade will take place at a price of \$0.6530 per Swiss franc.

*To learn all about the euro, the currency of the "new" Europe, go to* http://europa.eu.int/euro/entry.html

An earlier example described a portfolio that contained CHF120,000 par value in 8.33 percent Swiss corporate bonds. These bonds come due next March, at which time the issuing Swiss firm will mail the bondholders their final checks. In this case, the check will be for CHF125,000: This is the CHF120,000 principal amount plus the final interest check of CHF5,000. These funds will most likely have to be converted into dollars before they can be reinvested unless the proceeds will be used to buy new Swiss securities.

If the spot rate for the Swiss franc is \$0.6051, CHF125,000 is currently worth \$75,638. Between now and next March, this value can go up or down as the dollar depreciates or strengthens. The bondholders do not know for certain the dollar value of the Swiss franc check they will receive next March.

---

[12]A principal economic distinction between futures contracts and forward contracts is that futures contracts provide for daily marking-to-the-market, whereas forward contracts do not (see the next section).

An investor who is uncomfortable with this uncertainty and wants to hedge the foreign exchange exposure can do so using the Swiss franc futures contract. Because the portfolio will be receiving Swiss francs, the manager wants to promise to deliver them to a buyer, and so goes short, or sells, in the futures market. By doing so she is promising to sell these Swiss francs for $0.6530 apiece, for a total value of $81,625.

In March there will be a gain or loss in the futures market that will offset the gain or loss experienced when the manager converts the deutsche marks to dollars. Suppose the spot exchange rate in March is $0.6600. At that time the check from the bond issuer is worth CHF125,000 × $0.66/CHF, or $82,500. This is $875 more than the value locked in with the hedge. The manager closed out the futures position at the spot price of $0.6600 by buying one contract. It was bought at $0.6600 and sold at $0.6530, so the manager lost $0.0070 on each of the CHF125,000 for a total loss of $875. The loss in the futures market exactly cancels out the gain in the spot market.

If the dollar depreciated by March and the spot exchange rate became $0.6000, the CHF check the bondholder received would be worth $75,000. The price locked in was $81,625; the check was worth $6,625 less than that. In the futures market, the manager sold at $0.6530 and bought at $0.6000; this is a gain of $6,625, which exactly cancels out the reduced value of the check received.

**Hedging with Foreign Currency Options.** Two types of **foreign currency options** exist. *Call options* give their owner the right to buy a set quantity of foreign exchange, and *put options* give their owner the right to sell a set quantity. The price at which you have the right to buy or to sell is the *striking price* or the *exercise price*. The terms are synonymous. These securities are essentially the same as options on shares of stock or on indexes.

*Foreign currency options are the same as ordinary stock options except for the fact that they give their owner the right to buy or sell a foreign currency.*

Two characteristics of currency options are especially noteworthy. First, a call option with an exercise price quoted in dollars that gives the purchaser the right to buy British pounds is the same as a put option on dollars with an exercise price quoted in pounds. Second, for those familiar with option pricing, the notion of put-call parity for foreign currency options is merely a restatement of the interest rate parity theorem.

If we will receive CHF125,000 in March (three months from now), we could buy put options on the Swiss francs. (We buy puts because we want to sell the Swiss francs we receive.) Swiss franc options are standardized at CHF62,500 per contract, so we would need to buy two of them to hedge CHF125,000.

As with options on other assets, foreign currency options have various *striking prices* and *expiration dates*. If the spot rate were $0.6400/CHF, we might choose an at-the-money put with a striking price of $0.64, and we probably would choose an expiration as close as possible to the bonds' maturity date.

*The disadvantage of hedging with foreign currency options is that the hedger must pay a premium to establish the hedge.*

The disadvantage of hedging this way is that we have to pay for the options we buy, and they can be expensive, depending on the behavior of the foreign exchange markets. It is quite possible that a three-month option with the terms described in the previous example could have a premium of three-fourths of a penny per Swiss franc. This means that two Swiss franc foreign currency calls would cost (CHF62,500/contract) × (2 contracts) × ($0.0075/CHF), or $937.50. The fund manager needs to decide whether the foreign exchange risk is severe enough to justify this expense.

Futures are not always preferable to options for hedging purposes. Options provide a greater degree of precision in altering a portfolio's risk and return characteristics.[13] Also, for some applications it is possible to hedge by writing calls rather than buying puts. Writing calls involves a cash inflow rather than a cost. Ideally, the portfolio manager will select the best hedging technique for a particular purpose rather than having a cookbook approach to the problem.

### *The Eurobond Market*

**Eurobonds** are debt agreements that are denominated in a currency other than that of the country in which they are held. For instance, a bond denominated in Japanese yen being sold in Great Britain is a Eurobond. This is in contrast to a **foreign bond,** which is denominated in the local currency but is issued by a foreigner. Perhaps three-fourths of Eurobonds are denominated in U.S. dollars.

Research has generally found that U.S. firms issuing dollar-denominated Eurobonds pay a slightly lower interest rate than they would pay in the United States. Most Eurobonds are *bearer bonds* and thus provide some opportunity for their owner to avoid the payment of taxes on the interest received. It is unlikely, though, that this is the principal reason for the yield differential.

Because of the lower cost of borrowing in the Eurobond market, purchasing Eurobonds is popular with corporate treasurers. From a portfolio manager's perspective, however, their lower yield keeps Eurobonds from being popular investments.

### *Combining the Currency and Market Decisions*

It is important to note in this discussion that the hedging decision is not merely whether or not to hedge foreign currency back into the home currency. It is also possible, and often desirable, to *cross-hedge* a foreign investment into a different currency, with this latter currency ultimately converted back into the investor's home currency. A U.S. investor might, for instance, invest in Japan, use the forward market to sell yen for British pounds, and expect to convert the pounds back to U.S. dollars.

Suppose a Wall Street investment house forecasts the information shown in Table 7-9. The table shows analysts' expectations for the various equity markets, anticipated changes in exchange rates, and the prevailing short-term interest rates in the Euromarket.[14]

**TABLE 7-9** FORECASTS OF MARKET AND CURRENCY RETURNS

| *Country* | *Forecasted Equity Returns (Local Currency)* | *Forecasted Change in the Exchange Rate* | *Local Forecasted Dollar Return* | *Euro-deposit Return* |
|---|---|---|---|---|
| United States | 9.5% | 0% | 9.5% | 5.0% |
| Japan | 8.0% | 2.5% | 10.5% | 2.0% |
| Switzerland | 10.0% | −1.5% | 8.5% | 4.5% |
| United Kingdom | 9.5% | 1.0% | 10.5% | 4.5% |
| France | 6.5% | 3.0% | 9.5% | 5.0% |

[13]Options and futures can theoretically accomplish the same purpose if used in the right amount. They come in discrete amounts, though; investors cannot buy one-half of a futures contract. For small portfolios or for modest hedging needs, options enable investors to make small adjustments; a single futures contract, in contrast, might be too powerful for the need at hand.

[14]The motivation for this example comes from a publication entitled *Global Asset Management and Performance Attribution* (Charlottesville, Va.: Research Foundation of the Institute of Chartered Financial Analysts) by Denis S. Karnosky and Brian D. Singer. This is part of a study material in the CFA program. It is an excellent resource for those who want to explore the international investment/currency hedging decision further.

Looking at the row for Japan, the analysts believe the broad Japanese stock market will advance by 8 percent with the yen appreciating by 2.5 percent against the U.S. dollar. Adding these two values means that the U.S. investor who buys Japanese stocks is looking, on average, at a 10.5 percent return after returning to U.S. currency. (This is the column labeled Local Forecasted Dollar Return.) The table also shows that a one-year "money market" investment in Japanese yen currently yields 2 percent and that the Swiss franc, forecast to be the weakest currency, is expected to lose 1.5 percent relative to the dollar.

At first glance it seems that Switzerland is the best stock market; it has a forecast return of 10 percent, the highest of the five countries. This is wrong; the important variable is the *risk premium*, not the absolute return. The best market is Japan, with its 6 percent risk premium over the Eurodeposit rate. (This comes from subtracting 2 percent from 8 percent.) Risk premia for the other countries are 4.5 percent for the United States, 5.5 percent for Switzerland, 5 percent for the United Kingdom, and 1.5 percent for France. France is the least attractive stock market.

The currency decision comes from a comparison of the forward premium or discount on the currencies and the expected change in the exchange rate. The currency return comes from the forward market premium or discount and the actual change in the exchange rate. Investing in Country A and hedging into the currency of Country B provides a net currency benefit equal to the interest rate in B minus the interest rate in A (this is the forward market premium/discount) plus the forecast exchange rate change. This logic is tricky and needs to be studied with some numbers.

Suppose an investor chooses to invest in Swiss stocks and then cross-hedges into yen. If all the expectations in Table 7-9 are exactly right, the investor would earn 10 percent in the Swiss stock market, would lose 2.5 percent from the forward market transaction (2 percent – 4.5 percent), and would benefit from the 2.5 percent appreciation of the yen against the dollar. This gives a net return of 10 percent.

If, instead, the investment was in Japan and hedged into pounds, the return would be 8 percent minus 2 percent plus 4.5 percent plus 1 percent for a net return of 11.5 percent. Another way to look at this is as the equity risk premium plus the Eurodeposit return in the country of the hedge plus (or minus) the appreciation (or depreciation) of the currency used to hedge.

Table 7-10 shows all possible combinations of market and currency decisions from the previous example. The optimum set of market and currency decisions in this example comes from investing in Japan and cross-hedging into euros. This leaves the investor with 14 percent, more than any other alternative.

Forecasting both exchange rates and interest rates is quite difficult and often fruitless. For this reason, many portfolio managers routinely deal with the currency decision by hedging 50 percent of their exposure. This is intuitively appealing. Failure to hedge (0 percent hedging) amounts to a bet that the underlying currency will

**TABLE 7-10** JOINT EQUITY MARKET/CURRENCY DECISIONS

| | *Currency* | | | | |
|---|---|---|---|---|---|
| ***Market*** | ***$*** | ***Yen*** | ***CHF*** | ***Pounds*** | ***Euros*** |
| United States | 9.5% | 9.0% | 7.5% | 10.0% | 12.5% |
| Japan | 11.0% | 10.5% | 9.0% | 11.5% | 14.0% |
| Switzerland | 10.5% | 10.0% | 8.5% | 11.0% | 13.5% |
| United Kingdom | 10.0% | 9.5% | 8.0% | 10.5% | 13.0% |
| France | 6.5% | 6.0% | 4.5% | 7.0% | 9.5% |

appreciate. Complete hedging (100 percent) amounts to a bet it will depreciate. If the manager does not know what exchange rates will do, 50 percent hedging is the safe position.

A number of firms routinely use a 50 percent currency hedge in their portfolios. A portfolio manager at one large U.S. company states he does not believe in currency forecasting and "anything but a 50-percent hedged policy implicitly states a view of currency direction." When a portfolio manager's investment performance is judged against an "average benchmark," 50 percent hedging may be the safest and most prudent option.

### *Key Issues in Foreign Exchange Risk Management*

For many portfolio managers, foreign exchange risk is a very modest, or even immaterial, component of total risk. Still, if foreign exchange risk is ignored, it should be ignored on purpose rather than through ignorance. The steps in good foreign exchange risk management are these:

1. Define and measure foreign exchange exposure.
2. Organize a system that monitors this exposure and exchange rate changes.
3. Assign responsibility for hedging.
4. Formulate a strategy for hedging.

## Investments in Emerging Markets

Emerging market investments[15] offer substantial potential rewards to the careful investor, both in added return and in portfolio risk reduction. Special risks accompany these benefits, however. Besides ordinary market risk, the foreign exchange risk may be unhedgeable, political and economic risk may be high, investment information may be lacking or unreliable, and trading costs may be more expensive. Wise decisions regarding investments in emerging markets can be made only if the investor understands both the potential rewards and the many dimensions to their risk.

Many market analysts project that the greatest future growth and the greatest returns to stock ownership lie in the world's emerging markets. While the term **emerging market** does not have a universally agreed-upon definition, one clear characteristic is the lack of a mature stock market or exchange mechanism. This means that special risks accompany the opportunities for profit.[16]

For many citizens of a developing nation, stock markets and the concepts of risk and return are new and incredibly exciting ideas. There are dangers, though, when novice investors (domestic or foreign) anticipate investment results that are not reasonable. After the dismantling of the Soviet Union, the short-term view many Russians took regarding their financial future was a major concern to the consultants helping the country establish a market economy. People expected immediate, positive results from their investments while the Russian leaders wanted to build markets that encouraged long-term investment rather than speculation. The public needed to learn that they could not invest their money today and pick up their

---

[15]Some of the material on emerging markets comes from Chapter 13 of the author's book *Practical Investment Management* (Mason, OH: Thomson/South-Western) and from his article "Atractivos y riesgos de la inversión de portafolio en mercados emergentes," *Gaceta de Economía*, Instituto Technológico Autónomo de México, Ano 3, Numero 6. Primavera 1998.

[16]The *Emerging Markets Factbook* is a good source of data.

"winnings" two weeks later. This required a substantial educational effort that has still not been entirely successful.

At an Association for Investment Management and Research symposium on emerging markets, one speaker stated this:

> Significant differences exist among emerging markets, but as a group, they share one primary similarity—change, change driven by the rising aspirations of their populations. This characteristic is producing the growth and tremendous opportunity investors in emerging markets are pursuing. Risks accompany the opportunities, but investors can foster success by seeking out economies that have or will soon have political stability, open markets, policies that encourage growth, strong institutional structures, clearly defined investment rules, equitable taxation, market liquidity, and satisfactory intermediaries.[17]

There is good evidence that knowledgeable investors and portfolio managers can improve investment results by including emerging market investments in their portfolios. These investments require more research than a domestic investment and are subject to special risks.

## Background

A lot of money is invested in emerging markets. According to the Emerging Markets Traders Association, $2.043 trillion in debt traded during the first half of 2004, with Brazilian debt the most frequently traded ($325 billion).[18] Respondents to this industry survey indicated that 85% of their Eurobond trading was in sovereign (government) issues, with the remainder corporate bonds. Eight percent of the sovereign issues were Brady bonds.

Trading activity was even higher in 1997, nearly $6 trillion. International investment in general and emerging market investment in particular dropped off sharply when the global markets experienced what some called the "perfect storm" of financial disasters a short while later. In quick succession we had the Asian financial crisis of 1997–98, the Russian banking crisis of 1998, and the bursting of the Internet bubble. It didn't help build confidence when Argentina defaulted on its debt in 2001.

There is action in emerging market equity, too. In 2003 the Morgan Stanley Capital International index rose an attention-grabbing 52% when compared with the 26% of the U.S. market and the 13% of Great Britain. Value investors were intrigued, too. In December 2003 the MSCI EMF index traded at a price-to-book ratio only one-half that of the S&P 500, a valuation that many investors find appealing.

Some international agencies refer to any low-income country as an emerging market.[19] Most people would include Argentina, Brazil, India, Mexico, China, Eastern Europe, and Russia on the list. Countries in most of Africa, Central America, and some of the former Soviet republics are called "pre-emerging markets" or "emerging emerging markets."

## Adding Value

Good evidence suggests that prices in developing markets often contain significant inefficiencies. This means money is to be made by being a good stock

---

[17] Jeremy Paulson-Ellis, "Introducing Emerging Markets," *Managing Emerging Market Portfolios* (Charlottesville, Va.: Association for Investment Management and Research, 1993).

[18] Emerging Markets Traders Association, "EMTA Survey: Emerging Markets Debt Trading at US$1 Trillion in Second Quarter 2004."

[19] Gray, Stuart. "Emerging Market Investments: Still the Star?" April 2004, *http://www.investorsoffshore.com/html/specials/april04_em_archive.html*

picker and by identifying those industries most likely to benefit from economic development.

At present, shares in emerging market companies tend to sell for lower price/earnings multiples than do firms in developed markets. Consider two firms with identical capital structures and earnings, one on the New York Stock Exchange and the other on the Brazilian Stock Exchange. Chances are that the Brazilian firm will sell at a "better" price from the perspective of a fundamental analyst. A recent study[20] compared 46 pairs of companies with each pair containing a U.S. firm and a "matched" developing country firm. For instance, the researchers paired a U.S. telephone company with the Brazilian phone company Telebràs, and a U.S. electronics firm with the Korean firm Samsung. After collecting consensus earnings estimates on the firms as well as market price data, the researchers found that the five-year expected earnings growth rate was 16.2 percent per year for the developing country group compared to 13.8 percent for the developed market firms. However, the average price/earnings multiple for the emerging market firms was 18.7 compared to 21.1 for the companies in developed markets. This means that not only do the emerging market firms have greater expected growth, but also they are cheaper. Results such as these attract global investors.

### Reducing Risk

While correlations among the developed markets are increasing, the same is not true of the emerging markets. They show little correlation with developed markets or with each other. Low correlations are attractive as a means of reducing the variability of portfolio return. This feature is a primary reason for the attractiveness of emerging markets as a portfolio component.

The stock market of an emerging country can be particularly volatile, especially by U.S. standards. Figure 7-4 shows the wide swing in the value of a country index over two adjacent periods of time. Mexico devalued its currency in mid-December 1994, and world markets reacted sharply to this news. Over the next three months, the emerging markets represented in the figure declined an average of 15.9 percent. On March 9, 1995, Mexico announced its recovery plan, which was well received, and over the next two months, these same emerging markets rose an average 16.6 percent.

Morgan Stanley began preparing an emerging market index in December 1987. Since that time the data indicate that the diversification benefits from emerging markets remain substantial. Table 7-11 shows some historic performance data on emerging markets and other MSCI indexes.

### Following the Crowd

Some professional money managers treat emerging markets as a separate asset class. They invest in these markets after careful analysis because of profit potential and portfolio risk reduction. Other managers have a more poorly developed rationale. Asset allocation is an important topic today, and some managers probably feel that they must invest in emerging markets because it is contemporary practice. They want to avoid answering supervisors' awkward questions about why they ignore these markets.

[20]Burton Malkiel and J.P. Mei, *Global Bargin Hunting: The Investor's Guide to Profits in Emerging Markets*, Simon and Schuster, 1998. Reported in "Go Where the Growth Is," *Bloomberg Personal*, November 1997, 60–69.

**FIGURE 7-4**

Growing Market Volatility December 16, 1994– May 12, 1995

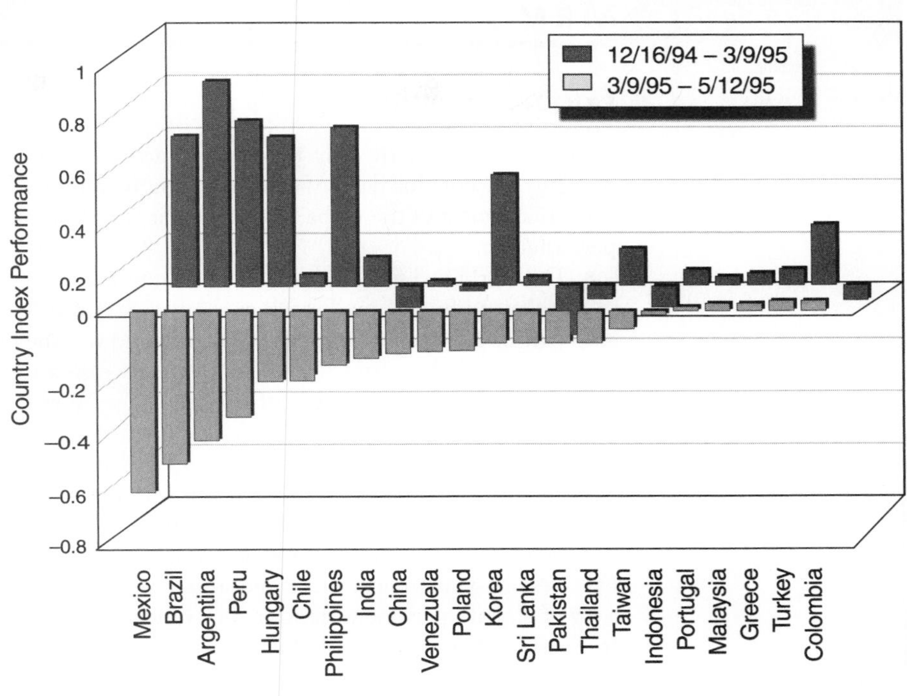


Source: *Barron's*, May 22, 1995, MW8.

**TABLE 7-11** MORGAN STANLEY CAPITAL INTERNATIONAL INDEXES DECEMBER 1987 – DECEMBER 2003

| *Index* | *Brief Description* | *Annualized Return* | *Standard Deviation* | *Correlation with U.S.* |
|---|---|---|---|---|
| MSCI Emerging Markets | 26 emerging markets | 12.61% | 23.58% | 0.58 |
| MSCI World Free | 23 developed countries | 8.20% | 14.62% | 0.83 |
| MSCI USA | 2500 U.S. stocks | 12.59% | 14.67% | 1.00 |
| MSCI Japan | Approximately 322 Japanese stocks | −1.25% | 23.53% | 0.35 |
| MSCI Europe | 16 developed countries | 10.41% | 16.17% | 0.69 |

Source: Morgan Stanley Capital International

## *Special Risks*

Investments in emerging markets face at least the same types of risks as any domestic investment; they also face several specific sources of uncertainty with the associated potential for loss. A potential investor needs to know about these.

**Incomplete Accounting Information.** There are significant problems with financial information sources in emerging markets. In general, the acquisition of reliable investment information requires an on-site security analyst. The managing

## PORTFOLIO MEMO

### Global Gloom

Diversifying internationally makes sense for a variety of reasons; it is a smart thing to do, but this does not make investors immune from market downturns. Sometimes most of the globe has a bad year with few markets turning in positive performance.

The world had such a year in 2001. Figure 7-5 shows the performance of most of the major international stock exchanges. Only seven stock markets of these thirty-three countries rose for the year. Finland was the big loser, down 37.83 ercent in U.S. dollar terms, while South Korea rose a spectacular 45.29 percent. Excluding the United States, the Dow Jones World Stock Index was down 21.02 percent for the year.

The September 11 terrorist attack in 2001 had a negative effect on virtually every securities exchange. Although this was not the sole reason for the market's global malaise, it clearly contributed to the year's substandard performance. Experienced portfolio managers know that international investment contributes to but does not guarantee positive investment results. For convenient access to a variety of global investment performance indexes, see the Morgan Stanley Capital International Website at *http://www.msci.com.*

**FIGURE 7-5** Stock Market Performance, 2001

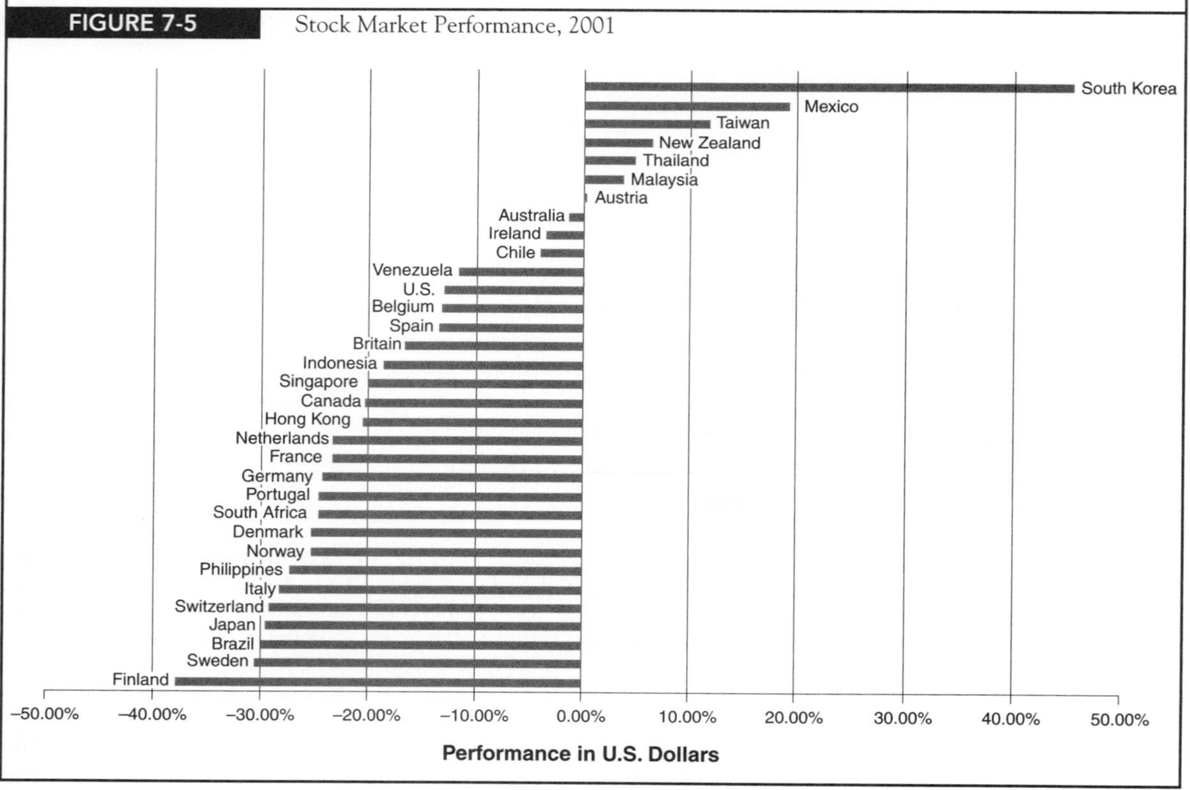

director and senior portfolio manager for the Montgomery Emerging Markets Fund states:

> We believe that conducting research locally and implementing portfolio decision making centrally is the key to consistency across emerging markets portfolios. . . . Members of our emerging markets team spend up to half their time abroad, and their research begins the moment they land.[21]

U.S. investors are accustomed to audited financial statements being available soon after the end of a company's fiscal year, with prompt interim statements available quarterly. In some countries, financial statements are more than six months old when they become available.

Accounting standards differ substantially across countries. The analyst unfamiliar with this fact can draw inaccurate conclusions from accounting documents. This is a problem even among the developed economies. U.S. firms, for instance, depreciate capital investments; German firms may expense them in the year of acquisition. Goodwill is a tax-deductible expense in Germany; it is *not* in the United States. German firms may increase the cost of goods sold by the level of their inventory reserves, thereby reducing reported profits. As a striking example of the net effect of these differences, Daimler-Benz once reported an annual loss (by U.S. accounting standards) of DM949 million. By German standards, however, the firm earned DM168 million.[22]

Good accounting information is frequently unavailable when considering an emerging market security. One emerging market portfolio manager states:

> In these markets, most analysts do not understand what a bottom-up, value-oriented investor is seeking. The analysts seem to think in terms of 90 days, not five years. Moreover, most of the analysts are inexperienced; the average analyst's age seems to be 23 years, and many do not know what a stock is until they are hired by the local brokerage firm.[23]

Many emerging market brokerage firms focus almost exclusively on the income statement but do not provide balance sheets to the potential investor. Intelligent investment decisions are difficult when the primary source of information is a single year's profit and loss statement, which may bear little relation to the firm's future prospects or the nature of its risk.

As markets develop, the number of financial institutions increases. Competition expands, expertise grows, and attention to detail becomes more important. The growth of financial intermediaries results in an increased level of information available to the potential investor. The financial market's own version of natural selection rewards success, and those engaged in good research reap the benefits. This takes time, however, and the fact remains that throughout the world's emerging markets, the lack of high-quality investment information is a serious impediment to capital formation.

**Foreign Currency Risk.** Securities traded on a foreign exchange are also denominated in something other than the investor's home currency. From the perspective

[21]Josephine Jimenez, "Silk Road Markets," *Bloomberg Personal*, November 1997, 35–38.

[22]Jeremy Paulson-Ellis, "Introducing Emerging Markets," *Managing Emerging Market Portfolios*, (Charlottesville, Va.: Association for Investment Management and Research, 1993.)

[23]Shaw B. Wagener, "Bottom-Up Investing in Emerging Markets," *Managing Emerging Market Portfolios* (Charlottesville, Va.: Association for Investment Management and Research, 1994.)

of an investor in another country, this produces *foreign exchange risk,* which is the chance of loss due to adverse changes in exchange rates.

Matsushita paid $6.1 billion for the U.S. firm MCA in late 1990. By summer 1995, the Japanese yen had appreciated by more than a third against the U.S. dollar. This means Matsushita experienced a currency translation loss of more than $2 billion. On the other hand, the Rolling Stones picked up an additional $2 million from their concert tour in Japan because their contract called for payment in yen. Foreign exchange risk is a very real component of the uncertainty in international investing.

In emerging markets, reducing foreign exchange risk by traditional hedging activities is complicated (or impossible) because reliable hedging vehicles in developing countries' currencies generally do not exist. Not every world currency has a futures market, currency option, or forward market. This means that a financial investment in an emerging market security carries the added risk of adverse foreign exchange fluctuations with little to be done to reduce it. Over the first eleven months of 1997, for instance, the currencies of Turkey, Indonesia, Thailand, Malaysia, the Philippines, South Korea, and Colombia all depreciated by over 20 percent relative to the U.S. dollar. Good hedging tools were lacking in these countries.

Mexico provides an excellent example of the interwoven nature of potential return and foreign exchange risk. In 1994 and 1995 the Mexican stock market declined substantially when the value of the peso plummeted. In May 1995, the exchange rate stabilized at around 5.9 pesos per U.S. dollar. Concurrently, Mexican three-month *cetes* offered an annualized yield of more than 50 percent. Short-term corporate borrowing rates topped 60 percent on an annualized basis. Such high rates are obviously attractive to potential investors, especially those accustomed to more modest rates of return. Anyone versed in the basics of investment finance, however, should realize that risk and expected return go hand in hand. These yields were so high because of the significant risk that the Mexican peso would again be devalued or that the country would default on its loans. Any investor who ignores such a risk does so at considerable peril.

Even in a well-developed market, the foreign currency hedging decision is a complicated one. An article in *Institutional Investor* states:

> An emerging consensus in the money management industry holds that currency risk may be safely ignored when it's a small part of a portfolio. Once international exposure passes a threshold of 10 to 20 percent, however, the currency risk becomes substantial and ought to be hedged in some form (depending on the fund's asset mix, time horizon, and tolerance for volatility).[24]

Another potential concern was seen in Asia in the fall of 1997. Shares of China Telecom H.K. went on sale in October 1997 as part of Asia's largest initial public offering (IPO).[25] Literally hundreds of thousands of Chinese citizens stood in line to buy these shares. Unfortunately, this IPO suffered unlucky timing and coincided with the Southeastern Asia currency crisis. The Hong Kong Hang Seng index fell 10 percent in a single trading session, and China Telecom declined 9 percent on its first trading day. In this instance, currency fluctuations bred market risk and led to massive changes in market value. IPOs are interesting to emerging market fund managers, but in this instance such an investor would have been hurt twice, once by the currency depreciation and once by market risk.

---

[24]Miriam Bensman, "Hedging on the Hedges," *Institutional Investor*, June 1996, 73–79.

[25]Biddy Chan, "High Hopes and Shaky Markets," *Bloomberg Personal*, November 1997, 52.

**Fraud and Scandals.** Emerging markets carry a substantial risk of fraud. This can range from accounting misstatements to counterfeit securities or "bucket" shops.[26] Many first-time Russian investors learned about securities fraud when they bought shares in the mammoth Russian firm MMM. Billed as a mutual fund taking advantage of the developing market in Russia, MMM turned out to be a pyramid scheme dependent on additional capital from new investors to make payments to existing investors. Once new investors stopped opening accounts, the firm had insufficient cash flow to pay existing investors. The collapse of this firm seriously hampered Russia's movement toward a market society by generating distrust among the investing public.

A major factor contributing to the problem of scandals is the fact that in an emerging economy, market participants do not fully understand the relationship among management, the work force, and the shareholders.[27] (This relationship is unclear even to many people in developed countries, but in a developed country, a regulatory and legal system is in place to protect the interests of the parties involved.) Redress available to victims of a scandal in a developing country may be inadequate, and this adds to the potential risk of its emerging market investment.

**Weak Legal System.** Investors dislike uncertainty. One source of uncertainty is the potential for untimely or inadequate legal redress in the event of a dispute regarding ownership interests or other financial matters. Investors will add an additional risk premium to the discount rate they apply to expected cash flows if a significant likelihood exists that the courts will not be helpful in the event of litigation. In some developing countries there is little confidence in the legal system, especially if the plaintiff is a foreigner. Such a situation does little to promote confidence in the financial markets or in the growth of business. As one analyst states:

> Although international investors prefer that countries not treat them differently from the way they treat domestic investors, a country's regulatory regime should also be judged by another factor: certainty. The reliability of government policymakers and regulators is frequently more important than the contents of the rules themselves.[28]

### *Asymmetric Correlations*

The potential for portfolio risk reduction is a widely stated motivation for international investment. In general, the returns in developing markets show relatively low correlation with returns from developed markets. Unfortunately, evidence suggests that the correlation is not the same during bull versus bear markets. Correlation *increases* when markets decline. This is opposite to what a portfolio manager would like, because it is during a down market that the benefits from diversification could be most useful. A recent study in the *Journal of Finance* by Longin and Solnik[29] found that although correlation increases during a declining market, it also decreases during large bull-market movements. This means that the extent of portfolio managers diversification depends on whether they are experiencing an up or a down market.

---

[26]A "bucket" shop is a firm that sometimes claims to have made a trade on a customer's behalf but in fact did *not* make the trade because of a feeling that the trade is ill advised. The firm is essentially betting against the customer.

[27]Paulson-Ellis, 1993.

[28]Rudolf van der Bigl, "Regulatory Environments in Emerging Markets," *Managing Emerging Market Portfolios* (Charlottesville, Va.: Association for Investment Management and Research, 1993).

[29]Francois Longin and Bruno Solnik, "Extreme Correlation of International Equity Markets," *Journal of Finance*, April 2001, 649–676.

## PORTFOLIO MEMO

### Country Effects

We know that low correlation exists across emerging markets, with obvious diversification implications. What is the situation with developed markets? Is one foreign market enough from the perspective of a U.S. portfolio manager? Barnes, Bercel, and Rothmann published research on this question.* They studied 3,709 securities from 23 developed countries over the period March 1992 through March 2000. They assigned securities to ten sectors according to the Morgan Stanley Capital Investments/Standard & Poor's global industry classification.

The authors draw several conclusions from their research:

- Country effects remain significant.
- Large stocks are influenced more by sectors.
- The opportunity to add value will continue to exist within countries due to the many obstacles that still work against convergence in the Euro zone.

This means that even though the marketplace is increasingly global, portfolio managers are still wise to consider country effects in their diversification strategy.

*Mark Barnes, Anthony Bercel, and Steven Rothmann, "Global Equities: Do Countries Still Matter," *Journal of Investing*, Fall 2001, 43–49.

Another consideration is the extent of the homogeneity *within* and *across* emerging markets. There is evidence[30] of a strong common influence in a given emerging market, much like an "industry effect" in a developed market. Within a single emerging market country, the securities tend to move as a group; this reduces the potential for useful diversification benefits *within* a country.

Emerging markets show low correlation across markets, however. The Longin and Solnik study found the average correlation across emerging markets to be only 0.07 compared to 0.49 for developed markets. In short, investment returns show *homogeneity within emerging markets* but *heterogeneity across them*. The implication is that investors should pick investments from different regions of the world.

### *Market Microstructure Considerations*

A collection of other types of risk relates to the nature of the financial markets and to the mechanics of trading in those markets. These *microstructure risks* may be less apparent to the individual investor, but they are significant to the institutional investor.

**Liquidity Risk.** Residents of a developing country typically have little money of their own to invest. This poses a special problem to the emerging market investor. If few local investors have funds committed to their home securities, most of the investors are foreign. This not only increases political risk but also sets the stage for a market collapse if everyone decides to pull out at once. A country may come into favor because of a prominent article in the financial press, but it could go on everyone's

[30]Arjun B. Divecha, Jame Drach, and Dan Stefek, "Emerging Markets: A Quantitative Perspective," *Journal of Portfolio Management*, Fall 1992, 41–50.

sell list just as quickly. Most of these markets have little depth, meaning that the bid/ask spread tends to be wide with only a minimal number of standing orders to buy and to sell. A large order to sell can be disruptive anytime, especially if numerous institutional orders are placed at about the same time.

An article in *Forbes* reported the comments of Ronald Chapman, head of international equities at the Dreyfus Corporation. Mr. Chapman indicated that he would like to invest in Thailand, but he cannot, basically because he has too much money. "It's pointless," Mr. Chapman says. "The largest stock in Thailand trades $900,000 per day. How is a large fund supposed to take a meaningful position in a market like that?"[31] *Forbes* states that "This lack of liquidity is a big problem because their buy or sell orders will quickly push prices away from them. For individual investors, it is an opportunity—a rare case of the small guy having an advantage."

**Trading Costs.** Foreign market investing is likely to involve trading costs at least 1 percent higher than those of domestic investing. Trading costs are usually higher in an emerging market than on a developed stock exchange. Total transaction costs can consume 5 percent of the value of a trade. Barings Securities estimates a bid/ask spread of 134 basis points (bp) in Brazil, 172 bp in Turkey, and 128 in Indonesia, with an average of 95.4 bp for its emerging market index.[32] Higher trading costs mean the investment must appreciate that much more to show a net return comparable to an otherwise identical domestic investment.

**Market Pressure.** Market pressure is an important but often forgotten component of trading costs. An institutional investor is not likely to invest just a few thousand dollars in a few hundred shares of a stock.[33] This pressure presents a potential problem with a small capitalization stock. An order to buy or sell a reasonable number of shares by U.S. standards might cause a substantial supply/demand imbalance so that the price moves adversely from the institution's perspective. For this reason, international investments in general and emerging market investments in particular should be viewed as long-term investments rather than a source of trading profits.

Judith Corchard, chief investment officer for Wright Investors' Service, says, "It's a whole different game outside the United States. On smaller exchanges a fund can constitute so much of the volume that it's almost impossible to tell if your own buying isn't driving the prices."[34]

A global trading cost study by Elkins/McSherry Company finds that worldwide the average market impact of an institutional trade is 27.5 basis points.[35] These costs range from a low of about 2.9 bp in Greece to a staggering 159 bp in South Korea. This compares to an estimated 21 bp for New York Stock Exchange trades.

**Marketability Risk.** Another concern in emerging market investment is the possibility that the investor will be unable to close out her position at a reasonable price. Chase Manhattan Bank lost nearly $200 million (pretax) during the 1997 Asian currency crisis because of a lack of marketability in some of its positions.[36]

---

[31] John H. Christy and Ronald Boone, Jr., "Opportunities in Asia," *Forbes*, May 4, 1998, 184.

[32] Information provided by Rosemary Macedo, vice-president of Quantitative Research at Bailard, Biehl, and Kaiser.

[33] Investing domestically, many institutions view a 10,000-share block as the minimum position.

[34] Jack Willoughby, "Trade Secrets," *Institutional Investor*, November 1997, 69–75.

[35] Ibid.

[36] Michael R. Sesit and Matt Murray, "Chase Manhattan Pounded in Emerging Markets," *The Wall Street Journal*, November 3, 1997, A4.

The bank held Brazilian and Russian bonds it wanted to sell but was unable to complete the trades. Partly because of this, the market value of the bank's stock fell nearly 4 percent in a single day during the crisis.

**Country Risk. Country risk** refers to a country's ability and willingness to meet its foreign exchange obligations. This is especially important in an emerging market. To meet its obligations, the country must be able to generate foreign exchange through profitable trading activity with other countries. When a country cannot sell its products, it has difficulty raising the foreign currencies necessary to honor its obligations. The two components of country risk are *political* risk and *economic* risk.

## Political Risk

*Political risk does not apply to U.S. firms doing business in the United States. It applies to U.S. firms doing business abroad.*

***Political risk*** is a measure of a country's willingness to honor its foreign obligations.[37] This term is not normally applied to U.S. firms doing business in the United States. This type of risk is largely a function of the stability of the government and its leadership. One leader may understand the importance of honoring contracts in global business, but his replacement may be motivated by other interests. Even if the country has the ability to pay its debts, a change in leadership may result in the government suddenly becoming unwilling to do so in a timely fashion. Other factors contributing to political risk are the attitudes of labor unions, the country's ideological background, and its past history with foreign investors.

*Political risk* is a selective category of risk; it applies only to firms with facilities in a foreign land. For example, a U.S. firm doing business in Japan faces political risk. Table 7-12 presents other characteristics of political risk.

*With real (or direct) foreign investment, the investor maintains control of the investment.*

*Portfolio (or financial) investment refers to the purchase of a foreign security.*

Foreign investments can be grouped into two large classes: *real investment* and *portfolio investment,* also called *direct* and *financial investments,* respectively. The key characteristic of **real investment** is that the investor retains control over the investment. For example, a manufacturing plant in Botswana built by a U.S. firm is direct investment. **Portfolio investment** refers to foreign investment via the securities markets. The purchase of shares of the Dutch firm Unilever by a U.S. investor constitutes portfolio investment. U.S. portfolio managers are primarily concerned with portfolio investment, the primary focus of this discussion.

**TABLE 7-12** AN EXPLANATION OF POLITICAL RISK

Political risk describes the situation where:

1. Periodic changes occur in the business environment.
2. These changes are difficult to anticipate.
3. The changes in the business environment stem from changes in the political environment.
4. The changes in the business environment have the potential to affect the profits of the firm significantly.

[37] In a broader international business context, political risk refers to the potential for a foreign government to require changes in the way a firm conducts its business. This might include a requirement that foreign nationals be promoted to supervisory positions, that a certain proportion of profits be reinvested locally, or that the business eventually must be sold to a local buyer.

Investments suffer from political risk to the extent that the potential exists for foreign government interference in the operation of the company issuing the investment security. This interference can be extreme, such as in the following situations:

- Government takeover of a company.
- Political unrest leading to work stoppages.
- Physical damage to facilities.
- Forced renegotiation of contracts.

The interference can also be more modest:

- Establishment of a requirement that a minimum percentage of supervisory positions be held by local nationals.
- Changes in operating rules.
- Restrictions on repatriation of capital.

We first consider the factors that contribute to political risk.

### Factors Contributing to Political Risk

**"Buy Local" Attitude.** Sometimes a form of moral suasion, the "buy local" attitude contributes to political risk. People are encouraged to purchase products made domestically and to avoid those produced outside the country. A U.S. conglomerate might have a foreign subsidiary in Germany, where it manufactures an item that competes with similar items produced by German firms. The buy local campaign would seek to make German consumers buy the German-produced item rather than the one produced by the U.S. subsidiary. An extensive buy local attitude can significantly affect sales and, ultimately, security value. Such an attitude prevailed in the United States in the early 1980s with regard to the purchase of foreign automobiles, particularly those from Japan.

*For an extensive coverage of country risk–related topics, see* http://www.duke.edu/~charvey/Country_risk/couindex.htm

**Public Attitude.** In less developed countries, people sometimes see little opportunity to improve their standard of living. The presence of a foreign manufacturing plant in rural Peru, for example, could send discouraging signals to the local citizens if the "foreigners" have air-conditioned cars, live in better homes than the Peruvians, have more money to spend, and exhibit these characteristics in an ostentatious fashion.

An important study by Harald Knudsen found that the single most significant factor contributing to political risk is the size of the gap between the public's aspirations and its expectations.[38] In other words, when people see what could be but realize that it probably never will be, the foreign firm tends to become a scapegoat. This may result in unfavorable action against it.

**Government Attitude.** When governments are unstable, the presence of foreign investors can become a volatile political issue. Foreign investors can be blamed for problems for which they have no responsibility. A foreign government could suspend a firm's ability to send funds back to its home country, instead forcing the firm to invest these funds locally.

---

[38]Harald Knudsen, "Explaining the National Propensity to Expropriate: An Ecological Approach," *Journal of International Business Studies*, Spring 1974, 51–69.

### *Subclasses of Political Risk*

**Macro Risk.** When a government takes an action that affects all foreign firms in a particular industry, **macro risk** exists. An example is Fidel Castro's confiscation of all foreign enterprises in Cuba in 1959 and 1960.

**Micro Risk.** The term **micro risk** refers to politically motivated changes in the business environment directed to selected fields of business activity or to foreign enterprises with specific characteristics. Expropriation of all public utilities is an example of micro risk. Macro risk is more dramatic, but micro risk is more prevalent.

### *Dealing with Political Risk*

Protection against political risk with foreign direct investment can be achieved by two principal means, which are not mutually exclusive. One approach is to seek a foreign investment guarantee from the Overseas Private Investment Corporation. This organization provides coverage against loss due to expropriation, nonconvertibility of profits, and war or civil disorder. The coverage is available only where the U.S. government has arranged a guarantee agreement with the host government of a less developed country.

The other approach is to avoid engaging in behavior that tends to stir up trouble with the host people or their government. Constructing flamboyant office buildings in poor areas or giving the impression of natural resource exploitation contrary to the host country's best interests are examples of behavior that should be avoided.

Political risk arising through portfolio investment is much less a problem than that arising through direct investment. The portfolio manager should consider the stability of the foreign capital markets before buying an international security, as well as estimate the likelihood that repatriation of profits or dividend checks could become impeded.

This aspect of risk assessment is sometimes called *country risk.* It exists even in the most developed countries. *Foreign Exchange Markets in the United States* makes the following statement: "At one time or another, virtually every country has interfered with international transactions in its currency. Interference might take the form of regulation of the local exchange market, restrictions on foreign investment by residents, or limits on inflows of investment funds from abroad."[39]

Two familiar examples of country risk occurred in the United States. After the Iranian hostage crisis in 1978, the U.S. government froze Iranian bank accounts and would not permit withdrawal of the substantial sums on deposit. In 1987, the U.S. government issued a ban on the importation of South African Krugerrands. Prior to the ban, this 1-ounce coin was the most popular form of individual gold ownership. Even after the government lifted the ban, the Krugerrand continued to sell at a discount to other world gold coins (such as the Canadian Maple Leaf or the Australian Koala), in spite of the fact that none of these coins has any collector's value, and all contain the same amount of gold.

**Economic Risk.** While political risk is a measure of the country's *willingness* to pay, economic risk is a measure of the country's *ability* to pay. Economic risk is more a function of the income statement than the balance sheet. A company's ability to pay is measured by indicators such as coverage ratios (like "times interest earned").

---

[39]Roger M. Kubarych, *Foreign Exchange Markets in the United States* (New York: Federal Reserve Bank of New York, 1978), 27.

When considering a nation at the macroeconomic level, comparable ratios include external debt divided by current account earnings or current account balance divided by gross domestic product. Prospects for future growth are not nearly as important as the ability to meet current debt payments.

In assessing country economic risk, it is important to consider the permanence of the country's capital base. Foreign aid is a temporary measure, not a long-term solution. When investment capital can leave the country as quickly as it came in, things can get complicated during bad times.

## Other Topics Related to International Diversification

### Multinational Corporations

If international investing makes sense, a logical question is this: Why not invest in a multinational firm? These firms can have subsidiaries all over the world, and it seems that the stock of such a company should provide a ready-made means of getting the risk-reduction benefits of international diversification.

How well this works is unclear. Studies by Rugman, Agarwal, Kohers, and Agmon and Lessard provide evidence that multinational corporations enjoy a lower cost of equity capital than one-country firms of similar risk.[40] Multinational corporations should be especially good investments, as a consequence.

Another study by two well-known researchers in international finance, Bertrand Jacquillat and Bruno Solnik, comes to a different conclusion. Their article's title is a clue to their results: "Multinationals Are Poor Tools for Diversification." The article concludes, "The multinational stock prices do not seem to be extensively affected by foreign factors and behave much like the stock price of a purely domestic firm."[41] Christophe and McEnally publish similar results in a recent article.[42]

Taking a slightly different tack, a recent article by Errunza, Hogan, and Hung[43] reports that it is possible to mimic a foreign index using only domestically available securities, implying that portfolio managers can enjoy the benefits of international diversification without investing in foreign stocks at all. Research continues in this area, and the literature will continue to expand. We clearly live and invest in a global marketplace; the question is how best to invest efficiently.

### American Depository Receipts

In the United States, investors can buy shares in Honda Motor Company if they choose to do so. Through a brokerage firm with a membership on the Tokyo Stock Exchange, investors can become the proud owners of stock certificates printed in

---

[40]Tamir Agmon, and Donald Lessard, "Investor Recognition of Corporate International Diversification," *Journal of Finance*, September 1977, 1049–1055; Alan M. Rugman, "Motives for Foreign Investment: The Market Imperfections and Risk Diversification Hypothesis," *Journal of World Trade Law*, September/October 1975, 567–573; Jamuna P. Agarwal, "Determinants of Foreign Direct Investment: A Survey," *Weltwirtschaftliches Archiv*, 4, 1980, 739–773; and Theodor Kohers, "The Effect of Multinational Operations on the Cost of Equity Capital of U.S. Corporations: An Empirical Study," *Management International Review*, 15, 2–3, 1975, 121–124.

[41]Bertrand Jacquillat and Bruno Solnik, "Multinationals Are Poor Tools for Diversification," *Journal of Portfolio Management*, Winter 1978, 12.

[42]Stephen E. Christophe and Richard W. McEnally, "U.S. Multinationals as Vehicles for International Diversification," *Journal of Investing*, Winter 2000, 67–75.

[43]Vihang Errunza, Ked Hogan, and Mao-Wei Hung, "Can the Gains from International Diversification Be Achieved without Trading Abroad?" *Journal of Finance*, December 1999, 2075–2107.

**TABLE 7-13** LARGEST AMERICAN DEPOSITORY RECEIPTS

| *Company* | *Ticker* | *Country* | *Industry* | *Market Capitalization ($millions)* |
|---|---|---|---|---|
| BP Plc | BP | U.K. | Oil/Gas Exploration | 136,430 |
| Nokia | NOK | Finland | Telecommunications | 128,530 |
| Petrobras | PBR | Brazil | Oil/Gas | 70,000 |
| América Móvil | AMX | Mexico | Telecommunications | 66,080 |
| Ericsson | ERICY | Sweden | Telecommunications | 55,430 |
| Royal Dutch/Shell | RD | Netherlands | Telecommunications | 54,690 |
| Elan | ELN | Ireland | Pharmaceuticals | 46,310 |
| Shanda Interactive | SNDA | China | Internet | 44,740 |
| Sanofi-Synthelabo | SNY | France | Pharmaceuticals | 38,470 |
| Teva Pharmaceuticals | TEVA | Israel | Pharmaceuticals | 37,640 |

Source: J. P. Morgan. Capitalization data as of February 4, 2005.

Japanese and registered in their names. Although this might be a nifty toy, it will become an inconvenience before long. What will these investors do with small dividend checks payable in Japanese yen? Will the investors' banks even know what the check says if it is printed in Japanese? Will the investors have to pay a hefty foreign exchange fee in order to cash it? Similar nuisances can arise when the investors decide to sell the shares. How will someone in the United States know what the certificate represents if it is printed in *kanji* (Japanese characters of Chinese origin)? What transfer agent is used to issue new certificates when shares trade hands?

*A comprehensive list of ADRs can be found at* http://www.wallstreeter.com/adrframe.htm

The way these problems are avoided is ingenious. Rather than buying shares of stock directly, investors buy **American depository receipts (ADRs).** These securities are actually receipts representing shares of stock that are held on the ADR holder's behalf in a bank in the country of origin. A person who buys Honda ADRs receives a certificate showing that actual Honda shares are held on her behalf at a bank in Japan. When she decides to sell the shares, she simply transfers her receipt to the purchaser, who gives her the appropriate amount of cash.

In early 1990 approximately forty foreign stocks were trading on the New York Stock Exchange via ADRs, and six were trading on the American Stock Exchange. About another 800 traded in the over-the-counter system. By 2004, about 2,200 ADRs from dozens of countries traded in the United States. Table 7-13 lists a few of the best known.[44]

From a practical standpoint, there is no difference between shares and ADRs. The ADR holder has the typical shareholder privileges: the right to vote, the right to receive dividends, and so on. Although ADRs are valued in dollars, they still have foreign exchange risk because their U.S. dollar value is determined by the exchange rate in addition to the investment value of the security.[45]

## International Mutual Funds

*For a list of international closed-end mutual funds, visit* http://www.closed-endfunds.com/scripts/cesearch_b.asp

Buying shares of multinational corporations may not be a good way to achieve international diversification, but buying shares in international mutual funds *is* a good way. Absolutely nothing prevents a portfolio manager from including a mutual fund investment in a collection of other securities.

[44]Good Websites on ADRs are *http://www.adr.com* and *http://www.bnyadr.com*.

[45]A good overview is provided in Dennis T. Officer and J. Ronald Hofmeister, "ADRs: A Substitute for the Real Thing?" *Journal of Portfolio Management*, Spring 1987, 61–65.

Mutual funds are classified according to their investment objective, such as capital appreciation, income, tax-free income, and so on. Some mutual funds have an additional feature: They invest only in securities issued outside the United States. Mutual funds serve as a useful approximation of the market portfolio for a great many individual investors. They permit diversification to an extent that would not otherwise be possible for the person with limited funds.

*Holding more than one mutual fund is a theoretically sound practice.*

It never occurs to some people that they can hold more than one mutual fund. From a theoretical standpoint, doing so is a good practice. The returns of any two funds are unlikely to be perfectly correlated, so holding them both has diversification benefits.

The same logic about additional holdings of common stock applies to mutual funds. If two are good, three are better. By strict finance theory, the theoretical "rational investor" of Table 7-2 who prefers mutual funds will hold shares in every mutual fund. To do otherwise would be irrational. As with stock portfolios, though, a trade-off exists between additional diversification benefits and the cost of obtaining those benefits. Managerial time is not free; it takes some effort to keep up with multiple investments, and the tax implications of mutual fund investing can be complicated.

A study in the *Economic Review* (a publication of the Federal Reserve Bank of Atlanta) offers an additional incentive to this method of investing internationally. The author, Paula Tkac, reports:

> the well-documented result that the average manager of a domestic fund does not outperform the U.S. market does not extend to the entire international fund market. A large percentage of managers of well-diversified international funds do outperform their passive MSCI benchmarks in a statistically significant manner. Managers of regional and country funds, however, do not show the same ability to outperform.[46]

## SUMMARY

Links among the capital markets of the world are increasing in number and improving in communications technology, yet these markets still maintain some unique characteristics. Consequently, international diversification of investments makes sense in that less-than-perfect correlation among the markets provides an opportunity for risk reduction in equity portfolios.

Although holding foreign securities reduces total risk, it introduces two new forms of risk. Foreign exchange risk arises through the uncertainty of relative exchange rates, particularly the price of a foreign currency in the home currency. This type of risk, if sufficiently large, can be hedged via the forward market, the foreign exchange futures market, or the foreign currency options market. Political risk arises from the potential for foreign governments to interfere with the operation of a company or with the free flow of investment capital or profits across international boundaries. This risk can be reduced by avoiding antagonistic international behavior, by monitoring country risk, and in some cases by obtaining government insurance.

---

[46]Paula Tkac, "The Performance of Open-End International Mutual Funds," *Economic Review*, Third Quarter 2001, 1–17.

Emerging markets likely will demonstrate substantial economic growth and excellent stock market returns in the future. Many investment managers are attracted to these markets because of the potential for high returns and for the portfolio risk reduction these investments may bring.

Emerging market investment has clear attractions, but there are important risks, too. Besides ordinary market risk, unavoidable foreign exchange risk may exist because finding a reliable way to hedge the currencies of these countries is difficult. Both political and economic risk measure the possibility that a country will be unwilling or unable to honor its foreign obligations.

Special emerging market risks include the absence of reliable accounting information, the potential for investment fraud, a weak legal system, poor liquidity and marketability on the exchanges, and higher trading costs. A strong market force affects the securities within a particular emerging market country, but heterogeneity exists in returns across emerging markets.

Many, if not most, investment managers believe that international securities comprise a separate asset class with a permanent place in the portfolio. Wise decisions regarding their use can be made only if the investor understands both the potential rewards and the unusual risk characteristics they carry.

Other methods for obtaining the benefits of international diversification are the purchase of shares in multinational corporations, the purchase of American depository receipts rather than foreign shares, and the purchase of mutual funds that invest globally.

## QUESTIONS

1. How would you determine when international diversification becomes superfluous? That is, how would you determine if the added cost of investing internationally is sufficiently rewarded?
2. The text indicates that on most world exchanges, the total risk of a typical security has a greater percentage of systematic risk than does a typical U.S. security. Elaborate on why this is the case.
3. If most people are rational, why do you think they fail to diversify properly? In particular, why do they fail to include foreign securities in their portfolios?
4. Comment on the following statement: If you have a lot of foreign holdings scattered around the world, foreign exchange risk is not much of a problem because the various translation gains and losses all average out to zero in the long run.
5. If you anticipated receiving a sum of a foreign currency in 90 days, why not hedge this transaction by using a 30-day forward contract and replacing it twice? Would this not give you greater flexibility over locking in the 90-day rate?
6. At present, 1 unit of Currency X equals 3 units of Currency Y. Interest rates are 6 percent in Country X and 8 percent in Country Y. Inflation in both countries suddenly rises by 3 percent. What effect would you expect this to have (a) on the respective interest rates and (b) on the relative exchange rates?
7. To a portfolio manager, why is economic exposure more important than either type of accounting exposure?
8. Do you think that a foreign investor would see any political risk in the United States? If so, in what respect?

9. Foreign exchange risk can be hedged; is there any way to hedge political risk?
10. Is a portfolio manager more concerned with real investment or with financial investment? Why?
11. Investor A holds three securities; Investor B holds twelve. For which investor would the addition of an international mutual fund to the portfolio make the most sense?
12. If you own a foreign security, are you more concerned with micro or macro political risk?
13. What is the advantage of American depository receipts over foreign shares?
14. You manage a $25 million portfolio for a very wealthy individual. This person brings in an article from *The Wall Street Journal* about a foreign mutual fund and expresses interest in it. How would you go about learning more about this fund for your client?
15. Comment on the following statement: I've never made any money in the currency forward market.
16. Do international securities have any place in a portfolio with the primary objective of growth of income?
17. How could you include the country risk ratings in an international stock valuation model?
18. Suppose you buy shares in a foreign company by purchasing American depository receipts rather than by buying shares on the foreign stock exchange where the security trades. Are you still concerned with foreign exchange risk? Why or why not?
19. This chapter deals with international equity diversification. Do you see any potential advantages to international diversification of a fixed-income portfolio?
20. In the *Forbes* article cited in the chapter, why could the lack of liquidity to institutional traders in emerging markets be an advantage to the individual investor?

## PROBLEMS

1. The current exchange rate is one U.S. dollar equal to 1.4456 units of Currency G. In the United States, the T-bill rate is 8.68 percent. The 60-day forward rate for Currency G is $0.7100/G. What Country G interest rate is implied in these prices?
2. Check *The Wall Street Journal* for 90-day forward prices on the Japanese yen. What is the forward premium or discount?
3. Using your answer to Problem 2 and assuming that 90-day T-bills yield 9 percent, what should a 90-day Japanese T-bill yield if both the Japanese and U.S. governments are considered equally risky?
4. Suppose a Canadian dollar costs 75 cents in U.S. money. If the market begins in equilibrium, what should the new exchange rate be if U.S. inflation is 1 percent higher than Canadian inflation?
5. Using data from a recent edition of *The Wall Street Journal*, find the U.S. and Canadian prime interest rates. Based on these values, what change does the market expect in the value of the Canadian dollar relative to the U.S. dollar during the next year?

**6.** You have ¥1,000,000 in bonds that will mature in 90 days. Using current data from *The Wall Street Journal*, show how you can hedge the foreign exchange risk by doing the following:

**a.** Using the forward market.

**b.** Using the futures market.

**7.** Show how you could hedge the exposure in Problem 6 using yen foreign currency options.

**8.** Suppose the U.S. prime interest rate is 7.75 percent, and the Japanese prime rate is 8 percent. The spot exchange rate for the Japanese yen is ¥136.15/$. If the 180-day forward rate is ¥135.90/$, is the market in equilibrium?

**9.** QUESTION 4 FROM THE 1995 CFA LEVEL III EXAM

Your discussion with Green has turned to the measurement of investment performance, particularly with respect to international portfolios.

***Table 4: Performance and Attribution Data***
***Annualized Returns for 5 Years Ended 12/31/94***

| *International Manager/Index* | *Total Return* | *Country/Security Return* | *Currency Return* |
|---|---|---|---|
| Manager A | –6.0% | 2.0% | –8.0% |
| Manager B | –2.0 | –1.0 | –1.0 |
| EAFE Index | –5.0 | 0.2 | –5.2 |

**a.** Assume that the Table 4 data for Manager A and Manager B accurately reflect investment skills and that both managers actively manage currency exposure. Briefly describe *one* strength and *one* weakness for *each* manager.

**(4 minutes)**

**b.** Recommend and justify a strategy that would enable the Fund to take advantage of the strengths of *each* of the two managers while minimizing their weaknesses.

**(6 minutes)**

Green is considering selling a portion of his Diversified Global Fund holding in order to create a portfolio that concentrates on country exposures. He now understands that an investor must look at both country/security returns and currency returns when deciding on a specific country in which to invest. You have developed the forecast returns shown in the first two columns of Table 5 below, along with the current one-year yields available to a U.S. investor in the several Eurodeposit markets.

***Table 5***

| | *Forecast Returns (Year Ending 6/30/96)* | | *Current Yields* |
|---|---|---|---|
| | *Local Market Returns* | *Exchange Rate Returns* | *One-Year Eurodeposits* |
| Germany (DM) | 6.0% | 2.0% | 4.0% |
| Japan (Yen) | 7.0 | –1.0 | 6.0 |
| U.S. ($) | 8.0 | 0.0 | 7.0 |

After examining the Table 5 data, Green suggests that an investment made in Japan, with the currency exposure hedged into Deutschmarks, would maximize his U.S. dollar return expectations. You disagree with Green's suggestion. Instead, you recommend that the investment be made in Germany with the currency exposure hedged into U.S. dollars.

**c.** Using Table 5 data, calculate the expected returns for *both* your proposal *and* Green's proposal. Show your work and briefly comment on the result.

**(8 minutes)**

Green says that the foregoing discussion was incomplete because it did not address the issue of temporary negative expectations about a given country's economic and/or market outlook. "Suppose," he says, "I am invested in Japanese stocks but want to eliminate my exposure to this market for a period of time. Can I accomplish this without the cost and inconvenience of selling out and buying back in again if my expectations change?"

**d.** Briefly describe a strategy to hedge *both* the local market risk *and* the currency risk of investing in Japanese stocks.

**(4 minutes)**

**e.** Briefly explain *two* reasons the hedge strategy you described in Part D might not be fully effective.

**(4 minutes)**

**10.** QUESTION 15 FROM THE 1996 CFA LEVEL III EXAM

The HFS Trustees have solicited input from three consultants concerning the risks and rewards of an allocation to international equities. Two of them strongly favor such action, while the third consultant commented as follows:

> The risk reduction benefits of international investing have been significantly overstated. Recent studies relating to the cross-country correlation structure of equity returns during different market phases cast serious doubt on the ability of international investing to reduce risk, especially in situations when risk reduction is needed the most.

**a. Describe** the behavior of cross-country equity return correlations to which the consultant is referring. Explain how that behavior may diminish the ability of international investing to reduce risk in the short run.

**(8 minutes)**

Assume the consultant's assertion is correct.

**b. Explain** why it might still be more efficient on a risk/reward basis to invest internationally rather than only domestically in the long run.

**(4 minutes)**

The HFS Trustees have decided to invest in non-U.S. equity markets and have hired Jacob Hind, a specialist manager, to implement this decision. He has recommended that an unhedged equities position be taken in Japan, providing the following comment and the Table 6 data to support his views:

> Appreciation of a foreign currency increases the returns to a U.S. dollar investor. Since appreciation of the Yen from 100¥/$U.S. to 98¥/$U.S. is expected, the Japanese stock position should not be hedged.

| *Table 6: Market Rates and Hind's Expectations* | | |
|---|---|---|
| | *U.S.* | *Japan* |
| Spot Rate (Yen per $U.S.) | n/a | 100 |
| Hind's 12-Month Currency Forecast (Yen per $U.S.) | n/a | 98 |
| 1-Year Eurocurrency Rate (% per Annum) | 6.00 | 0.80 |
| Hind's 1-Year Inflation Forecast (% per Annum) | 3.00 | 0.50 |

Assume that the investment horizon is one year and that there are no costs associated with currency hedging.

c. **State** and **justify** whether Hind's recommendation (not a hedge) should be followed. **Show** any calculations.

**(6 minutes)**

11. QUESTION 31 FROM THE 2000 CFA LEVEL II EXAM

Omni Advisors, an international pension fund manager, plans to sell equities denominated in Swiss Francs (CHF) and purchase an equivalent amount of equities denominated in South African Rands (ZAR).

Omni will realize net proceeds of 3 million CHF at the end of 30 days and wants to eliminate the risk that the ZAR will appreciate relative to the CHF during this 30-day period. Exhibit 31-1 shows current exchange rates between the ZAR, CHF, and the U.S. dollar (USD).

***Exhibit 31-1***
***Currency Exchange Rates***

| | *ZAR/USD* | | *CHF/USD* | |
|---|---|---|---|---|
| ***Maturity*** | ***Bid*** | ***Ask*** | ***Bid*** | ***Ask*** |
| Spot | 6.2681 | 6.2789 | 1.5282 | 1.5343 |
| 30-day | 6.2538 | 6.2641 | 1.5226 | 1.5285 |
| 90-day | 6.2104 | 6.2200 | 1.5058 | 1.5115 |

A. i. **Describe** the currency transaction that Omni should undertake to eliminate currency risk over the 30-day period.

ii. **Calculate** the following:

- The CHF/ZAR cross currency rate Omni would use in valuing the Swiss equity portfolio.
- The current value of Omni's Swiss equity portfolio in ZAR.
- The annualized forward premium or discount at which the ZAR is trading versus the CHF.

**(11 minutes)**

One year later Omni gathers the financial information in Exhibit 31-2:

***Exhibit 31-2***
***Financial Information***

| | |
|---|---|
| Base price level | 100 |
| Current U.S. price level | 105 |
| Current South African price level | 115 |
| Base Rand spot exchange rate | $0.175 |
| Current Rand spot exchange rate | $0.158 |
| Expected annual U.S. inflation | 7% |
| Expected annual South African inflation | 5% |
| Expected U.S. one-year interest rate | 10% |
| Expected South African one-year interest rate | 8% |

Omni uses the concepts of purchasing power parity (PPP) and the International Fisher Effect (IFE) to forecast spot exchange rates.

**B. Calculate** the following exchange rates:

i. The current ZAR spot rate in USD that would have been forecast by PPP.
ii. Using the IFE, the expected ZAR spot rate in USD one year from now.
iii. Using PPP, the expected ZAR spot rate in USD four years from now.

**(9 minutes)**

## INTERNET EXERCISES

Use the *Currency Rate Exchanger* at *http://www.jeico.com/currency1.html* to find the currency exchange rates between the US dollar and two other currencies of your choice. Compute the implied cross rate between these two foreign currencies and verify the result by checking the rate between the currencies using the *Currency Rate Exchanger*. Is there a possible arbitrage (profit-making) opportunity?

## FURTHER READING


Agarwal, Jamuna P. "Determinants of Foreign Direct Investment: A Survey." *Weltwirtschaftliches Archiv* 4, 1980, 739–773.

Agmon, Tamir, and Donald Lessard. "Investor Recognition of Corporate International Diversification." *Journal of Finance*, September 1977, 1049–1055.

Aharoni, Yair. *The Foreign Investment Decision Process*. Boston: Harvard Graduate School of Business Administration, Division of Research, 1966.

Akdogan, Haluk. "A Suggested Approach to Country Selection in International Portfolio Diversification." *Journal of Portfolio Management*, Fall 1996, 33–39.

Aliber, Robert Z. "The Interest Rate Parity Theorem: A Reinterpretation." *Journal of Political Economy*, December 1973, 1451–1459.

Barnes, Mark A., Anthony Bercel, and Steven H. Rothmann. "Global Equities: Do Countries Still Matter." *Journal of Investing*, Fall 2001, 43–49.

Barry, Christopher B., John W. Peavy III, and Mauricio Rodriguez. *Emerging Stock Markets: Risk, Return, and Performance*. Charlottesville, Va.: Research Foundation of the ICFA, 1997.

Cornell, Bradford. "Spot Rates, Forward Rates and Exchange Market Efficiency." *Journal of Financial Economics*, May 1977, 56–65.

Daniels, John D., Ernest W. Ogram, and Lee H. Radebaugh. *International Business: Environments and Operations*. Reading, Mass.: Addison-Wesley, 1976.

Eiteman, David K., Arthur I. Stonehill, and Michael H. Moffett. *Multinational Business Finance*, 6th ed. Reading, Mass.: Addison-Wesley, 1992.

Errunza, Vihang, Ked Hogan, and Mao-Wei Hung. "Can the Gains from International Diversification Be Achieved without Trading Abroad?" *Journal of Finance*, December 1999, 2075–2107.

Evans, John L., and Stephen Archer. "Diversification and the Reduction of Dispersion: An Empirical Analysis." *Journal of Finance*, December 1968, 561–571.

Finnerty, J.E., and K.P. Nunn, Jr. "The Determinants of Yield Spreads on U.S. and Eurobonds." *Management International Review* 2, 1985, 23–33.

Fouse, William L. "Allocating Assets Across Country Markets." *Journal of Portfolio Management*, Winter 1992, 20–27.

Gastineau, Gary L. "The Currency Hedging Decision: A Search for Synthesis in Asset Allocation." *Financial Analysts Journal*, May/June 1995, 8–17.

Gorman, Stephen A. *The International Equity Commitment*. Charlottesville, Va.: Research Foundation of the ICFA, 1998.

Grubel, Herbert G. "Internationally Diversified Portfolios: Welfare Gains and Capital Flows." *American Economic Review*, December 1968, 1299–1314.

Grubel, Herbert G., and Kenneth Fadner. "The Interdependence of International Equity Markets." *Journal of Finance*, March 1971, 89–94.

Hakkio, Craig S. "Is Purchasing Power Parity a Useful Guide to the Dollar?" *Economic Review*, Federal Reserve Bank of Kansas City, Third Quarter 1992.

Hammond, Dennis R.. "Equity Diversification Internationally." *Journal of Investing*, Summer 1996, 36–42.

Jacque, Laurent L. "Management of Foreign Exchange Risk: A Review Article." *Journal of International Business Studies*, Spring/Summer 1981, 81–99.

Jacquillat, Bertrand, and Bruno Solnik. "Multinationals Are Poor Tools for Diversification." *Journal of Portfolio Management*, Winter 1978, 8–12.

Karnosky, Denis S., and Brian D. Singer. *Global Asset Management Performance Attribution*. Charlottesville, Va.: Research Foundation of the ICFA, 1997.

Kidwell, David S., M. Wayne Marr, and G. Rodney Thompson. "Eurodollar Bonds: Alternative Finance for U.S. Companies." *Financial Management*, Winter 1985, 18–27.

Knudsen, Harald. "Explaining the National Propensity to Expropriate: An Ecological Approach." *Journal of International Business Studies*, Spring 1974, 51–69.

Kohers, Theodor. "The Effect of Multinational Operations on the Cost of Equity Capital of U.S. Corporations: An Empirical Study." *Management International Review* 15, 2–3, 1975, 121–124.

Kritzman, Mark P., and Katrina F. Sherrerd, eds. *Managing Currency Risk*. Charlottesville, Va.: Institute of Chartered Financial Analysts, 1989.

Kubarych, Roger M. *Foreign Exchange Markets in the United States*. New York: Federal Reserve Bank of New York, 1978.

Levy, Haim, and Marshall Sarnat. "International Diversification of Investment Portfolios." *American Economic Review*. September 1970, 668–692.

Levy, Haim, and Z. Lerman. "The Benefits of International Diversification in Bonds." *Financial Analysts Journal*, September/October 1988, 56–64.

Logue, Dennis, and George S. Oldfield. "What's So Special about Foreign Exchange Markets?" *Journal of Portfolio Management*, Spring 1977, 19–24.

Longin, Francois, and Bruno Solnik. "Extreme Correlation of International Equity Markets." *Journal of Finance*, April 2001, 649–676.

MacDonald, John G. "French Mutual Fund Performance: Evaluation of Internationally-Diversified Portfolios." *Journal of Finance*, December 1973, 1161–1180.

Madura, Jeff. "Influence of Foreign Markets on Multinational Stocks: Implications for Investors." *International Review of Economics and Business*, October 1989, 1009–1018.

———. *International Financial Management*, 3d ed. St. Paul: West Publishing, 1992.

Michaud, Richard O., Gary L. Bergstrom, Ronald D. Frashure, and Brian K. Wolahan. "Twenty Years of International Equity Investing," *Journal of Portfolio Management*, Fall 1996, 9–22.

Officer, Lawrence H. "The Purchasing Power Parity Theory of Exchange Rates: A Review Article." *IMF Staff Papers*, March 1976, 1–60.

Patro, Dilip Kumar. "Return Behavior and Pricing of American Depository Receipts." *Journal of International Financial Markets, Institutions, and Money*, January 2000, 43–67.

Peavy, John W. III, ed. *Managing Emerging Market Portfolios* Charlotteville, Va.: Research Foundation of the ICFA, 1994.

Rodriguez, Rita, and Eugene Carter. *International Financial Management*. Englewood Cliffs, N.J.: Prentice-Hall, 1976.

Rugman, Alan M. *International Diversification and the Multinational Enterprise*. Toronto: Lexington Books, 1979.

———. "Motives for Foreign Investment: The Market Imperfections and Risk Diversification Hypothesis." *Journal of World Trade Law*, September/October 1975, 567–573.

———. "Risk Reduction by International Diversification." *Journal of International Business Studies* 7, no. 2, 1976, 75–80.

Saunders, Anthony, and Richard S. Woodworth. "Gains from International Portfolio Diversification: U.K. Evidence 1971–1975." *Journal of Business Finance and Accounting*, Autumn 1977, 299–309.

Senchak, Andrew, and W.L. Beedles. "Is Indirect International Diversification Desirable?" *Journal of Portfolio Management*, Winter 1980, 49–57.

Solnik, Bruno. *International Investments*, 4th ed. Reading, MA: Addison-Wesley, 2000.

———. "International Parity Conditions and Exchange Risk: A Review." *Journal of Banking and Finance*, August 1978, 281–293.

———. "Why Not Diversify Internationally?" *Financial Analysts Journal*, July/August 1974, 48–54.

Stokes, Houston H., and Hugh Neuberger. "Interest Arbitrage, Forward Speculation and the Determination of the Forward Exchange Rate." *Columbia Journal of World Business*, Winter 1979, 86–98.

Tkac, Paula. "The Performance of Open-End International Mutual Funds." *Economic Review*, Third Quarter 2001, 1–17.

Tucker, Alan L., Jeff Madura, and Thomas C. Chiang. *International Financial Markets*. St. Paul: West, 1991.

Zychowicz, Ed. "The Development and Performance of Central European Markets." The Merrill Lynch Center for the Study of International Financial Services and Markets, Hofstra University Business Development Center, Fall 1997.

# 8 The Capital Markets and Market Efficiency

*"No matter how many winners you've got, if you either leverage too much or do anything that gives you the chance of having a zero in there, it'll all turn into pumpkins and mice."**

**Warren Buffett**

## Key Terms

chaos theory
chartist
continuous pricing function
day-of-the-week effect
economic function
efficient market hypothesis (EMH)
fair price function
informational efficiency
inside information
January effect
low PE effect
neglected firm effect
operational efficiency
optimum trading range
random walk
runs test
semi-efficient market hypothesis (SEMH)
small firm effect
technical analyst

## Introduction

Before explaining how people *should* behave, it is important to know how they *do* behave. Much of capital market theory springs from the notion that people like return and do not like risk and that dispersion around an expected return is a reasonable measure of risk.

## Role of the Capital Markets

Capital markets trade securities with lives of more than one year and are the hallmark of the capitalist system. Why is there a New York Stock Exchange (NYSE), an American Stock Exchange (AMEX), a Chicago Board of Trade, or a Chicago

*This and the margin quotations in this chapter come from "Living Legends," *CFA Magazine*, Jan–Feb 2003, 20–26.

Board Options Exchange (CBOE)?[1] This chapter begins with a review of the three principal functions of capital markets.

## Economic Function

The most important function of the capital markets is the **economic function.** Broadly speaking, this mechanism facilitates the transfer of money from savers to borrowers. Consider the secondary market for home mortgages. In many small communities in the United States, the residents are ordinary people with modest savings accounts. Still, the houses they buy are expensive, and most of the residents could not afford one without borrowing part of the cost. Suppose the area is a newly built bedroom community. Most residents will establish a local banking relationship for the convenience that checking and savings accounts offer. One person goes to the local bank and is successful in getting a $75,000 loan. Fifty other families do the same thing shortly thereafter. Very quickly, however, the entire savings of the town will be loaned out. The bank cannot loan money it does not have.

Does this mean that no one else in town can buy a house? Fortunately, it does not. Elsewhere in the United States are people who want to lend money rather than borrow it. Anytime someone buys a government or corporate bond or makes a deposit into a savings account she is lending money in the financial system. The system makes it easy to match up those who want to borrow with those who want to lend. The local banks that hold the mortgage certificates can sell these mortgages to someone else, and they routinely do so. Government agencies such as the Government National Mortgage Association and the Federal National Mortgage Association help facilitate these sales. Once the local bank sells a mortgage, it receives an inflow of money that can be used to finance someone else's home loan. The bank may subsequently sell this new mortgage, too, and the cycle goes on. A small $25 million bank with $25 million in assets could easily provide more than $250 million in mortgage financing this way.

*The economic function of the capital markets involves facilitating the flow of capital from savers to borrowers.*

Similarly, corporations sell stocks and bonds to the public. The U.S. government sells Treasury bonds to buyers all over the world. Individuals who own stock and suddenly need to raise cash can sell their shares to someone else. These are all examples of the *economic function of the capital markets*: facilitating the flow of capital from those who have it and wish to invest it to those who need it and want to borrow it.

## Continuous Pricing Function

*The continuous pricing function enables market participants to get accurate, up-to-date price information.*

A second function of the capital markets is the **continuous pricing function.** This means precisely what the name indicates: Prices are available moment by moment. This is a tremendous advantage to the security investor. Consider the case of antiques, for instance. How much is the old grandfather clock you inherited worth? How about your Chinese porcelain, or your 50 acres of southern pine timberland?

Determining the value of these items is not always conceptually easy, nor can the task be accomplished quickly. An appraiser must check authenticity and condition. Having established this, recent sales of other comparable items provide additional evidence of value. This might involve researching catalogs or auction reports, Internet research, or making numerous telephone calls. Whatever is necessary will take time and will be a nuisance.

[1]Since the opening of Eastern and Central Europe to a market economy, most U.S. college campuses routinely have students from the former Soviet Union eager to learn how the U.S. security markets work and how lessons learned here might be applied in their homeland.

This problem is much simpler with financial assets such as stocks or bonds. In most cases, we can quickly discover their prices during the business day. People routinely call their broker and ask, "How's Microsoft? How about Amazon.com?" They fully expect (and have come to take for granted) an instant reply. Alternatively, one can always check *The Wall Street Journal* or other newspaper with a business section, or get on the Internet for a quick price quotation.

Some securities do not trade very often, and investors are less confident in their ability to get a quick quotation on a firm that is too small to be carried in the electronic price-reporting system. Nonetheless, an analyst could come up with a close estimate for it more quickly than for an attic full of uncategorized art.

### Fair Price Function

*The fair price function removes the fear of buying or selling at an unreasonable price.*

The third function of the capital markets is the **fair price function.** Some people consider it the most important because of the anxiety it removes from them. This function means that an investor can trust the financial system. He can tell his broker to sell his stock at the going price and be assured of getting a fair price.

This is not the case with most of the things sold outside an organized trading ground. You would never, for instance, go to the automobile classified ads in the paper and pay whatever someone wanted for a particular car that interested you; there would be a very real chance that you would pay considerably more than necessary.

The reason capital market prices are fair stems from the fact that many players are in the game. These people are, in a sense, competing for the same business. If an investor has stock to sell, thousands of people are willing to bid on it. The markets ensure that the investors will sell it to the highest bidder. Conversely, buyers encounter numerous potential sellers, but the system ensures that the seller's order is matched up with the "best price," which from the buyers' perspective is the lowest price. The more participants and the more formal the marketplace, the more assurance the seller has that he is getting a good price.

*The more participants and the more formal the marketplace, the greater the likelihood that the buyer is getting a fair price.*

Consider a well-established local grocery store that is part of a national chain. Are customers comfortable doing their shopping there without much hesitation, or do they worry about not getting a good deal? Chances are that the prices prevailing in the store are competitive and fair. So many people pass through the area that stores with "unfair" high prices simply will not survive.

As another example, say that a person owns an especially valuable rare coin. One way to sell the coin would be to go to a regional coin show and take it from dealer table to dealer table to collect individual offers on it. An alternative is to offer it for sale at a coin auction. The latter choice will almost certainly result in a higher price. When many dealers simultaneously look at a particular coin, the market is much more efficient than when the dealers look at the coin individually.

There is an old joke among academic people about the business professor who was asked what his consulting fee was. He replied, "$2,000 per hour." When asked how much consulting he did, he replied "None, but that is my rate." Any price can be set, but when comparable services are available, the highest price will not get any action from the buyers.

The reverse is also true: if a price is too low, the market will quickly force it up. I was once in a discount department store and saw a shopping basket full of about three hundred rolls of cellophane tape carrying an obviously incorrect price tag. I found a clerk and asked if the tape was marked with the correct price; I was assured it was. I then informed the clerk that I would take all the store would sell me at that price—the three hundred rolls plus whatever was still in inventory in the back. The clerk returned a few minutes later with a manager, who announced that the tape was priced incorrectly and apologized for the inconvenience. I could have made a fuss but I didn't.

A discussion of fair pricing inevitably leads to the **efficient market hypothesis (EMH),** which is the theory supporting the notion that market prices are in fact fair. You can argue that this is the single most important paradigm in finance.

## Efficient Market Hypothesis

### *Types of Efficiency*

The efficient market hypothesis is a critical element of finance theory. Market efficiency influences many different subfields of finance, and anyone involved in the securities business should be familiar with the meaning and implications of market efficiency.

*The efficient market hypothesis deals with informational efficiency, which is a measure of how quickly and accurately the market digests new information.*

The two types of efficiency are *operational efficiency* and *informational efficiency*. **Operational efficiency** measures how well things function in terms of speed of execution and accuracy. At a stock exchange, operational efficiency is a function of the number of orders that are lost or filled incorrectly and the elapsed time between the receipt of an order and its execution. All market participants are concerned with these matters, but this is not the type of efficiency referred to in the EMH.

The EMH relates to **informational efficiency**, a measure of how quickly and accurately the market reacts to new information.[2] Eugene Fama, Professor of Finance at the University of Chicago, is probably the best-known advocate of the efficient market hypothesis. He has contributed to a great deal of the literature on this topic. He sums up the gist of this notion in one of his earliest writings, where he states, "In an efficient market at any point in time the actual price of a security will be a good estimate of its intrinsic value."[3] New data constantly enter the marketplace via such things as economic reports, company press releases, political statements, or public opinion surveys. What does all this information mean? Is rising unemployment in Germany good or bad for holders of U.S. Treasury bonds? How about Company XYZ's announcement that it intends to split its stock 5 for 1? Suppose the price of gold jumps $10 an ounce in one day; what effect will this likely have on stocks, if any?

*For a summary of EMH and related links, visit* http://www.investorhome.com/emh.htm

The market is informationally very efficient: Security prices adjust rapidly and accurately to new information without the need to digest it very long. Sometimes the speed of adjustment is remarkably fast. I was once sitting in the boardroom of a brokerage firm punching up my current stocks on the computer terminal. One of my holdings at the time was common stock in the MGM Grand Hotel, symbol GRH on the New York Stock Exchange. The stock was trading at 10.25 as I watched. The bell rang, and the red light flashed on the Dow Jones News Service monitor, indicating "hot news." I got up to see what it was and, to my dismay, read the following headline: "Fire at MGM Grand Hotel." In the seconds it took me to return to the computer, GRH was down to 7.50, which is approximately where it remained the rest of the day.

Anyone with common sense would realize that a hotel fire is bad news. In an informationally efficient market, prices are going to react fast, and they did. We could

[2]The *market* is a colloquial term referring to all the players: individuals, institutions, foreigners, and so on. We talk about the market behaving a certain way as if it were a single entity.

[3]Fama, Eugene, "Random Walks in Stock Market Prices," *Financial Analysts Journal*, Nov/Dec 1965, 55–59.

not expect to read about the fire in *The Wall Street Journal* the following day, to think "Well, I'll bet that hammers the stock; I'd better sell," and to find that the market was still trying to sort the news out. Prices had dropped long before.

The market is very efficient; it deciphers the news quickly, and prices adjust. Students in an investments class are sometimes disappointed to learn that they cannot take a stock market course giving them the power to read the financial pages, casually picking stocks here and there that will certainly double in price by next week. Things do not work that way.

Still, the market is not completely efficient. There are indeed rewards for the person who processes the news better than the next. For one thing, not everyone has access to the same news, nor does everyone receive the news in a timely fashion. Because of this, it is common to talk about three forms of the EMH, each of which is based on the availability of a different level of information. These are discussed next.

## Weak Form

*The weak form of the EMH states that charts are of no use in predicting future stock prices.*

The least restrictive form of the EMH is the *weak form*. It states that it is impossible to predict future stock prices by analyzing prices from the past. In other words, charting techniques are of no use.

Consider Figure 8-1. According to the weak form of the EMH, how a stock arrived at its current price makes no difference. It could have followed the route of Stock A, or it could have behaved like Stock B. The only thing that matters is the current price. The current price already includes any information contained in the past price series.

**FIGURE 8-1**

Which Stock Is Best?

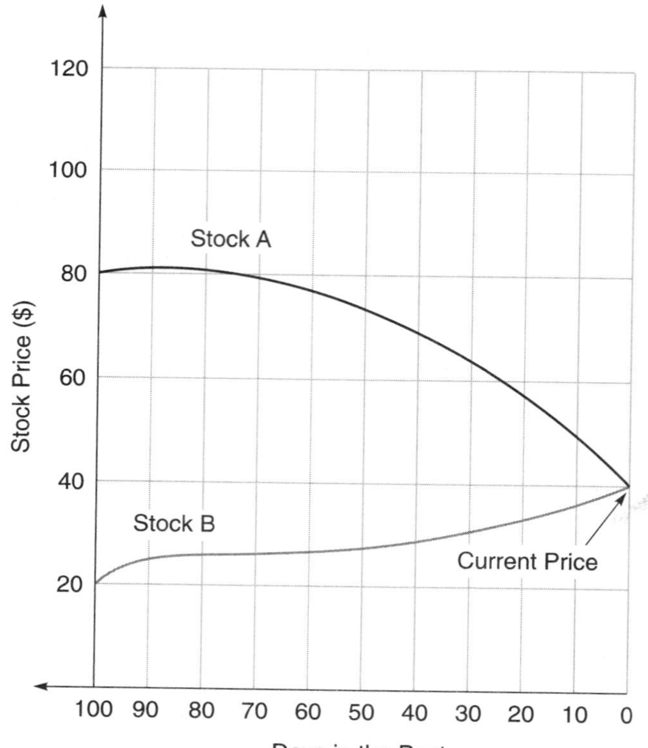

This is a difficult pill for most people to swallow. If we were to survey our friends and neighbors, virtually everyone would identify Stock B as clearly a better buy than Stock A. After all, B is rising while A is falling. Who would want to buy a declining stock?

*Past prices do not matter; future ones do.*

The point this logic misses is simple: Past prices do not matter; future ones do. Everyone has access to past price information, although some people can get these prices more conveniently than others. According to the EMH, so many people are looking at these same numbers that any free lunches have already been consumed. The current price is a fair one that considers any information contained in the past price data.

**Charting.** There are hundreds of books about charting. We refer to people who study charts as **technical analysts** or **chartists.** Just as we find identifiable forms in the clouds or in constellations of stars, our brains are creative enough to find patterns in a sequence of stock prices. Technical analysts learn what they consider important patterns through folklore or their own experience.

Consider the four graphs making up Figure 8-2. Are these random patterns, or does one or more of them tell something? Some technical analysts would look at

**FIGURE 8-2** Predicting the Future with Charts

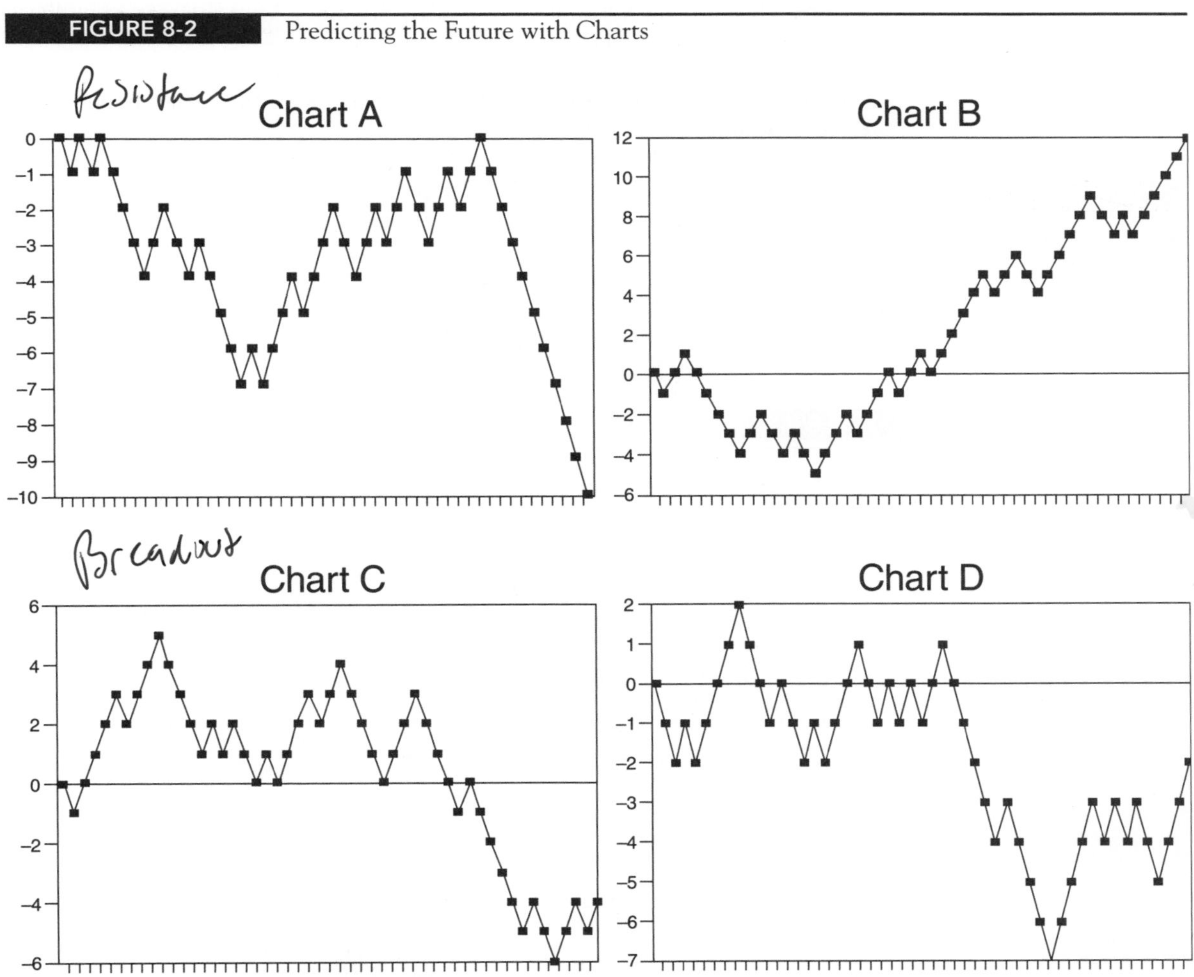

Chart A and see a stock that has been unsuccessful in penetrating a "resistance level" at 0. Its failure to rise above this after several attempts is followed by a major downturn in the stock price. Chart B shows a pattern that certainly looks good. This stock is on a sustained rise. Chart C shows another bearish situation. Here a stock has penetrated its "support level" at 0, resulting in a significant decline to the –5 area. A technical analyst would call this a "breakout on the downside." Chart D shows "congestion" in the –2 to +1 range, followed by a sharp break to a new equilibrium level around –4.

What should we make of all this? Would we be more inclined to buy one of these stocks than the others? Is one clearly inferior to the others? Here is the kicker: Each of these figures was created using the random number–generating function of a spreadsheet package. These are four successive random graphs, but with a different seed number to start each series. In all four graphs, the observation is either one unit higher than the previous observation or one unit lower, and each of the two possible outcomes has a 50 percent probability of occurring. Are these graphs useful in predicting what the spreadsheet will select next? Probably not.

Still, charts are likely to remain a permanent part of the investment landscape. They have a behavioral element that we do not fully understand. One of the foremost researchers in behavioral finance is Meir Statman. After the market pullback in September 1998, he stated

> If the market is going up, people expect it to continue to go up. But if it goes up for, say, six months without a correction, people get nervous. They kind of expect the market will go up over time, but not straight up. They find a correction a relief. So the next time the market gets up to the 8,000 level, people will feel we are on solid ground. We've had a correction. The prices are more reasonable.[4]

**Runs Test.** To be able to test the likelihood that a series of price movements such as these occurred by chance is handy. One way to do this is with a nonparametric statistical technique called a **runs test.** Table 8-1 shows the details.[5]

**TABLE 8-1** THE RUNS TEST

$$Z = \frac{R - \bar{x}}{\sigma}$$

where $R$ = number of runs;

$$\bar{x} = \frac{2n_1 n_2}{n_1 + n_2} + 1$$

$$\sigma^2 = \frac{2n_1 n_2 (2n_1 n_2 - n_1 - n_2)}{(n_1 + n_2)^2 (n_1 + n_2 - 1)}$$

$n_1$, $n_2$ = number of observations in each category; and

$Z$ = standard normal variable.[a]

[a]The standard normal variable comes from a normal distribution with a mean of 0 and a standard deviation of 1. Approximately 95 percent of the distribution lies within two standard deviations of the mean. Z statistics with large absolute values do not often occur by chance.

[4]Barry B. Burr, "What Happened? Nobody Knows," *Pensions and Investments*, September 7, 1998.

[5]Table 8-1 shows the Wald-Wolfowitz runs test. Although it is a useful test any time, it is best suited to cases where $n_1$ and $n_2$ are both greater than 20.

FIGURE 8-3

Counting Runs

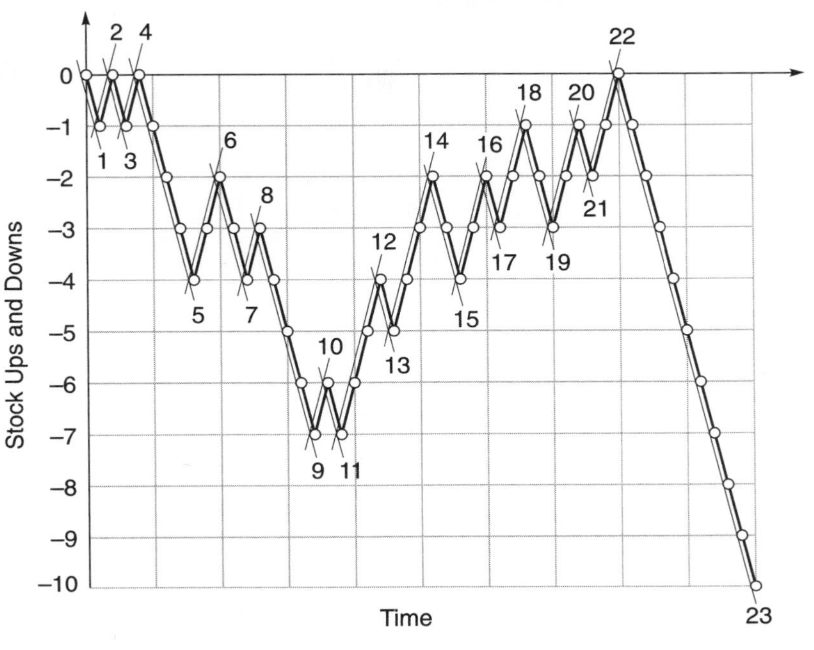


*A runs test measures the likelihood that a series of two variables is a random occurrence.*

A *run* is an uninterrupted sequence of the same observation. A coin-flipping experiment, for instance, might yield the following sequence of heads (H) and tails (T):

HHH TT H T HHH TTT H TT HH

Let us do a runs test on the stock price pattern in Chart A of Figure 8-2. Figure 8-3 reproduces Chart A and annotates it with runs. Each time the price change reverses sign, a new run begins. Figure 8-3 shows 23 runs in this series of 50 stock price changes, with 20 "ups" and 30 "downs."

Suppose we took fifty pennies and arranged them in a row. Then we turn them so that twenty of them are heads (or "up stock prices") and thirty are tails ("down stock prices"). We can arrange these coins in many different orders. We could have all the heads first and then all the tails, giving us only two runs. We could also alternate the heads and tails until the heads run out, giving us forty-one runs. Neither of these patterns would be expected to occur by chance. The results of the runs test indicate the likelihood of the various combinations of heads and tails. Table 8-2 shows the statistics for this experiment. The runs test calculates the number of ways the observed number of runs could occur given the relative number of heads and tails in the sample and the probability of this number.

Elementary probability theory teaches that about 95 percent of the area under the normal curve lies within 1.96 standard deviations of the mean. Our Z statistic of –0.595 is close to the standard normal distribution mean of 0. The likelihood of observing a Z statistic near 0 is very high.[6] We cannot be 95 percent certain that our observed stock prices did not happen by chance unless we get a Z statistic whose absolute value is 1.96 or greater.

[6]Using the Runs file on the text Website, you will find a 27.56 percent chance of getting 23 runs when $n_1$=20 and $n_2$=30.

**TABLE 8-2** RESULTS OF RUNS TEST

Number of runs = $R$ = 23
Number of ups = $n_1$ = 20
Number of down = $n_2$ = 30

$$\text{Mean number of runs} = \bar{x} = \frac{2 \times 20 \times 30}{50} + 1 = 25$$

$$\sigma = \left\{ \frac{2 \times 20 \times 30[(2 \times 20 \times 30) - 20 - 30]}{(20+30)^2(20+30-1)} \right\}^{1/2} = 3.36$$

$$Z = \frac{23-25}{3.36} = -0.595$$

## Semi-Strong Form

*The semi-strong form of the EMH states that security prices fully reflect all relevant publicly available information.*

The weak form of the efficient market hypothesis states that security prices fully reflect any information contained in the past series of stock prices. The *semi-strong form* takes the information set a step further and includes *all publicly available information.*

A plethora of information of potential interest to investors is available. In addition to past stock prices, such things as economic reports, brokerage firm recommendations, and investment advisory letters abound. Although no one person sees every one of these items, "the market" does, and prices move as people make decisions to buy and sell based on what they learn from the information set available to them.

The news item about the MGM Grand Hotel fire was not past price data; however, it was publicly available, and the stock did decline because of it. According to the semi-strong form of the EMH, this is exactly what is expected.

According to Michael J.C. Roth, former executive vice-president of USAA Investment Management,

> We recognize that the market is pretty efficient. We have seen time after time that when we get the word that a Wall Street firm is now recommending a stock, that stock is already up a point-and-a-half. The market is that efficient. As soon as anyone gets wind of a firm's recommendation—boom—people are buying it, and that stock's price goes up. By then, the value is diminished.[7]

Extensive academic research supports this version of the efficient market hypothesis. Studies have investigated the extent to which people can profit by acting on various corporate announcements such as stock splits, cash dividends, and stock dividends. An occasional paper shows that very small profits could have been made in a particular case, but the general result is consistent: The market reacts to public information very efficiently, and investors are seldom going to beat the market by analyzing public news, especially if they incur trading fees to buy and sell.

Burton Malkiel, author of the well-known stock market book *A Random Walk Down Wall Street*, says, "When you look at the evidence, you find that consistently, from year to year, two-thirds of professionally managed portfolios are beaten by a

---

[7]Reprinted from *Aide Magazine*, December 1989. ©1989, USAA, San Antonio, Texas.

low-cost index fund."[8] This troubling but persistent result suggests that securities are accurately priced and that in the long run returns will be consistent with the level of systematic risk taken. The implication is that active managers will underperform by the amount of their transaction costs. The industry does not like this part of academic research.

### *Strong Form*

*The strong form of the EMH says that security prices fully reflect all relevant public and private information.*

The most extreme form of the efficient market hypothesis is the *strong form*. This version states that security prices fully reflect all public and private information. Figure 8-4 sums up the three forms of the efficient market hypothesis. According to the strong form, even corporate insiders cannot make abnormal profits by exploiting *inside information* about their company.[9]

**Inside information** is factual information not available to the general public that will most likely influence security prices once it becomes public.

**FIGURE 8-4** The Forms of Market Efficiency

[8]Trammel, Susan, "The Great Debate," *CFA Magazine*, Nov–Dec 2003, 29.

[9]An abnormal profit is a return that is higher than that predicted by financial theory. That is, the return is higher than expected, given the level of risk of the investment. If someone could consistently earn abnormal returns using publicly available information, it would invalidate the semi-strong form of the efficient market hypothesis.

**PORTFOLIO MEMO**

## Short Your Competitor

Security laws are very strict about corporate insiders trading in the securities of their own firm. Inside information is technically called material, nonpublic information. (*Material* means that the information, if known, could logically be expected to move the security price.) People go to jail every year for trading on inside information. In determining what is legal, however, the law makes a distinction between individual and institutional investors. If you know your company is about to announce its intent to acquire another company, as a corporate officer you are not allowed to personally buy shares in the target before the public announcement of the acquisition; this is illegal. The corporation, however, is free to do so. It intends to buy the shares and can go about this almost anyway it wishes.

Sometimes the corporate boardroom knows it is about to do something that is likely to hurt a competitor. As an article in *Forbes* pointed out, "Jet Blue's entry into the Atlanta market wasn't good news for Delta."* Jet Blue's announcement could logically have been expected to depress the Delta Air Lines stock price. There is nothing in security law to prevent Jet Blue from speculating on this and selling Delta short, hoping to profit on the price decline. The *Forbes* article states,

> When economists Robert Hansen and John Lott asked the Securities and Exchange Commission if it would be legal for Company A to trade in Company B's shares on the basis of information generated by Company A: "All [eight securities lawyers] said that 1) it is legal to trade rivals' stock; 2) even at its most imperious, the SEC has never suggested that this is illegal; and 3) they had never heard of such a case being brought, or even episodes of such trading questioned."

Trading on this inside information is perfectly legal.

---

*Ayres, Ian and Barry Nalebuff, "Don't Sell Us Short," *Forbes*, February 2, 2004, 57.

The evidence does not support the strong form of the EMH. Insiders (even Martha Stewart) obviously can make a profit trading on their knowledge. Every year people go to jail, are fined, or are suspended from trading for doing so. Inside information gives an unfair advantage that can be used to extract millions of dollars from the marketplace. Where did these millions in profit come from? They came from the pockets of individual investors who did not have access to the confidential corporate news. Our society does not believe this is fair; consequently, insider trading is illegal.

### *Semi-Efficient Market Hypothesis*

*The semi-efficient market hypothesis states that some stocks are priced more efficiently than others.*

The EMH has a thought-provoking cousin. The essence of the **semi-efficient market hypothesis (SEMH)** is the notion that the market prices some stocks more efficiently than others. This is a very appealing idea to many market analysts. Consider two very different companies, such as International Business Machines (IBM) and a hypothetical start-up firm called Emergent Chip Technology. Everyone has heard of IBM, which trades on the New York Stock Exchange and many regional exchanges. Thousands of portfolios contain its shares, and virtually all security analysts watch it. The likelihood that an investor can find a free lunch in the shares of IBM is extremely small. The stock is priced fairly, and if she buys some she probably will earn a long-term return consistent with the stock's level of risk.

*"I have learned that the great opportunities are the places that have been neglected, where other people are not looking."*
John Templeton

According to the SEMH, fewer people will be watching Emergent Chip Technology, and consequently, its shares will more likely be undervalued. In other words, the stock might not be priced as efficiently as the shares of IBM or those of other well-known companies.

This idea is sometimes used to support the thesis that the market has several tiers, or that a security pecking order exists. The first tier contains IBM and the like.

## PORTFOLIO MEMO

### Fibonacci Numbers: Market Folklore

Leonardo Fibonacci (1170–1240) is familiar to many market technical analysts. He was a notable medieval mathematician, now famous for identifying the sequence of numbers that bears his name. The Fibonacci Sequence is shown here:

1 1 2 3 5 8 13 21 34 55 89 . . .

After the initial unit values, each succeeding *Fibonacci number* is defined as the sum of the two previous numbers: 3 + 5 = 8; 5 + 8 = 13; and so on. After the first few numbers, the ratio of each Fibonacci number to its predecessor is 1.618. This ratio continues infinitely for higher numbers:

| | | | | | | | | | | |
|---|---|---|---|---|---|---|---|---|---|---|
| | 1 | 2 | 3 | 5 | 8 | 13 | 21 | 34 | 55 | 89 |
| | ÷1 | ÷1 | ÷2 | ÷3 | ÷5 | ÷ 8 | ÷13 | ÷21 | ÷34 | ÷55 |
| = | 1 | 2 | 1.5 | 1.667 | 1.6 | 1.625 | 1.615 | 1.619 | 1.618 | 1.618 |

Fibonacci ratios use this "magic" 1.618 number, as follows:

| | | | | | | | | |
|---|---|---|---|---|---|---|---|---|
| | 0.618 | 1 | 0.618 | 1 | 1.618 | 2.618 | 4.236 | 6.853 |
| | ÷1.618 | ÷1.618 | ×1.618 | ×1.618 | ×1.618 | ×1.618 | ×1.618 | × 1.618 |
| = | 0.382 | 0.618 | 1 | 1.618 | 2.618 | 4.236 | 6.853 | 11.089 |

According to one trader, most advocates of Fibonacci numbers use the .382 and .618 ratios to "compute retracement levels of a previous move."* For example, if a stock falls from $100 to $70 (a 30 percent drop), it will encounter resistance to further advances after it recoups 38.2 percent of its loss, or until it reaches $81.46.

Fibonacci discovered these numbers while exploring the reproduction rates of rabbits. The remarkable thing is the frequency with which Fibonacci numbers occur in nature. The number and pattern of seed rows in a sunflower, the structure of pinecones, the chambers of a nautilus, and the topology of spiraling galaxies all share Fibonacci numbers (Figure 8-5).

One floor trader at the Chicago Mercantile Exchange told me she does not believe in Fibonacci numbers but had to follow them because so many other people did, and the market would react "strangely" when it approached a Fibonacci milestone.

*George Slezak, "How Fibonacci Can Forecast Stock Market Resistance Levels," *Futures*, July 1989, 36–37.

PORTFOLIO MEMO

## Fibonacci Numbers: Market Folklore, continued

FIGURE 8-5 Fibonacci Numbers and Bees*

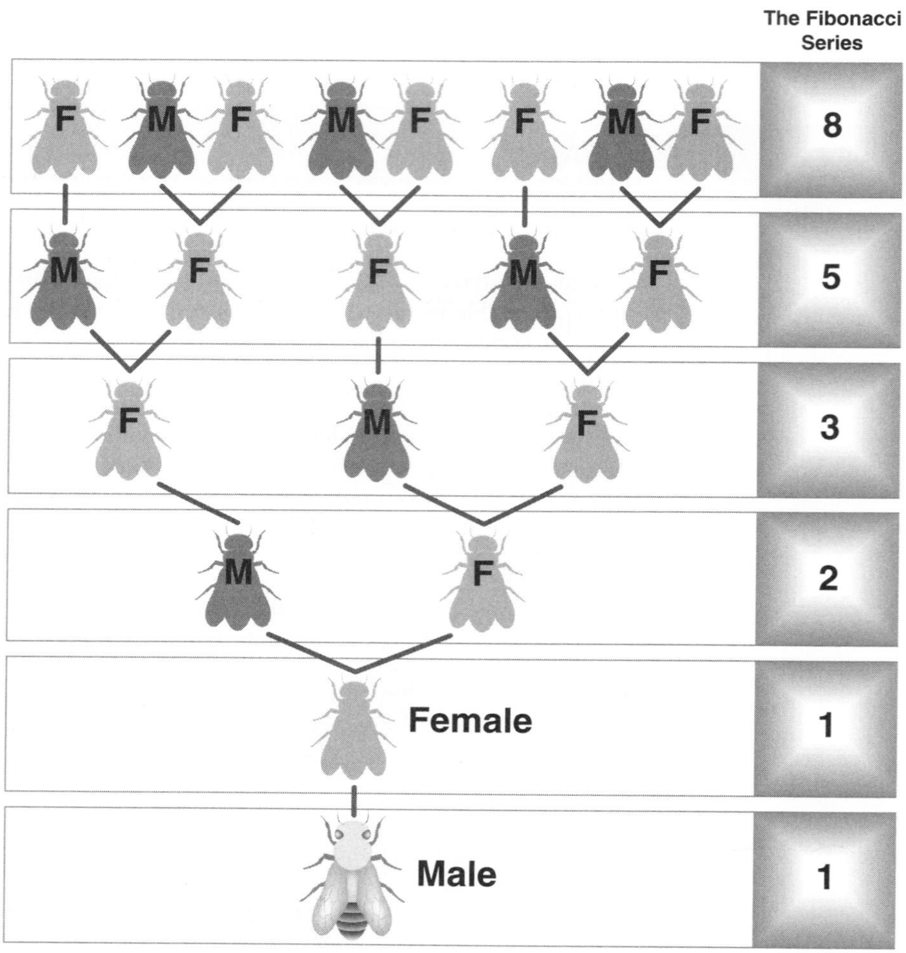

The Fibonacci Series

F M F M F F M F — 8

M F F M F — 5

F M F — 3

M F — 2

Female — 1

Male — 1

*Male bees come from an unfertilized egg and have only a mother. A female bee has both a mother and a father.

The second tier might contain lesser-known but well-established companies such as many of those that trade on the American Stock Exchange. The third tier might be companies such as Emergent Chip Technology. The farther down the tier list you go, the less efficient the pricing is, or so the reasoning goes.

It is probably safe to say that most students of the market are generally sympathetic to the logic of the semi-efficient market hypothesis. It is not possible to follow every security. Analysts *need* to follow the big names, and they simply do not have time to research the ever-expanding list of emerging companies.

### Security Prices and Random Walks

The efficient market hypothesis states that the current stock price fully reflects relevant news information. Although we can anticipate some of the news, much of it is unexpected. Some days the news is good; some days it is bad. The unexpected portion of the news, by definition, follows a *random walk*. The **random walk** idea says that news arrives randomly, and, because markets are efficient, security prices adjust to the arrival of the news. In general, we cannot forecast specifics of the news very accurately.

Substantial uncertainty surrounds even news that seems reasonably predictable. An article in *Forbes* reported the results of a study showing that over the period 1973 to 1990, the average error made by security analysts in forecasting the next quarter's corporate earnings for the firms they covered was 40 percent. On an annual basis, the average error was never less than 25 percent. From 1985 to 1990, the average error was 52 percent, indicating that the analysts' forecasting ability had not improved over the 18-year period.[10]

When the news relevant to a particular stock is good, people adjust their estimates of future returns upward, or they reduce the discount rate they attach to these returns. Either way, the stock price goes up. Conversely, when the news is bad, the stock price goes down.

*The random walk idea says that news arrives randomly, not that stock prices move randomly.*

Many people misunderstand what the random walk idea means. It does not say that stock prices move randomly. Rather, it says that the unexpected portion of the news arrives randomly, and that stock prices adjust to the news, whatever it is.

A famous analogy compares security prices to the path of a drunk staggering from lamppost to lamppost. The drunk has a beginning point and a target destination. The path of the drunk shows a trend from one post to the next. Along the way, however, the path is erratic. The drunk wanders right and left, perhaps occasionally out into the street or into the wall of a building.[11] An observer cannot accurately predict the precise route. The same is true of a security price and its consequent return. Over the long run, security returns are consistent with what we expect given their level of risk. In the short run, however, many ups and downs cloud the long-run outlook.

The stock price behaviors shown in the four charts of Figure 8-2 are random walks. Each succeeding observation is just as likely to be up as down.

## Anomalies

In finance, *anomaly* usually refers to unexplained results that deviate from those expected under finance theory, especially those related to the efficient market hypothesis. The best-known anomalies are the *low PE effect*, *low-priced stock performance*, *small firm effect*, *neglected firm effect*, *overreaction effect*, *January effect*, and *day-of-the-week effect*.

*"I'd like to make a pitch for low price-earnings ratio investing, which has been my prevailing philosophy . . . It just seems so much the easy way to go for somebody who's willing to work a bit at it and take on the marketplace."*

John Neff, CFA

### Low PE Effect

Numerous academic studies have uncovered evidence that stocks with low price/earnings ratios (PEs) provide higher returns than stocks with higher PEs. This is called the **low PE effect.** Studies by Basu, Breen, and Nicholson (among others) show this result.[12] None of these studies, however, used a risk-adjusted methodology.

[10] David Dremen, "Flawed Forecasts," *Forbes*, December 9, 1991, 342.
[11] The technical analyst would correctly identify the building as a "resistance level."
[12] See Further Reading at the end of the Chapter.

PORTFOLIO MEMO

## Profiting From Analysts' Forecasts

Many brokerage firms have an in-house research staff providing recommendations on individual securities. Are these helpful to investors? If they can make above-average profits by following an analyst's advice, this seems to be in contradiction to the efficient market hypothesis.

Many studies have investigated security analysts' forecasting ability, and the evidence is generally embarrassing for the analysts. A recent study in the *Journal of Finance** reviewed 360,000 buy/sell recommendations from 4,300 analysts over the period 1986–1996. The research concluded that after accounting for transaction costs, a strategy of buying the most highly rated stocks and selling those rated the lowest failed to produce a risk-adjusted return greater than zero, exactly what the efficient market hypothesis would predict.

*Brad Barber, Reuven Lehavy, Maureen McNichols, and Brett Trueman, "Can Investors Profit from the Prophets? Security Analyst Recommendations and Stock Returns," *Journal of Finance*, April 2001, 531–563.

A subsequent study by Basu *was* risk adjusted,[13] and even then the excess returns associated with low PE stocks persisted. Because this seems to conflict directly with the capital asset pricing model and the theory behind it, this Basu study is noteworthy.

### Low-Priced Stocks

*Some evidence indicates that low PE stocks outperform higher PE stocks of similar risk.*

Many people believe that certain stock price levels are either too high or too low. Equivalently, they believe that an **optimum trading range** for the price of stock exists. By finance theory, the stock price should be merely a marker and of no value in comparing firms. The size (and value) of a piece of pie depends on the number of pieces into which the pie is cut.

Still, folklore about stock prices abounds. As early as 1936 the academic literature showed evidence that low-priced common stock tended to earn higher returns than stock with a "high" price.[14] In their classic investment book, Graham and Dodd state, "It is a commonplace of the market that an issue will rise more steadily from 10 to 40 than from 100 to 400."[15]

---

[13]S. Basu, "Investment Performance of Common Stocks in Relation to Their Price-Earnings Ratios: A Test of the Efficient Market Hypothesis," *Journal of Finance*, June 1977, 663–682.

[14]L.H. Fritzmeier, "Relative Price Fluctuation of Industrial Stocks in Different Price Groups," *Journal of Business*, April 1936, 113–154.

[15]B. Graham and D.L. Dodd, *Security Analysis* (New York: McGray-Hall, 1962), 649. In a 1976 speech, Benjamin Graham backed off from this statement: "I am no longer an advocate of elaborate techniques of security analysis in order to find superior value opportunities. This was a rewarding activity, say, forty years ago, when our textbook 'Graham and Dodd' was first published; but the situation has changed a good deal since then. In the old days any well-trained security analyst could do a good professional job of selecting undervalued issues through detailed studies; but in the light of the enormous amount of research now being carried on, I doubt whether in most cases such extensive efforts will generate sufficiently superior selections to justify their cost. To that very limited extent I'm on the side of the 'efficient market' school of thought now generally accepted by the professors." (Cited in John Train, *Money Masters* (New York: Harper & Row, 1987, 103).

Consider the following question: Is it easier for a stock to rise from $5 to $6 than it is for it to rise from $50 to $60? The vast majority of people who play the market seem to believe this. If this *were* the case (which theory and empirical evidence dispute), every firm whose stock sold for $50 should split 10 for 1 so that its share price would advance faster.

### Small Firm and Neglected Firm Effects

Like the low PE effect, the *small firm effect* and the *neglected firm effect* are two important market anomalies that influence the stock selection of some investors (and some portfolio managers).

**Small Firm Effect.** The theory of the **small firm effect** maintains that investing in firms with low market capitalization[16] will, on average, provide superior risk-adjusted returns. Solid financial research supports this hypothesis. Important studies on this topic include those by Reinganum and Banz.[17] These and other research studies clearly provide evidence that small-capitalization firms outperform larger ones.

The Banz study divided all New York Stock Exchange firms into five groups based on their capitalization and determined the average annual performance of the five groups. Returns of the smallest group were almost 20 percent larger than those of the largest group. This is a thought-provoking result and a reason many investors find small caps so intriguing.

The obvious implication of this is that portfolio managers should give small firms particular attention in the security selection process. We do not know why the small firm effect exists, but it seems to persist. In the past, some anomalies tended to disappear soon after they were reported. The small firm effect is still with us.

*Visit* http://www.investorhome.com/anomaly.htm *for a sample of stock market anomalies.*

**Neglected Firm Effect.** The **neglected firm effect** is a cousin of the small firm effect. Institutional investors are sometimes limited to the larger-capitalization firms. As a consequence, security analysts do not pay as much attention to firms that are unlikely portfolio candidates. Arbel, Carvell, and Strebel investigated 510 firms over a ten-year period and found, as expected, that the smaller firms outperformed those that institutions widely held.[18] The authors postulated that institutions might perceive more risk with the smaller firms, and hence they ignore them. Arbel and Strebel show other evidence that the attention of security analysts does affect share prices and that if analysts neglect a firm, it has a systematic impact on the share value.[19]

The implication is the same as with the small firm effect: neglected firms seem to offer a free lunch with surprising regularity. When the Arbel, Carvell, and Strebel study appeared in 1983, the authors closed by stating that the effect was "unlikely to persist over time." Neglected firms, however, continue to be an important research area that we have not yet figured out.

---

[16] *Market capitalization* refers to the number of shares of stock outstanding multiplied by the current stock price.

[17] Mark R. Reinganum, "Portfolio Strategies for Small Caps vs. Large," *Journal of Portfolio Management*, Winter 1983, 29–36, and other references in Further Reading; R. Banz, "The Relationship between Return and Market Value of Common Stock," *Journal of Financial Economics*, March 1981, 3–18.

[18] Avner Arbel, Steven Carvell, and Paul Strebel, "Giraffes, Institutions, and Neglected Firms," *Financial Analysts Journal*, May/June 1983, 57–63.

[19] Avner Arbel and Paul Strebel, "Pay Attention to Neglected Firms," *Journal of Portfolio Management*, Winter 1983, 37–42.

*"I've learned that extreme dislocations in markets inevitably occur, and they also inevitably correct themselves. One needs to learn from that the discipline of being patient and having the conviction of one's own analysis."*
Gary Brinson, CFA

## Market Overreaction

Another area of research interest lies in the observed tendency for the market to overreact to extreme news, with the general result that investors can sometimes predict systematic price reversals. For instance, if stocks fall dramatically, they seem to have a tendency to perform better than their betas indicate they should in the following period. De Bondt and Thaler have written several important articles dealing with this subject.[20]

Experimental psychologists know that people often rely too heavily on recent data at the expense of the more extensive set of prior data. At a racetrack, for instance, success by the house handicapper on the previous race significantly influences the betting pattern on the following race, even if the handicapper was largely inaccurate on previous races. Based on this known result, De Bondt and Thaler

> conjectured that, as a consequence of investor overreaction to earnings, stock prices may also temporarily depart from their underlying fundamental values. With prices initially biased by either excessive optimism or pessimism, prior "losers" would be more attractive investments than prior "winners."

In their studies, De Bondt and Thaler found "systematic price reversals for stocks that experience extreme long-term gains or losses: Past losers significantly outperform past winners."[21]

Brown and Harlow, writing in the *Journal of Portfolio Management*, found that the overreaction was stronger to bad news than to good news during the period of their study.[22] After an especially large drop, security returns over the following period were unusually large and persistent.

An article appearing in *Financial Management* specifically investigated an earnings announcement by Intel on September 21, 2000.[23] The company issued a press release stating that third quarter revenue would be significantly lower than analysts' expectations. The stock subsequently fell 29 percent in the next three days. Using a discounted cash flow model, the article shows that the stock could not have been efficiently priced both before and after the announcement.

## January Effect

*Stock returns are inexplicably high in January, and small firms' stocks do better than large firms' stock.*

Another well-known anomaly is the **January effect.** Numerous studies show persuasive evidence that stock returns are inexplicably high in January and that small firms do better than large firms early in the year.[24] This is especially true for the first five trading days in January.

---

[20]Werner F.M. DeBondt and Richard H. Thaler, "Does the Stock Market Overreact?" *Journal of Finance*, July 1985, 793–805, and "Further Evidence on Investor Overreaction and Stock Market Seasonality," *Journal of Finance*, July 1987, 557–581.
[21]Ibid.
[22]Keith C. Brown and W.V. Harlow, "Market Overreaction: Magnitude and Intensity," *Journal of Portfolio Management*, Winter 1988, 6–13.
[23]Bradford Cornell, "Is the Response of Analysts to Information Consistent with Fundamental Valuation? The Case of Intel," *Financial Management*, Spring 2001, 113–136.
[24]Good overviews of the topic are provided by Richard Roll in the *Journal of Portfolio Management* and by Richard Rogalski and Shea M. Tinic, "The January Size Effect: Anomaly or Risk Mismeasurement?" *Financial Analysts Journal*, November/December 1986, 63–70.

PORTFOLIO MEMO

## Market Efficiency and Japan

The direct relationship between risk and expected return is a fundamental of finance. Persistent deviations from this are rare. The capital markets of Japan, however, have become a notable exception. Writing in the *Journal of Investing*, Baytas and Cakici found that over the period 1980–1997, equity investments, as a group, earned less than either bonds or convertible bonds.* Eighteen years is a long time for this anomalous result to persist.

Japan may be unusual because of the tendency there for firms to hold substantial numbers of each other's shares. Nonetheless, this result is troubling, and inconsistent with market efficiency and rational investor behavior.

*Ahmet Baytas and Nusret Cakici, "Do Stocks Really Provide the Highest Return in the Long Run?" *Journal of Investing*, Fall 1999, 89–96.

In his 1983 study, Richard Roll begins by reporting, "For 18 consecutive years, from 1963 through 1980, average returns of small firms have been larger than average returns of large firms on the first trading day of the calendar year."[25] Comparing AMEX stocks (which are generally smaller firms) with those on the NYSE, Roll found that the average return differential was 1.16 percent in favor of the small firms, and that the $t$-statistic for significance of the difference was a whopping 8.18.

This phenomenon has possible explanations. Branch proposes that the superior January performance comes from tax-loss trading late in December.[26] Rogalski and Tinic probably provide a better explanation, showing evidence that the risk of small stocks is not constant over the year and tends to be especially high early in the year.[27] The reason for this phenomenon of higher risk is itself unexplained. In any event, January tends to be a good month for the stock market.

Avner Arbel has studied numerous market anomalies, including the performance of neglected firms in January. In one study he formed stocks into four groups. Three groups come from S&P 500 stocks, divided into highly researched, moderately researched, and neglected, depending on the extent to which there was analyst coverage. The fourth group contained non-S&P 500 stocks.[28] Table 8-3 shows the results of his study.

The data in the table are compelling for both the neglected firm effect and the January effect. The less the research coverage, the higher the return, with this result especially pronounced in January. Note from the bottom row of the table that in January, non-S&P 500 firms earn 10.72 percent more than in an average month. The general thrust of the results persists even after adjusting for market risk.

[25]Richard Roll, "Vas ist Das?" *Journal of Portfolio Management*, Winter 1983, 18–28.

[26]Ben Branch, "A Tax Loss Trading Rule," *Journal of Business*, April 1977, 198–207.

[27]Rogalski and Tinic, 1986.

[28]Avner Arbel, "Generic Stocks: The Key to Market Anomalies," *Journal of Portfolio Management*, Summer 1985, 4–13.

**TABLE 8-3** THE JANUARY EFFECT ON SELECTED STOCKS

| | *Average January Return* | *Average January return minus average monthly return during the rest of the year* | *Average January return after adjusting for systematic risk* |
|---|---|---|---|
| **S&P 500 Companies** | | | |
| Highly Researched | 2.48% | 1.63% | –1.44% |
| Moderately Researched | 4.95% | 4.19% | 1.69% |
| Neglected | 7.62% | 6.87% | 5.03% |
| **Non-S&P 500 Companies** | | | |
| Neglected | 11.32% | 10.72% | 7.71% |

Source: Avner Arbel, "Generic Stocks: The Key to Market Anomalies," *Journal of Portfolio Management*, Summer 1985, 4–13.

## Day-of-the-Week Effect

Mondays are historically bad days for the stock market. Wednesdays and Fridays are historically good. Tuesdays and Thursdays are a mixed bag.[29] These results persist over various time periods and for periods of varying lengths. From July 1978 to December 1978, for instance, the average Monday return for the S&P 500 portfolio was –0.134 percent. This is a one-day return, so on an annualized basis, this corresponds to an aggregate loss of over 33 percent.

This should not happen in an efficient market. Once someone reports a recurring profitable trading opportunity, the actions of investors should cause it to disappear. Researchers discovered the **day-of-the-week effect** in the early 1980s, and it continues today. After accounting for trading fees, the economic significance of the anomaly is lower, but it remains nonetheless. No satisfactory theory explains why the phenomenon exists in the first place, nor is the reason that it seems to continue clear, despite all that has been published about it.

## Turn-of-the-Calendar Effect

Another interesting anomaly deals with calendar turning points. A study by Keim[30] finds that over a period of time, the bulk of the return comes from the last trading day of the month and the first few days of the following month. For the rest of the month, the ups and downs approximately cancel out.

## Persistence of Technical Analysis

*Technical analysis* refers to any technique in which past security prices or other publicly available information is employed to predict future prices. Market efficiency tests, especially those dealing with the weak form, have routinely found that investors cannot profitably exploit any evidence of market inefficiency after including

[29]See, for instance, Michael Gibbons and Patrick Hess, "Day-of-the-Week Effects and Asset Returns," *Journal of Business*, October 1981, 579–596; and Donald Keim and Robert F. Stambaugh, "A Further Investigation of the Weekend Effect in Stock Prices," *Journal of Finance*, July 1984, 819–835.

[30]Donald B. Keim, "Trading Patterns, Bid-Ask Spreads, and Estimated Security Returns: The Case of Common Stocks at Calendar Turning Points," *Journal of Financial Economics*, November 1989, 75–98.

the effects of transaction costs. Still, an immense amount of literature appears each year based in varying degrees on technical techniques that, if the EMH is true, should be useless.

Even finance professors seem less than totally committed to the EMH paradigm. In one national survey, 40 percent of the respondents with doctorates in finance believed that advance/decline lines (a popular tool of the technical analyst) were "useful" or "very useful." One-fourth agreed that "charts enhance investment performance."[31]

It is safe to say that we do not fully understand the theory or practice of technical analysis. Its techniques are generally imprecise and do not lend themselves to rigorous statistical testing. Certain phenomena from the clinical psychology literature seem to be at least partially operative in the stock market.[32] At a casino craps table, for instance, shooters throw the dice harder when trying for a high number. Low numbers, of course, require an easier toss. Although the random number that occurs and the strength of the toss obviously have no connection, a psychological illusion of control exists. Similarly, humans suffer from hindsight bias. With trading techniques, people tend to remember their successes and repress their failures. The author once had a neighbor who owned two hundred shares of a common stock. He was a graduate student, and this was his only investment. On days when the stock was up a point, he would brag, "I made $200 today." On days when the stock was down, he said nothing. Later, when the stock rose a point again, in his view, he "made another $200." He made that same $200 many times.[33]

## Chaos Theory

*For an interesting series on chaos theory see* www.mathjmendal.org/chaos/

At recent finance conferences, a few researchers have presented studies on *chaos theory* as applied to the stock market. **Chaos theory** is a growing field in physics that studies instances in which apparently random behavior is, in fact, quite systematic or even deterministic. This theory already has applications in weather prediction, population growth forecasts, and fisheries biology. As an example of the latter application, it is not true that a given volume of ocean water, left free from human interference, will reach an equilibrium population of the various fish species that inhabit it. As the fish grow and get bigger, they consume the smaller fry (of their own or a different species) in increasing numbers. Fewer young fish are left to mature; this, coupled with the natural death of the older fish, eventually results in a sudden drastic reduction in fish population, causing dismay to those who fish and excitement in the local media. At the same time, this phenomenon results in reduced predation and food competition by the surviving fry, so the population begins to grow dramatically, and the cycle continues. Interactions between species add complexity to the process.

Many physicists have found that they can ply their trade in Wall Street's most prestigious investment houses. Someone coined the term econophysics to refer to the application of physics principles in the analysis of stock market behavior. *Risk* magazine reports on a French investment fund with an automated investment strategy based in part on the studies of turbulence in wind tunnels. One of the principals

---

[31]Robert A. Strong, "A Behavioral Investigation of Three Paradigms in Finance," *Northeast Journal of Business and Economics*, Spring/Summer 1988, 1–28.

[32]George Racette and Susan Worcester, "Possible Psychological Explanations for the Persistence of Technical Analysis," paper presented at the annual meeting of the Financial Management Association, Denver, 9–12 October 1985.

[33]This is a good example of someone getting nonfinancial utility from his investments.

## PORTFOLIO MEMO

### Investor Irrationality

The notion of market efficiency assumes that investors behave rationally. That is, they prefer more return to less, less risk to more, and will not purchase a dominated security. In practice, good evidence suggests that investors are routinely overconfident and that this overconfidence generates some pricing momentum for growth stocks. Daniel and Titman provide some evidence on this subject. They propose that although investors use analytical methods, they also employ subjective hunches and act on gut feeling.*

Clinical psychologists note the *illusion of control* phenomenon at play in the stock market. People like to believe they are influencing events even when they clearly are not. The winning lottery number, for instance, is purely a random variable. Many lottery ticket vending machines provide an option for the machine to randomly select numbers, or the buyer can choose them. Very few people choose the random option; they want to pick their own numbers. Statistically, the winning number is completely independent of how the purchaser picks it. Similarly, market efficiency suggests that charting will not work; successive price changes are independent. Charts are appealing, however, and they give some people the sense that they are influencing their investment performance.

*Kent Daniel and Sheridan Titman, "Market Efficiency in an Irrational World," *Financial Analysts Journal*, November/December 1999, 28–40.

of the fund, Jean-Philippe Bouchaud, states, "It became clear that the velocity-velocity correlations found in wind tunnel experiments were similar, at least qualitatively, to the volatity-volatility correlations observed in financial markets."[34]

Attempts to find a pattern in stock market behavior have been associated with investments since the origin of the exchanges. There is much we do not know about how the market arrives at security prices, and chaos theory may eventually provide some partial answers. If the apparent randomness of security price changes can be shown to be nonrandom, much of the theory of finance would need revision.

## SUMMARY

The U.S. capital markets are extremely efficient, both informationally and operationally. They are the envy of much of the world, and many developing nations emulate them. They are not perfect, however. The vast number of securities traded on the exchanges, the rapid introduction of new financial products, and the globalization of world economies provide a fair but complicated financial battleground. Much about the markets, security pricing, and utility remains undiscovered.

Explanations will eventually emerge for the current anomalies, and any free lunches will disappear as they always have. One of the indirect societal benefits of security analysts and the activities of finance professors is that these people help keep the market efficient.

[34]Novroz Patel, "Econophysics—Does it Work?" *Risk*, March 2001, 32–34.

The capital markets serve three primary functions: economic, continuous pricing, and fair price.

The efficient market hypothesis (EMH) relates to informational efficiency and the fair price function, not to operational efficiency. The essence of the EMH is that so many people watch the marketplace that it is unlikely any individual can consistently make windfall profits by picking stocks better than the next person.

The EMH has three forms. The weak form says that past prices, or charts, are of no value in predicting future stock price performance. The semi-strong form says that security prices already fully reflect all relevant publicly available information. The strong form of the EMH extends the semi-strong form to include private, inside information as well. We know that insiders *can* make illegal profits, so this form of the EMH doesn't hold up.

The random walk theory does not state that security prices move randomly. Instead, it maintains that news arrives randomly and that, in accordance with the EMH, security prices rapidly adjust to the random arrival of news.

Anomalies are occurrences in the market that finance theory cannot explain. Stocks with low price/earnings ratios tend to show unusually higher returns; January is a good month for the stock market; and small firms tend to do better than large firms in January. Monday is a bad day for the stock market while Wednesdays and Friday have historically been good.

Technical analysis is diametrically opposed to the efficient market hypothesis, yet it has many advocates, including well-educated finance professors and practitioners. Chaos theory has the potential to explain at least partially some of these issues.

## QUESTIONS

1. If the stock market is efficient, what good is security analysis?
2. At a job interview with a Wall Street firm, you are asked if you believe in the efficient market hypothesis. How do you think you should answer this question?
3. What is the difference between the semi-strong form of the efficient market hypothesis and the semi-efficient market hypothesis?
4. How does the random walk notion tie in with the concept of market efficiency?
5. Make up a question that could be tested via a runs test.
6. Why is charting inconsistent with the weak form of the efficient market hypothesis?
7. Explain the difference between *informational* and *operational* efficiency.
8. Explain the difference between the *continuous pricing* function and the *fair price* function of capital markets.
9. How can finance professors justify their general criticism of technical analysis techniques (such as charting) when so many members of the investment community practice these methods?
10. Suppose that you estimate beta for a stock over an extended period, and your regression results yield a statistically positive intercept. Does this contradict the efficient market hypothesis?
11. What role do commissions play in a test of market efficiency?
12. What information do you think the price/earnings ratio provides? Should it be high, low, or in between?

13. Suppose a stock sells for $2.50. Do you have any preconceptions about this firm based just on the price?
14. What implications do you think the small firm effect has for modern portfolio management?
15. Someone decides to conduct a test of the January effect. Would this be a weak form test or a strong form test of the efficient market hypothesis?
16. In a Goldman Sachs research publication entitled *Making the Most of Value and Growth Investing*, the report states that "the excess returns from value stocks tend to follow a period of significant underperformance, making early identification and purchase of value stocks counterproductive as a general strategy."
Explain why the early purchase of value stocks might be counterproductive.

17. FROM THE 1993 LEVEL I CFA EXAM:

**a.** List and briefly describe the three *forms* of the Efficient Market Hypothesis.

**(6 minutes)**

**b.** Discuss the role of a portfolio manager in a perfectly efficient market.

**(9 minutes)**

18. FROM THE 1995 LEVEL II CFA EXAM:

**a.** Briefly explain the concept of the *efficient market hypothesis* (EMH) and each of its three forms—*weak, semistrong, and strong*—and briefly discuss the degree to which existing empirical evidence supports each of the three forms of the EMH.

**(8 minutes)**

**b.** Briefly discuss the implications of the efficient market hypothesis for investment policy as it applies to:

i. technical analysis in the form of charting, and
ii. fundamental analysis

**(4 minutes)**

**c.** Briefly explain *two* major roles or responsibilities of portfolio managers in an efficient market environment.

**(4 minutes)**

**d.** Briefly discuss whether active asset allocation among countries could consistently outperform a world market index. Include a discussion of the implications of *integration versus segmentation* of international financial markets as it pertains to portfolio diversification, but ignore the issue of stock selection.

**(6 minutes)**

## PROBLEMS

1. A psychic reader guesses "red" or "black" as fifteen cards are drawn from a deck. His success rate follows (R = right; W = wrong):

R R R W R R W W R R R R W R W

Test his accuracy using a runs test.

2. Follow the Dow Jones Industrial Average for one month, and do a runs test on up days versus down days. What do you conclude from your results?
3. OEX is the ticker symbol for the S&P 100 stock index. You can download free historical values of the OEX index at *http://quote.yahoo.com*. Select fifty days beginning as near your birthday as possible. Do a runs test on up versus down days.
4. Collect information from the Dividend News section of *The Wall Street Journal* for twenty NYSE–listed stocks. Also collect their betas from the Internet. On the ex-dividend date for each of your securities, calculate the actual percentage change in the stock price, the percentage change in the S&P 500 index, and the percentage change in stock price predicted by the securities' betas. Investigate whether or not it would have been profitable to buy the stock on the day prior to the ex-dividend date.
5. Using historical data on an actively traded, volatile stock such as Microsoft or Intel, see whether you can find any evidence to support the "retracement levels" claim reported in the chapter's Portfolio Memo on Fibonacci numbers. (This is done best by preparing a graph of the stock price behavior over the period and then visually identifying a likely time period to investigate.)

## INTERNET EXERCISE

Conduct a technical analysis of any stock of your choice at *http://www.traders.com*. Use whatever techniques you wish to, but explain your logic. Also compare a 100-day exponential moving average to a 10-day EMA. Does the stock seem more or less attractive when you consider the longer period?

## FURTHER READING

Ambachtsheer, Keith P. "Active Management That Adds Value: Reality or Illusion?" *Journal of Portfolio Management*, Fall 1994, 89–93.

Arbel, Avner. "Generic Stocks: The Key to Market Anomalies." *Journal of Portfolio Management*, Summer 1985, 4–13.

Arbel, Avner, Steven Carvell, and Paul Strebel. "Giraffes, Institutions, and Neglected Firms." *Financial Analysts Journal*, May/June 1983, 57–63.

Arbel, Avner, and Paul Strebel, "The Neglected and Small Firm Effect." *Financial Review*, November 1982, 201–218.

———. "Pay Attention to Neglected Firms." *Journal of Portfolio Management*, Winter 1983, 37–42.

Arnott, Robert, and Todd Miller. "Surprise! TAA Can Work in Quiet Markets." *Journal of Investing*, Fall 1997, 33–45.

Banz, R. "The Relationship Between Return and Market Value of Common Stock." *Journal of Financial Economics*, March 1981, 3–18.

Barber, Brad, Reuven Lehavy, Maureen McNichols, and Brett Trueman. "Can Investors Profit from the Prophets? Security Analyst Recommendations and Stock Returns." *Journal of Finance*, April 2001, 531–563.

Basu, S. "The Information Content of Price-Earnings Ratios." *Financial Management*, Summer 1975, 53–64.

———. "Investment Performance of Common Stocks in Relation to Their Price-Earnings Ratios: A Test of the Efficient Market Hypothesis." *Journal of Finance*, June 1977, 663–682.

Baytas, Ahmet and Nusret Cakici. "Do Stocks Really Provide the Highest Return in the Long Run?" *Journal of Investing*, Fall 1999, 89–96.

Beard, Craig G., and Richard W. Sias. "Is There a Neglected-Firm Effect?" *Financial Analysts Journal*, September/October 1997, 19–23.

Black, Fisher, Michael Jensen, and Myron Scholes. "The Capital Asset Pricing Model: Some Empirical Tests." In *Studies in Theory of Capital Markets*, ed. M.C. Jensen. New York: Praeger, 1972.

Bogle, John C. "Whether Markets Are More Efficient or Less Efficient, Costs Matter," *CFA Magazine*, Nov–Dec 2003, 6–7.

Breen, William. "Low Price-Earnings Ratios and Industry Relatives." *Financial Analysts Journal*, July/August 1968, 125–127.

Brown, Keith C., and W.V. Harlow. "Market Overreaction: Magnitude and Intensity." *Journal of Portfolio Management*, Winter 1988, 6–13.

Chen, N., R. Roll, and S. Ross. "Economic Forces and the Stock Market," *Journal of Business*, July 1986, 383–403.

Cornell, Bradford. "Is the Response of Analysts to Information Consistent with Fundamental Valuation? The Case of Intel." *Financial Management*, Spring 2001, 113–136.

Daniel, Kent, and Sheridan Titman. "Market Efficiency in an Irrational World." *Financial Analysts Journal*, November/December 1999, 28–40.

De Bondt, Werner F.M., and Richard H. Thaler. "Does the Stock Market Overreact?" *Journal of Finance*, July 1985, 793–805.

———. "Further Evidence on Investor Overreaction and Stock Market Seasonality." *Journal of Finance*, July 1987, 557–581.

Fabozzi, Frank J., Christopher K. Ma, William T. Chittenden, and R. Daniel Pace. "Predicting Intraday Price Reversals." *Journal of Portfolio Management*, Winter 1995, 42–53.

Fama, Eugene, "Random Walks in Stock Market Prices," *Financial Analysts Journal*, Nov/Dec 1965, 55–59.

French, Kenneth. "Stock Returns and the Weekend Effect." *Journal of Financial Economics*, March 1980, 55–69.

Fritzmeier, L.H. "Relative Price Fluctuation of Industrial Stocks in Different Price Groups." *Journal of Business*, April 1936, 113–154.

Gibbons, Michael, and Patrick Hess. "Day of the Week Effects and Asset Returns." *Journal of Business*, October 1981, 579–596.

Janjigian, Vahan. "*Forbes* Special Situation Survey: A Study in Market Efficiency." *Journal of Investing*, Summer 1997, 65–70.

Jegadeesh, Narasimhan. "Evidence of Predictable Behavior of Security Returns." *Journal of Finance*, July 1990, 881–898.

Jensen, Gerald R., Robert R. Johnson, and Jeffrey M. Mercer. "The Inconsistency of Small-Firm and Value Stock Premiums." *Journal of Portfolio Management*, Winter 1998, 27–36.

Keim, Donald B. "Trading Patterns, Bid-Ask Spreads, and Estimated Security Returns: The Case of Common Stocks at Calendar Turning Points." *Journal of Financial Economics*, November 1989, 75–98.

———. and Robert F. Stambaugh. "A Further Investigation of the Weekend Effect in Stock Prices. *Journal of Finance*, July 1984, 819–835.

Kim, Sun-Woong. "Capitalizing on the Weekend Effect." *Journal of Portfolio Management*, Spring 1988, 59–63.

Larson, Glen A., Jr. and Gregory D. Wozniak. "Market Timing Can Work in the Real World." *Journal of Portfolio Management*, Spring 1995, 74–81.

Lintner, J. "Security Prices, Risk and Maximal Gains from Diversification." *Journal of Finance*, December 1965, 587–615.

Lo, Andrew M., and A. Craig MacKinlay. "Data-Snooping Biases in Tests of Financial Asset Pricing Models." *Review of Financial Studies*, Winter 1990, 431–468.

McWilliams, James D. "Prices, Earnings, and P-E Ratios." *Financial Analysts Journal*, May/June 1966, 137–142.

Miller, Edward. "Why a Weekend Effect?" *Journal of Portfolio Management*, Summer 1988, 43–48.

Nicholson, Francis. "Price-Earnings Ratios," *Financial Analysts Journal*, July/August 1960, 43–45.

———. "Price Ratios in Relation to Investment Results," *Financial Analysts Journal*, January/February 1968, 105–109.

Peavy, John W. III, and David A. Goodman "The Significance of P/Es for Portfolio Returns." *Journal of Portfolio Management*, Winter 1983, 43–47.

Reinganum, Marc R. "Abnormal Returns in Small Firm Portfolios." *Financial Analysts Journal*, March/April 1981, 52–56.

———. "Misspecification of Capital Asset Pricing: Empirical Anomalies Based on Earnings' Yields and Market Values," *Journal of Financial Economics* 9, no. 1, 1981, 19–46.

———. "Portfolio Strategies for Small Caps vs. Large." *Journal of Portfolio Management*, Winter 1983, 29–36.

Rogalski, Richard, and Seha M. Tinic. "The January Size Effect: Anomaly or Risk Mismeasurement?" *Financial Analysts Journal*, November/December 1986, 63–70.

Roll, Richard. "Vas ist Das?" *Journal of Portfolio Management*, Winter 1983, 18–28.

———. "A Possible Explanation of the Small Firm Effect." *Journal of Finance*, September 1981, 879–888.

Stephenson, Kevin. "Just How Bad Are Economists At Predicting Interest Rates? (And What Are the Implications for Investors?)" *Journal of Investing*, Summer 1997, 8–10.

Strong, Robert A. "Do Share Price and Stock Splits Matter?" *Journal of Portfolio Management*, Fall 1983, 58–64.

# 9 Picking the Equity Players

*You buy a stock, and when it goes up, you sell it.*
*If it doesn't go up, don't buy it.*

**Will Rogers**

## Key Terms

blue chip
cash dividend
cyclical stock
defensive stock
dividend discount model
dividend reinvestment plan
forward split
fundamental analyst
growth investor
growth stock
income stock
multi-stage dividend discount model
odd lot-generating split
payout ratio
penny stock
property dividend
required rate of return
retention ratio
reverse split
signaling
speculative stock
spin-off
stock dividend
stock split
street name
technical analyst

## Introduction

This is a book about portfolio construction and management. As stated in Chapter 1, today's focus in investments is away from individual security analysis and toward the overall characteristics of the portfolio. Harry Markowitz showed how proper security selection enables the portfolio manager to reduce risk without sacrificing expected return. This book leaves detailed coverage of the many aspects of security analysis to other texts. This chapter and the next review important principles behind the security selection process that are especially relevant in the construction and management of a portfolio.

Confusion can arise when people use familiar investment terms incorrectly. One objective of this chapter is to explain the principal categories of common stock, especially the investment characteristics that make a category of stock suitable for one portfolio but not for another. This chapter also looks at dividends and the reason dividend checks do not increase the shareholders' wealth. Many people who should know better misunderstand this important point.

## Stock Selection Philosophy: Fundamental and Technical Analysis

There are two schools of thought in the business of stock picking. A **fundamental analyst** tries to discern the logical worth of a security based on its anticipated earnings stream. To do this, the analyst considers the firm's financial statements, industry conditions, and prospects for the economy. The analyst may find an outstanding company, call it XYZ, with excellent management and good future prospects but still not recommend it for purchase because the current stock price is too high. It may be attractive at $30 per share but not at $42.

The **technical analyst** thinks the financial statements and market conditions are of secondary importance. What matters is the price that people are willing to pay. Who is to say that XYZ is not worth $42 if that is what people are currently paying for it? The technical analyst is firmly convinced that supply and demand determine prices, that changes in supply and demand cause changes in prices, and that the changes in supply and demand can be predicted by observing the past series of stock prices.

A brokerage firm with a research capability usually has both types of analysts on its staff. Security analysis is a fascinating subject about which much is written, but, as stated earlier, this is not the focus of this book. This chapter is limited to several especially important aspects of individual stock characteristics and price behavior.

## Dividends and Why They Really Do Not Matter

By law, if a company pays dividends, it must pay them in proportion to the number of shares a person owns in that company. The holder of 200 shares of Harley Davidson, for example, will receive twice as many dividends as the holder of 100 shares.

A corporate distribution for which this is not the case is a *gift*. For instance, at one time Wrigleys sent one carton of Juicy Fruit chewing gum to each of its shareholders regardless of the number of shares they held. Because everyone received the same amount, the gum was a gift.

### *Types of Dividends*

Corporations may pay three types of dividends to their shareholders: *cash dividends* (the most common kind), *stock dividends*, and *property dividends*.

**Cash Dividends.** Most firms have an established dividend payment schedule through which a portion of the firm's profits are returned to the shareholders. These dividends may be received as **cash dividends** (via a check from the company), or they can sometimes be reinvested in additional shares of stock in the firm. This latter option occurs via a **dividend reinvestment plan** (DRIP), which always provides for the purchase of fractional shares and sometimes allows shareholders to buy these shares at a slight discount from the prevailing market price.

Securities may be held in your name or in a **street name.**[1] If you buy stock registered in a street name, your name is not on the stock certificate; it bears the name

[1]A *street name* refers to a "Wall Street" name. Instead of actually taking receipt of stock certificates, most investors choose to receive a monthly statement showing the securities the brokerage firm holds for them. "Merrill Lynch" appears on the stock certificate rather than "Sally Jones."

PORTFOLIO MEMO

## Good Companies and Good Investments

Many investors recognize that there is a difference between a good *company* and a good *investment*. They evaluate a stock the same way they evaluate any other purchase: See if the value received is worth the price paid.

You might be shopping for a new winter coat and find one that catches your eye. The styling appeals to you, the fabric is wonderful, and the brand has a good reputation. The $400 price tag, however, turns you off. It may be a great piece of clothing, but you are not going to pay that much for it. Conversely, you may be in a bargain discount store and buy some smoke-damaged goods dirt cheap. The quality is not there, but the price is right.

This is exactly what should happen in the stock market. Someone might sing the praises of a company because of its excellent working conditions, high-quality products, and future promise: You hear it described as a "good company." You cannot tell if it is a good investment, however, until you see the stock price. Many folks learned this lesson the hard way during the dot.com bubble a few years ago; few stocks are really worth a price/earnings ratio of 200. Similarly, in the investment community, plenty of bottom fishers are always on the lookout for beaten-down stocks that are selling for bargain prices.

In the behavioral finance literature, this phenomenon is an example of the "representativeness heuristic." People tend to think a good company represents a good investment.

of a Wall Street firm. Your brokerage firm holds the shares, and allocates the one large dividend check it gets on behalf of perhaps thousands of individual shareholders. Most brokerage firms automatically transfer any excess cash in an account into a money market fund of some type. This is a good arrangement because it reduces to a minimum the unproductive time for the dividends.

If, instead, the portfolio manager receives dividend checks directly, she needs a temporary haven for these funds until they accumulate sufficiently to finance the purchase of more securities or until they are paid as income to the fund beneficiary. Most portfolio managers have some money market instrument available for this purpose.

*A list of recent corporate dividend announcements is at* http://www.stocksmart.com

**Stock Dividends.** **Stock dividends** are paid in additional shares of stock rather than in cash. Firms typically announce these as a percentage, such as a "10 percent stock dividend." This means that if you hold 1,000 shares, you would receive an additional stock certificate for 100 shares. The person who holds 100 shares will get 10 more.

If you hold an odd lot, you will receive a check for the value of the fractional shares that cannot be distributed. You might, for instance, hold 221 shares. A 10 percent stock dividend would result in your receiving an additional 22 shares and a small check for the value of the remaining 1/10 share.

*Stock dividends are often paid to placate shareholders when the firm is unable to pay cash dividends.*

It is not completely clear why firms issue stock dividends, but we do know several things about them. First, they are popular when a firm lacks the funds to pay a cash dividend. They are especially common in the infancy or adolescent stages of a firm's life cycle. Second, many shareholders seem to like them. It is common for a firm to establish a regular pattern of paying both a cash dividend and a stock dividend.

**Property Dividends.** As the name implies, a **property dividend** is the distribution of physical goods (such as a firm's products) to shareholders, with each shareholder receiving an amount proportional to his stock holding. Property dividends are rare. They were more popular in the early days of our capital markets, when the number of shareholders in a particular company was likely to be small and the company produced something that could conveniently be distributed.

**Spin-Offs.** In some respects, a **spin-off** is like a property dividend. With a spin-off, a parent firm divests itself of a subsidiary, but rather than selling the subsidiary to some other firm, it distributes all shares in the subsidiary proportionally to the parent firm's shareholders. In effect, the parent has given away the subsidiary, and the shareholders are free to keep or sell the shares as they see fit.

Britain's Cadbury Schweppes (CSG, *NYSE*), for instance, is the parent company of Snapple. People who own shares of Cadbury indirectly are part owners of Snapple. CSG's management could decide it wanted out of the fruit drink business, and, instead of selling the subsidiary, could give it away to the Cadbury shareholders to sell themselves if they so desired. This would be a spin-off. In this case, each CSG shareholder would receive a Snapple stock certificate in the mail, or her broker would receive them on her behalf. The number of shares each stockholder received would be determined by her percentage holding of the Cadbury Schweppes stock.

Like property dividends, spin-offs are rare. When they do occur, the portfolio manager considers the investment merits of keeping the new stock or selling it and using the proceeds for some other purpose.

**Rights.** Shareholders sometimes have the ability to maintain the same percentage share of ownership in a corporation whenever the firm sells new shares to the public.[2] This is their preemptive right. If this privilege exists, the firm gives existing shareholders rights to buy any new shares offered by the company. These rights allow shareholders to buy the new stock at an advantageous price; they function like store coupons. If shareholders have the coupons, they can buy at a discount from the market price.

*Rights usually expire within a few weeks of issuance.*

Rights are actual securities that investors can buy or sell. They have a limited life, however, usually expiring a few weeks after they are issued. Figure 9-1 is an example of a right that expired on December 30, 1926.

When shareholders receive rights, they can do three things with them. They can sell the rights to someone else, they can use them to buy more shares, or they can allow them to expire. The last option is inappropriate because it amounts to throwing away money. Rights are valuable and should be exercised if the shareholder wants more stock. Otherwise, the shareholder should sell them.

With the proliferation of online trading, many investors do not have a handholding stockbroker watching over their accounts. Rights show up in their accounts with an accompanying instruction letter in the mail. These are confusing securities to many investors, and too often people decide to deal with the matter later. Rights usually have a life of just a few weeks; after that, their value is lost and cannot be recovered. If, instead, the account is with a full service brokerage firm and the investor has securities registered in a street name, the rights will be sent to the brokerage house, and a broker will make sure that customers do not inadvertantly allow them to expire.

---

[2]The corporate charter might provide that the shares trade *without* preemptive rights. This is becoming increasingly common and in some states is the default option in boilerplate corporate charter documents.

**FIGURE 9-1** A Sample Stock Right (Fractional Subscription Warrant)

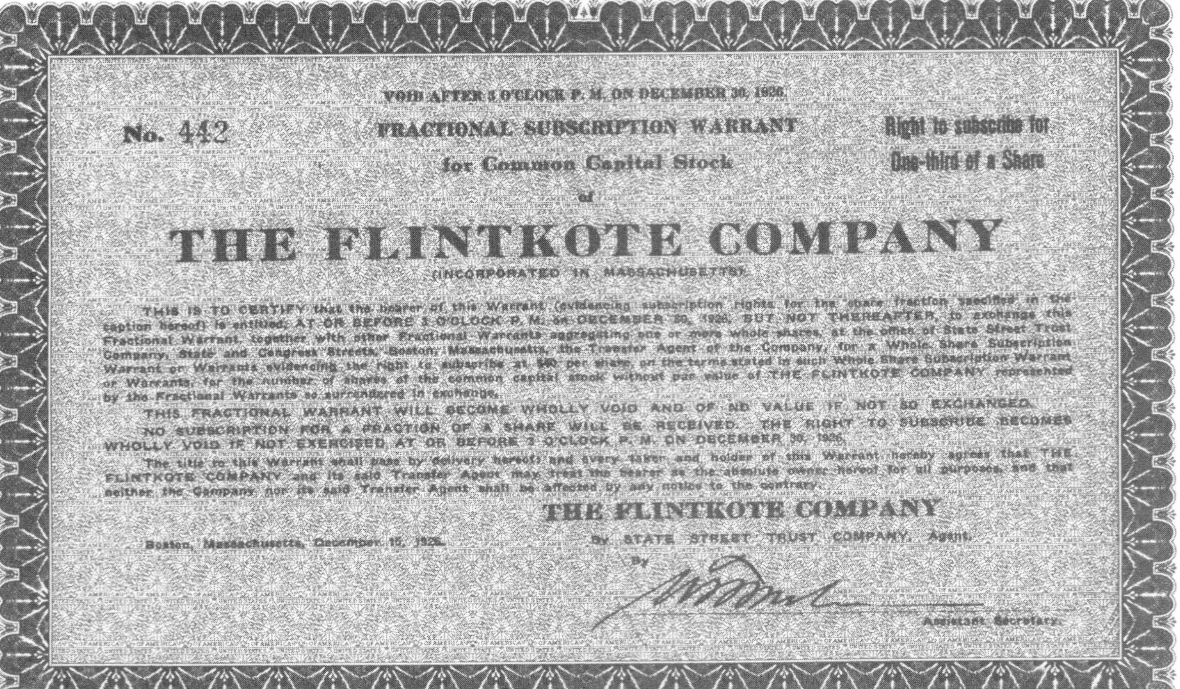

VOID AFTER 3 O'CLOCK P. M. ON DECEMBER 30, 1926.

No. 442

FRACTIONAL SUBSCRIPTION WARRANT
for Common Capital Stock
of

Right to subscribe for
One-third of a Share

THE FLINTKOTE COMPANY
(INCORPORATED IN MASSACHUSETTS)

THIS IS TO CERTIFY that the bearer of this Warrant (evidencing subscription rights for the share fraction specified in the caption hereof) is entitled, AT OR BEFORE 3 O'CLOCK P. M. on DECEMBER 30, 1926, BUT NOT THEREAFTER, to exchange this Fractional Warrant, together with other Fractional Warrants aggregating one or more whole shares, at the office of State Street Trust Company, State and Congress Streets, Boston, Massachusetts, the Transfer Agent of the Company, for a Whole Share Subscription Warrant or Warrants evidencing the right to subscribe at $40 per share, on the terms stated in such Whole Share Subscription Warrant or Warrants, for the number of shares of the common capital stock without par value of THE FLINTKOTE COMPANY represented by the Fractional Warrants so surrendered in exchange.

THIS FRACTIONAL WARRANT WILL BECOME WHOLLY VOID AND OF NO VALUE IF NOT SO EXCHANGED.

NO SUBSCRIPTION FOR A FRACTION OF A SHARE WILL BE RECEIVED. THE RIGHT TO SUBSCRIBE BECOMES WHOLLY VOID IF NOT EXERCISED AT OR BEFORE 3 O'CLOCK P. M. ON DECEMBER 30, 1926.

The title to this Warrant shall pass by delivery hereof; and every taker and holder of this Warrant hereby agrees that THE FLINTKOTE COMPANY and its said Transfer Agent may treat the bearer as the absolute owner hereof for all purposes, and that neither the Company nor its said Transfer Agent shall be affected by any notice to the contrary.

THE FLINTKOTE COMPANY

Boston, Massachusetts, December 15, 1926.

By STATE STREET TRUST COMPANY, Agent.

By

Assistant Secretary.

AMERICAN BANK NOTE COMPANY.

**Dividend Growth Rates.** Corporations like to establish a predictable dividend payout pattern to include an annual increase in the dollar amount of the dividend. Some people feel that predictable dividends help reduce the uncertainty surrounding the future cash flows to which shareholders are entitled. The dividend growth rate is an important variable used by many fundamental analysts; these are people who seek to determine value by studying the financial statements and other information about a firm that would logically influence its value.

A share of stock potentially has an infinite life. If the dividends increase by a known percentage rate each year, we can value a stock as a growing perpetuity. We cannot use the ordinary present/future value tables for a growing perpetuity, but fortunately a mathematical identity makes the task a simple one. Equation 9-1 shows a famous relationship known as the **dividend discount model:**

$$P_0 = \frac{D_0(1+g)}{k-g} = \frac{D_1}{k-g} \tag{9-1}$$

In this equation, $D_0$ is the current dividend; $D_1$ is the dividend to be paid next year; $g$ is the expected dividend growth rate; and $k$ is the discount factor according to the riskiness of the stock. $P_0$ is the current stock price (the stock price at time 0).

**TABLE 9-1** SAMPLE STOCK INFORMATION

| *Dividend History* | | | | | | | |
|---|---|---|---|---|---|---|---|
| **2004** | **2003** | **2002** | **2001** | **2000** | **1999** | **1998** | **1997** |
| 0.81 | 0.77 | 0.73 | 0.64 | 0.57 | 0.49 | 0.42 | 0.36 |

Current stock price = $37.48

The model assumes that the dividend stream is perpetual and the long-term growth rate is constant.[3]

You can use the dividend discount model to get an idea of how risky the market thinks a particular stock is at the moment. In Equation 9-1, you can observe the current stock price and the current dividend. You can calculate the historic dividend growth rate and observe analysts' estimates of its future long-term value. From these values you can form an estimate of the future growth rate. The one variable you cannot observe is the discount rate, $k$. You can calculate this value, however, if you know the other variables in the equation.

Suppose we have collected the Table 9-1 dividend history on General Electric. We can rearrange Equation 9-1 to get the following:

$$k = \frac{D_0(1+g)}{P_0} + g \tag{9-2}$$

*Dividend growth rates should be calculated using the geometric mean rather than the arithmetic mean.*

Before solving for $k$, we need to determine the dividend growth rate, $g$. We can start by computing the historical growth rate. There is a right and a wrong way to do this. The wrong way is to take the arithmetic average of the seven annual percentage changes in dividends. (Recall the discussion in Chapter 2 showing that the arithmetic average of a set of percentages is not always a useful statistic.) The rate that connects a beginning value with an ending value is a geometric mean; this is the rate a financial calculator will produce from its time value of money functions.

We want to know the growth rate that, when applied to a starting value of $0.36 (the 1997 dividend), will result in an ending value of $0.81 (the 2004 dividend). Here is the general equation for solving such a problem:

$$D_0(1+g)^n = D_n \tag{9-3}$$

Using our dividend data,

$$0.36(1+g)^7 = 0.81$$

Rearranging,

$$\begin{aligned}(1+g)^7 &= 0.81/0.36 = 2.2500\\ 1+g &= \sqrt[7]{2.2500} = 1.1228\\ g &= 12.28\%\end{aligned}$$

Over the past seven years, the dividend growth rate has been 12.28%.

[3]The dividend discount model assumes that the long-term growth rate is constant, but the periodic growth rate can vary. If the dividend growth rate were to be constant and known, there would be no uncertainty about the stock's price, and consequently no risk. An investment that bears no risk, however, should earn only the riskless rate.

PORTFOLIO MEMO

## Analysts' Growth Rate Estimates

Many firms publish their security analysts' estimates of future growth rates for revenue and earnings. According to financial theory, if a firm's dividend payout ratio remains constant, in the long run a firm's earnings growth and dividend growth are identical. Several firms collect these analyst estimates and publish consensus figures. First Call, I/B/E/S, and Zacks are the best-known. (I/B/E/S, the Institutional Brokerage Estimate System, is now part of First Call.)

Suppose an investor is following General Electric (*GE, NYSE*), a retail grocery store chain. At the First Call Website* he finds the following long-term growth rate estimates:

| *# Analysts* | *High* | *Low* | *Median* |
|---|---|---|---|
| 7 | 15.00% | 7.30% | 10.00% |

This shows that seven analysts have published estimates. (Many other analysts are likely following GE, but they do not forecast the growth rate.) The estimates range from a low of 7.30 percent to a high of 15.00 percent, with a median of 10.00 percent. The investor plans to use these forecasts in conjunction with the actual historical data to come up with his own estimate for use in the dividend discount model.

*A good source for this information is the "estimates" tab at *http://money.cnn.com*. that appears after getting a stock quote.

The Portfolio Memo shows that the median analyst estimate for General Electric's long-term growth rate is 10.00 percent, a rate below the historical rate from the past seven years. It always makes sense to consider reasons why the past may not be representative of the future. Doing a little more math, we find the historical rate from the past five years is 10.58 percent, a value closer to the median analyst estimate. Given this, suppose we settle on a projected dividend growth rate of 10.5 percent for valuation purposes. With the current stock price of $37.48 we can solve for $k$:

$$k = \frac{0.81(1.105)}{37.48} + 0.105$$

$$k = 0.1289 = 12.89\%$$

The variable $k$ is sometimes called the shareholders' **required rate of return.**

Sometimes it is reasonable to expect a firm's earnings to grow dramatically for a few years followed by more "normal" behavior subsequently. An analyst may, for instance, expect dividends to grow at 15 percent for the next three years, followed by a sustained 4 percent growth rate. Time value of money calculations can easily accommodate such an event. The valuation equation would look like this:

$$P_0 = \frac{D_0(1+.15)}{1+k} + \frac{D_0(1+.15)^2}{(1+k)^2} + \frac{D_0(1+.15)^3}{(1+k)^3} + \frac{\frac{D_0(1+.15)^3(1+.04)}{k-.04}}{(1+k)^3}$$

Such a model is a **multi-stage dividend discount model.** The final term in this equation is just the perpetual DCF model discounted back three years.

### *Why Dividends Do Not Matter*

When people are first told that dividends do not matter, they are skeptical. How can a check that they can cash and spend not matter?

Suppose I appear before a group of thirty skeptical finance students and announce that I am about to prove that dividends do not matter. I produce a shoe box, set it on the table in front of me but do not show the contents (if any). I do, however, get an outsider to verify that there is nothing "bad" in the box. This is essentially the role of an outside auditor. As the students watch, I count out one hundred $1 bills into the shoe box. Now I place a lid on the box and announce that I intend to terminate my ownership interest in the shoe box by "going public" and issuing 100 shares. If a student buys all 100 shares, she will own the entire "company." Naturally, I want to sell my company for as much as I can, but the marketplace will determine how much the box is worth. Each share must be worth at least $1. If it were worth less, a riskless profit would exist because a buyer could be certain of receiving the $100 (at least) contents of the box for less than this amount.

In practice, the shares will sell at a slight premium over $1, but suppose that the students are leery of this bizarre exercise and will pay only $1 exactly for a share. Some students buy one share, others buy more, and some will not buy any. Collectively, though, they acquire all 100 shares. I take the $100 they paid, issue them shares, and no longer own the shoe box or its contents.

Now the board of directors of the shoe box decides to pay a cash dividend of 10 cents per share. Our outside auditor reaches into the box, takes out ten $1 bills, exchanges them for two rolls of dimes, and proceeds to distribute the dimes to the students according to the number of shares they own. Folks who bought one share get one dime; those who bought five shares get five dimes. The 100 dimes are distributed this way.

How will the marketplace view this activity? Will the shares in the shoe box still command a price of $1? They will not, of course, because there may be only $90 left in the box; the students do not know precisely *what* is in the box, but they know that its value is less now than it was before the payment of the dividend. Similarly, an investor may not know exactly what he is going to get when he buys shares of stock in a real company, but he does know that the firm is worth less after it distributes cash.

*Paying dividends reduces the amount in a firm's checking account, and hence the shares are worth less.*

What will happen is that the market price of the shoe box shares will fall by the amount of the dividend. Shares that previously sold for $1 will now sell for 90 cents. This is generally what happens in the real world. Dividends do not fall from the sky; they are real money paid from the firm's checking account. If the firm gives money away in this fashion, it is simply not worth as much after paying the money.

*"I simply don't understand it. Every time this stupid stock pays a dividend, its value goes down. You would think it would go up." A lament around ex-dividend days.*

I once heard a fellow say, "I don't understand it; every time this stupid stock pays a dividend, it goes down. You would think it would go up." He obviously had not heard the shoe box story.

*On the ex-dividend date, share prices tend to fall by about the amount of the dividend.*

The ex-dividend date determines whether or not you get the dividend; consequently, on the ex-dividend date the price of a share of stock tends to fall by about the amount of the dividend to be paid. Research into this question is also confounded by the fact that many other things affect the price of the stock, and it is difficult to isolate a pure dividend effect.

An extreme example further illustrates why the share price falls after the payment of a dividend. In late 1987, UAL Corporation (the parent of United Airlines) decided to sell its three nonairline subsidiaries: Hertz Car Rental, Hilton International Hotels, and Westin Hotels. This was an extraordinary transaction from an accounting point of view, and it resulted in a large, one-time cash inflow. The board of directors subsequently announced its intent to pay a $50 special dividend to the shareholders. With nearly 22 million shares outstanding, payment of such a dividend would result in a sizable reduction in the firm's assets, and the value of the firm would be expected to fall.[4]

### *Theory Versus Practice*

*Unexpected changes in dividends can result in significant price changes in the associated common stock.*

The shoe box example shows why dividends theoretically do not matter. The payment of dividends simply changes the form in which the investor holds wealth, from "shares" to "shares worth less and some cash." Dividend policy, however, is one of the many areas in finance about which a great deal is yet to be discovered. It is very important in practice, and unexpected changes in dividend policy can result in significant changes in the market price of the associated common stock.

The market continually reacts to new information, and it does so in rather efficient fashion, as we have seen. Dividend information is potentially as important as any other information. Sometimes a dividend announcement carries specific news, particularly when the dividend amount is different from what security analysts had expected.

We know that firms try to establish a regular dividend payout pattern. This makes the shares easier to analyze, reduces the uncertainty about cash flows associated with stock ownership, and consequently may cause analysts to reduce the discount rate they apply to the firm's shares. Lowering the discount rate makes the shares a more attractive investment. If management breaks the anticipated dividend pattern, the level of uncertainty might go up, and analysts may lower their opinion of the stock.

Even an increase in a dividend is not necessarily good news. Most firms increase their dividend on an annual basis, and the market *expects* this. If management does not increase the dividend as expected, the market views this as bad news. Reducing or omitting a dividend is a very bad signal. Firms avoid reducing dividends like the plague because of the penalty the market attaches to this signal of management's opinion about future prospects for the firm. Conversely, an increase in dividends above what the market expects is a good signal. We know firms do not like to cut their dividends, and they consequently would not raise them if they did not expect to be able to maintain this higher level forever.

---

[4]To reduce the tax liability that shareholders would face on receipt of such a large dividend, the firm ultimately decided to buy back some of its own shares at a premium price rather than pay the dividend. This enabled many shareholders to take advantage of the capital gains tax break in effect at the time.

PORTFOLIO MEMO

## When Dividends Do Matter

In the year 1715, after the death of King Louis XIV, France was in financial trouble. To government, a simple solution to budget problems is the holy grail. John Law, a Scottish economist, had an idea that we now know as the Mississippi Bubble. With luck and clever scheming, in August 1717 he acquired a controlling interest in the Mississippi Company by selling shares to the public and financing the purchase with government debt. The company had a monopoly on trade in the French colony of Louisiana, where visions of gold and silver were dancing in European speculators' heads. The shares promised an annual dividend yield of 120 percent. This means "invest $10, get $12 in income and still have the shares." Such a rate is clearly unsustainable, but financial sophistication was even less two centuries ago than it is today. John Law's promises caused the share value to rise dramatically. It did not take long for it to became apparent there was no gold in Louisiana, and the share value vanished as quickly as it appeared.

Signaling *is a general term that refers to the indirect transmission of stock information.*

A significant portion of the finance literature deals with **signaling,** a general term referring to information conveyed in indirect fashion. It is a challenging research area, and one about which we know relatively little. A significant body of literature deals with signaling as it relates to dividends. Given that a firm's board of directors should know as much about the true prospects for the firm as anyone, changes in payout patterns may provide clues as to how the board views these prospects. As stated, firms do not like to reduce their dividends, so presumably management raises dividends only when the firm anticipates being able to maintain this higher level.

An increasing number of firms choose not to pay dividends. Fama and French[5] report that from 1978 to 1999, the proportion of publicly traded firms paying dividends fell from 66.5 percent to 20.8 percent. Although the demographic characteristics of firms changed over this period (i.e., from smokestack to technology), the research finds that firms have a lower propensity to pay dividends. That is, after controlling for corporate characteristics, management today is less inclined to use cash for dividends than they were twenty years ago.

### *Stock Splits Versus Stock Dividends*

Stock splits and stock dividends occur frequently in investment portfolios. Still, widespread misinformation is associated with them. It is important to understand the mechanics of splits and why they are not windfall gains.

**Stock Splits.** A **stock split** occurs when a firm changes the number of shares of its capital stock without changing the aggregate value of these shares. A stock split is also generally a neutral occurrence; it clearly is not a windfall gain for the recipient.

Stock splits are either *forward splits* or *reverse splits*. In a **forward split** (also called a *regular way split* or a *direct split*), shareholders end up with more shares than

[5]Eugene Fama and Kenneth R. French, "Disappearing Dividends: Changing Firm Characteristics or Lower Propensity to Pay?" *Journal of Financial Economics*, April 2001, 3–43.

before the split. The vast majority of stock splits are of this type. Two-for-one splits are especially common. In such a split, the holder of 2,300 shares before the split will be credited with another 2,300, making the total holdings 4,600 shares. A **reverse split**, in contrast, reduces the number of existing shares. Reverse splits are stated as "1 for 5," "1 for 10," and so on. With a 1-for-10 split, the holder of 1,000 shares will be left with only 100. Reverse splits are rare. A study by J. Randall Woolridge and Donald R. Chambers found that from 1962 to 1981, the NYSE, AMEX, and over-the-counter firms combined declared only about twenty reverse splits per year.[6]

*To see the stock split announcements of the last week, visit* http://www.stocksmart.com/

Recently, however, there have been more. *The Wall Street Journal* reported that through the first half of 2001, at least 86 companies had submitted proxy filings for reverse splits[7]. Many of these were dot.coms, including Excite@Home, Egghead.com, and Tickets.com, whose stock prices were well off their previous highs. The *WSJ* columnist wrote, "If history is any guide, these efforts—which are designed to have both practical and psychological effects—usually fail to save struggling companies their ultra-depressed stocks."

Either type of split may be an **odd lot–generating split,** which is a stock split likely to result in many small investors holding odd lots. A 3-for-2 split would fall in this category. The holder of 100 shares would end up with 150, the holder of 300 with 450, and so on.

*The primary motivation for a stock split is usually a desire to reduce the share price.*

The primary motivation for stock splits is usually to reduce the price of the shares. There is some evidence of an optimum trading range for the value of common stock, although the jury is still out on this subject. Theoretically, the price of the stock is unimportant; the wealth represented by the stock is the issue. For example, 100 shares of a $100 stock should be worth just as much as 1,000 shares of a $10 stock.

We do know, however, that many investors shy away from "high-priced" stocks. People prefer to buy round lots, and higher per-share prices make this more difficult. If a firm's stock is selling for $100 and management decides this is too high, it can split the stock, perhaps 4-for-1, and reduce the share price to around $25. This lower price may attract investors who previously passed the security by because of its steep price.[8]

**Why Stock Splits Do Not Matter.** Like cash dividends, a stock split neither increases nor decreases an investor's wealth. This can be seen best via an analogy. Imagine a perfect pie made from Maine blueberries. Mom cuts the pie into fourths and intends to dish out a piece to you and each of your three friends. Would it make any difference if the pie were cut into eight pieces and each of you received two? In either case you have precisely the same amount of pie. It does not matter into how many pieces it is cut; you cannot increase the total amount available for consumption by increasing the number of pieces.

*You cannot increase the value of a firm by splitting its shares.*

The same is true with the value of the firm. Its ownership is represented by all the shares of stock. Simply doubling the number of shares does not change the company's value.[9] As a consequence, after the split the share price adjusts to reflect the

---

[6]J. Randall Woolridge and Donald R. Chambers, "Reverse Splits and Shareholder Wealth," *Financial Management*, Autumn 1983, 5–15.

[7]Aaron Elstein, "Reverse Splits Seldom Can Reverse Fortune," *The Wall Street Journal*, June 21, 2001, C17.

[8]One firm that is apparently not concerned about its share pricing being too high is Warren Buffett's firm Berkshire Hathaway. In December 2004 its NYSE–listed shares sold for about $84,300.

[9]If the firm increased the number of its shares by selling more, the value of the firm *would* increase. This is not the case with a stock split; no additional shares are sold.

stock split ratio. With a 2-for-1 split, the share price falls to approximately half. A portfolio that previously held 50,000 shares valued at $40 each will now own 100,000 shares worth $20 each. In each case the total value is $2,000,000.[10]

*Stock splits can be used to artificially alter share price.*

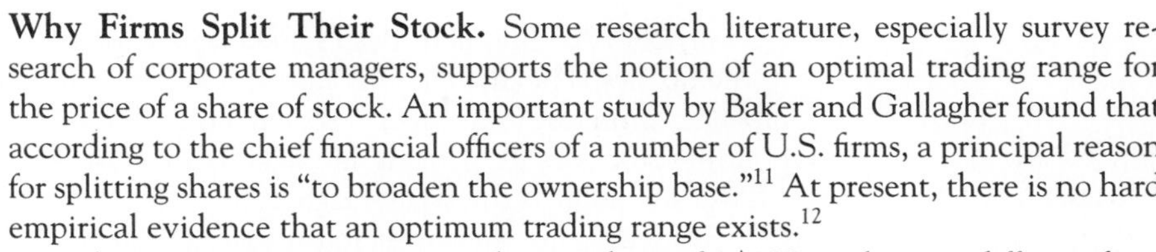

**Why Firms Split Their Stock.** Some research literature, especially survey research of corporate managers, supports the notion of an optimal trading range for the price of a share of stock. An important study by Baker and Gallagher found that according to the chief financial officers of a number of U.S. firms, a principal reason for splitting shares is "to broaden the ownership base."[11] At present, there is no hard empirical evidence that an optimum trading range exists.[12]

There is no economic reason why one share of a $100 stock is any different from 100 shares of a $1 stock, but many people believe that any stock selling for $1 per share must be risky or a loser. Similarly, some people will be uncomfortable paying $100 per share. As a consequence, firms sometimes use stock splits as a way to artificially alter their share price. If management believes that its current stock price of $120 scares off potential investors, the board of directors may choose to split the stock, perhaps 4-for-1, to reduce the price to the $30 range. A different company whose shares sold for $1 might have a 1-for-15 reverse split to raise the share price to $15.

Reverse splits are also occasionally used to reduce the number of outstanding shareholders. A large reverse split, such as 1 for 200, eliminates the ownership interest of everyone who owns fewer than 200 shares; after the split, these people would be left with less than a full share and would receive cash for their holdings rather than a new stock certificate. Management has done this in the past when it wanted to consolidate control of a company or perhaps take it private.

**Stock Dividends.** The financial pages sometimes report that a firm has announced a "100 percent stock dividend." This means that for every share you own, you will receive another one. How is this different from a 2-for-1 stock split? Similarly, how is a 5-for-4 stock split different from a 25 percent stock dividend?

In practical terms, it is not different at all. From an investor's perspective, the impact is exactly the same. The difference between a stock split and a stock dividend is purely an accounting phenomenon. With a stock split, the accountants alter the par value of the stock as carried on the firm's books. A stock dividend, however, does not affect the par value; new shares are issued. Par value is not a meaningful statistic from an investment point of view. It is an accounting artifact of no importance.

---

[10]There is some evidence that firms tend to raise their cash dividends at the same time they split their shares. Although the dividends themselves may not be a plus for reasons already discussed, the market looks to changes in dividends as signals about management's view of the future. Firms do not like to reduce dividends, and if they are raised, management probably expects to be able to continue the new payout rate. This bodes well for the future and may cause the stock price to be bid up. See Eugene Fama, Lawrence Fisher, Michael Jensen, and Richard Roll, "The Adjustment of Stock Prices to New Information," *International Economic Review*, February 1969, 1–21.

[11]H. Kent Baker and Patricia L. Gallagher, "Management's View of Stock Splits," *Financial Management*, Summer 1980, 75.

[12]In fact, at least one study shows that stock dividends or splits may degrade liquidity. See Dennis Murray, "Further Evidence on the Liquidity Effects of Stock Splits and Stock Dividends," *Journal of Financial Research*, Spring 1985, 59–67.

PORTFOLIO MEMO

## Tax Cuts and Stock Prices

On May 28, 2003 President Bush signed legislation providing significant changes to the tax law. The dividend tax rate dropped from as much as 38.6% to 15%. A brokerage firm research report* predicted that this alone would increase the price of utility stocks by 10 percent and lead to an average price/earnings ratio in the 11.5– 14.5 range. Is the analyst right?

To investigate, we can establish some initial conditions and see how things should change. Suppose the initial stock price is $10.00, the forward-looking annual dividend is $0.50, and the expected dividend growth rate is 5.5 percent. Assume also that the stock trades at a constant price/earnings ratio of 13, the midpoint of the range cited in the analyst's report. The analyst predicts the stock price will rise 10 percent, to $11.00. Let's see what logically should happen.

From these starting values we can determine a few other things:

$$\frac{\text{price}}{\text{earnings per share}} = 13 \quad \Rightarrow \text{eps} = \frac{\$10.00}{13} = \$0.77$$

payout ratio = $0.50/$0.77 = 65%
earnings retention rate = 1 − payout ratio = 35%
growth rate = retention rate × return on equity

$$\text{ROE} = \frac{5.5\%}{35\%} = 15.71\%$$

Table 9-2 uses these statistics to project earnings, dividends, equity, and stock price over the next five years. Panel A shows the initial scenario without any tax considerations. The initial equity value of $4.90 is a consequence of an ROE of 15.71 percent and earnings per share of $0.77. The stock price is a constant 13 times projected earnings. With no loss of generality this example assumes the investor will sell the shares at the end of the fifth year. The valuation equation shows that these numbers imply a discount rate of 10.52 percent. This traditional shareholders' required rate of return is a before-tax value. It is very close to the 10.50 percent value predicted by equation 9-2, the sum of the forward dividend yield and the growth rate.

Panel B of Table 9-2 incorporates the tax effects on both the dividends and the capital gain the investor experiences when he sells the stock in year five. The purpose of this panel is to find the investor-determined after-tax discount rate that is embedded in the current market price. The final term in the valuation equation assumes the investor pays capital gains taxes at the current 15 percent rate and pays them on a $3.08 gain (the difference between the year-five sales price and the initial $10.00 price). The after-tax discount rate is 8.31 percent.

We can now use this rate to find what the new stock price should be as a consequence of the reduction in the dividend tax. Panel C shows this. In this instance we know the future after-tax cash flows from the dividends, but continue to have an unknown in the last term where we figure the capital gains tax because we do not know the initial stock price. This becomes an algebraic exercise with

*A.G. Edwards, *Gas Utilities Quarterly Review*, July 6, 2004, 5.

## Tax Cuts and Stock Prices (continued)

one equation and one unknown, and fortunately Microsoft Excel makes short work of it. The implied stock price is $10.37, not the $11.00 proposed by the A.G. Edwards analyst. This corresponds to a DCF cost of equity of

$$\frac{.50}{10.37} + 0.055 = 10.32\%$$

**TABLE 9-2** THE EFFECT OF THE DIVIDEND TAX RATE CHANGE ON COST OF EQUITY

*Panel A*
*Initial Scenario (before tax)*

| *Year* | 0 | 1 | 2 | 3 | 4 | 5 | 6 |
|---|---|---|---|---|---|---|---|
| EPS | | $ 0.77 | $ 0.8122 | $ 0.8569 | $ 0.9040 | $ 0.9537 | $1.0061 |
| Dividend | | 0.50 | 0.5279 | 0.5570 | 0.5876 | 0.6199 | — |
| Contribution to retained earnings | | 0.27 | 0.2843 | 0.2999 | 0.3164 | 0.3338 | — |
| Equity | $ 4.90 | 5.17 | 5.4543 | 5.7542 | 6.0706 | 6.4044 | — |
| Stock price | $10.00 | 10.56 | 11.14 | 11.75 | 12.40 | 13.08 | — |
| Price/book | 2.04 | 2.04 | 2.04 | 2.04 | 2.04 | 2.04 | — |

$$\$10.00 = \frac{0.50}{(1+R)} + \frac{0.5279}{(1+R)^2} + \frac{0.5570}{(1+R)^3} + \frac{0.5876}{(1+R)^4} + \frac{0.6199+13.08}{(1+R)^5}$$

$R = 10.52\%$ (before tax)

*Panel B*
*Implied After-Tax Cost of Equity*
*(30% dividend tax, 15% capital gains tax)*

| *Year* | 0 | 1 | 2 | 3 | 4 | 5 |
|---|---|---|---|---|---|---|
| Dividend | | 0.50 | 0.5279 | 0.5570 | 0.5876 | 0.6199 |
| – tax | | 0.15 | 0.1584 | 0.1671 | 0.1763 | 0.1860 |
| Dividends after tax | | 0.35 | 0.3695 | 0.3899 | 0.4113 | 0.4339 |
| Stock price | $10.00 | 10.56 | 11.14 | 11.75 | 12.40 | 13.08 |

$$\$10.00 = \frac{0.35}{(1+R)} + \frac{0.3695}{(1+R)^2} + \frac{0.3899}{(1+R)^3} + \frac{0.4113}{(1+R)^4} + \frac{0.4339+(13.08-.15(13.08-10.00))}{(1+R)^5}$$

$R = 8.31\%$ (after tax)

*Panel C*
*Implied New Stock Price*
*(Given 8.31% cost of equity, 15% dividend tax, 15% capital gains tax)*

| *Year* | 0 | 1 | 2 | 3 | 4 | 5 |
|---|---|---|---|---|---|---|
| Dividend | | 0.50 | 0.5279 | 0.5570 | 0.5876 | 0.6199 |
| – tax | | 0.0750 | .0792 | .0836 | .0881 | .0930 |
| Dividends after tax | | .4250 | .4487 | .4735 | .4995 | .5269 |
| Stock price | *P* | 10.56 | 11.14 | 11.75 | 12.40 | 13.08 |

$$P = \frac{0.425}{(1.0831)} + \frac{0.4487}{(1.0831)^2} + \frac{0.4735}{(1.0831)^3} + \frac{0.4995}{(1.0831)^4} + \frac{0.5269+(13.08-.15(13.08-P))}{(1.0831)^5}$$

$P$ = implied new stock price = $10.37

## Investment Styles

Stock investors tend to follow one of two styles: they are either value investors or *growth* investors. They may also focus on firms of a particular market *capitalization.*

### *Value Investing*

A value investor likes to buy $1 worth of stock for fifty cents. Such an investor pays close attention to the firm's earnings history and its balance sheet and places much

PORTFOLIO MEMO

### A History of One Company's Stock Splits and Stock Dividends

**1957**—You buy 100 shares of Community Engineering for $1 per share. Community Engineering is a newly formed public corporation in State College, Pennsylvania.

**1960**—Community Engineering changes its name to C-Cor Manufacturing and spins off three shares of Centre Video for each share of C-Cor held. Your holdings: 100 C-Cor; 300 Centre Video.

**1969**—C-Cor splits 5-for-1, and Centre Video splits 6 for 1. Your holdings: 500 C-Cor; 1,800 Centre Video.

**1971**—Telecommunications, Inc. (*TCOM*), takes over Centre Video and gives 2.13 shares of TCOM for each share of Centre Video held. (Telecommunications is currently the largest operator of cable television systems in the United States.) Your holdings: 500 C-Cor; 3,834 TCOM.

**1979** (August 1)—Telecommunications reclassifies its common stock into Class A and pays a 100 percent stock dividend of Class B for each share of Class A held. Class B stock gets ten votes per share, whereas Class A gets only one. Your holdings: 500 C-Cor; 3,834 TCOM.A; 3,834 TCOM.B.

**1979** (August 31)—Telecommunications pays a 100 percent stock dividend of Class B for each share of Class A held. Your holdings: 500 C-Cor; 3,834 TCOM.A; 7,668 TCOM.B.

**1980**—Telecommunications pays a 100 percent stock dividend of Class A for each share of Class A held and one share of Class A for each share of Class B held. Your holdings: 500 C-Cor; 15,336 TCOM.A; 7,668 TCOM.B.

**1981**—C-Cor declares a 28-for-1 stock split. Your holdings: 14,000 C-Cor; 15,336 TCOM.A; 7,668 TCOM.B.

**1983**—TCOM.A splits 2-for-1. Your holdings: 14,000 C-Cor; 30,672 TCOM.A; 7,668 TCOM.B.

**1986**—TCOM.A and TCOM.B both split 2-for-1. Your holdings: 14,000 C-Cor; 61,344 TCOM.A; 15,336 TCOM.B.

**1987**—TCOM.A and TCOM.B both split 3-for-2. Your holdings: 14,000 C-Cor; 92,016 TCOM.A; 23,004 TCOM.B.

## A History of One Company's Stock Splits and Stock Dividends (continued)

**1989**—C-Cor, TCOM.A, and TCOM.B all split 2-for-1. Your holdings: 28,000 C-Cor; 184,032 TCOM.A; 46,008 TCOM.B.

**1994**—C-Cor splits 2-for-1. Your holdings: 56,000 C-Cor; 184,032 TCOM.A; 46,008 TCOM.B.

**1995**—Telecommunications spins off 1/4 share of Liberty Media (*LBTYA*) for each share of Class A and Class B stock held. TCOM.B also pays a $6 per share cash dividend. Your holdings: 56,000 C-Cor; 184,032 TCOM.A; 46,008 TCOM.B; 57,510 LBTYA; $276,048 in cash.

**1997**—Liberty Media pays a $9.50 per share cash dividend. Your holdings: 56,000 C-Cor, 184,032 TCOM.A; 46,008 TCOM.B; 57,510 LBTYA; $822,393 in cash.

**1998**—Liberty Media splits 3-for-2. Your holdings: 56,000 C-Cor, 184,032 TCOM.A; 46,008 TCOM.B; 86,265 LBTYA; $822,393 in cash.

**1999**—C-Cor changes its name to C-Cor.net and its ticker to *CCBL*. AT&T (ticker symbol *T*) acquires Telecommunications by exchanging 0.7757 shares of T for each share of TCOM.A and 0.8533 shares of T for each share of TCOM.B. Each share of LBTYA is exchanged for one share of Liberty Media Group Series A, a tracking stock (symbol *LMG.A*) of AT&T. LMG.A splits 2 for 1. T splits 3 for 2. Your holdings: 56,000 CCBL, 273,018 T, 172,530 LMG.A, $822,393 in cash.

**2000**—LMG.A and CCBL both split 2-for-1. T pays $0.26 per share in dividends. Your holdings: 112,000 CCBL, 273,018 T, 345,060 LMG.A, $893,378 in cash.

**2001**—AT&T splits off LMG.A; the new symbol is *LMC.A*. Later in the year, the symbol is again changed, this time to *L*. T pays dividends of $5.68 per share. Your holdings: 112,000 CCBL, 273,018 T, 345,060 L, $2,444,120 in cash.

**2002**—AT&T has a 1-for-5 reverse stock split and pays a special dividend of $8.485 per share in addition to its regular quarterly dividend. Your holdings: 112,000 CCBL, 54,604 T, 345,060 L, $2,948,825 in cash.

**2003**—AT&T pays dividends of $0.852 per share. Your holdings: 112,000 CCBL, 54,604 T, 345,060 L, $2,995,348 in cash.

**2004**—AT&T pays dividends of $0.952 per share. Your holdings: 112,000 CCBL, 54,604 T, 345,060 L, $3,047,331 in cash.

**TABLE 9-3** MARKET VALUE AS OF FEBRUARY 5, 2005

| *Stock* | *Shares* | *Price per Share* | *Value* |
|---|---|---|---|
| CCBL | 112,000 | $ 8.40 | $ 940,800 |
| T | 54,604 | 19.80 | 1,081,159 |
| L | 345,060 | 10.48 | 3,616,229 |
| Cash | | | $3,047,331 |
| | | Total | $8,685,519 |

more emphasis on known facts rather than conjecture. Two financial ratios that are particularly helpful in doing this are the price/earnings ratio and the price/book ratio.

**Price/Earnings Ratio.** The price/earnings ratio, or PE, is the firm's stock price divided by its earnings per share. If you use forecasted earnings, you have a *forward-looking PE*; if you use earnings that have already occurred, this is a *trailing PE*. You can use a combination of the two by combining earnings from the last two quarters with forecasted earnings for the next six months. Regardless of how you calculate the ratio, as a value investor you want this figure to be low. If you are about to buy a stock, you want a low stock price (the numerator) and high earnings (the denominator).

**Price/Book Ratio.** This is the firm's current stock price divided by its book value per share. Book value is the same as equity or net asset value: the firm's total assets minus its liabilities. Dividing book value by the number of shares outstanding gives book value per share.

PORTFOLIO MEMO

## What Do You Mean By "Earnings?"

A firm's earnings are arguably the single most important statistic in determining share value. This is the reason so many investors look at a firm's PE ratio. What the term *earnings* means, however, is increasingly complex. At their simplest, earnings are what is left at the bottom of a firm's income statement: the difference between revenue and expenses. An analyst might call this figure *accounting earnings*. Alternatively, the analyst might refer to *operating earnings,* also called *pro forma earnings*. This is a fuzzy concept one reporter calls "earnings before the bad stuff." Operating earnings might exclude extraordinary or nonrecurring charges that do not really measure a firm's "true" performance. Other analysts use phrases such as *economic earnings*, *core earnings*, or *ongoing earnings*. There is no universal definition of any of these terms. According to *The Wall Street Journal*, "More than 300 companies in the S&P 500 now exclude some ordinary expenses, as designed by GAAP, from the operating earnings numbers they feed to investors and analysts."*

Even before firms publish their earnings there is uncertainty. Earnings and growth rates are important in security analysis. Missing an earnings estimate is a problem that in recent years can really pound a stock. To reduce the likelihood of "missing earnings," firms sometimes provide earnings guidance that is a bit on the low side. That is, management might publicly say the firm expects to earn 26 cents per share in the upcoming quarter when it probably will earn 27 cents. Increasingly, the market calls this latter number the whisper number. As the whisper number phenomenon proliferated, a new corporate problem arose: The stock could exceed the published analysts' estimates, but it would still get pummeled if it misses the whisper number. On July 18, 2000, shares of Copper Mountain Networks (*CMTN, Nasdaq*) fell from $123.6875 to $94.1875 (a 24 percent drop) when it announced earnings higher than estimates but below the whisper number. Corporate treasurers may discover that honesty in earnings is the best policy after all.

*Jonathan Weil, "What's the P/E Ratio? Well, Depends on What Is Meant by Earnings," *The Wall Street Journal*, August 21, 2001, A1.

Book value is a ratio that must be taken with a grain of salt. Very often the market value of a firm's assets are quite different from their book value. Consider an office building. The accounting rules prescribe a depreciation method for the building whereby its value as shown on the balance sheet declines every year. In reality, however, the value of the building probably *rises*. Analysts and appraisers seeking to value a company usually adjust book value by restating assets at their market value if they can.

Value investors like a low price-to-book ratio. Sometimes it is below 1.0. This means that if you as a value investor were to buy all of a firm's stock and then sell all of the firm's assets at their carrying value, you would have more money than you started with. The December 14, 2004, edition of the *Value Line Investment Analyzer* covered 7,905 stocks, 827 of which sold for less than their book value. These would be particularly interesting to a value investor.

Note that the PE ratio is an income statement statistic, and the price/book ratio is a balance sheet calculation.

## Growth Investing

**Growth investors want price momentum.** They prefer stocks that are in favor and whose prices have been advancing. In this respect, growth and value investors are exactly opposite. Value investors prefer stock that is out of favor (hence cheap) while growth investors are willing to "pay up" for a stock that the market is likely to propel even higher. During the dot.com craze, many growth investors freely admitted that the "valuations were crazy" but continued to buy them because that was where the action was. Value investors who stuck to their guns showed unremarkable performance during this period but looked good when the Internet bubble burst in 2000.

Because the market tends to move through cycles, favoring value over growth and then reversing itself, many managers (and individual investors) try to hold both value and growth stocks in their portfolios. It is difficult to maintain the discipline of continuing to hold value stocks when they are not going anywhere, but because of the difficulty in predicting "style turning points," there is much to be said for this practice.

Figure 9-2 shows the relative performance of the S&P Barra *Value* (ticker SVX) and the S&P Barra *Growth* (SGX) indices. Consistent with the notion of systematic risk, these two subsets of stocks tend to both be up or both be down in a given year, but there are exceptions. When the Internet bubble burst in 2000, the technology stocks took a nosedive, but value stocks held their own. They were a powerful portfolio diversifier that year. It is hard to predict when value will outperform growth or vice versa, so many money managers diversify by holding both.

## Capitalization

In the context of equity investing, *capitalization* refers to the aggregate value of a company's common stock. The industry typically groups stock into large cap, mid cap, and small cap groups. Although there is no universally agreed upon break point when a firm moves from small cap to mid cap or mid cap to large cap, there are some general trends.

Many firms consider a large cap stock to be from a firm with equity capitalization more than around $1 billion.[13] A mid cap stock might be in the $500 million

[13]Doing a quick Internet search, I found one firm that had a large cap breakpoint of $3 billion and another that used $9 billion. There is no quantitative consensus on this point.

FIGURE 9-2

S&P Barra Value and Growth Indices

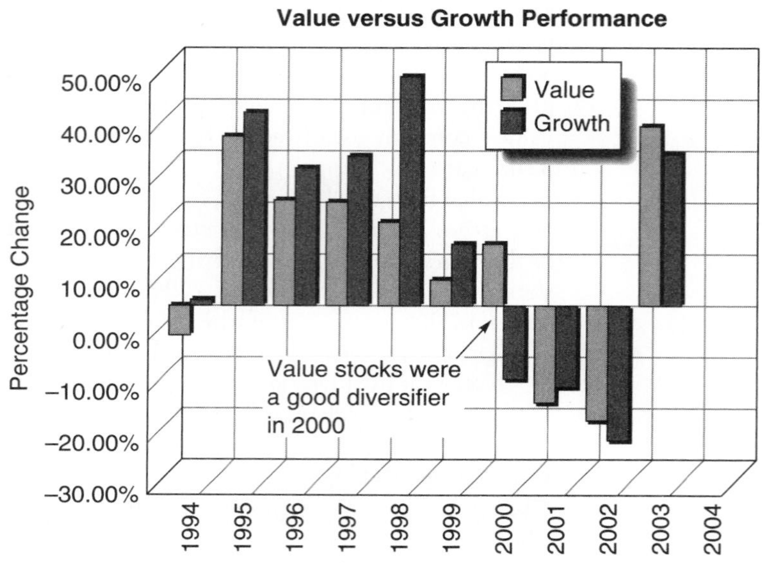


TABLE 9-4

| *Size* | *# of years as top performer* | *# of years as bottom performer* |
|---|---|---|
| Large cap | 10 (late 90s) | 11 |
| Mid cap | 4 (consistent middle) | 3 |
| Small cap | 11 (early 80s and 2000s) | 11 |

Source: Fifth Third Bankcorp

to $1 billion range, with a small cap stock being under $500 million. The term *micro cap*, referring to the smallest firms, is also used. As with the value versus growth debate, in some periods large cap stocks outperform small caps and mid caps, and the opposite occurs in other periods.

As with value and growth styles, there are periods of time when large cap stocks outperform small cap stocks, and vice versa. It is not likely that anyone has discovered a reliable way of telling when the current favorite will give way to the other. There is some interesting evidence showing that if you rank large, mid, and small caps in order of performance that the mid-cap stocks tend to stay in the middle. This suggests that if you can only buy one group, you might be best putting your money on the "average-sized" companies rather than the large or small.

Table 9-4 shows this result over the twenty-five years from 1979–2003. Large caps were the top or bottom performer 21 times, small caps were the top or bottom performer 22 times, with the mid-caps in the middle 18 times.

Figure 9-3 shows the performance of three Standard & Poor's indices: the S&P 600 (small cap), the S&P 400 (mid cap), and the S&P 500 (large cap) since January 1996. If you recall from Chapter 2 the examples showing how the geometric mean punishes dispersion, it may not be surprising that the "consistently in the middle" mid cap stocks show the highest terminal value. As with many things in the stock market, however, it would be dangerous to assume this is how the future will always play out.

FIGURE 9-3

Small, Mid, and Large Cap Performance

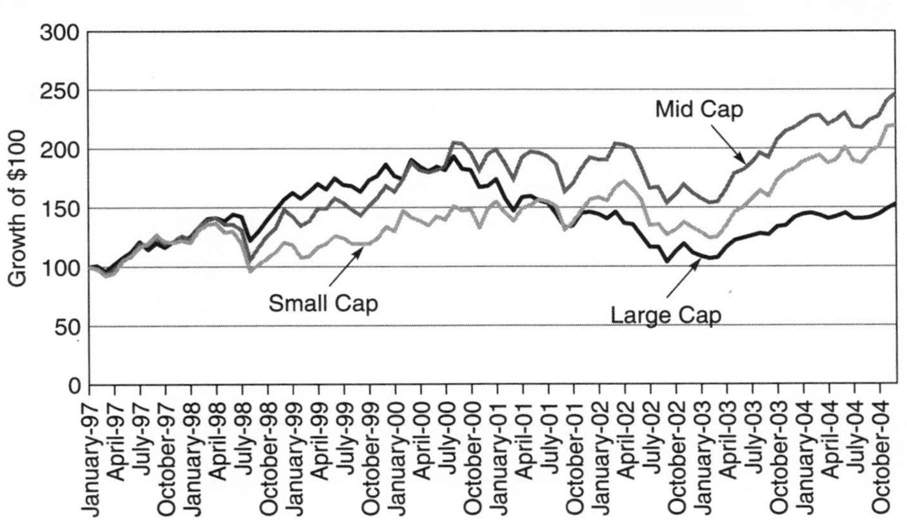


TABLE 9-5 STOCK PORTFOLIO

| *Stock* | *Ticker* | *Shares* | *Price* | *Value* |
|---|---|---|---|---|
| ARKANSAS BEST | ABFS | 300 | $27.80 | $ 8,340 |
| APPLIED FILMS | AFCO | 500 | 26.08 | 13,040 |
| AOL TIME WARNER | AOL | 100 | 30.69 | 3,069 |
| CENDANT | CD | 500 | 19.15 | 9,575 |
| CIENA | CIEN | 200 | 14.64 | 2,928 |
| CLARENT | CLRNE | 1,000 | 5.35 | 5,350 |
| FAIRCHILD SEMICONDUCTOR | FCS | 200 | 28.00 | 5,600 |
| HOME DEPOT | HD | 150 | 50.46 | 7,569 |
| HARLEY DAVIDSON | HDI | 200 | 52.72 | 10,544 |
| HEALTH MANAGEMENT ASSOCIATES | HMA | 300 | 17.96 | 5,388 |
| IVAX | IVX | 300 | 20.63 | 6,189 |
| OMI | OMM | 2,000 | 3.69 | 7,380 |
| OAKLEY | OO | 200 | 15.65 | 3,130 |
| ROUSE | RSE | 200 | 28.73 | 5,746 |
| SICOR | SCRI | 500 | 16.40 | 8,200 |
| SERVICE CORP INTERNATIONAL | SRV | 1,000 | 5.38 | 5,380 |
| TETRA TECH | TTEK | 500 | 19.94 | 9,970 |
| USINTERNETWORKING | USIX | 1,000 | 0.15 | 150 |
| | | | TOTAL | $117,548 |

## Integrating Style and Size

Because of the historical evidence regarding value versus growth and small versus large, many money managers hedge their bets and distribute their investment assets across the spectrum. One handy method for monitoring a portfolio is via the Morningstar style box found at the Morningstar website, *http://www.morningstar.com*. Consider the stock portfolio in Table 9-5.

FIGURE 9-4

Morningstar Style Box Diversification

| | Valuation | | |
|---|---|---|---|
| Value | Blend | Growth | |
| 11 | 0 | 15 | Large |
| 5 | 5 | 24 | Medium |
| 18 | 0 | 22 | Small |

Morningstar provides a number of handy analytical services, many of them free over the Internet. One such tool is the *portfolio X-Ray*. You can input a portfolio similar to the one in Table 9-5 and the X-Ray function will show the portfolio distribution across the value/growth and market capitalization dimensions. Figure 9-4 is the analysis of this portfolio.

Summing the figures in the "value" column, 34 percent of this portfolio is in value stocks. Similarly, 61 percent is in growth stocks, with the other 5 percent in between, classified as "blend." On the size dimension, the portfolio is more evenly distributed, with 26 percent large cap, 34 percent mid cap, and 40 percent small cap. The Morningstar classification system is convenient, and many investment professionals use it frequently.

## Categories of Stock

Classifying stock is a subjective process, and the categories are not necessarily mutually exclusive. The following section describes the most widely used categories.

### *Blue Chip Stock*

Of all the categories of stock, the **blue chips** might be the best known. The firms in this category are among the most familiar to the investment community. Given this, it is odd that the term *blue chip* lacks precise meaning. Investment professionals all believe that they know what a blue chip stock is, but most cannot come up with a fluent definition without using examples.

One common definition of a blue chip is a company with a long, uninterrupted history of dividend payments. This is probably not a perfect definition, but it fits a great many of the consensus blue chips. Table 9-6 shows a number of U.S. companies that satisfy the conditions of this definition. What constitutes a "long history"? This question has no specific answer, but each of the firms in Table 9-6 would surely qualify.

**TABLE 9-6** SAMPLING OF BLUE CHIP STOCKS

| *Company* | *Ticker Symbol* | *Dividends Paid Each Year Since* |
|---|---|---|
| American Express | AXP | 1870 |
| Coca-Cola | KO | 1893 |
| General Mills | GIS | 1898 |
| Ingersoll-Rand | IR | 1910 |
| Johnson Controls | JCI | 1887 |
| Lilly (Eli) | LLY | 1885 |
| Mellon Financial | MEL | 1895 |
| Union Pacific | UNP | 1900 |

Source: *Standard & Poor's Stock Guide*, November 2004

**TABLE 9-7** EXAMPLES OF INCOME STOCKS

| *Company* | *Ticker Symbol* | *Dividend Yield (%)* | *Payout Ratio (%)* |
|---|---|---|---|
| Predmont Natural Gas | PNY | 7.4 | 74 |
| Consolidated Edison | ED | 5.1 | 79 |
| Great Plains Energy | GXP | 5.4 | 73 |
| Empire District Electric | EDE | 5.8 | 99 |
| Duquesne Light | DQE | 5.5 | 96 |

Source: Value Line Investment Analyzer, December 2004.

Blue chip has become a colloquial term meaning "high quality." We speak of blue chip high school football prospects, for instance. Although *high quality* is itself a difficult term to define in the investment business, many high-quality stocks do not meet the criterion of uninterrupted dividend history.

### Income Stocks

By law, dividends must be paid out of a firm's earnings; they cannot be paid from borrowed funds. The bottom-line profit a firm makes is called *net income after taxes* (*NIAT*). From this amount the firm's board of directors may pay a dividend if they so choose. NIAT may be retained in its entirety within the firm, or the entire amount may be paid out. More typically, a portion of these earnings might be retained and a portion paid out. The proportion of NIAT that is paid as a dividend is the firm's **payout ratio.** The proportion retained is, not surprisingly, the **retention ratio.**

**Income stocks** are those that historically have paid a larger-than-average percentage of their NIAT as dividends to their shareholders. The best examples of income stocks are stocks of public utilities, such as electric companies, telephone companies, and natural gas companies. Table 9-7 lists a few income stocks with their recent payout ratios.

### Cyclical Stocks

Stocks whose fortunes are directly tied to the state of the overall national economy are called **cyclical stocks.** When the economy is booming, these stocks do well. During a recession, they do poorly. The term *cyclical* has nothing to do with a chart pattern, nor does it imply that the stocks are more predictable than other issues. They are cyclical in the sense that they follow the business cycle.

**TABLE 9-8** CYCLICAL STOCKS

| *Company* | *Ticker Symbol* | *Principal Business* |
|---|---|---|
| Dow Chemical | DOW | Chemicals, metals, plastics |
| Oregon Steel Mills | OS | Specialty and commodity steel |
| Alcoa | AA | Aluminum |
| International Aluminum | IAL | Building materials |
| Masco | MAS | Home improvement |

**TABLE 9-9** DEFENSIVE STOCKS

| *Company* | *Ticker Symbol* | *Principal Business* |
|---|---|---|
| Anheuser-Busch | BUD | Largest U.S. brewer |
| Winn-Dixie Stores | WIN | Supermarkets |
| Sysco Corporation | SYY | Food distribution |
| Altria Group | MO | Cigarettes, brewing |
| Red HookAle | HOOK | Brewery |

Good examples of cyclical stocks are found in the "smokestack industries," such as steel companies, industrial chemical firms, and perhaps the automobile producers. Table 9-8 lists a few of these.

### Defensive Stocks

The opposite of a cyclical stock is a **defensive stock.** These shares are largely immune to changes in the macroeconomy and tend to have low betas. Regardless of whether the overall market is bullish or bearish, defensive stocks continue to sell their products. As they do with cyclical stocks, people often misunderstand this term. Defensive stocks have nothing to do with the national defense.

There are four especially good examples of defensive industries. The best example is retail food chains. People shop at grocery stores in both good times and bad. Two of the other categories can be lumped under the heading "vice stocks." Tobacco and alcohol firms continue to sell their products regardless of interest rates, inflation, unemployment, or any other macroeconomic indicator. The final group includes the utilities. Even when people are out of work they use the telephone, turn on the lights, and draw water from the faucet. Other defensive products include cosmetics, drugs, soap, and health-care products. See Table 9-9 for some defensive stocks.

### Growth Stocks

*Growth stocks reinvest most of their earnings rather than paying them out as dividends.*

Income stocks pay out a relatively high percentage of their earnings as dividends, but *growth stocks* do not. Instead, the company reinvests most of its earnings into profitable investment opportunities that management expects to increase the value of the firm, and therefore the value of the firm's stock. Many growth stocks do pay dividends, but they generally retain a high percentage of their earnings.

Growth stocks are in the eye of the beholder. Many firms have never paid dividends and publicly state they have no plans to do so. By default, it seems these should be growth stocks because a stock that pays no dividends and does not increase in value would not be a very attractive investment. Few experienced investors, however, would be happy with this "by default" definition of a growth stock. A great deal of a stock analyst's time is spent trying to discover little-known growth stocks. A better definition of a **growth stock** might be a stock that is expected to show above-average capital appreciation in the future. Still, this is a subjective call, and one person's growth stock is another person's dog.

### Speculative Stocks

Another imprecise category is called *speculative stock*. A direct relationship exists between risk and expected return, as we have seen. *Speculation*, by definition, involves a short time horizon, and **speculative stocks** are those that have the potential to make their owners a lot of money quickly. At the same time, though, they carry an above-average level of risk.

Some analysts consider speculative stocks to be growth stocks at the far end of the risk spectrum. For example, most people would consider IBM a growth stock rather than a speculative stock. However, many analysts would consider a newly formed computer software company that paid no dividends and had no track record to be a speculative stock rather than a growth stock. Most speculative stocks are relatively new companies with heavy representation in the technology, bioresearch, and pharmaceutical industries.

### Penny Stocks

The catchall category **penny stock** refers to inexpensive shares. Most investors would consider any stock selling for less than $1 per share to be a penny stock.

I once knew a graduate student who owned 250,000 shares of a small over-the-counter company. This was an impressive statistic until I discovered that every time he mailed a letter to the firm, the stamp cost him the equivalent of 960 shares. This firm would satisfy anyone's definition of a penny stock.

### Categories Are Not Mutually Exclusive

The stock categories are not mutually exclusive. It is very possible for either an income stock or a growth stock also to be a blue chip. Potomac Electric Power (an income stock) had a dividend yield of around 4.8 percent in late 2004. The company has paid dividends continuously since 1904. It certainly meets the requirements of both categories. Similarly, defensive or cyclical stocks can be growth stocks. Albertsons is a successful retail food company (defensive stock) that weathers recessions and has good growth potential. Dow Chemical is a cyclical growth stock.

Can a stock be both a growth stock and an income stock? Your first impression is probably that this would be like having your cake and eating it, too, but the question defies an answer because of the subjective nature of the categories. Occidental Petroleum (OXY, *NYSE*) is a good example. This large diversified energy company appears in many investment portfolios with various objectives. It is highly likely that the demand for energy products will continue. This should mean that the future capital appreciation prospects for the stock are good. Occidental Petroleum, however, had a high dividend yield for many years—about 11.4 percent in December 1990.[14] This is higher than the rates shown for the income stocks in Table 9-7.

[14]The rate was lowered in early 1991 after the death of the firm's patriarch. Armand Hammer.

PORTFOLIO MEMO

## Massively Confused Investors Making Conspicuously Ignorant Choices

The prestigious *Journal of Finance* recently published an interesting article* looking at the comovements of stocks with similar ticker symbols. The author studied daily returns on MCI Communications (ticker symbol *MCI*) and Massmutual Corporate Investors (ticker symbol *MCIC*) over a three-year period from 1994 to 1997. The study found "unusually high correlation in returns between two stocks with similar ticker symbols." The author continues, "It is possible that as many as one percent of the MCIC trades that investors intend to make incorrectly result in an MCI transaction."

The article reports other examples of ticker confusion. On April 15, 1997, the Castle Convertible Fund (*CVF, AMEX*) had an unusually volatile day in response to a *Financial Times* article about troubles at the Czech Value Fund, abbreviated in the story as CVF. In a positive recommendation for the Morgan Stanley Asia Pacific Fund (*APF, NYSE*) *Barron's* once incorrectly listed the ticker as *APB*, actually the symbol for the Barings Asia Pacific Fund. This dramatically increased the trading volume for *APB* on that day and temporarily caused a trading delay. In another instance related to the "Stock Splits" Portfolio Memo in this chapter, when AT&T announced its intent to purchase Tele-Communications, Inc., the stock in *TCI* jumped to more than 37 times its daily average. *TCI*, however, is the ticker symbol for Transcontinental Realty Investors. The Tele-Communications, Inc., symbol was *TCOMA* (for the A shares) and *TCOMB* (for the B shares). As a consequence, the director of investor relations at TCI said, "I just hope this doesn't mean some people will realize they've owned the wrong stock for all these years."

---

*Michael S. Rashes, "Massively Confused Investors Making Conspicuously Ignorant Choices (MCI–MCIC)," *Journal of Finance*, October 2001, 1911–1927.

### *A Note on Stock Symbols*

Stock symbols show up on the ticker tape you see on some cable television stations, in financial center bars, and in brokerage firm offices. They are the identification codes you need to retrieve current price information from the Internet, Palm Pilots, and cell phones.

Stock symbols usually have one to four letters. A symbol of one, two, or three letters denotes a listed stock that trades on either the New York Stock Exchange or the American Stock Exchange. There is no particular meaning to a one-digit stock symbol versus a three-digit symbol, although there may be some prestige to a single digit.

Four-digit symbols are used for firms that trade in the Nasdaq stock market or the over-the-counter system. An exception to this general rule is for listed shares that have more than one class of stock, such as Class A and Class B. Liberty Media, for instance, has both Class A and Class B, with symbols L (for the class A) and LMCB (for the class B), both trading on the New York Stock Exchange. When multiple classes of stock exist, differences in voting rights are usually the only substantive dissimilarities in the shares.

Many firms try to obtain stock symbols that have a logical association with their products. Anheuser-Busch, for example, is *BUD*, in recognition of its famous beer. Some symbols are more subtle, such as Southwest Airlines's *LUV*. If you live in Texas, you probably know about Luv Field, where this airline frequently lands. A few other notable ticker symbols are *OO* for Oakley (the manufacturer of sunglasses), *EYE* for VISX, Inc. (laser eye surgery), *EAR* for HearUSA (hearing aid centers), *CAKE* (for the Cheesecake Factory), and *YUM* for Yum! Brands (the PepsiCo spin-off that owns Pizza Hut, KFC, and Taco Bell).

You can quickly find a stock symbol via the Internet. A good site is *http://finance.yahoo.com*, which has a "symbol lookup" option.

## SUMMARY

Dividends are an important part of the investment business, but not because they increase the shareholder's wealth. Dividends do not grow on trees; they come from the issuer's checking account, and they reduce the firm's value when the treasurer issues the checks. Dividends do provide current income, but they do so at the expense of future growth. A precise chronology of events surrounds the payment of a dividend. The ex-dividend date convention eliminates uncertainty regarding entitlement to forthcoming dividends.

Predictable dividends make the business of security valuation easier. The dividend discount model is a commonly used analytical tool to value shares of stock, and the dividend growth rate is the critical input to this model.

Stock splits, like dividends, do not alter the collective wealth of the shareholders. They are analogous to cutting pieces of a pie into smaller slices; the total amount of pie does not change as the serving size changes.

Stock has historically been placed into largely subjective categories, including blue chip, income, cyclical, defensive, growth, speculative, and penny. These categories are not mutually exclusive, nor are they precise.

## QUESTIONS

1. Explain why a stock dividend does not increase an individual investor's wealth.
2. If a firm is unable to pay a cash dividend, is it economically sound to pay a stock dividend?
3. Would you expect a property dividend to affect the value of a share of stock in the same fashion as a cash dividend?
4. Comment on the following statement: Dividends do matter; it is dividend policy that does not matter.
5. Suppose you were asked to empirically determine whether Goodyear Tire and Rubber is a cyclical stock. How would you proceed?
6. Comment on the following statement: A stock with a low payout ratio should appreciate more than an otherwise similar stock with a high payout ratio.
7. Common stock is a perpetual security. How, then, can a stock that does not pay dividends, such as Cisco Systems, have any value?
8. Why do you think firms avoid reducing or omitting dividends, even during unprofitable years?
9. Why does a reduction in the discount rate an analyst uses for a particular stock increase its investment appeal?

10. Using an analogy of tickets to a football game, explain an investor's options regarding what to do with stock rights.
11. A firm's board of directors is supposed to ensure that the firm seeks to "maximize share value." Given that most stock splits reduce the value of a share, how can they be reconciled with the board's responsibility?

## PROBLEMS

1. Consider the following information. How many shares do you hold today if you bought 1,000 shares of this stock at the beginning of 1975?
   1976—10 percent stock dividend
   1977—10 percent stock dividend
   1978—25 percent stock dividend
   1979—100 percent stock dividend
   1984—2-for-1 stock split
   1998—100 percent stock dividend
2. Suppose you believe that Coca-Cola (*KO, NYSE*) and PepsiCo (*PEP, NYSE*) are equally risky. Using the dividend discount model and data from the Internet, which of the two stocks is more attractive?
3. Explain why the following statement is *not* true. "If a firm's stock price goes up but the dividend does not change, this must mean that the expected dividend growth rate has increased."
4. Select any company included in the Dow Jones Industrial Average, and calculate its dividend growth rate over the last ten years.
5. Ten years ago a stock paid a $0.30 dividend. Since then it has split 2-for-1 twice. The current dividend is $0.16. If you have a required rate of return of 14 percent, what is the most you can pay for this stock?
6. Suppose you bought 100 shares of CenturyTel (*CTL, NYSE*) in December 1995 at $31.75.
   a. How many shares would you own today?
   b. If you sold it today, what would be your approximate holding period return?
7. A relatively new firm has the dividend payment history shown in Table 9-10. Suppose this stock sells for $8 per share. Estimate the shareholders' required rate of return using the dividend discount model with the following:
   a. The dividend growth rate calculated over the firm's entire history.
   b. The growth rate calculated over the actual dividend paying history only.
   Why are the two answers different? Which do you think is most meaningful?

**TABLE 9-10** DIVIDEND PAYMENT HISTORY

| *Year* | *Dividends Paid* |
|---|---|
| 1997 | $0 |
| 1998 | 0 |
| 1999 | 0 |
| 2000 | 0 |
| 2001 | 0.10 |
| 2002 | 0.13 |
| 2003 | 0.15 |
| 2004 | 0.18 |

## INTERNET EXERCISE

Using the screening tool at *screen.finance.yahoo.com/newscreener.html*, identify companies that do not pay any dividends (i.e., Max Dividend Yield = 0%) and have provided a five-year earnings growth rate over 100 percent. Of the top five (those with the greatest earnings growth rate), which do you believe would be most attractive to a growth investor? Explain.

## FURTHER READING


Baker, H. Kent, and Aaron L. Phillips. "Why Companies Issue Stock Dividends." *Financial Practice and Education*, Fall 1993, 29–37.

Baker, H. Kent, and Patricia L. Gallagher. "Management's View of Stock Splits." *Financial Management*, Summer 1980, 73–77.

Barker, C. Austin. "Effective Stock Splits." *Harvard Business Review*, January/February 1956, 101–106.

Copeland, Thomas E. "Liquidity Changes Following Stock Splits." *Journal of Finance*, March 1979, 115–141.

Eisemann, Peter C. "Stock Dividends: Management's View." *Financial Analysts Journal*, July/August 1978, 77–80.

Elgers, Pieter T., and Dennis Murray. "Financial Characteristics Related to Managements' Stock Split and Stock Dividend Decisions." *Journal of Business Finance and Accounting*, Winter 1985, 543–551.

Fama, Eugene, Lawrence Fisher, Michael Jensen, and Richard Roll. "The Adjustment of Stock Prices to New Information." *International Economic Review*, February 1969, 1–21.

——— and Kenneth R. French. "Disappearing Dividends: Changing Firm Characteristics or Lower Propensity to Pay?" *Journal of Financial Economics*, April 2001, 3–43.

Ferguson, Robert. "Making the Dividend Discount Model Relevant for Financial Analysts." *Journal of Investing*, Summer 1997, 53–64.

Frankfurter, George M., and William R. Lane. "The Perception of Stock Dividends." *Journal of Investing*, Summer 1998, 32–40.

Houseman, R., R. West, and J.A. Largan. "Stock Splits, Price Changes, and Trading Profits: A Synthesis." *Journal of Business*, January 1971, 69–77.

Johnson, Keith B. "Stock Splits and Price Change." *Journal of Finance*, December 1966, 675–686.

Kimball, Peter, and D. Robert Papera. "Effects of Stock Splits on Short-Term Market Prices." *Financial Analysts Journal*, May/June 1964, 75–80.

Millar, James A., and Bruce D. Fielitz. "Stock Split and Stock Dividend Decisions." *Financial Management*, Winter 1973, 35–45.

Murray, Dennis. "Further Evidence on the Liquidity Effects of Stock Splits and Stock Dividends." *Journal of Financial Research*, Spring 1985, 59–67.

Szewczyk, Samuel, and George P. Tsetsekos. "Do Dividend Omissions Signal Future Earnings or Past Earnings." *Journal of Investing*, Spring 1997, 40–53.

Woolridge, J. Randall, and Donald R. Chambers. "Reverse Splits and Shareholder Wealth." *Financial Management*, Autumn 1983, 5–15.

# 10 Security Screening

*Never tell people how to do things. Tell them what to do and they will surprise you with their ingenuity.*

***General George S. Patton***

## Key Terms

best of class investing
Compustat
Mergent, Inc.
screen
socially responsible investing
Standard & Poor's Corporation
thin trading
*Value Line Investment Survey*

## Introduction

Security screening is an important part of the portfolio construction process, but one about which relatively little is written. *Screening* involves whittling the security universe down to a manageable size before doing more detailed research.

Picking stocks is an art rather than a science; there is no single best way to choose individual investments. Everyone who participates in the capital markets uses some type of **screen**—a procedure for reducing a large set of alternatives to a more manageable number.

This chapter does not go into great detail about individual stock analysis. Techniques such as ratio analysis, comparison with industry averages, and income statement sensitivity analysis help in learning about a company, but these are topics for another book. We will, however, review some common screening statistics that can provide fast information about a company's likely future price behavior; the relationship between a firm's return on assets and its return on equity is especially important. Nonetheless, recall that Chapter 1 said the modern trend in investment management is away from stock analysis and toward portfolio management. Remember also the Evans and Archer research, which provides evidence that it is better to select a few stocks randomly than to pick a single favorite.

## Why Screening Is Necessary

### Time Constraints

*Lack of time is the primary motivation for screening.*

The primary reason screening is necessary is the limited amount of time available for making decisions. In the investment business, there simply is not time to analyze every security and process the associated information.

The New York Stock Exchange and the American Stock Exchange list thousands of potential investments, with thousands more trading in the Nasdaq market. Suppose you spend five minutes looking at each of 500 possible picks. Ignoring trips to the refrigerator and to the bathroom, this means you will spend 2,500 minutes, or more than a whole 40-hour workweek, checking out this subset of a much larger security universe. As obvious as this is, many people never develop a well-conceived way to deal with the data overload problem.

### Everyday Examples of Screens

Screens are not restricted to the investment business. People use them consciously and subconsciously every day. Consider a few examples.

**University Admission Tests.** Most universities have more people applying for admission than they are able (or willing) to accept. How are decisions on granting admission made? Most institutions use two steps: an initial screen and, for those passing this round, closer individual scrutiny.

As an example, a high school senior whose Scholastic Aptitude Test (SAT) scores totaled 1,450 would have little difficulty gaining admission to the majority of U.S. universities. Colleges always want the best and brightest, and high SAT scores are a good indicator of intellectual ability, although not a perfect one. Conversely, a student whose SAT scores totaled only 600 would in all likelihood have a difficult time in college. Many schools would decline to admit a person with scores this low and would give the student's complete file only cursory, if any, further attention.

College athletics periodically gets bad publicity when someone discovers a gifted athlete who, after four (or five) years at a prestigious university, cannot read at a high school level or solve basic math problems. The controversial Proposition 42 of the National Collegiate Athletic Association (NCAA) sought to reduce the number of academically unprepared athletes entering college. It stipulated that scholarships could not be given to players who fail to maintain a C average in eleven high school core subjects and fail to score at least 700 (on a scale of 400 to 1,600) on the SAT exam or 15 (on a scale of 1 to 36) on the American College Test (ACT) exam. This screen was widely denounced as racist because of the disproportionate number of African American athletes who do poorly on these standardized tests. The appropriateness of a screen is very important and will be discussed in a moment.

**The Football Team.** Sports teams normally have more players trying to join them than their rosters can carry. In a game such as football, with its specialized positions, coaches might use a number of initial screens to find in which position, if any, a prospective player might shine. Coaches might have players who want to be running backs run the 40-yard dash. Players who cannot cover this distance in less than 6 seconds may lack the speed to excel in this position. Offensive linemen might go to the weight room and bench press 250 pounds. Some coaches might consider this a minimum standard for the position. Split ends or receivers might be tested in both the 40-yard dash and the standing vertical jump.

All these tests are screens. Although not perfect, they are good indicators of the likelihood of success in a particular position.

## What Constitutes a Good Screen?

The idea of screening is appealing, and most screens are logical. But what constitutes a good screen? Is the 40-yard dash really an accurate measure of what kind of running back someone might make? The following sections discuss some characteristics of a good screen.

### *Ease of Administration*

Managerial aids are helpful only if you use them. The best mathematical model, computer program, or college textbook is of no value if you do not use it. The same is true with any screen.

Suppose, for instance, that I want to select a historical novel from the library to take with me on an intercontinental flight. I could select a book by finding one with the late James Michener's endorsement on the dust jacket. I like the historical novels Michener writes, and if he recommends a book, I suspect I would enjoy it. This would be a very inefficient screen. For one thing, there is no convenient way to find all the books that meet this criterion other than methodically going through every shelf in the library. Even the electronic card catalog does not have this information.

Alternatively, I could attempt to correspond with Michener's literary agent and ask for a recommendation, but this method would not produce results quickly and might be totally unproductive. Another approach would be to use a computer search at Amazon.com to gather information on historical novels. I could probably find an interesting book rather quickly just via the keyword "history." This would be a much easier way to find a suitable book than the other methods.

Now consider the stock market. I might go on an investment hunt looking for an attractive but thinly traded stock. **Thin trading** is a subjective term referring to a security with a relatively small number of shareholders and a general lack of trading volume. I could begin by identifying firms with fewer than 5,000 shareholders. As far as I know, there is no good way to do this. I would have to look up each individual company in one of the Standard & Poor's or Mergent publications, or I could search the vast research resources of the Internet. Even with a battalion of assistants, this would take days.

A better approach would be to check trading volume figures. I could take a random copy of *The Wall Street Journal*, run down the stock listings on the various exchanges and the Nasdaq market, and note firms with a previous day's volume of less than, say, 1,000 shares. There is no quantitative definition of thin trading, but a volume this small certainly qualifies as thin. This method would be much more efficient than checking the number of shareholders, and it would accomplish essentially the same purpose. From this list of thinly traded securities, I could apply further screens in my hunt for an attractive investment.

### *Relevance and Appropriateness*

Screens should also logically have something to do with the ultimate objective. You might say, "I am going to invest in a good company whose name begins with the letter A." This probably does not make any sense.

Now consider a slightly different situation. You want to identify a promising company but do not want to spend hours poring through the financial pages. You might instead decide to start at the top of the NYSE listing and find something in the early part of the alphabet. You could just as easily start at the end of the alphabet, or in the middle. This latter technique is more logical than the former. Assuming there is no systematic relationship among good/bad investments and the letters of the alphabet, those beginning with the letter A should be a random sample of the total security universe. Intentionally choosing a stock that begins with the letter A is probably not an appropriate screen; selecting one from the early part of the financial pages is probably okay. The point is that the first letter in a company's name is not really a decision variable, should not be material, and is consequently an inappropriate screening device.

### Acceptance by the User

*Screens should be:*
*1. Easy to administer.*
*2. Relevant and appropriate.*
*3. Acceptable to the user.*

Screens lose much of their value if the people who are affected by the screen fundamentally disagree with it. SAT scores, as stated earlier, are used as part of the academic eligibility criteria for college athletes. Not all coaches, however, believe this is reasonable. There is some evidence of cultural bias in the wording and general makeup of these exams, and some people believe they are an inappropriate screen.

### Ordinal Ranking of Screening Criteria

When you employ a multiple-stage screening process, it is important to establish a screen pecking order. The first screening criterion should be the one that will eliminate the most alternatives. This is also often the most important criterion, although not necessarily. The second criterion should eliminate the next highest number of alternatives, and so on. If you do not follow this approach, you run the risk of wasting considerable time making passes over extensive data that have no chance of selection.

Consider the problem of selecting a dessert from the dessert cart in a restaurant. I know someone who is terribly allergic to nuts. In choosing a dessert, she has to be extremely careful to select something completely nut free. Her first screen of the dessert tray will exclude anything that obviously has nuts, whether blended in it (pistachio ice cream), cooked in it (pecan pie), or decorating the top (many pastries). It would not make sense for her to go through the whole process and end up with pecan pie, only to discover, "Wow, I can't eat this; it has nuts." Eliminating alternatives with nuts should obviously be the first screening criterion.

## Sources of Information

As mentioned earlier, this book focuses on portfolio management rather than security selection. Many other books are available if you want detailed information about the analysis of financial statements and other factors that influence the value of a particular investment. This section briefly describes several well-known and readily accessible sources of information that can be very helpful in gathering quick information about unfamiliar securities.

### Value Line

One of the best-known subscription services is the ***Value Line Investment Survey.*** This weekly publication from Value Line, Inc., follows 1,700 different common stocks and rates each of them in two categories: timeliness and safety. *Timeliness* refers to precisely what you would expect: the advisability of buying this stock now. *Safety* is a measure of potential risk with a stock. It is a function of price stability and

**TABLE 10-1** VALUE LINE RANKING SYSTEM

| *Ranking* | *Number of Stocks with This Ranking* | *Meaning* |
|---|---|---|
| 1 | 100 | Best |
| 2 | 300 | Above average |
| 3 | 900 | Average |
| 4 | 300 | Below average |
| 5 | 100 | Worst |

Rankings are assigned to both timeliness and safety.

financial strength. Value Line assigns a ranking in each of these categories according to the schedule listed in Table 10-1.

It is common to hear someone make a statement like the following: "Value Line rates the stock 1 and 2." We usually state the timeliness ranking first, so this means Value Line ranks this particular stock 1 for timeliness and 2 for safety. In other words, Value Line feels the future price appreciation of this stock will rank in the top 100 of the 1,700 stocks followed in the survey; the safety ranking indicates that the firm's future performance is less uncertain than average.

The quality of Value Line's research is excellent. A great many market analysts attach considerable significance to the Value Line report on a stock.[1] Figure 10-1 is a sample Value Line report.

Value Line also prepares an electronic product called the *Value Line Investment Analyzer*. This service provides substantial financial information on about 7,500 stocks and closed-end investment companies. This provides for very efficient screening of many mid- and small-cap companies.

## Standard & Poor's

**Standard & Poor's Corporation** publishes a wide variety of reports on the economy, industries, and individual stocks. Two of these reports are especially useful to portfolio managers.

**Stock Report.** The S&P *Stock Report* is a one-page document that contains a surprisingly thorough description of a company and an estimate of what the future holds for it. S&P updates these reports quarterly; most public libraries have them. The report contains financial statement information in addition to dividend payment dates, beta, and other risk measures. Figure 10-2 is a sample *Stock Report.*

**Stock Guide.** The S&P *Stock Guide* (a companion to the *Bond Guide*) is a monthly publication containing summary statistics on thousands of common stocks, convertible preferred stocks, warrants, and mutual funds. This publication is small enough to be carried conveniently in a briefcase or coat pocket. Many brokers receive a dozen or so of these each month and provide them to customers who request them. Figure 10-3 shows a sample page.

## Mergent

**Mergent, Inc.**, formerly known as Moody's Financial Information Services, publishes another widely used set of investment information. Long-time users will likely continue to refer to these volumes as "Moody's manuals" for years.

---

[1]Clark Holloway found that because of transaction costs, gains from weekly adjustments to Value Line recommendations were not as profitable as yearly. See the Further Reading.

FIGURE 10-1 Sample Value Line Report

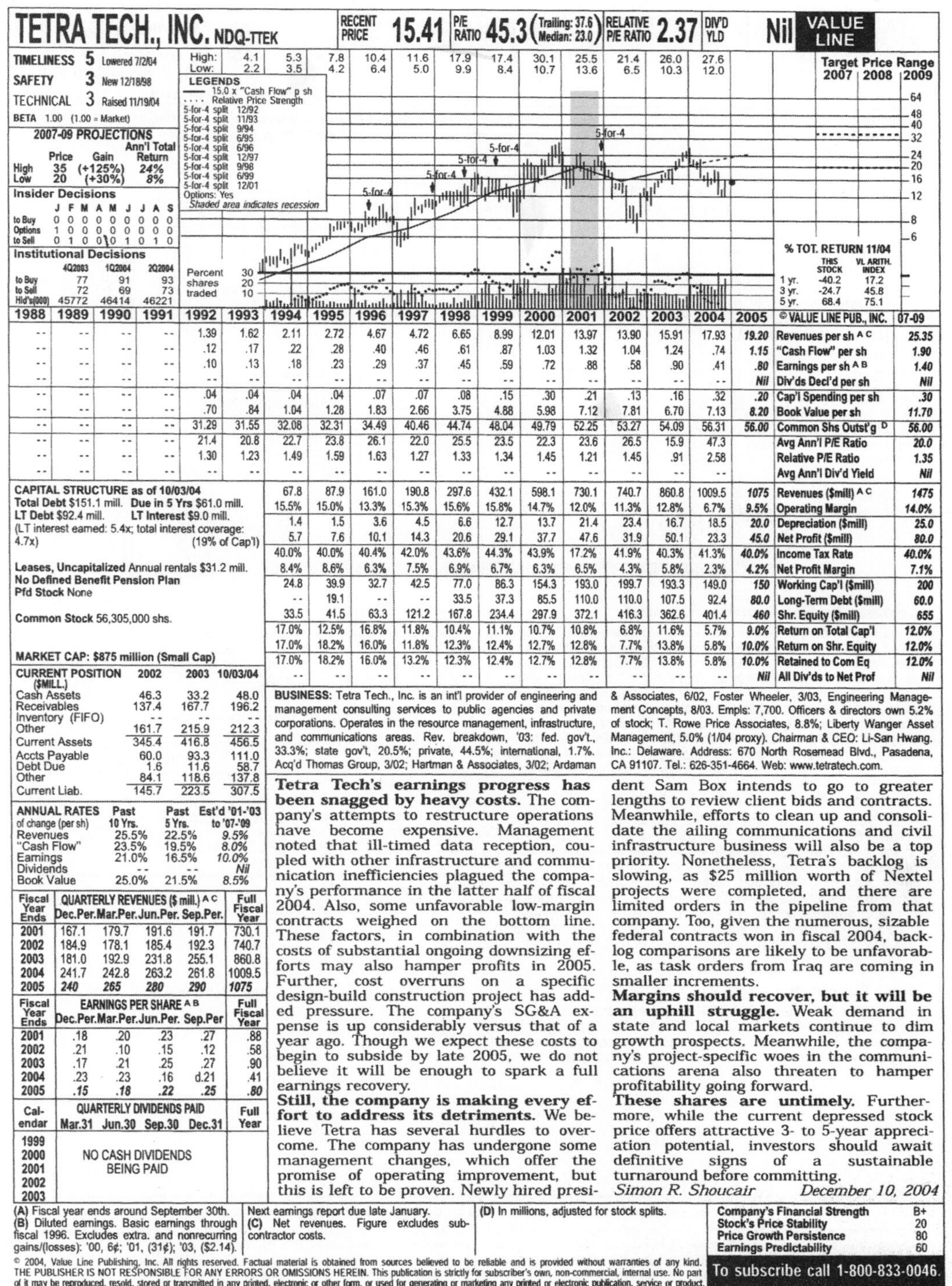

# TETRA TECH., INC. NDQ-TTEK

RECENT PRICE 15.41 | P/E RATIO 45.3 (Trailing: 37.6 Median: 23.0) | RELATIVE P/E RATIO 2.37 | DIV'D YLD Nil | VALUE LINE

TIMELINESS 5 Lowered 7/2/04
SAFETY 3 New 12/18/98
TECHNICAL 3 Raised 11/19/04
BETA 1.00 (1.00 = Market)

| | 1992 | 1993 | 1994 | 1995 | 1996 | 1997 | 1998 | 1999 | 2000 | 2001 | 2002 | 2003 | 2004 |
|---|---|---|---|---|---|---|---|---|---|---|---|---|---|
| High: | 4.1 | 5.3 | 7.8 | 10.4 | 11.6 | 17.9 | 17.4 | 30.1 | 25.5 | 21.4 | 26.0 | 27.6 | |
| Low: | 2.2 | 3.5 | 4.2 | 6.4 | 5.0 | 9.9 | 8.4 | 10.7 | 13.6 | 6.5 | 10.3 | 12.0 | |

Target Price Range 2007 | 2008 | 2009

**2007-09 PROJECTIONS**

| | Price | Gain | Ann'l Total Return |
|---|---|---|---|
| High | 35 | (+125%) | 24% |
| Low | 20 | (+30%) | 8% |

**Insider Decisions**

| | J | F | M | A | M | J | J | A | S |
|---|---|---|---|---|---|---|---|---|---|
| to Buy | 0 | 0 | 0 | 0 | 0 | 0 | 0 | 0 | 0 |
| Options | 1 | 0 | 0 | 0 | 0 | 0 | 0 | 0 | 0 |
| to Sell | 0 | 1 | 0 | 0 | 0 | 1 | 0 | 1 | 0 |

**Institutional Decisions**

| | 4Q2003 | 1Q2004 | 2Q2004 |
|---|---|---|---|
| to Buy | 77 | 91 | 93 |
| to Sell | 72 | 69 | 73 |
| Hld's(000) | 45772 | 46414 | 46221 |



**% TOT. RETURN 11/04**

| | THIS STOCK | VL ARITH. INDEX |
|---|---|---|
| 1 yr. | -40.2 | 17.2 |
| 3 yr. | -24.7 | 45.8 |
| 5 yr. | 68.4 | 75.1 |

| 1988 | 1989 | 1990 | 1991 | 1992 | 1993 | 1994 | 1995 | 1996 | 1997 | 1998 | 1999 | 2000 | 2001 | 2002 | 2003 | 2004 | 2005 | © VALUE LINE PUB., INC. | 07-09 |
|---|---|---|---|---|---|---|---|---|---|---|---|---|---|---|---|---|---|---|---|
| -- | -- | -- | -- | 1.39 | 1.62 | 2.11 | 2.72 | 4.67 | 4.72 | 6.65 | 8.99 | 12.01 | 13.97 | 13.90 | 15.91 | 17.93 | 19.20 | Revenues per sh A C | 25.35 |
| -- | -- | -- | -- | .12 | .17 | .22 | .28 | .40 | .46 | .61 | .87 | 1.03 | 1.32 | 1.04 | 1.24 | .74 | 1.15 | "Cash Flow" per sh | 1.90 |
| -- | -- | -- | -- | .10 | .13 | .18 | .23 | .29 | .37 | .45 | .59 | .72 | .88 | .58 | .90 | .41 | .80 | Earnings per sh A B | 1.40 |
| -- | -- | -- | -- | -- | -- | -- | -- | -- | -- | -- | -- | -- | -- | -- | -- | -- | Nil | Div'ds Decl'd per sh | Nil |
| -- | -- | -- | -- | .04 | .04 | .04 | .04 | .07 | .07 | .08 | .15 | .30 | .21 | .13 | .16 | .32 | .20 | Cap'l Spending per sh | .30 |
| -- | -- | -- | -- | .70 | .84 | 1.04 | 1.28 | 1.83 | 2.66 | 3.75 | 4.88 | 5.98 | 7.12 | 7.81 | 6.70 | 7.13 | 8.20 | Book Value per sh | 11.70 |
| -- | -- | -- | -- | 31.29 | 31.55 | 32.08 | 32.31 | 34.49 | 40.46 | 44.74 | 48.04 | 49.79 | 52.25 | 53.27 | 54.09 | 56.31 | 56.00 | Common Shs Outst'g D | 56.00 |
| -- | -- | -- | -- | 21.4 | 20.8 | 22.7 | 23.8 | 26.1 | 22.0 | 25.5 | 23.5 | 22.3 | 23.6 | 26.5 | 15.9 | 47.3 | | Avg Ann'l P/E Ratio | 20.0 |
| -- | -- | -- | -- | 1.30 | 1.23 | 1.49 | 1.59 | 1.63 | 1.27 | 1.33 | 1.34 | 1.45 | 1.21 | 1.45 | .91 | 2.58 | | Relative P/E Ratio | 1.35 |
| -- | -- | -- | -- | -- | -- | -- | -- | -- | -- | -- | -- | -- | -- | -- | -- | -- | | Avg Ann'l Div'd Yield | Nil |

| 1994 | 1995 | 1996 | 1997 | 1998 | 1999 | 2000 | 2001 | 2002 | 2003 | 2004 | 2005 | | 07-09 |
|---|---|---|---|---|---|---|---|---|---|---|---|---|---|
| 67.8 | 87.9 | 161.0 | 190.8 | 297.6 | 432.1 | 598.1 | 730.1 | 740.7 | 860.8 | 1009.5 | 1075 | Revenues ($mill) A C | 1475 |
| 15.5% | 15.0% | 13.3% | 15.3% | 15.6% | 15.8% | 14.7% | 12.0% | 11.3% | 12.8% | 6.7% | 9.5% | Operating Margin | 14.0% |
| 1.4 | 1.5 | 3.6 | 4.5 | 6.6 | 12.7 | 13.7 | 21.4 | 23.4 | 16.7 | 18.5 | 20.0 | Depreciation ($mill) | 25.0 |
| 5.7 | 7.6 | 10.1 | 14.3 | 20.6 | 29.1 | 37.7 | 47.6 | 31.9 | 50.1 | 23.3 | 45.0 | Net Profit ($mill) | 80.0 |
| 40.0% | 40.0% | 40.4% | 42.0% | 43.6% | 44.3% | 43.9% | 17.2% | 41.9% | 40.3% | 41.3% | 40.0% | Income Tax Rate | 40.0% |
| 8.4% | 8.6% | 6.3% | 7.5% | 6.9% | 6.7% | 6.3% | 6.5% | 4.3% | 5.8% | 2.3% | 4.2% | Net Profit Margin | 7.1% |
| 24.8 | 39.9 | 32.7 | 42.5 | 77.0 | 86.3 | 154.3 | 193.0 | 199.7 | 193.3 | 149.0 | 150 | Working Cap'l ($mill) | 200 |
| -- | 19.1 | -- | -- | 33.5 | 37.3 | 85.5 | 110.0 | 110.0 | 107.5 | 92.4 | 80.0 | Long-Term Debt ($mill) | 60.0 |
| 33.5 | 41.5 | 63.3 | 121.2 | 167.8 | 234.4 | 297.9 | 372.1 | 416.3 | 362.6 | 401.4 | 460 | Shr. Equity ($mill) | 655 |
| 17.0% | 12.5% | 16.8% | 11.8% | 10.4% | 11.1% | 10.7% | 10.8% | 6.8% | 11.6% | 5.7% | 9.0% | Return on Total Cap'l | 12.0% |
| 17.0% | 18.2% | 16.0% | 11.8% | 12.3% | 12.4% | 12.7% | 12.8% | 7.7% | 13.8% | 5.8% | 10.0% | Return on Shr. Equity | 12.0% |
| 17.0% | 18.2% | 16.0% | 13.2% | 12.3% | 12.4% | 12.7% | 12.8% | 7.7% | 13.8% | 5.8% | 10.0% | Retained to Com Eq | 12.0% |
| -- | -- | -- | -- | -- | -- | -- | -- | -- | -- | -- | Nil | All Div'ds to Net Prof | Nil |

**CAPITAL STRUCTURE as of 10/03/04**
**Total Debt** $151.1 mill. **Due in 5 Yrs** $61.0 mill.
**LT Debt** $92.4 mill. **LT Interest** $9.0 mill.
(LT interest earned: 5.4x; total interest coverage: 4.7x) (19% of Cap'l)

**Leases, Uncapitalized** Annual rentals $31.2 mill.
**No Defined Benefit Pension Plan**
**Pfd Stock** None

**Common Stock** 56,305,000 shs.

**MARKET CAP: $875 million (Small Cap)**

| CURRENT POSITION ($MILL.) | 2002 | 2003 | 10/03/04 |
|---|---|---|---|
| Cash Assets | 46.3 | 33.2 | 48.0 |
| Receivables | 137.4 | 167.7 | 196.2 |
| Inventory (FIFO) | -- | -- | -- |
| Other | 161.7 | 215.9 | 212.3 |
| Current Assets | 345.4 | 416.8 | 456.5 |
| Accts Payable | 60.0 | 93.3 | 111.0 |
| Debt Due | 1.6 | 11.6 | 58.7 |
| Other | 84.1 | 118.6 | 137.8 |
| Current Liab. | 145.7 | 223.5 | 307.5 |

| ANNUAL RATES of change (per sh) | Past 10 Yrs. | Past 5 Yrs. | Est'd '01-'03 to '07-'09 |
|---|---|---|---|
| Revenues | 25.5% | 22.5% | 9.5% |
| "Cash Flow" | 23.5% | 19.5% | 8.0% |
| Earnings | 21.0% | 16.5% | 10.0% |
| Dividends | -- | -- | Nil |
| Book Value | 25.0% | 21.5% | 8.5% |

| Fiscal Year Ends | QUARTERLY REVENUES ($ mill.) A C Dec.Per. | Mar.Per. | Jun.Per. | Sep.Per. | Full Fiscal Year |
|---|---|---|---|---|---|
| 2001 | 167.1 | 179.7 | 191.6 | 191.7 | 730.1 |
| 2002 | 184.9 | 178.1 | 185.4 | 192.3 | 740.7 |
| 2003 | 181.0 | 192.9 | 231.8 | 255.1 | 860.8 |
| 2004 | 241.7 | 242.8 | 263.2 | 261.8 | 1009.5 |
| 2005 | 240 | 265 | 280 | 290 | 1075 |

| Fiscal Year Ends | EARNINGS PER SHARE A B Dec.Per. | Mar.Per. | Jun.Per. | Sep.Per | Full Fiscal Year |
|---|---|---|---|---|---|
| 2001 | .18 | .20 | .23 | .27 | .88 |
| 2002 | .21 | .10 | .15 | .12 | .58 |
| 2003 | .17 | .21 | .25 | .27 | .90 |
| 2004 | .23 | .23 | .16 | d.21 | .41 |
| 2005 | .15 | .18 | .22 | .25 | .80 |

| Cal-endar | QUARTERLY DIVIDENDS PAID Mar.31 | Jun.30 | Sep.30 | Dec.31 | Full Year |
|---|---|---|---|---|---|
| 1999 | | | | | |
| 2000 | NO CASH DIVIDENDS BEING PAID | | | | |
| 2001 | | | | | |
| 2002 | | | | | |
| 2003 | | | | | |

**BUSINESS:** Tetra Tech., Inc. is an int'l provider of engineering and management consulting services to public agencies and private corporations. Operates in the resource management, infrastructure, and communications areas. Rev. breakdown, '03: fed. gov't., 33.3%; state gov't, 20.5%; private, 44.5%; international, 1.7%. Acq'd Thomas Group, 3/02; Hartman & Associates, 3/02; Ardaman & Associates, 6/02, Foster Wheeler, 3/03, Engineering Management Concepts, 8/03. Empls: 7,700. Officers & directors own 5.2% of stock; T. Rowe Price Associates, 8.8%; Liberty Wanger Asset Management, 5.0% (1/04 proxy). Chairman & CEO: Li-San Hwang. Inc.: Delaware. Address: 670 North Rosemead Blvd., Pasadena, CA 91107. Tel.: 626-351-4664. Web: www.tetratech.com.

**Tetra Tech's earnings progress has been snagged by heavy costs.** The company's attempts to restructure operations have become expensive. Management noted that ill-timed data reception, coupled with other infrastructure and communication inefficiencies plagued the company's performance in the latter half of fiscal 2004. Also, some unfavorable low-margin contracts weighed on the bottom line. These factors, in combination with the costs of substantial ongoing downsizing efforts may also hamper profits in 2005. Further, cost overruns on a specific design-build construction project has added pressure. The company's SG&A expense is up considerably versus that of a year ago. Though we expect these costs to begin to subside by late 2005, we do not believe it will be enough to spark a full earnings recovery.

**Still, the company is making every effort to address its detriments.** We believe Tetra has several hurdles to overcome. The company has undergone some management changes, which offer the promise of operating improvement, but this is left to be proven. Newly hired president Sam Box intends to go to greater lengths to review client bids and contracts. Meanwhile, efforts to clean up and consolidate the ailing communications and civil infrastructure business will also be a top priority. Nonetheless, Tetra's backlog is slowing, as $25 million worth of Nextel projects were completed, and there are limited orders in the pipeline from that company. Too, given the numerous, sizable federal contracts won in fiscal 2004, backlog comparisons are likely to be unfavorable, as task orders from Iraq are coming in smaller increments.

**Margins should recover, but it will be an uphill struggle.** Weak demand in state and local markets continue to dim growth prospects. Meanwhile, the company's project-specific woes in the communications arena also threaten to hamper profitability going forward.

**These shares are untimely.** Furthermore, while the current depressed stock price offers attractive 3- to 5-year appreciation potential, investors should await definitive signs of a sustainable turnaround before committing.

*Simon R. Shoucair December 10, 2004*

(A) Fiscal year ends around September 30th.
(B) Diluted earnings. Basic earnings through fiscal 1996. Excludes extra. and nonrecurring gains/(losses): '00, 6¢; '01, (31¢); '03, ($2.14).
Next earnings report due late January.
(C) Net revenues. Figure excludes subcontractor costs.
(D) In millions, adjusted for stock splits.

| | |
|---|---|
| Company's Financial Strength | B+ |
| Stock's Price Stability | 20 |
| Price Growth Persistence | 80 |
| Earnings Predictability | 60 |



Source: The Value Line Investment Survey, December 10, 2004. Copyright © 2004 by Value Line Publishing, Inc.: used by permission. For subscription information to the Value Line Investment Survey, please call (800) 634-3583.

**FIGURE 10-2** Sample S&P *Stock Report*

STANDARD &POOR'S

STOCK REPORTS

# Tetra Tech

**December 25, 2004**

NASDAQ Symbol **TTEK**

**In S&P SmallCap 600**

TTEK has an approx. 0.17% weighting in the S&P SmallCap 600

**GICS Sector:** Industrials
**Sub-Industry:** Diversified Commercial Services
**Peer Group:** Business Services

**Summary:** TTEK provides specialized management consulting and technical services in three principal areas: resource management, infrastructure and communications.

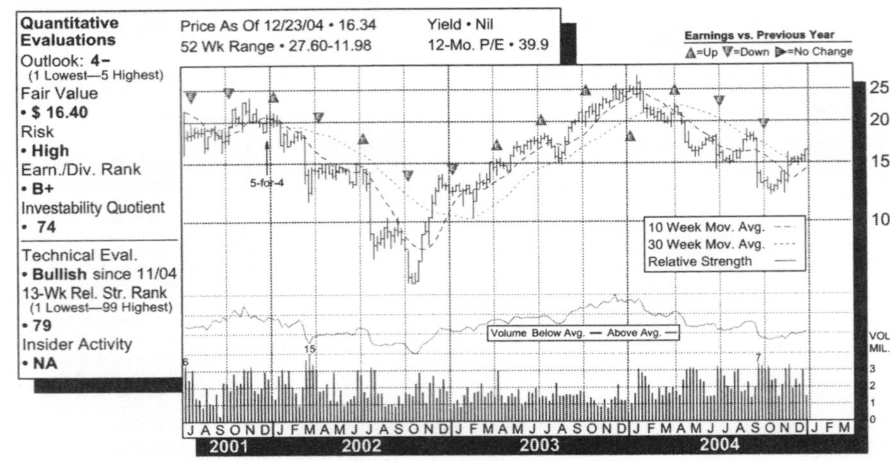


## Business Profile - September 23, 1999

A significant part of Tetra Tech's growth strategy is to acquire other companies which complement its lines of business or that broaden its geographic presence. It purchased 10 companies in five separate transactions in FY 98 (Sep.). During the first nine months of FY 99, WATR acquired seven companies. In September 1999, the company was awarded a three-year contract valued at up to $46 million by the U.S. Environmental Protection Agency (EPA) for the Office of Water's National Watershed Protection Program. Tetra Tech's shares were split 5-for-4 in each of the past seven years.

## Operational Review - September 23, 1999

Net revenues for the nine months ended July 4, 1999, advanced 53%, year to year, with all client sectors contributing to the gain. Revenue gains from commercial clients as well as revenues contributed by acquired companies bolstered 1999 revenues. Profitability was restricted by higher expenses related to acquisitions as well as a 71% increase in depreciation and amortization charges. After taxes at 43.2%, versus 43.5%, net income rose 45%, to $20,392,000 ($0.52 a share, based on 8.3% more average shares) from $14,064,000 ($0.39, adjusted).

## Stock Performance - Dec 23, 2004

In the past 30 trading days, TTEK's shares have increased 24%, compared to a 2% rise in the S&P 500. Average trading volume for the past five days was 357,104 shares, compared with the 40-day moving average of 604,134 shares.

## Key Stock Statistics

| | | | |
|---|---|---|---|
| Dividend Rate/Share | Nil | Shareholders | 2,864 |
| Shs. outstg. (M) | 56.2 | Market cap. (B) | $0.919 |
| Avg. daily vol. (M) | 0.455 | Inst. holdings | 90% |
| Tang. Bk. Value/Share | 2.32 | | |
| Beta | 0.97 | | |

Value of $10,000 invested five years ago: $ 13,982

## Fiscal Year Ending September 30

| | 2004 | 2003 | 2002 | 2001 | 2000 | 1999 |
|---|---|---|---|---|---|---|
| **Revenues (Million $)** | | | | | | |
| 1Q | 241.7 | 181.0 | 184.9 | 167.1 | 129.2 | 89.25 |
| 2Q | 331.4 | 192.9 | 178.1 | 234.3 | 138.8 | 96.96 |
| 3Q | 375.5 | 313.6 | 185.4 | 250.1 | 203.8 | 157.1 |
| 4Q | 392.1 | 255.1 | 192.3 | 191.7 | 173.6 | 125.1 |
| Yr. | 1,436 | 860.8 | 740.7 | 730.1 | 598.1 | 432.1 |
| **Earnings Per Share ($)** | | | | | | |
| 1Q | 0.23 | 0.17 | 0.21 | 0.18 | 0.15 | 0.12 |
| 2Q | 0.23 | 0.21 | 0.10 | 0.20 | 0.16 | 0.13 |
| 3Q | 0.16 | 0.25 | 0.15 | -0.07 | 0.19 | 0.17 |
| 4Q | -0.21 | 0.28 | 0.13 | 0.27 | 0.28 | 0.18 |
| Yr. | 0.41 | 0.90 | 0.58 | 0.57 | 0.78 | 0.59 |

**Next earnings report expected: late-January**

**Dividend Data**

No cash dividends have been paid.

**FIGURE 10-2** Sample S&P *Stock Report, Continued*

STANDARD &POOR'S

STOCK REPORTS

# Tetra Tech, Inc.

**December 25, 2004**

**Business Summary - November 22, 2004**

Tetra Tech is a leading provider of consulting, engineering and technical services in the areas of resource management and infrastructure. As a consultant, the company assists clients in defining problems and developing innovative and cost-effective solutions. These services span the life cycle of a project, and include research and development, applied science and technology, engineering design, construction management, and operations and maintenance. TTEK's clients include a diverse base of governmental and commercial organizations located in the U.S., and, to a lesser extent, internationally.

Prior to FY 03 (Sep.), the company operated in three areas: infrastructure, communications, and resource management. However, due to consolidation of the marketplace, management merged the communications and infrastructure segments during the first quarter of FY 03.

The resource management division (58% of FY 03 revenue, and 63% of operating profits; 12% margins) supports high priority government programs for water quality improvement, environmental restoration, productive reuse of defense facilities, and strategic environment resource planning. The unit provides services that include research and development, applied science and technology, engineering design, construction management, and operations and maintenance. Over the past five years, segment margins averaged 13%.

In the infrastructure area (41%, 33%; 8.6%), TTEK focuses on the development of water infrastructure projects, institutional facilities, commercial, recreational and leisure facilities; transportation projects; and communications infrastructure projects. Over the past five years, margins for the segment averaged 10%.

The company provides services to a diverse base of federal (33.4% of FY 03 revenue), state and local government agencies (20.4%), and commercial (44.5%) and international clients (1.7%).

TTEK enters into three types of service contracts: fixed-price (38% of FY 03 revenue); time-and-materials (41%); and cost-plus (21%). Fixed price contracts call for the client to pay a specified price. Time-and-materials contracts call for the client to pay for labor and other expenses at hourly rates. Cost-plus contracts require the client to reimburse the company for allowable costs and fees, which may be fixed or performance-based.

Since December 2000, the company has made a number of acquisitions, at a total cost of about $218 million. In 2003, it acquired certain assets of Foster Wheeler Environmental Corp. and Hartman Consulting Corp. These entities provide engineering and program management services throughout the U.S. The total purchase price was about $68 million. TTEK also acquired Engineering Management Concepts, Inc. (EMC), an engineering and management firm that provides information technology and weapons test range and systems logistical support services. The total purchase price was about $19 million.

| **Per Share Data ($)**<br>**(Year Ended September 30)** | **2004** | **2003** | **2002** | **2001** | **2000** | **1999** | **1998** | **1997** | **1996** | **1995** |
|---|---|---|---|---|---|---|---|---|---|---|
| Tangible Bk. Val. | NA | 2.63 | 2.56 | 2.43 | 2.16 | 1.54 | 1.32 | 0.94 | 1.18 | 0.84 |
| Cash Flow | NA | 1.20 | 1.00 | 0.96 | 1.04 | 0.85 | 0.60 | 0.49 | 0.39 | 0.36 |
| Earnings | 0.41 | 0.90 | 0.58 | 0.57 | 0.78 | 0.59 | 0.46 | 0.37 | 0.29 | 0.23 |
| S&P Core Earnings | NA | 0.82 | 0.56 | 0.50 | NA | NA | NA | NA | NA | NA |
| Dividends | Nil | Nil | Nil | Nil | Nil | Nil | Nil | Nil | Nil | Nil |
| Payout Ratio | Nil | Nil | Nil | Nil | Nil | Nil | Nil | Nil | Nil | Nil |
| Prices - High | 27.60 | 25.97 | 21.40 | 25.50 | 30.05 | 17.20 | 17.92 | 11.57 | 10.44 | 7.78 |
| - Low | 11.98 | 10.26 | 6.47 | 13.60 | 10.70 | 8.40 | 9.85 | 5.01 | 6.38 | 4.19 |
| P/E Ratio - High | 67 | 29 | 37 | 45 | 39 | 29 | 39 | 31 | 36 | 33 |
| - Low | 29 | 11 | 11 | 24 | 14 | 14 | 22 | 13 | 22 | 18 |
| **Income Statement Analysis (Million $)** | | | | | | | | | | |
| Revs. | NA | 861 | 741 | 730 | 598 | 432 | 298 | 191 | 161 | 87.9 |
| Oper. Inc. | NA | 110 | 83.8 | 70.6 | 88.0 | 68.1 | 46.4 | 29.1 | 21.3 | 13.7 |
| Depr. | NA | 16.7 | 23.4 | 21.4 | 13.7 | 12.7 | 6.59 | 4.51 | 3.61 | 1.89 |
| Int. Exp. | NA | 10.2 | 9.34 | 9.63 | 7.36 | 3.56 | 2.33 | 0.32 | 1.08 | Nil |
| Pretax Inc. | NA | 83.9 | 55.0 | 40.7 | 67.2 | 52.3 | 37.9 | 24.6 | 17.0 | 12.6 |
| Eff. Tax Rate | NA | 40.3% | 41.9% | 24.3% | 39.8% | 44.3% | 42.0% | 42.0% | 40.4% | 40.0% |
| Net Inc. | NA | 50.1 | 31.9 | 30.8 | 40.4 | 29.1 | 20.6 | 14.3 | 10.1 | 7.55 |
| S&P Core Earnings | NA | 45.5 | 30.7 | 27.3 | NA | NA | NA | NA | NA | NA |
| **Balance Sheet & Other Fin. Data (Million $)** | | | | | | | | | | |
| Cash | NA | 33.2 | 46.3 | 16.2 | 7.56 | 8.19 | 4.89 | 12.3 | 6.13 | 13.1 |
| Curr. Assets | NA | 417 | 345 | 316 | 297 | 195 | 142 | 80.9 | 57.9 | 72.3 |
| Total Assets | NA | 693 | 672 | 607 | 526 | 380 | 267 | 160 | 88.5 | 92.9 |
| Curr. Liab. | NA | 223 | 146 | 123 | 143 | 109 | 65.3 | 38.3 | 25.2 | 32.4 |
| LT Debt | NA | 107 | 110 | 112 | 85.5 | 37.3 | 33.5 | Nil | Nil | 19.0 |
| Common Equity | NA | 363 | 416 | 359 | 284 | 221 | 152 | 108 | 63.3 | 41.5 |
| Total Cap. | NA | 470 | 526 | 471 | 370 | 258 | 186 | 121 | 63.3 | 60.5 |
| Cap. Exp. | NA | 8.42 | 7.17 | 11.0 | 14.7 | 7.00 | 3.50 | 2.60 | 2.40 | 1.50 |
| Cash Flow | NA | 66.8 | 55.3 | 52.2 | 54.2 | 41.8 | 27.2 | 18.8 | 13.7 | 9.45 |
| Curr. Ratio | NA | 1.9 | 2.4 | 2.6 | 2.1 | 1.8 | 2.2 | 2.1 | 2.3 | 2.2 |
| % LT Debt of Cap. | NA | 22.9 | 20.9 | 23.7 | 23.1 | 14.4 | 18.0 | Nil | Nil | 31.4 |
| % Net Inc.of Revs. | NA | 5.8 | 4.3 | 4.2 | 6.8 | 6.7 | 6.9 | 7.5 | 6.3 | 8.6 |
| % Ret. on Assets | NA | 7.3 | 5.0 | 5.4 | 8.9 | 9.0 | 9.7 | 11.5 | 11.1 | 10.5 |
| % Ret. on Equity | NA | 12.9 | 8.1 | 9.6 | 16.0 | 15.6 | 15.8 | 16.7 | 19.3 | 20.1 |

Data as orig reptd.; bef. results of disc opers/spec. items. Per share data adj. for stk. divs.; EPS diluted. E-Estimated. NA-Not Available. NM-Not Meaningful. NR-Not Ranked. UR-Under Review.

**Office**—3475 East Foothill Boulevard, Pasadena, CA 91107. **Telephone**—626-351-4664. **Email**—ir@tetratech.com **Website**—http://www.tetratech.com **Chrmn & CEO**—L. Hwang. **Pres**—J. Jaska. **EVP, CFO & Treas**—D.W. King. **EVP & Secy**—R. Lemmon. **VP & General Counsel**—J.B. Salin. **Investor Contact**—M. Bieber 626-351-4664. **Dirs**—H. Grant, P. C. Haden, L. Hwang, J. Jaska, J. C. Lewis, J. J. Shelton, R. H. Truly, D. A. Whalen. **Founded**—in 1966. **Domicile**—Delaware. **Empl**— 8,900. **S&P Analyst:** Anthony M. Fiore, CFA /MF/BK

Source: Standard & Poor's Stock Guide (New York: Standard & Poor's Corporation, 2004): Reprinted with permission.

**FIGURE 10-3** Sample Page from the S&P *Stock Guide*

## 204 UNI-UTI

Standard & Poor's

¶ S&P 500 · # MidCap 400 · ✣ SmallCap 600 · • Options

| Index | Ticker | Name of Issue (Call Price of Pfd. Stocks) | Market | Com. Rank. & Pfd. Rating | Inst. Hold Cos | Inst. Hold Shs. (000) | Principal Business | Price Range 1971-02 High | 1971-02 Low | 2003 High | 2003 Low | 2004 High | 2004 Low | Oct. Sales in 100s | October, 2004 Last Sale Or Bid High | Low | Last | %Div Yield | P-E Ratio | EPS 5 Yr Growth | % Annualized Total Return 12 Mo | 36 Mo | 60 Mo |
|---|---|---|---|---|---|---|---|---|---|---|---|---|---|---|---|---|---|---|---|---|---|---|---|
| ✣1 | USPI | United Surgical Ptnrs | NNM | NR | . . | . . . | Oper surgical centers | 34.65 | 13.35 | 34.50 | 14.29 | 41.15 | 31.63 | 63263 | 36.00 | 31.63 | 35.01 | . . . | 12 | . . . | 17.1 | 18.0 | . . . |
| ¶2•[1] | UTX | ✓United Technologies | NY,B,C,Ch,P,Ph | A+ | 1919 | 401052 | Aerospace,climate ctrl sys | 87.50 | 1.29 | 96.75 | 53.51 | 97.84 | 80.67 | 412094 | 96.41 | 88.48 | 92.82 | 1.5 | 17 | 12 | 20.6 | 28.1 | 11.9 |
| 3 | UU | United Utilities ADS[51] | NY,Ph | NR | 37 | 2735 | Utility:water & electric | 32.37 | 16.56 | 21.93 | 15.40 | 21.54 | 17.40 | 20146 | 21.54 | 19.92 | 21.44 | 7.6 | 11 | −10 | 42.9 | 19.7 | 13.0 |
| 4•[1] | UCOMA | ✓UnitedGlobalCom Inc'A' | NNM | C | 437 | 332432 | Intl multi-channel TV svcs | 114.62 | 0.50 | 9.00 | 2.20 | 10.90 | 5.80 | 259094 | 7.87 | 7.18 | 7.48 | . . . | 3 | NM | 19.4 | 86.7 | −27.9 |
| ¶5•[2] | UNH | ✓UnitedHealth Group | NY,Ph,P | A | 1888 | 584347 | Manages health maint svcs | 50.50 | 0.16 | 58.67 | 39.20 | 75.19 | 55.45 | 1076868 | 75.19 | 64.61 | 72.40 | 0.0 | 19 | 37 | 42.6 | 30.2 | 45.2 |
| 6 | UTL | UNITIL Corp | AS | B+ | 33 | 893 | Hldg co: elec utility in N.H. | 38.56 | 5.96 | 26.34 | 23.05 | 28.50 | 25.33 | 434 | 28.15 | 27.15 | 27.90 | 4.9 | 19 | −1 | 19.1 | 10.6 | 6.0 |
| #7 | UTR | ✓Unitrin Inc | NY | B | 292 | 20494 | Ins hldg:life,accid&hlth,prop | 42.80 | 12.25 | 42.50 | 21.50 | 44.95 | 36.72 | 23986 | 43.95 | 39.77 | 43.18 | 3.8 | 14 | −19 | 21.6 | 11.5 | 9.3 |
| 8 | UCO | ✓Univl Compression Hldgs | NY | NR | 247 | 19369 | Nat'l gas compression svc | 40.50 | 14.60 | 27.00 | 15.36 | 36.22 | 25.49 | 34792 | 36.22 | 33.61 | 34.58 | . . . | 21 | 33 | 57.3 | 7.3 | . . . |
| #9 | UVV | ✓Univl Corp | NY,B,Ch,Ph,P | A | 334 | 22246 | Leaf tobacco/building prod | 49.50 | 1.35 | 44.51 | 35.11 | 53.72 | 42.01 | 20227 | 46.80 | 43.04 | 45.78 | 3.4 | 10 | −1 | 8.3 | 15.4 | 16.4 |
| 10 | PANL | ✓Univl Display | NNM,Ph | NR | 57 | 9534 | Dvp stg:electronics R&D | 38.50 | 3.00 | 15.81 | 6.20 | 18.87 | 6.80 | 11172 | 10.48 | 8.31 | 9.83 | . . . | d | −12 | −14.7 | 5.3 | 21.3 |
| ✣11 | UFPI | ✓Univl Forest Products | NNM | A | 272 | 13045 | Mfr,dstr lumber products | 27.80 | 5.87 | 32.98 | 15.01 | 38.65 | 26.36 | 15046 | 38.65 | 33.80 | 36.63 | 0.3 | 15 | 12 | 24.5 | 29.7 | 20.9 |
| 12 | UHT | Univl Health Realty | NY,Ch | A− | 137 | 3771 | Real estate investment trust | 28.50 | 8.25 | 30.79 | 23.90 | 34.09 | 24.15 | 4461 | 31.88 | 29.61 | 31.42 | 6.4 | 15 | 6 | 20.0 | 16.0 | 23.1 |
| #13•[3] | UHS | ✓Univl Health Svs'B' | NY,Ph | B+ | . . | . . . | Acute care hospitals | 57.50 | 0.75 | 54.75 | 32.05 | 56.95 | 39.55 | 131848 | 44.70 | 39.55 | 41.56 | 0.8 | 15 | 23 | −11.9 | −3.3 | 29.0 |
| 14 | UUU | Univl Security Instr | AS | C | 4 | 2 | Mfr security prod,telecom dev | 33.00 | 0.25 | 14.81 | 5.06 | 15.25 | 10.00 | 276 | 11.20 | 10.35 | 10.88 | . . . | 8 | NM | −8.5 | 130 | 60.2 |
| 15 | UTI | Univl Tech Institute | NY | NR | 174 | 16496 | Auto repair education svcs | . . . . | . . . . | 30.40 | 20.50 | 48.50 | 24.26 | 17504 | 33.61 | 29.48 | 32.81 | . . . | 32 | . . . | . . . | . . . | . . . |
| ¶16•[4] | UVN | ✓Univision Communic'A' | NY,Ch,Ph | NR | 949 | 240054 | Spanish-language TV brodcg US | 62.68 | 5.75 | 39.95 | 21.83 | 40.05 | 28.38 | 263971 | 32.10 | 29.22 | 30.96 | . . . | 42 | 10 | −8.8 | 7.4 | −6.2 |
| ¶17•[3] | UCL | ✓Unocal Corp | NY,B,C,Ch,P,Ph | B | 902 | 222885 | Oil & gas explor,dvlp,prod'n | 46.62 | 3.40 | 37.08 | 24.97 | 44.17 | 34.18 | 314293 | 44.17 | 40.56 | 41.75 | 1.9 | 10 | 30 | 38.3 | 14.1 | 5.6 |
| 18•[5] | UNA | ✓UNOVA Inc | NY | NR | 270 | 50642 | Indl automation systems | 24.00 | 2.15 | 25.23 | 4.42 | 26.63 | 13.59 | 119002 | 15.64 | 13.90 | 15.35 | . . . | 77 | 15 | −29.3 | 69.0 | 2.9 |
| ¶19•[2] | UNM | ✓UnumProvident Corp | NY | B | 713 | 276989 | Disablilty/life/hlth insur | 56.87 | 1.80 | 19.54 | 5.91 | 16.85 | 11.41 | 1032891 | 15.97 | 11.41 | 13.66 | 2.2 | 8 | Neg | 5.6 | −11.7 | −10.9 |
| 20 | UNN | UnumProvident Corp 7.25%'PINES' | NY | . . .[56] | . . | . . . | Public Income Notes | 25.04 | 19.70 | 25.79 | 14.50 | 26.24 | 21.20 | 2378 | 25.50 | 23.71 | 24.85 | 7.3 | . . | . . . | 6.8 | . . . | . . . |
| 21 | UPM | ✓UPM-Kymmene Corp ADS[58] | NY | NR | 66 | 14174 | Mfr paper/forest pds | 22.25 | 11.31 | 20.25 | 12.30 | 20.45 | 17.55 | 12668 | 20.35 | 19.12 | 19.86 | 3.9 | 15 | −13 | 10.9 | 12.5 | 10.3 |
| 22 | UQM | ✓UQM Technologies | AS | C | 26 | 1175 | R&D electric motor tech | 11.75 | 1.55 | 3.88 | 2.05 | 3.60 | 2.00 | 7178 | 2.55 | 2.00 | 2.33 | . . . | d | 5 | −30.9 | −20.3 | −9.4 |
| #23•[6] | URBN | ✓Urban Outfitters | NNM | B+ | 446 | 50439 | Retail/wholesale apparel,gifts | 9.30 | 1.60 | 20.64 | 4.18 | 41.47 | 18.33 | 182822 | 41.47 | 34.01 | 41.00 | . . . | 39 | 35 | 146 | 133 | 49.4 |
| 24 | URT | Urecoats Industries | AS | NR | 4 | 234 | Recycled sealing pds | 56.25 | 0.20 | 1.28 | 0.30 | 2.00 | 0.35 | 1986 | 0.60 | 0.35 | 0.47 | . . . | d | 14 | 23.7 | −48.8 | −19.0 |
| ✣25 | URS | ✓URS Corp | NY,B,Ch,P,Ph | B+ | 309 | 38964 | Engin'g & architectural svcs | 230.00 | 2.25 | 26.00 | 7.95 | 31.34 | 22.12 | 46156 | 27.63 | 25.98 | 27.60 | . . . | 15 | −7 | 26.1 | 7.2 | 8.9 |
| 26 | UBA | ✓Urstadt Biddle Properties'A' | NY | B | 148 | 8082 | RE inv tr:purch/lease back | 12.18 | 6.75 | 14.57 | 11.00 | 16.81 | 12.51 | 6965 | 16.81 | 15.05 | 16.10 | 5.3 | 21 | 5 | 25.7 | 28.1 | 26.2 |
| 27 | UBP | Com | NY,Ch,Ph | B | 33 | 783 | | 13.87 | 4.50 | 13.99 | 11.95 | 15.94 | 12.89 | 591 | 15.94 | 14.45 | 15.40 | 5.1 | 22 | 6 | 23.2 | 28.2 | 25.2 |
| 28 | UDW | US Dataworks | AS | NR | 5 | 486 | Financial ind software prd | 22.81 | 0.30 | 4.84 | 0.50 | 3.68 | 0.80 | 36025 | 1.46 | 1.07 | 1.23 | . . . | d | 50 | −62.0 | 5.4 | . . . |
| 29•[7] | CLEC | ✓US LEC Corp'A' | NNM | NR | 25 | 2949 | Telecommunication svcs | 48.00 | 1.49 | 8.60 | 1.85 | 8.20 | 3.00 | 14439 | 3.95 | 3.00 | 3.35 | . . . | d | Neg | −36.6 | −4.2 | −34.5 |
| 30 | USAK | ✓USA Truck | NNM | B | 20 | 3969 | General commodities truck'g | 20.25 | 4.87 | 12.35 | 6.01 | 13.00 | 9.05 | 1025 | 12.99 | 11.85 | 12.31 | . . . | 21 | 31 | 14.5 | 19.9 | 7.2 |
| 31 | USNA | ✓USANA Health Sciences | NNM | B | 152 | 8879 | Mfr nutritional/hlth prd | 12.06 | 0.43 | 39.49 | 5.75 | 36.59 | 22.89 | 49442 | 36.15 | 29.29 | 29.83 | . . . | 22 | 57 | −10.6 | 236 | 48.5 |
| 32 | UBH | ✓U.S.B. Holding | NY | A | 104 | 3238 | Commercial bkg,New York | 21.06 | 1.86 | 19.19 | 13.33 | 27.50 | 18.31 | 6288 | 27.50 | 25.04 | 27.18 | s1.9 | 20 | 12 | 55.6 | 37.2 | 20.9 |
| 33•[8] | USU | ✓USEC Inc | NY,Ph | NR | 179 | 60117 | Uranium fuel enrichment svcs | 16.31 | 3.43 | 9.00 | 5.20 | 11.14 | 6.88 | 102566 | 11.14 | 9.35 | 9.66 | 5.7 | . . | −46 | 38.8 | 22.7 | 10.1 |
| ✣34•[3] | USFC | ✓USF Corp | NNM | B+ | . . | . . . | Trucking-gen'l commodities | 52.00 | 9.33 | 36.25 | 22.27 | 38.70 | 27.51 | 34831 | 38.70 | 34.30 | 35.84 | 1.0 | 17 | −26 | 13.7 | 8.1 | −2.9 |
| 35•[9] | USG | USG Corp | NY,P | D | 227 | 30814 | Gypsum base bldg products | 65.00 | 2.80 | 23.72 | 3.78 | 23.89 | 12.30 | 206973 | 23.89 | 18.24 | 22.39 | . . . | 4 | NM | 33.7 | 60.8 | −14.2 |
| 36 | USIH | ✓U.S.I. Holdings | NNM,Sg,Mo | NR | 189 | 39688 | Insurance/financial svcs | 11.75 | 9.60 | 13.70 | 9.68 | 16.70 | 9.52 | 135541 | 14.00 | 9.52 | 9.71 | . . . | 14 | . . . | −23.8 | . . . | . . . |
| ¶37•[10] | UST | ✓UST Inc | NY,B,Ch,P | A− | 657 | 139484 | Snuff,tobacco,wine,spirits | 41.35 | 0.45 | 37.79 | 26.73 | 41.48 | 34.00 | 176065 | 41.48 | 39.56 | 41.16 | 5.1 | 13 | −31 | 21.3 | 12.5 | 13.0 |
| 38 | UTMD | Utah Medical Products | NNM,Ch | B+ | 27 | 1973 | Mfr medical devices/supplies | 23.50 | 0.62 | 26.30 | 17.41 | 27.19 | 16.02 | 4604 | 18.87 | 17.50 | 17.97 | 3.3 | 8 | 22 | −22.5 | 17.8 | 23.1 |
| 39 | UTK | UTEK Corp | AS | NR | 3 | 36 | Business dvlp co | 8.75 | 5.25 | 11.14 | 5.40 | 17.15 | 11.00 | 921 | 15.44 | 14.70 | 15.20 | . . . | 7 | . . . | 57.5 | 26.8 | . . . |
| 40 | UTIW | ✓UTi Worldwide | NNM | NR | 239 | 16864 | Freight forwarding svcs | 26.45 | 11.16 | 38.82 | 22.00 | 67.25 | 37.65 | 30136 | 67.25 | 56.00 | 65.00 | 0.1 | 38 | 16 | 89.0 | 73.5 | . . . |

**Uniform Footnote Explanations-See Page 1. Other:** [1]ASE,CBOE,P,Ph:Cycle 2. [2]ASE,CBOE,P:Cycle 3. [3]CBOE,P:Cycle 1. [4]ASE,CBOE:Cycle 3. [5]CBOE:Cycle 3. [6]P:Cycle 3. [7]ASE:Cycle 1. [8]ASE,CBOE:Cycle 1. [9]CBOE,P:Cycle 2. [10]ASE,CBOE,P:Cycle 1. [51]Ea par L ADS rep 2 Ord. [52]Incl $20.573 proceeds from sale of rights. [53]Excl subsid pfd. [54]Fiscal Jun '02 & prior. [55]12 Mo Mar'04:Fiscal Jun'03 earn $4.34. [56]Rated'A-'by S&P. [57]Total Issue Amt. [58]Ea ADS rep 1 ord shr FIM10. [59]Approx. [60]Reported in Euros. [61]Pfd in $M. [62]Fiscal Jun'01 & prior. [63]12 Mo Dec'02:Fiscal Jun'02 earn $0.20. [64]Incl liabs subj to compromise.

## FIGURE 10-3 Sample Page from the S&P *Stock Guide*, *Continued*

## Common and Convertible Preferred Stocks

**UNI-UTI** 205

| Splits ◆ Index | Cash Divs. Ea. Yr. Since | Dividends: Latest Payment | | | Dividends: Total $ | | | Financial Position: Mil-$ | | | | Capitalization | Shs. 000 | | Earnings $ Per Shr.: Years | | | | | | | Interim Earnings | $ per Shr. | | |
|---|---|---|---|---|---|---|---|---|---|---|---|---|---|---|---|---|---|---|---|---|---|---|---|---|---|
| Index | Since | Period $ | Date | Ex. Div. | So Far 2004 | Ind. Rate | Paid 2003 | Cash& Equiv. | Curr. Assets | Curr. Liab. | Balance Sheet Date | Lg Trm Debt Mil-$ | Pfd. | Com. | End | 2000 | 2001 | 2002 | 2003 | 2004 | Last 12 Mos. | Period | 2003 | 2004 | Index |
| 1 | .... | None Since Public | | | ... | Nil | .... | 43.2 | 162 | 118 | 6-30-04 | 306 | ... | 28328 | Dc | vpd0.58 | v□d0.26 | v0.75 | v1.06 | .... | 2.97 | 9 Mo Sep | v0.74 | v2.65 | 1 |
| 2 | 1936 | Q0.35 | 12-10-04 | 11-17 | 1.40 | 1.40 | 1.13½ | 2340 | 14677 | 11670 | 9-30-04 | 4254 | ... | 511043 | Dc | v3.55 | v3.83 | v4.42 | v4.69 | E5.60↑ | 5.39 | 9 Mo Sep | v3.53 | v4.23 | 2 |
| 3 | 1999 | 1.07 | 9-7-04 | 6-30 | 1.605 | 1.62 | [52]3.576 | 1932 | 2872 | 2530 | 3-31-04 | 8073 | ... | 711800 | Mr | v2.19 | v1.38 | v1.57 | v1.92 | .... | 1.92 | | | | 3 |
| 4 | .... | None Since Public | | | ... | Nil | .... | 1389 | 1892 | 874 | 6-30-04 | 4036 | ... | ±784323 | Dc | ±vd13.24 | vΔd45.76 | Δ□vd3.23 | v±7.41 | .... | 2.57 | 6 Mo Jun | v±4.51 | v±d0.33 | 4 |
| 5◆ | 1990 | A0.03 | 4-16-04 | 3-30 | 0.03 | 0.03 | 0.015 | 3509 | 7028 | 9372 | 6-30-04 | 2250 | ... | 664698 | Dc | v1.10 | v1.40 | v2.13 | v2.96 | E3.92↑ | 3.68 | 9 Mo Sep | v2.13 | v2.85 | 5 |
| 6 | 1908 | Q0.34½ | 11-15-04 | 10-28 | 1.38 | 1.38 | 1.38 | 3.82 | 27.3 | 45.1 | 9-30-04 | 111 | [53]... | 5539 | Dc | v1.47 | v□1.01 | v1.23 | v1.58 | .... | 1.46 | 9 Mo Sep | v1.12 | v1.00 | 6 |
| 7 | 1990 | Q0.415 | 8-27-04 | 8-12 | 1.245 | 1.66 | 1.66 | Total Assets $8869.2M | | | 9-30-04 | 502 | ... | 68571 | Dc | v1.32 | v5.60 | vd0.12 | v1.82 | .... | 3.07 | 9 Mo Sep | v1.17 | v2.42 | 7 |
| 8 | .... | None Since Public | | | ... | Nil | .... | 38.1 | 250 | 135 | 6-30-04 | 791 | ... | 31455 | Mr | v0.34 | v1.65 | v1.08 | v0.98 | E1.62↑ | 1.41 | 3 Mo Jun | vd0.06 | v0.37 | 8 |
| 9 | 1927 | Q0.39 | 11-8-04 | 10-6 | 1.56 | 1.56 | 1.44 | 52.7 | 1796 | 1013 | 6-30-04 | 769 | ... | 25532 | Mr | v3.77 | v4.08 | v[54]4.00 | v[55]3.80 | E4.75 | 3.66 | 3 Mo Jun | v0.94 | v0.80 | 9 |
| 10 | .... | None Since Public | | | ... | Nil | .... | 54.8 | 56.4 | 4.50 | 6-30-04 | .... | 500 | 27495 | Dc | vd0.62 | vd1.11 | vd1.71 | vd0.82 | .... | d0.78 | 6 Mo Jun | vd0.37 | vd0.33 | 10 |
| 11 | 1993 | S0.05 | 12-15-04 | 11-29 | 0.10 | 0.10 | 0.09½ | 19.2 | 487 | 205 | 9-25-04 | 247 | ... | 17905 | Dc | v1.49 | v1.63 | v1.97 | v2.18 | .... | 2.46 | 9 Mo Sep | v1.85 | v2.13 | 11 |
| 12 | 1987 | Q0.50 | 9-30-04 | 9-13 | 1.49½ | 2.00 | 1.96 | Total Assets $209M | | | 6-30-04 | 50.4 | ... | 11747 | Dc | v1.81 | v1.74 | v1.84 | v2.07 | .... | 2.12 | 9 Mo Sep | v1.39 | v1.44 | 12 |
| 13◆ | 2003 | 0.08 | 9-15-04 | 8-30 | 0.24 | 0.32 | 0.08 | 36.3 | 711 | 474 | 6-30-04 | 849 | ... | ±58185 | Dc | v±1.50 | v±□1.62 | v±2.74 | v±3.20 | E2.80↓ | 2.89 | 9 Mo Sep | v±2.45 | v±2.14 | 13 |
| 14◆ | .... | 0.10 | 7-5-78 | 6-14 | ... | Nil | .... | 0.05 | 6.38 | 1.90 | 6-30-04 | .... | ... | 1581 | Mr | vd0.62 | v0.21 | v1.54 | v1.49 | .... | 1.42 | 3 Mo Jun | v0.51 | v0.44 | 14 |
| 15 | .... | None Since Public | | | ... | Nil | .... | 8.93 | 31.8 | 61.0 | 6-30-04 | 0.03 | ... | 27772 | Sp | ... | ... | ... | v0.79 | .... | 1.02 | 9 Mo Jun | v0.58 | v0.81 | 15 |
| 16◆ | .... | None Since Public | | | ... | Nil | .... | 79.7 | 591 | 294 | 6-30-04 | 1351 | ... | ±322564 | Dc | v±0.57 | v□0.23 | v±0.34 | v±0.55 | E0.74 | 0.67 | 6 Mo Jun | v±0.21 | v±0.33 | 16 |
| 17 | 1916 | Q0.20 | 11-12-04 | 10-7 | 0.80 | 0.80 | 0.80 | 939 | 2542 | 2102 | 6-30-04 | 3340 | ... | 264749 | Dc | v3.08 | v2.50 | v1.34 | v□2.76 | E4.30↑ | 4.16 | 9 Mo Sep | v□2.08 | v3.48 | 17 |
| 18 | .... | None Since Public | | | ... | Nil | .... | 191 | 772 | 398 | 6-30-04 | 109 | ... | 60870 | Dc | vd0.71 | vd5.14 | v0.04 | vd0.33 | .... | 0.20 | 6 Mo Jun | vd0.27 | v0.26 | 18 |
| 19 | 1925 | Q0.07½ | 11-19-04 | 10-21 | 0.30 | 0.30 | 0.29¾ | Total Assets $48504M | | | 6-30-04 | 3089 | ... | 296406 | Dc | v2.33 | v□2.39 | v□1.68 | vΔd1.54 | E1.74 | d2.84 | 6 Mo Jun | vd0.58 | vd1.88 | 19 |
| 20 | 2002 | Q0.453 | 9-15-04 | 9-10 | 1.359 | 1.813 | 1.813 | Co opt redm fr 6-25-2007 at $25 | | | | [57]150 | ... | ... | Dc | ... | ... | ... | .... | .... | .... | Due 6-15-2032 | | | 20 |
| 21◆ | 1998 | 0.766 | 4-12-04 | 3-25 | 0.766 | 0.77 | [59]0.686 | 388 | 3031 | 2288 | [60]12-31-03 | 3993 | ... | 260116 | Dc | □v2.22 | v1.72 | v1.10 | v0.88 | .... | 1.37 | 6 Mo Jun | v0.31 | v0.80 | 21 |
| 22 | .... | None Since Public | | | ... | Nil | .... | 2.89 | 4.60 | 1.36 | 6-30-04 | 1.07 | ... | 19575 | Mr | vd0.18 | vd0.49 | vd0.19 | vd0.25 | .... | d0.27 | 3 Mo Jun | vd0.02 | vd0.04 | 22 |
| 23◆ | .... | None Since Public | | | ... | Nil | .... | 102 | 222 | 83.0 | 7-31-04 | .... | ... | 80945 | Ja | v0.15 | v0.22 | v0.35 | v0.60 | E1.06↑ | 0.85 | 6 Mo Jul | v0.20 | v0.45 | 23 |
| 24◆ | .... | None Paid | | | ... | Nil | .... | 0.10 | 1.59 | 8.66 | 6-30-04 | 0.02 | 63 | 28947 | Dc | vd0.50 | □vd0.06 | vd0.66 | vd0.55 | .... | d0.26 | 6 Mo Jun | vd0.40 | vd0.11 | 24 |
| 25 | .... | 5%Stk | 9-11-87 | 8-26 | ... | Nil | .... | 38.5 | 977 | 507 | 7-31-04 | 523 | ... | 43499 | Oc | v2.27 | v2.41 | v2.03 | v1.76 | E1.90 | 1.49 | 9 Mo Jul | v1.18 | v0.91 | 25 |
| 26 | 1999 | Q0.21½ | 10-15-04 | 9-28 | 0.86 | 0.86 | 0.84 | Total Assets $396M | | | 7-31-04 | 108 | 550 | ±25777 | Oc | v0.55 | v0.97 | v0.87 | v0.73 | .... | 0.76 | 9 Mo Jul | v0.54 | v0.57 | 26 |
| 27 | 1970 | Q0.19½ | 10-15-04 | 9-28 | 0.78 | 0.78 | 0.76 | .... | ... | ... | | .... | ... | 7142 | Oc | v0.49 | v0.88 | v0.78 | v0.66 | .... | 0.70 | 9 Mo Jul | v0.48 | v0.52 | 27 |
| 28◆ | .... | None Paid | | | ... | Nil | .... | 3.59 | 5.20 | 1.44 | 6-30-04 | 0.04 | 630 | 26653 | Mr | vd0.95 | vd0.95 | vd0.25 | vd0.38 | .... | d0.26 | 3 Mo Jun | vd0.17 | vd0.05 | 28 |
| 29 | .... | None Since Public | | | ... | Nil | .... | 42.1 | 109 | 113 | 6-30-04 | 92.3 | [61]253 | 30074 | Dc | vd4.57 | v±d2.83 | vd2.26 | vd1.08 | .... | d0.88 | 6 Mo Jun | vd0.61 | vd0.41 | 29 |
| 30 | .... | None Since Public | | | ... | Nil | .... | 1.43 | 56.9 | 59.7 | 9-30-04 | 100 | ... | 9341 | Dc | v0.01 | v0.12 | v0.28 | v0.36 | .... | 0.59 | 9 Mo Sep | v0.24 | v0.47 | 30 |
| 31◆ | .... | None Since Public | | | ... | Nil | .... | 13.8 | 32.7 | 19.3 | 7-03-04 | .... | ... | 19010 | Dc | v0.15 | v0.12 | v0.41 | v0.98 | .... | 1.37 | 9 Mo Sep | v0.66 | v1.05 | 31 |
| 32◆ | 1996 | Q0.13 | 10-15-04 | 9-29 | s0.435 | 0.52 | s0.367 | Total Deposits $1877M | | | 6-30-04 | 156 | ... | 20349 | Dc | v0.95 | v1.01 | v1.29 | v1.39 | .... | 1.34 | 9 Mo Sep | v1.08 | v1.03 | 32 |
| 33 | 1998 | Q0.138 | 12-15-04 | 11-23 | 0.55 | 0.55 | 0.55 | 32.4 | 1373 | 334 | 6-30-04 | 500 | ... | 84286 | Dc | v0.10 | v[62]0.97 | v[63]d0.04 | v0.13 | .... | 0.06 | 6 Mo Jun | v0.08 | v0.01 | 33 |
| 34 | 1992 | Q0.093 | 10-6-04 | 9-17 | 0.373 | 0.373 | 0.373 | 143 | 512 | 286 | 7-03-04 | 250 | ... | 27781 | Dc | v3.61 | v1.43 | v0.11 | v□1.60 | E2.08↑ | 1.30 | 9 Mo Sep | v□0.92 | v0.62 | 34 |
| 35 | .... | Div Omitted 5-9-01 | | | ... | Nil | .... | File bankruptcy Chapt 11 | | | | [64]2241 | ... | 43015 | Dc | vd5.62 | v0.36 | □v3.22 | v□3.19 | .... | 6.34 | 9 Mo Sep | v□2.13 | v5.28 | 35 |
| 36 | .... | None Since Public | | | ... | Nil | .... | 16.0 | 300 | 270 | 6-30-04 | 139 | ... | 48949 | Dc | ... | pvd3.42 | vd2.43 | v0.77 | .... | 0.71 | 9 Mo Sep | v0.38 | v0.32 | 36 |
| 37 | 1912 | Q0.52 | 12-31-04 | 12-13 | 2.08 | 2.08 | 2.00 | 444 | 1125 | 606 | 6-30-04 | 840 | ... | 165223 | Dc | v2.70 | v2.97 | vd1.61 | v1.90 | E3.16↓ | 2.15 | 9 Mo Sep | v2.17 | v2.42 | 37 |
| 38 | 2004 | 0.15 | 1-5-05 | 12-14 | 0.30 | 0.60 | .... | 22.0 | 29.9 | 4.82 | 6-30-04 | .... | ... | 4520 | Dc | v0.90 | v1.14 | v1.36 | vΔ1.50 | .... | 2.22 | 9 Mo Sep | v1.13 | v1.85 | 38 |
| 39 | .... | None Since Public | | | ... | Nil | .... | Total Assets $28.5M | | | 6-30-04 | .... | ... | 5502 | Dc | v§2.24 | §v2.53 | v0.69 | v0.04 | .... | 2.15 | 6 Mo Jun | vd0.72 | v1.39 | 39 |
| 40 | 2001 | A0.11½ | 5-21-04 | 4-28 | 0.11½ | 0.095 | 0.09½ | 141 | 513 | 332 | 4-30-04 | 7.43 | ... | 30739 | Ja | v0.88 | v0.75 | v1.11 | v1.42 | .... | 1.71 | 6 Mo Jul | v0.62 | v0.91 | 40 |

**◆Stock Splits & Divs By Line Reference Index** [5]2-for-1,'00,'03. [13]2-for-1,'01. [14]4-for-3,'04. [16]2-for-1,'00. [21]2-for-1,'03. [23]2-for-1,'03,'04. [24]1-for-10 REVERSE,'02. [28]1-for-5 REVERSE,'03. [31]2-for-1,'03. [32]10%,'02:Adj for 5%,'04.

Source: Standard and Poor's *Stock Guide* (New York: Standard & Poor's Corporation, 2004). Reprinted with permission.

**Mergent's Manuals.** Most needs for quick information can be satisfied by either the *Stock Report* or the *Stock Guide*, but at times you may not find what you need in these two sources. *Mergent's Manuals* are good places to turn next. This publication contains seven sets of volumes covering industrial firms, public utilities, over-the-counter industrials, transportation issues, and bank/finance issues. Another Mergent publication, *Company Archives Manual*, provides data on defunct companies since 1996.

An especially common problem arises when you seek information about a company that, unknown to you, does not have stock that trades publicly. The firm may be a subsidiary of another company or may not be publicly held. *Mergent's Manuals* contain a cross-reference of subsidiaries. If you look up Pizza Hut, for instance, you will find that this firm is a subsidiary of Yum! Brands, spun off from PepsiCo in October 1997. Further attempts to find specific financial information about Pizza Hut are most likely going to be fruitless.

*Mergent's Manuals* contain more detailed news reports about a firm, more detailed financial statements, and other relevant information that cannot be included in the *Stock Report* because of space limitations.

**Mergent Dividend Record.** When it is necessary to investigate the recent dividend history of a company (payment dates, ex-dividend dates, and so on), *Mergent Dividend Record* is one of the most convenient places to get this information quickly. The reference room in most public libraries carries this service.

### *Brokerage Information*

Your broker can be another noteworthy information source. All full-service brokerage firms (and some discount firms) have the ability to provide their customers with stock research. You can request a report on a particular company or give your broker a list of securities of interest and ask that you receive reports on these firms as they become available.

### *Internet*

The volume and quality of information freely available over the Internet is growing exponentially. Numerous sites have excellent, user-friendly research interfaces. These days a listing of Internet sites can quickly become outdated, but a few reliable popular sites include *http://finance.yahoo.com*, *http://www.smartmoney.com*, *http://www.morningstar.com*, *http://www.fool.com*, and *http://www.bloomberg.com*.

It seems certain that the amount of information available over the Internet will continue to increase and become even more accessible. Data that was expensive to obtain just a few years ago is now free from numerous sources via your home computer. Competition is always good, and you should enjoy product improvements from the various information vendors.

## Screening Processes

### *Multiple-Stage Screening*

In most investment applications, it is necessary to use several stages of screening, because no one variable can capture all the relevant information the portfolio manager or private investor needs in order to make a buy/do not buy decision. A few examples will help illustrate this.

*By itself, the earnings-per-share figure is not very meaningful.*

Suppose you hear the following statement: "LBZ and CXD are both ranked 1 and 2 by Value Line, but LBZ has earnings per share of $4.50 compared with $3.22

for CXD. The way I see it, LBZ has to be a better buy." This is not a logical argument for one very important reason and a host of other minor ones. Holding constant expected future growth and required rate of return, higher-priced stocks *should* have higher earnings per share than lower-priced stocks. Here we know nothing about the relative prices of the two stock issues or their prospects for future growth. The point is that by itself, earnings per share is not a very useful screening device. This reasoning, in fact, is the primary purpose for calculating price/earnings ratios and reporting them in the financial press. The PE ratio "normalizes" the earnings by relating them to the cost of acquiring them.

Another good example of the need for multiple-stage screening comes from concern about the dividend yield of a growth stock. In choosing a growth stock, would it make sense to search initially for those with the highest dividend yield? Probably not, because of the following logic:

- Growth stocks, by definition, retain most of their earnings.
- No company likes to reduce its dividend payout.
- A high dividend yield, therefore, either means that the stock price has fallen considerably or that most of the company's earnings are not being retained in order to avoid cutting the dividend. If this is the case, it has ceased to be a growth stock.

### *Subjective Screening*

Not all reasonable screens need to be quantitative. Clients often provide instructions regarding certain subjective investment characteristics they desire or want to avoid. They can include a variety of investment criteria. The Social Investment Forum defines the term **socially responsible investing** this way:

> "Integrating personal values and societal concerns with investment decisions is called Socially Responsible Investing (SRI). SRI considers both the investor's financial needs and an investment's impact on society. With SRI, you can put your money to work to build a better tomorrow while earning competitive returns today."[2]

Socially responsible investing means that the investor established subjective constraints in the list of eligible investments. Seventeenth-century Quakers may have been the first social screeners. They could not reconcile their religious beliefs with the ownership of slaves, so they didn't own any, even though slavery was generally accepted practice at the time.

The Sullivan Principles and the MacBride Principles are examples from the more recent past. The Sullivan Principles deal with "Codes of Conduct for Companies Operating in South Africa." These were first drawn up by the Reverend Leon Sullivan in an attempt to expedite the end of apartheid in South Africa. The MacBride Principles call on U.S. companies with operations in Ireland to promote fair employment practices there.

Clients might indicate that they do not want to invest in a company that does not adhere to the Sullivan Principles. This is a subjective criterion but one that a great many individuals and institutions employ.

In early 1991, three health-care workers' pension funds passed resolutions regarding the MacBride Principles. The $1.6 billion Health Care Employees Pension Fund of New York, the $36 million New England Health Care Employees Pension

---

[2]*http://www.socialinvest.org/Areas/SRIGuide/*

Fund, and the $8.6 million Connecticut Health Care Associates Pension Fund adopted resolutions urging their investment managers to support proxy resolutions implementing the MacBride Principles.[3] Portfolio managers obviously need to pay attention to these actions. In 2003 there was about $2.2 trillion invested in some form of socially responsible investing.

Socially responsible investing screening criteria that are common today include restrictions against investing in tobacco stocks, electric utilities that use nuclear power, or firms that do not adhere to the CERES Principles. This latter set of rules is promulgated by the Coalition of Environmentally Responsible Economies and is a general call for environmental accountability. Those who adopt the principles commit to work toward protection of the biosphere, sustainable natural resource use, safe products, and several other goals.[4]

Other criteria that may appear in social screening are animal testing, labor relations, gambling, defense/weapons, community investment, the environment, human rights, product safety, contraception, non-marital partner benefits, biotechnology, pornography, employment equality, and others. You could probably make a case, in fact, for excluding about everything for one reason or another.[5] The smaller your security universe gets, however, the more difficulty you have in diversifying properly.

Subjective screening is not an issue to be taken lightly. If someone wants to use such a screen, this fact needs to be spelled out in careful detail in a policy statement. As an example, in July 1991, a lawsuit was filed against the $1.8 billion Board of Pensions of the Evangelical Lutheran Church of America alleging that "the board breached its fiduciary responsibility by using social criteria to determine its investment policies."[6] The plaintiffs in the lawsuit asked the courts to rule on the prudence of socially directed investments and on the separation of the management of the church and the management of the church pension fund.

The topic of socially responsible investing is multifaceted, quite interesting in many respects, and something that is likely to be with us for a long time. If you are interested in studying the matter further, the Winter 1997 issue of the *Journal of Investing* deals entirely with the topic of socially responsible investing. The journal contains articles by many notable investment professionals engaged with the topic.

**Best of class investing** is a relatively new development in the world of socially responsible investing. This practice recognizes that it is possible to find a reason to fault virtually all companies in some socially sensitive area, such as the environment, hiring practices, or the nature of their product. Recognizing the importance of diversification, it wouldn't make sense to dramatically limit investments to just a few types of businesses.

Instead, some managers who are sympathetic to the SRI movement opt to look for "role models" within each industry and select them, even if some part of their business will still be offensive to some constituencies. Light Green Advisors, for

---

[3]See Joel Chernoff, "MacBride Principles Taken to Heart by Funds," *Pensions & Investments*, June 10, 1991, 30.

[4]There is more on the CERES Principles in Chapter 18.

[5]For example, CEO salary is too high, simultaneously laying off employees and paying dividends to shareholders, lack of cumulative voting at annual meetings, political campaign contributions, predatory lending.

[6]See Sabine Schramm, "Church Sued over Fund Investment Criteria," *Pensions & Investments*, September 2, 1991, 35.

MEMO

## What Does "Socially Responsible" Mean?

According to the Social Investment Forum, socially responsible investing is "a process that considers the social and environmental consequences of investments, both positive and negative, within the context of rigorous financial analysis." Some people argue that a socially responsible fund offers a "triple bottom line": financial return, social return, and environmental return. All of this sounds good.

However, in an article in *Common Ground* magazine, Paul Hawken states that "the term 'socially responsible investing' is so broad it is meaningless. . . . SRI mutual funds have no common standards, definitions, or codes of practices."* This conclusion is the result of a study** by the Natural Capital Institute on the practice of socially responsible investing (SRI) across the globe. A spokesperson for the Social Investment Forum agrees: "Mr. Hawken is correct that there are no rigid standards dictated for SRI funds to follow in the United States. SRI funds offer a wide range of options for investors in order to meet diverse ethical and investing criteria."[†]

Among the findings of the Natural Capital Institute study are these:

1. The cumulative investment portfolio of the combined SRI mutual funds is virtually no different than the combined portfolio of conventional mutual funds.
2. SRI fund advertising caters to people's desires to improve the world by avoiding bad actors in the corporate world, but it can be misleading and oftentimes has little correlation to portfolio holdings.
3. The environmental screens used by portfolio managers are loose and do little to help the environment.
4. The language used to describe SRI mutual funds, including the term "SRI" itself, is vague and indiscriminate and leads to misperception and distortion of investor goals.

Over 90% of the companies in the Fortune 500 are included in somebody's SRI portfolio. The important thing for a portfolio manager (and for an investor) to know is that the very notion of SRI investing is ambiguous. It is not an easily compartmentalized topic. If someone tells you "We invest in a socially responsible portfolio," it probably means they don't hold any tobacco stocks but doesn't tell you much else.

---

*Hawken, Paul. "Is Your Money Where Your Heart Is?" *Dragonfly Media.* Online at *http://www.dragonflymedia.com/portal/featured_stores/200410/hawken_paul.html*

**The survey results are available online at *http://www.naturalcapital.org/images/NCI_SRI_10-04.pdf*

[†]KLD Research and Analytics, Inc., "Paul Hawken Critiques Socially Responsible Investment: Is He On Target or Off Base?" Online at *http://www.kld.com/article.cgi?id-1564*

instance, states that it does not compare companies across industry lines or exclude whole industry sectors:

> LGA recognizes that the economy is built on interdependence. For instance, the software industry cannot exist without computer hardware, and hardware requires plastics, metals and energy. All industries rely on one another.

> LGA has developed and uses a new quantitative model of corporate environmental behavior and investment performance to select the "best of class" in every major industry sector except tobacco products.[7]

In other words, the firm determines which companies are the most environmentally responsible within their industry. These get "extra credit" in the portfolio construction process. Many investment managers and clients alike agree with this logic, and increasingly are using the best of class notion to simultaneously "make a statement" and manage money in accordance with modern portfolio theory.

### *Screening with the Popular Press Only*

Not everyone is skilled at Internet searches or has the time to head to the local library's reference room to gather extensive information about possible investments. Many people begin the whole process with the financial pages of their local newspaper or with news items in *The Wall Street Journal.* Fortunately, it is possible to do some very effective screening with just this limited information. Table 10-2 lists decision variables that an investor might conveniently use for screening.

**Price/Earnings Ratio.** Considerable folklore exists regarding the meaning of a stock's price/earnings ratio. One perspective is that low PEs are good because this means the investors pay a little to get a lot. On the face of things, this seems reasonable. Earnings are good, and the more cheaply they can be bought, the better. The problem with this is that past earnings do not contribute to the future economic value of a share of stock; they contribute only to market psychology, which does influence current value but can also change in a flash. Future earnings are the economic engine behind share value. The financial pages generally report past earnings,[8] or a *trailing PE ratio.* This fact is what causes another group of investors to argue that high PE ratios are better because they mean that the efficient marketplace anticipates that future earnings will be higher than those of the past. If the market is efficient, stock prices are appropriate given their expected earnings, and the price/earnings ratio as a screen is irrelevant. Although this dilemma has not been resolved to everyone's satisfaction, the PE ratio is a common screening statistic.

*Newspaper price/earnings ratios are calculated on the basis of past earnings, whereas future earnings are what matter.*

**Dividend Yield.** We have seen that even though the payment of a dividend does not materially alter a recipient's wealth, people like to get them. Receiving a check in the mail is reassuring, and dividends stroke egos and give shareholders a sense of importance. Of course, some people have *income* or *growth of income* as their primary investment objective and are particularly concerned about getting part of their return in spendable form.

**TABLE 10-2** POSSIBLE SCREENING VARIABLES FOR COMMON STOCK USING ONLY DATA FROM THE FINANCIAL PRESS

| |
|---|
| PE ratio |
| Dividend yield |
| Stock price |
| Exchange listing |
| Familiarity |
| Relation of current price to 52-week high and low |

[7]Best of Class Investing," http://www.lightgreen.com/best-of-class.htm

[8]Some publications base the PE ratio on the past six months' actual earnings and the forecast earnings for the next six months. This is a blend of a trailing and a "market forecast" PE.

**Stock Price.** As mentioned earlier, some people believe in an optimum trading range for stock prices. According to finance theory, the cost of a share should be merely a marker and of no value in comparing firms. As we saw in an earlier example, the size (and value) of a piece of pie depends on the number of pieces into which the pie is cut.

Many people prefer to avoid odd lots during the screening process, although there is no longer any good reason to do so. Suppose someone wants to add $3,000 to his individual retirement account. A round lot of 100 shares means that the share price cannot be more than $30. To avoid getting an odd lot, the IRA investor might include this price restriction as part of the screen.

**Exchange Listing.** Many excellent companies are listed on the American Stock Exchange or trade in the Nasdaq market. A client, however, might choose to restrict equity picks to Big Board (NYSE) stocks.

**Familiarity.** Another very reasonable criteria for some clients is *familiarity*. This means that you, as a portfolio manager, will restrict your portfolio components to securities of companies with which your client is familiar. People feel good knowing that they are partial owners of a large, respected corporation, especially one about which they know something. This is a subjective criterion, and one that is perfectly okay.

**52-Week Trading Range.** People often make statements such as this: "The stock is trading at the low end of its annual high and low." Such a statement is dangerous because it implies that the stock is predictable, rising from the low to the high and back again every year. Stock does not behave this way.

The 52-week trading range listed in the newspaper merely reports the highest and lowest price levels of the stock during the previous year. If prices are efficient, this information is of no value in predicting future prices. More technically, the research of Roger Ibbotson and Rex Sinquefield in *Stocks, Bonds, Bills, and Inflation* finds the first-order autocorrelation of annual capital gains on common stocks to be essentially 0.[9] This is further evidence that what the stock has done in the past does not help determine what it is likely to do in the future.

Nonetheless, many investors watch the trading range figures, and it is reasonable to argue that a stock near "its high" or "its low" is somehow different than others near the middle. Such assessments are on shaky ground, but they, too, are part of market folklore. If someone wants to include these data in the screening process, it probably does no harm.

**Options Availability.** Some people know how versatile stock options can be in a portfolio and try to invest in equity issues that have options available. This information is contained in the financial press, but not on the same newspaper page as the stock listing. If they understand the option listings, however, they can quickly find out whether options trade on a given stock. The S&P *Stock Report, Stock Guide*, and Internet also carry this information.

---

[9]Roger G. Ibbotson and Rex A. Sinquefield, *Stocks, Bonds, Bills, and Inflation: Historical Returns (1926–1987)*, (Charlottesville, Va.: Research Foundation of the Institute of Chartered Financial Analysts, 1989).

**TABLE 10-3** A SIMPLE FINANCIAL PAGES STOCK SCREEN

| |
|---|
| PE ratio less than 20 and more than 0 |
| Dividend yield more than 1 percent |
| Stock price less than $35 |
| Stock price more than $5 |
| NYSE stock |

**An Example Screen.** Suppose we construct the screen listed in Table 10-3 and use it on *The Wall Street Journal* extract in Figure 10-4. This clipping shows 100 securities. As a general rule, the first screening pass should be with the criterion that will eliminate the most alternatives or save the most time. In this example, we have information only from the New York Stock Exchange, so we do not need to do anything else with this criterion. If we had the whole newspaper, however, we would certainly restrict our search to the pages with NYSE prices. It would make no sense to go through AMEX or Nasdaq listings when we know they are ineligible alternatives.

We might begin by using the stock price criterion. Crossing out entries with share prices higher than $35 reduces the list by 42 securities, and 58 now remain. We also stipulate that the share price should be above $5. This eliminates two more.

Forty of the remaining stocks have a PE ratio above 20 or less than zero. Removing them leaves sixteen potentially eligible picks.[10] Finally, five of these have a dividend yield under 1 percent, so we remove them from further consideration.

Eleven stocks remain from the original 100, and the administration of this screen took less than five minutes. Table 10-4 shows details on the eleven stocks that passed all the screens.

At this point, we may want to look at the final group to see if we should make any more modifications. BRT Realty Trust is a real estate investment trust, and we might not be interested in such an investment. Also, its high dividend yield might make us uncomfortable. Perhaps we decide to remove this security from further consideration purely on the basis of subjective feeling. We might also eliminate Bairnco with its

**TABLE 10-4** STOCKS FROM FIGURE 10-4 THAT PASS THE SCREEN

| *Symbol* | *Company* | *Dividend Yield (%)* | *PE Ratio* | *Share Price* |
|---|---|---|---|---|
| BRT | BRT Realty Trust | 7.7 | 16 | $24.91 |
| BZ | Bairnco | 2.2 | 3 | 10.98 |
| BXS | BancorpSouth | 3.2 | 16 | 24.01 |
| BKH | Black Hills | 4.1 | 20 | 30.23 |
| BTH | Blyth | 1.3 | 16 | 28.61 |
| BGP | Borders Group | 1.5 | 14 | 23.70 |
| BK | Bank of New York | 2.4 | 18 | 32.95 |
| BNS | Bank of Nova Scotia | 3.9 | 12 | 32.50 |
| B | Barnes Group | 2.9 | 18 | 27.74 |
| BLS | BellSouth | 3.8 | 12 | 28.22 |
| BMS | Bemis | 2.2 | 18 | 28.55 |

[10]If the entry under the PE listing shows three dots (...), the PE is not meaningful because it is negative or very large. A company whose stock sold for $20 and that had earnings per share of $0.02, for instance, would have a PE ratio of 1,000. The financial press usually will not print a PE higher than 100.

**FIGURE 10-4**

Sample Stock Listing

**B**

| | | | | | | | | | | | |
|---|---|---|---|---|---|---|---|---|---|---|---|
| | 24.0 | 70.57 | 48.09 | BASF ADS | **BF** | 1.72e | 2.5 | ... | 419 | 69.12 | 1.27 |
| | 9.0 | 43.25 | 33.02 | BB&T Cp | **BBT** | 1.40 | 3.3 | 16 | 9424 | 42.13 | 0.30 |
| | −25.6 | 9.47 | 4.39 | BcoFran ADS | **BFR** | .45e | 7.2 | ... | 1448 | 6.28 | 0.28 |
| | 5.5 | 24.64 | 18.67 | BCE Inc | **BCE** | 1.20g | ... | ... | 1686 | 23.60 | −0.12 |
| | 33.0 | 35.40 | 24.90 | BG Gp ADS | **BRG** | .32e | .9 | ... | 3313 | 34.64 | 0.63 |
| | 29.2 | 24.38 | 14.61 | BHPBilton ADS | **BHP** | .36e | 1.5 | ... | 7818 | 23.59 | 0.29 |
| | 33.1 | 23.81 | 15.22 | BHPBilton PLC | **BBL** | .36e | 1.5 | ... | 52 | 23.23 | 0.53 |
| | 21.4 | 32 | 19.91 | BJs WhslClb | **BJ** | | ... | 17 | 11393 | 27.87 | −0.58 |
| | 31.2 | 54.65 | 34.85♣ | BJ Svc | **BJS** | .16e | .3 | 22 | 15313 | 47.10 | −0.31 |
| ↑ | 48.3 | 35.85 | 24.40 | BKF CapGp | **BKF** | .33e | .9 | dd | 441 | 36.60 | 1.15 |
| | −2.6 | 21.87 | 13.70 | BMC Sftwr | **BMC** | | ... | cc | 7481 | 18.16 | −0.30 |
| ↑ | 18.6 | 37.10 | 29.89 | BOC Gp ADS | **BOX** | 1.45e | 3.9 | ... | 115 | 36.86 | −0.02 |
| | 19.1 | 62.10 | 46.65♣ | BP Plc ADS | **BP** | 1.71e | 2.9 | 14 | 18301 | 58.79 | 0.43 |
| | 73.0 | 50.50 | 22.50 | BP Prudhoe | **BPT** | 3.82e | 7.7 | ... | 1229 | 49.30 | −0.38 |
| | 22.3 | 42.54 | 29.90 | BRE Prop | **BRE** | 1.95 | 4.8 | 42 | 2268 | 40.85 | −0.80 |
| | −13.7 | 29.35 | 19 | BRT RltyTr | **BRT** | 1.92 | 7.7 | 16 | 140 | 24.91 | 0.36 |
| | 80.3 | 11.90 | 5.75 | Bairnco | **BZ** | .24f | 2.2 | 3 | 38 | 10.98 | −0.01 |
| | 34.7 | 45.30 | 30.40 | BakrHughs | **BHI** | .46 | 1.1 | 32 | 17900 | 43.31 | 0.53 |
| | 20.6 | 28.75 | 21.32♣ | BaldorElec | **BEZ** | .60f | 2.2 | 30 | 1456 | 27.55 | −0.53 |
| | 48.6 | 45.20 | 28.26 | Ball Cp | **BLL** s | .40 | .9 | 17 | 3492 | 44.25 | 0.77 |
| | −49.1 | 8.04 | 2.95 | BallyTtlFit | **BFT** | | ... | dd | 3538 | 3.56 | 0.01 |
| | 16.3 | 29.75 | 22.93 | BancoBilbao | **BB** | .66e | 2.3 | ... | 23 | 28.96 | 0.25 |
| | 22.2 | 17 | 12 | BcoBilViz | **BBV** | .50e | 3.0 | ... | 1701 | 16.93 | 0.11 |
| | 34.5 | 75.19 | 35 | BncoBrdsco | **BBD** s | 3.18 | 4.5 | ... | 891 | 71.04 | −0.44 |
| ↑ | 35.5 | 37.80 | 25.30 | BcoDeChli | **BCH** | 1.89e | 5.0 | ... | 9 | 37.94 | 1.09 |
| | 47.7 | 73.60 | 35.34 | BancoItau ADS | **ITU** | 2.64e | 3.7 | ... | 1293 | 72 | −0.24 |
| | −3.5 | 19.99 | 13.90 | BcoLatin | **BLX** | 1.20e | 6.5 | ... | 1171 | 18.55 | ... |
| ↑ | .35.2 | 32.05 | 22.85 | BcoSantChile ADS | **SAN** | 1.90e | 5.9 | ... | 2194 | 32.15 | 0.15 |
| | 0.0 | 12.40 | 9.14 | BcoSantdr | **STD** | .39e | 3.2 | ... | 3096 | 12.01 | 0.19 |
| ↑ | 132.0 | 12.78 | 5.01 | Bancol ADS | **CIB** | .41e | 3.3 | ... | 1137 | 12.39 | −0.06 |
| | 1.2 | 25.25 | 19.35 | Bncpsouth | **BXS** | .76f | 3.2 | 16 | 1041 | 24.01 | 0.10 |
| | 17.0 | 51.30 | 38.32 | Bandag | **BDG** | 1.32f | 2.7 | 15 | 611 | 48.21 | −0.14 |
| | 8.7 | 47.71 | 35.38 | Bandag A | **BDGA** | 1.32f | 3.0 | 13 | 32 | 43.92 | −0.22 |
| | 13.2 | 47.47 | 38.51 | BankAm | **BAC** s | 1.80 | 4.0 | 12 | 87566 | 45.52 | 0.32 |
| | 17.7 | 50.73 | 40.97 | Bk Hawaii | **BOH** | 1.32f | 2.7 | 17 | 3650 | 49.66 | 0.14 |
| | 17.2 | 65.75 | 46.99 | BkIrlnd ADS | **IRE** | 2.18e | 3.4 | ... | 129 | 64.40 | 0.03 |
| | 11.7 | 49.26 | 35.67 | BkMntrl | **BMO** | 1.76g | ... | ... | 325 | 46.12 | 0.46 |
| | −0.5 | 34.85 | 27.25 | BankNY | **BK** | .80 | 2.4 | 18 | 15961 | 32.95 | −0.22 |
| | 28.4 | 32.93 | 23.75 | BkNovaScotia | **BNS** s | 1.28fg | 3.9 | 12 | 94 | 32.50 | 0.39 |
| ↑ | 39.3 | 19.76 | 13.35 | BkAtlBcp A | **BBX** | .14 | .7 | 17 | 4522 | 19.54 | −0.12 |
| | 11.0 | 36.64 | 30.25 | Bknorth | **BNK** | .80 | 2.2 | 16 | 5447 | 36.10 | −0.26 |
| | 8.8 | 47.50 | 36.74 | BantaCp | **BN** | .68 | 1.5 | 19 | 1625 | 44.05 | −0.44 |
| ↑ | 22.9 | 44.95 | 32.78 | Barclays ADS | **BCS** | 1.62e | 3.6 | ... | 1227 | 44.69 | 0.34 |
| | 56.4 | 64.63 | 39.42 | Bard CR | **BCR** s | .48 | .8 | 27 | 6407 | 63.53 | −0.37 |
| | 30.3 | 32.16 | 20.04 | BarnesNoble | **BKS** | | ... | 15 | 7395 | 30.85 | −0.37 |
| | −14.1 | 33.57 | 24.20♣ | BarnesGp | **B** | .80 | 2.9 | 18 | 287 | 27.74 | 0.12 |
| | −11.8 | 53.99 | 32.01♣ | BarrPharm | **BRL** s | | ... | 35 | 5553 | 45.25 | 0.33 |
| | 3.7 | 25.52 | 18.04 | BarckGld | **ABX** | .22 | .9 | 76 | 15382 | 23.56 | 0.29 |
| | 25.1 | 69 | 50.30 | BauschLomb | **BOL** | .52 | .8 | 22 | 2891 | 64.92 | −0.08 |
| | 9.1 | 34.84 | 27.10 | BaxterInt | **BAX** | .58 | 1.7 | 31 | 24232 | 33.30 | −0.20 |
| | 0.3 | 57.97 | 49.14 | BaxterInt un | | 3.50 | 6.3 | ... | 780 | 55.43 | −0.20 |
| | −3.7 | 47.61 | 13.91 | BayVwCap | **BVC** | 5.00e | 31.7 | ... | 431 | 15.75 | 0.19 |
| | 14.3 | 34.20 | 23.52 | Bayer ADS | **BAY** | .61e | 1.8 | ... | 760 | 33.61 | 0.36 |
| | 30.7 | 109.85 | 75.35 | BearStearn | **BSC** | 1.00f | 1.0 | 11 | 7137 | 104.50 | −0.03 |
| | −23.8 | 11.30 | 7.22 | BearingPt | **BE** | | ... | dd | 72450 | 7.69 | 0.10 |
| | 48.0 | 148.39 | 86.43 | BeazerHm | **BZH** | .40 | .3 | 8 | 5021 | 144.51 | −0.34 |
| | 30.6 | 68.07 | 48.03 | BeckmnCoultr | **BEC** | .52 | .8 | 20 | 3295 | 66.39 | −0.01 |
| ↑ | 38.3 | 58.08 | 39.70 | BectonDksn | **BDX** | .72f | 1.3 | 32 | 10227 | 56.89 | −0.94 |
| | 0.9 | 32.10 | 26.15 | BedfdPrpty | **BED** | 2.04 | 7.1 | 26 | 531 | 28.88 | 0.03 |
| | 28.8 | 24.48 | 15.56♣ | BeldenCDT | **BDC** s | .10e | .4 | dd | 1597 | 23.15 | −0.25 |
| | −0.3 | 31 | 24.46 | BellSouth | **BLS** | 1.08 | 3.8 | 12 | 38843 | 28.22 | 0.08 |
| | −9.9 | 29.90 | 18 | Belo | **BLC** | .40f | 1.6 | 25 | 2643 | 25.54 | −0.31 |
| ↑ | 14.2 | 28.75 | 23.24♣ | Bemis | **BMS** s | .64 | 2.2 | 18 | 3372 | 28.55 | 0.22 |
| | −5.3 | 40.45 | 23.61 | BenchmkElec | **BHE** | | ... | 22 | 4354 | 32.97 | −0.50 |
| | 9.2 | 25.32 | 20.60 | Benetton | **BNG** | .92e | 3.6 | ... | 28 | 25.20 | 0.32 |
| | −23.8 | 14.76 | 8.35 | BntlyPhrm | **BNT** | | ... | 41 | 877 | 10.14 | −0.34 |
| ↑ | 31.9 | 46.24 | 31.95 | Berkley | **BER** | .28 | .6 | 10 | 2577 | 46.09 | 0.07 |
| | 2.4 | 95700 | 81150 | BerkHathwy A | **BRKA** | | ... | 21 | z450 | 86300 | 1100 |
| | 2.1 | 3195 | 2685 | BerkHathwy B | **BRKB** | | ... | ... | z9640 | 2873 | 11.93 |
| ↑ | 144.5 | 49.37 | 18.22♣ | BerryPete A | **BRY** | .48 | 1.0 | 20 | 1683 | 49.42 | 0.46 |
| | 8.8 | 62.20 | 43.87 | BestBuy | **BBY** | .44 | .8 | 21 | 27303 | 56.82 | 0.27 |
| | 2.7 | 9.41 | 5.83 | BeverlyEnt | **BEV** | | ... | 15 | 8586 | 8.82 | −0.17 |
| | −19.3 | 15.62 | 11.05 | BigLots | **BLI** | | ... | 25 | 6281 | 11.47 | 0.01 |
| | 14.6 | 35 | 27.49 | BillBarrett | **BBG** n | | ... | ... | 2554 | 33.30 | −0.11 |
| | 1.0 | 16.30 | 14.50 | BiminiMtg | **BMM** n | .54p | ... | ... | 2201 | 15.51 | −0.13 |
| ↑ | 41.3 | 21.75 | 15.75 | BiomdRltyTr | **BMR** n | 1.08 | 4.8 | ... | 1980 | 22.46 | 0.92 |
| | −26.0 | 26.01 | 14.30 | Biovail | **BVF** | | ... | ... | 7190 | 15.91 | ... |
| | 7.1 | 18.75 | 12.13 | BisysGp | **BSG** | | ... | 30 | 2777 | 15.93 | −0.14 |
| | 74.4 | 86.68 | 48.07 | BlackDeck | **BDK** | .84 | 1.0 | 16 | 3821 | 86.01 | 0.35 |
| | 1.3 | 32.49 | 26.52 | BlackHills | **BKH** | 1.24 | 4.1 | 20 | 1738 | 30.23 | −0.08 |
| | 42.3 | 78.24 | 51.41 | BlkRk A | **BLK** | 1.00 | 1.3 | 37 | 414 | 75.60 | −1.40 |
| | −12.4 | 61 | 44.16 | BlockHR | **HRB** | .88 | 1.8 | 15 | 7006 | 48.51 | 0.06 |
| | −9.4 | 11.87 | 6.50 | Blkbstr A | **BBI** s | .08a | .8 | dd | 21618 | 9.96 | −0.01 |
| | 29.3 | 9.85 | 6.31 | Blkbstr B | **BBIB** n | | ... | ... | 7550 | 9.18 | −0.02 |
| | 114.1 | 18.50 | 7.45 | BlountInt | **BLT** | | ... | dd | 4448 | 16.85 | −0.10 |
| | −13.5 | 13.46 | 9.26 | BlSqIsrael | **BSI** | 1.48e | 15.0 | ... | 48 | 9.89 | −0.13 |
| | 204.5 | 19.88 | 6.10 | Bluegreen | **BXG** | | ... | 15 | 2048 | 19 | −0.11 |
| | −2.8 | 14 | 13 | BluelinxHldgs | **BXC** n | | ... | ... | 3351 | 13.12 | −0.13 |
| | −11.2 | 36 | 27.85♣ | Blyth | **BTH** | .38f | 1.3 | 16 | 1773 | 28.61 | −0.38 |
| | 26.3 | 55.48 | 38.04 | Boeing | **BA** | 1.00f | 1.9 | 15 | 23371 | 53.22 | 0.12 |
| | −34.3 | 8.75 | 4.47 | Bombay | **BBA** | | ... | dd | 2683 | 5.35 | −0.01 |
| | 8.1 | 25.34 | 21.11 | BordersGrp | **BGP** | .36f | 1.5 | 14 | 4502 | 23.70 | 0.16 |
| ↑ | 20.1 | 51.64 | 38.35 | BorgWarner | **BWA** s | .56f | 1.1 | 14 | 3484 | 51.10 | −0.25 |
| | 18.2 | 27.95 | 16.40 | BostBeer | **SAM** | | ... | 23 | 440 | 21.45 | −0.01 |
| | 31.8 | 63.82 | 42.99 | BostProp | **BXP** | 2.60 | 4.1 | 24 | 1983 | 63.50 | 0.20 |
| | −3.4 | 46.10 | 31.25 | BosSci | **BSX** | | ... | 34 | 25290 | 35.50 | 0.03 |
| | −5.8 | 48 | 34.15 | Bowater | **BOW** | .80 | 1.8 | dd | 4444 | 43.64 | −0.17 |
| | 13.6 | 17.99 | 11.11♣ | Bowne | **BNE** | .22 | 1.4 | cc | 1612 | 15.40 | −0.09 |
| ↑ | 141.6 | 38.19 | 15.74 | BoydGaming | **BYD** | .34 | .9 | 38 | 9301 | 38.99 | 1.68 |
| | −3.5 | 4.60 | 2.20 | Boyds | **FOB** | | ... | 37 | 687 | 4.10 | 0.06 |

TABLE 10-5 COMPARISON OF ROA AND ROE FOR TWO STOCKS

| *Year* | *Emery Air Freight (EAF)* | | *Johnson & Johnson (JNJ)* | |
|---|---|---|---|---|
| | **ROA** | **ROE** | **ROA** | **ROE** |
| 1976 | 19.1 | 33.1 | 12.5 | 16.7 |
| 1977 | 20.5 | 36.2 | 13.2 | 17.7 |
| 1978 | 19.8 | 36.5 | 13.4 | 18.6 |
| 1979 | 19.0 | 35.8 | 13.3 | 18.9 |
| 1980 | 16.8 | 30.6 | 12.8 | 18.7 |
| 1981 | 9.2 | 24.7 | 13.0 | 19.4 |
| 1982 | 3.6 | 13.2 | 13.0 | 19.5 |
| 1983 | 7.8 | 24.6 | 11.2 | 16.7 |
| 1984 | 8.8 | 21.6 | 11.7 | 17.7 |
| 1985 | 4.2 | 10.2 | 12.7 | 19.5 |

suspicious PE of 3. The remaining nine stocks now warrant careful attention, and we may decide to conduct some security analysis on them, perhaps by seeing whether Value Line covers them or by reading their S&P *Stock Report*.

### *A Quick Risk Assessment Screen with the Stock Report*

**ROA and ROE.** As we have seen, the S&P *Stock Report* is a useful source of information. Most libraries and brokerage firms carry this publication. When asked about an unfamiliar stock, you can often learn something useful by a five-second comparison of the return on assets (ROA) and return on equity (ROE) figures for the company over the ten-year period which the *Stock Report* provides. *ROA* equals a firm's net income after taxes (NIAT) divided by its total assets; *ROE* is NIAT divided by equity. If a firm has any debt, its total assets always exceed its equity, so ROE will be greater than ROA (assuming earnings are positive).

**Evaluating ROA and ROE.** In general, the proverbial "good, safe investment" has a history of stable ROA and ROE figures, with ROE somewhat higher than ROA. If the ROE is substantially higher than the ROA, the firm is heavily leveraged and therefore risky. Much debt works to a firm's advantage when it accurately selects positive net present value projects. If, however, the projects do not turn out to be profitable, the firm must still pay the interest on its debt, resulting in a reduction in NIAT. Furthermore, high variance in these figures (ROE especially) is a sure indication of a risky company. Some analysts, in fact, use variance of ROE instead of variance of stock price returns in their assessment of company risk.

The data contained in Table 10-5 are actual figures for two very different companies from 1976 to 1985. It is readily apparent that over this period, *JNJ* had a much more stable ROA and ROE pattern than *EAF*. *EAF* shows rapid growth initially, followed by a slowdown. *JNJ* shows the type of dependable pattern security analysts love. From these figures we might conclude that *JNJ* is a "safer" stock.

## Examples of Commercial Screens

### *Published Paper Data*

**Value Line Publications.** One of the most widely used screens in security selection is the information contained in the timeliness and safety rankings of the *Value Line Investment Survey*, which have already been mentioned. This ranking system began in 1965 and since that time has developed a widespread following in the investment community.

Subscribers to the *Value Line Investment Survey* receive, in addition to the company reports, a summary of the ratings on the 1,700 Value Line stocks, a very useful screening device. Figure 10-5 shows a sample page from this portion of the Value Line service. Investors can use this information to sort through a large number of stocks quickly.

We might be Value Line fans and decide to limit our picks to stocks rated either 1 or 2 for timeliness. Reading down the list in Figure 10-5, we find twenty stocks that satisfy this criterion. We might overlook some good ones by excluding those ranked 3, 4, or 5, but the twenty that remain stand a very good chance of being desirable portfolio candidates.

Elsewhere in the *Value Line Investment Survey* we find opinions about timely industries, including an industry ranking and a listing of stocks rated 1 or 2 for timeliness within a timely industry. These are "timely stocks in timely industries." Figure 10-6 is an example.

Identifying attractive stocks or related groups of stocks is a process called sector screening**.** Figure 10-6 indicates that at the time of this Value Line report, the company considered basic chemicals to be the most attractive of the approximately 100 industry groups.

It is also reasonable for many people to begin their screening by choosing only those stocks ranked 1 for timeliness. Value Line also segregates this information; Figure 10-7 is an example.

Value Line provides other information that some people might wish to include in a screen. Noteworthy examples include listings of stocks that sell at a discount to book value, stocks that have the highest dividend yield, and stocks that have the highest and lowest price/earnings ratios.

## *Computerized Data*

**Value Line Investment Analyzer.** The PC-based version of Value Line is extremely useful. Users can screen the 7,500-security database by any or all of more than 300 variables, including up to twenty that they can define themselves and have the program calculate for them. Table 10-6 shows the grouping of the screening variables, the number of variables within each category, and an example of each. A group of stocks or the entire database can be screened any number of times using different sets of variables and values. The package also permits the preparation of statistical summaries and detailed tabular reports. Weekly updates are quickly available to subscribers via the Value Line web page at *http://www.valueline.com*.

**Compustat.** Academic researchers know the S&P **Compustat** tapes well. Both mainframe computer and microcomputer versions of this information source exist. Both types enable the user to screen thousands of stocks for specific financial statement information. The screen can include anything from familiar statistics, such as the current ratio or retained earnings, to less frequently used values, such as unfunded pension liabilities. This service is often used in conjunction with tests of the market's response to accounting changes.

## FIGURE 10-5 Value Line Summary of Advices and Index

**December 24, 2004** **SUMMARY AND INDEX • THE VALUE LINE INVESTMENT SURVEY** **Page 3** **AD-AN**

**PAGE NUMBERS**
Bold type refers to Ratings and Reports; *italics to Selection & Opinion*

| *Selection & Opinion* | Ratings & Reports | NAME OF STOCK | Ticker Symbol | Recent Price | Timeliness | Safety | Technical | Beta | 3-5 year Target Price Range | and % appreciation potential | Current P/E Ratio | % Est'd Yield next 12 mos. | Est'd Earns. 12 mos. to 6-30-05 | (f) Est'd Div'd next 12 mos. | Industry Rank | Qtr. Ended | Earns. Per sh. | Year Ago | Qtr. Ended | Latest Div'd | Year Ago | Do Options Trade? |
|---|---|---|---|---|---|---|---|---|---|---|---|---|---|---|---|---|---|---|---|---|---|---|
| | 1922 | ADVO, Inc. | AD | 36.09 | 5 | 3 | 3 | .90 | 30- 50 | (N- 40%) | 23.1 | 1.2 | 1.56 | .44 | 36 | 9/30 | .41 | .46 | 12/31 | .11 | NIL | |
| | 1202 | AEGON Ins. Group | AEG | 13.51 | 3 | 3 | 3 | 1.65 | 20- 30 | (50-120%) | 11.4 | 4.4 | 1.19 | .60 | 34 | 6/30 | .61(p) | .61(p) | 12/31 | ◆NIL | NIL | YES |
| | 1710 | Aeropostale | ARO | 30.00 | 1 | 3 | 4 | 1.55 | 35- 50 | (15- 65%) | 19.1 | NIL | 1.57 | NIL | 72 | 10/31 | .55 | .37 | 12/31 | NIL | NIL | YES |
| | 1297 | Aether Systems | AETH | | | | | | SEE FINAL SUPPLEMENT - PAGE 1297 | | | | | | | | | | | | | |
| | 629 | Aetna Inc. | AET | 126.20 | 1 | 3 | 3 | .95 | 130-195 | (5- 55%) | 16.4 | NIL | 7.70 | .04 | 19 | 9/30 | 1.75 | 1.27 | 12/31 | .04 | .04 | YES |
| *2044* | 2170 | Affiliated Computer | ACS | 58.50 | 1 | 3 | 1 | 1.10 | 80-125 | (35-115%) | 18.9 | NIL | 3.10 | NIL | 9 | 9/30 | .72 | .60 | 12/31 | NIL | NIL | YES |
| | 2130 | Affiliated Managers | AMG | 66.50 | 3 | 3 | 3 | 1.55 | 70-105 | (5- 60%) | 27.1 | NIL | 2.45 | NIL | 65 | 9/30 | .55 | .50 | 12/31 | NIL | NIL | YES |
| 1464 | 181 | Affymetrix Inc. (NDQ) | AFFX | 36.23 | 1 | 4 | 4 | 1.50 | 35- 55 | (N- 50%) | 33.2 | NIL | 1.09 | NIL | 40 | 9/30 | .25 | .10 | 12/31 | NIL | NIL | YES |
| 1986 | 125 | Agilent Technologies | A | 24.18 | 3 | 3 | 3 | 1.55 | 40- 60 | (65-150%) | 32.2 | NIL | .75 | NIL | 70 | 10/31 | .15 | .03 | 12/31 | NIL | NIL | YES |
| | 1024 | Agilysys, Inc. (NDQ) | AGYS | 16.99 | 2 | 3 | 3 | 1.05 | 17- 25 | (N- 45%) | 19.3 | 0.7 | .88 | .12 | 59 | 9/30 | .13 | d.04 | 12/31 | .03 | .03 | YES |
| | 1216 | Agnico-Eagle Mines | AEM | 13.68 | 3 | 3 | 2 | .40 | 15- 25 | (10- 85%) | 31.1 | 0.2 | .44 | .03 | 53 | 9/30 | .12 | d.14 | 3/31 | .03 | .03 | YES |
| 990 | 477 | Agrium, Inc. | AGU | 16.46 | 2 | 3 | 1 | .80 | 25- 35 | (50-115%) | 10.2 | 0.7 | 1.61 | .11 | 44 | 9/30 | .43 | .17 | 3/31 | ◆.055 | .055 | YES |
| | 1515 | Ahold ADR | AHO | | | | | | SEE LATEST REPORT | | | | | | | | | | | | | |
| | 1962 | Air Products & Chem. | APD | 57.82 | 3 | 3 | 2 | .95 | 55- 85 | (N- 45%) | 19.7 | 2.0 | 2.94 | 1.16 | 32 | 9/30 | .73 | .58 | 3/31 | .29 | .23 | YES |
| | 478 | Airgas Inc. | ARG | 25.85 | 3 | 3 | 2 | 1.05 | 30- 45 | (15- 75%) | 19.6 | 0.8 | 1.32 | .20 | 44 | 9/30 | .30 | .26 | 12/31 | .045 | .04 | YES |
| 1462 | 255 | Alaska Air Group | ALK | 32.38 | 2 | 3 | 2 | 1.35 | 35- 50 | (10- 55%) | 39.5 | NIL | .82 | NIL | 42 | 9/30 | 2.08 | 1.52 | 12/31 | NIL | NIL | YES |
| | 1334 | Albany Int'l 'A' | AIN | 34.13 | 4 | 3 | 3 | 1.05 | 45- 65 | (30- 90%) | 14.8 | 0.9 | 2.30 | .32 | 47 | 9/30 | .42 | .50 | 3/31 | .08 | .07 | |
| | 1243 | Albany Molecular (NDQ) | AMRI | 11.23 | ▲3 | 3 | 3 | 1.10 | 11- 17 | (N- 50%) | 21.2 | NIL | .53 | NIL | 69 | 9/30 | .11 | .26 | 12/31 | NIL | NIL | |
| | 1963 | Albemarle Corp. | ALB | 40.08 | 3 | 3 | 2 | .90 | 45- 70 | (10- 75%) | 20.9 | 1.5 | 1.92 | .60 | 32 | 9/30 | .48 | .35 | 3/31 | ▲.15 | .145 | YES |
| | 816 | Alberto Culver | ACV | 47.55 | 3 | 1 | 3 | .70 | 60- 75 | (25- 60%) | 19.9 | 0.9 | 2.39 | .45 | 51 | 9/30 | .61 | .51 | 12/31 | .10 | .07 | YES |
| | 1516 | Albertson's, Inc. | ABS | 23.56 | 2 | 3 | 3 | .80 | 30- 45 | (25- 90%) | 14.5 | 3.2 | 1.62 | .76 | 83 | 10/31 | .29 | .25 | 12/31 | .19 | .19 | YES |
| 1982 | 1224 | Alcan Inc. | AL | 47.32 | 3 | 3 | 3 | 1.10 | 40- 65 | (N- 35%) | 18.1 | 1.3 | 2.62 | .60 | 48 | 9/30 | .41 | .44 | 12/31 | .15 | .15 | YES |
| | 769 | Alcatel ADR(g) | ALA | 15.07 | 2 | 4 | 3 | 1.85 | 14- 25 | (N- 65%) | 35.9 | NIL | .42 | NIL | 26 | 9/30 | .08 | d.25 | 12/31 | NIL | NIL | YES |
| | 1225 | Alcoa Inc. | AA | 31.30 | 4 | 3 | 3 | 1.35 | 45- 65 | (45-110%) | 16.8 | 1.9 | 1.86 | .60 | 48 | 9/30 | .34 | .33 | 12/31 | .15 | .15 | YES |
| | 277 | Alexander & Baldwin (NDQ) | ALEX | 44.74 | 3 | 3 | 3 | .90 | 45- 65 | (N- 45%) | 19.7 | 2.0 | 2.27 | .90 | 25 | 9/30 | .58 | .52 | 12/31 | .225 | .225 | YES |
| 1982 | 586 | Alleghany Corp. | Y | 285.00 | ▼4 | 1 | 3 | .55 | 405-495 | (40- 75%) | 33.6 | NIL | ▼8.48 | NIL | 39 | 9/30 | d6.69 | NA | 12/31 | NIL | NIL | |
| | 155 | Allegheny Energy | AYE | 19.55 | 2 | 5 | 2 | 1.60 | 20- 40 | (N-105%) | 17.9 | NIL | 1.09 | NIL | 88 | 9/30 | .37 | d.41 | 12/31 | NIL | NIL | YES |
| | 1226 | Allegheny Technologies | ATI | 22.26 | 2 | 4 | 1 | 1.50 | 19- 30 | (N- 35%) | 37.7 | 1.1 | .59 | .24 | 48 | 9/30 | .09 | d.32 | 12/31 | .06 | .06 | YES |
| | 1244 | Allergan, Inc. | AGN | 79.98 | 3 | 2 | 5 | .75 | 95-125 | (20- 55%) | 26.2 | 0.5 | 3.05 | .38 | 69 | 9/30 | .67 | .57 | 12/31 | .09 | .09 | YES |
| | 696 | ALLETE | ALE | 35.38 | – | 2 | – | NMF | 25- 30 | (N- N%) | 26.6 | 3.4 | 1.33 | 1.20 | 89 | 9/30 | .36 | NA | 12/31 | .30 | NIL | YES |
| | 2131 | Alliance Capital Mgmt. | AC | 40.94 | 4 | 3 | 3 | 1.35 | 45- 65 | (10- 60%) | 17.0 | 6.1 | 2.41 | 2.50 | 65 | 9/30 | .52 | .57 | 12/31 | .52 | .57 | YES |
| | 1054 | Alliance Semiconductor (NDQ) | ALSC | 3.52 | 4 | 4 | 4 | 1.85 | 5- 8 | (40-125%) | NMF | NIL | d.63 | NIL | 66 | 9/30 | d.29 | d.18 | 12/31 | NIL | NIL | YES |
| | 697 | Alliant Energy | LNT | 27.77 | 3 | 3 | 3 | .80 | 25- 35 | (N- 25%) | 15.4 | 3.8 | 1.80 | 1.05 | 89 | 9/30 | .76 | .78 | 12/31 | ▲.263 | .25 | YES |
| | 545 | Alliant Techsystems | ATK | 66.11 | 3 | 3 | 3 | .70 | 75-115 | (15- 75%) | 16.2 | NIL | 4.09 | NIL | 22 | 9/30 | .78 | .93 | 12/31 | NIL | NIL | YES |
| | 2132 | Allied Capital Corp. | ALD | 28.01 | 3 | 2 | 4 | .85 | 40- 60 | (45-115%) | 12.2 | 8.1 | 2.30 | 2.28 | 65 | 9/30 | .66 | .28 | 12/31 | .57 | .57 | YES |
| | 349 | Allied Waste | AW | 9.08 | 4 | 3 | 4 | 1.10 | 10- 15 | (10- 65%) | 22.1 | NIL | .41 | NIL | 82 | 9/30 | .12 | .14 | 12/31 | NIL | NIL | YES |
| | 587 | Allmerica Financial | AFC | 32.24 | 3 | 3 | 4 | 1.50 | ▲40- 60 | (25- 85%) | 13.0 | NIL | 2.48 | NIL | 39 | 9/30 | .37 | .50 | 12/31 | NIL | NIL | YES |
| 529 | 2225 | Alloy, Inc. (NDQ) | ALOY | 6.50 | 2 | 4 | 3 | 1.20 | 17- 30 | (160-360%) | NMF | NIL | .03 | NIL | 8 | 10/31 | .04 | d.17 | 12/31 | NIL | NIL | YES |
| | 588 | Allstate Corp. | ALL | 51.35 | 3 | 2 | 3 | .95 | 60- 80 | (15- 55%) | 12.1 | 2.3 | 4.26 | 1.18 | 39 | 9/30 | .08 | .91 | 3/31 | .28 | .24 | YES |
| | 723 | ALLTEL Corp. | AT | 58.25 | 3 | 2 | 3 | 1.00 | 70- 95 | (20- 65%) | 17.2 | 2.7 | 3.38 | 1.56 | 57 | 9/30 | .92 | .77 | 3/31 | ▲.38 | .37 | YES |
| 1796 | 182 | ALPHARMA Inc. | ALO | 16.78 | 3 | 3 | 4 | .85 | 25- 40 | (50-140%) | 24.0 | 1.1 | .70 | .18 | 40 | 9/30 | d.09 | .10 | 12/31 | .045 | .045 | YES |
| | 1055 | Altera Corp. (NDQ) | ALTR | 20.41 | 3 | 3 | 3 | 1.65 | 30- 50 | (45-145%) | 24.0 | NIL | .85 | NIL | 66 | 9/30 | .22 | .11 | 12/31 | NIL | NIL | YES |
| 1800 | 1575 | Altria Group | MO | 60.80 | 4 | 3 | 3 | .75 | 60- 95 | (N- 55%) | 12.6 | 4.9 | 4.81 | 2.97 | 97 | 9/30 | 1.29 | 1.22 | 12/31 | .73 | .68 | YES |
| | 2226 | Amazon.com (NDQ) | AMZN | 41.00 | 2 | 4 | 2 | 1.65 | 50- 80 | (20- 95%) | 36.0 | NIL | 1.14 | NIL | 8 | 9/30 | .15 | .07 | 12/31 | NIL | NIL | YES |
| | 2133 | Ambac Fin'l Group | ABK | 84.42 | 3 | 2 | 3 | 1.10 | 80-110 | (N- 30%) | 12.9 | 0.6 | 6.52 | .50 | 65 | 9/30 | 1.65 | 1.45 | 12/31 | .125 | .11 | YES |
| | 1227 | AMCOL Int'l | ACO | 19.27 | 3 | 3 | 1 | .90 | 18- 25 | (N- 30%) | 20.9 | 1.9 | .92 | .36 | 48 | 9/30 | .27 | .22 | 3/31 | .09 | .12 | YES |
| | 323 | Amdocs Ltd. | DOX | 26.25 | 3 | 4 | 4 | 1.45 | 25- 45 | (N- 70%) | 20.2 | NIL | 1.30 | NIL | 46 | 9/30 | .31 | .23 | 12/31 | NIL | NIL | YES |
| 1610 | 407 | Amerada Hess | AHC | 85.09 | 3 | 3 | 3 | .90 | 70-100 | (N- 20%) | 11.4 | 1.4 | 7.46 | 1.20 | 15 | 9/30 | 1.74 | 1.30 | 3/31 | .30 | .60 | YES |
| | 698 | Ameren Corp. | AEE | 49.70 | 4 | 1 | 3 | .75 | 40- 50 | (N- N%) | 18.4 | 5.1 | 2.70 | 2.54 | 89 | 9/30 | 1.20 | 1.70 | 12/31 | .635 | .635 | YES |
| | 794 | Amer. Axle | AXL | 29.26 | 5 | 3 | 3 | 1.15 | 40- 60 | (35-105%) | 8.4 | 2.4 | 3.50 | .70 | 95 | 9/30 | .68 | .71 | 12/31 | .15 | NIL | YES |
| | 1711 | Amer. Eagle Outfitters (NDQ) | AEOS | 45.53 | 1 | 3 | 4 | 1.40 | 50- 70 | (10- 55%) | 17.4 | 0.5 | 2.61 | .24 | 72 | 10/31 | .77 | .25 | 3/31 | .06 | NIL | YES |
| | 699 | Amer. Elec. Power | AEP | 34.83 | 3 | 3 | 3 | 1.15 | 30- 40 | (N- 15%) | 14.6 | 4.1 | 2.38 | 1.43 | 89 | 9/30 | .80 | .89 | 12/31 | .35 | .35 | YES |
| | 2134 | Amer. Express | AXP | 56.14 | 3 | 2 | 3 | 1.50 | 50- 70 | (N- 25%) | 19.2 | 0.9 | 2.92 | .48 | 65 | 9/30 | .69 | .59 | 3/31 | .12 | .10 | YES |
| | 589 | Amer. Financial Group | AFG | 32.16 | 2 | 3 | 4 | 1.00 | 40- 55 | (25- 70%) | 11.1 | 1.6 | 2.89 | .50 | 39 | 9/30 | .53 | .73 | 12/31 | .125 | .125 | YES |
| | 927 | Amer. Greetings | AM | 27.60 | 3 | 3 | 2 | .95 | 20- 35 | (N- 25%) | 15.8 | 0.9 | 1.75 | .24 | 38 | 8/31 | .10 | d.15 | 12/31 | ▲.06 | NIL | YES |
| | 630 | Amer. Healthways (NDQ) | AMHC | 34.78 | 1 | 3 | 2 | 1.30 | 30- 45 | (N- 30%) | 35.1 | NIL | .99 | NIL | 19 | 8/31 | .27 | .15 | 12/31 | NIL | NIL | YES |
| 1299 | 2135 | Amer. Int'l Group | AIG | 64.72 | – | 3 | – | 1.20 | 115-170 | (80-165%) | 13.8 | 0.5 | 4.70 | .30 | 65 | 9/30 | .97 | .98 | 3/31 | .075 | .065 | YES |
| | 1482 | Amer. Italian Pasta | PLB | 20.37 | 5 | 3 | 3 | .70 | 19- 30 | (N- 45%) | 97.0 | 3.7 | .21 | .75 | 79 | 9/30 | d.15 | .69 | 12/31 | .188 | NIL | YES |
| | 1109 | Amer. Power Conv. (NDQ) | APCC | 20.80 | 4 | 3 | 1 | 1.25 | 25- 35 | (20- 70%) | 21.7 | 1.9 | .96 | .40 | 23 | 9/30 | .28 | .26 | 12/31 | .10 | .08 | YES |
| | 1378 | Amer. Standard | ASD | 41.44 | 3 | 3 | 3 | .95 | 35- 50 | (N- 20%) | 17.8 | NIL | 2.33 | NIL | 56 | 9/30 | .65 | .55 | 12/31 | NIL | NIL | YES |
| | 1421 | Amer. States Water | AWR | 25.47 | 4 | 3 | 2 | .70 | 20- 30 | (N- 20%) | 18.5 | 3.5 | 1.38 | .90 | 94 | 9/30 | .52 | .51 | 12/31 | ▲.225 | .221 | |
| | 978 | Amer. Superconductor (NDQ) | AMSC | 15.07 | 3 | 5 | 3 | 1.30 | 18- 35 | (20-130%) | NMF | NIL | d.82 | NIL | 78 | 9/30 | d.15 | d.30 | 12/31 | NIL | NIL | YES |
| | 724 | Amer. Tower 'A' | AMT | 18.36 | 3 | 5 | 3 | 2.00 | 16- 30 | (N- 65%) | NMF | NIL | d.58 | NIL | 57 | 9/30 | d.25 | d.18 | 12/31 | NIL | NIL | YES |
| | 852 | Amer. Woodmark (NDQ) | AMWD | 44.25 | 2 | 3 | 3 | .95 | 40- 60 | (N- 35%) | 18.1 | 0.3 | 2.45 | .12 | 60 | 10/31 | .67 | .50 | 12/31 | .03 | .025 | |
| | 183 | AmerisourceBergen | ABC | 63.05 | 3 | 3 | 5 | .75 | 90-135 | (45-115%) | 16.0 | 0.2 | 3.94 | .10 | 40 | 9/30 | .82 | 1.05 | 12/31 | .025 | .025 | YES |
| | 2227 | AmeriTrade Holding (NDQ) | AMTD | 13.81 | 3 | 4 | 3 | 1.80 | 20- 35 | (45-155%) | 17.7 | NIL | .78 | NIL | 8 | 9/30 | .14 | .13 | 12/31 | NIL | NIL | YES |
| | 853 | Ameron Int'l | AMN | 37.46 | 5 | 3 | 3 | .85 | 45- 65 | (20- 75%) | 11.3 | 2.1 | 3.32 | .80 | 60 | 8/31 | .72 | .94 | 12/31 | .20 | .20 | |
| | 1379 | Ametek, Inc. | AME | 34.74 | 2 | 2 | 2 | 1.05 | 30- 40 | (N- 15%) | 20.2 | 0.7 | 1.72 | .24 | 56 | 9/30 | .42 | .33 | 12/31 | .06 | .03 | YES |
| | 667 | Amgen (NDQ) | AMGN | 63.54 | 1 | 2 | 3 | .95 | 80-110 | (25- 75%) | 24.8 | NIL | 2.56 | NIL | 75 | 9/30 | .60 | .46 | 12/31 | NIL | NIL | YES |
| 1297 | 1094 | Amkor Technology (NDQ) | AMKR | 6.18 | 4 | 5 | 4 | 1.85 | 4- 8 | (N- 30%) | NMF | NIL | d.73 | NIL | 64 | 9/30 | d.13 | .04 | 12/31 | NIL | NIL | YES |
| 1559 | 575 | Ampco-Pittsburgh | AP | 13.59 | 4 | 3 | 3 | .60 | 20- 30 | (45-120%) | NMF | 2.9 | ▲d.06 | .40 | 2 | 9/30 | d.19 | .11 | 3/31 | ◆.10 | .10 | |
| | 2102 | AmSouth Bancorp. | ASO | 25.47 | 3 | 2 | 3 | .95 | 30- 45 | (20- 75%) | 12.7 | 3.9 | 2.00 | 1.00 | 76 | 9/30 | .48 | .45 | 3/31 | ▲.25 | .24 | YES |
| | 1931 | Anadarko Petroleum | APC | 67.37 | 2 | 3 | 3 | .90 | 70-110 | (5- 65%) | 10.0 | 0.8 | 6.76 | .56 | 7 | 9/30 | 1.58 | 1.09 | 12/31 | .14 | .14 | YES |
| | 1056 | ANADIGICS Inc. (NDQ) | ANAD | 3.29 | 4 | 5 | 3 | 1.95 | 9- 16 | (175-385%) | NMF | NIL | d.75 | NIL | 66 | 9/30 | d.25 | d.41 | 12/31 | NIL | NIL | YES |
| | 1057 | Analog Devices | ADI | 37.99 | 3 | 3 | 4 | 1.70 | 50- 70 | (30- 85%) | 27.1 | 0.6 | 1.40 | .24 | 66 | 10/31 | .34 | .23 | 12/31 | .06 | .04 | YES |
| 837 | 126 | Analogic Corp. (NDQ) | ALOGE | 46.39 | 4 | 3 | 3 | .65 | 35- 55 | (N- 20%) | 37.1 | 0.7 | 1.25 | .32 | 70 | 7/31 | .32 | .12 | 3/31 | .08 | .08 | |
| | 747 | Andrew Corp. (NDQ) | ANDW | 12.98 | 4 | 3 | 5 | 1.40 | 17- 25 | (30- 95%) | 44.8 | NIL | .29 | NIL | 52 | 9/30 | NIL | .06 | 12/31 | NIL | NIL | YES |
| 1796 | 1245 | Andrx Group (NDQ) | ADRX | 20.81 | 4 | 4 | 5 | 1.15 | 45- 75 | (115-260%) | 21.5 | NIL | .97 | NIL | 69 | 9/30 | .16 | .16 | 12/31 | NIL | NIL | YES |
| | 324 | Angelica Corp. | AGL | 27.55 | 4 | 3 | 3 | .70 | 25- 35 | (N- 25%) | 26.7 | 1.6 | 1.03 | .44 | 46 | 10/31 | .29 | .25 | 3/31 | .11 | .11 | |
| | 1217 | AngloGold Ashanti ADR | AU | 36.75 | 4 | 3 | 2 | .55 | 30- 45 | (N- 20%) | 29.4 | 2.1 | 1.25 | .76 | 53 | 3/31 | NA | NA | 12/31 | ◆NIL | NIL | YES |
| | 1535 | Anheuser-Busch | BUD | 50.30 | 3 | 1 | 3 | .60 | 75- 90 | (50- 80%) | 17.6 | 1.9 | 2.85 | .98 | 43 | 9/30 | .85 | .80 | 12/31 | .245 | .22 | YES |
| | 1174 | Annaly Mortgage Mgmt. | NLY | 20.22 | 3 | 3 | 3 | .65 | 15- 25 | (N- 25%) | 10.1 | 9.6 | 2.01 | 1.95 | 96 | 9/30 | .53 | .30 | 12/31 | .50 | .28 | YES |

(•) All data adjusted for announced stock split or stock dividend. See back page of Ratings & Reports.
◆ New figure this week.
(b) Canadian Funds.
d Deficit.
(f) The estimate may reflect a probable increase or decrease. If a dividend boost or cut is possible but not probable, two figures are shown, the first is the more likely.
(g) Dividends subject to foreign withholding tax for U.S. residents.
(h) Est'd Earnings & Est'd Dividends after conversion to U.S. dollars at Value Line estimated translation rate.
(j) All Index data expressed in hundreds.
(p) 6 months (q) Asset Value
N=Negative figure NA=Not available NMF=No meaningful figure





Source: *The Value Line Investment Survey*, December 24, 2004. Copyright © 2004 Value Line Publishing, Inc.: used by permission.

**FIGURE 10-6** Value Line Timely Stocks in Timely Industries



## STOCKS MOVING DOWN IN TIMELINESS RANK

| Stock Name | Old Rank | New Rank | Reason for Change | Earnings Est. 12 months to 6-30-05 |
|---|---|---|---|---|
| Tektronix, Inc. | 3 | 4 | Surprise factor, earnings reversal. Management forecasts 26-30¢ for the Feb. period vs. year ago 33¢. Our estimate was 37¢. | 1.50 |
| Waters Corp. | 1 | 2 | Dynamism of the ranking system. | |

(A) New full-page report in this week's Ratings & Reports.
(B) Supplementary report in this week's Ratings & Reports.

## TIMELY STOCKS IN TIMELY INDUSTRIES

| Page No. | Industry (Industry Rank) | Recent Price | Ranks: Timeliness | Ranks: Safety | Ranks: Technical | Beta | Current P/E Ratio | % Est'd Yield | Est'd. 3-5 Year Price Apprec. |
|---|---|---|---|---|---|---|---|---|---|
| | **Chemical (Basic) (INDUSTRY RANK 1)** | | | | | | | | |
| 1236 | Du Pont | 48.39 | 2 | 1 | 3 | 1.00 | 19.8 | 2.9 | 25- 55% |
| 1237 | Georgia Gulf | 53.70 | 1 | 3 | 2 | 1.00 | 13.6 | 0.7 | N- 30% |
| 1238 | Lyondell Chemical | 29.13 | 1 | 4 | 3 | 1.25 | 31.3 | 3.1 | N- 35% |
| 1240 | Olin Corp. | 22.50 | 1 | 3 | 2 | 0.85 | 21.2 | 3.6 | N- 10% |
| | **Steel (General) (INDUSTRY RANK 2)** | | | | | | | | |
| 576 | Carpenter Technology | 58.77 | 1 | 3 | 2 | 1.30 | 21.0 | 0.7 | N- N% |
| 577 | Cleveland-Cliffs | 49.93 | 2 | 3 | 2 | 1.05 | 20.1 | 0.8 | N- N% |
| 578 | Commercial Metals | 21.93 | 1 | 3 | 1 | 0.95 | 9.5 | 0.9 | 35-105% |
| 579 | Nucor Corp. | 53.50 | 1 | 3 | 3 | 1.20 | 7.0 | 1.0 | 30-105% |
| 580 | Quanex Corp. | 45.33 | 2 | 3 | 3 | 1.00 | 15.2 | 1.2 | 10- 55% |
| 581 | Ryerson Tull | 15.93 | 2 | 3 | 3 | 1.15 | 7.7 | 1.3 | 25- 90% |
| 582 | Steel Technologies | 24.40 | 1 | 3 | 2 | 0.65 | 6.7 | 0.8 | 25- 85% |
| 583 | Worthington Inds. | 19.81 | 2 | 3 | 2 | 0.95 | 10.2 | 3.3 | 50-100% |
| | **Homebuilding (INDUSTRY RANK 3)** | | | | | | | | |
| 867 | Beazer Homes USA | 147.27 | 2 | 3 | 3 | 1.20 | 7.6 | 0.3 | N- 5% |
| 869 | Horton D.R. | 41.36 | 2 | 3 | 4 | 1.30 | 10.0 | 0.8 | N- 10% |
| 870 | Hovnanian Enterpr. 'A' | 48.60 | 2 | 3 | 3 | 1.15 | 7.7 | NIL | 15- 75% |
| 871 | KB Home | 105.50 | 2 | 3 | 2 | 1.15 | 8.7 | 1.4 | N- 15% |
| 872 | Lennar Corp. | 56.35 | 2 | 3 | 3 | 1.15 | 9.4 | 1.0 | N- 35% |
| 873 | M.D.C. Holdings | 87.01 | 2 | 3 | 3 | 1.20 | 7.6 | 0.7 | N- 20% |
| 874 | NVR, Inc. | 754.50 | 1 | 3 | 3 | 1.10 | 10.2 | NIL | N- 25% |
| 875 | Pulte Homes | 64.99 | 2 | 3 | 3 | 1.20 | 8.2 | 0.3 | 15- 70% |
| 876 | Ryland Group | 57.10 | 2 | 3 | 3 | 1.30 | 8.5 | 0.4 | N- 15% |
| 877 | St. Joe Corp. | 58.43 | 2 | 1 | 2 | 0.80 | 50.8 | 1.0 | N- N% |
| 878 | Standard Pacific Corp. | 65.08 | 2 | 3 | 3 | 1.25 | 6.8 | 0.5 | N- 25% |
| 879 | Toll Brothers | 66.02 | 1 | 3 | 3 | 1.20 | 11.8 | NIL | N- 15% |
| | **Retail Building Supply (INDUSTRY RANK 4)** | | | | | | | | |
| 881 | Building Materials | 38.22 | 1 | 3 | 2 | 0.80 | 11.6 | 0.8 | N- 20% |
| 882 | Fastenal Co. | 62.43 | 2 | 3 | 2 | 1.20 | 33.4 | 0.8 | N- 45% |
| 883 | Home Depot | 42.49 | 1 | 2 | 3 | 1.30 | 18.4 | 0.8 | 90-160% |
| 885 | Lowe's Cos. | 57.92 | 2 | 3 | 3 | 1.15 | 19.1 | 0.3 | 80-170% |
| | **Coal (INDUSTRY RANK 5)** | | | | | | | | |
| 525 | Joy Global | 38.35 | 1 | 3 | 2 | 1.15 | 21.4 | 1.2 | 5- 55% |
| 526 | Massey Energy | 34.26 | 2 | 3 | 3 | 1.30 | 38.1 | 0.5 | N- 30% |
| 527 | Peabody Energy | 78.78 | 1 | 3 | 2 | 1.00 | 21.8 | 0.8 | N- 35% |
| | **Trucking (INDUSTRY RANK 6)** | | | | | | | | |
| 266 | Arkansas Best | 44.10 | 1 | 3 | 1 | 1.05 | 14.0 | 1.2 | N- 35% |
| 268 | Forward Air | 45.88 | 2 | 3 | 3 | 1.05 | 27.0 | NIL | 10- 65% |
| 269 | Heartland Express | 21.50 | 1 | 3 | 2 | 0.90 | 24.2 | 0.4 | N- N% |
| 270 | Hunt (J.B.) | 41.55 | 1 | 3 | 3 | 1.30 | 18.5 | 1.2 | N- 30% |
| 275 | Yellow Roadway | 54.00 | 1 | 3 | 1 | 1.20 | 11.7 | NIL | 10- 55% |
| | **Petroleum (Producing) (INDUSTRY RANK 7)** | | | | | | | | |
| 1931 | Anadarko Petroleum | 67.37 | 2 | 3 | 3 | 0.90 | 10.0 | 0.8 | 5- 65% |
| 1932 | Apache Corp. | 51.67 | 2 | 3 | 2 | 0.85 | 9.0 | 0.6 | 15- 75% |
| 1933 | Berry Petroleum 'A' | 47.50 | 1 | 3 | 2 | 0.70 | 14.4 | 1.0 | N- N% |
| 1934 | Burlington Resources | 44.42 | 2 | 3 | 2 | 0.80 | 11.5 | 0.8 | N- 15% |
| 1936 | Forest Oil | 32.27 | 2 | 3 | 2 | 1.00 | 13.0 | NIL | N- 25% |
| 1937 | Noble Energy | 61.54 | 2 | 3 | 2 | 0.90 | 12.0 | 0.3 | N- N% |
| | **Internet (INDUSTRY RANK 8)** | | | | | | | | |
| 2225 | Alloy, Inc. | 6.50 | 2 | 4 | 3 | 1.20 | NMF | NIL | 160-360% |
| 2226 | Amazon.com | 41.00 | 2 | 4 | 2 | 1.65 | 36.0 | NIL | 20- 95% |
| 2228 | CNET Networks | 11.43 | 2 | 5 | 4 | 2.05 | 63.5 | NIL | 5- 75% |
| 2229 | CheckFree Corp. | 37.99 | 2 | 4 | 3 | 1.65 | 76.0 | NIL | 20- 95% |
| 2231 | E*Trade Fin'l | 14.97 | 2 | 3 | 3 | 2.00 | 15.3 | NIL | 65-135% |
| 2232 | EarthLink, Inc. | 11.75 | 2 | 4 | 3 | 1.15 | 14.9 | NIL | 20-115% |
| 2233 | eBay Inc. | 117.39 | 1 | 3 | 4 | 1.45 | 79.9 | NIL | N- 45% |
| 2237 | priceline.com | 23.91 | 2 | 4 | 5 | 2.30 | 21.7 | NIL | 130-295% |
| 2240 | VeriSign Inc. | 35.96 | 2 | 4 | 2 | 1.90 | 41.8 | NIL | N- 40% |
| 2241 | Yahoo! Inc. | 38.29 | 1 | 3 | 3 | 1.80 | 89.0 | NIL | N- 5% |
| | **Computer Software/Svcs (INDUSTRY RANK 9)** | | | | | | | | |
| 2169 | Adobe Systems | 62.65 | 1 | 3 | 3 | 1.45 | 34.0 | 0.1 | N- 20% |
| 2170 | Affiliated Computer | 58.50 | 1 | 3 | 1 | 1.10 | 18.9 | NIL | 35-115% |
| 2171 | Anteon Int'l | 42.22 | 1 | 3 | 2 | 0.65 | 24.5 | NIL | 20- 65% |
| 2173 | Autodesk, Inc. | 34.81 | 1 | 3 | 3 | 1.15 | 45.2 | NIL | N- N% |
| 2175 | BMC Software | 19.03 | 2 | 3 | 3 | 1.60 | 42.3 | NIL | 5- 60% |
| 2176 | BearingPoint | 8.48 | 2 | 3 | 3 | 1.55 | 22.9 | NIL | 90-195% |
| 2177 | Borland Software | 11.63 | 2 | 4 | 3 | 1.25 | 30.6 | NIL | 20-115% |
| 2178 | CACI Int'l 'A' | 68.46 | 1 | 3 | 1 | 0.80 | 25.4 | NIL | N- 25% |
| 2179 | Cadence Design Sys. | 14.30 | 2 | 3 | 2 | 1.50 | 18.1 | NIL | 75-145% |
| 2181 | Citrix Sys. | 25.82 | 1 | 3 | 2 | 1.80 | 28.7 | NIL | 15- 75% |
| 2182 | Cognizant Technology | 40.57 | 1 | 3 | 1 | 1.05 | 48.3 | NIL | N- 25% |
| 2183 | Cognos Inc. | 43.32 | 1 | 3 | 3 | 1.25 | 32.3 | NIL | 15- 75% |
| 2185 | Computer Sciences | 56.80 | 2 | 3 | 2 | 1.10 | 17.8 | NIL | 30- 95% |
| 2188 | DST Systems | 50.45 | 2 | 3 | 3 | 1.20 | 19.9 | NIL | N- 60% |
| 2189 | Electronic Data Sys. | 22.53 | 2 | 4 | 1 | 1.50 | 44.2 | 0.9 | 10- 80% |
| 2192 | Fiserv Inc. | 38.51 | 2 | 3 | 4 | 1.10 | 18.9 | NIL | 95-185% |
| 2193 | Henry (Jack) & Assoc. | 19.35 | 2 | 3 | 3 | 1.20 | 24.2 | 0.8 | 55-135% |
| 2198 | Macromedia, Inc. | 31.00 | 1 | 3 | 4 | 1.50 | 35.6 | NIL | 15- 75% |
| 2200 | McAfee, Inc. | 32.71 | 2 | 4 | 2 | 1.55 | 42.5 | NIL | N- 20% |
| 2202 | Mercury Interactive | 45.61 | 1 | 3 | 4 | 1.80 | 38.0 | NIL | 20- 85% |
| 2204 | Moldflow Corp. | 13.44 | 2 | 4 | 3 | 0.95 | 26.9 | NIL | 20- 85% |
| 2207 | Oracle Corp. | 14.09 | 1 | 3 | 3 | 1.15 | 23.5 | NIL | 20- 75% |
| 2209 | Parametric Technology | 5.98 | 2 | 5 | 4 | 1.55 | 23.0 | NIL | N-100% |
| 2213 | RSA Security | 20.88 | 1 | 4 | 3 | 1.60 | 35.4 | NIL | 20- 90% |
| 2215 | SEI Investments | 42.56 | 1 | 3 | 3 | 1.45 | 25.8 | 0.5 | 5- 65% |
| 2220 | Symantec Corp. | 27.38 | 1 | 3 | 3 | 1.05 | 33.8 | NIL | N- 45% |
| | **Steel (Integrated) (INDUSTRY RANK 10)** | | | | | | | | |
| 1415 | AK Steel Holding | 13.43 | 1 | 4 | 1 | 1.30 | 8.4 | NIL | 20- 85% |
| 1419 | U.S. Steel Corp. | 51.50 | 2 | 3 | 1 | 1.30 | 6.2 | 1.0 | N- 35% |
| | **Information Services (INDUSTRY RANK 11)** | | | | | | | | |
| 375 | Advisory Board | 37.34 | 1 | 3 | 4 | 1.00 | 29.4 | NIL | 20- 75% |
| 377 | ChoicePoint Inc. | 44.05 | 2 | 3 | 3 | 0.90 | 25.2 | NIL | 25- 80% |
| 378 | Corporate Executive | 66.47 | 2 | 3 | 3 | 1.25 | 42.9 | 0.6 | 15- 65% |
| 381 | Equifax, Inc. | 28.22 | 2 | 3 | 3 | 1.10 | 17.2 | 0.4 | 5- 60% |
| 382 | FactSet Research | 49.37 | 1 | 3 | 3 | 1.25 | 25.1 | 0.6 | 20- 70% |
| 385 | Getty Images | 68.25 | 2 | 3 | 3 | 1.65 | 36.7 | NIL | N- 10% |
| 386 | Interactive Data | 21.44 | 2 | 3 | 3 | 1.05 | 23.6 | NIL | N- 40% |
| 387 | Moody's Corp. | 83.98 | 2 | 2 | 3 | 0.80 | 28.2 | 0.4 | N- 15% |
| | **Oilfield Svcs/Equip. (INDUSTRY RANK 12)** | | | | | | | | |
| 1942 | Baker Hughes | 43.34 | 2 | 3 | 3 | 1.00 | 25.3 | 1.1 | N- 40% |
| 1943 | Cal Dive Int'l | 41.50 | 1 | 3 | 3 | 1.00 | 20.6 | NIL | N- 35% |
| 1945 | Diamond Offshore | 37.82 | 2 | 3 | 3 | 1.05 | 61.0 | 0.7 | 5- 60% |
| 1947 | Global Inds. | 8.22 | 2 | 4 | 2 | 1.10 | 28.3 | NIL | N- 10% |
| 1949 | Halliburton Co. | 40.18 | 2 | 3 | 3 | 1.25 | 23.5 | 1.2 | N- 35% |
| 1951 | Input/Output | 8.00 | 2 | 4 | 4 | 0.95 | 27.6 | NIL | 75-215% |
| 1955 | Schlumberger Ltd. | 66.13 | 2 | 3 | 3 | 1.05 | 31.2 | 1.1 | N- 45% |
| 1959 | Transocean Inc. | 40.27 | 2 | 3 | 3 | 1.10 | 56.7 | NIL | N- 25% |
| 1960 | Weatherford Int'l | 53.11 | 2 | 3 | 3 | 1.10 | 28.6 | NIL | N- 40% |
| | **Natural Gas (Div.) (INDUSTRY RANK 13)** | | | | | | | | |
| 439 | Devon Energy | 40.17 | 2 | 3 | 1 | 0.85 | 9.3 | 0.5 | 10- 60% |
| 441 | EOG Resources | 73.26 | 2 | 3 | 2 | 0.90 | 14.2 | 0.3 | N- N% |
| 443 | Energen Corp. | 58.64 | 2 | 3 | 2 | 0.70 | 15.5 | 1.3 | N- 10% |
| 446 | Kinder Morgan | 71.87 | 2 | 3 | 3 | 0.80 | 18.5 | 3.3 | 10- 65% |
| 449 | Newfield Exploration | 60.86 | 2 | 3 | 3 | 0.90 | 10.7 | NIL | 25- 90% |
| 452 | Questar Corp. | 49.32 | 2 | 2 | 2 | 0.85 | 17.2 | 1.7 | N- 40% |
| 453 | Southwestern Energy | 52.24 | 1 | 3 | 1 | 0.80 | 17.9 | NIL | N- 5% |
| 455 | Vintage Petroleum | 23.11 | 2 | 3 | 3 | 0.90 | 12.6 | 1.0 | N- 10% |
| 457 | Williams Cos. | 16.40 | 2 | 5 | 2 | 2.40 | 23.4 | 1.2 | 5- 85% |
| 458 | XTO Energy | 33.68 | 1 | 3 | 2 | 0.80 | 13.2 | 0.6 | 20- 65% |
| | **Foreign Electronics (INDUSTRY RANK 14)** | | | | | | | | |
| 1559 | Canon Inc. ADR | 52.01 | 2 | 2 | 3 | 0.90 | 16.4 | 1.0 | 15- 55% |
| 1561 | Hitachi, Ltd. ADR | 65.15 | 2 | 3 | 3 | 1.00 | 29.5 | 1.4 | 60-145% |
| 1562 | Kyocera Corp. ADR | 71.86 | 2 | 3 | 3 | 1.00 | 17.3 | 0.8 | 40-110% |
| 1563 | Matsushita Elec. ADR | 15.42 | 2 | 2 | 2 | 0.95 | 70.1 | 0.9 | N- 25% |



Source: *The Value Line Investment Survey*, December 24, 2004. Copyright © 2004 Value Line Publishing, Inc.: used by permission.

FIGURE 10-7 Value Line Timely Stocks



# Timely Stocks

## Stocks Ranked 1 (Highest) for Relative Price Performance (Next 12 Months)

| Page No. | Stock Name | Ticker | Recent Price | Ranks: Safety | Ranks: Technical | Current P/E Ratio | % Est'd Yield | Industry Group | Industry Rank |
|---|---|---|---|---|---|---|---|---|---|
| 1415 | AK Steel Holding | AKS | 13.43 | 4 | 1 | 8.4 | NIL | Steel (Integrated) | 10 |
| 2169 | Adobe Systems | ADBE | 62.65 | 3 | 3 | 34.0 | 0.1 | Computer Software/Svcs | 9 |
| 375 | Advisory Board | ABCO | 37.34 | 3 | 4 | 29.4 | NIL | Information Services | 11 |
| 1710 | Aeropostale | ARO | 30.00 | 3 | 4 | 19.1 | NIL | Retail (Special Lines) | 72 |
| 629 | Aetna Inc. | AET | 126.20 | 3 | 3 | 16.4 | NIL | Medical Services | 19 |
| 2170 | Affiliated Computer | ACS | 58.50 | 3 | 1 | 18.9 | NIL | Computer Software/Svcs | 9 |
| 181 | Affymetrix Inc. | AFFX | 36.23 | 4 | 4 | 33.2 | NIL | Medical Supplies | 40 |
| 1711 | Amer. Eagle Outfitters | AEOS | 45.53 | 3 | 4 | 17.4 | 0.5 | Retail (Special Lines) | 72 |
| 630 | Amer. Healthways | AMHC | 34.78 | 3 | 2 | 35.1 | NIL | Medical Services | 19 |
| 667 | Amgen | AMGN | 63.54 | 2 | 3 | 24.8 | NIL | Biotechnology | 75 |
| 2171 | Anteon Int'l | ANT | 42.22 | 3 | 2 | 24.5 | NIL | Computer Software/Svcs | 9 |
| 1110 | Apple Computer | AAPL | 65.26 | 3 | 2 | 56.3 | NIL | Computers/Peripherals | 23 |
| 266 | Arkansas Best | ABFS | 44.10 | 3 | 1 | 14.0 | 1.2 | Trucking | 6 |
| 546 | Armor Holdings | AH | 47.55 | 3 | 4 | 18.4 | NIL | Aerospace/Defense | 22 |
| 2173 | Autodesk, Inc. | ADSK | 34.81 | 3 | 3 | 45.2 | NIL | Computer Software/Svcs | 9 |
| 1714 | Bed Bath & Beyond | BBBY | 40.33 | 2 | 3 | 24.3 | NIL | Retail (Special Lines) | 72 |
| 1933 | Berry Petroleum 'A' | BRY | 47.50 | 3 | 2 | 14.4 | 1.0 | Petroleum (Producing) | 7 |
| 193 | Biosite Inc. | BSTE | 59.77 | 4 | 3 | 25.9 | NIL | Medical Supplies | 40 |
| 118 | Black & Decker | BDK | 85.64 | 3 | 2 | 15.2 | 1.0 | Home Appliance | 80 |
| 1583 | Bright Horizons Family | BFAM | 66.20 | 3 | 2 | 31.5 | NIL | Educational Services | 77 |
| 881 | Building Materials | BMHC | 38.22 | 3 | 2 | 11.6 | 0.8 | Retail Building Supply | 4 |
| 2178 | CACI Int'l 'A' | CAI | 68.46 | 3 | 1 | 25.4 | NIL | Computer Software/Svcs | 9 |
| 326 | C.H. Robinson | CHRW | 54.53 | 3 | 2 | 31.7 | 1.1 | Industrial Services | 46 |
| 297 | CKE Restaurants ■ | CKR | 13.95 | 4 | 3 | 18.9 | NIL | Restaurant | 63 |
| 1943 | Cal Dive Int'l | CDIS | 41.50 | 3 | 3 | 20.6 | NIL | Oilfield Svcs/Equip. | 12 |
| 286 | Can. National Railway | CNI | 60.27 | 3 | 1 | 15.5 | 1.1 | Railroad | 20 |
| 576 | Carpenter Technology | CRS | 58.77 | 3 | 2 | 21.0 | 0.7 | Steel (General) | 2 |
| 1381 | Cendant Corp. | CD | 22.70 | 3 | 3 | 13.2 | 1.6 | Diversified Co. | 56 |
| 2181 | Citrix Sys. | CTXS | 25.82 | 3 | 2 | 28.7 | NIL | Computer Software/Svcs | 9 |
| 2182 | Cognizant Technology | CTSH | 40.57 | 3 | 1 | 48.3 | NIL | Computer Software/Svcs | 9 |
| 2183 | Cognos Inc. | COGN | 43.32 | 3 | 3 | 32.3 | NIL | Computer Software/Svcs | 9 |
| 578 | Commercial Metals | CMC | 21.93 | 3 | 1 | 9.5 | 0.9 | Steel (General) | 2 |
| 634 | Community Health | CYH | 28.12 | 3 | 2 | 16.4 | NIL | Medical Services | 19 |
| 1677 | Costco Wholesale | COST | 48.36 | 3 | 3 | 23.9 | 0.8 | Retail Store | 41 |
| 1063 | Cree, Inc. | CREE | 40.82 | 4 | 2 | 31.2 | NIL | Semiconductor | 66 |
| 201 | Cytyc Corp. | CYTC | 28.44 | 4 | 3 | 32.0 | NIL | Medical Supplies | 40 |
| 1112 | Dell Inc. | DELL | 42.19 | 3 | 3 | 30.6 | NIL | Computers/Peripherals | 23 |
| 1967 | Eastman Chemical | EMN | 56.80 | 3 | 4 | 19.2 | 3.1 | Chemical (Diversified) | 32 |
| 2233 | eBay Inc. | EBAY | 117.39 | 3 | 4 | 79.9 | NIL | Internet | 8 |
| 382 | FactSet Research | FDS | 49.37 | 3 | 3 | 25.1 | 0.6 | Information Services | 11 |
| 1011 | Garmin Ltd. | GRMN | 56.85 | 3 | 1 | 26.7 | 0.9 | Electrical Equipment | 17 |
| 1237 | Georgia Gulf | GGC | 53.70 | 3 | 2 | 13.6 | 0.7 | Chemical (Basic) | 1 |
| 1032 | Harman Int'l | HAR | 125.00 | 3 | 2 | 40.3 | NIL | Electronics | 59 |
| 984 | Headwaters Inc. | HDWR | 29.17 | 3 | 1 | 13.9 | NIL | Power | 78 |
| 269 | Heartland Express | HTLD | 21.50 | 3 | 2 | 24.2 | 0.4 | Trucking | 6 |
| 883 | Home Depot | HD | 42.49 | 2 | 3 | 18.4 | 0.8 | Retail Building Supply | 4 |
| 270 | Hunt (J.B.) | JBHT | 41.55 | 3 | 3 | 18.5 | 1.2 | Trucking | 6 |
| 136 | II-VI Inc. | IIVI | 42.48 | 3 | 2 | 28.3 | NIL | Precision Instrument | 70 |
| 1034 | Intermagnetics Gen'l | IMGC | 29.97 | 3 | 1 | 28.5 | NIL | Electronics | 59 |
| 1441 | Internet Security | ISSX | 24.13 | 4 | 2 | 43.9 | NIL | E-Commerce | 16 |
| 512 | Itron Inc. | ITRI | 22.19 | 3 | 4 | 18.5 | NIL | Wireless Networking | 18 |
| 525 | Joy Global | JOYG | 38.35 | 3 | 2 | 21.4 | 1.2 | Coal | 5 |
| 758 | Juniper Networks | JNPR | 27.60 | 4 | 2 | 49.3 | NIL | Telecom. Equipment | 52 |
| 1685 | Kohl's Corp. | KSS | 46.68 | 3 | 4 | 20.6 | NIL | Retail Store | 41 |
| 1292 | Korn/Ferry Int'l | KFY | 21.61 | 3 | 1 | 28.8 | NIL | Human Resources | 55 |
| 139 | Kronos Inc. ■ | KRON | 49.58 | 3 | 3 | 30.8 | NIL | Precision Instrument | 70 |
| 556 | L-3 Communic. Hldgs. | LLL | 74.50 | 3 | 3 | 20.1 | 0.5 | Aerospace/Defense | 22 |
| 1238 | Lyondell Chemical | LYO | 29.13 | 4 | 3 | 31.3 | 3.1 | Chemical (Basic) | 1 |
| 2198 | Macromedia, Inc. | MACR | 31.00 | 3 | 4 | 35.6 | NIL | Computer Software/Svcs | 9 |
| 760 | Marvell Technology | MRVL | 35.40 | 3 | 3 | 69.4 | NIL | Telecom. Equipment | 52 |
| 918 | MeadWestvaco | MWV | 32.92 | 3 | 2 | 21.4 | 2.8 | Paper/Forest Products | 29 |
| 2202 | Mercury Interactive | MERQ | 45.61 | 3 | 4 | 38.0 | NIL | Computer Software/Svcs | 9 |
| 874 | NVR, Inc. | NVR | 754.50 | 3 | 3 | 10.2 | NIL | Homebuilding | 3 |
| 1530 | Nash Finch Co. | NAFC | 37.67 | 4 | 1 | 11.4 | 1.5 | Food Wholesalers | 30 |
| 1125 | Network Appliance | NTAP | 34.64 | 4 | 3 | 58.7 | NIL | Computers/Peripherals | 23 |
| 289 | Norfolk Southern | NSC | 35.66 | 3 | 2 | 15.4 | 1.1 | Railroad | 20 |
| 579 | Nucor Corp. | NUE | 53.50 | 3 | 3 | 7.0 | 1.0 | Steel (General) | 2 |
| 280 | OMI Corp. | OMM | 18.70 | 3 | 1 | 4.8 | 1.5 | Maritime | 25 |
| 1240 | Olin Corp. | OLN | 22.50 | 3 | 2 | 21.2 | 3.6 | Chemical (Basic) | 1 |
| 2207 | Oracle Corp. ■ | ORCL | 14.09 | 3 | 3 | 23.5 | NIL | Computer Software/Svcs | 9 |
| 309 | P.F. Chang's | PFCB | 56.75 | 3 | 3 | 38.9 | NIL | Restaurant | 63 |
| 1399 | Park-Ohio | PKOH | 25.15 | 4 | 3 | 11.8 | NIL | Diversified Co. | 56 |
| 527 | Peabody Energy | BTU | 78.78 | 3 | 2 | 21.8 | 0.8 | Coal | 5 |
| 1690 | Penney (J.C.) | JCP | 40.00 | 3 | 3 | 16.7 | 1.4 | Retail Store | 41 |
| 762 | Qualcomm Inc. | QCOM | 44.34 | 3 | 3 | 37.9 | 0.6 | Telecom. Equipment | 52 |
| 1755 | Quiksilver Inc. | ZQK | 29.58 | 3 | 3 | 20.0 | NIL | Retail (Special Lines) | 72 |
| 2213 | RSA Security | RSAS | 20.88 | 4 | 3 | 35.4 | NIL | Computer Software/Svcs | 9 |
| 517 | Research in Motion Ltd | RIMM | 82.60 | 4 | 3 | 51.0 | NIL | Wireless Networking | 18 |
| 1020 | Rockwell Automation | ROK | 47.78 | 2 | 1 | 24.4 | 1.4 | Electrical Equipment | 17 |
| 2215 | SEI Investments | SEIC | 42.56 | 3 | 3 | 25.8 | 0.5 | Computer Software/Svcs | 9 |
| 2164 | SLM Corporation | SLM | 53.55 | 1 | 3 | 23.0 | 1.4 | Financial Svcs. (Div.) | 65 |
| 1447 | Sapient Corp. | SAPE | 7.85 | 4 | 3 | 31.4 | NIL | E-Commerce | 16 |
| 453 | Southwestern Energy | SWN | 52.24 | 3 | 1 | 17.9 | NIL | Natural Gas (Div.) | 13 |
| 316 | Starbucks Corp. | SBUX | 58.68 | 3 | 3 | 53.3 | NIL | Restaurant | 63 |
| 1891 | Station Casinos | STN | 54.55 | 3 | 4 | 25.7 | 1.5 | Hotel/Gaming | 58 |
| 582 | Steel Technologies | STTX | 24.40 | 3 | 2 | 6.7 | 0.8 | Steel (General) | 2 |
| 2220 | Symantec Corp. | SYMC | 27.38 | 3 | 3 | 33.8 | NIL | Computer Software/Svcs | 9 |
| 714 | TXU Corp. | TXU | 63.91 | 3 | 3 | 15.4 | 3.5 | Electric Util. (Central) | 89 |
| 1021 | Thomas & Betts | TNB | 30.80 | 3 | 3 | 20.8 | NIL | Electrical Equipment | 17 |
| 1449 | TIBCO Software | TIBX | 12.00 | 4 | 3 | 41.4 | NIL | E-Commerce | 16 |
| 879 | Toll Brothers | TOL | 66.02 | 3 | 3 | 11.8 | NIL | Homebuilding | 3 |
| 563 | United Industrial Corp. | UIC | 39.33 | 3 | 2 | 20.3 | 1.0 | Aerospace/Defense | 22 |
| 652 | UnitedHealth Group | UNH | 86.23 | 2 | 3 | 19.3 | NIL | Medical Services | 19 |
| 1767 | Urban Outfitters | URBN | 44.10 | 3 | 2 | 37.4 | NIL | Retail (Special Lines) | 72 |
| 792 | Walgreen Co. | WAG | 39.00 | 1 | 3 | 26.2 | 0.5 | Pharmacy Services | 45 |
| 1452 | Websense Inc. | WBSN | 52.40 | 4 | 2 | 46.4 | NIL | E-Commerce | 16 |
| 742 | Western Wireless 'A' | WWCA | 28.75 | 5 | 4 | 15.5 | NIL | Telecom. Services | 57 |
| 458 | XTO Energy | XTO | 33.68 | 3 | 2 | 13.2 | 0.6 | Natural Gas (Div.) | 13 |
| 2241 | Yahoo! Inc. | YHOO | 38.29 | 3 | 3 | 89.0 | NIL | Internet | 8 |
| 275 | Yellow Roadway | YELL | 54.00 | 3 | 1 | 11.7 | NIL | Trucking | 6 |

■ **Newly added this week.**

**Rank 1 Deletions:**
Chattem Inc.; Exxon Mobil Corp.; Waters Corp.

**Rank removed–see supplement or report:**
None.





Source: *The Value Line Investment Survey*, December 24, 2004. Copyright © 2004 Value Line Publishing, Inc.: used by permission.

TABLE 10-6 VALUE LINE INVESTMENT ANALYZER SCREENING VARIABLES

| *Category* | *Number of Variables* | *Sample Criterion* |
|---|---|---|
| Analyst alerts | 66 | Return on Common Equity Increased |
| General business | 18 | Industry |
| Income statement | 14 | Operating Income |
| Balance sheet | 22 | Total Assets |
| Other annual data | 3 | Free Cash Flow |
| Annual ratios | 20 | Dividend Payout |
| Per share | 9 | Cash Flow per Share |
| Per share ratio | 6 | Average Annual Dividend Yield |
| Estimate | 16 | Estimated Earnings per Share |
| Growth rates | 15 | Dividend Growth, 10 years |
| Latest quarter | 20 | Sales Latest Quarter |
| Bank/Thrift | 11 | Loan Loss Provisions |
| Insurance | 8 | Insurance in Force |
| Brokerage | 4 | % Commissions |
| Retail store | 2 | Number of Stores |
| Total returns | 10 | Total Return YTD |
| Annual returns | 10 | Total Return 2003 |
| Trading volume | 12 | 3 Month Relative Strength |
| MPT statistics | 9 | Beta 3-year |
| Earnings per share | 14 | EPS 1 QTR Ago |
| Projections | 11 | Proj Dividend Growth Rate |
| Ratings | 10 | Industry Rank |
| Identification | 10 | Options Listing |
| User-Defined statistics | 20 | Cash Flow/Price |

## SUMMARY

Stock screening is necessary to reduce the huge number of possible investments to a smaller number for careful investigation. The lack of time for decision making is the primary reason that screening is an important part of the portfolio management process.

Screens are used in everyday life; they are not limited to the investment business. Universities use SAT scores as an admission screen, football coaches use physical tests, and shoppers develop their own screening criteria when they select purchases.

Screens often have more than one criterion. In establishing a screen, the first pass should be with the variable that is either the most important or that will save the most time. Making several screening passes over extensive data that have no chance of selection wastes time. Subjective screening criteria are an important part of modern investment management. Concerns about South African investment, the use of nuclear power, and so on are very real and should be included in the security selection process if they are material for a client.

Very serviceable screens can be established using only the information published in the newspaper. The PE ratio, the dividend yield, the stock price, and the 52-week trading range are common screening criteria.

Final selection of securities can be assisted by a quick comparison of return on assets and return on equity over the ten-year period shown in the S&P *Stock Report*. High volatility in the ROE statistic is good evidence of investment risk.

In addition to published paper data, computerized data sources are available to screen very large security universes quickly.

## QUESTIONS

1. The text states that by itself, the level of earnings per share is not a very good screening variable. Can you think of an exception to this?
2. A firm's ROA is equal to its ROE. What does this probably indicate about the firm's capital structure?
3. Suppose that you work in a university admissions office and are told that SAT scores may no longer be used as an entry criterion. How would you screen the approximately 12,000 applications you get annually?
4. Why are there potential dangers in using just the dividend yield of a stock as a screening variable, regardless of your investment objective?
5. Suppose you are assembling something in your house and need a screwdriver. Your tools are kept outside in the garage. Write down a screen that indicates the logic you follow in determining which screwdriver or screwdrivers to bring inside.
6. Does a subjective screen need to make any sense if it eliminates possibilities? For instance, is it okay to listen to a client who says, "I do not want to invest in any automobile companies?"
7. What information do you think the price/earnings ratio provides? Should the P/E be high, low, or in between?
8. Suppose a stock sells for $2.50. Do you have any preconceptions about this firm based just on the price?
9. You develop a set of criteria to meet a client's investment objectives. However, even though you have an extensive computerized data base, you find that no stock is able to pass all the screens. How would you proceed from here?
10. Would you expect to find a positive relationship between a stock's beta and the variance of its ROE?
11. Is it possible for a firm's ROE to be less than its ROA?
12. Is it possible for a stock to have a price/earnings ratio of 0? If so, how?

## PROBLEMS

1. You decide to buy a lawnmower. Set up a reasonable screen that will help you make a selection.
2. Using the *Value Line Investment Survey,* establish a screen that will help you construct a $50,000, ten-security common stock portfolio with a beta of about 1.20 for someone whose primary investment objective is growth and whose secondary objective is growth of income.
3. Go to a recent issue of *The Wall Street Journal*. Using common stock beginning with the letter C, identify all securities that pass the following screen:
   - PE between 6 and 15.
   - Stock price between $5 and $25.

- Positive dividend yield.
- Listed on NYSE or AMEX.
- Current price in lower half of 52-week trading range.

4. From the securities you identified in Problem 3, identify the single security you find the most appealing of those that passed the screen.
5. Using a current issue of the *Value Line Investment Survey*, prepare a table showing the number of securities that are present in each stage of the following screen (the numbers in parentheses indicate the number of securities that meet the listed criteria):
   a. Covered by the *Value Line Investment Survey* (1,700).
   b. Rated 1 or 2 for timeliness (400).
   c. Also rated 1 or 2 for safety (?).
   d. Stock price less than $50 (?).
   e. Dividend yield more than 2.0 percent (?).
   f. PE less than 35 (?).
   g. Options available (?).
6. For the stocks that passed all stages of the screen in Problem 5, prepare a table showing the arithmetic average ROA and ROE over the past ten years for each of the firms. Get this information from the S&P *Stock Report* or from the *Value Line Investment Survey*.
7. Repeat Problem 3 using the letter *F*.
8. Using *Moody's Manual of Investments*, find the parent firm of each of the following subsidiaries:
   a. Taco Bell.
   b. Frito Lay.
   c. Wilson Sporting Goods.
   d. Burger King.
9. Refer to Figure 10-4. Make a list of the securities that pass the following screen:
   - Stock price less than 30.
   - PE ratio between 10 and 25.
   - Dividend yield more than 2 percent.
10. Use the screening feature of the Thomson Investor site or some other Internet-based screening tool. Develop a logical screen that leaves you with about a dozen companies in which you personally might invest.

##  INTERNET EXERCISE

Using *Stockscreener* at *http://screen.finance.yahoo.com/newscreener.html*, create a portfolio of five equities. Develop a set of personal screening criteria to narrow the security universe to these final five securities.

##  FURTHER READING

Guerard, John B., Jr. "Additional Evidence on the Cost of Being Socially Responsible in Investing," *Journal of Investing*, Winter 1997, 31–36.

Holloway, Clark. "Testing an Aggressive Investment Strategy Using Value Line Ranks." *Journal of Finance*, March 1981, 263–270.

Kinder, Peter D., and Amy L. Domini. "Social Screening: Paradigms Old and New." *Journal of Investing,* Winter 1997, 12–19.

McWilliams, James D. "Prices, Earnings, and P-E Ratios." *Financial Analysts Journal,* May/June 1966, 137–142.

Moskowitz, Milton. "Social Investing: The Moral Foundation." *Journal of Investing,* Winter 1997, 9–11.

Nicholson, Francis. "Price-Earnings Ratios." *Financial Analysts Journal,* July/August 1960, 43–45.

———. "Price Ratios in Relation to Investment Results." *Financial Analysts Journal,* January/February 1968, 105–109.

Peavy, John W. III, and David A. Goodman. "The Significance of P/Es for Portfolio Returns." *Journal of Portfolio Managemen,t* Winter 1983, 43–47.

Strong, Robert A. "Do Share Price and Stock Splits Matter?" *Journal of Portfolio Management,* Fall 1983, 58–64.

# 11 Bond Pricing and Selection

*We cannot gamble with anything so sacred as money.*
***William McKinley***

## Key Terms

accrued interest
annuity
assessment bond
balloon loan
bearer bond
bond beta
book entry form
call premium
call protection
call risk
collateral trust bond
consol
convenience risk
conversion price
conversion ratio
conversion value
convertible bond
credit risk
current yield
debenture
default risk
duration
equipment trust certificate
expectations theory
full faith and credit issue
general obligation issue
income bond
indenture
inflation premium theory
interest rate risk
investment grade
investment horizon
junk bond
legal list
level of interest rates
liquidity preference theory
liquidity premium
Malkiel's interest rate theorems
marketability risk
mortgage
municipal bond
premium over conversion value
rating agency
realized compound yield
registered bond
reinvestment rate risk
revenue bond
sinking fund
spot rate
subordinated debenture
term structure of interest rates
Treasury Direct System
variable rate bond
yield curve
yield spread
yield to maturity
zero coupon bond

## Introduction

Some people consider bonds dull and boring. Actually, the investment characteristics of bonds range completely across the risk/return spectrum. They can be extremely safe or extremely risky.

As part of a portfolio, bonds provide both stability and periodic income. It is possible to have some capital appreciation if bonds are purchased at a discount or if interest rates fall, but this is not normally a motive in acquiring them. The first part of this chapter reviews basic principles of bonds, especially their risk and the nature of their return. The second part deals with selecting bonds for a portfolio.

## Review of Bond Principles

We first review basic principles of bonds before moving on to the topic of bond pricing.

### Identification of Bonds

*Bonds are identified by issuer, coupon, and maturity.*

In November 2004, 26 different debt issues were trading on Household Finance.[1] An investor identifies a specific bond by stating the issuer, the coupon, and the maturity. For instance, a broker might receive an order to buy five Household Finance "eights of 10." This is an order to purchase $5,000 face value of the Household Finance bonds with an 8 percent stated interest rate and a maturity in the year 2010. The financial press would list this bond as "Household Finance 8s10." The *s* does not stand for anything, but it is pronounced when identifying the bond.[2] One of the other Household Finance bonds pays 7.04 percent per year and matures in 2012. These are the "seven point zero fours of twelve": HF 7.04s12.

### Classification of Bonds

A legal document called the **indenture** describes the details of a bond issue. This pamphlet gives a complete description of the loan, including terms of repayment, collateral, protective covenants, and default provisions.

**Issuer.** One method of classifying bonds is by the nature of the organization initially selling them. Bonds are sold by corporations; by federal, state, and local governments; by government agencies; and by foreign corporations or governments.[3] There are subcategories of corporate bonds according to the principal business of the issuer as Table 11-1 shows. Railroads once appeared in the list but are not particularly important anymore.

**Security.** The security of a bond refers to what backs the bond, or what collateral reduces the risk of the loan.

---

[1]Household Finance is a subsidiary of Household International.

[2]It is possible that at one time the *s* indicated that the coupon payments were semiannual. Today, virtually all bonds pay their interest semiannually. Neither *The Wall Street Journal* nor the Standard and Poor's monthly *Bond Guide* identifies any purpose of the letter *s* in their listings. *The Wall Street Journal Guide to Understanding Money and Markets* by Richard Saul Wurman, Alan Siegel, and Kenneth M. Morris (Access Press/Prentice-Hall, 1990) indicates the *s* is not a meaningful symbol but is used merely to separate the interest rate figures from the following figures, especially when the interest rate does not include a fraction.

[3]Bonds sold by state and local governments are called *municipal bonds*. Government agencies selling bonds includes the Federal National Mortgage Association (Fannie Mae), the Student Loan Marketing Association (Sallie Mae), the Government National Mortgage Association (Ginnie Mae), and the Federal Home Loan Bank, among others.

**TABLE 11-1** CLASSIFICATION OF BONDS BY ISSUER

| *Government* | *Corporation* | *Other* |
|---|---|---|
| U.S. Treasury | Industrial | Foreign governments |
| Federal agency | Utility | Foreign corporations |
| State | Financial | World Bank |
| Local | Transportation | |

**TABLE 11-2** TREASURY BILLS, NOTES, AND BONDS

| *Type* | *Maturity* | *Minimum Purchase* | *Issue Schedule* |
|---|---|---|---|
| Bills | 13, 26, or 52 weeks | $1,000 | 3- and 6-month bills, weekly; 12-month bills, issued every 4 weeks |
| Notes | 2, 3, 5, 10 years | $1,000 | 2-year notes, monthly; 3-, 5-, and 10-year notes, generally quarterly |
| Bonds | Over 10 years | $1,000 | February, August, and November |

***Unsecured Debt.*** All debt of the U.S. Treasury Department is secured by the ability of the federal government to make principal and interest payments from general tax revenues. No specific assets are listed as collateral for federal debt.

Table 11-2 shows the details of securities issued by the U.S. Treasury. These securities are backed by the credit of the U.S. government. State and local governments can also issue debt without specific assets pledged against it. These bonds are **full faith and credit issues,** or **general obligation issues.** Like obligations of the federal government, they are backed by the taxing power of the issuer.

Financially sound corporations frequently issue **debentures,** which are really just signature loans backed by the good name of the company.[4] If a company issues a second set of unsecured bonds, these are **subordinated debentures,** meaning that in the event of financial distress, the issuer must pay off the original debenture issue before sending any money to the holders of subordinated debentures.

***Secured Debt.*** There are many ways to provide specific security for a risky debt issue. Municipal issues may be *revenue bonds* or *assessment bonds*. A **revenue bond** is a bond whose interest and principal are repaid from revenue generated by the project financed by the bond. **Assessment bonds** benefit a specific group of people, who pay an assessment to help pay principal and interest. Revenue bonds might be used to finance a turnpike or a bridge across a river, with user fees being the primary source of debt repayment.[5] Assessment bonds might pay for projects that benefit a specific group of people. The installation of streetlights in a residential area is an example. People who directly and routinely benefit from this improvement would be assessed a higher property tax.

[4]Not all debentures are safe investments, however. In times of economic trouble, previously issued debentures may be attractive only to speculators.

[5]A good argument can also be made that revenue bonds are not secured because failure of a toll bridge (for instance) is comparable to the failure of a city to provide sufficient tax revenues to support its general obligation bonds. The bridge is not pledged as collateral on a revenue bond.

Corporate secured debt comes in many forms. **Mortgages** are well-known securities that use land and buildings as collateral. Many public utilities' debt issues are mortgages. **Collateral trust bonds** are backed by other securities, such as investments held by the firm or the stock of a subsidiary. **Equipment trust certificates** provide physical assets, such as a fleet of trucks, as collateral for the loan.[6] Airlines use them widely to finance the purchase of new airplanes, and railroads use them to finance the purchase of boxcars. In both cases the collateral may be easily transported to a new purchaser if the bondholder wishes to liquidate the collateral in the aftermath of a bankruptcy.

**Term.** The final common debt classification is by term, the original life of the debt security. Short-term securities are those with an initial life of less than one year, such as U.S. Treasury bills. Intermediate-term securities, such as U.S. Treasury notes, have lives ranging from one year to perhaps ten years; there is no precise demarcation between intermediate term and long term. Long-term securities, such as U.S. Treasury bonds, have maturities longer than ten years.

Loan arrangements may also be open ended, similar to a corporate line of credit at a commercial bank or an individual's home equity loan. These loans, however, are seldom readily marketable and usually cannot be sold to another lender.

### *Terms of Repayment*

All bonds have specific provisions for the payment of interest and repayment of principal.

**Interest Only.** With most marketable debt, the periodic payments are entirely interest. The principal amount of the loan is repaid in its entirety at maturity.

**Sinking Fund.** A **sinking fund** (which may be required by a bond indenture) requires the establishment of a cash reserve for the ultimate repayment of the bond principal. In some circumstances lenders may require that the borrower provide for the eventual retirement of the debt by setting aside a portion of the principal amount of the debt each year. For instance, a $10 million 20-year debt issue might provide that after five years the borrower must deposit $1 million every third year into a special escrow account to partially offset the eventual burden of debt repayment.

Alternatively, the debt might provide that after a period of time, the borrower must call a certain number of the bonds each year. This means that a portion of the debt must be paid off early each year according to the call schedule contained in the bond indenture.

**Balloon. Balloon loans** may partially amortize the debt with each payment but repay the bulk of the principal at the end of the life of the debt. Most balloon loans are not marketable.

**Income Bonds.** The key characteristic of an **income bond** is that the issuer must pay the interest only if the firm earns it. This means if you, as the issuer, do not earn enough money to pay the interest, you do not have to pay it. An income bond might be used to finance an income-producing property, perhaps a parking garage. If the facility is unprofitable in the first few years, the interest does not have to be paid. It may or may not accumulate, depending on the specifications of the bond indenture.

---

[6]The assets backing equipment trust certificates are not owned by the firm until the certificate is paid off.

A number of income bonds traded a century ago, but in 2005, they are certainly on the endangered securities list and may be extinct.

## *Bond Cash Flows*

Relative to other types of securities, nonconvertible bonds produce cash flows that an analyst can predict with a high degree of accuracy. The structure of these cash flows falls into one of four groups: *annuities*, *zero coupon bonds*, *variable rate bonds*, and *consols*.

**Annuities.** Most bonds are annuities plus an ultimate repayment of principal. An **annuity** promises a fixed amount on a regular periodic schedule for a finite length of time. A 9 1/2 percent coupon bond with semiannual interest payments might currently sell for $900 and come due eight years from today. At maturity the bond returns $1,000 to the bondholder. We know the bond's present value ($900), its term (eight years), and the future cash flows ($47.50 every six months for eight years and a single $1,000 payment in eight years). This is a simple present value/future value problem with the only unknown in the valuation equation being the discount rate. The discount rate that equates the present value of the future cash flows with the current price of the bond is the bond's yield to maturity (the same as its internal rate of return).

**Zero Coupon Bonds.** A **zero coupon bond** has a specific maturity date when it returns the bond principal, but it pays no periodic income. In other words, the bond has only a single cash inflow, the par value at maturity. An investor might pay $450 for a bond that promises to return $1,000 in seven and one-half years. The valuation equation for such a security is the simplest possible: the current market price is equal to the discounted par value of the bond.

**Variable Rate Bonds.** Some securities do not carry a fixed interest rate but allow the rate to fluctuate in accordance with a market index; these are **variable rate bonds.** U.S. Series EE savings bonds are a good example. The interest on these is 90 percent of the average five-year Treasury securities rate from the preceding six months. If market rates move higher, the income earned on these bonds increases, and vice versa.

**Consols.** A **consol** pays a level rate of interest perpetually; the bond never matures, and the income stream lasts forever. Bonds of this type trade in Europe and Canada but are not prevalent in the United States.

## *Convertible Bonds*

*The conversion feature is a security holder right, not an obligation.*

Some debt instruments have a valuable conversion option. The bondholder has the right, but not the obligation, to exchange **convertible bonds** for another security or for some physical asset. The conversion option is a one-way street. Once conversion occurs, the security holder cannot elect to reconvert and regain the original debt security. The two types of convertible debt securities are those that are *security* backed and those that are *commodity* backed.

**Security-Backed Bonds.** Security-backed convertible bonds are convertible into other securities, usually common stock of the company that issued the bonds. Occasionally, though, the conversion terms provide for the exchange of the bond for preferred stock, for shares in a subsidiary company, or for common shares in another firm.

**Commodity-Backed Bonds.** Commodity-backed bonds are convertible into a tangible asset such as silver or gold. Perhaps the most famous commodity-backed convertible bonds were those of the Sunshine Mining Company, one of the largest silver mines in the United States. These bonds were convertible into 50 ounces of silver at the bondholder's request.

### *Registration*

There are three ways to record the ownership of a bond: as a *bearer* bond, a *registered* bond, or a *book entry* bond.

**Bearer Bonds.** Bonds that do not have the name of the bondholder printed on them are **bearer bonds**. They belong to whoever legally holds them. These bonds have actual coupons around the perimeter that the bondholder must clip with scissors as interest payment dates arrive. Because of this characteristic, bearer bonds are also called *coupon bonds*. Each coupon bears a date and a currency amount. Once clipped, the coupons can usually be deposited into the bondholder's bank account as cash at any teller window. Banks have special envelopes for the deposit of bond coupons.

*New debt may no longer be issued in bearer form.*

In the United States, firms may no longer issue debt in this form.[7] The Internal Revenue Service (IRS) is largely responsible for this fact, because bearer bonds have for years been a popular method of tax evasion. Interest earned on bearer bonds is difficult for the IRS to trace, and history tells us that over the years, millions of dollars of interest has gone unreported on individual income tax returns.

**Registered Bonds.** Bonds that *do* show the bondholder's name are **registered bonds.** Rather than clipping coupons, holders of registered bonds receive interest checks in the mail from the issuer.

**Book Entry Bonds.** The U.S. Treasury and some corporations issue bonds in **book entry form** only. Until recently it was possible to buy a Treasury note or bond and actually take delivery of the security. Now, however, people who want to buy these securities on their own must open accounts through the **Treasury Direct System** at a Federal Reserve Bank. Rather than issuing a bond certificate, the Treasury Department opens an account on the buyer's behalf, crediting interest as earned and principal upon maturity. A buyer can open an account via the Internet by visiting the U.S. Treasury website at *http://www.publicdebt.treas.gov*.

Rather than using the Treasury Direct System, many investors buy government securities through their brokerage firm in the same way they buy corporate bonds. They pay a commission[8] to do this but hopefully benefit from good advice from the broker.

## Bond Pricing and Returns

As with any application of the fundamental time value of money principle, a deterministic relationship exists between the current price of the security, its promised future cash flows, and the riskiness of those cash flows. The current price is the market's estimation of what the expected cash flows are worth in today's dollars.

[7]Bearer bonds are very popular outside the United States, however.

[8]Brokerage firms often quote bonds on a "net" basis, meaning the price quoted to a potential buyer includes a markup in lieu of a commission. The confirmation statement may show no commission, but the purchase price reflects a trading fee.

## Valuation Equations

Several widely used mathematical relationships are particularly relevant in pricing a debt security.

**Annuities.** Consider a typical bond that pays interest semiannually. Assume also that it has just made an interest payment. Equation 11-1 shows the valuation equation used for published bond yields.

$$P_0 = \sum_{t=1}^{N} \frac{C_t}{[1+(R/2)]^t} \tag{11-1}$$

where $N$ = term of the bond in semiannual periods; $C_t$ = cash flow at time $t$, paid semiannually; $R$ = annual yield to maturity; and $P_0$ = current price of the bond.

The bond-pricing relationship is customarily expressed in terms of the number of semiannual payment periods. An eight-year bond, for example, has sixteen semiannual payments. This procedure also requires dividing the annual yield to maturity ($R$) by 2 to turn it into a semiannual equivalent.

Equation 11-1 can be separated into two parts, one for the interest component and one for the principal:

$$P_0 = \underbrace{\sum_{t=1}^{N} \frac{C}{[1+(R/2)]^t}}_{\text{Interest}} + \underbrace{\frac{\text{Par}}{[1+(R/2)]^{2N}}}_{\text{Principal}} \tag{11-1a}$$

where C = coupon payment; no subscript $t$ is needed because all the coupon payments are identical.

Suppose a bond currently sells for \$900, pays \$95 per year (interest paid semiannually), and returns the par value of \$1000 in exactly eight years. What discount rate is implied in these numbers? To find out, we solve the following valuation equation:

*It is customary to express the bond-pricing relationship in terms of semiannual periods.*

$$\$900 = \underbrace{\left[\sum_{t=1}^{16} \frac{\$47.50}{[1+(R/2)]^t}\right]}_{\text{Interest}} + \underbrace{\left[\frac{\$1{,}000}{[1+(R/2)]^{16}}\right]}_{\text{Principal}} \tag{11-2}$$

The valuation equation contains only one unknown; you can solve it using time value of money tables, a financial calculator, or a software package such as Microsoft Excel. In this example, $R$ is 11.44 percent.

The investor in this bond receives return from two sources: (1) periodic interest and (2) the return of the bond principal in eight years. You can value these two components separately once you solve for the interest rate. Using 11.44 percent, the present value of the interest component is \$489.40 and is \$410.60 for the principal.

**Zero Coupon Bonds.** The investor who buys the zero coupon bond described earlier pays \$450 today and receives \$1,000 in seven and one-half years. This is a simple present value/future value problem.

We want to know the compound growth rate that will cause \$450 to grow to \$1,000 in seven and one-half years. To find this interest rate, use Equation 11-3:

$$P_0 = \frac{\text{Par}}{(1+R)^t} \tag{11-3}$$

Substituting our numbers,

$$\$450 = \frac{\$1,000}{(1+R)^{7.5}} \qquad R = 11.23\%$$

Following the convention of using semiannual periods complicates the problem only slightly:

$$\$450 = \frac{\$1,000}{[1+(R/2)]^{15}} \qquad R = 10.94\%$$

**Variable Rate Bonds.** You cannot determine the precise present value of the cash flows associated with a variable rate bond because you do not know the future cash flows in advance. The valuation equation must allow for the variable cash flows and the fact that the interest rate implied in the equation may change each time the cash flow stream is altered. Assuming interest is paid semiannually, the following pricing relationship exists:

$$P_0 = \sum_{t=1}^{N} \frac{C_t}{(1+R_t)^t} \qquad \textbf{(11-4)}$$

where $R_t$ = interest rate at time $t$. This equation looks similar to the valuation equation for an annuity, but it is not the same. An annuity provides a constant dollar payout; a variable rate security does not. Also, the annuity equation had only one discount rate. This equation provides for more than one, as shown by the $t$ subscript on $R$.

**Consols.** In Equation 11-1, suppose that $t$ equals infinity. In other words, the cash flows go forever. An annuity that provides a constant dollar amount forever is a *level perpetuity*. With $t = \infty$, Equation 11-2 reduces to the mathematical identity in Equation 11-5.

$$P_0 = \sum_{t=1}^{\infty} \frac{C}{(1+R)^t} = \frac{C}{R} \qquad \textbf{(11-5)}$$

A consol might sell for $800 and pay $80 per year forever. Its rate of return, then, is $80/$800 = 10.00%. This is a very intuitive result. If you invest $800 and earn 10 percent on your money, each year you receive $80 in income without touching the original principal. Thus, $800 invested at 10 percent generates $80 per year and can do so forever if the interest rate remains at 10 percent.

### Yield to Maturity

*The yield to maturity calculation carries an assumption that coupon proceeds are reinvested at the yield to maturity.*

*If a bond pays periodic interest, it is not possible to lock in a prescribed yield to maturity.*

In the previous valuation equations, $R$ is the yield to maturity. **Yield to maturity** is precisely the same concept as internal rate of return in corporate finance applications. Yield to maturity captures the total return (from income and capital gains/losses) associated with the investment. This is the rate of return for an investor who buys a bond and holds it until maturity, with each of the semiannual interest payments reinvested at the yield to maturity. The latter point is a source of considerable confusion to beginning market analysts.

It is possible to buy a bond at a price that promises a certain yield to maturity but, in fact, results in a much lower benefit to the pocketbook than expected. Consider

**TABLE 11-3** EFFECTS OF DIFFERENT REINVESTMENT RATES: FUTURE VALUE OF TWENTY SEMIANNUAL $50 PAYMENTS

| *Annual Rate* | *Semiannual Rate* | *FVIF*[a] | *FV of $50 Annuity* |
|---|---|---|---|
| 0.0% | 0.0% | 20.00 | $1,000.00 |
| 7.0 | 3.5 | 28.28 | 1,414.00 |
| 10.0 | 5.0 | 33.07 | 1,653.50 |
| 13.0 | 6.5 | 38.83 | 1,941.50 |

[a]FVIF = future value interest factor (twenty periods).

the following example. An investor buys a $1,000, 10-year Treasury note carrying a 10 percent coupon. Because the purchase price equals the bond's par value, its yield to maturity equals its coupon of 10 percent. The investor might say that she has locked in a 10 percent rate of return by buying this bond. This is not the case; the actual return can be more or less than this.

To see this, consider the T-note in comparison with another security, a 10-year zero coupon bond. This bond has a par value of $1,000, which will be returned upon maturity in ten years. For this bond to have a yield to maturity of 10 percent, it must have a current market price of $376.89. The T-note also has a yield to maturity of 10 percent. As stated previously, though, this is predicated on the reinvestment of the coupon proceeds at a 10 percent rate. If the investor is unable to reinvest at this rate, her actual yield will be different from 10 percent.

Consider Table 11-3. To earn a 10 percent annual return, a $1,000 investment must grow to $2,653.50 after ten years (this assumes semiannual compounding). The table indicates that if the $50 annuity (from the coupon payments) is reinvested at 10 percent, its future value is $1,653.50. Added to the $1,000 return of principal in year 10, the investment grows to exactly the right amount to yield a 10 percent return: $2,653.50. At other reinvestment rates, the terminal value can be significantly different from the target figure. It is apparent that the reinvestment rate has an impact on the ultimate value of your investment.

### *Realized Compound Yield*

We frequently need to compare an interest-bearing bond (that virtually always pays twice a year) with some competing investment paying interest on a different time schedule. By convention we use semiannual periods in determining a bond's yield to maturity and then double the result to convert it into an annual percentage.

If you are comparing bonds with other securities, it is best to compute the effective annual rate for all of them to reduce the likelihood of comparing apples and oranges. Equation 11-6 shows how to compute the effective annual rate.

$$\text{Effective annual rate} = [1 + (R/x)]^{x} - 1 \qquad \textbf{(11-6)}$$

where $R$ = yield to maturity and $x$ = number of payment periods per year.

Recall the bond from an earlier example: current price = $900; annual interest = 9.5 percent (paid semiannually); and time remaining until maturity = 8 years. We determined a yield to maturity of 11.44 percent. This bond's effective annual rate is 11.77 percent:

$$\begin{aligned}\text{Effective annual rate} &= [1 + (0.1144/2)]^{2} - 1\\ &= 1.1177 - 1\\ &= 11.77\%\end{aligned}$$

**TABLE 11-4** CASH FLOWS FROM A 9.5 PERCENT, 8-YEAR BOND

| *Time* | *Cash Flow* | *Present Value* | |
|---|---|---|---|
| | | **At 11.44%** | **At 11.77%** |
| 0.5 | $47.50 | $ 45.00 | $ 44.93 |
| 1.0 | 47.50 | 42.62 | 42.50 |
| 1.5 | 47.50 | 40.38 | 40.20 |
| 2.0 | 47.50 | 38.25 | 38.02 |
| 2.5 | 47.50 | 36.23 | 35.97 |
| 3.0 | 47.50 | 34.32 | 34.02 |
| 3.5 | 47.50 | 32.51 | 32.18 |
| 4.0 | 47.50 | 30.80 | 30.44 |
| 4.5 | 47.50 | 29.17 | 28.79 |
| 5.0 | 47.50 | 27.64 | 27.23 |
| 5.5 | 47.50 | 26.18 | 25.76 |
| 6.0 | 47.50 | 24.80 | 24.36 |
| 6.5 | 47.50 | 23.49 | 23.05 |
| 7.0 | 47.50 | 22.25 | 21.80 |
| 7.5 | 47.50 | 21.08 | 20.62 |
| 8.0 | 1,047.50 | 440.38 | 430.08 |
| | Total | $915.10 | $899.95 |
| | Market price of the bond = $900.00 | | |

Table 11-4 shows the cash flows associated with this bond and their present values when discounted at 11.44 percent and when discounted at 11.77 percent.

The yield to maturity of a bond is the interest rate that equates the current price of the bond with the present value of the expected interest and principal payments. In this example, the future cash flows discounted at 11.44 percent total $915.10, a sum higher than the current price of the bond. This means that the discount rate is too low; we need to reduce the value of the future cash flows. The interest rate that satisfies the equation is the effective annual yield, or **realized compound yield** (11.77 percent in this example).[9] Mathematically, 11.44 percent compounded semiannually equals 11.77 percent compounded annually.

### *Current Yield*

If an investor holds a bond until it matures, the yield to maturity measures the investor's total return.[10] The **current yield**, in contrast, measures only the return associated with the interest payments. This measure does not include the anticipated capital gain or loss resulting from the difference between par value and the purchase price.

The previous section determined the yield to maturity for a 9.5 percent coupon bond selling for $900 and maturing in eight years. The current yield for this bond is simply the annual interest divided by the current price, or $95/$900 = 10.56%.

Current yield is an important statistic for someone who is primarily concerned about spendable income from investments. The fact that the long-run rate of return may be different is not as important. A zero coupon bond, for instance, has a zero current yield. It would be an inappropriate investment for a retired person who needed routine interest checks for living expenses.

[9]Rounding errors cause the total in Table 11-4 to differ slightly from the $900 market value of the bond.
[10]This assumes the investor reinvests the coupon proceeds at the yield to maturity.

It is important to note that for bonds selling at a discount, the yield to maturity is always more than the current yield. Conversely, for bonds selling at a premium, the yield to maturity will be less than the current yield.

## *Term Structure of Interest Rates*

**Yield Curve.** The bond investor is particularly concerned with two aspects of interest rates: the *level of interest rates* and the *term structure of interest rates*. Rather than the formal phrase **term structure of interest rates,** we usually say **yield curve.** It is well known in financial economics that the term structure of interest rates is related to other macroeconomic variables such as the stock market.

*To retrieve the current term structure of the U.S. Treasury Securities interest rates, go to* http://www.ustreas.gov/offices/domestic-finance/debt-management/interest-rate/yield.html

Figure 11-1 shows a "typical" yield curve for U.S. Treasury securities, although some economists would argue that there is no such thing. We usually see long-term interest rates higher than rates for shorter terms, and we also usually see the yield curve get flatter the farther out in time we go.

If the **level of interest rates** changes, the yield curve shifts up or down. Sometimes long-term rates change more than short-term rates and vice versa. The special situation when interest rates rise or fall by the same amount across the entire maturity spectrum is called a *parallel shift* in the yield curve. In Figure 11-1, if the economy saw a 1 percent parallel shift upward in the yield curve, the entire diagram would simply rise by 1 percentage point along the y-axis.

A precept of finance is that riskier securities have higher expected returns. As a consequence, if we superimposed the term structure associated with, say, AAA or

FIGURE 11-1

Typical Yield Curve

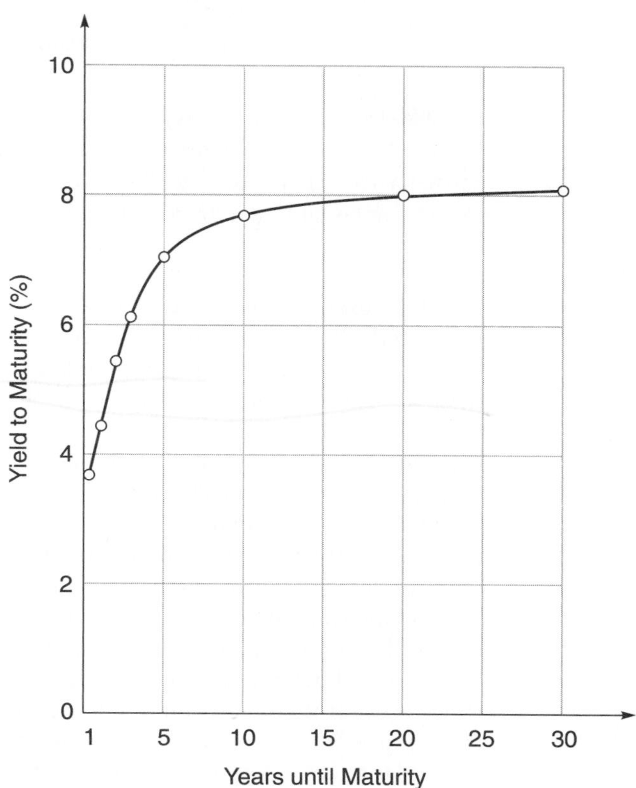

BBB corporate bonds over that of U.S. Treasury securities, we would find that they plotted above the corresponding yield for the less-risky government securities. Their structure might be parallel to that of Treasury securities, but their level would certainly be higher.

*See the dynamic "living yield curve" from the Smartmoney.com website at:* http://www.smartmoney.com/onebond/index.cfm?story=yieldcurve

**Theories of Interest Rate Structure.** Most of the time, long-term interest rates are higher than short-term rates. When this is the case, people say the yield curve is upward sloping. The steepness of the slope, however, changes markedly over time. Three leading theories seek to explain why the term structure of interest rates changes.

***Expectations Theory.*** Suppose an investor must choose between two investment alternatives. Alternative A is an investment in a 2-year certificate of deposit at a rate of 9 percent. Alternative B is an investment in a 1-year CD at a rate of 8 3/4 percent, with the opportunity to reinvest the funds after one year at the prevailing 1-year CD interest rate, whatever it may be at that time.

Given these alternatives, a *forward rate* is implied in the 2-year CD: It is the 1-year CD rate that is expected to prevail one year from now. In academic literature, the forward rate from time 1 to time 2 is usually designated as ${}_1f_2$. By definition, then, the following relationship holds:

$$(1 + R_2)^2 = (1 + R_1)(1 + {}_1f_2) \quad \textbf{(11-7)}$$

In this example, the 1-year forward rate ${}_1f_2$ is

$$1 + {}_1f_2 = \frac{(1+R_2)^2}{1+R_1} = \frac{(1+0.09)^2}{1+0.0875} = 1.0925 \therefore {}_1f_2 = 9.25\%$$

The essence of the **expectations theory** of interest rates is that wealth-maximizing people are smart enough to figure out how to earn the maximum return on their investment, and given Equation 11-7, the forward rate must be what people expect the 1-year rate to be in one year. Mathematically,

$${}_1f_2 = E({}_1R_2) \quad \textbf{(11-8)}$$

If the expectations theory of interest rates is accurate, the only explanation for an upward-sloping yield curve is an expectation that interest rates will continually increase in the future. This seems unlikely, and past evidence does not support this theory. For this reason, the expectations theory of interest rates has few advocates.

***Liquidity Preference Theory.*** Continuing with the example, Alternative A involves a single security, the certificate of deposit. With Alternative B, the investor has a CD plus an option to obtain a new CD in a year's time. Options are always valuable; you can exercise the option if you wish, but you are not obliged to do so. If interest rates rise sharply, you will fare better if you hold Alternative B than Alternative A because you can reinvest the funds at the higher rate after one year. With Alternative A, the funds remain committed to the lower rate for another year.

Financial institutions influence the flow of funds from depositors by the way in which they set their rates of interest. If they want to attract long-term investments, they increase their long-term investment rates. Conversely, if they do not want to lock in long-term interest payment obligations (perhaps because the institutions expect rates to fall), they offer attractive short-term rates.

Proponents of the **liquidity preference theory** believe that investors, in general, prefer to invest short term rather than long term and that borrowers must entice lenders to lengthen their investment horizon by paying a premium for long-term money. This **liquidity premium** means that forward rates are actually higher than the expected interest rate in a year's time. Projecting this logic across the maturity spectrum results in an upward-sloping yield curve.

***Inflation Premium Theory.*** The principal tenet of the **inflation premium theory** is that risk comes from the uncertainty associated with future inflation rates. The degree of uncertainty about inflation is a function of how far into the future one looks. Next year's inflation rate is much easier to estimate than the rate ten years from now.

Investors who commit their funds for long periods of time are bearing more purchasing power risk than short-term investors, and rational investors do not willingly accept added risk unless they are compensated for doing so. More inflation risk, therefore, means that longer-term investments will carry a higher yield than those with shorter terms, and consequently the yield curve is upward sloping.

## Spot Rates

For a given issuer, all bonds of a particular maturity do not have the same yield to maturity, even if they have the same default risk. If you look at *The Wall Street Journal*, you can always find several U.S. Treasury bonds maturing at approximately the same time but with different reported yields to maturity. This happens because the yield to maturity is a statistic calculated *after* learning the bond price; the market does not find the value of a bond by using the yield to maturity. Instead, it values each of the bond's cash flows using the appropriate spot rate.

A **spot rate** is the yield to maturity of a zero coupon security. There is a one-month spot rate, a one-year spot rate, an eighteen-month spot rate, a 75-month spot rate, and so on. The yield to maturity is the *single* interest rate that, when applied to the stream of cash flows associated with a bond, causes the present value of those cash flows to equal the bond's market price. The yield to maturity is a useful hip-pocket statistic, but it does not have any clear economic meaning other than being an average of the various spot rates over the security's life. Figure 11-2 illustrates this.

The market, however, does not *value* a bond using the yield to maturity concept. Rather, the yield to maturity is a statistic derived after the bond value is known. Stated another way, you get the bond price first and then solve for the yield to maturity, not the other way around.

For valuation purposes, you should think of a bond as a *package* of zero coupon securities, each providing a single cash flow and each valued using the appropriate spot rate. The market determines bond value by discounting each component at a specific rate rather than by some average rate. For instance, in determining the yield to maturity of a 3-year, 7-percent Treasury note selling for 110, the valuation equation is

$$110.0 = \frac{3.5}{(1+r/2)} + \frac{3.5}{(1+r/2)^2} + \frac{3.5}{(1+r/2)^3} + \frac{3.5}{(1+r/2)^4} + \frac{3.5}{(1+r/2)^5} + \frac{103.5}{(1+r/2)^6}$$

Properly valuing the bond requires using *spot* rates, with each discount rate $r$ potentially different:

$$110.0 = \frac{3.5}{(1+r_1/2)} + \frac{3.5}{(1+r_2/2)^2} + \frac{3.5}{(1+r_3/2)^3} + \frac{3.5}{(1+r_4/2)^4} + \frac{3.5}{(1+r_5/2)^5} + \frac{103.5}{(1+r_6/2)^6}$$

FIGURE 11-2

Yield to Maturity and the Spot Rate Curve

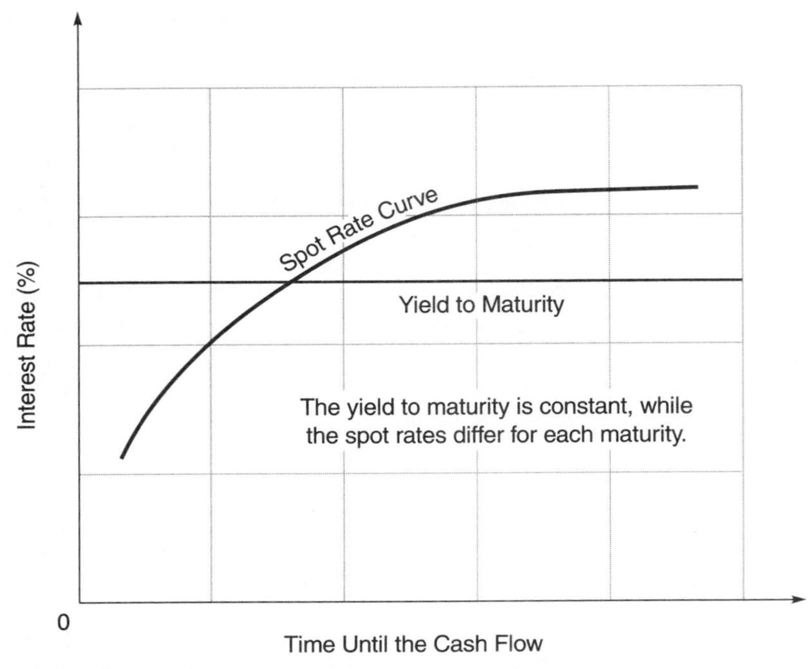


Finding the spot rates is a more complicated algebraic exercise than finding the yield to maturity, so you can relegate this task to the computer. Still, you improve your understanding of bond valuation if you know the mechanics of finding the spot rates.

You can get the six-month spot rate directly by looking at the Treasury bill listing in the financial press or on the Internet. Suppose the rate associated with a six-month T-bill is 5.26 percent. You then want to determine the one-year spot rate. Suppose also that a one-year Treasury note with a 6 1/2 percent coupon sells for 101. Valuing the bond in dollar form rather than percentages, the equation is:

$$1{,}010 = \frac{32.50}{(1 + r_1/2)} + \frac{1{,}032.50}{(1 + r_2/2)^2}$$

You know the six-month spot rate, $r_1$, is 5.26%. Inserting this into the equation, you are left with a single unknown, $r_2$:

$$1{,}010 = \frac{32.50}{(1 + .0526/2)} + \frac{1{,}032.50}{(1 + r_2/2)^2}$$

Solving the equation, you find $r_2 = 5.46\%$. You can use this same technique, called bootstrapping, to find each of the other spot rates.

The important point to remember is that the market values a bond by adding the present value of each of its cash flows, with a different discount rate normally used at each point in time. Having determined the proper bond price, if you wish, you can then determine the one *single* interest rate (the yield to maturity) that will cause the present value of the future cash flows to equal the market price of the bond.

## Why Deflation May Be Bad

Inflation is a general rise in the price of household purchases. It results in an increase in the cost of living. One of the monetary policy objectives of the Federal Reserve Board is to keep inflation in check. *Deflation* occurs when the price level declines rather than increases. For investors, deflation can be just as bad as inflation.

Prices in Japan have been declining for over a decade, and that economy is in terrible shape. (In early 2005, the Japanese stock market was lower than it was 20 years earlier.) During the Great Depression in the United States, prices fell approximately 7 percent each year from 1929 to 1933; it took the country years to recover.

In a deflationary period, a firm has little ability to raise its prices. It will lose business to competitors who keep their prices lower. In fact, firms may have to reduce their prices to attract business. Customers recognize this and delay purchases, waiting for prices to fall even more. These falling prices mean that corporate profit margins narrow, making it more difficult to pay interest on existing debt. Lower profits and less ability to service debt put downward pressure on stock, making portfolios less valuable as collateral. Some firms inevitably default on their debt, attracting the attention of bankers who become less inclined to approve marginal loans or to grant accommodations to existing borrowers.

Working and investing in an inflationary economy is difficult, but the economy's occasional bouts of deflation can be just as troublesome.

### *The Conversion Feature*

Convertible bonds give their owners the right to exchange the bonds for a prespecified amount of some other asset, normally shares of stock.

Hilton Hotels, for instance, issued bonds with a 5 percent coupon that matured in 2006. Each bond was convertible at any time into 45.115 shares of Hilton common stock. The number of shares the bondholder receives when the bond is converted is measured by the **conversion ratio.** For this bond, the conversion ratio is 45.115. The par value of the bond divided by the conversion ratio is the **conversion price:**[11]

$$\frac{\$1{,}000/\text{bond}}{45.115 \text{ shares/bond}} = \$22.166/\text{share}$$

The net effect is that the bondholder had the right to buy 45.115 shares of Hilton common stock at $22.166 per share for each $1,000 bond held.

Fractional shares of stock are not allowed. As a consequence, most bondholders who exercise their conversion privilege receive a small check along with their new shares. The check reflects the value of the fractional shares. In this example, the holder of $10,000 par value of the bonds would receive a stock certificate for 451 shares and a check for the value of 0.15 of a share: (0.15)($22.166) = $3.32.

[11]The conversion price is sometimes called the *effective price of conversion*. The conversion price is *not* a fee that must be paid to convert the bond.

**TABLE 11-5** CONVERTIBLE BOND ARBITRAGE

Bond price: $1,250 (assumed)
Conversion price: $22.165
Conversion ratio: 45.115 shares
Stock price: $30
Conversion value: Conversion ratio × Stock price = 45.115 shares × $30/share = $1,353.45

To Take Advantage of the Arbitrage:

1. Buy as many bonds as you can afford at $1,250 each.
2. Convert each bond into stock worth $1,353.45.
3. Sell the stock, making a $103.45 profit on each bond.
4. Buy more bonds, and repeat the process.

As the price of the underlying common stock rises above the conversion price, the bond begins to act more and more like the stock itself. The current stock price multiplied by the conversion ratio is called the **conversion value.**

The market price of a convertible bond will never be less than its conversion value. If this did happen, arbitrage would occur. *Arbitrage* is the existence of a riskless profit (such as finding a $5 bill on the sidewalk); such a situation does not last very long. Consider the example in Table 11-5. This situation constitutes a money machine, and it will be short-lived. Arbitrageurs buying the bonds will force prices up, and the selling pressure on the stock might push its price down. The bond price and the stock price will quickly move back in line so that the arbitrage is gone.

*Bonds should never sell for less than their conversion value.*

It is quite possible, however, for a bond to sell for more than its conversion value. Suppose Hilton Hotels common stock sold for $30. The conversion value would be $30.00 × 45.115 = $1,353.45. A $1,000 par Hilton convertible bond should not sell for less than this. It could easily sell for $1,400, though; there is no arbitrage if the bond sells for more than the conversion value. The difference between the bond price and the conversion value is the **premium over conversion value,** which reflects the potential for future increases in the common stock price.

A few convertible bonds have a mandatory conversion feature. These *mandatory convertibles* convert automatically into common stock after three or four years. Rating agencies tend to view these as common stock equivalents, so they have less impact on a firm's credit rating.

### The Matter of Accrued Interest

Bondholders earn interest each calendar day they hold a bond. This is unlike the situation with common stock for which the dividend is an all-or-nothing item.[12] Despite this, firms mail interest payment checks only twice a year. Someone might buy a bond today and receive a check for six months' interest just two weeks from now. This would be a substantial return in two weeks' time. Things do not work this way, however, for the story is incomplete.

When buying a bond, the buyer pays the *accrued interest* to the seller of the bond. **Accrued interest** refers to interest that has accumulated since the last interest payment date but which the issuer has not yet paid. Similarly, the bond seller receives accrued interest from the bond buyer. One day's interest accrues for each day

[12]If an investor buys stock before an ex-dividend date, he gets the entire forthcoming dividend. If he buys it on the ex-dividend date or later, he is not entitled to the next dividend.

FIGURE 11-3

Accrued Interest

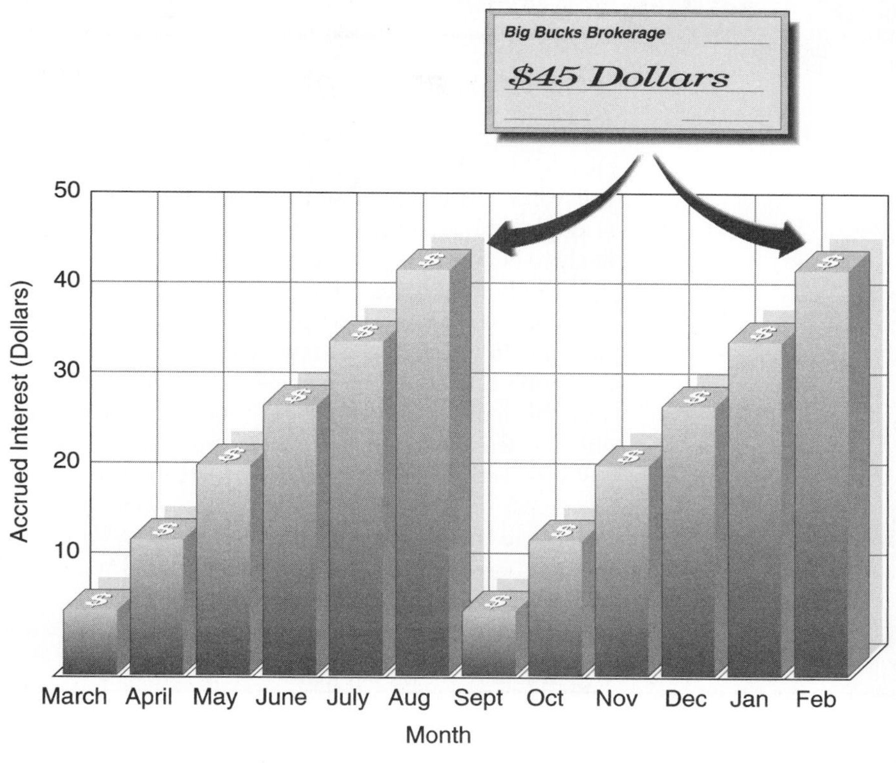


9 percent interest payable February 1 and August 1.

the bond is held.[13] At the end of the interest payment period, the bond issuer sends one check for the entire six months' interest to the current bondholder.

Figure 11-3 shows how bond interest accrues over the calendar year.[14] This example is for a U.S. Treasury bond with a 9 percent coupon that pays interest on the first day of February and the first day of August. A 9 percent coupon bond pays $90 in interest each year. This amounts to $0.2466 per day. A person who buys $1,000 of these bonds on May 5, for instance, acquires the bond ninety-four days into the interest cycle. The buyer must pay $0.2466/day × 94 days = $23.18 in accrued interest to the seller of the bond. If the purchase price is 95 (meaning 95 percent of par value), the buyer would pay $950 (the principal) plus $23.18 (the accrued interest) for a total of $973.18. On top of this would be any brokerage commission.

At the end of the calendar year, bond investors must report the amount of interest they have earned to the Internal Revenue Service. Interest income equals the interest checks received from the company plus accrued interest received from bonds sold minus accrued interest paid during the year.

[13]With corporate bonds, the industry convention is to calculate accrued interest on the basis of twelve 30-day months, for a 360-day year. With U.S. government bonds standard practice is to use a full 365-day year.

[14]By tradition, the market calculates accrued interest on U.S. government securities based on actual days, as in this example. With *corporate* bonds, however, we assume there are twelve thirty-day months in the year and calculate accrued interest accordingly.

PORTFOLIO MEMO

## The Importance of the Coupon

While the price of an individual bond will fluctuate over time as the yield curve changes and the bond's credit rating shifts, it is extremely likely that the bond will eventually be retired at par. In the long run, the ups and downs of the bond price probably won't matter. This means that the bulk of the investor's return is likely to be from the income stream generated by the bond's coupon.

The BondsOnline Advisor* points out that from 1950 to 2004 bonds earned an annual average of 6.3 percent. During this 55-year period there were only five instances in which interest rates fell enough to cause bonds' percentage price appreciation to exceed their income yield. If you dissect the total return from bonds over this lengthy period, 6.1 percent of the total came from the coupon, with only 0.2 percent coming from price appreciation.

It is certainly possible to use bonds to *speculate* on rating changes, turnaround situations, or changes in interest rates. Bond speculation invariably looks to changes in the bond price because of some anticipated event. To the long-term *investor*, however, the bond price plays second fiddle to the coupon.

*Taub, Stephen, "Don't Underestimate the Power of the Coupon," *BondsOnline Advisor*, December 2004.

# Bond Risk

This common belief is not accurate: "Stock is risky; bonds are not." Bonds do carry risk, although the forms of the risk differ from those associated with equity securities. To manage bonds properly in any portfolio, you must understand the types of risk they bear.

## Price Risks

The price of a bond can change every day; this means that bonds are subject to price risk. Price risk has two components: **interest rate risk** and **default risk.**

**Interest Rate Risk.** *Interest rate risk* is the chance of loss because of changing interest rates. If someone buys a bond with a 10.4 percent yield to maturity and market interest rates rise a week later, the market price of this bond will fall. This happens because risk-averse investors always prefer a higher yield for a given level of risk. Newly issued, equally risky bonds will yield more after the interest rate rise, and the only way investors will want to purchase the old bonds is if they can buy them for a lower price. Relative to the purchase price, the bondholder has a paper loss after the rise in interest rates. If the bond were to be sold at this point, there would be a realized loss.

Small certificates of deposit at a bank are not negotiable, and we do not usually refer to interest rate risk with retail CDs. The CD investor still faces this type of risk, however. If you buy a CD with an effective yield of 6.45 percent and the bank raises its rate a week later to 6.60 percent, your ultimate return would have been higher had you waited a week to make the purchase.

**TABLE 11-6** STANDARD & POOR'S BOND RATINGS

| *Investment Grade* | *Junk* | *Special Ratings* |
|---|---|---|
| AAA | BB | CI (obsolete, for income bonds) |
| AA | B | D (bonds in default) |
| A | CCC | |
| BBB | CC | |
| | C | |

Ratings AA through CCC can carry a plus or minus.

Similarly, a home buyer must usually issue a mortgage to finance the property.[15] It is certainly possible that mortgage loan rates could go down after a loan committal. Even a small difference in interest rates on a mortgage can amount to thousands of dollars over the term of the loan. The difference in total repayments on a $100,000 thirty-year loan at 10.00 percent versus 9.75 percent, for instance, is $6,631.

**Default Risk.** *Default risk* measures the likelihood that a firm will be unable to pay the principal and interest on a bond in accordance with the bond indenture. Standard & Poor's Corporation and Moody's Investors Service are the two leading advisory services monitoring the default risk of bonds.[16]

Standard & Poor's rates bonds on a scale of AAA (least risk) to D (bonds in default). The ratings from AA through CCC can also carry a plus or minus. The complete set of ratings is shown in Table 11-6. Bonds are either **investment grade** or **junk bonds;** there is no middle ground. Bonds rated below BBB are junk bonds. Statutory law limits many fiduciaries to investment grade bonds.

Standard & Poor's has a separate description for each of the ratings AAA, AA, A, and BBB. The junk bond definitions all speak to varying degrees of "vulnerability to nonpayment."[17] BB-rated bonds have the least vulnerability; C-rated bonds have the highest. Consistent with the familiar trade-off between risk and expected return, the lower the grade of a bond, the higher its yield to maturity, everything else being equal.

## Convenience Risks

**Convenience risk** refers to added demands on management time because of bond calls, the need to reinvest coupon payments, or the difficulty in trading a bond at a reasonable price because of its low marketability. Convenience risks make up another category of risks associated with bond investments. These risks may not be easily measured in dollars and cents, but they still have a cost.

**Call Risk. Call risk** refers to the inconvenience to the bondholder associated with a company retiring a bond early. The bond issuer frequently has the option to pay its debts off ahead of schedule if it so desires. If the company makes the decision to do so, it *calls* the bond. This can be a nuisance for the bondholder whose portfolio

---

[15]The borrower issues the mortgage; the lender acquires the mortgage. A mortgage is an asset to the lender and a liability to the borrower.

[16]Standard and Poor's indicates that its ratings are a function of three factors: (1) the likelihood of default; (2) the nature and provisions of the obligation; and (3) the protection afforded by, and the relative position of, the obligation in the event of bankruptcy or reorganization.

[17]Standard and Poor's *Bond Guide*, "Issue Credit Rating Definitions," October 1998, 12.

acquired good-quality bonds when interest rates were at an all-time high. As interest rates come down, the issuer is going to seek to refinance this debt at the new, lower rates.[18]

As an example, suppose a firm borrows $50 million with a 9 percent, 20-year bond issue. Perhaps after one year, market interest rates fall and the firm can now borrow at 8.80 percent. If the firm is able to call the first bond issue and issue new bonds with the lower rate, the total interest savings over the next nineteen years at the new rate would be (9% – 8.8%) × $50 million × 19 years = $1.9 million.[19] This figure does not consider the time value of money, but the point remains. Falling interest rates provide a significant incentive for the firm to call its existing bonds and issue new ones at a lower rate.

If your bonds are called, you will no longer receive the high rate you expected. This is also an inconvenience to the portfolio manager, because he will have to select another issue to replace these bonds in the portfolio. This involves both management time and trading fees.

*The higher the coupon on a bond, the higher its reinvestment rate risk.*

To provide some protection to the bondholder against call risk, many bond issues have some degree of *call protection* and may provide a *call premium*. **Call protection** is a period of time after the issuance of a bond when the issuer cannot call it. A 20-year bond might have five years of call protection. After the call protection expires, bondholders frequently receive a **call premium** ("inconvenience" compensation) if the issuer calls the bond. This often begins at an amount equal to one year's interest and then gradually declines to zero as the bond maturity approaches.

PORTFOLIO MEMO

## Bond Sector Bets

Bonds are not just for "widows and orphans." Some of Wall Street's foremost investors have gained or lost millions of dollars by their portfolio allocation to this asset class.

In April 1997 the legendary Warren Buffet bought $1 billion worth of 20–23 year zero coupon bonds. Thirty-year Treasury bonds were yielding about 7.09 percent at that time. By August 1998 the 30-year yield was down to 5.54 percent, resulting in a $400 million gain for his portfolio.

In December 1995 Jeffrey Vinik was the manager of the $55 billion Fidelity Magellan mutual fund. That month he put 32.1 percent of the fund into 30-year T-bonds, yielding about 6.06 percent at that time. During the first half of 1996, interest rates rose and bond prices plummeted. In June 1996 the 30-year rate was up a full percentage point from where Vinik bought them. Vinik resigned from Fidelity that month to start his own firm.

Long-term bonds, even U.S. government bonds, are not for you if you are faint of heart. You will likely get exactly what you were promised if you hold them until maturity, but they can be very volatile along the way. For some investors the consequences of that volatility are unacceptable.

---

[18] A homeowner may do the same thing if mortgage rates decline significantly. Refinancing a mortgage involves calling the original loan prior to issuing a new mortgage.

[19] There would also be flotation costs (the expense of selling a new security) with the new debt, and these should be considered when determining whether or not calling the old debt is advisable.

**Reinvestment Rate Risk.** Even if a bond issue is not called when rates decline, you, as a bondholder, still face the fact that you cannot reinvest the interest checks at a rate as high as the bond's original yield to maturity. Consider two bonds, both with a yield to maturity of 13 percent. One is a zero coupon bond, and the other has a 16.5 percent coupon. The former is a pure discount security, generating no cash flows to reinvest before maturity; consequently, it carries no *reinvestment rate risk*. **Reinvestment rate risk** refers to the uncertainty surrounding the rate at which coupon proceeds can be put back to work. The latter bond must sell at a premium because its yield to maturity is less than its coupon rate. Most of the return on this bond comes via the interest checks, which the bondholder does need to reinvest. Unfortunately for you, unless you accept more default risk, the interest checks will be reinvested at a rate below the bond's 16.5 percent coupon rate. Reinvestment rate risk is high with this bond. In general, the higher the coupon on the bond, the higher the reinvestment rate risk.

**Marketability Risk.** Most bonds do not trade in an active secondary market. The majority of bond buyers intend to hold the securities until maturity rather than trade them like shares of stock. This means that although thousands of corporate and government bonds exist, many of those issues are not offered for sale. Similarly, numerous analysts maintain a constant watch on a company's stock but probably pay less attention to the firm's specific bond issues. **Marketability risk** refers to the difficulty of trading a bond. Bonds with low marketability usually carry a wider bid-ask spread than that of a more liquid issue, or a higher risk premium implied in the lower price a potential buyer is willing to pay for the bond.[20]

### Malkiel's Interest Rate Theorems

Any good portfolio manager knows *Malkiel's theorems*. Portfolio managers who are unfamiliar with them are likely to remain minor league players. **Malkiel's interest rate theorems** provide information about how bond prices change as interest rates change.

*Bond prices move inversely with yields.*

**Theorem 1.** *Malkiel's Theorem 1* is familiar: Bond prices move inversely with yields. If the general level of interest rates rises, the price of an existing bond goes down. Conversely, if the level of interest rates declines, the price of an existing bond increases. The reason this happens stems directly from the effect of the time value of money on the bond's income stream.

Suppose that in March 2005 investors will pay $1,000 for a ten-year, BB-rated bond that carries a 9 percent coupon. The owner of this bond will receive $90 per year (actually $45 every six months) until the bond matures. Two months later the prime rate increases one-half point. This generally results in an upward shift in the entire yield curve. Newly issued BB-rated bonds might carry a 9.5 percent coupon, providing $95 per year in interest. Given two BB-rated bonds of equal maturity, one of which pays $90 per year and the other pays $95 per year, it is easy to see that these bonds are not going to sell for the same price. The bond paying $95 per year is preferable, and people are going to be willing to pay more for it.

For the 9 percent coupon bond to compete in this higher interest rate market, its price must fall. In practice, the price of the lower coupon bond falls so that its

---

[20]A higher risk premium, of course, means that the market price of the bond is lower.

yield to maturity becomes 9.5 percent. This new price is $968.17, but because corporate bonds trade in eighths of a percent of par, the financial press will show this price as 96 3/4. At this price its investment appeal is comparable to the new 9.5 percent coupon bonds.

*Longer term bonds have more interest rate risk.*

**Theorem 2.** If two bonds are similar in every respect except for the time remaining until they mature, the bond with the longer life will fluctuate most as interest rates change. *Malkiel's Theorem 2* states that long-term bonds have more interest rate risk.

One way to get intuition into this result is to consider the extremes and the middle: a bond that matures tomorrow, another bond that is a consol (no expiration), and a third that is a "normal" bond. Bond A is BBB rated, carries a 9 percent coupon, and matures tomorrow. Bond B is BBB rated, carries a 9 percent coupon, and is a consol. Bond C is BBB rated, carries a 9 percent coupon, and matures in one year. Regardless of what interest rates do, Bond A is worth $1,000 tomorrow. It makes no difference whether market rates go up or down; changing interest rates do not affect Bond A. The holder of Bond B, in contrast, is very concerned about interest rate movements. If interest rates rise, the holder of Bond B will be stuck with a security paying a below-market rate, conceivably forever. There is no maturity date to eventually pull the bond price up. The holder of Bond C faces a situation that lies between these extremes. If interest rates rise tomorrow, Bond C will fall in value because it will pay a below-market rate for the next twelve months. In one year, though, it will be redeemed at par. In this sense there is no loss from the fall in the bond price because the loss disappears by maturity.

*Higher coupon bonds have less interest rate risk.*

**Theorem 3.** *Malkiel's Theorem 3* states that higher coupon bonds have less interest rate risk. This theorem is a time value of money cousin of the "bird in the hand" argument. Money in hand is a sure thing while the present value of an anticipated future receipt is risky.

The yield on a bond comes from two sources: the interest received and the return of the principal at maturity. Earlier we looked at a 9.5 percent bond, maturing in eight years, selling for $900, with a yield to maturity of 11.44 percent. This is $R$ in the following equation, where $t$ = time period:

$$\$900 = \underbrace{\left|\sum_{t=1}^{16} \frac{\$47.50}{(1 + R/2)^t}\right|}_{\text{Interest}} + \underbrace{\left|\frac{\$1,000}{(1 + R/2)^{16}}\right|}_{\text{Principal}} \tag{11-9}$$

Consider another bond maturing in eight years with a yield to maturity of 11.44 percent but with a zero coupon. Its valuation equation is:

$$\$410.66 = \underbrace{\left|\sum_{t=1}^{16} \frac{\$0}{(1+R/2)^t}\right|}_{\text{Interest}} + \underbrace{\left|\frac{\$1,000}{(1+R/2)^{16}}\right|}_{\text{Principal}} \tag{11-10}$$

This bond provides no annuity stream and consequently sells for a very low price.

Suppose that there is a downward, parallel shift in the yield curve and that eight-year bonds of similar risk now yield just 11.00 percent. What happens to the prices of the two bonds? To find out, change the value of $R$ in Equations 11-9 and 11-10 and then solve for the new bond price. The 9.5 percent coupon bond will rise by $21.53 (2.4 percent of its market value) to $921.53, whereas the zero coupon bond will rise

**TABLE 11-7** 10 PERCENT COUPON BOND PRICE CHANGES

| *YTM (%)* | *Bond A* | *Bond B* | *Bond C* | *Bond D* |
|---|---|---|---|---|
| | | *Bond Maturity* | | |
| | 3 Years | 5 Years | 20 Years | 22 Years |
| | | *Bond Market Price* | | |
| 11 | $975 | $962 | $920 | $918 |
| 12 | 951 | 926 | 850 | 846 |
| | $ 24 | $ 36 | $ 70 | $ 72 |

A – B difference, $12; C – D difference, $2.

by $13.92 (3.4 percent of market value) to $424.58. As expected, the change in interest rates affected the higher coupon bond the least.

**Theorem 4.** Theorem 2 indicates that the longer the bond has until its maturity, the more its price will fluctuate. *Malkiel's Theorem 4* tells us that when comparing two bonds, the relative importance of Theorem 2 diminishes as the maturities of the two bonds increase.

Suppose you have two bonds with identical coupons. Bond A matures in three years; Bond B matures in five. If interest rates rise, you know from Theorem 1 that the price of both bonds will fall. Theorem 2 tells you that Bond B, with its longer time until maturity, will fall in price the most.

Consider two other bonds, Bonds C and D. Bond C matures in twenty years, whereas Bond D matures in twenty-two. Rising interest rates will cause the prices of these two bonds to fall also, and Bond D will fall more than Bond C. Theorem 4 tells you that the price differential will be larger between Bonds A and B than between Bonds C and D. In other words, the two-year difference in maturity is more important with the short-term bonds than with the long-term bonds.

An example helps show this. Table 11-7 indicates that if market interest rates rise from 11 to 12 percent, the prices of all four bonds fall. Note that the longer the term of the bond, the greater the price decline. Bonds A and B are two years apart in their maturities; the difference in their price declines is $12. Bonds C and D are also two years apart, but the difference in their price changes is only $2. As Theorem 4 indicates, the extra two years make little difference for long-term bonds.

**Theorem 5.** *Malkiel's Theorem 5* states that capital gains from an interest rate decline exceed the capital loss from an equivalent interest rate increase. The last theorem does not influence the portfolio manager's decisions. It is simply a mathematical fact of life.

In Table 11-7 Bond A initially sells for $975. If interest rates rise by 1 percent (from 11 to 12 percent), the price of the bond declines by $24. If, instead, interest rates fall by 1 percent (to 10 percent), Bond A would sell for its par value of $1,000. This is a price rise of $25. The capital gain from a 1 percent drop in interest rates exceeds the capital loss from a 1 percent rise in interest rates.

### Duration as a Measure of Interest Rate Risk

*Duration* is a direct measure of interest rate risk; it combines Malkiel's theorems into a single statistic so that you can readily determine the relative risk of a set of bonds. Fixed income security pricing is incomplete without a discussion of duration.

**The Concept of Duration.** **Duration** is probably the central concept in modern fixed income security management.[21] Business school courses in bank management and investments normally cover the calculation of duration. However, many people never get beyond the black-box stage with this statistic. That is, they can crunch the numbers, solve for it, and give its definition, but they still lack a thorough understanding of the result.

*For a good discussion of risk in general, see* http://www.contingencyanalysis.com

Frederick R. Macaulay coined the term *duration* in 1938 when he suggested studying the time structure of a bond by measuring its average term to maturity.[22] For a security with no embedded options (e.g., noncallable), the duration statistic is the weighted average number of years necessary to recover the initial cost of the bond where the weights reflect the time value of money. Duration's principal value to the financial manager or industrial engineer is that it is a direct measure of interest rate risk; the higher the duration, the higher the interest rate risk.

**Calculating Duration.** Equation 11-11 presents the traditional duration calculation:

$$D = \frac{\sum_{t=1}^{N} \frac{C_t}{(1+R)^t} \times t}{P_0} \qquad \textbf{(11-11)}$$

where $D$ = duration; $C_t$ = cash flow at time $t$; $R$ = yield to maturity of the bond; $P_0$ = current price of the bond; $N$ = years until bond maturity; and $t$ = time at which a cash flow is received.

Equation 11-11 provides some intuition into the duration statistic in that it shows time weighted by the present value of the cash flows received in each time period, but the calculation is unwieldy. Fortunately, there is a simpler method: Equation 11-12 shows the closed-form formula for duration.

$$D = \frac{C\left[\frac{(1+R)^{N+1} - (1+R) - RN}{R^2(1+R)^N}\right] + \frac{F \times N}{(1+R)^N}}{P_0} \qquad \textbf{(11-12)}$$

where $C$ = coupon payment per period; $F$ = face (par) value of the bond; $N$ = number of periods until maturity; $R$ = yield to maturity of the bond per period; and $P_0$ = current market price of the bond.

*Duration is the weighted average number of years necessary to recover the initial cost of the bond.*

**Applying Duration.** Duration is especially useful in determining the relative riskiness of two or more bonds when visual inspection of their characteristics makes it unclear which is most vulnerable to changing interest rates. Consider, for instance, the two bonds in Table 11-8.

We will first confirm Bond A's duration using the closed-form equation. We have the following information: $C = \$47.50$; $F = \$1{,}000$; $P_0 = \$900$; $R = 11.44\%$ per year, or 5.72% per half-year period; and $N = 8$ years, or 16 half- year periods.

[21]Duration is discussed in more technical detail in Chapters 14 and 21.

[22]Frederick R. Macaulay, *Some Theoretical Problems Suggested by the Movements of Interest Rates, Bond Yields, and Stock Prices in the United States Since 1856* (New York: National Bureau of Economic Research, 1938).

**TABLE 11-8** USING DURATION TO COMPARE TWO BONDS

| Bond | Annual Interest | Remaining Life | Current Price | Yield to Maturity |
|---|---|---|---|---|
| A | $ 95 | 8 years | $900 | 11.44% |
| B | $110 | 9 years | $950 | 11.92% |

Duration of A = 5.64 years. Duration of B = 5.85 years. Bond B has more interest rate risk.

$$D = \frac{47.5\left[\dfrac{(1+0.0572)^{17} - (1.0572) - (0.0572 \times 16)}{0.0572^2(1.0572)^{16}}\right] + \dfrac{1{,}000 \times 16}{(1.0572)^{16}}}{900}$$

$$= 11.29 \text{ semiannual periods, or } 5.64 \text{ years}$$

This is the value that Table 11-8 shows.

Malkiel's theorems indicate that the prices of bonds with higher coupons fluctuate less than those of bonds with lower coupons, and that bonds with shorter maturities fluctuate less than bonds with longer maturities. With Bonds A and B, though, it is not immediately obvious which will fluctuate most with changing interest rates because the higher coupon bond also has the longest time remaining until maturity. Calculation of the durations indicates that Bond B (with a duration of 5.85) has more risk than Bond A (with a duration of 5.64).

Later in this chapter we will see that matching a bond's duration to a particular investment horizon offsets both reinvestment rate risk and interest rate risk. This is one of duration's most important uses to some institutional investors.

## The Meaning of Bond Diversification

*Bond price risk is composed of default risk and interest rate risk.*

It is important to diversify a bond portfolio. However, bond diversification serves a different purpose from the diversification associated with equity securities. The Evans and Archer results show how holding a portfolio rather than a single security reduces unsystematic risk. The mathematics of diversification prove that total risk normally declines when you add an equity security to the portfolio provided the new stock is less than perfectly correlated with the existing portfolio. Things are a bit different with bonds. You do not refer to systematic or unsystematic risk with debt securities. Rather, you worry about two other types of risk: *default risk* and *interest rate risk*. These two types of risk are what we seek to diversify in a fixed income portfolio.

### Default Risk

*Rating agencies such as Standard & Poor's and Moody's function as the credit bureaus for bond issuers.*

*Default risk* refers to the likelihood that a firm will be unable to repay the principal and interest of a loan as agreed in the bond indenture. **Credit risk** is the equivalent of this term for an individual consumer. Credit bureaus provide information about a borrower's past credit history. Retail lending officers at a bank find this information useful when they consider someone's credit application. Similarly, credit bureaus monitor the financial condition and past credit history of corporations. We call these commercial credit bureaus **rating agencies.** Standard & Poor's Corporation, Moody's Investors Service, and Dun & Bradstreet are a few prominent rating agencies.

*Diversifying default risk requires the purchase of bonds from a number of different issuers.*

Even though there is no unsystematic risk to diversify away, it is not wise to place a sizable percentage of a fund's assets in any single security, regardless of how safe that security is.[23] No matter how much default risk an investor can bear, it is prudent to spread the investment funds over bonds from a number of different issuers. A firm might have several bond issues, some of which Standard & Poor's rates AAA and others rated A. Buying some of each does not accomplish the task of diversifying the default risk, however, because if the issuer defaults on one issue, this will affect all of the firm's debt issues. Enron had about twenty different bond issues when it went into bankruptcy. An investor who owned ten of them was probably in worse shape than someone who owned just one.

*In general, the longer the time a bond has until its maturity, the higher its yield to maturity.*

## Dealing with the Yield Curve

The fundamental interest rate yield curve decision deals with the familiar trade-off between risk and return. Most of the time the yield curve is upward sloping, with uncertainty about future rates increasing with the time horizon. Everything else being equal, the longer a fixed-income security has until maturity, the higher the return it will have in order to compensate investors for bearing this added risk.

Before the portfolio manager begins the process of selecting specific bonds, he or she needs to determine the degree of interest rate risk the fund's owner will tolerate. The longer the average duration of the fund, the higher its expected level of return, but the greater the damage that can occur if interest rates move adversely.

Consider an individual investor about to invest $2,500 in a certificate of deposit at a local bank. Assume the rate for a one-year CD is 4.10 percent while a five-year CD pays 4.25 percent. Although a bank certificate of deposit will not go down in value, the depositor faces an interest penalty[24] if it becomes necessary to withdraw the funds before the CD's maturity date. The question is this: Does the extra yield of 15 basis points adequately compensate for the added risk of locking the money up for five years rather than for just one year? Many investors would not think so and would invest their money for the shorter period, making a new investment decision after one year.

The same thing happens with the selection of our favored point on the yield curve. We can usually get a higher yield by holding a 20-year Treasury bond rather than short-term debt, but does the higher yield justify the substantially increased level of risk? If interest rates were to rise, the high-duration 20-year bonds would fall dramatically, whereas the shorter-term bonds would be hit less hard. A portfolio manager in conjunction with the client and the statement of investment policy needs to determine the appropriate level of interest rate risk that the portfolio should carry.[25]

---

[23]U.S. Treasury securities are probably an exception to this rule.

[24]The penalty is often three months' worth of interest.

[25]The author once had a conversation with a fund manager about this very subject in regard to an income-oriented $800,000 portfolio. AAA-rated bonds were yielding about 20 basis points less than A-rated bonds of the same maturity. On a portfolio of $800,000, this difference in yield amounts to $1,600 per year. In this particular case, the author thought the extra dollars were worth the modest increase in risk.

### Bond Betas

We have seen that according to finance theory, the market prices securities according to their their level of risk relative to the market average (their beta). Market risk does affect bonds, but most investors are much more concerned with default risk and interest rate risk.

The idea of **bond betas** has never become fully accepted. A flurry of academic research on this topic occurred some years ago, but little became of it. Beta is not an especially useful concept with securities that have a finite life such as bonds, stock options, or Treasury bills. Other types of risk are more pertinent to these securities.[26]

## Choosing Bonds

In selecting bonds, a manager should consider a number of factors. Attention to them will save time and will reduce aggravation.

### Client Psychology and Bonds Selling at a Premium

*Premium bonds held to maturity are expected to pay higher coupon rates than the market rate of interest.*

The purchase of bonds selling at a premium can be awkward to discuss with a customer. This is more of a psychological problem than a real one, but from the fund manager's perspective, it becomes a real problem if the client is unhappy about it.

Suppose a corporate bond matures in seven years and sells for 125. This means that each bond costs 125 percent of par, or $1,250. Bonds sell for a premium when they have a coupon rate higher than the required rate of return on other bonds with equivalent maturities and default risk.[27]

http://www.investinginbonds.com *is a comprehensive Website that covers fixed income–related issues.*

High coupon rates are useful when it is necessary to generate income in a portfolio. There is a trade-off, though. The fact that the bond sells for a premium means that its market price will trend downward toward the par value as the bond moves toward its maturity date. This leaves the fund manager open to misplaced criticism from people who do not understand this issue. A client might say, "Why would I buy something that I know is going to go down in value?" In this example, the fund manager knows that the bond bought for $1,250 will decline in value by $250 over the next seven years. The client is asking a legitimate question, and although there is absolutely nothing wrong with buying bonds selling at a premium, a fund manager might want to avoid having to answer questions of this sort.

---

[26]Mathematically, the bond beta is this:

$$\beta_i = \frac{-\text{Duration} \times \{\text{COV}[E(R_{i,t+1} - R_{it})/(1 + R_{it}), R_{mt}]\}}{\sigma_m^2}$$

In words, the beta of a bond is equal to minus its duration multiplied by the covariance between the change in interest rate divided by 1 plus the original interest rate and the return on the market index, all divided by the variance of return on the market index. The important implication here is that a bond's beta is directly proportional to its duration. Higher durations mean higher betas (in absolute values).

[27]This could actually be an advantage to a tax-exempt investor such as a pension fund. High coupons mean high interest receipts, which are fully taxable. The marketplace often prices tax considerations, and premium bonds (with their high coupons) consequently may be "penalized" in their market prices. If this is the case, they should be especially attractive to tax-exempt investors.

PORTFOLIO MEMO

## Do Bondholders Really Gain When Rates Fall?

*Bank CFO:* The recent decline in interest rates has resulted in our investment portfolio containing a number of bonds that sell for a premium. We had a nice gain on them, and we decided to take it.
*Bank Director:* Why take the gain if you have to pay taxes on it?
*Bank CFO:* We were able to offset the gains with losses elsewhere in the portfolio. As it worked out, there will be no tax liability at all from the bond sale.
*Bank Director:* I'm sure you know it, but just so everyone understands, there is a reason a bond sells for a premium: Its coupon is above average in the current market. If you sell the bond and take the capital gain, you give up the higher income stream in the future. The appreciation on these bonds is not like the appreciation of a stock, and people who consider the appreciation a windfall gain are mistaken. Bond price appreciation is really a neutral event in an economic sense; you can take the gain now and give up the future income or you can keep the bond and get more income than you otherwise would.
*Bank CFO:* You are exactly right, of course, and we did consider that. We found that we could replace the bonds we sold with others of comparable grade and do so at a net present value just above zero. Also, we were about to lose some tax loss carryforward amounts, so it made especially good sense to make the trade.

### Call Risk

*Call risk* is a type of convenience risk. Bonds cease to earn interest when the issuer calls them. A portfolio manager needs to get these funds back to work as quickly as possible. Fund managers sometimes have "favorite" bonds that find their way into many of their managed portfolios. If these bonds are callable, the fund managers run the risk of having to make adjustments to many portfolios all at one time.

*Avoid making extensive use of a single callable bond issue.*

There is no reason to exclude callable bonds categorically from the list of eligible securities. You will unnecessarily limit your options if you do so. However, it is good practice to avoid making wholesale use of a particular callable bond issue. If a called bond appears in two of your portfolios, it is not a problem. If the bond issue appears in seventy-five of your portfolios, however, you have a real inconvenience on your hands, especially if the portfolios are part of a duration-matching scheme or some other structured strategy.

### Constraints

Guidance from the investor or a formal statement of investment policy often dictates that the bond portfolio conform to certain constraints.

*The expected return on a bond portfolio can be raised by choosing lower ratings, longer maturities, or both.*

**Specifying Return.** The expected return on a security is a function of the security's riskiness. For bonds, the pertinent risks are those arising from the possibility of default and from changing interest rates. You can raise the expected return on a bond portfolio by including riskier bonds (those with lower S&P ratings), by choosing bonds with longer maturities, or by doing both.

For funds with income as the primary objective, you, as a fund manager, seek to earn as much income as possible within certain limits. You should not, for instance, choose the riskiest bonds you can find merely because you know they are likely to have a high current yield. Junk bonds occasionally default, and if you hold one of these, it will not help your client or your reputation.

**Specifying Grade.** Limiting choices to bonds rated at or above a certain rating is a very common constraint. Many organizations have a **legal list.** Securities on this list are the only eligible investments.

Limiting a fund to the purchase of *investment grade* bonds is a common constraint. Bonds rated below BBB have a higher yield, but they carry more default risk. According to the records maintained by Standard & Poor's, over a five-year horizon, bonds rated BB have a default experience almost five times that of bonds rated BBB.[28] A portfolio manager will not take on the added risk of noninvestment grade bonds unless the yield pickup is substantial. Many organizations are even more conservative and specify that they will accept only U.S. government or the highest-rated corporate bonds (AAA) in their portfolios. Alternatively, a fund may be limited to no more than a certain percentage of non-AAA bonds or have some other limitation.

*The rating agencies do not assign a rating to U.S. government securities.*

**Specifying Average Maturity.** Another common constraint is *average maturity*. Someone might indicate a desire to limit investments to bonds with maturities of five years or less. The motivation for this is usually concern about rising rates in the future and a desire to keep interest rate risk low.

Specifying a maximum average duration would be a better approach, but the duration concept is unfamiliar to nonprofessionals. With a little work you can educate your client about the merits of duration over maturity, but sometimes this is not practical. If you are told to keep maturities under five years, it is a good idea to do so and not try to explain how you technically met the constraint through careful monitoring of the average duration.

**Periodic Income.** Some funds have periodic income needs that allow little or no flexibility. A recently retired worker might elect to take a lump-sum retirement benefit of $500,000. Perhaps you have been asked to manage these funds, and you propose investing them in high-grade corporate bonds. With a current yield of about 6 percent, you tell your client that this sum can be expected to generate at least $30,000 per year.

Bonds pay interest twice a year, but your client likely will want to receive checks more frequently than this, probably monthly, or even twice a month. By carefully selecting the bonds in the portfolio, you can arrange for your client to receive regular checks from the U.S. Treasury according to a predetermined schedule. This issue is examined more closely in the next part of this chapter.

**Maturity Timing.** Occasionally a portfolio manager needs to construct a bond portfolio so that it matches a particular *investment horizon*. The **investment horizon** is the period of time over which funds are expected to be committed to a particular investment portfolio. For example, you might want to assemble securities to fund a

[28]Reza Bahar, Leo Brand, and Krishnan Nagpal, "Credit Ratings and Recovery Experience: An Overview," *Investment Guide for Plan Sponsors—Risk Budgeting: A Cutting Edge Guide to Enhancing Fund Management* (New York: Institutional Investor, 2000), 45–52.

PORTFOLIO MEMO

## The Taxable/Tax-Exempt Spread

Bonds issued by state and local governments are generally exempt from tax. Because of the tax advantage, these ***municipal bonds*** have lower yields than their taxable counterparts in the corporate sector. For a given maturity, the difference between a taxable yield and a tax-exempt yield is the **yield spread,** a value that frequently changes. Investors and portfolio managers both should watch this number and move between sectors as appropriate.

Suppose an investor is in a combined federal and state tax bracket of 38 percent. On December 3, 2000, the average rate on taxable money market funds was 6.15 percent, with tax-free money market funds paying 3.60 percent* for a yield spread of 255 basis points (2.55 percent). If the investor earned a taxable 6.15 percent before tax, he would be left with $(100\% - 38\%) \times 6.15\% = 3.81\%$ after tax. Because this rate exceeds that on the tax-exempt bond, he is better off holding the taxable fund.

On December 3, 2001, following a long series of Federal Reserve Board discount rate cuts, the spread had narrowed considerably. Taxable funds yielded 1.83 percent and tax-free funds earned 1.29 percent, for a spread of only fifty-four basis points. From the investor's perspective, the tax-free fund is now a better investment. The after-tax yield on the taxable fund is 1.13 percent, not as good as the alternative.

Another alternative was a slightly longer maturity municipal. Also as of December 3, 2001 a five-year municipal yielded an average 3.30 percent. This was nearly triple the after-tax rate on an ordinary money market mutual fund at that time. Many investors would find this higher yield an appealing alternative.

*Source: Salomon Smith Barney Fixed Income Research.

specific, preestablished set of payment obligations over the next ten years.[29] Perhaps you need to generate income of $10,000 per year for ten years (after which the fund is dissolved), and you are to construct a portfolio of U.S. Treasury securities to accomplish the task. Ideally, you would make an initial investment in carefully selected securities and then be able to collect interest payments and principal repayments so that you satisfy the income needs and wind up with a zero balance in the account at the end of the ten-year period. To do this, you would want to avoid buying anything with a maturity more than ten years out.[30]

This is a different constraint than that of specifying average maturity. The constraint of specifying average maturity is really a specification about the duration you want, which is a statement about the acceptable level of interest rate risk. Maturity timing is the issue of having income generated as needed.

[29]Duration matching is a variation on this theme.

[30]Note that specifying that all bonds mature by the end of an investment horizon effectively rules out most immunization techniques. Imposing such a constraint may raise the cost of structuring the portfolio.

**Socially Responsible Investing.** The issue of socially responsible investing is as pertinent to fixed income investing as it is to the selection of equity securities. Some clients will ask that certain types of companies not be included in the portfolio. Common examples include companies involved in the use of nuclear power, the manufacture of military hardware, or the production of "vice" products such as alcohol or cigarettes.

## Example: Monthly Retirement Income

### *The Problem*

Consider a hypothetical situation. Someone has come to you with $1,100,000 to put into the market and indicates that the fund must provide at least $4,000 income per month. This monthly income is an inviolable constraint. After further discussion, you determine that the client's primary objective is growth of income with income as a secondary objective. The fund will be split approximately 50–50 between common stocks and debt securities to meet these objectives.

You subsequently decide to include ten common stocks in the equity portion and to make the stocks approximately equally weighted but without using odd lots. The equity selections appear in Table 11-9. Assume that you incurred $1,500 in brokerage commissions when these stocks were purchased.

The current quarterly dividends on the stocks total $3,010. Dividend payment dates can be determined quickly from either the S&P *Stock Guide* or *Value Line*.[31] On an annual basis, the stocks will pay $3,010 × 4, or $12,040. Based on a market value of $494,000, this means the dividend yield on the equity portion of the portfolio is about 2.44 percent. The generation of $4,000 per month means that the total fund must yield $4,000 × 12 = $48,000 per year, for an annual income yield of $48,000/$1,100,000 = 4.36 percent. If the fund is split 50–50 between stocks and bonds, the bonds need to have a current yield of at least 6.28 percent to generate the required monthly income.

**TABLE 11-9** EQUITY PORTION OF SAMPLE PORTFOLIO

| *Stock* | *Value* | *Quarterly Dividend* | *Payment Month* |
|---|---|---|---|
| 3,000 AAC | $ 51,000 | $ 380 | Jan/April/July/Oct |
| 1,000 BBL | 50,000 | 370 | Jan/April/July/Oct |
| 2,000 XXQ | 49,000 | 400 | Feb/May/Aug/Nov |
| 5,000 XZ | 52,000 | 270 | March/June/Sept/Dec |
| 7,000 MCDL | 53,000 | 0 | — |
| 1,000 ME | 49,000 | 370 | Feb/May/Aug/Nov |
| 2,000 LN | 51,000 | 500 | Jan/April/July/Oct |
| 4,000 STU | 47,000 | 260 | March/June/Sept/Dec |
| 3,000 LLZ | 49,000 | 290 | Feb/May/Aug/Nov |
| 6,000 MZN | 43,000 | 170 | Jan/April/July/Oct |
| Total | $494,000 | $3,010 | |

[31]It is the date of payment, not the ex-dividend date or the date of record, that is important in this problem. You are concerned about when the money is actually in hand.

Part of the initial $1,100,000 deposit will be lost to transaction costs such as the payment of commissions and accrued interest on the bonds you buy. The bonds will actually have to yield somewhat more than 6.28 percent, then, for everything to work out.

## *Unspecified Constraints*

*As with equity selection, we can construct a bond portfolio that produces desired income with the least possible risk.*

How do you pick the bonds? Your ultimate objective is to select them to meet all constraints of the problem. You also want to meet the logical unspecified constraints. For instance, you probably are not going to choose CC-rated bonds to maximize the income you generate, nor are you going to focus on the longest maturities you can find because of their higher yields. Just as with equity security selection, the task here is meeting the minimum required expected return with the least possible risk.

## *Using S&P's* Bond Guide

Standard & Poor's *Bond Guide* is a very helpful tool in working toward a solution to problems like this. You must meet the monthly income constraint, so you need to know in which months the bonds pay interest. You are also interested in knowing the default risk rating. The *Bond Guide* gives both data.

Figure 11-4 is an excerpt from the *Bond Guide*. The column at the far left identifies the bond by issuer, coupon, and maturity. The next column, labeled Interest Dates, indicates when interest is paid. The two letters indicate which months, with

**FIGURE 11-4** Example from Standard & Poor's Bond Guide

Corporate Bonds **ELI-ENR** 81

| Title-Industry Code & Co. Finances (In Italics) | Ind | Fixed Charge Coverage 1995 | 1996 | | 1997 | Year End | Cash & Equiv. (Million $) | Curr. Assets (Million $) | Curr. Liab. (Million $) | Balance Sheet Date | L. Term Debt (Mil $) | | Capitalization (Mil $) | Total Debt % Capital | | | | | | |
|---|---|---|---|---|---|---|---|---|---|---|---|---|---|---|---|---|---|---|---|---|
| Individual Issue Statistics — Exchange | Interest Dates | S&P Rating | Date of Last Rating Change | Prior Rating | Eligible | Bond Form | Redemption Provisions — Regular Price | Regular (Begins) Thru | Sinking Fund Price | Sinking Fund (Begins) Thru | Refund/Other Restriction Price | Refund/Other Restriction (Begins) Thru | Outst'g (Mil $) | Underwriting Firm | Underwriting Year | Price Range 1998 High | Price Range 1998 Low | Mo. End Price Sale(s) or Bid | Curr. Yield | Yield to Mat. |
| ***Elizabethtown Water** (Cont.)* | | | | | | | | | | | | | | | | | | | | |
| Deb 8s 2022 | mS | A | | | X | BE | 105.60 | 8-31-99 | Z100 | .... | .... | .... | 15.0 | S1 | '92 | 106⅛ | 104⅜ | 105¾ | 7.57 | 7.48 |
| Deb 7¼s 2028 | mN | A | | | X | BE | 105.44 | (11-1-98) | Z100 | (11-1-98) | .... | .... | 50.0 | S1 | '93 | 104⅜ | 100 | 104⅜ | 6.95 | 6.90 |
| ***Emerson Electric*** | ***23c*** | *13.85* | *13.68* | | *15.74* | *Sp* | *221.0* | *4717* | *3842* | *9-30-97* | *571.0* | | *7436* | *27.1* | | | | | | |
| Nts 6.30s 2005 | mN | AA+ | | | X | R | NC | .... | .... | .... | .... | .... | 250 | G1 | '95 | 107 | 100⅝ | 107 | 5.89 | 5.11 |
| ***Empire District Electric*** | ***72a*** | *3.10* | *3.05* | | *2.97* | *Dc* | *1.69* | *44.70* | *15.00* | *6-30-98* | *246.0* | | *498.0* | *49.4* | | | | | | |
| 1st[1] 8⅛s 2009 | mN | A− | | | X | R | NC | .... | .... | .... | .... | .... | 20.0 | S1 | '94 | 120¾ | 112½ | 120¾ | 6.73 | 5.59 |
| 1st 7.60s 2005 | Ao | A− | | | X | R | NC | .... | .... | .... | .... | .... | 10.0 | S1 | '95 | 112½ | 106⅜ | 112½ | 6.76 | 5.30 |
| 1st 7½s 2002 | jJ | A− | 5/94 | A | X | R | NC | .... | .... | .... | .... | .... | 37.5 | S1 | '92 | 108 | 104¾ | 108 | 6.94 | 5.13 |
| 1st 6½s 2010 | Ao | A− | | | X | BE | NC | .... | .... | .... | .... | .... | 50.0 | S4 | '98 | 106⅝ | 98½ | 106⅝ | 6.10 | 5.71 |
| 1st 7s 2023 | aO | A− | 5/94 | A | X | R | 103.26 | (10-1-03) | .... | .... | .... | .... | 45.0 | S1 | '93 | 105¼ | 98¾ | 105¼ | 6.65 | 6.57 |
| 1st 7¾s 2025 | Jd | A− | | | X | BE | 103.875 | (6-1-05) | .... | .... | .... | .... | 30.0 | S1 | '95 | 112⅜ | 105½ | 112⅜ | 6.90 | 6.74 |
| 1st[2] 7¼s 2028 | Jd | A− | 5/94 | A | X | R | 104 | 5-31-99 | .... | .... | .... | .... | 14.5 | J2 | '93 | 104¾ | 100¾ | 104⅛ | 6.96 | 6.92 |
| ***Energen Corp*** | ***73b*** | *2.95* | *2.91* | | *2.40* | *Sp* | *8.20* | *160.0* | *184.0* | *3-31-98* | *378.0* | | *724.0* | *52.5* | | | | | | |
| Deb[3] 8s 2007 | Fa | A | | | X | BE | 104 | 1-31-99 | .... | .... | .... | .... | 20.0 | J2 | '92 | 104⅝ | 103⅝ | 103⅝ | 7.72 | 7.41 |
| ***Engle Homes*** | ***13h*** | *n/a* | *n/a* | | *n/a* | *Oc* | | | | *4-30-98* | *140.0* | | *293.0* | *47.8* | | | | | | |
| Sr Nts[4] 9¼s 2008 | Fa | B | | | Y | BE | 104.625 | (2-1-03) | .... | .... | [5]Z109.25 | 2-1-01 | 150 | Exch. | '98 | 102¼ | 94 | 96½ | 9.59 | 9.83 |
| ***Engelhard Corp*** | ***44a*** | *6.16* | *5.62* | | *4.96* | *Dc* | *44.30* | *1396* | *1443* | *6-30-98* | *502.0* | | *1332* | *37.7* | | | | | | |
| Nts 7s 2001 | fA | A | | | X | BE | NC | .... | .... | .... | .... | .... | 150 | M5 | '96 | 104⅞ | 102½ | 104⅞ | 6.67 | 5.13 |
| Nts 7⅜s 2006 | fA | A | | | X | BE | [6]Z100 | .... | .... | .... | .... | .... | 100 | M5 | '96 | 111⅞ | 106⅝ | 111⅞ | 6.59 | 5.49 |
| Nts 6.95s 2028 | Jd | A | | | X | BE | [7]Z100 | .... | .... | .... | .... | .... | 120 | M5 | '98 | 100⅝ | 97¾ | 100⅝• | 6.91 | 6.90 |
| ***Enhance Financial Svcs Grp*** | ***35*** | *12.32* | *14.90* | | *12.64* | *Dc* | | | | *6-30-98* | *75.00* | | *752.0* | *18.5* | | | | | | |
| • Deb 6¾s 2003 | Ms | A+ | | | X | BE | NC | .... | .... | .... | .... | .... | 75.0 | S1 | '93 | No Sale | | 105½ | 6.40 | 5.34 |
| ***Enron Corp[8]*** | ***73e*** | *3.80* | *3.73* | | *1.78* | *Dc* | *170.0* | *4669* | *4412* | *12-31-97* | *6254* | | *9702* | *46.8* | | | | | | |
| Sr Deb 7s 2023 | fA15 | BBB+ | 12/95 | BBB | X | R | 102.575 | (8-15-03) | .... | .... | .... | .... | 100 | M2 | '93 | 101½ | 95⅛ | 99¾ | 7.02 | 7.02 |
| Sr Nts[9] 9.65s 2001 | Mn15 | BBB+ | 12/95 | BBB | X | R | NC | .... | .... | .... | .... | .... | 100 | P4 | '89 | 111½ | 108⅞ | 110⅞ | 8.70 | 5.16 |
| [10]Nts[11] 9½s 2001 | Jd15 | BBB+ | 12/95 | BBB | X | R | NC | .... | .... | .... | .... | .... | 100 | B7 | '89 | 111⅛ | 108⅝ | 110¾ | 8.58 | 5.19 |
| Nts 6.45s 2001 | mN15 | BBB+ | | | X | BE | NC | .... | .... | .... | .... | .... | 300 | S1 | '97 | 103½ | 100¼ | 103½ | 6.23 | 5.22 |
| Nts 6½s 2002 | fA | BBB+ | | | X | BE | [7]Z100 | .... | .... | .... | .... | .... | 150 | L3 | '97 | 104⅛ | 100⅝ | 104⅛ | 6.24 | 5.29 |
| Nts 9⅛s 2003 | Ao | BBB+ | 12/95 | BBB | X | R | NC | .... | .... | .... | .... | .... | 200 | M6 | '91 | 115¼ | 111¼ | 115¼ | 7.92 | 5.28 |
| Nts 9⅞s 2003 | Jd15 | BBB+ | 12/95 | BBB | X | R | NC | .... | .... | .... | .... | .... | 100 | F1 | '88 | 119 | 114⅞ | 119 | 8.30 | 5.26 |
| Nts 6⅝s 2003 | aO15 | BBB+ | | | X | BE | [7]Z100 | .... | .... | .... | .... | .... | 100 | C1 | '97 | 105⅝ | 101½ | 105⅝ | 6.27 | 5.34 |
| Nts 6¾s 2004 | mS | BBB+ | | | X | R | NC | .... | .... | .... | .... | .... | 100 | N1 | '97 | 106⅞ | 101 | 106⅞ | 6.32 | 5.38 |
| Nts 7⅝s 2004 | mS10 | BBB+ | 12/95 | BBB | X | R | NC | .... | .... | .... | .... | .... | 200 | M2 | '92 | 111⅝ | 106 | 111⅝ | 6.83 | 5.32 |
| Nts 6¾s 2004 | mS15 | BBB+ | 12/95 | BBB | X | R | NC | .... | .... | .... | .... | .... | 50.0 | S1 | '95 | 107¼ | 101⅛ | 107¼ | 6.29 | 5.31 |
| Nts 6⅝s 2005 | mN15 | BBB+ | | | X | BE | NC | .... | .... | .... | .... | .... | 250 | M6 | '97 | 106 | 99⅞ | 106 | 6.25 | 5.59 |
| Nts 6.40s 2006 | jJ15 | BBB+ | | | X | BE | [7]Z100 | .... | .... | .... | .... | .... | 250 | C1 | '98 | 104⅝ | 99¼ | 104⅝ | 6.12 | 5.66 |
| Nts 7⅛s 2007 | Mn15 | BBB+ | 12/95 | BBB | X | R | NC | .... | .... | .... | .... | .... | 150 | G1 | '95 | 109¾ | 103⅜ | 109¾ | 6.49 | 5.68 |
| Nts 6⅞s 2007 | aO15 | BBB+ | 12/95 | BBB | X | R | NC | .... | .... | .... | .... | .... | 100 | M2 | '95 | 108⅛ | 101¾ | 108⅛ | 6.36 | 5.71 |
| Nts 6¾s 2009 | fA | BBB+ | | | X | R | Z100 | .... | .... | .... | .... | .... | 200 | C5 | '97 | 107⅞ | 100⅝ | 107⅞ | 6.26 | 5.76 |
| Nts 6.95s 2028 | jJ15 | BBB+ | | | X | BE | [7]Z100 | .... | .... | .... | .... | .... | 250 | C1 | '98 | 99⅝ | 97⅜ | 97½ | 7.13 | 7.15 |
| Sr Sub Deb 6¾s 2005 | jJ | BBB | 12/95 | BBB− | X | R | NC | .... | .... | .... | .... | .... | 200 | L3 | '93 | 106¾ | 100¾ | 106¾ | 6.32 | 5.54 |
| Sr Sub Deb 8¼s 2012 | mS15 | BBB | 12/95 | BBB− | X | R | NC | .... | .... | .... | .... | .... | 150 | B7 | '92 | 122 | 113⅛ | 122 | 6.76 | 5.91 |
| ***Enron Oil & Gas*** | ***49*** | *n/a* | *9.27* | | *4.62* | *Dc* | *13.60* | *245.0* | *239.0* | *6-30-98* | *851.0* | | *2151* | *39.6* | | | | | | |
| Nts 6.70s 2006 | mN15 | A− | | | X | BE | NC | .... | .... | .... | .... | .... | 150 | M5 | '96 | 108 | 101⅞ | 108 | 6.20 | 5.47 |
| Nts 6½s 2007 | jD | A− | | | X | BE | NC | .... | .... | .... | .... | .... | 100 | G1 | '97 | 106½ | 100½ | 106½ | 6.10 | 5.58 |

**Uniform Footnote Explanations-See Page 1.** Other: [1] (HRO)On 11-1-01 at 100. [2] Death red benefit,ltd,as defined. [3] (HRO)At 100,ltd as defined. [4] (HRO)On Chge of Ctrl at 101. [5] Max $50M red w/proceeds of Pub Eq Off'g. [6] Greater of 100 or amt based on formula. [7] Red at greater of 100 or amt based on formula. [8] See InterNorth. [9] (HRO)On 5-15-96 at 100. [10] Credit Sensitive Nts. [11] Int(9.2%-14%)subj to chge.

Source: Standard & Poor's *Bond Guide* (New York: Standard & Poor's Corporation, 1998). Reprinted with permission.

the capital letter corresponding to the month in which the bond ultimately matures. If interest is paid on the first of the month, only the first letters of the months are shown. If interest is paid on the fifteenth of the month, the number 15 appears after the second letter.[32]

In Figure 11-4, Enron Corporation has some notes with a 6.40 percent coupon maturing in the year 2006. The Interest Dates column shows jJ15. The company pays interest every six months, so jJ must correspond to January and July. June cannot be one of the months because the other payment month would then have to be December, which does not begin with *J*. The 15 indicates that the interest payment date is the fifteenth of the month. The actual maturity date of the bond is *July* 1, 2006, because the second *J* is capitalized.

The next column shows that S&P rates this bond BBB+, so it is an investment grade bond. The far three columns contain other useful information for the problem at hand. Here you find a recent market price for the bond, the current yield based on this market price, and the yield to maturity.

### *Solving the Problem*

The information contained in Figure 11-4 is only a small extract of the total bond universe from which you can pick. There are enough choices here, though, for you to come up with a reasonable solution to this portfolio construction problem.

You have two constraints: to choose bonds rated BBB or higher and to try to keep average maturities below fifteen years.

*Dividend increases should not be relied upon to meet a specific income requirement.*

Your task will be easier if you prepare a worksheet like the one in Table 11-10. Note that this table covers only the first six months of the year. This happens because the dividend and interest payments for the second half of the year will be the same as those from the first half. Bonds pay interest twice a year, and the first payment is the same amount as the second.[33] Similarly, most stocks pay dividends quarterly. Although firms do try to raise their dividends annually, it is not a good

**TABLE 11-10** MONTHLY INCOME REQUIREMENT WORKSHEET

| *Security* | *Price* | *Jan.* | *Feb.* | *March* | *April* | *May* | *June* |
|---|---|---|---|---|---|---|---|
| | | | *Equities* | | | | |
| 3,000 AAC | $ 51,000 | $ 380 | | | $ 380 | | |
| 1,000 BBL | 50,000 | 370 | | | 370 | | |
| 2,000 XXQ | 49,000 | | $ 400 | | | $ 400 | |
| 5,000 XZ | 52,000 | | | $270 | | | $270 |
| 7,000 MCDL | 53,000 | | | | | | |
| 1,000 ME | 49,000 | | 370 | | | 370 | |
| 2,000 LN | 51,000 | 500 | | | 500 | | |
| 4,000 STU | 47,000 | | | 260 | | | 260 |
| 3,000 LLZ | 49,000 | | 290 | | | 290 | |
| 6,000 MZN | 43,000 | 170 | | | 170 | | |
| Equities Subtotal | $494,000 | $1,420 | $1,060 | $530 | $1,420 | $1,060 | $530 |

[32]A few bonds have payment dates other than the first or the fifteenth, but this is rare.

[33]Actually, the two payments could differ by a penny. If a bond's coupon rate is not evenly divisible by 2, the payments will differ. A bond with a coupon of 8 1/8 percent, for instance, would have payments of $40.62 and $40.63 six months apart.

idea to count on a dividend increase to meet some income-need constraint.[34] The best practice is to assume that the dividends paid in the first two quarters will be repeated in the second two quarters until the company announces a change.

When you are finished with your portfolio, the total income generated in each of these months must be at least $4,000. For this customer, you should assume it is unacceptable to have $4,500 in one month and $3,500 the next, even though these two payments add up to an average of $4,000 per month.

The author of this book knows a portfolio manager who once prepared a portfolio similar to the one above to supplement a client's other income. In the client's case, the budgeted monthly income was $1,000. The manager's initial recommendation contained bonds that paid $2,000 in interest in April, but nothing in May. The client asked, "How am I supposed to live on nothing in May?" Attempts to explain the need to save part of April's check met with deaf ears. The client said, "You really cannot expect someone to be able to save part of April's check; no one has that much self-control." The portfolio manager wound up having to redo the portfolio to meet the monthly income requirement that had been specified in the first place.[35]

**Dealing with Accrued Interest and Commissions.** As we have seen, when you buy bonds, you must pay both a commission and any accrued interest that is due on them. Brokerage firms often maintain an inventory of bonds for resale to their customers and do so on a "net" basis. This means that the price you pay for the bond already includes a markup representing compensation to the broker. The trade confirmation shows no specific commission amount. In this example, assume that all bond prices are net prices.

Calculating accrued interest can be burdensome. If you wish, you can calculate accrued interest to the day, yielding a precise dollar amount. This is a tedious job, though, and it is seldom necessary to go to this much trouble.

An easier approach is to use the *mid-term heuristic*. When you finish your portfolio, interest will be generated fairly uniformly over the calendar year. This effectively means that some bonds will have just paid their interest, and you will have to pay very little accrued interest. Others will be just about to pay their interest, so the accrued interest bill will be large. Still other bonds will be near the middle of the interest rate cycle and will require payment of about one-half of an interest check. On average, you can assume that any given bond is midway through the payment cycle and that you have to pay half of one interest payment as accrued interest. In other words, if you buy a $10,000 par value bond with a 7 percent coupon, you assume that you must pay accrued interest of $7\% \times \$10{,}000 \times 1/2 \times 1/2 = \$175.00$. This is so because a 7 percent, $10,000 bond pays $700 per year, or $350 every six months. You should set aside half of this, or $175, to cover the "average" accrued interest bill.

**Choosing the Bonds.** The data in the worksheet in Table 11-10 show how much monthly income must be generated by the bonds to receive a total of at least

---

[34]Dividends, of course, also could decrease. Companies avoid reducing dividends if at all possible, so this normally occurs only during financial distress.

[35]He could also have used some type of money market account as a temporary haven for excess funds, paying them out the following month. The only disadvantage of this is the added managerial time required to make the withdrawal and issue the check.

**TABLE 11-11** BOND DATA ON THE INTERNET

- Bureau of the Public Debt Online (*http://www.publicdebt.treas.gov*). This site enables the purchase of U.S. government securities directly via the Treasury direct system.
- ConvertBond.com (*http://www.convertbond.com*). This is a Morgan Stanley Dean Witter site offering a variety of information sources on convertible bonds, including a pricing analysis on numerous issues. This is a fee service.
- Investing in Bonds.com (*http://www.investinginbonds.com*). This is an elementary educational site that provides a good overview of the fixed income market.
- Tradebonds.com (*http://www.tradebonds.com*). *Forbes* magazine calls this site "E-Trade for bonds." It provides an online brokerage for fixed income securities and includes a search feature by bond characteristic.
- Numa Web (*http://www.numa.com*). This site contains a handy convertible bond calculator.

Source: "Bonds," *Forbes*, 26 Feb 2001, 72.

$4,000 per month. Using the *Bond Guide*, you can select securities with the right payment months and BBB ratings or higher. Keep in mind the potential dangers of buying bonds that sell at a premium. Table 11-11 shows several useful Internet sources of bond data.

Table 11-12 presents one solution to the problem.[36] This portfolio meets the constraints, but can you improve it? The answer is yes. For one thing, all the bonds you bought sell at a slight premium. This means that their value will decline as maturity approaches. Whether or not this is a material consideration depends on the specific situation and the attitude of the client. In this example, assume that this is not cause for concern.

Another likely criticism is that you have not included very many different bond issues. Many fund managers would prefer to generate the income for a given month by using several different bond issues rather than a single one. If you check ten experienced fund managers, you will find that they do not all agree on whether or not this is a problem.

One definite problem is the fact that you failed to invest the entire amount you were given. Things do not always work out exactly even, but you began with $1,100,000 and still have $39,520 in cash. You might decide this is too much and that you need to buy more of something.

You essentially have two choices: buy more stock or buy more bonds. The primary objective of this portfolio is growth of income, and you meet the minimum income constraint. So it is probably best to spend the extra cash on something with growth potential rather than using it to generate more current income. Suppose you buy one more stock issue, leaving you with the final portfolio shown in Table 11-13.

This portfolio is clearly preferable to the initial solution, and it probably still could be improved. Someone might point out that the addition of the 2,000 shares of ERT moves the equity portion of the fund further from an equally weighted stock fund. This happens because the investment in ERT is somewhat less than the typical investment in the other issues.

[36]The table lists the par value purchased and the market value of each bond. For instance, $8,000 par of the Enron 6 5/8s03 with a market value of $8,450 indicates that each bond costs $1,056.25 and would be listed in the financial pages at a price of 105 5/8. Indicating par value and market value is a common convention in brokerage account statements.

**TABLE 11-12** INITIAL PROBLEM SOLUTION

| *Security* | *Price* | *Income Earned* | | | | | |
|---|---|---|---|---|---|---|---|
| | | *Jan.* | *Feb.* | *March* | *April* | *May* | *June* |
| | | ***Equities*** | | | | | |
| 3,000 AAC | $ 51,000 | $ 380 | | | $ 380 | | |
| 1,000 BBL | 50,000 | 370 | | | 370 | | |
| 2,000 XXQ | 49,000 | | $ 400 | | | $ 400 | |
| 5,000 XZ | 52,000 | | | $270 | | | $270 |
| 7,000 MCDL | 53,000 | | | | | | |
| 1,000 ME | 49,000 | | 370 | | | 370 | |
| 2,000 LN | 51,000 | 500 | | | 500 | | |
| 4,000 STU | 47,000 | | | 260 | | | 260 |
| 3,000 LLZ | 49,000 | | 290 | | | 290 | |
| 6,000 MZN | 43,000 | 170 | | | 170 | | |
| Equities subtotal | $494,000 | $1,420 | $1,060 | $530 | $1,420 | $1,060 | $530 |
| | | ***Bonds*** | | | | | |
| $80,000 Empire District Electric 7½s02 (A-) | $ 86,400 | $3,000 | | | | | |
| $80,000 Energen 8s07 (A) | 82,900 | | $3,200 | | | | |
| $100,000 Enhance Financial Services 6¾s03 (A+) | 105,500 | | | $3,370 | | | |
| $80,000 Enron Corp. 6⅝s03 (BBB+) | 84,500 | | | | $2,650 | | |
| $90,000 Enron Oil and Gas 6.7s06 (A-) | 97,200 | | | | | $3,010 | |
| $100,000 Englehard 6.95s28 (A) | 100,630 | | | | | | $3,470 |
| Bonds subtotal | $557,130 | $3,000 | $3,200 | $3,370 | $2,650 | $3,010 | $3,470 |
| Total Income Generated | | $4,420 | $4,260 | $3,900 | $4,070 | $4,070 | $4,000 |
| Portfolio Cost: | | | | | | | |
| Stock | | $ 494,000 | | | | | |
| Bonds | | $ 557,130 | | | | | |
| Accrued Interest | | 9,350 | | | | | |
| Stock Commissions | | 1,500 | | | | | |
| Total Cost | | $1,060,480 | | | | | |

**TABLE 11-13** FINAL PROBLEM SOLUTION

| *Security* | *Price* | | | *Income Earned* | | | |
|---|---|---|---|---|---|---|---|
| | | *Jan.* | *Feb.* | *March* | *April* | *May* | *June* |
| | | | | *Equities* | | | |
| 3,000 AAC | $ 51,000 | $ 380 | | | $ 380 | | |
| 1,000 BBL | 50,000 | 370 | | | 370 | | |
| 2,000 XXQ | 49,000 | | $ 400 | | | $ 400 | |
| 5,000 XZ | 52,000 | | | $270 | | | $270 |
| 7,000 MCDL | 53,000 | | | | | | |
| 1,000 ME | 49,000 | | 370 | | | 370 | |
| 2,000 LN | 51,000 | 500 | | | 500 | | |
| 4,000 STU | 47,000 | | | 260 | | | 260 |
| 3,000 LLZ | 49,000 | | 290 | | | 290 | |
| 6,000 MZN | 43,000 | 170 | | | 170 | | |
| 2,000 ERT | 30,000 | | | 200 | | | 200 |
| Equities subtotal | $524,000 | $1,420 | $1,060 | $730 | $1,420 | $1,060 | $730 |
| | | | | ***Bonds*** | | | |
| $80,000 Empire District Electric 7½s02 (A-) | $ 86,400 | $3,000 | | | | | |
| $80,000 Energen 8s07 (A) | 82,900 | | $3,200 | | | | |
| $100,000 Enhance Financial Services 6¾s03 (A+) | 105,500 | | | $3,370 | | | |
| $80,000 Enron Corp. 6⅝s03 (BBB+) | 84,500 | | | | $2,650 | | |
| $90,000 Enron Oil and Gas 6.7s06 (A-) | 97,200 | | | | | $3,010 | |
| $100,000 Englehard 6.95s28 (A) | 100,630 | | | | | | $3,470 |
| Bonds subtotal | $557,130 | $3,000 | $3,200 | $3,370 | $2,650 | $3,010 | $3,470 |
| Total Income Generated | | $4,420 | $4,260 | $4,100 | $4,070 | $4,070 | $4,200 |
| Portfolio Cost: | | | | | | | |
| Stock | | $ 524,000 | | | | | |
| Bonds | | $ 557,130 | | | | | |
| Accrued Interest | | 9,350 | | | | | |
| Stock Commissions | | 1,600 | | | | | |
| Total Cost | | $1,092,080 | | | | | |

PORTFOLIO MEMO

## Enron Bonds and Company Risk

You probably noticed that Figure 11-4 shows a number of Enron bonds with their BBB+ investment grade bond rating. This S&P *Bond Guide* extract is from 1998. Three years later Enron was an infamous household name representing the largest corporate bankruptcy in U.S. history. The fact that a respected rating agency such as Standard & Poor's blesses a bond does not immunize an investor from loss. *Company risk* is a term used to capture the chance of loss due to unanticipated, company-specific events. In early 2002 it was common for people to ask their portfolio manager, "Did we have any Enron in the portfolio?" If the answer was yes, most of the time an informed investor did not find fault with the portfolio manager. This was simply bad luck, just like owning stock in the company that insured the World Trade Center. You cannot completely eliminate investment risk unless you quit the game, and that is not a good long-term strategy.

A manager can virtually always improve an investment portfolio as time passes, and the next time you rebalance this fund, it would make sense to think about doing something about the relative proportion of ERT. For now, this is a reasonable solution.

**Overspending.** Fund managers should avoid overspending in the account. If a client gives you $1,100,000 to invest, it is not going to sit well if you announce a week later than you need another $5,000 because the portfolio cost slightly more than the client deposited with you.

*Never ask your client for more money.*

It does not matter why you overspent. You can tell your client about the need to pay accrued interest on the bonds and try to weasel out of the situation by explaining that she will get this money back with the next interest check. Chances are your client will still be irritated by the fact that you want more money. The money she gives you establishes another constraint in the portfolio construction problem. The total of all costs associated with the portfolio should not exceed this amount.

**What about Convertible Bonds?** Can convertible bonds have a place in a portfolio like the one you just completed? The answer is definitely yes. This portfolio's primary objective is growth of income. It needs to produce income, but the level of income it produces should increase each year.

Convertible bonds have a slightly lower coupon rate than otherwise comparable, nonconvertible issues. Investors are willing to take a reduced current yield in exchange for the possibility of capital gains resulting from appreciation in the value of the underlying security.[37]

People buy convertible bonds in hopes of price appreciation. This is the same reason you buy many stock issues. As long as you meet the income constraints in the

[37]Convertible bonds, for all practical purposes, come with a call option that gives their owner the right to buy shares of stock at a predetermined price (called the *conversion price*). This right becomes especially valuable if the value of the stock rises above the conversion price.

portfolio, convertible bonds can serve a useful role. In fact, some investors believe they should never buy stock without first checking to see whether there is an attractive convertible bond issue as an alternative.

## SUMMARY

Investors identify bonds by their issuer, their coupon, and their maturity year. They are classified according to the nature of the issuer and the security behind them. Some bonds provide a conversion feature whereby the bondholder can exchange them for another asset, usually shares of common stock in the same company.

The income stream associated with most bonds contains two components: an annuity stream and a principal repayment at maturity. The discount rate that equates the present value of the future cash flows with the current price of the bond is the bond's yield to maturity, a concept identical to the internal rate of return.

The yield to maturity calculation assumes that the bondholder can reinvest coupon proceeds at the bond's yield to maturity. If the reinvestment rate is different from this, the rate of return ultimately realized will be different.

When comparing bonds with investments that do not make semi-annual payments, the effective annual yield (or realized compound yield) helps make a meaningful comparison.

Bond investors watch both the level of interest rates and their term structure. These two values together describe the yield curve.

Bond risk has two major classifications. Price risks refer to the chance of monetary loss due to (1) the likelihood of the firm's defaulting on its loan payments and (2) the variability of interest rates. Convenience risks refer to additional demands on management time because of bond calls, because of the need to reinvest interest checks, or because of poor marketability of a particular issue.

Malkiel's interest rate theorems provide information about how bond prices change as interest rates change. The concept of duration is essential in understanding fixed income securities. Duration is a measure of interest rate risk; it combines Malkiel's theorems into a single statistic so that you can readily determine the relative risk of a set of bonds.

It is important to diversify the bond portion of a portfolio, but not for the same reasons you diversify an equity portfolio. Bonds are subject to market risk, but effects from default risk and interest rate risk overwhelm the effect of market risk.

You can diversify default risk by choosing several different bond issuers. Choosing a number of bonds issued by the same company does not accomplish this purpose because if the company defaults on one of these bonds, all of its bonds will be adversely affected.

Interest rate yield curves are normally upward sloping; the longer the term of a security, the higher is its yield, everything else being equal. Choosing longer maturities can increase expected return. Doing so also increases the amount of interest rate risk carried.

There is nothing wrong with buying callable bonds, but as a manager, you should avoid making wholesale use of a single issue. If a particular callable bond issue appears in many of the portfolios under management, a bond call results in considerable managerial time replacing the security.

In the selection of specific bonds for inclusion in a portfolio, common constraints include minimum yield, minimum grade, average maturity, periodic income needs, maturity timing requirements, and a desire to invest in a "socially responsible" manner.

When constructing a portfolio, you may need to choose components so that income is received according to a monthly schedule. You should not spend more than the amount received to invest and must remember the need to pay accrued interest when buying bonds.

## QUESTIONS

1. Is it possible to calculate the yield to maturity of a variable rate security? Why or why not?
2. Security A is a 7 percent Treasury bond that has four years of life remaining from its original term of twenty-five years. Security B is a 7 percent Treasury note that has four years of life left from its original term of five years. Is there any reason the two securities should not sell for the same price?
3. Comment on the following statement: In valuing a bond, it makes no difference how old the security is. All that matters is how much time is left until maturity.
4. What is the difference between a Treasury bond and a Treasury note?
5. What is meant by *convenience risk*? Is this important to the bond investor?
6. Comment on the following statement: Having a bond called is always good news because you realize a capital gain from retiring the bond at par.
7. Explain the term *parallel shift* as it applies to the yield curve.
8. Why should a convertible bond never sell for less than its conversion value?
9. The Sunshine Mining Company bonds mentioned in the chapter were convertible into 50 ounces of silver. What was the conversion price of these bonds?
10. Of what importance is the accrued interest phenomenon to a bond investor?
11. Standard & Poor's changes the rating of a particular bond from A to BBB. What effect would you expect this to have on the price of the bond?
12. What is the relationship between yield to maturity and realized compound yield?
13. Explain in 250 words or less why someone who buys a 14 percent coupon security at par has not locked in a 14 percent rate of return, even if the security makes all payments as promised.
14. The Standard & Poor's *Bond Guide* has a column entitled "Stock Value of Bond" in the convertible bond section. What do you think this means?
15. Why do you think the conversion feature of a bond is a one-way street?
16. Why is there no arbitrage if a bond sells for more than its conversion value?
17. In constructing a portfolio whose primary objective is income, which are you most concerned with, a bond's current yield or its yield to maturity?
18. Two bonds have identical durations. Would you expect them to have the same yield to maturity? Why or why not?
19. You look in *The Wall Street Journal* and see that a bond price has risen since last week. List four possible reasons for this.
20. Why is it okay to buy bonds selling at a premium? What caveats should be included with this statement?
21. Briefly explain the issue of buying callable bonds.

22. Do you think it is possible for an investor to lose money if a bond is called?
23. AA-rated bonds have higher expected returns than AAA-rated bonds. Similarly, A-rated bonds have higher returns than AA-rated bonds. How do you help a client decide how much default risk to take?
24. A bond is rated AA by Standard & Poor's. Its duration is 5.56 years. To understand this bond's riskiness, do you need to know the issuer?
25. What is the relationship between a bond's duration and its beta?
26. Why might bonds selling at a premium be especially advantageous to a pension fund?
27. Why do convertible bonds have lower coupons than otherwise similar nonconvertible bonds?
28. Are bond betas positive or negative? Explain your answer logically.
29. If a bond portfolio pays out all the income it generates, is reinvestment rate risk a concern? Why or why not?
30. When selecting bonds for a portfolio, what factors should be considered before choosing specific maturities and quality ratings?
31. Comment on the following statement: "In evaluating the suitability of a bond for a portfolio, I don't care about its maturity. Duration is all that matters."
32. Comment on the following statement: "I virtually never include AAA-rated bonds in portfolios I manage. AA-rated bonds are virtually as safe, and they yield more."
33. Callable bonds have a characteristic known as *negative convexity*. This is the characteristic of a bond whose price appreciation will be less than its price depreciation for a large change in yield. (This is opposite to the way noncallable bonds behave.) Thinking about a bond selling for near its call price, explain why it would have negative convexity.

## PROBLEMS

Assume that all bonds are $1,000 par value.

1. A person buys a 5-year, $1,000 certificate of deposit that carries a nominal rate of 9 percent, compounded semiannually. Six months after this purchase, a 4 1/2-year CD at the same bank offers a 9.5 percent annual rate, also compounded semiannually. How much difference is there in total interest paid by the two competing investments?
2. A seven-year bond with an 8 percent coupon rate has a yield to maturity of 9.15 percent. What is the current bond price?
3. Calculate the duration of the bond in Problem 2 using the following methods:
   **a.** The traditional method (Equation 11-11).
   **b.** The closed-form method (Equation 11-12); the Duration file on the text Website can be used to check your answer.
4. A zero coupon bond matures in eight years and sells for $500.
   **a.** Without doing any calculations, estimate its yield to maturity.
   **b.** Calculate the exact yield to maturity.
5. An 8 percent coupon bonds sells for $800 and matures in seven years. Calculate its yield to maturity, assuming the following:
   **a.** The bond pays a single annual interest payment.
   **b.** The bond pays interest semiannually.

6. A 7 1/4 percent bond is purchased 43 days after the most recent interest payment. How much accrued interest must be paid by the bond purchaser?
7. A 7 1/2 percent coupon bond matures in twenty-one years and sells for $750. What percentage of the bond's current value comes from the interest the bond pays over its remaining life?
8. Use the Duration file on the Strong Software for this problem: A consol that sells for par carries a 6 percent interest rate. What is its duration? (*Hint*: The answer is not infinity.)
9. A certain mortgage security has a yield to maturity of 13.5 percent but makes payments monthly. What is its effective annual yield?
10. The Chock Full O' Nuts (*CHF*) 7s2012 bonds have a conversion price of $9.54. What is their conversion ratio?
11. Suppose Chock Full O' Nuts common stock sells for $10 per share. What is the minimum value for which the bond in Problem 10 should sell?
12. If the *CHF* 7s2012 bond in Problem 10 sells for $1,100 when the common stock is at $10, what is the bond's premium over conversion value?
13. Using current data from *The Wall Street Journal*, construct the yield curve for U.S. Treasury securities.
14. Choose an interest-paying corporate bond from the financial pages. Calculate the proportion of its current value that comes from (a) interest and (b) principal repayment.
15. Smith invests $10,000; five years later she has $16,105.10. Jones invests $10,000 and withdraws $1,000 at the end of each of the next five years. Both claim to have earned 10 percent on the investment. How can this be if Smith earned $6,105.10 in interest whereas Jones received only $5,000?
16. Mr. Kenduskeag bought five of the *CHF* bonds described in Problem 10 on May 9, 2005. These pay interest on April 1 and October 1. He sold them on November 1, 2005. How much interest must he report to the Internal Revenue Service?
17. Two bonds both sell for par. One has a 10 percent yield to maturity and matures in four years. The other has an 11 percent yield to maturity and matures in two years.

    **a.** If you put half your money in each bond, what is your portfolio yield to maturity? (*Hint*: It is not 10.5 percent.)

    **b.** Under what circumstance would a portfolio split evenly between a 10 percent yield to maturity bond and an 11 percent yield to maturity bond have a portfolio yield to maturity of 10.5 percent?
18. Using recent prices for U.S. Treasury securities from *The Wall Street Journal*, calculate the forward interest rate, ${}_1f_{1.5}$.
19. Get a recent copy of the S&P *Bond Guide*, and using the yields to maturity shown in the guide, prepare a yield curve out to twenty years for (a) AAA-rated bonds, (b) BBB-rated bonds, and (c) CCC-rated bonds.
20. This problem uses the Bondport file on the Strong Software on the text Website. Given $200,000 to invest in a 100 percent bond portfolio with income as the primary objective, set up an investment grade portfolio that will generate as much income as possible but at least $1,000 per month.
21. You buy $5,000 par value of U.S. government 10¼s09 bonds at a price of 99 seventy-three days into the interest period. If you pay a commission to your broker of $40, how much does the trade cost you, including accrued interest?
22. You construct a $500,000 bond portfolio that yields 8.5 percent annually. Approximately one-twelfth of the annual income is received each month.

Using the heuristic mentioned in the chapter, how much accrued interest will you have to pay to assemble this portfolio?

23. Prepare a worksheet like Table 11-9 showing ten stocks that pay dividends semiannually.
24. Using current market prices, invest $500,000 in a growth of income/capital appreciation portfolio in which the asset allocation is 70 percent stock and 30 percent bonds.
    a. Calculate the portfolio beta.
    b. Use the Duration file on the Strong Software to calculate the duration of the bond portion.
    c. Estimate the annual income from the portfolio.
25. Repeat Problem 24 with the additional requirement that all stocks have a price/earnings ratio less than 20.
    a. Using *Value Line* data, what is your estimate of the total income the portfolio will produce five years from today?
    b. What average dividend growth rate is implied by your answer to Part a?
26. Repeat Problem 24 with the additional requirement that the portfolio generate at least $1,500 per month in income.
27. Construct a portfolio consisting of 100 percent convertible bonds with income as the primary objective and capital appreciation as the secondary objective. Prepare a table showing the size of each position, the bond rating, the market price, the conversion price, the current stock price, the current yield, and the yield to maturity.
28. Given $1 million to invest, construct a portfolio of at least five zero coupon bonds that mature in the year 2010.
    a. Estimate duration for this portfolio.
    b. What will be the approximate value of the portfolio at the end of the year 2010?
    c. What compound annual growth rate does your answer to Part b imply?
29. Assume commissions are $8 per $1,000 par value. Suppose you are given $525,000 to invest in a junk bond portfolio. Using 15 different bonds and the mid-term accrued interest heuristic, build the portfolio and show:
    a. Its income schedule.
    b. Its average duration.
    c. Its total cost.
30. Go to the website *http://www.tradebonds.com*. Using the search feature, identify three bonds with a maturity of between 10 and 12 years that are rated BB or B. Rank order these as an investment and explain your reasoning.
31. A client's federal tax rate is 28 percent; his state tax rate is 8 percent.

| | *Treasury Bond* | *Corporate Bond* | *Municipal Bond* |
|---|---|---|---|
| | *(Yield 5.5%)* | *(Yield 6.5%)* | *(Yield 3.3%)* |
| Federal tax | Taxable | Taxable | Tax Exempt |
| State tax | Tax Exempt | Taxable | Tax Exempt |

Which of the three bonds would produce the most after-tax income for the customer?

32. Using the website *http://www.tradebonds.com* or some other data source, determine the yield spread between
    a. Twenty-year Treasury bonds and ten-year Treasury bonds.

b. Twenty-year Treasury bonds and one-year T bills.
c. Five-year Treasury bonds and five-year AAA municipal securities.
d. Five-year AAA corporate bonds and five-year BBB corporate bonds.

33. Use the dynamic yield curve tool at *http://www.stockcharts.com/charts/YieldCurve.html* to identify a period when the yield curve was
    a. unusually steep.
    b. relatively flat.
    c. inverted (some short-term rates higher than longer-term ones).

## INTERNET EXERCISE

Compute the current market price of a bond with the following features: face value = $1,000, coupon rate = 5.25%, current market rate = 3.5%, months until maturity = 30. Use the Web-based *Smart Money* calculator at *http://www.smartmoney.com/onebond/index.cfm?story=bondcalculator* to do this. After entering these inputs, determine the effect of a 2 percent up/down interest rate move on the bond price.

Go to the convertible bond calculator at *http://www.numa.com/derivs/ref/calculat/cb/calc-cba.htm*. Notice the input fields as determinants of the value of a convertible bond. Compute the price of a convertible bond using the default values in the input fields. How much of the value of this bond is attributed to the existence of the call feature?

## FURTHER READING


Alexander, Gordon J. "Applying the Market Model to Long-Term Corporate Bonds." *Journal of Financial and Quantitative Analysis*, December 1980, 1063–1080.

Altman, Edward I., and Scott A. Nammacher. *Investing in Junk Bonds*. New York: Wiley, 1987.

Ang, James S., and K.A. Patel. "Bond Rating Methods: Comparison and Validation." *Journal of Finance*, May 1975, 631–640.

Babcock, Guilford C. "Duration as a Link between Yield and Value." *Journal of Portfolio Management*, Summer 1984, 58–65.

Best, Peter, Alistair Byrne, and Antti Ilmanen. "What Really Happened to U.S. Bond Yields." *Financial Analysts Journal*, May/June 1998, 41–49.

Bierwag, G.O. "Immunization, Duration, and the Term Structure of Interest Rates." *Journal of Financial and Quantitative Analysis*, December 1977, 725–742.

Bierwag, G.O., George Kaufman, and Alden Toevs. "Duration: Its Development and Use in Bond Portfolio Management." *Financial Analysts Journal*, July/August 1983, 15–35.

Bierwag, G.O., George G. Kaufman, Robert L. Schweitzer, and Alden Toevs. "The Art of Risk Management in Bond Portfolios," *Journal of Portfolio Management*, Spring 1981, 27–36.

Chua, Jess H. "A Closed-Form Formula for Calculating Bond Duration." *Financial Analysts Journal*, May/June 1984, 76–78.

Dialynas, Chris P. "Bond Yield Spreads Revisited." *Journal of Portfolio Management*, Winter 1988, 57–62.

Fabozzi, Frank J., and Irving M. Pollack, eds. *The Handbook of Fixed Income Securities*. Homewood, Ill.: Dow Jones–Irwin, 1987.

Fair, Ray C., and Burton G. Malkiel. "The Determinants of Yield Differentials between Debt Instruments of the Same Maturity." *Journal of Money, Credit and Banking*, November 1971, 733–749.

Fielitz, Bruce D. "Calculating the Bond Equivalent Yield for T-Bills." *Journal of Portfolio Management*, Spring 1983, 58–60.

Fisher, Lawrence. "Determinants of Risk Premiums on Corporate Bonds." *Journal of Political Economy*, June 1959, 217–237.

Fuller, Russell J., and John W. Settle. "Determinants of Duration and Bond Volatility." *Journal of Portfolio Management*, Summer 1984, 66–72.

Homer, Sidney, and Martin Liebowitz. *Inside the Yield Book: New Tools for Bond Market Strategy*. Englewood Cliffs, N.J.: Prentice-Hall, 1972.

Hopewell, Michael H., and George Kaufman. "Bond Price Volatility and Term to Maturity: A Generalized Respecification." *American Economic Review*, September 1973, 749–753.

Howe, Jane Tripp. *Junk Bonds: Analysis and Portfolio Strategies*. Chicago: Probus Publishing, 1988.

Jahankhani, Ali, and George E. Pinches. "Duration and the Nonstationarity of Systematic Risk for Bonds." *Journal of Financial Research*, Summer 1982, 151–160.

Jones, Charles P. "Probable Bond Returns: The Lessons of History." *Journal of Investing*, Fall 1996, 69–73.

Kalotay, A.J. "On the Structure and Valuation of Debt Refundings." *Financial Management*, Spring 1982, 41–42.

Kane, Edward J., and Burton G. Malkiel. "The Term Structure of Interest Rates: An Analysis of a Survey of Interest Rate Expectations." *Review of Economics and Statistics*, August 1967, 343–355.

Macaulay, Frederick R. *Some Theoretical Problems Suggested by the Movements of Interest Rates, Bond Yields, and Stock Prices in the United States since 1856*. New York: National Bureau of Economic Research, 1938.

Malkiel, Burton G. "Expectations, Bond Prices, and the Term Structure of Interest Rates." *Quarterly Journal of Economics*, May 1962, 197–218.

McConnell, J.J., and G.G. Schlarbaum. "Returns, Risks, and Pricing of Income Bonds, 1956–1976 (Does Money Have an Odor?)." *Journal of Business*, January 1981, 33–64.

Percival, John. "Corporate Bonds in a Market Model Context," *Journal of Business Research*, October 1974, 461–467.

Pogue, Thomas F., and Robert M. Soldofsky. "What's in a Bond Rating?" *Journal of Financial and Quantitative Analysis*, June 1969, 201–228.

Reilly, Frank K., and Michael D. Joehnk. "The Association between Market-Determined Risk Measures for Bonds and Bond Ratings." *Journal of Finance*, December 1976, 1387–1403.

Reilly, Frank K., and Rupinder Sidhu. "The Many Uses of Bond Duration." *Financial Analysts Journal*, July/August 1980, 58–72.

Reilly, Frank K., David J. Wright, and Kam C. Chan. "Bond Market Volatility Compared to Stock Market Volatility." *Journal of Portfolio Management*, Fall 2000, 82–92.

Sharpe, William F. "Bonds vs. Stocks: Some Lessons from Capital Market Theory." *Financial Analysts Journal*, November/December 1973, 74–80.

Stigum, Marcia, and Frank J. Fabozzi. *Bond and Money Market Instruments*. Homewood, Ill.: Dow Jones–Irwin, 1987.

Van Horne, James C. "Called Bonds: How Does the Investor Fare?" *Journal of Portfolio Management*, Summer 1980, 58–61.

Weinstein, Mark I. "The Systematic Risk of Corporate Bonds." *Journal of Financial and Quantitative Analysis*, September 1981, 257–278.

# 12 The Role of Real Assets

*Gold still represents the ultimate form of payment in the world.*

***Alan Greenspan***

## Key Terms

assessed value
biological risk
bullion
cap rate
developed property
discounted cash flow (DCF) approach
economic risk
equity REIT
fee simple value
financial asset
gold certificate
hybrid REIT
intrinsic value
investment value
leased fee value
leasehold value
liquidity risk
London fix
management risk
market comparables approach
market value
mortgage REIT
product class shift
productivity risk
real asset
real estate investment trust (REIT)
regulatory risk
replacement cost approach
stumpage
TIMO
troy ounce
undeveloped (raw) property

## Introduction

Modern investment decisions involve much more than traditional stocks and bonds issues. Falling in love with the status quo can be fatal to a portfolio manager. As an example, evidence indicates a significant factor in the problems of the U.S. savings and loan industry during the 1990s was due to the failure of many of these institutions to keep up with developments in modern finance. Some investors made millions of dollars during the dot.com craze by thinking outside the box while others lost most of their investments by ignoring traditional principles of valuation. Ignorance of concepts such as duration and how futures and options can help manage risk contributed to the demise of these institutions. Today's executives must keep pace with changes in the industry if they want to survive, or if they hope to take their firm past the "mom-and-pop" stage. A firm's rationalization of waiting for someone else to do it first because it sees itself as a "conservative institution" is no longer valid.

This chapter looks at real estate and gold, with special attention to the potential of timberland. Not every portfolio can or should invest in these. The evidence is clear, though, that assets like these are assuming an increased role in some of the country's largest pension funds and in private investor portfolios. As stated in an article in *Forbes*, "Rather than prohibiting trustees from putting money into so-called 'speculative' investments, . . . the American Law Institute's new guidelines allow trustees greater freedom to diversify investments across the entire spectrum of possibilities."[1]

Fifteen years ago the finance literature had virtually nothing on the topic of timberland. Since then, articles have appeared in academic publications such as the *Financial Analysts Journal* and in trade journals such as *Pensions and Investments*. Papers on timberland have been presented at the annual meetings of many academic associations.

Before considering specific information about these investment alternatives, it is useful to note the distinction between *financial assets* and *real assets*. Most portfolio investments are **financial assets.** These are familiar securities such as shares of common stock, corporate bonds, and bank certificates of deposit.

If someone buys one hundred shares of General Motors (GM) stock, this is an asset on his personal balance sheet. These same shares, however, show up on the right-hand side of the GM corporate balance sheet in the Shareholders' Equity section. They are not assets from GM's perspective. Similarly, if you deposit $1,000 in your bank and buy a certificate of deposit, the CD is an asset to you; it is a liability for the bank. The key characteristic of a financial asset is that for each such asset, somewhere a corresponding liability exists. Financial assets are on two balance sheets, as an asset for someone and as a liability for someone else.

*Financial assets have a corresponding liability; real assets do not.*

**Real assets**, in contrast, do not have a corresponding liability, although one may be created to finance the purchase of the asset. If an investor owns 100 acres of land or 100 troy ounces of gold, these are assets to the investor but not liabilities to anyone else. If the investor borrows money to finance the purchase, however, the debt contract is a financial asset to the lender.

Real estate purchases are normally leveraged, and the investor might need a mortgage in order to buy the land. The mortgage is an asset to the bank and a liability to the borrower. The investor issued the mortgage for her own convenience; it is not an essential part of the ownership of real assets.

# Real Estate in General

## *Investment Characteristics*

Tradition and folklore widely acclaim real estate as a good investment.[2] Until the recession of 1991, property values in many parts of the country rose with such regularity that it seemed real estate investment had approached the mythical sure bet.[3]

[1]"From Grave to Cradle," *Forbes*, October 1, 1990, 86.

[2]While *real estate* is the term in popular jargon, *real property* is preferable. Real estate is the tangible asset, whereas real property is a legal interest in real estate. We own real property. The value of our real property is a function of our interest in the property, which may be less than fee simple. This becomes important with syndications, common and undivided ownership, timber rights, easements, and so on.

[3]Try telling this to someone in the Southwest or the Northeast in early 1992, however, or to the savings and loans and commercial banks that invested heavily in commercial property at the start of the economic slowdown.

FIGURE 12-1

Land Distribution in the United States (2002 Data)

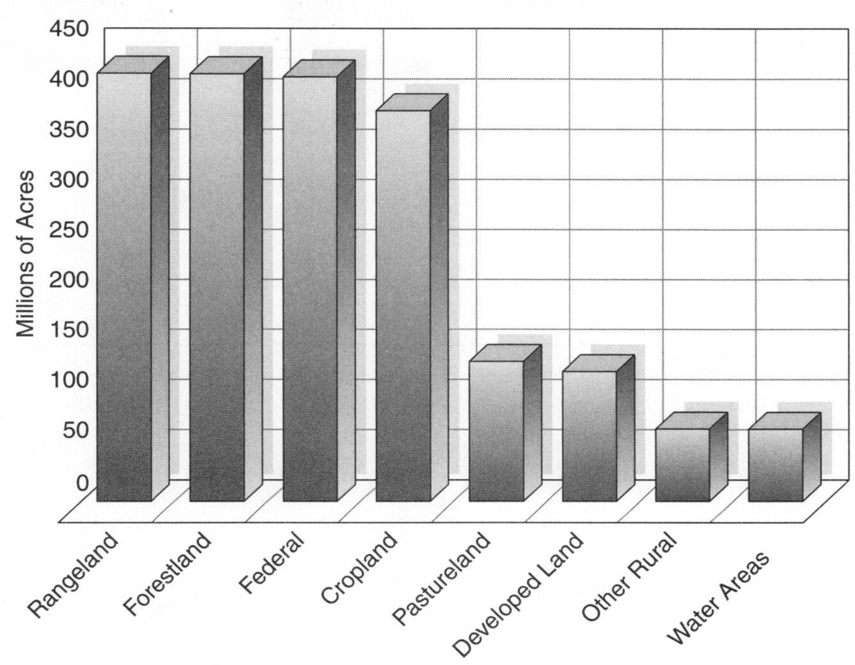


Source: U.S. Bureau of the Census, *Statistical Abstract of the United States*, 2004–2005.

*Buy land. They ain't making any more of the stuff.*
Will Rogers

Most real estate textbooks cite three fundamental characteristics of land early in the discussion. Land is (1) immobile, (2) indestructible, and (3) nonfungible.[4] Land obviously cannot be moved. It has historically been considered indestructible, although our casual attitude toward trash and toxic waste has made some areas unusable for most purposes. Land is also nonfungible, meaning that every plot is unique. The house lot next door is not equivalent to yours, nor is your garden identical to mine, even though they are exactly the same size and grow the same vegetables. Figure 12-1 shows the distribution of land by usage category throughout the United States.

Investors typically think of land as a long-term investment, although it does not have to be. Small firms often buy timberland, hoping to liquidate the timber and sell the land over a fairly short time horizon. This is especially true when the highest and best use of the land is not as timberland but for development or the extraction of minerals. Institutional timberland owners are seldom liquidators. The majority of them look for a mix of annual cash flows and long-term price appreciation. Table 12-1 shows five general categories of real estate: residential, commercial, industrial, farm, and special purpose.

## Developed and Undeveloped Property

Real estate is either *developed property* or *undeveloped property*. **Developed property** is land with improvements on it; **undeveloped (raw) property** has no improvements. Investors generally purchase developed property for its income-producing characteristics

[4]Note that while these characteristics apply to land, they do not apply to real estate in general, which includes bridges, buildings, fences, and so on.

**TABLE 12-1** CATEGORIES OF REAL ESTATE

| *Residential* | *Commercial* | *Industrial* | *Farm* | *Special Purpose* |
|---|---|---|---|---|
| Owner occupied | Office buildings | Light manufacturing | Timberland | Cemeteries |
| Rental | Store properties | Heavy manufacturing | Pastureland | Churches |
| | Lofts | Mining | Ranches | Government properties |
| | Theaters | | Orchards | Golf courses |
| | Garages | | Farmland | Parks |
| | Hotels and motels | | | Public buildings and streets |

**FIGURE 12-2**

Pension Fund Investment in Real Estate

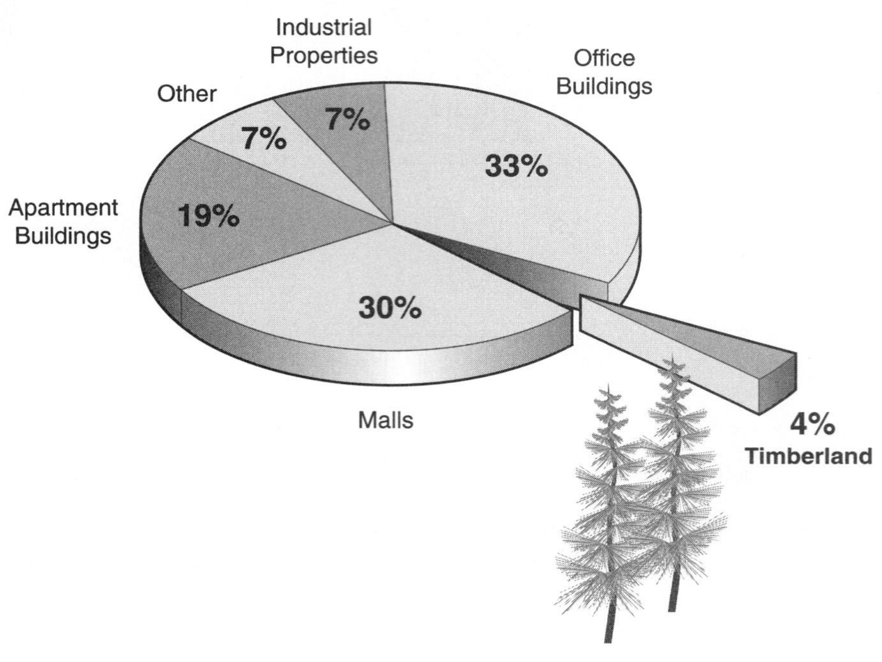


Source: *Southern Journal of Supplied Forestry* by Harris/DeForest/Futch/Cubbage. © 1989 by Society of American Foresters. Reproduced with permission of Society of American Foresters in the format Textbook via Copyright Clearance Center.

and for the tax advantage stemming from depreciation of buildings on the land. Shopping malls, apartment complexes, and office buildings are good examples. Most real estate limited partnerships invest primarily in developed property.

The motives for the purchase of undeveloped property are more varied. They include outright speculation; timber, crop, or livestock production; and the actual production of subdivided lots for resale or development. A person who buys coastal property in the expectation of rising property values is speculating via the acquisition of undeveloped property and probably believes that someday it will be developed.

### *Pension Fund Investment in Real Estate*

The U.S. pension fund industry has nearly $100 billion invested in one form or another of real estate. Figure 12-2 shows the approximate distribution of pension fund real estate investments by type of asset.

Pension funds often acquire real estate when their cash inflows are larger than expected. Ronald R. Roessler, the head of real estate investing for AT&T, sharply increased the fund's property buying in 1980 when "$200 million a month was coming in to invest. We had no place to put the money."[5]

In 1990 the average pension fund had about 4 percent of its assets invested in real estate. Ten years later the percentage for many funds was closer to 20 percent. A popular and convenient method of real estate investment is via a **real estate investment trust (REIT)**, which is essentially a closed-end investment company that purchases real property and divides the ownership interest into shares. Many REITs trade on the New York Stock Exchange. There is more on this later in the chapter.

In many respects timberland is the epitome of undeveloped property. What could be more undeveloped than the woods? Timberland as a pure investment, however, can definitely be income producing, as we will see.

## Timberland in Particular

Timberland is an often overlooked but very viable form of real estate for most large portfolios. It is also an interesting asset because there is so much of it. The United States encompasses about 2.27 billion acres, of which about 20.9 percent are timberland.[6] This asset has real potential to account for a major share of the expected increased investment in real estate.

There is a technical distinction between *timberland* and *forestland*. The federal definition of forestland is "land of at least one acre which is at least 10% stocked by forest trees." Timberland is "land covered by forest capable of producing twenty cubic feet per acre of industrial wood annually." Timberland is more important that forestland as an investment asset because the investor is mostly interested in the income stream that comes from the periodic harvest of some of the trees.

### *Institutional Interest in Timberland*

Institutional interest in timberland ownership is clearly on the rise. Investment houses and other corporations have designed innovative forms of ownership to make timberland ownership more convenient. John Hancock, The Campbell Group, UBS, Forest Investment Associates, and TimberVest are among the major players offering public limited partnerships and closed-end investment companies in timberland. A few major insurance companies offer separate timber accounts to pension funds, and securitized units of the timberlands of forest product companies are available. (An asset is *securitized* when it can be traded via a marketable certificate showing ownership of the asset.)

A November 1987 survey of 1,500 pension funds and other tax-exempt funds identified twenty-two that collectively owned approximately $222 million worth of timberland.[7] These funds indicated that they expected to hold their investment for an average of 10 to 15 years. In 1995 financial institutions held $3.5 billion in timberland. Two years later the figure was up 57 percent to $5.5 billion. The 2004 figure was about $10.0 billion.

[5]"Land Ho! Pensions Race for Real Estate," *The Wall Street Journal*, September 19, 1989, C1.

[6]*Statistical Abstract of the United States 2004–2005*.

[7]Reported in Thomas Harris, Jr., Christopher DeForest, Scott Futch, and Frederick Cubbage. "A Survey of Pension Fund Investments in Timberland." *Southern Journal of Applied Forestry* 13, no. 4, 1989, 188–192.

*We need to be able to explain timberland to potential investors in exactly the same terms as stocks, bonds, and other investments.*
Clark S. Binkley, Hancock Timber Resource Group

A *Pension Fund News* report on timberland describes the "new respectability" of timberland investments.[8] The article reports that several timberland investment managers routinely receive requests for information about this investment, whereas in years past timberland was an alternative about which they had to educate and convince potential investors.

Late in 2001 Harvard Management (which manages the Harvard University endowment fund) voted to put 6 percent of its $18.3 billion portfolio, or about $1.1 billion, into timberland. According to Jack Meyer, president of Harvard Management Company, "Harvard is interested in timber because it has provided an attractive rate of return over the years, and it gives the portfolio added diversification."[9] Contemporaneously, the Massachusetts Pension Reserves Investment Management Board voted to put 2 percent of its $29 billion portfolio in timber.

Several examples of public timberland investment funds are the John Hancock ForesTREE funds I–V, the U.S. Timberlands Company LP (*TIMBZ, Nasdaq*), and Plum Creek (*PCL, NYSE*). Plum Creek is an *REIT* invested predominantly in timberland operations. It is as close to a pure play timberland investment as an individual investor with limited capital will find.

Among the institutions in the Hancock funds are the Oregon Public Employees Retirement System, the Fire and Police Association of Colorado, and the Orange County (California) Retirement System.[10] People in the know often refer to timberland funds by the acronym **TIMO** for timberland investment management organization. A TIMO is similar to a closed-end investment company, although they are very illiquid because of the long investment horizon associated with timber. They usually involve a minimum investment of around $5 million per investor. In 2004, TIMOs managed timberland worth about $14.4 billion.

## A Timberland Investment Primer

This section is a primer on the varying aspects of timberland as an asset, on its risks and potential returns, and on its special appeal as a risk-reducing portfolio component.

**Timberland As an Asset.** The different motivations for timberland investment generally fall into one of three groups: timberland as collateral, timberland as a strategic investment, or timberland as a pure investment.

***Timberland As Collateral.*** The use of timberland as collateral has a long heritage. Life insurance companies and the Federal Land Bank both routinely secure loans, either partially or fully, with timberland, and they have done so for many years. In fact, the first leveraged buyout probably occurred with timberland, the forest itself being used as collateral for the loan used to acquire the land.

*Timberland is a strategic investment when owning it helps ensure the long-term viability of a company.*

***Timberland as a Strategic Investment.*** Timberland serves as a strategic investment when owning it helps ensure the long-term viability of a company or reduces the volatility of its cash flows. This motivation is especially evident in regions where the forest industry is strong and depends heavily on assured raw material supplies. In Maine, for instance, the forest industry employs 7 percent of the total work force and constitutes 12 percent of the gross state product. The state is 88 percent forested, the highest percentage in the nation. Approximately 8.5 million acres of commercial

---

[8]Richard F. Stolz. "Sponsors Eye Timberland Investments." *Pension Fund News*, May/June 1989.

[9]Dave Kovaleski. "Harvard, MassPRIM Put Funds Into Forest." *Pensions and Investments*, October 15, 2001, 19.

[10]Terry Williams, "Interest in Timberland Growing," *Pensions and Investments*, May 11, 1992, 22.

timberland (50 percent of the state total) is owned by forest product companies such as Bowater, Scott Paper, and Champion International. This ownership helps ensure a constant supply of timber for the company's mills.

Timberland contributes peripherally to another important Maine industry: tourism. Forest product companies own most of Maine's deep woods. These firms maintain logging roads and means of access to some of the country's most pristine salmon streams and wilderness camping areas. If this forestland were in the hands of private individuals or nonforest product firms, land ownership likely would be fragmented into many smaller parcels. Substantial amounts of these parcels would be unavailable for harvest, and much more subdivision and development would occur. More waterfront camps would be built, Ford pickups would be displaced by BMWs, and the special appeal of the area would diminish.

*For further in-depth information about the investment characteristics of timber, refer to http://www.campbellgroup.com/timber_invest/default.htm*

*Timberland can be purchased as collateral, as a strategic investment, or as a pure portfolio investment.*

***Timberland as a Pure Investment.*** The fund manager is most concerned with timberland as a pure investment. This means the property is held for its own investment merits rather than as part of a strategic plan or to assist in project financing. This is the focus of the following discussion.

**Timberland Investors.** Table 12-2 shows how the relative ownership of timberland has changed since 1952. The largest current holders of timberland for pure investment purposes are the California Public Employees Retirement System ($1.25 billion), John Hancock Financial Services ($2.5 billion), and the New Hampshire State Employees Retirement System.

**Timberland Returns.** There is a distinction between *timber* and *land*. Timber grows on the land and is sold and renewed. While still growing, timber is referred to as **stumpage.** The owner can also sell the land, but that is a final step.

*The value of a tree comes from its volume, its diameter, and the market price for its species.*

Three components make up the value of a particular stand of timber: (1) the volume of wood on the acreage, (2) the size and quality of the trees, and (3) the market price of the species of forest products. Small-diameter or defective trees are suitable only for fuel, pulpwood, and making fiberboard. Medium-sized trees that can be used for sawtimber can be four or more times as valuable as a comparable volume of pulpwood. The largest and best-quality trees can be used for veneer, and these sell for a substantial premium over younger trees. The market price of the forest products is not particularly volatile, but it obviously affects the value of standing timber.

A timberland investor's return is a function of four principal factors. First, as with any investment, the acquisition cost and selling price are the most important. Second, site productivity, or the ability of a site to grow timber, is determined by weather, soil conditions, microsite factors, and other natural phenomena. *Microsite*

**TABLE 12-2** TIMBERLAND OWNERSHIP IN THE UNITED STATES (THOUSANDS OF ACRES)

| *Owner Class* | *1952* | *1970* | *2002* |
|---|---|---|---|
| Federal | 103,124 | 107,108 | 147,278 |
| State, County, and Municipal | 27,216 | 29,010 | 37,559 |
| Forest Industry, Farmer Owned, and Other Private | 358,269 | 363,576 | 356,261 |
| Total Timberland | 488,609 | 499,697 | 541,098 |
| Total Forestland | 664,194 | 753,549 | 748,923 |

Source: "Agricultural Statistics" 1956, 1976, 2004, United States Department of Agriculture, U.S. Government Printing Office.

*factors* refer to conditions that make a section of land different from the surrounding terrain. Common examples include coves, where the soil tends to be deeper, moist, and well drained; frost pockets, which are deleterious to plant growth; and depressions, which provide protection from prevailing winds. The timber on some mature forestland in remote parts of the country has little harvest value because of the extraordinary costs (such as those involved in making a road) the owner would incur to get it to market.

Substantial price differences occur by geographic region, too. In the United States there are three timberland regions: the Pacific Northwest, the Northeast, and the South. Property in the Pacific Northwest is worth much more than property in the other two regions because the temperate rainforest is a much better climate for tree growth, and so the trees grow faster. All else being equal, this fundamental difference results in an acre of timberland in Oregon selling for perhaps eight times as much as an otherwise similar acre in Maine.

*Timberland is often measured in hectares. A hectare is 10,000 square meters, or 2.47 acres.*

Third, management competence is an important factor in return on investment because optimum silvicultural practices and management strategies can greatly affect returns. Finally, market price ultimately determines the return, but unlike most agricultural products, timber involves substantial investor discretion in regard to time of harvest. If the market price is low, the trees can usually be left to get larger (and more valuable) until the market price rises. Most high-quality timber investments increase in volume by at least 3 percent annually.

It is important to consider the importance of the biological growth rate of timber as it affects the investor's total return. For instance, if timber prices fall by 5 percent one year but the volume of timber in a particular stand increases by 5 percent, the aggregate value of the investment has not materially changed.[11] The fact that timberland produces more of itself (it is its own factory) is a very attractive characteristic of the investment. Like any factory, though, timberlands have costs such as taxes and management expenses.

The price of timber is also a function of the relative size of the trees on the land. Small trees may be useful only for firewood or paper pulp. Slightly larger trees can be used for chair legs, spindles, and other small carpentry or furniture applications. As the trees get larger, they move into the sawtimber class and are cut into planks and dimension lumber. The largest trees are in the veneer class and are used in the finest furniture.

A trained forest appraiser knows to look for trees undergoing a **product class shift,** which occurs when trees are at the upper end of one class and are about to move into the next, more valuable class. The difference in price for a given volume of veneer-class timber versus sawtimber can be as much as 4 to 1. Investors who purchased timberland at sawtimber prices and resold at veneer prices a few years later have made significant profits (Figure 12-3).

One of the largest portfolio investors in timberland is the John Hancock Mutual Life Insurance Company. This firm has invested in timberland for over fifty years. This type of investment may provide certain tax advantages. In general, expenses incurred in the management of timberland can be used to offset nontimber income. Also, the income from the investment is deferred until a time chosen by the investor, when the forest is cut.

Forestland also can be an inflation hedge. Over the long run, the returns to forestland have exceeded the inflation rate. One study indicates that the real rate of return on an "all forest products" index over the period 1870 to 1973 was 1.39 percent.

[11]This assumes the product composition has not changed. Larger trees are usually worth more per unit volume.

FIGURE 12-3 Components of Timberland Total Return

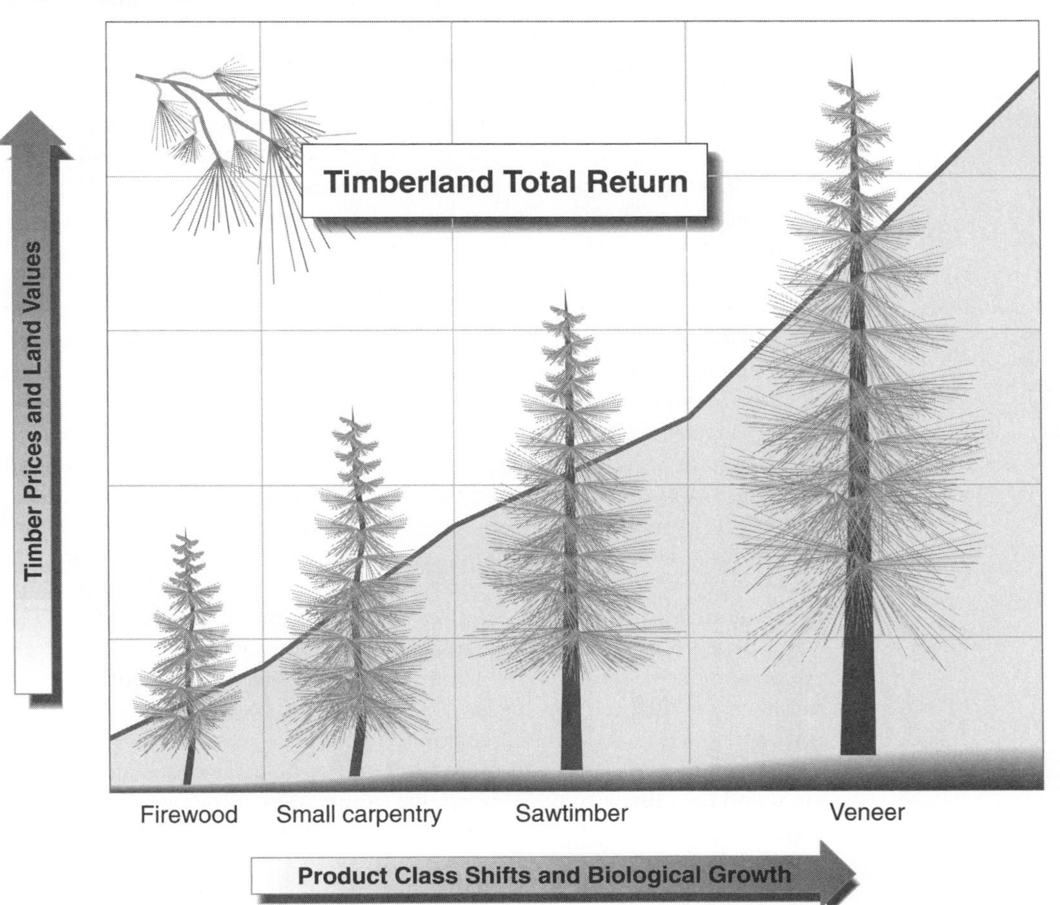


**Timberland Risks.** Timberland risks fall into two groups. **Biological risks** include fire, insects, disease, productivity, and wind. **Economic risks** cover quality, liquidity, demand, price, management practices, and changes in the regulatory environment.

***Biological Risks.*** One obvious risk to timberland is loss due to a natural event. Losses from fire, drought, windstorms, disease, or insect damage are generally uninsurable. This possibility is troubling to the potential investor, but fortunately it is not generally a problem on well-managed land.

The Weyerhaeuser Company, for instance, operates 700,000 acres in Mississippi and Alabama. Its average annual losses from biological risks have been less than 2 percent.[12] A study commissioned by the Weyerhaeuser Corporation found that timberland losses due to fire, insects, and disease total less than 0.2 percent per year.

[12]James F. Webb. "Risks Associated with Timberland Investments and the Timing of the Investment to Minimize the Risk." Paper presented at the Forest Products Research Society Conference, Milwaukee, April, 1987, 27–29.

Compare this with commercial real estate, where vacancy rates average between 5 and 10 percent. According to an article in *Smartmoney*, even after the eruption of Mount St. Helens, landowners were still able to sell 80 percent of the damaged timber. In short, biological risk is minimal.

**Productivity risk** refers to the possibility that a stand of timber will not produce the anticipated volume of wood. This may be because of biological factors such as species competition, drought, or disease. The proliferation of hardwood species in a spruce or pine plantation, for instance, would be a significant deterrent to productivity. Their presence inhibits the growth of the softwoods, and reducing the hardwood competition can be costly.

*Pacific Northwest timber prices climbed 60.5 percent and 27.3 percent in 1992 and 1993, respectively, when the U.S. government retired federal forest reserves in order to preserve spotted owl habitat.*

***Economic Risks.*** Liquidity risks relate to management, liquidity, and regulatory risk. One economic risk for timberland is substantial **management risk.** This means that poor management practices can seriously erode the value of timberland. In parts of the Northeast, for example, the soil is shallow and rocky. If trees depend on mutual canopy support to stay erect and someone then partially cuts (thins) the forest in an inappropriate fashion, the overhead support is lost, and the first heavy windstorm may cause most of the remaining timber to blow down and be lost.[13]

**Liquidity risk** is a very real concern, largely because of the relatively limited market for timber and timberland. This is exacerbated in premerchantable stands that must grow for years before the trees can be converted to forest products. Also, the nonfungible character of the asset makes investment analysis difficult: Investors cannot simply look in *The Wall Street Journal* to learn what a stand of trees is worth. A comparable sale analysis, which appraisers perform for residential real estate, is not always available. This means that substantial uncertainty exists regarding the true market value of premerchantable timberland.

**Regulatory risk** stems from statutes and ordinances that limit forest management and land use options. This risk has grown in importance recently to become a major concern among investors. Examples include the issues of the spotted owl, bans on clear-cutting, and wetland zoning.

*The lack of a standard index for timberland values was a historic impediment to portfolio investment in timberland, but this has changed.*

**Problem of Lack of Information.** Until recently there was relatively little publicly available quantitative information about timberland performance. There is a potential apples and oranges problem, too. Timberland is not a fungible asset, and its characteristics vary in different parts of the country. Figure 12-4 shows timberland returns by region since 1960.

Wachovia Timberland Investment Management began publishing an index called the *Timberland Performance Index (TPI)* in 1994. This index consists of weighted quarterly returns from property that Wachovia and its competitors manage. Wachovia reports the index back to 1991, and since 1996 the Warnell School of Forest Resources at the University of Georgia maintains and updates the Timber Mart South (Southern United States) index. Information is available at *http://www. tmart-south.com/tmart. Log Lines* publishes a separate index for the Pacific Northwest. The National Council of Real Estate Investment Fiduciaries (NCREIF) also publishes a timberland index based on property values rather than investment fund values.

Timberland indexes also have a functional problem. It is inappropriate to prepare an index based on a past series of market prices for timber. This is so because

[13]This fact is part of the motivation for clear-cutting, which is a complicated social and environmental issue. Clear-cutting is sometimes the best way to manage portions of a forest.

FIGURE 12-4

Regional Timberland Performance

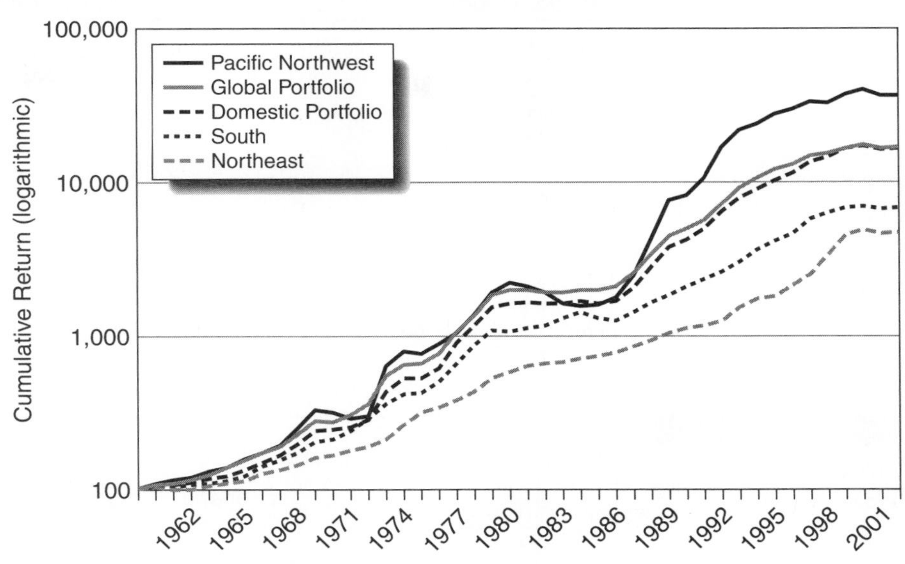


Source: Hancock Timber Resource Group

such an index would ignore the return associated with the growth in timber volume as well as the low volatility associated with the land component. Focusing on timber prices alone biases the return downward and biases volatility upward. Thus, First Wachovia has two indexes, one for timber and the other for timber plus land. Each index accounts for both timber prices and volume growth.

Preparing an index based on changes in timberland's per acre value over time also is not possible. This is so because of the substantial differences in the trees, the land, and the market for different acreages. Per acre values are influenced by at least the following: local timber market prices, timber species, site productivity, timber volume by product category such as pulpwood and sawtimber, a site's past management history, bare land value in local markets, and tract size of the investment.[14]

**Timberland as a Portfolio Component.** Despite the problems stemming from the lack of a standard index, interest in the risk-reduction potential that timberland offers is growing. We have seen that portfolios should contain assets whose returns are poorly correlated. Low correlation reduces the volatility of a portfolio without necessarily affecting the expected level of return. Virtually all studies of timberland price behavior find very low or negative correlation between timberland and other investment alternatives. Table 12-3 contains data from the period 1960 to 2002. Figure 12-5 is a traditional risk/return plot.

Robert Conroy and Mike Miles constructed efficient frontiers using various asset classes.[15] They reported that portfolios constrained with an investment of 25 percent

[14]Jon R. Caulfield. "Assessing Timberland Investment Performance." *Real Estate Review*, Spring 1994, 76–81.

[15]Robert Conroy and Mike Miles. "Commercial Forestland in the Pension Portfolio: The Biological Beta." *Financial Analysts Journal*, September/October 1989, 46–54.

**TABLE 12-3** TIMBERLAND CORRELATION COEFFICIENTS, 1960–2002

| *Investment* | *Correlation Coefficient* |
|---|---|
| Timberland | 1.00 |
| Commercial real estate | –0.08 |
| S&P 500 index | –0.17 |
| Small cap equities | –0.10 |
| International equities | –0.14 |
| Treasury bills | 0.04 |
| Long-term corporate bonds | –0.32 |
| Inflation | 0.39 |

Source: Data from Hancock Timber Resource Group. "Timberland as a Portfolio Diversifier," Research Notes, 2003.

**FIGURE 12-5**

Risk and Return 1983–2002

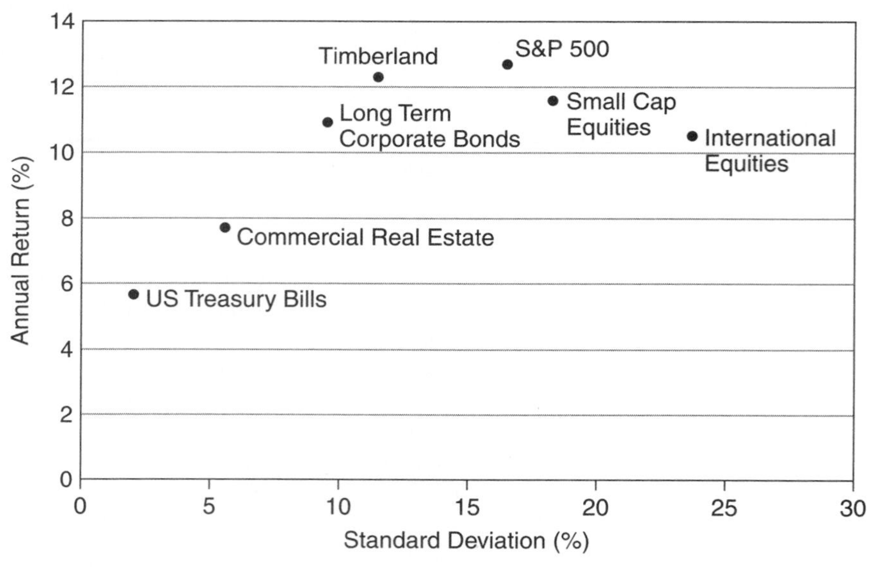


Source: Hancock Timber Research Group, "Timberland as a Portfolio Diversifier," *Research Notes*, 2003.

in both large-capitalization stocks and long-term bonds, with less than 10 percent in small-capitalization stocks and with a monthly expected return of 1.00 percent, were most efficient with 6.44 percent of the assets in timberland.

*The Performance Presentation Standards of the Association for Investment Management and Research require that investment managers perform a real estate valuation at least quarterly.*

**Future Prospects.** The outlook for timber investors is very promising. Asset allocation strategies are in vogue among portfolio managers, and it seems likely that an increasing number of portfolio managers will discover timberlands.[16] Conroy and Miles state, "Commercial forestland in the United States is unique enough in terms of risk/return profile and large enough in terms of aggregate value to warrant consideration for inclusion as a distinct asset class in the pension asset allocation process."[17] Large pension funds will probably continue to be the principal private investors outside the forest products industry.

[16]Asset allocation is discussed in Chapter 25.

[17]Conroy and Miles, 1989, 46.

PORTFOLIO MEMO

## Appraisals and Valuations

TimberVest, a well-known timberland investment management organization, publishes the newsletter *Tree Talk*. In a recent issue, the firm comments on the frequent blurring of the terms *appraisal* and *valuation*. The firm describes an appraisal as "an independent, third-party opinion of the property's present market value."* An appraisal involves an extensive survey of the property to determine wood volume by type and size of tree. Data collected during the process serve as inputs to techniques such as a discounted cash flow analysis or a comparable sales methodology. The appraiser couples site-specific information with current market prices for timber to arrive at an estimate of value.

Periodic *valuations* occur between appraisals (which might be done every five years). A valuation begins with the previous appraisal and makes adjustments based on projected tree growth, product class shifts, and the market price for timber. These adjustments lead to a new estimate of market value. A valuation is less involved than an appraisal.

*TimberVest, "The Issue of Appraisal-Based Returns, Part II," *Tree Talk*, 4, no. 1.

***Index Problems.*** Reliable information about timberland returns is a relatively new phenomenon. The fact that timberland is not an exchange-traded product, coupled with regional variations and a general lack of liquidity, makes continuous pricing (in the securities markets sense) impossible. Appraisals are useful, but traditional investors are more comfortable with market-determined prices rather than the opinion of an expert. This has historically been the single biggest deterrent to the expanded use of timberland as a portfolio component.

*The lack of a consistent timberland index is perhaps the single biggest barrier to increased timberland investment by pension funds.*

The short history and appraisal-based nature of timber indexes may continue to inhibit complete acceptance of forestland as a viable portfolio component. Nonetheless, the mounting evidence of its powerful diversification benefits, in addition to its long-term returns, will continue to win converts.

***Social Risk.*** The issue of social risk also is applicable. The timber industry considers forestland to be a renewable resource, yet many environmentalists do not. Although landowners can plant trees (and many timber harvesters routinely do so), it can take considerable time for a true forest to reappear.

Readers need to consider carefully any statistics about how long reforestation takes because the numbers vary widely. An Australian eucalyptus forest, for instance, will completely rejuvenate only six years after cutting. Southern pine from Alabama or Georgia takes 25 to 35 years to develop to economic maturity. Commercial forests in the Northeast may take 60 to 80 years, whereas forests in the West need 50 to 100 years. Redwood, Douglas fir, and western red cedar can take 400 years to reach "old growth" proportions. The consequences of clearing redwood obviously differ from those associated with cutting eucalyptus. Regardless of species, a virgin forest can never be replaced. Disagreement over fundamental issues such as those associated with cutting old trees has the potential to result in adverse public perception of the earth citizenship of a portfolio's sponsor.

## Real Estate Investment Trusts

A real estate investment trust, or *REIT,* is a convenient means of investing in a portfolio of real estate properties. It is essentially a closed-end investment company holding real estate. A REIT owns and usually operates a variety of forms of income-producing real estate such as shopping centers, office buildings, hotels, and apartment complexes. The phrase "and operates" is important; a REIT does not speculate in property by buying it and looking to sell it for a quick profit. In early 2005 there were approximately 180 exchange-listed REITs registered with the SEC, mostly trading on the New York Stock Exchange, with assets in excess of $400 billion. Another 800 were not SEC registered and not listed on an exchange.

*For details on REIT investing, see the* REIT Fact Book *published by the National Association of Real Estate Investors.*

While this form of investment dates to the 1880s, the modern version was born in 1960 when Congress passed the Real Estate Investment Trust Act, authorizing this form of ownership in order to make this asset class more accessible to individual investors. As long as the REIT distributes at least 90 percent of its taxable income to its shareholders, the firm is able to deduct the dividends from its corporate taxable income. (Normally firms cannot deduct dividends.) Most REITs distribute all their income and pay no federal tax.[18] The legislation lays down certain requirements for the REIT to enjoy this tax advantage. Among these are the requirements that the REIT must:

- be an entity taxable as a corporation;
- be managed by a board of directors;
- have shares that are transferable;
- have at least 100 shareholders;
- have no more than 50 percent of its shares held by five or fewer people; and
- invest at least 75 percent of its assets in real estate.

For technical reasons, there were barriers to pension fund investment in REITs until 1993. These restrictions are now gone. Today, most pension funds invest in real estate, and REITs are a common way of doing so.

### *Types of REITs*

There are three types of REITs: equity, mortgage, and hybrid. An **equity REIT** owns and operates income-producing real estate. This is probably the most popular and common type. Most equity REITs specialize in a particular type of property such as apartment houses, office buildings, or even self-storage facilities. Income comes primarily from rent. A **mortgage REIT** buys mortgages or lends money directly to property purchasers. Income comes primarily from loan interest. A **hybrid REIT** owns and operates properties as well as engaging in the financing of property. Income is a combination of rent and interest.

## Types of Real Estate Value

While this textbook does not go into great detail about security selection, there are some aspects of real estate valuation that you should understand when considering investment in this asset class. Investment real estate is sometimes described as a bond

[18]An REIT is not a partnership; it is a corporation. An REIT investor receives an IRS form 1099 at the end of the year rather than the form K-1 that a partnership interest receives.

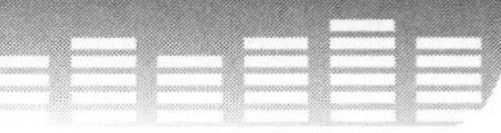


## Real Estate Valuation Methods

Someone who seeks to determine the market value of a piece of property is likely to use three methods to help arrive at the estimate: the market comparables approach, the discounted cash flow approach, and the replacement cost approach.

The **market comparables approach** to valuation is also called the sales comparison approach. In this method, the analyst selects one or more financial ratios such as price/sales and price/earnings in conjunction with a group of generally comparable properties. If this "peer group," for instance, has an average price/sales ratio of 3.0 and the property you are valuing has annual sales of $2 million, this suggests a value of $6 million for the firm.

The **discounted cash flow (DCF)** or income approach values the property by determining the present value of the anticipated future cash flows. The analyst estimates the future cash flows, determines an appropriate discount rate, and does the math. This method usually gets the most weight in a valuation analysis. Recalling the formula for a growing perpetuity, $PV = C_1/(k - g)$, real estate people refer to the quantity $(k - g)$ as the capitalization rate, or just the **cap rate.** For example, with a 20 percent required rate of return and an anticipated 5 percent growth rate in the cash flows, the cap rate is 15 percent. The reciprocal of this is 6.67. If the property under scrutiny will generate a cash flow of $500,000 next year, the DCF model indicates that the property is worth 6.67 times this, or $3,335,000.

The **replacement cost approach,** also called the cost approach, determines what it would cost to replace the building. This method typically receives the least weight in a valuation because a property's market value and its replacement cost are often quite different.

An appraiser will often use all three methods and weight them based on the special circumstances of the property of interest. He might, for instance, assign 50 percent weight to the DCF approach, 40 percent to the market comparables approach, and 10 percent to the replacement cost approach.

with inflation-protected principal and a coupon that might be zero, might be fixed, or might be variable. There may be no income (zero coupon), there may be a constant monthly rent (fixed coupon), or the rent may be adjusted periodically according to the prevailing prime interest rate (variable coupon).

The "value" of a real estate property is a more nebulous concept than the value of a share of stock or a bond. There are different meanings to "value" depending on your purpose or your point of view. These are all important and are part of the language of real estate investing. **Market value** is defined by the Federal Home Loan Bank as "the most probable price which a property would bring in a competitive and open market under all conditions requisite to a fair sale, the buyer and seller acting prudently, knowledgeably and assuming the price is not affected by undue stimulus."[19] Other definitions speak of "fair market value" as an "arm's-length transaction" in which neither party is under any compulsion to sell and in which both parties understand the relevant facts about the investment.

[19]Federal Home Loan Bank Board, *Appraisal Policies and Practices of Insured Institutions and Service Corporations*, Federal Register, Volume 52, Number 94, May 15, 1987.

**Fee simple value** is a measure of what a property would be worth if there were no leases encumbering it. An existing lease affects the value of a property. An empty office building won't sell for the same price as an identical building fully rented out under a ten-year lease. In contrast, a **leased fee value** is the value of the property given its existing leases. **Leasehold value** is basically the value of the lease, although this is not as simple as it might seem. You cannot just subtract the leased fee value from the fee simple value to arrive at the leasehold value. If the lease terms are attractive to the tenant, the lease terms are likely to be below market from the perspective of the property owner. The reverse is true if the lease payment is higher than the rate otherwise prevailing in the marketplace. Sometimes an investor buys property that is already leased to someone else and buys out the lease because they want to use the property themselves. Such a person might pay more for the lease than the cash flows would suggest is appropriate.

This leads to another definition of value, **investment value.** This is the value of a property to a particular investor, and may be more or less than market value. While not a perfect example, this concept prevails when a home-shopping couple offers a seller more than the asking price for a home because they really want it and don't want to be outbid by someone else. The flip side is the property that is for sale for $1 million, but your calculations suggest it is not worth more than $800,000 to you. From your perspective, $800,000 is the investment value.

**Assessed value** is the basis on which the city levies property taxes. There is no consistent relationship between assessed value and market value, although cities periodically try to adjust assessments to bring them generally into line. Political and regulatory issues often make this difficult.

## Gold

In varying degrees, just about all of us are intrigued by gold. Throughout history, humans have been influenced by the heraldic metal. We have envied those who have had it, pitied those who did not, moved to where it could be mined, and fought or robbed one another to obtain more of it. Many of us wear some of it every day of our adult lives.

### *Motivation for Gold Investment*

*People often buy gold because of the security it is expected to provide during times of trouble.*

In a nutshell, perhaps the most important general investment characteristic of gold is this: People buy it primarily because of the security it provides against times of trouble. *Forbes* magazine points out that gold's "main value is as an insurance policy against inflation."[20] About one-third of the world's gold is held as government reserves by central banks.

Nowhere is the security function of gold more evident than in Europe, where there is a particular fondness for gold ownership as a hedge against bad times. Many Europeans purchase small amounts of gold on a regular monthly basis through some sort of savings plan offered at a local bank. Throughout Europe, especially in Germany and Switzerland, children often receive small gold bars as presents for birthdays or other special occasions. Over the long run, gold has been a good store of value, whereas national currencies have been devastated by inflation or government bankruptcy.

[20]"Annual Fund Rating," *Forbes*, September 3, 1990, 160.

FIGURE 12-6

Global Private Investor Gold Stocks

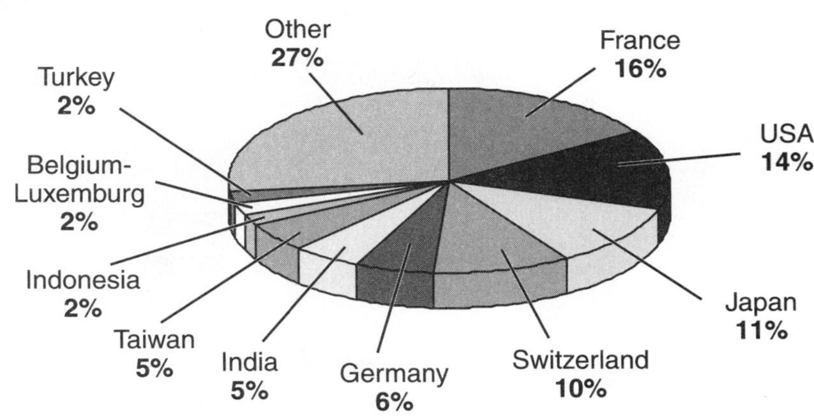


*Some analysts refer to gold as the "currency without a country."*

*"Including gold within an existing portfolio could improve investment performance by either increasing returns without increasing risk, or by reducing risk without adversely affecting returns."*
Ray E. Lombra, Professor of Economics, Pennsylvania State University

Paul Henshaw said, "Gold is how you survive when everything else is down the drain."[21] Largely as a consequence of these lessons from history, French citizens, who have suffered through many wars, own much of the privately held gold in the world, mostly in the form of coins. The World Gold Council estimated that in 2001 the above-ground stock of gold was 142,600 metric tons,[22] with 15 percent of that in private hands. About half of the total stock is in jewelry. Figure 12-6 shows the estimated distribution of privately held gold worldwide.

Numerous factors can make gold an attractive investment. Like timberland, gold has often demonstrated returns that are unrelated or even opposite to those of the stock market as a whole. This *sometimes* makes gold a powerful diversifying agent in a portfolio. Figure 12-7 shows the price movements of the Philadelphia Stock Exchange's gold and silver index (ticker symbol *XAU*) and the S&P 500 stock market index (ticker symbol *SPX*) since 1986. The correlation in the annual returns is –0.04, a very attractive value for portfolio risk reduction.

## Determinants of the Price of Gold

Gold is a popular trading commodity among speculators because of its price volatility. It is popular with hedgers because of its risk-reduction characteristics. When gold starts to move, it sometimes does so in a hurry. For instance, during most of 1986, gold traded in a narrow range, generally between $325 and $355 per **troy ounce,** which weighs 9.7 percent more than the standard ounce. In late summer, gold prices rapidly escalated, rising by $19 an ounce in one day (August 11). Near the end of the year gold was at about $400. Several major factors influence the price of gold:

*As the values of national currencies decline, the price of gold rises.*

- *The strength of the U.S. dollar.* The European and Middle Eastern investment communities often view investments in gold and the U.S. dollar as mutually exclusive. They sell one when they buy the other. As concerns rise over such factors as the trade balance and protectionism, investors dump dollars and buy gold, providing upward pressure on gold prices.
- *The strength of foreign currencies.* As foreign currencies grow stronger relative to the U.S. dollar, the price of gold as measured in the home currency declines

[21] *New West* 1:11 July 5, 1976.
[22] A metric ton is 1,000 kilograms, or about 2,200 pounds.

FIGURE 12-7 S&P 500 and Gold

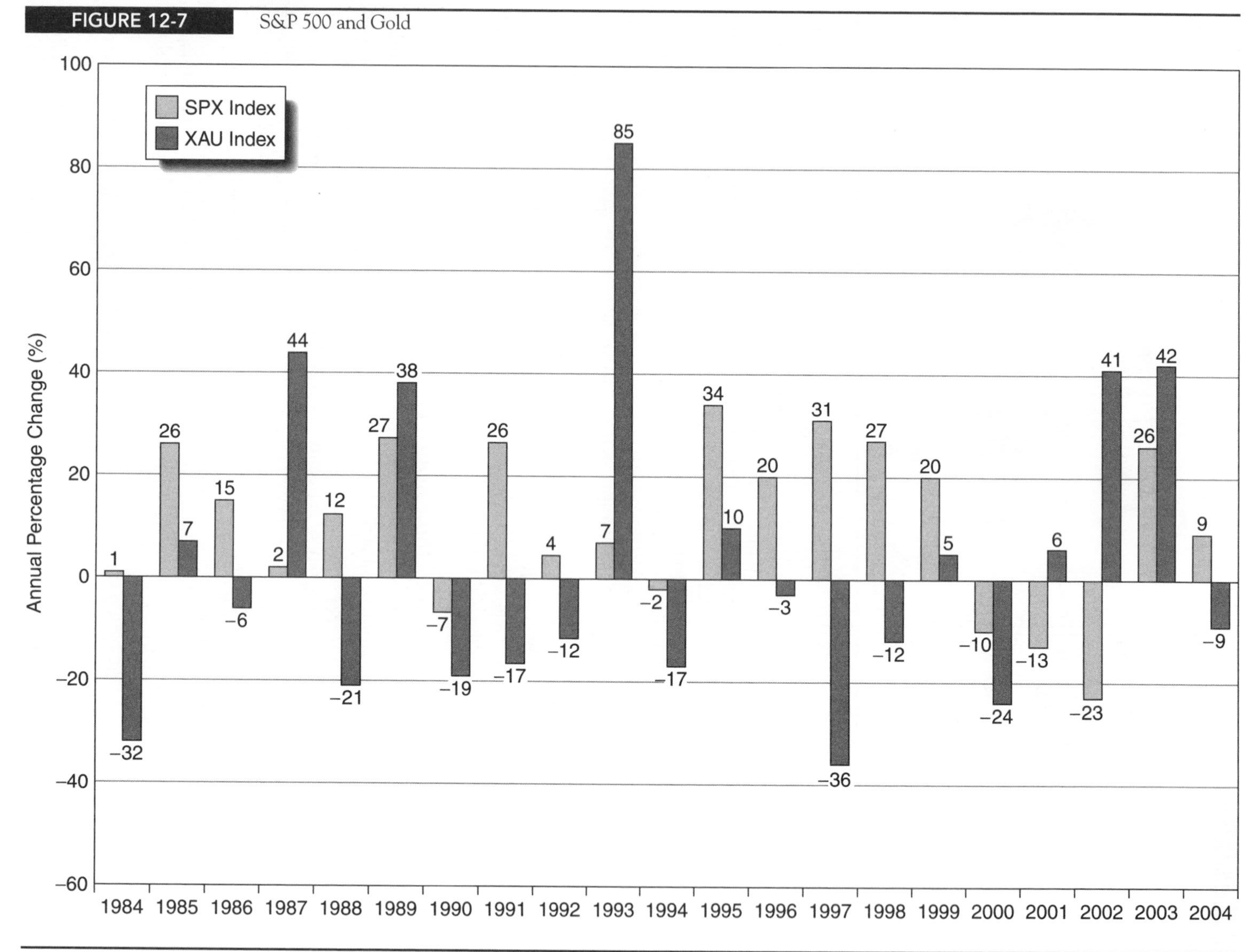

FIGURE 12-8

American Eagle Bullion Sales

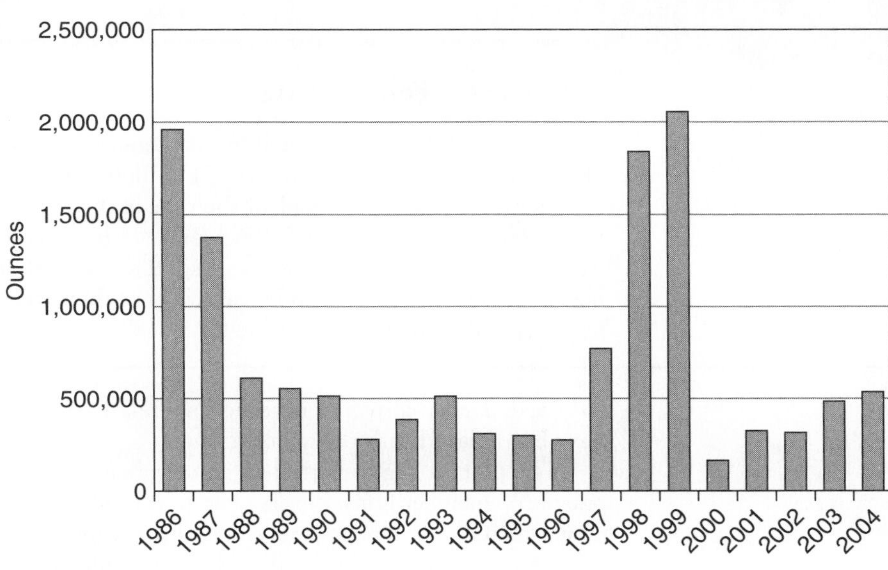


Source: United States Mint

for the foreign investor. This traditionally prompts significant purchases of gold by the Japanese, the Germans, and the Swiss.

- *Inflation and rising oil prices.* No one likes inflation. Historically, gold has been a useful inflation hedge, and an increase in the price of oil raises fears of inflation.
- *International finance uncertainty.* Third-world loans, mounting debt, and the emergence of the United States as the world's largest debtor nation worry many investors. These investors again turn to gold for stability during times of uncertainty.

*Supply is generally not the driving force behind gold price movements.*

Figure 12-8 shows annual sales of all denominations of American Eagle bullion coins by the United States mint. Note the dramatic increase in sales in the latter part of the 1990s. The specter of a Y2K disaster, with computers across the world potentially being confused by the three zeros in the year 2000, led many pundits to predict a global financial meltdown at the turn of the century. This possibility attracted national attention and led to a "bomb shelter" mentality in some communities. In anticipation of this, many people returned to gold as a safe-haven hedge against times of trouble. When the new year passed without major problems, interest in gold dropped dramatically. Sales in the next twelve months were at an all-time low.

### The London Fix

Basic principles of supply and demand determine the actual price of gold. However, a ninety-year-old ritual establishes the price that is quoted by the news services and the financial press. Twice each day, at 10:30 A.M. and 3 P.M. London time, representatives of the five member firms of the London Gold Market gather in an office of the London banking firm N.M. Rothschild & Son Ltd. to "fix" the price of gold. The members at these meetings are in constant telephone communication with their firms to search for a gold price that will clear the market, meaning that at that price supply and demand will be in balance. This price, called the **London fix** and stated

PORTFOLIO MEMO

## Japanese Gold Coins

In November 1986, Japan issued special commemorative coins to mark Emperor Hirohito's sixty-year reign. At least 14 million of these coins were minted. Each coin contains 20 grams of gold; at the time of their issuance, the coins had a face value equivalent of U.S. $650. The coins are legal tender, although virtually all were purchased as mementos. An especially attractive feature to those who bought them is that they can be cashed in at their face value regardless of what happens to the price of gold in the future.

in U.S. dollars by convention, reflects the relative balance of buy and sell orders that have been placed with the member firms.

The process begins with a suggested price from a designated representative of one of the member firms. Buyers react to this price, followed by sellers. If the orders do not match, a new price is suggested. Buyers and sellers move in or out as the proposed fix price varies. Usually the process is completed within fifteen minutes of the first suggested price. The record for the longest session was set one afternoon in 1980, when it took ninety-nine minutes to achieve balance. News of the fix is flashed around the world within minutes of its determination.

Although the London fix is an important price, it is not the only price. Gold is continuously bought and sold on organized exchanges throughout the world, with trading tracking the sun from London to markets in Singapore, Australia, Hong Kong, the United States, and elsewhere. Prices are constantly changing in response to economic and political news.

### *Investing in Gold*

An individual or an institution can invest in gold in four principal ways: bullion, gold certificates, mining company shares, and coins.

**Bullion.** The rare individual may have the money and inclination to buy gold bars (**bullion**) and stack them in the basement. Investors can acquire smaller quantities as 1-ounce bars, nuggets, or gold dust. Table 12-4 shows some of the weight measures used throughout the world for gold. These investments may be exotic, but they have obvious shortcomings. First, they have a significant risk of theft. Second, they produce no income until sold. Third, they lack marketability.

**TABLE 12-4** POPULAR SIZES OF GOLD BARS

| *Unit of Weight* | *Region Where Used* | *Equivalent Troy Ounces* |
|---|---|---|
| One Troy Ounce | USA, United Kingdom, Australia | — |
| 100 Grams | Globally | 3.2151 |
| 10 Tola | India, Pakistan, Middle East, Singapore | 3.75 |
| 5 Tael | Hong Kong, Taiwan, China | 6.017 |
| 10 Baht | Thailand | 4.901 |
| 5 Chi | Vietnam | 0.603 |
| 10 Dons | Korea | 1.206 |

Source: World Gold Council

Despite these factors, at least eight pension funds invest in gold bullion to diversify their other investments. The manager of one fund cites the threat of renewed inflation as a primary motive for holding gold. As a point of interest, the Rhode Island Hospital Trust National Bank is second only to the U.S. Treasury in the amount of gold it keeps on deposit.

**Gold Certificates.** Investors also can purchase documents representing ownership of gold bullion that is kept by someone else on their behalf. A number of banks in the United States and Canada issue these **gold certificates,** which are obligations of the issuer to deliver gold upon demand. If you purchase these, you can actually take delivery any time you wish. Most likely the bullion is kept in a vault at a bank, investment house, or coin dealership. Certificates are registered in your name, which adds a bit of security to the investment. Certificates may also be readily sold back to the dealer from whom you bought them, although you will lose a few percentage points in the dealer's bid-ask spread. You generally pay no sales tax when you buy gold this way; state laws vary on whether you have to pay this tax if you buy gold bullion and take it home.

*Convenience is the primary advantage of gold certificates over the bullion itself.*

The primary advantage of gold certificates over the bullion itself is convenience. You are freed from worry about storage, delivery, and insurance. These certificates do carry the risk that there is no gold backing them, but if you deal through a major bank or brokerage firm, this risk is minimal (or nonexistent with insurance from the Federal Deposit Insurance Corporation or the Security Investor Protection Corporation).

**Shares in Mining Companies.** Perhaps the most popular form of gold ownership in the United States is through the purchase of shares in gold-mining companies, either directly or through a mutual fund. Homestake Mining is the largest U.S. gold-mining company, and it is a popular investment for those seeking to speculate in gold. For Homestake Mining, a $5 per ounce increase in the price of gold amounts to about a $1 million increase in earnings.

*An advantage to investing in shares in mining companies is the potential for periodic income via dividends.*

Several mutual funds specialize in gold or other precious metals: Indirectly owning gold in this form has major advantages over other forms of ownership in that shares are instantly marketable and can generate some income through dividends.

It is also possible to invest in shares of South African mining companies. Investors can find prices for these companies in the "Foreign Markets" section of *The Wall Street Journal.*

*It is important to distinguish between a gold coin's bullion (intrinsic) value and its numismatic (collector's) value.*

**Coins.** Gold coins are popular with both collectors and gold speculators. It is important to distinguish between a coin's *intrinsic value* and its numismatic value. A coin's **intrinsic value** is the higher of its bullion value or its fiat value (the value assigned to it by the issuing government). Collectors may be willing to pay more than the value of gold contained in a coin because the coin is rare or popular. Some people find it difficult to be both coin collectors and investors in gold. It is easy to fall in love with the coins bought for their bullion value.

*In 1986 Japan imported 565 tons of gold, about half of which was used to mint the Hirohito gold coin. Japan set the previous record for gold imports the year before by importing 197 tons.*

Table 12-5 lists the most popular coins for investing in gold bullion. The South African Krugerrand, once again a most popular gold coin, was spurned by many investors during the apartheid days of the South African government. The convenience of bullion coins has increased the popularity of gold investments in the United States.

**TABLE 12-5** POPULAR COINS FOR GOLD INVESTMENT

| |
|---|
| American Eagles |
| Australian Nugget |
| Austrian Philharmonic |
| Canadian Maple Leaf |
| Mexican Peso |
| South African Krugerrand |
| Generally available in 1/20, 1/10, 1/4, 1/2, 1 oz. and 1 kilogram sizes. |

## SUMMARY

Portfolio managers should keep abreast of new developments in their field and not exclude potential investments simply because "no one else does it." Many worthy portfolio components are ignored because of a lack of understanding of their merits.

Timberland is an increasingly popular investment with the nation's largest pension funds. Its historic returns have been at least as high as those of common stocks, and timberland offers significant portfolio risk-reduction benefits because of its low correlation with other financial assets. Real estate in general, and timberland in particular, are expected to make up a much larger percentage of managed portfolios in the next five years.

Many investors consider gold to be a good hedge against times of uncertainty, as well as against inflation. Gold is an especially popular investment in Europe and is becoming more so in the United States. There are various ways to invest in gold, some of them very convenient.

## QUESTIONS

1. What is the difference between a financial asset and a real asset?
2. How do the investment characteristics of developed and undeveloped land differ?
3. What is the difference between real property and real estate?
4. Name the five major categories of real estate.
5. Why is land nonfungible?
6. What are the three classic motivations for timberland investment?
7. Which components make up the value of a stand of timber?
8. Timberland returns are a function of what four principal factors?
9. What is the distinction between biological and economic risks with timberland?
10. Suppose you were asked to propose an index for timberland that would satisfy the needs of pension fund managers. What characteristics should the index possess?
11. One of the concerns facing the timberland investor is management risk. Is this risk unique to timberland?
12. What is meant by *product class shift*?
13. Why is it inappropriate to prepare a timberland investment index based on the market price of timber?

14. List the major factors influencing the price of gold.
15. What are the principal means by which someone can invest in gold?
16. What is the London fix?
17. Comment on the following statement: Gold is a dangerous investment because its pricing is controlled by a European cartel of banks.
18. As shown in the chapter, gold often shows countercyclical behavior with the broad stock market averages. Given this, do you think a pension fund manager can justify using gold futures as a portfolio component? (If you are unfamiliar with futures contracts, their principles are discussed in Chapter 21.)

##  INTERNET EXERCISE

*http://www.goldinstitute.org/markets/1833tab.html* contains average gold price data since 1833. Identify the trend in the price of gold between 1994 and 1998. What can you conclude about the price performance of gold mutual funds during the same time period based on the gold price trends?

##  FURTHER READING

Baumgartner, David C., and Carol A. Hyldahl. "Using Price Data to Consider Risk in the Evaluation of Forest Management Investments." *U.S. Department of Agriculture General Technical Report* NC-144, 1991.

———. "Price Risk Analysis for Private Nonindustrial Forest Management." *Northern Journal of Applied Forestry*, June 1992, 55–57.

Bodie, Z., and V.I. Rosansky. "Risk and Return in Commodity Futures." *Financial Analysts Journal*, May/June 1980, 27–39.

Brennan, M.J. "Evaluating Natural Resource Investments." *Journal of Business* 58, 1985, 135–157.

Caulfield, Jon P. "Assessing Timberland Investment Performance." *Real Estate Review*, Spring 1994, 76–81.

Conroy, Robert, and Mike Miles. "Commercial Forestland in the Pension Portfolio: The Biological Beta." *Financial Analysts Journal*, September/October 1989, 46–54.

Dasso, Jerome, and Alfred A. Ring. *Real Estate: Principles and Practices*, 11th ed. Englewood Cliffs, N.J.: Prentice-Hall, 1989.

Harris, Thomas Jr., Christopher DeForest, Scott Futch, and Frederick Cubbage. "A Survey of Pension Fund Investments in Timberland." *Southern Journal of Applied Forestry* 13, no. 4, 1989, 188–192.

Haynes, W.N. "The Forest Products Industry—A Long-Range Outlook." *Forest Products Journal* 35, no. 10, 1985, 18–20.

Howard, T.E., and S.E. Lacy. "Forestry Limited Partnerships." *Journal of Forestry* 84, no. 12, 1986, 39–43.

Ibbotson, R.G., and C.L. Fall. "The United States Market Wealth Portfolio: Components of Capital Market Values and Returns, 1947–1978." *Journal of Portfolio Management*, Fall 1979, 82–92.

Irwin, S., and D. Landa. "Real Estate, Futures, and Gold as Portfolio Assets." *Journal of Portfolio Management*, Fall 1987, 29–34.

"Land Ho! Pensions Race for Real Estate." *The Wall Street Journal*, September 19, 1989, C1.

Johnson, Robert, and Luc Soenen. "Gold as an Investment Asset: Perspectives from Different Countries." *Journal of Investing*, Fall 1997, 94–99.

Manthy, R.S. "Scarcity, Renewability, and Forest Policy." *Journal of Forestry* 75, 1977, 201–205.

Mills, W.L. "Forestland: Investment Attributes and Diversification Potential." *Journal of Forestry*, January 1988, 19–24.

———. *Risk/Return Tradeoff among Forest and Nonforest Investments*. West Lafayette, Ind.: Purdue University Press, 1980.

Pease, D.A. "Longterm Loans Secured by Managed Timberlands." *Forest Industry*, November 1982, 33.

Rinehart, J.A. "Institutional Investment in U.S. Timberlands." *Forest Products Journal* 35, no. 5, 1985, 13–18.

Stolz, Richard F. "Sponsors Eye Timberland Investments." *Pension Fund News*, May/June 1989.

Strong, Robert A., and Bret P. Vicary. "A Growing Interest in Timberland." *Explorations* (published by the University of Maine), Winter 1990, 36–40.

Thomson, Thomas A. "Evaluating Some Financial Uncertainties of Tree Improvement Using the Capital Asset Pricing Model and Dominance Analysis." *Canadian Journal of Forest Resources* 19, 1989, 1380–1388.

———. "Financial Maturity: A Binomial Options Pricing Approach." Paper presented at the Symposium on Systems Analysis in Forest Resources, Charleston, March 3–7, 1991.

———. "Efficient Combinations of Timber and Financial Market Investments in Single-Period and Multiperiod Portfolios." *Forest Science*, June 1991, 461–480.

———. "Risk and Return from Investments in Pine, Hardwoods, and Financial Markets." *Southern Journal of Applied Forestry* 16, 1992, 20–24.

U.S. Department of Agriculture, U.S. Forest Service. "Analysis of the Timber Situation in the United States, 1952–2030." For. Res. Rept. No. 23. Washington, D.C.: Government Printing Office, 1982.

Webb, James F. "Risks Associated with Timberland Investments and the Timing of the Investment to Minimize the Risk." Paper presented at the Forest Products Research Society Conference, Milwaukee, April, 1987, 27–29.

Wiegner, K.W. "A Growing Investment?" *Forbes*, November 8, 1982, 50–55.

Zinkhan, F. Christian. "Forestry Products, Modern Portfolio Theory, and Discount Rate Selection." *Southern Journal of Applied Forestry* 12, 1988, 132–135.

———. "Timber Analysis Perplexing." *Pensions & Investment Age* 1, May 1989, 47–48.

———. "Timberland as an Asset for Institutional Portfolios." *Real Estate Review*, Winter 1990, 69–74.

———, and Kossuth Mitchell. "Timberland Indexes and Portfolio Management." *Southern Journal of Applied Forestry* 14, 1990, 119–124.

PART THREE

# Portfolio Management

# 13 Revision of the Equity Portfolio

*An individual can make a difference; a team can make a miracle.*
***1980 U.S. Olympic hockey team***

## Key Terms

| | | |
|---|---|---|
| active management | dollar cost averaging | reactive strategy |
| anticipatory strategy | exposure range | rebalancing |
| asset class appraisal | floor value | round lot |
| buy and hold | indexing | static strategy |
| churning | market impact | stop order |
| constant beta portfolio | mix range | swing component |
| constant mix strategy | multiplier | tactical asset allocation |
| constant proportion portfolio insurance | naive strategy | tender offer |
| crawling stop | normal mix | tracking error |
| discount brokerage firm | odd lot | window dressing |
| | passive management | |

## Introduction

Construction of a portfolio is only one part of the manager's duties. Portfolios need maintenance and periodic revision. The needs of the beneficiary and the relative merits of the portfolio components will change over time, and the portfolio manager must react to these changes. Portfolio management usually requires periodic revision of the portfolio in accordance with the statement of investment policy and the associated management strategy. This chapter reviews the principal considerations involved in revising the equity portion of the portfolio. The following chapter discusses revision of the fixed-income components.

## Active Management versus Passive Management

An **active management** policy is one in which the composition of the portfolio is dynamic. That is, the manager periodically changes the portfolio components or their proportion within the portfolio. In contrast, a strategy of **passive management** is one in which the portfolio, once established, is largely left alone. Before selecting one of these approaches, it is important for you to understand the choices and their costs.

### The Manager's Choices

**Leave the Portfolio Alone.** One obvious choice facing the portfolio manager is to leave the portfolio alone, and a great many people choose it. A **buy and hold** strategy means that as a portfolio manager, you simply select your investments and hang on to them. This is a passive strategy. It is also a **naive strategy** in that it requires very little thinking to implement. A naive strategy, however, is not necessarily a poor one. To an individual investor, the primary advantage of the buy and hold strategy may be that it reduces the psychological anxiety involved with portfolio management.[1] Among these worries is the investors' question of when to sell stock they own. There is more on this later in the chapter. If they *do not* sell, they have certainly eliminated the dilemma over *when* to sell.[2]

*Naive strategies are not necessarily poor ones.*

Another point in favor of the policy of leaving the portfolio alone is the great amount of academic research showing that, on a risk-adjusted basis[3] portfolio managers very often fail to outperform a simple buy and hold strategy. One of the oldest studies (now a classic) of professional investment management is the Michael C. Jensen study that reviewed the performance of 115 mutual fund managers over the period 1955 to 1964.[4] On a risk-adjusted basis, the average mutual fund return before management expenses was 0.1 percent less than that which could have been achieved by an investment of comparable risk in T-bills and the market index. Jensen's study found no evidence that any portfolio manager was able to consistently outperform the market.

Morningstar, Inc., a Chicago-based mutual fund reporting service, conducted a study of 278 U.S. mutual funds over the ten-year period ending April 30, 1990. The service found that when funds were ranked by their portfolio turnover rates, the funds ranking in the bottom 25 percent (those with the lowest turnover) earned an annual average return of 15.8 percent compared with an overall market average of 15.1 percent. This is further evidence that high portfolio turnover rates do not necessarily generate good performance, and they may hinder it.[5]

Elton, Gruber, Das, and Hlavka provide additional evidence in a 1993 article. They find that managers with low turnover outperform managers with high turnover. They indicate that the difference in performance is likely due to the added transaction costs associated with higher turnover.

The same results seem to prevail with individual investors. Barber and Odean[6] obtained six years' worth of data on 78,000 customers from a large discount brokerage firm. They divided the customers into three categories: *active traders* (who made more than 48 trades per year, comprising 7.7 percent of the total), *affluents* (who had more than $100,000 in equity but fewer than 48 trades), and *general* (everyone else).

---

[1]Professional money managers are seldom paid to practice buy and hold strategies. They are expected to manage their accounts actively.

[2]You may, however, create other worries. Even portfolios managed through a buy and hold strategy can sometimes be improved by intervention.

[3]Risk adjusting involves simultaneous consideration of the realized return from a portfolio and the level of risk contained in the portfolio. Techniques for doing this are a central theme of Chapter 17.

[4]Michael C. Jensen, "The Performance of Mutual Funds in the Period 1955–1964," *Journal of Finance*, May 1968, 389–416.

[5]A naive strategy also usually involves lower transaction costs than an active one.

[6]Brad M. Barber and Terrance Odean, "The Common Stock Investment Performance of Individual Investors," Working paper, Graduate School of Management, University of California, Davis, 1998.

**TABLE 13-1** INDIVIDUAL INVESTOR PERFORMANCE (MONTHLY RETURNS)

| *Category* | *Gross Return* | *Net Return* |
|---|---|---|
| Active Trader | 1.54% | 1.19% |
| Affluent Trader | 1.52 | 1.42 |
| General Trader | 1.39 | 1.22 |

Source: Barber and Odean.

Table 13-1 shows some of the results. The table indicates that the investors who traded the most had the lowest net return.

Another bit of thought-provoking evidence in favor of buy and hold comes from the startling decline in portfolio performance if the portfolio manager is out of the market on the wrong days. Over the period 1982–1990 the average compound annual return on the S&P 500 stock index was about 18 percent. If the manager was out of the market on the ten best days over this nine-year period, the average return drops to 12 percent. Take out the best 20 and the return drops to 8 percent. Take out the best 30 and the return is only 5 percent.[7] The fear of missing the boat is clearly on the mind of a portfolio manager who chooses to temporarily get out of the market.

It is easy to replicate a study like this over other time periods now that historical data is readily available on the Internet. The results are persistent: take out a few of the best trading days, and the aggregate performance drops sharply. Missing out on the big "up days" is arguably even more important in a bear market. Over the five-year period from January 2000 through December 2004 the S&P 500 index fell from 1469.25 to 1211.92, for an average annual return of –4.70 percent per year. Take out the three best days and the return drops to –8.15 percent. Take out the ten and twenty best and the aggregate return is –14.59 percent and –21.79 percent, respectively.[8]

Despite this somewhat disturbing indictment of portfolio manager performance, the financial press is full of advertisements for computer software, investment advisory letters, charting services, and similar products that allege to enable an investor to beat the market. When tested statistically, however, trading systems do not have a good long-term batting average. Why pay for investment advice if it is of no value?

**Rebalance the Portfolio.** **Rebalancing** a portfolio is the process of periodically adjusting it to maintain certain of its original conditions.

**Asset Allocation and Rebalancing within the Aggregate Portfolio.** When a portfolio contains both stocks and bonds, there are two principal rebalancing strategies, called *constant mix* and *constant proportion portfolio insurance*.

***Constant Mix Strategy.*** A **constant mix strategy** is one in which the manager makes adjustments to maintain the relative weighting of the asset classes within the portfolio as their prices change.

Suppose a portfolio has a market value of $3 million. The associated statement of investment policy specifies a target asset allocation of 70 percent stock and 30 percent bonds, with rebalancing every three months. Table 13-2 shows the initial

[7]Charles D. Ellis, *Investment Policy*, 2nd ed., Chicago: Irwin, 1993.

[8]Another study reports that if you were out of the market for the three best days each year from 1963–1993 you would have missed 95% of the total return!

**TABLE 13-2** CONSTANT MIX STRATEGY

| Date | Portfolio Value | Actual Allocation | Stock | Bonds | Action | Revised $ Allocation |
|---|---|---|---|---|---|---|
| 1 Mar | $3,000,000 | 70%/30% | $2,100,000 | $900,000 | None | — |
| 1 Jun | $3,400,000 | 73%/27% | $2,480,000 | $920,000 | Stock: Sell $100,000 Bonds: Buy $100,000 | Stock: $2,380,000 Bonds: $1,020,000 |
| 1 Sep | $3,750,000 | 72%/28% | $2,700,000 | $1,050,000 | Stock: Sell $75,000 Bonds: Buy $75,000 | Stock: $2,625,000 Bonds: $1,125,000 |
| 1 Dec | $3,100,000 | 68%/32% | $2,100,000 | $1,000,000 | Stock: Buy $70,000 Bonds: Sell $70,000 | Stock: $2,170,000 Bonds: $930,000 |

portfolio value and its value three, six, and nine months later, with the indicated managerial action.

At the end of the first quarter, the portfolio value has risen 13.3 percent, largely due to appreciation of the stocks. Before any action, the actual portfolio allocation is 73 percent stock and 27 percent bonds. To get back to the target 70 percent/30 percent ratio, the manager needs to sell stock and buy bonds. The situation repeats itself three months later, and the manager again sells shares and buys bonds.

During the next three months the market pulls back with the stock percentage falling to 68 percent. Now the stock percentage is below the target figure. The manager needs to sell bonds and buy stock.

Note in each instance that the actual allocation differed from the target by only a few percentage points. Whether or not the deviation is large enough to correct depends on the individual portfolio and the indicated constraints. The investment policy statement may say that the stock component can range between 65 percent and 75 percent, or it might state 70 percent with no range indicated. There is a cost with portfolio revision, and the portfolio manager should not make adjustments that are not economically feasible.

Many people find it bizarre that constant mix rebalancing requires the purchase of securities that have performed poorly and the sale of those that have performed the best. The manager should always consider this method of rebalancing as one choice but not necessarily the best one. An alternate, and fundamentally different, strategy is constant proportion portfolio insurance.

***Constant Proportion Portfolio Insurance.*** A **constant proportion portfolio insurance** (CPPI) strategy requires the manager to invest a percentage of the portfolio in stocks according to the following formula:

$$\$ \text{ in stocks} = \text{Multiplier} \times (\text{Portfolio value} - \text{Floor value})$$

Suppose the statement of investment policy behind the $3 million portfolio in the previous example established a floor value of $2 million and a multiplier of 2.5. The initial stock allocation, then, would be

$$2.5\ (\$3 \text{ million} - \$2.0 \text{ million}) = \$2.5 \text{ million}$$

**TABLE 13-3** S&P 500 STOCK INDEX

| *Month End* | *Closing Index* |
|---|---|
| Jan 1998 | 980.28 |
| Feb 1998 | 1,049.34 |
| Mar 1998 | 1,101.75 |
| Apr 1998 | 1,111.75 |
| May 1998 | 1,090.82 |
| Jun 1998 | 1,133.84 |
| Jul 1998 | 1,120.67 |
| Aug 1998 | 957.28 |
| Sep 1998 | 1,017.01 |
| Oct 1998 | 1,098.67 |
| Nov 1998 | 1,163.63 |
| Dec 1998 | 1,229.63 |

Source: *http://finance.yahoo.com*

**TABLE 13-4** CPPI PORTFOLIO REBALANCING

| *Date* | *Change in SPX from prior Quarter* | *Portfolio Value* | *$ in Equity* | *$ in Bonds* | *Actual Asset Mix* | *Desired Equity Position* | *Action* | *Ending Asset Mix* |
|---|---|---|---|---|---|---|---|---|
| Feb | — | $3,000,000 | $2,500,000 | $500,000 | 83%/17% | $2,500,000 | None | 83%/17% |
| May | +3.95% | 3,098,824 | 2,598,824 | 500,000 | 84%/16% | 2,747,060 | Move $148,236 into stock | 89%/11% |
| Aug | −12.24 | 2,762,524 | 2,410,760 | 351,764 | 87%/13% | 1,906,310 | Move $504,450 into bonds | 69%/31% |
| Nov | +21.56 | 3,173,446 | 2,317,310 | 856,136 | 73%/27% | 2,933,615 | Move $616,305 into stock | 92%/8% |

Table 13-3 shows the S&P 500 stock index over the period January to December 1998.

Suppose the portfolio manager established this portfolio the last day of February 1998 with an initial $2.5 million allocation to equity and anticipates quarterly adjustments to the portfolio. Assume that the stock portion has a beta of 1.0 and that the value of the bonds does not change. Table 13-4 shows the subsequent rebalancing of the portfolio each quarter.

Table 13-4 indicates that from the end of February until the end of May, the stock market rose 3.95 percent. The associated increase in the portfolio value means that a higher percentage of the assets should be in stock. The indicated action is to sell $148,236 from the bond portfolio and move these funds into stock.

The following quarter was a down period. The allocation to stock at the end of the period was down to 69 percent. During the next three months the market recovered its losses and rose further, ending with an equity allocation of 92 percent.

One of the consequences of following a CPPI strategy is that market movements can result in the portfolio being 100 percent invested in either stock or bonds. In this example, for instance, the **floor value**, a set value beyond which a portfolio's value must not fall, of $2 million means the portfolio will be 100 percent in bonds when the portfolio value falls to \$2 million. The 2.5 multiplier means it will be 100 percent in stock when the portfolio value rises to \$3,333,333.[9] A **multiplier** is a measure of aggressiveness in a constant proportion portfolio insurance strategy.

***Relative Performance of Constant Mix and CPPI Strategies.*** It is important to note the fundamental difference in the constant mix and the CPPI rebalancing strategies: A constant mix strategy *sells* stock as it rises, and a CPPI strategy *buys* stock as it rises. Similarly, a constant mix strategy *buys* stock as it falls, and a CPPI strategy *sells* stock as it falls.

*A constant mix strategy sells stock as it rises; a CPPI strategy buys stock as it rises.*

Because of this fundamental difference in these two rebalancing schemes, their performance can be quite different. Consider four different scenarios: a rising market, a declining market, a flat market, and a volatile market.

In a *rising market*, the CPPI strategy outperforms constant mix. This happens because the portfolio manager is buying stock in a rising market, action that is logically a moneymaker. The constant mix strategy continually sells shares to maintain the desired asset allocation; this lowers the portfolio return over the period of rising prices.

The same is true during a *declining market*. Buying stock that continues to fall is not attractive, but that is what the constant mix strategy does. The CPPI strategy, in contrast, gradually reverts to 100 percent bonds if the market declines enough.

If the market is essentially *flat*, neither strategy has an obvious advantage over the other because few portfolio adjustments are necessary. Both strategies remain in neutral until there is a price movement large enough to trigger rebalancing.

The equity market frequently is *volatile*. This means that prices rise for a period, then fall, and then rise again. This is precisely what the constant mix strategist hopes for because this portfolio benefits on market reversals. As the stock market falls, the constant mix strategy requires the manager to buy more stock. When it begins to rise again, the manager must reduce the equity holding. This is a winning solution because the manager buys stock at low prices and then sells it at high prices.

Market volatility does not benefit the CPPI manager. She would buy stock as the market rises only to see it fall back and then sell it. Similarly, stock is sold as it falls only to rise again and cause frustration.

It is not possible to categorically say that either of these strategies is clearly preferable to the other. Their relative performance depends on the performance of the market during the evaluation period. In the very long run, it is probably safe to say that the market is going to rise, which seems to favor the CPPI strategy. During most shorter periods, however, it is quite safe to predict that the market will fluctuate (i.e., be volatile). This argues in favor of the constant mix strategy. The choice of strategy depends largely on the portfolio's investment horizon and the importance of the "floor value" concept.

**Rebalancing within the Equity Portion.** An all-equity portfolio (or within the equity portion of a larger portfolio) has three classic strategies: *constant proportion*, *constant beta*, and *indexing*.

***Constant Proportion.*** Consider the information in Table 13-5. Initially, the portfolio contains ten stocks. Approximately 10 percent of the portfolio is invested in each of these securities, making this an approximately equally weighted portfolio.

---

[9]You can solve this algebraically. If $S$ is the dollar investment in stock and $B$ is the dollar investment in bonds, $S + B$ is the total portfolio value. When the portfolio is 100 percent in stock, $B = 0$ and the following equation would hold: $S = 2.5(S - \$2 \text{ million})$. Solving for $S$, we get \$3.333 million.

**TABLE 13-5** INITIAL PORTFOLIO VALUE

| *Stock* | *Beta* | *Price* | *Shares* | *Value* | *Percentage of Total Portfolio* |
|---|---|---|---|---|---|
| FC | 1.15 | 22 | 400 | $ 8,800 | 8.80 |
| HG | 1.20 | 13.50 | 700 | 9,450 | 9.45 |
| YH | 0.95 | 50 | 200 | 10,000 | 10.00 |
| LO | 1.00 | 67 | 150 | 10,050 | 10.05 |
| QWS | 1.10 | 20.38 | 500 | 10,190 | 10.19 |
| GTY | 1.05 | 66 | 150 | 9,900 | 9.90 |
| LOL | 0.90 | 11.88 | 800 | 9,504 | 9.50 |
| POE | 1.00 | 106 | 100 | 10,600 | 10.60 |
| ZR | 1.15 | 44 | 250 | 11,000 | 11.00 |
| EDT | 1.12 | 31.38 | 300 | 9,414 | 9.41 |
| Cash | 0.00 | | | 1,092 | 1.10 |
| Total | | | | $100,000 | 100.00 |

*Many investors try to avoid odd lot transactions.*

The manager could, of course, have come much closer to a 10 percent investment in each security. If the portfolio manager bought 319 shares of EDT instead of 300, this security would represent 10.01 percent of the portfolio. Why, then, did the manager not do so? The reason is probably mostly psychological. Many investors try to avoid **odd lots,** share quantities that are not multiples of 100.[10] Lots of 507 or 46 shares are odd lots. (In contrast, 200 shares, 1,000 shares, or 1,200 shares are examples of **round lots.**)

Nothing is wrong with buying odd lots, although at some brokerage firms such a trade might involve a slightly higher commission cost when figured on a percentage basis. Using the published commission schedule from one major full-service brokerage firm, for example, the trade of 100 shares of a $25 stock incurs a $72.75 commission. Two 50-share trades of the same stock would cost $92.76, whereas ten 10-share trades would cost $375. Many portfolio managers have learned that their clients prefer to avoid odd lots, and consequently managers often instinctively behave in accordance with this perspective for all of their clients.[11] With the ease of Internet trading and low flat-rate commissions, though, using odd lots has few real impediments.

*Constant proportion rebalancing requires selling "winners" and buying "losers."*

In any event, suppose that after a period of time, the value of the portfolio has appreciated from $100,000 to $120,000, as Table 13-6 shows. Three of the securities declined in value; the advance of the other seven was sufficient to yield an overall portfolio gain of 20 percent. The portfolio will probably also receive some dividend income over time; Table 13-6 shows an increase in portfolio cash from $1,092 to $2,150. Because the ten-security portfolio is now worth $120,000, one-tenth of this amount, or $12,000, should be invested in each of the ten securities to maintain equal weighting. It will be necessary to sell some of the shares that have performed the best and to buy more of the securities that have performed the worst. Table 13-6 indicates one possible approach to the rebalancing problem.

[10]In the case of high-priced shares of common stock or preferred stock, round lots are often 50 shares or sometimes even as low as 10 shares.

[11]If stock options are used in the portfolio, however, there is a rationale for preferring round lots: options can be written only in round lots. The use of stock options as portfolio components is discussed in Chapter 16, "Option Overwriting."

**TABLE 13-6** CONSTANT PROPORTION REVISION AT TIME 1

| *Stock* | *Price* | *Before Revision* | | *After Revision*[a] | |
|---|---|---|---|---|---|
| | | *Value* | *Percentage* | *Action* | *Value* |
| 400 FC | $ 20 | $ 8,000 | 6.67 | Buy 200 | $ 12,000 |
| 700 HG | 15 | 10,500 | 8.75 | Buy 100 | 12,000 |
| 200 YH | 90 | 18,000 | 15.00 | Sell 50 | 13,500 |
| 150 LO | 55 | 8,250 | 6.88 | Buy 50 | 11,000 |
| 500 QWS | 30 | 15,000 | 12.50 | Sell 100 | 12,000 |
| 150 GTY | 80 | 12,000 | 10.00 | None | 12,000 |
| 800 LOL | 13 | 10,400 | 8.67 | Buy 100 | 11,700 |
| 100 POE | 126 | 12,600 | 10.50 | None | 12,600 |
| 250 ZR | 60 | 15,000 | 12.50 | Sell 50 | 12,000 |
| 300 EDT | 27 | 8,100 | 6.75 | Buy 100 | 10,800 |
| Cash | | 2,150 | 1.79 | Use $1,750 | 400 |
| Total | | $120,000 | 100.00 | | $120,000 |

[a]This assumes no commission costs.

**TABLE 13-7** INITIAL PORTFOLIO BETA CALCULATION

| *Stock* | *Beta* | *Initial Value* | *Contribution to Portfolio Beta* |
|---|---|---|---|
| 400 FC | 1.15 | $ 8,800 | 0.1012 |
| 700 HG | 1.20 | 9,450 | 0.1134 |
| 200 YH | 0.95 | 10,000 | 0.0950 |
| 150 LO | 1.00 | 10,050 | 0.1005 |
| 500 QWS | 1.10 | 10,188 | 0.1121 |
| 150 GTY | 1.05 | 9,900 | 0.1039 |
| 800 LOL | 0.90 | 9,500 | 0.0855 |
| 100 POE | 1.00 | 10,600 | 0.1060 |
| 250 ZR | 1.15 | 11,000 | 0.1265 |
| 300 EDT | 1.12 | 9,413 | 0.1055 |
| Cash | 0.00 | 1,099 | 0.0000 |
| Total | | $100,000 | 1.0496 rounded to 1.05 |

***Constant Beta Portfolio.*** The **constant beta portfolio** in Table 13-5 has a beta of approximately 1.05, as Table 13-7 shows. As time passes, the values of the portfolio components change, and the values of the component betas may also change. This may cause the overall portfolio beta to change as well.

*Beta must be estimated, and the estimate is clouded with substantial uncertainty.*

It is important to remember that beta is a statistic that is estimated, and these estimates are far from perfect. Substantial uncertainty is associated with a beta taken from a regression model or scatter diagram. Practically speaking, this means portfolio analysts cannot quote beta to four decimal places meaningfully nor can they even be confident that a beta of 1.05 is different from a beta of 1.07. Beta is a useful measure of risk, but keep in mind the limitations on the ability to estimate it.

Rebalancing a portfolio to maintain a constant beta can be much simpler than maintaining a constant mix. This is so because usually the portfolio manager can alter the beta appropriately by altering only a few of the portfolio components.

The portfolio in Table 13-7 has a beta of about 1.05. (We normally should not express beta with more than two decimals.) Assume that this is the target beta that the portfolio manager has selected. Over time the values of the portfolio components will change, which can cause the portfolio beta to shift.

**TABLE 13-8** CONSTANT BETA REVISION AT TIME 1

| *Stock* | *Beta* | *Before Revision* | | *After Revision*[a] | |
|---|---|---|---|---|---|
| | | *Value* | *Contribution to Portfolio Beta* | *Action* | *Contribution to Portfolio Beta* |
| 400 FC | 1.15 | $ 8,000 | 0.0767 | | 0.0767 |
| 700 HG | 1.20 | 10,500 | 0.1050 | | 0.1050 |
| 200 YH | 1.40[b] | 18,000 | 0.2100 | Sell 100 | 0.1050 |
| 150 LO | 1.00 | 8,250 | 0.0688 | | 0.0688 |
| 500 QWS | 1.45[b] | 15,000 | 0.1813 | Sell 200 | 0.1088 |
| 150 GTY | 1.05 | 12,000 | 0.1050 | | 0.1050 |
| 800 LOL | 0.90 | 10,400 | 0.0780 | Buy 400 | 0.1170 |
| 100 POE | 1.00 | 12,600 | 0.1050 | Buy 50 | 0.1575 |
| 250 ZR | 1.15 | 15,000 | 0.1438 | | 0.1438 |
| 300 EDT | 1.12 | 8,100 | 0.0756 | | 0.0756 |
| Cash | 0.00 | 2,150 | 0.0000 | | 0.0000 |
| Total | | $120,000 | 1.1492 | | 1.0632 |

[a]This assumes no commission costs.
[b]New value.

Consider the information in Table 13-8. The portfolio beta has risen to 1.15, and we see that the portfolio manager has revised the beta estimate for stocks YH and QWS. The manager can reduce the portfolio beta to the 1.05 target in the following ways:

1. *Shift money into the stock portfolio and hold cash.* Diluting a stock portfolio with cash reduces the beta because cash has a beta of zero. This may not be feasible, however, because equity portfolios should be made up largely of equity securities. Cash should be a temporary visitor to the portfolio rather than a long-term resident.
2. *Shift money into the equity portfolio and buy stocks with a beta lower than the target figure.* This avoids the criticism of holding cash in a stock portfolio, but it still is not always a reasonable solution. It means obtaining money somewhere else, and this is not always possible.
3. *Sell high-beta stocks and hold cash.* As with the first alternative, this reduces the equity holdings, which is not necessarily appropriate.
4. *Sell high-beta stocks and buy low-beta stocks.* The stocks bought could be new additions to the portfolio or additions to existing positions.

This example uses the fourth alternative: Sell some stock with a beta higher than the target figure of 1.05, and buy more of one of the stocks with a beta lower than 1.05.

The calculations show that selling 100 shares of YH and 200 shares of QWS (whose beta values have risen substantially) and investing some of the proceeds in 400 more shares of LOL and 50 more of POE reduces the portfolio beta nearly to the target. This also increases the amount of cash on hand by $3,500 because the cost of the securities purchased ($11,500) is less than the proceeds from the securities sold ($15,000).

*The presence of some cash in an equity portfolio is appropriate and expected.*

Holding some cash in the equity portion of the portfolio is actually a good idea because of the flexibility it gives the portfolio manager in maintaining constant mixes or constant betas. The fact that most stocks pay periodic dividends is one reason cash is present in the first place.

**Change the Portfolio Components.** Another portfolio revision alternative is to change the portfolio components. Risk is an inherent part of the marketplace. Events sometimes deviate from what the manager expects, and sometimes those differences translate into a dollar loss.

*If markets are efficient, there is no such thing as an overvalued or undervalued stock.*

If an investment turns sour, the portfolio manager should do a bit of soul-searching. This is one time that a portfolio manager must either become a stock analyst or rely on in-house research recommendations. If markets are efficient, of course, the current stock price—whatever it is—properly accounts for expected future events, and there is no such thing as an overvalued or undervalued stock.

If you were the portfolio manager and an efficient markets agnostic to boot, you might believe that if LO were a good buy at its original price of $67, it should be an even better buy at its current price of $55. If this is really the case, then buy more. The presumption, of course, is that your estimate of LO's future promise is more accurate than that of the market as a whole. If yours is a minority view, it is not obvious that LO is truly undervalued. The level of wealth contained in a share of LO has fallen, and your client is going to want an explanation as to why you plan to buy more of this loser. Admit that your expectations were faulty, be forthright about it, and look for a replacement security, if need be. Some of the best advice ever given about situations like this came from Admiral James T. Kirk, of the *Starship Enterprise*: "If I can have honesty, I can forgive mistakes."

Perhaps after some thought, the portfolio manager decides that sticking with LO is an ill-advised choice. She sells LO and replaces the stock with HJY, currently selling for $29. The other two losers to date, EDT and FC, have not declined as much, and the manager decides to keep them. After the sale of LO and subsequent rebalancing, the portfolio appears as in Table 13-9.

While constant beta portfolio management was in vogue a number of years ago, it is unusual today to find a portfolio manager who actively manages a portfolio with a beta *objective*. It is much more common to view beta as a *constraint* emanating from the statement of investment policy. The statement, for instance, may speak of managing the equity portion of the account such that its risk is "between 85 and 120 percent of the market average." This implies a portfolio beta of between 0.85 and 1.2. As long as the portfolio remains in that range it is in compliance with investment policy, and that is what today's manager is most interested in.

**TABLE 13-9** AMENDED PORTFOLIO AFTER REBALANCING

| *Stock* | *Price* | *Value* |
|---|---|---|
| 600 FC | $ 20 | $ 12,000 |
| 800 HG | 15 | 12,000 |
| 350 HJY (added) | 29 | 10,150 |
| 150 YH | 90 | 13,500 |
| 0 LO (sold) | | 0 |
| 400 QWS | 30 | 12,000 |
| 150 GTY | 80 | 12,000 |
| 900 LOL | 13 | 11,700 |
| 100 POE | 126 | 12,600 |
| 200 ZR | 60 | 12,000 |
| 400 EDT | 27 | 10,800 |
| Cash | | 1,250 |
| Total | | $120,000 |

*Extensive information and advocacy for index mutual funds are available at:* http://www.indexfundsonline.com

*Indexing is a policy of attempting to mimic the returns of some market index.*

**Indexing.** Some managers are in charge of funds that seek to mirror the performance of a market index such as the S&P 500 or the Russell 1000; we call this form of portfolio management **indexing.** These portfolios (often mutual funds) tend to be large and, as part of their marketing efforts, often advertise their intent to track a market index.

If such a fund accomplishes its objective, it eliminates concern about outperforming the market because, by design, it seeks to behave just like the market averages. The fund manager makes no decisions about timing or relative security value but attempts to maintain some predetermined characteristics of the portfolio, such as a beta of 1.0 with a high $R^2$. The high $R^2$ increases the likelihood that the fund will follow the index closely. The term **tracking error** refers to the extent to which a portfolio deviates from its intended behavior.

## Tactical Asset Allocation

**Tactical asset allocation (TAA)** is a modern name for an old idea. Its practice, however, has become much more formal than it was in the past. Anyone actively managing a portfolio that contains more than one asset class (such as stocks, bonds, and real property) practices some form of TAA. Today's portfolio managers should be able to speak intelligently about the relative merits of this practice.

### *What Is Tactical Asset Allocation?*

*Asset class appraisal is the hardest part of tactical asset allocation.*

In a nutshell, TAA managers seek to improve the performance of their funds by shifting the relative proportion of their investments into and out of asset classes as the relative prospects of those asset classes change. If stocks are expected to outperform bonds, the manager increases the proportion of the investment in stocks. A manager who expects bonds to outperform stocks will decrease stock investment and increase the investment in bonds. This process, called **asset class appraisal,** is the most difficult part of TAA. Asset class appraisal is the process of determining the relative merits of common stock, bonds, Treasury bills, or other asset classes, given current economic conditions. The problem, of course, is correctly anticipating which asset class will perform best in the coming period. We know that over the long run, a buy-and-hold strategy for stocks will outperform an investment in bonds, but TAA tries to take advantage of short-term deviations from the long-term trend. This is not an easy task.

**Intuitive versus Quantitative Techniques.** The two approaches to tactical asset allocation are the intuitive approach and the quantitative approach. The intuitive approach is the old-fashioned seat-of-the pants method. Decisions are based on personal opinion and gut feeling. For instance, if you as a manager became bearish on the stock market, you would reduce your exposure to the equity market by shifting your funds elsewhere (or by using futures or options to reduce your market risk). How much money you move depends on the extent of your market pessimism and the constraints under which the TAA program operates.

A problem with the intuitive approach stems from a psychological fact of life known as *hindsight bias*. Clinical psychologists know the human tendency to be selective in our memory. Fund managers might remember the times they were correct in their market forecasts but have dimmer recollections of their errors. This makes it difficult to assess how well an imprecisely defined TAA program has worked.

**FIGURE 13-1**

Portfolio Strategies and Tactical Asset Allocation

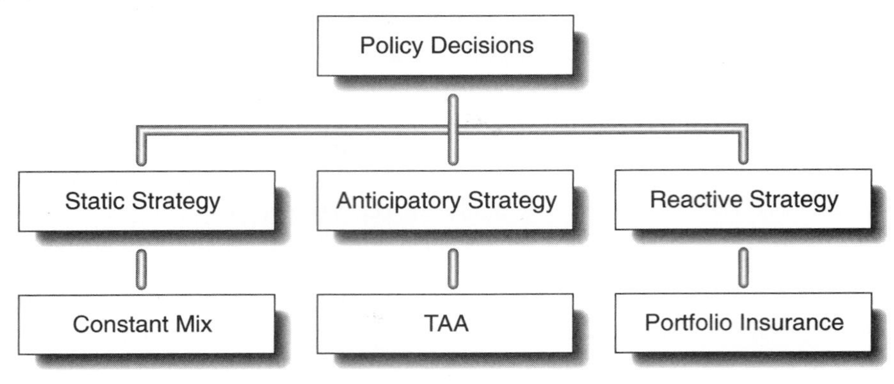


In most modern TAA plans, though, some type of quantitative system is involved in the decision making. Fund managers usually use both an analytical assessment of the merits of each asset class and some system for implementing precise portfolio changes. As a manager, you might measure the gap between the dividend yield on the S&P 500 index and the average yield on AAA corporate bonds. Based on your historical study of these figures, you might establish a policy of increasing your equity exposure when the gap rises above a certain point or reducing your equity when the gap narrows sufficiently. All managers have their own favorite techniques for quantitative analysis.

**Overview of the Technique.** Figure 13-1 shows how a policy decision leads to the choice of a strategic "theme" and to specific portfolio management techniques.

**Policy Decisions.** The first step, a policy step, is the decision to use a TAA program in the first place and then the establishment of the extent to which it will be used in fund management. A related decision is the number of asset classes to employ. Many firms limit this number to three: stocks, bonds, and cash equivalents (usually T-bills). There is no reason, however, that other investment assets, such as gold, could not be included. Timberland could be included, but this asset class does not lend itself to frequent sales and repurchases. It is also possible to subdivide a principal asset class. The General Board of Higher Education and Ministry of the United Methodist Church, for instance, had, in 1998, a policy specifying 60 percent in equities, plus or minus 10 percent.[12] Of the equity allocation, 20 percent was to be held in small capitalization stocks. This means that within the aggregate portfolio, the small-cap investment could range between 10 percent and 14 percent.

*Tactical asset allocation is not an all-or-nothing strategy.*

A second requirement is to establish a constraint regarding how extensive the TAA management is to be. Tactical asset allocation is not an all-or-nothing strategy, as we will see shortly. A fund manager might decide to employ TAA on 25 percent of a particular portfolio, whereas another portfolio with different objectives or different client needs might be 100 percent subject to TAA shifts.

**Strategy.** Portfolio management can take three alternative strategic directions. One option, the **static strategy,** maintains a static portfolio mix. Many fund managers

[12]Reported in the *Not-For-Profit Adviser*, Fleet Financial Group, July 1998.

have learned through experience the difficulty in successful market timing and, consequently, no longer try it. Rather, they employ a constant mix of the portfolio's assets, such as 60 percent stock and 40 percent bonds. In an efficient market context, we would not expect any market timing strategy to outperform a buy-and-hold strategy consistently. This is the justification for a static mix strategy.

Alternatively, a fund manager might use a **reactive strategy,** in which he makes decisions based on events that have already occurred. A portfolio insurance program where he sells stock as it falls or buys it as it rises is an example of a reactive strategy. Regardless of whether portfolio insurance is accomplished via futures, options, or dynamic hedging, decisions are made in response to some specific price movement in the equity market. These movements cause the portfolio manager to alter the relative proportion of equities.

*Strategies can be static, reactive, or anticipatory.*

The best technique is an **anticipatory strategy.**[13] The manager shifts funds before the markets move. Someone who is able to predict correctly which asset class will outperform the others over a forthcoming period is more valuable than another manager who merely seeks to reduce damage, which is essentially what portfolio insurance does.

### How TAA Can Benefit a Portfolio

The goal of an anticipatory strategy is to outperform the portfolio without TAA. That is, if you as a fund manager normally hold 50 percent stock and 50 percent bonds, your portfolio under TAA management should outperform this static mix.

In considering a TAA program, it is important for the manager not to lose sight of the basic principle of finance that states that a direct relationship exists between risk and expected return. Stocks, on average, are riskier than bonds, which is the reason their long-term performance exceeds that of bonds. A TAA program that is usually heavily oriented toward equities *should* outperform another asset mix where equities play a more minor role. Simply saying that a TAA program outperformed some static mix does not accomplish much. As always, return must be discussed within a risk/return framework.

The potential gains to a clairvoyant fund manager from a tactical asset allocation program are enormous. With hindsight, it is always easy to see what the optimum investment strategy would have been. Table 13-10 compares the results of

**TABLE 13-10** IMPACT OF TACTICAL ASSET ALLOCATION, 1926 TO 1998

| *Investment Vehicle* | *Compound Annual Return* | *Ending Value of $1.00* |
|---|---|---|
| Treasury bills | 3.77% | $15 |
| Corporate bonds | 5.80 | 61 |
| S&P 500 | 11.22 | 2,353 |
| Static mix: | | |
| 60% stocks, 40% bonds | 9.50 | 754 |
| 70% stocks, 30% bills | 9.37 | 693 |
| Optimum monthly shifts | 40.34 | 55,510,318,361 |

Source: Ensign Peak Advisors, Inc., Salt Lake City, UT 84150.

[13]The anticipatory strategy is ideal, of course, only if the fund manager is correct in what he or she anticipates.

several strategies over the period 1926 to 1998. The figures indicate that a manager who had bought and held U.S. Treasury bills over this period would have earned a compound annual return of 3.77 percent. Bonds, stocks, and the two static mix combinations would have earned more. A seer, knowing in advance which asset class would perform the best in the following month, could have achieved extraordinary returns. By shifting funds each month to earn the highest subsequent return, an initial $1 investment would have grown to over $55 billion.

*Even partial success with TAA asset class shifting can significantly improve a portfolio's performance.*

There are untold stories here, of course. Commissions and taxes would have gobbled up much of the potential profit, and no one can consistently predict the future. Suppose, though, that a manager was *occasionally* able to anticipate correctly the asset class that would perform best in the following period. Intuition suggests that even partial accuracy would significantly improve long-run investment performance. This is precisely the motivation for tactical asset allocation.

Remember however that the fund manager might be wrong more often than right in the asset class shifts. If shuffling funds around fails to outperform a buy-and-hold strategy, the manager can be accused of churning and poor management.

### Designing a TAA Program

*To see tactical asset allocation (TAA) in action, visit* http://www.harrell.com/itaa.htm

Two preliminary steps are necessary before the fund manager can successfully implement a TAA program. In conjunction with the client, she must establish the portfolio's *normal mix* and its *mix range* (also called *exposure range*). These two figures produce a third value, called the *swing component*. The **normal mix** is the benchmark proportion each asset class constitutes in its portfolio.[14] The **mix range,** or **exposure range,** specifies how much the current mix can deviate from the normal mix.

Perhaps a fund has a normal mix of 50 percent equities and 50 percent bonds. The mix range might permit the proportion of equity investments to drop as low as 40 percent and to rise as high as 60 percent. This obviously means that the bond proportion can range from a low of 40 percent (when the stock investment is 60 percent) to a high of 60 percent (when the stock investment is lowest). These values create a swing component of 20 percent. (The **swing component** is the percentage of the total portfolio whose composition by asset class may change.) This is so because each component can be reduced by 10 percent or increased by 10 percent, for a 20 percent overall permissible range. Figure 13-2 shows these values.

*The key element of TAA is properly investing the swing component.*

The job of the TAA fund manager sounds simple, but it is not. "All" that needs to be done is to determine how to invest the swing component. If stocks look good, shift the swing component toward more equity. If, instead, the manager expects bonds to outperform stock, the swing component is heavy on bonds. If the manager anticipates a "normal" market, he should invest the swing component in accordance with the normal mix of the rest of the portfolio.

### Caveats Regarding TAA Performance

*TAA programs implicitly assume it is possible to outperform a buy-and-hold strategy by shifting asset classes.*

**Efficient Market Implications.** The fundamental criticism of tactical asset allocation programs is their implicit assumption that some people can time the market and hence outperform a buy-and-hold strategy. This is inconsistent with the precepts of the efficient market hypothesis.

Still, there is much we do not know about the workings of the marketplace and how security prices are determined. Some fund managers do have good records with

[14]Many fund managers seem to have established 60 percent/40 percent as the standard stocks/bonds asset mix. There is nothing magic about these proportions, but they are widely employed on the street as a starting point in the construction of a wide variety of growth-oriented portfolios.

FIGURE 13-2

Tactical Asset Allocation

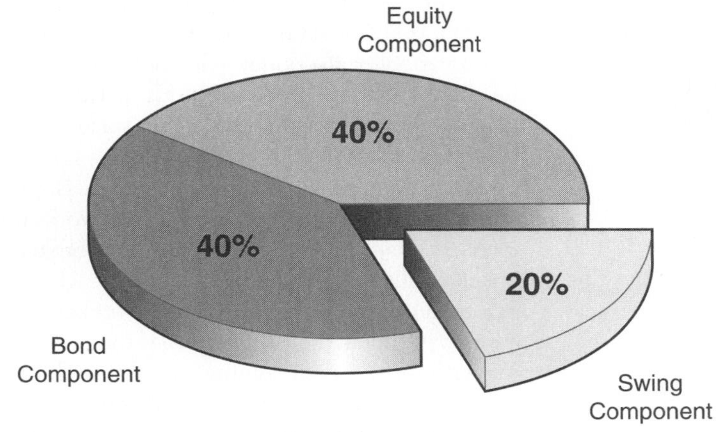


This figure assumes a normal mix of 50 percent stock and 50 percent bonds.

their TAA programs; whether this reflects skill or just luck probably is impossible to determine unambiguously.

Individual investors have practiced their own version of TAA for many years by using the switching option provided by many mutual fund families. An investor might own shares in a capital appreciation fund that permits funds to be shifted into a bond or money market fund at the account holder's wish. Taking advantage of such an option in order to capitalize on expected market movements amounts to tactical asset allocation. Although few formal studies of the long-term success of mutual fund switching have been done, some mutual fund managers specifically recommend against it in the fund prospectus, pointing out that few investors have historically been able to beat a long-term buy-and-hold strategy.

**Impact of Transaction Costs.** Buying and selling securities is not costless. The portfolio incurs trading fees each time a trade occurs. If the marginal gains from the TAA switching do not exceed the dollar costs and managerial time employed to earn them, the TAA program has not been an effective portfolio management tool.

### *Costs of Revision*

Revising a portfolio is not without costs. These costs can be direct dollar costs, can result from the consumption of management time, can stem from tax liabilities, and can result from the creation of an image problem that may spring from a perception of unnecessary trading activity.

**Trading Fees.** A U.S. phenomenon is that virtually every time property legally changes hands, someone pays a fee. If you buy something at a hardware store, you probably pay a sales tax. If you sell real estate, you pay a transfer tax. If you leave property to someone in a will, your estate is liable for a federal estate tax, and your state may require the beneficiaries to pay an inheritance tax. You also incur fees when you sell securities. The most important of these are brokerage commissions.

***Commissions.*** The public cannot conveniently buy or sell shares directly because we are not members of the exchanges where these shares trade. Unless we are able to find a willing partner to a desired trade via a newspaper ad or some other method, we must find someone who is a member of the appropriate exchange to act as our agent and make the trade for us. Stockbrokers perform this agency function, and we pay them a fee for their efforts. Investors pay commissions both to buy and to sell shares.

*Commissions are normally a function of the dollar amount of the trade and the number of shares involved.*

At a traditional brokerage firm, commissions with shares of stock are a function of two variables: the dollar value of the trade and the number of shares involved in the trade. At most brokerage firms, a 1,000-share trade of a $10 stock involves a higher commission than a 100-share trade of a $100 stock, even though both trades have a value of $10,000.

*Brokers can discount their commissions if they choose to do so.*

The commission on a particular trade is split between the broker who takes the order and the firm for which the broker works. Brokers with a high level of production keep a higher percentage than a new broker. Percentages vary by firm, but a new broker might keep about one-third of each commission dollar generated while a high producer might keep half. Some brokers discount their commissions with their more active clients. This means that they voluntarily reduce the size of the commission with the discount coming out of their share of the total commission. An undiscounted commission, for instance, might be $120, with the individual broker keeping $40. If the broker chooses, he can reduce the total commission to $100, giving up $20 from his own compensation. Precise negotiated commission arrangements between clients and brokers should be clearly established to avoid confusion.

Investors also can trade through **discount brokerage firms,** either over the telephone or the Internet. These firms offer substantially reduced commission rates but few ancillary services, such as market research or periodic newsletters. The largest discount brokers have an institutional desk where portfolio managers can enjoy even higher commission savings through quantity discounts.

A good rule of thumb for retail commission costs at a full-service firm is that most trades average about 2 percent of the stock value, with a minimum commission of $35 or so. On large, actively managed institutional portfolios, the percentage rate might be half this amount or even less; even so, these costs can be significant. The portfolio revision steps outlined in Table 13-2 would cost about $455 at a 2 percent commission rate. This may not seem like much on a six-figure portfolio, but these costs do add up over the course of a year, especially if rebalancing occurs frequently.

If you refer to Table 13-6, you will note that the investments in each of the ten securities range from $10,800 to $13,500. A portfolio that was truly equally weighted would have $12,000 in each of the ten securities. In our example, the manager probably decided that the portfolio in Table 13-6 is adequate and that further refinement would involve too many odd lots and too much more commission expense.

***Transfer Taxes.*** Some states impose taxes on the transfer of securities. These fees are usually very modest and are more of a nuisance tax than anything else. In one state, the tax on a trade of 300 shares of a $30 stock amounts to a paltry 16 cents. Transfer taxes are not normally a material consideration in the portfolio management process, but the manager should be able to explain what they are.

**Market Impact.** Another cost of trading is the **market impact** of placing the trade. This is the change in market price purely because of executing the trade. A stock might have last traded at $50 with a bid price of $49.95 and an ask price of $50.05. An individual investor who placed a market order to buy 100 shares would likely pay a total of $5,005. An institutional order to buy 50,000 shares at the market, however, could easily bump the stock price up by 25 cents or more. If the 50,000 share trade was filled at an average price of $50.20, this extra 20 cents per share is a portfolio cost of $10,000. The stock price went up because of the trade. Market impact is a very real cost of trading, especially with shares that have modest average daily volume.

## Changing Commission Schemes

Since the earliest days of the brokerage industry, brokers have worked on a commission basis. A customer made a trade and paid a commission, with the broker keeping part of the fee for her services. An element of conflict of interest in such a payment scheme has always existed because the broker has an incentive to encourage trading activity. **Churning,** or unnecessary trading to generate commissions, is an unethical and potentially illegal practice. Most brokers have their customers' best interests at heart and are sensitive to the propriety of the trading activity they recommend, but the conflict remains.

The subjective nature of the word *unnecessary* means that charges of churning are not always easy to prove. When is a trade unnecessary? This is an arguable point, but fund managers must be aware of the issue and make sure that their actions are well conceived and justifiable should they ever have to explain the activity in an account.

The proliferation of online trading firms and "commission wars" has caused brokerage firms to take a hard look at their traditional method of earning revenue. There is a growing trend to compensate brokers on the dollar value of the assets they bring under management rather than on the level of their customers' trading activity. Also, at many firms, individual investors may now choose to pay a single annual fee on their account and trade as much as they like rather than pay a fee with each trade. Both of these developments help reduce the conflict of interest inherent in a compensation scheme based on trading activity. After the Internet bubble burst, brokerage firms began actively seeking to increase their fee-based income. These are amounts earned automatically based on the dollar value of an account regardless of its turnover. This type of revenue stream provides greater earnings stability during market downturns when trading activity usually dries up.

**Management Time.** The majority of portfolio managers handle more than one account. It is common for a single person to have responsibility for thirty or forty half-million-dollar portfolios. Even a relatively simple rebalancing problem like the one in this example takes time. Rebalancing several dozen portfolios, each containing fifteen or twenty securities, is time consuming. Automation can help with rebalancing to a certain extent, but the manager must still review the proposed changes before implementing them.

**Tax Implications.** The selling of securities may have income tax implications. Nonprofit organizations, such as community endowments and pension funds, need not worry about this because they are usually tax exempt. Individual investors and some corporate clients, however, are concerned about taxes. In our example, YH rose from \$50 to \$90. The sale of 50 shares of YH (as proposed in Table 13-6) yields a realized \$2,000 gain that is taxable that year to the fund owner. Even in the average 28 percent tax bracket, this results in a \$560 liability that is a direct cost of the trade. Tax implications are complicated and should be addressed when the portfolio comes under management.

PORTFOLIO MEMO

## Dollar Cost Averaging: Panacea for the Small Investor

**Dollar cost averaging** is a compelling investment technique individual investors frequently use. Although some mutual fund sales personnel like to pretend that their firm thought up the idea, dollar cost averaging is a simple mathematical phenomenon that anyone can exploit.

The idea is to invest a fixed amount at a regular interval into the same security regardless of current market conditions. Dollar cost averaging eliminates the need to time the market and requires only selecting an appropriate security (usually a mutual fund) for investment.

Consider the three situations in Figure 13-3. Suppose an individual invests $100 per month over nine months into a common stock mutual fund. This means a total of $900 is invested.

In Scenario A, the shares purchased in March cost $10 each. The share price rises by $1 each month through November, when they are worth $18. Over this period the investor accumulates 66.614 shares. Worth $18 apiece in November, their combined value is $1,199.05. Scenario B shows the reverse situation: The shares are initially worth $18 and decline by $1 per month. A total of 66.614

FIGURE 13-3 Dollar Cost Averaging

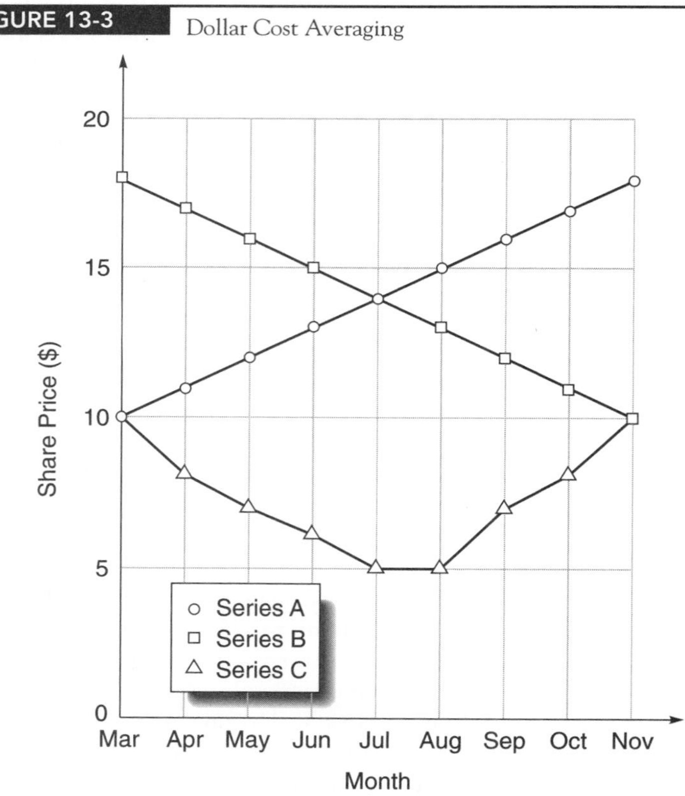


Each month, $100 is invested.

PORTFOLIO MEMO

## Dollar Cost Averaging (continued)

shares also accumulate, and in November 66.614 shares at $10 each are worth $666.14. Finally, Scenario C shows a fluctuating market, where share prices decline from their initial $10 value to $5, bottom out at this price and then rise back to their starting value of $10. Here 130.239 shares accumulate with an ending value of $1,302.39.

Table 13-11 summarizes the account transactions in each of the three situations. Many people are surprised to see that Scenario C (fluctuating market) is preferable to Scenario A (steadily rising market) in a dollar cost averaging scheme. The reason for this is the increased number of shares the $100 investment buys at the lower prices.

Dollar cost averaging fails to earn a positive return in only two situations. One is when the chosen security trends down over the investment period. (Dollar cost averaging makes money even if the stock price movement is level, provided it fluctuates.) The second possibility for a loss is when the investor bails out at a low price or decides to skip an investment because prices are too low. (One of the curious psychological aspects of investing is that the public seems especially prone to buy when the market is steadily advancing and prices approach all-time highs. Conversely, the public sells when the market falls and prices are low. This is inconsistent with our buying behavior with other products.)

**TABLE 13-11** SHARES ACQUIRED VIA DOLLAR COST AVERAGING WITH A $100 PURCHASE EACH MONTH

| *Month* | *Scenario A* | *Scenario B* | *Scenario C* |
|---|---|---|---|
| March | 10.000 | 5.556 | 10.000 |
| April | 9.091 | 5.882 | 12.500 |
| May | 8.333 | 6.250 | 14.286 |
| June | 7.692 | 6.667 | 16.667 |
| July | 7.143 | 7.143 | 20.000 |
| August | 6.667 | 7.692 | 20.000 |
| September | 6.250 | 8.333 | 14.286 |
| October | 5.882 | 9.091 | 12.500 |
| November | 5.556 | 10.000 | 10.000 |
| Total | 66.614 | 66.614 | 130.239 |
| Value | $1,199.05 | $666.14 | $1,302.39 |

*Window dressing describes cosmetic changes to a portfolio near the end of a reporting period.*

*"If you have to eat a frog, it is best not to look at it too long." Mark Twain*

**Window Dressing. Window dressing** refers to largely cosmetic changes made to a portfolio near the end of some reporting period. A fund manager, for instance, may provide a detailed portfolio statement twice a year, on June 30 and December 31. This statement usually has two parts. One part itemizes the assets contained in the portfolio at that point in time. This is analogous to a balance sheet and tends to be the part of the report that receives the most attention. Many users of the report focus on the net change in market value over the reporting period. The second part of the portfolio statement is often longer and reports all activity in the fund since the previous report. Dividends received, securities bought and sold, management fees paid, and so on are reported here. This part is like a daily accounting journal.

At http://screen.morningstar.com/FundSelector.html?hnav=fundsSelect *you can screen mutual funds by ten different criteria, including expense ratios, manager's tenure, asset size, and returns.*

Say you are a fund manager who has one particularly poor performer like LO in our example. You could show this loser on your fund balance sheet, but it might be less stressful to sell it, getting it off the early pages of the report and relegating it to the second part. Window dressing is a real-world phenomenon; people do not want to attract attention to their mistakes. The key thing to remember is your fiduciary responsibility to act in the best interest of your clients. Do not sell stock without a well-conceived rationale that you would be comfortable explaining to the fund owner.

**Rising Importance of Trading Fees.** As a final note, the prevalence and impact of trading fees is receiving increased attention in the investment community. Investment banking scandals, lawsuits regarding churning, and incomplete prospectus information are attracting attention from regulatory bodies, consumer groups, and financial columnists. Someone pays the cost of trading securities, and that someone is the individual or institution that has entrusted the portfolio manager with money. Flippancy regarding commission costs is clearly unethical and sometimes illegal.

### *Contributions to the Portfolio*

Another part of the portfolio management process deals with periodic additional contributions to the portfolio from either internal or external sources. Although this is not a complicated activity, it is an important one. Accumulating a pile of uncashed interest or dividend checks is obviously not in the client's best interest. It is important to get dividends back to work as soon as possible after receiving them. An uncashed check earns no return, and a casual attitude toward these checks is unsound fiduciary practice.

If an account holds its securities in a street name, dividends go to the brokerage firm holding the securities on the client's behalf. Most brokerage firms have arrangements whereby any excess cash in an account is automatically transferred into an interest-bearing fund of some type. This is a good arrangement because it reduces to a minimum the unproductive time of the dividends.

If instead the portfolio manager receives the dividend checks, there needs to be some temporary haven (such as a money market fund) for these funds until they accumulate sufficiently to finance the purchase of more securities or until they are paid as income to the fund beneficiary.

## When Do You Sell Stock?

Knowing when to sell a particular stock is perhaps one of the toughest parts of the investment business. One of the questions most commonly asked by the layperson concerns when to sell the stock. Behavioral evidence suggests that the typical investor sells winners too soon and keeps losers too long.[15] This section deals with thoughts on the sale of equity securities.

### *Rebalancing*

As we have seen, rebalancing a portfolio because of changing security values can cause the portfolio manager to sell shares but not necessarily because they are doing

[15]See, for instance, the Barber and Odean article listed in the Further Reading section at the end of this chapter.

poorly. In the example presented in Table 13-6, rebalancing required the sale of some of the shares of YH, QWS, and ZR, even though these three securities were winners. Profit taking with winners is a logical consequence of portfolio rebalancing.

## Upgrading

Investors should also sell shares when their investment potential has deteriorated to the extent that they no longer merit a place in the portfolio. In Table 13-9, we saw that stock LO had taken a dive and that the manager decided to suffer the consequences and sell the stock. Shares of HJY were purchased instead. It is difficult to take a loss, but it is even worse to hang on to a loser and have the loss (or opportunity loss) grow even worse.[16] The sale of LO and its replacement with HJY is an example of upgrading.

## Sale of Stock via Stop Orders

*Stop orders activate a market order if shares trade at the stop price. The use of a stop order does not guarantee a certain sales price.*

*Stop orders* are extremely useful investment tools, yet surprisingly few individual or institutional investors routinely use them. Most **stop orders** are sell stops, which activate a market order to sell a set number of shares if shares trade at the stop price. Stop orders can be used to minimize losses or to protect a profit.

**Using Stops to Minimize Losses.** Suppose you buy 1,000 shares of a stock at $23, and the share price declines to $19. You might decide that if it falls another dollar, you are going to sell it, take your loss, and find a replacement. To do this, you could place a stop order to sell 1,000 shares and set the stop price at $18.[17] This means that if the stock trades at $18 per share or less, your stop order will be activated and become a market order to sell your shares. You are not guaranteed $18 per share, however, because a market order indicates a desire to sell for the best available price. In a volatile market, your trade might occur at $17.75 or even less.

Stop orders—or stop-loss orders, when used this way—can make some of your when-to-sell decisions automatically. You might routinely place stops 15 percent below the current market price of each equity security. If a security declines in value this much, it will be sold via the stop order. You file stop orders with the stock specialist at the exchange, so you do not have to rely on a broker to track the order.

**Using Stops to Protect Profits.** Stop orders also can be used to protect profits. In many respects this is their more important use. Suppose you purchased stock at $33, and it is now at $48. You have a nice gain in the stock and are tempted to take the profit. But you also think there is a good chance that the stock will continue to advance, and you would hate to miss out on the additional gain. You are also troubled by the fact that many people take profits too soon.

*Crawling stops are used to protect profits rather than to minimize losses.*

Instead of selling the stock, you place a $45 stop order to sell the shares. This is $3 below the current market price. If the stock retreats to $45, your shares are sold, and you will still be left with a nice profit. If the stock continues to run up, however, you can simply move the stop up behind it. Some people refer to this as a **crawling stop.** As an example, suppose that three weeks later your stock has advanced another $5, to $53. You call your broker and move the stop price up to

[16]Hard as it may be to your ego, you must continually recall that there are no losers in an efficient market. The current price is a fair one; what has happened in the past does not matter.

[17]You could also place a stop order to sell only part of your shares, or you could place several stops at different stop prices on portions of your holdings.

**FIGURE 13-4**

Using a Crawling Stop

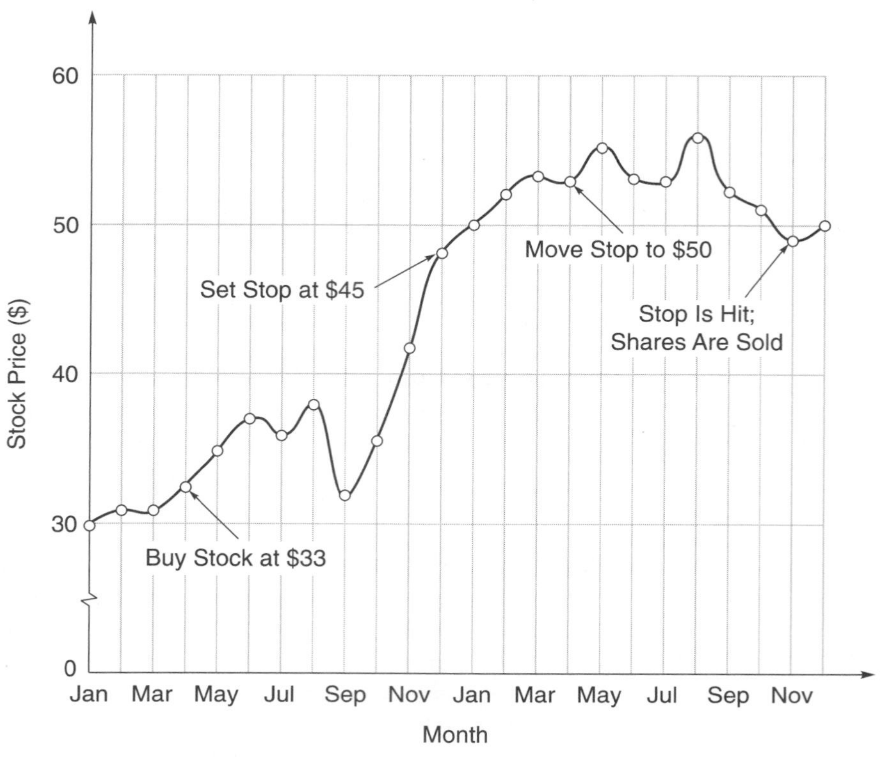


perhaps $50. Now if the stock retreats, you have protected another $5 per share in profits. Figure 13-4 summarizes this example.

Stop orders do not cost anything to place. You pay a commission only if the order results in a trade.

### *Extraordinary Events*

Unexpected occurrences can also make it necessary for the portfolio manager to sell shares of stock.

**Change in Client Objectives.** Occasionally the client's investment objectives change. For example, a church may be about to undertake a major renovation and need to generate additional income to pay for it. The church decision-making board may decide to change the endowment fund's primary objective to income from growth of income. This will probably cause the portfolio manager to reduce the percentage of the portfolio that is in equities.

**Change in Market Conditions.** When the portfolio manager's outlook for the stock market turns bearish, it is often appropriate to reduce equity holdings in favor of fixed-income securities. Many fund managers actively seek to time the market. In many respects this is the essence of tactical asset allocation strategies.

**Buy-Outs.** A fund manager might learn of a **tender offer** for one of the fund's holdings. This means that someone is offering to purchase the shares of a company,

PORTFOLIO MEMO

### The Adverse Psychology of Passive Trading Rules

Trading stock is much more fun than following a buy and hold strategy, even when confronted with the historical evidence. According to *Forbes* magazine, "Over the past decade the average holding period for equities has fallen from 28 months to 16. Mutual fund customers stay put for 2.9 years, down from 5.5. For exchange-traded funds, those index-fund substitutes ideal for long-term investors, the average holding time is 2.5 days."[*] This increased trading activity is all the more remarkable when you overlay the fact that over an extended period, the unmanaged S&P 500 index has outperformed 90 percent of the actively managed U.S. investment funds.[+]

Similarly, to some portfolio managers, passive strategies such as constant proportion have lost their appeal. Fleet Investment Advisors writes, "When your equity holdings are climbing through the roof while your fixed income portfolio seems stuck in the celler, it can feel like a fool's game to sell the stuff that's doing well in order to buy the stuff that isn't."[†] The vice president for investments at one major U.S. university says, "An automatic rebalancing system based on preset percentages is what I call a brainless approach. It's something a sixth-grader could do. It tends to penalize high-performing asset classes and reward poor performing asset classes."[#]

Every portfolio manager hopes to "outperform" the market, and every year many will, but more will not. We have both a brain and finance theory, and we should use both in making investment decisions.

[*] Neil Weinberg and Michael Maiello, "Stand Fast," *Forbes*, July 23, 2001, 150–151.
[+] Ibid., 151.
[†] Ann Monroe, "Striking a Balance," *The Not-For-Profit Advisor*, January 2001, 6–7.
[#] Ibid., 6.

normally for a premium over the previous market price. It is difficult to pass up most tender offers, and it is generally in the client's best interest to sell the stock to the would-be acquirer.

**Caprice.** Sometimes there is really no compelling reason to sell shares beyond some inexplicable gut feeling or a desire to do something. Portfolio managers need to be careful about making unnecessary trades in a managed account, but they also must pay attention to their experience, intuition, and professional judgment. An experienced portfolio manager who is worried about a particular holding or who thinks the portfolio needs a change probably should make the switch.

### *Final Thoughts*

Unfortunately, there is no easy answer to the question, When do I sell stock? Psychologically, the portfolio manager is torn between a desire to protect profits or minimize further losses and the potential for price appreciation.

In an efficient market context, the current stock price is an extremely important number, one that accurately reflects the information available to the investing community. This means the current price is a fair price. Still, an investor logically can sell shares in an efficient market framework as utility curves or consumption decisions change. As a portfolio manager, the important thing is to know why you are about to do something. Everything you do must be logically justifiable at the time you do it. Hindsight is an inappropriate perspective for investment decision making.

## SUMMARY

Portfolio management strategies can be either passive or active. Buy and hold is the most obvious of the passive strategies. A naive strategy is one that requires very little thinking to implement, but such a strategy is not necessarily a poor one.

Rebalancing involves adjusting the relative proportion of each portfolio component according to some target proportion. This may appear to require selling winners and buying losers. Popular methods of rebalancing include maintaining a constant mix of the portfolio components, maintaining a constant beta, or matching the performance of some stock market index (called *indexing*).

Another managerial consideration is the handling of contributions to the portfolio (from both internal and external sources). Dollar cost averaging is a useful method of periodically adding to a portfolio without the need for extensive security analysis. Deciding when to sell shares of stock, particularly ones that are doing well, can be complicated. Stop orders are useful in protecting profits from stocks that continue to have good prospects.

Tactical asset allocation (TAA) is a rapidly growing topic in the field of portfolio management. Basically, a TAA program seeks to shift the relative asset proportions of a portfolio as the prospects for the various asset classes change. It is unusual to have more than three asset classes (stocks, bonds, and cash), although there is no reason why other assets, such as timberland or hard assets, could not be included. The essence of the TAA program is making a decision about how to invest the swing component of the portfolio. This amounts to an attempt to time the market. Even with only modest success, the marginal gains can be substantial.

## QUESTIONS

1. Portfolio management is really a process of continual portfolio revision. Do you agree with this statement?
2. What is the point of portfolio rebalancing? Why not just leave the portfolio alone?
3. Why is portfolio revision not free of cost?
4. Show how a crawling stop order can be used to protect a profit.
5. Although stop orders can be quite useful, surveys show that very few individual investors ever use them. Why do you think this is?
6. A portfolio manager finds that a particular collection of securities has a correlation coefficient of 0.96 with the S&P 500. If the objective is to mimic the S&P 500 index, would it make sense to try to increase the correlation by adding more securities? What are the pros and cons of doing so?

7. A portfolio has a primary objective of capital appreciation and a secondary objective of growth of income. If you feel bearish about the stock market as a whole, is it appropriate for you to reduce your equity holding to zero? Why or why not?
8. The text mentions that an investor could routinely place stops 15 percent below the current price of each equity position. Is there any reason not to do this?
9. How would you determine whether a fund manager is guilty of churning?
10. Is it feasible to organize an all-equity fund so that it is managed as an equally weighted, constant beta portfolio?
11. Consider the following statement: As time passes, the beta of a self-contained stock portfolio often declines. This statement is true. Why do you think this is so?
12. Suppose you have a very accurate, reliable estimate for a security's long-term expected return, this estimate has very little variance, and the expected return is commensurate with the security's risk. Explain why it makes sense to buy more of this security if it fails to earn this expected return in the next period.
13. How does the idea of tactical asset allocation tie in with the efficient market hypothesis?
14. What is meant by asset class appraisal?
15. Is there a cost to tactical asset allocation other than commission costs and managerial time?
16. How does TAA fit in with the portfolio objectives discussed in Chapters 3 and 4?
17. Is TAA appropriate for a fixed-income portfolio?
18. Why does a tactical asset allocator need to be concerned with the potential for charges of churning?

## PROBLEMS

1. Make up an example showing how dollar cost averaging makes a profit even in a flat market, in which a security is not trending up or down but fluctuates around a mean of zero.
2. On March 1, an all-equity portfolio you manage is equally weighted. On June 1, it has changed as shown in the following table. What specific steps should you take to rebalance the portfolio, assuming no security position is completely eliminated?

| *Stock* | *Value on March 1* | *Value on June 1* |
|---|---|---|
| 1,000 JUI | $ 10,000 | $ 11,750 |
| 500 LLO | 10,000 | 9,500 |
| 2,300 KI | 10,000 | 12,000 |
| 1,200 NMB | 10,000 | 17,875 |
| 500 ERW | 10,000 | 8,875 |
| 1,700 OP | 10,000 | 10,625 |
| 900 XXC | 10,000 | 12,455 |
| 1,200 PPM | 10,000 | 13,800 |
| 2,500 PPU | 10,000 | 9,500 |
| 1,500 WQE | 10,000 | 11,000 |
| Total | $100,000 | $117,380 |

3. Consider the information in the following table:

| *Stock* | *Beta* | *Value* |
|---|---|---|
| 1,000 JUI | 1.07 | $ 11,750 |
| 500 LLO | 0.92 | 9,500 |
| 2,300 KI | 1.10 | 12,000 |
| 1,200 NMB | 1.22 | 17,875 |
| 500 ERW | 1.10 | 8,875 |
| 1,700 OP | 0.88 | 10,625 |
| 900 XXC | 1.00 | 12,455 |
| 1,200 PPM | 1.03 | 13,800 |
| 2,500 PPU | 1.22 | 9,500 |
| 1,500 WQE | 1.14 | 11,000 |
| Total | | $117,380 |

a. What is the beta of this portfolio?
b. What (specifically) would you do to bring this portfolio back to a target beta of 1.10?

4. A portfolio consists of $250,000 in stock and $10,000 in cash. The beta of the portfolio is 1.10. Show how the beta of the portfolio can be reduced to 0.95 by shifting the equity/cash proportions.
5. Consider the portfolio in Problem 3 (before any adjustments). Estimate the value of each of the components if the S&P 500 index rises from 1,400.00 to 1,500.00.
6. Suppose the variance of the market is 0.04. What is the approximate variance of the portfolio in Problem 3? (Refer to the statistical relationships in Chapter 5.)
7. Consider the following mutual fund history:

| *Date* | *Fund A* | *Fund B* |
|---|---|---|
| January | 12.00 | 11.53 |
| February | 11.47 | 11.22 |
| March | 12.21 | 11.98 |
| April | 12.33 | 12.05 |
| May | 12.44 | 12.61 |
| June | 13.17 | 12.93 |
| July | 12.76 | 13.08 |

a. Calculate the variance of return for each of the two mutual funds.
b. If you had employed a dollar cost averaging program by making monthly investments of $250, in which fund would you have the most money at the end of July?

8. Suppose an investor put $125 per month into both Funds A and B in Problem 7. Calculate the variance of the two-security portfolio over this period.
9. In Problem 2, assume that on March 1, each of the stocks had a dividend yield of 4 percent and that each paid dividends quarterly. If you can earn 6 percent in a money market account, approximately how much interest would you lose if you accumulated one year's worth of uncashed dividend checks?

10. FROM THE 1995 LEVEL III CFA EXAM (Question 11)
The Board is concerned about the pension portfolio's downside risk and wants to adopt a formal policy for rebalancing the plan's assets in response to fluctuations in market values. Donovan asks you to review the major strategies that

the Board should consider. You are aware of three strategies used to reallocate between higher-risk and lower-risk assets: "Constant Mix," "Constant Proportion," and "Buy and Hold."

**A.** Describe the primary characteristics of *each* of these *three* strategies as they relate to changes in market values. Identify the market environment in which *each* strategy should provide the best relative performance.

**(12 minutes)**

**B.** Recommend *one* strategy for the Board's consideration, taking their concerns into account. Justify your choice.

**(4 minutes)**

11. Using the "historical quotes" feature at the Website *http://finance.yahoo.com*, determine the total return on the S&P 500 index for 2001 if an investor was:
    - **a.** In the market the *whole year*,
    - **b.** Out of the market on the ten *best* days;
    - **c.** Out of the market on the twenty *best* days;
    - **d.** Out of the market on the ten *worst* days.
12. Using data from the previous 20 trading days, calculate the growth in a $1 investment for which the optimum daily switches were made between two asset classes: Treasury bills and the S&P 500 stock index. Ignore commissions.

## INTERNET EXERCISE

Go to the Morningstar Website at *http://www.morningstar.com* and pick a mutual fund. You can also identify a particular fund using the "Fund Selector." Then retrieve a "*Quicktake*" report for this mutual fund and check the portfolio composition. Note which holdings in the portfolio are new, which have increased in weight, and which have shrunk since the last portfolio.

## FURTHER READING


Ambachtsheer, K.P., and James Farrell. "Can Active Management Add Value?" *Financial Analysts Journal*, November/December 1979, 39–47.

Barber, Brad M., and Terrance Odean. "The Courage of Misguided Convictions." *Financial Analysts Journal*, November/December 1999, 41–55.

Bogle, John C. "When to Index and When Not to Index." *Pension World*, April 1980 (Part 1), May 1980 (Part 2).

Brealey, R.A., and S.D. Hodges. "Dynamic Portfolio Selection." *Financial Analysts Journal*, March/April 1973, 50–65.

Elton, Edwin J., Martin J. Gruber, Sanjiv Das, and Matthew Hlavka. "Efficiency with Costly Information: A Reinterpretation of Evidence from Manager Portfolios." *Review of Financial Studies* 6, 1, (1993), 1–23.

Jensen, Michael C. "The Performance of Mutual Funds in the Period 1955–1964." *Journal of Finance*, May 1968, 389–416.

McEnally, Richard W. "Latané's Bequest: The Best of Portfolio Strategies." *Journal of Portfolio Management*, Winter 1986, 21–30.

———. "Time Diversification: The Surest Route to Lower Risk?" *Journal of Portfolio Management*, Summer 1985, 24–26.

Markowitz, Harry M. "Portfolio Selection." *Journal of Finance*, March 1952, 77–91.

———. *Portfolio Selection: Efficient Diversification of Investments*, New Haven, Conn.: Yale University Press, 1959.

Perold, Andre F., and William F. Sharpe. "Dynamic Strategies for Asset Allocation." *Financial Analysts Journal*, January/February 1988, 16–27.

Rudd, Andrew. "Optimal Selection of Passive Portfolios." *Financial Management*, Spring 1980, 57–65.

Schreiner, John. "Portfolio Revision: A Turnover-Constrained Approach." *Financial Management*, Spring 1980, 67–75.

Sharpe, William F. "Are Gains Likely from Market Timing?" *Financial Analysts Journal*, March/April 1975, 60–69.

Snigaroff, Robert G. "The Economics of Active Management." *Journal of Portfolio Management*, Winter 2000, 16–24.

Sorensen, Eric H., Keith L. Miller, and Vele Samak, "Allocating between Active and Passive Management," *Financial Analysts Journal*, September/October 1998, 18–31.

Statman, Meir. "A Behavioral Framework for Dollar-Cost Averaging." *Journal of Portfolio Management*, Fall 1995, 70–78.

Walkling, Ralph A., and Robert O. Edmister. "Are There Commission Cost Side-Effects from Portfolio Management Decisions?" *Financial Analysts Journal*, July/August 1983, 52–59.

# 14 Revision of the Fixed-Income Portfolio

*There are no permanent changes because change itself is permanent. It behooves the industrialist to research and the investor to be vigilant.*

**Ralph L. Woods**

## Key Terms

barbell strategy
bond swap
bullet strategy
confidence index
convexity
flight to quality
laddered strategy
Macaulay duration
modified duration
yield curve inversion

## Introduction

The fixed-income component of a portfolio needs periodic revision, as does its equity counterpart. Whether the chore is more difficult with bonds than with stock depends on to whom you speak. The price behavior of bonds is arguably more predictable than that of stock because bond prices converge on their par values as maturity approaches. Also, with some bond strategies, we know certain necessary aspects of the revision process years in advance.

To some extent, managing a bond portfolio involves forecasting future interest rates, just as managing a stock portfolio may require an assessment of near-term market movements. In an efficient market context, of course, nobody can accurately predict the future. What managers can do, however, is manage the risk they face. Equity managers face market risk, whereas bond managers face interest rate, default, and reinvestment rate risks. Fixed-income security management is largely a matter of altering the level of risk the portfolio faces, especially interest rate risk as measured by duration.

This chapter presents several well-known bond portfolio strategies that require periodic revision. It also reviews how the fund manager can adjust the portfolio to be consistent with these strategies.

## Passive versus Active Management Strategies

### *Passive Strategies*

The two passive bond strategies are (1) buy and hold and (2) indexing.

*"Although buy-and-hold is a realistic option for investors who buy equities, it is an act of wanton imprudence for investors in debt securities. Ultimately, of course, a debt security reverts to cash, and thereafter earns nothing for its owner. Well before the maturity date, however, its entire pattern of market behavior changes with the passage of time. This means that active management of fixed income securities is an inescapable responsibility."*
Peter L. Bernstein, former editor, *Journal of Portfolio Management*

**Buy and Hold.** You can build a portfolio of common stock and not touch it again for decades. This is *passive management* taken to an extreme, but it is common practice with perpetual securities such as common stock. Things are different with bonds because they have a maturity date, after which their investment merit ceases. If you discover ten GHY 8s of 1967 in a forgotten family safe, each of these bonds is probably worth $1,040 (the $1,000 principal and the last coupon amount of $40). These bonds were also worth $1,040 on their maturity day in 1967, so the money might as well have been buried in the backyard the past few decades. This implies that a passive bond strategy still requires the periodic replacement of bonds as they mature.

**Indexing.** Another passive approach to bond management involves an attempt to replicate the investment characteristics of a popular measure of the bond market. In the United States there are more than 400 indexes to measure the performance of fixed-income securities. These are published predominately by Salomon Brothers, Lehman Brothers, and Merrill Lynch. Two of the best-known bond indexes are the Salomon Brothers Corporate Bond Index and the Lehman Brothers Long Treasury Bond Index.

The rationale for indexing comes from the pioneering work on the concept of market efficiency with equity securities. *Market efficiency* means that managers are unable to predict market movements and that attempts to time the market are, on average, fruitless.

*"The universe of bonds is broader and more diverse than that of stocks."*
Frank Reilly and David Wright in the *Handbook of Fixed Income Securities*

Securities held in the two best-known bond indexes are primarily high-grade issues, which yield less than lower-grade issues. A manager can normally outperform the return on a bond index by including enough lower-grade issues in the portfolio under management to crank up its return. The proper comparison should be between the index and a managed portfolio of comparable risk to the index. *Comparable risk* means both similar default risk and similar interest rate risk (duration). It does not make sense to compare a twenty-five-year BBB-rated bond portfolio with a five-year AAA-rated portfolio without addressing the risk differential.

Merrill Lynch and Salomon Brothers have prepared high-yield bond indexes since the mid-1980s when junk bonds became widespread. These are reported in *The Wall Street Journal* and elsewhere in the financial press.

*"The only thing worse than a passive strategy is an unsuccessful active one. The results are bad and the costs are excessive."*
Henry B. Spencer, senior vice-president, Guardian Life Insurance

Investments in bond index funds have increased from less than $500 million in 1980 to $100 billion today. A bond index fund is a collection of securities that seeks to mimic the performance of a published measure of bond returns. One likely reason for the increase is the fact that professionally managed bond funds have generally failed to outperform bond averages. In the two-year period ended September 30, 1990, only 16 percent of 637 professionally managed bond portfolios managed to outperform the Salomon Brothers investment grade bond index. None of these portfolios beat the index in each year of this period. Bond managers do not do any better beating the market than their equity counterparts.

### *Active Strategies*

Two classic and well-known active bond management strategies are the *laddered strategy* and the *barbell strategy*, although they require so little effort to implement that some people would classify them as passive.

FIGURE 14-1

Laddered Bond Portfolio

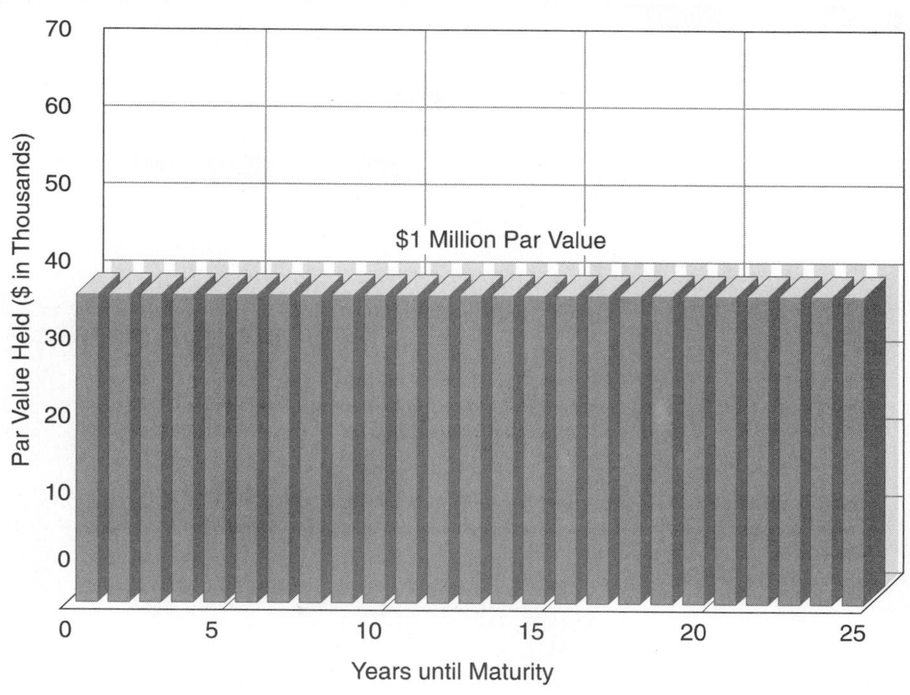


**Laddered Portfolio.** Fixed-income securities with long maturities usually carry the highest yields to maturity, but they also have the most interest rate risk. Rather than try to second-guess interest rate changes, a popular alternative is to use a **laddered strategy,** which distributes the fixed-income dollars throughout the yield curve. Consider the example in Figure 14-1. Here bonds have been selected to spread their maturities uniformly over the next twenty-five years. The manager could have chosen twenty or thirty years rather than twenty-five; there is nothing magic about the twenty-five-year period.

Tending a laddered portfolio is simple. The portfolio in Figure 14-1 consists of bonds worth $1 million in par value, with one-twenty-fifth of this ($40,000) invested in each maturity from one to twenty-five years. Each year $40,000 par value matures, and the portfolio manager uses the proceeds from these bonds to buy other bonds with a twenty-five year maturity. The remaining bonds move "one place to the left" until ultimately they mature and a new twenty-five year bond enters the portfolio. The manager's only decision is which specific twenty-five year bonds to buy with the proceeds from the matured bonds. See Figure 14-2.

**Barbell Portfolio.** A barbell strategy is the other classic active bond management strategy. The **barbell strategy** differs from the laddered strategy in that there is less investment in the middle maturities. Figure 14-3 shows one example of a bond portfolio managed via a barbell strategy. As in Figure 14-1, the twenty-five year maximum maturity is arbitrary. The horizon could just as easily be twenty or thirty years. In this example, the largest investments are in bonds with maturities of one to five years and twenty-one to twenty-five years. Initially, there is an investment of $70,000 par value

FIGURE 14-2

Revision of a Laddered Bond Portfolio

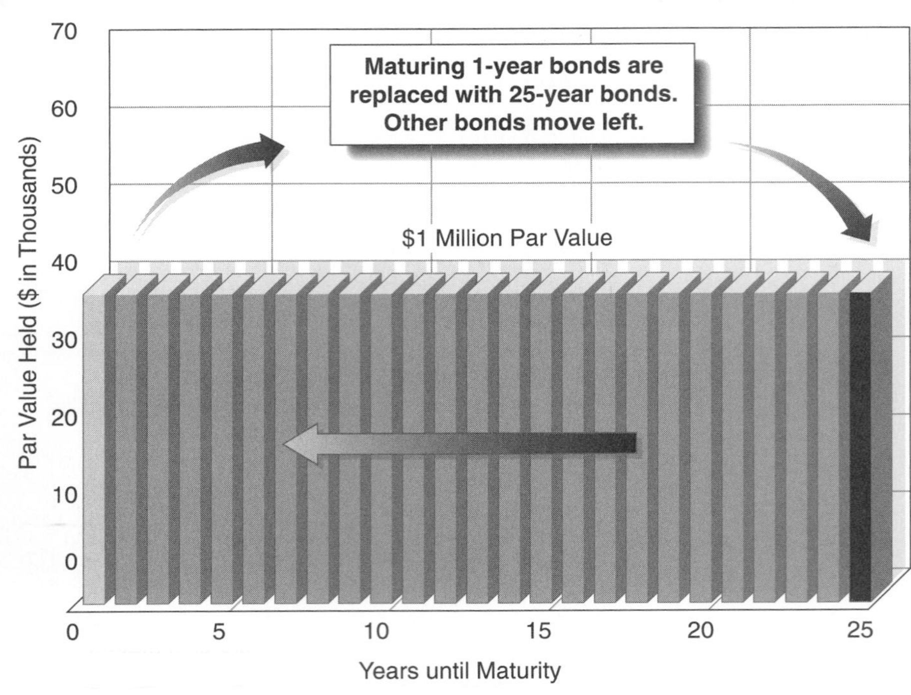


FIGURE 14-3

Barbell Bond Portfolio

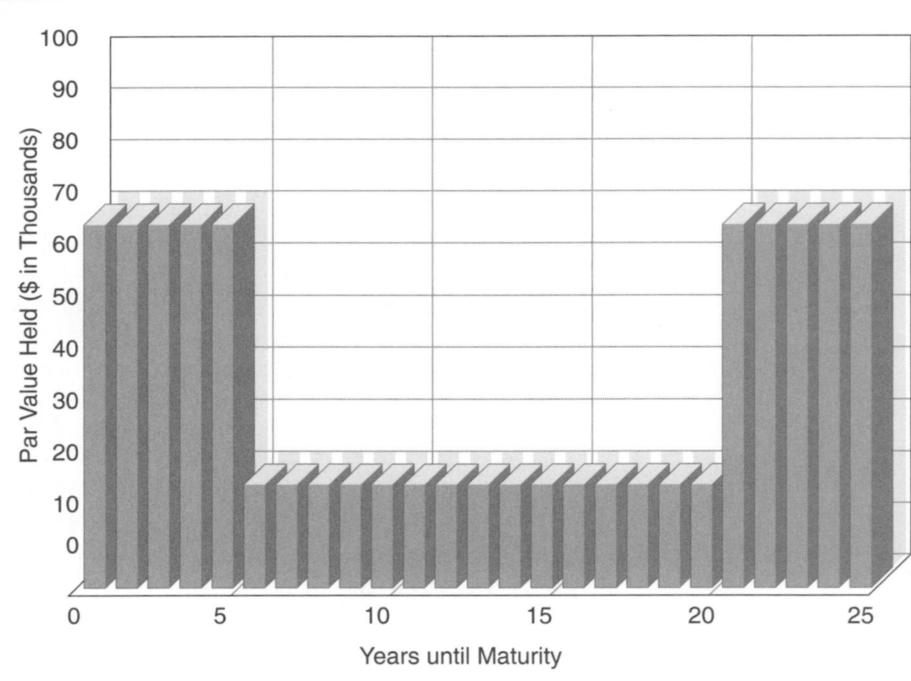

FIGURE 14-4

Revision of a Barbell Bond Portfolio

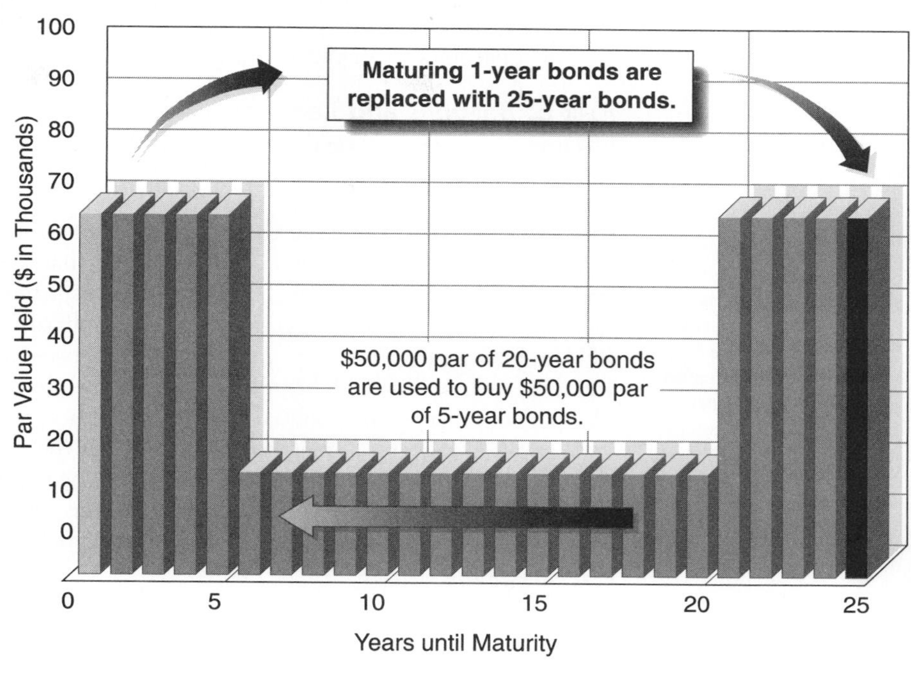


in bonds with each of these maturities and $20,000 par value in each maturity from six to twenty years.[1]

Managing a barbell portfolio is slightly more involved than managing a laddered portfolio because each year the manager must replace *two* sets of bonds. The one-year bonds mature, and the proceeds are used to buy new twenty-five year bonds. The twenty-one year bonds become twenty-year bonds, and it is necessary to sell $50,000 par value of these. The manager then applies this cash toward the purchase of $50,000 par value of five-year bonds (see Figure 14-4).

**Other Active Strategies.** The bread and butter for some fixed-income investment houses is identifying bonds that are likely to experience a rating change in the near future. An increase in the bond rating pushes the price up; a downgrade does the opposite.

The price impact can be significant. On January 12, 2005, according to http://www.bondsonline.com the average yield on a 10-year, BBB-rated corporate bond was 5.98 percent. For a bond with a 4 percent coupon, this corresponds to a bond price of 85.26 percent. Also on this date, the average yield on a 10-year, A-rated bond was 5.42 percent. With a 4 percent coupon, this bond would sell for 89.15 percent. This is a price differential of 4.56 percent. An astute bond manager who correctly identified a BBB-rated bond that was about to be upgraded to single A would substantially improve the portfolio's performance for the year by purchasing such a bond in advance of the upgrade.

[1]The number of weights on each end of the bar is also arbitrary. Instead of five weights, the barbell might carry three or eight weights. The diameter of the bar can also vary. The name *barbell* simply refers to the general shape of the maturity distribution.

A variation on this theme is finding BB bonds with the potential to move up to investment grade. An extra price boost is often associated with this particular upgrade because it becomes an eligible investment for many more institutional investors.

### Risk of Barbells and Ladders

It is important to recognize that the relative risks of the barbell and laddered strategies are not the same for two reasons.

*"Institutional investors increasingly are turning to passive money management in response to what they consider to be high fees for active managers whose returns often don't outperform the indexes."* Editorial opinion, Pensions and Investment Age, *29 May 1989, 10.*

**Interest Rate Risk.** Suppose the two portfolios shown in Figures 14-1 and 14-3 contain bonds with a 10 percent coupon rate and that the prevailing yield curve is a traditional, upward-sloping one with one-year securities yielding 9.0 percent. Assume that for each additional year until maturity up to twenty-one years, the bonds yield an additional ten basis points (for example, two-year bonds yield 9.1 percent, and three-year bonds yield 9.2 percent). Maturities after twenty-one years are flat at 11.0 percent. Figure 14-5 shows the durations of these securities.

Duration increases as maturity lengthens, but the increase is not linear. This is exactly what Malkiel's theorem about the decreasing importance of lengthening maturity means. A noticeable difference exists in the durations of one- and two-year bonds, but not much relative difference in the durations of twenty-four- and twenty-five year bonds.

The duration of a bond portfolio is simply a weighted average of the component durations.[2] For the barbell portfolio, the duration is 6.05 years. For the laddered

**FIGURE 14-5**

Component Durations

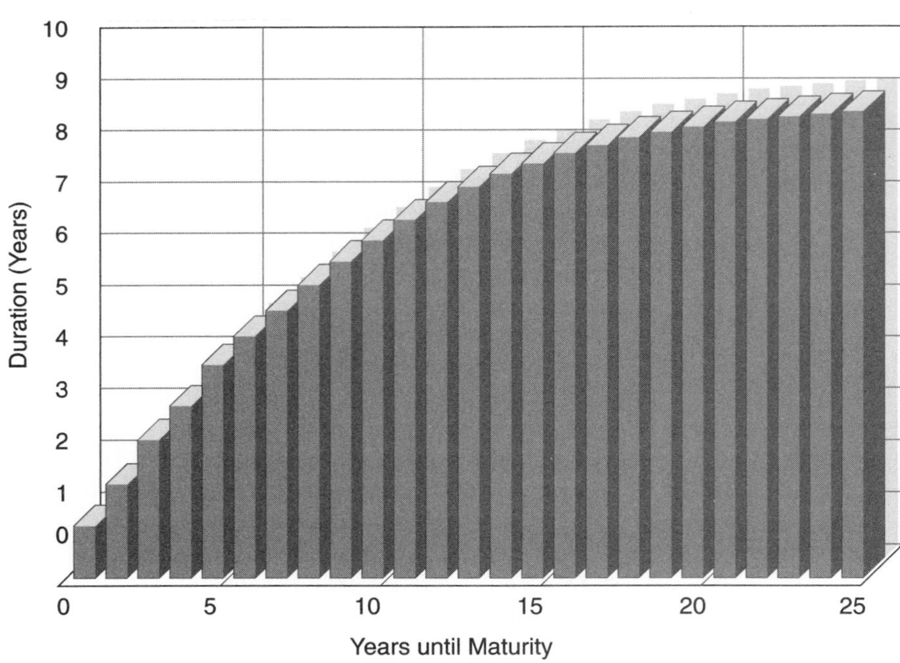


[2]Actually, this is an arguable statement. If you calculate the yield to maturity of a bond portfolio as if it were a single security and use this value to calculate the duration of the "single security," you will get a slightly different answer than if you use the weighted average approach. Given the bid-ask spread of bond prices and the uncertainty of their precise purchase price, this difference is usually ignored in practice. The weighted average approach is much simpler to employ.

**TABLE 14-1** RISK COMPARISON WITH LADDERED AND BARBELL STRATEGIES

| | *Rising Interest Rates* | *Falling Interest Rates* |
|---|---|---|
| Interest Rate Risk | Barbell favored | Laddered favored |
| Reinvestment Rate Risk | Barbell favored | Laddered favored |

(This assumes the duration of the laddered portfolio is greater than the duration of the barbell portfolio.)

portfolio, the duration is 6.53 years. Duration measures interest rate risk, so this particular laddered portfolio is riskier than the barbell portfolio.

**Reinvestment Rate Risk.** Both the laddered and barbell portfolios have a face value of $1 million; all bonds in both portfolios have a 10 percent coupon rate. This means that both portfolios will generate $100,000 per year in income. The barbell portfolio requires the reinvestment each year of $70,000 in par value, whereas the laddered portfolio requires the reinvestment of $40,000. If interest rates fall, the lost interest will be more with the barbell strategy than with the laddered strategy. This is so because the barbell strategy results in $30,000 more being reinvested at a lower rate. Rising rates, of course, would favor the barbell strategy because more funds would be available each year for investment at the new, higher rates available.

**Reconciling Interest Rate and Reinvestment Rate Risks.** Table 14-1 summarizes the relevant points in the comparison. During a period of falling interest rates, the laddered portfolio fares better than the barbell portfolio. The opposite is true when interest rates are rising.

Note, however, that the results in Table 14-1 do not apply in every comparison of barbell and laddered portfolios. It is possible, for instance, to construct a barbell portfolio with a longer duration than a laddered portfolio by carefully selecting the coupon rates of the components. The lower the coupon rates, the higher the duration, everything else being kept constant. If the bonds in Figure 14-3 were all zero coupon bonds, for instance, the portfolio duration would be 13.0 years. Such a portfolio would have no reinvestment rate risk but substantial interest rate risk.

*Duration is a pure measure of interest rate risk only for parallel shifts in the yield curve.*

Table 14-1 also does not apply during periods when the yield curve is inverting (**yield curve inversion** occurs when short-term rates are rising faster than long-term rates). The yield curve is inverted when 90-day T-bills yield more than U.S. government bonds. Duration as a pure measure of interest rate risk works only for parallel shifts in the yield curve. This means that if the rate for a six-month T-bill rises by half a percentage point, the average rates for all other maturities also rise by half a percentage point. When the yield curve is in the process of inverting, its shifts are not parallel.

The implication of this is that a barbell strategy is safer than a laddered strategy when the yield curve is inverting. The prices of the long-term securities in a barbell portfolio are relatively constant because long-term rates are not changing much, whereas the short-term securities are not changing much because they are short term. A laddered strategy loses more than a barbell strategy during periods of yield curve inversion.

The opposite is true during periods of falling interest rates. In fact, an ambitious manager might then create a reverse barbell, with most maturities middle term and fewer securities short and long term.

### Bullets versus Barbells

Another important bond portfolio comparison is the bullet strategy versus the barbell strategy. A **bullet strategy** is one in which the bond maturities cluster around one particular maturity on the yield curve. It is possible to construct two portfolios, one a bullet and one a barbell, with the same durations but with substantially different responses to changes in interest rates. This is so because the yield curve seldom undergoes a parallel shift, and duration is an inaccurate predictor when the shift is not parallel.

While it is not an infallible rule, some people follow a heuristic stating that the barbell strategy will outperform a bullet strategy when the yield curve flattens, and, conversely, the bullet strategy will outperform a barbell strategy when the yield curve steepens. This is not an exact relationship because it depends on *how much* the yield curve flattens or steepens. For small movements, though, the rule is generally accurate.

### Swaps

A portfolio manager's exchange of an existing bond or set of bonds for a different issue is a **bond swap.**[3] Bond swaps are usually intended to do one of four things:

1. Increase current income.
2. Increase yield to maturity.
3. Improve the potential for price appreciation with a decline in interest rates.
4. Establish losses to offset capital gains or taxable income.

There are four main types of swaps.[4]

*Profitable substitution swaps are inconsistent with the notion of market efficiency.*

**Substitution Swap.** In a substitution swap, the investor finds an opportunity to increase current yield by exchanging one bond for another of similar risk and maturity and pick up a few basis points in the process. For example, an investor might sell a thirty-year, 8 percent bond selling at par and replace it with another thirty-year, 8 percent coupon bond selling for $980. This increases the current yield by 16 basis points ($80/$980 = 0.0816).[5] Securities that promise the same return and have the same risk level normally sell for the same price, so obvious opportunities for substitution swaps are not common.

*A set of bond portfolio management strategies is provided at* http://www.finpipe.com/bondstr.htm

**Intermarket or Yield Spread Swap.** The intermarket or yield spread swap involves bonds that trade in different markets, such as government bonds versus corporate bonds. Small differences in these markets sometimes cause similar bonds to behave differently in response to changing market conditions. Speculators may look for bonds with different yields to maturity because they expect that the spread between the two yields to maturity will widen or narrow.

---

[3]Much of the material in this section comes from Robert A. Strong and Chiara Hall, "Speculating with Bonds," *American Association of Individual Investors Journal*, July 1986, 9–12.

[4]Numerous other types of swaps deal with balance sheet management. In corporate finance, for instance, it is common for two firms to exchange the payments on their debt when one firm pays a floating rate and the other pays a fixed rate. There is an example of this in Chapter 21.

[5]Commissions are especially material in examples of this type. If it costs $8 to trade $1,000 par of a bond issue, the advantages to the swap in this example disappear.

For instance, when the economic situation of the country is expected to deteriorate, there is often a **flight to quality** as investors become less willing to hold risky bonds. As investors buy safe bonds (perhaps those rated AAA) and sell more risky bonds (perhaps BBB), the spread between their yields widens. In essence, the value of risky bonds falls during a flight to quality.

One way of measuring this phenomenon is via a *confidence index*, such as the one published weekly in *Barron's*. The **confidence index** is the ratio of the yield on AAA bonds to the yield on BBB bonds. This ratio has a theoretical upper boundary of 1.0 because the yield on safe bonds should never exceed the yield on risky bonds. The more confident people are about the future, the more willing they are to accept risk. As investors buy risky bonds, their prices rise, their yields decline, and the confidence index increases.

**Bond-Rating Swap.** A bond-rating swap is really a form of the intermarket swap. It might be used by an investor who understands the historical data on the yield spreads between bonds of different ratings and who feels able to forecast the movements of these yield spreads in the marketplace. Bonds with higher quality ratings should have a lower yield to maturity than more risky bonds. If an investor anticipates a change in the yield spread, it may be possible to swap bonds with different ratings so that the swap produces a capital gain with a minimal increase in risk.

*"The problem with trying to nail down today's yields for the long run is that timing the bond market is notoriously difficult."*
Tom Herman, *The Wall Street Journal*

**Rate Anticipation Swap.** Someone who anticipates lower interest rates might swap long-term bonds selling at a premium for long-term discount bonds—a rate anticipation swap. Premium bonds are less volatile than discount bonds, and the anticipated decline in interest rates should generate a higher capital gain with the discount bonds. Conversely, if an investor expected rates to rise, she might exchange discount bonds for premium bonds or swap longer-term bonds for short-term bonds.

### Forecasting Interest Rates

Despite what the public likes to think, few professional money managers have a good batting average when it comes to timely prediction of changes in interest rates. Still, changing interest rates are a fact of investment life, and substantial rewards await those who do successfully predict a change.

We know from Malkiel's theorems that rising interest rates cause market participants to bid down the prices of existing bonds and vice versa. We also know that long-term bonds are more volatile than short-term bonds and that low-coupon bonds are more volatile than high-coupon bonds. Duration captures the combined volatility effects of maturity and coupon rate.

The active bond manager who anticipates falling interest rates will want to increase the duration of the portfolio. This way, the value of the portfolio rises the most when rates decline. Of course, this is a two-edged sword; if the manager is wrong about the direction of interest rates, increasing the duration will magnify the paper losses the portfolio suffers. A portfolio manager who expects rates to rise should shorten duration to minimize the impact.

The fixed-income parallel to the question, "What do you think the stock market is going to do?" is "Do you think interest rates are going up or down?" The media frequently ask the country's leading economists about their expectations for future interest rates, and the divergence in their forecasts can be astounding. The theories of the yield curve discussed previously are useful in understanding why the term structure of interest might take on a particular shape, but predicting changes in the yield curve is another matter entirely. This is a formidable task beyond the scope of this book.[6]

### *Volunteering Callable Municipal Bonds*

Many bonds are *callable*, meaning that the issuer can force their early redemption. The bond indenture states precise terms of the call feature. A vice president of a national brokerage firm once described to the author a method his firm had used for years to earn extra profits via the call feature of small municipal bond issues. Consider this example. A municipality has an outstanding issue of 5 percent bonds that mature in fifteen years. The bond indenture requires the city treasurer to retire $100,000 par of these bonds each year by calling for their redemption at par ($1,000).

Suppose that this bond issue sells in the marketplace for 90 percent of par and that a portfolio you manage contains $50,000 par of these bonds. Knowing that the treasurer has to call $100,000 par value of these bonds in a few months, you volunteer your $50,000 holding at a price of 95 percent of par, or $47,500. This is a win–win situation. Rather than having to retire one hundred bonds at $1,000 each, the city treasurer is able to retire half of the necessary number at only $950, for a savings of $50 each. This saves the town a total of $2,500. In addition, the bond portfolio has an instant capital gain of $2,500, which is to the client's benefit.

Successfully employing such a strategy requires careful understanding of numerous bond indentures and probably a working relationship with municipal finance officers. Nonetheless, the strategy can work if the portfolio manager has a strong enough desire to implement it.

There is no reason in principle that this tactic would not also work with corporate bonds. In practice, however, corporate bond issues are much larger and often prescribe some specific lottery method for calling bonds as required. It is far less likely that a corporate treasurer would be able to accommodate such a request.

## Bond Convexity (Advanced Topic)

*For an interesting discussion of convexity go to* http://www.investopedia.com/university/advancedbond/advancedbond6.asp

*Bond convexity is the difference between the actual price change of a bond and that predicted by the duration statistic.*

*The importance of convexity increases as the magnitude of rate changes increases.*

Bond convexity is an advanced topic that many books on investments or portfolio management choose not to cover. Some instructors will choose to skip it here as well. The author has included it for two reasons. First, it is a concept of increasing importance that is getting more attention in the literature. Second, an understanding of convexity adds significantly to an understanding of the uses (and limitations) of the duration statistic.

### *The Importance of Convexity*

For a given interest rate change, **convexity** is the difference between the actual price change in a bond and that predicted by the duration statistic. In practice, the effects of convexity are minor. Understanding the concept of convexity, however, makes duration a more user-friendly statistic.

Using calculus terminology, *duration* is the first derivative of the bond-pricing equation with respect to the yield, whereas convexity is the second derivative. It is easiest to see the importance of this statistic using a graph. Figure 14-6 indicates that the yield to maturity of a bond is not a direct linear function of the bond's price. The

[6]It may well be beyond the scope of every book, given what we currently know about the efficiency of the securities markets.

FIGURE 14-6

Comparative Bond Convexity

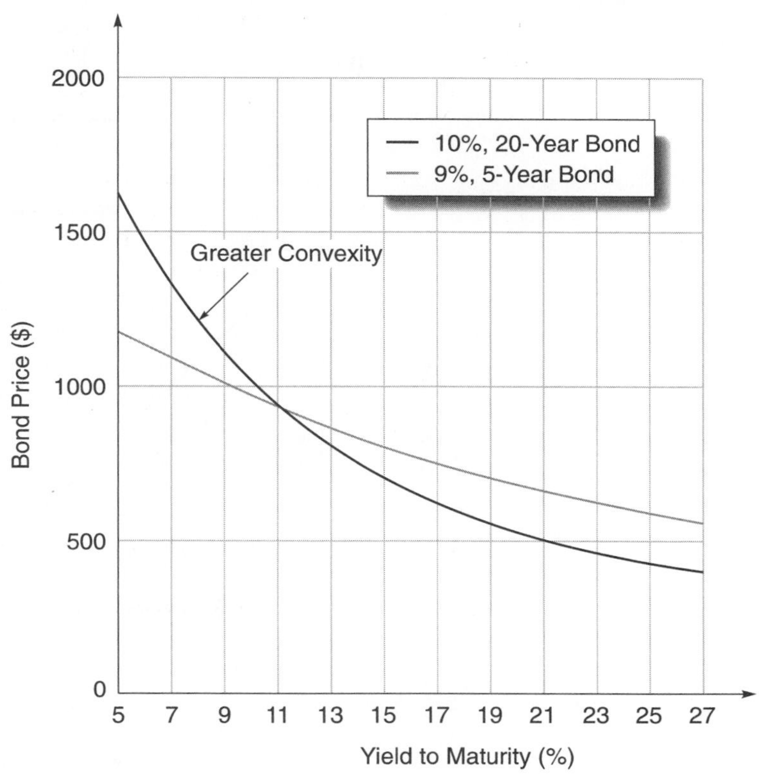


first derivative of price with respect to yield is negative (evident from the downward-sloping curves), but there is also a second derivative that is positive. That is, the decline in bond price as yield increases is decelerating. The shape of this curve is the bond's convexity. The sharper the curve, the greater the convexity.

The implication of this is shown in Figure 14-7, showing the yield to maturity and price relationship for a 10 percent, twenty-year bond that sells for $750 and has a yield to maturity of 13.7 percent. The tangent line corresponds to the price change predicted by duration. As the bond's yield moves up or down, there is a divergence from the actual price change (the curved line) and the duration-predicted price change (the tangent line). The more pronounced the curve, the greater the price difference. Similarly, the greater the yield change, the more important convexity becomes. Duration can measure price change accurately for an infinitesimally small change in interest rates, but as the rate change increases, the importance of convexity grows.

### *Calculating Convexity*

In his excellent book *Bond Markets, Analysis and Strategies*, Frank J. Fabozzi uses calculus to show that you can approximate the actual price change of a bond as

$$dP = \left[\frac{dP}{dR}dR\right] + \left[\frac{1}{2} \times \frac{d^2P}{dR^2}(dR)^2\right] + \text{Error} \quad (14\text{-}1)$$

FIGURE 14-7

Bond Convexity

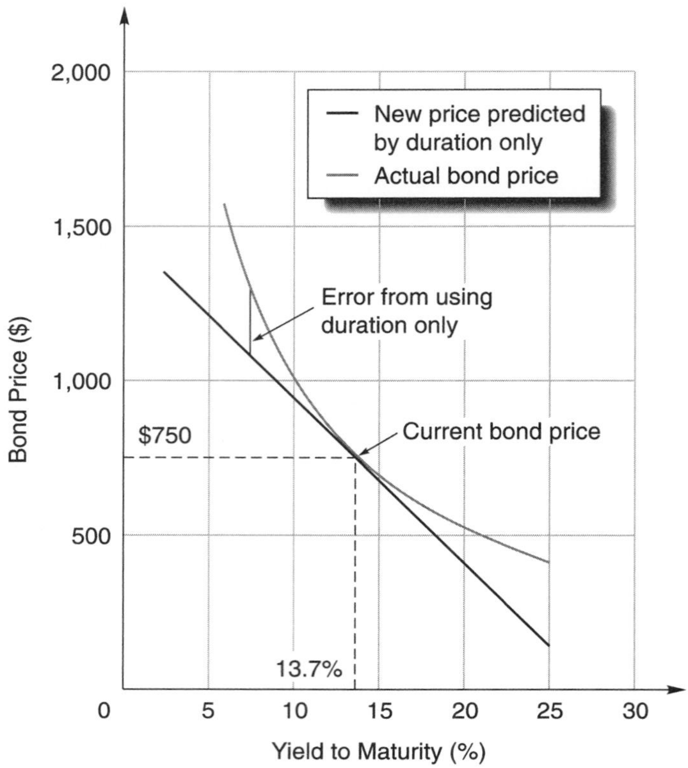


where $P$ = bond price and $R$ = yield to maturity.[7] In words, price change = $f$ (duration, convexity, error). The first term on the right side of Equation 14-1 is the price change in the bond as a consequence of the bond's duration; the second term is the price change as a consequence of its convexity.

Equation 14-1 shows the change in the bond price associated with a change in the bond's yield to maturity. To get the *percentage* change, it is necessary to divide each term by the bond's price:

$$\frac{dP}{P} = \left[\frac{1}{P} \times \frac{dP}{dR} dR\right] + \left[\frac{1}{2P} \times \frac{d^2P}{dR^2}(dR)^2\right] + \frac{\text{Error}}{P} \tag{14-2}$$

The second term of Equation 14-2 contains the bond convexity:

$$\text{Convexity} = \frac{1}{2P} \times \frac{d^2P}{dR^2}(dR)^2 \tag{14-3}$$

[7]This equation comes from a Taylor series expansion of the bond-pricing equation. The Taylor series is useful for approximating many mathematical functions.

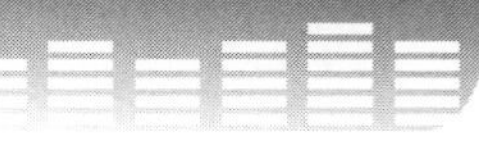

PORTFOLIO MEMO

## Two Derivatives: Speed and Acceleration

Some readers of this book will be unfamiliar with calculus concepts such as first and second derivatives. The idea behind them is not difficult. Calculus is largely about rates of change, in particular how one variable in an equation changes if another variable in the equation changes by a small amount.

Suppose you are traveling in an automobile at thirty miles per hour. How far will you travel in two minutes? Based just on this information, there is no way to tell. It depends on how your speed is changing. Perhaps you are traveling at a *constant* speed of thirty miles per hour. Because there are sixty minutes in an hour, you will travel one mile in two minutes. *Speed is the first derivative of distance traveled with respect to time.*

Alternatively, you might have been traveling at highway speed of sixty-five mph and be braking to a stop. At some point you will be traveling exactly thirty mph. In the next two minutes, however, you may travel only one hundred feet, much less than a mile. The converse is true when accelerating. After blasting off, how far does the space shuttle travel in the two minutes after its speed is exactly thirty mph? *Acceleration is the second derivative of distance with respect to time.* Equivalently, it is the *first derivative of speed with respect to time.* That is, how does speed change with the passage of time?

Knowing only that you are traveling at exactly thirty mph is insufficient information to determine how far you will travel in a period of time.

The analogy holds true with bonds. Duration is the first derivative of the bond price with respect to the yield. Convexity is the second derivative. We have a good idea how much a bond price will change if the yield moves from 5.00 percent to 5.0005 percent, just as we can predict reasonably well how far the space shuttle travels in the 0.0005 seconds after its speed was thirty mph. If the bond yield changes from 5 percent to 6 percent or if we increase the space shuttle's travel time by two minutes, the first derivative alone will predict an inaccurate result. Duration works well for small changes in yield, but for a significant jump in rates, we should include the effects of convexity.

Suppose we have a bond that pays three cash flows: $C_1$, $C_2$, and $C_3$. Equation 14-4 shows this bond's pricing equation:

$$P = \frac{C_1}{(1+R)^1} + \frac{C_2}{(1+R)^2} + \frac{C_3}{(1+R)^3} \qquad \textbf{(14-4)}$$

We can restate this as Equation 14-5:

$$P = C_1(1+R)^{-1} + C_2(1+R)^{-2} + C_3(1+R)^{-3} \qquad \textbf{(14-5)}$$

Now we take the first derivative with respect to the yield to maturity, $R$:

$$\frac{dP}{dR} = -C_1(1+R)^{-2} - 2C_2(1+R)^{-3} - 3C_3(1+R)^{-4}$$

$$= \frac{-C_1}{(1+R)^2} - \frac{2C_2}{(1+R)^3} - \frac{3C_3}{(1+R)^4}$$

$$= \frac{-1}{(1+R)} \times \left[\frac{C_1}{(1+R)^1} + \frac{2C_2}{(1+R)^2} + \frac{3C_3}{(1+R)^3}\right]$$

More generally, for any number of time periods $t$:

$$\frac{dP}{dR} = \frac{1}{(1+R)} \times \sum_{\text{All } t} \frac{-t \times C_t}{(1+R)^t} \quad \textbf{(14-6)}$$

This gives the actual price change in the bond. If we want to know the percentage price change, we divide through by the price of the bond, $P$:

$$\frac{dP}{dR} \times \frac{1}{P} = \frac{1}{(1+R)} \times \sum_{\text{All } t}\left[\frac{-t \times C_t}{(1+R)^t} \times \frac{1}{P}\right] \quad \textbf{(14-7)}$$

The portion of this equation in brackets is the duration measure we saw in Chapter 11, called **Macaulay duration** after the researcher who coined the term. Making a minor time value of money adjustment to Macaulay duration, as in Equation 14-7, results in **modified duration.** Because most bonds pay interest semiannually, we usually calculate modified duration as the traditional Macaulay duration discounted by one-half the annual yield to maturity:

$$\text{Modified duration} = \frac{\text{Macaulay duration}}{\left[1 + (\text{Annual yield to maturity}/2)\right]}$$

### *An Example*

Modified duration is related to the percentage change in the price of a bond for a given change in the bond's yield to maturity. Specifically, the percentage change in the bond price is equal to the negative of modified duration multiplied by the change in yield. (The negative sign is necessary because bond prices move inversely with interest rates.) A 10 percent, twenty-year bond selling for $750 has a duration of 7.57 years and a yield to maturity of 13.70 percent. Half the annual yield to maturity is 6.85 percent, and modified duration is therefore (7.57/[1 + 0.0685]) = 7.09 years.

Now suppose market interest rates change, and our bond's yield to maturity falls to 12.70 percent. Its new market price will be $805.50, and its new duration will be 7.94 years (modified duration = 7.47 years).

The price change predicted by duration is equal to the negative of modified duration multiplied by the yield change: −7.09 × −0.01 = 7.09%. The actual price change was (805.50 − 750)/750 = 7.40%. This is a difference of thirty-one basis points, amounting to $31,000 on a $10 million bond portfolio.

Including bond convexity gives a better forecast. This requires the calculation of the second derivative of the bond price with respect to the yield (the second term on the right side of Equation 14-1). Table 14-2 shows this calculation.

**TABLE 14-2** SECOND DERIVATIVE OF BOND-PRICING EQUATION

$$P = \sum_{t=1}^{n} \frac{C_t}{(1+R)^t} = \sum_{t=1}^{n} C_t (1+R)^{-t}$$

$$\frac{dP}{dR} = \sum_{t=1}^{n} -tC_t (1+R)^{-t-1}$$

$$\frac{d^2P}{dR^2} = \sum_{t=1}^{n} -t(-t-1)C_t (1+R)^{-t-2}$$

$$= \sum_{t=1}^{n} \frac{t(t+1)C_t}{(1+R)^{t+2}}$$

Table 14-3 is a worksheet to use to solve for the numerical value of convexity. It is important to be consistent with periods when calculating duration and convexity. That is, you do not want to mix up semiannual periods with annual periods. To annualize duration it is necessary to divide by the square of the number of periods per year. The bottom of Table 14-3 shows the calculations needed to move from the second derivative to convexity in years.

To estimate the percentage price change due to convexity, we see from Equation 14-1 that we multiply convexity by one-half the square of the change in the bond's yield to maturity: $86.73 \times 0.5 \times (-0.01)^2 = 0.0043 = 0.43\%$. The total percentage price change (from duration and from convexity) is then estimated to be 7.09 + 0.43% = 7.52%. We saw earlier that the actual price change was 7.40 percent. Our estimate using convexity differs from this by twelve basis points, whereas our estimate using duration alone was off by thirty-one basis points.

Therefore, although duration is a useful measure of interest rate risk, it is an imperfect one for nontrivial changes in interest rates. If you find yourself playing the "what-if" game regarding changing interest rates and their effect on your portfolios, your forecasting accuracy can be improved by including the effects of convexity along with those of duration.

Two general rules concerning convexity are useful to remember:

1. The higher the yield to maturity, the lower the convexity, everything else being equal.
2. The lower the coupon, the greater the convexity, everything else being equal.

### *Using Convexity*

The preceding discussion covered the definition and calculation of convexity. What, however, is its practical meaning? How can portfolio managers use their understanding of this statistic to make better investment decisions?

Figure 14-8 shows two bonds, both of which have a 10 percent yield to maturity, a current market price of $1,000, and a duration of eleven years. One bond is a 10 percent perpetuity, whereas the other is a zero coupon bond with a par value of $2,853. The figure indicates that no matter what happens to interest rates, the bond with the greater convexity fares better. It has a higher price at any new yield to maturity than the bond with the lower convexity. In language reminiscent of efficient portfolios, the investment in the zero coupon bond dominates the competing investment.[8]

[8]In an efficient market, then, no one would purchase the competing investment, and its price would have to decline until it reached the equilibrium price.

**TABLE 14-3** CALCULATION OF CONVEXITY

| *Period* | *Cash Flow* | $1/(1+R)^{t+2}$ | $t(t+1)CF$ | |
|---|---|---|---|---|
| 1 | 50 | 0.8197 | 100 | 81.9741 |
| 2 | 50 | 0.7672 | 300 | 230.1564 |
| 3 | 50 | 0.7180 | 600 | 430.8029 |
| 4 | 50 | 0.6720 | 1000 | 671.9746 |
| 5 | 50 | 0.6289 | 1500 | 943.3429 |
| 6 | 50 | 0.5886 | 2100 | 1236.0131 |
| 7 | 50 | 0.5508 | 2800 | 1542.3655 |
| 8 | 50 | 0.5155 | 3600 | 1855.9114 |
| 9 | 50 | 0.4825 | 4500 | 2171.1645 |
| 10 | 50 | 0.4515 | 5500 | 2483.5241 |
| 11 | 50 | 0.4226 | 6600 | 2789.1707 |
| 12 | 50 | 0.3955 | 7800 | 3084.9720 |
| 13 | 50 | 0.3702 | 9100 | 3368.3987 |
| 14 | 50 | 0.3464 | 10500 | 3637.4487 |
| 15 | 50 | 0.3242 | 12000 | 3890.5795 |
| 16 | 50 | 0.3034 | 13600 | 4126.6481 |
| 17 | 50 | 0.2840 | 15300 | 4344.8564 |
| 18 | 50 | 0.2658 | 17100 | 4544.7038 |
| 19 | 50 | 0.2487 | 19000 | 4725.9437 |
| 20 | 50 | 0.2328 | 21000 | 4888.5461 |
| 21 | 50 | 0.2179 | 23100 | 5032.6632 |
| 22 | 50 | 0.2039 | 25300 | 5158.6004 |
| 23 | 50 | 0.1908 | 27600 | 5266.7890 |
| 24 | 50 | 0.1786 | 30000 | 5357.7638 |
| 25 | 50 | 0.1671 | 32500 | 5432.1424 |
| 26 | 50 | 0.1564 | 35100 | 5490.6072 |
| 27 | 50 | 0.1464 | 37800 | 5533.8901 |
| 28 | 50 | 0.1370 | 40600 | 5562.7589 |
| 29 | 50 | 0.1282 | 43500 | 5578.0055 |
| 30 | 50 | 0.1200 | 46500 | 5580.4357 |
| 31 | 50 | 0.1123 | 49600 | 5570.8607 |
| 32 | 50 | 0.1051 | 52800 | 5550.0899 |
| 33 | 50 | 0.0984 | 56100 | 5518.9243 |
| 34 | 50 | 0.0921 | 59500 | 5478.1512 |
| 35 | 50 | 0.0862 | 63000 | 5428.5403 |
| 36 | 50 | 0.0806 | 66600 | 5370.8401 |
| 37 | 50 | 0.0755 | 70300 | 5305.7745 |
| 38 | 50 | 0.0706 | 74100 | 5234.0413 |
| 39 | 50 | 0.0661 | 78000 | 5156.3100 |
| 40 | 1050 | 0.0619 | 1722000 | 106537.6307 |
| | | | Total | 260193.3162 |

Second derivative = 260,193.32

$$\text{Convexity in years} = \frac{\text{Second derivative}}{\text{Bond price (Periods per year)}^2}$$

$$= \frac{260{,}193.32}{750(2)^2} = 86.73$$

FIGURE 14-8

Convexity and Dominance

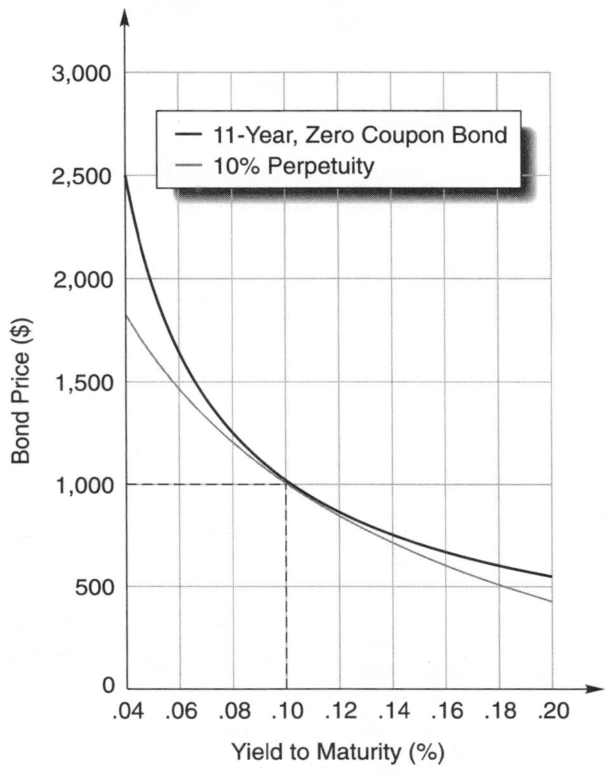


Duration = 11 years.

Given a choice, then, managers should seek high convexity while meeting the other constraints in their bond portfolios. By doing so, they minimize the adverse effects of interest rate volatility for a given portfolio duration.

In fairness, it must be pointed out that in many applications, convexity is a minor issue. The effects of convexity are visually apparent for only rather large changes in interest rates. On large bond portfolios, however, the small effect may translate into a significant number of dollars.

## SUMMARY

Portfolio management strategies can be either passive or active. Buy and hold is the most obvious of the passive strategies, but it is not a feasible strategy with bonds because they mature and must be replaced. Barbell and laddered strategies are passive, but they still require periodic attention by the portfolio manager. Active management strategies with bonds include buying bonds in anticipation of a credit upgrade, various types of swaps, and adjusting the portfolio duration in accord with an attempt to forecast interest rate changes.

The price change of a bond as a consequence of changing interest rates can be more accurately forecasted by using bond convexity along with the duration statistic. Convexity measures the second derivative of the bond price with respect to its yield, whereas duration is a first derivative.

## QUESTIONS

1. Why is pure passive management not possible with a bond portfolio?
2. What is a nonparallel shift in the yield curve?
3. Once the securities have been selected, it is easier to manage a stock portfolio than a bond portfolio. Do you agree with this point of view?
4. What role does default risk play in both barbell and laddered bond strategies?
5. How do you tell if the yield curve is inverted?
6. Zero coupon bonds are preferable to coupon bonds in an immunization strategy. Do you agree?
7. Does the existence of a profitable yield swap imply market inefficiency? Why or why not?
8. Why is a buy and hold strategy for a bond portfolio an act of "wanton imprudence"?
9. Why is the value of *Barron's* confidence index theoretically limited to 1.0?
10. In general, does a portfolio manager want bond convexity to be high or low (everything else being equal)?
11. Why is bond price prediction still not perfect if you use convexity in addition to duration?

## PROBLEMS

The Duration file on the text Website will be helpful, but not necessary, for some of these problems.

1. A person wins $1 million in the state lottery. Actually, the person receives $50,000 per year for twenty years. The present value of this is considerably less than $1 million. Using a 10 percent discount rate, what is the duration of this cash flow stream?
2. Using the bonds in the following table, calculate the duration of a portfolio consisting of one each of the bonds using the following approaches:
   a. The dollar weighted average approach.
   b. The single-security approach.

| *Company* | *Maturity (Years)* | *Coupon (%)* | *Price* | *Yield to Maturity (%)* |
|---|---|---|---|---|
| ABC | 4 | 10 | 98 | 10.63 |
| DEF | 8 | 9 | 87 | 11.53 |
| GHI | 22 | 11 | 102 | 10.76 |
| JKL | 28 | 10 | 90 | 11.17 |

All bonds pay interest on March 1 and September 1.

3. Calculate the convexity of the ABC bond from Problem 2.
4. Suppose market interest rates change by 50 basis points. Estimate the new price of the ABC bond from Problem 2 using the following:
   a. Duration only.
   b. Duration and convexity.
5. Construct a ten-year laddered portfolio consisting of 100 bonds from Problem 2 so that the portfolio pays at least $800 per month in income.
6. Consider the bond portfolio shown in Figure 14-9 on page 433. Would you say this portfolio contains more or less interest rate risk than the barbell portfolio shown in Figure 14-3? Explain your answer.

FIGURE 14-9

Bond Portfolio

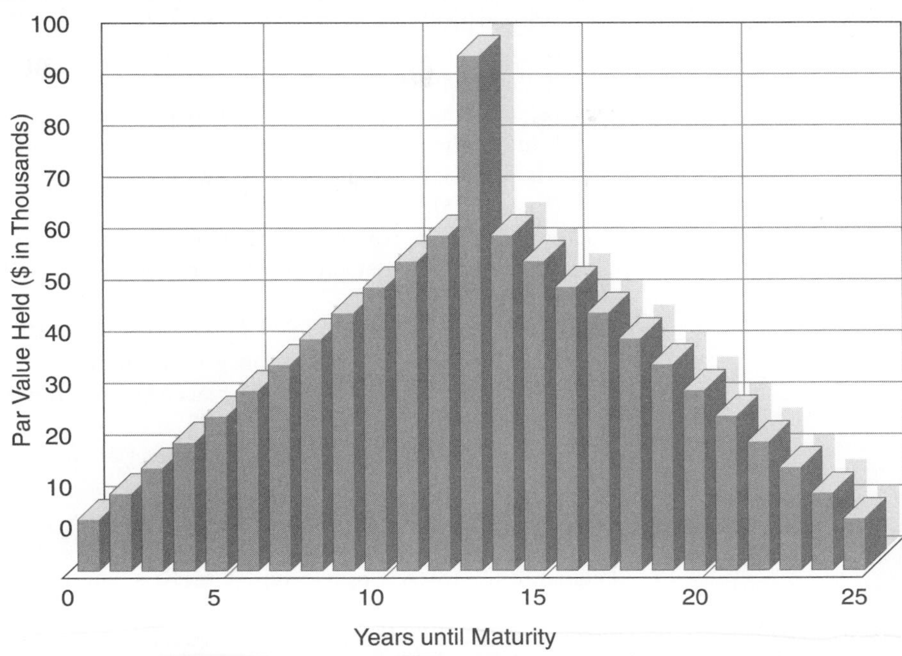


7. Figure 14-8 indicates that the duration of a 10 percent consol that sells for par is eleven years. What is the duration of a 10 percent consol that sells for 90 percent of par?
8. Make up an example showing how a barbell portfolio can have a shorter duration than that of a laddered portfolio.
9. Suppose you had to construct a barbell portfolio that provided a fixed monthly payment to a client. How would you do this? Show an example.
10. A bond matures in ten years and sells for 94 percent of par. It has a yield to maturity of 11 percent, a duration of 6.4 years, and convexity of 125. If the prime interest rate is lowered one-half point and the yield curve follows suit, what do you predict the new price of the bond will be?

## INTERNET EXERCISE

Go to the Morningstar Website at *http://www.morningstar.com* and pick a bond mutual fund. You can identify a particular bond fund using the "*Fund Selector*." Then retrieve a "*Quicktake*" report for this mutual fund and check the portfolio composition. Note which bond holdings in the portfolio are new, which have increased in weight, and which have shrunk since the last portfolio.

## FURTHER READING

Abdullah, F.A., and V.L. Bean. "At Last, a Swaps Primer," *Financial Executive*, July/August 1988, 53–57.

Altman, Edward I., and Scott A. Nammacher. *Investing in Junk Bonds*. New York: John Wiley & Sons, 1987.

Bierman, Harold. "Investors in Junk Bonds." *Journal of Portfolio Management*, Winter 1990.

Bierwag, G.O. *Duration Analysis: Managing Interest Rate Risk*. Cambridge, Mass.: Ballinger, 1987.

Bierwag, G.O., G.G. Kaufman, and Alden Toevs. "Recent Developments in Bond Portfolio Immunization Strategies." *Innovations in Bond Portfolio Management*, ed. by G.G. Kaufman, G.O. Bierwag, and A. Toevs. (Greenwich, Conn.: JAI Press, 1983).

Buetow, Gerald W., Ronald Sellers, Donald Trotter, Elaine Hunt, and Willie Whipple. "The Benefits of Rebalancing." *Journal of Portfolio Management*, Winter 2002, 23–32.

Choie, Kenneth S. "A Simplified Approach to Bond Portfolio Management: DDS." *Journal of Portfolio Management*, Spring 1990.

Cornyn, Anthony G., ed. *Controlling and Managing Interest Rate Risk*. New York: New York Institute of Finance, 1997.

Fabozzi, F.J. *Bond Markets, Analysis and Strategies*, 3d ed. Englewood Cliffs, N.J.: Prentice-Hall, 1996.

Fabozzi, F.J., ed. *Handbook of Fixed Income Securities*, 5th ed. Chicago: Irwin Professional Publishing, 1997.

Felgran, S.D. "Interest Rate Swaps: Use, Risk, and Price." *New England Economic Review*, November/December 1987, 22–32.

Garbade, K.D. "Bond Convexity and Its Implications for Immunization." *Topics in Money and Securities Markets*, March 1985.

Hegde, S.P., and K.P. Nunn. "Non-infinitesimal Rate Changes and Macaulay Duration." *Journal of Portfolio Management*, Winter 1988, 69–73.

Homer, Sidney, and Martin L. Leibowitz. *Inside the Yield Book: New Tools for Bond Market Strategy*. Englewood Cliffs, N.J.: Prentice-Hall, 1972.

Kopprasch, Robert, John McFarlane, Janet Showers, and Daniel Ross. "The Interest-Rate Swap Market: Yield Mathematics, Terminology, and Conventions." *The Handbook of Fixed Income Securities*, 3d ed., ed. Frank J. Fabozzi. Homewood, Ill.: Business One—Irwin, 1991.

Lacy, Nelson, and Sanjay K. Nawalkha. "Convexity, Risk, and Returns." *Journal of Fixed Income*, December 1993, 72–79.

Leibowitz, Martin L., William S. Kraske, and Ardavan Nozari. "Spread Duration: A New Tool for Bond Portfolio Management." *Journal of Portfolio Management*, Spring 1990.

Plaxco, Lisa, and Robert D. Arnott. "Rebalancing a Global Policy Benchmark." *Journal of Portfolio Management*, Winter 2002, 9–22.

Smith, C.W., C.W. Smithson, and L.M. Wakeman. "The Market for Interest Rate Swaps." *Financial Management*, Winter 1988, 34–44.

Strong, Robert A., and Richard Borgman. "Portfolio Duration." *Journal of Business and Economic Studies*, Fall 1999, 67–81.

Strong, Robert A., and Chiara Hall. "Speculating with Bonds." *American Association of Individual Investors Journal*, July 1986, 9–12.

Wall, L.D., and J.J. Pringle. "Interest Rate Swaps: A Review of the Issues." *Economic Review*, November/December 1988, 22–40.

# 15 Principles of Options and Option Pricing

*We sent the first draft of our paper to the* Journal of Political Economy *and promptly got back a rejection letter. We then sent it to the* Review of Economics and Statistics *where it also was rejected.*

*Merton Miller and Eugene Fama at the University of Chicago then took an interest in the paper and gave us extensive comments on it. They suggested to the* JPE *that perhaps the paper was worth more serious consideration. The journal then accepted the paper.*

***Fischer Black, on his journal article with Myron Scholes that gave birth to the Black-Scholes Option Pricing Model***

## Key Terms

American option
asked price
at the money
bid price
Black-Scholes Option Pricing Model (OPM)
call option
closing transaction
crowd
delta
European option
exercise
fungibility
in the money
intrinsic value
marketmaker
opening transaction
Options Clearing Corporation (OCC)
order book
out of the money
premium
put option
specialist
striking price
time value
underlying security
wasting asset
writing an option

## Introduction

Stock options are fascinating. Innovations in their use and discoveries about their pricing have been among the most important developments in the field of finance during the last twenty years. Many professional students of the marketplace spend a good deal of their time investigating the relationship between option prices and other economic and psychological variables.

The cornerstone of option pricing is the Black-Scholes Option Pricing Model (OPM). This model has been tested empirically many times, and it is an excellent representation of reality. To the portfolio manager, *delta* is the best-known of the OPM's progeny; this statistic plays a central role in sophisticated portfolio protection plans and in risk management applications. It is discussed later in the chapter. It is necessary to gain some insight into the OPM to make it less mysterious.

## Option Principles

### Why Options Are a Good Idea

Today's financial world is complicated. We face many sources of risk that were not present in the mid-nineteenth century. Today's communication technology provides us almost instantaneous information about events such as the war on terrorism, developments with Enron, political posturing, international trade disputes, airline labor strikes, and Fed announcements. All of these bits of news can affect the value of our investments.

Experienced investors are seldom 100 percent bullish or 100 percent bearish. Investment decision trees have many branches and many decision nodes. The constant arrival of new information affecting investments means that for the portfolio manager, the investment process is dynamic: Positions need to be constantly reassessed and portfolios adjusted.

Managers have learned much about the behavior of security prices and the interaction of the security markets. This knowledge makes it possible and prudent to fine-tune their investment strategy to deal with the many possible future states of the world.

Managers frequently trade stock to refine the portfolio's investment characteristics. Options are much more convenient (and less expensive) to use than wholesale purchases or sales of shares of stock each time a risk adjustment is appropriate. Using an appropriate option strategy, the manager can transfer that risk to some other market participant who, for a price, is willing to bear it.

Options provide financial leverage, and this is one of the primary reasons some investors (or speculators) buy them. As an example, you, as an investor, may believe that XYZ Corporation (selling for $65) is an excellent takeover candidate and suspect that the price of the common stock is about to take off. If you were to buy 100 shares of this stock, it would cost $6,500. As an alternative, you could speculate on the takeover rumors using a single stock option selling for perhaps $300. With this position, you would benefit from a sharp increase in the stock price but would have only a modest amount of money at risk. The worst that could happen with the option is that you would lose all $300; if you bought the stock, you could lose much more than that if the stock plummeted.

Some people use options as a means of generating additional income from their investment portfolio. Endowment funds, pension funds, and individuals routinely use options for this purpose. The next chapter covers this use of options in detail.

In short, options give the marketplace opportunities to adjust risk or alter income streams that would otherwise not be available. An economist would call this phenomenon "enhanced spanning" of the market.

### What Options Are

*The option premium is the price of the option.*

Two types of options exist: *call options* and *put options*. Call options are easier to understand, so let's look at these first.

**Call Options.** Although you may not be familiar with call options, you probably are familiar with the call option concept. Suppose that while shopping in a department store, you find a leather coat that you cannot live without. Today is the last day of a sale, and your checkbook is nearly on empty. You also left your credit cards at home. Perhaps the sale price of the coat is $225. You might find the store manager and ask if the store would keep the coat for you and guarantee you the sale price until next Friday, which is your payday. If the manager agrees, the store has created a **call option:** You have the right (but not the obligation) to buy one coat at a predetermined price ($225) any time between now and next Friday, when the option expires. The store gave you this option at no charge. With any stock option, the amount you pay for the option is called the **premium.** In this example, the premium was zero.

*A call option gives you the right to buy but is not a promise to buy.*

It is important to recognize that you have not promised to buy the coat. If you should find an identical coat at a lower price in another store, you can simply abandon your option with the original store and buy it at the cheaper location. The owner of a call option has the *right* to buy within a specified time period. In exchange for this right, the owner of the option pays a cash premium to the option seller.

*A put option gives you the right to sell.*

**Put Options.** A call gives you the right to *buy*; a put gives you the right to *sell.* **Put options** are conceptually difficult for many people, because the right to sell something is not as intuitive as the right to buy something, particularly when people learn it is not necessary to own the asset before acquiring the right to sell it.

One large real estate agency gives a put option to homeowners who list their homes for sale with the agency. After the real estate agent and the homeowner agree on a reasonable listing price for the house, the agency makes the usual attempts to sell it. In the event that a buyer is not found, the homeowner has the right to sell the house to the agency at 70 percent of the original listing price. Again, the homeowner is not obliged to sell the house to the agency at this price; if circumstances warrant, however, the homeowner can exercise the right to do so.

### Standardized Option Characteristics

All exchange-traded options have standardized expiration dates.[1] For most options, this is the Saturday following the third Friday of certain designated months. Individual investors typically view the third Friday of the month as the expiration date because the exchanges are closed to public trading on Saturday. Saturday is reserved for bookkeeping operations among the brokerage firms whose clients have dealt in the just-expiring options.

The **striking price** of an option is the predetermined transaction price. These are established at multiples of $2.50 or $5.00, depending on the current stock price. In general, stocks priced at $25.00 or below have the $2.50 multiple, whereas higher-priced stocks have the $5.00 multiple.[2] Shifts in the price of a stock result in the creation of new striking prices. As a matter of policy, there is usually at least one striking price above and at least one below the current stock price.

Both puts and calls are based on 100 shares of the **underlying security,** which is the security that the option gives you the right to buy or sell. If you buy a call option on the stock of a particular company, you are purchasing the right to buy 100 shares of stock. It is not possible to buy or sell odd lots of options.

---

[1]Exchange-traded options are those publicly traded on a formal exchange. Some options are private arrangements between an investor and a brokerage firm. These can have any terms the two parties choose. Such an arrangement is called an *over-the-counter option.*

[2]Stocks with unusually high prices, such as some of the Internet stocks in early 1999, have option striking prices set at $10 multiples.

### *Where Options Come From*

If you buy an option, someone has to sell it to you; two parties must participate in the trade. Unlike more familiar securities such as shares of stock, no set number of put or call options exists. In fact, the number in existence changes every day. Options can be created, and they can be destroyed. This unusual fact is crucial to understanding the options market.

**Opening and Closing Transactions.** The first trade someone makes in a particular option is an **opening transaction.** When you subsequently terminate a position by closing it out with a second trade, this latter trade is a **closing transaction.** Purchases and sales can be either type of transaction.

The owner of an option will ultimately do one of three things with it:

1. Sell it to someone else.
2. Let it expire.
3. Exercise it.

This is easy to explain using tickets to a Saturday hockey game at a local university. Suppose you buy two tickets for a premium of $15 each. This is analogous to an opening transaction. The ticket gives you the right, but not the obligation, to go to the game. If you choose, you can (1) sell your tickets to someone else before the game or (2) decide to watch the game on local television and leave the tickets in your desk drawer, where they will expire worthless. Finally, you can (3) use the tickets and go to the game. No matter which of these courses of action you choose, it is analogous to a closing transaction. Game day is analogous to expiration day, and the tickets are worthless when the game ends. (See Figure 15-1.)

*Selling an option as an opening transaction is called* writing *the option.*

Buying something as an opening transaction is perhaps easier to understand than selling something as an opening transaction. The university created the tickets and sold them; this was an opening transaction for the university. *Writing an option* refers to the sale of an option as an opening transaction.

*The option writer keeps the option premium no matter what happens in the future.*

No matter what the owner of an option does, the writer of the option keeps the option premium that the option buyer paid. Returning to the hockey game example, the university keeps the $30 paid for the two tickets regardless of whether you go to the game or not.

**FIGURE 15-1**

Buying a Call Option

## Buying a Call Option

**Is like buying a ticket to a University of Maine hockey game. Having bought the ticket, I can do the following:**

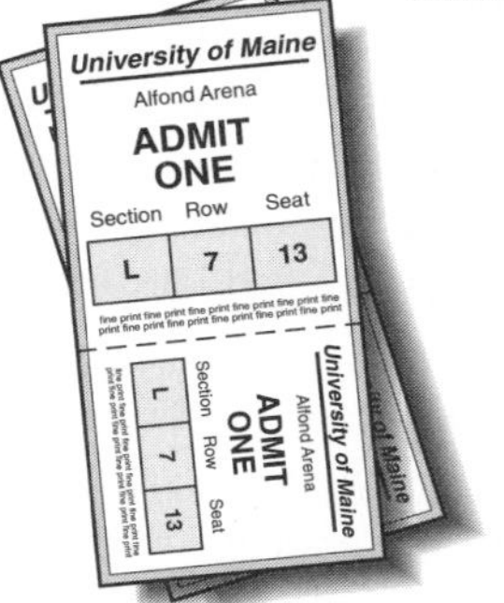


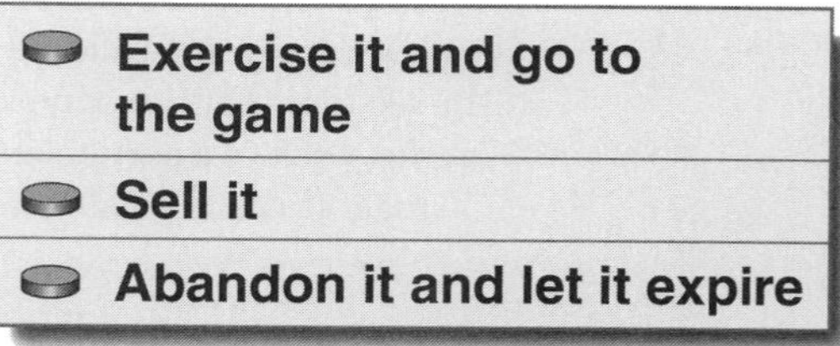


The university wrote the option and gets to keep the premium (the ticket cost) no matter which alternative I choose.

Options have an important characteristic called **fungibility,** which refers to the ability of participants in the futures and options markets to reverse their positions by making offsetting trades. This means that for a given company, all options of the same type with the same expiration and striking price are identical. Fungibility is particularly important to the option writer. For example, you may write an option and receive a premium for doing so. **Writing an option** means you create the option and sell it. If market conditions change a week later, you can buy an option on the same company with the same contract terms, and this gets you out of the market: Writing an option and buying a similar one are two transactions that cancel out in your brokerage account. You have to pay for the option you buy, and the amount you pay may be more or less than the amount you received when you wrote it. The important point is that you do not have to buy the option back from the specific person to whom you sold it because the options are fungible.[3]

**Role of the Options Clearing Corporation.** The presence of the **Options Clearing Corporation (OCC)** is an important feature of the options market. This organization positions itself between every buyer and seller and acts as a guarantor of all option trades. When people buy or sell options, they are actually buying them from, or selling them to, the OCC. The OCC also regulates the trading activity of members of the various options exchanges, setting minimum capital requirements and providing for the efficient transfer of funds among members as gains or losses occur. The OCC publishes a booklet entitled *Characteristics and Risks of Standardized Options*, which every potential option user receives upon opening an options account. These are available from any brokerage firm or over the Internet from the Website of the Chicago Board Options Exchange (CBOE): *http://www.cboe.com.*

## Where and How Options Trade

In the United States, options trade on five principal exchanges: the CBOE, the American Stock Exchange (AMEX), the Philadelphia Stock Exchange, the Pacific Stock Exchange, and the International Securities Exchange.

Trading on the Philadelphia Stock Exchange and the AMEX is via the *specialist* system, whereas trading on the CBOE and the Pacific Stock Exchange is via the *marketmaker* system. Under the **specialist** system, all orders to buy or sell a particular security must pass through a single individual. The specialist keeps an **order book** with standing orders from investors all over the country and tries to maintain the market in these securities in a fair and orderly fashion. If no private individual has placed an order to buy the option that you want to sell, the specialist must buy the option from you at a price close to the current price. This is part of the specialist's job, and it helps contribute to the ease of entry and exit from the marketplace.[4]

Under the **marketmaker** system, instead of a single specialist, competing marketmakers trade in a specific location. The number of marketmakers can range from a small handful to more than 500 in some cases. These people compete against one another for the public's business by attempting to be there first with the best price to take an order.

In both the specialist and marketmaker systems, an option actually has two prices at any given time: a *bid price* and an *asked price*. The **bid price** is the highest

---

[3]You might note that hockey tickets, in general, are not fungible because all seats are not equally desirable.

[4]These same comments apply to specialists on the stock exchanges.

price anyone is willing to pay for a particular option; the **asked price** is the lowest price at which anyone is willing to sell. By definition, at any moment there are only one bid price and one asked price.

Marketmakers must be quick to react to arriving orders if they want any business. Their bread and butter is buying options at the bid price and then selling at the asked price to someone else as quickly as possible. If, for instance, a particular marketmaker buys ten option contracts (options on 1,000 shares) at $4 each and sells them thirty seconds later for $4.15, a $150 profit results. The result of this constant competition for the public business is that investors can be confident that they will get a market-determined, rather than capricious, price when they trade.

Marketmakers in a particular option assemble in a specified part of the exchange floor near an individual called the *order book official*. This person has numerous duties; one of particular importance is making sure that small public orders to buy or sell are not ignored and, in fact, receive priority from the trading crowd at the exchange. The **crowd** is the colloquial term for the people in a trading location. The exchange sometimes censures a marketmaker for failure to pay attention to the price information quoted by the order book official or for making a trade with another individual on the exchange floor when a public order was "on the book" at the identical price.

## The Option Premium

*Intrinsic value + Time value = Option premium.*

**Intrinsic Value and Time Value.** The price of an option (the premium) has two components: *intrinsic value* and *time value*. **Intrinsic value** for a call option equals the stock price minus the striking price and for a put is the striking price minus the stock price. By convention, intrinsic value cannot be less than zero. **Time value** equals the premium minus the intrinsic value.

If an option has no intrinsic value, it is said to be **out of the money.** If it does have intrinsic value, it is **in the money.** In the special case in which an option's striking price exactly equals the price of the underlying security, the option is **at the money.**[5]

**The Financial Page Listing.** Table 15-1 is a hypothetical extract from the financial press that illustrates some of the basic characteristics of stock options. The extract shows the listing for Nile.com, an imaginary on-line bookseller and direct competitor of Amazon.com. Nile.com appears in many of the examples that follow.

The number *116* listed below the company name is the current price of one share of Nile.com common stock. The next column lists striking prices from 90 to 125. (Note that the stock price of $116 is repeated by each striking price.) The next six columns are actually two sets of three columns: three for calls and three for puts. At the top of each of these columns is the expiration month. The numbers below the expiration months are the option premiums.

An investor identifies a stock option by company, expiration, striking price, and type of option (generally in that order), as Figure 15-2 shows. The financial pages list the price for an option on a single share. Because "one option" really means an option on 100 shares, an individual who buys one Nile.com FEB 115 call @ $8 would actually pay $8 per share × 100 shares, or $800.

The right to buy at $115 is valuable when the stock price is $116, so the Nile.com FEB 115 call is in the money. For a call option, intrinsic value is the stock price minus the striking price: in this case, $116 – $115 = $1. We know the option premium, and we know the intrinsic value, so we can solve for the time value: Time value = Premium – Intrinsic value, or $8 – $1 = $7.

[5]Options that are almost at the money are sometimes called *near the money*.

**TABLE 15-1** SAMPLE STOCK OPTIONS LISTING

| *Stock & New York Close* | *Striking Price* | *Calls* | | | *Puts* | | |
|---|---|---|---|---|---|---|---|
| | | JAN | FEB | APR | JAN | FEB | APR |
| Smith Electronics | 60 | 6.38 | 8.25 | 9 | 0.06 | 0.75 | 0.88 |
| 66.38 | 65 | 2.50 | 4.88 | 6.75 | 0.69 | 2.25 | 3.50 |
| 66.38 | 70 | 0.43 | 2.25 | 2.75 | 3.63 | 5 | 6 |
| 66.38 | 75 | 0.06 | 1.13 | 2.50 | 8.38 | 9 | 9.75 |
| Western Oil | 50 | 17.25 | 17.75 | 18.13 | 0.06 | 0.88 | 1.38 |
| 66.75 | 55 | 12 | 14.75 | 15.50 | 0.13 | 1.75 | 2.50 |
| 66.75 | 60 | 7.50 | 11.25 | 13 | 0.63 | 3.38 | 4.50 |
| 66.75 | 65 | 4 | 8.38 | 10 | 2.38 | 6 | 6.75 |
| 66.75 | 70 | 2 | 5.75 | 7.75 | 5 | 8.25 | 9 |
| 66.75 | 75 | 0.69 | 4.13 | 5.75 | 8.88 | 10 | 11 |
| 66.75 | 80 | 0.38 | 3 | 4.50 | 14 | 14.88 | 16 |
| Nile.com | 90 | 26 | 26.38 | 27 | 0.06 | 0.13 | 0.50 |
| 116 | 95 | 22.25 | 24.13 | 25 | 0.06 | 0.50 | 0.75 |
| 116 | 100 | 18 | 19.38 | 21 | 0.06 | 0.75 | 1.13 |
| 116 | 105 | 12.50 | 14.75 | 16 | 0.06 | 0.88 | 2 |
| 116 | 110 | 8.13 | 10 | 13 | 0.38 | 2.63 | 4 |
| 116 | 115 | 3.50 | 8 | 10 | 1.63 | 4.25 | 6 |
| 116 | 120 | 1.38 | 6 | 7.25 | 5 | 7.25 | 8.50 |
| 116 | 125 | 0.50 | 4.63 | 5.50 | 9.13 | 10 | 11.13 |

**FIGURE 15-2**

Identifying an Option

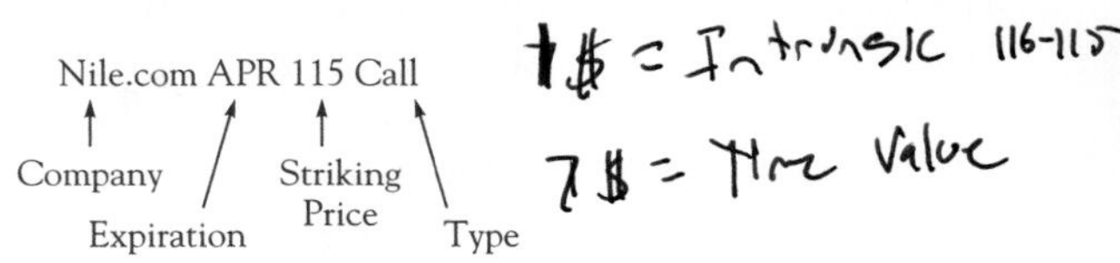


The Nile.com FEB 115 put is out of the money because there is no incentive to sell at $115 when the market price of the stock is more than this. Even though this option has no intrinsic value, it does have time value: $4.25. This helps illustrate an important point: Prior to their expiration, out-of-the-money options are not worthless.

Stock prices change continuously, and, consequently, so can the option premium. Even if a stock price remains constant, the option premium can still change. One reason for this is the change in time value. The longer an option has until expiration, the more it is worth.[6] This is so because the stock price has more time to fluctuate and could therefore rise or fall more with more time. If you look again at the premiums shown in Table 15-1, you will see that for a given striking price, option premiums increase for more distant expirations.

[6]This is true with an American option (exercisable anytime prior to expiration). With a European option (exercisable only at maturity), more time does not necessarily mean more value. In the extreme case, consider a European option with a perpetual life. It could never be exercised, so it would be worthless.

As an option moves closer to expiration, its time value decreases. Option traders refer to this phenomenon as *time value decay*. Everything else being equal, the value of an option declines over time. This fact makes an option a **wasting asset,** an often misunderstood term. Football tickets are also wasting assets because at some point in time they cease to have any value. Anyone who has observed activities around a football stadium knows the price that scalpers get for tickets begins to decline at the kickoff. By the end of the first half, the price has fallen substantially. The fact that something is a wasting asset, however, does not mean that it is not useful.

### *Sources of Profits and Losses with Options*

**Option Exercise.** Options give you the right to buy or sell. With an **American option,** this right can be exercised at any time prior to the expiration of the option. **European options,** in contrast, can be exercised only at expiration.

Although American options can be exercised any time, it is advantageous to exercise them early in very few situations. Doing so essentially amounts to abandoning any time value remaining in the options. Consider the Nile.com FEB 115 call selling for $8 while the underlying stock sells for $116. If an investor exercised this option, he would buy stock for $1 less than its market price; the option would have intrinsic value of $1. By exercising he recovers this intrinsic value but throws away the remaining $7 of option premium.

*The option premium is not a down payment on the option terms.*

**Exercise Procedures.** An investor who decides to **exercise** an option notifies her broker of her desire to do so. An investor who exercises a call option with a striking price of $25 must put up a full $25 per share for the 100 shares covered by the contract, or $2,500. The option premium is not a down payment on the option terms; the cost of the option does not count toward the total. Remember that the option writer keeps the option premium no matter what happens. Similarly, someone who intends to exercise a put must acquire 100 shares of stock for each put he intends to exercise. The premium paid for the put does not count toward the cost of the stock.

The writer of a call option must be prepared to sell 100 shares of the underlying stock to the call owner if the call owner decides to exercise. If the writer does not own any shares of the stock, he must purchase them in the open market at the current price before delivering them. Similarly, the writer of a put option must be prepared to buy shares of stock if the put holder decides to exercise and sell them.

*The option holder, not the option writer, decides when and whether to exercise. In general, you should not buy an option with the intent of exercising it.*

An important point to note is the fact that the ball is in the option holder's court. The option holder, not the option writer, decides when and whether to exercise. Because options are fungible, the option writer can reverse a position if it is profitable to do so. Then the consequences of exercise are someone else's concern.

Many people are surprised that an option should generally never be purchased with the intent of exercising it; instead, the option buyer anticipates selling the option at a profit. We have already seen that options are not normally exercised until just before they expire because earlier exercise amounts to discarding the remaining time value. If you exercise a call near the end of its life, you must come up with the money to pay for the stock, which might be inconvenient. You will also have to pay your broker a commission to exercise the call. When you sell the stock, you will pay another commission. The same thing is true with puts. Unless you already own the stock, you will have to buy shares in the open market (paying a commission) and pay another commission when you exercise the put. You can recover the full value contained in any option simply by selling it. This way you do not have to come up with any more money; you pay a single commission, and you are out of the market.

## Option Pricing

It is important for the option user to understand why some options sell for more than others and the information that the option premium provides about the underlying security.

### *Determinants of the Option Premium*

**Market Factors.** Six variables significantly influence the option premium. We have already seen two of these: the striking price and the time until option expiration. Because a call option lets you buy at a predetermined price, it seems logical that the lower the price at which you can buy, the more the option should be worth. This is exactly what we observe in the financial pages. Table 15-1 shows that as the striking price becomes lower for a given company's call options, the option premium goes up. We have also seen that the longer the option has until expiration, the more it is worth. Table 15-1 shows that for both puts and calls, the option premium increases as we look at more distant expirations.

A third factor influencing the call premium is also easy to understand: the current stock price. The higher the stock price, the more a given call option is going to be worth and the less a put option will be worth. Remember that a primary reason many people buy call options is to benefit from a rise in the price of the stock. If the stock price goes up, so will the value of the call option.

*The more volatile a security, the higher its option premium.*

The other three factors influencing the option premium may be less obvious. They are the volatility of the underlying stock, the dividend yield on the underlying security, and the risk-free interest rate.

Assets that show price volatility lend themselves to option trading.[7] This is the fourth factor determining the option premium: *The greater an asset's price volatility, the higher is its option premium.* It is not uncommon to look in the financial pages and find options on two different companies with the same current stock prices and, for instance, FEB 40 calls. These two options might sell for very different premiums. Because the intrinsic value of an option is a calculated value that does not depend on anything other than the current stock price and the option striking price, differences in the premium for these two options must be caused by differences in the time value of the option.

A fifth factor that influences the call option premium is the *dividend yield on the underlying common stock.* A company's board of directors announces that a dividend will be paid on a certain date (the date of payment) to the stockholders as of a certain cutoff date (the date of record). To eliminate uncertainty about such things as processing time and mail delays in determining exactly who is listed on the company's shareholder list on the date of record, the brokerage industry establishes an *ex-dividend date,* which is two business days before the date of record. People must buy stock before the ex-dividend date to qualify for the dividend that is about to be paid. People who buy the stock on the ex-dividend date do not receive the dividend, and this provides downward pressure on the price of the stock. If it were possible to hold constant all the other factors influencing stock prices, we would expect the value of a share of stock to fall by about the amount of the dividend on the ex-dividend date.

A person who buys a call option does not want the price of the stock to fall, yet the payment of a dividend will do just that. The higher the dividend, the more the

[7]They may also lend themselves to futures market trading.

PORTFOLIO MEMO

## Profit and Loss Diagrams

Profit and loss diagrams are a convenient way to illustrate the possibilities associated with a particular option position. The standard diagram has Stock Price at Option Expiration on the horizontal axis and Profit or Loss on the vertical axis. For any stock price on expiration day, then, you can immediately see whether the option position will result in a gain or loss. Figures 15-3 through 15-6 show diagrams for the four basic option positions. The option premium comes from the values for Smith Electronics in Table 15-1.

Figure 15-3 shows that the maximum profit is unlimited when someone buys a call option (is long), while the maximum loss is known and limited. The converse is true when someone writes a naked call (is short), as shown in Figure 15-4.

FIGURE 15-3 Long Call Option

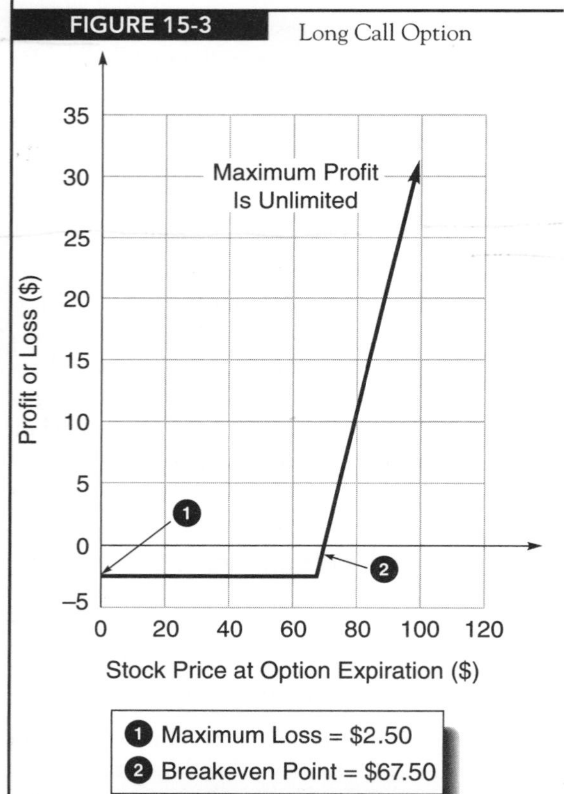


Option premium = $2.50; strike price = $65; expiration = JAN

FIGURE 15-4 Short Call Option

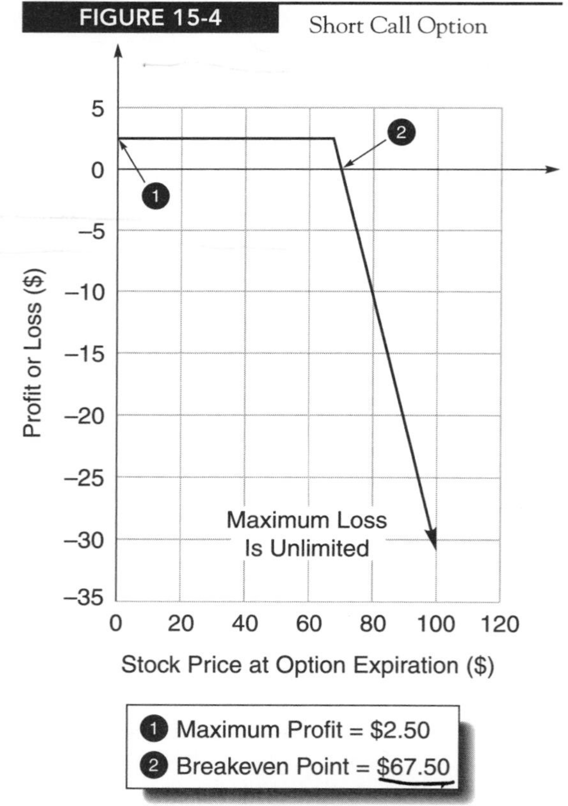


Option premium = $2.50; strike price = $65; expiration = JAN

# PORTFOLIO MEMO

## Profit and Loss Diagrams (continued)

Purchasing a put (Figure 15-5) also involves a known and limited maximum loss with large profits possible if the stock price declines sharply. The naked put writer (Figure 15-6) suffers a large loss if stock prices decline but earns the option premium if prices rise above the striking price. In every instance, the bend in the profit and loss diagram occurs at the option striking price.

A useful rule of thumb to remember in constructing these diagrams is the fact that any bend in the diagram always occurs at the striking price.

**FIGURE 15-5** Long Put Option

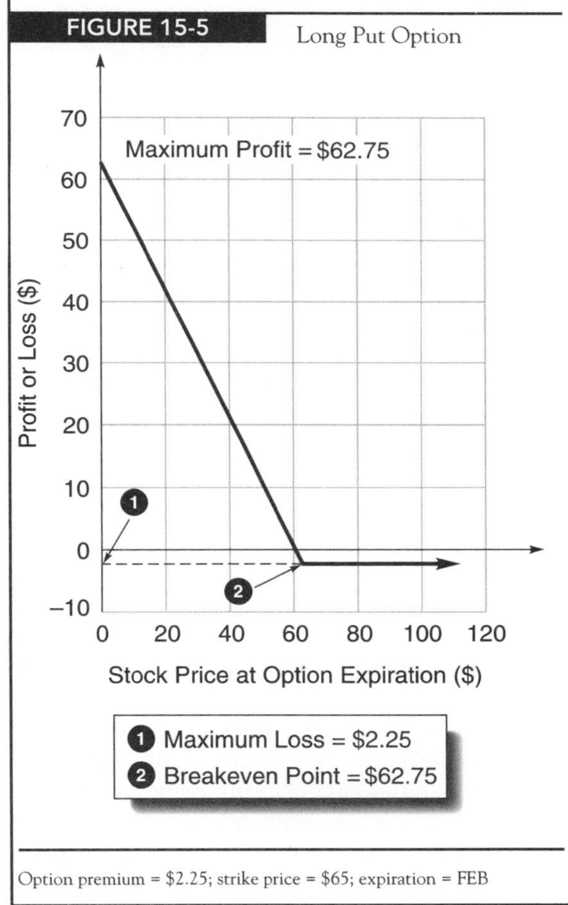


Option premium = $2.25; strike price = $65; expiration = FEB

**FIGURE 15-6** Short Put Option

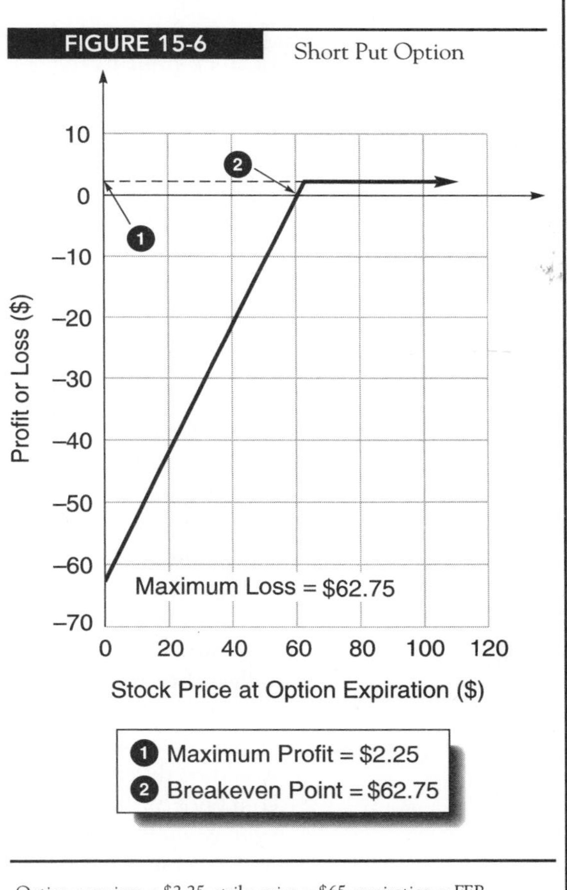


Option premium = $2.25; strike price = $65; expiration = FEB

price will fall. With a listed stock option there is no adjustment to the contract terms because of a cash dividend.

The key point of this discussion is that, all other things being equal, companies that pay large dividends have a smaller call option premium than companies with low dividend yields. This is easy to understand if we consider an extreme example in which a firm announces its intent to pay a liquidating dividend and go out of business. After the company pays this dividend, the firm's shares will be worthless, as will the associated call options. People who own these calls and do not exercise them before the last ex-dividend date will lose 100 percent of their investment.

The sixth factor that influences option premiums is the risk-free interest rate. The higher this interest rate, the higher the call option premium, everything else being equal. To understand this factor, remember that exercise of the call option requires you to pay for the underlying stock. Because exercise will occur in the future, the time value of money is a consideration. The higher the interest rate, the lower the present value of the exercise price to be paid in the future, and consequently the higher the value of the call option.

*Call premium* =

$$f\left(\overset{-}{K}, \overset{+}{T}, \overset{+}{S}, \overset{+}{V}, \overset{-}{D}, \overset{+}{R}\right)$$

*where*
*K = option striking price*
*T = time until option expiration*
*S = current stock price*
*V = stock volatility*
*D = stock dividend yield*
*R = current risk-free interest rate.*

**Accounting Factors.** *Exchange-traded options* are adjusted for stock splits or stock dividends. The most common event necessitating an adjustment is a stock split. Two-for-one splits are common; this means that a shareholder who owns 100 shares of stock prior to the split will own 200 afterward. Similarly, a 4-for-1 split would mean the holder of 100 presplit shares would have 400 postsplit shares. Sometimes the split ratio is not a whole number (2 or 4, for example). In a 3-for-2 split, the holder of 100 shares would have 150 after the split. Splits of this type are often called odd-lot generating because they result in many people holding shares that are no longer in multiples of 100.

It is important to recognize that a stock split does not inherently increase the shareholders' wealth. The firm is worth some specific dollar amount, and it does not matter into how many pieces the pie is cut. If you eat one piece of a pie cut into four pieces, you have eaten exactly the same amount of pie that you would have eaten had you been given two pieces of a pie cut into eighths. The stock market is not fooled by stock splits. If you own 100 shares of stock worth $50 each and the firm splits 2 for 1, after the split you will have 200 shares each worth about $25. Your total wealth has not changed.

Suppose you own one Nile.com FEB 120 call, and Nile.com then splits 2 for 1. The Options Clearing Corporation would dictate the following adjustment to all outstanding options on Nile.com: The striking price would be reduced by the split ratio, and the number of options you own would be increased by the split ratio. In this case, you would discover on your monthly brokerage account statement that you now owned two Nile.com FEB 60 calls. The dollar amount represented by these two calls is the same as the dollar amount represented by your original single call option ($2 \times \$60 = \$120$).

If Nile.com were to have an odd-lot–generating split, say 3 for 2, the adjustment would be different. Listed options are written only on multiples of 100 shares; you could not have an option to buy 50 shares. In this case, the striking price of the option would be reduced by the split ratio (as in the first example). Instead of increasing the number of options you owned, the number of shares covered by your option would be increased by the split ratio. This means that after the 3-for-2 split, you would own one Nile.com 80 call, and that one call would give you the right to buy 150 shares. As before, the dollar amount represented by the call is the same before and after the split.

## Black-Scholes Option Pricing Model

One of the most useful developments in finance during the last thirty years is the **Black-Scholes Option Pricing Model (OPM).** This model is a useful representation of how the marketplace determines an option premium. Virtually all option analysts use some form of the Black-Scholes OPM to assist them in their decision making.

**TABLE 15-2** BLACK-SCHOLES OPTION PRICING MODEL

$$C = S[N(d_1)] - Ke^{-Rt}[N(d_2)]$$

$$d_1 = \frac{\ln(S/K) + [R + (\sigma^2/2)]t}{\sigma\sqrt{t}}$$

$$d_2 = d_1 - \sigma\sqrt{t}$$

where $C$ = theoretical call premium
$S$ = current stock price
$t$ = time in years until option expiration
$K$ = option striking price
$R$ = risk-free interest rate
$\sigma$ = standard deviation of stock returns
$N(x)$ = probability that a value less than "x" will occur in a standard normal distribution
ln = natural logarithm
$e$ = base of natural logarithms (2.7183)

Table 15-2 presents this famous model. Suppose you have the following information on stock XYZ: $S = \$30$; $K = \$25$; $t = 3$ months $= 0.25$ year; $R = 5\%$; and $\sigma = 0.45$. The first thing you need to do is calculate $d_1$ and $d_2$, the arguments for the standard normal functions, $N(x)$:

$$d_1 = \frac{\ln(S/K) + [R + (\sigma^2/2)]t}{\sigma\sqrt{t}}$$

$$= \frac{\ln(30/25) + [.05 + (.45^2/2)].25}{.45\sqrt{.25}}$$

$$= \frac{.1823 + [.05 + .1013].25}{(.45)(.5)}$$

$$= 0.978$$

$$d_2 = d_1 - \sigma\sqrt{t}$$

$$= 0.978 - (.45)(.5)$$

$$= 0.753$$

Now that you have the two arguments, $d_1$ and $d_2$, you can determine the values for the normal probability functions $N(d_1)$ and $N(d_2)$. To do this you must look up the appropriate values from a probability table similar to Table 15-3. Read down the columns in the table until you find a value of $x$ that corresponds to the value you want. You may not find the exact number needed; if this is the case, you either interpolate or use the closest entry. (You can also get this figure from the NORMSDIST function in Microsoft Excel.) In this example, the value of $N(0.978)$ is approximately 0.836, and $N(0.753)$ is about 0.774.

Now you can continue with your efforts to find a theoretical Black-Scholes value for this call option. Returning to the formula, you can plug in the values you just determined:

$$C = \$30[0.836] - \$25e^{-(.05)(0.25)}[0.774]$$

$$= \$6$$

**TABLE 15-3** CUMULATIVE NORMAL PROBABILITY DISTRIBUTION

| | 0.00 | 0.01 | 0.02 | 0.03 | 0.04 | 0.05 | 0.06 | 0.07 | 0.08 | 0.09 |
|---|---|---|---|---|---|---|---|---|---|---|
| −3.00 | 0.0014 | 0.0013 | 0.0013 | 0.0012 | 0.0012 | 0.0011 | 0.0011 | 0.0011 | 0.0010 | 0.0010 |
| −2.90 | 0.0019 | 0.0018 | 0.0018 | 0.0017 | 0.0016 | 0.0016 | 0.0015 | 0.0015 | 0.0014 | 0.0014 |
| −2.80 | 0.0026 | 0.0025 | 0.0024 | 0.0023 | 0.0023 | 0.0022 | 0.0021 | 0.0021 | 0.0020 | 0.0019 |
| −2.70 | 0.0035 | 0.0034 | 0.0033 | 0.0032 | 0.0031 | 0.0030 | 0.0029 | 0.0028 | 0.0027 | 0.0026 |
| −2.60 | 0.0047 | 0.0045 | 0.0044 | 0.0043 | 0.0041 | 0.0040 | 0.0039 | 0.0038 | 0.0037 | 0.0036 |
| −2.50 | 0.0062 | 0.0060 | 0.0059 | 0.0057 | 0.0055 | 0.0054 | 0.0052 | 0.0051 | 0.0049 | 0.0048 |
| −2.40 | 0.0082 | 0.0080 | 0.0078 | 0.0075 | 0.0073 | 0.0071 | 0.0069 | 0.0068 | 0.0066 | 0.0064 |
| −2.30 | 0.0107 | 0.0104 | 0.0102 | 0.0099 | 0.0096 | 0.0094 | 0.0091 | 0.0089 | 0.0087 | 0.0084 |
| −2.20 | 0.0139 | 0.0136 | 0.0132 | 0.0129 | 0.0125 | 0.0122 | 0.0119 | 0.0116 | 0.0113 | 0.0110 |
| −2.10 | 0.0179 | 0.0174 | 0.0170 | 0.0166 | 0.0162 | 0.0158 | 0.0154 | 0.0150 | 0.0146 | 0.0143 |
| −2.00 | 0.0228 | 0.0222 | 0.0217 | 0.0212 | 0.0207 | 0.0202 | 0.0197 | 0.0192 | 0.0188 | 0.0183 |
| −1.90 | 0.0287 | 0.0281 | 0.0274 | 0.0268 | 0.0262 | 0.0256 | 0.0250 | 0.0244 | 0.0239 | 0.0233 |
| −1.80 | 0.0359 | 0.0351 | 0.0344 | 0.0336 | 0.0329 | 0.0322 | 0.0314 | 0.0307 | 0.0301 | 0.0294 |
| −1.70 | 0.0446 | 0.0436 | 0.0427 | 0.0418 | 0.0409 | 0.0401 | 0.0392 | 0.0384 | 0.0375 | 0.0367 |
| −1.60 | 0.0548 | 0.0537 | 0.0526 | 0.0516 | 0.0505 | 0.0495 | 0.0485 | 0.0475 | 0.0465 | 0.0455 |
| −1.50 | 0.0668 | 0.0655 | 0.0643 | 0.0630 | 0.0618 | 0.0606 | 0.0594 | 0.0582 | 0.0571 | 0.0559 |
| −1.40 | 0.0808 | 0.0793 | 0.0778 | 0.0764 | 0.0749 | 0.0735 | 0.0721 | 0.0708 | 0.0694 | 0.0681 |
| −1.30 | 0.0968 | 0.0951 | 0.0934 | 0.0918 | 0.0901 | 0.0885 | 0.0869 | 0.0853 | 0.0838 | 0.0823 |
| −1.20 | 0.1151 | 0.1131 | 0.1112 | 0.1094 | 0.1075 | 0.1057 | 0.1038 | 0.1020 | 0.1003 | 0.0985 |
| −1.10 | 0.1357 | 0.1335 | 0.1314 | 0.1292 | 0.1271 | 0.1251 | 0.1230 | 0.1210 | 0.1190 | 0.1170 |
| −1.00 | 0.1587 | 0.1563 | 0.1539 | 0.1515 | 0.1492 | 0.1469 | 0.1446 | 0.1423 | 0.1401 | 0.1379 |
| −0.90 | 0.1841 | 0.1814 | 0.1788 | 0.1762 | 0.1736 | 0.1711 | 0.1685 | 0.1660 | 0.1635 | 0.1611 |
| −0.80 | 0.2119 | 0.2090 | 0.2061 | 0.2033 | 0.2005 | 0.1977 | 0.1949 | 0.1922 | 0.1894 | 0.1867 |
| −0.70 | 0.2420 | 0.2389 | 0.2358 | 0.2327 | 0.2297 | 0.2266 | 0.2236 | 0.2207 | 0.2177 | 0.2148 |
| −0.60 | 0.2743 | 0.2709 | 0.2676 | 0.2644 | 0.2611 | 0.2579 | 0.2546 | 0.2514 | 0.2483 | 0.2451 |
| −0.50 | 0.3085 | 0.3050 | 0.3015 | 0.2981 | 0.2946 | 0.2912 | 0.2877 | 0.2843 | 0.2810 | 0.2776 |
| −0.40 | 0.3446 | 0.3409 | 0.3372 | 0.3336 | 0.3300 | 0.3264 | 0.3228 | 0.3192 | 0.3156 | 0.3121 |
| −0.30 | 0.3821 | 0.3783 | 0.3745 | 0.3707 | 0.3669 | 0.3632 | 0.3594 | 0.3557 | 0.3520 | 0.3483 |
| −0.20 | 0.4207 | 0.4168 | 0.4129 | 0.4091 | 0.4052 | 0.4013 | 0.3974 | 0.3936 | 0.3897 | 0.3859 |
| −0.10 | 0.4602 | 0.4562 | 0.4522 | 0.4483 | 0.4443 | 0.4404 | 0.4364 | 0.4325 | 0.4286 | 0.4247 |
| −0.00 | 0.5000 | 0.4960 | 0.4920 | 0.4880 | 0.4841 | 0.4801 | 0.4761 | 0.4721 | 0.4681 | 0.4642 |

Choose units and tenths vertically; select hundredths horizontally.

According to the Black-Scholes Option Pricing Model, a three-month call option on this stock should sell for $6.

## *Development and Assumptions of the Model*

The actual development of the Black-Scholes model is complicated. Many of the steps used in building it come from physics, mathematical shortcuts, and arbitrage arguments. Fischer Black had been working on a valuation model for stock warrants, a type of security closely related to call options. After taking a derivative to measure how the discount rate of a warrant varies with time and the stock price, the resulting differential equation was similar to a well-known heat equation from physics. Myron Scholes joined Black in working on the problem, and the result is the model used throughout finance today.

For many option professionals the model has become a trusted black box, but you should be aware of some assumptions in the model as you use it.

**The Stock Pays No Dividends during the Option's Life.** The Black-Scholes model assumes that the underlying security pays no dividends during the life of the

**TABLE 15-3** CUMULATIVE NORMAL PROBABILITY DISTRIBUTION (CONTINUED)

| | 0.00 | 0.01 | 0.02 | 0.03 | 0.04 | 0.05 | 0.06 | 0.07 | 0.08 | 0.09 |
|---|---|---|---|---|---|---|---|---|---|---|
| +0.00 | 0.5000 | 0.5040 | 0.5080 | 0.5121 | 0.5159 | 0.5199 | 0.5239 | 0.5279 | 0.5319 | 0.5358 |
| 0.10 | 0.5398 | 0.5438 | 0.5478 | 0.5517 | 0.5557 | 0.5596 | 0.5636 | 0.5675 | 0.5714 | 0.5753 |
| 0.20 | 0.5793 | 0.5832 | 0.5871 | 0.5909 | 0.5948 | 0.5987 | 0.6026 | 0.6064 | 0.6103 | 0.6141 |
| 0.30 | 0.6179 | 0.6217 | 0.6255 | 0.6293 | 0.6331 | 0.6368 | 0.6406 | 0.6443 | 0.6480 | 0.6517 |
| 0.40 | 0.6554 | 0.6591 | 0.6628 | 0.6664 | 0.6700 | 0.6736 | 0.6772 | 0.6808 | 0.6844 | 0.6879 |
| 0.50 | 0.6915 | 0.6950 | 0.6985 | 0.7019 | 0.7054 | 0.7088 | 0.7123 | 0.7157 | 0.7190 | 0.7224 |
| 0.60 | 0.7257 | 0.7291 | 0.7324 | 0.7356 | 0.7389 | 0.7421 | 0.7454 | 0.7486 | 0.7517 | 0.7549 |
| 0.70 | 0.7580 | 0.7611 | 0.7642 | 0.7673 | 0.7703 | 0.7734 | 0.7764 | 0.7793 | 0.7823 | 0.7852 |
| 0.80 | 0.7881 | 0.7910 | 0.7939 | 0.7967 | 0.7995 | 0.8023 | 0.8051 | 0.8078 | 0.8106 | 0.8133 |
| 0.90 | 0.8159 | 0.8186 | 0.8212 | 0.8238 | 0.8264 | 0.8289 | 0.8315 | 0.8340 | 0.8365 | 0.8389 |
| 1.00 | 0.8413 | 0.8437 | 0.8461 | 0.8485 | 0.8508 | 0.8531 | 0.8554 | 0.8577 | 0.8599 | 0.8621 |
| 1.10 | 0.8643 | 0.8665 | 0.8686 | 0.8708 | 0.8729 | 0.8749 | 0.8770 | 0.8790 | 0.8810 | 0.8830 |
| 1.20 | 0.8849 | 0.8869 | 0.8888 | 0.8906 | 0.8925 | 0.8943 | 0.8962 | 0.8980 | 0.8997 | 0.9015 |
| 1.30 | 0.9032 | 0.9049 | 0.9066 | 0.9082 | 0.9099 | 0.9115 | 0.9131 | 0.9147 | 0.9162 | 0.9177 |
| 1.40 | 0.9192 | 0.9207 | 0.9222 | 0.9236 | 0.9251 | 0.9265 | 0.9279 | 0.9292 | 0.9306 | 0.9319 |
| 1.50 | 0.9332 | 0.9345 | 0.9357 | 0.9370 | 0.9382 | 0.9394 | 0.9406 | 0.9418 | 0.9429 | 0.9441 |
| 1.60 | 0.9452 | 0.9463 | 0.9474 | 0.9484 | 0.9495 | 0.9505 | 0.9515 | 0.9525 | 0.9535 | 0.9545 |
| 1.70 | 0.9554 | 0.9564 | 0.9573 | 0.9582 | 0.9591 | 0.9599 | 0.9608 | 0.9616 | 0.9625 | 0.9633 |
| 1.80 | 0.9641 | 0.9649 | 0.9656 | 0.9664 | 0.9671 | 0.9678 | 0.9686 | 0.9693 | 0.9699 | 0.9706 |
| 1.90 | 0.9713 | 0.9719 | 0.9726 | 0.9732 | 0.9738 | 0.9744 | 0.9750 | 0.9756 | 0.9761 | 0.9767 |
| 2.00 | 0.9772 | 0.9778 | 0.9783 | 0.9788 | 0.9793 | 0.9798 | 0.9803 | 0.9808 | 0.9812 | 0.9817 |
| 2.10 | 0.9821 | 0.9826 | 0.9830 | 0.9834 | 0.9838 | 0.9842 | 0.9846 | 0.9850 | 0.9854 | 0.9857 |
| 2.20 | 0.9861 | 0.9864 | 0.9868 | 0.9871 | 0.9875 | 0.9878 | 0.9881 | 0.9884 | 0.9887 | 0.9890 |
| 2.30 | 0.9893 | 0.9896 | 0.9898 | 0.9901 | 0.9904 | 0.9906 | 0.9909 | 0.9911 | 0.9913 | 0.9916 |
| 2.40 | 0.9918 | 0.9920 | 0.9922 | 0.9925 | 0.9927 | 0.9929 | 0.9931 | 0.9932 | 0.9934 | 0.9936 |
| 2.50 | 0.9938 | 0.9940 | 0.9941 | 0.9943 | 0.9945 | 0.9946 | 0.9948 | 0.9949 | 0.9951 | 0.9952 |
| 2.60 | 0.9953 | 0.9955 | 0.9956 | 0.9957 | 0.9959 | 0.9960 | 0.9961 | 0.9962 | 0.9963 | 0.9964 |
| 2.70 | 0.9965 | 0.9966 | 0.9967 | 0.9968 | 0.9969 | 0.9970 | 0.9971 | 0.9972 | 0.9973 | 0.9974 |
| 2.80 | 0.9974 | 0.9975 | 0.9976 | 0.9977 | 0.9977 | 0.9978 | 0.9979 | 0.9979 | 0.9980 | 0.9981 |
| 2.90 | 0.9981 | 0.9982 | 0.9982 | 0.9983 | 0.9984 | 0.9984 | 0.9985 | 0.9985 | 0.9986 | 0.9986 |
| 3.00 | 0.9986 | 0.9987 | 0.9987 | 0.9988 | 0.9988 | 0.9989 | 0.9989 | 0.9989 | 0.9990 | 0.9990 |

option. If you try the model on securities that have different dividend yields but are similar in every other respect, the model will predict the same price because the OPM does not consider dividends. We have already seen, however, that the higher the dividend yield, the lower the call premium, and the financial pages would most likely not reflect the same premium for these two options.

Most stocks do pay dividends. This does not mean the OPM is useless for these securities. It is possible to make an adjustment that helps account for the effect of the dividend payment. A common way of doing this is to subtract the discounted value of a future dividend from the current stock price before you solve for the value of the call. For instance, if a 50 cent cash dividend will be earned eighty-two days from today, you can turn this future value into a present value equivalent the same way as in other financial applications. Suppose the XYZ stock is expected to go ex-dividend by 50 cents in eighty-two days.

It is common practice to discount the dividend from the ex-dividend date rather than the date of payment because the stock that the call owner has the right to buy materially changes on the ex-dividend date. Before that date, the stock comes with the dividend; on that date and after, the purchaser is not entitled to the dividend.

The use of the natural logarithm in the OPM assumes continuous compounding of interest. You should be consistent in your dividend adjustment, so you discount the 50 cents on a continuous basis as well. Eighty-two days is 82/365 of a year, or 0.2247. The present value of the dividend payment then equals $e^{-(0.05)(0.2247)}$($0.50) = 0.989(0.50) = $0.49 where $e$ is the base of natural logarithms. The adjusted stock price is then $30.00 – $0.49, or $29.51, and the adjusted call premium becomes $5.55.

**European Exercise Terms.** Another assumption of the OPM is that the option is of the European variety. Unlike American options, European options can be exercised only on the expiration date. American options are more valuable than European options because the flexibility of exercise is valuable. This is not a major pricing consideration, however, because very few calls are ever exercised prior to the last few days of their lives.

**Markets Are Efficient.** The Black-Scholes OPM also assumes that the stock market is informationally efficient; people cannot, as a rule, predict the direction of the market or of an individual stock. Market efficiency is a central paradigm in modern investment theory. However, market efficiency should always be taken with a grain of salt. What good, for instance, would Black-Scholes prices have been on October 19, 1987, the day the market crashed? To paraphrase a famous quotation about democracy, market efficiency may not be a very good explanation of investor behavior, but it is head and shoulders above any other theory we have.

**No Commissions.** Another important assumption of the OPM is that market participants do not have to pay any commissions to buy or sell, but you know this is not true. Even floor traders pay fees that finance the administration and self-regulation of the exchanges. The commissions paid by individual investors are more substantial and can significantly affect the true cost of an option position. These trading fee differentials cause slightly different effective option prices for different market participants.

**Constant Interest Rates.** Another assumption of the Black-Scholes model is that the interest rate ($R$) in the model is constant and known. *Risk-free interest rate* is a common term in finance, but there actually is no such rate. In option pricing, it is common to use the discount rate on a U.S. Treasury bill that has a maturity approximately equal to the remaining life of the option as a proxy for this important interest rate, but even this can change on a daily basis. During a period of rapidly changing interest rates, the use of a single rate to calculate the value of a six-month option, for instance, might not be advisable. Many people spend much time looking for ways to value options when the parameters of the traditional Black-Scholes model are not known or are changing.

**Lognormal Returns.** The Black-Scholes model also assumes that the logarithms of the returns of the underlying security are normally distributed. This is a reasonable assumption for most assets on which options are available.

### *Insights into the Black-Scholes Model*

We can partition the Black-Scholes OPM into two parts, as follows:

$$C = \underbrace{S[N(d_1)]}_{\text{Part A}} - \underbrace{Ke^{-Rt}[N(d_2)]}_{\text{Part B}}$$

A call is valuable if, upon its exercise, the stock received is worth more than the striking price paid. If you are looking at an option that still has time until it expires, the important question for you today is whether the value of the stock you would receive on expiration day is higher than the present value of the striking price you would have to pay to exercise the option. In Part A of the OPM equation, $S$ is the current stock price, which, by finance theory, is the discounted value of the expected stock price at any future point. (If this were not the case, the markets would not be in equilibrium.) In option pricing theory, $N(d_1)$ is called a *pseudo-probability;* it is the probability of the option being in the money at expiration, adjusted for the *depth* the option is in the money.[8] Part B of the equation can be viewed as the present value of having to pay the exercise price on expiration day. $N(d_2)$ is the *actual* probability the option will be in the money on expiration day. The value of a call option, then, is the difference between the expected benefit from acquiring the stock and paying the exercise price on expiration day.

At expiration, calls are valuable only if the stock price is higher than the option striking price. As you contemplate the stock market, you also know that the higher the volatility of the underlying security, the greater the likelihood that the security will reach a distant striking price. This is the primary reason that option models are so sensitive to the estimate of volatility used in the model and that many analysts in the securities business make a career of studying volatilities.

The previous pages indicate that calculating Black-Scholes values can be tedious. Fortunately, it is not necessary to do so by hand. As with any financial model, it is not a good idea to use it as a "black box" that generates magic numbers. Investors and portfolio managers who use the Black-Scholes model generally understand what the model does and the factors that influence the premium.

One very convenient way to get a theoretical option value is via the *options calculator* available at the Chicago Board Options Exchange Website. You can download the calculator by visiting http://www.cboe.com/LearnCenter/Software.aspx. Elsewhere on the CBOE Website you will find some very helpful educational information regarding options and their intelligent use in an investment portfolio.

## Delta

When option traders or analysts talk shop, they almost certainly use the term *delta* frequently in their conversation. Deltas are an important by-product of the Black-Scholes model, and they provide particularly useful information to people who use options in portfolios.[9] **Delta** is the change in option premium expected from a small change in the stock price, all other things being the same. Symbolically,

$$\Delta = \frac{\partial C}{\partial S}$$

where $\partial C/\partial S$ is the first partial derivative of the call premium ($C$) with respect to the stock price ($S$). This value is useful because it allows us to determine how many options are needed to mimic the returns of the underlying stock.

Fortunately, the Black-Scholes OPM makes the determination of delta a simple task: It exactly equals $N(d_1)$. Delta for a call option is always less than 1 and more

[8] For a very intuitive explanation of this and other points related to option pricing, see the article by Grant, Vora, and Weeks listed in the Further Reading section of this chapter.

[9] Delta applications are discussed in Chapter 22 of this book. For a detailed discussion of the calculation and utility of the derivatives of the OPM, see Alan L. Tucker, *Financial Futures, Options and Swaps* (Minneapolis/St. Paul: West, 1991), chap. 13.

**TABLE 15-4** PUT/CALL PARITY ARBITRAGE TABLE

| *Activity* | *Cash Flow* | *Stock Price at Option Expiration* | |
|---|---|---|---|
| | | *Value if $S_1 < K$* | *Value if $S_1 > K$* |
| Write call | $+C$ | 0 | $K - S_1$ |
| + Buy stock | $-S_0$ | $S_1$ | $S_1$ |
| + Buy put | $-P$ | $K - S_1$ | 0 |
| + Borrow | $K/(1 + R)^T$ | $-K$ | $-K$ |
| = Sum | $C - P - S_0 + [K/(1 + R)^T]$ | 0 | 0 |

where

$C$ = call premium
$P$ = put premium
$S_0$ = stock price now
$S_1$ = stock price at option expiration
$K$ = striking price
$R$ = risk-free interest rate
$T$ = time until option expiration

than 0, because $N(d_1)$, the area under the normal curve, ranges from 0 to 100 percent. In the hypothetical example following Table 15-2, we determined a value of 0.836 for $N(d_1)$, the option delta. This means that for a $1 change in the price of the underlying stock price, the option would change by about 84 cents.

### Theory of Put/Call Parity

One of the most important academic papers on the pricing of options was Hans Stoll's paper on the idea of put/call parity (the basic relationship between put and call option prices).[10] The essence of this theory is that the price of a put, the price of a call, the value of the underlying stock, and the riskless rate of interest form an interrelated securities complex. If you know the value of three of these assets, you can solve for the value of the fourth. An understanding of the theory of put/call parity can be a big help in understanding the implications of the Black-Scholes OPM.

Consider the put/call parity arbitrage in Table 15-4. Arbitrage is present when there is a riskless profit opportunity. If an investment position must equal zero for any future stock price, the initial cost of the investment should also be zero. Table 15-4 shows that with European options and a nondividend-paying stock, an investor can combine a long stock position with a short call and a long put and have no position in the market. No matter what happens to future stock prices, the position will be worth zero at option expiration.

A similar proof shows that the combination of three positions on the other side of the market (a short stock position, a long call, and a short put) also yields no position. If someone has no position in the market, the position is riskless, and riskless investments should earn the riskless rate of interest.

Suppose an investor borrows money to buy stock and simultaneously writes a call and buys a put, where both options are at the money. The investor then holds this position until option expiration. This results in a theoretically perfect

[10]Hans Stoll, "The Relationship between Put and Call Option Prices," *Journal of Finance*, December 1969, 801–824.

hedge, and a bank should be willing to lend money at the riskless rate of interest (theoretically). Arbitrage profits should equal zero, so we anticipate that

$$C - P - \frac{SR}{(1+R)} = 0 \tag{15-1}$$

with all variables as previously defined; additionally, $S$ = value of the stock, and $SR$ = interest charge.

Put/call parity comes from the following logic. There is one cash inflow (from writing the call) and there are two cash outflows (paying for the put and paying the interest on the bank loan). The inflow from the loan can be ignored because it is spent as soon as it is received. The interest on the bank loan is paid in the future: It needs to be discounted to a present value. That is the reason the interest charge ($SR$) is divided by the quantity $1 + R$.

We can rearrange the equation as follows:

$$C - P = \frac{SR}{(1+R)} \tag{15-2}$$

Dividing both sides of the equation by the value of the stock ($S$), we get

$$\frac{C}{S} - \frac{P}{S} = \frac{R}{(1+R)} \approx R \tag{15-3}$$

The quantity $R/(1 + R)$ is very close to $R$.[11] This shows that relative put and call prices differ by the risk-free rate of interest. For at-the-money options, the call premium should exceed the put premium, and the difference will increase as the price of the stock goes up.

Suppose you do as before: write the call, buy the put (with the same striking price as the call), and buy stock—but instead of borrowing the current stock value, you borrow the present value of the striking price of the options discounted from the option expiration date. If the options are at the money, the stock price equals the option striking price. It is necessary to discount the striking price because this amount is paid in the future, and dollars today are not the same as dollars tomorrow. This yields the profit/loss contingency table for the combined positions shown in Table 15-4.

The theory of put/call parity indicates that relative call prices should exceed relative put prices by about the riskless rate of interest when the options are at the money and the stock pays no dividends.

Regardless of whether the stock price at option expiration is above or below the exercise price, the net value of the combined positions is zero. This results in the put/call parity relationship.[12] The put/call parity model is

$$C - P = S - \frac{K}{(1+R)^T}$$

A numerical example shows the reason the put/call parity model must hold true. In the absence of arbitrage, equivalent financial claims should sell for the same price. Suppose stock and option prices are as shown in Table 15-5. No matter what

[11]For instance, if $R$ = 5.5%, then 0.055/1.055 = 0.052, or 5.2%.

[12]This relationship holds exactly for European options only.

**TABLE 15-5** ARBITRAGE VIA OPTION MISPRICING

Stock price ($S$) = \$50
Option striking price ($K$) = \$50
Time until expiration = 0.5 year
Annual T-bill interest rate = 6%
Call premium = \$4.75
Put premium = \$3

Theoretical put value (given the call value):

$$P = \$4.75 - \$50 + [\$50/(1.06)^{0.5}] = \$3.31$$

This means the actual call price (\$4.75) is too high or that the put price (\$3) is too low.

***To Exploit the Arbitrage:***

Write 1 call at \$4.75
Buy 1 put at \$3
Buy 1 share at \$50
Borrow \$48.56 at 6 percent for six months
This nets a certain arbitrage profit of \$0.31, as shown below.

| ***Profit/(Loss) from*** | ***Stock Price at Option Expiration*** | | |
|---|---|---|---|
| | \$ 0.00 | \$50.00 | \$100.00 |
| Call | 4.75 | 4.75 | (45.25) |
| Put | 47.00 | (3.00) | (3.00) |
| Loan | (1.44) | (1.44) | (1.44) |
| Stock | (50.00) | 0.00 | 50.00 |
| Total | \$ 0.31 | \$ 0.31 | \$ 0.31 |

the stock price at option expiration, the activities described yield a certain profit. If the put price had been too high relative to the call price, the arbitrageur would have written the put, bought the call, sold a share of the stock short, and invested the proceeds from the short sale at the 6 percent interest rate.

## Stock Index Options

A stock index option is the option exchanges' most successful innovation. The first of these, the S&P 100 index option (ticker symbol OEX), began trading on the CBOE in March 1983. Since that time, index options now trade on the American, Philadelphia, and Pacific stock exchanges as well as the CBOE.

Index options are similar to traditional stock options with one important difference: Index options have no delivery mechanism. All settlements are in cash. It is not practical to deliver share certificates for each component of the index.

When an index option is in the money at expiration, a *cash* transfer occurs between the option buyer and the option writer rather than a *securities* transfer. The owner of an in-the-money call receives the difference between the closing index level and the option striking price multiplied by the option multiplier (usually 100). With an in-the-money index put option, the option holder receives the difference between the striking price and the index level. The cash settlement feature makes index options versatile tools for portfolio management because they permit risk adjustments with little disruption of the underlying portfolio.

## SUMMARY

The two types of options are puts and calls. Calls give investors the right to buy; puts give them the right to sell. All options have a predetermined expiration day and a predetermined buying/selling price, called the *striking price*.

The first trade an individual makes in a particular option is an opening transaction; when the position is closed out, the trade is a closing transaction. The sale of options as an opening transaction is called *writing the option*.

Options have both intrinsic value and time value. Intrinsic value changes every time the value of the underlying security changes, and time value declines as the expiration date approaches.

Six important market factors determine the option premium: the option striking price, the time remaining until the option expires, the stock price, the volatility of the underlying asset, the dividend yield on the underlying asset, and the level of interest rates.

The Black-Scholes Option Pricing Model (OPM) is a very useful explanation of how the option premium is determined in the marketplace. Delta is the first derivative of the OPM with respect to the price of the underlying asset. It measures how the price of an option changes with small changes in the value of the underlying asset.

Option pricing is based on arbitrage arguments. The price of an asset, the prices of puts and calls on that asset, and the riskless rate of interest form an interrelated securities complex. If we know the value of three of these factors, we can solve for the value of the fourth. The basic relationship between put and call option prices is called *put/call parity*, and related logic leads to the Black-Scholes OPM.

Index options are extremely popular. They trade the same way that ordinary equity options do, except that they are cash-settled.

## QUESTIONS

1. In general, does a person who buys a call option want prices to go up or down?
2. Buying a call is exactly the same as writing a put. True or false, and why?
3. Why are options considered wasting assets?
4. If one thousand people own XYZ put options, then one thousand people wrote XYZ puts. True or false, and why?
5. Why do most people sell their valuable options rather than exercising them?
6. How is it possible for an options contract to disappear without expiring or being exercised?
7. Suppose you are bullish on a stock. What are the relative advantages and disadvantages of buying a call versus writing a put?
8. Refer to Table 15-1. Give an example of an option that is near the money.
9. Refer to Table 15-1, and look at the section pertaining to Nile.com. Using the striking prices listed as a clue, do you think the price of Nile.com common stock has risen or fallen in the weeks prior to these prices?
10. Why do you think some options have more striking prices listed than others?
11. Would you expect an American option on a particular stock always to sell for at least as much as a European option with the same exercise terms? Why or why not?

12. Comment on the following statement: An option that is out of the money must have time value.
13. Comment on the following statement: An option that is in the money must have intrinsic value.
14. Comment on the following statement: Options are nothing more than a side bet on the direction stock prices are going to move.
15. Briefly explain why the following statement is wrong: If you buy an XYZ JUN 25 call option in March, the only way you can make a profit is if the price of XYZ closes above 25 on expiration day in June.
16. An at-the-money option has time value equal to its intrinsic value. True or false?
17. Briefly explain how it is possible for an out-of-the-money put option on XYZ to sell for more than an in-the-money put option on XYZ.
18. Why do many people believe that buying a put is preferable to selling short shares of the underlying stock?
19. If you sell an option as an opening transaction, this is called *writing the option*. But just because you wrote an option does not mean it was an opening transaction. True or false, and why?
20. The number of XYZ call options in existence is always a constant. True or false?
21. Why is writing an in-the-money put riskier than writing an out-of-the-money put?
22. Suppose someone buys five XYZ FEB 40 puts and also buys five XYZ FEB 30 puts. Is this the same as buying ten XYZ FEB 35 puts?
23. Suppose you look in the newspaper and see that an option has changed price since yesterday, but the stock price has remained the same. Explain three factors that can cause the option premium to change while the stock price remains unchanged.
24. Suppose the general level of interest rates in the economy rises. What effect would this have on call premiums? Why do interest rates matter at all in option pricing?
25. Briefly explain why stock splits do not adversely affect the holder of a stock option.
26. Why is it not possible for the delta of a call option to be more than one or less than zero? Explain this using intuition rather than mathematics.
27. Suppose interest rates rise. Will an option's delta change if the stock price remains unchanged?

## PROBLEMS

1. Using Table 15-1, answer the following questions:
   **a.** How much time value is in a Smith Electronics (SELE) FEB 60 call option?
   **b.** What is the intrinsic value of a SELE JAN 65 call?
   **c.** What is the intrinsic value of a SELE APR 75 put?
   **d.** Suppose you write a Western Oil (WO) FEB 65 call. What is your maximum profit?
   **e.** Suppose you buy a Nile.com FEB 115 put for the price listed. At expiration, Nile.com stock sells for $85.38. What is your profit or loss?
   **f.** What is your maximum possible profit if you buy a WO FEB 70 call?

2. Suppose you simultaneously buy 400 shares of SELE and write two FEB 70 puts. What is your gain or loss if, at option expiration, the common stock of SELE sells for $57.38?
3. In Problem 2, what is your profit or loss if SELE stock is $77.38 at option expiration?
4. Suppose an investor engages in three simultaneous transactions: (1) she buys 100 shares of Nile.com (NIL) common stock, (2) writes a FEB 115 put, and (3) buys a FEB 110 put. Does this strategy make any sense?
5. In Problem 4, what is the investor's profit or loss if NIL is unchanged at option expiration?
6. Use the Black-Scholes OPM for this problem: A stock currently sells for $43.50 and pays no dividends. A call option (striking price = $45) on this security expires in 67 days. At present, U.S. Treasury bills are yielding 5.3 percent per year. You estimate the past volatility of the stock returns to be 44 percent. According to the Black-Scholes OPM, what is the value of this call?
7. Suppose you own ten FEB 60 puts on XYA, and the company splits the stock 3 for 2. What are your option holdings after the split adjustments are made to the contract terms?
8. Use the Black-Scholes OPM for this problem: A stock sells for $25. A put option with a $25 striking price has 145 days until expiration. If the volatility of the underlying stock is 0.20 and interest rates are 5 percent, what is the delta of this put option?
9. Use the Black-Scholes OPM for this problem: Suppose you do not know the volatility of the underlying asset in Problem 8, but you do know that the put premium is $1.38. How can you find the put delta?

Use the data in Table 15-1 for Problems 10 through 14.

10. Draw a profit and loss diagram for the purchase of a FEB 80 WO call option.
11. Draw a profit and loss diagram for the purchase of a FEB 70 WO put option.
12. Draw a profit and loss diagram for a short SELE FEB 70 call option.
13. Draw a profit and loss diagram for a short FEB 60 WO put option.
14. Suppose a call option sells for $2.50, a put option sells for $2.00, both options have a $25.00 striking price, the current stock price is $25.50, and the options both expire in forty-six days. Using the put-call parity model, calculate the rate of interest implied in these numbers.

## INTERNET EXERCISE

Use the option price calculator at *http://www.cboe.com/LearnCenter/Software.aspx* to price the option in Problem 6.

## FURTHER READING

Bittman, James B. *Options for the Stock Investor.* Chicago: Irwin, 1996.

Black, Fischer. "Fact and Fantasy in the Use of Options." *Financial Analysts Journal,* July/August 1975, 36–72.

Black, Fischer, and Myron Scholes. "The Pricing of Options and Corporate Liabilities." *Journal of Political Economy,* May 1973, 637–659.

Bookstaber, Richard. "The Use of Options in Performance Structuring." *Journal of Portfolio Management,* Summer 1985, 36–50.

Cox, John, and Mark Rubenstein. *Options Markets.* Englewood Cliffs, N.J.: Prentice-Hall, 1985.

Degler, W. "How to Survive the First Few Months of Options Trading." *Futures,* April 1986, 52–53.

Gastineau, Gary. *The Options Manual,* 3d ed. New York: McGraw-Hill, 1988.

———, and A. Mandansky "Simulation Is No Guide to Option Strategies." *Financial Analysts Journal,* September/October 1979, 61–76.

Gladstein, M., Robert Merton, and Myron Scholes. "The Returns and Risks of Alternative Put Option Portfolio Investment Strategies." *Journal of Business,* January 1982, 1–55.

Grant, Dwight, Gautam Vora, and David Weeks. "Teaching Option Valuation: from Simple Discrete Distributions to Black/Scholes via Monte Carlo Simulation." *Financial Practice and Education,* Fall/Winter 1995, 149–155.

Malkiel, Burton, and Richard Quandt. *Strategies and Rational Decisions in the Securities Options Markets.* Cambridge, Mass.: MIT Press, 1969.

Merton, Robert. "Theory of Rational Option Pricing." *Bell Journal of Economics and Management Science,* Spring 1973, 141–183.

Ritchken, Peter. *Options: Theory, Strategy, and Applications.* Glenview, Ill.: Scott, Foresman, 1987.

Stoll, Hans. "The Relationship between Put and Call Option Prices." *Journal of Finance,* December 1969, 801–824.

Strong, Robert A. *Derivatives: An Introduction,* 2d edition. Mason, Oh: South-Western, 2005.

———, and Amy Dickinson. "Forecasting Better Hedge Ratios." *Financial Analysts Journal,* January/February 1994, 70–72.

# 16 Option Overwriting

*What's a good way to raise the blood pressure of an Investor Relations Manager?*
*Answer: Talk about the pros and cons of stock options.*
***Eilene H. Kirrane, Boston chapter of the National Investor Relations Institute***

## Key Terms

cash settlement
covered call
deep in the money
fiduciary put
hedging
improving on the market
index option
long position
margin
naked call
overwriting

## Introduction

Option *overwriting* is an increasingly popular portfolio activity. **Overwriting** refers to creating and selling stock options in conjunction with a stock portfolio.

The option overwriter usually has one of two motives in mind. One is to generate additional portfolio income; this is clearly the most common purpose. A second is to purchase or sell stock at a better-than-market price.

Oppenheimer Capital is one of the largest U.S. managers of options programs for institutional investors, with responsibility for more than $3 billion. Its most popular offering is an options overwriting program that is independent of a client's equity holdings, so the option trading never affects the underlying portfolio.

This chapter assumes that you are familiar with the basic principles of stock options and their markets covered in Chapter 15.

## Using Options to Generate Income

The most popular use of options by both individual investors and institutions is to generate additional portfolio income. Investors can do this by writing either puts or calls, with calls being much more popular for this purpose. The examples that follow use data from Table 15-1.

*The option strategy guide at* http://www.numa.com/derivs/ref/os-guide/os-0.htm *outlines 17 distinct strategies including covered call writing.*

### *Writing Calls to Generate Income*

**Writing Covered Calls.** Writing covered calls is the most common use of stock options by both individual and institutional investors. Investors usually write call options against stock they already own. When this is the case, the call is a **covered call.** It is important to note that a covered call is exactly the same as any other call option except that the owner simultaneously owns the stock.[1]

As illustrated in Chapter 15, a profit and loss diagram helps in determining the consequences of various stock prices at option expiration. First consider a profit and loss diagram for a long stock position. A **long position** is simply an asset that someone owns. Table 15-1 shows that the common stock of the Nile.com Corporation sells for $116 per share. If someone buys one share at this price, the maximum *loss* is the full investment of $116. This happens if the stock becomes worthless. The stock investor's maximum *gain* is theoretically unlimited because the stock price can rise to any level. If the stock price remains unchanged from its current level, the investor breaks even (ignoring commissions and dividends). Figure 16-1 shows this situation.

If an investor writes a call option, he is giving someone else the right to purchase his stock at the striking price. Regardless of how much the stock advances over the life of the option, he has an obligation to sell it at the striking price if the holder of the call option exercises.

Suppose someone owns 100 shares of Nile.com and chooses to write a February 120 call against it. The option writer gets the premium ($600, in this case) right away, which the writer keeps no matter what happens to the stock price.[2] At any stock price above $120, however, the stock will be called away.[3]

**FIGURE 16-1**

Long Stock Position Purchased at $116

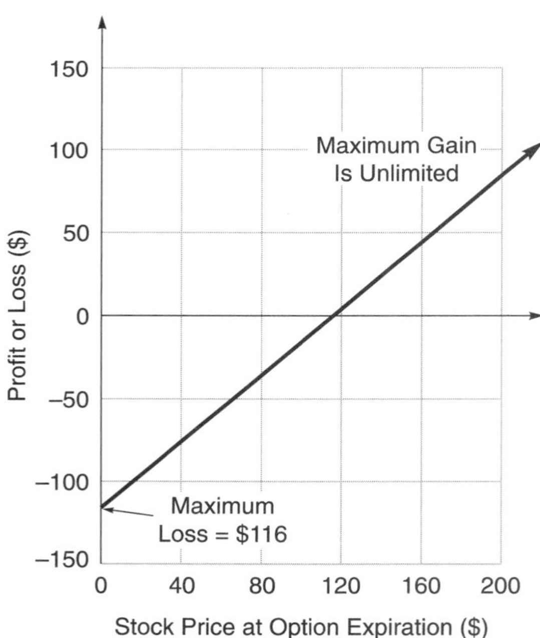


[1]If you own shares of stock, you are said to be *long*. The term has nothing to do with time.

[2]See Table 15-1; 100 × $6 = $600.

[3]Option exercise normally occurs just before the option expires. Exercise can, however, conceivably occur at any time with an American option.

**TABLE 16-1** PROFIT AND LOSS WORKSHEET FOR A COVERED CALL

| | *Stock Price at Option Expiration* | | | | | | |
|---|---|---|---|---|---|---|---|
| | *0* | *50* | *100* | *116* | *120* | *125* | *150* |
| Long stock | −116 | −66 | −16 | 0 | +4 | +9 | +34 |
| Short call | +6 | +6 | +6 | +6 | +6 | +1 | −24 |
| Total | −110 | −60 | −10 | +6 | +10 | +10 | +10 |

Stock price = $116; FEB 120 call = $6.

A Website fully dedicated to covered option strategies can be found at http://www.coveredcall.com

Table 16-1 is a profit and loss worksheet showing various possible outcomes for this covered call. (We typically prepare these worksheets on the basis of a single share rather than 100.) The table shows that if stock prices decline, the call premium cushions the loss by $6. Even if the stock drops to zero, the writer still keeps the option premium, so the net loss is "only" $110 (rather than $116, as in Figure 16-1). The maximum gain is $10, which occurs at stock prices of $120 and above. The writer always gets to keep the $6 premium regardless of future prices. At a price of $120, the stock is up $4 from its initial price of $116; the total gain to the covered call writer, then, is $10 at this point. At any stock price above $120, the stock will be called away, and additional gains in the stock will belong to the person holding the call.

*The opportunity cost associated with option exercise is the principal disadvantage of covered call writing.*

At a stock price of $150, for instance, the call will be exercised: It gives its holder the right to buy stock worth $150 for the exercise price of $120, and the call writer has to sell her stock to the call holder. She incurs a $30 opportunity cost when she sells; this is the principal disadvantage of writing covered calls.

In actual dollars, she makes a $10 profit per share if the stock price is $150 at option expiration. She sells her shares for $120, resulting in a $4 gain from the original $116 price in this example. Also she keeps the $6 premium for writing the option. At any stock price above the striking price, she earns this maximum gain of $10. Figure 16-2 shows the situation.

Consider another example from your perspective as a portfolio manager. Perhaps one of your managed accounts contains 2,000 shares of Nile.com. In late December, the stock sold for $116 as shown in Table 15-1. The beneficiary of this account encounters an unexpected need for additional income in the next few weeks. You notice that a FEB 125 call on Nile.com sells for $4.63 or $463 on 100 shares. If you write twenty of these call contracts against the 2,000 shares of Nile.com, this would generate $9,260 in immediate income.

The worst thing that could happen would be for the stock of Nile.com to fall to zero. This, of course, could happen regardless of whether or not you used the options market. If prices advance above the striking price of $125, the stock will be called away and sold to the owner of the call option for $125 per share, regardless of the current stock price. This should not be viewed as a disaster, though, because the position shows a nice profit. The stock rose from $116 to $125, which, on 2,000 shares, results in a gain of $18,000; furthermore, you received the $9,260 premium when you sold the option.[4]

Calculating the annualized rate of return in this situation is an interesting exercise because it illustrates one dimension to the performance evaluation issue to be covered in Chapter 17. You can approach this calculation in two ways. One way is

[4]From your perspective, $125 is the ceiling on the share price because you will have to sell it for $125 at any share price above that.

**FIGURE 16-2**

Writing a Covered Call

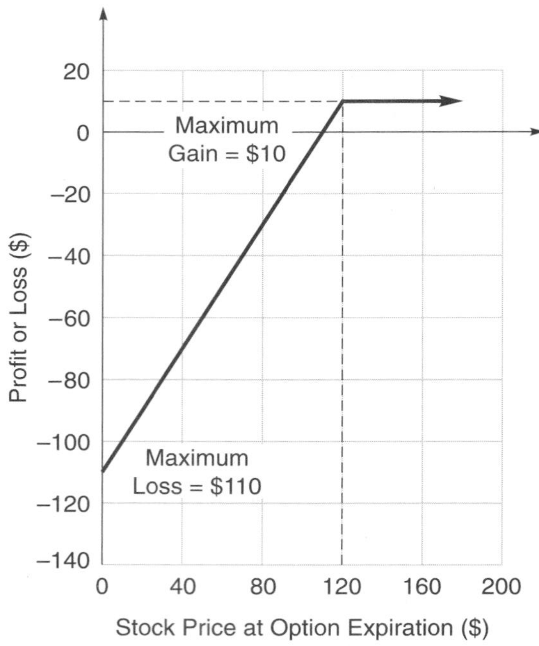


Stock price = $116; $120 call = $6.

to assume that you held 2,000 shares of Nile.com, initially worth a total of $232,000. From December 30 to option expiration in February is about 50 days. You earned a capital gain of $18,000 from the rise in the value of the stock, and you received the option premium of $9,260. Your annualized rate of return is then

$$\frac{\$18,000 + \$9,260}{\$232,000} \times \frac{365}{50} = 86\%$$

Suppose, however, you buy the 2,000 shares and simultaneously write the calls. The premium income you receive can be used to reduce the size of your initial investment. If you view the problem this way, the calculation yields a substantially different result:

$$\frac{\$18,000}{\$232,000 - \$9,260} \times \frac{365}{50} = 59\%$$

The difference lies in the *time value of money*: Dollars today are not the same as dollars tomorrow. The holding period return makes no distinction as to when you receive the funds. You would obviously prefer to receive the option premium at the beginning of the investment period rather than receive the same amount at the end. The correct measure of return would be a time-value–adjusted rate that accurately reflected when dollars were paid and when they were received.

*Writing covered calls is the most popular use of stock options by both individual and institutional investors.*

Writing covered calls is an attractive way to generate income. It is a very popular strategy with foundations, pension funds, and other portfolios that need to produce periodic cash payments. A need for income, however, is not necessarily the motivation for covered call writing. In relatively stable or slightly declining markets, writing these options can simply serve to enhance investment returns.

**Writing Naked Calls.** Writing a call that is covered by stock already in the portfolio is one thing; writing one that is *uncovered,* or *naked,* is a whole new ball game. Writing a **naked call** involves a potentially unlimited loss. The reason for this is easy to see. When you write a call, someone has the right to buy shares of stock from you. If you do not own these shares, option exercise means you must buy them in the open market before delivering them to the call option holder. The stock price might be much higher than the striking price of the option. Buying stock at a high price and selling it at a low price is clearly a losing proposition.

Despite this, some institutional heavyweights engage in continuous naked call writing as a means of generating income. Writing naked calls is a common strategy at the options desk of some large brokerage houses. These firms are writing the options not for clients but for themselves in an attempt to make money for the firm. Let's see how this might work.

Table 15-1 indicates that the premium for a JAN 80 call on Western Oil is \$0.38, whereas Western Oil's stock sells for \$66.75. Suppose these prices are from the end of December. This means that the January option has only about three weeks until it expires. A brokerage firm may believe that it is extremely unlikely that Western Oil will rise to \$80 per share by option expiration in January, and consequently the firm may choose to write 100 of these calls (options on 10,000 shares). If it is able to do this at the listed premium of \$0.38, the firm experiences a cash inflow of \$0.38/share × 10,000 shares, or \$3,800. The firm receives the money now, and as long as the stock price stays below \$80, nothing else happens. But if the stock were to rise dramatically, the firm could sustain a large loss. Brokerage firms monitor the market carefully, and if rumors or favorable news regarding Western Oil began to circulate, the firm would close its option positions by buying them back.

Individual investors can write naked options, too, but brokerage firms discourage small investors from doing so by enforcing minimum account balance requirements (often \$20,000 minimum equity) before permitting this type of speculative activity.

*Private foundations can lose their tax-exempt status if they engage in any activity that could jeopardize their ability to carry out their exempt purpose.*

A fiduciary must be extremely careful about writing naked calls for a client, even if the client fully understands the riskiness of the strategy. Private foundations can lose their tax-exempt status if they engage in certain proscribed behaviors, one of which is investing in anything that jeopardizes the carrying out of the exempt purposes of a private foundation.

The fact that naked calls theoretically can result in an unlimited loss means that writing naked calls could jeopardize a private foundation's ability to continue its tax-exempt purposes. For this reason, writing naked calls on individual securities is almost certainly inappropriate for a charitable portfolio.

### *Writing Puts to Generate Income*

**Fiduciary Puts.** Any time you write an option, you generate income, but you also create a contingent liability on the account's balance sheet. When you write a call, you must sell stock if instructed to do so by the Options Clearing Corporation (OCC). When you write a put, you must buy stock if instructed to do so. In a naked option position, you do not have another related security position that would cushion losses from price movements that adversely affect your short option position.

The term *covered put* is not used very often. According to the Chicago Board Options Exchange *Options Reference Manual,*

> A short put option is "covered" if the account has on deposit cash or cash equivalents whose market value equals 100% of the aggregate strike price.
>
> Regulation T, Section 220.8(3)(ii) defines cash equivalents to be any of the following instruments provided they mature in one year or less: securities issued or guaranteed by the United States or its agencies, negotiable bank certificates of deposit, or bankers' acceptances issued and payable in the United States. In both instances the broker has access to what is needed to meet any assignment obligation of the short options: either physical possession (or rights thereto) of the underlying security for short calls or cash to purchase the underlying for short puts.[5]

A covered put is better called a *fiduciary put* or a cash-secured put. This put option differs from any other only in that the writer of a covered put deposits the striking price of the option in an interest-bearing account or holds the necessary cash equivalents. This deposit provides collateral against the possibility of exercise. The writer of a **fiduciary put** already has the money needed to buy the stock if exercise occurs.

Figure 16-3 shows the profit and loss diagram for a short put position. This diagram shows the writing of a Nile.com FEB 120 put option for $7.25. At any stock price above the striking price of $120, the put will expire worthless. This is what the speculative put writer wants to happen. At prices below $120, the holder of the put will exercise the option, and the put writer will have to purchase shares at $120 apiece. A fiduciary put will earn interest on the amount deposited; thus, the intercepts on the graph will shift a bit, depending on the time until expiration of the option and the associated interest earned.

**FIGURE 16-3**

Writing a Put at $7.25

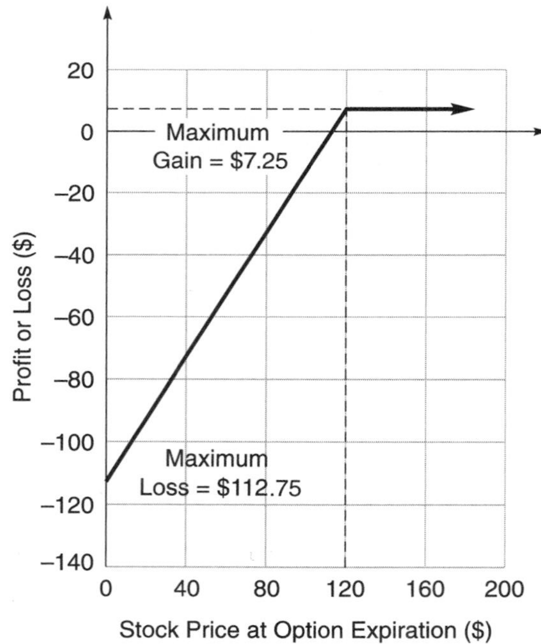


Strike price = $120.

[5]Chicago Board Options Exchange, *Options Reference Manual: A Guide for Institutional Investors* (Chicago: CBOE, January 1990), M2.

*Fiduciary puts and covered calls have similar profit and loss characteristics.*

Note that no major differences exist in the profit and loss diagrams for the covered call and the fiduciary put; this is important. For certain accounts, writing fiduciary puts probably makes more sense than buying stock and immediately writing calls against it. Certainly, the commission costs are lower with fiduciary puts.

*Put overwriting involves being simultaneously long stock and short puts on the same stock.*

**Put Overwriting.** Another important option strategy involves owning shares of stock and writing *put* options against them. Because owning shares and writing puts are both bullish strategies, put overwriting is also a bullish strategy. Remember that any time an investor writes an option, the largest possible gain is the option premium; losses can be large, however, if prices move against the investor.

An investor might simultaneously buy shares of Nile.com at $116 and write a Nile.com FEB $115 put. Table 16-2 is a profit and loss worksheet for this strategy, and Figure 16-4 is the associated profit and loss diagram. Figure 16-4 indicates that if prices rise above the option striking price, the put will expire worthless, and dollar-for-dollar profits will be enjoyed on the stock rise. But if prices fall, the investor's loss is double because the stock is depreciating and he incurs progressively larger liabilities on the short put position.

**TABLE 16-2** PUT OVERWRITING WORKSHEET

| | *Stock Price at Option Expiration* | | | | |
|---|---|---|---|---|---|
| | *0* | *$75* | *$115* | *$116* | *$150* |
| Long stock | −116 | −41 | −1 | 0 | +34 |
| Short put | −110.75 | −35.75 | +4.25 | +4.25 | +4.25 |
| | −226.75 | −76.75 | +3.25 | +4.25 | +38.25 |

Buy stock at $116; write $115 put at $4.25.

**FIGURE 16-4**

Put Overwriting

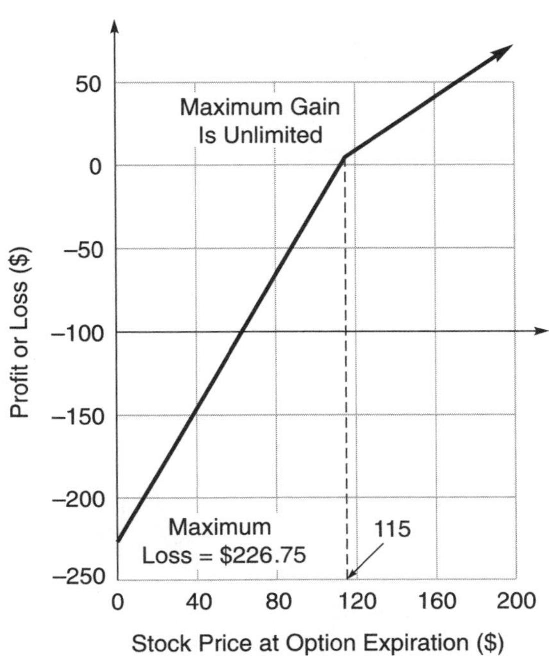


Buy stock at $116; write 115 put at $4.25.

Put overwriting may be appropriate for a portfolio manager who needs to generate additional income from the portfolio but does not want to write calls for fear of opportunity losses in a bull market. If the portfolio does continue to increase in value, the puts will expire worthless, the portfolio will benefit from the premium income received, and the portfolio will remain intact. In contrast, if stock prices turn down and the portfolio manager does not trade out of the put positions quickly, the overall effect on the portfolio could be disastrous.

Figure 16-5 shows the results of a strategy of continuous put overwriting on a portfolio of twenty-five securities over a 239-week period from 1977 to 1982. An equal dollar amount was invested in each of the original twenty-five common stocks on which put options were available. The initial portfolio value begins at $10,000 for ease in interpreting the results over the period. A portfolio overwritten with in-the-money put options must increase in value for the puts to expire worthless. With out-of-the-money puts, the value of the stock in the portfolio can decline to the striking price without the risk of exercise by the put holder. Writing in-the-money puts is a riskier strategy, and Figure 16-5 indicates that over the long run, the riskiest strategy shows a higher realized return than the other two (as expected by finance theory). During some intermediate periods, though, writing in-the-money puts results in major portfolio losses.

**FIGURE 16-5**

A Brief History of Put Overwriting

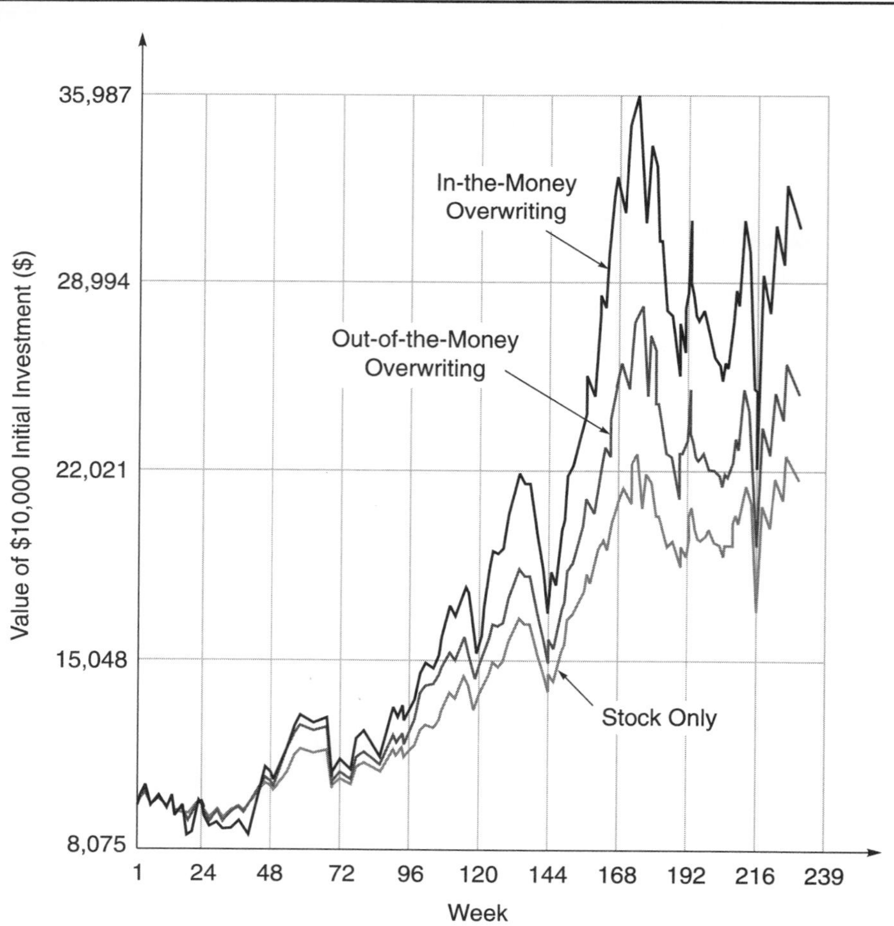

An analyst must investigate any investment strategy carefully because it is crucial to consider overall market behavior during the period of investigation. Over the 239-week period shown in Figure 16-5, though, it is apparent that put overwriting would have significantly improved the returns of this portfolio.

### Writing Index Options

An **index option** is one of the most successful financial innovations of all time. Two especially popular indexes are those on the S&P 100 index and the S&P 500 index, both trading on the Chicago Board Options Exchange. The trading symbols for these two indexes are OEX and SPX, respectively, and this is how investors refer to these option products. Table 16-3 shows a few of the most popular indexes on which options trade.

Detailed information on these and many other indexes is available via the exchanges' Websites: *http://www.cboe.com*, *http://www.amex.com*, and *http://www.phlx.com*.

*Index options have little unsystematic risk.*

One advantage of index options is that they have little unsystematic, or company-specific, risk. The OEX index has one hundred securities, enough to provide thorough diversification. (A manager can lower the *systematic* risk of a portfolio by writing index calls or buying index puts.)

Say you are the manager of a $5 million, well-diversified stock portfolio containing fifty individual securities and it becomes necessary to generate more income from this portfolio. One solution is to write call options against the individual components

**TABLE 16-3** INDEXES WITH LISTED OPTIONS

| *Index* | *Symbol* | *Exchange* | *Description* |
|---|---|---|---|
| S&P 100 | OEX | CBOE | 100 stocks from a broad range of industries |
| S&P 500 | SPX | CBOE | 500 stocks from a broad range of industries |
| NASDAQ-100 | NDX | CBOE | 100 of the largest nonfinancial stocks listed on the NASDAQ stock market |
| Dow Jones Industrials | DJX | CBOE | 30 of the largest, most liquid NYSE stocks |
| Russell 2000 | RUT | CBOE | Bottom 2,000 of the 3,000 largest stocks in the United States |
| Institutional Index | XII | AMEX | 75 stocks held in the greatest dollar amount among all publicly traded issues in institutional portfolios larger than $100 million |
| Japan Index | JPN | AMEX | 210 large capitalization Japanese stocks |
| Morgan Stanley Hi-tech | MSH | AMEX | 35 electronics-based stocks from nine industry sub-sectors |
| Gold/Silver | XAU | Philadelphia | 10 widely held companies in the gold and silver mining industry |
| Oil Service | OSX | Philadelphia | 15 companies that provide oil drilling and production services, oil field equipment, support services, and geophysical/reservoir services |
| Semiconductor | SOX | Philadelphia | 16 U.S. companies that are primarily involved in the design, distribution, manufacture, and sale of semiconductors |

**TABLE 16-4** S&P 100 INDEX OPTION LISTING

| | Calls | | | Puts | | |
|---|---|---|---|---|---|---|
| *Strike Price* | *Feb* | *Mar* | *Apr* | *Feb* | *Mar* | *Apr* |
| 600 | 37.50 | 51 | — | 9.13 | 17.25 | 22.50 |
| 610 | 30 | 41.75 | 49.75 | 11.75 | 21.38 | 23.50 |
| 620 | 24 | 37.88 | 44.50 | 15 | 24 | — |
| 625 | 29.50 | 34.75 | — | 16.75 | 24.50 | 32.38 |
| 630 | 16.75 | 27 | 34.50 | 24 | 30 | — |
| 640 | 11.88 | 21.88 | 32.50 | 26 | 32 | — |
| 650 | 8 | 20.25 | 27.50 | 30.75 | 34.88 | 37 |
| 660 | 5 | 13.75 | — | 39.50 | — | — |
| 670 | 2.75 | 10.25 | — | — | — | — |
| 680 | 1.44 | 7 | 13 | — | — | — |
| 690 | 0.75 | 5.50 | — | — | — | — |

Closing level of index = 626.01

in the portfolio. If the portfolio contains 5,000 shares of IBM, you could write 50 IBM calls. If the portfolio has 10,000 shares of General Motors, you could write 100 GM calls, and these would be covered. Each option transaction costs you a commission. If you write calls against all fifty stocks in the portfolio, you will pay fifty commissions. You also run the risk that one or more of the stocks will be called away because of a takeover, unexpected good news, or some other company-specific event.

Another solution is to write index calls instead of traditional equity calls. Table 16-4 shows prices when the level of the OEX index was 626.01. FEB 690 calls sold for $0.75, or $75 per contract of 100 "shares." The call options become in the money once the OEX index goes above 690; this converts to a 10.2 percent increase in the market in one month, a change that is certainly possible but not a frequent occurrence.

With equity options, you know how many options you can write and still have them covered by your stock: You can write one option contract for each 100 shares you own. What about index options? How many FEB 690 calls can you write? The next section answers this more complicated question.

*The use of a margin account does not necessarily involve borrowing money or paying any interest.*

**Margin Considerations in Writing Index Call Options.** The term **margin** has caused innumerable problems for fund managers over the years. Many individual investors are familiar with margin accounts as a means of getting leverage in investments by borrowing money from a broker to buy securities. Tax-exempt funds generally cannot borrow money to invest without incurring some tax liability, so they seldom choose to use a margin account for this purpose. The use of a margin account, however, is not prima facie evidence of borrowing money. In fact, many charitable funds or fiduciary accounts have employed margin accounts for years and have never used them to borrow; their purpose is to provide the fund manager with added flexibility in managing the account.

In our example, the current level of the OEX index is 626.01. Because one contract contains 100 "indexes," the value of one contract is $62,601. Assume again you have a stock portfolio worth $5 million.

**Using a Cash Account.** A portfolio manager can write index options in a cash account, but there are stringent rules regarding the "collateral" that she must post. Despite what one might expect, "*Regulation T and exchange margin rules do not permit*

*For current margin requirements, see the CBOE* Margin Manual *at* http://www.cboe.com/LearnCenter/pdf/margin2-00.pdf

*short index calls in a cash account to be covered by a deposit of the underlying components with the broker.* Market index–covered call writing on a cash account basis can be effected only if a custodian bank were to issue to the broker an OCC index option escrow receipt."[6] See Figure 16-6 for a sample index option escrow receipt. In this escrow receipt, a bank certifies that it holds collateral sufficient to cover the writing of a certain number of index call options. The writer can provide the necessary collateral by the deposit of cash, cash equivalents, marginable stock, or any combination of these.[7] The collateral must total the full closing value of the underlying index on the trade date.

A \$5 million portfolio could be used to provide the collateral for writing 79 OEX index calls in a cash account: \$5 million/\$62,601 per contract = 79.87 contracts. Writing 79 FEB 690 contracts would generate immediate cash of 79 × \$75, or \$5,925. If more income were needed, the manager could investigate using a lower striking price or a longer time until maturity. Alternatively, she could use a margin account; this is the next topic.

**FIGURE 16-6** Sample Index Option Escrow Receipt

**THE OPTIONS CLEARING CORPORATION**

**Index Option Escrow Receipt** **Date**

**To: (Clearing Member name)** **and (Broker name)**

**and The Options Clearing Corporation:**

The undersigned (the "Bank"), having an office at ____________________, hereby represents and warrants that (a) it is a bank or trust company organized under the laws of the United States or a state thereof and supervised and examined by state or federal authority having supervision over banks or trust companies, (b) the equity attributable to all outstanding shares of capital stock issued by the Bank is not less than \$20,000,000; and (c) the total amount of cash and securities (at current market value) held by it pursuant to outstanding escrow receipts and guarantee letters collateralizing put and call options does not exceed a dollar amount equal to 25% of the equity attributable to all outstanding shares of capital stock issued by the Bank.

The Bank certifies that it holds the cash and/or securities hereinafter described (the "Deposit") in the United States of America as custodian for the account of ____________________ (the "Customer"), and that the Customer or its agent has specifically authorized the Bank to file this Escrow Receipt with you and to hold this Deposit as an escrow deposit pursuant to the Rules of The Options Clearing Corporation (the "Corporation") in respect of the Customer's position ("short position") as a writer of the following index call option contracts:

| Trade Date: | | Underlying Index: | |
|---|---|---|---|
| | | Option Series | |
| Number of Contracts | Aggregate Closing Index Value Per Contract at Trade Date | Expiration Month/Year | Aggregate Exercise Price Per Contract |
| | | | |

The Bank further certifies that:

(i) The Deposit consists of (a) cash, (b) cash equivalents meeting the requirements of §220.8(a)(3)(ii) of Regulation T of the Board of Governors of the Federal Reserve System (the "FRB"), (c) common stocks listed on a national securities exchange or included in the current List of OTC Margin Stocks published by the FRB, or (d) any combination thereof;

(ii) The total market value of the Deposit as of the trade date indicated above (valuing cash equivalents and common stocks at their closing sale prices, if subject to last sale reporting, or at their most recent bid prices, if not subject to last sale reporting) was not less than the product of (a) the number of contracts indicated above and (b) the aggregate closing index value per contract at trade date indicated above (such product being hereinafter referred to as the "Initial Position Value"):

(iii) To the extent that the Deposit includes securities, the Bank has by book entry or otherwise identified as being included within the Deposit: (a) specific certificates for such securities in the Bank's possession, (b) a quantity of such securities that constitutes or is part of a fungible bulk of securities in the Bank's possession, (c) a quantity of such securities that constitutes or is part of a fungible bulk of securities credited to the account of the Bank on the books of a "financial intermediary" (as defined in §8-313(4) of the Delaware Uniform Commercial Code), or (d) any combination thereof;

(iv) To the extent that the Deposit includes securities described in clause (iii)(a) or (iii)(b) above, such securities are in good deliverable form (or the Bank has the unrestricted power to put such securities into good deliverable form) in accordance with the requirements of the primary market for such securities;

(v) The Customer or its agent has duly authorized the Bank to liquidate any securities included in the Deposit to the extent necessary to perform the Bank's obligations hereunder;

(vi) The Bank will not subject nor permit the Customer to subject the Deposit or any portion thereof to any lien or encumbrance, or cause or permit the Deposit or any portion thereof to be applied to or used in satisfaction of any claim of The Bank (in any capacity whatsoever) against the Customer or any other person or entity or used by the Bank as an offset in whole or in part in any manner whatsoever, and the Bank will promptly notify the Corporation, the Clearing Member named above (the "Clearing Member") and the Broker, if any, named above (the "Broker") if any notice of lien, levy, court order or other process which may or purports to affect the Deposit or any portion thereof is served upon it;

(vii) The Bank maintains a written affirmation from the Customer or its agent stating that all index call options written for the Customer's account and covered by escrow receipts issued by the Bank are written against a diversified stock portfolio.

Upon the instructions of the Customer or its agent, the Bank may from time to time substitute cash, cash equivalents described in clause (i)(b) above, or common stocks described in clause (i)(c) above, for any property theretofore included in the Deposit, provided that (a) the current market value of the substituted property is at least equal to

(continued)

[6]Chicago Board Options Exchange, January 1990, M2.

[7]A stock is marginable if it is eligible for purchase in a margin account. Most stock is marginable. Exceptions include shares priced below \$5 and securities of firms in financial distress.

**FIGURE 16-6** Sample Index Option Escrow Receipt (continued)



that of the property for which it is substituted, and (b) the representations made in clauses (iii), (iv) and (v) above remain true and correct after giving effect to such substitution.

Upon the request of the Corporation, the Clearing Member, or the Broker (collectively, the "Beneficiaries") at any time while this Escrow Receipt remains outstanding, the Bank will promptly provide such Beneficiary with a written listing of the cash, cash equivalents, and/or common stocks then included within the Deposit. If the total market value of the Deposit shall at any time be less than 55% of the product of (a) the number of contracts indicated above and (b) the "aggregate current index value" of the underlying index (as defined in article XVII of the By-Laws of the Corporation), the Bank shall promptly notify the Customer or its agent thereof and request that the Deposit be supplemented. If the total market value of the Deposit shall at any time be less than 50% of said product (whether or not a request to the Customer for supplementation is then pending), the Bank will immediately advise the Beneficiaries in writing thereof. If any cash equivalent included in the Deposit shall cease to meet the requirements of clause (i)(b) above, or if any common stock included in the Deposit shall cease to meet the requirements of clause (i)(c) above, such cash equivalent or stock shall be assigned a value of zero for the purpose of any computation of total market value hereunder.

The Bank agrees that it will hold the Deposit in accordance with the terms hereof until this Escrow Receipt is released or the Bank is directed to make payment as hereinafter provided. Upon presentation of this Escrow Receipt with the Endorsement of Release below duly executed on behalf of each of the Beneficiaries, the Bank will release the Deposit to the Customer or its agent. Upon presentation of this Escrow Receipt (i) by the Corporation, with the Payment Order below duly executed on its behalf, (ii) by the Clearing Member, with the Payment Order below duly executed on its behalf and the Endorsement of Release below duly executed on behalf of the Corporation, or (iii) by the Broker, with the Payment Order below duly executed on its behalf and the Endorsement of Release below duly executed on behalf of the Corporation and the Clearing Member, the Bank will promptly pay to the order of the party presenting this Escrow Receipt, out of the Deposit or the proceeds thereof, an amount in cash equal to the aggregate "exercise settlement amount" of the number of index option contracts indicated above or such lesser number of contract as shall be specified in the Payment Order, plus all applicable commissions and other charges. As used herein, the term "exercise settlement amount" means the amount by which the aggregate current index value" of the underlying index (as defined in Article XVII of the By-Laws of the Corporation) on the date of exercise exceeds the price per contracted indicated above.

In the event that the Bank is presented with a Payment Order for a lesser number of index option contracts than the number indicated above, the Bank will issue to the party presenting the Payment Order, in exchange for this Escrow Receipt, an identical Escrow Receipt for the number of contracts indicated above minus the number of contracts covered by the Payment Order.

The Bank has been authorized by the Customer or its to confirms that (i) if the short position described above is closed out, it is the Customer's responsibility to ensure that this Escrow Receipt is released and until this Escrow Receipt is duly withdrawn from the corporation by the Clearing Member the Corporation will retain the right to demand payment in accordance herewith upon the assignment of an exercise notice to any short position in a series of indexes of all options identified above carried in the Clearing Member's customers' account with the Corporation: and (ii) exercise notices assigned by the Corporation to short positions for which escrow receipts have been deposited by the Clearing Member are allocated to particular customers by the Clearing Member or by their respective brokers, and if the Clearing Member is suspended by the Corporation and the Corporation cannot promptly determine the identities of the assigned customers, the Corporation will reallocate such exercise notices and such reallocation shall be binding on the Customer, notwithstanding any contrary notice or confirmation which the Customer may have received from the Clearing Member or the Customer's broker.

If the Customer is the Bank acting in a fiduciary or similar capacity, or a trust or custodial or similar account maintained with the Bank, it is nonetheless understood that in issuing this Escrow Receipt and functioning as escrowee and bailee of the Deposit hereunder, the Bank is acting in a wholly separate capacity, and not in any particular capacity set forth above. Nothing herein shall be deemed to require the Bank to make payment in contravention of any court order or judgment binding on the Bank in its capacity as escrowee and bailee hereunder, which on its face affects the Deposit: or the proceeds thereof.

(Bank) ______________________________

By: ______________________________

**Endorsement of Release**

The undersigned hereby release(s) all rights with respect to this Escrow Receipt.

The Options Clearing Corporation

By ______________________________ Date ______________

Clearing Member

By ______________________________ Date ______________

Broker

By ______________________________ Date ______________

**Payment Order**

The undersigned hereby certifies to the above-named Bank that an exercise notice for ______________ index call option contracts of the series indicated below filed with The Options Clearing Corporation on ________________, 20_____ has been assigned to the short position of the above-named Clearing Member which includes the above option contract(s), and demands payment of the amount indicated below, which constitutes the aggregate exercise settlement amount for the contracts comprising the assigned short position plus all applicable commissions and other charges.

Assigned Series ______________________ ______________________ $ ______________________

(Index, Exp. Mo., Ex. Price) Amount payable

☐ The Options Clearing Corporation ☐ Clearing Member ☐ Broker

By ______________________________ Date ______________

Source: Reprinted by permission of the Options Clearing Corporation, 440 S. La Salle St., Chicago IL 60605.

**Using a Margin Account.** When someone writes index calls in a margin account, the required funds equal *the market value of the options plus 15 percent of the index value times the index multiplier less any out-of-the-money amount*: (Market value of options) + (0.15 × index × Multiplier) – (Amount out of the money). This margin requirement is also subject to a minimum amount equal to the market value of the options plus 10 percent of the market value of the index times the index multiplier.

The required funds can be in various forms, and some forms "count more" than others. The precise rules occasionally change, but Table 16-5 provides a general guideline. Table 16-6 calculates the maximum number of index calls that can be written using each of these alternative forms of providing margin.

**TABLE 16-5** MARGIN EQUIVALENTS

| | |
|---|---|
| Cash: | 100% |
| U.S. Treasury securities: | 96% |
| Nonconvertible corporate debt trading at par: | 80% |
| Stock: | 50% |

**TABLE 16-6** MAXIMUM NUMBER OF INDEX CALLS THAT CAN BE WRITTEN AGAINST A $5 MILLION STOCK PORTFOLIO

| | | |
|---|---|---|
| | ***Using Cash*** | |
| 15% of index value: | 15% × $626.01 × 100 × N = | $9,390.15N |
| | Plus | |
| Market value of options: | N × $0.75 × 100 = | $75.00N |
| | Minus | |
| Out-of-the-money amount: | ($690 – $626.01) × 100 × N = | ($6,399.00N) |
| | Total | $3,066.15N |
| | $5 million = $3,066.15N | |
| | N = 1,630 contracts | |
| | Using Treasury bonds (96% of cash level) | |
| | 1,630 contracts × 96% = 1,564 contracts | |
| | Using corporate bonds (80% of cash level) | |
| | 1,630 contracts × 80% = 1,304 contracts | |
| | Using stock (50% of cash level) | |
| | 1,630 contracts × 50% = 815 contracts | |

This table uses FEB 690 OEX calls at $0.75; OEX = 626.01. N = maximum permissible number of contracts.

The margin account alternatives obviously provide portfolio managers the opportunity to generate much more income than if they were limited to a cash account. A portfolio manager who posts cash to a margin account and writes the maximum 1,630 contracts generates 1,630 contracts × $75.00/contract = $122,250 in income.[8] This is over twenty times as much as would be possible in a cash account.

**The Risk of Index Calls.** The risk in using index calls is that the index will rise above the chosen striking price. The lower the striking price, the more income the portfolio receives, but the greater is the likelihood that the option will end up in the money.

*Index options are cash settled.*

If the index calls do end up in-the-money, the index option *cash settlement* provision keeps this from becoming a major inconvenience. **Cash settlement** means that option exercise results in the transfer of dollars rather than securities. The call writer owes the call holder the intrinsic value of the call at option expiration. If a manager writes 79 FEB 690 OEX calls and the index is at 691.00 on expiration day, they must pay (691.00 – 690.00) × $100 × 79 contracts = $7,900 to the holder or holders of the call options.

[8] Even though the rules permit writing 1,630 option contracts, this probably involves more leverage, and consequently more risk, than many portfolio managers acting as fiduciaries would be willing to bear.

Presumably, the value of the stock portfolio rose as well, and this gain will at least partially offset the option liability. In any event, the portfolio always retains the proceeds from writing the options.

Under current rules, the composition of the portfolio is irrelevant in determining the equity requirement for covered index call writing. Conceivably, an investor with $1 million in a single security could use it as collateral for index options.

**What Is Best?** Is writing index options preferable to writing calls on the portfolio components? Many people think so, but there is no universal consensus. In any case, many managers of large funds use index options almost exclusively. Index options have several obvious advantages:

1. They require only a single option position instead of many.
2. They vastly reduce aggregate commission costs.
3. They carry much less company-specific risk.
4. There is less disruption of the portfolio when calls expire in-the-money and are exercised.

Options are a difficult concept for many people, and the concept of options on an "imaginary" asset such as an index can be even more confusing. Also, a little knowledge is usually a dangerous thing. It is not difficult to imagine someone who knows a little about options questioning the prudence of writing "naked" index options in a fiduciary account. The portfolio manager probably is going to have to explain why the index option writing strategy is covered, is appropriate, and is preferable to traditional equity call writing.

### *A Comparative Example*

This next example shows the gains or losses associated with four strategies discussed in this chapter: covered equity call writing, covered index call writing, writing fiduciary puts, and put overwriting. The example considers three market scenarios: an advance of 5 percent, no change, and a decline of 5 percent. It is important to recognize that these four strategies are not substitutes for one another. Writing fiduciary puts and put overwriting are bullish strategies, for instance, whereas writing covered calls is less so and may even be done in anticipation of declining prices. Assume we have a portfolio of five stocks (see Table 16-7).

**Covered Equity Call Writing.** In the strategy of covered equity call writing, individual equity call options are written against each of the five securities in the portfolio. Various striking prices and expirations could be chosen, depending on the manager's intent. Table 16-8 shows the manager's selection of options and the performance of the portfolio under each of the three scenarios.

The portfolio makes money in each of these scenarios. It makes the most money when the market advances, but in this situation all of the options are in the money

**TABLE 16-7** STOCK PORTFOLIO

| *Stock* | *Price* | *Shares* | *Value* | *Beta* |
|---|---|---|---|---|
| Atlantic Richfield (ARC) | 61.13 | 500 | $ 30,565 | 1.10 |
| Bell Atlantic (BEL) | 70 | 400 | 28,000 | 0.80 |
| International Paper (IP) | 76.63 | 400 | 30,652 | 1.10 |
| Upjohn (UPJ) | 93.88 | 300 | 28,164 | 1.00 |
| Federal Express (FDX) | 63.50 | 500 | 31,750 | 1.20 |
| Total | | | $149,131 | 1.05 |

**TABLE 16-8** COVERED EQUITY CALL WRITING

| | | |
|---|---|---|
| Write 5 ARC APR 60 calls at 3.25 | = | $1,625 income |
| Write 4 BEL APR 70 calls at 2.75 | = | $1,100 income |
| Write 4 IP APR 75 calls at 5.25 | = | $2,100 income |
| Write 3 UPJ APR 95 calls at 7 | = | $2,100 income |
| Write 5 FDX APR 65 calls at 4 | = | $2,000 income |
| Total | | $8,925 income |

*Market Up 5%*

| *Stock* | *Theoretical Price* | *Stock Gain* | *Option Income* | *Total* |
|---|---|---|---|---|
| ARC | 64.49[a] | –$565 | $1,625 | $1,060 |
| BEL | 72.80[a] | 0 | 1,100 | 1,100 |
| IP | 80.84[a] | –652 | 2,100 | 1,448 |
| UPJ | 98.57[a] | 336 | 2,100 | 2,436 |
| FDX | 67.31[a] | 750 | 2,000 | 2,750 |
| Total | | | | $8,794 |

*Market Unchanged*

| *Stock* | *Price* | *Stock Gain* | *Option Income* | *Total* |
|---|---|---|---|---|
| ARC | 61.13[a] | –$565 | $1,625 | $1,060 |
| BEL | 70.00 | 0 | 1,100 | 1,100 |
| IP | 76.63[a] | –652 | 2,100 | 1,448 |
| UPJ | 93.88 | 0 | 2,100 | 2,100 |
| FDX | 63.50 | 0 | 2,000 | 2,000 |
| Total | | | | $7,708 |

*Market Down 5%*

| *Stock* | *Theoretical Price* | *Stock Gain* | *Option Income* | *Total* |
|---|---|---|---|---|
| ARC | 57.80 | –$1,665 | $1,625 | –$40 |
| BEL | 67.20 | –1,120 | 1,100 | –20 |
| IP | 72.40 | –1,692 | 2,100 | 408 |
| UPJ | 89.20 | –1,404 | 2,100 | 696 |
| FDX | 59.70 | –1,900 | 2,000 | 100 |
| Total | | | | $1,144 |

[a]The stock would be called because the call option expires in the money.

at expiration, all would be exercised, and the portfolio would lose all five securities to call notices. Two securities, ARC and IP, also are called away when the market is unchanged. The options on these securities were in the money when they were written. A market decline of 5 percent results in all five options expiring worthless. The option income of $8,925 mitigates the effect of the decline in market value of the five stocks, resulting in an overall modest gain for the portfolio.

**Covered Index Call Writing.** In this strategy the manager writes covered index calls rather than individual equity call options. Table 16-9 shows the results of this strategy under the same three scenarios. Using index calls, the greatest gain occurs if the market advances 5 percent. Because of the cash settlement, the manager does not have to sell any of the stocks. However, the 5 percent rise in the market caused the APR 620 call to rise in value. The cash settlement of this option results in a cash outflow from the portfolio that reduces the net benefit of writing the options.

**TABLE 16-9** COVERED INDEX CALL WRITING

Write 1 APR 620 OEX call at $44.50 = $4,450 income
Initial value of OEX index = 626.01

*Market Up 5% (Index = 657.31)*

| *Stock* | *Theoretical Price* | *Gain* | *Options* | |
|---|---|---|---|---|
| ARC | 64.50 | $1,685 | Loss on cash settlement (620 – 657.31) × 100 | = –$3,731 |
| BEL | 72.80 | 1,120 | | |
| IP | 80.80 | 1,668 | | |
| UPJ | 98.60 | 1,416 | Income received | = 4,450 |
| FDX | 67.30 | 1,900 | | |
| | Stock gain | $7,789 | Net option gain | $ 719 |
| | | **Net gain = $8,508** | | |

*Market Unchanged (Index = 626.01)*

| *Stock* | *Price* | *Gain* | *Options* | |
|---|---|---|---|---|
| ARC | 61.13 | $0 | Loss on cash settlement (620 – 626.01) × 100 | = –$ 601 |
| BEL | 70 | 0 | | |
| IP | 76.63 | 0 | | |
| UPJ | 93.88 | 0 | Income received | = 4,450 |
| FDX | 63.50 | 0 | | |
| | Stock gain | $0 | Net option gain | $3,849 |
| | | **Net gain = $3,849** | | |

*Market Down 5% (Index = 594.71)*

| *Stock* | *Theoretical Price* | *Gain* | *Options* | |
|---|---|---|---|---|
| ARC | 57.80 | –$1,665 | Cash settlement: | |
| BEL | 67.20 | –1,120 | Options expire worthless | |
| IP | 72.40 | –1,692 | | |
| UPJ | 89.20 | –1,404 | Income received | = $4,450 |
| FDX | 59.70 | –1,900 | | |
| | Stock loss | –$7,781 | Net option gain | $4,450 |
| | | **Net loss = –$3,331** | | |

**Writing Fiduciary Puts.** In the strategy of writing fiduciary puts, there are no shares of stock. Instead, the portfolio's cash resides in an interest-bearing account. The manager writes index put options in anticipation of the underlying stocks rising in value.[9] Table 16-10 shows the hypothetical results of this strategy.

**Put Overwriting.** The final strategy, put overwriting, is the most aggressive. Put overwriting can result in significant losses if security prices decline, as we see in the example in Table 16-11.

[9]Individual equity put options could be used instead of index puts.

**TABLE 16-10** WRITING FIDUCIARY INDEX PUTS

Write 2 APR 650 OEX puts at $37 = $7,400 income
(Assume $149,126 in cash is invested at 5% for 3 months, yielding $1,864 in interest.)

***Market Up 5% (Index = 657.31)***

| | | |
|---|---|---|
| Options expire out-of-the-money: | | |
| Option premium | = | $7,400 |
| Interest received | = | 1,864 |
| Total | | $9,264 |

***Market Unchanged (Index = 626.01)***

| | | |
|---|---|---|
| Options expire in-the-money: | | |
| Options loss is ($626.01 – $650.00) × 200 | = | –$4,798 |
| Option premium received | = | 7,400 |
| Net gain on options | = | $2,602 |
| Interest received | = | 1,864 |
| Total | | $4,466 |

***Market Down 5% (Index = 594.71)***

| | | |
|---|---|---|
| Options expire in-the-money: | | |
| Options loss is ($594.71 – $650.00) × 200 | = | –$11,058 |
| Options premium received | = | 7,400 |
| | Total | –$3,658 |
| Interest received | | 1,864 |
| | Total | –$1,794 |

**Risk/Return Comparisons.** Figure 16-7 shows the relative profits and losses resulting from the four strategies. Put overwriting has the largest potential losses and gains; the other strategies are more conservative. (These examples ignore commission costs. They would affect covered equity call writing and put overwriting the most.)

The writing of covered equity calls is not always superior to the writing of covered index calls. Any example is sensitive to the market conditions used in its illustration. Here the use of equity calls dominates index calls in each scenario, but this need not be the case.

## Combined Hedging/Income Generation Strategies

Two important strategies have both *hedging* and *income generation* aspects. (**Hedging** refers to any activity that reduces risk.) These are not the best means of hedging nor the best means of generating income, but they may serve certain purposes quite well.

### *Writing Calls to Improve on the Market*

Occasionally, someone decides to sell shares of stock but has no immediate need of the cash proceeds from the sale. This person can sometimes increase the amount received from the sale of the stock by writing *deep-in-the-money calls* against the stock position. The term **deep in the money** is subjective; it describes any option that has "substantial" intrinsic value.

Suppose that on December 30 an institution holds 1,000 shares of Nile.com and votes to liquidate the entire position. Table 15-1 in Chapter 15 shows that the

**TABLE 16-11** PUT OVERWRITING

| | |
|---|---|
| Write 5 ARC APR 65 puts at 5.25 | = $2,625 income |
| Write 4 BEL APR 70 puts at 2.50 | = $1,000 income |
| Write 4 IP APR 75 puts at 2.75 | = $1,100 income |
| Write 3 UPJ APR 95 puts at 5.50 | = $1,650 income |
| Write 5 FDX APR 65 puts at 4.13 | = $2,065 income |
| Total | $8,440 income |

*Market Up 5%*

| *Stock* | *Theoretical Price* | *Stock Gain* | *Option Income* | *Total* |
|---|---|---|---|---|
| ARC | 64.50 | $1,685 | $2,375[a] | $ 4,060 |
| BEL | 72.80 | 1,120 | 1,000 | 2,120 |
| IP | 80.80 | 1,670 | 1,100 | 2,770 |
| UPJ | 98.60 | 1,418 | 1,650 | 3,068 |
| FDX | 67.30 | 1,900 | 2,065 | 3,965 |
| Total | | | | $15,983 |

*Market Unchanged*

| *Stock* | *Price* | *Stock Gain* | *Option Income* | *Option Loss* | *Total* |
|---|---|---|---|---|---|
| ARC | 61.13 | $0 | $2,625 | –$1,938 | $ 687 |
| BEL | 70 | 0 | 1,000 | 0 | 1,000 |
| IP | 76.63 | 0 | 1,100 | 0 | 1,100 |
| UPJ | 93.88 | 0 | 1,650 | –338 | 1,312 |
| FDX | 63.50 | 0 | 2,065 | –750 | 1,315 |
| Total | | | | | $5,414 |

*Market Down 5%*

| *Stock* | *Price* | *Stock Gain* | *Option Income* | *Option Loss* | *Total* |
|---|---|---|---|---|---|
| ARC | 57.80 | –$1,665 | $2,625 | –$3,600 | –$2,640 |
| BEL | 67.20 | –1,120 | 1,000 | –1,120 | –1,240 |
| IP | 72.40 | –1,690 | 1,100 | –1,040 | –1,630 |
| UPJ | 89.20 | –1,404 | 1,650 | –1,740 | –1,494 |
| FDX | 59.70 | –1,900 | 2,063 | –2,650 | –2,487 |
| Total | | | | | –$9,491 |

[a]ARC did not rise above the put striking price of 65. Therefore, the puts would be exercised, resulting in a loss of $0.50 × 5 × 100 = $250, which partially offsets the $2,625 income received.

premium for a JAN 100 call on Nile.com is $18, whereas the current market price of Nile.com stock is $116. The institution could simply sell the shares outright and receive $116 per share × 1,000 shares, or $116,000. The institution would receive this money, minus selling commissions, on the third business day after the sale.

*You can often sell stock at a "better" price if you write deep-in-the-money calls.*

**Improving on the market** is a market colloquialism for writing options in the hope that they are exercised, thereby enabling the writer to buy or sell stock at a "better" price than the current one. The portfolio manager might consider writing 10 JAN 100 calls on Nile.com. If these could be sold for the newspaper price of $18 each, the institution would receive $18,000 in premium income the next day. These calls are in the money by $16. As long as Nile.com is above $100 per share on the third Friday in January, the holder of the call options will exercise them. At that time the portfolio

FIGURE 16-7

Comparison of Four Strategies

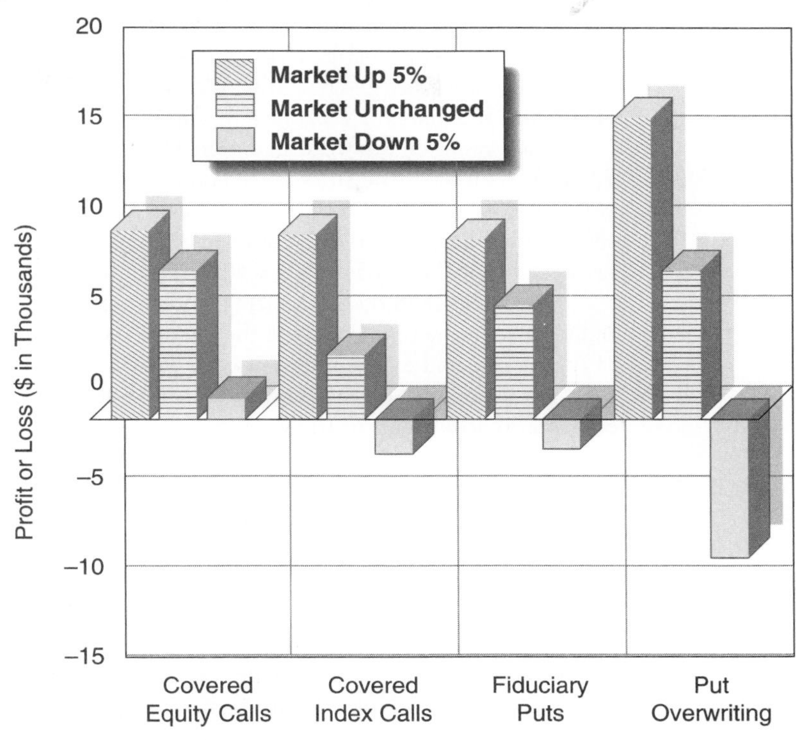


manager would have to sell 1,000 shares of Nile.com for $100 each and would receive $100,000. The total received by the institution in this case is $18,000 + $100,000, or $118,000. This is $2,000 more than would have been received had the stock simply been sold. This strategy involves two commissions, one to write the calls and one to sell the stock. There is also a modest time value of money difference. In any case, the firm ends up with more money than had options not been used.

This strategy may look attractive, but consider several things before embracing it. First, there is some risk that would not be present if the portfolio manager simply sold the stock. Selling stock results in cash in hand. Although unlikely, Nile.com certainly could fall by 14 percent and drop below the striking price of $100 per share, in which case the options would not be exercised. The option premium received means this strategy would break even at a stock price of $98. At this price, the stock is down by $18, but you would still have the $18 premium from writing the call. The two amounts exactly cancel each other. If the stock fell below $98, the manager would have fared better if he had sold the share outright.

Experienced option traders know that they need to be careful about relying on option prices listed in the financial pages. It may not be possible for them actually to trade at the stated premium of $18; the current market price may be less than this. But they can be assured that there is *some* time value associated with these deep-in-the-money options, and they can capture it with the strategy described here.

*You can often buy stock cheaper if you acquire it by writing in-the-money put options.*

### *Writing Puts to Acquire Stock*

It is also possible to improve on the market when buying stock. This involves writing in-the-money *put* options.

Perhaps you, a portfolio manager, have decided to buy 500 shares of Western Oil (WO). Table 15-1 indicates that the current price of WO is $66.75; January 70 puts sell for $5. These options are in the money because the striking price of $70 is above the current stock price. Their intrinsic value is $70 – $66.75, or $3.25. Instead of buying the 500 shares of WO outright, suppose you write 5 WO JAN 70 puts instead.

As always when you write an option, you receive the option premium ($5 × 500 = $2,500). As long as the stock price stays below $70, the put will be exercised, and you must pay $70 each for the 500 shares. Subtracting the option means the net share cost is $65. This is less than the original stock price, and it results in a total savings of ($66.75 – $65) × 500 = $875.00.[10]

Again, this method of acquiring stock is not riskless. If the stock rises substantially between the time you write the put and its expiration, the put might move out of the money and expire unexercised. You still keep the option premium, but you have not accomplished the primary objective of buying the 500 shares of WO. An opportunity loss occurs in this case.

### *Writing Covered Calls for Downside Protection*

Another motivation for writing covered calls is to protect a security position against market downturns. Sometimes an investor who owns shares of stock suspects that the market will turn down in the next few weeks but really does not want to sell the shares at the moment. She might consider using covered calls to provide some cushion against losses.

Referring to the Table 15-1 prices for Nile.com, the investor might decide to hedge against the risk of a declining market by writing a FEB 120 call. The $6 premium received means that no actual cash loss occurs until Nile.com falls below the current price ($116) minus the premium received ($6), or $110. Of course, if the investor's suspicion about the market is wrong and Nile.com advances above $120, she has the risk of the stock's being called before she makes a closing transaction to remove the option position.

This strategy provides some downside protection but is not a particularly effective hedge. In general, an individual who needs protection against falling stock prices is better off buying put options or using some form of portfolio insurance (covered in Part Four of this book).

## Multiple Portfolio Managers

Sometimes more than one portfolio manager has day-to-day responsibilities for a fund. When this is the case, there needs to be a clear-cut understanding of individual responsibilities and of how accountability is determined.

### *Separate Responsibilities*

The term *overwriting* originated as the result of the phenomenon by which one manager assembled a portfolio of stock in accordance with a client's investment objective, and a different person used this portfolio for a program of writing covered options. The principal feature of this type of overwriting program is that the option manager is responsible for replacing any stock that is lost as a consequence of call options being exercised as well as for disposing of any stock acquired from the exercise of puts. The option writer seeks to generate sufficient income to offset the trading fees associated with the options and the sale or replacement of the underlying stock

[10]An extra commission would reduce the benefit slightly.

positions. Losses from closing out option positions unprofitably are also the responsibility of the option manager. Overwriting is not intended to be a break-even strategy, however, so the option manager must make enough money after paying these trading costs to make the overwriting program worthwhile.

The key operational issues are the separation of the two managers and the recognition that management of the stock portfolio is the most important concern. The option writing should not hinder the stock manager in any way. The stock portfolio simply provides the equity used to cover short option positions and satisfy margin requirements.

Index options eliminate the concern over stock being called or being "put in an account" (this is where the name "put" comes from). Index options provide for a straightforward cash settlement.

### Distinction Between Option Overwriting and Portfolio Splitting

Option overwriting is usually distinct from portfolio splitting. *Portfolio splitting* means managing a portfolio in accordance with more than one objective. For instance, half of a portfolio might be restricted funds that have growth of income as an objective. The other half might be managed for capital appreciation.

Option overwriting seeks to generate additional profits for the fund through the receipt of option premiums. Management of the underlying portfolio is in accordance with the objective decided upon by the client.

It would be possible, though, to manage a stock portfolio to achieve capital appreciation (probably with a low dividend yield) and simultaneously use stock options to generate income (making up for the lost dividend yield). This could be done by a single portfolio manager or separate individuals.

### Integrating Options and Equity Management

Index options are very important in managing market risk. Equity options enable the manager to hedge company-specific risk.

**Hedging Company-Specific Risk.** To hedge company-specific risk as a manager, you must first identify the fact that it exists to an unacceptable degree. Security analysis is complicated. If you manage thirty portfolios that contain a total of fifty different equity positions, you have much homework to do to keep up with all the news on these firms. Thus, a clear trend in fund management is away from security selection and toward pure portfolio management.

The essence of portfolio theory is that a well-diversified basket of stocks will contain very little nonmarket risk. Given this, it is not necessary to spend much time studying the portfolio components. Manage the portfolio according to its market risk (as measured by beta) and the level of market risk you are comfortable with, given current economic conditions.

Still, in some situations, you want to hedge a company-specific risk while leaving the rest of the portfolio intact. You can do this using individual equity options rather than options on a market index. A company, for instance, might be in the final stages of some litigation proceedings. An adverse outcome would seriously affect the stock price of the company in question. Equity options can reduce this risk.

Sometimes you, as a manager, can employ options based on an industry index, such as the oil and gas index or the computer technology index prepared by the American Stock Exchange. These options have not always met with the popularity the exchanges hoped, but in theory, such options can be used to hedge industry risk.

Rather than spending time choosing which stocks to write options against or going to the trouble (and expense) of writing options against all of the stocks, it is much simpler to write index options. This avoids the need for company analysis, is easily accomplished, and accomplishes the same objective.[11]

**Unity of Command.** Unity of command is a principle of leadership. Index options increase the feasibility of using a single portfolio manager—one who has responsibility for both equity and option positions. The exercise of an index option does not require the transfer of securities, so this problem disappears. The time requirement to overwrite with index options is minimal, and competent portfolio managers can learn most of what they need to know about index options in a short time. Furthermore, the manager who has the flexibility that index options offer also can exercise more creativity.

## SUMMARY

The most common use of stock options by both individuals and institutions is writing covered calls, which involves writing call options against stock already owned.

Writing puts against a portfolio is called *put overwriting*. This strategy generates additional portfolio income but involves substantial added risk if stock prices decline. Writing deep-in-the-money calls can be an effective way to sell stock at a slightly higher than current price. This is called *improving on the market*.

A portfolio manager can write put options to acquire stock at a below-market cost. The effective stock price is the put striking price minus the option premium received. This strategy carries with it the risk of an opportunity loss if prices rise sharply before the option expires.

Option overwriting programs may employ a separate manager who uses the existing stock portfolio to cover any short option positions. The option manager may not interfere with the management of the underlying portfolio, but instead should seek to generate additional portfolio income. A growing trend, however, is toward a single portfolio manager with responsibility for both equity and option management. This trend is in large part due to the utility of index options, which eliminate the problems of company-specific risk and the time requirements of extensive security analysis.

## QUESTIONS

1. What should a portfolio manager consider before embarking on a put overwriting program during a bear market?
2. Refer to Table 15-1. You are considering improving on the market by writing covered calls with an April expiration against shares of Smith Electronics that you own. Is there any relative advantage of the APR 70 call over the APR 75 call?
3. Why is writing an in-the-money put riskier than writing an out-of-the-money put?

[11]A technical point should be mentioned here. Option pricing theory shows that everything else being equal, the higher the volatility of the underlying asset, the higher is the option premium. We know that diversification reduces volatility and that a portfolio will have a lower volatility than the average volatility of its components. This means that index options will tend to have lower premiums than equity options. If you write options, you want to receive a high premium. Depending on the level of transaction costs you must pay, writing equity calls rather than index calls could result in a higher net level of income to the fund.

4. Someone's primary portfolio objective is capital appreciation. Would it ever make sense for this person to write covered calls?
5. How do index options simplify operational problems with option overwriting?
6. A fund manager wants to hedge against a market downturn. Would it make sense to write index calls and use the proceeds to buy index puts?
7. How can writing calls potentially jeopardize a tax-exempt fund's ability to carry out its charitable purpose?
8. Write a 250-word paragraph explaining the word *margin*. Assume the paragraph is for the business column of your local newspaper.
9. Under what circumstances is a short put option covered?
10. Suppose someone recommends a change in the rules so that a short put is also covered if the put writer is simultaneously short of shares of the underlying stock. Does this make sense to you?
11. How is the risk of a fiduciary put different from the risk of a nonfiduciary short put?
12. Comment on the following statement: Writing covered index calls is always preferable to writing covered equity calls.
13. Write a 250-word article explaining the relative merits (and the potential risk) of improving on the market by writing deep-in-the-money covered calls.
14. Suppose someone decides to use puts to acquire stock. Would he or she normally use in-the-money or out-of-the-money put options?
15. The text indicates that option buyers seldom acquire options with the intent of exercising them. Why, then, would stock ever be called away?

## PROBLEMS

1. Draw a profit and loss diagram for writing a Western Oil APR 70 put option. Refer to Table 15-1 as necessary.
2. Suppose you simultaneously buy 400 shares of Exxon at 70 and write 2 APR 70 puts at $2.50. What is your gain or loss if, at option expiration, the common stock of Exxon sells for $77.38?
3. Draw a profit and loss diagram for the simultaneous purchase of 100 shares of International Paper at $76.68 and the writing of an APR 80 call at $2.75.
4. Draw a profit and loss diagram for the simultaneous purchase of 100 shares of Western Oil and the writing of an APR 65 put. Refer to Table 15-1 as necessary.
5. You buy 1,000 shares of XYZ at $27 on February 1. On April 2, you write 10 JUL 30 calls for $3 each. The options are exercised on April 20, and you sell your shares at the exercise price.
   a. What is your holding period return?
   b. What is the true rate of return (that is, the internal rate of return)?
6. You manage a $10 million endowment fund and would like to write index calls to generate some income. Suppose the OCT 320 OEX call sells for $1.13, and the current level of the index is 315.66. How much income can you generate
   a. In a cash account?
   b. In a margin account using cash equivalents?
   c. In a margin account using common stock?
7. Suppose you write 50 OCT 320 calls in Problem 6. What are the dollars and cents implications to you if, at option expiration, the level of the OEX index is 334.96?

8. Draw a profit and loss diagram for the purchase of 200 shares of Nile.com stock and the writing of 1 APR 120 covered call *and* writing of 1 APR 125 covered call. (*Hint*: Remember that any bend or bends in the diagram occur at the striking price.) Refer to Table 15-1 as necessary.
9. You manage a $5 million stock portfolio, which is held in a margin account. How much income can you generate by writing FEB 600 OEX puts from Table 16-4?
10. Refer to Table 16-4. You hold $2 million in stock with a portfolio beta of 1.15. You write 2 APR 650 OEX calls and write 2 APR 600 OEX puts. Estimate the total portfolio gain if, at option expiration, the S&P 100 index is 660.00.
11. Repeat Problem 9 using APR 610 puts.
12. Repeat Problem 9 using MAR 680 OEX calls.

## INTERNET EXERCISE

Go to the "*Most Active*" listing at *http://www.cboe.com*. There identify the equity call option contract with the greatest volume on the previous day. Draw a profit and loss diagram for the purchase of 100 shares of the underlying stock and the writing of a covered call. (You can get yesterday's stock price at *http://finance.yahoo.com*.)

## FURTHER READING

Black, Fischer. "Fact and Fantasy in the Use of Options." *Financial Analysts Journal*, July/August 1975, 36–72.

Black, Fischer, and Myron Scholes. "The Pricing of Options and Corporate Liabilities." *Journal of Political Economy*, May 1973, 637–659.

Bookstaber, Richard. "The Use of Options in Performance Structuring." *Journal of Portfolio Management*, Summer 1985, 36–50.

Chicago Board Options Exchange. *Options Reference Manual: A Guide for Institutional Investors*. Chicago: CBOE, January 1990.

Dawson, F. "Risks and Returns in Continuous Option Writing." *Journal of Portfolio Management*, Winter 1978, 58–63.

Degler, W. "How to Survive the First Few Months of Options Trading." *Futures*, August 1986, 52–53.

Gastineau, Gary. *The Options Manual*. 3d ed. New York: McGraw-Hill, 1988.

Gladstein, M., Robert Merton, and Myron Scholes. "The Returns and Risks of Alternative Put Option Portfolio Investment Strategies." *Journal of Business*, January 1982, 1–55.

Merton, R., M. Scholes, and M. Gladstein. "The Returns and Risks of Alternative Call Option Portfolio Investment Strategies." *Journal of Business*, April 1978, 183–242.

Pounds, H. "Covered Call Writing: Strategies and Results." *Journal of Portfolio Management*, Winter 1977, 31–42.

Yates, J., and R. Kopprasch. "Writing Covered Call Options: Profits and Risks." *Journal of Portfolio Management*, Fall 1980, 74–79.

# 17 Performance Evaluation

*And with that they clapped him into irons and hauled him off to the barracks. There he was taught "right turn," "left turn," and "quick march," "slope arms," and "order arms," how to aim and how to fire, and was given thirty strokes of the "cat." Next day his performance on parade was a little better, and he was given only twenty strokes. The following day he received a mere ten and was thought a prodigy by his comrades.*

***On Candide's forcible impressment into the Bulgarian army, from Voltaire's Candide***

## Key Terms

alpha
dollar-weighted rate of return
incremental risk-adjusted return (IRAR)
Jensen measure
residual option spread (ROS)
Sharpe measure
time-weighted rate of return
Treynor measure

## Introduction

Performance evaluation is a critical and often poorly handled aspect of the portfolio management process. The principal problem with performance evaluation is the human tendency to focus on the return a portfolio earned over a period of time with little regard to the risk taken in achieving that return. Proper performance evaluation should involve a recognition of both the return and the riskiness of the investment.

## Importance of Measuring Portfolio Risk

The importance of associating a security's return with a measure of the risk of that return is a principle of finance that is well known to students of the capital markets. Yet as recently as the 1950s, academic journals contained articles in which returns were discussed in the absence of a risk perspective. As stated earlier, in their classic *Security Analysis*, Graham and Dodd assert, "It is a commonplace of the market that an issue will rise more steadily from 10 to 40 than from 100 to 400."[1]

[1]Benjamin Graham and David Dodd, *Security Analysis*, 5th ed. (New York: McGraw-Hill, 1988).

What is lacking here is the *risk dimension*. Are $10 stocks, on average, riskier than $100 stocks? If this is the case, then we would expect them (on average) to rise faster. Graham and Dodd said nothing about *relative* risk in their statement, but we cannot talk meaningfully about return without also considering the associated level of risk.

A precept of finance theory is the concept of utility maximization: Given the choice, people avoid distasteful events and seek out satisfying phenomena. They try to maximize the expected utility associated with their decisions. Investors must choose between investment alternatives when the future performance of the competing investment choices is uncertain. It is a well-established fact that for most investors, the expected utility of an investment $[E(U)]$ is a positive function of the expected return of the investment, $E(\tilde{R})$, and a negative function of the variance of these returns, $\sigma^2$:

$$E(U) = f[E(\tilde{R}), -\sigma^2]$$

This result leads to the tradition in finance of using the variance or, equivalently, the standard deviation of return as a quantitative measure of risk.[2]

One of the ironies of investment management is the widely held attitude that risk matters only if it hurts the investor. Suppose a portfolio manager doubles the value of one of her funds in a year's time. Is this good performance? Many people would say yes, but we really cannot make any judgment without knowing how she achieved the return.

At a casino's roulette wheel, a player who correctly bets that the ball will stop on a red number wins $1 for every dollar bet. The gambler loses the entire bet if the ball stops on a black number. If someone places a bet on red and wins on three consecutive spins of the wheel, does that mean he is an excellent roulette player because he doubled his money three times in three tries? Although there were substantial gains, there was also a substantial risk in the process. The gambler's ship came in, so to speak, but it could have sunk just as easily.

*The essence of performance evaluation is associating a measure of risk with the realized return.*

The essence of performance evaluation is associating a measure of risk with the portfolio return. Did the fund manager essentially play roulette with the invested funds, or was the return achieved by steady growth in a well-diversified portfolio?

Baseball batting averages provide another good example of the need to look beyond the numbers. If a player has a batting average of .500, is this good? It seems so, because someone with a batting average of "only" .300 is a premium player. In contrast, what if the .500 hitter has been at bat only twice, struck out once, and beat out an infield single the other time? This gives him a .500 average, but it is not nearly as impressive as if he had been at bat two hundred times.

## A Lesson from History: The 1968 Bank Administration Institute Report

The need for consistent performance measurement of investment funds is not a new problem. In 1968 the Bank Administration Institute (a trade association) published a research report entitled *Measuring the Investment Performance of Pension Funds*. A blue-chip panel of academicians (including James Lorie, Kalman Cohen, Joel Dean, David Durand, Eugene Fama, Lawrence Fisher, and Eli Shapiro) participated in this study. Its purpose was to develop an improved way of measuring the investment

[2]Risk is actually a qualitative concept that is impossible to completely measure. Research has discovered, however, that a quantitative measure of dispersion (like variance or standard deviation) is a very good proxy.

performance of pension funds and pension fund managers. Among the conclusions of the study are these:

1. Performance of a fund should be measured by computing the actual rates of return on a fund's assets.
2. These rates of return should be based on the market value of the fund's assets.
3. Complete evaluation of the manager's performance must include examining a measure of the degree of risk taken in the fund.
4. Circumstances under which fund managers must operate vary so greatly that indiscriminate comparisons among funds might reflect differences in these circumstances rather than in the ability of the managers. Some special circumstances could include the defined purpose of the fund, specific restrictions, contractual arrangements with the trustor and trustee, and technical characteristics of the fund.

As you will see, little has occurred in the intervening years to make these recommendations obsolete. They are still the backbone of proper performance measurement.

## A Lesson from a Few Mutual Funds

Table 17-1 shows annual returns earned by two very different common stock mutual funds over the period 1975 to 1988. At first glance, the mean returns of both of these funds seem noble. Mutual Shares appears to have performed slightly better because its mean annual return is about 4 percentage points higher than that of 44 Wall Street. Closer investigation, however, reveals a very significant difference in the performance of these two funds. Figure 17-1 shows the end-of-the-year value of an initial $10,000 investment in each of the funds. At the end of 1988, the Mutual Shares investment was worth $174,476; the 44 Wall Street investment was worth only $28,891. In fact, the 44 Wall Street investment was worth $28,410 at the end of 1975, and over the next thirteen years appreciated in value by only $481. This is obviously thought provoking as well as a material consideration for a potential investor.

*Two key points with performance evaluation:*
*1. The arithmetic mean is not a useful statistic in evaluating growth.*
*2. Dollars are more important than percentages.*

You can learn two lessons from this comparison. One is that the arithmetic mean is not a useful statistic in evaluating growth rates. The other is that dollars matter more than percentages.

**TABLE 17-1** SELECTED MUTUAL FUND RETURNS

| *Year* | | *44 Wall Street* | *Mutual Shares* |
|---|---|---|---|
| 1975 | | +184.1% | +24.6% |
| 1976 | | +46.5 | +63.1 |
| 1977 | | +16.5 | +13.2 |
| 1978 | | +32.9 | +16.1 |
| 1979 | | +71.4 | +39.3 |
| 1980 | | +36.1 | +19.0 |
| 1981 | | −23.6 | +8.7 |
| 1982 | | +6.9 | +12.0 |
| 1983 | | +9.2 | +37.8 |
| 1984 | | −58.7 | +14.3 |
| 1985 | | −20.1 | +26.3 |
| 1986 | | −16.3 | +16.9 |
| 1987 | | −34.6 | +6.5 |
| 1988 | | +19.3 | +30.7 |
| | Mean | +19.3% | +23.5% |

Change in net asset value, January 1 through December 31.

**FIGURE 17-1**

Mutual Fund Performance, 1975 to 1988, with a $10,000 Initial Investment

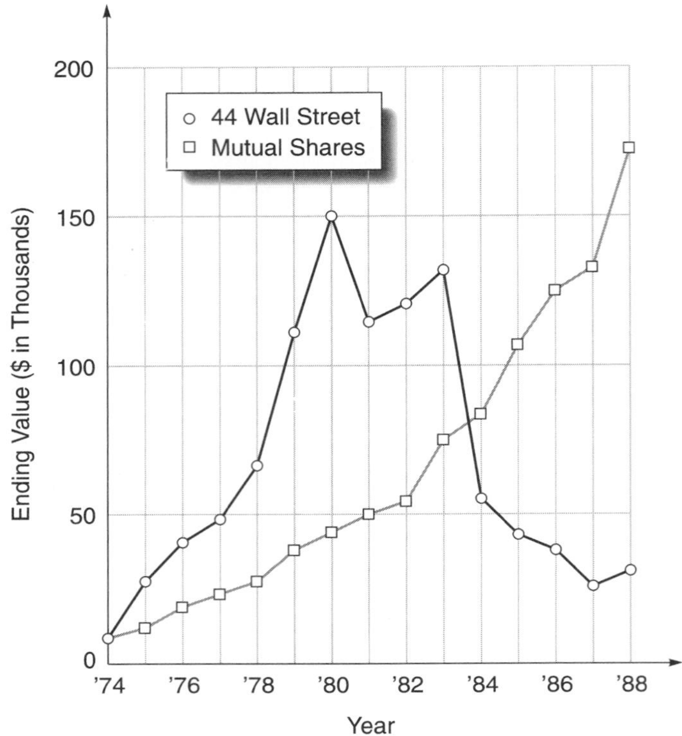


### *Why the Arithmetic Mean Is Often Misleading: A Review*

Consider a simple example. An initial $100 investment falls by 50 percent in one period and rises by 50 percent in the following period. What is the average return? The first inclination is to just add the two returns and divide by 2, for an average return of 0. This, however, is not the right answer. In the first period, the $100 investment fell to $50, and in the second period, it rose to be worth $75. The math shows that if something falls in value by 50 percent, it must rise in value by 100 percent to get back to its starting point.

The proper measure of average investment return over time, as we have seen, is the geometric mean (GM) return . The following is its formula:

$$GM = \left[ \prod_{i=1}^{n} R_i \right]^{1/n} - 1$$

where $R_i$ = the return relative in Period $i$.[3] The capital Greek letter pi stands for "product summation." This means that instead of adding values together, you multiply them.

An investment that falls in value by 50 percent has a return relative for that period of $-0.50 + 1.0 = 0.50$. In the second period, when it rises by 50 percent, the return relative is $0.50 + 1.0 = 1.50$. The geometric mean return is the square root of the product of these two return relatives, or $(0.5 \times 1.5)^{1/2} - 1 = -13.40\%$. Rather than breaking even, this investment lost 13.4 percent per period.

[3]Recall that a return relative is the return plus 1. This measure is useful because it eliminates negative signs.

You can check this result. A $100 investment that loses 13.4 percent declines to $86.60. If it loses another 13.4 percent, its value declines to $75.00. This is the value determined earlier.

*An interactive annualized geometric return calculator is featured at* http://www.morningstar.com

The geometric mean returns for 44 Wall Street and Mutual Shares are 7.9 and 22.7 percent, respectively. This illustrates the very significant difference in the returns of these two funds over this fourteen-year period.

You can also get very different performance numbers, depending on when you begin and end your examination period. Any economic researcher knows how sensitive results can be to the data period used. Table 17-1 shows the mean return for 44 Wall Street of 19.3 percent over the period 1975 to 1988. If, however, you considered the period 1976 to 1987, the average return falls to 5.5 percent, a much less impressive number.

### Why Dollars Are More Important Than Percentages

Someone might manage two separate investment funds; one earned 12 percent last year, and the other earned 44 percent. What rate of return did the manager average? The wrong way to figure this out is to take the average of the two returns: (44% + 12%)/2 = 28%.

Suppose the fund earning 12 percent was a $40 million pension fund, whereas the 44 percent rate was earned on a $250,000 individual portfolio. Weighting the returns by the dollars involved, this manager's average performance is much closer to 12 percent than it is to the average of 28 percent. In fact, 99.38 percent of the $40.25 million managed by this person earned 12 percent. Only 0.62 percent earned the higher rate. The weighted average return, then, is (0.9938 × 12%) + (0.0062 × 44%) = 12.20%.

## Traditional Performance Measures

### Sharpe and Treynor Measures

William F. Sharpe and Jack Treynor designed the two leading portfolio performance measures, which are similar.[4] See Figure 17-2. The only mathematical difference in the two measures is in their denominators. The *Sharpe measure* uses the standard

**FIGURE 17-2**

Sharpe and Treynor Performance Measures

$$\text{Sharpe measure} = \frac{\bar{R} - R_f}{\sigma}$$

$$\text{Treynor measure} = \frac{\bar{R} - R_f}{\beta}$$

Where $\bar{R}$ = average return

$R_f$ = risk-free rate

$\sigma$ = standard deviation of returns

$\beta$ = beta

[4]See William F. Sharpe, "Mutual Fund Performance," *Journal of Business*, January 1966, 119–138; and Jack Treynor, "How to Rate Management of Investment Funds," *Harvard Business Review*, January–February 1965, 63–75.

TABLE 17-2 SAMPLE INVESTMENT RESULTS

| | Returns | | | | | Excess Returns | | | |
|---|---|---|---|---|---|---|---|---|---|
| | A | B | C | S&P | T-bill | A | B | C | S&P |
| January | 2.53 | 2.07 | 3.00 | 2.30 | 0.67 | 1.86 | 1.40 | 2.33 | 1.63 |
| February | –4.40 | –3.90 | –6.00 | –4.00 | 0.69 | –5.09 | –4.59 | –6.69 | –4.69 |
| March | –1.32 | –1.08 | –1.44 | –1.20 | 0.67 | –1.99 | –1.75 | –2.11 | –1.87 |
| April | 2.42 | 1.98 | 2.64 | 2.20 | 0.70 | 1.72 | 1.28 | 1.94 | 1.50 |
| May | 1.43 | 1.17 | 1.56 | 1.30 | 0.71 | 0.72 | 0.46 | 0.85 | 0.59 |
| June | 0.50 | 3.40 | 0.48 | 0.40 | 0.69 | –0.19 | 2.71 | –0.21 | –0.29 |
| July | –0.33 | –1.30 | 2.00 | –0.30 | 0.73 | –1.06 | –2.03 | 1.27 | –1.03 |
| August | 3.00 | 2.34 | 3.90 | 2.60 | 0.75 | 2.25 | 1.59 | 3.15 | 1.85 |
| September | 4.00 | 4.79 | 4.00 | 3.10 | 0.75 | 3.25 | 4.04 | 3.25 | 2.35 |
| October | –5.00 | –4.50 | –3.72 | –3.10 | 0.77 | –5.77 | –5.27 | –4.49 | –3.87 |
| November | 3.19 | 2.61 | 4.48 | 2.90 | 0.74 | 2.45 | 1.87 | 3.74 | 2.16 |
| December | 5.28 | 4.32 | 5.76 | 4.80 | 0.75 | 4.53 | 3.57 | 5.01 | 4.05 |
| Mean % | 0.94 | 0.99 | 1.39 | 0.92 | 0.72 | 0.22 | 0.27 | 0.67 | 0.20 |
| Standard deviation | 3.07 | 2.91 | 3.36 | 2.53 | 0.03 | 3.07 | 2.91 | 3.36 | 2.53 |
| Beta | | | | | 0.00 | 1.20 | 1.06 | 1.29 | 1.00 |
| Sharpe measure | | | | | | .073 | .094 | .200 | .079 |
| Treynor measure | | | | | | .183 | .255 | .519 | .200 |

Monthly figures are in percentages.

deviation of periodic security returns, whereas the *Treynor measure* uses the security (or portfolio) beta.[5]

*The Treynor performance measure is appropriate for single securities and for portfolios. The Sharpe measure should be used only for portfolios.*

Despite their mathematical similarity, these two measures have an important conceptual difference. The **Treynor measure** evaluates the return relative to beta, a measure of systematic risk. It ignores any unsystematic risk that might be present. Finance theory indicates that expected return is a function of necessary risk (systematic risk) only, and therefore the Treynor measure should be an appropriate risk measure for single securities as well as portfolios.

The **Sharpe measure,** in contrast, evaluates return relative to total risk. In a well-diversified portfolio, total risk is predominately from systematic risk factors. The Sharpe measure is therefore appropriate for use with a portfolio. A single security, however, contains substantial unsystematic risk. It would not be appropriate to apply the Sharpe measure in this case.

*Read a detailed exposition of the Sharpe measure by William Sharpe at* http://www.stanford.edu/~wfsharpe/art/sr/sr.htm

Table 17-2 presents hypothetical return statistics over a year's time. The table shows both mean returns and mean excess returns (e.g., with the prevailing Treasury bill rate subtracted). The table shows two different risk measures: (1) the standard deviation of return and (2) beta, the measure of systematic risk. Both the Sharpe and Treynor measures compute excess return per unit of risk. Return is "good" and risk is "bad," so the higher this ratio, the better. Table 17-2 shows that Fund C has the best risk-adjusted performance because its ratio is higher than that of either Fund A or Fund B with both the Sharpe and Treynor measures.

Figures 17-3 and 17-4 illustrate these results. The upward-sloping line in each figure shows the combinations of risk and return that finance theory predicts. Combinations that lie above this line are better than expected, and points below are substandard. Over the hypothetical year of Table 17-2, Funds B and C outperformed the

[5]The Capital Asset Pricing Model is a one-period model. For theoretical reasons, the return used in these performance measures is the statistical mean return rather than a geometric average.

FIGURE 17-3

Risk-Adjusted Performance (Sharpe)

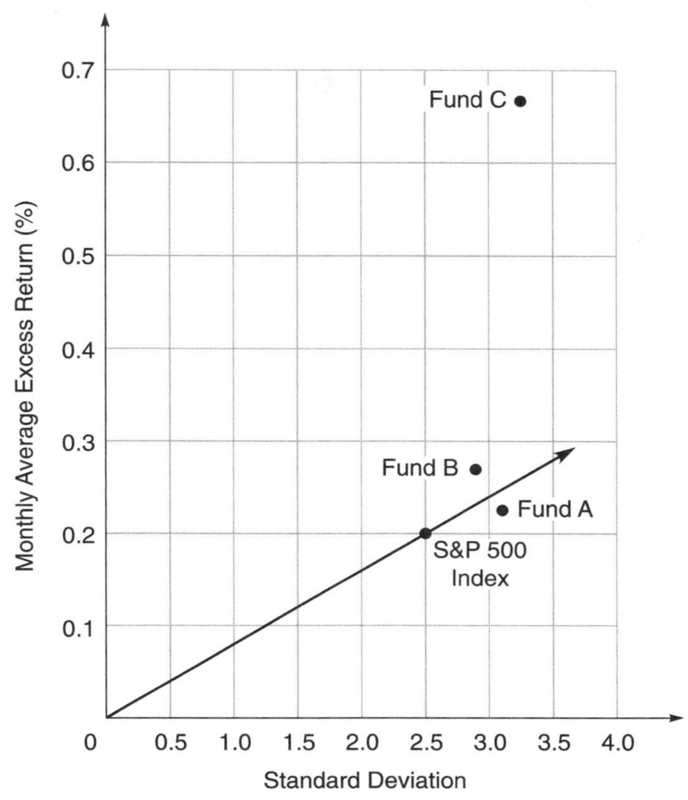


overall market as represented by the S&P 500 stock market index, whereas Fund A underperformed the market.

Now consider another example. Table 17-3 shows the first six years of data from Table 17-1. Over this period, 44 Wall Street shows an annual mean return of 64.6 percent, which is considerably higher than the 29.2 percent earned by Mutual Shares. It is easy to jump to the conclusion that 44 Wall Street showed superior performance over these six years. It is certainly true that the fund made handsome gains over this period. This perspective, however, considers only the return. It ignores the volatility of the fund. To compare the two funds properly, risk must be part of the overall picture.

For the sake of this example, assume that the T-bill rate was a constant 10 percent per year over this period.[6] With this assumption, we can calculate risk-adjusted performance using the Sharpe measure (see Figure 17-5). Mutual Shares shows a higher return per unit of risk than 44 Wall Street during this six-year period. This means that its risk-adjusted performance is superior to that of the other fund, even though 44 Wall Street showed average annual returns that were more than twice as high.

Despite all of this, many people take risk-adjusted performance measurement with a grain of salt. You would have a difficult time convincing everyone that Mutual Shares outperformed 44 Wall Street over the period 1975 to 1980. The attitude

[6]Interest rates were very volatile over this period. We were experiencing double-digit inflation, and it is consequently difficult to arrive at an average T-bill rate.

**FIGURE 17-4**

Risk-Adjusted Performance (Treynor)

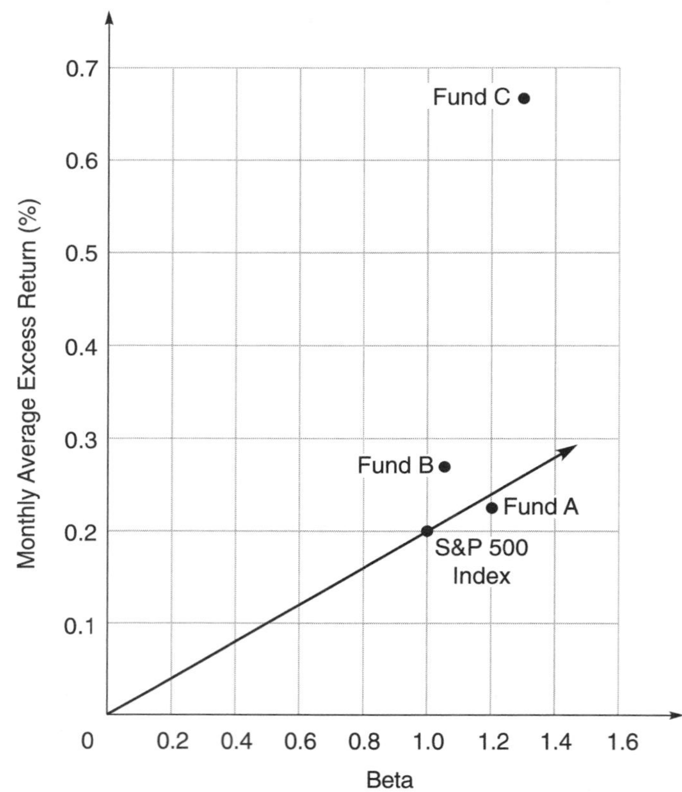


**FIGURE 17-5**

Risk-Adjusted Performance, 1975 to 1980, as Determined by the Sharpe Measure

$$\text{44 Wall Street: } \frac{0.646 - 0.100}{0.560} = 0.975$$

$$\text{Mutual Shares: } \frac{0.292 - 0.100}{0.173} = 1.110$$

**TABLE 17-3** COMPARATIVE MUTUAL FUND RETURNS

| *Year* | | *44 Wall Street* | *Mutual Shares* |
|---|---|---|---|
| 1975 | | +184.1% | +24.6 |
| 1976 | | +46.5 | +63.1 |
| 1977 | | +16.5 | +13.2 |
| 1978 | | +32.9 | +16.1 |
| 1979 | | +71.4 | +39.3 |
| 1980 | | +36.1 | +19.0 |
| | Mean | +64.6% | +29.2% |
| | Standard deviation | 56.0% | 17.3% |

Change in net asset value, January 1 through December 31.

that risk matters only if it hurts the investor prevails in the subconscious minds of most people. The words of a philosopher seem especially relevant here: "To prove a thing is not enough; you must convince someone to accept it."

### Jensen Measure

Another traditional performance measure, the **Jensen measure,** is important to know, although it is seldom used today as a formal measure of risk-adjusted performance. It stems directly from the implications of the Capital Asset Pricing Model:

$$R_{it} - R_{ft} = \alpha + [\beta_i(R_{mt} - R_{ft})]$$

*The safest way to double your money is to fold it over once and put it in your pocket.*
Frank McKinney Hubbard

Finance theory requires that the excess return on a security and the excess return on the market portfolio be directly related to the beta of the security, and that securities with a beta of zero should have an excess return of zero. This means that in the previous equation, the constant term $\alpha$ should be zero. If this term is positive, it indicates the presence of an upward trend in security prices that is unexplainable by finance theory. If it is negative, it indicates a downward trend.

Michael Jensen proposed using this **alpha** term as a measure of performance.[7] If a portfolio manager is a better-than-average stock picker and consistently earns returns higher than those predicted by beta, the alpha of the portfolio will be positive. Subsequent research has revealed several statistical and theoretical problems with the

PORTFOLIO MEMO

## Problems with the Sharpe Measure

Writing in *Risk & Reward,** Hillary Till points out several problems with unquestioning use of the Sharpe measure. The Long-Term Capital Management (LTCM) hedge fund failure in late 1997 nearly caused a collapse of the world financial system. Till reports that a year earlier, with thirty-one months of operation under its belt, LTCM boasted a spectacular 4.35 Sharpe measure even after deducting fees. She correctly observes, "With the benefit of hindsight, we can say that LTCM's realised Sharpe ratio after two and a half years of operation did not give a meaningful indication of how to evaluate its investments."

Also, Chapters 15 and 16 in this textbook show how the presence of options in a portfolio alters its return distribution. Writing covered calls, for instance, skews the return distribution to the left, making the standard deviation more difficult to interpret in a CAPM or Sharpe ratio sense. According to Till, "An investor can seem to 'outperform' under CAPM by accepting negatively skewed returns in exchange for improving the mean or variance of the investment. As a matter of fact, Hayne Leland of UC–Berkeley has shown that a strategy of selling fairly valued options can produce a positive alpha." Writing covered calls should not automatically make a manager an above-average performer.

We have numerous analytical tools and we have a brain; we should use both in evaluating the performance of a portfolio.

*Hillary Till, "Life at Sharpe's End," *Risk & Reward*, September 2001, 39–43.

[7]Michael Jensen, "The Performance of Mutual Funds in the Period 1945–1965," *Journal of Finance*, May 1968, 389–416.

Jensen measure, and it is generally out of favor with today's managers and academic researchers. You still frequently hear managers speak of the search for "positive alpha," however, meaning above-average investment results. Some of the reference sources available on the Internet report an investment's alpha over past periods of time.[8]

### *Performance Measurement in Practice*

**Academic Issues.** A controversy is growing in academia about the value of the traditional portfolio measures. No one questions the need to view asset returns in a risk-adjusted framework. The issue is that their use relies on the Capital Asset Pricing Model as the correct view of the world, yet evidence continues to accumulate that may ultimately lead to displacement of the CAPM paradigm. Efforts to develop the arbitrage pricing model, multi-factor CAPMs, and an inflation-adjusted CAPM have implications for proper performance evaluation. Until someone discovers a better technique, however, the Sharpe and Treynor measures are likely to continue as popular methods in academic research.

**Industry Issues.** Virtually everyone who ever studied investment theory in a university classroom has read about the merits of the traditional performance measures. The sobering fact is that the investment industry has never really adopted them. A 1987 survey of three thousand investment practitioners found that more than 80 percent agreed with the following statement: "Portfolio managers are hired and fired largely on the basis of realized investment returns with little regard to risk taken in achieving the returns."[9]

In actual practice, formal performance measurement usually involves (among other things) a comparison of the fund's performance with that of some benchmark. For instance, an all-equity fund might have the S&P 500 index as its benchmark, whereas a fund composed of both stocks and bonds might use as its benchmark some weighted average of the S&P 500 and the Shearson Lehman Bond Index. Such practice has intuitive appeal but can still lead to misleading results if client and manager do not both pay careful attention to comparative beta and duration statistics.

In considering investment performance, it can be instructive to see *why* an investment performed better or worse than expected. One method for doing so is "Fama's Return decomposition," named for Eugene Fama, a finance professor at the University of Chicago. He shows how to segregate realized investment performance into several components that give more information on what the manager actually did.[10]

Figure 17-6 shows the performance of a manager whose portfolio had a set target level of systematic risk, $\beta_{target}$. Such a level of beta has a corresponding level of expected return, $R_{target}$. The portfolio actually earned the level of return shown by point X and reflected systematic risk of $\beta_{actual}$, which is higher than the target.

Because the investor chose to take some risk, the investor *should* earn a return higher than the risk-free rate. This increment is labeled "Return from Investor's Risk." The manager, we see, took on more risk than the target level, so again we

---

[8]*http://finance.yahoo.com*, for instance, reports alpha for mutual funds under the risk selection.

[9]Robert A. Strong, "A Behavioral Investigation of Three Paradigms in Finance," *Northeast Journal of Business and Economics*, Spring/Summer 1988, 1–28.

[10]See Chapter 24 of Edwin J. Elton and Martin J. Gruber, *Modern Portfolio Theory and Investment Analysis*, 5th ed., for an excellent amplification of this aspect of performance evaluation (New York: Wiley, 1995).

**FIGURE 17-6**

Fama's Return Decomposition

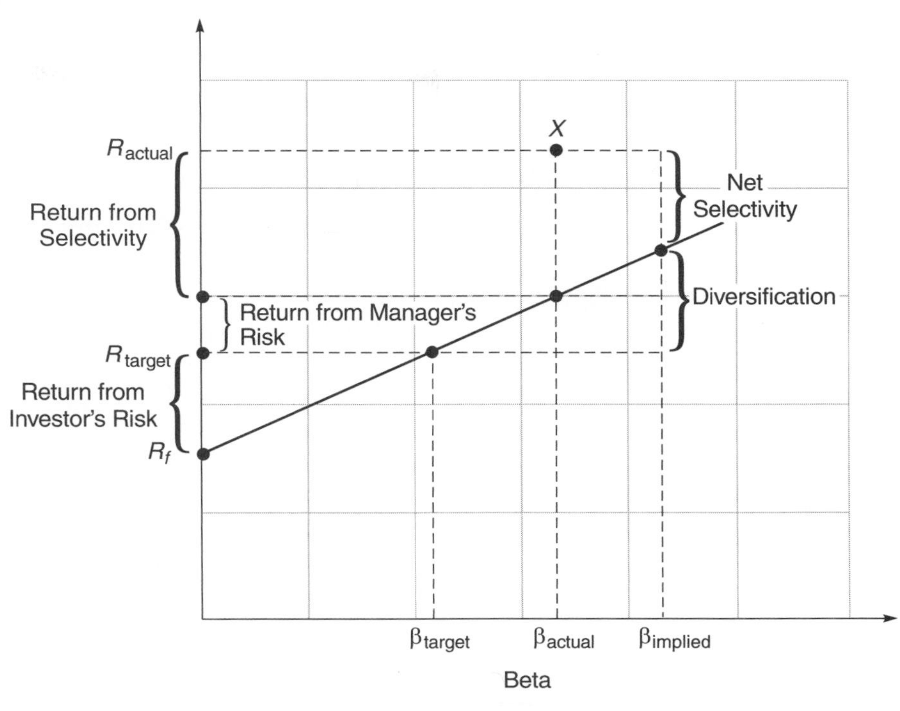


Source: Adapted from Eugene Fama, "Components of Investment Performance," *Journal of Finance*, June 1972, 551–567.

expect the actual return to be higher than the target. The level of systematic risk, marked $\beta_{implied}$, corresponds to a portfolio with the same level of total risk as the actual portfolio. You can find this value by remembering (from Chapter 5) that

$$\sigma^2_{portfolio} = \beta^2_{portfolio}\,\sigma^2_{market}$$

*For an excel file that will perform the Fama Return decomposition, visit* http://clem.mscd.edu/~mayest/FIN4600/Files/famadcmp.xls

We see that the actual return, then, has three components: the return the investor chose to take, the added return the manager chose to seek, and return from the manager's good selection of securities.

On the right-hand side of Figure 17-6 we see values labeled "diversification" and "net selectivity." Diversification is the difference between the return corresponding to the beta implied by the total risk of the portfolio and the return corresponding to its actual beta (systematic risk). Diversifiable risk decreases as portfolio size increases, so if the portfolio is well diversified the "diversification return" should be near zero, because the actual and implied betas will be approximately equal. Net selectivity measures the portion of the return from selectivity in excess of that provided by the "diversification" component.

Suppose we want to investigate the performance of a portfolio that earned 16 percent in the past year. The statement of investment policy indicated a beta range of 0.85–1.25 with a target beta of 1.0; the actual portfolio beta was 1.20. The S&P 500 index and portfolio had standard deviations of 12 percent and 20 percent, respectively, and the market index earned 10 percent for the year. Using the equation on the previous page, the beta of a naively constructed but well-diversified

FIGURE 17-7

Return Decomposition

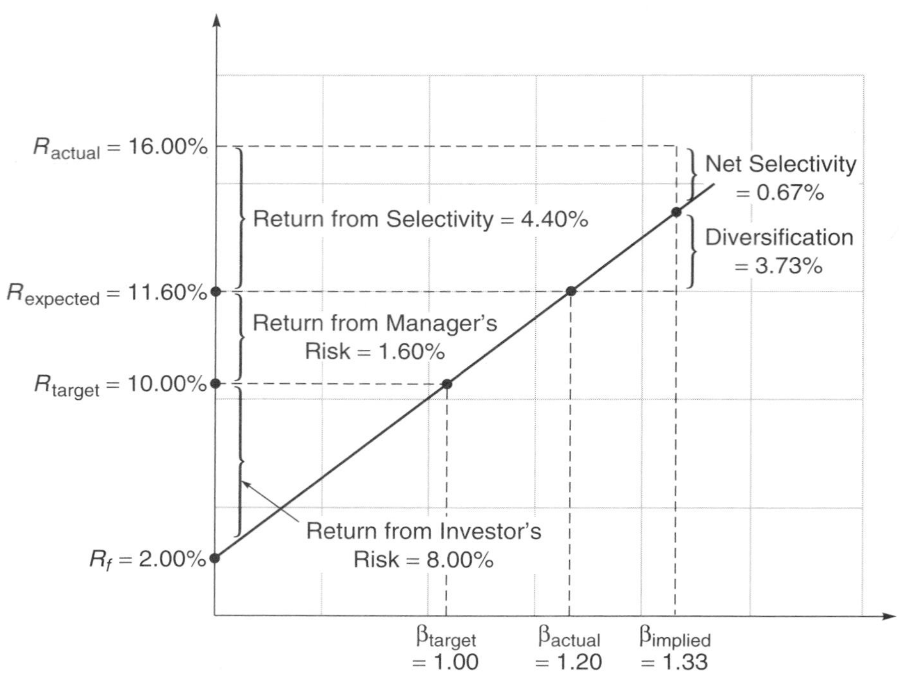


portfolio with a standard deviation of 0.20 is

$$\frac{\sigma_p}{\sigma_m} = \frac{0.20}{0.12} = 1.67$$

Figure 17-7 shows the return decomposition. The portfolio did very well, earning 16 percent compared to the 10 percent earned by the S&P 500. Two percent of the return comes from the risk-free rate. The market average earned 8 percent more than this. By increasing the portfolio beta, the manager should have earned an additional 1.60 percent from taking on more risk (manager's risk). The portfolio was less than completely diversified because the standard deviation implied a beta greater than the actual value. This concentration in fewer securities paid off, however, because the diversification component is 3.73 percent to the good. In addition, good security selection added another 0.67 percent (net selectivity). This makes the return from selectivity a total of 4.40 percent.

## DOLLAR-WEIGHTED AND TIME-WEIGHTED RATES OF RETURN

We have previously seen that the arithmetic mean can be misleading when talking about the average performance of an investment. Remember that "up 50 percent, down 50 percent" does not result in a breakeven situation. There is a related concern when a money manager is in charge of a portfolio for which there can be inflows and outflows beyond his control, such as deposits or withdrawals directed by the client.

We will see how to deal with this in a moment. First, though, it is important to distinguish between two general methods of determining return: dollar weighted and time weighted. The **dollar-weighted rate of return** is analogous to the concept of internal rate of return in corporate finance. It is the rate of return that makes the present value of a series of cash flows equal to the cost (or initial value) of the investment. In other words, the investment has a zero net present value when its cash flows are discounted at the internal rate of return. The dollar-weighted rate of return is the value $R$ in the equation below:

*The dollar-weighted rate of return is the same as the internal rate of return.*

$$\text{cost} = \frac{C_1}{(1+R)} + \frac{C_2}{(1+R)^2} + \frac{C_3}{(1+R)^3}$$

where $C_t$ represents the cash flow at time $t$. We saw a similar formula earlier in the book when we looked at the yield to maturity of a bond.

The **time-weighted rate of return** measures the compound growth rate of an investment. This method eliminates the effect of cash inflows and outflows by computing a return for each period and linking them. This is the same as the geometric mean return. If we have four quarterly returns, for instance, the formula for the annual time-weighted return would be

*The time-weighted rate of return is the same as the compound growth rate.*

$$\text{time-weighted return} = (1+R_1)(1+R_2)(1+R_3)(1+R_4) - 1$$

where $R_t$ = return for quarter $t$. The time-weighted rate of return and the dollar-weighted rate of return will be equal if there are no inflows or outflows from the portfolio.

## Performance Evaluation with Cash Deposits and Withdrawals

Consider the following scenario. You invest $1,000 in a mutual fund on January 1. Each month thereafter you add another $100 to your account. On December 31, the fund is worth $2,300. How do you measure how well it performed? Your fund is worth substantially more than at the beginning of the year, but much of that increase comes from your contributions rather than from increased share value.

Similarly, you might have deposited $100 each month but also might have withdrawn $500 from the fund in the summer. At the end of the year, the fund might be worth $1,500. Did the fund perform well? These are realistic concerns that complicate the problem of performance evaluation. See the Portfolio Memo on the Beardstown Ladies; their investment performance should not have taken credit for the dues they paid.

This is a common situation in most portfolios. The owner of the fund takes periodic distributions from the portfolio, and may occasionally add to it. The established way to calculate portfolio performance in this situation is via a time-weighted rate of return.

The Association for Investment Management and Research Performance Presentation Standards require calculating the time-weighted rate of return using at least quarterly portfolio valuations, with daily valuation being preferred. Two common methods of doing so are the daily valuation method and the modified BAI method.

PORTFOLIO MEMO

## The Beardstown Ladies

In 1996, a group of women from Illinois, with an average age of around 70, wrote and published a financial "how-to" book titled *The Beardstown Ladies' Common-Sense Investment Guide*. These women quickly became media favorites in that their reported annual investment performance of 23.4 percent over the prior decade exceeded that of virtually all professional investment managers over the same period. Representatives of the investment club appeared on television, were interviewed repeatedly, and had great fun enjoying their popularity in the media. The book sold more than 800,000 copies.

Unfortunately for the ladies, things took a turn for the worse when someone discovered that the performance figures "took credit" for the monthly dues the members paid. During the evaluation period, members collectively paid about $400 per month, or a total of $4,800 per year into the fund. Given this, you would expect the value of the fund to grow. For part of this time, in fact, the total value of the fund was less than $40,000. The dues alone added 10 percent to the increase in the portfolio value.

After the word was out, the accounting firm Price Waterhouse "audited" the fund performance and reported that its true performance (after taking into account the dues payments) was an annual rate of 9.1 percent, a figure below the market average. The mistake was an honest but embarrassing one.

It is good when an investment portfolio increases in value, but it is important not to confuse an increase in asset value with good investment performance.

### *Daily Valuation Method*

The daily valuation method calculates the exact time-weighted rate of return but is cumbersome because it requires determining a value for the portfolio each time any cash flow occurs. Cash flows might be dividends, interest, or additions to or withdrawals from the fund. It is cumbersome also because it requires a value of the portfolio any time a cash flow occurs whether generated internally or from an outside agency. Still, it is the preferred method. The daily valuation method solves for $R$ in Equation 17-1.

$$R_{\text{daily}} = \prod_{i=1}^{n} S_i - 1 \tag{17-1}$$

where $S = \dfrac{MVE_i}{MVB_i}$

and $MVE_i$ = market value of the portfolio at the end of period $i$ *before any cash flows in period i but including accrued income for the period.*

$MVB_i$ = market value of the portfolio at the beginning of period $i$ *including any cash flows at the end of the previous subperiod and including accrued income.*

We will look at an example after seeing the other approach, the modified BAI method.

## PORTFOLIO MEMO

### Performance Attribution

Investment committees want two principal pieces of information: 1) Did the manager do what we hired her to do? and 2) How well did she do it? In answering the second question it is also useful to learn the *reasons* for the performance, regardless of whether it was good or bad.

Figure 17-8 shows one way in which Putnam Institutional Management answers this question for the firm's clients in its international equity portfolio. The figure shows that for the first quarter of 2000 the Putnam International Trust earned a return 613 basis points above its benchmark (the Morgan Stanley Capital Investments European/Australian/Far East Index). The chart shows how Putnam attributes the performance across five areas: market selection, translation effect, stock selection, currency hedging, and the effect of cash. Over this time period the excellent performance was largely due to the manager's *stock selection;* good "stock picking" accounted for 529 basis points of the total excess returns. This means the manager tended to pick stocks with above-average performance relative to their local markets, e.g. Swiss stocks that outperformed Swiss market averages.

The manager added another 78 basis points by *market selection:* this reflects the effective over- or underweighting of various country markets based on the manager's outlook for that part of the world.

**FIGURE 17-8**

Performance Attribution

**Market selection**
- Positive impact from market selection in Europe: underweights to the U.K. and Belgium; overweights to Sweden, France, and Finland.

**Translation effect**
- Underweight to weakening Euro (down 4.5%) helped performance.

**Stock selection**
- Significant gains from stock selection in France, Switzerland, and Australia exceeded negative stock selection in Japan.
- Additionally, careful stock selection in the financial, health care and consumer staples sectors was positive.

**Currency hedging**
- No hedges in the current quarter

**Cash**
- Minimal impact from transactional cash balances

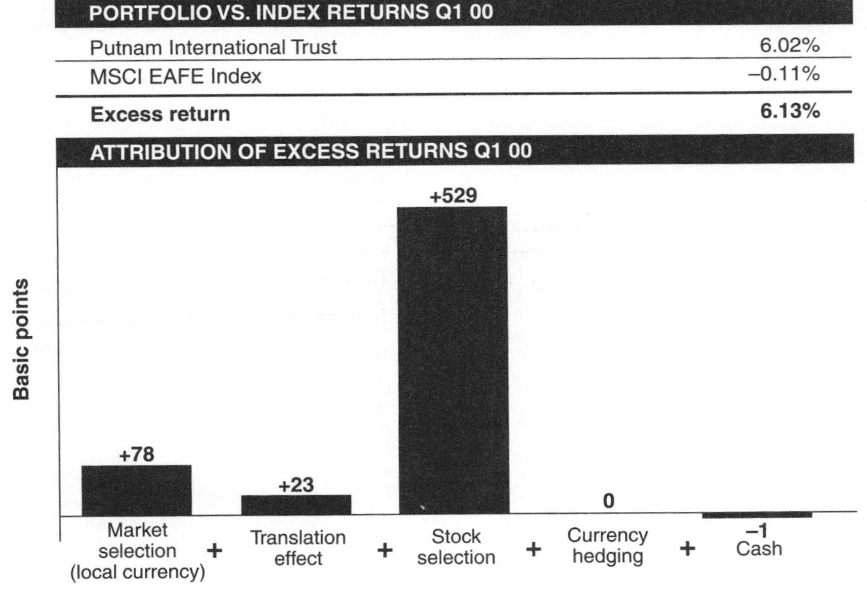

| PORTFOLIO VS. INDEX RETURNS Q1 00 | |
|---|---|
| Putnam International Trust | 6.02% |
| MSCI EAFE Index | –0.11% |
| **Excess return** | **6.13%** |



Variance due to intra-month effect and compounding.

This graphical technique makes it easy to explain the source of the fund's performance. In addition, the attribution detail gives the client confidence that the manager is technically competent and knows the portfolio well.

### Modified Bank Administration Institute (BAI) Method

The modified BAI method approximates the internal rate of return for the investment over the period in question. It is the value of $R$ that satisfies Equation 17-2.

$$MVE = \sum_{i=1}^{n} F_i (1 + R)^{w_i} \tag{17-2}$$

where F = the sum of the cash flows during the period (with opposite signs for inflows and outflows)

$MVE$ = market value at the end of the period, including accrued income

$F_0$ = market value at the start of the period

$w_i = \dfrac{CD - D_i}{CD}$

$CD$ = total number of days in the period

$D_i$ = number of days since the beginning of the period in which cash flow $F_i$ occurred.

The modified BAI method is an approximation of the true internal rate of return. Solving for the exact value can be quite complicated with a large portfolio, which might conceivably have a cash flow every day. The relevant equation would be an enormous polynomial. Precision is always desirable, but the Association for Investment Management and Research (AIMR)[11] standards permit reasonable approximations when required.

### An Example

These calculations may look complicated, but they are easier than they seem. An example will clarify the two methods. Suppose you are an investor who has an account with a mutual fund, and "dollar cost averages" by putting $100 per month into the fund. Table 17-4 shows the activity and results over a seven-month period.

Table 17-5 organizes the cash flows and values for solution via the daily valuation method. The solution is a return of 40.6 percent.

**TABLE 17-4** MUTUAL FUND ACCOUNT VALUE

| *Date* | *Description* | *$ Amount* | *Price* | *Shares* | *Total Shares* | *Value* |
|---|---|---|---|---|---|---|
| January 1 | balance fwd | | $7.00 | | 1,080.011 | $7,560.08 |
| January 3 | purchase | 100 | $7.00 | 14.286 | 1,094.297 | $7,660.08 |
| February 1 | purchase | 100 | $7.91 | 12.642 | 1,106.939 | $8,755.89 |
| March 1 | purchase | 100 | $7.84 | 12.755 | 1,119.694 | $8,778.40 |
| March 23 | liquidation | 5,000 | $8.13 | 615.006– | 504.688 | $4,103.11 |
| April 3 | purchase | 100 | $8.34 | 11.990 | 516.678 | $4,309.09 |
| May 1 | purchase | 100 | $9.00 | 11.111 | 527.789 | $4,750.10 |
| June 1 | purchase | 100 | $9.74 | 10.267 | 538.056 | $5,240.67 |
| July 3 | purchase | 100 | $9.24 | 10.823 | 548.879 | $5,071.64 |
| August 1 | purchase | 100 | $9.84 | 10.163 | 559.042 | $5,500.97 |

August 1 account value 559.042 × $9.84 = $5,500.97

[11]The Association for Investment Management and Research recently changed its name to the CFA Institute, but the performance rules are likely to be called the AIMR Standards for some time.

**TABLE 17-5** DAILY VALUATION WORKSHEET

| *Date* | *Sub Period* | *MVB* | *Cash Flow* | *Ending Value* | *MVE* | *MVE/MVB* |
|---|---|---|---|---|---|---|
| January 1 | | | | $7,550.08 | | |
| January 3 | 1 | $7,560.08 | $100 | $7,660.08 | $7,560.08 | 1.0 |
| February 1 | 2 | $7,660.08 | $100 | $8,755.89 | $8,655.89 | 1.13 |
| March 1 | 3 | $8,755.89 | $100 | $8,778.04 | $8,678.04 | 0.991 |
| March 23 | 4 | $8,778.04 | –$5,000 | $4,103.11 | $9,103.11 | 1.037 |
| April 3 | 5 | $4,103.11 | $100 | $4,309.09 | $4,209.09 | 1.026 |
| May 1 | 6 | $4,309.09 | $100 | $4,750.10 | $4,650.10 | 1.079 |
| June 1 | 7 | $4,750.10 | $100 | $5,240.67 | $5,140.67 | 1.082 |
| July 3 | 8 | $5,240.67 | $100 | $5,071.64 | $4,971.64 | 0.949 |
| August 1 | 9 | $5,071.64 | $100 | $5,500.97 | $5,400.97 | 1.065 |

Product of *MVE/MVB* values = 1.406; → R = 40.6%

**TABLE 17-6** MODIFIED BAI METHOD WORKSHEET (USING INTEREST RATE OF 42.1%)

| | *Day* | *Weight* $\frac{(214 - days)}{214}$ | *Cash Flow* | $(1.421)^{weight}$ × *cashflow* |
|---|---|---|---|---|
| January 1 | 0 | 1.0000 | $7,560.08 | $10,741.36 |
| January 3 | 2 | 0.9907 | $100 | $141.62 |
| February 1 | 31 | 0.8551 | $100 | $135.03 |
| March 1 | 60 | 0.7196 | $100 | $128.75 |
| March 23 | 83 | 0.6121 | –$5,000 | ($6,199.20) |
| April 3 | 94 | 0.5607 | $100 | $121.77 |
| May 1 | 123 | 0.4252 | $100 | $116.11 |
| June 1 | 153 | 0.2850 | $100 | $110.53 |
| July 3 | 185 | 0.1355 | $100 | $104.87 |
| August 1 | 214 | 0.0000 | $100 | $100 |
| | | | Total | $5,500.84 |

Solving via the modified BAI method requires a computer unless you are a real whiz with algebra. Even the "simplified" polynomial expression can be quite complicated, and it is much better to let a spreadsheet package such as Microsoft Excel® do the work.

To set the problem up it is necessary to determine the number of calendar days between the various cash flows. Table 17-6 shows these numbers. The table shows that using an interest rate of 42.1 percent, the total of the compounded $F_i$ cashflows is approximately equal to the ending value of the account.

## An Approximate Method

The American Association of Individual Investors proposes an approximate method for determining the rate of return when inflows and/or outflows are associated with the portfolio. Equation 17-3 shows this heuristic.

$$R = \frac{P_1 - 0.5(\text{net cash flow})}{P_0 + 0.5(\text{net cash flow})} - 1 \tag{17-3}$$

In this equation, net cash flow is the sum of the inflows and outflows; inflows have a positive sign and outflows a negative sign.

In Table 17-6, we showed deposits into the fund of \$800 and a withdrawal of \$5,000. The net cash flow is \$4,200 leaving the fund. Plugging the values into the equation, we get

$$R = \frac{5,500.97 - 0.5(-4,200)}{7,550.08 + 0.5(-4,200)} = 1.3947 \Rightarrow 39.5\%$$

This differs by about one percentage point from the 40.6 percent value determined earlier. Depending on the calculation's purpose, the approximate version may be sufficiently accurate.

## Performance Evaluation When Options Are Used

One of the assumptions underpinning much of financial theory is statistical normality of the security returns. We assume that an average, or mean, return exists for a particular security or portfolio and that we can measure the security's risk by the symmetrical dispersion of possible returns around that mean return.

The problem is that inclusion of options in a portfolio usually shifts the return distribution so that the returns are *not* normal. Writing covered calls, for instance, causes the distribution to be substantially skewed to the left. This happens because the striking price of the option creates an upper limit on returns for the option writer. Skewness is zero in a normal distribution.

How material this fact is depends on the purpose for investigating the portfolio. Beta and standard deviation lose their theoretical appeal if the return distribution is nonsymmetrical. In most ordinary performance evaluation applications, the departure from normality that a well-diversified portfolio experiences because of the use of options is modest. In technical financial research, however, the nonnormality is an important consideration in hypothesis testing.

Yair Aharoni makes a good statement about assumptions in economic theory:

> Economic theory does not pretend to mirror reality. It only claims, by a process of simplification, to isolate some significant strands in economic causal sequences, and to describe how these strands operate. Economic theory, therefore, is rarely either right or wrong: it is only more or less useful, depending upon whether the necessary simplification constitutes a very large or very small departure from reality.[12]

With these thoughts in mind, we consider two alternative methods of performance evaluation in portfolios when options are used.

### Incremental Risk-Adjusted Return from Options

The **incremental risk-adjusted return (IRAR)** is a single performance measure indicating the contribution of an options program to overall portfolio performance. This approach has intuitive appeal; a positive IRAR indicates above-average performance; a negative IRAR indicates that the portfolio would have fared better without the options program. Figure 17-9 shows how to calculate IRAR.

[12]Yair Aharoni, *The Foreign Investment Decision Process* (Cambridge, Mass.: Harvard University Press, 1986), ix.

FIGURE 17-9

Incremental Risk-Adjusted Return (IRAR) from Options

$$IRAR = (SH_o - SH_u)\sigma_o$$

where $SH_o$ = Sharpe measure of the optioned portfolio

$SH_u$ = Sharpe measure of the unoptioned portfolio

$\sigma_o$ = standard deviation of the optioned portfolio

FIGURE 17-10

Incremental Risk-Adjusted Return (IRAR) from Options

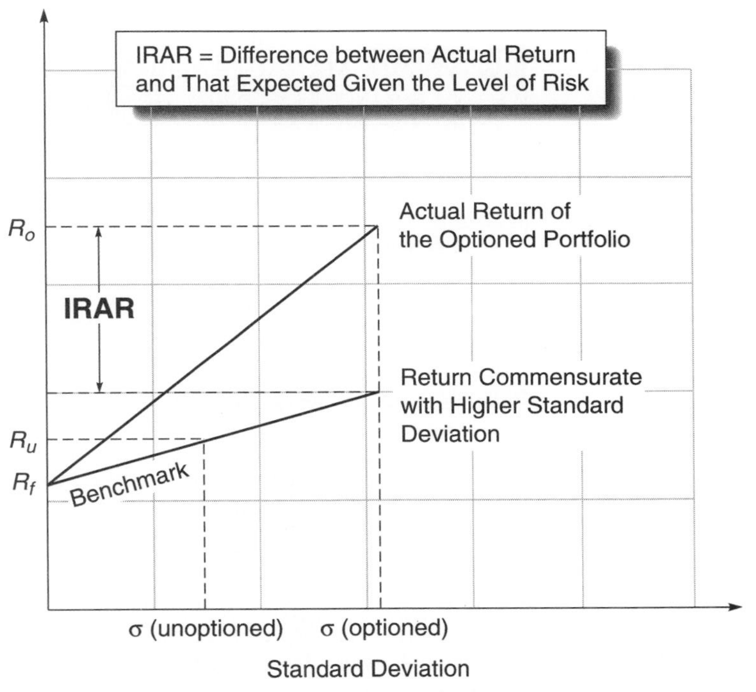


Figure 17-10 helps show how the IRAR fits in with finance theory, which postulates a direct relationship between risk and return. If a manager is able to earn a return higher than expected for a given level of risk, this is superior performance. The unoptioned portfolio can be used as a benchmark; we know its realized return, risk, and the risk-free rate. A line connecting these two points indicates the expected return per unit of risk. A portfolio with higher risk (higher standard deviation) should earn a higher return, and vice versa. Appropriate values all lie on the benchmark line in Figure 17-10. A point that lies above this benchmark line results from superior performance, and the higher than expected return is the IRAR.

**An IRAR Example.** Consider a portfolio manager who periodically writes S&P 100 index call options in the account to take advantage of anticipated market

PORTFOLIO MEMO

## The M2 Performance Measure

In 1985 Franco Modigliani won the Nobel Prize in Economics. He and his granddaughter Leah attracted attention in 1997 with their proposal for a new performance measurement technique they called M2.

Suppose you are a portfolio consultant working with an investment committee as it reviews the performance of its managers over the past year. You distribute the data in Table 17-7.

**TABLE 17-7** MANAGER PERFORMANCE LAST 12 MONTHS

| *Risk-Free Rate ($R_f$) = 5.20%* | | | |
|---|---|---|---|
| | *Return* | *Standard Deviation* | *Sharpe Measure* |
| Alpha Source Partners | 12.07% | 0.205 | 0.335 |
| Loon Securities | 10.87 | 0.169 | 0.335 |
| Jones Investments | 14.56 | 0.366 | 0.256 |
| S&P 500 | 12.15 | 0.230 | 0.302 |

Imagine how awkward the following conversation could be to you as the consultant:

*Board Member:* I see Jones knocked everybody's socks off this year; they earned almost 15 percent and beat the market by three points.

*You:* Actually, on a risk-adjusted basis, they underperformed both the S&P 500 and your other two managers.

*Board Member:* What do you mean? They beat the market and have better returns than either Alpha or Loon.

*You:* Not exactly; you need to consider risk-adjusted performance. See the Sharpe Measure column in the table. That measures return per unit of risk. The higher the ratio, the better.

*Board Member:* You're telling me that Alpha and Loon, neither of which even kept up with the market, did better than Jones?

*You:* Actually, sir, both Alpha and Loon did *better* than the market. Their Sharpe measures are better than the S&P.

*Board Member:* I see that number you are focusing on is the same for both Alpha and Loon. Are you telling me that Loon's 10.87 percent is just as good as Alpha's 12.07 percent?

*You:* Yes, sir. Alpha and Jones were your best managers, even though their returns are below the market average.

*Board Member to the Committee:* This just doesn't pass the straight face test. I'll take 15 percent over 12 percent anytime.

The M2 performance measure seeks to reduce this confusion by expressing relative performance in risk-adjusted basis points. The key is to ensure that the portfolio being evaluated and the benchmark have the same standard deviation.

PORTFOLIO MEMO

## The M2 Performance Measure (continued)

To do this we calculate a risk-adjusted portfolio return using Equation 17-4:

$$R_{\text{risk adjusted portfolio}} = \frac{\sigma_{\text{benchmark}}}{\sigma_{\text{portfolio}}} R_{\text{actual portfolio}} + \left(1 - \frac{\sigma_{\text{benchmark}}}{\sigma_{\text{portfolio}}}\right) R_f \qquad (17\text{-}4)$$

Performing the calculations, we find

**Alpha Source Partners**

$$R_{\text{Alpha}} = \frac{0.230}{0.205} 12.07\% + \left(1 - \frac{0.230}{0.205}\right) 5.20\% = 12.91\%$$

**Loon Securities**

$$R_{\text{Loon}} = \frac{0.230}{0.169} 10.87\% + \left(1 - \frac{0.230}{0.169}\right) 5.20\% = 12.91\%$$

**Jones Investments**

$$R_{\text{Jones}} = \frac{0.230}{0.366} 14.56\% + \left(1 - \frac{0.230}{0.366}\right) 5.20\% = 11.08\%$$

**S & P 500**

$$R_{\text{S\&P}} = \frac{0.230}{0.230} 12.15\% + \left(1 - \frac{0.230}{0.230}\right) 5.20\% = 12.15\%$$

These results show no difference in the returns of Alpha and Loon, both of which outperformed the S&P 500 benchmark by 76 basis points (12.91% – 12.15%). This is exactly what the Sharpe measure shows, too. Jones Investments underperformed the benchmark by 107 basis points and underperformed Alpha and Loon by 183 basis points.

Rather than presenting the data as in Table 17-7, as the portfolio consultant you might be more comfortable presenting the results in the format of Table 17-8:

**TABLE 17-8** RELATIVE PERFORMANCE

| *Portfolio* | *Risk-Adjusted Return* | |
|---|---|---|
| Alpha Source Partners | 12.91% | Above average performance |
| Loon Securities | 12.91 | Above average performance |
| S&P 500 Index | 12.15 | Market average |
| Jones Investments | 11.08 | Below average performance |

The inquisitive board member would begin his conversation from a very different perspective if his perspective came from this alternate presentation of the facts.

**TABLE 17-9** IRAR EXAMPLE

| Week | *Unoptioned Portfolio* | *Long Stock Plus Option Premiums* | – | *Short Options*[a] | = | *Optioned Portfolio* |
|---|---|---|---|---|---|---|
| 0 | $200,000 | $214,112 | | $14,112 | | $200,000 |
| 1 | 190,000 | 203,406 | | 8,868 | | 194,538 |
| 2 | 195,700 | 209,508 | | 10,746 | | 198,762 |
| 3 | 203,528 | 217,888 | | 14,064 | | 203,824 |
| 4 | 199,457 | 213,530 | | 11,220 | | 202,310 |
| 5 | 193,474 | 207,124 | | 7,758 | | 199,366 |
| 6 | 201,213 | 215,409 | | 10,614 | | 204,795 |
| 7 | 207,249 | 221,871 | | 13,164 | | 208,707 |

[a]Option values are theoretical Black-Scholes values based on an initial OEX value of 300, a striking price of 300, a risk-free interest rate of 8 percent, an initial life of 90 days, and a volatility of 35 percent. Six OEX calls are written.

**TABLE 17-10** IRAR WORKSHEET

| *Unoptioned Portfolio* | *Return Relative* | *Optioned Portfolio* | *Return Relative* |
|---|---|---|---|
| $200,000 | | $200,000 | |
| 190,000 | 0.9500 | 194,538 | 0.9727 |
| 195,700 | 1.0300 | 198,762 | 1.0217 |
| 203,528 | 1.0400 | 203,824 | 1.0255 |
| 199,457 | 0.9800 | 202,310 | 0.9926 |
| 193,474 | 0.9700 | 199,366 | 0.9854 |
| 201,213 | 1.0400 | 204,795 | 1.0272 |
| 207,249 | 1.0300 | 208,707 | 1.0191 |
| | Mean = 1.0057 | | Mean = 1.0063 |
| | Standard deviation = 0.0350 | | Standard deviation = 0.0206 |

Risk-free rate = 8%/year = 0.15%/week

$$SH_u = \frac{0.0057 - 0.0015}{0.0350} = 0.1200 \qquad SH_o = \frac{0.0063 - 0.0015}{0.0206} = 0.2330$$

IRAR = (0.2330 – 0.1200) × 0.0206 = 0.0023 per week, or about 12% per year

movements. Table 17-9 shows some hypothetical values of the portfolio, both with and without the options. This table assumes that the stock portfolio has a beta of 1.0, that the portfolio was initially worth $200,000, and that the premiums received from writing the options were invested into more shares of stock.

Was it productive to write these index calls? The first impression probably indicates that it was because the optioned portfolio (the far right column) appreciated more than the unoptioned portfolio. The IRAR calculations appear in Table 17-10. The results show that the options program was successful at adding about 12 percent per year to the overall performance of the fund. The fund manager knew what he was doing, during this time period at least.

**IRAR Caveats.** The IRAR is a potentially useful measure of performance, but someone might use it inappropriately. A portfolio manager, for instance, might use puts to protect against a large fall in stock prices. (We will look at this strategy in Chapter 20.) Such an insurance strategy sets a floor on the possible holding period

FIGURE 17-11

Residual Option Spread (ROS)

$$ROS = \prod_{t=1}^{n} G_{ot} - \prod_{t=1}^{n} G_{ut}$$

$$\text{where } G_t = V_t / V_{t-1}$$

$$V_t = \text{value of portfolio in Period } t$$

Subscripts *u* and *o* denote unoptioned and optioned portfolios, respectively.

FIGURE 17-12

Residual Option Spread Worksheet

***Unoptioned portfolio***

(0.95)(1.03)(1.04)(0.98)(0.97)(1.04)(1.03) = 1.03625

***Optioned portfolio***

(0.9727)(1.0217)(1.0255)(0.9926)(0.9854)(1.0272)(1.0191) = 1.04351

ROS = 1.04351 – 1.03625 = 0.00726

Given an initial investment of $200,000, the ROS translates into a dollar differential of $200,000 × 0.00726 = $1,452.

return and severely truncates the return distribution for the portfolio. In this case, the standard deviation of the optioned portfolio is probably a poor measure of risk. This is especially true if the portfolio manager is catering to a client who values the ability to set a floor return on investments. These same concerns apply to the residual option spread, the next topic.

### Residual Option Spread

The **residual option spread (ROS)**, shown in Figure 17-11, is an alternative performance measure used with portfolios containing options. Figure 17-12 calculates the residual option spread for the optioned and unoptioned portfolios example in Table 17-9. In the formula for the ROS, $G_t$ is merely the return relative for Period *t*, so we have this from Table 17-9.

A positive residual option spread indicates that at the end of the observation period, the use of options resulted in more terminal wealth than would have resulted from merely holding the stock.[13] A positive ROS does not mean, however, that the incremental return is appropriate, given the new level of risk of the optioned portfolio.

This is not necessarily a problem, though. Covered call writing always reduces the variance of return of a portfolio, so a positive ROS is always evidence of superior risk-adjusted performance in a covered call-writing program. In contrast, put overwriting always increases the portfolio return variance. No general statement can be made about a positive ROS here. (We can say that a negative ROS is prima facie evidence of poor performance in a program of put overwriting. If the ROS is positive, the IRAR needs to be calculated before conclusions can be reached in this case.)

[13]Table 17-9 shows an ending difference in terminal values of $1,458 rather than $1,452, as in Figure 17-12, due to rounding.

### Final Comments on Performance Evaluation with Options

People use options in portfolios for many reasons. The IRAR and ROS both focus on whether an optioned portfolio outperforms an unoptioned portfolio. Such measurements can easily overlook important subjective considerations involved in the decision to use options. Using options as insurance, for instance, sets a floor on the possible holding period return, severely truncating the returns distribution. This means that the standard deviation of the optioned portfolio is a poor measure of risk for this portfolio. Insurance has a value, to be sure, but whether we can really measure what we want to measure using only quantitative methods is unclear.

## SUMMARY

Performance evaluation is a critical part of the portfolio management process. The central issue is coupling a measure of risk with the return of a portfolio. The measurement of risk is often neglected.

Average returns over time should be measured using a geometric growth rate. The arithmetic mean gives misleading results and should not be used to compare competing investment funds.

The Sharpe and Treynor measures are the two leading performance indicators. Their calculations are similar, except that the Sharpe measure uses the standard deviation of returns as a risk measure whereas the Treynor measure uses beta.

When a portfolio has frequent cash deposits and withdrawals, it is best to calculate performance via a time-weighted rate of return. AIMR performance presentation standards require this.

If a portfolio includes options, the incremental risk-adjusted return (IRAR) helps to investigate the performance of the options program. The residual option spread (ROS) may also be useful but not with every type of option activity.

## QUESTIONS

1. Why does risk matter if it does not hurt the investor? Given that an investment made money, what difference does it make how the money was earned?
2. Give a general explanation of the concept of risk-adjusted performance measurement.
3. Why is expected utility, $E(U)$, a *negative* function of the variance of return?
4. Suppose an investment is known to have doubled in value. Name two things you would need to know before deciding whether this is good performance.
5. The 1968 Bank Administration Institute report contains a warning about the "varying circumstances" under which fund managers must operate. List some specific features of a fund management contract that could affect the measurement of the manager's performance.
6. Look at the return information in Table 17-1. Suppose an investor had held shares in either of these funds for the entire period from 1975 to 1988. Does it

make any difference in which order the annual rates of return were earned? For instance, would it make any difference if the +184.1 percent return were earned in 1988 rather than in 1975?

7. Would you use the arithmetic or the geometric mean to measure each of the following?
   a. Average total assets of a fund at the end of the calendar year.
   b. Your average salary increase over the last ten years.
   c. Your average annual increase in weight since you were one year old.
8. Briefly explain why it is necessary to use return relatives in the calculation of the geometric mean.
9. Suppose you are looking at the risk-adjusted performance of the stock of a particular company. Does it make any difference if you use the Sharpe measure as opposed to the Treynor measure?
10. Why does covered call writing always reduce the variance of return of a portfolio?

## PROBLEMS

1. Consider the following three investments. Assume that T-bills yielded a constant 3 percent. Calculate the risk-adjusted performance of each of the funds, using the Sharpe measure.

| *Year* | A | B | C |
|---|---|---|---|
| 2001 | +5% | +4% | +6% |
| 2002 | +0 | +1 | −1 |
| 2003 | −5 | −4 | −10 |
| 2004 | +8 | +10 | +18 |
| 2005 | +5 | +5 | +7 |

2. Using the data in Problem 1, calculate the risk-adjusted performance of an equally weighted portfolio of all three funds, and plot the results in risk/return space.
3. Using the data in Problem 1, calculate the geometric mean return for the three funds and for the three-security, equally weighted portfolio. Rank the investments *by descending order* of geometric mean. Does this technique give you the same ranking order as the Sharpe measure calculated in Problem 1?
4. Calculate the time-weighted rate of return for the monthly account activity shown here:

| *Cash Flow* | *Month* | *Ending Value* |
|---|---|---|
| | Balance forward | $23,000 |
| +200 | January | 23,556 |
| +200 | February | 24,556 |
| −500 | March | 23,965 |
| −500 | April | 23,100 |
| +200 | May | 22,900 |

5. Using the data in Table 17-9, show the IRAR graphically, as in Figure 17-10.

6. Using the data in Problem 1 and assuming that Investment B is an optioned version of Investment A, calculate the incremental risk-adjusted return from options.
7. A church's endowment fund was established with growth of income as its primary objective. At the beginning of the calendar year the fund's market value was $783,000. Over the year, the church withdrew $54,600 from the fund in equal monthly installments. The market value at the end of the year was $773,000. What was the fund's rate of return for the year?
8. Select an out-of-the-money call option on IBM that has about three months until expiration. Collect daily values of the stock price and the option premium over the next twenty trading days. From these data, calculate the following:
   a. The IRAR.
   b. The ROS.

   Explain in 250 words what your answers to Parts a and b mean.
9. Using the data in Table 17-6, assume the investor had deposited $300 per month instead of $100. Redo the calculations using
   a. The time-weighted rate of return.
   b. The approximate method.
10. Consider the following information.
    Riskfree rate = 2.5%
    Market return = 12%
    Market standard deviation = 0.14
    Portfolio return = 14%
    Portfolio target beta = 1.1
    Actual portfolio beta = 1.2
    Portfolio standard deviation = 0.18

Prepare a figure like Figure 17-7 showing Fama's return decomposition.

##  INTERNET EXERCISE

Retrieve the annual return data for Fidelity Magellan Fund (FMAGX) for the last five years from *www.morningstar.com*. Calculate the Sharpe Measure for Magellan. Use the current one year T-bond rate from *www.bloomberg.com/markets* as the risk-free rate.

##  FURTHER READING

Association for Investment Management and Research. *AIMR Performance Presentation Standards Handbook*, 2d ed., Charlottesville, Va.: AIMR, 1996.

Bailey, Jeffrey V. "Are Manager Universes Acceptable Performance Benchmarks?" *Journal of Portfolio Management*, Spring 1992, 170–174.

Bank Administration Institute. *Measuring the Investment Performance of Pension Funds*. Park Ridge, Ill.: BAI, December 1968.

Bowen, John J., and Meir Statman. "Performance Games." *Journal of Portfolio Management*, Winter 1997, 8–15.

Chang, E.C., and W.G. Lewellen. "Market Timing and Mutual Fund Performance." *Journal of Business*, 1984, 57–72.

Connor, Gregory, and Robert A. Korajczyk. "The Attributes, Behavior, and Performance of U.S. Mutual Funds." *Review of Quantitative Finance and Accounting* I, 1991, 5–26.

Cumby, Robert, and Jack D. Glen. "Evaluating the Performance of International Mutual Funds." *Journal of Finance*, June 1990, 497–521.

Evnine, Jeremy, and Andrew Rudd. "Option Portfolio Risk Analysis." *Journal of Portfolio Management*, Winter 1984, 23–27.

Fama, Eugene. "Components of Investment Performance." *Journal of Finance*, June 1972, 551–567.

Galai, Dan, and Robert Geske. "Option Performance Measurement." *Journal of Portfolio Management*, Spring 1984, 42–46.

Golec, J. "Do Mutual Fund Managers Who Use Incentive Compensation Outperform Those Who Don't?" *Financial Analysts Journal* 44, no. 6, 1988, 75–79.

Grinblatt, M., and S. Titman. "Portfolio Performance Evaluation: Old Issues and New Insights." *Review of Financial Studies*, 1989, 393–421.

Henriksson, Roy D. "Market Timing and Mutual Fund Performance: An Empirical Investigation." *Journal of Business*, January 1984, 73–96.

——— and Robert C. Merton. "On Market Timing and Investment Performance: II. Statistical Procedures for Evaluating Forecasting Skills." *Journal of Business*, October 1981, 513–534.

Ippolito, Richard A. "Efficiency with Costly Information: A Study of Mutual Fund Performance, 1965–1984." *Quarterly Journal of Economics*, February 1989, 1–23.

Jensen, Michael. "The Performance of Mutual Funds in the Period 1945–1965." *Journal of Finance*, May 1968, 389–416.

———. "Risk, the Pricing of Capital Assets, and the Evaluation of Investment Portfolios." *Journal of Business*, April 1969, 167–247.

Kon, Stanley J., and Frank C. Jen. "The Investment Performance of Mutual Funds: An Empirical Investigation of Timing, Selectivity, and Market Efficiency." *Journal of Business*, 52, no. 2, 1979, 263–289.

———. "The Market-Timing Performance of Mutual Fund Managers." *Journal of Business* 56, no. 3, 1983, 323–347.

Lakonishok, J. "Performance of Mutual Funds versus Their Expenses." *Journal of Business Research*, Summer 1981, 110–114.

Lee, Cheng-few, and Shafiqur Rahman. "Market Timing, Selectivity, and Mutual Fund Performance: An Empirical Investigation." *Journal of Business* 63, no. 2, 1990, 261–278.

———. "New Evidence on Timing and Security Selection Skill of Mutual Fund Managers." *Journal of Portfolio Management*, Winter 1991, 80–83.

Lehmann, Bruce N., and David M. Modest. "Mutual Fund Performance Evaluation: A Comparison of Benchmarks and Benchmark Comparisons." *Journal of Finance*, June 1987, 233–265.

Modigliani, Franco, and Leah Modigliani. "Risk-Adjusted Performance." *Journal of Portfolio Management*, Winter 1997, 45–54.

Muralidhar, Arun S. "Risk Adjusted Performance: The Correlation Correction." *Financial Analysts Journal*, September/October 2000.

Prakash, A.J., and R.M. Bear. "A Simplifying Performance Measure Recognizing Skewness." *The Financial Review* (February 1986), 135–144.

Sharpe, William F. "Mutual Fund Performance." *Journal of Business*, January 1966, 119–138.

———. "Morningstar's Risk-Adjusted Ratings." *Financial Analysts Journal*, July/August 1998, 21–33.

Stein, David M. "Measuring and Evaluating Portfolio Performance after Taxes." *Journal of Portfolio Management*, Winter 1998, 117–124.

Treynor, Jack. "How to Rate Management of Investment Funds." *Harvard Business Review*, January–February 1965, 63–75.

# 18 Fiduciary Duties and Responsibilities

*The scientific advances provided by modern portfolio theory, together with the evolving prudent expert standard, virtually require that fiduciaries base their investment actions on a total portfolio approach. Although the legal establishment has been regrettably slow to provide leadership in this direction, investment managers and other fiduciaries must recognize and apply these theoretical advances, particularly in drafting investment policy statements and considering the asset classes to be included in a potential asset mix. No particular asset or strategy should be per se excluded from consideration.*

**William G. Droms**

## Key Terms

- CERES Principles
- cumulative voting
- diversification rule
- documents rule
- due diligence
- duty of care
- duty of loyalty
- ERISA
- exclusive purpose rule
- fiduciary
- indicia of ownership rule
- legal list
- party in interest
- proxy statement
- prudent expert standard
- Sarbanes–Oxley Act
- social investing
- soft dollars
- sole interest of the beneficiary rule
- Uniform Management of Institutional Funds Act
- Uniform Prudent Investor Act

## Introduction

*A fiduciary is a person or an institution that manages money and/or business affairs for another person or institution.*

A **fiduciary** is a person or an institution (such as a bank trust department or a private money management firm) managing money and/or business affairs for another person or institution. A fiduciary might be a stockbroker, a certified public accountant, an attorney, a financial planner, a bank trust department, or a private money management firm. A person who represents herself to the public as an "expert" on money management matters may well assume a fiduciary responsibility by default.

Note that an accountant, stockbroker, or attorney is not automatically a fiduciary. It depends on the relationship between the professional and the client. If a person has *discretion* in the management of someone's funds, he assumes a fiduciary duty and must act accordingly. A stockbroker who merely executes a client's orders, however, is not acting in a fiduciary capacity. That same broker, though, may have complete control over another client's investment assets and clearly is acting as a fiduciary in that case.

Historically, brokers have avoided describing themselves as having a fiduciary duty to their clients. Executing orders for clients involves much less potential liability than giving advice. These days, however, brokers routinely call themselves financial consultants, so it is increasingly clear that they often do assume a fiduciary duty to their clients. One investment advisor says "Anyone providing advice to the public, and certainly those that are marketing themselves as providing advice are deemed fiduciaries."[1]

Fiduciary duty is not a responsibility to take lightly. The courts have little patience with professional malpractice or managers who put their own personal interests ahead of those of their clients. This chapter reviews the key principles of case and statutory law dealing with fiduciary duties and highlights facts an investment professional should know about the legal aspects of money management.

## History

Fiduciary law is a developing field.[2] Legal precedent is often slow to evolve, a fact that has frustrated many portfolio managers when they found that financial practice and the requirements of the law were inconsistent. In fact, in the mid-1850s, court decisions held trustees responsible for *any* loss resulting from a decline in value of an investment portfolio. In *King v. Talbot,*[3] decided in 1869, the New York Court of Appeals ruled that the entire asset class known as *common stock* was an imprudent investment. More than a century later, it is difficult for us to imagine a court offering such an opinion. Fortunately, things are better today, but it is useful to know how we arrived at the present set of rules.

### Prudent Man Rule

The prudent man rule[4] is probably the origin of modern fiduciary standards. This standard comes from the court case *Harvard College v. Amory*, familiar to anyone who has studied fiduciary law. The issue in this case was whether a trustee could invest in the stock of manufacturing and insurance corporations. In the early 1800s, English courts limited trustees to investing in government securities.[5] In its decision the court rejected the English rule and stated:

> All that can be required of a trustee to invest is, that he shall conduct himself faithfully and exercise a sound discretion. He is to observe how men of prudence, discretion and intelligence manage their own affairs, not in regard to speculation, but in regard to the permanent disposition of their funds, considering the probable income, as well as the probable safety of the capital to be invested.[6]

[1]Wallell, Melanie. "What's In a Name?" *Investment Advisor,* August 2003, 91–93.

[2]Some material in this section comes from Robert A. Strong, *The Prudence of Put Option Writing by Tax Exempt Organizations*, doctoral dissertation, Pennsylvania State University, 1983.

[3]40 NY 76 (1869).

[4]Some politically correct writers have begun to refer to this as the prudent *investor* rule.

[5]Scott, *The Law of Trusts*, § 227.4 (4th ed. 1988 and Supplement 1990).

[6]*Harvard College v. Amory*, 9 Pick. 446 (Mass. 1830).

This means that fiduciaries do not need to be clairvoyant. They do, however, need to use good judgment and make long-term decisions for other people in a manner consistent with how reasonable people manage their own money.

*There is no legal definition of speculation.*

One of the problems stemming from this case is the word *speculation*. The language from the case provides a subtle disapproval of speculation but nowhere defines it. Various activities have been labeled speculative in the trust literature: buying on margin, the purchase of shares in new organizations, using trust property in a business enterprise, and buying property for resale. To this day, there is no legal definition of speculation although policymakers often condemn it. This lack of clarification on what constitutes a speculative activity certainly made fiduciaries reluctant to try anything novel or that otherwise lacked precedent. Fiduciaries move into new territory slowly. As the African proverb says, "Only a fool tests the water with both feet."

In 1889 the New York legislature passed a bill limiting trust investments to government bonds and mortgage securities unless the trust documents specifically permitted other investments. This is probably the first instance of what we now call a **legal list**, which is a statement of eligible investments. Other states followed the New York lead, generally blessing fixed income investments and leaving common stock off the list. Legal lists were widely accepted until the 1940s, when states began passing legislation offering more flexibility to investment managers.

Over one hundred years after *Harvard College v. Amory*, another complication arose with language in the standard reference source *Restatement (Second) on Trusts*, which contains this passage:

> No man of intelligence would make a disposition of property where in view of the price the risk of loss is out of proportion to the opportunity for gain. Where, however, the risk is not out of proportion a man of intelligence may make a disposition which is speculative in character with a view to increasing his property instead of merely preserving it. Such a disposition is not a proper trust investment, because it is not a disposition which makes the preservation of the fund a primary consideration.[7]

A reasonable person could interpret these words to mean that speculation is the assumption of added risk in hope of higher returns rather than for principal preservation. This, of course, is inconsistent with why people buy securities at all: They hope to earn a return greater than they could have by keeping their money in cash. The language indicates that added risk in the quest for higher return is acceptable for a man of intelligence but not for a trust investment. This passage from the authoritative trust reference source complicated life for investment managers. The American Stock Exchange sums things up this way:

> The main problem may be that although speculative investments are condemned by all, it may be impossible to legally define the term "speculative." If prudence is to be based on needs of the beneficiary, an investment that is speculative for one account may be a sound investment in another, due to such factors as tax considerations, age of the beneficiary and duration of the trust. Even if such a definition were possible, it may only be appropriate in the context of a particular economic climate because investment philosophies change according to economic conditions.[8]

[7] *Restatement (Second) on Trusts*, Comment e. on §227 (1959).

[8] American Stock Exchange. *Options for Institutions: The Prudent Man Rule*, 1978.

### *The Spitzer Case*

Financial theory made some legal headway in the 1973 court case *Spitzer v. Bank of New York.*[9] M. James Spitzer, the guardian of a trust, alleged imprudence on the part of the bank in the administration of the trust. Specifically, he disputed four security issues that resulted in a total loss of $238,000 over four years. The aggregate portfolio, however, showed a gain of $1.7 million over the same period.

This case has two key outcomes. First, the court of appeals dismissed the bank's contention that the mere fact that the portfolio showed a reasonable rate of return was a defense against imprudence. The court stated that "to hold to the contrary would in effect be to assure fiduciary immunity in an advancing market." As an extreme example, the portfolio manager cannot roll the dice at a craps table with a customer's life savings and argue that no harm was done because the throw turned out to be a winner. Gambling with a client's account is fundamentally wrong; the fact that the manager made money does not make the action prudent.

Note that the Bank of New York was *not* gambling with the client's money. The bank was probably managing things quite well. The court merely rejected the bank's contention that the fact the account made money means everything was handled appropriately. This is the first legal point that makes the *Spitzer* case so noteworthy.

*The Spitzer case recognized that securities should be considered part of a portfolio.*

The second outcome of the case is the court's ruling that each portfolio component must be judged on the extent to which it contributes to overall portfolio characteristics and the resulting likelihood that the portfolio will serve the beneficiary well. The New York Court of Appeals stated:

> focus of inquiry . . . is on the individual security as such and factors relating to the entire portfolio are to be weighed only along with others in reviewing the prudence of the particular investment decision.

Here we have recognition that securities are normally part of a portfolio and that the characteristics of the portfolio have some bearing on whether or not a particular asset is a good portfolio component. The decision also provides support for the "total return concept."

The former director of the SEC's Special Study of Option Markets commented on the *Spitzer* case in *The Review of Securities Regulation*:

> Common law, however, never demanded investment infallibility nor held a fiduciary to prescience in investment decisions. Moreover, testimony of experts in financial affairs is admissible on the soundness of a particular investment.[10] Consequently, recognition by the investment management community of an investment method as valid has been given great weight.[11] Evidence of what other professional money managers are doing is also relevant in determining the prudence of a particular course of action.[12]

Also in the *Spitzer* case, the court held that hindsight is an inappropriate perspective from which to judge the prudence of an investment decision. Citing from

---

[9]*Spitzer v. Bank of New York* 43 A.D. 2d 105, 349 N.Y.S. 2d 747 (1st Dept. 1973), aff'd 35 N.Y. 2d 512, 364, N.Y.S. 2d 164 (1974).

[10]3 Scott on Trusts § (1967)..

[11]Dickenson's Appeal, 152 Mass. 184, 25 N.E. 99 (1890).

[12]Mindonick, *State's Changing Prudent Man Rule,* N.Y. Law J, Nov. 15, 1976.

Scott's *Law of Trusts*:

> In determining the propriety of the securities held by the trustee, it is important to consider the portfolio as a whole, and not merely each individual security. As we shall see, it is important to consider whether there has been a proper diversification of investments.[13]

The dual notions that prudence is determined before the fact and that characteristics of the portfolio partly determine whether or not an investment is prudent set the stage for a major revision of the prudent man rule, the prudent *expert* standard.

## Prudent Expert Standard

*ERISA established the prudent expert standard.*

The **prudent expert standard** comes from Section 404 of the Employee Retirement Income Security Act, commonly known as **ERISA.** This act came about because Congress was concerned with private pension plans and what happens when a large firm fails. For instance, Studebaker closed its plant in 1963. The company pension plan was substantially underfunded, and more than 4,000 company employees were without their promised retirement funds. Passed in 1974, ERISA establishes a national, uniform set of requirements for fiduciary conduct with pension funds. Although this act deals with pension fund management, courts and legislatures widely apply its provisions in other fiduciary settings. The important section states that a pension fiduciary shall discharge his duties

> with the care, skill, prudence and diligence under the circumstances then prevailing that a prudent man acting in a like capacity and familiar with such matters would use in the conduct of an enterprise of a like character and with like aims.[14]

This standard does not refer to an "ordinary person." Instead, it refers to someone who is *familiar with such matters* and is acting in a *like capacity* for a *similar institution* with a *similar investment policy*. In other words, what do the experts think about the investment vehicle or the investment activity? The lay opinion is insufficient; the manager must ask someone who is up to speed on current practice.

## Uniform Management of Institutional Funds Act

The National Conference of Commissioners of Uniform Laws enacted The **Uniform Management of Institutional Funds Act** in 1972 in recognition of the need for clarity and definitive guidelines in the management of charitable investment funds such as public foundations[15] and endowments. This is the act that officially blessed the total return concept described in the earlier chapter on investment policy. This eliminates undue concern with individual investment performance, concentrating instead on the performance of the aggregate portfolio.

## Uniform Prudent Investor Act

In 1994 the same National Conference approved the **Uniform Prudent Investor Act.**[16] The American Bar Association formally approved it in 1995. This act is

---

[13]2 A. Scott, *Law of Trusts* § 1809, 1840 (1959).

[14]ERISA §404 (a) (1) (B).

[15]Section 4944 of the Internal Revenue Code applies to *private* foundations.

[16]Copies of the act are available from the National Conference of Commissioners on Uniform State Laws, 676 North St. Clair Street, Suite 1700, Chicago, IL 60611. (312) 915-0195

**FIGURE 18-1**

Provisions of the Uniform Prudent Investor Act

- "The standard of prudence is applied to any investment as part of the total portfolio, rather than to individual investments. In the trust setting the term 'portfolio' embraces all the trust's assets." UPIA § 2(b)
- "The tradeoff in all investing between risk and return is identified as the fiduciary's central consideration." UPIA § 2(b)
- "All categoric restrictions on types of investments have been abrogated; the trustee can invest in anything that plays an appropriate role in achieving the risk/return objectives of the trust and that meets the other requirements of prudent investing." UPIA § 2(e)
- "The long familiar requirement that fiduciaries diversify their investments has been integrated into the definition of prudent investing." UPIA § 9
- "The much criticized former rule of trust law forbidding the trustee to delegate investment management functions has been reversed. Delegation is now permitted, subject to safeguards." UPIA § 9

*To see an extensive summary of the Uniform Prudent Investor Act, go to* http://www.nccusl.org/nccusl/uniformact_summaries/uniformacts-s-upia.asp

subject to state by state adoption; it is not a federal mandate. In a preliminary note, the Conference states:

> Over the quarter century from the late 1960s the investment practices of fiduciaries experienced significant change. The Uniform Prudent Investor Act (UPIA) undertakes to update trust investment law in recognition of the alterations that have occurred in investment practice. These changes have occurred under the influence of a large and broadly accepted body of empirical and theoretical knowledge about the behavior of capital markets, often described as "modern portfolio theory."

This act formally embraces what business schools teach in the classroom. The UPIA makes five fundamental alterations in the former criteria for prudent investing. Figure 18-1 lists them.

*The practical effect of the UPIA is that portfolio managers may handle fiduciary accounts in accordance with current financial theory and best investment practice.*

The UPIA is a grandchild of the prudent man rule; it is related but substantially different. The practical effect of the UPIA is that portfolio managers may handle fiduciary accounts in accordance with current financial theory and best investment practice.

## Fiduciary Duties

Although ERISA deals with the management of pension funds, it has influence throughout the investment community. Most managers know about the prudent expert rule, agree with it, and follow it. ERISA also outlines two primary fiduciary duties: *reasonable care* and *undivided loyalty*. Again, although ERISA focuses on pension plans, much of the legal literature on proper investment manager conduct deals with some aspect of these duties. The **duty of care** deals with prudent decisions while the **duty of loyalty** seeks to minimize conflicts of interest.

*The two primary fiduciary duties are reasonable care and undivided loyalty.*

### *Care*

These are the four elements of the duty of care.

**Prudent Expert.** As stated previously, ERISA fiduciaries are subject to the prudent expert standard. It is not enough to manage money the way ordinary people do; the ERISA manager must be familiar with and practice modern investment methods.

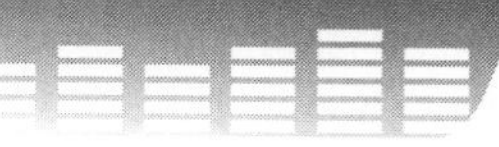


MEMO

## The Sarbanes–Oxley Act of 2002

Few congressional acts have attracted as much boardroom attention as the **Sarbanes–Oxley Act** of 2002, dubbed Sarbox by many who are affected by it. Spawned largely by the accounting debacles of Enron, Global Crossing, and others, the act seeks to reform accounting practice, board behavior, and the practice of security analysis. While the Act is complicated, some of the basic provisions are below:

- There must be a "financial expert" on the audit committee of a Board of Directors. Companies must disclose the name of this expert, as well as the expert's qualifications.*
- Both the company CEO and Chief Financial Officer must personally attest to the accuracy of the firm's financial statements. False certification may result in a $1 million fine and 10 years in jail.
- Tampering with corporate records is a crime punishable by up to 10 years in jail.
- Accounting firms providing the audit function may generally not provide other services (such as bookkeeping) to the firm while performing the audit.
- Sarbanes–Oxley established an oversight board called the Public Company Accounting Oversight Board (known as peekaboo).

It is no exaggeration to say that this act more than any other in recent memory has changed corporate governance in practice. It certainly has made directors much more aware of their fiduciary responsibilities.

*According to Nell Minnow, founder and editor of the Corporate Library, in the early 1990s O. J. Simpson was a member of the two-person audit committee of Infinity Broadcasting, and "the other guy didn't know any more about accounting than O. J. did."

**Diversification Rule.** Under ERISA, the **diversification rule** requires that pension plans be diversified, which in this sense means exactly what it does elsewhere in finance: Assets should be selected to reduce the risk of the portfolio.

The law requires diversification unless under the circumstances it is clearly prudent not to do so. An obvious question thus arises: When is it clearly prudent not to diversify? A corollary might be "Can prudent people disagree on the prudence of current diversification?" Fortunately, the law does not require that money managers be infallible. Documentation and intentional action provide a safe harbor in most situations. As long as a manager documents the well-conceived rationale for an investment decision, armchair quarterbacks generally cannot fault the manager. If your analysis as a manager leads to the conclusion that diversification is not a good idea at the moment, as long as you document your thought process and are not grasping at straws, your decision is usually legally defensible.

**Documents Rule.** The **documents rule** requires that the investment manager handle the fund in accordance with the documents that govern the plan unless it violates the duties of care or loyalty. There is an important caveat here, however: The governing document may not violate ERISA or state law fiduciary rules. The pension plan document at Microsoft, for instance, could not require the manager to select stocks from the computer industry only. This would violate the diversification rule.

**Indicia of Ownership Rule.** The **indicia of ownership rule** generally requires that documents relating to asset ownership must be under the jurisdiction of the U.S. court system. It would be difficult to hold a set of St. Barthelemy Caribbean villas in the pension fund as a real estate holding. St. Barth is a province of France, with the property deed subject to French law rather than the laws of the United States.

### *Loyalty*

These are the two elements to the duty of loyalty.

**Sole Interest of Beneficiary Rule.** The **sole interest of the beneficiary rule** means that the customer's best interest comes ahead of the best interest of the fiduciary. ERISA states:

> A fiduciary shall discharge his duties with respect to a plan solely in the interest of the participants and beneficiaries and for the exclusive purpose of: (i) providing benefits to participants and their beneficiaries; and (ii) defraying reasonable administrative expenses of administering the plan.[17]

Suppose a client holds 10,000 shares of ABC Electric and wonders whether XYZ Electric is a better investment. Suppose also that you as the portfolio manager (and fiduciary) consider each firm as a substitute for the other, neither having an investment advantage over the other. You might personally get some benefit (such as a commission) from making the switch. Under the sole interest rule, you have an obligation to tell the client that you do not believe the exchange is in her best interest even though such a statement means less money to you.

This standard does not mean that the fiduciary does the task for free. It is reasonable to incur trading fees and to compensate the portfolio manager. The UPIA states in section 7:

> In investing and managing trust assets, a trustee may only incur costs that are appropriate and reasonable in relation to the assets, the purposes of the trust, and the skills of the trustee.

The act goes on to state that the key thing is to not waste money. The fiduciary needs to make cost comparisons and ensure that the "customer" is getting appropriate value for his dollar. The law does *not* require the fiduciary to deal with the broker offering the lowest commission schedule. It *does* require a fiduciary paying more than the minimum fee available to obtain some additional value commensurate with the higher cost.

**Exclusive Purpose Rule.** The **exclusive purpose rule** requires a fiduciary to do her job for the single task of providing benefits to the beneficiary. The rule does provide, however, that the fund may be used to defray reasonable expenses that the fiduciary incurs in carrying out these duties.

---

[17]ERISA Section 404(a)(1)(A).

### Prohibited Transactions

*In addition to the standards of care and loyalty, ERISA defines four prohibited transactions.*

In addition to the standards of care and loyalty, ERISA defines four prohibited transactions.[18] Engaging in any of these constitutes a violation of law regardless of whether or not the act results in any actual loss to the client.

**Specific Transaction Restrictions.** These restrictions preclude a fiduciary from making a trade between the pension plan and a party in interest. A **party in interest** is a person or organization who has some relationship to the pension plan. For instance, a fund manager could not buy property owned by a corporate executive for inclusion in the portfolio, even if the property were a good investment in its own right. Similarly, it would be dangerous for a pension fund to buy bonds issued by a company for which a member of the corporate board of directors serves as an officer. The law wants security transactions to be arms-length trades, free of even the appearance of a conflict of interest.

**General Transaction Restrictions.** These restrictions prohibit the transfer of any plan assets to a party in interest. The pension fund, for instance, could not sell shares to a beneficiary of the fund. There is little practical distinction between the general and specific transaction restrictions of ERISA.

**Fiduciary Conduct Restrictions.** The essence of these restrictions is precluding the fiduciary from somehow using the plan assets for his own benefit. As an example, a fiduciary cannot direct trades to a particular brokerage firm because that firm "kicks back" part of the commission to the fiduciary. (The issue of "soft dollars" is tricky; we will turn to it in a moment.)

**Property Restrictions.** ERISA limits pension fund investments to marketable debt and equity securities and to "qualifying employer real property." This latter category is generally property that is leased to the plan sponsor, who then makes lease payments to the pension fund.

## Emerging Areas

In several important areas, best practices are still developing. These are *due diligence*, *social investing*, *proxy voting*, and *soft dollars*.

### Due Diligence

According to *Black's Law Dictionary*, **due diligence** is

> Such a measure of prudence, activity, or assiduity, as properly exercised by a reasonable and prudent man under the particular circumstances; not measured by any absolute standard, but depending on the relative facts of the case.

Fiduciaries frequently need to exercise due diligence in the conduct of their duties. Obviously, you need to carefully consider investment decisions and ensure that the information on which you base your decisions is accurate, but other situations also call for due diligence. For instance, some employees handle clients' money and

[18]The material in this section relies heavily on the article by William G. Droms, "Fiduciary Responsibilities of Investment Managers and Trustees," *Financial Analysts Journal*, July/August 1992, 58–64.

securities. It is prudent to conduct a credit check on them to reduce the potential for theft. Due diligence is also necessary in real estate purchases, certain client representations, and securities underwriting. This means that you need to make a reasonable effort to gather facts and ensure their accuracy before making a decision that could affect a beneficiary. Investing on a "hot tip" overheard in the elevator, for instance, is not a prudent investment action.

It is also not prudent to buy a stock because you read in *Forbes* that Merrill Lynch recommends it. The *Forbes* article might be wrong, or it might be untimely. Some articles are written months before they are published. You, as a fiduciary, have an obligation to confirm the report rather than accept it secondhand.

You can go a long way with due diligence by following the statement of investment policy. Does the intended investment contribute to the diversification of the portfolio? If you do not know what the company does, it would be hard for you to say. Is the price of the investment consistent with its potential return? Again, without some research, you cannot answer the question. Any appearance of a conflict of interest clouds the issue.

### *Social Investing*

The legal status of **social investing** requirements is somewhat cloudy. It is easy to understand how an investor might prefer to stay away from companies that pollute or manufacture products she considers disagreeable, but the question of how this restriction affects investment performance remains unanswered. The academic research is ambiguous. A fiduciary should always listen to the wishes of the beneficiaries and, when prudent to do so, seek to satisfy them. If the investment manager's favorite electric utility uses some nuclear power, it is usually not difficult to find a substitute utility

PORTFOLIO MEMO

## Shareholder Proposals

One of the rights a shareholder has is the ability to submit a proposal to be voted upon at the corporation annual meeting. A decade ago these were largely a corporate nuisance, with few ever receiving enough votes to pass. Things are changing. Both the number of proposals submitted and the percentage of votes these proposals receive are going up. According to the Corporate Library, there were 668 shareholder proposals on the ballot in 2003, up 87% from the 358 in 2000. In 2003 the number of shareholder proposals receiving more than 50% of the vote (159) nearly tripled from the 54 proposals receiving at least 50% in 2000.*

According to the Social Investment Forum, between 2002 and 2003 the number of corporate governance resolutions grew from 499 to 746. Executive compensation proposals on the ballot tripled in this same period.** Much of this increased shareholder activism is certainly related to the corporate governance and accounting scandals of the Enron ilk that have marred the financial profession. The corporation has always belonged to the shareholders, not to management. When management gets greedy or acts illegally it is natural for the owners to step in.

*Kim, Queena Sook, "Corporate Gadflys Are the Buzz," *Wall Street Journal*, June 10, 2004, C1.

**Aschkenasy, Janet, "Change of Heart?", *Plan Sponsor*, March 2004, 39–42.

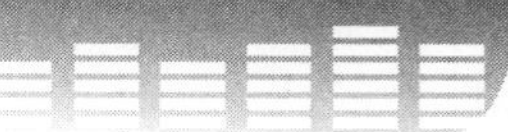

## PORTFOLIO MEMO

### Trading Errors and Directed Trades

A portfolio manager calls one of your traders to place a buy order for 100,000 shares of Automatic Data Processing. Your trader calls brokerage firm XYZ and orders "100,000 shares ADP at the market." The XYZ trader later confirms the purchase of "100,000 shares of Allied Product at xx and 1/4." Your trader says that he wanted to buy Automatic Data Processing, not Allied Product. The XYZ trader explains that the "ADP" symbol is used by Allied Product and that Automatic Data Processing's symbol is "AUD." The market on Allied Product is now off by 1/4, so your trader asks XYZ to sell the shares and cover the $25,000 loss. XYZ agrees but says it will need to recoup the loss in additional trades. In the ensuing week, your trader directs a sufficient number of trades to XYZ to compensate for the loss. Perhaps without realizing it, your firm may have violated numerous regulations or laws.*

SEC rules do not permit a broker-dealer to "strike a deal" in order to correct a trading error. Dealers (and investment managers) are fully responsible for their own errors and must bear the cost. Directing trades to a particular broker or investment house in order to compensate for an error may violate the Exclusive Purpose rule or the Sole Interest of the Beneficiary rule when acting in a fiduciary capacity. For members of the Association for Investment Management and Research, directing trades to make up for errors may also violate provisions of Standard IV (B.3) *Fair Dealing* and Standard IV(A.3) *Independence and Objectivity* of the AIMR Standards of Practice.

*Fred P. Boy, General Counsel, Lynch, Jones & Ryan, Inc., "Compensation for Trading Errors," *AIMR Standards Reporter*, September/October 1998, 1.

that does not. If a client wants you to avoid firms that use nuclear power, you should do so if you prudently can. Such a decision does not violate any fiduciary duty.

On the other hand, a request not to invest outside the investor's home state on the grounds that "I want to benefit local people" would be more difficult for the investment manager to accept. The benefits of diversification are clear, should not be lightly discarded, and are likely much more difficult to achieve if you restrict the security universe to stock from your own part of the country.

URL

*For the premier site for Internet proxy voting, go to* http://www.proxyvote.com

### *Proxy Voting*

One of the rights of shareholders is the right to vote on matters of importance at the annual meeting. Most individual investors do not particularly care about this right. The legendary economist John Kenneth Galbraith describes the typical corporate annual meeting as "perhaps our most elaborate exercise in popular illusion," the illusion being that stockholders have any significant role to play in the important decisions a corporation makes.[19]

Although many investors do not choose to exercise this right, they have it nonetheless. Shareholders who are unable to attend the annual meeting for any

[19]Victor F. Morris, "Reclaiming Shareholder Power," *Financial Analysts Journal*, May/June 1997.

**FIGURE 18-2**

Obstacles to Effective Proxy Voting

- Lack of a clear policy and support from the management of the investment firm.
- The perception that many proxies are routine.
- Uncertainty about voting responsibilities for passively managed funds.
- Overzealous management attempts to influence owners.
- Increasing international investment.
- Delegation of voting authority.
- The proxy distribution system.

reason have the right of proxy voting. A **proxy statement** is a legal document allowing the shareholder to cast an absentee ballot.

**Proxy Voting and the Law.** Most of the time the formal votes at a corporation's annual meeting are routine. The two most common items to vote on are (1) ratifying the board of directors' choice of an auditor and (2) electing members of the board of directors. Many investors consider these decisions inconsequential and do not vote.

*The right to vote is an asset of the organization; fiduciaries cannot abandon it.*

Recent court decisions have established that a fiduciary does not have the option not to vote. The courts say that the right to vote is an asset of the organization, and the investment manager breaches a fiduciary duty if he fails to exercise it. The manager could argue that failing to vote shares violates the sole interest of the beneficiary rule. The fiduciary who fails to vote chooses personal convenience over the interest of the beneficiary. A fiduciary may believe the votes are trivial, but that is not his decision to make. As of August 31, 2004, mutual funds are required to disclose their actual proxy votes.

*For a comprehensive proxy voting policy, see the California Public Employee Retirement System policy at* http://www.calpers-governance.org/principles/global/globalvoting.pdf.

**Establishing a Proxy Voting Policy.** Many money management firms have no clear policy on proxy voting. This is likely to change because, as stated previously, the courts assert that proxy voting is not optional for a fiduciary. A survey[20] by the Association for Investment Management and Research found that investment managers frequently cite a number of obstacles to effective proxy voting. Figure 18-2 lists the reasons that managers most commonly cited.

Securities and Exchange Commission rule 206(4)-6 provides certain requirements on investment advisors and proxy voting. Among the most important are these:

- Adopt proxy voting rules in the best interest of the customer;
- Disclose these voting rules to clients;
- Disclose how clients can find out how the investment advisor has voted proxies.

The rule states that "Advisers that have implicit as well as explicit voting authority must comply with rule 206(4)-6." The rule further states that

> The federal securities laws do not specifically address how an adviser must exercise its proxy voting authority for its clients. Under the Advisers Act, however, an adviser is a fiduciary that owes each of its clients duties of care and loyalty with respect to all services undertaken on the client's behalf, including proxy voting. The duty of care requires an adviser with proxy voting authority to monitor corporate events and to vote

[20] *Establishing a Proxy Voting Policy for Professional Investors*, AIMR, 1992.

> the proxies. To satisfy its duty of loyalty, the adviser must cast the proxy votes in a manner consistent with the best interest of its client and must not subrogate client interests to its own.

The key point is that proxy voting is not optional; investment advisors have a fiduciary responsibility to vote, and to vote in the best interest of the customer.

Another issue that frequently appears on the proxy statement is **cumulative voting.** Suppose you own 1,000 shares of a company and there are five matters to vote on. Under noncumulative voting, you could cast 1,000 votes for or against each of the five questions. If the company's bylaws permit cumulative voting, you are entitled to 5,000 votes that you can cast any way you choose. You might cast all 5,000 in favor of question 1 and not vote on the other four, or you could cast 3,000 for question 1 and 500 for each of the other four questions. A cumulative voting provision makes it easier for an outsider to elect someone to the corporate board of directors.

A shareholder presented such a proposal at the 1998 annual meeting of Chrysler Corporation. Her proposal stated:

> RESOLVED: That the stockholders of Chrysler, assembled in Annual Meeting in person and by proxy, hereby request the Board of Directors to take the necessary steps to provide for cumulative voting in the election of directors, which means each stockholder shall be entitled to as many votes as shall equal the number of shares he or she owns multiplied by the number of directors to be elected, and he or she may cast all of such votes for a single candidate, or any two or more of them as he or she may see fit.[21]

In her statement in support of the resolution, the shareholder presenting the resolution argued that many states have mandatory cumulative voting, many corporations have adopted it on their own, and at the previous annual meeting of Chrysler, 22.44 percent of the shares voting voted in favor of it.

The company recommended a vote against the proposal, saying

> Your directors recommend a vote AGAINST this proposal. Your Board of Directors believes that cumulative voting for directors would not serve any useful purpose and would be contrary to the best interests of Chrysler and its shareholders.[22]

Although shareholder proposals recommending cumulative voting are common, they rarely pass. Shareholders as a group seldom vote against the recommendation of management.

*Detailed information about CERES and the list of participating companies can be seen at* http://www.ceres.org

Another common shareholder proposal is endorsement of the **CERES Principles**, formally called the *CERES Principles for Public Environmental Accountability*. CERES stands for the Coalition for Environmentally Responsible Economies. Companies endorsing these principles commit to working for (1) protection of the biosphere, (2) sustainable natural resource use, (3) waste reduction and disposal, (4) energy conservation, (5) risk reduction, (6) safe products/services, (7) environmental restoration, (8) informing the public, (9) management commitment, and (10) audits and reports. Detailed explanations of these ten points are available directly from CERES.[23]

These principles seem reasonable, and you might wonder why someone would not support them. Chrysler also had a CERES Principles shareholder proposal at its

---

[21]Chrysler Corporation, "Notice of Annual Meeting of Stockholders," April 17, 1998, 26.
[22]Ibid.
[23]CERES, 711 Atlantic Avenue, Boston, MA 02110. (617) 451-0927.

1998 annual meeting. The Board of Directors recommended a vote against it for the following reasons:

> Your directors recommend a vote AGAINST this proposal. The Company formally adopted a policy on environmental principles in 1992. The policy reflects the Company's commitment to the environment and its goal of integrating sound environmental practices, materials and technology into the Company's products and manufacturing processes. The policy's objectives include: resource conservation; pollution prevention; recycling improvements; efficient energy use; and continuous improvement.
>
> In furtherance of that policy, Chrysler's environmental staff conducts or oversees periodic audits of each operating unit to assess their environmental performance. The company believes that such audits are effective in enabling management to identify areas of concern and prevent or remedy potential problems.
>
> Since many of the topics covered by this proposal are already included in the extensive reports the Company is required to prepare under federal and state law, the Proposal would burden the company with additional reporting obligations and their associated costs in connection with a mandatory annual E\CERES Report. The Company also believes that endorsing the CERES Principles would impose unnecessary costs on the Company of obligating it to pay an annual fee to CERES of $25,000.
>
> In summary, the Company believes that the costs and uncertainties associated with the proposal outweigh any potential environmental benefits which might result from its adoption.[24]

This particular proposal is a good example of the need for due diligence. The fact that a "yes" vote would commit the company to an annual cost of $25,000 might very well be a material matter. Before voting against management, it is important to know what you are doing and to document your decision.

Other matters that frequently appear as shareholder resolutions include eliminating staggered terms for the directors, compensation limits for officers, diversity and hiring practices, and social investing issues.

Fiduciary law requires you as a fiduciary to vote proxies in the best interest of the beneficiary, which is not necessarily the same as the best interest of the company. Many firms establish a proxy voting policy that segregates routine from nonroutine actions. The choice of an auditor, for instance, is routine, and the policy might require you to always vote in favor of management's recommendation. There should be some mechanism whereby somebody, perhaps a committee, looks at more complicated issues and tries to determine what makes the best sense for the beneficiary. Finally, there should be some policy for corresponding with management prior to a decision to vote against their recommendation. This latter point is especially true for fiduciaries controlling a large number of shares when their votes might materially influence the vote.

**Mechanics of Voting.** You might vote shares at an annual meeting in four ways. First, you could attend the meeting and vote in person. This is generally impractical because of geographic separation, but may occasionally be feasible if you operate your business from a financial center.

A second option is to fill out the paper proxy that comes with the annual report and mail it back. A neutral outside party electronically reads these. This is a relatively expensive option for the corporation. The firm must pay all the postage costs plus the fee of the firm that tabulates the results.

---

[24]Chrysler Corporation, "Notice of Annual Meeting of Stockholders," April 17, 1998, 29.

*You may vote proxies over the Internet.*

The industry is moving toward the electronic distribution of stockholder information. In a desire to cut costs, firms now actively encourage shareholders (and their fiduciaries) to vote in one of the remaining two ways: over the Internet or via a touch-tone telephone. The proxy statement has a control number printed on it. By going to the indicated Website or dialing the designated toll-free phone number and entering this control number, the shareholder can quickly and efficiently vote the shares.

### Soft Dollars

*The SEC requires investment advisors to disclose soft dollar arrangements to their clients.*

In a sweeping report entitled *Disclosure by Investment Advisers Regarding Soft Dollar Practices*, the Securities and Exchange Commission defines **soft dollars** as "arrangements under which products or services other than execution of securities transactions are obtained by an adviser from or through a broker-dealer in exchange for the direction by the adviser of client brokerage transactions to the broker-dealer."[25] Because of the potential for a conflict of interest, the SEC requires investment advisers to disclose soft dollar arrangements to their clients.[26]

*The Securities Exchange Act of 1934 specifically allows an investment fiduciary to use soft dollars to acquire research services.*

**Soft Dollars and Research.** Many investment professionals immediately associate soft dollars with research service. According to the SEC, "Soft dollar arrangements have developed as a link between the brokerage industry's supply of research and the money management industry's demand for research."[27] Section 28(e) of the Securities Exchange Act of 1934 creates a "safe harbor" for advisers using soft dollars to pay for research. The act protects an adviser from a claim that she breached a fiduciary duty by using soft dollars for this purpose.

Many broker-dealers provide more than execution of trades: they often also provide research that they develop internally or they acquire from another information vendor. A bank trust department, for instance, might direct some of its trades to a particular broker-dealer in exchange for monthly research reports in addition to the trade execution. It may be economical for the trust department to use someone else's research rather than developing its own, and a portion of the client's trading fees pay for it.

Presumably, the research is of such a quality that it results in better returns for the trust clients. If this is not the case, it is not clear that the fiduciary is managing the account wisely. The key issue is whether the customer is getting value for the price paid. Again citing from the SEC report,

> Under traditional fiduciary principles, a fiduciary cannot use assets entrusted by clients to benefit itself. As the Commission has recognized, when an adviser uses client commissions to buy research from a broker-dealer, it receives a benefit because it is relieved from the need to produce or pay for the research itself. In addition, when transactions involving soft dollars involve the adviser "paying up" or receiving executions at inferior prices, advisers using soft dollars face a conflict of interest between their need to obtain research and their clients' interest in paying the lowest commission rate available and obtaining the best possible execution.[28]

---

[25]*Disclosure by Investment Advisers Regarding Soft Dollar Practices*, *Advisors Act Release No. 1469*, February 14, 1995.

[26]The SEC requires this disclosure regardless of whether the use of the soft dollars falls under the protective harbor provisions of section 28(e) of the Securities and Exchange Act of 1934.

[27]*Disclosure by Investment Advisors Regarding Soft Dollar Practices*, *Advisors Act Release No. 1469*, February 14, 1995.

[28]Ibid.

Using soft dollars to pay for acquired research is an established practice in the brokerage industry. When the fiduciary uses soft dollars to buy other services or to buy assets, he starts looking for trouble.

**Soft Dollars and Nonresearch Acquisitions.** Using soft dollars to acquire assets or services other than research is potentially a violation of a fiduciary's duty. There are many gray areas here. For instance, is a computer devoted exclusively to investment research a reasonable use of soft dollars? Such a question does not always have an obvious answer. The SEC study revealed numerous nonresearch uses (and abuses) of soft dollars, as shown in Figure 18-3. Table 18-1 shows the complete breakdown of how the industry was using soft dollars during the period of the study.

**SEC Recommendations for Soft Dollar Arrangements.** As a result of its recent study, the SEC's Office of Compliance, Inspections and Examinations made four

**TABLE 18-1** CATEGORIZATION OF PRODUCTS PURCHASED WITH SOFT DOLLARS

| | | |
|---|---|---|
| ***Research*** | | |
| Reports | 53.5% | |
| News | 13.6 | |
| Pricing Services | 5.5 | |
| Computer Hardware | 2.9 | |
| Portfolio Management | 1.8 | |
| Miscellaneous | 1.2 | |
| Computer—Other | 1.1 | |
| | | 79.7% |
| ***Mixed Use*** | | |
| Portfolio Management | 1.8 | |
| Reports | 1.7 | |
| Computer—Other | 1.3 | |
| Computer—Hardware | 1.2 | |
| Miscellaneous | 1.0 | |
| Pricing Services | 0.6 | |
| News | 0.4 | |
| | | 7.9% |
| ***Non-Research*** | | |
| Miscellaneous | 1.7 | |
| Pricing Services | 0.2 | |
| Computer—Other | 0.2 | |
| News | 0.1 | |
| | | 2.2% |
| ***Trade Assistance*** | | |
| Pricing Services | 5.7 | |
| Miscellaneous | 4.1 | |
| Computer—Hardware | 0.2 | |
| Computer—Other | 0.1 | |
| | | 10.2% |
| | | 100.0% |

Source: "Inspection Report on the Soft Dollar Practice of Broker-Dealers, Investment Advisers, and Mutual Funds," Appendix C, Securities and Exchange Commission, September 22, 1998.

**FIGURE 18-3**

Nonresearch Items Paid for with Soft Dollars

- Paying the salary of an adviser's research employee.
- Paying for an adviser's nonresearch information technology purchases.
- Paying for travel, airfare, hotels, meals, and other expenses of a research consultant.
- Paying for research services provided by a "consultant" operating out of the adviser's office.
- Paying for an adviser's office rent and equipment, cellular phone service, and personal expenses.

Source: "Inspection Report on the Soft Dollar Practice of Broker-Dealers, Investment Advisers, and Mutual Funds," Section IV B 1, Securities and Exchange Commission, September 22, 1998.

**TABLE 18-2** SEC RECOMMENDATIONS REGARDING SOFT DOLLARS

1. We noted many examples of advisers claiming the protection of the safe harbor without meeting its requirements. We also found that industry participants were not uniformly following prior Commission guidance with respect to soft dollars. As a result, we recommend that the Commission publish this report to reiterate guidance with respect to the scope of the safe harbor and to emphasize the obligations of broker-dealers, investment advisers and investment companies that participate in soft dollar arrangements. We also recommend that the Commission reiterate and provide further guidance with respect to the scope of the safe harbor, particularly concerning (a) the uses of electronically provided research and the various items used to send, receive and process research electronically, and (b) the uses of items that may facilitate trade execution;
2. Many broker-dealers and advisers did not keep adequate records documenting their soft dollars activities. We believe that the lack of adequate recordkeeping contributed to incomplete disclosure, using soft dollars for non-research purposes without disclosure, and inadequate mixed-use analysis. We recommend that the Commission adopt recordkeeping requirements that would provide greater accountability for soft dollar transactions and allocations. Better recordkeeping would enable advisers to more easily assure compliance and Commission examiners to more readily ascertain the existence and nature of soft dollar arrangements when conducting inspections;
3. We noted many instances where advisers' soft dollar disclosures were inadequate or wholly lacking—especially with respect to non-research items. We recommend that the Commission modify Form ADV to require more meaningful disclosure by advisers and more detailed disclosure about the products received that are not used in the investment decision-making process. In addition, the Commission should require advisers to provide more detailed information to clients upon request; and
4. In light of the weak controls and compliance failures that we found, we recommend that the Commission publish this report in order to encourage advisers and broker-dealers to strengthen their internal control procedures regarding soft dollar activities. We suggest that advisers and broker-dealers review and consider the controls described in this report, many of which were observed as effective during examinations.

Source: "Inspection Report on the Soft Dollar Practice of Broker-Dealers, Investment Advisers, and Mutual Funds," Appendix C, Securities and Exchange Commission, September 22, 1998.

recommendations to the full commission. These recommendations, presented in Table 18-2, are designed to clarify acceptable soft dollar practices. This is likely to be an area of particular SEC interest in the next few years. Investment managers and fiduciaries will need to be much more aware of the presence of soft dollars and should make a special effort to disclose their use to beneficiaries as required by law.

## SUMMARY

A fiduciary is a person who is responsible for the business affairs of another. Modern fiduciary law began with the prudent man rule in the 1830 court case *Harvard College v. Amory* and has progressed to the prudent expert rule, which requires a fiduciary to make investment decisions the way experts do. The law requires diversification, consideration of total return, and consideration of a potential investment as a portfolio component. For many years, investment managers acting in a fiduciary manner were constrained by a legal list identifying the types of assets in which they could invest.

The Employee Retirement Income Security Act, commonly called *ERISA*, governs the management of pension plans but has become a widely used standard in the management of other portfolios, too. Several standards for prudent investing are found in The Uniform Prudent Investor Act, which focuses on charitable investment funds.

The two principal fiduciary duties are care and loyalty. There are four elements of the duty of care and two elements of the duty of loyalty. The courts have held that these duties require a fiduciary to vote proxies in the best interest of the beneficiary. As a consequence, money managers should establish a formal voting policy for proxies received.

Soft dollar arrangements involve exchanging security trades for research services. These arrangements are allowable provided the fund receives adequate value for the commission. The use of soft dollars to pay for assets or other services is potentially a violation of fiduciary law and is an issue the Securities and Exchange Commission is reviewing carefully.

## QUESTIONS

1. Define the term *fiduciary*.
2. What is the significance of the court case *Harvard College v. Amory*?
3. **a.** What does the prudent man rule say about speculation?
   **b.** How does the rule define speculation?
4. Briefly explain two major results of the *Spitzer v. Bank of New York* case.
5. The *Spitzer* case can be considered a *threat* to modern portfolio management or an *endorsement* of it. Explain how it can be interpreted in these two different ways.
6. Explain the prudent expert standard from ERISA.
7. List three main features of the Uniform Prudent Investor Act.
8. What are the two central fiduciary duties?
9. Distinguish between the *documents rule* and the *indicia of ownership rule* contained in ERISA.
10. Under what circumstances can a pension fund manager choose to violate the plan document?
11. Explain the term *party in interest*.
12. Given the *sole interest of the beneficiary rule*, how can a trustee justify paying more than the lowest possible brokerage commissions?
13. Explain the term *due diligence*.
14. How should a trustee deal with a request that the fund not invest in tobacco, alcohol, defense, or electric utility stocks if they have any nuclear power generation?

15. An investment management firm's policy states that when acting as a trustee, the firm should "vote all proxies received." You learn that this statement is inadequate regarding proxy voting. How should it be amended?
16. Explain the term *CERES Principles*.
17. Create an example showing how cumulative voting makes it easier for a group to elect someone to a board of directors.
18. Explain four ways in which someone might vote shares at a corporate annual meeting.
19. Explain the term *soft dollars*.
20. According to the SEC's survey of the investment industry, what are the three most common uses of soft dollars?
21. Rent a movie dealing with the stock market, such as *Other People's Money*, *Wall Street*, or *Trading Places* and identify possible breaches of fiduciary duty that occur in the plot.
22. Obtain a proxy statement that contains a shareholder proposal and comment on the proposal from the perspective of a fiduciary.
23. 
FROM THE 1995 LEVEL III CFA EXAM (Question 7)

QUESTION 7 HAS FOUR PARTS FOR A TOTAL OF 30 MINUTES

Your discussion of ethics with Green now turns to "fiduciary duty." Green asks you to give examples of this fundamental concept. You show him a series of statements that might be made by an AIMR member who is an investment manager for a pension plan operating under the provision of ERISA, the Employee Retirement Income Security Act of 1974. This U.S. legislation established guidelines and requirements for fiduciary conduct and sets standards for many aspects of all private and some public pension plans in the United States. Together with the AIMR Code of Ethics and Standards of Practice, the ERISA prescriptions may serve as a model for appropriate fiduciary conduct worldwide.

Note to candidates: Respond to the following statements as if you were a "plan fiduciary" under the provisions of ERISA and an AIMR member whose conduct is governed by its Code and Standards. Your job as an investment professional gives you full investment authority over the portion of the pension portfolio you manage.

**A.** Evaluate the validity of *each* of the two statements below. In each evaluation, include a discussion of *two* relevant fiduciary duties pertaining to the statements.

(i) "A decision to invest in a company entails a responsibility to vote proxies."

(ii) "You have breached your fiduciary duty as a manager if you have caused an account under your control to 'pay up' (i.e., pay a brokerage commission in excess of that charged for a trade done on a 'best execution' basis) on a transaction for the account."

**(14 minutes)**

**B.** "Social investing" in a pension fund context may be defined as the investment of plan assets not only to provide retirement benefits to plan beneficiaries, but also to promote social goals and policies deemed to be worthy and/or to withhold investment in the securities of companies deemed to be socially irresponsible.

Evaluate the validity of the statement below. Include in your evaluation *two* relevant reasons that support your position.

"Social investing is inconsistent with the requirements of ERISA."

**(7 minutes)**

**C.** Evaluate the validity of the underlined "Prudent Expert Rule" portion of the statement appearing directly below. Include in your response reference to *three* specific components of that rule.

"Adverse investment outcomes may trigger inquiry into a fiduciary's conduct and may influence a court's judgment as to prudence and the extent of any liability. Nevertheless, ERISA's 'Prudent Expert Rule' is more properly termed a rule of conduct than a rule of investment performance."

**(6 minutes)**

**D.** Evaluate the validity of the statement below, and briefly explain the basis for your conclusion.

"An investment manager's responsibilities as defined by ERISA take precedence over the plan documents and objectives in the event of conflict between these and the ERISA requirements."

**(3 minutes)**

## INTERNET EXERCISE

Retrieve a proxy statement for any company from the Web by running a search engine on the keywords "proxy statement."

## FURTHER READING


Arnott, Robert, and Peter L. Bernstein. "The Right Way to Manage Your Pension Fund." *Harvard Business Review*, January/February 1988.

Association for Investment Management and Research. *Standards of Practice Handbook*, 7th ed. Charlottesville, VA: AIMR, 1996.

Crawford, George. "Case Study: A Fiduciary Duty to Use Derivatives?" *Stanford Journal of Law, Business and Finance*, Spring 1995.

Droms, William G. "Fiduciary Responsibilities of Investment Managers and Trustees." *Financial Analysts Journal*, July/August 1992, 58–64.

*Establishing a Proxy Voting Policy for Professional Investors*. Charlottesville, VA: AIMR, 1992.

Gertner, Marc. "DOL Enhances Enforcement of Pension Investments." *Pension World*, December 1990, 18–20.

Hamilton, Sally, Hoje Jo, and Meir Statman. "Doing Well While Doing Good? The Investment Performance of Socially Responsible Mutual Funds." *Financial Analysts Journal*, November/December 1993, 62–66.

Logue, Dennis E., and Jack S. Rader. *Managing Pension Plans*. Boston: Harvard Business School Press, 1998.

Morris, Victor F. "Reclaiming Shareholder Power." *Financial Analysts Journal*, May/June 1997.

Pozen, R.C. "The Prudent Person and ERISA: A Legal Perspective." *Financial Analysts Journal*, March/April 1977.

# PART FOUR

# Portfolio Protection and Emerging Topics

# 19 Principles of the Futures Market

*As near as I can learn, and from the best information I have been able to obtain on the Chicago Board of Trade, at least 95% of the sales of that Board are of this fictitious character, where no property is actually owned, no property sold or delivered, or expected to be delivered but simply wagers or bets as to what that property may be worth at a designated time in the future. . . . Wheat and cotton have become as much gambling tools as chips on the farobank table. The property of the wheat grower and the cotton grower is treated as though it were a "stake" put on the gambling table at Monte Carlo. The producer of wheat is compelled to see the stocks in his barn dealt with like the peas of a thimblerigger, or the cards of a three-card-monte man. Between the grain-producer and loaf eater, there has stepped in a "parasite" between them robbing them both.*

***Senator William D. Washburn (D–Minn.), before Congress, July 11, 1892***

## Key Terms

- Acapulco trade
- basis
- cash price
- clearing corporation
- commodities trading advisor
- Commodity Futures Trading Commission
- contango market
- daily price limit
- day trader
- delivery month
- expectations hypothesis
- full carrying charge market
- good faith deposit
- hedger
- inverted market
- locals
- long hedge
- managed futures
- marked to market
- market variation call
- normal backwardation
- open interest
- open outcry
- outtrade
- pit
- position trader
- price discovery
- scalpers
- settlement price
- speculator
- spot price

## Introduction

The futures market is a very useful, but often misunderstood, part of our economic system. This and the next two chapters show how the futures market enables various businesses, financial institutions, and farmers to lessen price risk, which is the risk of loss because of an uncertain future price for a commodity or a financial asset.

As with options, the two major groups of futures market participants are hedgers and speculators, with the former transferring some or all of the price risk they bear to the latter. Futures contracts trade on a wide variety of assets. This chapter gives examples using both agricultural commodities and foreign currencies. Other financial futures, like those traded on Treasury bonds and stock indexes, have been an extremely popular and fast-growing segment of the futures market. Chapters 20 and 21 discuss them.

First we look at the economic role of futures markets. These markets developed to meet the needs of agriculture, and understanding these original applications is helpful in learning what the market can and cannot do. Then we will see how the trading system actually functions and review some basic principles of futures contract pricing.

## Futures Contracts

### What Futures Contracts Are

*A futures contract is a promise to buy or to deliver a certain quantity of a standardized good by a specific date.*

*Futures contracts* are promises; the person who initially sells the contract promises to deliver a quantity of a standardized commodity to a designated delivery point during a certain month, called the **delivery month.** The other party to the trade promises to pay a predetermined price for the goods upon delivery. The person who promises to buy is said to be long; the person who promises to deliver is short.[1]

There are some analogies between a futures contract and an option contract. Both involve a predetermined price and contract duration. An option, however, is precisely that: an option. The person holding an option has the *right* but not the *obligation* to exercise the put or the call. If an option has no value at its expiration, the option holder will allow it to expire unexercised. But with futures contracts, a trade must occur if someone holds the contract until its delivery deadline. Futures contracts do not expire unexercised. One party has promised to deliver a commodity that another party has promised to buy.[2]

For instance, a trader may purchase a July soybean contract at the Chicago Board of Trade. The purchase price might be $6.22 per bushel. This contract calls for the delivery of 5,000 bushels of No. 2 yellow soybeans to a specially designated regular warehouse at an approved delivery point by the last business day in July. Upon delivery, the purchaser of the contract must pay $6.22 for each of the 5,000 bushels, or a total of $31,100. If the current price (**spot price,** or **cash price**) for soybeans is higher than $6.22, the purchaser of the contract will make a profit. A spot price of $6.33 would result in a profit of $0.11 on each of 5,000 bushels, or $550. In contrast, if the spot price were only $6.15, the buyer would lose $0.07 per bushel, or $350.

An important concept to keep in mind with futures is that the purpose of the contracts is not to provide a means for the transfer of goods. Stated another way, people cannot transfer property rights to real or financial assets with futures contracts. Futures contracts do, however, enable people to reduce some of the risks they assume in their business.

*Most futures contracts are eliminated before the delivery month.*

Most futures contracts are eliminated before the delivery month. Similarly, people who buy puts or calls do not usually intend to exercise them; valuable options

[1]As with options, *long* and *short* in this context have nothing to do with time.

[2]It is also possible for one or both parties to the trade to transfer their half of the promise to someone else via an offsetting trade.

are sold before expiration day. An individual speculator who is long a corn futures contract does not want to take delivery of 5,000 bushels of the commodity. A farmer who has promised to deliver wheat through the futures market may prefer to sell the crop locally rather than deliver it to an approved delivery point. In either case, the contract obligation can be satisfied by making an offsetting trade, or trading out of the contract. The speculator with a long position would sell a contract, which would cancel the long position. The farmer with a short position would buy. Both individuals would be out of the market after these trades.

### Why We Have Futures Contracts

Perhaps no other part of the financial marketplace has received as much scrutiny as the futures market. Unlike other markets, where tangible items change hands (stock certificates, diamonds, real estate, and so on), the participants in the futures market deal in promises. A trader can buy or sell thousands of bushels of wheat or tons of soybean meal and have absolutely no intention of ever growing the commodity or taking delivery of it. In fact, fewer than 2 percent of the commodities underlying all futures contracts are ever actually delivered. It is possible for the quantity of a commodity as represented by the total number of futures contracts actually to exceed the available supply worldwide. These odd facts help explain why the commodity markets are frequently attacked by would-be reformers.

*Fewer than 2 percent of futures contracts actually result in delivery.*

Let us look at an example of how the futures market benefits college students. Many graduating seniors buy themselves class rings made of gold. These usually have to be ordered months prior to the actual graduation date. When seniors order the rings, they want a firm price quotation from the ring manufacturer; they do not want to hear that it "depends on the price of gold when we make your ring." A company like Jostens or Balfour can lock in the price it has to pay for gold by appropriate trades in the futures market. Because the firm wants the gold, it buys gold futures, promising to pay a set price for the gold when it is delivered. A gold-mining company, in contrast, would sell contracts, promising to deliver the gold. Perhaps the trade occurs at a price of $475.50 per ounce, with delivery set for December.

*I'm not a gambler, I'm not in a crapshoot...I'm a speculator. Here's the difference. In gambling, you create the risk. In speculating, you assume the risk.*

Lee Stern, owner of the Chicago Sting soccer team and member of the Chicago Board of Trade

There are 100 troy ounces of gold in one futures contract. This means that the mining company will deliver 100 ounces and receive $47,550 for it regardless of the price of gold at delivery time. The suppliers of gold know their ultimate selling price, and the manufacturers of the rings know their major materials cost. If these two companies were not able to lock in the future price of gold, the price to the consumer would be significantly higher in order to account for the added price risk faced by both the miner and the manufacturer.

Unfortunately, some influential people still share Senator Washburn's views of the futures market. Fortunately, they are in the minority. The commodity exchanges are continually adding new products, and the number of people and organizations who find useful opportunities with futures is increasing. The basic function of the commodity futures market is to transfer risk from some businessperson (the *hedger*) to someone who is willing to bear it (the *speculator*). The speculator assumes this risk because of the opportunity for profit. We will discuss these people in greater detail later.

### How to Fulfill the Futures Contract Promise

*The clearing corporation ensures the integrity of each futures contract by interposing itself between each buyer and seller.*

You might ask, "What happens if someone decides not to pay for the commodity as promised or if a particular farmer is unable to deliver the wheat?" This is a good question. If it were possible for people to back out of the trade without fulfilling their parts of the promises, the futures system would not work. People would lose confidence in the system, and it would not be attractive to either hedgers or speculators. Eliminating this uncertainty is the role of the **clearing corporation.**

Each exchange has a clearing corporation performing a critical duty: ensuring the integrity of the futures contract. Although trades originate between two specific individuals or institutions, the trades actually become sales to or by the clearing corporation. By interposing itself between buyer and seller, the clearing corporation becomes a party to every trade.

Futures contracts are promises, and promises must be kept. On active trading days, some individual accounts may fluctuate in value by more than a million dollars. Misfortune or incompetence sometimes forces an exchange member into bankruptcy, yet that member's positions still constitute promises with other exchange members. It is the clearing corporation that assumes the responsibility for those positions when a member is in financial distress. If this were not the case, the integrity of the trading system would break down, and members would tend to trade only with the other members who were financially strongest. In such a situation, market prices probably would become less competitive.

It is difficult to overstate the value of a sound clearing system at a commodities exchange. The Chicago Mercantile Exchange publishes a short document entitled *The Financial Safeguard System of the Chicago Mercantile Exchange*. One section of this paper deals with the financial integrity of the marketplace:

> The accounts of individual members and non-member customers doing business through the facilities of the CME must be carried and guaranteed by a clearing member. *In every matched transaction executed through the Exchange's facilities, the Clearing House is substituted as the buyer for the seller and the seller for the buyer.* The Clearing House is an operating division of the Exchange and all rights, obligations and/or liabilities of the Clearing House are rights, obligations, and/or liabilities of the CME. Clearing members assume full financial and performance responsibility for all transactions executed through them and all positions they carry. The Clearing House, dealing exclusively with clearing members, holds each clearing member accountable for every position it carries regardless of whether the position is being carried for the account of an individual member, for the account of a non-member customer or for the clearing member's own account. Conversely, as the contraside to every position, the Clearing House is held accountable to the clearing members for performance on all open positions.[3]

*The clearing corporation guarantees the integrity of the contracts trading within the jurisdiction of the rules and bylaws of the exchange.*

Because of the possibility that the collective members of the clearing corporation might have to absorb large losses due to the default of one or more members, stringent financial conditions are a condition of membership. The clearing corporation strictly enforces these requirements. **Good faith deposits** (or performance bonds) are required from each member on each contract to help ensure the member's financial capacity to meet the obligations in bad times.[4] The good faith deposit is the initial equity requirement that must be deposited with an opening transaction in a futures contract.

---

[3]Chicago Mercantile Exchange, *The Financial Safeguard System of the Chicago Mercantile Exchange* (Chicago: CME, March 1988), 1.

[4]In practice, the good faith deposit is usually called a *margin deposit* or *margin requirement*. As with the margin requirement of certain option overwriting strategies, this use of the term *margin* does not imply that money is borrowed or that interest is paid.

MEMO

## Futures Regulation

Legally, futures contracts are not securities, so they are not under the jurisdiction of the Securities and Exchange Commission (SEC). The regulatory agency for futures is the **Commodity Futures Trading Commission (CFTC).** Congress created the CFTC in 1974 as an independent agency to regulate commodity futures and option markets in the United States. According to the Commission's mission statement, "The agency protects market participants against manipulation, abusive trade practices and fraud. Through effective oversight and regulation, the CFTC enables the markets to serve better their important functions in the nation's economy—providing a mechanism for price discovery and a means of offsetting price risk."*

Companies and individuals that offer advice about futures or who handle futures trades must also register with a CFTC-approved self-regulatory organization, the National Futures Association (NFA). The CFTC Website states, "The CFTC also seeks to protect customers by requiring registrants to disclose market risks and past performance information to prospective customers, by requiring that customer funds be kept in accounts separate from those maintained by the firm for its own use, and by requiring customer accounts to be adjusted to reflect the current market value at the close of trading each day. In addition, the CFTC monitors registrant supervision systems, internal controls and sales practice compliance programs. Further, all registrants are required to complete ethics training."+

In December 2000 Congress passed the Commodity Futures Modernization Act authorizing the CFTC for an additional five years. It also resolved some regulatory turf battles between the SEC and the CFTC with regard to the trading of futures contracts on single stocks.

*http://www.cftc.gov/cftc/cftcglan.htm.
+Ibid.

# Market Mechanics

Let us turn now to a discussion of how a futures contract is actually established on the exchanges.

### *The Marketplace*

The visitor to a commodity exchange is often struck by the apparent confusion in the exchange.[5] Trades are made by **open outcry** of the floor traders, meaning that traders shout out their offers to buy and sell. To the uninitiated, the cacophony of normal business seems like a furious argument. Traders do not stand in line or use computerized order entry; they stand in a sunken area called the **pit** and bark their offers to buy or sell to others within the trading circle. In addition to spoken offers,

[5]There are many commodity exchanges in the United States. Among the best known are the Chicago Board of Trade, the Chicago Mercantile Exchange, the New York Mercantile Exchange, and the New York Board of Trade.

*To visit the world's largest futures exchange, go to* http://www.cbot.com

traders use a series of hand signals to indicate their willingness to buy or sell, as well as the quantity and price at which they want to trade.

Only members of the exchange are allowed in the trading pit itself. The Chicago Board of Trade has more than 3,600 members, including 1,402 full members with the right to trade in any of the commodities at the exchange. Associate members have more limited trading privileges. An associate membership allows an individual to trade the financial instrument futures and certain other designated markets. "IDEMs" may trade all futures contracts in the index, debt, and energy markets category. "COMs" may trade all options contracts listed in the commodity options market category. The price of a membership is determined by the market and can vary daily. As an example, a full membership at the Chicago Board of Trade sold for $530,000 on October 6, 1987. The first sale of a seat after the market crashed on October 19 was on October 29, at a price of $321,000. On February 2, 1999, a full membership sold for $540,000, with an IDEM membership selling for $30,000 the following day. Three years later on March 28, 2002, a full membership sold for $310,000. In February 2005, the bid price for a full membership was $1,225,000. Many newcomers to the exchange choose to lease a membership from someone while trying to develop the expertise and capital to warrant acquiring their own memberships.

Next to each trading pit is a raised structure called a *pulpit,* where representatives of the exchange's market report department enter all price changes into the price-reporting system. The walls surrounding the trading area are covered with a massive electronic wallboard reflecting price information about the commodities being traded. Current prices, as well as the two previous prices, are shown, along with the high and low prices at which a particular contract has traded during its life. This wallboard also powers a global network of price information to which investors and brokerage firms worldwide subscribe.

Hundreds of order desks line the perimeter of the exchange trading floor; here telephone and teletype personnel from member firms receive orders from clients and relay order confirmations. Most telephone clerks tape their conversations to protect themselves against alleged order errors. The Chicago Mercantile Exchange has approximately 1,200 workstations and 153,600 telephone lines.

At one time the Chicago Board of Trade building housed more computer screens than any other building in the world except the National Aeronautics and Space Administration (NASA) headquarters. Because of the amount of activity within the building, in the history of the exchange, it has seldom been necessary to turn on the heat!

Visitors to any of the exchanges note the colorful display of trading jackets worn by people on the trading floor. Exchange policy requires every employee to wear either a business suit or a trading jacket. The Chicago Mercantile Exchange provides red jackets to any member who desires one and, for a nominal fee, will provide a freshly laundered one every Wednesday. At all exchanges, brokers from a particular firm have the option of wearing a distinctive jacket color to make it easier for their messengers and clerical people to locate them. At the Chicago Board of Trade, messengers wear yellow jackets; royal blue signifies telephone/teletype people; tan jackets are worn by price-reporting supervisors; and dark brown jackets are worn by price reporters.

Certain commodities have designated areas within the pit for the trading of a particular delivery month. The pit itself is either octagonal or polygonal, with steps descending into the center. The edge of the pit is approximately waist high to an observer outside. Each trader in the pit wears a large badge containing a two- or three-letter (up to four letters at the Chicago Mercantile Exchange) personal identification code and an indication of which firm he or she works for (or clears trades through; more on this later).

As in most professions, there is a pit lingo, with which people on the trading floor quickly become familiar. On days when there is little trading activity, people say they can "see through the pit." An unusually large trade by someone who normally trades just a few contracts at a time is called an **Acapulco trade,** presumably because if the trader is successful with the trade it will finance a trip to exotic places. When traders incorrectly assess the market and lose all their trading capital, they have "busted out," or gone to "Tapioca City." A sudden rush of pit activity for no apparent reason is called a "fire drill." A big price move is a "lights-out" move. Traders who are riding a winning streak joke about establishing an "O'Hare spread," referring to O'Hare Airport. The O'Hare spread is "Sell Chicago, Buy Mexico."

The trading floor occasionally observes a moment of silence from 11:00 to 11:01 A.M. This acknowledges events such as the death of a longtime member of the exchange or a national or world disaster (such as the *Challenger* space shuttle accident or the Chernobyl nuclear power plant explosion).

### Creation of a Contract

Suppose trader ZZZ sells five contracts of September Treasury bonds to trader Dan Hennebry at 77 $^{31}/_{32}$.[6] The price of 77 31/32 means 77 31/32 percent of par, or $77,968.75. A price change of 1/32 would be the equivalent of $31.25. The two traders confirm the trade verbally and with the hand signals appropriate to the U.S. Treasury bond pit. Each of them then fills out a card recording this information. See Figure 19-1 for an example. One side of the card is blue, which is for buy trades. The other side is red for sales. Each commodity has a symbol, and each delivery month has a letter code. Table 19-1 lists these symbols for commodities traded at the Chicago Board of Trade. Hennebry's card notes that he bought five contracts of September U.S. Treasury bonds at a price of 77 31/32 from trader ZZZ at Firm 000.

The letter A is circled and written in at the far right of the card. This is the time block at which the trade occurred. The first thirty minutes of trading constitutes block A; the second thirty minutes, block B; and so on until the close of trading. Normally, a trader either circles the letter or writes it in, but not both. The time block helps to ensure that orders are correctly matched during the clearing process. This card also shows a second, independent trade with TTT for two contracts of September T-bonds at a price of 78 6/32.

At the conclusion of trading, each trader submits his cards (called the *deck*) to the clearinghouse, where all the cards are matched and errors identified. The role of the clearing operation is crucial to a well-functioning exchange and is discussed shortly. First, let us look at the principal players in the futures market.

### Market Participants

Two types of participants are needed in a successful futures market: hedgers and speculators. Without hedgers, the market would not exist, and speculators would perform no economic function.

*Hedgers transfer price risk to speculators, who are willing to bear it.*

**Hedgers.** In the context of the futures market, a **hedger** is defined as someone engaged in some type of business activity with an unacceptable level of price risk. For instance, a farmer must decide each winter what crops to put in the ground in

---

[6]The trading unit for Treasury bonds is $100,000 par value of U.S. Treasury bonds that have a remaining maturity of at least fifteen years.

**FIGURE 19-1**

A Trader's Card

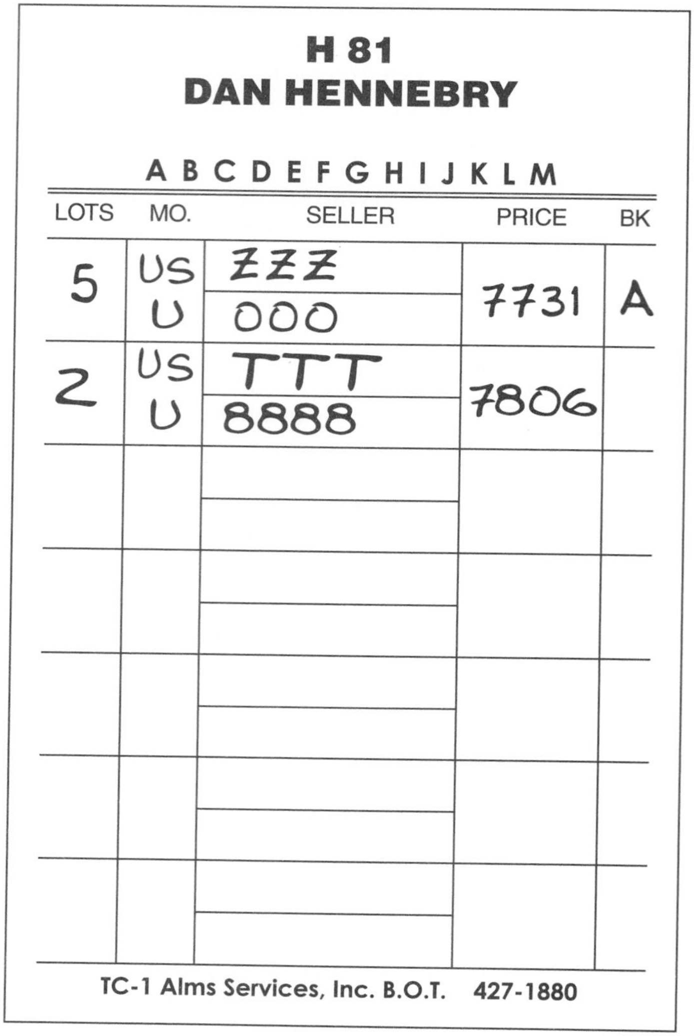

**H 81**
**DAN HENNEBRY**

**A B C D E F G H I J K L M**

| LOTS | MO. | SELLER | PRICE | BK |
|---|---|---|---|---|
| 5 | US<br>U | ZZZ<br>OOO | 7731 | A |
| 2 | US<br>U | TTT<br>8888 | 7806 | |
| | | | | |
| | | | | |
| | | | | |
| | | | | |
| | | | | |

**TC-1 Alms Services, Inc. B.O.T. 427-1880**

the spring. The farmer knows about such things as crop rotation but still may face a decision between soybeans and wheat, for instance. To a large extent, the welfare of the farmer's family or business depends on the price of the chosen commodity at harvest. If the price is high, the farmer will earn a nice profit on the crop. Overabundance or reduced demand, however, may cause prices to fall so much that the farmer cannot even recover operating costs.

To reduce this risk, the farmer may choose to hedge in the futures market. In essence, the farmer transfers the risk he or she is unwilling to bear to the speculator, who is willing to bear it.

In March, for instance, September soybeans may be selling for \$5.80. The farmer may find this price attractive because it would provide a reasonable profit level and eliminate the price risk associated with the commodity. The farmer can hedge the price risk by promising to sell all or part of the crop through the futures market to someone who is willing to pay \$5.80 per bushel for it. As long as the

**TABLE 19-1** SELECTED COMMODITY SYMBOLS AT THE CHICAGO BOARD OF TRADE

| | | | | | |
|---|---|---|---|---|---|
| | | ***Commodity*** | | | |
| AG | 1,000 oz Silver | | FV | 5-year Treasury notes | |
| SV | 5,000 oz Silver | | TU | 2-year Treasury notes | |
| S | Soybeans | | C | Corn | |
| SM | Soybean meal | | US | Treasury bonds | |
| BO | Soybean oil | | W | Wheat | |
| O | Oats | | RR | Rough Rice | |
| TY | 10-year Treasury notes | | DJ | CBOT DJIA index | |
| | | ***Delivery Month*** | | | |
| | | ***Current Year*** | | | |
| F | January | K | May | U | September |
| G | February | M | June | V | October |
| H | March | N | July | X | November |
| J | April | Q | August | Z | December |
| | | ***Following Year*** | | | |
| A | January | E | May | P | September |
| B | February | I | June | R | October |
| C | March | L | July | S | November |
| D | April | O | August | T | December |

Note: These symbols may vary by information vendor.

farmer is able to grow the crop and deliver it, she will receive the agreed-upon $5.80 per bushel.

*The futures market cannot provide protection against crop failure.*

It is important to recognize that the farmer cannot eliminate the risk of a poor crop through the futures market; only price risk can be eliminated. Crop insurance may help protect against such an eventuality, but the futures market cannot.

With agricultural futures, the hedger normally goes *short* in the futures market because the farmer wants to deliver something. This is a short hedge. The farmer promises to deliver, whereas the speculator goes long (promising to pay). It is also possible for a hedger to go *long* to protect some economic interest. This is a **long hedge.** Consider the manufacturer of college class rings mentioned earlier. Should the price of gold rise dramatically after the price quotation on the rings, the manufacturer could see the entire profit eroded. This risk could be hedged by the manufacturer's going long sufficient gold contracts to guarantee a supply of gold at reasonable prices.

*In some respects, speculators sell insurance.*

**Speculators.** For the hedger to eliminate unacceptable price risk, someone must be found who is willing to assume that risk in the hedger's place. This person is the speculator.[7] The **speculator** has no economic activity requiring the use of futures contracts but finds attractive investment opportunities there and takes positions in futures in hopes of making a profit rather than protecting one. In certain respects, the speculator performs the same role that insurance companies perform when they prepare policies. The person who buys insurance is unwilling to bear the full risk of economic loss should an accident occur and consequently chooses to transfer that risk to the insurance company. The insurance company is willing to bear the risk

[7]It could also be another hedger. Depending on needs, hedges can be either short or long.

because it believes there is a profit to be made by providing this coverage in exchange for the insurance premium. One pricing theory holds that the hedger does, in fact, pay a premium for "insurance"; this will be examined later in the section on pricing principles.

As already indicated, the speculator normally goes long. As with other types of securities, it is conceptually easier for most investors to envision price rises than price declines, but speculators may also go short if they believe that the current level of prices is too high. A speculator might promise to deliver 5,000 bushels of wheat at $4 for September delivery if he feels that wheat will not sell for that much at delivery time. The speculator cannot conveniently deliver wheat, because he is not in the business of growing it; this does not matter, however, because the speculator can easily exit the market by buying a September wheat contract to cancel out the previous position. The difference in price on the two trades will be the speculator's profit or loss.

Speculators are either *position traders* or *day traders*. A **position trader** routinely maintains futures positions overnight and sometimes keeps a contract open for weeks. **Day traders** close out all of their positions before trading closes for the day, taking whatever profits or losses they have incurred.

**Scalpers.** **Scalpers** are really speculators, too, but they are important enough to warrant their own classification. These people trade for their own accounts, making a living by buying and selling contracts in the pit. Studies have shown that the most successful trades the scalper makes are those that have less than thirty seconds between the purchase and sale of the contract. Scalpers may buy and sell the same contract many times during a single trading day. The value of their accounts can change drastically on days with wide price swings.

In Figure 19-1 we saw that Hennebry bought five contracts of September Treasury bonds from ZZZ. ZZZ is also a scalper, and what she wants to do after this trade is buy five contracts at a lower price as quickly as she can. Suppose a customer telephones his broker and places a market order to sell five September Treasury bond contracts. When this order reaches the pit, the scalpers will all attempt to provide the other side of the trade at a favorable price. Suppose ZZZ is able to get this trade, and she buys the five contracts at 77 29/32. Having sold five contracts earlier at 77 31/32, this is a gain of 2/32 on each of five contracts, so the total profit she just made is

$$\frac{2}{32}\% \times \frac{\$100{,}000}{\text{Contract}} \times 5 \text{ contracts} = \$312.50$$

Three hundred dollars for a minute's work is not bad!

Scalpers are also called **locals,** meaning that they are "part of the neighborhood," people with whom it is desirable to maintain good relations. It is important to recognize that the scalpers play a crucial role in the economic functioning of the futures markets. Their active trading with one another helps keep prices continuous and accurate, which is the hallmark of the U.S. financial system. The futures market would be much less liquid without the scalpers.

## The Clearing Process

Integrity, honesty, and accuracy are crucial features of a viable trading system. Each day at the Chicago Board of Trade, more than 600,000 futures contracts change hands, with a total dollar value in the billions. Large sums of money are made and lost each minute in the trading pits; it is imperative that a mechanism be in place to ensure that the promises made are, in fact, kept, even when large transfers of money occur. Making sure promises are kept is one role of the clearing process.

All traders in the pit prepare trading cards on their transactions. The clearing process begins when attempts are made to match up the cards describing a particular trade. In Figure 19-1, we saw Hennebry's trade of five September U.S. Treasury bond contracts at 77 31/32 with seller ZZZ of Firm 000. Somewhere in the system there should also be a card from ZZZ showing a sale to Hennebry with similar terms. When these two cards are matched, a futures contract exists. In addition to matching trades, the clearing process performs other functions: supervising the accounting for performance bonds, handling intramarket settlements, establishing settlement prices, and providing for delivery. The following sections will examine each of these functions in greater detail.

## Matching Trades

All traders on the floor are responsible for ensuring that their decks are promptly entered into the clearing process. Every trade must be cleared through a member firm of the Board of Trade Clearing Corporation. Scalpers make arrangements with a member firm to process their decks after trading each day. A scalper normally uses only one clearinghouse, and the name of this organization is displayed on her trading jacket. This name is the firm name that is entered on trading cards filled out by parties to the scalper's trades.

Brokers are people in the pits who are members of the exchange trading for their own accounts and whatever public accounts they choose to accept. They can also be hired by brokerage houses such as Merrill Lynch to handle the firm's transactions on the exchange floor. These people also fill out trading cards, but they often submit them periodically during the course of trading rather than turning in their decks at the end of the day. A visitor to the exchange is usually amazed by the accuracy with which people in the pit can sail the heavy cardboard trading cards across the room to their firms' trading desks. This is a distance of 10 yards or more, and desk reporters can usually catch the cards without leaving their posts. This practice is against exchange rules, but it happens on busy days.

While the clearing corporation is associated with the Board of Trade, it is an independent organization with its own officers and rules. Some members of the Board of Trade are also members of the clearing corporation. These people can clear their own trades and, for a fee, sometimes clear trades for nonmembers. Scalpers might pay $1.50 per trade to a member firm for clearing their trades. All trades must go through the clearing process.

After a clearing corporation receives a member's trading cards, the information on them is edited and checked by computer. Cards with missing information are returned to the clearing member for correction. Once all cards have been edited, the computer attempts to match cards for all trades that occurred on the exchange that day.

*Unmatched trades are called outtrades and must be resolved by the parties involved.*

Sometimes it is not possible to match all trades exactly. These mismatches are **outtrades** and result in an Unmatched Trade Notice being sent to each of the clearing corporation members. It is the responsibility of the traders themselves to sort out their outtrades and arrive at a solution to the mismatches. A price out—where the two traders wrote down different prices for a given trade—sometimes occurs when one person writes down a price that is away from the market or far from the current trading range. For instance, soybeans might be trading between $5.97 and $6.01 during time block C on a given day. Writing a price of $5.01 rather than $6.01 would result in an outtrade that is easily reconciled by the two participants to the trade. Where the error is not obvious, such as a price of $5.97 1/4 and a potential match with a price of $5.97 1/2, the two traders often compromise by splitting the difference. It is possible that neither of them can remember the precise instant when that particular trade occurred.

Another mismatch is the *house out*, where the trading card lists an incorrect member firm. This is normally easy to rectify, since there will likely be two trades that do match except for the clearing firm identification. A *quantity out* occurs when the number of contracts in a particular trade is in dispute. A trader may think he bought eight contracts, whereas the seller sold eighteen. *Strike outs* and *time outs* occur primarily with futures options, when errors occur with either the striking price or the delivery month. The worst of all outtrades is the *sides out*, when both cards indicate the same side of the market (that is, both indicate buy or both indicate sell). These are difficult to reconcile and do not happen very often.

Regardless of the reason for the Unmatched Trade Notice, it is the trader's individual responsibility to resolve the error. On the rare occasions when this cannot be done, the dispute may be taken to arbitration with the clearing corporation.

At the Chicago Board of Trade, outtrades account for 1 or 2 percent of daily volume. Although this number is small, the impact of outtrades can be substantial. It is estimated that floor brokers lose between 10 and 17 percent of gross billings to outtrades.

A preliminary computer run is completed by 5 P.M. each trading day. The clearinghouse distributes a listing of unmatched trades to each firm, with apparent outtrades, from this preliminary run. Many entries on the listing are simply clerical errors. Firms have until 8 P.M. to make corrections. Large firms, which clear for many scalpers, sometimes have preliminary run listings several inches thick. Trade checkers attempt to resolve mismatches by checking order cards and calling clearing clerks in other firms. Any mistakes discovered are submitted to the clearinghouse, and another computer run then occurs. According to the market report department at the Chicago Board of Trade, about 90 percent of all outtrades are cleared by the second computer run. The remainder must be cleared the following morning by the individual traders involved before they begin trading for the day. Price disputes are frequently settled by simply splitting the difference.

The exchanges employ outtrade clerks to assist in the process of reconciling trades. This is a stressful job, since outtrades are no fun, and the parties involved are not always in the best of moods. These people wear green jackets at the Chicago Mercantile Exchange and are well paid.

Once all outtrades have been resolved, the computer prints a daily trade register showing a complete record of each clearing member's trades for the day. Within this register are subsidiary accounts for each customer clearing through the firm. These accounts show all positions in each commodity and delivery month, much like other types of brokerage statements.

### Accounting Supervision

The performance bonds deposited by the member firms remain with the clearing corporation until the member closes out her positions either by making an offsetting trade or by delivery of the commodity. When successful delivery occurs, good faith deposits are returned to both parties, payment for the commodity is received from the buyer and remitted to the seller, and the warehouse receipt for the goods is delivered to the buyer.

On a daily basis, the accounting problem is formidable even when no deliveries occur. Unlike most other types of investment accounts, futures contracts are **marked to market** every day, meaning that funds are transferred from one account to another on the basis of unrealized (or paper) gains and losses. For instance, if the initial deposit in a member's account is $2,000 on a purchase of a soybean contract at $6.00 per bushel, a decline in the price of the soybeans to $5.99 would result in a $50 paper loss, and the member's account would show only $1,950 remaining from the $2,000 deposit. At the end of each trading day, the clearing corporation makes these transfers and prepares a summary of positions and cash in the account for each member.

**Open interest** is a measure of how many futures contracts in a given commodity exist at a particular time.[8] There is no set number of option or futures contracts. Someone who writes an option creates a new contract. Similarly, someone who decides to go short a futures contract has created a new contract. The number of futures promises can increase or decrease every day, depending on the relative proportion of opening and closing transactions.

Open interest increases by one every time two opening transactions are matched, and it decreases by one every time two closing transactions are matched. If a trade involves a closing transaction by one participant and an opening transaction by the other, open interest will not change: The number of promises remains unchanged, although the players may change. This is a consequence of the fungibility of futures contracts. If trader A owes $10 to trader B, and trader B owes $10 to trader C, then trader B does not need to be in the picture; the clearing corporation can close out trader B and instruct trader A to pay trader C.

The clearinghouse maintains information about open interest and publishes it in the financial pages on a daily basis. Large open interest figures are desirable to ensure a competitive market.

Open interest is not the same as trading volume. A single futures contract might be traded many times during its life. A bank that hedges interest rate risk by buying Treasury bond futures might keep this position for several months. The speculators who take the other side of this trade, however, might exchange their half of the promise a hundred times before the delivery date.

### *Intramarket Settlement*

On rare occasions, commodity prices move so much in a single day that good faith deposits for many members are seriously eroded even before the day ends. When deemed necessary, the president of the clearing corporation may call on a member to deposit more funds into his account during the day. This is a **market variation call,** and these funds must be deposited within one hour from the time the call is issued. This procedure also helps ensure the integrity of commodity futures contracts.

### *Settlement Prices*

When the bell rings, signaling the end of the trading day in the commodity pits, it is difficult to tell precisely what the last trade was. Because all commodity accounts are marked to market at the close of each day, it is essential that a price be established so that funds can be transferred among accounts. The **settlement price** is analogous to the closing price on the stock exchanges, and this is the figure that will appear in the next morning's financial pages. Procedures vary slightly from commodity to commodity, but the settlement price is normally an average of the high and low prices during the last minute or so of trading. Establishment of the official settlement price is another of the clearing corporation's functions.

---

[8]This same concept exists with put and call options.

*The prices of some futures contracts are constrained by daily price limit restrictions.*

Unlike the prices established on most exchanges, many commodity futures prices are constrained by a **daily price limit.** This means that the price of a contract is not allowed to move by more than a predetermined amount each trading day. For instance, if the daily price limit for soybeans is 30 cents, today's settlement price cannot be more than 30 cents higher or 30 cents lower than yesterday's settlement price. Commodities are said to be *up the limit* or *down the limit* when a big move like this occurs. Trading will simply stop for the day once a limit move has occurred. It may take several days for prices to work their way to a new equilibrium price.

### Delivery

Although the clearing corporation interposes itself between every buyer and seller, it never actually takes or makes delivery of any commodity. However, it does provide the framework that ensures accurate delivery. Let us look at the delivery procedure for a grain contract at the Chicago Board of Trade.

A seller who decides to deliver the commodity promised fills out a Notice of Intention to Deliver with the clearing corporation. This indicates the intention of delivering the commodity on the next business day. Delivery can occur any time during the delivery month, and the first business day prior to the first day of the delivery month is called *first notice day*.

On the day prior to first notice day, all members with long positions in their accounts must submit a Long Position Report to the Clearing Corporation. This document indicates all members' long positions and their dates of purchase. This document must also be updated each day during the delivery month. The date when this report is required is known as *position day*. On the next day, *intention day*, the clearing corporation may assign delivery to the member with the oldest long position in the particular commodity. The price of the delivered commodity is adjusted for quality differentials and any other associated costs, such as temporary storage or transportation.

As a rule, speculators and their brokers do not like to handle deliveries. Delivery can occur any time in the delivery month, and consequently speculators tend to move out of the market a few days prior to first notice day. Delivery procedures vary somewhat among the exchanges and are quite different with financial futures.[9]

## Principles of Futures Contract Pricing

*Check out the contract specifications for almost every futures contract traded in the world at* http://www.gammafutures.com/news/specframe.htm

In considering what makes a futures contract valuable and what makes the price of the contract fluctuate from day to day, it is important to remember that a futures contract is a promise to exchange certain goods at a future date. You must keep your part of the promise unless you get someone to take the promise off your hands (that is, you make a closing transaction). The promised goods are valuable now, and their value in the future may be more or less than their current worth. Prices of commodities change for many reasons, such as new weather forecasts, the availability of substitute commodities, psychological factors, and changes in storage or insurance costs. These factors all involve shifts in demand for a commodity, changes in the supply of the commodity, or both.

General principles of futures pricing are included in this chapter. Chapters 20 and 21 give specific examples of pricing with stock index and interest rate futures.

[9]At the Chicago Mercantile Exchange, for instance, both buyers and sellers of its Treasury bill contract may initiate delivery, and delivery must occur on a single, predetermined day of the delivery month.

MEMO

## Managed Futures*

The term **managed futures** refers to investment management in which futures contracts are used as an asset class, especially for their profit potential rather than for their risk-reduction benefits. Money managers who deal in futures are formally called **commodities trading advisors,** or CTAs.

There is some evidence that futures as a group have low or even negative return correlation with stock and bond markets. If this is the case, it makes them excellent portfolio components. The managed futures industry got a significant shot in the arm in 1983 when a Harvard professor, John Lintner, reported on his research showing that futures have an important role to play in investment management. At the 1983 Annual Conference of the Financial Analysts Federation in Toronto, Canada, Professor Lintner presented a paper entitled "The Potential Role of Managed Commodity-Financial Futures Accounts (and/or Funds) in Portfolios of Stocks and Bonds."

The paper reported that "the improvements from holding an efficiently-selected portfolio of managed accounts or funds are so large—and the correlation between returns on the futures portfolios and those on the stock and bond portfolio are so surprisingly low (sometimes even negative)—that the return/risk tradeoffs provided by augmented portfolios . . . clearly dominate the tradeoffs available from portfolios of stocks alone or from portfolios of stocks and bonds."

In early 2005 about $40 billion was invested in managed futures accounts. As with investment managers in any asset class, the performance of the CTAs varies. Some have lost most of their capital, while others have made their clients very happy. For many large institutional investors, especially endowments and foundations, managed futures have become an important part of the portfolio.

*This material comes from the author's book *Derivatives: An Introduction*, Cincinnati, Ohio: South-Western, 2002, p. 391.

Three main theories of futures pricing exist: (1) the expectations hypothesis, (2) normal backwardation, and (3) a full carrying charge market. These are discussed in the following sections.

### *Expectations Hypothesis*

Remember Senator Washburn's comments about "fictitious" contracts? The contracts are, in fact, very real, with brokerage houses and the clearinghouse to enforce compliance with their terms. Because a futures contract calls for delivery of a specified good in the future, it seems likely that one of the major determinants of the futures contract's value is the current value of the commodity in the cash market. This is exactly what we find.

One of the most simple generalizations we can make about this relationship is the **expectations hypothesis.** This states that the futures price for a commodity is what the marketplace expects the cash price to be when the delivery month arrives. If September soybeans are selling in the futures market for $5 per bushel, this means that $5 is what the marketplace expects soybeans to sell for in September. There is evidence that the expectations hypothesis is a reasonably accurate description of the way things happen. This is a very important fact for the user of the futures market, because it provides an important source of information about what the future is likely to bring. If I want to know what people expect the price of heating oil to be this fall, I can look in *The Wall Street Journal* for the price of a heating oil futures contract and know that this figure is a reliable estimate based on current information. (Of course, the price for the retail customer would be somewhat higher than the price that a wholesale distributor would pay.)

The information provided through futures prices is so important that one of the major functions of the futures market is normally listed as **price discovery.** Price discovery is a function of the futures market that indicates the market's consensus about likely future prices for a commodity. Nowhere in finance do people like uncertainty; wherever possible, people seek to resolve the unknown. The futures market serves a useful role when people ponder the price of important commodities at a future date. You may be interested in knowing what the market thinks the price of gold or Euros will be a year from now. According to the expectations hypothesis, the best place to look for an estimate is in the financial pages. Simply look at what a futures contract with a delivery month one year hence settled at yesterday.

### Normal Backwardation

Remember that investors do not like risk, and that they will take a risk only if they think they will be properly rewarded for bearing the risk. If the futures price is what people think the cash price will be at delivery time, why would anyone be interested in speculating? It seems that the hedger can get rid of the price risk without any cost and that the speculator agrees to take the risk off the hedger's back for nothing. This seems improbable in real life.

The concept of **normal backwardation** is attributed to economist John Maynard Keynes. Like much of good economics, the idea is simple and very logical. A hedger who uses the futures market is essentially buying insurance. Price risk is eliminated by locking in a future price that is acceptable. When people obtain insurance, they pay for it because the insurance company could not remain in business if it offered this protection at no cost. Keynes argues that this means the futures price must be a downward-biased estimate of the future cash price. In other words, the cash price prevailing at delivery time will actually be somewhat higher than the price predicted by the futures market. This is so because the speculator must be rewarded for taking the risk that the hedger was unwilling to bear. The hedger might really believe that the cash price of soybeans in September will be about $5.04 but also might be perfectly willing to take $5.00 per bushel for certain. Even though the hedger is taking a bit less than she thinks the beans will sell for, the hedger is uncomfortable taking the risk that the soybean market might collapse to $4.75 or less. The hedger can live with the peace of mind that $5.00 per bushel brings.

The speculator, in contrast, has access to the same information as the hedger and might agree that $5.04 is a good estimate for the cash price of beans in September. Remember that one contract of soybeans is 5,000 bushels, so if the speculator can promise to pay $5.00 per bushel and turn around and sell them for $5.04, this is a $200 gain. The high leverage associated with futures contracts can make this an impressive rate of return when annualized. However, prices could take a dive and result in big losses for the speculator (but not for the farmer, because his risk was transferred away).

The concept of normal backwardation does not really mean that the expectations hypothesis is wrong. Keynes agrees that the futures market provides useful information about the future. With the logic of normal backwardation, though, we may be able to fine-tune our estimate of future cash market prices.

### Full Carrying Charge Market

A **full carrying charge market** is one where the prices for successive delivery months reflect the cost of holding the commodity or financial instrument. Commodities can be bought in the cash market and stored for later consumption. As we have seen, the person who performs the storage function gets a fee for this service. It is necessary to keep grains dry, to protect them against fire, to keep the rat population to a minimum, and to provide insurance on the stored commodities. Insurance is necessary to protect against loss of the goods because of tornado damage, floods, fire, and even explosions. Every few years we read of spectacular blowups of a grain elevator. The dust and fine seed particles that can get suspended in the air will ignite with a vengeance under certain circumstances.

We can say that in a world of certainty, the futures price ($FP$) is equal to the current cash price ($CP$) plus the carrying charges ($c$) until the delivery month: $FP = CP + c$. All participants in the futures market are very concerned with the concept of *basis*. **Basis** is the difference between the futures price of a commodity and the current cash price. Normally, the futures price exceeds the cash price; this is a **contango market.** If the futures price is less than the cash price, we have an **inverted market.** As the gap between the futures price and the cash price narrows, we say that the basis has strengthened; the basis weakens if the gap gets wider.

*Basis is the difference between the futures price and the cash price.*

Although we do not live in a world of certainty, the difference between a futures price and the cash price is very often quite close to the carrying costs between the two points in time. Such a market has important implications for the speculator. Suppose that in early September it costs 2 1/2 cents per bushel per month to store soybeans, and current prices are as follows: cash price for soybeans = \$4.85; futures price in November = \$4.90, in January = \$4.95, and in March = \$5.00. A speculator might be trying to decide between the January and March delivery months. Speculators who want to go long (thinking that soybean prices will increase) should buy the near delivery month (January). Those who want to go short (anticipating a downturn in prices) should sell the far delivery month (March). The reason for this can be readily seen.

Arbitrage exists if someone can buy a commodity, store it at a known rate, and get someone to promise to buy it later at a price that exceeds the cost of storage. In a full carrying charge market like the one in this example, the basis must either stay the same or strengthen; it cannot weaken because that would produce an arbitrage situation. In other words, the difference between a January and a March contract could become less than 5 cents, but it should never be more.[10] If it were more, you could buy January, sell March, take delivery in January, pay a nickel storage for two months, deliver the beans in March, and be ahead without having taken any risk.[11]

Although there is never certainty in any investment, speculators who buy the near contract can be very confident of one of two things. If they are right and the price of soybeans does go up, then January soybeans should rise by at least as much as March soybeans. If they are wrong and soybean prices fall, then January soybeans should fall no more than March soybeans. In either case, speculators are better off buying the near delivery month.

---

[10]This assumes that monthly storage costs remain constant.

[11]This example also assumes that the arbitrageur can deliver the soybeans in the grade required.

The logic holds in reverse for speculators who are bearish. They want to go short the far contract because it will either fall in value more or rise in value less than the near delivery month.[12]

### *Reconciling the Three Theories*

The three theories of futures pricing are actually quite compatible. The differences in them are somewhat like the fable of the chicken and the egg: It may not be easy to decide which comes first. The expectations hypothesis says that a futures price is simply the expected cash price at the delivery date of the futures contract. People know about storage costs and other costs of carry (insurance, interest, and so on), and we would not expect these costs to surprise the market when they are incurred. It therefore seems logical that people would expect these costs to determine the futures price in part.

The essence of normal backwardation is that the hedger is willing to take a bit less than the actual expected future cash price for the peace of mind that comes with insurance. Given that the hedger is obtaining price insurance with futures, it is logical that there be some cost to the insurance. The hedger perhaps expects a higher price but is willing to accept a lower price to reduce risk.

## Foreign Currency Futures

If you understand the basic principles of hedging and speculating, you will have no trouble applying those concepts to futures contracts on foreign currencies.

### *Hedging and Speculating with Foreign Currency Futures*

We have seen that with the appropriate hedging strategy, farmers can reduce price risk. In the world of international business, another significant risk is foreign exchange risk, or the risk of loss due to shifting relative values in national currencies. The next two chapters will discuss how the futures market enables a portfolio manager to minimize market risk and how bankers can reduce the interest rate risk they face. The major players in the foreign exchange market are people representing commercial interests, such as major retailing firms, international banks, and multinational businesses. Locals have a smaller role in the foreign currency markets.

When business transactions occur between two countries, the goods or services traded must be valued in some currency. A U.S. importing firm, for instance, might agree to buy a large shipment of wood carvings, clocks, and candles from a German manufacturer. Suppose the total cost of the items is €20 million, handshakes occur on June 1, and the German firm promises to deliver the goods in early September. Payment is to be made upon delivery.

Before the U.S. importer accepted the €20 million price, it checked the relative value of the U.S. dollar and the Euro to make sure the Euro price translated into an acceptable U.S. dollar price. Presumably it did, or the transaction would not have occurred.

Although the cost of the goods is fixed in Euros, the price that counts is the U.S. dollar price, and this will almost certainly change before payment occurs. The world political situation, changes in international interest rates, and inflationary fears all

[12]This relationship is less obvious with financial futures. The interest rate yield curve is seldom flat, and this means that the average cost of carry varies according to the time span covered. The shape of the yield curve can change in such a fashion that the strategy just described was, in fact, not the best when viewed after the fact.

contribute to daily fluctuation in relative exchange rates worldwide. From the U.S. importer's perspective, two transactions must occur to complete this sale. First, it is necessary to buy the Euros; second, it is necessary to pay for the imported goods. The price of the second transaction is fixed in the sales agreement; the price of the Euros will change over time.

Fortunately, this foreign exchange risk can be hedged away in the futures market. Table 19-2 shows a set of sample Euro futures prices. The U.S. importer needs to acquire Euros, so it is necessary to buy futures contracts. Payment will be made in September, so the September futures contract is the one to use. The newspaper indicates that yesterday's price of Euros for September delivery was about $1.35 cents per Euro. There are €125,000 in one contract. Because the importer needs to hedge €20 million, it needs exactly 160 contracts. The importer would go long 160 contracts.

Once September arrives, the hedger (the importer) can do one of two things. It needs the Euros, so one approach would be simply to sit back and wait for delivery to occur. When it received the Euros, it could then transfer them to the German manufacturer. Or the importer could trade out of the contracts by selling them before receiving a delivery notice.

If the Euros appreciated from June to September (that is, their cost increased), the hedger would have a gain in the futures market that offsets the higher cost of the Euros in the cash market. In contrast, if the Euros depreciated, the lower cost in the cash market would be offset by a loss in the futures market. As in any hedging application, the hedge serves as insurance against some specific type of risk. The fact that the importer did not need the insurance (the Euros fell in value) should not be interpreted to mean that hedging was a bad investment.

### Pricing of Foreign Exchange Futures Contracts

Futures prices are a function of the cash price plus a cost of carrying the particular asset or financial instrument. With foreign currency, the cost of holding one currency rather than another is really an opportunity cost measured by differences in the interest rates prevailing in the two countries. Figure 19-2 presents a basic pricing model for foreign currency futures contracts.

**TABLE 19-2** SAMPLE EURO FUTURES PRICES

| *Month* | *High* | *Low* | *Settle* | *Change* | *Open Interest* |
|---|---|---|---|---|---|
| March | 1.3419 | 1.3480 | 1.3455 | +29 | 79304 |
| June | 1.3449 | 1.3510 | 1.3484 | +29 | 104583 |
| September | 1.3501 | 1.3553 | 1.3492 | +29 | 1596 |

€125,000 per contract; priced in $ per Euro.

**FIGURE 19-2**

Foreign Exchange Futures Pricing

$$P_f = \text{spot rate} \times \left[1 + (I_{ed} - I_k) \times \frac{\text{days to delivery}}{365}\right]$$

where $P_f$ = futures price

$I_{ed}$ = Eurodollar rate

$I_k$ = local currency rate

Note: A 360-day year is used to calculate Euro, Japanese yen, and Swiss franc rates.

The local currency rate is the risk-free interest rate prevailing in the country of concern. Suppose that in the land of Leptonia, interest rates are 10.00 percent, and the current dollar price of a lepton is \$0.4817. Also suppose that the current Eurodollar deposit rate is 7.50 percent.[13] For how much should a 90-day futures contract sell? Using the formula in Figure 19-2, we find that the equilibrium price is

$$0.4817 \times \left[1 + (0.075 - 0.100) \times \frac{90}{365}\right] = 0.4787$$

This means that the futures price for leptons should be less than their cost in the spot market.

The market prices foreign exchange futures this way because of the theory of *interest rate parity*. This states that securities with similar risk and maturity should differ in price by an amount equal to (but opposite in sign from) the difference between national interest rates in the two countries. In this example, Leptonia's interest rate is 2.5 percent (on an annual basis) higher than the U.S. rate. For ninety days, or one-fourth of a year, Leptonia's rates are 0.625 percent higher. Therefore, leptons for delivery in ninety days should sell at a 0.625 percent discount from their spot value, and this is exactly what we find.

Foreign exchange futures contracts all call for delivery of the foreign currency in the country of issuance to a bank of the clearinghouse's choosing. Let us look at one more example. Suppose that I sell a Country X foreign currency futures contract to someone residing in Country X. By selling a contract as an opening transaction, I have promised to deliver a certain quantity of foreign currency. Assume that the contract calls for delivery in six months, and that the interest rates in my country are higher than the interest rates in Country X. I can invest the currency until I must deliver it. Similarly, the buyer of the futures contract can invest the funds that will be used to pay for the foreign exchange. Because my interest rates are relatively higher than those of the Country X resident, I have an advantage: I will earn more interest. This differential is reflected in compensation to the Country X futures contract buyer via a discounted futures contract price. Any futures price is a function of the cash price and the carrying costs associated with holding the commodity or financial instrument.

## SUMMARY

Futures contracts are promises to buy or deliver a certain quantity of a carefully defined commodity by a certain date. Futures contracts enable farmers, bankers, or anyone else with economic interests in a particular commodity to hedge price risk. The futures market, however, cannot provide protection against crop failure or against making bad investments. To ensure the integrity of the contract, all trades are actually sales to or purchases from the clearing corporation. Both hedgers and speculators post good faith deposits to show their capacity to sustain any losses that might accrue to them.

Three main theories of futures pricing exist: the expectations hypothesis, the concept of normal backwardation, and the concept of a full carrying charge market. Rather than being competing philosophies, these three theories are different

[13]A Eurodollar is a U.S. dollar on deposit outside the United States. These are not subject to Federal Reserve Board reserve requirements, are more valuable to lenders, and consequently carry slightly higher interest rates than domestic time deposits.

perspectives on the fundamental result that futures prices are primarily determined by today's cash price, by expectations about how the cash price is likely to change in the future, and by the cost of storing and transporting commodities.

Foreign exchange futures are used to reduce foreign exchange risk or the risk of loss due to shifting relative values in national currencies. These contracts are priced according to the theory of interest rate parity, which is really just another version of the cost-of-carry pricing model shown in Figure 19-2.

## QUESTIONS

1. How is it possible for the trading volume in a particular futures contract to exceed the open interest in that commodity?
2. Why is a delivery mechanism essential to a well-functioning futures market?
3. Do you think that daily price limits make sense?
4. Under current rules, hedgers must post a smaller good faith deposit than speculators. Do you feel this is a reasonable rule?
5. Explain how it is possible for a hedger to benefit from a narrowing basis in a particular commodity.
6. Explain how yesterday's volume for a futures contract could have been 20,000 contracts, yet open interest rose by only 1,484 contracts.
7. Closing all futures exchanges would probably be inflationary because of the added risk the producers would have to bear. Do you agree?
8. Suppose you were on a commission that was evaluating several proposals for new futures contracts. What would you want to know before you could make a decision on whether or not the proposals should be approved?
9. Do you think it would be possible for futures contracts to trade via the specialist system rather than the marketmaker system? Why or why not?
10. Commodities whose prices are particularly volatile lend themselves to futures trading. Lettuce is usually considered to be the grocery store commodity whose price is most uncertain. One day it is 47 cents a head, and the next day it is 99 cents. Some people argue that futures contracts would never work for perishable commodities like lettuce. Do you agree?
11. A farmer anticipates having 50,000 bushels of wheat ready for harvest in September. What would be the implications of hedging by doing the following?
    a. Selling eight contracts of September wheat.
    b. Selling ten contracts of September wheat.
    c. Selling twelve contracts of September wheat.
12. Give examples of someone who might profitably use a long hedge in the following:
    a. Corn.
    b. Gold.
    c. Soybeans.
13. Briefly explain why prices for futures contracts on grains are generally higher for more distant delivery months.
14. How might someone use foreign exchange futures in a short hedge?
15. Suppose you are a speculator in yen futures, and you are currently long three contracts. You hear a rumor about interest rates rising in Japan. Is this good news for you?

## PROBLEMS

1. Suppose two weeks ago a speculator purchased four contracts of September soybeans at $6.30 1/2. The price today is $6.32 per bushel. What is the person's gain or loss?
2. A farmer anticipates harvesting 50,000 bushels of wheat in September. How much money would the farmer receive from hedging by selling eight contracts of September wheat at a settlement price of $6.32 per bushel (a) today and (b) at delivery?
3. Refer to a current issue of *The Wall Street Journal*. According to the expectations hypothesis, what is the best estimate for the wholesale price of heating oil next December?
4. A U.S. importer anticipates a need for €8 million in several months. How many futures contracts would this person need to buy or sell to hedge this requirement completely?
5. Refer to the example on the land of Leptonia interest rates in the chapter. Suppose Leptonia's interest rates rise to a 3.0 percent premium over the U.S. rate. What should the new exchange rate be?
6. Refer to Table 19-2. A speculator previously bought three March Euro contracts at 0.5600. If these were sold at the settlement price shown in the table, what would be the profit or loss?
7. A hedger goes short eight Euro futures contracts at a price of 0.5622; at the same time, the spot $/€ rate is 0.5599. A month later the futures contracts are satisfied by delivery of the Euros, and the spot rate is 0.5610. Show this person's gain or loss (including opportunity loss) in both the futures and spot markets, along with the net gain or loss in the two positions combined.

## INTERNET EXERCISE

Retrieve the latest Australian dollar futures prices from *http://futures.tradingcharts.com/castletrading/chart/AD*. Do the prices across maturities exhibit backwardation or contango?

## FURTHER READING

Black, Fischer. "The Pricing of Commodity Contracts." *Journal of Financial Economics*, January/March 1976, 167–179.

Carlton, D. "Futures Markets: Their Purpose, Their History, Their Successes and Failures." *Journal of Futures Markets*, Fall 1984, 237–271.

Chicago Board of Trade. *Commodity Trading Manual*. Chicago: Chicago Board of Trade, 1999.

Edwards, Franklin R. "The Clearing Association in Futures Markets: Guarantor and Regulator." *Journal of Futures Markets*, Fall 1984, 369–392.

Hilley, J., C. Beidleman, and J. Greenleaf. "Does Covered Interest Arbitrage Dominate in Foreign Exchange Markets?" *Columbia Journal of World Business*, Winter 1979, 99–107.

Kamara, A. "The Behavior of Futures Prices: A Review of Theory and Evidence." *Financial Analysts Journal*, July/August 1984, 68–75.

Kolb, Robert. *Futures, Options, and Swaps*, 4th ed. Maldon, MA: Blackwell Publishers, 2002.

Raynaud, J., and J. Tessier. "Risk Premiums in Futures Markets: An Empirical Investigation." *Journal of Futures Markets*, Summer 1984, 189–211.

Rockwell, Charles. "Normal Backwardation, Forecasting, and the Returns to Commodity Futures Traders." *Food Research Institute Studies*, supplement 7, 1967, 107–130.

Seidel, Andrew D., and Philip M. Ginsberg. *Commodities Trading*. Englewood Cliffs, N.J.: Prentice-Hall, 1983.

Silber, W. "Marketmaker Behavior in an Auction Market: An Analysis of Scalpers in Futures Markets." *Journal of Finance*, September 1984, 937–953.

Tamarkin, Bob. *The New Gatsbys*. New York: Quill NY, 1985.

Teweles, Richard, Charles Harlow, and Herbert Stone. *The Commodity Futures Game: Who Wins? Who Loses? Why?* New York: McGraw-Hill, 1977.

Working, Holbrook. "The Theory of Price of Storage." *American Economic Review*, December 1949, 1262.

# 20 Benching the Equity Players

*Don't be discouraged by a failure. It can be a positive experience. Failure is, in a sense, the highway to success, inasmuch as every discovery of what is false leads us to seek earnestly after what is true, and every fresh experience points out some form of error which we shall afterwards carefully avoid.*

**John Keats**

## Key Terms

basis
basis convergence
delta
dynamic hedging
hedge ratio
position delta
protective put

## Introduction

Portfolio protection is a relatively new concept in portfolio management and is getting more press and more converts in the marketplace. The basic idea involves adding components to a portfolio in order to establish a floor value for the portfolio below which it should not fall. Three popular techniques to do so are using equity or stock index put options, futures contracts, or dynamic hedging.

## Using Options

Options enable the portfolio manager to adjust the characteristics of a portfolio without disrupting it. This can be done with brute force—by using options in a 1-to-1 ratio with stock holdings—but there is a better method. This, however, requires an understanding of the basics of option pricing. Portfolio protection aside, knowledge in this specialized area substantially improves the portfolio manager's professional competence. In some firms, fluency in the fundamentals of option pricing is essential for anyone anticipating a career in portfolio management. The first part of this chapter reviews key aspects of this topic.

## *Equity Options with a Single Security*

**Importance of Delta.** A group of sophisticated users of stock options would find communication substantially impaired if they could not refer to *delta*. The importance of this concept in the sophisticated use of options is hard to overstate.

*Delta enables us to determine the number of options necessary to mimic the returns of the underlying security.*

**Delta** is a measure of the sensitivity of the price of an option to changes in the price of the underlying asset. Mathematically, delta is the partial derivative of the option premium with respect to the stock price:

$$\text{Delta} = \Delta = \frac{\partial P}{\partial S}$$

where $P$ = option premium and $S$ = stock price. For the person using options to hedge a portfolio, delta is useful in allowing us to determine how many options are needed to mimic the returns of the underlying security.

Delta equals $N(d_1)$ in the Black-Scholes Option Pricing Model. Suppose an option has a delta of 0.836. This means that a $1.00 movement in the stock price will result in an $0.84 approximate change in the option premium. The absolute value of delta is always between 0 and 1; call deltas are positive, put deltas are negative.[1]

**Protective Puts.** Someone who owns shares of stock has a long position in the security. In the investment business, the term *long* simply means that a person owns something; it has nothing to do with a time span.

*A protective put is not a special kind of option; it is the simultaneous holding of a long stock position and a put option on that stock.*

Situations occasionally arise in which investors anticipate a decline in the value of some of their investments but do not want to sell them because of tax considerations or other reasons. These investors might consider using *protective puts*.[2] A **protective put** is not a special kind of put option; it is a descriptive term given to a long stock position combined with a long put position. If someone owns shares of a particular stock and buys a put on that same stock (regardless of striking price or expiration), the put is a protective put.

**Protective Put Profit and Loss Diagram.** The option premiums from Table 20-1 are used in the examples that follow. Suppose, for instance, that a person buys one

**TABLE 20-1** HYPOTHETICAL OPTION PREMIUMS FOR ZZX CORPORATION

| *Striking Price* | *Calls* | | | *Puts* | | |
|---|---|---|---|---|---|---|
| | *Jun* | *Jul* | *Sep* | *Jun* | *Jul* | *Sep* |
| 40 | 10.25 | 10.50 | 11.25 | 0.06 | 0.13 | 0.25 |
| 45 | 5.50 | 6.13 | 7.13 | 0.13 | 0.50 | 1 |
| 50 | 1.13 | 2.75 | 4 | 1.50 | 2.13 | 2.75 |
| 55 | 0.38 | 0.88 | 2 | 5 | 5.25 | 5.63 |

Current ZZX stock price = $50.

[1]For options that are substantially in- or out-of-the-money, delta is also approximately equal to the probability that an option will be in the money at expiration. For some research on this question, see the Strong and Dickinson article from the *Financial Analysts Journal* in the Further Reading section of this chapter.

[2]The term *protective put* was probably coined by Robert C. Pozen in an article, "The Purchase of Protective Puts by Financial Institutions," *Financial Analysts Journal*, July/August 1978, 47–60.

**FIGURE 20-1**

Long Stock Position

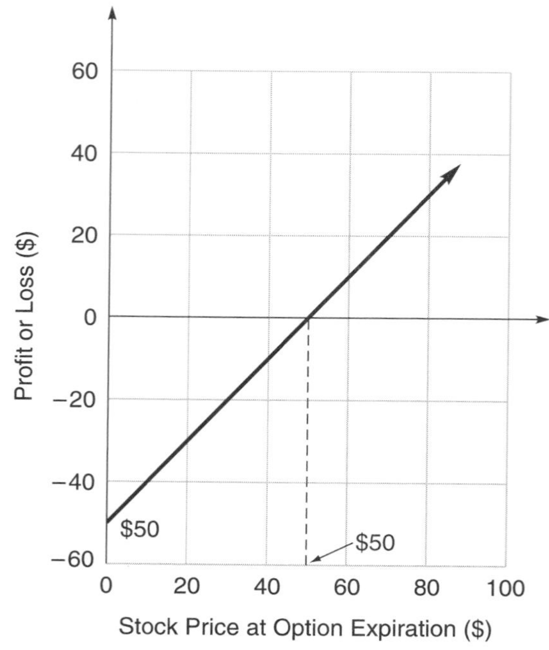


Stock purchased at $50.

share of stock in the ZZX Corporation for $50. This is a simple situation. The most that can be lost is $50, and this occurs if the stock price falls to 0. The most that can be made is unlimited because theoretically the stock price can rise infinitely. Figure 20-1 shows these results.

Figure 20-2 is a profit and loss diagram for the purchase of a ZZX put with a premium of $1 and a striking price of $45. The largest possible profit from holding this position is $44. This occurs when the stock declines to 0 because the owner of the put could sell worthless stock for $45. The $1 paid for the option is a sunk cost, however, so the net gain is $44. The most the put buyer can lose is the amount paid for the put, or $1.

*Extensive portfolio protection strategies using options are provided at* http://www.cboe.com/protection

Figure 20-3 is the combination of Figures 20-1 and 20-2; it shows the protective put with its $6 maximum possible loss and a potentially unlimited maximum gain. The $6 maximum loss comes from the fact that the stock price can decline by $5 before the "insurance policy" becomes effective (the deductible is $5 and the investor had to pay $1 to get the insurance).

Continuing with this analogy, a protective put is like the collision insurance policy on an automobile. The car is valuable, and the owner would suffer if it were damaged in an accident. To protect against this potential for loss, the owner can buy insurance, fully expecting to "lose" all the money he paid for it. He should not feel discouraged if the year goes by and he does not have an accident and gets no chances to use the insurance. The insurance also carries a deductible amount; he must personally assume the risk of loss up to the deductible amount, perhaps $250.

When you as an investor select the striking price for a protective put, you are selecting the deductible you want for your stock insurance. The more protection you

FIGURE 20-2

Long 45 Put Purchased at $1

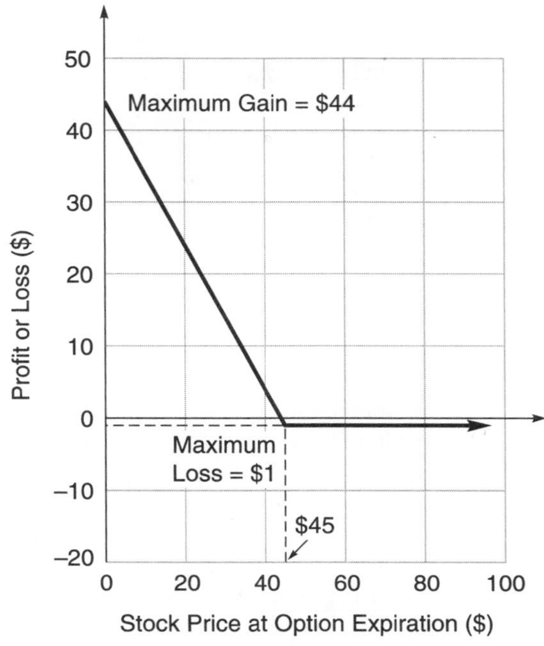


FIGURE 20-3

Protective Put

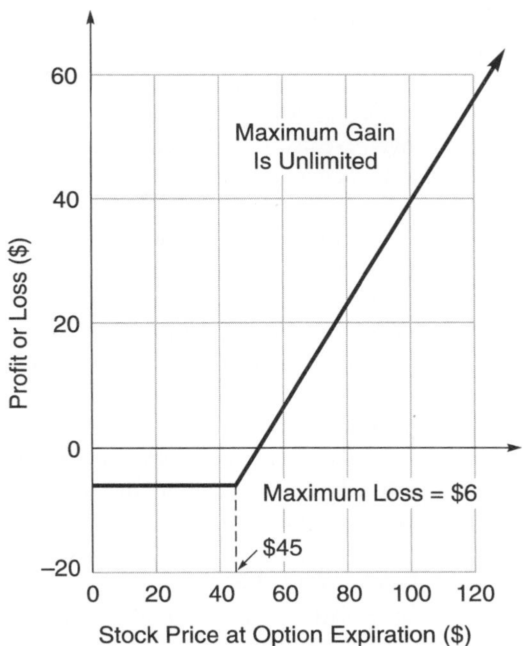


Stock bought at $50; 45 put bought at $1.

**TABLE 20-2** ANALOGIES BETWEEN AN INSURANCE POLICY AND A PROTECTIVE PUT

| *Insurance Policy* | *Put Option* |
|---|---|
| Premium | Time value |
| Value of insured property | Stock price |
| Policy face value | Option striking price |
| Deductible | Stock price minus striking price |
| Term | Time until option expiration |
| Likelihood of loss | Stock volatility |

Source: Adapted from Nicholas Hansen, "Portfolio Insurance," *Institutional Options Update*, July/August 1986.

want, the higher the premium you are going to pay. This is exactly the same as with the automobile insurance. Coverage for the first dollar of body damage has a very high premium. In contrast, an owner who is willing to assume the risk of the first $500 and buys insurance against just major damage pays a much lower insurance premium. Larger deductibles mean a lower premium, which is also true in the options market.

Returning to Table 20-1, you might decide to buy a ZZX JUN 50 put to protect your long stock position. You pay the option premium of $150 to the person who wrote the put and hope that your stock continues to rise. In other words, you fully expect to lose all the money you paid for the protective put. It may seem odd that you would ever buy a security while expecting to lose money on the investment, but remember the motivation for buying fire insurance on a home or collision insurance on a car. The situations are quite similar. Table 20-2 shows analogies between a protective put and an insurance policy.

*Writing covered calls is an imperfect form of portfolio protection because it provides only limited protection.*

**Writing Covered Calls.** Sometimes an investor is long shares of stock and suspects that the market will turn down in the next few weeks but really does not want to sell the shares at the moment. As an alternative to buying puts, she might consider using covered calls to provide some cushion against losses from a falling market. Writing covered calls is an imperfect form of portfolio protection because it provides only limited coverage. Still, it is useful to understand the risk reduction nature of covered call writing.

Return to the prices for ZZX in Table 20-1. Someone might decide to hedge against the risk of a declining market by writing a JUL 50 call for $2.75. The premium received means that no actual cash loss occurs until ZZX falls below the current price ($50) minus the premium received ($2.75), or $47.25. Of course, if the investor's feeling about the market is wrong and ZZX advances above $50, he faces the risk of the stock's being called until he makes a closing transaction to get rid of the option position.

This strategy provides some downside protection, but it is not a particularly effective hedge. In general, an individual who needs protection against falling stock prices and wants to use options is better off buying put options.

## Index Options

Table 20-3 shows sample OEX prices with the current level of the index at 327.19. As with equity options, the OEX contract is based on 100 times the option premium listed in the newspaper.

Consider the OEX OCT 315 put, listed at 3.25. One of these contracts costs 100 × $3.25, or $325.00. This is the maximum money at risk unless the option is

**TABLE 20-3** SAMPLE S&P 100 STOCK INDEX OPTION LISTING

| *Strike* | *Calls* | | | *Puts* | | |
|---|---|---|---|---|---|---|
| | *Sep* | *Oct* | *Nov* | *Sep* | *Oct* | *Nov* |
| 310 | 18 | ... | ... | 0.63 | 2.38 | 3.63 |
| 315 | 13.63 | 17.75 | ... | 1 | 3.25 | 4.13 |
| 320 | 9.25 | 14 | 16.25 | 1.75 | 4.38 | 6.38 |

Index: High 327.20 Low 326.02 Close 327.19 +0.49

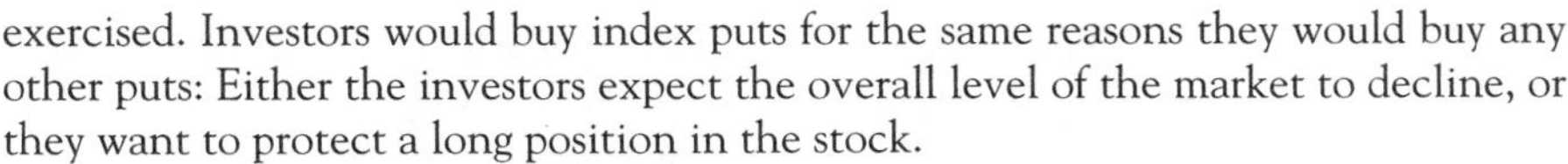

exercised. Investors would buy index puts for the same reasons they would buy any other puts: Either the investors expect the overall level of the market to decline, or they want to protect a long position in the stock.

Suppose that your motivation for buying a put is the latter: You want to protect a diversified portfolio of common stock against an anticipated market downturn. If market prices do decline, you hope to have a gain on your puts that will largely offset the losses on your stock portfolio.

*See the Options Toolbox at* www.cboe.com

Two questions quickly arise: (1) How many puts do you need to buy? (2) How do you decide which striking price to pick? In principle, you could use any of the puts, although the relative costs of using them would differ markedly. The key to determining the appropriate number of puts to buy comes from delta. Delta measures how an option price changes for a given small change in the underlying stock (or index) value, so it can be used to determine how many puts are necessary to cancel exactly any price movements in the stock.

To calculate delta, you need to know all the inputs to the Black-Scholes Option Pricing Model and solve for the $N(d_1)$ function (see Table 15-2). Deltas for puts are negative because puts increase in value as stock prices go down. Suppose that the delta for the OCT 315 put is –0.235.[3] This means that for each point (or dollar) decline in the S&P 100 index, the value of this put increases by 0.235 (or $0.235). For strict accuracy, delta must be recalculated every time the index changes.

With this information, you calculate a *hedge ratio (HR)*. The **hedge ratio** is a calculated value indicating the amount of an asset necessary to eliminate a certain type of risk with an investment position. The formula is as follows:

$$\text{HR} = \frac{\text{Portfolio value}}{\text{Contract "value"}} \times \text{Portfolio beta} \times \frac{1}{|\text{Delta}|}$$

$$(\text{Contract value} = \text{Strike price} \times 100)$$

Suppose the portfolio to be hedged has a market value of $125,000 and a beta of 1.10. The number of puts needed to hedge is then

$$\frac{\$125{,}000}{\$31{,}500} \times 1.10 \times \frac{1}{0.235} = 18.57$$

[3]In the absence of previous values for the OEX index, solving for delta in this example first requires determination of the option's implied volatility. This is the volatility estimate that causes the Black-Scholes model to predict the current price. When this estimate of the standard deviation is included in the pricing model, $N(d_1)$ will be the option delta. The Sigma file in the Strong Software on the text Website will solve for the implied volatility of a call option.

You would buy nineteen OEX OCT 315 puts to hedge this portfolio. This number should cause any decline in the value of the stock portfolio to be offset by an increase in the value of the put options.

Suppose that immediately after you buy nineteen of these puts, the market falls by 0.25 percent. This means that the OEX index drops to 326.37. The portfolio, with a beta of 1.10, should fall by (0.25 percent × 1.10) = 0.275 percent to a value of $124,656. This is a portfolio loss of $344.

Declining market prices increase the value of the puts. The new Black-Scholes price for the puts is $3.44. You purchased nineteen of these at $3.25 each, so you have a gain of 19 × 100 × ($3.44 – $3.25) = $361. The gain on the puts cancels the loss on the stock.

Note that the gain on the puts is actually a bit more than enough to cover the loss on the stock. One reason is that more puts were purchased than technically necessary because of the round-lot limitation on option contracts. In addition, delta changes as the stock price changes and as time passes; as a consequence, the hedge ratio changes, too. To maintain the portfolio protection precisely, it is necessary to monitor the hedge ratio and adjust the option position by buying or selling puts as needed (or by including other options in the portfolio).

In this example, assume that the OEX index remains at 326.37 at the end of the day. The OEX OCT 315 put delta is now –0.240, and the hedge ratio changes to

$$\frac{\$124{,}656}{\$31{,}500} \times 1.10 \times \frac{1}{0.240} = 18.1$$

To maintain the hedge, you should sell one of the nineteen puts.

When options are used for hedging applications in multimillion-dollar portfolios, the hedge ratio should be constantly monitored; many firms adjust their option holdings daily.

## Using Futures Contracts

### *Importance of Financial Futures*

The number of underlying assets on which futures contracts are available seems to grow every year. The exchanges virtually always have a proposal for a new futures contract pending regulatory approval.

Financial futures are the fastest-growing segment of the futures market. In 1972, physical commodities such as agricultural products, lumber, and metals made up more than 95 percent of all the futures volume. Today, these combined contracts amount to only about one-third of the total futures volume. The financial futures contracts are extremely important in the United States and globally.

### *Stock Index Futures Contracts*

Stock index futures contracts are similar to the traditional agricultural contracts except for the matter of delivery. The first thing to understand about an index futures contract is the nature of the underlying asset. What is it that people are promising to deliver or buy? Someone can hold a handful of soybeans or corn, but what about the Standard & Poor's 500 index? How can someone buy or sell a stock index? These are reasonable questions asked somewhere in the United States every day by banks, retirement funds, and individual investors who are learning the potential role these contracts have in their own portfolios.

## S&P 500 Stock Index Futures Contract

Standard and Poor's Corporation began publishing the S&P 500 index in 1917; it was originally intended as a standard against which portfolio managers and investment advisers might be judged. Initially, the index comprised only two hundred stocks, with expansion to five hundred in 1957. Of the five hundred companies, four hundred are industrial firms, forty are public utilities, forty are financial companies, and twenty are transportation firms. The stock of these five hundred companies adds up to about 80 percent of the total value of securities traded on the New York Stock Exchange. The S&P 500 index is currently one of the Commerce Department's leading indicators.

S&P weights the index to give greater importance to larger companies. In calculating the index, each of the five hundred share prices is multiplied by the number of outstanding shares in that particular firm. These figures are then added together and compared with an arbitrary starting value of 100.00 established during a 1941–1943 base period.

Like other futures contracts, a stock index future is a promise to buy or sell the standardized units of a specific index at a fixed price by a predetermined future date. Figure 20-4 lists the characteristics of the S&P 500 stock index futures contract.

*Stock index futures have no delivery mechanism; all closing contracts are settled in cash.*

Unlike most other commodity contracts, there is no actual delivery mechanism at expiration of the stock index futures contract. All settlements are in cash. It is not practical to have speculators or hedgers deliver five hundred different stock certificates in the appropriate quantities to satisfy the requirements of the contract. We know the value of the index at delivery time, and it is much more convenient to credit or debit accounts with accrued gains or losses.

## Hedging with Stock Index Futures

We have looked at the principles of hedging. These same rules hold true for hedging with financial futures. A hedger seeks to reduce or eliminate price risk; using the S&P 500 futures contract, a portfolio manager can attenuate the impact of a decline in the value of the portfolio components.

For a hedge to be effective, the hedging device chosen should be as similar as possible to the commodity at risk. Farmers do not hedge their wheat crop by using corn futures, nor should an equity manager hedge stock holdings with a bond index. The S&P 500 index is a good representative of a well-diversified portfolio and is

**FIGURE 20-4**

Characteristics of S&P 500 Stock Index Futures

Contract size = $250 × index value.

Minimum price change is 0.10 ($25).

Initial good faith deposit for a speculator is $20,625 (subject to change).

Contracts are marked to market daily.

Delivery of stocks does not occur; contracts are settled in cash.

The contracts do not earn dividends.

Trading hours: 9:30 A.M. to 4:15 P.M. EST.

Settlement months and ticker symbols:

Futures: SP    Cash index: SPX

MAR (H)    JUN (M)    SEP (U)    DEC (Z)

Expiration: Third Friday of contract month at 4:15 P.M. EST.

These contracts are nicknamed SPOOZ in the trading pit.

effective in hedging the investment portfolio of an endowment fund, mutual fund, or other broad-based portfolio. Futures on the Dow Jones Industrial Average might be used to hedge a blue chip portfolio, while futures on the Nasdaq index would be better suited to hedging a technology portfolio.

Suppose you are the portfolio manager for a $75 million fund. You anticipate a downturn in the market in the near future but remain bullish for the long term. You are concerned that a declining portfolio value would look bad in the end-of-year report your fund will provide to its interested parties. What can you do?

One obvious alternative is to sell everything before prices fall. This solution would protect your gains, but the trading costs would be expensive. Also, you do not want to suffer the embarrassment of managing a fund containing only cash equivalents. Anyone can manage a fund like that, and it is unlikely that the fund beneficiaries will feel that you are earning your fee.

Another approach is to hedge the stock portfolio using the futures market. Futures hedging involves taking a position in the futures market that offsets a position you hold in the "cash" market. If you are long stock, logically you should be short futures. Just as the farmer needs to determine how many contracts to sell, the portfolio manager must calculate the number of contracts necessary to counteract likely changes in the portfolio value.

Three pieces of information are needed to make this calculation:

1. The value of the appropriate futures contract.
2. The dollar value of the portfolio to be hedged.
3. The beta of your portfolio.

The first of these is easy to determine. The Chicago Mercantile Exchange sets the size of an S&P 500 futures contract at $250 times the value of the S&P 500 index. Table 20-4 is a set of sample S&P 500 stock index futures contract prices. It indicates that the prior day's closing value for the S&P 500 index was 348.76 and that the DEC S&P 500 futures contract settled at 353.00. The value of the futures contract is therefore $250 × 353.00, or $88,250. The difference between a particular futures price and the current index itself is referred to as the **basis**. For the December S&P 500 futures contract, the basis is 353.00 – 348.76, or 4.24 points.

Second, we already know the portfolio value, $75 million in this example. Finally, we need the portfolio beta. Many portfolio management software packages provide this statistic, along with other market information on the portfolio components.

As we have seen, properly diversifying a portfolio can eliminate the unsystematic risk. In fact, one of the principal results of capital market theory is the fact that investors are not rewarded for bearing unsystematic risk. The market assumes that investors have been smart enough to reduce risk through diversification as much as possible for a given level of anticipated return.

Systematic risk is measured by beta. In our example, we can assume that our large $75 million portfolio contains securities from many industries and that

**TABLE 20-4** S&P 500 STOCK INDEX FUTURES

| | *Open* | *High* | *Low* | *Settle* | *Change* |
|---|---|---|---|---|---|
| SEP | 348.40 | 350.20 | 345.70 | 348.50 | +0.20 |
| DEC | 353.20 | 354.80 | 350.20 | 353.00 | +0.20 |
| MAR | 358.00 | 359.00 | 355.00 | 357.60 | +0.20 |

Index: High 349.18 Low 345.74 Close 348.76 +0.41

unsystematic risk is essentially zero. Beta is also a measure of the relative risk of a portfolio compared with a benchmark portfolio such as the S&P 500 index. By definition, the benchmark has a beta of 1.0. Portfolios that are riskier than the benchmark have a beta greater than 1.0, whereas more conservative portfolios have a beta less than 1.0. Suppose your portfolio has a beta of 0.92. This means that for every 1 percent change in the value of the S&P 500 index, your portfolio should change in value by 0.92 percent.

### *Calculating a Hedge Ratio*

As with options, a futures hedge ratio indicates the number of contracts needed to mimic the behavior of the portfolio. The hedge ratio has two components. First is a *scale factor*, which deals with the dollar value of the portfolio relative to the dollar value of the futures contract. The larger the portfolio, the more futures contracts will be necessary.

The second component of the hedge ratio comes from the *level of systematic risk* of the stock portfolio. Futures contracts have a beta of 1.0, whereas the stock portfolio can have a beta much higher or lower than this. If the stock portfolio has a beta greater than 1.0, it changes in value faster than the futures contract, and more contracts are necessary to offset these changes. A beta less than 1.0 means the hedge requires fewer contracts.

The hedge ratio for our example is

$$HR = \frac{\text{Dollar value of portfolio}}{\text{Dollar value of S\&P contract}} \times \text{Beta}$$

$$= \frac{\$75 \text{ million}}{\$250 \times \$353} \times 0.92 = 782 \text{ contracts}$$

The stock portfolio manager who chooses to hedge wants to establish positions that will offset one another, ideally eliminating market risk for a period of time. To do this, it is necessary to have equivalent dollar investments in the stock market and in the futures market.

The hedge ratio incorporates the relative value of the stocks and futures and accounts for the relative riskiness of the two "portfolios." One portfolio (the S&P 500 index) has a beta of 1.0 by definition, and the second portfolio (the stocks) may be more or less risky than this. If it is less risky, fewer futures contracts are necessary to hedge. If the stock portfolio has a beta greater than 1.0, more futures contracts are necessary.

To hedge a long position, the manager needs to go short the futures contracts. Because these are not available in fractional amounts, the portfolio manager must round to a whole number. Some managers have a policy of rounding down to avoid overhedging, which might be considered speculating by some regulators.

Let's see what would happen to the aggregate value of the portfolio under several different market scenarios when the futures contracts expire. (Dividends are ignored in these examples; they would be the same in each scenario.)

**The Market Falls.** Perhaps the market falls as expected. This creates a loss in the stock portfolio and a gain in the futures market. Suppose the S&P 500 index falls from 348.76 to 325.00, for a decline of 6.81 percent. This means the portfolio should have fallen by 6.81% × 0.92 = 6.27%, or $4,698,900. This is a loss.

**FIGURE 20-5**

S&P 500 Index Falls from 348.76 to 325.00

***Portfolio:***

–6.81% × 0.92 × $75 million = $4,698,900 loss

***Futures:***

(353 – 325) × 782 × $250 = $5,474,000 gain

***Net Effect:***

$775,100 gain

**FIGURE 20-6**

S&P 500 Index Rises from 348.76 to 365.00

***Portfolio:***

4.66% × 0.92 × $75 million = $3,215,400 gain

***Futures:***

(365 – 353) × 782 × $250 = $2,346,000 loss

***Net Effect:***

$869,400 gain

In the futures market, the manager has a gain. She sold 782 contracts short at 353.00. At the expiration of the futures contract, she can close out her 782 short contracts by buying 782 contracts at 325.00. (At expiration, the price of the futures contract should exactly equal the index itself.) This gives her a gain of 28.00 points × 782 contracts × $250 = $5,474,000. The combined positions (cash and futures market) leave a gain of $775,100 (see Figure 20-5).

**The Market Rises.** Suppose the index rises from 348.76 to 365.00. In this scenario the market moved in the opposite direction from what was expected. A market rise of 4.66 percent means the portfolio should rise by 4.29 percent, or $3,215,400.

The manager will lose money on the futures position because she sold the futures short, and they rose to 365.00 at expiration. The loss is (365.00 – 353.00) × 782 × $250 = $2,346,000. The combined positions yield a gain of $869,400 (see Figure 20-6).

**The Market Is Unchanged.** If the market is unchanged, the manager has no gain on the stock portfolio, but does have a gain in the futures. The basis will deteriorate to 0 at expiration, so she will have a gain of (353.00 – 348.76) × 782 × $250 = $828,920 (see Figure 20-7).

### *Hedging in Retrospect*

In practice, a hedge of this type is never perfect: Usually some relatively small profit or loss occurs when the manager lifts the hedge. There are two reasons for this. First, it is usually not possible to hedge exactly because the futures contracts are available in integer quantities only, so the portfolio manager must round to the nearest whole number. Second, stock portfolios seldom behave exactly as their betas say they should. In the previous example, the portfolio should change by 92 percent as much as the

**FIGURE 20-7**

S&P 500 Index
Unchanged at 348.76

*Portfolio:*

0% × 0.92 × $75 million = $0

*Futures:*

(353.00 – 348.76) × 782 × $250 = $828,920 gain

*Net Effect:*

$828,920 gain

## What Is Speculation?

The late Professor Merton Miller (Nobel laureate from the University of Chicago) told a story of a conversation he had with the treasurer of a Chicago oil company. In the aftermath of the Persian Gulf war, the price of oil dropped sharply and the value of the firm's oil inventory declined substantially. Merton told the man that it ". . . served him right for speculating on oil prices."

"But we didn't speculate," the man said. "We didn't use the futures markets at all."

Merton replied, "That's the point; by not hedging your inventory, you gambled that the price of oil would not drop. You guessed wrong, and you lost."

If you do not hedge, you are a *de facto* speculator.

Source: Conversation between the author and Merton Miller, February 7, 1992, North Miami Beach, Florida.

overall market. In practice, it may change by more or less than this amount. Any deviation from the expected figure yields a less-than-perfect hedge after the fact.

*Convergence of the futures contract with the cash index works to the advantage of the short hedger.*

If you examine the results in each of these scenarios carefully, you will note that the basis works to the advantage of the short hedger. Even if the market remains unchanged, the value of the futures contracts will decline as the delivery month approaches. On the last day of a futures contract's life, its market price should equal the spot price. This means that the basis becomes zero. This phenomenon is called **basis convergence.**

The gains earned from the deteriorating basis are large in dollar amounts but modest in percentage terms. In the scenario where the market is unchanged, there was a combined gain of $828,920. On a $75 million portfolio, this represents a percentage return of only 1.11 percent over about fifteen weeks, or 3.83 percent per year. This hedging is also not a free lunch; in the scenario where the market advances, the manager would have earned more money had the hedge not been used.

It is by no means necessary for a portfolio manager to hedge the entire portfolio. Instead of using 782 contracts, as in the examples, the manager might decide to hedge only 80 percent of the portfolio, using 626 contracts. This allows greater upside appreciation if the portfolio manager was wrong about a forthcoming downturn but would still provide substantial protection against a declining market.

## Dynamic Hedging

**Dynamic hedging** strategies attempt to replicate a put option by combining a short position with a long position to achieve a position delta equal to that which would be obtained via protective puts. This sounds cryptic but is really not complicated.

Part of the logic of the Black-Scholes Option Pricing Model stems from the fact that at a particular point in time, an investor can replicate a stock option by some combination of the underlying asset and Treasury bills. The relative proportion of

### PORTFOLIO MEMO

### Synthetic T-Bills and Synthetic Index Portfolios

Investors may receive *dividends* on their stock portfolios. A speculator in a stock index futures contract earns *interest* on the good faith deposit but receives no dividends. The essence of stock index futures pricing is capturing the relative difference between the interest and dividend payments. In equilibrium, the futures price equals the dollar value of the index plus the short-term interest rate minus the dividend yield received. The formula for pricing stock index futures is

$$F = Se^{(R-D)t}$$

where

$F$ = futures price
$S$ = level of the index
$e$ = base of natural logarithms
$R$ = T-bill rate
$D$ = dividend yield of index
$t$ = time until futures delivery date

The portfolio manager views this formula as a simple three-security relationship:

[Long T-bills] + [Long stock index futures] = [Long index portfolio]

This relationship is important to large institutional investors because they can replicate a well-diversified stock portfolio by simply holding a long position in stock index futures and using Treasury bills to satisfy the good faith deposit requirement. A manager who does this creates a synthetic index portfolio.

Conversely, a manager holding a stock portfolio can turn it into a synthetic Treasury bill by selling stock index futures. We simply move the futures position to the other side of the equals sign. (Subtracting stock index futures means selling them.)

[Long T-bills] = [Long Index portfolio] – [Stock index futures]

This makes it very easy to alter the portfolio allocation between T-bills and stock. Rather than wholesale purchases or sales of individual securities, the portfolio manager can make a single futures trade, thereby saving trading fees and managerial time.

each of these assets will constantly change as time passes or the price of the underlying asset changes.

A short position in the underlying asset is necessary to replicate a put because both puts and short positions become more valuable as the stock price declines. A short position in the proper proportion to the rest of the portfolio, at a specific moment in time, exactly replicates a certain put option. This means their deltas will be equal at that moment.

### Dynamic Hedging Example

Refer to the price information in Table 20-1. Assume that you own 1,000 shares of ZZX and are interested in buying a JUL 50 put for downside protection. Assume also that this option expires in sixty days, that T-bills yield 8 percent, that ZZX pays no dividends, and that you estimate the stock's volatility at 30 percent. Using this information, the put delta is –0.435. If you hold your 1,000 shares of ZZX and also buy ten puts (remember that one put option contract covers 100 shares), you have a **position delta** of (1,000 × 1.0) + (1,000 × –0.435) = 565. A position delta is the sum of all the deltas in a portfolio.

*Position delta is the sum of all the deltas in a portfolio. It is a measure of bullishness.*

Stock has a delta of exactly 1.0 because it "behaves exactly like itself." A stock and options portfolio with a position delta of 565 behaves like a stock-only portfolio composed of 565 shares of the underlying stock. In this example, the original position delta was 1,000 (1.0 for each of the 1,000 shares of stock). After including the puts, the position delta is 565. With the puts, the portfolio is 56.5 percent as bullish as it was without them.

There is another way to achieve a position delta of 565. You could sell 435 shares short. To check this, observe that (1,000 × 1.0) + (435 × –1.0) = 565. (A short position in a stock has a delta of exactly –1.0 because it is the mirror image of a long position.) By selling short the proper number of shares, you achieve precisely the same result as if you had purchased the JUL 50 put.

### The Dynamic Part of the Hedge

As time passes and the price of ZZX stock changes, the delta of your chosen put also changes. Suppose that after one week, the price of the stock is down to $49 per share from the original price of $50. The JUL 50 put now has a delta of –0.509, and the position delta has changed to (1,000 × 1.0) + (1,000 × –0.509) = 491.

To continue to replicate the characteristics of the put via dynamic hedging, it is necessary to sell short another 74 shares, making a total of 509 sold short. The position delta is then (1,000 × 1.0) + (509 × –1.0) = 491. This is the same value determined using the put option.

In contrast, if the stock price had risen to $51, the put delta would have changed to –0.371, and the position delta would be (1,000 × 1.0) + (1,000 × –0.371) = 629. This means that you would need to cover 64 of the 435 shares you initially sold short. Subsequent to this, your dynamically hedged position delta would be (1,000 × 1.0) + (371 × –1.0) = 629.

### Dynamic Hedging with Futures Contracts

If a portfolio is large enough, it becomes appropriate to hedge via stock index futures contracts rather than individual stock options or short sales. Stock index futures move in tandem with a well-diversified portfolio of stock, so they have a delta of +1.0.

Assume that an equity portfolio with a beta of 1.0 has $52.5 million in market value and that a particular futures contract sells for 700. The futures contract has a

PORTFOLIO MEMO

## Position Delta

A position delta is the sum of the component deltas in a portfolio. A portfolio might contain 10,000 shares of a particular common stock. Shares have a delta of +1.0, so this position contributes 10,000 delta points to the portfolio.

The manager might decide to reduce the size of this position by 25 percent. This could be done by selling 2,500 shares or by using options. Assuming a risk-free interest rate of 8 percent, market volatility of 20 percent, and a current stock price of $45, the Black-Scholes OPM gives the following values:

3-month $50 call: delta = 0.209; premium = $0.51

3-month $40 put: delta = –0.078; premium = $0.16

Writing an option causes its delta to change sign because the delta essentially is being subtracted rather than added.

Figure 20-8 shows that if the manager writes 100 of these call contracts against the shares and buys 53 put contracts, the position delta is equivalent to a long position of 7,497 shares, approximately 75 percent of the original number. The premium received from writing the calls is more than enough to pay for the puts; in fact, $4,252 in net income is generated by the transactions (ignoring commission costs).

Options are widely used in risk management applications of this sort. The position delta concept is extremely important to the sophisticated risk manager.

FIGURE 20-8

Position Delta

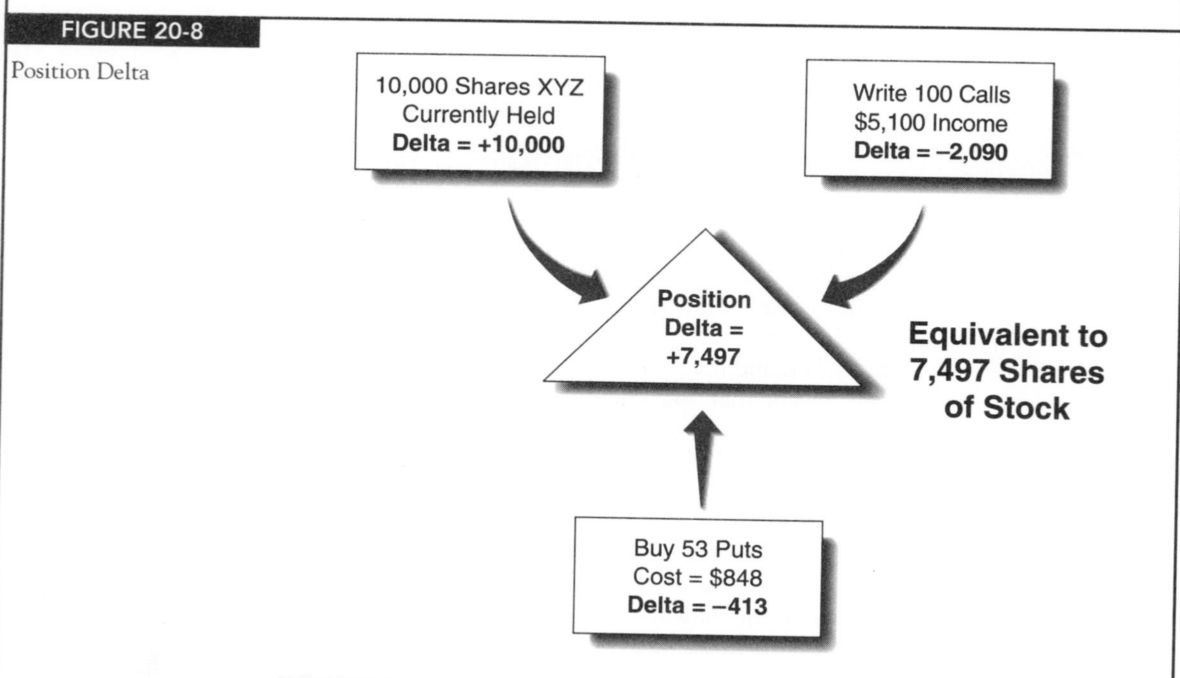

dollar value of $250 × 700.00 = $175,000. Three hundred futures contracts, then, have a dollar value equal to that of the portfolio.

We might wish to replicate a particular put option with a delta of –0.400, thereby creating a protective put when coupled with our stock portfolio. This would leave us with a position delta of 1.0 – 0.400 = 0.600. To do this, we simply sell enough futures contracts to pull our position delta down to the desired level.

Earlier we saw how to calculate a hedge ratio to eliminate market risk:

$$HR = \frac{\text{Dollar value of portfolio}}{\text{Dollar value of futures contract}} \times \text{Beta}$$

With our $52.5 million portfolio, the hedge ratio is

$$\frac{\$52.5 \text{ million}}{\$250 \times 700} \times 1.0 = 300.0 \text{ contracts}$$

If we sell three hundred S&P 500 contracts short, the position delta will be 0. In this example, however, the target is a position delta of 0.600, so we do not need 300 contracts. Logically, in order to keep 60 percent of the market exposure, we eliminate 40 percent of it. This means we use 40 percent of the hedge ratio, or 120 contracts.

As time passes, the value of both the futures contract and the portfolio will change, causing the hedge ratio to change as well. For instance, if the value of our portfolio falls to $47.5 million and the futures contract falls to 624.00, the new hedge ratio is

$$\frac{\$47.5 \text{ million}}{\$250 \times 624} \times 1.0 = 304.5 \text{ contracts}$$

Forty percent of this is 121.8, or approximately 122 contracts. To maintain the position delta, we must sell two more contracts.

## SUMMARY

Portfolio protection involves adding components to a portfolio with the intent of ensuring that the value of the portfolio will not fall below a predetermined floor value. Options, futures contracts, and dynamic hedging can be used to do this.

Sophisticated hedging with options requires some familiarity with principles of option pricing. The Black-Scholes Option Pricing Model is very useful in this regard. The first derivative of this model with respect to the stock price is called *delta*; this statistic measures how an option premium changes as the stock price changes.

A protective put is a long put position held in conjunction with a long position in the underlying stock. This is like an insurance policy on stock. The owner selects the deductible and the policy term and pays a premium for the insurance.

Stock index futures can be used to reduce the systematic risk associated with a well-diversified stock portfolio. When hedging this way, it is necessary to know the value of the chosen futures contract, the portfolio value, and its beta.

Dynamic hedging strategies attempt to replicate a put option by combining a short position with a long position to achieve a position delta equal to that which would be obtained via protective puts.

## QUESTIONS

1. What is the purpose of portfolio protection?
2. What does it mean to say that options enable you to technically adjust the characteristics of a portfolio?
3. Why is delta important in portfolio hedging applications?
4. Give an example of a situation in which someone might buy an option and fully expect to lose all his money in the option position.
5. Explain how it is possible to have options on an intangible item such as a stock market index.
6. Someone wants to hedge a stock portfolio against a market decline. Are there any relative advantages to hedging using covered call writing as opposed to buying protective puts?
7. Explain how futures contracts can be used to alter the position delta of a stock portfolio.
8. Could an S&P 500 stock index futures contract be used to hedge a portfolio of only five stocks?
9. What role does beta play in the construction of a hedge ratio for a stock portfolio?
10. What does it mean to say that convergence of the futures contract with the cash index works to the advantage of the short hedger?
11. Explain how it is possible to replicate a put option by selling shares of stock short.
12. Briefly explain the concept of dynamic hedging.
13. At one time dynamic hedging was called *portfolio insurance*. Why do you think portfolio *insurance* is now normally called portfolio *protection?*
14. In hedging a portfolio, is there anything philosophically wrong with hedging only part of it?
15. Why might overhedging be considered speculation?

## PROBLEMS

Consider the following information for Problems 1 through 3:

| | |
|---|---|
| Stock price = \$33.50 | Striking price = \$30 |
| Risk-free rate = 8.00% | Time until expiration in June = 77 days |
| Dividends = \$0 | Volatility = 33% |
| Put premium = \$0.50 | Call premium = \$4.50 |
| Put delta = –0.181 | Call delta = 0.819 |

1. Suppose you own 10,000 shares of this stock, and you buy 50 of these JUN 30 puts (puts on 5,000 shares). What is your position delta?
2. If you have a position delta of zero, you are delta neutral. How many puts do you have to buy to become delta neutral? What would this cost?
3. Suppose you write 100 JUN 30 covered calls against your stock.
   a. What is your position delta?
   b. How many JUN 30 puts must you buy to become delta neutral?
4. You want to hedge your stock portfolio using OEX index puts. Your portfolio is worth \$2.5 million and has a beta of 1.12; the current level of the OEX index

is 315.55. The 325 OEX puts you have selected have a delta of –0.223. How many of these OEX puts do you need to buy?

5. In Problem 4, suppose that after a few weeks, the value of your stock portfolio is $2.45 million, the OEX index is 313.56, and the put delta is –0.245. What do you need to do to get your portfolio back to a delta neutral position?
6. Refer to the data in Problem 4. Suppose you want to hedge the portfolio using the MAR S&P 500 stock index futures contracts shown in Table 20-4. How many of these contracts do you need to buy or sell?
7. Create an example related to Problem 6 showing why dynamic hedging requires you to sell futures when the market is falling or to buy them when the market is rising.

The Strong Software on the text Website is helpful for solving Problems 8, 9, 10, and 11. You can also use the options calculator at the CBOE Website *http://www.cboe.com/TradTool/OptionCalculator.asp*.

8. Refer to a current edition of *The Wall Street Journal*. Calculate the number of puts (near-the-money with about three months until expiration) needed to hedge 1,000 shares of IBM common stock. Assume a volatility of 0.15. List any other assumptions you need to make.
9. Redo Problem 8 using implied volatility for IBM rather than the assumed figure.
10. Prepare a plot showing the behavior of the following statistics as time passes. Assume the price of the underlying asset does not change.
    a. In-the-money call.
    b. Out-of-the-money call.
    c. In-the-money put.
    d. Out-of-the-money put.
11. What is the relationship between the delta of a call option and the delta of a put when both options have a common expiration and striking price?

##  INTERNET EXERCISE

Use the Options Calculator at *http://www.cboe.com/TradTool/OptionCalculator.asp* to verify the price, delta, and other "greeks" for the call option in Problem 1.

##  FURTHER READING

Ansbacher, M. *The New Stock Index Market*. New York: Walker and Company, 1983.

Bittman, James B. *Options for the Stock Investor*. Chicago: Irwin, 1996.

Black, F., and M. Scholes. "The Pricing of Options and Corporate Liabilities." *Journal of Political Economy*, May 1973, 637–659.

Bookstaber, Richard. *Option Pricing and Strategies in Investing*. Reading, Mass.: Addison-Wesley, 1981.

Brennan, M.J., and E.S. Schwartz. "Arbitrage in Stock Index Futures." *Journal of Business*, January 1990, S7–S31.

Brenner, M. *Option Pricing*. Lexington, Mass.: Lexington Books, 1983.

Choie, K.S., and F. Novemstky. "Replication of Long-Term with Short-Term Options." *Journal of Portfolio Management*, Winter 1989, 17–19.

Cox, J., and M. Rubenstein. *Options Markets*. Englewood Cliffs, N.J.: Prentice-Hall, 1985.

Fabozzi, F., and G. Kipnis. *Stock Index Futures*. Homewood, Ill.: Dow Jones–Irwin, 1984.

Figlewski, Stephen. *Hedging with Financial Futures for Institutional Investors*. Cambridge, Mass.: Ballinger Publishing, 1986.

———. "Hedging with Stock-Index Futures: Theory and Application in a New Market." *Journal of Futures Markets*, Summer, 1985, 183–199.

Gastineau, Gary. *The Options Manual*, 3d ed. New York: McGraw-Hill, 1988.

Gould, F.J. "Stock Index Futures: The Arbitrage Cycle and Portfolio Insurance." *Financial Analysts Journal*, January/February 1988, 48–62.

Halford, Richard. "The Art of Trading Stock Index Futures." *Journal of Investing*, Fall 1997, 87–93.

Hill, Joanne, and Tom Schneeweis. "Reducing Volatility with Financial Futures." *Financial Analysts Journal*, November/December 1984, 34–40.

Jarrow, Robert A., and Andrew Rudd. *Option Pricing*. Homewood, Ill.: Irwin, 1983.

Loosigan, Allan. *Stock Index Futures*. Reading, Mass.: Addison-Wesley, 1985.

Moriarty, E., S. Phillips, and P. Tosini. "A Comparison of Options and Futures in the Management of Portfolio Risk." *Financial Analysts Journal*, January/February 1981, 61–67.

Nordhauser, F., "Using Stock Index Futures to Reduce Market Risk." *Journal of Portfolio Management*, Spring 1984, 56–62.

Ritchken, P. *Options: Theory, Strategy, and Applications*. Glenview, Ill.: Scott, Foresman, 1987.

Schwartz, Edward, Joanne Hill, and Thomas Schneeweis. *Financial Futures*. Homewood, Ill.: Irwin, 1986.

Stoll, H. "The Relationship between Put and Call Option Prices." *Journal of Finance*, December 1969, 801–824.

Stoll, Hans R., and Robert E. Whaley. *Futures and Options*. Cincinnati, Ohio: South-Western, 1993.

Strong, Robert A. *Derivatives: An Introduction*. 2d ed. Mason, Ohio: South-Western, 2005.

———, and Amy Dickinson. "Predicting Better Hedge Ratios." *Financial Analysts Journal*, January/February 1994, 70–72.

# 21 Removing Interest Rate Risk

*The first mistake is usually the cheapest mistake.*

***A trader adage***

## Key Terms

bond equivalent yield
bullet immunization
cheapest to deliver
counterparty risk
deliverable bond
Eurodollars
funds gap
immunization
interest rate sensitivity
interest rate swap
invoice price
notional amount
position day

## Introduction

Chapter 20 showed how an investor can remove much of the worry about adverse stock market fluctuations by hedging that risk away using stock index futures. Many portfolios, however, especially those with income as a primary objective, contain a large percentage of securities that have high **interest rate sensitivity**. That is, their value can be adversely affected if market interest rates rise. Corporate and government bonds, for instance, are interest rate sensitive. Chapter 11 ("Bond Pricing and Selection") showed that bond prices move inversely with interest rates. This means that the value of a bond portfolio will decline if market interest rates increase. A passbook savings account, in contrast, is not interest rate sensitive. The principal value of such an account cannot decline regardless of what happens to interest rates. The rate of interest paid on the account can change, but the value of the account will never decline unless money is taken out of it.

This chapter considers several methods of reducing the level of interest rate risk associated with a portfolio of rate-sensitive assets. The most efficient method requires the use of interest rate futures, so we begin with a discussion of the characteristics of these financial futures contracts.

## Interest Rate Futures Contracts

Interest rate futures contracts[1] have enjoyed the same success as stock index futures. These contracts are the most successful futures contracts in the world if success is measured by trading volume. Daily volume on T-notes and T-bonds combined is usually more than 1 million contracts, of which between 4 and 5 percent will ultimately be settled by delivery. Many financial institutions routinely hedge interest rate risk or lock in yields using these products.

### *Categories of Interest Rate Futures Contracts*

We group interest rate futures contracts into *short-term*, *intermediate-term*, and *long-term* categories.

*The term* Eurodollars *refers to any dollar-denominated deposit outside the United States.*

**Short-Term Contracts.** The two principal short-term contracts are Eurodollars and U.S. Treasury bills. **Eurodollars** (EDs) are simply U.S. dollars on deposit in a bank outside the United States. At least one trillion such dollars exist; they are the most popular form of the short-term futures contract. Eurodollars came about in the 1950s during the cold war between the United States, the Soviet Union, Eastern Europe, and China. The communist countries feared the evolution of circumstances that might cause the U.S. government to freeze or confiscate their deposits in New York's money center banks. (This was indeed done with Iranian assets following the hostage crisis in 1979.) To avoid this possibility, these communist countries transferred their dollar balances to banks in Europe.

Today, the term *Eurodollars* applies to any U.S. dollar deposit outside the jurisdiction of the U.S. Federal Reserve Board. Financial institutions often prefer Eurodollar deposits to domestic deposits because EDs are not subject to reserve requirement restrictions. This means that every ED received by a bank can be reinvested somewhere else. This bank preference for EDs translates into a slightly higher interest rate on ED deposits.

*Eurodollars are not the same as Euros. Euros are the currency adopted by the twelve member states of the European Union. Eurodollars are U.S. dollars outside the United States.*

Although EDs have this important advantage, they also carry more risk than a domestic deposit. They could be confiscated or frozen by the government of a foreign country, and there may not be any deposit insurance where the deposits are located.

**Intermediate- and Long-Term Contracts.** The contract on U.S. Treasury notes is the only member of the intermediate-term category of interest rate futures contracts. The contract on Treasury bonds is the principal player in the long-term category. Contracts are also available on municipal bonds and on a U.S. dollar index, but these are special-purpose contracts and have a limited following. The mechanics of using the long- and intermediate-term contracts for hedging or speculating are similar.

### *U.S. Treasury Bills and Their Futures Contracts*

**Characteristics of U.S. Treasury Bills.** Unlike most other fixed-income instruments, U.S. Treasury bills are sold at a discount from their par, or face, value. The government sells 91-day (13-week) and 182-day (26-week) T-bills at a weekly

[1]Avoid referring to futures contracts as *securities*. They are *contracts* and are regulated by the Commodity Futures Trading Commission rather than the Securities and Exchange Commission.

auction. The more an investor pays for a Treasury bill, the lower its yield to her, and the lower interest the government must pay.

An investor might pay \$9,852 for a \$10,000 T-bill that matures in ninety-one days. At maturity, the investor receives \$10,000, meaning the investor earned \$148 in interest. Treasury bills do not carry a stated interest rate. Their rate of return is a function of the time until maturity and the price paid for the bills.

Although T-bills are simple discount securities, years of tradition have resulted in several alternative ways of measuring their yield or calculating their price. Using traditional present value/future value notions, the pricing relationship for these simple discount securities seems to be straightforward:

$$\text{Price} = \frac{\text{Par value}}{(1+R)} \tag{21-1}$$

where $R$ = yield to maturity. For the Treasury bill described previously, we can quickly solve for the yield to maturity:

$$\$9{,}852 = \frac{\$10{,}000}{(1+R)}$$

Rearranging terms,

$$R = (\$10{,}000 / \$9{,}852) - 1 = 0.01502 = 1.502\%$$

URL

*Current quotes for U.S. Treasury securities can be found at* http://www.smartmoney.com/bondmarketup/

This rate is for one-fourth of a year. To annualize the rate and make it more easily interpreted, it is necessary to multiply by 4, giving a yield to maturity of 6.01 percent.

Industry practice is slightly different. The following is the standard convention:

$$\text{T-bill price} = \text{Face value} - \text{Discount amount} \tag{21-2}$$

$$\text{Discount amount} = \text{Face value} \times (\text{Days to maturity}/360) \times \text{Ask discount}$$

With an *ask discount* of 6.01 percent, we find a discount amount of $\$10{,}000 \times 91/360 \times 6.01\% = \$152$.[2] The T-bill price is then $\$10{,}000 - \$152 = \$9{,}848$. This differs slightly from the previous value of \$9,852, because in the first example we multiplied by 4 rather than by 360/91.

The financial press also calculates T-bill yields on a *bond equivalent* basis, as follows:

$$\text{Bond equivalent yield} = \frac{\text{Discount amount}}{\text{Discount price}} \times \frac{365}{\text{Days to maturity}} \tag{21-3}$$

If the T-bill sells for \$9,852, the **bond equivalent yield** is

$$\frac{\$148}{\$9{,}852} \times \frac{365}{91} = 6.025\%$$

The bond equivalent yield adjusts for two things: (1) the fact that there are 365 (not 360) days in a year and (2) the fact that the discount price is the required investment, not the face value. This measure enables an investor to compare more directly the yield on T-bills with competing investment alternatives.

[2]Like other securities, T-bills have a bid price and an ask price. The price is quoted on either a discount basis or as a percentage of par.

**TABLE 21-1** DECEMBER T-BILL FUTURES INFORMATION

| | | | | | Discount | | |
|---|---|---|---|---|---|---|---|
| *Open* | *High* | *Low* | *Settle* | *Change* | *Settle* | *Change* | *Open Interest* |
| 93.69 | 93.69 | 93.64 | 93.64 | −.09 | 6.36 | +.09 | 221 |

Alternatively, we could use $(1 + R)^{0.25}$ in the denominator of Equation 21-1, changing the answer to 6.15 percent. This method assumes that the interest can be compounded into subsequent T-bills, thereby earning a higher effective rate.

**Treasury Bill Futures Contracts.** Treasury bill futures contracts call for the delivery of $1 million par value of 90-day T-bills on the delivery date of the futures contract. This means that on the day someone delivers the Treasury bills, they mature in ninety days.

*Daily settlement prices for various interest rate futures contracts can be accessed at* http://www.cme.com/trading/prd/ir/index.html

Table 21-1 is an extract of prices from the financial pages. Note that the paper presents contract prices both as a percentage *of* par and as a discount *from* par. The settlement price of 93.64 represents 93.64 percent of 100, or a discount of 100.00% – 93.64% = 6.36% from par. This figure of 6.36 percent is the market's best estimate of what 90-day T-bills will yield near the end of December.

Remember that 6.36 percent for ninety days is not the same as 6.36 percent for one year. The rate published in *The Wall Street Journal* is an annual rate; it is necessary to convert the price in the paper to the bill's actual cost.

Suppose someone buys a DEC T-bill futures contract at a price of 93.64. What specifically does this mean in dollars and cents? To find out, we must convert the annual yield into the true yield for the life of the T-bill (in this case, ninety days). By custom we use 360-day years in this computation. So 6.36 percent per year becomes 90/360 × 6.36% = 1.5900% for ninety days. When someone buys a T-bill futures contract at 93.64, he is promising to buy $1 million in T-bills, and the price he is promising to pay is

$$\frac{\$1 \text{ million}}{1.015900} = \$984,348.85$$

Suppose that by December, interest rates have risen to 7.00 percent. In this case, *The Wall Street Journal* price will be 93.00. The new price of the futures contract is

$$90/360 \times 0.0700 = 0.0175$$

$$\frac{\$1 \text{ million}}{1.0175} = \$982,800.98$$

This means that a speculator who bought a T-bill at 93.64 lost money:

| | |
|---|---|
| $982,800.98 | Received |
| –984,348.85 | Paid |
| $ 1,547.87 | Loss[3] |

The price of a fixed-income security moves inversely with market interest rates. In this example, the speculator was long a T-bill contract, and interest rates rose. Consequently, the speculator lost money.

[3]The futures contract holder, in all likelihood, will not pay or receive nearly this much. Instead the holder will trade out of the contract before the delivery month. The account will then be credited or debited with the gain or loss on the futures market transaction.

Small movements in the relative level of interest rates translate into significant amounts of money. A change of one basis point (0.01 percent) in the price of a T-bill futures contract results in a $25 change in the value of the contract.

*Speculators buy T-bill contracts when they expect short-term rates to fall and sell contracts when they expect rates to rise.*

Now consider another example, this time from a hedger's perspective. Suppose you learn that an educational foundation whose assets you manage will receive $10 million from an estate in three months. As the portfolio manager, you would like to be able to invest the money now because you believe that interest rates are trending downward. With sums of money this large, even a few basis points translate into a lot of dollars.

*To lock in a current interest rate, buy T-bill futures.*

Using the futures market, you can lock in the current interest rate. To do this, it is necessary to buy T-bill futures because you want the T-bills. If you had the money, you would buy them now; but you will not receive the money for another three months. The previous example showed that you are promising to pay $984,348.85 for $1 million in T-bills if you buy a futures contract at 93.64. You will receive $10 million from the estate, so perhaps you decide to buy 10 DEC T-bill futures contracts. (Ten of these contracts have a market value of slightly less than $10 million.)

Three months later you receive the money as expected. Now you can remove your hedge by selling the futures contracts. Suppose that interest rates did fall and that 90-day T-bills now yield 5.5 percent. $1 million in T-bills would cost

$$90/360 \times 0.055 = 0.01375$$

$$\frac{\$1 \text{ million}}{1.01375} = \$986,436.50$$

This is $2,087.65 more than the price at the time you established the hedge. You are buying $10 million face value in T-bills, so the total added cost to your fund is $20,876.50.

In the futures market, however, you have a gain that will offset the higher purchase price. A yield of 5.5 percent means the futures contracts will be quoted in the paper as 94.50. When you close out these futures positions, you will sell your contracts for more than you paid for them. In fact, your gain in the futures market will be $20,876.50—exactly equal to your opportunity cost from the decline in interest rates.

## Treasury Bonds and Their Futures Contracts

**Characteristics of U.S. Treasury Bonds.** U.S. Treasury bonds are similar to corporate bonds in virtually every respect. They pay semiannual interest, have a maturity date of up to thirty years from time of issuance,[4] and trade readily in the capital markets. The two differences between a Treasury bond and a Treasury note are that (1) T-notes, by definition, have a life of less than ten years at the time they are initially offered and (2) T-bonds are callable fifteen years after they are issued, whereas T-notes are not.

*Treasury bonds may be callable after fifteen years.*

The Treasury Department issues new bonds and notes in book entry form only, with the owner's name recorded in Washington. There are no longer any actual bond certificates. Despite the fact that registered bonds do not require the bondholder to clip a coupon, we still refer to a bond's *coupon rate*. This is the stated interest rate that determines the dollar amount of interest the bond pays. If a $1,000 par bond has a

[4]The Treasury Department has discontinued issuing 30-year T-bonds. This is probably not a permanent change.

coupon rate of 8½ percent, the bond will pay 8½ percent of par value per year, or $85. In actual practice, this would be paid in two $42.50 installments six months apart.

As we have seen, bonds are identified by the issuer, the coupon, and the year of maturity. We might refer, for instance, to the U.S. Government "6 and one quarters of 23." This means the Treasury bonds with a 6.25 percent coupon rate come due in 2023.

**Treasury Bond Futures Contracts.** The Treasury bond futures contract calls for the delivery of $100,000 face value of U.S. Treasury bonds that have a minimum of fifteen years until maturity (and, if callable, have a minimum of fifteen years of call protection). Bonds that meet these criteria are said to be **deliverable bonds.**

Defining the underlying commodity for the T-bond futures contract, however, is more involved than with other commodities. An important feature of all commodity contracts is fungibility. Hedgers and speculators both want to be able to trade out of their contracts without having to go through the delivery process.

Some commodity traders consider the T-bond pit to be the most sophisticated arena at the exchange. It is one of the largest and most difficult for an observer to follow; sometimes more than seven hundred people are in the pit at the opening bell.

As with the T-bill contract, speculators buy T-bond contracts when they expect interest rates to fall and go short when they expect them to rise.[5]

Whereas an exchange-inspected bushel of wheat is the same as any other such bushel, a Treasury bond with a 9 percent coupon and twelve years until maturity is not the same as another bond with a 4 percent coupon and twenty-three years to maturity. Unlike stock index futures, delivery *does* actually occur with Treasury bill, bond, and note futures, although most contracts are closed via an offsetting trade. Only about 4 percent of Treasury bond contracts, for instance, are settled by delivery.

*Conversion factors are used to "standardize" bonds for futures delivery.*

To "standardize" the $100,000 face value T-bond contract traded on the Chicago Board of Trade, an adjustment factor is used to convert all deliverable bonds to bonds yielding 6 percent. These adjustment factors (or *conversion factors*, as they are also called) are published by the Chicago Board of Trade.[6] They are a function of the remaining life of a particular bond and its coupon rate. Bonds that have coupons higher than 6 percent are more valuable than bonds with lower yields, so these bonds count extra if delivered. Similarly, bonds with yields less than 6 percent have adjustment factors less than 1. Table 21-2 shows some sample conversion factors.

The exchange standardizes bonds by multiplying the settlement price by the conversion factor and then adding any accrued interest to yield an invoice price.

**TABLE 21-2** SAMPLE CHICAGO BOARD OF TRADE CONVERSION FACTORS FOR T-BONDS

| *Remaining Life (Years/Months)* | *Coupon Rate (%)* | | | |
|---|---|---|---|---|
| | 5 | 6 | 6.5 | 8.25 |
| 16–0 | 0.8981 | 1.0000 | 1.0510 | 1.2294 |
| 18–6 | 0.8902 | 0.9999 | 1.0548 | 1.2467 |
| 20–9 | 0.8836 | 0.9999 | 1.0580 | 1.2616 |

[5]They also buy when they expect a smaller drop than the rates implied in the futures contract, and vice versa.

[6]Adjustment factors can also be calculated using the CONVFACT file on the Strong Software at the text Website. (Prior to the March 2000 contract, the futures benchmark was 8 percent rather than 6 percent.)

(The buyer pays accrued interest to the seller of the bonds, just as we saw in Chapter 11. This occurs when bond delivery is between interest payment dates.) The **invoice price** is the amount that the deliverer of the bond receives when a particular bond is delivered against a futures contract. Equation 21-4 shows how to calculate the invoice price.

$$\text{Invoice price} = (\text{Settlement price on position day} \times \text{Conversion factor}) + \text{Accrued interest} \quad \textbf{(21-4)}$$

**Position day** is the day the bondholder notifies the clearinghouse of an intent to deliver bonds against a futures position. This occurs two business days prior to the day the bonds are delivered. Delivery occurs by wire transfer between accounts; funds are transferred the same way.

Suppose, for instance, someone wants to deliver a 7 percent bond with twenty years and eleven months remaining in its life, and the settlement price for the T-bond futures contract on position day is 101-00 (meaning 101 and 0/32 percent of par). The remaining maturity is rounded down to the nearest quarter, giving twenty years and three quarters (twenty years and nine months). The invoice price is then

| | | |
|---|---|---|
| | 1.0100 | Futures settlement price |
| × | $100,000.0000 | Contract size |
| × | 1.1162 | Conversion factor |
| | $112,736.2000 | |
| + | 588.3300 | Accrued interest[7] |
| | $113,324.5300 | Invoice price |

*The bond cheapest to deliver is normally the eligible bond with the longest duration.*

At any given time, several dozen bonds usually are eligible for delivery on the T-bond futures contract. Normally, only one of these bonds will be **cheapest to deliver.** As we have seen, the yield on a bond is a function of the bond price, the coupon, and the time until maturity. Bonds with coupons of 6 percent, for instance, may yield more or less than 6 percent, depending on their price. Only if they sell for par will they yield 6 percent exactly. Other bonds, perhaps with a coupon of 7 percent, may also yield 8 percent, but this means they sell for less than their par value. The conversion factors make all bonds equally attractive for delivery only when the bonds under consideration yield 6 percent. If they yield more or less than this, one of the bonds will have the lowest adjusted price and, hence, be cheapest to deliver.

A reasonably quick way to determine the bond cheapest to deliver is to divide the deliverable bonds' market prices by their respective conversion factors. Whichever bond has the lowest ratio is the cheapest to deliver. In the calculation of cheapest to deliver, Chicago Board of Trade policy requires that the remaining life of the bond be rounded down to the nearest quarter of a year.

Consider an example using the information in Table 21-3 to illustrate the meaning of cheapest to deliver. If I have to buy bonds to deliver against a futures contract, I want to acquire these bonds as cheaply as possible. Table 21-3 indicates that if I use the 7.25s2025, they will cost me $76,910.04. The other bond would cost more: $77,697.74. The 7.25s are cheapest to deliver.

The way the delivery system actually works is slightly different from this example. If I am short ten T-bond futures contracts, I promise to deliver $1 million face value of bonds. I will deliver 100 bonds; I cannot deliver fractional bonds. Consequently, the conversion factor adjustment influences the amount I receive from the

[7]The bond matures in twenty years and eleven months. This means it is one month into the interest rate cycle. Accrued interest on one bond is therefore 1/6 × $35, or $5.83. On $100,000 par, the total is $583.33.

**TABLE 21-3** CALCULATION OF BOND CHEAPEST TO DELIVER

| *Bond* | *Price* | *Duration* | *Conversion Factor* |
|---|---|---|---|
| 7.25% of MAY 2025 | 89 16/32 | 11.14 | 1.1637 |
| 8.125% of AUG 2028 | 99 11/32 | 10.92 | 1.2786 |

7.25% of May 2025
Time until maturity = 26 years, 4 months → 26 years, 1 quarter
Conversion factor = 1.1637
Cost of buying 100 bonds to deliver:
100 bonds/1.1637 = 85.933 bonds
85.933 bonds × $895.00/bond = $76,910.04

8.125% of Aug 2028
Time until maturity = 26 years, 7 months → 26 years, 2 quarters
Conversion factor = 1.2786
Cost of buying 100 bonds to deliver:
100 bonds/1.2786 = 78.211 bonds
78.211 bonds × $993.4375/bond = $77,697.74

Date of calculation is January 15, 1999.

person who receives the bonds I deliver. The lower the coupon on the bond I deliver, the less I receive for it. The buyer pays an invoice price calculated via Equation 21-4. In practice, theoretical calculations regarding T-bond futures and their hedge ratios are all based on the characteristics of the cheapest to deliver bond.

## Concept of Immunization

*It is seldom possible to eliminate interest rate risk completely.*

**Immunization** means precisely what the term implies. If a bond portfolio is immunized, it is largely protected from damage due to fluctuations in market interest rates. It is seldom possible to eliminate interest rate risk completely, just as there is always a possibility of developing a disease after being vaccinated against it.

Completely immunizing a fixed-income portfolio is a very technical chore. If it is necessary to be absolutely precise in the process, a number of fine points must be considered, all of which complicate the process considerably. The Further Reading section at the end of this chapter lists published work regarding theoretical immunization issues. Managers involved in fixed-income security management should continue their education by learning about the assumptions of the various immunization techniques.

### *Duration Matching*

The two general classes of immunization problem are those involving independent portfolios and those involving asset/liability management.

**An Independent Portfolio.** Bullet immunization is one method of reducing the interest-rate risk associated with an independent portfolio.

*Bullet immunization is concerned with getting the effects of interest rate risk and reinvestment rate risk to cancel one another out.*

**Bullet Immunization Example.** The technique of **bullet immunization** seeks to ensure that a set sum of money will be available at a specific point in the future. The effects of interest rate risk and reinvestment rate risk should cancel each other out. If market interest rates rise, this benefits the portfolio when the manager reinvests coupon proceeds, but the increase in interest rates reduces the value of the portfolio's bond holdings. Proper immunization ensures that the dollars-and-cents effects of these two sources of risk net to zero.

As a simple example, suppose that we are required to invest $936 and ensure that it will grow at a 10 percent compound rate over the next six years, at which time the funds will be withdrawn. This means that in six years the fund needs to be worth $1,658.18: $\$936 \times (1.10)^6 = \$1,658.18$.

Over the six-year period, interest rates will most likely change. If they go up, our reinvested coupons will earn more interest, but the value of any bonds we buy will go down. The account will be liquidated at the end of six years, so we are concerned about the possibility that a capital loss on the bonds may cause our account to end up with a value below our target.

This risk can be reduced by the proper selection of bonds in which to invest. Specifically, we want to invest $936 in some asset or portfolio of assets so that its yield to maturity is 10 percent and its duration is 6.00 years.

One possibility is the single bond used in the example in Table 21-4. This bond has a coupon of 8.8 percent, a maturity in eight years, and a current price such that its duration is 6.00 years. We can immunize using this security. For the sake of simplicity, the example assumes that the bond pays its interest annually and that market interest rates change only once, at the end of the third year. Table 21-4 shows two changes: rates falling from 10 to 9 percent, and rates rising from 10 to 11 percent.

If interest rates remain constant, at the end of year 6 the value of the accumulated (and reinvested) interest proceeds plus the value of the bond equals the amount we targeted (rounding errors ignored).[8] If rates fall to 9 percent, the interest accumulated is $14.54 less than in the constant rate scenario, but the bond price is $17.30 higher. Rising rates increase the interest received by $13.50, but the bond price falls by $16.90.

You will note in the two scenarios in which interest rates change that the resulting portfolio value does not exactly equal the target figure of $1,658.18. Why not? The reason is that the effects of convexity were ignored. Duration is a first-derivative statistic, and it works well for small changes in interest rates. Larger changes result in a divergence between actual price changes and those predicted by duration. Although the dollar difference is not great in this example, the error would be more important if we were investing $936 million rather than the modest sum here.

*If interest rates are expected to rise, bond portfolio managers can reduce the anticipated damage by lowering the duration of the portfolio.*

**Expectation of Changing Interest Rates.** *Duration* is a measure of interest rate risk. The higher the duration, the higher the level of interest rate risk. Faced with the prospect of rising interest rates, the bond portfolio manager might choose to reduce the duration of the portfolio. Duration declines with shorter maturities and higher coupons. This means the portfolio manager wants to sell long-term bonds and replace them with short-term bonds, and sell bonds with low coupons, replacing them with bonds carrying higher coupons. If the manager knows the bonds' durations, the task can be accomplished in one step: Sell bonds with high durations and replace them with bonds of lower duration.

Suppose we have a portfolio like the one in Table 21-5. This portfolio has a market value of $273,746; based on this market value, its average duration is 5.55 years. What can we do if interest rates are expected to rise? The obvious answer is to reduce duration. An extreme approach is to sell all these bonds and replace them with the shortest-duration securities we can find. One solution would be 30-day

[8]We must solve for the bond value: Given an 8.8 percent coupon, a 10 percent yield to maturity, and two years of remaining life, the bond value is $979.20.

**TABLE 21-4** EFFECTS OF IMMUNIZATION

Requirement: Invest $936 at a guaranteed rate of 10% per year for 6.00 years. No cash withdrawals until year 6, when the entire amount is withdrawn.
Solution: Invest $936 in a security (or portfolio of securities) with a yield to maturity of 10.00% and a duration of 6.00 years. One possibility is an investment in the following single bond:
Bond price = $936
Bond annual coupon = 8.8%
Bond maturity = 8 years
Bond yield to maturity = 10.00%

***Interest Rates Remain Constant at 10%***

| | ***Reinvestment Rate at End of Year*** | | | | | |
|---|---|---|---|---|---|---|
| | **10%** | **10%** | **10%** | **10%** | **10%** | — |
| ***Year*** | **1** | **2** | **3** | **4** | **5** | **6** |
| | $88.00 | $ 96.80 | $106.48 | $117.13 | $128.84 | $ 141.72 |
| | | 88.00 | 96.80 | 106.48 | 117.13 | 128.84 |
| | | | 88.00 | 96.80 | 106.48 | 117.13 |
| | | | | 88.00 | 96.80 | 106.48 |
| | | | | | 88.00 | 96.80 |
| | | | | | | 88.00 |
| Total | $88.00 | $184.80 | $291.28 | $408.41 | $537.25 | $678.97 |
| | + Bond value at end of year 6 | | | | | 979.20 |
| | Total portfolio value | | | | | $1,658.17 |

***Interest Rates Fall to 9% After Three Years***

| | ***Reinvestment Rate at End of Year*** | | | | | |
|---|---|---|---|---|---|---|
| | **10%** | **10%** | **9%** | **9%** | **9%** | — |
| ***Year*** | **1** | **2** | **3** | **4** | **5** | **6** |
| | $88.00 | $ 96.80 | $105.51 | $115.01 | $125.36 | $ 136.64 |
| | | 88.00 | 96.80 | 105.51 | 115.01 | 125.36 |
| | | | 88.00 | 95.92 | 104.55 | 113.96 |
| | | | | 88.00 | 95.92 | 104.55 |
| | | | | | 88.00 | 95.92 |
| | | | | | | 88.00 |
| Total | $88.00 | $184.80 | $290.31 | $404.44 | $528.84 | $664.43 |
| | + Bond value at end of year 6 | | | | | 996.50 |
| | Total portfolio value | | | | | $1,660.93 |

***Interest Rates Rise to 11% After Three Years***

| | ***Reinvestment Rate at End of Year*** | | | | | |
|---|---|---|---|---|---|---|
| | **10%** | **10%** | **11%** | **11%** | **11%** | — |
| ***Year*** | **1** | **2** | **3** | **4** | **5** | **6** |
| | $88.00 | $ 96.80 | $106.48 | $118.19 | $131.19 | $ 145.63 |
| | | 88.00 | 96.80 | 107.45 | 119.27 | 132.39 |
| | | | 88.00 | 97.68 | 108.42 | 120.35 |
| | | | | 88.00 | 97.68 | 108.42 |
| | | | | | 88.00 | 97.68 |
| | | | | | | 88.00 |
| Total | $88.00 | $184.80 | $291.28 | $411.32 | $544.56 | $692.47 |
| | + Bond value at end of year 6 | | | | | 962.30 |
| | Total portfolio value | | | | | $1,654.77 |

"Total" shows end-of-year value of reinvested coupon proceeds. Coupons are received at the end of the year.

TABLE 21-5 BOND PORTFOLIO

| *Par* | *Company* | *Coupon* | *Maturity* | *Price* | *Yield* | *Duration* |
|---|---|---|---|---|---|---|
| $ 50,000 | XYZ | 10 1/8 | 2012 | $ 50,860 | 9.80% | 5.28 |
| 75,000 | DEF | 8 | 2017 | 63,728 | 10.13 | 7.41 |
| 40,000 | ALQ | 9 1/2 | 2013 | 40,376 | 9.34 | 5.84 |
| 60,000 | LLG | 7 7/8 | 2020 | 48,810 | 10.29 | 8.14 |
| 70,000 | FFQ | 7 | 2007 | 69,972 | 7.01 | 2.08 |
| $295,000 | | | | $273,746 | | 5.55 |

TABLE 21-6 SIMPLE NATIONAL BANK BALANCE SHEET, JANUARY 1, 2005

| | | | |
|---|---|---|---|
| Rate-sensitive assets | $273,746 | Nonrate-sensitive liabilities | $ 26,000 |
| Nonrate-sensitive assets | 500,000 | Rate-sensitive liabilities | 400,000 |
| | | Net worth | 347,746 |
| Total assets | $773,746 | Total liabilities and net worth (L&NW) | $773,746 |

Treasury bills. Others would be bank repurchase agreements or short-term certificates of deposit.

**An Asset Portfolio with a Corresponding Liability Portfolio.** The previous example showed how an independent bond portfolio can have its interest rate reduced by lowering the average duration of the portfolio. The problem is slightly different if we simultaneously have interest-sensitive liabilities on our balance sheet. This kind of problem is the bank immunization case.

Banks have their own investment officers. In addition to managing portfolios like anyone else, the bank investment officer often is also concerned with certain balance sheet effects associated with changes in the value of the bank's assets and liabilities. Books on the management of financial institutions go into this topic in much greater detail than we will here.

Assume that the bond portfolio shown in Table 21-5 is part of the bank's balance sheet shown in Table 21-6. A bank's **funds gap** is defined as its rate-sensitive assets (RSA) minus its rate-sensitive liabilities (RSL). If the bank wants to immunize itself from the effect of interest rate fluctuations, it must reorder its balance sheet so that the following condition holds:

$$\$_A \times D_A = \$_L \times D_L$$

where $\$_{A,L}$ = dollar value of rate-sensitive assets and liabilities, and $D_{A,L}$ = dollar-weighted average duration of assets and liabilities.

Assume that our bank's interest-sensitive assets are limited to the bonds we looked at previously; the duration of this bond portfolio is 5.55 years (as determined in Table 21-5). Assume also that the interest-sensitive liabilities have a duration of 1.00 years.[9]

We see from these numbers that at the moment, the bank is not immunized from interest rate risk:

$$\$273{,}746 \times 5.55 \text{ years} = 1{,}519{,}290.30 \text{ \$–years}$$

$$\$400{,}000 \times 1.00 \text{ years} = 400{,}000 \text{ \$–years}$$

$$1{,}519{,}290.30 \neq 400{,}000$$

[9]These might be the bank's own bonds that the bank had previously issued in the capital market.

This has important implications. The dollar-duration value of the asset side of the portfolio exceeds that of the liability side. If market interest rates rise, the value of the rate-sensitive assets (RSA) and rate-sensitive liabilities (RSL) will both fall. However, the decline in RSA will exceed the decline of the RSL. The balance sheet must balance, which means that net worth must also decline. Net worth is what determines the value of shares of stock, and management clearly wants to take action to keep the share price from falling if possible. From a pure banking point of view, declining net worth will also cause problems with capital adequacy ratios of the type that bank examiners watch.

To immunize, this bank needs to do one or more of the following:

1. Get rid of some RSA.
2. Reduce the duration of the RSA.
3. Issue more RSL.
4. Raise the duration of the RSL.

Practical considerations make some of these alternatives more attractive than others. Issuing more debt, for instance, is not something that a bank can do quickly, nor can it sell new bonds without significant selling costs. Selling new bonds is also not something that a bank can do very often without causing concern in the capital market. Alternative 3 is probably not a feasible alternative most of the time. Similarly, it is generally not possible to alter the duration of the existing liabilities. This eliminates Alternative 4.

*Banks usually make duration adjustments by altering the left side of the balance sheet.*

This leaves us with the left side of the balance sheet. We could sell some of the investment bonds we hold from the list in Table 21-5 and put the proceeds into non-RSA. The other alternative is to put the proceeds from the sale of high-duration bonds into lower-duration bonds.

This leaves us with one equation and two unknowns (the dollar amount of RSA and their duration). Consequently, the problem theoretically has an infinite number of solutions. In practice, the fact that bonds are sold in increments of $1,000 par value limits the number of possibilities.

If we look carefully at the existing bond portfolio (Table 21-5), we see that our ultimate solution will require us to reduce our RSA. The lowest-duration bond we have is the FFQ 7s07, with a duration of 2.08 years. If we sold all the other bonds and invested the proceeds in more FFQ bonds, the $-years value would be $273,746 × 2.08 years = 569,392 $-years, which is still more than the target value of 400,000 $-years. This means that we have to reduce the size of our RSA.

Note that reducing our RSA does not mean that we are throwing anything away. We have plenty of other assets (such as cash, overnight federal funds, and non-negotiable certificates of deposit) that are not rate sensitive. We will shift RSA money into these as needed.

A good computer programmer could prepare an algorithm that would search the possible ways to rearrange our portfolio and give us a list of the most desirable options. In the absence of such a program, we can still solve the problem without spending too much time on it.

One reasonable solution to the problem is to sell all the bonds except those of XYZ and FFQ, the bonds with the lowest duration. This changes the portfolio, as shown in Table 21-7. This portfolio consists of $120,832 of RSA with an average duration of 3.42, for a total of $120,832 × 3.42 years = 413,245 $-years. This is relatively close to the target figure of 400,000 $-years.

### Immunizing with Interest Rate Futures

Some of the largest users of the T-bond futures contract are financial institutions that use them to hedge interest rate risk on their longer-term securities. A commercial

TABLE 21-7 MODIFIED BOND PORTFOLIO

| Par | Company | Coupon | Maturity | Price | Yield | Duration |
|---|---|---|---|---|---|---|
| $50,000 | XYZ | 10⅛ | 2012 | $ 50,860 | 9.80% | 5.28 |
| 70,000 | FFQ | 7 | 2007 | 69,972 | 7.01% | 2.08 |
| | | | Total RSA | 120,832 | | 3.42 |
| Cash equivalents (non-RSA) | | | | 152,914 | | |
| | | | | $273,746 | | |

bank like the one in the previous example usually maintains a substantial portion of its assets in government securities such as Treasury bonds. If interest rates were to rise, the market value of these bonds would fall, resulting in a reduction in equity on the right side of the balance sheet. Faced with such a prospect, the institution could go short T-bond contracts to hedge this risk.

To effectively implement such a hedge, the manager requires a hedge ratio, much as is necessary with stock index futures. But instead of using beta as a measure of market sensitivity, it is necessary to know the portfolio duration (a measure of interest rate sensitivity).[10]

Suppose a bank portfolio manager holds $10 million face value in government bonds that have a current market price of $9.7 million. Assume also that the weighted average duration of this portfolio is 9.0 years and that the 7.25s25 T-bonds (from Table 21-3), with a duration of 11.14 years, are the cheapest to deliver. The manager can hedge the risk of rising rates via a futures-based immunization strategy.

The hedge ratio is

$$HR = CF_{ctd} \times \frac{P_b \times D_b}{P_f \times D_f} \tag{21-5}$$

where $P_b$ = price of bond portfolio as a percentage of par; $D_b$ = duration of bond portfolio; $P_f$ = price of futures contract as a percentage of 100%; $D_f$ = duration of cheapest-to-deliver bond eligible for delivery against the futures contract; and $CF_{ctd}$ = conversion factor for the cheapest-to-deliver bond.

The hedger wants to select a quantity of futures contracts with characteristics such that

$$P_{c2} - P_{c1} + HR(P_{f2} - P_{f1}) = 0 \tag{21-6}$$

where $P_{ct}$ = price of cash portfolio at time $t$, and $P_{ft}$ = price of futures contracts at time $t$. The whole purpose behind immunization is getting the change in value of one set of assets to offset the change in value of another set.

The cheapest-to-deliver bonds have a duration of 11.14. Suppose the portfolio manager chooses to hedge using a futures contract with a recent settlement price of $90^{22}/_{32}$ percent of par, or 0.906875. The hedge ratio is then

$$HR = 1.1637 \times \frac{0.97 \times 9.0}{0.906875 \times 11.14} = 1.0056$$

Because the portfolio manager is concerned about rising interest rates, and rising rates cause bond prices to fall, the manager needs to go short futures contracts.

[10]Many different strategies exist for hedging interest rate risk. This duration-based example is just one of them.

The number sold depends on the portfolio size and the hedge ratio, as follows:

$$\text{Number of contracts} = \frac{\text{Portfolio value}}{\$100{,}000} \times HR \tag{21-7}$$

$$= \frac{\$9.7 \text{ million}}{\$100{,}000} \times 1.0056$$

$$= 97.54 \text{ contracts} \rightarrow 98 \text{ contracts}$$

This procedure is analogous to the computations used with stock index futures.

A word of caution is in order here. Financial futures are sophisticated financial instruments. Their pricing has many nuances that have not been covered here, including assumptions about yield curve behavior, delivery procedures, and so on. For instance, at least five other ways of calculating the appropriate hedge ratio with financial futures exist. If you want to learn more about these contracts in terms of strategy and application, review some of the books on financial futures in this chapter's Further Reading section.

### *Immunizing with Interest Rate Swaps*

An **interest rate swap** is a popular tool with bankers, corporate treasurers, and portfolio managers who need to manage interest rate risk. As with futures, a swap enables the manager to alter the level of risk without disrupting the underlying portfolio.

Some interest-bearing assets carry a fixed rate; that is, the level of income they produce does not vary with changes in the general level of interest rates. Other assets have a variable (floating) rate. Typically, the floating rate is linked to a market rate such as the London Interbank Offer Rate (LIBOR) or the U.S. prime interest rate.

Of the two participants in the swap, one is currently paying a fixed rate and the other is paying a floating rate. Suppose The Fifth National Bank currently has variable rate loans totaling $100 million as assets on its balance sheet; the bank is currently receiving a variable rate. At the same time, Sojourners Insurance Company holds $100 million in corporate bonds, with an average fixed rate coupon of 7.00 percent; it is receiving a fixed rate. The investment manager at Sojourners is pretty sure that interest rates are going to rise, which will cause the value of its bond investments to fall. To deal with this, the manager wants to reduce the duration of the interest-sensitive assets. (For the sake of this example, assume the bank has no interest-sensitive liabilities.)

The people at Fifth National do not share the interest rate outlook of the folks at Sojourners: in fact, they believe rates are going down. These two institutions are good candidates for an interest rate swap.

The essence of the arrangement is simple: Sojourners agrees to pay a fixed rate on $100 million to Fifth National in exchange for receiving a variable rate on $100 million. Figure 21-1 shows the net effect of the cash flows from the perspectives of the two institutions. Initially, Sojourners receives a fixed rate and is subject to interest rate risk. After the swap, Sojourners passes the fixed rate it receives from its bonds on to Fifth National. Sojourners is left receiving a variable rate and has essentially eliminated the risk.

The *price* of a swap is the fixed rate to which the two parties agree.[11] Suppose in this example that the agreed-upon fixed rate is 8.50 percent. The variable rate is set as

[11]The chosen fixed rate will be the interest rate that causes the swap to have a net present value of zero from the perspective of both parties. It is easy to solve for this rate from the spot rate curve, and both parties will determine the same fixed rate value. Because the swap initially has no value to either party, it is not an asset and does not appear on either firm's balance sheet except as a footnote.

FIGURE 21-1 Interest Rate Swap

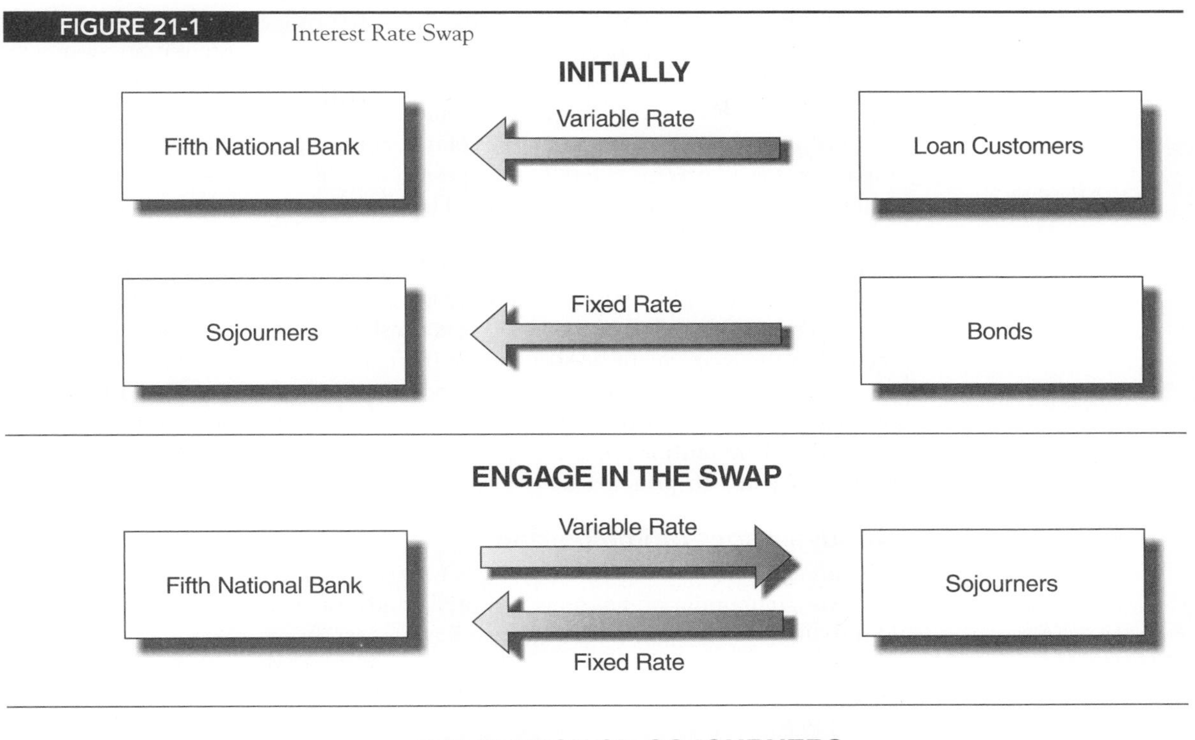


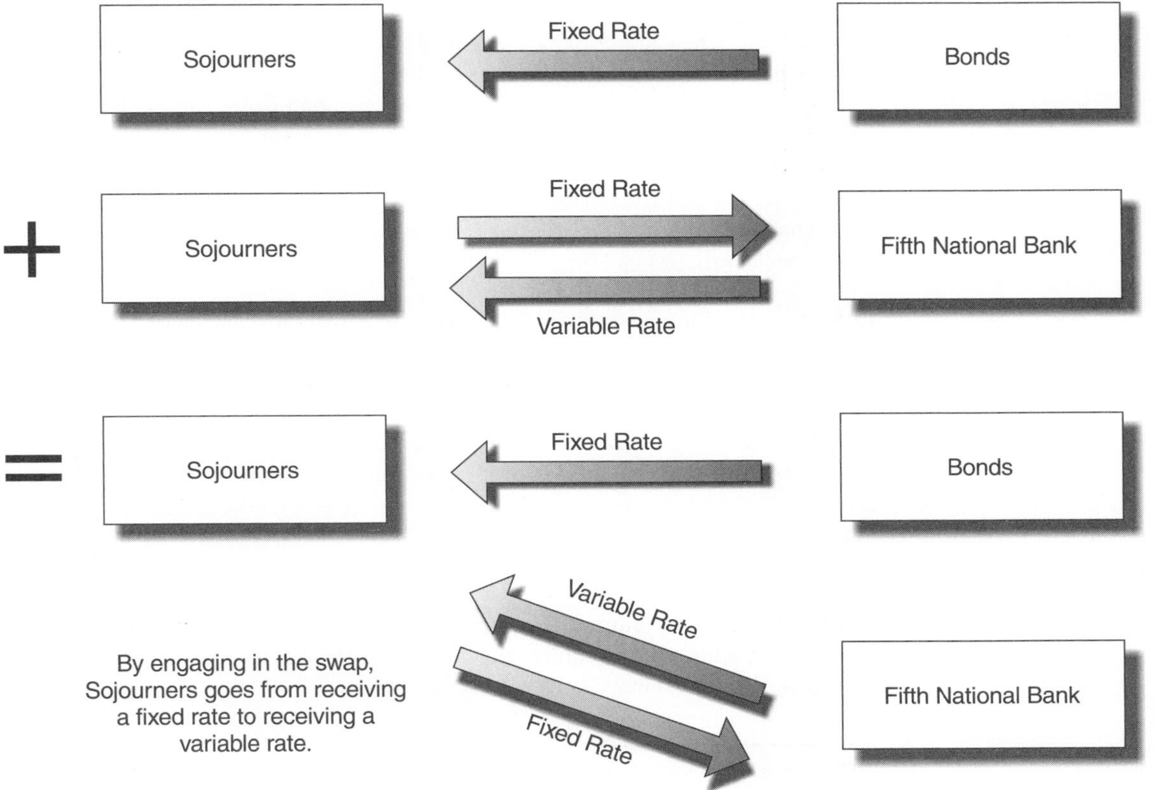

LIBOR plus 100 basis points. Figure 21-2 shows the cash flows the two parties exchange based on hypothetical changes in interest rates. In an interest rate swap such as this, only the net cash flow changes hands; there is no need for both parties to deliver cash. The party owing the larger amount pays the excess over what it is owed.[12]

Using a swap introduces a new type of risk, **counterparty risk.** Because no clearinghouse is guaranteeing the trade, the possibility exists that one party to the swap will not honor its part of the agreement. The consequences of this are not as severe as they might initially seem. If Fifth National fails to pay Sojourners, it is not likely that Sojourners will go ahead and pay Fifth National. The amount at risk is just the net amount owed plus the opportunity cost of not completing the swap arrangement. (Presumably the party *receiving* the net cash flow will not default on the agreement, but the *payer* might do so.) We see in Figure 21-2 that the actual cash flows are much less than $100 million. It would not be reasonable to interpret this swap as putting $100 million at risk. This is the reason the size of the swap is referred to as the **notional amount;** it is just the reference point for determining how much interest is to be paid; the principal amount never changes hands.[13]

### Disadvantages of Immunizing

*Continuous immunization is probably not an optimum strategy.*

If immunization is a good idea, why doesn't everyone do it? Ignorance is a prime reason. Also, immunization has some potential disadvantages. It is probably not a good idea to immunize continuously for the following reasons.

**Opportunity Cost of Being Wrong.** Immunization strategies are based on certain assumptions about the future direction of interest rates, or they may simply be based on the assumption that future rates will be volatile. If the market is efficient, forecasting changes in interest rates is very difficult. With an incorrect forecast, immunized portfolios can suffer an opportunity loss.

Consider the sample bank balance sheet in Table 21-6. This bank has more $-years in RSA than in RSL. We went through an exercise to get these two figures approximately equal because if interest rates had risen, the bank would have suffered a decline in its net worth.

Suppose, however, that contrary to our expectations, interest rates declined. Then, if we had left the balance sheet alone, the value of the RSA would have risen more than the value of the RSL did. This would have resulted in an increase in the bank's net worth.

**Lower Yield.** Immunization usually results in a lower level of income generated by the funds under management. The typical yield curve is upward sloping. This means that everything else being equal, the longer the term of a fixed-income security, the higher its yield.

By reducing the duration (either via asset shifting or interest rate futures), the fund characteristics will shift to the left on the yield curve, normally resulting in a lower level of income for the fund beneficiary. It is a fundamental of finance that lower risk means a lower expected return. This principle holds for immunization strategies as with other investment activities.

**Transaction Costs.** Immunization is also not a costless activity. Selling certain bonds and buying others requires the payment of brokerage commissions. For some investors, these sales may also result in tax liabilities.

---

[12]There are standardized agreements for swaps that spell out exactly how interest is calculated and paid.

[13]Foreign currency swaps are different; the principal amount does change hands in such a swap.

FIGURE 21-2 Interest Rate Swap Cash Flows

**Interest Rate Swap Cash Flows**

Fifth National Bank and Sojourners Insurance agree to swap interest payments on $100 million notional value based on a fixed rate of 8.5% and a floating rate of LIBOR plus 100 bp.

**6 months later:**
**LIBOR = 7.00%**

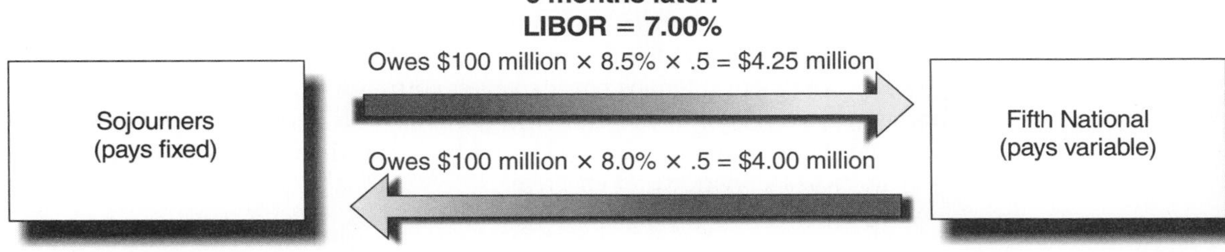


**NET: Sojourners pays Fifth National $250,000**

**12 months later:**
**LIBOR = 6.75%**

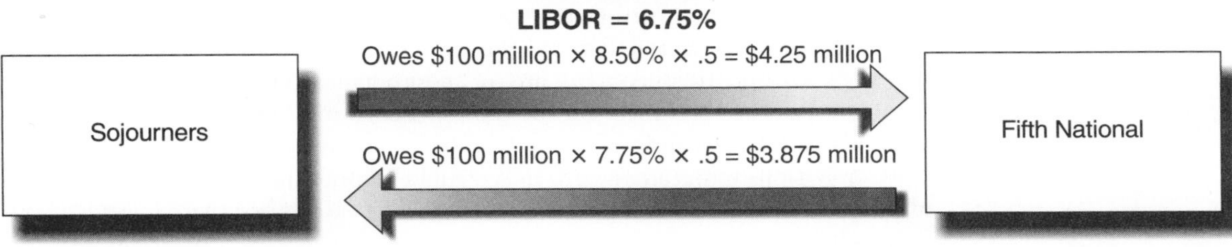


**NET: Sojourners pays Fifth National $375,000**

**18 months later:**
**LIBOR = 7.50%**

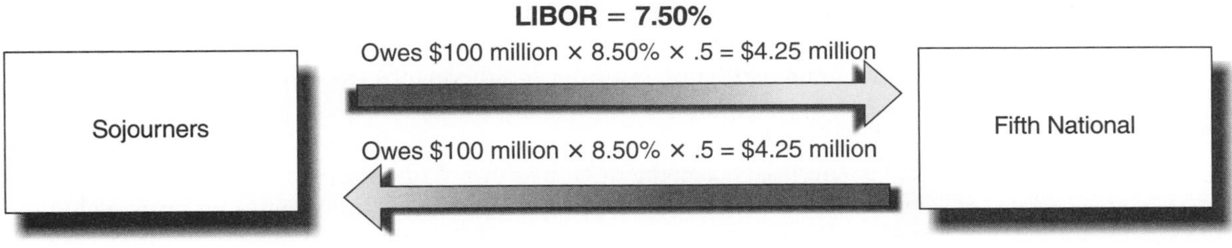


**NET: No cash changes hands**

**24 months later:**
**LIBOR = 7.75%**

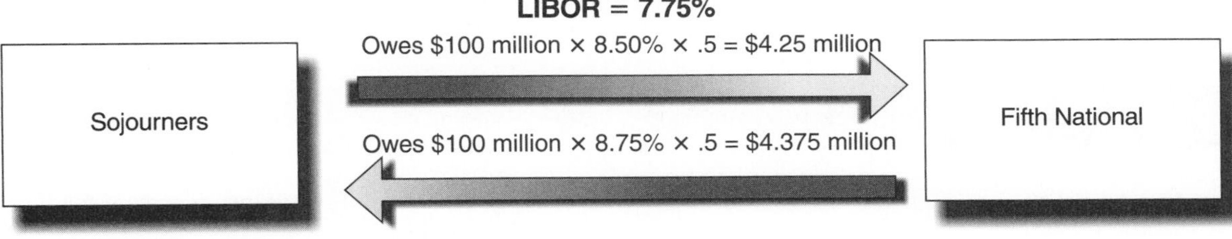


**NET: Fifth National pays Sojourners $125,000**

Commissions are also associated with the futures market, but they are much lower than those resulting from the wholesale replacement of bonds. In fact, this is one of the primary reasons that the futures market is the method of choice for immunization strategies among many portfolio managers.

*Immunization is neither a costless nor a permanent portfolio adjustment.*

**Immunization Is Instantaneous Only.** A portfolio theoretically is immunized only for an instant. With each day that passes, durations change, yields to maturity change, and market interest rates change. The effects of convexity manifest themselves as an increasing level of error between what we expect to happen and what actually occurs unless we periodically readjust the portfolio. This means that the hedge ratio (for futures) or the $-years value (for asset shifting) also changes.

It is not practical for any but the largest portfolios to make daily adjustments to account for changing immunization needs. Smaller portfolios may be initially immunized and revised only after weeks have passed or when conditions have changed enough to make revision cost effective.

## SUMMARY

We group interest rate futures contracts into short-term, intermediate-term, and long-term contracts. Eurodollars are the most popular short-term futures contract. Treasury notes and Treasury bonds are the most popular in the latter two categories, respectively. These contracts can be used to hedge interest rate risk such as that faced by financial institutions.

Conversion factors are used to turn eligible T-bonds into equivalents for futures delivery. Bonds with coupons above 6 percent count extra; bonds with lower coupons do not count as much.

Treasury bonds are priced on the basis of a bond that is the cheapest to deliver. When long-term market interest rates are above 6 percent, the bond with the highest duration is normally the cheapest to deliver.

Immunization is a technique designed to eliminate much of the interest rate risk inherent in a bond portfolio or the net interest rate risk on a balance sheet. The essence of immunization is turning long-term securities into short-term securities or security equivalents.

Hedging with financial futures requires a hedge ratio. With stock index futures, beta is a necessary component of this ratio. With interest rate futures, duration is the key component. A portfolio manager can also use an interest rate swap to alter the level of interest rate risk within the portfolio.

Immunization is not a costless activity. It usually results in an opportunity loss if the direction of interest rates is not correctly forecasted; it lowers the expected return of a portfolio, and it results in higher transaction costs. Immunization also is an instantaneous strategy that requires frequent revision.

## QUESTIONS

1. Briefly explain why it is necessary to translate all bonds into 6 percent equivalents in the delivery process for Treasury bond futures.
2. What is the purpose of calculating the bond equivalent yield with Treasury bills?

3. Suppose you are the manager of a money market mutual fund. Would it matter if you hedged interest rate risk using Treasury bond futures instead of T-bill futures?
4. Why is it necessary to include the provision about call protection in the definition of bonds eligible for delivery against the T-bond futures contract?
5. Who might logically use T-bills or Eurodollars in a hedge designed to reduce interest rate risk?
6. Why is immunization not a costless activity?
7. Do you think that the need to hedge short-term interest rates is as important as the need to hedge long-term rates?
8. Could a bank portfolio manager hedge the risk of a bond portfolio by using T-bill futures? If so, how?
9. Explain why the cheapest-to-deliver bond has the lowest ratio of market price to conversion factor.
10. For a bank to be immunized, the duration of the left side of its balance sheet must equal the duration of the right side. True or false, and why?
11. Look at a current issue of *The Wall Street Journal*. Compare the settlement prices of the different Treasury bill futures contracts. Why do you think they are different?

## PROBLEMS

1. The newspaper price for a T-bill futures contract is 93.33. What is the value of the T-bills promised at delivery based on this price?
2. A speculator goes long four T-bill contracts at 93.34 and closes them out three weeks later at 93.40. Calculate this person's gain or loss in dollar terms.
3. Zero coupon bonds are securities that pay no periodic interest. They have one cash flow: the return of principal at maturity. What is the duration of a zero coupon bond?
4. A $10,000 T-bill comes due in eighty-eight days and sells for $9,800. Calculate the following:
   a. The ask discount.
   b. The bond equivalent yield.

Problems 5 through 10 use the Convfact file on the Strong Software on the text Website.

5. You deliver 16-year T-bonds with a 7 percent coupon on an interest payment date against a futures contract position. If the T-bond settlement price on position day is 92, what is the invoice price?
6. Make up a bullet immunization example using two of the bonds in Table 21-5. Prepare a summary like the one in Table 21-4. Assume the bonds pay interest annually.
7. A Treasury bond matures in twenty-one years and has a coupon of $7\frac{5}{8}$ percent. What is its conversion factor?
8. A Treasury bond matures in twenty-one years and has a coupon of 9 percent. What is its conversion factor?
9. On position day, a T-bond futures contract settles at 92. The hedger chooses to deliver bonds with a $6\frac{1}{2}$ percent coupon that mature in twenty-four years, five months. If delivery occurs exactly halfway through an interest payment cycle, what is the invoice price?

10. Refer to Problem 9. Suppose, instead, the bond chosen for delivery is a 9 percent, 20-year bond. The other conditions remain the same. What is the invoice price?
11. Refer to Table 21-5. Instead of a par value of $295,000, suppose this portfolio was scaled up in size by a factor of 10. Suppose also that the cheapest-to-deliver bond sells for 92 and has a duration of 10.5, and that the relevant futures settlement price is 90½. How many Treasury bond futures contracts are necessary to immunize the portfolio?
12. A 10 percent bond sells for 110 percent of par and matures in exactly sixteen years. Calculate its conversion factor.
13. You expect to receive $4.5 million to invest in Treasury bills in one month. Using current price information from *The Wall Street Journal,* show specifically how to lock in a current interest rate using Treasury bill futures.
14. Repeat Problem 13, except lock in a long-term rate using Treasury bond futures.

## INTERNET EXERCISE

Go to the Chicago Board of Trade Website at *http://www.cbot.com*. Investigate the "publications" section and order some free material dealing with interest rate risk hedging.

## FURTHER READING


Arak, Marcelle, and Laurie S. Goodman. "How to Calculate Better T-Bond Hedge Ratios." *Futures*, February 1986.

———, and Susan Ross. "The Cheapest to Deliver Bond on the Treasury Bond Futures Contract." *Advances in Futures and Options Research* 1, B (1986): 49–74.

Arditti, F. "Interest Rate Futures: An Intermediate Stage toward Efficient Risk Allocation." *Journal of Bank Research,* Autumn 1978, 146–150.

Bacon, P., and R. Williams. "Interest Rate Futures: New Tool for the Financial Manager." *Financial Management,* Spring 1976, 32–37.

Bierwag, G.O. "The Art of Risk Management in Bond Portfolios." *Journal of Portfolio Management,* Spring 1981, 27–36.

———. "Dynamic Portfolio Immunization Policies." *Journal of Banking and Finance,* April 1979, 23–41.

———. "Immunization, Duration, and the Term Structure of Interest Rates." *Journal of Financial and Quantitative Analysis*, December 1977, 725–742.

Chance, Don. "Futures Contracts and Immunization." *Review of Research in Futures Markets*, March 1986, 124–140.

———. "An Immunized-Hedge Procedure for Bond Futures." *Journal of Futures Markets*, Fall 1982, 231–242.

*Chicago Board of Trade Conversion Factors*. Brookline, Mass.: Financial Publishing, 1985.

*Commodity Trading Manual*. Chicago: Chicago Board of Trade, 1994.

Figlewski, Stephen. *Hedging with Financial Futures for Institutional Investors*. Cambridge, Mass.: Ballinger Publishing, 1986.

Geske, Robert L., and Dan R. Pieptea. "Controlling Interest Rate Risk and Return with Futures." *Review of Futures Markets*, May 1987, 64–86.

Hilliard, Jimmy. "Hedging Interest Rate Risk with Futures Portfolios under Term Structure Effects." *Journal of Finance*, December 1984, 1547–1569.

Kolb, Robert W. *Interest Rate Futures*. Richmond, Va.: Robert F. Dame, 1982.

———, and Raymond Chiang. "Duration, Immunization, and Hedging with Interest Rate Futures." *Journal of Financial Research*, Summer 1982, 161–170.

Labuzewski, John W. "Examining Duration, 'Hedge Ratio,' and Basis Risk to Hedge Securities." *Futures*, May 1989, 50–51.

Little, Patricia Knain. "Financial Futures and Immunization." *Journal of Financial Research*, Spring 1986, 1–12.

Sinkey, Joseph F. *Commercial Bank Financial Management*. New York: Macmillan, 1983.

Toevs, Alden, and David P. Jacob. "Futures and Alternative Hedge Ratio Methodologies." *Journal of Portfolio Management*, Spring 1986, 60–70.

# 22 Integrating Derivative Assets and Portfolio Management

*Life wasn't designed to be risk-free. The key is not to eliminate risk, but to estimate it accurately and manage it wisely.*

***William A. Schreyer, former chairman and CEO, Merrill Lynch & Company***

## Key Terms

away from the money
Black Option Pricing Model
cash drag
futures option
nonsynchronous trading
position delta

## Introduction

This chapter is an extended example focusing on risk management and income generation. It pays special attention to the integration of futures and options into the portfolio management process.

## Setting the Stage

Regardless of whether a portfolio manager uses derivative assets, portfolio objectives must be set. The fund manager can use futures and options to adjust the characteristics of the fixed-income portfolio, the equity portfolio, or both to keep the portfolio in line with those objectives.

### *Portfolio Objectives*

Assume that you have been given responsibility for the management of a corporation's in-house scholarship fund. The fund previously had no specific objectives stated; there was no statement of investment policy. The fund is composed entirely of corporate and government bonds and several large bank certificates of deposit. It seems the fund has income as its objective by default.

The CDs have recently matured, and the corporation has decided to get the account under professional supervision. After discussion with a subcommittee of the board of directors (which has fiduciary responsibility for the fund), the board determined that growth of income was the fund's primary objective, with capital appreciation as its secondary objective. A one-time need also requires that the portfolio generate at least $75,000 in income during the next year. There will be future draws on the portfolio for subsequent scholarships, but the board set no specific dollar amount. That has been left to your professional judgment.

The account will be opened with a deposit of cash and the existing fixed-income securities, for a total value of about $1.5 million. The foundation has a small, separate trust fund (not under management by your firm), and you have been told that trading fees will be paid from this source. This means that you do not need to consider these charges as you construct the portfolio.

### Portfolio Construction

**Fixed-Income Securities.** The fund currently holds ten separate fixed-income securities. You are pleasantly surprised to find that there is some rhyme and reason to this portfolio. Table 22-1 shows current statistics for these issues.

**Stocks.** The decision has been made to include twenty common stocks in the portfolio so that the portfolio beta is between 1.05 and 1.15. You do not want to invest a substantial amount of the funds available for equity purchase into any single security, so you decide to try to constrain the investment in each stock to between 4 and 7 percent of the total.

Such a problem lends itself to a solution by linear programming. The linear programming model in Figure 22-1 is one way that you as a manager might approach the problem. Linear programming is most often a tool to find the *optimum* solution to a problem. Here it is used to find a *feasible* solution to an otherwise cumbersome problem. You could adjust the proportions of the individual stocks using a trial-and-error approach, but a linear program will make short work of the task.

Some objective function must be specified in a linear program, but this application has no obvious variable to maximize or minimize. The program in Figure 22-1 seeks to maximize the portfolio beta but also constrains the portfolio beta to be within 1.05 and 1.15. This linear program was solved using the Statistical Analysis

**TABLE 22-1** FIXED INCOME SECURITIES

| *Par* | *Issue* | *Price(%)* | *YTM(%)* | *Market Value* | *Annual Income* | *Duration* |
|---|---|---|---|---|---|---|
| $ 50,000 | US6s05 | 100 | 6.00 | $ 50,000 | $ 3,000 | 5.13 |
| 50,000 | US7s06 | 105 | 6.10 | 52,500 | 3,500 | 5.69 |
| 50,000 | US7s07 | 105 | 6.20 | 52,500 | 3,500 | 6.31 |
| 50,000 | US7s08 | 104¾ | 6.30 | 52,375 | 3,500 | 6.88 |
| 50,000 | US5.5s09 | 90⅝ | 6.80 | 45,313 | 2,750 | 7.69 |
| 50,000 | AB6.3s10 | 94⅝ | 7.00 | 47,313 | 3,150 | 8.01 |
| 50,000 | CD7.1s11 | 100 | 7.10 | 50,000 | 3,550 | 8.27 |
| 50,000 | EF7.3s12 | 100⅞ | 7.20 | 50,438 | 3,650 | 8.63 |
| 50,000 | GH7¼s13 | 99½ | 7.30 | 49,750 | 3,625 | 9.01 |
| 50,000 | IJ6¼s14 | 89⅝ | 7.40 | 44,813 | 3,125 | 9.63 |
| $500,000 | | | | $495,002 | $33,350 | 7.48* |

*Value-weighted average.

**FIGURE 22-1**

Linear Program for Construction of the Stock Portfolio

$$\text{MAX} \sum_{i=1}^{20} \frac{x_i \beta_i}{\text{stock portfolio value}} \text{ (maximum portfolio beta)}$$

subject to

$$(1) \sum_{i=1}^{20} x_i = \$1{,}000{,}000 \text{ (invest all the money)}$$

$$(2) \sum_{i=1}^{20} = \frac{x_i \beta_i}{\$1{,}000{,}000} \leq 1.15 \text{ (beta less than or equal to 1.15)}$$

$$(3) \sum_{i=1}^{20} = \frac{x_i \beta_i}{\$1{,}000{,}000} \geq 1.05 \text{ (beta greater than or equal to 1.05)}$$

$$(4) \frac{x_i}{\$1{,}000{,}000} < 0.07 \text{ (maximum individual investment of 7\%)}$$

$$(5) \frac{x_i}{\$1{,}000{,}000} > 0.04 \text{ (minimum individual investment of 4\%)}$$

$x_i$ = dollars invested in Security $i$

$\beta_i$ = beta of Security $i$

**FIGURE 22-2** SAS Linear Program

```
DATA;
INPUT P1-P20 T $ R @@;
CARDS;
 .011 .0097 .0123 .0131 .0086 .0121 .01 .0105 .0107 .0111 .0092
 .0087 .107 .01 .0106 .0127 .0109 .0095 .0105 .0110 MAX .
 .011 .0097 .0123 .0131 .0086 .0121 .01 .0105 .0107 .0111 .0092
 .0087 .0107 .01 .0106 .0127 .0109 .0095 .0105 .0110 LE 1.15
 .011 .0097 .0123 .0131 .0086 .0121 .01 .0105 .0107 .0111 .0092
 .0087 .0107 .01 .0106 .0127 .0109 .0095 .0105 .0110 GE 1.05
1 1 1 1 1 1 1 1 1 1 1 1 1 1 1 1 1 1 1 1 EQ 100
4 4 4 4 4 4 4 4 4 4 4 4 4 4 4 4 4 4 4 4 LOWERBD .
7 7 7 7 7 7 7 7 7 7 7 7 7 7 7 7 7 7 7 7 UPPERBD .
PROC LP;
VAR P1-P20;
RHS R;
TYPE T;
```

The values under the CARDS statement are the individual security betas divided by 100. This program is based on a total portfolio expenditure of $100; values can be scaled linearly for larger portfolios.

System (SAS) LP procedure; the complete program is listed in Figure 22-2. Table 22-2 shows the results of the initial run (for a $1 million portfolio).

You wish to avoid the wholesale use of the odd lots suggested by the linear program, so you round the share purchases to the nearest hundred, making one or two other small adjustments to stay within the capital constraints. Table 22-3 shows the final stock portfolio, annotated with other details. The complete listing of the portfolio (stocks and fixed-income securities) appears in Table 22-4 on page 600.

**TABLE 22-2** INITIAL PORTFOLIO SOLUTION

| *Stock* | *Price* | *Shares* | *Beta* |
|---|---|---|---|
| SEC1 | $11 | 5,454 | 1.10 |
| SEC2 | 22 | 1,818 | 0.97 |
| SEC3 | 16.50 | 4,242 | 1.23 |
| SEC4 | 7 | 10,000 | 1.31 |
| SEC5 | 23.13 | 2,162 | 0.86 |
| SEC6 | 14 | 5,000 | 1.21 |
| SEC7 | 17 | 2,353 | 1.00 |
| SEC8 | 21 | 1,905 | 1.05 |
| SEC9 | 46 | 870 | 1.07 |
| SEC10 | 28 | 2,500 | 1.11 |
| SEC11 | 7.75 | 5,161 | 0.92 |
| SEC12 | 9 | 4,444 | 0.87 |
| SEC13 | 14 | 2,857 | 1.07 |
| SEC14 | 21 | 1,905 | 1.00 |
| SEC15 | 16 | 2,500 | 1.06 |
| SEC16 | 19.50 | 3,590 | 1.27 |
| SEC17 | 47 | 851 | 1.09 |
| SEC18 | 66 | 606 | 0.95 |
| SEC19 | 34 | 1,176 | 1.05 |
| SEC20 | 56 | 1,250 | 1.10 |

**TABLE 22-3** FINAL STOCK PORTFOLIO

| *Stock* | *Price* | *Shares* | *Value* | *Annual Dividends* | *Beta* |
|---|---|---|---|---|---|
| SEC1 | $11 | 5,500 | $ 60,500 | $ 1,210 | 1.10 |
| SEC2 | 22 | 1,800 | 39,600 | 634 | 0.97 |
| SEC3 | 16.50 | 4,200 | 69,300 | 1,455 | 1.23 |
| SEC4 | 7 | 10,000 | 70,000 | 0 | 1.31 |
| SEC5 | 23.13 | 2,200 | 50,886 | 3,307 | 0.86 |
| SEC6 | 14 | 5,000 | 70,000 | 1,190 | 1.21 |
| SEC7 | 17 | 2,400 | 40,800 | 816 | 1.00 |
| SEC8 | 21 | 1,900 | 39,900 | 758 | 1.05 |
| SEC9 | 46 | 900 | 41,400 | 662 | 1.07 |
| SEC10 | 28 | 2,500 | 70,000 | 490 | 1.11 |
| SEC11 | 7.75 | 5,200 | 40,300 | 1,733 | 0.92 |
| SEC12 | 9 | 4,400 | 39,600 | 2,020 | 0.87 |
| SEC13 | 14 | 2,900 | 40,600 | 568 | 1.07 |
| SEC14 | 21 | 1,900 | 39,900 | 998 | 1.00 |
| SEC15 | 16 | 2,500 | 40,000 | 1,880 | 1.06 |
| SEC16 | 19.50 | 3,600 | 70,200 | 772 | 1.27 |
| SEC17 | 47 | 800 | 37,600 | 1,918 | 1.09 |
| SEC18 | 66 | 600 | 39,600 | 1,069 | 0.95 |
| SEC19 | 34 | 1,200 | 40,800 | 1,306 | 1.05 |
| SEC20 | 56 | 1,000 | 56,000 | 2,240 | 1.10 |
| | | | $ 996,986 | $25,026 | 1.08* |
| | Uninvested cash | | $ 3,014 | | |
| | Total value | | $1,000,000 | | |

*Value-weighted average.

**TABLE 22-4** FINAL PORTFOLIO

***Fixed-Income Securities***

| *Par* | *Issue* | *Price* | *YTM* | *Market Value* | *Annual Income* | *Duration* |
|---|---|---|---|---|---|---|
| $ 50,000 | US6s05 | $100 | 6.00 | $ 50,000 | $ 3,000 | 5.13 |
| 50,000 | US7s06 | 105 | 6.10 | 52,500 | 3,500 | 5.69 |
| 50,000 | US7s07 | 105 | 6.20 | 52,500 | 3,500 | 6.31 |
| 50,000 | US7s08 | 104¾ | 6.30 | 52,375 | 3,500 | 6.88 |
| 50,000 | US5.5s09 | 90⅝ | 6.80 | 45,313 | 2,750 | 7.69 |
| 50,000 | AB6.3s10 | 94⅝ | 7.00 | 47,313 | 3,150 | 8.01 |
| 50,000 | CD7.1s11 | 100 | 7.10 | 50,000 | 3,550 | 8.27 |
| 50,000 | EF7.3s12 | 100⅞ | 7.20 | 50,438 | 3,650 | 8.63 |
| 50,000 | GH7¼s13 | 99½ | 7.30 | 49,750 | 3,625 | 9.01 |
| 50,000 | IJ6¼s14 | 89⅝ | 7.40 | 44,813 | 3,125 | 9.63 |
| $500,000 | | | | $495,002 | $33,350 | 7.48* |

***Stock Portfolio***

| *Stock* | *Price* | *Shares* | *Value* | *Annual Dividends* | *Beta* |
|---|---|---|---|---|---|
| SEC1 | $11 | 5,500 | $ 60,500 | $ 1,210 | 1.10 |
| SEC2 | 22 | 1,800 | 39,600 | 634 | 0.97 |
| SEC3 | 16.50 | 4,200 | 69,300 | 1,455 | 1.23 |
| SEC4 | 7 | 10,000 | 70,000 | 0 | 1.31 |
| SEC5 | 2.13 | 2,200 | 50,886 | 3,307 | 0.86 |
| SEC6 | 14 | 5,000 | 70,000 | 1,190 | 1.21 |
| SEC7 | 17 | 2,400 | 40,800 | 816 | 1.00 |
| SEC8 | 21 | 1,900 | 39,900 | 758 | 1.05 |
| SEC9 | 46 | 900 | 41,400 | 662 | 1.07 |
| SEC10 | 28 | 2,500 | 70,000 | 490 | 1.11 |
| SEC11 | 7.75 | 5,200 | 40,300 | 1,733 | 0.92 |
| SEC12 | 9 | 4,400 | 39,600 | 2,020 | 0.87 |
| SEC13 | 14 | 2,900 | 40,600 | 568 | 1.07 |
| SEC14 | 21 | 1,900 | 39,900 | 998 | 1.00 |
| SEC15 | 16 | 2,500 | 40,000 | 1,880 | 1.06 |
| SEC16 | 19.50 | 3,600 | 70,200 | 772 | 1.27 |
| SEC17 | 47 | 800 | 37,600 | 1,918 | 1.09 |
| SEC18 | 66 | 600 | 39,600 | 1,069 | 0.95 |
| SEC19 | 34 | 1,200 | 40,800 | 1,306 | 1.05 |
| SEC20 | 56 | 1,000 | 56,000 | 2,240 | 1.10 |
| | | | $996,986 | $25,026 | 1.08* |

| Total portfolio value: | Fixed income | $ 495,002 |
|---|---|---|
| | Cash | 3,014 |
| | Stock | 996,986 |
| | | $1,495,0[illegible]2 |

*Value-weighted average.

## Meeting an Income Constraint

Derivative assets can increase the income generated by a portfolio and reduce the levels of market or interest rate risk the portfolio faces. Index options are especially well suited to increasing portfolio income.

### Determining Unmet Income Needs

The portfolio shown in Table 22-4 contains about 67 percent stock and 33 percent bonds. (The percentage held in cash is essentially zero.) These proportions are consistent with the primary and secondary objectives of growth of income and capital appreciation, respectively.

A contractual commitment the corporation previously made necessitates the generation of at least $75,000 in income for the forthcoming calendar year. The portfolio as it stands should yield $33,350 from the bonds and at least $25,026 in dividends, for an annual total of $58,376. This is a total portfolio yield of 3.9 percent and a shortfall of $16,624 relative to the $75,000 goal.

### Writing Index Calls

Suppose the manager decides to write stock index call options to make up the difference. Although the exercise of index calls does not result in the actual delivery of stock certificates because index options are cash settled, exercise is still an inconvenience to be avoided. The index call writer can reduce the likelihood of exercise by writing short-term out-of-the-money options but sacrifices option premium by doing so.[1]

As shown in Chapter 15, for options that are substantially in or out of the money, the option delta is approximately equal to the likelihood that the option will expire in the money.[2] Calculating delta requires knowledge of the anticipated option volatility over the life of the option, and you can extract this from the current option prices by determining the volatility implied in Black-Scholes prices.

It is best to estimate implied volatility using a near-the-money option with a remaining life equal to the desired time horizon. Suppose that after consideration of the risk and return characteristics of the various choices, you narrow the choices down to the index options shown in Table 22-5, all of which have an August expiration. The table indicates the current level of the index is 298.96, so the appropriate option to use in the calculation of implied volatility is the AUG 300 call with a

**TABLE 22-5** AUGUST INDEX OPTION DATA

| *Striking Price* | *Premium* | *Delta* |
|---|---|---|
| 305 | 4.13 | 0.435 |
| 310 | 3 | 0.324 |
| 315 | 1.75 | 0.228 |
| 320 | 1 | 0.151 |

Current Level of the Index = 298.96

[1]This is consistent with the fundamental trade-off of risk and return.

[2]See the article by Baz and Strong in the Further Reading section of this chapter to learn more about this heuristic.

premium of 7.50. Assume there are 59 days until expiration for the sake of this example. Using the assumed T-bill rate of 6.0 percent gives an implied volatility of 13.77 percent.[3]

Now you must decide which option(s) in the August series to write. To make an informed decision, you must consider both the likelihood of option exercise and the level of income generated. Once you have determined implied volatility, you can calculate the option deltas. Table 22-5 shows the out-of-the-money August call deltas.

As shown in Chapter 15, the number of index option contracts that the manager can write depends on the nature of the equity provided for the short calls. In this situation, the equity comes from the existing stocks and bonds. Table 16-6 shows that the first step in the determination is the calculation of the number of contracts that can be written using cash as collateral. Table 22-6 calculates this value for striking prices from 305 to 320.

**TABLE 22-6** MAXIMUM PERMISSIBLE AUGUST INDEX CALL CONTRACTS USING CASH AS COLLATERAL

| *Strike Price = 305* | | |
|---|---|---|
| 15% of index: 0.15 × $298.96 × 100 × *N* | = | $4,484.40*N* |
| Plus market value: *N* × $4.875 × 100 | = | 487.50*N* |
| Minus out-of-the-money amount: ($305 – $298.96) × 100 × *N* | = | (604.00*N*) |
| | | $4,367.90*N* |
| $1,495,002 = $4,367.90*N* | | |
| *N* = 342 contracts | | |
| *Strike Price = 310* | | |
| 15% of index: 0.15 × $298.96 × 100 × *N* | = | $4,484.40*N* |
| Plus market value: *N* × $3.00 × 100 | = | 300.00*N* |
| Minus out-of-the-money amount: ($310 – $298.96) × 100 × *N* | = | (1,104.00*N*) |
| | | $3,680.40*N* |
| $1,495,002 = $3,680.40*N* | | |
| *N* = 406 contracts | | |
| *Strike Price = 315* | | |
| 15% of index: 0.15 × $298.96 × 100 × *N* | = | $4,484.40*N* |
| Plus market value: *N* × $1.75 × 100 | = | 175.00*N* |
| Minus out-of-the-money amount: ($315 – $298.96) × 100 × *N* | = | (1,604.00*N*) |
| | | $3,055.40*N* |
| $1,495,002 = $3,055.40*N* | | |
| *N* = 489 contracts | | |
| *Strike Price = 320* | | |
| 15% of index: 0.15 × $298.96 × 100 × *N* | = | $4,484.40*N* |
| Plus market value: *N* × $1.00 × 100 | = | 100.00*N* |
| Minus out-of-the-money amount: ($320 – $298.96) × 100 × *N* | = | (2,104.00*N*) |
| | | $2,480.40*N* |
| $1,495,002 = $2,480.40*N* | | |
| *N* = 603 contracts | | |

[3]The value would be slightly different if the dividends on the OEX index were included. The index itself pays no dividends, but the underlying securities do, and this information can be used to adjust Black-Scholes estimates. (Recall that the Black-Scholes model assumes no dividends.)

**TABLE 22-7** AUGUST INDEX CALL DELTA

| *Striking Price* | *Wall Street Journal Premium* | *Delta* | *Maximum Contracts** | *Income* |
|---|---|---|---|---|
| 305 | 4.875 | 0.435 | 171 | $83,362 |
| 310 | 3.00 | 0.324 | 203 | 60,900 |
| 315 | 1.75 | 0.228 | 244 | 42,700 |
| 320 | 1.00 | 0.151 | 301 | 30,100 |

*Using stock as collateral.

Table 22-7 presents the option delta with the maximum number of contracts that can be written using stock as collateral. The number of contracts that can be written using stock is only half the number permissible using cash, and it constitutes the most restrictive condition (see Table 16-5). The portfolio at hand contains some government and corporate bonds that carry more generous margin rules. As Table 22-7 shows, however, the number of contracts that can be written using the most restrictive requirements (those for stock) are more than enough to satisfy the additional income need of $16,624.

After reviewing the choices, you decide to write 56 contracts of the AUG 310 index calls. The use of these options rather than a more out-of-the-money option is advantageous principally in that it requires writing fewer contracts. The AUG 310 calls, if sold for $3 each, generate additional portfolio income of $16,800, which will be received immediately and can be transferred to the fund beneficiary. With a delta of 0.324, it is likely that these options will expire worthless and require no further activity by the fund manager.

## Risk Management

The risk management function requires that the portfolio manager deal with the stock portfolio and the fixed-income portfolio separately.

### *Stock Portfolio*

*Writing calls will reduce a portfolio's beta.*

Table 22-4 indicates that the beta of the stock portfolio alone is about 1.08. Writing call options against a portfolio always reduces the portfolio beta because short calls carry negative deltas.[4] Even when the task at hand does not directly involve adjusting the risk level of the portfolio, it is important to know the risk level.

It is possible, for instance, to write index call options in a quantity so that the overall portfolio has a negative position delta, is therefore bearish, and will benefit more from declining market prices than from a rise. If your position delta is negative, it is certainly important to be aware of the fact.

You chose to write 56 of the AUG 310 calls, and this will reduce the portfolio beta. The options contribute $56 \times 100 \times -0.324 = -1{,}814$ to the portfolio position delta. But how is this figure combined with the knowledge that the portfolio beta is 1.08?

[4]Writing calls also always reduces the position delta.

The answer lies in turning the portfolio into index equivalents, much as was done when hedge ratios were calculated for stock index futures contracts in Chapter 20. There the hedge ratio was determined as follows:

$$HR = \frac{\text{Portfolio value}}{\text{Contract value}} \times \text{Beta}$$

In the current example, you know the stock portfolio value, the portfolio beta, and the value of the index. This gives a hedge ratio of

$$HR = \frac{\$996{,}975}{\$298.96 \times 100} \times 1.08 = 36.02$$

The stock portfolio shown in Table 22-4 is theoretically equivalent to 36.02 at-the-money contracts of the index. Although no index contract has a striking price of 298.96, you can still calculate the delta of such a hypothetical contract. This merely requires substituting 298.96 for the striking price in the Black-Scholes model. Doing so, you find a delta of 0.578.

You can now estimate the stock portfolio position delta as shown in Table 22-8. The stock portfolio has a beta of 1.08 and is equivalent to 36.02 at-the-money index contracts, which have a delta contribution of 2,081.96. After writing the calls, the position delta is only 267.56. You can then approximate the resulting portfolio beta by a simple proportional relationship, as shown here:[5]

$$\frac{\text{Initial portfolio delta}}{\text{Initial portfolio beta}} = \frac{\text{Final portfolio delta}}{\text{Final portfolio beta}}$$

$$\frac{2{,}081.96}{1.08} = \frac{267.56}{\text{Beta}}$$

$$\text{Beta} = 0.14$$

These results indicate that the stock portfolio, combined with the short index calls, has a positive position delta and a slightly positive beta, meaning that the complete package is slightly bullish. In other words, the portfolio will benefit from rising market prices and will suffer from falling prices. An example will illustrate this, but first a word needs to be said about trusting prices from the financial press and from theoretical pricing models.

**TABLE 22-8** CALCULATION OF POSITION DELTA

| | | *Stock Portfolio* | | |
|---|---|---|---|---|
| *INDEX Equivalent* | | *Delta* | | *Contribution* |
| 36.02 | × | 0.578 × 100 | = | 2,081.96 |
| | | ***AUG 310 Calls*** | | |
| *Contracts* | | *Delta* | | *Contribution* |
| 56 | × | (−0.324) × 100 | = | −1,814.40 |
| | | | Position delta | 267.56 |

[5]As a first derivative, delta is most accurate for small changes in the price of the underlying asset. With a large change in market prices, this proportional estimate of beta will be inaccurate.

**Caveats about Prices from the Popular Press.** *The Wall Street Journal* and other daily financial publications are widely thought to include the closing prices for securities traded on the exchanges. In fact, the paper shows the last price at which a security traded during the day. The same is true of an Internet price quotation; you retrieve the last price, whenever it was. It may or may not have been at the close of trading. For an actively traded issue, the last trade is likely to have occurred very near the closing bell. For less actively traded issues, however, including deep in-the-money or deep out-of-the-money options, this price may have been determined hours before the close. The phenomenon whereby comparative prices come from different points in time is called **nonsynchronous trading.** Consequently, when you consider strategies that involve the use of options that are **away from the money** (that is, they are not near the money), you should avoid taking the calculations too far without verifying the actual bid/ask prices for a security using a Quotron screen or other electronic source.

In the example at hand, *The Wall Street Journal* price for the AUG 310 call is shown as $3.00; using an implied volatility of 13.77 percent, the Black-Scholes price is $3.40. This is a substantial difference in premium, and the differential adds up quickly when options are written in quantity. It is likely, in fact, that at the close of the market, when the information in Table 22-5 was compiled, the $3.00 price reported in the financial press was not current. The true price was probably closer to the theoretical value.

**Caveats about Black-Scholes Prices for Away-from-the-Money Options.** Another issue compounds the problem at hand. The Black-Scholes Option Pricing Model works very well for options that are near the money. The model works less accurately for options that are substantially in the money or out of the money, however.[6] Investigating the reasons for the lack of fit is an ongoing area of options research. The implied volatility we found using a near-the-money option was 13.77 percent. This value, coupled with the other parameters, yields a theoretical value for the AUG 320 call of $1.27 rather than $1.00, as shown in the newspaper.[7]

*Implied volatility is a catchall statistic.*

Given our current understanding of options pricing, implied volatility is really a catchall statistic. Unknown factors that influence the option premium are all captured in the volatility estimate, which is the one Black-Scholes variable that cannot be directly observed.

When it is necessary to calculate parameters such as delta for away-from-the-money options, it is sometimes preferable to abandon the near-the-money estimate of implied volatility and instead use the "catchall" implied volatility from the option you are investigating. If, for instance, you assume that the $1 premium (as shown in *The Wall Street Journal*) is correct, it yields an implied volatility of 12.78 percent. Although this may not seem to be significantly different from the best value of 13.77 percent, it makes a 27 percent difference in the calculated option premium.

The estimation of likely future values of inexpensive out-of-the-money options, especially those that are nearing expiration, is an imprecise business. Nonetheless,

---

[6]The Black-Scholes model tends to underprice out-of-the-money options and to overprice deep in-the-money options.

[7]It is dangerous to rely too heavily on option prices as shown in the financial press. Nonsynchronous pricing between the option and the underlying assets may indicate pricing relationships suggesting arbitrage or other inconsistencies.

**TABLE 22-9** NEW PORTFOLIO VALUES FROM A 0.5 PERCENT MARKET RISE OR FALL

| | *Market Rises by 0.5%* | | | |
|---|---|---|---|---|
| Stock: | \$996,975 × .005 × 1.08 | = | \$5,384 | gain |
| Calls: | 56 × 100 × (\$3.40 – 3.90*) | = | 2,800 | loss |
| | Net effect | = | \$2,584 | gain |
| | *Market Falls by 0.5%* | | | |
| Stock: | \$996,975 × (–.005) × 1.08 | = | \$5,384 | loss |
| Calls: | 56 × 100 × (\$3.40 – 2.53*) | = | 4,872 | gain |
| | Net effect | = | \$ 512 | loss |

*New Black-Scholes value.

suppose that we use the 12.78 percent implied volatility as a proxy for all of this uncertainty and use this value to estimate delta and future option premiums. The revised calculation gives a delta of 0.133.

**Evidence That a Positive Position Delta Is Bullish.** Assume that the actual price for the AUG 310 index call is exactly its Black-Scholes value, \$3.40. Then consider two different scenarios in which the market (1) instantaneously rises by 0.5 percent and (2) instantaneously falls by 0.5 percent. Because you know the portfolio beta, you can easily forecast what the new stock portfolio value is likely to be. It is also possible to calculate a new Black-Scholes call value based on the new level of the index. Table 22-9 shows the results. The portfolio appreciates if stock market prices rise and declines if the market falls.

### *Hedging Company Risk*

In the previous example, index options generated income for the portfolio; this action also lowered the portfolio beta. Suppose that one of the companies in the portfolio (Security 9) is in the midst of an ugly lawsuit that could involve a substantial legal judgment if the firm loses. Such a risk is company specific; it is in addition to overall market risk. You can hedge this risk using equity options.

**Buying Puts.** Suppose you expect a verdict in the litigation within two weeks. As shown in Table 22-3, the 900 shares of Security 9 currently sell for \$46 each. The theoretical Black-Scholes value for a 30-day put option with a \$45 striking price is \$0.32, with a delta of –0.26. (This uses a riskless interest rate of 6.0 percent and a volatility estimate of 15 percent.)

You may choose to hedge your 900-share position against a share price decline, but first you need to make a decision about the precise risk you want to hedge against. If you are worried about the possibility of a steep price decline, say 20 or 25 percent, then you could buy 9 protective put contracts in the manner described in Chapter 20. Owning 9 puts would give you the right to sell your 900 shares at the striking price regardless of how low the stock price went.

Alternatively, you might also be interested in hedging against a smaller price decline. This is best understood via an example. As Table 22-3 shows, Security 9 sells for \$46 per share. Suppose we consider a 30-day put with a \$45 striking price. With a riskless rate of 6 percent and a volatility of 15 percent, such an option has a theoretical value of \$0.33 and a delta of –0.27.

Now let the stock fall by 1 percent, to $45.54. On 900 shares, this is a decline of $414. The decline in the stock price will increase the put premium. Assuming the option still has 30 days until expiration, the new Black-Scholes premium is $0.47. On the 9 put contracts, this is a gain of 9 × 100 × ($0.47 –$0.33) = $126. The loss on the stock is more than three times this, so while the 9 puts mitigated the loss they did not eliminate it.

To hedge against a small price change we have to do things differently. First, we determine how many option contracts are necessary to bring the **position delta** to zero. Position delta is the total of the deltas in Security 9 and its options. A share of stock has a delta of 1.0 by definition; the put in this example has a delta of –0.27. The required number of put contracts is a simple ratio:

$$\#\,\text{contracts} = \frac{\text{shares} \times 1.0}{|\text{put delta}| \times 100}$$

(The absolute value is necessary because of the negative sign on a put delta.) In this example, the number of contracts we need is

$$\frac{900 \times 1.0}{|-0.26| \times 100} = 34.6 \approx 35$$

Buying 35 put contracts, we have a position delta of (900 × 1.0) + [35 × 100 × (–0.27)] =–45. Because options are only available in lots of 100 we cannot get to zero exactly.

If we had purchased 35 put contracts at $0.33 and seen them rise to $0.47 after the stock fall, we would have had a gain on them of 35 × 100 × ($0.47 – $0.33) = $490. This would more than offset the loss in the stock price.

A thorough discussion of "delta hedging" techniques is beyond the scope of this book. The option delta is a first derivative, which only gives accurate predictions for relatively small changes in variables. The point for the discussion here is that a portfolio manager who uses options to reduce risk may very well use options covering more shares than are in the portfolio.

**Buying Puts and Writing Calls.** Hedging a long stock position involves adding negative deltas to the positive deltas from the shares. Long puts have negative deltas, and so do short calls.

Suppose you choose to combine covered calls on Security 9 with long puts to reduce the cash outlay required to obtain the needed protection. A 30-day, $45 call on Security 9 has a theoretical Black-Scholes value of $1.53 and a delta of 0.740. If you write these calls, the portfolio has a cash inflow, which can help pay for the long puts. One effective combination of long puts and short calls comes from the solution to the pair of simultaneous equations shown in Table 22-10.

As with other option applications, major market movements up or down can result in significantly different ending portfolio values for the puts-only scenario compared with the puts-and-calls alternative. Risk management is a dynamic process; it is not good practice to include options in a portfolio and then ignore them. If market conditions change significantly, the derivative assets business virtually always has a course of action preferable to doing nothing.

### *Fixed-Income Portfolio*

As shown in Table 22-1, the fixed-income portfolio has a market value of $495,002 (99 percent of par) and a value-weighted duration of 7.48 years. The current yield of

**TABLE 22-10** ONE POSSIBLE COMBINATION OF LONG PUTS AND SHORT CALLS

Let $X$ = number of puts purchased (delta = –0.26)
$Y$ = number of calls written (delta = –0.74)

Establish position delta of 0:

$$-0.26X - 0.74Y + 900 = 0 \quad \text{(A)}$$

Zero cash outlay:

$$-\$0.32X + \$1.53Y = 0 \quad \text{(B)}$$

Solving Equations A and B simultaneously,

$$Y = 453.90 \text{ and } X = 2169.64$$

Round to 5 call and 21 put contracts.

***Resulting Position Delta***

| *Stock* | | *Calls* | | *Puts* | | *Total* |
|---|---|---|---|---|---|---|
| (900 × 1.0) | + | (–500 × 0.74) | + | [2,100 × (–0.26)] | = | –16 |

***Option Cash Flows***

| *Calls* | | *Puts* | | *Net Outlay* |
|---|---|---|---|---|
| [500 × (–$1.53)] | + | (2,100 × $0.32) | = | $93 |

the portfolio is 6.7 percent, found by dividing the annual income ($33,350) by the market value ($495,002).

**Hedging the Bond Portfolio Value with T-Bond Futures.** If market interest rates rise, the value of a fixed-income portfolio declines. The extent of the decline in the portfolio value can be calculated from the bond-pricing equations reviewed in Chapter 11, or it can be estimated via the duration statistic.[8]

Table 22-11 shows net portfolio values for the various bonds if rates rise by 1 percent. Note that duration also changes as the yields to maturity and market prices change.[9] Duration is the first derivative of the bond-pricing equation with respect to the yield to maturity. This means that the duration statistic measures how a bond price changes as the interest rate changes. If rates rise by 1 percentage point, a portfolio with a duration of 7.48 is expected to fall by about 7.48 percent.

The fixed-income portfolio fell in market value from $495,002 to $460,995. This is a decline of $34,007, representing a 6.87 percent reduction in the value of the portfolio, which is approximately that predicted by the duration statistic.

Chapter 21 showed how to use Treasury bond futures to reduce interest rate risk by reducing portfolio duration. Predicting future interest rates is risky business, but a portfolio manager who anticipated the increase in rates could have hedged the portfolio by using Treasury bond futures.

Suppose the cheapest-to-deliver T-bond sells for 94 percent of par, matures in sixteen years, and has a 7.5 percent coupon. Such a bond has a yield to maturity of 8.18 percent, a duration of 9.36 years, and a Chicago Board of Trade conversion

[8]The change can be estimated more precisely if the convexity statistics are also known. See the optional discussion on convexity in Chapter 14.

[9]It is not common to speak of a portfolio yield to maturity because portfolio components seldom all have the same maturity. It is possible to calculate a value-weighted yield to maturity, which may be useful in some situations, but the resulting statistic must be used carefully.

**TABLE 22-11** FIXED-INCOME SECURITIES AFTER A 1 PERCENT PARALLEL SHIFT UPWARD IN THE YIELD CURVE

| *Par* | *Issue* | *Price(%)* | *YTM(%)* | *Market Value* | *Annual Income* | *Duration* |
|---|---|---|---|---|---|---|
| $ 50,000 | US6s99 | 95.17 | 7.00 | $ 47,585 | $ 3,000 | 5.10 |
| 50,000 | US7s00 | 99.46 | 7.10 | 49,730 | 3,500 | 5.65 |
| 50,000 | US7s01 | 98.80 | 7.20 | 49,400 | 3,500 | 6.25 |
| 50,000 | US7s02 | 98.05 | 7.30 | 49,025 | 3,500 | 6.80 |
| 50,000 | US5.5s03 | 84.23 | 7.80 | 42,115 | 2,750 | 7.59 |
| 50,000 | AB6.3s04 | 87.72 | 8.00 | 43,860 | 3,150 | 7.87 |
| 50,000 | CD7.1s05 | 92.42 | 8.10 | 46,210 | 3,650 | 8.10 |
| 50,000 | EF7.3s06 | 92.89 | 8.20 | 46,445 | 3,650 | 8.43 |
| 50,000 | GH71/4s07 | 91.40 | 8.30 | 45,700 | 3,625 | 8.77 |
| 50,000 | IJ61/4s08 | 81.85 | 8.40 | 40,925 | 3,125 | 9.36 |
| $500,000 | | | | $460,995 | $33,450 | 7.33* |

*Value-weighted average.

factor of 1.1529. If you choose to use a futures contract selling for 92, the hedge ratio (as shown in Equation 21-5) is then 0.9914:

$$HR = CF_{ctd} \times \frac{P_b \times D_b}{P_f \times D_f}$$

$$= 1.1529 \times \frac{0.9900 \times 7.48}{0.9200 \times 9.36} = 0.9914$$

where $P_b$ = price of bond portfolio as a percentage of par; $D_b$ = duration of bond portfolio; $P_f$ = price of futures contract as a percentage of 100%; $D_f$ = duration of cheapest-to-deliver bond eligible for delivery against the futures contract; and $CF_{ctd}$ = conversion factor for the cheapest-to-deliver bond.

The fixed-income portion of the portfolio has a market value of $495,002. The number of T-bond contracts that need to be sold to hedge completely is then five contracts, as shown in Equation 21-7:

$$\text{Number of contracts} = \frac{\text{Portfolio value}}{\$100{,}000} \times HR$$

$$= \frac{\$495{,}002}{\$100{,}000} \times 0.9914$$

$$= 4.91 \text{ contracts} \rightarrow 5 \text{ contracts}$$

*A futures call gives its owner the right to go long; a futures put gives its owner the right to go short.*

**Hedging the Bond Portfolio with Futures Options.** It is also possible to hedge the bond portfolio using **futures options.** A futures option is an option giving its owner the right to buy or "sell" a futures contract. A futures call gives its owner the right to go long a futures contract; a futures put carries the right to go short.

Futures options received a less-than-overwhelming initial reception when they first began trading. To the uninitiated, futures and options are complicated enough

TABLE 22-12 SAMPLE T-BOND FUTURES OPTIONS

| *Strike* | *Calls* | | | *Puts* | | |
|---|---|---|---|---|---|---|
| | *Nov* | *Dec* | *Mar* | *Nov* | *Dec* | *Mar* |
| 96 | 3–58 | 3–63 | 3–63 | 0–02 | 0–09 | 0–59 |
| 98 | 2–02 | 2–20 | 2–44 | 0–10 | 0–30 | 1–39 |
| 100 | 0–42 | 1–06 | 1–44 | 0–50 | 1–14 | 2–36 |
| 102 | 0–08 | 0–26 | 1–00 | 2–16 | 2–33 | 3–52 |

Contract size $100,000 par value; priced in points and 64ths of par.

in themselves. Given this, the concept of an option on a futures contract can be truly befuddling. As futures options developed some history, however, hedgers learned how useful they can be. As with equity or index options, the buyer of a futures option has a known and limited maximum loss, whereas the buyer of the futures contract itself can realize large losses from an adverse price movement in the underlying asset. Nor do futures options require the good faith deposit associated with a futures contract. A futures option has time value, intrinsic value, a premium, and a delta value, just like other options. Once a potential user understands this, futures options become less intimidating.

Rather than going short T-bond futures to hedge the bond portfolio, T-bond futures options can be used instead. If you buy T-bond futures puts, you acquire the right to go short, which you can exercise if you need to. Alternatively, as with other option applications, you can sell the options and recover the wealth contained therein.

Table 22-12 shows sample information on U.S. Treasury bond futures options. As seen previously, the T-bond futures contract is based on the delivery of $100,000 par value of T-bonds, and the contract is priced as a percentage of par. The option premium is quoted in the financial press as a percentage (in points and sixty-fourths of a point) of $100,000 par. The premium for a MAR 100 call, for instance, is shown in Table 22-12 as 1–44. This means 1 44/64 percent of $100,000, or $1,687.50. A person buying the call pays this amount; the option writer receives the premium, keeping it no matter what happens to interest rates in the future.[10]

Hedging with futures options shares many of the same principles as hedging with equity or stock index options. Best results are achieved by using a delta-based hedge ratio that considers the number of option contracts needed to replicate the underlying asset. Doing so requires modeling the bond portfolio as if it were one bond instead of a package of many.

The fixed-income portfolio shown in Table 22-1 has a coupon yield of 6.67 percent, a duration of 7.48 years, and a market price equal to 99 percent of par. If these statistics were associated with a single security, that security would have a yield to maturity of 6.8 percent and a maturity date ten years in the future. The associated Chicago Board of Trade (CBT) conversion factor for T-bond delivery is approximately 1.0521.

[10]Futures options expire in the month prior to the delivery month of the underlying asset. A March T-bond option, for instance, expires in February. Unlike equity or index options, there is no consistent "third Friday of the month" rule. Expirations differ by commodity. T-bond options expire at noon on the last Friday of the month, preceding by at least five trading days the first notice day for the corresponding T-bond futures contract.

**FIGURE 22-3**

Black Option Pricing Model

$$C = e^{-rt}\left[FN(a) - KN(b)\right]$$

$$\text{where } a = \frac{\ln(F/K) + \sigma^2 \times \frac{t}{2}}{\sigma\sqrt{t}}$$

$$b = a - \sigma\sqrt{t}$$

$C$ = futures call option premium
$e$ = base of natural logarithms
$r$ = risk-freeinterest rate
$t$ = time until option expiration
$K$ = option striking price
$F$ = futures price
$\sigma$ = annual volatility of the futures price
ln = natural logarithm

**FIGURE 22-4**

Put Pricing Model Based on Put/Call Parity

$$P = C - e^{-rt}(F - K)$$

where $P$ = put premium.

All variables are as defined in Figure 22-3.

*A detailed history of the developments that led to the conception of the Black-Scholes Option Pricing Model is at* http://www.summithq.com/newsroom/pdf/Black-Scholes_Oct03.pdf

Assume you decide to use the MAR 98 T-bond call option to hedge against the risk of rising interest rates. Fischer Black developed a variant of the Black-Scholes Option Pricing Model, known as the **Black Option Pricing Model,** which is useful for pricing futures options. The Black model is given in Figure 22-3. A put pricing model (based on put/call parity) is shown in Figure 22-4.

Using the Black model and assuming the option has 150 days until expiration, a volatility of 8.6 percent, and a riskless rate of interest of 6 percent, the delta of the MAR 98 T-bond call is 0.583.[11] The appropriate hedge ratio is

$$HR = CF \times \frac{\text{Portfolio value}}{\$100{,}000} \times \frac{1}{\text{Delta}}$$

Substituting the appropriate values,

$$HR = 0.91 \times \frac{\$495{,}002}{\$100{,}000} \times \frac{1}{0.583}$$

$$= 7.7264$$

[11]If you are familiar with calculus, you can see from Table 22-13 and Figure 22-3 that delta for futures options is slightly different from delta for equity or index options. The derivative of the option price with respect to the futures price is $e^{-rt}N(a)$ for calls and $e^{-rt}N(-b)$ for puts.

**TABLE 22-13** EFFECTS OF T-BOND OPTION HEDGE

| *Time* | *Bond Portfolio* | *Futures* | *Futures Options* |
|---|---|---|---|
| Initially | $495,002 | 99–03 | 9 at 2–44 = $24,187.50 |
| At expiration | 460,995 | 90–01 | Expire worthless |
| | $ 34,007 Loss | | $24,187.50 Gain |
| | Net effect: $9,819.50 loss | | |

As with other options, fractional contracts are not allowed with futures options, so perhaps you decide to write 9 MAR 98 T-bond calls. Table 22-12 shows these listed with a premium of 2–44, which means 2 44/64 percent of $100,000, or $2,687.50. Writing nine of these generates income of $24,187.50.

*Option hedges are not completely effective unless they are periodically adjusted.*

Table 22-13 shows the results of the hedge if interest rates move up by 1 full percentage point. The table points out something important: Option hedges are not perfect. Delta measures how the option premium changes for small changes in the underlying asset. Large moves in the underlying asset, however, require adjustment of the hedge. If the hedge is not adjusted, it will be less than completely effective.

Despite the fact that the hedge in this instance is not perfect, overall losses were attenuated significantly. In actual practice, they could have been reduced much further by manager intervention over the period of the hedge. The most likely adjustment would have been the writing of additional T-bond futures call option contracts.

## Managing Cash Drag*

Money managers know that their performance is periodically judged relative to some market index. They also know that if they appear to underperform, they will lose clients and find it difficult to get new ones. A portfolio suffers **cash drag** when it is not fully invested. Cash drag can detract from portfolio performance.

Consider the case of an all-equity mutual fund manager whose benchmark is the S&P 500 index. Suppose the fund's assets total $500 million, with 5 percent routinely held in cash equivalents. A mutual fund needs to keep a certain amount of cash on hand to accommodate investor share redemption requests, something that occurs daily. The fund receives additional deposits from existing customers and checks from new accounts on a daily basis as well. Over long periods of time, the evidence is clear that equity securities earn a higher return than cash. It is difficult enough for a money manager to "beat the market" without having a downward bias in relative fund performance because part of the portfolio is being invested in an asset likely to earn a below-market rate.

Suppose the equity portion of the portfolio has a beta of 1.0 and that over a six-month period, the broad market rises by 11.50 percent, with cash earning 2.50 percent. The return on this portfolio is then $(0.95 \times .1150) + (0.05 \times 0.0250) = 11.05$ percent. Relative to the S&P benchmark, the manager underperformed by 45 basis

*This section on cash drag comes from the author's textbook *Derivatives: An Introduction*, SouthWestern, 2005.

FIGURE 22-5

Neutralizing Cash

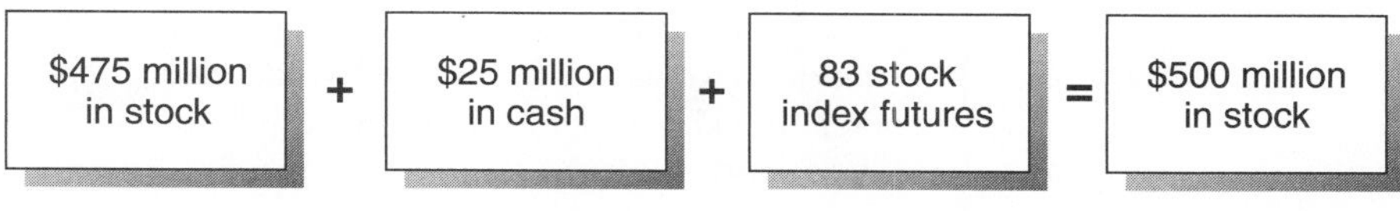


points. This may not seem like much of a shortfall, but no manager wants to face comments of the type "didn't even match the market average."

Many fund managers deal with this situation by holding a long position in stock index futures that will offset the cash position. Suppose a distant SPX futures contract settled at 1200.00. The fund manager wants to buy enough of these to bring up the market exposure of the fund assets from 95 percent to 100 percent. Solving for the hedge ratio,

$$HR = \frac{\text{Portfolio size}}{\text{Futures size}} \times \text{Beta}$$

The "portfolio size" we want to add is 5% of $500 million:

$$HR = \frac{0.05 \times \$500 \text{ million}}{1200.00 \times \$250} \times 1.0 = 83.33$$

If the portfolio manager buys 83 SPX futures and mixes them with the existing stock/cash portfolio, it should behave very much like a 100 percent equity index fund. See Figure 22-5. The same procedure works with a bond fund. The manager can offset the "cash drag" on fund performance by holding a long position in interest rate futures.

## SUMMARY

This chapter showed how a portfolio manager can logically incorporate the use of derivative assets in the portfolio management process. After setting portfolio objectives, she selects fixed income and equity securities that are consistent with those objectives. A mathematical aid such as linear programming can simplify this process enormously.

Regardless of whether the manager uses derivative assets, portfolio objectives must be set. The fund manager can use futures and options to adjust the characteristics of the fixed-income portfolio, the equity portfolio, or both.

If income needs remain unmet, writing index call options is a popular means of generating the required funds. The fund manager wants to be sure to stay within the fiduciary rules for writing covered calls and to monitor the likelihood of option exercise. Knowledge of the option delta is useful for the latter point. Company-specific risk should be hedged using equity options rather than index options. Doing this properly also requires determination of the option delta. In the chapter example, we wrote calls in such a quantity as to offset the cost of the puts we bought, also ensuring that the resulting position delta was what we wanted.

Derivative assets can increase the income generated by a portfolio and reduce the levels of market or interest rate risk the portfolio faces. Index options are especially well-suited to increasing portfolio income. Stock index or Treasury bond futures are especially useful for lowering portfolio risk.

Futures options can also be used to generate income or to adjust risk. Employing them requires knowledge of the relevant statistics such as option deltas, T-bond conversion factors, and the duration of the cheapest-to-deliver bond. Hedges constructed using options lose their effectiveness over time unless they are periodically adjusted.

The final hedged portfolio should still be consistent with the portfolio objectives, meet the specified income need, and be properly protected against risk.

## QUESTIONS

1. Does writing index calls limit the maximum price appreciation of a stock portfolio?
2. List the advantages and disadvantages of the various index call option striking prices from the perspective of a call writer.
3. In the example in the chapter, how else could additional portfolio income have been generated? Assume there are no legal restrictions constraining your choices.
4. Why might a speculator choose to use an individual equity option rather than an S&P 100 (OEX) option?
5. Do you think that the margin requirements for writing index options should be different from those for equity options? Why or why not?
6. Suppose the holder of a diversified portfolio decided to hedge against a market downturn by buying OEX puts instead of writing OEX calls. Explain the steps the person would take to do this.
7. Remembering that the purchase of a futures contract requires only a good faith deposit (which can be satisfied by the deposit of interest-bearing Treasury bills), and using the formula for put/call parity from Chapter 15, what relationship would you expect between the prices of at-the-money futures puts and calls on the same underlying commodity?
8. Explain why writing calls reduces a portfolio's beta.
9. In Table 22-9, why are the gain/loss components not of equal size?

## PROBLEMS

1. Use an SAS linear program similar to that in Figure 22-2 to construct a ten-security stock portfolio with a beta greater than 1.00 and less than 1.50. Also, ensure that some investment is made into each of the ten securities and that no more than 20 percent of the fund is in any single security. Finally, select the potential stocks from the list of those that *Value Line* currently ranks 1 for timeliness. (Security betas are shown in the *Value Line* report.)
2. Refer to the information in Table 22–7. Suppose the fund manager used AUG 315 index calls to make up the income shortfall. How many would be required?
3. Given your answer to Problem 2, what is the maximum possible portfolio value?

4. Consider the information in Table 22-9. If the overall market (a) advances by 10 percent or (b) falls by 10 percent in the next thirty days, what is a likely aggregate portfolio value in each instance just before option expiration?
5. Using the BSOPM file and current prices from the Internet, estimate the delta of a near-the-money OEX call option with about two months until expiration.
6. With the Black and Sigma files, and using current prices from the Internet, estimate the delta of a near-the-money S&P 500 futures put option.
7. The BSOPM, Sigma, and Black files are helpful in solving this problem. Alternatively, use the options calculator at the CBOE Website. Suppose you have a \$10 million stock portfolio with a beta of 1.10. Using current data from the Internet, determine the number of contracts necessary to hedge this position completely, using the following:
   **a.** An S&P 500 futures contract.
   **b.** OEX call options.
   **c.** OEX put options.
   **d.** S&P 500 futures calls.
   **e.** S&P 500 futures puts.
   In each instance, indicate which specific option or contract you selected.
8. This problem uses the Black file. Assume that the cheapest-to-deliver Treasury bond sells for par. Also assume that the riskless rate of interest is 5 percent and that the options in Table 22-12 expire in 30, 60, and 150 days for the NOV, DEC, and MAR expirations, respectively. Assuming volatility to be 9 percent, prepare a delta table for the options shown in Table 22-12.
9. An at-the-money futures call sells for \$2 and expires in one month. What should a futures put sell for? (You can determine this without any calculations.)
10. In Problem 9, suppose the option striking price is 99 and the underlying asset sells for 100; the riskless interest rate is 5 percent. What is the theoretical put value?
11. You manage a \$223 million S&P 500 index portfolio that currently is 3.5 percent in cash. Show how you could eliminate the cash drag using an SPX futures contract that settled at 1300.00.
12. FROM THE 1995 LEVEL III CFA EXAM (Question 16)

QUESTION 16 HAS TWO PARTS FOR A TOTAL OF 24 MINUTES

The manager of BI's fixed-income portfolio has shown exceptional security selection skills, and has produced returns consistently above those on BI's fixed-income benchmark portfolio. The Board wants to allocate more money to this manager and to further enhance the fund's alpha. This action would increase the proportion allocated to fixed income and decrease the proportion in equities. However, the Board wants to keep the present fixed income/equity proportions unchanged.

**A.** **Identify** *two* distinct strategies using derivative financial instruments that the Board could use to increase the fund's allocation to the fixed-income manager without changing the present fixed-income/equity proportions. **Briefly explain** how *each* of these *two* strategies would work.

**(8 minutes)**

**B.** **Briefly discuss** *one* advantage *and one* disadvantage of *each* of the strategies you identified in Part A above. **Present** your discussion in

terms of the *effect(s)* of these advantages and disadvantages on the portfolio's:
(i) *risk* characteristics; and
(ii) *return* characteristics.

**(16 minutes)**

## INTERNET EXERCISE

Go to the Chicago Board of Trade Website at *http://www.cbot.com*. Find the page dealing with products on the Dow Jones Industrial Average. Using current price data from this site, show how someone could completely hedge a $1 million stock portfolio (beta = 0.90) using DJIA futures calls and/or puts.

## FURTHER READING

Baz, Jamil, and Robert A. Strong. "The Bias in Delta as an Indicator of the Likelihood of Option Exercise." *Financial Practice and Education*, Spring/Summer 1997, 91–94.

Bierwag, G.O., George Kaufman, and Alden Toevs. "Duration: Its Development and Use in Bond Portfolio Management." *Financial Analysts Journal*, July/August 1983, 15–35.

Chance, Don. "Futures Contracts and Immunization." *Review of Research in Futures Markets* 5, no. 2, 1986, 124–140.

Geske, Robert L., and Dan R. Pieptea. "Controlling Interest Rate Risk and Return with Futures." *Review of Futures Markets* 6, no. 1, 1987, 64–86.

Kolb, Robert, and Raymond Chiang. "Duration, Immunization, and Hedging with Interest Rate Futures." *Journal of Financial Research*, Summer 1982, 161–170.

McEnally, Richard. "How to Neutralize Reinvestment Rate Risk." *Journal of Portfolio Management*, Spring 1980, 59–63.

Toevs, A., and D. Jacobs. "Futures and Alternative Hedge Ratio Methodologies." *Journal of Portfolio Management*, Spring 1986, 60–70.

# 23 Contemporary Issues in Portfolio Management

*There are clearly some real bad people out there who have done bad things, but there are also 15,000 companies out there, the great majority of which are run by honest people. Having said that, there has been a general erosion of professional standards [fueled by] an attitude that "everybody else is doing it" and a perceived need to meet quarterly earnings numbers. We've got to get back to an honest approach and a broad-gauged concept of what we really mean by management performance.*

**William Donaldson, Chairman, Securities & Exchange Commission**

## Key Terms

alternative asset
Chartered Financial Analyst program
cover a short
DOT
hedge found
hypothecation agreement
long/short portfolio
managed futures
merger arbitrage
program trading
Regulation FD
short sale
stock lending
stock loan finder

## Introduction

Some of the most important emerging areas in the field of portfolio management are controversial. Security analyst objectivity has been the subject of numerous Congressional hearings. Stock lending and program trading can be useful activities for institutional investors, but both suffer from an image problem. Earlier chapters have shown how useful futures and options can be in portfolio management, but there are still many portfolios for which investment policy does not permit the use of derivative assets. "Alternative investments" are an increasingly popular asset class in institutional portfolios. This chapter looks at these and other contemporary issues of interest to money managers.

## Security Analyst Objectivity*

In theory there has always been a "fire wall" between the investment banking function of an investment house and its research department. This is because of the potential for a conflict of interest that might arise if an investment bank is courting a firm for some underwriting business at the same time that its analysts are developing an investment opinion on the potential customer's stock. A "sell" or "hold" rating could cause the client to take their business elsewhere. In the late 1990s, of the entire population of security analyst opinions on stocks, less than 2 percent were "sell."[1] The vast majority implied some degree of bullishness.

*"The goal is to try to get back the public perception that analysts are independent and call stocks as they see them."*
Mark Lackritz, President, Securities Industry Association

In 2001 and early 2002 the security analyst community received some very bad publicity stemming from a few highly visible breaches of this fire wall, in which brokers were publicly singing the praises of shares while internal memos indicated that the firm's research department thought they were dogs.

In March of 2002 the National Association of Securities Dealers filed rules with the SEC that address this lack of objectivity. Among other things, the rules

- Improve the investment banking/research fire wall;
- Separate analyst compensation from investment banking deals;
- Improve disclosure of investment banking relationships;
- Require a firm to prepare a performance graph showing how its investment recommendations have done over the past 3 years; and
- Reduce the ability of analysts to engage in "front running," or making trades in advance of those anticipated by the investing public.[2]

The President of the Association for Investment Management and Research (now the CFA Institute) testified before Congress on this issue. He educated the committee members on the CFA Institute Code of Ethics, and the fact that not all security analysts are Institute members and subject to the code. The CFA Institute subsequently issued a document on Research Objectivity Standards for public comment, anticipating that, when finalized, these standards would complement the existing Code of Ethics and Standards of Practice, reinforcing the need to keep investment advice objective.

*"No matter how expert some Wall Street analysts may be, they are not equipped, and should not be expected, to detect fraud. Managements who lie have the ability to—and do—fool even the most astute and sophisticated of investors."*
Thomas Bowman, CFA, President, AIMR

The SEC adopted Regulation Analyst Certification ("Reg AC") in April 2003. This rule requires analysts to certify that their reports reflect their opinions and not someone else's, as well as disclosing any compensation they receive related to their recommendations. One related requirement is that firms must establish a compensation committee that reviews and approves each analyst's compensation based solely on the quality of analysts' research, their track record, and their productivity.

## Stock Lending

**Stock lending** is a little-known but lucrative part of the securities business. It is the practice by which one institution loans stock to another institution, often so that a

---

*Some of the material in this section comes from the author's textbook *Practical Investment Management*, 3rd edition, page 536, also published by Thomson.

[1]Hill, Chuck, "Correcting Abuses of the Past," *CFA Magazine*, Jan/Feb 2003, 5.

[2]"U.S. Regulators Propose Strict New Rules for Sell-Side Analysts and Firms," *AIMR Advocate*, May/June 2002, 1.

customer of the second institution can sell them short. A firm can earn substantial income with very little risk via a stock-lending program.

The practice of stock lending is similar to a repurchase agreement. In a repurchase agreement, an investor approaches a bank and indicates a desire to invest a sum of money for a relatively short period of time, often just a single day. The bank produces securities that the investor buys and promises to buy these securities back at a price agreed upon at the time the agreement is entered into. There is no price risk from the investor's perspective; she knows the current and future prices exactly. The securities that the investor buys can be equities or fixed income securities, and the bank may use its own investments or borrow them from another institution.

With a stock loan, the institution wanting to borrow the stock puts up collateral, usually cash, and agrees to return the securities at a later date. The lender can earn interest on the cash collateral. Normally, the required collateral is about 102 percent of the value of the securities lent.

At any given time at least $300 billion worth of securities are probably on loan. While anyone can loan securities, the predominant players are large "trust" banks (such as Bank of New York, Bankers Trust, Mellon, and State Street), pension funds, mutual funds, insurance companies, and, to a lesser extent, corporate treasurers.

Selling short is central to understanding stock lending, so we will first review the mechanics of the *short sale*.

## Mechanics of a Short Sale

*Short selling involves the sale of borrowed shares.*

The notion that a person can profitably and legitimately sell something he does not own has troubled participants in the security markets since the early 1600s, when Dutch authorities attempted to outlaw short selling.[3] In a nutshell, the **short sale** involves borrowing securities from someone, selling them to another market participant, eventually purchasing shares in the same company from another market participant, and returning these substitute shares to the original lender. Although this procedure may be conceptually awkward, it need not be viewed as an egregious, un-American act (which is how some people view the practice).

The short sale is normally motivated by a bearish sentiment toward a particular stock. If the short seller is able to borrow shares and sell them at $25, the repurchase of these shares a few months later at $19 yields a $6 profit to the investor. Instead of buying at a low price and then selling at a higher price, the short seller has simply reversed the order of the two transactions.

*Brokerage firms receive interest on shares they loan to another firm.*

The actual lender of the shares is normally an unknowing participant in the entire matter. For instance, investors with margin accounts at their brokerage houses may be involved in the process. When an investor opens a margin account she signs a **hypothecation agreement** giving the broker the right to lend the shares to someone else. This is of no real concern to the investor, because she can still trade the shares and continues to earn dividends. The brokerage firm itself also may lend shares from its own corporate account to another brokerage firm. In such a case, the borrower pays interest to the lender at approximately the broker's call money rate.

Over the years many discussions on the merits of short selling have taken place; these conversations have occurred on the floor of Congress and in the smallest boardroom. Those in favor of short selling point out that margin trading encompasses two

[3]The material in this section is taken from Robert A. Strong, "A Short Guide to the Mechanics of a Short Sale," *AAII Journal*, July 1985, 18–20.

activities: buying on margin and selling short. People have little trouble with the leveraged purchase of shares; why find fault with a related procedure on the other side of the market?

Short selling's samurai quickly remind us that it was margin buyers who were largely responsible for the events leading to the Great Crash of 1929 and that because speculative buying forces prices up, margin buying is inflationary. Short selling helps offset this influence.

The opposition is quick to point out that short selling has a checkered heritage and has, on occasion, been destabilizing to the market. Traders have a long memory for manipulation, corners, and "short squeezes," such as the 1862 Harlem Railroad incident starring Cornelius Vanderbilt and Boss Tweed, or the Piggly Wiggly market corner in 1923. Also, people traditionally want the market to advance; few actively root for a price decline. And, so the logic goes, because the downward pressure induced by short sellers runs contrary to the public interest, short selling must be evil.

Regardless of where your opinion lies in this respect, short selling is a fact of life and worth understanding. Figure 23-1 outlines the steps of a simple short sale with common stock. Short sellers recognize that because they are selling on margin, they must meet a margin requirement. Selling 100 shares of a stock short at $60 requires the deposit of 50 percent of this amount, or $3,000, into a special account with the short seller's brokerage firm. An old Wall Street saying is that "bulls pay interest; the bears don't." When a person buys on margin he pays interest; when he sells short, he does not because he has not borrowed any money. In fact, he must deposit funds.

**FIGURE 23-1** The Steps in a Short Sale

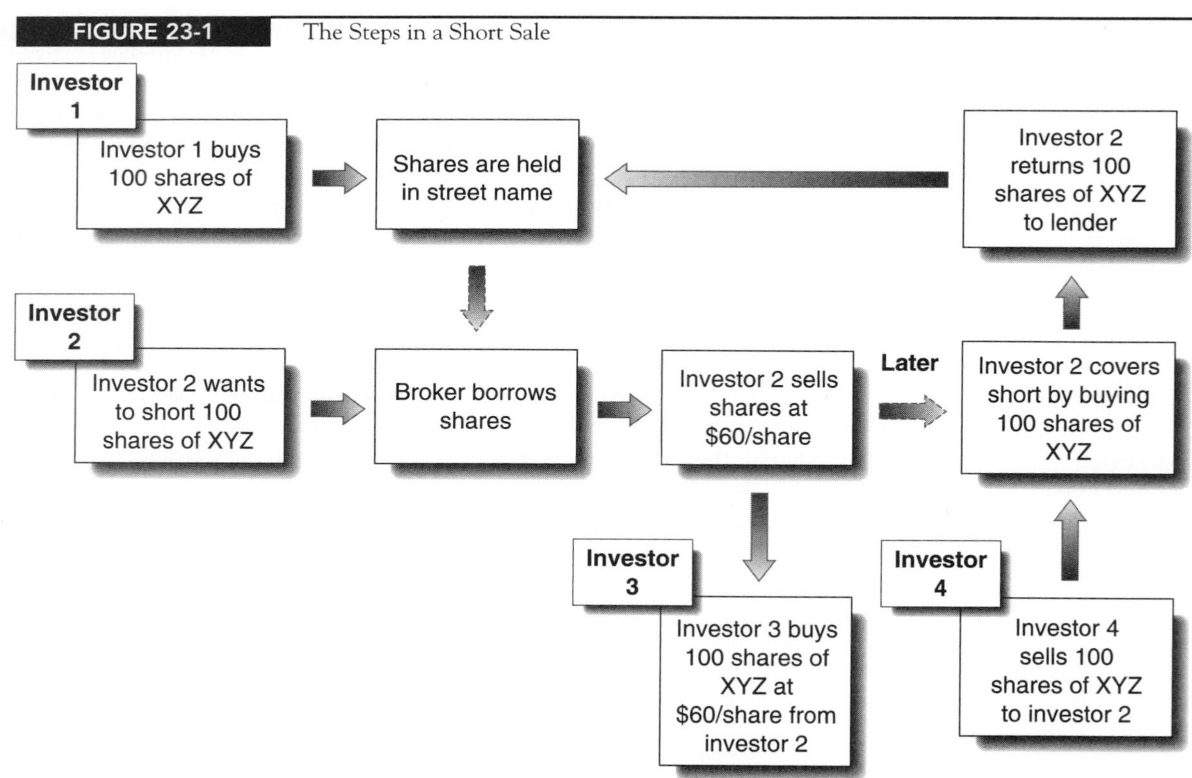


Source: Robert A. Strong, "A Short Guide to the Mechanics of a Short Sale," *AAII Journal*, July 1985.

*The short seller has an obligation to eventually replace the borrowed shares.*

Suppose that a Merrill Lynch customer buys 100 shares of XYZ in a margin account and that Merrill subsequently lends these shares to another of its clients, who wants to sell them short. The short seller then might sell these shares to an account at UBS Paine Webber. An important point here is that the Merrill Lynch customer does not care who bought the shares nor is the customer informed. The short seller simply has an obligation to return what was borrowed sometime in the future (hence another Wall Street jingle, "He who sells what isn't his'n must buy it back or go to prison").

*Short sellers must pay any dividends to the person from whom the stock was borrowed.*

At this point, two investors believe that they own shares in XYZ: the lender (who bought the shares in a margin account) and the person who bought the shares from the short seller. Dividends are not a problem because the short seller, by industry practice, must pay them to the lender. The short seller does not mind this, though, because the stock price will be pressured downward on the ex-dividend day by about the amount of the dividend, and this is beneficial from the short seller's perspective.

At some point in the future, the short seller **covers the short** by repurchasing shares (it does not matter from whom) to replace the shares borrowed earlier. If she buys these shares at a price lower than that at which they were sold, she makes a profit. Of course, if she buys these shares at a higher price, she suffers a loss.

It is important to note that although selling short is a legitimate investment activity, it is not always the best way to accomplish a purpose. On a single security, for instance, the purchase of a put option is often preferable to selling short. A short sale involves losses that are potentially unlimited, whereas the purchase of a put option involves a loss no greater than the premium paid for the put. The potential profit from a put is nearly identical to that from the short sale, and buying an option has no margin requirement.

### How a Stock Lending Transaction Works

Suppose that a customer of Hot Tip Brokerage decides that XYZ stock is overvalued at $25 per share. He places an order to sell short 10,000 shares. To process the customer's order, Hot Tip must locate 10,000 shares to sell. The firm first checks its own accounts to see if any of its other customers have XYZ shares on deposit in their margin accounts. If so, the firm borrows and sells these shares on the short seller's behalf.

*Stock loan finders facilitate the borrowing of shares.*

Sometimes, though, sufficient shares are not on hand, and the brokerage firm must seek to borrow them from someone else. This may be done directly with another brokerage firm or may be done using the services of a **stock loan finder.**[4] The stock loan finder, for a fee, uses its own contacts in the securities industry to track down someone who has and is willing to lend the needed shares. We assume in this example that Hot Tip employs the stock lending firm of Normal Equities to facilitate the short sale and that Normal Equities arranges for Custom Portfolios to lend the shares to Hot Tip.

Once Hot Tip receives the needed shares, the Hot Tip customer is able to sell them short. We will assume that the short sale occurs at the market price of $25. Hot Tip Brokerage must now deposit collateral worth the value of the shares with the stock lender (Custom Portfolios). The collateral may be provided by Treasury bills or cash. In this example, the requirement is $250,000. Hot Tip receives this amount from the short sale, and these funds finance the T-bills or cash equivalents that Hot Tip must deliver to Custom Portfolios. As long as the loan is outstanding, Custom

[4]In late 2000 the California Public Employees Retirement System and Old Mutual PLC established a Web-based securities lending company (eSecLending LLC) to provide the marketplace with a more efficient system for security lending programs. See *http://www.eSecLending.com/*.

Portfolios earns interest on the collateral provided. Typically, part of the interest earned is shared with Normal Equities as a finder's fee.

Eventually, the customer must cover the short position by buying shares to replace those that were sold short earlier. When the short is covered, Hot Tip forwards the purchased shares to Custom Portfolios. The collateral is returned, and the stock loan is satisfied.

All the institutional participants benefit in this situation. Hot Tip was able to satisfy the customer who wanted to sell short. Normal Equities earned a finder's fee, and Custom Portfolios earned a "free" return on idle stock certificates. The short selling customer would have benefited if the short position were covered at a price lower than that at which the shares were sold, but that is outside the stock lending issue.

There is also an increasing amount of international fixed-income securities lending. Fixed-income securities are widely used as collateral in bond futures transactions. According to an article in *Pensions and Investments*, foreign bond lending can add between 40 and 200 basis points to a fixed-income portfolio. The California Public Employees' Retirement Fund has more than $5 billion in international equities and nearly $3 billion in foreign bonds, and it has a lending program with both types of securities. The article also reports that several custodian banks reported that "the use of international bond lending is a natural progression for investors sophisticated enough to be investing in international securities or to be doing any sort of securities lending."[5]

### *Stock Lending's Lucrative Nature*

**Advantages of Stock Lending.** Stock lending is a very lucrative business for financial institutions. In 1994, the California Public Employees Retirement fund made $21 million from lending securities; the Illinois Teachers' Retirement System made $3 million. The six largest master trust banks made more than $600 million in income on a lending pool of $155 billion in 1994.[6] It is unlikely that anyone knows exactly what the grand total is in a given year, but in 1999 the total income to stock lenders probably approached $1 billion.

Stock lending is particularly popular when our markets see increased merger and acquisition activity, such as occurred during the 1980s. During such periods **merger arbitrage** is a popular activity. Typically this involves buying shares of likely takeover candidates and selling short those of the anticipated acquirers. Wholesale short selling increases the demand for the services of the stock lender.

Stock lending is also advantageous to the brokerage firm as a way of financing the margin purchases of its customers. Under current rules, a customer need put up only 50 percent of the value of the securities purchased. The remainder can be borrowed from the broker, and the customer pays interest on these borrowed funds. The customer's brokerage firm can either obtain a bank loan to finance the other 50 percent of the purchase, or the shares the customer bought can be lent. In the latter case, the stock borrower deposits sufficient funds as collateral to finance the margin purchase internally. This is certainly cheaper than borrowing from the bank.

**Disadvantages of Stock Lending.** The stock lender really gives up very little. The customer whose shares were borrowed still receives dividends as they are earned. (The short seller is responsible for their payment.) Stock dividends, subscription rights, or other recapitalizations also continue to belong to the lender. The customer

[5]"Security Lending Spreads," *Pensions and Investments*, April 1, 1991, 2.

[6]Paul G. Barr and Barry B. Burr, "Securities Lending Not Riskless," *Pensions and Investments*, August 8, 1994, 3.

can also sell the shares whenever desired. The fact that a particular customer's shares are on loan is merely an inconvenience for the customer's brokerage firm; it does not prevent the customer from selling. The firm makes an accounting entry essentially transferring shares from another customer's account to the account of the customer who wants to sell.

The one thing the customer does potentially give up is the right to vote on shareholder matters. After shares are sold short, there are two apparent shareholders, the person whose shares were borrowed and the person who bought the shares when they were sold. The short seller is, practically speaking, a negative owner, but people cannot cast negative votes. By tradition, the person holding the certificate is the one who gets to vote.[7] To most shareholders, this is a modest concession. The typical shareholder seldom is interested in which firm audits the books, who the directors are, and what the minor bylaw changes are.

Some people believe that significant risk is associated with the possibility that the stock borrower might not return the securities.[8] This is not much of a risk. Stock loans are "marked to market" in the same way that futures contracts are. Should the stock rise in value, the borrower must deposit additional collateral with the lender. In the event of default, the lender's liability is the extent to which the stock's market value exceeds the value of the collateral.

### Regulatory Concerns

*Stock lending has some serious image problems on Wall Street.*

The increased stock lending activity has not gone unnoticed by the various regulatory agencies that keep an eye on Wall Street. According to an article in *Business Week*, the chief financial officer of a major securities firm says stock lending is "the dirtiest business in the entire brokerage business. . . . It's the business nobody wants to talk about."[9]

*"The stock lending area is one that has not been adequately supervised over the years."*
Ira Lee Sorkin, former head of the New York Securities and Exchange Commission

Technically, stock-lending activities are not subject to the jurisdiction of the Securities and Exchange Commission because a stock loan does not involve the purchase or sale of a security. Still, many market observers believe that there is some abuse in the practice of stock lending. One possible area of abuse lies in the lending of shares held in a cash account. People who open margin accounts sign hypothecation agreements that explicitly give their brokers the authority to loan their shares. Shares held in a cash account, however, may not be loaned without the customer's specific approval.

*People who open margin accounts sign hypothecation agreements that explicitly give their brokers the authority to loan their shares.*

In late 1989 the federal government announced an intent to probe the stock-lending programs of major brokerage firms.[10] Federal prosecutors began investigating potential theft, money laundering, and kickbacks in the stock-lending departments of a number of brokerage firms.

### Certificateless Trading

Global efforts are underway to speed up the settlement process for security transactions. International investment is widespread, and the difference in settlement procedures across countries can cause significant problems. In the United States, trades

---

[7]Companies do not normally issue actual stock certificates anymore. They are expensive to produce and are not necessary in a world of electronic commerce. The corporate transfer agent maintains ownership records in book entry form.

[8]See Ralph Vitale, "Lending Securities for Pocket Money," *Treasury and Risk Management*, March/April 1994, 38–39.

[9]"The Business Nobody Wants to Talk About," *Business Week*, September 25, 1989, 196.

[10]See Leonard J. Hollie, "Program on Hold: Stock Lending Probe Delays Start," *Pensions and Investment Age*, September 18, 1989, 1, 62.

PORTFOLIO MEMO

### Social Security and 401(k) Plans

Social Security reform was a front burner topic at the start of President George W. Bush's second term. The public got a crash course on asset classes and their relative risks from the talk shows and the news magazines. Just a few years earlier people read of the thousands of employees whose retirement savings were depleted when their company's stock (perhaps Enron) declined sharply and most of their 401(k) consisted of these shares. *The Wall Street Journal* reported, "In the 23 years since 401(k) plans were first created, many people have made obvious mistakes in investing their own money, such as putting too much money into low-yield savings accounts or betting the house on their own company's stock."* A study by the Employee Benefit Research Institute found that 53 percent of 401(k) accounts had more than 10 percent of their assets in company stock. More than 10 percent of the accounts had over 90 percent of their assets in their company stock.**

Just because it is your own company's stock it does not mean that the rules of diversification don't apply. You still need to spread the money around, and a large concentration of funds in any single security is always dangerous. The public's mishandling of its 401(k) accounts is ammunition for those who oppose President Bush's plan for personal retirement accounts in which citizens may direct part of the social security into the stock market. It is also why even the proponents indicate that an equity investment would have to be in a diversified mutual fund rather than individual equity positions.

*Lauricella, Tom, "A Lesson for Social Security: Many Mismanage Their 401 (k)s", *Wall Street Journal*, 1 December 2004, A1.
**Ibid.

typically settle three business days after the trade date. In Hong Kong, it is one day after the trade date; in Australia, there is no set period, but it usually takes between five and ten business days. In contrast, in Italy it can be as long as five weeks, and in France up to six weeks.

Computer automation makes it possible to process some types of financial activity (such as electronic funds transfer) almost immediately. Newly issued U.S. Government bonds and notes are registered in book entry form only and can be transferred from buyer to seller with a few strokes at the keyboard. Paper stock certificates, however, are a hindrance to automated stock trades, and there are increasing efforts to discontinue them.

## Program Trading

*Program trading* is a much maligned computerized technique for making automatic investment decisions to take advantage of inefficiencies (arbitrage) in the marketplace. The practice is really an automated version of a longstanding investment house practice.

*A Website dedicated to program trading issues is located at* http://www.programtrading.com

*Program trading is*
*1. Portfolio trading.*
*2. Computerized trading.*
*3. Computer decision making.*

Although it is not easy to define, the term **program trading** can be used to mean any computer-aided buying or selling activity in the stock market. Other people view program trading as synonymous with stock index futures arbitrage. *The Wall Street Journal* defines program trading as the simultaneous purchase or sale of at least 15 different securities with a total value of $1 million or more.[11]

Hans Stoll and Robert Whaley have described some of the confusion regarding program trading, and propose that program trading has three key characteristics:

1. It is portfolio trading, meaning that an entire portfolio of stocks is traded via a single order.
2. It is computerized trading done with small individual lots of stock rather than large blocks.
3. It is computer decision making when the decisions are triggered by the existence of mispricing (arbitrage).[12]

One of the fundamental principles of finance is that arbitrage opportunities will be short lived. When security prices deviate from their true value so that riskless profits can be made, some market observers will find the arbitrage, exploit it, and quickly eliminate it.

Many program trading systems are designed to take advantage of temporary imbalances between stock prices as determined at the New York Stock Exchange and the price of stock index futures contracts as determined at the Chicago Mercantile Exchange. A deterministic relationship exists between the value of the stocks making up the Standard & Poor's 500 index and the value of a futures contract on this index. Normally, the futures contract sells for more than the level of the S&P 500 index. This is true so long as the yield on Treasury bills exceeds the dividend yield on the S&P 500 stock index. If the gap between stock prices and the futures price (the futures basis) is theoretically too small, arbitrageurs will buy futures and sell stock because they expect the basis to widen. Conversely, if the basis is too large, they will buy stock and sell futures. Either way, the trades are made on the expectation that the basis will return to its "proper" level.

*Arbitrageurs help keep the market efficient.*

Arbitrageurs in the marketplace perform a very useful function: their activities help keep the market efficient, ensuring that prices do not deviate from their proper values for very long. Similarly, arbitrageurs usually are not hurting for pocket change, particularly if they act in markets that are popular with the investing public.

Burton Malkiel, dean of the Yale School of Organization and Management, is one of the best-known researchers on Wall Street and in academia. He sums up the benefits of arbitrage this way: "The benefits of arbitrage are twofold. First, by increasing trading in both underlying stocks and derivative products, liquidity in both markets is enhanced. Second, arbitrage trades link markets and ensure that both the underlying securities and the derivative instruments are appropriately priced."

Computers have made the lives of both the arbitrageur and the institutional investor simpler and more profitable. Using the New York Stock Exchange's Designated Order Turnaround system, called **DOT** or *SuperDOT*, market orders for less than 2,100 shares of a stock may be placed with a stock specialist electronically rather than through a floor broker. With high-speed, online computers, it is much easier to identify those instances when arbitrage is present.

---

[11] "Program Trading," *The Wall Street Journal*, June 14, 1991, C5.
[12] Hans Stoll and Robert Whaley, "Program Trading and the Monday Massacre," Working Paper, November 4, 1987, unpublished.

It is not accurate to say that these watchful computers call the shots on which way stock prices are to move next. The computer identifies situations in which an opportunity for arbitrage appears to be present, but it does not cause the situation.

Groups of arbitrageurs often identify profitable opportunities almost simultaneously, and they take advantage of these computer-identified opportunities on a grand scale by collectively buying or selling hundreds of thousands of shares in minutes. Contrary to popular belief, however, this extra volume is mostly from numerous small institutional trades rather than massive 100,000-share transactions. Given that the arbitrage situation normally works in only a single direction (for example, everyone buys or everyone sells), this large influx of orders can cause prices to change drastically. Program trading is also the generic term used to describe any strategy that instantaneously recommends buy or sell orders because of apparent arbitrage.

*Program trading is the generic term used to describe any strategy that instantaneously recommends buy or sell orders because of apparent arbitrage.*

At present, program traders normally fall into one of two groups: (1) institutions that buy stock index futures and Treasury bills to create the equivalent of an index portfolio (long stock index futures + long T-bills = long index portfolio) and (2) institutions that combine a well-diversified stock portfolio with short positions in stock index futures to create synthetic Treasury bills (long index portfolio + short stock index futures = long T-bills). A synthetic T-bill is a collection of securities whose price return performance mimics that of a Treasury bill. Most synthetic T-bill positions are a combination of a long stock position and a short position in stock index futures contracts. If traders find that they can synthetically create an index fund that yields more than the actual index portfolio, or create synthetic T-bills that yield more than actual T-bills, they are going to jump at the chance. In doing so, they may collectively buy or sell thousands of shares in the blink of an eye.

Program trading suffers from a bad name because of the alleged impact these programs have on security prices. If the market takes a real tumble or if it is unusually volatile, someone often puts the blame on program trading. The stock specialist needs to match buy and sell orders as they arrive, and if program trading leads to the rapid arrival of numerous DOT orders at once, the specialist can have difficulty maintaining a fair and orderly market. This situation can lead to increased volatility, which is not desirable.

On September 11, 1986, for instance, the Dow Jones Industrial Average fell 86.61 points (4.61 percent); the following day it continued to decline, and the total drop was 120 points in two days, or a decline of about 6.4 percent. In early 2005, with the Dow Jones Industrial Average around 11,000, this corresponds to a drop of 507 points. On January 23, 1987, there was an intraday swing of 152 points in the Dow Jones Industrial Average, representing about a 7.25 percent range. Program trading was blamed for the disturbing market behavior on both occasions. Many fingers still point at program trading as the culprit behind the crash of 1987, although portfolio insurance probably played a larger role. For all investors, large one-day changes in the DJIA are thought provoking. Some people panic and dump their stocks whenever the market takes a dive. These people often lose money and declare, "That's it; back to the CDs at the bank."

It is easy to forget that a 100-point drop in the DJIA when it is over 10,000 is not the same as an 80-point drop when it is under 2,000. Some longtime market participants still subconsciously think of 50-point movements in the DJIA as a major change. Gary Gastineau, author of the *Stock Options Manual*, points out that the market decline of 41.91 points on April 30, 1986, was the largest one-day point decline on record at that time. However, that 2.3 percent decline had been exceeded at least 362 times over the previous five years, or an average of once every two months.[13]

Many professional traders and investment managers believe that program trading benefits the public. W. Gordon Binns, vice-president and chief investment funds officer of General Motors (GM), told a congressional panel that the use of program trading enabled GM to reduce average commission costs for the company pension fund from between 7 and 10 cents per share to between 2 and 3 cents per share. This is clearly to the benefit of the many retirees receiving checks from the fund.

To investigate program trading and the effect that futures and options may have on the cash (stock) markets, the Federal Reserve Board, the Commodity Futures Trading Commission, and the SEC jointly commissioned a study. This study reports that futures and options markets do not destabilize cash market prices.

Investor relations officers seem to have another view. The trade publication *Pensions and Investments* periodically reports on surveys regarding attitudes toward current portfolio management issues. According to a National Investor Relations Institute study described in that publication, 89 percent of the 300 respondents said program trading contributes to market volatility.[14]

Still another point of view is presented in the trade publication *Investing*. In an article aptly entitled "Program Trading, Futures, and Other Indictments," Douglas A. Love concludes, "No relation exists between program trading intensity and daily market volatility."[15]

## Alternative Investments

There is a relatively new asset class on the scene that has come to be called **alternative assets.** While there is no precise definition, the category includes about anything outside the ordinary stock, bonds, cash, and real estate asset classes. Endowments and foundations are the leaders in the use of this asset class. Three especially popular versions of alternative investing are *long/short portfolios*, *hedge funds*, and *managed futures*.

### Long/Short Portfolios

*The important thing in a long/short portfolio is for the long stock to outperform the short stock.*

Short selling is an essential element of an increasingly popular hedging strategy called building a **long/short portfolio**, which combines elements of speculation, fundamental stock analysis, and hedging to reduce risk.

The research department of a firm might identify a collection of stocks it believes are undervalued and another set of stocks it believes are overvalued. In its simplest form, the long/short strategy buys the undervalued shares and sells short the overvalued shares. Assuming that the portfolio had sufficient initial assets to fund the purchase of the undervalued shares, the proceeds from the short sale are used to buy Treasury bills. If the market goes up, the shares probably all rise, but the undervalued shares should rise more than the overvalued shares. Conversely, if the market falls, the overvalued shares (which were sold short) should fall more than the undervalued

[13]Gary Gastineau, *Arbitrage, Program Trading, and the Tail of the Dog* (Chicago: Chicago Board Options Exchange, 1986).

[14]"Program Trading Curbs Supported," *Pensions and Investments*, February 5, 1990, 8.

[15]Douglas A. Love, "Program Trading, Futures, and Other Indictment," *Investing*, Winter 1990, 18–21.

shares. Interest would be earned on the Treasury bills, and (if the stock analysis were accurate) the long/short portfolio would make money in either instance.

J.P. Morgan is reported to have put $250 million into long/short portfolio strategies such as this. At least one state employee pension fund has made a similar (although smaller) commitment.

### *Hedge Funds*

There is no completely satisfactory definition of a **hedge fund.** Some definitions include the words "sophisticated hedging and arbitrage techniques" in describing the fund's activities. A hedge fund, however, may not be involved in anything even remotely related to hedging in the traditional risk-reduction sense. We can say they are largely unregulated investment funds, usually with less than 100 investors and generally with a substantial minimum investment (at least $100,000 but sometimes $1 million or more). They do not register with the SEC and are often organized as a partnership. Investors are limited partners, with the hedge fund manager the general partner. The general partner faces unlimited liability and, as a consequence, typically earns a fee of about 1 percent plus 20 percent of the profits the fund makes. Most hedge funds make consistency of return their objective rather than maximum capital appreciation.

Sections 3(c)(1) and 3(c)(7) of the Investment Company Act of 1940 enable hedge funds to avoid registration and regulation as investment companies. Section 4(2) and Rule 506 of Regulation D of the Securities Act of 1933 enable the funds to avoid registering the securities they offer with the SEC. These regulations, however, prohibit a hedge fund from advertising in the traditional sense. New partners are acquired via referral and word of mouth.

Probably the first such fund was formed in 1949, and used short sales to offset the market risk of other equity positions. According to the Hedge Fund Association (*www.thehfa.org*), in early 2005 this was a $934 billion industry with approximately 8,050 funds. Foundations owned about 8 percent of the total, pension funds 9 percent, and other institutional investors 15 percent. Nearly 44 percent was owned by individuals.

Many funds use leverage to (hopefully) magnify returns, but seldom by more than a 2:1 ratio of debt to equity. A famous exception was Long Term Capital Management, the hedge fund involving two Nobel prize winners and other Wall Street luminaries that had a leverage ratio of 100:1 before its demise.[16]

Hedge funds often advertise some specialized investment style. Some make substantial use of long/short portfolios, often referred to as a market neutral strategy. In 2004 the Yale University Endowment had 26 percent of its $12.7 billion portfolio in a market neutral strategy.[17] (Yale was the first institutional investor to use this asset class, putting 15 percent of its portfolio into such a strategy in 1990.) If your stock picking skills are good and you buy undervalued securities and short those that are overvalued it doesn't make any difference what the market does. You have removed systematic risk and are left only with a positive alpha (if you are right). Other funds seek to take advantage of discrepancies in cross-currency exchange rates via a currency overlay strategy or exploit interest rate differentials between countries. Another strategy is convertible arbitrage, which

---

[16]The television series *Nova* produced an excellent show entitled "Trillion Dollar Bet" on the activities of Long Term Capital Management.

[17]*http://www.yale.edu/investments/Yale_Endowment_04.pdf*

typically buys convertible bonds or convertible preferred stock and shorts the common shares. Still another hedge fund style is buying securities in distressed companies, especially the debt that may sell for pennies on the dollar but ultimately be settled for much more than that when the firm's bankruptcy settlement is approved.

### Managed Futures

Another category of alternative investments are **managed futures.** As the name implies, this asset class includes a portfolio of long or short speculative futures contracts. The manager buys that which he feels is cheap, sells that which is expensive, and may do both to somehow hedge the aggregate risk. Morgan Stanley describes managed futures as "an industry in which professional money managers direct investments in the global currency, interest rate, equity, metal, energy and agricultural markets. They do this through the use of futures, forwards and options."[18] There are many versions of this strategy; a Google search will produce over 1 million hits on the words "managed futures." In early 2005 the Harvard Endowment Fund had over 13 percent of its portfolio invested in commodities.

## Role of Derivative Assets

*"I think the things that are keeping people from using these are a lack of understanding of what they are, and a fear that they are more speculative, more risky, than using regular securities."*
Jeanne Gustafson,
Evaluations Associates, Inc.

Futures and options can be extremely versatile tools for the investment manager. Unfortunately, many institutions are not permitted to use them in the management of their accounts. Sometimes this happens because the fund manager lacks the skill to do so, but more often it happens because these derivative assets are distrusted and misunderstood by people in policy-making roles. The answer to this problem lies in more education for practitioners and policy makers.

### Process of Education

Ways in which derivative assets such as options and futures can benefit a portfolio are now well established. These securities and contracts are used successfully in pension funds, in insurance portfolios, at commercial banks, and by government agencies such as the Federal National Mortgage Association. Still, futures and options have an image problem. People hear the words and immediately cry, "Speculative! Risky! Inappropriate!" As a result, many potential users of these products do not use them because of a misunderstanding of their economic purpose.

To help alleviate this problem, the various exchanges offer excellent seminars throughout the country to present information about ways in which derivative assets can be used in conservative portfolios. Especially notable among these are the risk management conferences sponsored by the Chicago Board Options Exchange, the Chicago Board of Trade, the Chicago Mercantile Exchange, and the London International Financial Futures Exchange. In addition, many brokerage firms have their own educational efforts in local seminars on the fundamentals of futures and options.

*The whole point of derivative asset education is to give people more choices.*

The exchanges historically have been very good at presenting their information in a generally unbiased fashion. As with any investment, it is important that a discussion about derivative assets include a clear statement of the risks along with the potential rewards. Derivative assets are not for everybody, but they are appropriate for a great many people or institutions that remain ignorant of this investment

[18] *www.morganstanleyindividual.com*

PORTFOLIO MEMO

## Beta: A Paradigm in Trouble?

The concept of beta is one of the central concepts in finance theory. For years people have been taught that there is a direct relationship between the expected rate of return on an investment and its undiversifiable risk (which is measured by beta).

Two of the most respected researchers in finance, Eugene Fama and Kenneth French, have presented preliminary evidence indicating that there may be more to the story. They studied the performance of thousands of stocks over a 30-year period and concluded that "beta as the sole variable explaining returns on stock is dead."

Fama and French find that long-term returns depend on company size and price-to-book ratios in addition to beta. Smaller companies and those with low price-to-book ratios showed historical returns greater than those predicted by beta alone.

Richard Roll, one of the original proponents of the arbitrage pricing theory, says these results prove what other academics have been talking about for some time. Arbitrage pricing suggests that returns are a function of several factors in addition to systematic risk.

It is likely that beta will continue to be a very useful statistic for many decades. It is easy to calculate and easy to interpret. Still, it is arrogant to assume that we know it all, and ongoing financial research indicates that some exciting discoveries about how securities are priced lie around the corner.

Source: *The New York Times*, 18 February 1992, C1.

alternative. The whole point of education is to give people more choices, and that is precisely what derivative asset education is all about.

Even for those who already employ futures and options, opportunities for further education abound. The pricing and optimum application of derivative assets is a very technical subject, and our understanding of this topic continues to improve each year. Popular practices go out of style as managers discover more efficient methods of accomplishing a particular end. This is the very essence of human innovation. The well-informed portfolio manager needs to keep up with developments in the field or risk becoming a dinosaur.

### *Getting Board Approval*

The battle does not end once the portfolio manager is convinced of the potential merits of futures and options, because very often the manager must convince someone else of these advantages. Boards of trustees, supervisors, or fund beneficiaries often share the preconception that these investments are speculative and inappropriate activities.

The fund manager who gets permission to begin a derivative asset program is usually one who can explain the merits of doing so in nontechnical, everyday language. In the words of a Gordon Lightfoot song, "Most of us hate anything we don't understand." This is certainly the case in the investment business. Until the decision maker fully comprehends how futures and options work, there will be latent suspicion of the program. Of course, if you are the person responsible for educating the board or your boss, it is essential that you be technically competent yourself. Technical competence is an extremely valuable leadership (and managerial) skill.

Finally, it is often best to speak about futures and options as risk management tools rather than as a way of enhancing return. It is certainly possible to speculate with futures or options, but that is not their primary role in most portfolios.

## The Chartered Financial Analyst Program

The *Chartered Financial Analyst (CFA)* designation is a prestigious credential for those involved in the money management business. Research reports emanating from brokerage houses are primarily the product of people who have completed the CFA program.[19] Some firms even make enrollment in the program a condition of employment.

### History

The **Chartered Financial Analyst program** began in 1959 with the formation of the Institute of Chartered Financial Analysts (ICFA). The objectives of this organization were to promote investment education and ethical behavior among security analysts, portfolio managers, and others involved in the investment business. The ICFA awarded the first CFA charter in 1963. Another organization, the Financial Analysts Federation (FAF), merged with the ICFA in 1990 to form the *Association for Investment Management and Research (AIMR)*. AIMR changed its name to the CFA Institute in 2004. The organization administers the annual CFA exams and develops the CFA curriculum. In many respects the CFA Institute is the mouthpiece for the intellectual component of the investment business. Figure 23-2 lists various statistics about the CFA program in 2005.

### The CFA Program Exams

To complete the program and earn the CFA designation, candidates must pass three separate exams taken at least a year apart. Each CFA exam is given only once per year, on the first Saturday in June.

The CFA program consists of three levels, numbered I, II, and III. The examination for each level is a six-hour exam broken into morning and afternoon sections. The Level I exam is multiple choice. Level II is entirely composed of item

**FIGURE 23-2**

Facts on the 2004–2005 CFA Program

- CFA candidates enrolled in 2004: 85,305
- Nations of residence of CFA candidates and charterholders: 150
- Number of CFA charterholders: 70,436
- Exam sites worldwide in 2005: 240 in 74 nations
- Average number of hours candidates study for each exam: 250
- Candidates from outside the United States and Canada in 2005: 52%
- Graders required for 2004 exam: 722

Source: *www.cfainstitute.org*

[19]The writers of these reports generally are not located locally. The community brokerage office receives the reports from the firm's research offices, probably in New York. Few retail stockbrokers complete the CFA program.

FIGURE 23-3

CFA Program Enrollment

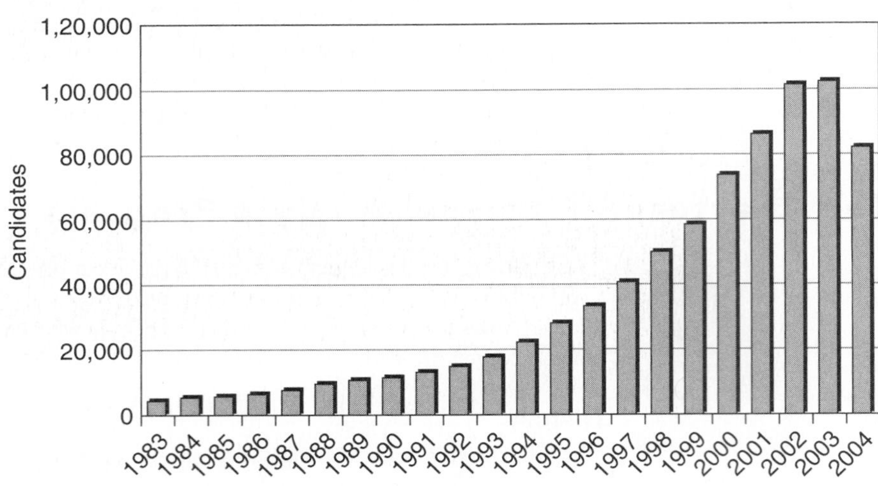


sets, which involve a vignette followed by six multiple-choice questions. Level III includes essay, valuation, analysis, and item sets. Level I covers basic tools and inputs to the investment valuation process. Much of this material will be familiar to someone with an undergraduate degree in finance, but a great deal will be new. There is, in the author's opinion, virtually no chance that someone can pass Level I without substantial study. The number of candidates passing Level I, for instance, has been below 50 percent the last four years. The combined pass rate for all three levels has been steadily declining since 1963.

Study is even more essential at Level II. Here the emphasis is on security valuation, including an understanding of the effect that different accounting standards (domestic and international) have on the interpretation of financial statements. Level II also includes specialized topics such as the valuation of closely held companies and the management of emerging market portfolios. Level III covers portfolio management. All three levels contain a heavy dose of professional standards case studies.

Historically, approximately 700 persons who have earned the CFA designation have assembled in Charlottesville, Virginia, in early summer to grade the essay portions of the exams. A group of about 130 senior graders review exams close to the passing mark, making a final determination on pass/fail. In 2004 the pass rates were 34 percent, 32 percent, and 64 percent for levels I, II, and III, respectively. Figure 23-3 shows the growth in the CFA Program enrollment. Note the exponential growth in the last decade.

## *CFA Program Themes*

There are four motivating factors behind the CFA program: increasing the *technical competence* of those in the investment business, the accurate *presentation* of investment results, adherence to *fiduciary duty*, and maintenance of a very high *ethical standard* of conduct.[20]

[20]The material in this section comes from my textbook *Practical Investment Management*, 3rd edition 2004, also published by Thomson/South-Western.

**Competence.** I have made the point elsewhere in this book that the modern investment world is far more complicated than it was a generation ago. Asset allocation, the proliferation of derivatives, and investment globalization all thicken the plot for investors and those who advise them.

Investors have a long-standing fear that they may not be acting in their own best interest. An investor wonders whom to trust, and fears that his or her financial adviser has a conflict of interest stemming from the connection between commissions and the level of trading activity (which is at least partially a function of the broker's recommendations). People who complete the CFA program are technically very competent and are likely to keep their noses clean during their professional careers. We expect our doctors and lawyers to be well schooled and current, and are rapidly coming to expect the same from our financial advisers.

**Presentation Standards.** The earlier chapter on performance presentation indicated that past results are sometimes described in misleading fashion by those who want to cast themselves in the best light, even if they skirt ethical borders in doing so. CFA candidates learn state-of-the-art standards and ideally prepare their own reports in accordance with the AIMR requirements. From a fiduciary perspective, compliance with AIMR requirements is on its way to being mandatory.

*From a fiduciary perspective, compliance with AIMR reporting requirements is becoming mandatory.*

**Fiduciary Duties.** People who are responsible for investing or giving advice regarding someone else's money have a fiduciary responsibility. This requires conduct that is in the individual client's best interest as well as being fair to the collective group of all clients. Understanding the priority of transactions, the disclosure of possible conflicts, and the importance of research reports is an important part of fiduciary duties.

**Ethics.** The Research Foundation of the Institute of Chartered Financial Analysts prepared a monograph on ethics in the investment profession.[21] In the introduction, the report cites a *Money* magazine/ABC poll[22] finding that more than two-thirds of Americans think financial advisers put their own interests ahead of those of their clients. The publication also reports on a survey[23] of members of the Financial Executives Institute, with that group choosing "ethics in the securities markets" as their *chief concern* from a list of 14 economic conditions and investment trends.

*According to a recent poll, more than two-thirds of Americans think financial advisers put their own interests ahead of those of their clients.*

The promotion of ethical conduct is a major objective of the CFA program. Investment professionals need to recognize that their decisions and recommendations can have very consequential effects on their clients' lives. The coverage of ethics in the CFA program is very useful and can be put directly to use by the investment professional; there is little "fluff" with the standards of practice.

For instance, it is important for a security analyst to clearly distinguish between fact and opinion. The analyst may *believe* something about a stock's future price behavior but not know for certain what it will do. Analysts should not give the investing public the impression that they have it all figured out. Similarly, research reports should be objective, unbiased, and have a reasonable basis supporting the conclusions developed. Managers with multiple clients must consider how to treat them all fairly without giving partial treatment to the biggest accounts.

---

[21]Theodore E. Veit and Michael R. Murphy, "Ethics in the Investment Profession: A Survey" (Charlotte, VA: Research Foundation of the Institute of Chartered Financial Analysts, 1992).
[22]Andrea Rock, "Financial Advice You Can Trust," *Money* 18, November 1989, 80–96.
[23]Mimi Deitsch, "The Economy and the Stock Market: Views of Financial Executives," *Financial Executive* 6, July/August 1990, 48–49.

MEMO

### The CFA Premium

The Association for Investment Management and Research (AIMR), predecessor to the CFA Institute, in conjunction with Russell Reynolds Associates, conducted a global compensation survey in 2001. More than 11,000 AIMR members completed the questionnaire. The survey provided convincing evidence of the value the marketplace puts on the chartered financial analyst designation. Among AIMR members with at least ten years of experience, those who had completed the CFA program earned, on average, 17 percent more than AIMR members who had not. Median total compensation for CFA charterholders was $245,000 compared to $210,000 for non-charterholders.

Source: James Cudahy, "Compensation Survey Goes Global: United Kingdom, Hong Kong, and Singapore Added to Biennial Study," *AIMR Exchange*, May/June 2001, 11.

Many people have studied ethics in school or elsewhere, but it is rare to find a curriculum that can immediately lead to positive change in behavior. The ethics portion of the CFA curriculum is not simple, but it will be fascinating to anyone in the money management business.

## Regulation Fair Disclosure

In August 2000 the Securities and Exchange Commission approved Regulation Fair Disclosure, commonly called **Regulation FD.** The principal provision of the rule prevents companies from giving material information to security analysts, mutual funds, or institutional investors unless the company simultaneously issues the same information to the general public.

### *The SEC Position*

In the published ruling, the SEC states its concerns and the motivation quite plainly:

> We have become increasingly concerned about the selective disclosure of material information by issuers. As reflected in recent publicized reports, many issuers are disclosing important nonpublic information, such as advance warnings of earnings results, to securities analysts or selected institutional investors or both, before making full disclosure of the same information to the general public. Where this has happened, those who were privy to the information beforehand were able to make a profit or avoid a loss at the expense of those kept in the dark.
>
> We believe that the practice of selective disclosure leads to a loss of investor confidence in the integrity of our capital markets. Investors who see a security's price change dramatically and only later are given access to the information responsible for that move rightly question whether they are on a level playing field with market insiders.
>
> Regulation FD is also designed to address another threat to the integrity of our markets: the potential for corporate management to treat material information as a commodity to be used to gain or maintain favor with particular analysts or investors. As noted in the Proposing Release, in the absence of a prohibition on selective disclosure, analysts may feel pressured to report favorably about a company or otherwise slant

their analysis in order to have continued access to selectively disclosed information. We are concerned, in this regard, with reports that analysts who publish negative views of an issuer are sometimes excluded by that issuer from calls and meetings to which other analysts are invited.[24]

In short, the purpose of the rule is to increase the quantity and quality of the information available to investors and to eliminate what some perceive as an unfair advantage historically enjoyed by Wall Street's big guns.

### The Industry Position

While the SEC anticipated that Regulation FD would increase the information available to the public, evidence indicates that precisely the opposite has occurred. Because of a fear of violating the rule, some companies are reluctant to answer a question that has not been publicly answered before. Similarly, companies in general have begun to provide less information between quarterly reports, again wanting to avoid any appearance of selective reporting to particular groups. Historically, for instance, a corporate executive who was a dinner speaker would almost always provide new information to the audience. A security analyst who visited a firm would return to his office with useful information about earnings prospects. After writing a research report, the analyst would often ask the company to review it for accuracy. With Regulation FD in place, these activities are much less likely to happen.

Another change is apparent in a firm's quarterly conference call with the brokerage industry. Rather than productive question and answer sessions, these have become scripted shows with less substance from the analysts' perspective.

### AIMR Response

As the foremost industry spokesman, the CFA Institute has also joined the conversation about the merits of Regulation FD. In sum, the Institute is not fond of the rule because it has reduced rather than increased the amount of information available to investors.

When the rule was first announced, the Institute formally studied its likely impact. The study group anticipated that "to avoid any possible SEC enforcement actions, corporations will reduce their communications to 'sound bites' and 'boilerplate' disclosures, which contain little information to analysts and the public at large."[25] It seems that the Institute was right. A year later, an industry survey on the effects of Regulation FD found that "while the overall goal of providing small investors and investment professionals with the same information is being achieved, it has been at the cost of *less* information in terms of quantity and quality."[26]

### The Future of the Regulation

The decision to adopt the rule was not unanimous. SEC Commissioner Laura Unger voted against it and in December 2001 published a study on the rule with recommendations regarding it. The study made three main points:

1. *The Commission should provide more guidance on materiality*. The rule states that firms may not selectively disclose "material" information but there is not universal consensus on the definition of *material*.

---

[24]Securities and Exchange Commission. 17 CFR Parts 240, 243, and 249 Release Nos. 33-7881, 34-43154, IC-24599, File No. S7-31-99, RIN 3235-AH82 Selective Disclosure and Insider Trading.
[25]AIMR Press Room, "NIRI Survey of Corporate IR Execs Shows SEC's Reg FD Would Curtail Disclosure, Analyst Group AIMR Says." *http://www.cfainstitute.org/pressroom/00releases/00regfdsurv.html*
[26]"Regulation FD Revisited," *AIMR Advocate*, January/February 2002, 3.

2. *The Commission should make it easier for issuers to use technology to comply with Regulation FD*. Many firms would like to make much more extensive use of the Internet to satisfy the requirements of the rule. The SEC position, however, has been that Website publication alone does not satisfy Reg FD's broad distribution requirement. Unger's report recommends, "The Commission should make clear that options such as adequately noticed website postings, fully accessible webcasts and electronic mail alerts would satisfy Regulation FD."[27]
3. *The Commission should analyze what issuers are saying post-FD*. There are widely different opinions on the effects of this regulation. Citing from Unger's report,

> Certain key questions have not yet been answered about whether Regulation FD has chilled corporate communications. On its face, Regulation FD has increased investor access to corporate information, but the regulation's impact on the amount and quality of information investors receive has not yet been quantified. Some issuers and investor representatives at the Roundtable believed that more information is now available, while sell-side analysts generally believed the opposite. As to the quality of information, some panelists found no change, while others believed that Reg FD has led to a decline in the quality of information. Panelists said that some issuers have used the rule as a shield to limit information flow and that issuers have generally retreated to scripted presentations.

Most parties generally agree with the spirit of the regulation, but the evidence indicates considerable disagreement about whether Regulation FD is a step in the right direction. There will be much more discussion about how best to amend this rule to improve the investment climate in the United States.

## SUMMARY

Stock lending is a very lucrative activity on Wall Street. It is not talked about much, nor is it generally well understood by the public. When individuals sell shares short, share certificates must be acquired to complete the short sale. When the certificates are not available in house, they must be borrowed. Stock loan finder firms facilitate this process and receive a fee for their services. Firms that lend the certificates earn interest on the share value at no real cost to themselves. The lent certificates come from the margin accounts of customers at the firm. Stock lending is outside the jurisdiction of the Securities and Exchange Commission because the activity does not involve the purchase or sale of a security.

Program trading is a much maligned computerized technique for making automatic investment decisions to take advantage of inefficiencies (arbitrage) in the marketplace. The practice is really an automated version of a longstanding investment house practice. There is some evidence that program trading contributes to increased volatility in the marketplace and an equal amount of evidence that argues the opposing view.

The economic function of derivative assets such as futures and options is not well understood by a great many people who must make consequential decisions

[27]Laura Unger, "Special Study: Regulation Fair Disclosure Revisited," available at *http://www.sec.gov/news/studies/regfdstudy.htm*

about investment policy. Futures and options have a reputation of being speculative, inappropriate investments for all but the very rich. In fact, these securities have their greatest value as risk management tools, and that is how they should be represented to people unfamiliar with them. Virtually all portfolios could occasionally benefit from the fine-tuning that futures and options can provide.

The CFA program is rapidly becoming a mandatory credential for new entrants to the money management field. Some firms make enrollment in the program a condition of employment. Major themes in the CFA program are professional competence, the presentation of data, understanding fiduciary duties, and adherence to a code of ethics.

## QUESTIONS

1. Someone once said, "Finance is the study of arbitrage." What does this statement mean?
2. Suppose that conclusive proof became available showing that program trading does increase the volatility of the security markets. What changes, if any, do you think would be called for?
3. Why is portfolio insurance called a reactive strategy?
4. Why do you think most brokerage firms have minimum equity requirements before a particular account is allowed to sell short?
5. If a person owns stock but holds it in a street name, does the person care if the stock certificates are lent or not?
6. Why do you think firms are not permitted to lend certificates held in a cash account?
7. What is the function of the stock loan finder?
8. Why is stock lending considered so lucrative?
9. If you were in charge of a Senate panel designated to investigate stock lending, what specific points would you want to address?
10. Write a 250-word explanation of program trading that could be printed in a local newspaper.
11. How does arbitrage fit in with program trading?
12. What is a derivative asset? Why do you think so many people have a hard time understanding this concept?
13. Why is default not a major concern in the stock lending business?

## PROBLEMS

1. Using library reference material, show the gap between the dividend yield on the S&P 500 and the yield on AAA corporate bonds today, one year ago, and five years ago.
2. You own 1,000 shares of XYZ and have purchased ten protective put contracts. The puts have a delta of –0.317.
   a. What is your position delta?
   b. Instead of buying puts, how many of your shares should you sell short to achieve the same result?
3. Investigate the 1862 Harlem Railroad short squeeze involving Cornelius Vanderbilt and Boss Tweed. What was the central issue in this case?

## INTERNET EXERCISE

Visit the Website *http://www.thomsoninvest.net/cgi-bin/fund_screener/mf_screener?PAGE1=* and identify the top ten performing asset allocation mutual funds. Then visit *http://quote.yahoo.com* and collect the Sharpe and Treynor performance measures on each of these funds. How did these funds perform relative to an index fund?

## FURTHER READING


Brush, John S. "Comparisons and Combinations of Long and Long/Short Strategies." *Financial Analysts Journal,* May/June 1997, 81–89.

"The Business Nobody Wants to Talk About." *Business Week,* September 25, 1989, 196, 198.

Grossman, Sanford J. "An Analysis of the Implications for Stock and Futures Price Volatility of Program Trading and Dynamic Hedging Strategies." National Bureau of Economic Research Working Paper No. 2357, August 1987.

———. "Program Trading and Market Volatility: A Report on Interday Relationships." *Financial Analysts Journal,* July/August 1988, 18–28.

Jacobs, Bruce I., Kenneth N. Levy, and David Starer. "Long-Short Portfolio Management: An Integrated Approach," *Journal of Portfolio Management,* Winter 1999, 23–32.

———. "On the Optimality of Long-Short Strategies." *Financial Analysts Journal,* March/April 1998, 40–51.

Love, Douglas A. "Program Trading, Futures, and Other Indictments." *Investing,* Winter 1990, 18–21.

Michaud, Richard O. "Are Long-Short Equity Strategies Superior?" *Financial Analysts Journal,* November/December 1993, 44–49.

Pessin, Allan H. *Fundamentals of the Securities Industry.* New York: New York Institute of Finance, 1985.

Strong, Robert A. "A Short Guide to the Mechanics of a Short Sale." *AAII Journal,* July 1985, 18–20.

# GLOSSARY

**absolute purchasing power parity** The fact that, because of the law of one price, equivalent assets in different countries should sell for the same price after adjusting for currency differences.

**Acapulco trade** An unusually large trade for a particular individual. Presumably, if the trade is profitable, the trader will go to Acapulco on a luxury vacation.

**accrued interest** Interest that has been earned on a bond but that has not yet been paid.

**active management** A dynamic investment policy that requires periodic action by the portfolio manager.

**alpha** A measure of the difference between a portfolio's actual performance and the performance expected by finance theory.

**alternative assset** Generally understood to mean any investment asset other than stocks, bonds, real estate, or cash.

**American depository receipts (ADRs)** Securities that are actually receipts representing shares of stock that are held on the ADR holder's behalf in a bank in the country of origin.

**American option** An option whose owner has purchased the right to buy or sell a set number of shares of common stock (normally 100 shares) at a set price (the striking, or exercise, price) from a specified person (the option writer) any time prior to the expiration of the option.

**annuity** A fixed sum of money paid for a fixed period of time.

**anticipatory strategy** A form of tactical asset allocation in which decisions are made in anticipation of a future economic event.

**arbitrage pricing theory (APT)** A pricing theory based on the absence of arbitrage and the notion that a security's expected return comes from a number of economic factors.

**arithmetic mean** The sum of a series divided by the number of elements in the series.

**asked price** The lowest price at which anyone has expressed a willingness to sell a particular asset.

**assessed value** The value of an asset used to determine property taxes.

**assessment bond** A debt instrument where the income needed to pay the interest is obtained via a billing process, such as income taxes or user fees.

**asset allocation** The proportion of funds distributed across a set of asset classes.

**asset class** A large subgroup of the investment universe such as common stocks, corporate bonds, or cash equivalents.

**asset class appraisal** The stage in a tactical asset allocation program in which a comparative analysis is made of broad groups of competing investment alternatives such as stocks, bonds, or timberland.

**at-the-money** An option where the striking price equals the current market price of the underlying security.

**away-from-the-money** An option with no intrinsic value whose striking price is distant from the current stock price.

**balloon loan** Any loan with a large payment due at the end of the life of the loan.

**barbell strategy** A leading passive bond strategy (along with the laddered strategy). The barbell strategy differs from the laddered strategy in that less investment is made in the middle maturities. See also *laddered* strategy.

**basis** The difference between the futures price of a commodity and the current cash price at a specific location.

**basis convergence** The pricing phenomenon whereby the difference between the price of a stock index futures contract and the level of the underlying stock index declines as time passes, everything else being equal.

**bearer bond** Another name for a coupon bond. A bearer bond is one which is not registered in the owner's name and is negotiable by whoever legally holds it. Bearer bonds have dated coupons which are clipped for the payment of interest.

**benchmark** A standard against which investment performance might be judged.

**beta** The sensitivity of a security to changes in a broad market index. A beta of 1.0 indicates average sensitivity. A beta greater than 1.0 indicates greater sensitivity, and therefore greater risk.

**bid price** The highest price at which anyone has expressed a willingness to buy a particular asset.

**best of class investing** The practice of identifying the most socially conscious (or least offensive) company within an industry and investing in that company even though some of its activities may be inconsistent with the manager's views of social responsibility.

**biological risk** The risk of insect, fire, wind, or disease damage to timberland.

**bivariate** Belonging to a random variable population in which the elements possess two characteristics of interest.

**Black Option Pricing Model** An option pricing model for use on futures options.

**Black-Scholes Option Pricing Model (OPM)** One of the most significant developments in the history of finance. This model provides an analytical framework for the evaluation of securities that provide a claim on other assets.

**blue chip** A subjective term for a good stock. Often used to refer to a stock with a long, uninterrupted history of dividend payments.

**bond beta** A little-used measure of the systematic risk of a bond.

**bond equivalent yield** The method of determining the interest rate on a Treasury bill that includes 365 days per year and recognizes the fact that the actual T-bill investment is less than the par value.

**bond swap** A portfolio manager's exchange of an existing bond or set of bonds for a different issue.

**book entry form** A method of registering securities in which no actual certificates are issued. A record of ownership is maintained by the issuer of the security. Purchases and sales are recorded by changing the names "on the books" rather than by transferring security certificates.

**borrowing portfolio** In the context of the capital market line, an efficient portfolio that involves purchasing the market portfolio on margin.

**bullet immunization** A technique appropriate for a client who has an initial sum of money to invest and wants to accumulate a predetermined sum on a specific future date. The technique involves assembling a basket of bonds whose collective holding period returns will match that of a hypothetical zero coupon bond.

**bullet strategy** A fixed income portfolio strategy in which most investments are made near a particular maturity or duration.

**bullion** Unworked gold, usually in bar form.

**buy and hold** A passive, naive investment strategy in which someone buys a security and maintains the security position without revision.

**call option** An option whose owner has purchased the right to buy a set number of shares of common stock (normally 100 shares) at a set price (the striking, or exercise, price) from a specified person (the option writer) anytime prior to a specified date (the expiration date).

**call premium** (1) The market price of a call option; (2) additional compensation that sometimes must be paid when a bond is redeemed prior to its maturity date.

**call protection** A period of time during which a bond issuer may not call a particular bond issue.

**call risk** The potential for inconvenience or economic loss associated with having a bond issue called.

**cap rate** The required rate of return minus the growth rate, especially in real estate valuation.

**capital appreciation** One of the four principal portfolio objectives, in which the fund manager seeks to increase the principal value of the fund rather than to generate income.

**Capital Asset Pricing Model (CAPM)** A theoretical model measuring the expected return of an asset in terms of its beta and the expected return on a broad market index.

**capital market line (CML)** A line drawn in expected return/standard deviation space from the risk-free rate to the market portfolio.

**cash dividend** A payment to shareholders of a portion of a firm's earnings.

**cash drag** Comparing a fund that is 95 percent in stock with an index that is 100 percent in stock results in a phenomenon called cash drag.

**cash matching** A form of portfolio dedication or immunization in which a basket of securities is assembled such that the basket generates income that arrives just in time and in just the right amount to pay a bill.

**cash price** The current price of an asset, particularly an asset on which futures contracts trade; also called the spot price.

**cash settlement** The settlement procedure used with stock index futures and options. No delivery of the underlying asset occurs with these securities.

**CERES principles** A set of principles espoused by The Coalition for Environmentally Responsible Economies which requires commitment to various measures designed to benefit the environment.

**chaos theory** A developing field in physics that seeks to find deterministic patterns in seemingly random events.

**Chartered Financial Analyst Program** A program administered by the Association for Investment Management and Research which leads to the Chartered Financial Analyst designation. This is a highly desirable credential within the portfolio management community.

**chartist** A technical analyst who believes that skillful interpretation of charts can improve investment performance.

**cheapest to deliver** The specific financial instrument that is most advantageous to use in delivery against a Treasury bond or Treasury note futures contract.

**churning** An illegal activity in which a broker makes, or advises a client to make, unnecessary trades in an account for the purpose of generating excess commissions.

**clearing corporation** A corporation whose role is to eliminate uncertainty about delivery in the futures and options markets. It does this by interposing itself between buyers and sellers. All trades are actually sales to, or purchases from, the clearing corporation.

**closing transaction** An option trade in which an investor eliminates a previously established option position. For the purchaser of an option, a closing transaction is a sale of the option. For an option writer, a closing transaction is a purchase of the option or the receiving of an exercise notice from the option holder.

**collateral trust bond** A bond backed by claims on other securities.

**commodities trading advisor** A broker who is licensed to trade futures contracts.

**Commodity Futures Trading Commission** A five-member U.S. government agency charged with supervising and regulating the futures exchanges.

**Compustat** A computerized data base covering most U.S. companies and containing a history of virtually all accounting variables.

**confidence index** The ratio of the yield on high-grade bonds to the yield on low-grade bonds, with the value of this ratio theoretically limited to 1.0.

**consol** A perpetual bond.

**constant beta portfolio** An investment portfolio in which the manager seeks to keep the portfolio's systematic risk (as measured by beta) constant.

**constant mix strategy** A portfolio rebalancing strategy that seeks to maintain the relative weighting of asset classes within the portfolio as the security prices change.

**constant proportion portfolio insurance** An investment portfolio in which the manager increases the proportion invested in stock as stock prices rise.

**consumption decision** The choice an investor makes between spending money today or investing it so as to be able to spend more later.

**contango market** The typical relationship with most futures contracts, in which the futures price exceeds the cash price.

**continuous** Based on an infinite number of time intervals rather than a discrete number. Continuous compounding of interest makes use of natural logarithms rather than "per period" compounding.

**continuous pricing function** One of the functions of the securities markets. This function ensures that assets listed on the exchange can always be traded quickly without the need to search for a buyer or seller.

**convenience risk** A nonquantifiable aspect of risk that measures the potential for added managerial time requirements because of events such as having to replace a called bond.

**conversion price** The price at which the holder of a convertible bond has the right to purchase the asset into which the bond is convertible.

**conversion ratio** The quantity of the underlying asset for which a convertible bond may be exchanged.

**conversion value** The current value of the assets for which a convertible bond may be exchanged.

**convertible bond** A debt instrument that can be exchanged at the holder's wish for another asset (usually shares of common stock).

**convexity** For a given interest rate change, the difference between the actual price change in a bond and that predicted by the duration statistic.

**corner portfolio** A portfolio generated by the Markowitz full covariance model, in which a new security enters the portfolio or an existing security leaves as portfolio risk changes.

**correlation** A statistical measure of the relationship between two variables.

**counterparty risk** The risk that the party with whom you have entered into a swap will be unable or unwilling to fulfill their side of the contract.

**country risk** An aspect of the risk assessment of foreign investments, particularly involving a measurement of political risk in a particular country.

**covariance** A measure of the relationship between two variables. Covariance is related to correlation by the standard deviations of the two variables.

**covariance matrix** A display of the covariances between all possible pairs of a set of variables. This term is usually associated with the Markowitz full covariance model.

**cover** The process of eliminating an existing investment position by taking an offsetting trade.

**cover a short** Eliminate a short position by buying securities identical to those sold short.

**covered call** A call option an investor has written against common stock owned. A call option is also considered covered if it is held in the same portfolio as a call option with the same expiration date but a lower striking price, or in the same portfolio as a call option of the same striking price but a later expiration date.

**covered interest arbitrage** A sequence of actions in the currency markets, currency forward markets, and in different money markets that results in a riskless profit because of these markets being out of equilibrium.

**crawling stop** A stop order used to protect a profit by continually raising the stop price behind a rising stock.

**credit risk** See *default risk*.

**crowd** The colloquial term used for the people in a trading pit.

**cumulative voting** A corporate voting procedure whereby a shareholder entitled to vote on, say, ten matters has the option of casting all ten votes for or against one single matter (and not voting on the others).

**current yield** The annual income generated by a security divided by its current price.

**cyclical stock** A stock whose earnings are particularly sensitive to trends in the overall economy.

**daily price limit** The restriction at a commodities exchange preventing the market price of a futures contract from rising or falling more than a set limit each day.

**day of the week effect** A market anomaly whereby Wednesdays and Fridays tend to be good days for the stock market, with Mondays being bad.

**day trader** A speculator who does not normally maintain an open position in any asset overnight.

**debenture** A debt issue secured only by the good name of the company.

**deep-in-the-money** A subjective description that applies to any option that has substantial intrinsic value.

**default risk** A measure of the likelihood that a borrower will be unable to repay principal and interest as agreed; also called credit risk.

**defensive stock** A stock whose earnings are largely independent to swings in the economy.

**defined contribution plan** A retirement plan in which the firm contributes a stated dollar amount on each employee's behalf on a regular basis, but with no guarantee as to the future value of those dollars.

**deliverable bond** A U.S. Treasury bond with at least fifteen years until maturity (or fifteen years of call protection).

**delivery date** The date that a commodity is due to be delivered in a futures contract.

**delivery month** The month specified in a futures contract by which delivery (or settlement) of the contract must be made unless the position is previously eliminated by an offsetting trade.

**delta** The change in option premium expected from a small change in the stock price.

**dependent variable** A variable whose value is determined by the value of other independent variables.

**Designated Order Turnaround (DOT)** The Designated Order Turnaround system at the New

York Stock Exchange; also called SuperDOT. This system allows trades of less than 2,100 shares to be placed directly with a specialist by electronic means.

**developed property** Property that has been improved by the construction of buildings.

**diminishing marginal utility of money** The notion that although more wealth is always preferred to less, each additional dollar contributes a smaller amount to the investor's aggregate level of satisfaction.

**discount brokerage firm** A firm that offers substantially reduced commission costs, usually at the expense of reduced services such as investment advice or research.

**discounted cash flow (DCF) approach** A valuation method that estimates the present value of future cash flows to be received from an investment.

**discrete** Based on a set of time intervals. Discrete compounding compounds interest based on a "per period" rate.

**distribution** The frequency with which particular random variables in a population are routinely observed.

**diversification rule** The ERISA requirement that pension plans be diversified.

**dividend discount model** The mathematical identity for the value of a growing perpetuity. This model is often used to estimate the intrinsic value of a common stock.

**dividend reinvestment plan** A program offered by many corporations in which shareholders can choose to have immediate reinvestment of their dividend checks in additional stock of the firm. These programs always provide for the purchase of fractional shares and often give a slight discount on the share price from the prevailing market price.

**documents rule** The ERISA requirement that a manager must handle a pension fund in accordance with the plan document unless the document violates ERISA or state law fiduciary rules.

**dollar cost averaging** A periodic investment program in which an investor makes regular purchases of the same dollar amount into the same security.

**dollar-weighted rate of return** The internal rate of return from an investment.

**dominance** The characteristic an investment alternative has when its risk and return characteristics are preferable to the alternatives.

**due diligence** The process of investigating something in a manner consistent with how a prudent person would conduct the investigation.

**duration** A measure of interest rate risk. Duration is generally a weighted average of the length of time required for cash flows to be received from a fixed-income security.

**duration matching** A form of portfolio dedication or immunization in which a basket of assets is assembled such that its present value and its duration match that of a liability or stream of liabilities.

**duty of care** An ERISA requirement that focuses on procedures designed to ensure that the manager makes prudent decisions.

**duty of loyalty** An ERISA requirement that seeks to minimize conflicts of interest and to ensure that the manager has the beneficiary's best interest in mind.

**dynamic hedging** A portfolio insurance technique that requires frequent revision of a hedge using stock index futures or options.

**economic exposure** A type of exposure that measures the risk that the value of a security will decline due to an unexpected change in relative foreign exchange rates.

**economic function** The characteristic of the capital markets that facilitates the matching of potential buyers and sellers.

**economic risk** The chance of loss due to adverse factors regarding quality, liquidity, demand, price, management, or regulation.

**efficient frontier** The collection of dominant portfolios for given levels of risk or return.

**efficient market hypothesis (EMH)** The theory that publicly available information is rapidly and accurately reflected in the price of securities, and that over the long run, realized returns will be consistent with their level of undiversifiable risk.

**efficient portfolio** A collection of securities whose risk and expected return combination plots on the efficient frontier.

**emerging market** An imprecise term referring to a country without a mature stock market or exchange mechanism.

**Employee Retirement Income Security Act (ERISA)** The Employee Retirement Income Security Act, designed to help ensure the safety of pension funds by establishing a uniform set of standards for fiduciary conduct.

**endowment fund** A perpetual, tax-exempt portfolio organized to benefit a nonprofit organization such as a church, library, or educational institution.

**equipment trust certificate** A bond backed by claims on equipment.

**equity option** An option in which common stock is the underlying security.

**equity REIT** A real estate investment trust that owns and operates income producing property.

**equity risk premium** The difference in the average return between stocks and some measure of the risk-free rate, usually either the Treasury bill rate or Treasury bond rate.

**Eurobond** A debt agreement that is denominated in a currency other than that of the country in which it is held.

**Eurodollar** A U.S. dollar located outside the United States. Eurodollars are the underlying asset for a popular short-term debt futures contract.

**European option** An option whose owner has purchased the right to buy or sell a set number of shares of common stock (normally 100 shares) at a set price (the striking or exercise, price) from a specified person (the option writer) *only* at the specified date (the expiration date).

**exchange-traded fund** A portfolio of securities that trades as a single basket on a stock exchange.

**exclusive purpose rule** The fiduciary requirement that an investment manager handle the funds for the sole benefit of the beneficiary.

**exercise** The act by which an option holder expresses an interest to sell shares to the option writer at the specified price (with puts) or to buy shares from the option writer at the specified price (with calls).

**expectations hypothesis** The theory that the futures price for a commodity is what the marketplace expects the cash price to be when the delivery month arrives.

**expectations theory** The explanation of the yield curve which requires forward rates to reflect the market expectation of future rates.

**expected return** The investment return predicted by financial theory.

**exposure range** A specification in a tactical asset allocation program of how much the mix range can deviate from the normal mix.

**fair bet** A lottery in which the expected pay-off is equal to the cost of playing.

**fair price function** The characteristic of the capital markets in which investors are able to trust the validity of the prevailing prices.

**fear of regret** The tendency for investment managers to avoid risk because they do not like having to apologize to clients.

**fee simple value** The value of a property in the absence of any encumbering leases.

**fiduciary** A person or institution responsible for the management of someone else's money.

**fiduciary put** A short put option in which the put writer deposits the striking price of the put into an interest-bearing account; also called a cash-secured put.

**financial asset** An asset for which a corresponding liability exists somewhere.

**flight to quality** What occurs when the economic situation of a country is expected to deteriorate and investors become less willing to hold risky bonds. The value of risky bonds falls during a flight to quality as safe bonds are purchased and risky bonds are sold.

**floor value** A set value below which a portfolio's value must not fall, especially with a constant proportion portfolio insurance strategy.

**foreign bond** A debt agreement that is denominated in the local currency but issued by a foreign corporation.

**foreign currency option** A listed option giving the holder the right to buy or sell a specified quantity of foreign currency. Foreign currency options are distinct from foreign currency futures options.

**foreign exchange risk** The chance of loss due to adverse fluctuations in exchange rates between national currencies.

**forward rate** A contractual rate between a commercial bank and a client for the future delivery of a specified quantity of foreign currency; the forward rate is normally quoted on the basis of one, two, three, six, and twelve months.

**forward split** A stock split in which shareholders receive additional shares and are left with a greater number of shares than before the split.

**foundation** An organization designed to benefit the arts, education, research, or community welfare in general.

**full carrying charge market** A futures market for a particular commodity in which the basis for successive delivery months reflects the cost of storing (or holding, in the case of financial futures) the commodity or financial instrument.

**full faith and credit issue** A debt issue which is backed only by the good reputation and perhaps the taxing power of the issuer.

**fundamental analyst** A person who studies earnings and relative value in determining the intrinsic value of a security.

**funds gap** The difference between a bank's rate-sensitive assets and its rate-sensitive liabilities.

**fungibility** The ability of participants in the futures and options markets to reverse their positions by making offsetting trades. This occurs because the individual contracts are standardized and interchangeable.

**futures contract** A legal, transferable, standardized contract that represents a promise to buy or sell a quantity of a standardized commodity by a predetermined delivery date.

**futures option** A type of option that gives the holder of a call the right to assume a long position in a futures contract and gives the holder of a put the right to go short a futures contract.

**general obligation issue** Bonds that are secured by the taxing power of a government.

**geometric mean** The *n*th root of the product of *n* observations.

**gold certificate** A document that represents ownership of gold bullion that is kept by someone else on the owner's behalf.

**good faith deposit** The initial equity requirement that must be deposited with an opening transaction in a futures contract. This is often called margin, although no money is borrowed.

**growing annuity** A finite series of cash flows which increase by a set percentage each period.

**growing perpetuity** An infinite series of cash flows which increase by a set percentage each period.

**growth** One of the four principal investment objectives, in which an investor seeks an increase in the principal value of a fund at the expense of current income.

**growth investor** An investor who prefers stocks that are in favor and whose prices have been advancing.

**growth of income** One of the four principal investment objectives, in which the level of income generated by a portfolio is expected to grow each year.

**growth stock** A stock in a company that retains a good portion of its earnings in anticipation of being able to reinvest them profitably in the company.

**hedge fund** An investment vehicle restricted to a small number of wealthy investors, with the fund employing some set of sophisticated hedging and arbitrage techniques.

**hedge ratio** A calculated value that indicates the quantity of an asset that must be acquired or sold to eliminate completely a certain type of risk with an investment position.

**hedger** A person who faces some type of economic risk and chooses to eliminate or reduce it by some type of offsetting transaction.

**hedging** The act of transferring unwanted risk to another market participant who is willing to bear it.

**holding period return** A comparison of the ending value of an investment with its original cost. The holding period return is insensitive to the length of the period.

**hybrid REIT** A real estate investment trust that owns and operates income producing property and also invests in mortgages.

**hypothecation agreement** A legal document that an investor must sign before opening a margin account at a brokerage firm. This document gives the broker permission to lend shares held in a street name.

**immunization** The process of removing interest rate risk by adjusting the duration of assets and liabilities via the futures market or portfolio rebalancing.

**improving on the market** The practice of writing deep-in-the-money covered calls to sell stock at a slightly above-market price, or writing in-the-money puts to acquire stock at a below-market price.

**in-the-money** An option that has intrinsic value based on the stock price and striking price. Calls are in-the-money when the striking price is less than the stock price; puts are in-the-money when the stock price is less than the striking price.

**income bond** A bond on which the interest is payable only if it is earned.

**income stock** A stock that pays out most of its earnings as dividends.

**inconsistent objectives** An impossible combination of primary and secondary portfolio objectives. A person cannot, for instance, couple capital appreciation with stability of principal.

**incremental risk-adjusted return (IRAR)** A performance measure used in portfolios that include option positions.

**indenture** The legal document describing the terms of a bond issue.

**independent variable** A variable that is measured without regard to other variables and is used to help determine the value of some dependent variable.

**index option** An option to buy or sell a hypothetical basket of securities whose value is determined by a market index: Index options are settled in cash; there is no delivery mechanism.

**indexing** The practice of continually adjusting a portfolio such that its characteristics match as nearly as possible those of some market index.

**indicia of ownership rule** The ERISA requirement that documents relating to asset ownership must be under the jurisdiction of the U.S. court system.

**industry effect** The tendency for firms sharing a similar line of business to experience similar movements in their earnings or stock prices.

**inflation premium theory** The rapidity with which prices are rising; it measures how rapidly the money standard is losing its purchasing power.

**informational efficiency** The aspect of the market considered by the efficient market hypothesis. Informational efficiency means that the market quickly and accurately reacts to the arrival of new information.

**inside information** Privately held news that, when released to the public, is likely to have an impact on the price of securities. Trading on the basis of inside information is illegal.

**interest rate parity** The theory that in the absence of market imperfections, international foreign currency exchange rates reflect differentials in the relative national interest rates.

**interest rate risk** The chance of loss because of adverse movement in the level or term structure of interest rates.

**interest rate sensitivity** The characteristic of an asset whose price will necessarily change if the level of interest rates changes.

**interest rate swap** A transaction between two institutional investors whereby one party agrees to pay a fixed interest rate on some notional amount in exchange for receiving a floating interest rate from the other party.

**intrinsic value** A characteristic of an option determined by the degree to which it is in-the-money.

**inverted market** A market in which the futures price is less than the cash price.

**investment grade** A description of bonds rated BBB or higher by Standard & Poor's.

**investment horizon** The period of time a particular investment is expected to be held.

**investment management** The actual practice of selecting securities and placing them in a portfolio.

**investment policy** A statement outlining the expectations of the portfolio manager and the constraints under which the manager must operate.

**investment strategy** Short-term activities that are consistent with established investment policy and that will contribute positively toward obtaining the objective of a portfolio.

**investment value** The value of property to a particular investor; this amount may be more or less than market value.

**invoice price** The amount that the buyer of an interest rate futures contract must pay when the securities underlying the futures contract are delivered.

**issuer** The organization that created a particular debt or equity security.

**January effect** A pricing anomaly in which stock returns (especially those of small firms) do abnormally well in January.

**Jensen measure** A seldom-used method of performance evaluation. A Jensen measure greater than 0 indicates that a security has shown an upward drift in its price that is unexplainable by its level of systematic risk.

**junk bond** Historically, any bond rated BB or below by Standard & Poor's.

**laddered strategy** One of two especially famous passive bond strategies (along with the barbell strategy). Rather than trying to second-guess interest rate changes, a popular alternative is to distribute the fixed-income dollars throughout the yield curve.

**law of one price** The fundamental finance principle that requires that equivalent assets sell for the same price.

**leased fee value** The value of a property given the existing leases on it.

**leasehold value** The value of the lease on a property.

**legal list** A limited security universe for a particular investor. Only securities on the legal list are eligible investments.

**lending portfolio** In the context of the capital market line, an efficient portfolio that is partially invested in the riskless interest rate.

**level of interest rates** The vertical placement of the yield curve as opposed to its slope.

**liability funding** Another name for portfolio dedication.

**liquidity** The extent to which something can be quickly converted into cash at approximately its market value.

**liquidity preference theory** The theory of interest rate behavior which states that investors, in general, prefer to invest short term rather than long term.

**liquidity premium** With the liquidity preference theory of interest rates, the result that forward rates are actually higher than the expected future interest rate.

**liquidity risk** The potential for loss because of an inability to convert an asset to cash at a reasonable price.

**locals** Marketmakers at a futures or options exchange who seek to take the other side of incoming orders and quickly trade these positions to brokers representing other incoming orders; also called *scalpers*.

**logreturn** The natural logarithm of an investment return.

**London fix** The price of gold determined twice a day in London by a group of bankers who seek to match buy and sell orders until equilibrium is found.

**long hedge** A transaction in which an asset is purchased as a hedge.

**long position** The most common investment position in which an asset is owned, as opposed to being borrowed or written.

**long/short portfolio** A strategy whereby a firm dedicates funds for the specific purpose of buying shares that are considered undervalued and selling short shares that are considered overvalued.

**low PE effect** The phenomenon whereby stocks with low price/earnings (PE) ratios often seem to outperform stocks with higher PE ratios.

**Macaulay duration** The traditional measure of duration. Duration is a measure of interest rate risk and a weighted average of the time it takes to recover the cost of a security.

**macro risk** An element of political risk that describes government action that affects all foreign firms in a particular industry.

**Malkiel's interest rate theorems** A set of relationships among bond prices, bond terms, and the level of interest rates.

**managed futures** A portfolio of long and/or short speculative futures contracts

**management fee** Compensation paid to an investment fund manager.

**management risk** The potential for financial loss because of poor management practice, especially with timberland investments.

**margin** The general term for good faith deposits or other cash deposits required to establish or maintain an investment position.

**margin call** The requirement to add equity to an investment account because of adverse price movements or new transactions.

**market comparables approach** A valuation approach that uses various price ratios to estimate the value of the property of interest.

**marked to market** The practice in the futures markets of transferring funds from one account to another each day on the basis of unrealized (or paper) gains and losses.

**market impact** Change in market price purely because of executing the trade.

**market model** A regression model relating the past series of excess returns on an investment to the past series of excess returns on a market index. The market model is often used to estimate beta for the Capital Asset Pricing Model.

**market portfolio** A theoretical construct of the Markowitz full covariance model which represents the tangent point of a line from the riskfree rate to the efficient frontier for risky securities.

**market price of risk** Measures the cost of expected return in terms of risk.

**market variation call** A margin call received during the day that requires that funds be deposited within one hour.

**marketability risk** The potential for loss because of the inability to convert an asset into cash at any price.

**marketmaker** One of a number of people who compete against one another for the public's business, thereby helping to ensure that the public receives a market-determined price for options.

**market value** The likely selling price of a property when neither the buyer nor the seller are under a compulsion to trade and when both parties to the trade have complete information about the property.

**Markowitz diversification** Diversification designed to exploit the covariances of the portfolio components.

**Markowitz model** The portfolio construction algorithm that requires knowledge of all the pairwise covariances between the potential portfolio components.

**mean** The arithmetic average.

**median** In a sample or a population, the value above which half the observations lie and below which half the observations lie. The median reduces the effect of outliers (data points which plot away from the pattern shown by most of the others).

**Mergent, Inc.** Formerly known as Moody's Financial Information Services, publishes a widely used set of investment information.

**merger arbitrage** The practice of buying shares of potential takeover targets and selling short the shares of the acquirer.

**micro risk** A term that refers to the direction of politically motivated changes in the business environment of selected fields of business activity, or to foreign enterprises with specific characteristics.

**minimum variance portfolio** The combination of assets from a security universe that has lower variance than any other possible combination.

**mix range** A measure of how much the relative mix can deviate from the normal mix; also called the exposure range.

**mode** The value that appears most frequently in a set of data.

**modified duration** The traditional Macaulay duration discounted by one-half the annual yield to maturity.

**mortgage** A debt security in which real estate is used as collateral.

**mortgage REIT** A real estate investment trust that buys mortgages or lends money to property purchasers.

**multi-index model** A theoretical representation of market prices in which price effects (such as industry effects) other than those from systematic risk are included.

**multiplier** A measure of aggressiveness in a constant proportion portfolio insurance strategy. A higher multiplier, in general, means a higher percentage of the portfolio will be invested in stock.

**multi-stage dividend discount model** A variation of a dividend discount model that allows for more than one anticipated future growth rate in the income stream

**multivariate** A distribution in which the variables have more than one characteristic of interest.

**municipal bond** A debt instrument issued by a city or state government.

**naive diversification** A method of achieving a reduction of portfolio risk by investing in several securities without particular regard for the individual security characteristics.

**naive strategy** Any investment strategy that follows a predetermined pattern regardless of future changes in the investment environment.

**naked call** A short call option in which the writer does not own, or have a claim to, the underlying security or asset.

**neglected firm effect** The tendency for lesser-known firms to perform better than they should according to financial theory.

**nonsynchronous trading** The phenomenon in which prices on related securities may have been determined at different points in time.

**normal backwardation** The theory of futures pricing that predicts that the futures price is downward biased in order to provide a risk premium to the speculators, who normally have a net long position.

**normal mix** The normal percentage of a portfolio that is invested in the various classes of assets (such as stocks, bonds, and cash) in the portfolio.

**notional amount** In a swap. the dollar amount on which the periodic interest payment is calculated.

**odd lot** A quantity of stock that is not evenly divisible by 100 shares.

**odd lot-generating split** A stock split that is not in a whole-number ratio like 2-for-1 or 4-for-1. For instance, in a 3-for-2 split, the holder of 100 shares would have 150 shares (an odd lot) after the split.

**open interest** A measure of how many futures contracts in a given commodity exist at a particular point in time.

**open outcry** The trading method used at the futures exchanges and at some of the options exchanges. Trades are made verbally among members of a trading crowd rather than through a single specialist.

**opening transaction** The establishment of an investment position. This position may be long or short.

**operational efficiency** A measure of the speed and accuracy with which orders are placed and confirmed at an exchange.

**opportunity cost** The benefit forgone in order to take advantage of some other opportunity.

**optimum trading range** The unproved notion that there is a best price range for stock.

**Options Clearing Corporation (OCC)** An organization that acts as a guarantor of all option trades between buyers and sellers. The OCC also regulates the trading activities of members of option exchanges.

**order book** A book in which a specialist keeps standing orders from all over the country to ensure that the market in these securities is maintained in a fair and orderly fashion.

**out-of-the-money** A description of an option that has no intrinsic value.

**outtrade** A mismatch in the trading cards of two brokers in a trading pit. The two brokers must resolve the misunderstanding (or error) before they can resume trading.

**overriding** The practice of writing options against an existing portfolio; also called overwriting. The person in charge of the option activity is often not the same as the portfolio manager, and in many cases the option writer may not alter the underlying portfolio.

**overwriting** See *overriding*.

**party in interest** An ERISA term referring to a person or organization who has some relationship to a firm's pension plan.

**passive management** A management strategy in which the investment manager does not take an active role in revising the portfolio components.

**payout ratio** A firm's dividends per share divided by its earnings per share.

**penny stock** A colloquial term for any low-priced stock.

**pit** The sunken trading arena of a futures or options exchange where members of that exchange engage in trades.

**plan sponsor** An employer who provides a retirement plan to employees.

**political risk** Risk that arises from the potential for foreign governments to interfere with the operation of a company or with the free flow of investment capital or profits across international boundaries.

**population** The complete set of a particular group of random variables.

**portfolio dedication** A portfolio strategy in which specific assets are earmarked to satisfy the needs of a known future cash outlay. Dedicated portfolios are normally immunized against interest rate risk.

**portfolio investment** Foreign investment via the securities markets; also known as financial investment.

**portfolio splitting** The practice of managing a portfolio in accordance with two separate sets of objectives. This involves breaking the portfolio into a subportfolio for each objective.

**position day** The date when a hedger notifies the clearinghouse of an intent to deliver bonds. This is two business days before the delivery date.

**position delta** The sum of the deltas in a portfolio. The position delta is a relative measure of bullishness or bearishness.

**position trader** A speculator who routinely maintains futures positions overnight, and sometimes keeps a contract open for weeks.

**premium** With options, the actual amount that is paid for an option; with futures, the situation in which a particular futures price is higher than some other price.

**premium over conversion value** The difference between the current market price of a convertible bond and its value if converted into common stock.

**price discovery** A function of the futures market that helps indicate the market's consensus about likely future prices for a commodity.

**price risk** The risk of loss because of an uncertain future price for a commodity or financial asset.

**primary objective** The principal goal of a portfolio; either capital appreciation, growth of income, income, or stability of principal.

**product class shift** With timberland, the phenomenon whereby a stand of trees grows sufficiently large to move from one primary use category (such as sawtimber) to another (such as veneer). Forests become more valuable as they undergo a product class shift.

**productivity risk** A risk associated with the future growth of timberland.

**program trading** A generic term used for any activity that involves the trading of portfolios via computers, where the decision to make a trade is also computer generated.

**property dividend** A proportional distribution to shareholders of some asset other than cash or securities.

**prospectus** The legal document that every potential investor into a mutual fund must receive before opening an account. It describes the intent of the fund, its charges, and its management.

**protective put** A long position in a put option held simultaneously with a long position in the same common stock. A protective put is a hedge.

**proxy statement** A document shareholders receive in advance of the annual meeting of the corporation that permits them to cast an absentee ballot.

**prudent expert standard** The modern version of the prudent man rule. This standard originated with ERISA and requires a fiduciary to act the way an expert would, not just in the fashion of an ordinary person.

**psychic return** Nonquantifiable benefits received from an investment activity.

**purchasing power parity (PPP)** The phenomenon in international finance whereby relative exchange rates reflect differences in the relative purchasing power of a currency in the two countries.

**put option** An option whose owner has purchased the right to sell a set number of shares of common stock (normally 100 shares) for a set price (the striking, or exercise, price) to a specified person (the option writer) any time prior to a specified date (the expiration date).

**quadratic programming** An extension of linear programming in which the objective function contains a second order term.

**qualitative** Not measurable by numerical techniques.

**quantitative** Measurable by numerical techniques.

**R squared** A measure of the goodness of fit around a regression line.

**random walk** A data series in which the next value is totally unpredictable.

**rating agency** An organization that provides an assessment of the default risk of a company or municipality.

**reactive strategy** A strategy for making a tactical asset allocation investment decision as a consequence of something that has already happened.

**real asset** An asset for which there is no corresponding liability.

**real estate investment trust (REIT)** A portfolio of real estate assets that trades like a closed end investment company.

**real investment** An investment in physical assets rather than securities, especially with international investments.

**real rate** Theoretically, the rate of return investors demand for giving up the current use of funds.

**realized compound yield** The effective rate of interest actually earned on an investment over a period of time, including the reinvestment of intermediate cash flows.

**rebalancing** The practice of adjusting the proportions held in various securities in accordance with a predetermined portfolio policy such as constant beta or equal weighting.

**registered bond** A bond which is imprinted with the owner's name and which pays interest (if any) via a check rather than clipped coupons.

**regulation FD** Regulation Fair Disclosure, which prevents companies from giving important corporate information to analysts or institutional investors in advance of making that same information available to the public.

**regulatory risk** The chance of loss due to adverse changes in the regulatory environment. The spotted owl issue is an example of regulatory risk from the perspective of a lumbering operation in the U.S. Northwest.

**reinvestment rate risk** The possibility of loss due to falling interest rates that would result in a reduction in the amount of income received through the compounding of interest. Reinvestment rate risk reduces the realized compound yield of an investment.

**relative purchasing power parity** The condition in which changes in exchange rates stem from changes in countries' inflation rates.

**replacement cost approach** A real estate valuation method that seeks to determine what it would cost to replace an existing building.

**required rate of return** The expected rate of return that must be associated with an investment (given its risk) in order to make it an acceptable investment.

**residual option spread (ROS)** A form of performance evaluation used with portfolios containing options. The residual option spread measures the difference between the realized return on the optioned portfolio and the realized return on the unoptioned portfolio.

**retention ratio** One minus the earnings retention ratio. Also called the *plowback ratio*.

**return** The benefit (financial or psychic) associated with an investment position.

**return on assets (ROA)** A profitability measure calculated as net income after taxes divided by total assets.

**return on equity (ROE)** A profitability measure calculated as net income after taxes divided by equity.

**return on investment (ROI)** An imprecise measure of profitability that usually means the same thing as return on assets. The term ROI should be avoided unless its meaning is clearly understood.

**return relative** The realized return plus 1. In calculating compound returns, return relatives are used because they eliminate negative signs.

**revenue bond** Any bond that will be repaid using proceeds from the project that the bond issue financed (such as a toll bridge or turnpike).

**reverse split** A recapitalization in which the number of shares of common stock is reduced rather than increased. After a reverse split, shareholders are left with fewer shares than before, but the price per share is higher.

**risk** Chance of loss.

**risk aversion** The general economic characteristic of investors whereby everything else being equal, investors prefer less risk.

**risk premium** The component of interest rates that is toughest to measure; the magnitude of the risk premium is a function of the perceived risk of a security.

**riskless rate of interest** The theoretical concept indicating that a rate of return should be earned on an asset with zero variance of return. U.S. Treasury bills are often used as a proxy for the riskless rate.

**round lot** A quantity of stock evenly divisible by 100 shares.

**runs test** A nonparametric statistical test signed to determine the likelihood of a binomial pattern's occurring by chance.

**St. Petersburg paradox** An illustration of the diminishing marginal utility of money whereby investors will not pay an infinite amount for an investment with an infinite expected return.

**S&P 500 stock index** A standard against which portfolio managers and investment advisors might be judged. It is currently one of the Commerce Department's twelve leading indicators.

**sales charge** A commission paid to buy shares in a mutual fund. No-load funds have no sales charge.

**sample** A collection of observations from a random variable population.

**sample statistic** A characteristic such as a mean or standard deviation of a set of sample data.

**Sarbanes-Oxley Act** An important corporate governance act passed in 2002 that seeks to improve financial reporting and the quality of board oversight of accounting records.

**scalpers** See *locals*.

**screen** A logical method of reducing the size of a population so that the remaining members can be examined closely.

**secondary objective** The traditional investment goal that is second in importance.

**security** A financial asset.

**security market line (SML)** A plot of the expected returns of securities against their betas.

**semi-efficient market hypothesis (SEMH)** The notion that there are various tiers of stocks, some of which are priced more efficiently than others.

**semi-variance** A method of measuring risk in which only deviations on the adverse side of the mean are considered. For instance, a very large one-day gain in the stock price would not be considered in the calculation of semi-variance for a stock buyer but would be considered by a short seller.

**settlement price** Normally, an average of the high and low prices during the last minute or so of trading. It is analogous to the closing price on the stock exchanges.

**Sharpe measure** A method of performance evaluation that calculates the ratio of a security's excess return to its standard deviation of return. The higher the Sharpe measure, the greater the risk-adjusted return and the better the performance.

**short sale** A sale in which sellers borrow stock from their brokers, sell it, and hope to buy similar shares in the future at a lower price to replace those borrowed.

**signaling** A theoretical area of finance that studies the extent to which the market interprets various activities of the firm (such as dividend increases) as management signals of likely future firm performance.

**single-index model** A model of security price behavior in which the preponderance of a security's price behavior is explained by one measure of overall market activity.

**sinking fund** An escrow type of account that a firm establishes for the eventual retirement of a bond issue. Annual payments are often required to be made into the fund.

**skewness** A statistical measure of the lack of symmetry of a distribution.

**small firm effect** The tendency for firms with low levels of capitalization to perform better than finance theory suggests they should.

**social investing** The practice of disallowing investment in certain industries or companies because of a desire to avoid their products or their manner of doing business. Recent examples of targeted firms include nuclear power, defense spending, environmental issues, and hiring practices.

**socially responsible investing** Integrating personal values and societal concerns with investment decisions.

**soft dollars** Arrangements under which products or services other than execution of securities transactions are obtained by an advisor in exchange for directing trades to the provider of the services.

**sole interest of the beneficiary rule** The ERISA requirement that the customers' best interest must come ahead of the best interest of the fiduciary.

**specialist** An individual at the American Stock Exchange and the New York Stock Exchange through whom all orders to buy or sell a particular security must pass. The specialist is charged with maintaining a fair and orderly market.

**speculative stock** A loose category of common stock that includes growth stocks with high betas or with little price history.

**speculator** In the futures market, a person who, for a price, is willing to bear the risk that the hedger does not want.

**spin-off** A recapitalization in which a firm reissues shares of a previously acquired subsidiary and ceases to be involved in the management of the subsidiary.

**spot price** The current price of a commodity for immediate delivery; also called the cash price.

**spot rate** The current exchange rate for two currencies; the rate that is posted on signs at international airports and in banking centers. The spot rate changes daily.

**stability of principal** An investment objective in which an investor indicates he or she wants no chance of any deterioration in the original principal value. This is the most conservative of the four traditional investment objectives.

**Standard & Poor's Corporation.** A company that publishes a wide variety of reports on the economy, industries, and individual stocks.

**standard error** The standard deviation divided by the square root of the number of observations.

**static strategy** A form of tactical asset allocation that maintains a constant mix of security classes.

**statistic** A characteristic of a sample or of a population of random variables.

**stochastic** Having a random nature. A stochastic process is not completely predictable.

**stochastic dominance** A theory of dominance based on the likelihood of realizing an outcome below a certain level. Regardless of the level chosen, the less the likelihood of earning less than this amount, the better.

**stock dividend** A distribution of more shares of stock to stockholders. Stock dividends generally do not increase or decrease a shareholder's wealth.

**stock lending** The practice of lending shares held in a margin account to another firm where someone wishes to sell them short. The stock lender earns interest on the value of the loaned shares.

**stock loan finder** A person or firm that facilitates the borrowing of shares to sell short by locating shares that can be borrowed.

**stock split** A recapitalization in which the number of shares in existence is increased by giving shareholders more shares for each share they own. This is also called a forward or regular way stock split.

**stop order** An order that becomes a market order when the stop price is touched during trading. Stop orders can be used to minimize losses or to protect profits.

**street name** The name of the brokerage firm that is holding securities on behalf of a client.

**striking price** See *exercise price*; the term *striking price* is generally used when describing options.

**stumpage** Timber that is still on the stump and growing.

**subordinated debenture** An unsecured bond issue that is lower in priority than other debt issues.

**suitability** The appropriateness of a particular investment asset for a particular investment purpose. Speculation in futures contracts, for instance, would not be suitable for a low-income retiree.

**superfluous diversification** Holding more securities than are reasonably required to reduce unsystematic risk to a practical minimum.

**surplus** The difference between the assets of a portfolio and the present value of the liabilities associated with that portfolio. This term is especially associated with insurance companies and with defined benefit retirement plans.

**swing component** The portion of a portfolio that, under a tactical asset allocation program, may be shifted among asset classes.

**systematic risk** The variance of a security's returns that stems from overall market movements and is measured by beta.

**tactical asset allocation (TAA)** A formal method of periodic portfolio revision in which the fund manager seeks to outperform the market by shifting funds into various asset classes as economic conditions change.

**target return** A quantitative rate of return objective such as 8 percent per year or a set percentage above the inflation rate.

**technical analyst** A security analyst who makes use of charts and technical indicators, believing that changes in price occur because of changes in supply and demand.

**tender offer** An offer by one firm to acquire the shares of another.

**term structure of interest rates** The shape and location of the yield curve.

**thin trading** Securities whose trading volume is low relative to other securities.

**time value** The amount by which the market price of an option exceeds its intrinsic value.

**time weighted rate of return** A return calculation that accounts for the actual period of time that funds were in the portfolio. It makes adjustments for deposits and withdrawals.

**TIMO** Timberland investment management organization.

**total return** The gain or loss in a portfolio taking into account both price changes and income received.

**total return concept** The practice of considering both the income and the capital appreciation of an investment in determining the level of payout from the investment.

**total risk** The sum of systematic and unsystematic risk. Variance of return (or standard deviation) is used to measure total risk.

**tracking error** The deviation of a portfolio's price behavior from the behavior of some other portfolio's behavior that it seeks to mimic.

**transaction exposure** The chance of loss with the purchase or sale of goods associated with changes in the exchange rate between two currencies.

**translation exposure** Exposure that stems from the holding of foreign assets and liabilities that are denominated in currencies other than U.S. dollars.

**Treasury Direct System** A book-entry account used to record ownership of U.S. Treasury securities.

**Treynor measure** A performance measure similar to the Sharpe measure except that the excess return is divided by beta rather than by the standard deviation of returns.

**troy ounce** The standard for gold weight. A troy ounce weighs 9.7 percent more than the standard ounce.

**uncertainty** The dispersion of possible outcomes of a future event.

**underlying security** The common stock or other asset that an option allows its holder to buy or sell.

**undeveloped (raw) property** Real estate on which no buildings exist.

**Uniform Management of Institutional Funds Act** A 1972 Act providing guidelines for the management of charitable investment funds such as public foundations and endowments.

**Uniform Prudent Investor Act** A 1994 act subject to state-by-state adoption outlining prudent investment management. This act allows portfolio managers to handle fiduciary accounts in accordance with financial theory and best investment practice.

**univariate** A population that contains only one characteristic of interest.

**unsystematic risk** Diversifiable risk that is unique to a particular company.

**utility** The economic satisfaction associated with some activity. Utility is a qualitative concept.

**Value Line Investment Survey** A popular investment advisory service widely known for its timeliness and safety ranking system.

**variable rate bond** An interest-bearing security on which the interest rate periodically changes.

**wasting asset** A property of an option such that, when everything else remains equal (that is, the stock price does not change), the value of the option will decline over time.

**window dressing** Cosmetic changes that are made to a portfolio, usually just prior to the preparation of periodic reports.

**writing an option** The act of selling options as an opening transaction.

**yield curve** The plot of yields to maturity associated with bonds of a particular risk class over the available maturities.

**yield curve inversion** The unusual (and usually short-lived) phenomenon in which short-term interest rates exceed long-term rates.

**yield spread** The difference between a taxable yield and a tax-exempt yield.

**yield to maturity** The true rate of return that will be earned on a debt instrument if the security is held until its maturity and all interest and principal are repaid as agreed. The calculation of yield to maturity assumes that it is possible to reinvest coupon returns at the yield to maturity.

**zero coupon bond** A debt security that pays no periodic income and is sold at a discount from its maturity value.

# INDEX

# Q



# R

# S



# T

# U



# V



# W



# Y



# Z